NCLC Cumulative Title Index, Vols. 1-231

"À Aimée d'Alton" (Musset) **150**:309
"À Albert Mérat" (Verlaine) **230**:163, 169
"À Alfred de M." (Sainte-Beuve) **5**:346
"À Arthur Rimbaud" (Verlaine) **230**:170
"À celle qui est trop gaie" (Baudelaire) **6**:109; **29**:73; **55**:60, 76
"À Charles Baudelaire" (Verlaine) **230**:162, 171
A. D. Baratynskoy (Pavlova) **138**:4, 33
"À Don Quichotte" (Verlaine) **230**:162
"À Elvire" (Lamartine)
See "Elvire"
"À Ernest Delahaye" (Verlaine) **230**:169
"À Eugénie" (Verlaine) **230**:166
"À Félix Guiliemardet" (Lamartine) **11**:272
"À Fontenay" (Sainte-Beuve) **5**:348
"À George Sand" (Musset) **150**:310
"A. I. Kaznacheevu" (Aksakov) **181**:61
"À Juana" (Musset) **150**:309
"À Julie" (Musset) **150**:322
"À la dérive" (Laforgue) **221**:44
"À la Malibran" (Musset) **150**:318
"À la manière de Paul Verlaine" (Verlaine) **51**:361; **230**:171
À la manière de plusieurs (Verlaine) **2**:623; **230**:191, 209
"À la mi-Carême" (Musset) **150**:309
"À la Princesse Roukhine" (Verlaine) **230**:211-12, 215
"À la promenade" (Verlaine) **2**:628; **51**:378, 380; **230**:164
"À la très-chère" (Baudelaire) **55**:29
"À l'éternelle madame" (Corbière) **43**:9
"À l'Etna" (Corbière) **43**:27
"À Lord Byron" (Lamartine) **11**:254, 268-69
"A Luigia Pallavicini caduto da cavello" (Foscolo) **8**:268, 270, 277
"À M.A. de L" (Desbordes-Valmore)
See "À Monsieur Alphonse de Lamartine"
"À M. Auguste le Prévost" (Sainte-Beuve) **5**:348
"À M. Léon Bruys d'Ouilly" (Lamartine) **190**:263
"A M. Victor Hugo" (Bertrand) **31**:48
"À M. Victor Hugo" (Musset) **7**:275
"À M. Viguier" (Sainte-Beuve) **5**:348
"À M. Wap" (Lamartine) **190**:225
"À ma bien-aimée" (Verlaine) **230**:170
"À ma femme" (Verlaine) **230**:166, 169
"À Mademoiselle" (Sainte-Beuve) **5**:348
A Major String Quartet, op. 18 (Beethoven)
See *String Quartet in A Major, op. 18*
A Minor String Quartet, op. 132 (Beethoven)
See *String Quartet in A Minor, op. 132*
"À mon âge, je sais . . ." (Verlaine) **230**:166, 172
"À mon ami Alfred T." (Musset) **150**:310
"À mon ami Edouard B" (Musset) **150**:310
"À mon ami Leroux" (Sainte-Beuve) **5**:348
"À mon ami Ulric Guttinguer" (Sainte-Beuve) **5**:348
"À mon cotre Le Négrier" (Corbière) **43**:28
"À némésis" (Lamartine) **11**:271, 289
"À Ninon" (Musset) **150**:309
"À Paul Bourget" (Laforgue) **221**:84
"À Pépa" (Musset) **150**:309
An a priori Autobiography (Brownson) **50**:27
"À quoi rêvent les jeunés filles" (Musset) **7**:260, 264, 268; **150**:301, 304-5, 315
"A. S. Pushkin" (Dobrolyubov) **5**:142
"À Sainte-Beuve" (Musset) **7**:275, 279
"À Ulric G." (Musset) **150**:232, 310
"À un dîner d' athées" (Barbey d'Aurevilly) **1**:70, 75, 77-78; **213**:16, 19, 63, 65-66, 68, 89
"À un poète mort" (Leconte de Lisle) **29**:222, 235
"À une demoiselle" (Corbière) **43**:13
"À une heure du matin" (Baudelaire) **155**:82
"À une jeune Arabe" (Lamartine) **11**:279
"À une madone" (Baudelaire) **55**:9, 43-4, 67
"À une mendiante Rousse" (Baudelaire) **6**:80; **55**:16, 35, 40
"À une passante" (Baudelaire) **6**:79; **29**:101; **55**:35, 40, 42
"A une raison" (Rimbaud) **35**:295-96, 322-23; **82**:232-33; **227**:238-41, 247, 309-10
A. W. Schlegels Vorlesungen über schöne Litteratur und Kunst (Schlegel) **15**:230
"A Zacinto" (Foscolo) **8**:279-80; **97**:57, 68
"Aaron Trow" (Trollope) **101**:233, 235
Abaellino, the Great Bandit (Dunlap) **2**:215
"L'Abbandonata" (Symonds) **34**:355
L'abbaye de Typhaines (Gobineau) **17**:79
"L'abbaye de Vallombreuse" (Lamartine) **11**:255
"The Abbé Aubain" (Mérimée) **6**:354, 364-5, 368-9, 371; **65**:47, 49, 54, 59, 63, 85, 101, 113
"The Abbé Delille and Walter Landor" (Landor) **14**:166, 195
The Abbess: A Romance (Trollope) **30**:319
"The Abbess of Castro" (Stendhal)
See *L'abbesse de Castro*
"L'Abbesse de Castro" (Stendhal)
See *L'abbesse de Castro*
L'abbesse de Castro (Stendhal) **23**:349, 381, 408-9, 413; **46**:307; **178**:173, 226
L'Abbesse de Jouarre (Renan) **26**:387-89, 415
"Abbey Asaroe" (Allingham) **25**:20
The Abbot (Scott) **15**:300, 312; **69**:303-04, 306, 313; **110**:233; **209**:182, 184-85, 229-30, 232-34, 236-38
"Abbot of Inisfalen" (Allingham) **25**:13
"The Abbot's Ghost; or, Maurice Treherne's Temptation" (Alcott) **58**:46; **83**:6
Abbotsford (Irving) **2**:373
"Abdala" (Martí) **63**:85, 102
Abdallah (Tieck) **5**:515, 517-18, 523, 527-28
Die Abderiten, eine sehr wahrscheinliche Geschichte (Wieland) **177**:234, 242, 245, 248, 251, 254, 256-57, 261, 287-88, 316-21, 330, 336
"Abdias" (Stifter) **41**:335, 366, 367, 391
Abdias (Stifter) **198**:283, 285, 288-89, 291-92, 294, 306-10, 315-17
"The Abdication of Fergus" (Ferguson) **33**:279-80, 293
The Abduction (Becque)
See *L'Enlèvement*
"Abecedarju" (Preseren) **127**:315
Abednego the Money-Leader (Gore) **65**:21
"La abeja y el zángano" (Lizardi) **30**:67
Abel (Alfieri) **101**:18-19
"Abel and Cain" (Baudelaire)
See "Abel et Caïn"
"Abel et Caïn" (Baudelaire) **6**:94
"Abel Jansen Tasman" (Clarke) **19**:231, 236
Aben Humeya (Martínez de la Rosa) **102**:230, 241-46
"Abencerrage" (Hemans) **29**:192
"The Abencerrage" (Hemans) **71**:276
"Abend" (Eichendorff) **225**:42
"Der Abend" (Grillparzer) **102**:174
"Der Abend" (Schiller) **39**:338-39, 355
"Abend auf Golgatha" (Keller) **2**:421
"Abendlied an die Natur" (Keller) **2**:421
"Abendlied unterm bestirntem Himmel," WoO 150 (Beethoven) **227**:32
"Abendlied-augen, meine Lieben Fensterlein" (Keller) **2**:421
"Abendphantasie" (Hölderlin) **16**:184
"Abendrot im Walde" (Meyer) **81**:205
"Abendständchen" (Brentano) **1**:102, 105
"Abendwolke" (Meyer) **81**:146
Aben-Hamet, the Last of the Abencerages (Chateaubriand) **3**:110, 117, 126
"Abenlied" (Claudius) **75**:190
"Die Abenteuer der Silvester-Nacht" (Hoffmann) **183**:248, 252-57
Die Abenteuer des Don Sylvio von Rosalva (Wieland)
See *Der Sieg der Natur über die Schwärmerei; oder, die Abenteuer des Don Sylvio von Rosalva*
Die Abenteuer in der Sylvesternacht (Hoffmann) **2**:348
Das aber kann ich nicht ertragen (Storm) **195**:20-21
"An Aberration" (Karamzin)
See "Strannost"
Abhandlung über den Ursprung der Sprache, walche den von der Königl (Herder) **8**:305, 314; **186**:13, 17-18, 20, 69-70, 72-73, 84, 86
"The Abjuration of St. Peter" (Baudelaire)
See "Le reniement de Saint-Pierre"
The Abolitionists (Channing) **17**:24, 32, 35
"L'aboma" (Leconte de Lisle) **29**:225
"Aboriginal Death Song" (Kendall) **12**:192, 201
"Abou Ben Adhem" (Hunt) **1**:414-15, 423; **70**:264
"About a Christmas Book" (Thackeray) **213**:327
"About Dolly" (Cooke) **110**:33
"About Goads: An Exhortation to the Children of [illegible]
See "[illegible]

"About How Ivan Ivanovič Quarreled with Ivan Nikiforovič" (Gogol)
See "The Tale of How Ivan Ivanovich Quarrelled with Ivan Nikiforovich"
"About Hunting" (Aksakov)
See "Ob okhote"
About Money and Other Things (Craik) **38**:127
"About Petukh and His Children. A Heraldic Casus" ("O Piemukhie i iego diemyakh. Gieralsoftdichieskij kazus") (Leskov) **174**:136, 138-39
About the Book—Restricted Action (Mallarmé)
See *L'Action restreinte*
"About the Magazine" (Prescott) **163**:19
"Abraham Davenport" (Whittier) **8**:509, 523; **59**:360-1
Abraham Lincoln: His Speeches and Writings (Lincoln) **201**:184-92, 216
"Abram Morrison" (Whittier) **8**:517
"El abrazo de Vergara" (Alarcón) **219**:45-46
Abrégé de l'histoire de la Régence (Genlis) **166**:26
"Abriß von den eropäischen Verhältnissen der deutschen Literatur" (Schlegel) **142**:307-8, 324
An Abridgement of Universal Geography, Together with Sketches of History (Rowson) **182**:254, 260-61, 333, 355
An Abridgment of Universal Geography: Together with Sketches of History (Rowson) **69**:114-16
Abroad (Saltykov) **16**:369
"Absalom" (Willis) **194**:304, 306
"Der Abschied" (Klopstock) **11**:237; **225**:296
"Abschied" (Lenau) **16**:269-70
"Abschied" (Mörike) **10**:453
"Abschied von der Utopie" (Heine) **54**:331
"Abschied von Gastein" (Grillparzer) **102**:174
Abseits (Storm) **1**:540; **195**:13, 21, 41, 67
"Absence" (Bowles) **103**:55
"L'Absence" (Dacre) **151**:148
"Absence" (Kemble) **18**:181
"The Absent" (Very) **9**:383-85
The Absentee (Edgeworth) **1**:257, 262-68, 270-72; **51**:77, 79, 88, 90-1, 93, 100, 102, 104-05, 117, 119; **158**:54, 57, 61
Les absents (Daudet) **1**:249
"Abt Vogler" (Browning) **19**:132, 153; **79**:106, 110-11
"Einem Abtrünnigen" (Heine) **147**:202
"Abu Midjan" (Lampman) **25**:188, 199
Abufar de Ducis (Heredia) **209**:119
"La abulea y la nieta" (Silva) **114**:311
"Abundance" (Meyer)
See "Fülle"
"Abuse of the gospel" (Cowper) **94**:72-3
The Abyss (Goncharov)
See *Obryv*
"The Academy of Death. A Fragement" (Freneau) **111**:134
"Acadia" (Longfellow) **103**:296
Accepted Addresses (Sala) **46**:237
"Account of Lord Byron's Residence" (Polidori) **51**:218
Account of New South Wales and the State of the Convicts (Dyer) **129**:115
"Account of Sappho" (Robinson) **142**:142
"An Account of Some Strange Disturbances in an Old House on Aungier Street" (Le Fanu)
See "Some Strange Disturbances in an Old House on Augier Street"
An Account of the Christian Faith on the Principles of the Evangelical Church (Schleiermacher)
See *Der christliche Glaube nach den Grundsäzen der evengelischen Kirche im Zusammenhange dargestellt*
"Account of the Rural Sentiment Which is Cultivated at the Country Seat of a Man of Fashion" (Mackenzie) **41**:191
"Les accroupissements" (Rimbaud) **35**:271, 282
"An Accursed Race" (Gaskell) **70**:189
"The Accuser Who Is the God of This World" (Blake) **13**:213
"Ach nimmer will es in dem Herzen schweigen" (Brentano) **191**:69
"Achan" (Kendall) **12**:192
"Achievements of the Genius of Scott" (Martineau) **26**:350; **137**:309
Achilleis (Goethe) **4**:207, 216
Der Achtzehnte Brumaire des Louis-Bonaparte (Marx) **17**:315, 322, 328, 335, 353, 355; **114**:8, 11, 37, 41, 46, 70
Acia (Turgenev)
See *Asya*
"Acknowledgment" (Lanier) **6**:246; **118**:202, 215
"Acme" (Rossetti) **50**:293
"Acontius and Cydippe" (Morris) **4**:442, 447
Acrobate (Feuillet) **45**:79
"L'acropole" (Rimbaud)
See "Villes II"
"Across the Pea-Fields" (Lampman) **25**:183-84, 209
Across the Plains, with Other Memories and Essays (Stevenson) **5**:410, 414, 419; **14**:331; **193**:206, 213-15, 220
"Across the Plains: Leaves from the Notebook of an Emigrant between New York and San Francisco" (Stevenson) **193**:356
An Act for Establishing Religious Freedom, Passed in the Assembly of Virginia in the Beginning of the Year 1786 (Jefferson) **11**:170-71, 189, 198, 209; **103**:263
Acté (Dumas) **71**:204
L'Acte Additionnel aux Constitutions de L'Empire (Constant) **182**:85, 211
Actes et paroles (Hugo) **3**:262
"Action at Stoney Creek" (Richardson) **55**:342
"L'Action restreinte" (Mallarmé) **210**:210, 226-28, 251, 262-64
L'Action restreinte (Mallarmé) **41**:233, 271, 282, 287
Les actionnaires (Scribe) **16**:394
Actions Speaks Louder (Tamayo y Baus)
See *Del dicho al hecho*
Actors and Acting (Lewes)
See *On Actors and the Art of Acting*
Les actrices (Goncourt and Goncourt) **7**:153, 174
"Acts and Scenes" (Landor) **14**:177
"The Acts of the Polish Nation since the Beginning of the World to Its Crucifixion" (Mickiewicz) **3**:390
"Actual and Ideal" (Alcott) **167**:75
"Ad Amicos" (Taylor) **89**:317
"Ad Angelo Mai quand'ebbe trovato i libri di Cicerone della Repubblica" (Leopardi) **129**:219, 266, 312, 314-15, 328-29, 346
"Ad Arimane" (Leopardi) **129**:252, 356
"Ad Criticum" (Boker) **125**:77
"Ad Hoc Poetic Art" (Verlaine)
See "L'art poétique ad hoc"
"Ad leones" (Norwid) **17**:379, 383
Ada Reis (Lamb) **38**:237, 251
Adam and Eve (Clough) **27**:56, 67, 91, 100
Adam and Eve (Prescott) **163**:58, 75, 78, 90
Adam Bede (Eliot) **118**:40, 43, 58-62, 103-4, 127, 147
Adam Bede (Eliot) **209**:4, 15, 54
"Adam Buff, the Man without a Shirt" (Jerrold) **2**:395
Adam Graeme of Mossgray (Oliphant) **221**:226, 244
Adam Greene of Mossgray (Oliphant) **11**:429, 432, 445
"Adam Smith as a Person" (Bagehot) **10**:58
"Adam, the Carrion Crow" (Beddoes) **3**:34
Adam's Tod (Klopstock)
See *Der Tod Adams: Ein Trauerspiel*
The Adams Papers (Adams) **106**:4
Adams-Jefferson (Jefferson) **103**:192
Addison (Macaulay) **42**:87
"Address" (Barnes) **75**:43
"Address" (Emerson)
See "The Divinity School Address"
"Address at Gettysburg" (Lincoln)
See "Gettysburg Address"
"Address at the Meeting of the Boston Whig Young Men's Club" (Adams) **175**:76-77
"Address Before the Free People of Color" (Garrison) **149**:229
"Address before the Springfield Scott Club, in Reply to Judge Douglas's Richmond Speech" (Lincoln) **201**:161-62
"Address before the Springfield Washington Temperance Society" (Lincoln) **201**:159, 196
"Address before the Wisconsin Agricultural Society" (Lincoln) **201**:169, 183
"Address before the Young Men's Lyceum of Springfield, Illinois" (Lincoln) **201**:185, 196, 203-4
"An Address Delivered at Lenox on the First of August, 1842, Being the Anniversary of Emancipation in the British West Indies" (Channing) **17**:25
"Address Delivered at the Opening of the New Theatre in Richmond, Va." (Timrod) **25**:363
Address Delivered before the Free People of Color (Garrison) **149**:246, 258-60
"An Address Delivered Before the Senior Class in Divinity College, Cambridge" (Emerson)
See "The Divinity School Address"
"An Address Delivered in the Court-house in Concord" (Emerson) **38**:155-56
Address delivered on the occasion of reading The Declaration of Independence, Fourth of July, 1821 (Adams) **175**:72
"An Address in Opposition to the Election of — —" (Brackenridge) **227**:117
"Address of a Water Nymph" (Darwin) **106**:182
"Address of Abraham Lincoln, on Taking the Oath of Office as President of the United States, March 4, 1861" (Lincoln) **201**:157, 165, 169-70, 172, 186, 198, 209, 219, 222, 225
Address of the Central Council of the Communist League (Marx) **114**:39
Address on the Present Condition, Resources, and Prospects of British North America (Haliburton) **15**:128
Address on the Question of Free Trade (Marx) **17**:333
"Address to a Child" (Wordsworth) **138**:229
"Address to a Lark" (Clare) **86**:155
"An Address to a Wild Deer" (Wilson) **5**:550
"Address to Certain Gold Fishes" (Coleridge) **90**:28
"Address to his auld dog Hector" (Hogg) **109**:202
"An Address to Lord Howe" (Paine) **62**:322
An Address to Miss Phillis Wheatly (Hammon) **5**:261-62, 264-65
"Address to Plenty" (Clare) **9**:72
"Address to the 'Bread and Cheese Club'" (Cooper) **203**:39
"An Address to the Deity" (Barbauld) **185**:32, 89, 138-39, 141
"An Address to the Fremment of Canada" (Moodie) **113**:308
"An Address to the Friends of Liberty" (Dyer) **129**:103, 129
An Address to the Government of the United States on the Cession of Louisiana (Brown) **74**:88, 170-73, 175; **122**:116, 119
An Address to the Irish People (Shelley) **18**:341; **93**:373
Address to the Muses (Baillie) **71**:54-5; **151**:123
An Address to the Negroes in the State of New York (Hammon) **5**:262
Address to the Night (Baillie) **71**:51

An Address to the Opposers of the Repeal of the Corporation and Test Acts (Barbauld) **185**:32, 43-44, 117-19, 121-22, 141, 156
An Address to the People of Great Britain on the Doctrine of Libels and the Office of Juror (Dyer) **129**:105-6, 113, 137
"Address to the People of South Carolina" (Calhoun) **15**:27
"Address to the People of the Free States of the Union" (Adams) **175**:75
Address to the People on the Death of the Princess Charlotte (Shelley) **93**:272-73; **143**:232; **175**:325
"Address to the Rural Muse" (Clare) **9**:79-80; **86**:160
"Address to the Senators and Representatives of the Free States" (Child) **73**:105
"Address to the Swilcar Oak" (Darwin) **106**:183
"Address to Working Men, by Felix Holt" (Eliot) **118**:37-38, 55-57, 64, 92, 130, 156-57, 160, 176, 180-81, 190
"Addressed to Ignorance, Occasioned by a Gentleman's desiring the Author never to assume Knowledge of the Ancients" (Yearsley) **174**:337-38
"Addressed to Messrs. Dwight and Barlow, On the Projected Publication of Their Poems in London" (Trumbull) **30**:350
Addresses (Schleiermacher) **107**:303-10, 313-14, 316
"Addresses on the Fundamental Features of the Present Age" (Fichte) **62**:19
Addresses to the German Nation (Fichte)
See *Reden an die deutsche Nation*
"Der Adel und die Revolution" (Eichendorff) **225**:62
"Adelaide" (Beethoven) **227**:32
"Adélaïde" (Gobineau) **17**:92-3, 103
Adelaide and Theodore (Staël-Holstein)
See *Adélaïde et Théodore*
Adélaïde de Brunswick (Sade) **47**:326
Adélaïde et Théodore (Staël-Holstein) **91**:322, 339
Adelchi (Manzoni) **29**:250-51, 261, 275, 278, 299, 302, 304; **98**:204, 209, 213, 215, 217, 219-20, 224-25, 228, 230, 245, 244, 276
Adèle et Théodore, ou Lettres sur l'éducation (Genlis) **166**:7-8, 14-19, 28-29, 31-33, 42, 49, 64
Adelgitha; or, The Fruits of a Single Error (Lewis) **11**:305-06
Adelheid von Wulfingen (Kotzebue) **25**:141
"Adeline" (Tennyson) **202**:334, 337
Adeline Mowbray; or, The Mother and Daughter (Opie) **65**:157, 168, 171-74, 179, 193-5, 201-2, 206-10, 212, 215, 217
Adelmorn, the Outlaw (Lewis) **11**:296, 302, 304-05
The Adelphi (Bird) **197**:32
Adelphi (Cowper) **94**:14, 94, 121, 125, 128
"El aderezo de esmeraldas" (Bécquer) **106**:98
"Adeus de Thereza" (Castro Alves) **205**:4
"Adeus, Meu Canto" (Castro Alves) **205**:10, 22, 25-26
"Adieu" (Balzac) **153**:88, 91-93, 149, 151
"L'adieu" (Lamartine) **11**:282
"Adieu" (Musset) **150**:309
"Adieu" (Rimbaud) **4**:466, 485; **35**:289-90, 293-94, 303-04, 306-07, 313-14, 320, 324; **82**:223, 229, 236-37, 241, 251-52, 254-55, 262; **227**:210, 278, 303, 305-6, 318, 325
"Adieu" (Verlaine) **230**:167
"Adieu mystères" (Maupassant) **83**:184
"Adieu to Belashanny" (Allingham)
See "The Winding Banks of Erne"
"Adieu!—Adieu!" (Moodie) **113**:348
"Adieux à la poésie" (Lamartine) **190**:200
"Adieux à Suzon" (Musset) **150**:309
Les adieux au comptoir (Scribe) **16**:393
Adini (Brown) **74**:7
"Adiós" (Castro) **3**:101; **78**:37, 40-41
"The Adirondacs" (Emerson) **1**:279; **38**:193; **98**:182-83
"Adivinase el dulce y perfumado" (Castro) **78**:41
"Adlercreutz" (Runeberg) **41**:312, 314
"Adlerskaya pesnya" (Bestuzhev) **131**:152
"Admetus" (Lazarus) **8**:411-14, 417-18, 420, 425; **109**:289-90, 294, 319
Admetus, and Other Poems (Lazarus) **8**:412-13, 417-18, 422, 425; **109**:289, 294, 319, 321
"Administrative Grace" (Leskov)
See "Administrativnaia gratsiia"
"Administrative Nihilism" (Huxley) **67**:64, 66, 97, 105
"Administrativnaia gratsiia" (Leskov) **174**:53
"Administrativnaja gracija" (Leskov)
See "Administrativnaia gratsiia"
Admiral Guinea (Stevenson) **5**:411, 421
Adolescent (Dostoevsky)
See *Podrostok*
"Adolf and Annette" (Coleridge) **90**:31, 33, 35-6
Adolphe: An Anecdote Found among Papers of an Unknown Person and Published by M. Benjamin de Constant (Constant) **6**:211, 213-22, 224-25, 228-29
Adolphe: An Anecdote Found among the Papers of an Unknown Person and Published by Benjamin de Constant (Constant)
See *Adolphe: Anecdote trouvée dans les papiers d'un inconnu et publiée par M. B. de Constant*
Adolphe: Anecdote trouvée dans les papiers d'un inconnu et publiée par M. B. de Constant (Constant) **182**:94-97, 126-30, 144, 146, 149, 151, 154-55, 159-61, 164, 166-67, 169-70, 172-75, 177-78, 185-92, 194, 215-24, 226-28
Adonai, or the Pilgrim of Eternity (Lippard)
See *The Entranced; or, the Wanderer of Eighteen Centuries*
Adonais (Shelley)
See *Adonais: An Elegy on the Death of John Keats*
Adonais: An Elegy on the Death of John Keats (Shelley) **18**:320, 329, 344, 349-51, 353-54, 361, 363-64, 373; **93**:322-29, 344; **175**:207, 245, 264, 310, 312, 314-15, 342
"The Adopted Child" (Hemans) **71**:264
"Adormeciendo a David" (Isaacs) **70**:311
Adrastea (Herder) **8**:307, 313; **186**:48
Adrian, the Neophyte (Lippard) **198**:134
Adrienne Lecouvreur (Scribe) **16**:389, 412-14
Adrift in New York; or, Tom and Florence Braving the World (Alger) **8**:43; **83**:114
The Adulateur (Warren) **13**:413-16, 419, 425-26, 428; **226**:253-55, 258, 260, 263, 267, 270, 277, 285-87, 290
L'adultera (Fontane) **26**:235-37, 241, 243-44, 259, 270-71, 275-76; **163**:162, 189, 197, 239-40, 250-51, 255
Adultera (Martí) **63**:84
Advance Notice (Gogol) **5**:233
"Advent" (Rossetti) **2**:559, 562-3; **50**:272; **66**:330; **186**:332
"An Adventure in the East Indies" (Bryant) **6**:181
"The Adventure of Lieutenant Jergounoff" (Turgenev)
See "Istoriya leytenanta Ergunova"
"The Adventure of My Aunt" (Irving) **19**:341
"The Adventure of Prince Florizel and a Detective" (Stevenson) **193**:255, 316
An Adventure of Richelieu (Tamayo y Baus)
See *Una aventura de Richelieu*
"Adventure of the Hansom Cabs" (Stevenson) **5**:394; **193**:252
"The Adventure of the Mysterious Stranger" (Irving) **2**:370; **19**:341
Adventures (Trelawny)
See *Adventures of a Younger Son*
The Adventures of a Brownie (Craik) **38**:122
The Adventures of a Naval Officer; or, Scenes and Adventures in the Life of Frank Mildmay (Marryat) **3**:318-19, 321-22
The Adventures of a Puppet (Collodi)
See *Le Avventure di Pinocchio*
Adventures of a Telegraph Boy (Alger)
See *Number 91; or, The Adventures of a New York Telegraph Boy*
Adventures of a Younger Son (Trelawny) **85**:314-16, 318-20, 324-25, 327, 330-37, 339, 342-44, 346-48
The Adventures of Arthur O'Leary (Lever)
See *Arthur O'Leary: His Wanderings and Ponderings in Many Lands*
The Adventures of Caleb Williams (Godwin)
See *Things As They Are; or, The Adventures of Caleb Williams*
The Adventures of Captain Bonneville (Irving) **2**:376-77; **95**:258-59
The Adventures of Captain Farrago (Brackenridge)
See *Modern Chivalry: Containing the Adventures of Captain John Farrago, and Teague O'Regan, His Servant*
"The Adventures of Frederick Pickering" (Trollope) **101**:235
The Adventures of Hugh Trevor (Holcroft) **85**:192-93, 206-07, 228-31, 236-38, 242-46
The Adventures of Major O'Regan (Brackenridge)
See *Modern Chivalry: Containing the Adventures of Captain John Farrago, and Teague O'Regan, His Servant*
Adventures of Nicholas Doświadczynski (Krasicki) **8**:399-401, 404-05
"The Adventures of Oliver Twist, or, The Parish Boy's Progress" (Dickens)
See *Oliver Twist*
The Adventures of Philip on His Way through the World; Shewing Who Robbed Him, Who Helped Him, and Who Passed Him By (Thackeray) **5**:466, 470, 472, 482, 484-85, 488; **169**:247, 298; **213**:232-39, 266
The Adventures of Pinocchio (Collodi)
See *Le Avventure di Pinocchio*
The Adventures of Robin Day (Bird) **1**:91; **197**:12, 68
The Adventures of the Last Abencérages (Chateaubriand)
See *Aben-Hamet, the Last of the Abencerages*
Adventures of Ulysses (Lamb) **10**:417
"Adventures on Salisbury Plain" (Wordsworth) **111**:267, 346-47
"Advertisement" (Keble) **87**:156, 199
"Advertisement" (Wordsworth) **206**:296, 341
"Advertisement to Lyrical Ballads" (Wordsworth) **111**:202, 213, 239, 244, 276, 293-94, 306, 314-15, 317, 337, 339, 354-57, 360, 363, 366, 368
"Advice of an Old Woman" (Mörike) **10**:446
"Advice; or, The Squire and the Priest" (Crabbe) **26**:93, 130, 134; **121**:65-6, 71, 73, 76
"Advice to a Raven in Russia" (Barlow) **23**:29-31; **223**:33
"Advice to Authors: By the late Mr. Robert Slender" (Freneau) **111**:81, 132, 156
"Advice to Ladies of a Certain Age" (Trumbull) **30**:349
Advice to the Privileged Orders (Barlow) **23**:17-18, 21-2, 27, 29, 41, 43
Advice to the Privileged Orders in the Several States of Europe, Resulting from the Necessity and Propriety of a General Revolution in the Principle of Government (Barlow) **223**:7, 9, 23-25, 27, 45-49, 57-58, 60-61, 67
Advice to Young Men and (Incidentally) to Young Women, in the Middle and Higher Ranks of Life (Cobbett) **49**:110, 114, 116,

119, 123, 140, 147-48, 150, 152-53, 159
"Aél" (Gómez de Avellaneda) **111**:4, 27
"Aeneid" (Morris) **4**:420, 441
"Æolian Harp" (Coleridge)
See "The Aeolian Harp"
"Aeolian Harp" (Allingham) **25**:18, 20
"The Aeolian Harp" (Coleridge) **99**:5, 38, 40-41, 59, 92, 101, 105; **177**:44; **231**:37, 68, 70-72, 77, 91, 110, 130-31, 135
"The Aeolian Harp" (Zhukovsky) **35**:393
"Aerial Omens" (Whittier) **8**:485
"Aes triplex" (Stevenson) **5**:425
Aesthetic Ideology (Schlegel) **226**:234
"Aesthetic Poetry" (Pater) **7**:305, 327, 333; **90**:241, 305-06, 326, 346
"The Aesthetic Validity of Marriage" (Kierkegaard) **125**:282
"Aesthetic Value of Greek Comedy" (Schlegel)
See "Vom ästhetischen Werte der griechischen Komödie"
"Aesthetics" (Laforgue)
See "Esthétique"
Aesthetics (Hegel)
See *Vorlesungen über die Aesthetik*
Æsthetics (Schleiermacher) **107**:285
The Aesthetics of Ugliness (Sacher-Masoch) **31**:302
Aëthra (Hayne) **94**:136
"Ætna" (Cowper) **94**:117
Af en endnu Levendes Papirer (Kierkegaard) **34**:218, 222, 267-69; **125**:203, 231
Afar in the Forest (Traill)
See *Lady Mary and Her Nurse; or, A Peep into the Canadian Forest*
"Afar Off, and Nigh by the Blood of Christ" (Parker) **186**:204
"L'affaire Champonathieu" (Hugo) **10**:378
L'affaire Clémenceau: Mémoire de l'accusé (Dumas) **9**:224, 228-29, 234
L'affaire Lerouge (Gaboriau) **14**:14, 16-17, 19-21, 23-4, 26-33
Affectation (Sheridan) **91**:243
"L'affichage céleste" (Villiers de l'Isle Adam) **3**:581, 590
"The Affliction of Margaret—of—" (Wordsworth) **12**:393, 430-31, 444
"L'Affreux Ivry . . ." (Verlaine) **230**:167
"Afinskaia zhizn" (Karamzin) **173**:309, 323
Afloat (Maupassant)
See *Sur l'eau*
Afloat and Ashore (Cooper)
See *Afloat and Ashore; or, The Adventures of Miles Wallingford*
Afloat and Ashore; or, The Adventures of Miles Wallingford (Cooper) **1**:221; **54**:258, 266, 276; **203**:75
Afoot with the Year (Lampman) **194**:79-80, 90
L'Africaine (Scribe) **16**:390, 401
The African (Murray) **63**:214
"African Blood" (Castro Alves)
See "Sangre de africano"
The African Woman (Scribe)
See *L'Africaine*
The Africans (Dunlap) **2**:211
Afsluttende uvidenskabelig Efterskrift (Kierkegaard) **34**:199-200, 203-05, 224, 238; **78**:123-25, 148, 154-55, 159-60, 162, 166, 189-90, 195, 197-98, 201, 215, 217, 228, 238, 240, 249-51; **125**:218, 250, 261-63, 265
Aftenen (Grundtvig) **158**:138
"After" (Browning) **79**:153
"After a Tempest" (Bryant) **6**:159, 176
After Breakfast (Sala) **46**:237
After Dark (Collins) **1**:173, 180, 186; **93**:46
After Dark—A Tale of London Life (Boucicault) **41**:49
"After Death" (Rossetti) **2**:557, 561; **50**:269, 289, 295-96; **186**:271, 304
"After Great Pain, a Formal Feeling Comes" (Dickinson) **21**:43; **171**:199-200
After London; or, Wild England (Jefferies) **47**:92-93, 95, 102, 104, 109, 112, 113, 124, 130-33, 142
"After Many Years" (Kendall) **12**:183, 187, 189, 198-99
"After Mist" (Lampman) **25**:210
"After Rain" (Lampman) **25**:169; **194**:53, 82, 84-86
After Reading Dante (Liszt)
See *Après une Lecture du Dante*
"After Snow" (Lampman) **194**:79
"After the Burial" (Lowell) **2**:511; **90**:193
"After the Camanches" (Cooke) **110**:9
"After the Death of John Brown" (Thoreau) **7**:406
"After the Deluge" (Rimbaud)
See "Après le déluge"
After the Dinner Comes the Reckoning (Ostrovsky)
See *Ne vse kotu maslenitsa*
"After the Flood" (Rimbaud)
See "Après le déluge"
"After the French Liberation of Italy" (Rossetti) **77**:297
"After the German Subjugation of France, 1871" (Rossetti) **77**:297
"After the Hunt" (Kendall) **12**:181, 191
"After the Picnic" (Rossetti) **186**:265
"After the Play" (Gogol)
See "Teatral'nyi raz'ezd posle predstavleniia novoi komedii"
"After the Pleasure Party" (Melville) **3**:363; **91**:184
"After the Shower" (Lampman) **25**:210
"After the Storm" (Herzen) **10**:337
"After the Supper and Talk" (Whitman) **31**:434
"After the Theater" (Gogol)
See "Teatral'nyi raz'ezd posle predstavleniia novoi komedii"
"After the Tornado" (Hayne) **94**:138
"After the Victory" (Isaacs)
See "Después da la victoria"
"After What I've Seen . . ." (Verlaine)
See "D'après ce que j'ai vu . . ."
After-Dinner Chat (Silva)
See *De sobremesa*
"Aftermath" (Longfellow) **2**:492; **45**:161, 187
"Afternoon at a Parsonage" (Ingelow) **39**:263-65
"Afternoon in February" (Longfellow) **45**:152; **103**:293
Afternoon of a Faun (Mallarmé)
See *L'après-midi d'un faune*
"After-Thought" (Wordsworth) **166**:205, 213
"Again a Springtime" (Bertrand) **31**:55
"Again His Voice Is at the Door" (Dickinson) **21**:58
Against Heavy Odds: A Tale of Norse Heroism (Boyesen) **135**:8, 15
"Against Inconsistency in our Expectations" (Barbauld) **50**:3; **185**:112, 153
Against the Dualism of Soul and Body, Flesh and Spirit (Feuerbach) **139**:290
Against the Little Accuser (Grundtvig) **158**:141
"Against widows" (Lonnrot) **53**:339
"Agamemnon" (Galt) **1**:327
Agamemnon and Orestes (Alfieri) **101**:32
Agamemnone (Alfieri)
See *Agamennone*
Agamemnon's Grave (Slowacki)
See *Grób Agamemnona*
Agamemnon's Tomb (Lazarus) **109**:294
Agamennone (Alfieri) **101**:4, 8, 32, 42, 73
Aganippe und Phiala (Klopstock) **225**:286
Agar (Staël-Holstein) **91**:359
"Agassiz" (Lowell) **90**:190, 193, 220
"Agatha" (Eliot) **13**:334
Agatha's Husband (Craik) **38**:110, 120, 128
Agathodämon (Wieland) **177**:244, 246, 287, 330, 334
Agathon (Wieland)
See *Geschichte des Agathon*
Agay-Han (Krasiński) **4**:305-06, 309
"Age d'or" (Rimbaud) **4**:484; **35**:269
The Age of Constantine the Great (Burckhardt)
See *Die Zeit Constantins des Grossen*
"The Age of Peace" (Jones) **222**:125, 158
The Age of Reason (Paine) **62**:259, 262, 264, 268-9, 271, 275, 278, 280, 285, 297-8, 309, 311-2, 314, 39, 345-6, 349, 368, 370, 373, 375-6, 379-80, 385-6, 389-93
"The Age of Steam" (Horne) **127**:253
The Age of the Despots (Symonds) **34**:318-19, 346-47, 349, 357, 360-63, 368, 370
Agemennone (Alfieri)
See *Agamennone*
"The Agency of Heaven in the Cause of Liberty" (Brackenridge) **7**:44
"The Ages" (Bryant) **6**:158, 161-62, 164, 171, 181, 189, 191; **46**:4, 15
The Ages of the World (Schelling)
See *Die Weltalter*
Agezylausz (Slowacki) **15**:371, 378
"Aggression in Egypt, and Freedom in the East" (Gladstone) **213**:112
Agide (Alfieri) **101**:13, 7, 39, 42
Agis (Alfieri)
See *Agide*
"The Agitation of the Socialist-Democratic Party in Austria" (Bakunin) **58**:133
"Aglauron and Laurie" (Fuller) **50**:258
"Agnes" (Mörike) **201**:252, 294, 302
Agnes (Oliphant) **61**:173, 188, 209
"Agnes asszony" (Arany) **34**:15, 20
Agnes Bernauer: Ein deutsches Trauerspiel in fünf Aufzügen (Hebbel) **43**:230, 234, 238-40, 244-45, 249, 251, 249, 261-62, 264, 269, 284, 287, 291, 297, 300, 301
Agnes Bernauerin (Ludwig) **4**:350
Agnes Grey: An Autobiography (Brontë) **4**:38-40, 42-43, 48-50, 52-55; **71**:73, 75, 78-82, 84-86, 88-91, 93, 98, 104-09, 111-13, 120, 122-28, 131-39, 144-46, 148, 150, 153-57, 159, 162-63, 165-66, 169, 171-79; **102**:3, 27
Agnes of Sorrento (Stowe) **3**:557, 559, 562, 568
Agnete and the Merman (Andersen) **79**:13, 78, 82
Agnete og Havmanden (Andersen) **214**:15
"Agnosticism" (Huxley) **67**:96
"Agnosticism and Christianity" (Huxley) **67**:41
"La agonía del héroe" (Isaacs) **70**:311
L'agonie de la Semillante (Daudet) **1**:247
Agonies (Flaubert) **19**:288
"The Agony of the Hero" (Isaacs)
See "La agonía del héroe"
Agrarian Justice (Paine) **62**:262, 271, 296, 301, 373
Agreement of Religion with Reason (Kant)
See *Religion within the Limits of Reason Alone*
"Agricultura de la zona tórrida" (Bello) **131**:103-4, 109-13, 119
"Agricultural Address" (Madison) **126**:329
"Agriculture" (Lincoln) **201**:166
"El agua y el fuego" (Rizal) **27**:425
Ah! (Wergeland) **5**:535
"Ah, I feel wretched . . ." (Bestuzhev)
See "Akh, toshno mnye . . ."
"Ah! May the Red Rose Live Alway" (Foster) **26**:298
"Ah, Peggie, since th'art gane away" (Hogg) **109**:200
"Ah Poverties, Wincings, and Sulky Retreats" (Whitman) **81**:315
"Ah! Sun-Flower" (Blake) **13**:181, 221; **37**:15, 26-7, 29, 43, 49, 51, 62, 92
"Ah What Is Love, Our Love, She Said" (Clough) **27**:106
Ahalya Baee (Baillie) **71**:3; **151**:46-8, 86
"Ahasver, der ewige Jude" (Lenau) **16**:279, 284
Ahavat Zion (Mapu) **18**:286-93, 295, 298-301, 303
Die Ahnen (Freytag) **109**:165, 170-73

Die Ahnfrau (Grillparzer) **1**:382-85, 387, 389, 397; **102**:81, 85, 100, 120-26, 146, 148, 176, 186
Ahnung und Gegenwart (Eichendorff) **8**:214-19, 222, 226-29; **225**:3, 5, 8, 12, 16, 18-19, 21-22, 24-25, 28, 30, 98, 100, 103
"Aho, Aho, Love's Horn Doth Blow" (Beddoes) **3**:34
Aiace (Foscolo) **8**:270
"Aideen's Grave" (Ferguson) **33**:278, 293, 305
"Aids to Reflection" (Coleridge) **9**:147, 155, 205; **54**:79, 107; **99**:112-16
Aids to Reflection in the Formation of a Manly Character on the Several Grounds of Prudence, Morality, and Religion: Illustrated by Select Passages from Our Elder Divines, Especially from Archbishop Leighton (Coleridge) **177**:106-7, 116; **197**:231, 241, 285-86; **231**:34, 40, 44, 82, 90, 121, 123
"L'aigle du casque" (Hugo) **3**:276
"Aileen" (Kendall) **12**:193
"Aileen Astore" (Darley) **2**:130
"The Ailing Muse" (Baudelaire)
See "La Muse malade"
"Ailleen" (Banim and Banim) **13**:129
"The Aim of Life" (Brontë) **217**:15-16
"Aimer Paris" (Banville) **9**:30
"The Aims of Education" (Bello) **131**:121
"Ainsi Va le Monde" (Robinson) **142**:173
"Ain't I A Woman" (Truth)
See "Ar'n't I a woman?"
"Air" (Boyesen) **135**:47
"Air de Biniou" (Laforgue) **221**:47
"Air:—spirituosi" (Darwin) **106**:182
"Airiños, airiños, aires" (Castro) **3**:100
"Äiti ja lapsi" (Kivi) **30**:51
"La ajorca de oro" (Bécquer) **106**:97, 108, 120-21, 130-31, 161
"Ajudah" (Mickiewicz) **3**:404
"Akatsuki Zukuyo" (Ichiyō) **49**:353
"Akbar's Dream" (Tennyson) **30**:283; **202**:191
Akëdysséril (Villiers de l'Isle Adam) **3**:583
"Akerman Steppes" (Mickiewicz)
See "Stepy Akermańskie"
"Akh, toshno mnye . . ." (Bestuzhev) **131**:149, 180-81
"Akhill" (Zhukovsky) **35**:398
Akinari ibun (Ueda Akinari) **131**:21
"The Akond of Swat" (Lear) **3**:296
"Akrivie Phrangopoulo" (Gobineau) **17**:80, 92-3, 103
"Al Aaraaf" (Poe) **1**:492, 514, 527; **16**:304; **55**:156; **94**:240; **117**:195-96, 216, 221, 225, 227-31, 233, 237, 239, 244, 260, 262, 264-70, 273, 275-78, 281, 301; **211**:249-51
Al Aaraaf, Tamarlane, and Minor Poems (Poe) **1**:492, 514; **117**:226, 305
"Al alzamiento de los griegos" (Heredia) **209**:131
"Al besar una flor de maravilla" (Manzano) **155**:307
"Al C. Andrés Quintana Roo" (Heredia) **209**:138
"Al escudo de armas de Nueva Granada" (Isaacs) **70**:313
"Al genio de la libertad" (Heredia) **209**:137
"Al mar" (Gómez de Avellaneda) **111**:30, 33, 56-7, 64-7
"Al mar!" (Isaacs) **70**:303, 313
"Al pie de la estatua" (Silva) **114**:261, 301-3
Al! prav se piše kaua ali kaʃha (Preseren)
See "Črkarska pravda"
"Al recibir el retrato de mi madre" (Heredia) **209**:138
"Al sol" (Espronceda)
See "Himno al sol"
"Al sol" (Heredia) **209**:119-20, 129
Al través de los libros amó siempre (Silva) **114**:263
Alaric at Rome: A Prize Poem (Arnold) **218**:155-56
Alarcos (Disraeli)
See *The Tragedy of Count Alarcos*
Alarcos (Schlegel) **45**:287, 327
"Alastor" (Browning) **79**:113
"Alastor; or, The Spirit of Solitude" (Shelley) **18**:326-27, 331, 334, 344, 358, 361, 363, 365, 369, 380, 383
Alastor; or, The Spirit of Solitude, and Other Poems (Shelley) **18**:313; **93**:275, 283, 287-88, 290-91, 356, 369-77; **143**:200; **175**:215, 246-47, 337
"Albanos Traum" (Jean Paul) **7**:234
"L'albatros" (Baudelaire) **55**:18, 48-51, 53, 55-6, 64; **155**:95
"Albert and Emily" (Beddoes) **3**:33; **154**:9-11, 54, 67-68
Albert Savarus (Balzac) **153**:8, 147
"Albert und Concordia" (Arnim) **159**:63
"Albertine's Wooers" (Hoffmann) **2**:342
Albertus, ou l'âme et le péché: légende théologique (Gautier) **1**:339, 342-43, 347, 350; **59**:17-19, 39, 70
Die Albigenser (Lenau) **16**:263, 266, 268-70, 272, 274-75, 277, 280-81
The Albigenses (Maturin) **6**:325-28, 332-34, 341
The Albigenses: A Romance (Maturin) **169**:10, 13, 24, 39-46, 50, 71, 73-74, 120, 122-23
"Albina M'Lush" (Willis) **194**:298-99
"Albion and Marina" (Brontë) **105**:54
"Albor" (Isaacs) **70**:311
"El album" (Larra) **17**:282
Album cubano de lo bueno y lo bello (Gómez de Avellaneda) **111**:7, 30, 33, 57, 64-6
"Album de la ciudad. El Fénix" (Casal) **131**:263
Album de vers et de prose (Mallarmé) **4**:376
Album de Vers et Prose (Mallarmé) **210**:264
Album d'un Voyageur (Liszt) **199**:304, 307
Album für die Jugend (Schumann) **143**:98
Album Verses, with a Few Others (Lamb) **10**:405; **113**:166, 283-84
Album zutique (Verlaine) **230**:171
"Albums" (Laforgue) **221**:82
"Alcaics" (Clough) **27**:104
Alcanor (Cumberland) **167**:158
"Alcedama Sparks; Or, Old and New" (Cooke) **110**:37, 43
"Alceo" (Foscolo)
See "Alceus"
"Alceus" (Foscolo) **8**:266, 268; **97**:51-52
"Alchemy of the Logos" (Rimbaud)
See "Alchimie du verbe"
"Alchemy of the Word" (Rimbaud)
See "Alchimie du verbe"
"Alchimie de la douleur" (Baudelaire) **55**:65
"Alchimie du verbe" (Rimbaud) **35**:268, 317-20; **82**:222-23, 227, 231, 237, 240-41, 245, 247; **227**:196, 210, 213, 278, 280-81, 293, 313, 315-16, 319, 327
"L'alchimiste" (Bertrand) **31**:48-9
L'Alchimiste (Dumas)
See *The Alchymist*
The Alchymist (Dumas) **11**:47; **71**:192-93
"Alciphron" (Moore) **6**:386
"Alcove" (Barbauld)
See "Verses Written in a Alcove"
Alcuin: A Dialogue (Brown) **22**:23, 45; **74**:7, 9, 14-15, 19, 28-30, 32, 47, 50, 54, 134, 151-57, 182
"Alcyone" (Lampman) **25**:186, 189, 193-94, 216-17, 219; **194**:47, 90
Alcyone and Other Poems (Lampman) **25**:169, 183-84, 199; **194**:24-25, 51-52, 62, 67, 69-70, 76-78, 120, 138
"La aldeana infiel" (Isaacs) **70**:306
Aldomen (Senancour) **16**:438, 445, 447-48
Aleid (Multatuli) **165**:345
"Alexander and Zenobia" (Brontë) **4**:44
Alexander the Kind (Eminescu) **33**:265; **131**:292
"Alexander von Humboldt" (Taylor) **89**:308
Alexandru Lăpuşneanu (Eminescu) **33**:265, 267; **131**:292
"Alexis und Dora" (Goethe) **90**:109
"Alfarabi" (Beddoes) **3**:33; **154**:53
"Alfieri and Italian Drama" (Lewes) **25**:285
"Az alföld" (Petofi) **21**:262, 285
"Alföldi utazás" (Madach) **19**:369
Alfonso, King of Castile (Lewis) **11**:302, 305
Alfonso Munio (Gómez de Avellaneda) **111**:4, 12, 24, 28
"Alfoxden, 1798" (Wordsworth) **206**:332
Alfoxden Journal (Wordsworth) **25**:396, 400, 404-06, 408-09, 411, 412, 416-17, 419
"Alfred and Jennet" (Bloomfield) **145**:159
Alfred Hagart's Household (Smith) **59**:295, 299, 314, 319, 332
The Algerine Captive; or, The Life and Adventures of Doctor Updike Underhill: Six Years Prisoner among the Algerines (Tyler) **3**:572-75, 577-78
Älgskyttarne (Runeberg)
See *Elgskyttarne*
The Alhambra (Irving) **2**:371, 377-80, 383-84, 387-88; **19**:332; **95**:239, 280
"Al-Hassan" (Mangan) **27**:284
"Alice Doane's Appeal" (Hawthorne) **17**:137; **39**:180-81; **95**:128, 132, 137, 139; **171**:270; **191**:276
"Alice Du Clos" (Coleridge) **177**:160
"Alice Fell" (Wordsworth) **12**:430; **111**:213
Alice in Wonderland (Dodgson)
See *Alice's Adventures in Wonderland*
Alice; or, the Mysteries (Bulwer-Lytton) **1**:140; **45**:21, 23, 28-9, 68
Alice Through the Looking Glass (Dodgson)
See *Through the Looking-Glass and What Alice Found There*
Alice's Adventures in Wonderland (Dodgson) **2**:106-15, 118-20; **53**:37-155; **139**:4, 7, 15, 22-26, 32-33, 35, 40, 43-45, 48, 50, 52, 57, 59, 64, 67-68, 72, 76, 80, 83-86, 88-90, 92-94, 96, 98-99, 101, 107-12, 114-21, 124, 126, 131-58
Alice's Adventures Under Ground (Dodgson) **139**:35, 44, 86, 108, 112, 138, 140-41, 147
Alide: An Episode of Goethe's Life (Lazarus) **8**:414, 425; **109**:289, 292, 297, 301, 323
"The Alien Boy" (Robinson) **142**:137, 249-50
Alien Bread (Turgenev)
See *Nakhlebnik*
The Alienated Manor (Baillie) **71**:64
"Alina" (Karamzin) **173**:266
Aline et Valcour (Sade) **3**:468, 478, 481, 491, 495-96; **47**:305, 309, 311, 314-16, 328, 335
Alix (Feuillet) **45**:75, 79
"All About Lovers" (Parton) **86**:367
"All Alone" (Robinson) **142**:137, 149-50, 152, 249-51, 278
"All Alone Along the Road I Am Walking" (Lermontov)
See "Alone I Go along the Road"
"All Along the Village Street" (Petofi)
See "A faluban utcahosszat"
"All' amica risanata" (Foscolo) **8**:265, 268, 270, 277
"All Heaven Is Blazing Yet" (Rossetti) **50**:314-5
"All in Honour" (Smith) **59**:257
All in the Dark (Le Fanu) **9**:302; **58**:271
All in the Family, or the Married Fiancée (Griboedov)
See *Svoia sem'ia, ili Zamuzhniaia nevesta*
"All in the Family Way" (Moore) **110**:172
All in the Wrong. A Comedy. As it is Acted at the Theatre-Royal in Drury-Lane. By Mr. Murphy (Murphy) **229**:222, 243-44
"All Men Are Born Free And Equal" (Crawford) **127**:222, 225, 227
All On a Summer's Day (Inchbald) **62**:143, 145, 147
All Religions Are One (Blake) **57**:89; **127**:5, 124; **173**:9; **190**:42; **201**:34
"All Saints" (Rossetti) **50**:312
"All Souls' Day" (Silva)
See "Día de difuntos"

"All the letters I can write" (Dickinson) **77**:145-46
All the World a Mask (Boker)
See *The World a Mask*
All the Year Round (Dickens) **187**:26
"All Things Are Current Found" (Thoreau) **7**:383
"Alla Luna" (Leopardi) **129**:350
"Alla musa" (Foscolo) **8**:280
"Alla primavera o delle favole antiche" (Leopardi) **129**:232, 246, 251, 328, 352-53, 357
"Alla sera" (Foscolo) **8**:279; **97**:67
"Alla sua donna" (Leopardi) **129**:290-91, 293, 295, 297, 350, 357
"Alla sua donna lontana" (Foscolo) **8**:278
"Alla vita abbozzata di Silvio Sarno" (Leopardi) **129**:335
"L'allée" (Verlaine) **2**:628; **51**:378, 380
"Une allée du Luxembourg" (Nerval) **67**:306
"The Allegash and East Branch" (Thoreau) **207**:254
Allegoric Vision (Coleridge) **231**:85, 88
"Allégorie" (Baudelaire) **6**:80; **55**:14, 74, 77
"Allégorie" (Verlaine) **230**:164
Allerhöchstdieselben (Börne) **193**:4
Allerlei Glück (Fontane) **163**:169
Allerley (Schumann) **143**:138
Allerton and Dreux; or, the War of Opinion (Ingelow) **39**:263
"An Alley in Flanders" (Desbordes-Valmore)
See "Une Ruelle de Flandres"
"Allez en paix" (Desbordes-Valmore) **97**:13
"Allgegenwart" (Grillparzer) **102**:174
"Die Allgegenwart Gottes" (Klopstock) **225**:308
Das Allgemaine Brouillon (Novalis) **178**:40, 86-88, 108, 117-18, 126-28
"Alligator Killing" (Thorpe) **183**:356
"All'Italia" (Leopardi) **129**:218-20, 316, 328, 330
"Allocution to Poetry" (Bello)
See "Alocución a la Poesia"
"Allouma" (Maupassant) **83**:201-02
"All's Well that Ends Well" (Lamb) **125**:304
"El alma cubana" (Martí) **63**:159-60
"El alma de la rosa" (Silva) **114**:299
"Alma Mater" (Levy) **59**:86
"Al-Mamon" (Gogol) **5**:227
The Almanach-Monger (Pushkin) **3**:434
Almanacks (Emerson) **66**:186-8, 190-5, 197, 221-2
Almansor (Heine) **147**:166-67
Almansur (Tieck) **5**:523
"Las almas muertas" (Silva) **114**:300
Las almas muertas (Silva) **114**:267
"Almeria" (Edgeworth) **1**:267; **51**:89-90
"Alnwick Castle" (Halleck) **47**:55-59, 64, 67, 69, 73, 79, 83, 86
Alnwick Castle and other Poems (Halleck) **47**:71
"Alocución a la Poesia" (Bello) **131**:93, 102-7, 109, 111, 113, 119
"Alone" (Osgood) **141**:334
"Alone" (Poe) **117**:225, 227, 268
"Alone I Go along the Road" (Lermontov) **5**:295; **126**:144
"Alone in the Forest" (Traill) **31**:328
"Alone Upon Zamorna's Plain" (Brontë) **109**:30
"Along the Pasig" (Rizal) **27**:425
"Along the River Rontanka" (Bestuzhev)
See "Vdol' Fontanki-reki"
"Alonzo the Brave and the Fair Imogene" (Lewis) **11**:297, 300, 311
Aloys und Imelde (Brentano) **1**:102; **191**:38
Der Alpenkönig und der Menschenfeind (Raimund) **69**:5, 8-10, 12-13, 18, 22, 25-6, 34-5, 38, 43-6, 48, 50, 53, 58-61
"Alphonse et Dalinde, ou la Féerie de l'Art et de la Nature" (Genlis) **166**:33, 36
"Alphonso of Castile" (Emerson) **98**:179
"An Alpimalyan Dialogue" (Turgenev) **21**:431
Alpine Roses (Boyesen)
See *Ilka on the Hill-Top*
"Alpine Spirit's Song" (Beddoes) **154**:47
The Alp-king and the Misanthropist (Raimund)
See *Der Alpenkönig und der Menschenfeind*
"The Alps" (Tyutchev) **34**:381
"The Alps at Daybreak" (Rogers) **69**:67
"Alpuhara" (Mickiewicz)
See "Alpujarra"
"Alpujarra" (Mickiewicz) **3**:398
La Alpujarra (Alarcon) **1**:12, 14; **219**:18, 28
Alroy (Disraeli)
See *The Wondrous Tale of Alroy*
"Als er sein Weib und's Kind an Ihrer Brust Schlafend Fand" (Claudius) **75**:192
Also a Philosophy of the History for the Education of Mankind (Herder)
See *Auch eine Philosophie der Geschichte zur Bildung der Menschheit*
"Also on Humor and Style Therein" (Almqvist)
See "Aven om humor och stil däri"
"Alt paa sin rette Plads" (Andersen) **79**:30, 54; **214**:56-57
"Altdeutsche Landsleute" (Arnim) **159**:63
Das alte Buch und die Reise ins Blaue hinein (Tieck) **5**:519
"Der alte Garten" (Eichendorff) **225**:45
Der alte Leibkutscher Peter des Dritten (Kotzebue) **25**:139-40
Der alte Mann mit der jungen Frau (Nestroy) **42**:230, 233
Das alte Siegal (Stifter) **41**:336, 379
"Das alte Siegel" (Stifter) **198**:259-60
"Der Alte Turmhahn" (Mörike) **10**:447, 453
Der alte Turmhahn: Idyll (Mörike) **201**:253, 267, 318, 349, 353, 366, 370
"Alte und neue Kirchenmusik" (Hoffmann) **183**:188, 224, 310
Der Alte vom Berge (Tieck) **5**:519
Altenglisches Theatre (Tieck) **5**:520; **46**:359
Älteste Urkunde des Menschengeschlechts (Herder) **186**:13, 18, 84-85, 87, 91-93, 98
"Although I put away his life-" (Dickinson) **77**:65
Altiora Peto (Oliphant) **47**:278-79, 281, 284-85
Alton Locke, Tailor and Poet (Kingsley) **35**:203-04, 209, 213-15, 220-23, 227, 228, 230-31, 233-34, 235-37, 240-41, 242, 244, 246-48, 249-53, 254-56
Altorf (Wright) **74**:363
"Ałushta at Night" (Mickiewicz)
See "Ałuszta w nocy"
"Ałushta in Daytime" (Mickiewicz)
See "Ałuszta w dzień"
"Ałuszta at Day" (Mickiewicz)
See "Ałuszta w dzień"
"Ałuszta at Night" (Mickiewicz)
See "Ałuszta w nocy"
"Ałuszta w dzień" (Mickiewicz) **3**:403
"Ałuszta w nocy" (Mickiewicz) **3**:403-04
The Alvareda Family (Caballero)
See *La familia de Alvareda: Novela original de costumbres populares*
"Always with You" (Isaacs)
See "Siempre contigo"
Alwin (Fouqué) **2**:267
Alwyn (Holcroft)
See *Alwyn, or The Gentleman Comedian*
Alwyn, or The Gentleman Comedian (Holcroft) **85**:206, 215, 218, 228, 234, 236-37, 239-40, 243
Alzuma. A Tragedy. As Performed at the Theatre-Royal in Covent-Garden (Murphy) **229**:259
"Am Brunnen vor dem Tore" (Muller) **73**:374, 380-85, 387, 391-92, 394
"Am drei: Sonntag nach Ostern" (Droste-Hülshoff) **3**:196
"Am Feierabend" (Muller) **73**:364, 370
"Am Feste Mariae Lichtmess" (Droste-Hülshoff) **3**:196
"Am Himmelstor" (Meyer) **81**:143, 162
"Am I" (Laforgue)
See "Suis-je"
Am Kamin (Storm) **1**:542, 544; **195**:70
"Am Neujahrstag" (Droste-Hülshoff) **3**:202
Am olam (Smolenskin) **30**:186-88, 192-93, 198
"Am Quell der Donau" (Hölderlin) **16**:175, 195
"Am Sylvester" (Meyer) **81**:157
"Am Tage der Freundschaftsfeier" (Hölderlin) **16**:174
"Am Turme" (Droste-Hülshoff) **3**:202
"Am Walde" (Mörike) **201**:285, 293
"Am Wassersturz" (Meyer) **81**:142
Amadis (Gobineau) **17**:83
Amadis of Gaul (Southey) **97**:267-68
"Amandar" (Cooke) **110**:43
"Les amants de Kandahar" (Gobineau) **17**:70, 92-3, 103
"Les Amants de Montmorency" (Vigny) **102**:368
Amaryllis (Jefferies)
See *Amaryllis at the Fair*
Amaryllis at the Fair (Jefferies) **47**:91-93, 95, 97, 101-06, 113, 116, 118, 120, 122, 134, 137, 140, 142-43, 145
The Amateur Emigrant from the Clyde to Sandy Hook (Stevenson) **5**:414; **47**:88, 90, 100-02, 111-12, 114, 121, 126-27, 133-34; **193**:220, 353, 356-57
"The Amateur Emigrant" (Stevenson) **193**:303-4, 310
"Amatsu otome" (Ueda Akinari) **131**:20-22, 55
Amaury (Dumas) **71**:204
"The Amazon" (Leskov)
See "Voitel' nica"
Ambarvalia (Clough) **27**:41, 43, 76-7, 91, 98, 104-7, 114
Ambarvalia (Prescott) **163**:32, 52, 54, 63, 84, 108, 136
The Ambassador's Wife (Gore) **65**:20
The Ambiguities (Melville)
See *Pierre; or, The Ambiguities*
L'ambitieux (Scribe) **16**:388, 414
"Ambition" (Lampman) **25**:201, 208, 220; **194**:15, 19
"The Ambitious Guest" (Hawthorne) **171**:342-43
The Ambitious Ones (Scribe)
See *L'ambitieux*
Ambras Américas (Sarmiento) **123**:268, 273, 275-77
"Ambrosio, of The Monk" (James)
See *The Monk, a Romance*
"Ambuscades" (Kirkland) **85**:265
"Ambush" (Mickiewicz)
See "Czaty"
"L'ame de la maison ou la vie et la mort d'un grillon" (Gautier) **59**:31
"L'ame du vin" (Baudelaire) **6**:129; **55**:2
"L'âme errante" (Desbordes-Valmore) **97**:29
"Ame et jeunesse" (Desbordes-Valmore) **97**:6
Amelia (Cumberland) **167**:136, 154
Amelia (Patmore) **9**:343
"Amelia Webster" (Austen) **119**:13
Amélie et Germaine (Constant) **6**:223; **182**:169
"Amen!" (Rossetti) **50**:268
Amenities of Literature, Consisting of Sketches and Characters of English Literature (D'Israeli) **217**:285-87, 295, 298-99, 301, 303, 333, 336
"América" (Bello) **131**:109
America: A Prophecy (Blake) **173**:152, 157; **190**:11, 14, 36, 123; **201**:21, 29, 41-46, 54, 57, 92-93, 122-23
America: A Prophecy, 1793 (Blake) **13**:159, 163, 167, 183, 214-15, 217, 222, 233, 251-52; **37**:4, 33, 51; **57**:56; **127**:11, 77-8
"America, Commerce, and Freedom" (Rowson) **182**:281-82, 313, 330-31, 353, 357
America Libera (Alfieri) **101**:48-50

"America; or, A Poem on the Settlement of the British Colonies" (Dwight) **13**:275, 277
America Revisited (Sala) **46**:234
"America to Great Britain" (Allston) **2**:21
"American Antiquities" (Barlow) **223**:52-55
"American civilization" (Emerson) **98**:43-4, 49, 171
"American Claimant" (Hawthorne) **39**:245
The American Crisis (Paine) **62**:247-8, 250, 265, 270, 281, 312, 321-2, 353, 364-71, 391
The American Democrat; or, Hints on the Social and Civic Relations of the United States of America (Cooper) **203**:49, 55, 72-73, 163
The American Democrat; or, Hints on the Social and Civil Relations of the United States of America (Cooper) **1**:216-17; **54**:256, 288-90, 300
An American Dictionary of the English Language . . . (Webster) **30**:391, 393-401, 407, 409-14, 419
"The American Drama" (Poe) **55**:172, 182
The American Frugal Housewife (Child) **6**:198-99; **73**:40, 50, 58, 66-7, 75, 86, 96, 129
The American Fugitive in Europe: Sketches of Places and People Abroad (Brown)
See *Three Years in Europe; or, Places I Have Seen and People I Have Met*
The American Gardener (Cobbett) **49**:110, 150, 156
"The American Ideal Woman" (Kirkland) **85**:270, 272
"American Independence" (Freneau) **111**:142
"The American Legend" (Taylor) **89**:302
"American Liberty" (Freneau) **111**:139
"American Literature" (Lazarus) **109**:295, 305
"American Literature" (Lippard) **198**:134
"American Literature, Its Position in the Present Time, and Prospects for the Future" (Fuller) **211**:92, 201, 203
"An American Love Ode" (Warton) **118**:356
American Notebooks (Hawthorne)
See *Passages from the American Note-Books of Nathaniel Hawthorne*
American Notes (Dickens)
See *American Notes for General Circulation*
American Notes for General Circulation (Dickens) **3**:143-44; **113**:145; **219**:64-65, 67, 72, 75-76, 83, 112, 134, 184-85, 188-93, 234
"The American Novelist and His Public" (Boyesen) **135**:20, 22
"The American Pantheon" (Cranch) **115**:22, 41
An American Primer (Whitman) **4**:576-77, 580; **31**:374; **81**:286, 309, 311, 326, 347
The American Republic (Brownson) **50**:35, 52-3, 65, 67-8
The American Rushlight (Cobbett)
See *The Rush-Light*
"The American Scholar" (Emerson) **1**:285-87, 299, 306-07; **38**:158, 186, 206, 208, 218-22; **98**:9, 12, 17-19, 21, 26-27, 63, 107, 113, 144, 150, 152-53, 160, 190
The American Scholar (Parker) **186**:192
An American Selection of Lessons in Reading and Speaking (Webster)
See *A Grammatical Institute, of the English Language, Comprising, an Easy, Concise, and Systematic Method of Education, Designed for the Use of English Schools in America*
The American Senator (Trollope) **6**:461, 466, 477, 518; **33**:363; **101**:251, 253, 257, 292, 309, 327; **215**:200, 210-11, 213, 215, 229, 232-33, 283
American Silvas (Bello)
See *Silvas Americanas*
"American Slavery" (Emerson) **98**:43, 45
"The American Soldier" (Freneau) **111**:124, 191
The American Spelling Book (Webster)
See *A Grammatical Institute, of the English Language, Comprising, an Easy, Concise, and Systematic Method of Education, Designed for the Use of English Schools in America*
"An American Tale" (Williams) **135**:315
The American Tar (Rowson) **69**:140-41
The American Tar, or the Press Gang Defeated (Rowson) **182**:281, 353
"The American Union" (Garrison) **149**:256
"The American Village" (Freneau) **1**:320, 324; **111**:100, 108, 139, 143, 146-51, 166
The American Woman's Home; or, Principles of Domestic Science (Beecher) **30**:15, 17, 22-4
American Women: Will You Save Your Country (Beecher)
See *The Duty of American Women to Their Country*
"American Writers" (Neal) **161**:307
Americans in England; or Lessons for Daughters (Rowson) **182**:281
Americans in England; or, Lessons for Daughters (Rowson) **69**:140-41
"America's Mightiest Inheritance" (Whitman) **81**:286-87, 292, 294-95
"Les ames du purgatoire" (Mérimée) **6**:360, 363, 366, 369-70; **65**:48-50, 53-9, 61, 63-4, 102, 105, 121
Les âmes vaillantes (Dumas) **71**:217, 221-22
"Âme vers Dieu, pensez à moi" (Verlaine) **230**:167
Améthystes (Banville) **9**:17, 28
"L'ami d'enfance" (Desbordes-Valmore) **97**:28
L'ami des femmes (Dumas) **9**:223-24, 226, 230-31, 245-46, 249, 253
An Amicable Division (Turgenev)
See *Zavtrak u predvoritelya*
An Amicable Settlement (Turgenev)
See *Zavtrak u predvoritelya*
"Amicus Redivivus" (Lamb) **10**:435-36
Amiel's Journal: The Journal Intime of Henri-Frédéric Amiel (Amiel)
See *Fragments d'un journal intime*
Les amies (Verlaine) **2**:621, 632; **51**:363; **230**:169, 178
"Les amies de pension" (Villiers de l'Isle Adam) **3**:588
"El amigo de la muerte" (Alarcón) **219**:18
"Amigos vellos" (Castro) **3**:101
Amistad funesta (Martí) **63**:85, 92
Ammalat-bek (Bestuzhev) **131**:152, 160-64, 186, 200
"Ammerkungen zum Antigonä" (Hölderlin) **187**:281
"Ammerkungen zum Oedipus" (Hölderlin) **187**:281-82
"Amnistie" (Desbordes-Valmore) **97**:30
Among Friends One Always Comes to Terms (Ostrovsky)
See *Svoi lyudi—sochtemsya!*
"Among Lowell Mill Girls" (Larcom) **179**:186, 190, 195
Among My Books (Lowell) **2**:509; **90**:219
"Among the Euganean Hills" (Symonds) **34**:352
"Among the Hills" (Whittier) **8**:521, 525; **59**:361, 371
Among the Hills, and Other Poems (Whittier) **8**:501; **59**:357, 360
"Among the Millet" (Lampman) **194**:58, 63
Among the Millet, and Other Poems (Lampman) **25**:160-61, 168-69, 176, 178, 180, 183, 192, 194-95, 199, 212; **194**:3, 5, 19, 22, 52-53, 55-61, 63, 67, 72-73, 76-77, 93, 95, 97, 115, 123, 128, 131, 133, 138
"Among the Multitude" (Whitman) **81**:329; **205**:219
"Among the Orchards" (Lampman) **25**:167
"Among the Timothy" (Lampman) **25**:160, 168, 183, 196, 198-200, 207, 219; **194**:14, 19, 23, 31, 42, 47-48, 50, 58, 63-66, 84, 88-89, 91, 93, 103, 139
"Among the Trees" (Bryant) **6**:168, 174, 187; **46**:15, 19
Amor con Amor se Paga (Martí) **63**:103
Amor de padre (Martínez de la Rosa) **102**:230, 245-47
"Amor en el claustro" (Casal) **131**:264
"Amor eterno" (Isaacs) **70**:307, 311
"Amor mundi" (Rossetti) **2**:562; **50**:272; **66**:305; **186**:272, 338
"Amor Vitae" (Lampman) **25**:218; **194**:76
L'amore delle tre melarance (Gozzi) **23**:107, 113-14, 117-20, 122-25, 127, 129
"Amore e Morte" (Leopardi) **129**:217, 219-20, 357, 360
"Amores catiros" (Castro) **78**:42
"Amores de Soledad" (Isaacs) **70**:306
Amorina (Almqvist) **42**:6, 10, 14, 16-17
Amoroso, King of Little Britain (Planché) **42**:272, 285
"Amos Barton" (Eliot)
See "The Sad Fortunes of the Rev. Amos Barton"
"L'Amour" (Desbordes-Valmore) **97**:5
"Amour" (Maupassant) **83**:174
L'amour (Michelet) **31**:214, 218, 222, 224-25, 260-62; **218**:303-4
Amour (Verlaine) **2**:618-19, 628, 632; **51**:351-2, 355, 359, 361-2, 266-8, 370, 372; **230**:160, 165, 167, 169, 171, 178, 183, 207-11
L'Amour Africain (Mérimée) **65**:52, 58, 62, 79, 82
L'amour au 18e siècle (Goncourt and Goncourt) **7**:165
"L'amour de mensonge" (Baudelaire) **29**:101; **55**:23
"L'amour et le crâne" (Baudelaire) **6**:80; **55**:27, 74, 80
L'amour et le grimoire (Nodier) **19**:379
L'amour impossible (Barbey d'Aurevilly) **1**:71; **213**:5, 30, 46, 96, 98-100
"Amour joie et fléau du monde" (Gautier) **59**:17
"L'amour multiforme et large" (Verlaine) **230**:169
"L'amour par terre" (Verlaine) **51**:378, 382
"L'amour suprême" (Villiers de l'Isle Adam) **3**:591
"Amoureuse du Diable" (Verlaine) **230**:167
Les amoureuses (Daudet) **1**:238, 243, 248-50
"Les Amours" (Laforgue) **221**:23
Amours de Gervais et d'Eulalie (Nodier) **19**:402
Les Amours de Philippe (Feuillet) **45**:83, 85, 91
"Les amours de Vienne" (Nerval) **67**:363
Amours de Voyage (Clough) **27**:42-3, 46-9, 52, 56-8, 62, 65-6, 71, 73, 77-82, 92, 97-8, 103, 108-10, 112-16
Amours de Voyage (Prescott) **163**:8-11, 27-29, 31-33, 36-37, 41, 50-53, 55-56, 58-59, 61-64, 69, 85, 89, 96, 109-10, 117, 126-27, 129-32, 135-37, 139, 144, 147-54
Les amours forcés (Balzac) **5**:84
Les amours jaunes (Corbière) **43**:2, 4-5, 7, 11, 13, 19, 22, 24, 26-33
"The Amours of Mr. Deuceace" (Thackeray) **213**:346
Amphitryon (Kleist) **2**:438-39, 442-43, 445, 450, 454, 456, 458; **37**:217, 225, 233, 237, 239, 243, 253, 255, 267, 271-4; **222**:186, 221-22, 228-29, 231, 236, 239, 256
"Ample Make This Bed" (Dickinson) **21**:80
"Der Amtschirurgus—Heimkehr" (Storm) **195**:44-45
The Amulet (Meyer)
See *Das Amulett*
Das Amulett (Meyer) **81**:183, 186-90
"Amusements" (Crabbe) **26**:121
"Amy" (Tennyson) **65**:369
"Amy Cranstoun" (Sedgwick) **19**:444
"Amy Wentworth" (Whittier) **8**:519; **59**:360, 370-1
Amymone, a Romance of the Days of Pericles (Linton) **41**:163, 165

"Amy's Cruelty" (Barrett Browning) **61**:7, 45, 76
"An Bodmer" (Klopstock) **11**:237
An die ferne Geliebte (Beethoven) **227**:31-32, 35
"An Done" (Klopstock) **11**:237
"An Ebert" (Klopstock) **11**:220, 237
An Ebert (Klopstock) **225**:282, 284, 289
"An Fanny" (Klopstock) **11**:237
An Fanny (Klopstock) **225**:294, 296, 316, 319
An Freund und Feind (Klopstock) **225**:288, 305-7, 311
"An Giske" (Klopstock) **11**:236
An Gleim (Klopstock) **225**:298
"An Gott" (Klopstock) **11**:237
An Gott (Klopstock) **225**:294, 296
An meine Freunde (Klopstock)
See *Wingolf*
"Anacaona" (Tennyson) **202**:188
"Anacreon by the Stove" (Derzhavin) **215**:19
Anacreon's Grave (Pushkin) **3**:415
Anacreontic Songs (Derzhavin)
See *Anakreonticheskiia pesni*
"Anactoria" (Blind) **202**:13
Anakreon und die Sogenannten Anakreontischen Lieder (Mörike) **10**:449
Anakreonticheskiia pesni (Derzhavin) **215**:11-12, 16, 22
Analysis of the Influence of Natural Religion on the Temporal Happiness of Mankind (Bentham) **38**:92, 97-9
Analytical Studies (Balzac)
See *Études analytiques*
Ananda math (Chatterji) **19**:204, 211, 213-16, 218-22, 224
Ānandamath (Chatterji)
See *Ananda math*
The Anarchiad: A New England Poem (Barlow) **223**:51-55, 57-61
The Anarchiad: A New England Poem (Trumbull) **30**:352, 375, 379
Anarchichal Fallacies: Being an Examination of the Declaration of Rights Issued During the French Revolution (Bentham) **38**:52
"Anarchism" (Adams) **33**:18, 24
"Anarchy and Authority" (Arnold) **126**:7, 23, 41, 44
The Anas (Jefferson) **11**:171, 173, 199
"Anastasius" (Chivers) **49**:50
"L'anathème" (Leconte de Lisle) **29**:221, 228, 231, 235
"L'Anatomiste" (Borel)
See "Don Andréa Vésalius l'anatomiste"
The Anatomy of Dandyism, with Some Observations on Beau Brummell (Barbey d'Aurevilly)
See *Du dandysme et de George Brummell*
"The Ancestral Footstep" (Hawthorne) **2**:324, 333, 335; **171**:261
The Ancestress (Grillparzer)
See *Die Ahnfrau*
"Anchar" (Pushkin) **3**:443
L'ancien régime (Taine) **15**:425, 430, 432-33, 439, 447, 466, 474
L'ancien régime et la révolution (Tocqueville) **7**:423, 427, 432-35, 445-46, 455, 458; **63**:282, 290, 292-3, 336, 340
"L'Ancien Régime; or, The Good Old Rule" (Thomson) **18**:391-92
"Ancient and Modern Church Music" (Hoffmann)
See "Alte und neue Kirchenmusik"
"Ancient and Modern Ideas of Purity" (Patmore) **9**:342
Ancient Ballads and Legends of Hindustan (Dutt) **29**:122-23, 125-30
"Ancient Feast" (Shevchenko)
See "Tryzna"
"Ancient Idols" (Horne) **127**:276
"The Ancient Mariner" (Coleridge)
See *The Rime of the Ancient Mariner: A Poet's Reverie*
The Ancient Mariner (Coleridge)
See *The Rime of the Ancient Mariner: A Poet's Reverie*
"The Ancient Mariner" (Lampman) **194**:30
Ancient Marinere (Coleridge)
See *The Rime of the Ancient Mariner*
"The Ancient Mystic" (Tennyson)
See "The Ancient Sage"
"The Ancient of Days" (Blake) **190**:83
"The Ancient Poets" (Thoreau)
See "Homer. Ossian. Chaucer."
"An Ancient Proverb" (Blake) **13**:240; **37**:35
"The Ancient Sage" (Tennyson) **30**:226-28, 250, 254, 269-70, 275; **65**:241; **115**:257, 335, 348; **202**:290, 293, 312
Ancient Spanish Ballads, Historical and Romantic (Lockhart) **6**:292-93, 295-97
"An Ancient Tale—Roman and Olda" (Bestuzhev)
See "Starinnaia povest'—Roman i Ol'ga"
"And ar'n't I a woman?" (Truth)
See "Ar'n't I a woman?"
"And Did Those Feet in Ancient Time Walk upon England's Mountains Green?" (Blake) **13**:205
"And If the Branches" (Eminescu) **33**:247, 249
And the Weary Are at Rest (Brontë) **109**:26, 29, 38
"L'Andalouse" (Musset) **150**:232
Andante favori (Beethoven) **227**:26
"Andenken" (Hölderlin) **16**:176; **187**:185, 213, 215-19, 224, 237, 282
André (Dunlap) **2**:210-18
André (Sand) **2**:587; **42**:319-20, 335, 353; **57**:312, 317-20, 332, 367; **174**:167, 225, 228
"André Chénier" (Pushkin) **83**:298-99, 301-06
André del Sarto (Musset) **7**:271, 281; **150**:226, 329, 335, 343-44, 350
André le Savoyard (Kock) **16**:245
"Andrea del Sarto" (Browning) **19**:117, 127, 132-33, 153; **79**:98, 106, 110-11, 163-64, 170
Andrea of Hungary (Landor) **14**:165
"Andréa Vésalius" (Borel)
See "Don Andréa Vésalius l'anatomiste"
Andrede an meine Zuhörer (Arnim) **159**:47
"Andrei Kolosov" (Turgenev) **21**:377, 414, 417, 431, 438; **37**:435; **122**:242, 247, 258, 266
"Andrei Mureşanu" (Eminescu) **33**:245, 264, 266
"Andrej Kolosov" (Turgenev)
See "Andrei Kolosov"
"Andrew Rykman's Prayer" (Whittier) **8**:496, 524; **59**:366
Andrey, knyaz' Pereyaslavskii (Bestuzhev) **131**:147, 151, 182
"Andrey Kolosov" (Turgenev)
See "Andrei Kolosov"
Andrey, Prince of Pereyaslavl' (Bestuzhev)
See *Andrey, knyaz' Pereyaslavskii*
"Andromeda" (Kingsley) **35**:211-212, 219, 232
Andromeda, and Other Poems (Kingsley) **35**:205-06, 249
Andy Blake (Boucicault) **41**:28
Andy Gordon (Alger) **8**:43-44
Andy Grant's Pluck (Alger) **8**:20
Andzhelo (Pushkin) **3**:461
"L'ane" (Banville) **9**:16
"L'ane" (Maupassant) **100**:181
"Anecdote" (Karamzin)
See "Anekdot"
"Anecdote for Fathers" (Wordsworth) **12**:387, 430, 446; **111**:202, 209, 223-25, 227, 251-52, 279-81, 316, 348, 358
"An Anecdote on Byron" (Pushkin) **83**:273
"Anecdotes" (Pushkin) **83**:270
Anecdotes and Egotisms (Mackenzie) **41**:187, 189-90, 190, 192, 195, 210
Anecdotes of Eminent Painters in Spain (Cumberland) **167**:121, 140, 148
Anecdotes of Sir Walter Scott (Hogg)
See *Familiar Anecdotes of Sir Walter Scott*
Anecdotes of the Late Samuel Johnson, LL.D., During the Last Twenty Years of His Life (Piozzi) **57**:241-2, 253, 259, 265-7, 270, 275, 285, 287-97, 299, 302-4
"Anekdot" (Karamzin) **173**:268
Anfangsgründe der Tugendlehre (Huxley) **67**:214
"L'ange exilé" (Beranger) **34**:43
"L'ange, fragment épique" (Lamartine) **11**:273
"L'Ange gardien" (Desbordes-Valmore) **97**:22
"L'ange mélancolique" (Banville) **9**:14
Ange Pitou (Dumas) **71**:232, 242-43
L'ange tutélaire; ou, Le démon femelle (Pixérécourt) **39**:274, 276-77, 279, 286
"The Angel" (Blake) **13**:221; **37**:4, 11, 13, 43, 51, 78, 92
"Angel" (Lermontov) **5**:288, 292-94, 299; **126**:129, 144, 214
"Angel and Daemon" (Eminescu) **33**:245, 247; **131**:295
"Angel and Demon" (Eminescu)
See "Angel and Daemon"
El angel de la guarda (Alarcón) **219**:4
"An Angel in the House" (Hunt) **70**:264
The Angel in the House (Patmore) **9**:335-57, 342-43, 345-49, 351-52, 354-56, 361-62, 364, 366
The Angel in the House, Book I: The Betrothal (Patmore) **9**:329-33, 335-36
The Angel in the House, Book II: The Espousals (Patmore) **9**:330-32
"The Angel of Patience" (Taylor) **89**:306-07
"The Angel of the Odd" (Poe) **117**:192, 195, 217, 221-22, 224, 237-38, 242-43, 260, 280-82, 297, 299, 309, 334, 336
"El ángel y el poeta" (Espronceda) **39**:86
Angela (Dumas)
See *Angèle*
Ángela (Tamayo y Baus) **1**:565-67, 571
Angela Borgia (Meyer) **81**:199
Angèle (Dumas) **11**:43, 48, 57, 67; **71**:193
"Angelic Guidance" (Newman) **38**:345
Angelika (Storm) **1**:536, 539-40; **195**:4, 20, 94
"Angelina" (Edgeworth) **1**:255; **51**:84, 86, 88, 90; **158**:7
Angelina (Robinson) **142**:184
Angélique (Nerval) **1**:485; **67**:332, 345-47, 358, 363-64, 366
Angelo (Hugo) **161**:255
Angelo (Pushkin) **83**:339
Angelo, Tyran de Padove (Hugo) **3**:256, 269
"Angels at the foot" (Rossetti) **186**:234-35
Angels of the Family (Desbordes-Valmore)
See *Les Anges de la famille*
"The Angel's Whisper" (Chivers) **49**:49
L'angélus (Maupassant) **1**:468; **83**:168, 177-81, 224
"L'Angelus du matin" (Verlaine) **51**:369-70; **230**:163
Angelus! Prière aux Anges Gardiens (Liszt) **199**:307
Les Anges de la famille (Desbordes-Valmore) **97**:12
L'Anglais mangeur d'opium (Musset) **7**:279
"The Angle of a Landscape" (Dickinson) **21**:75
"The Angler" (Irving) **19**:327
"The Anglers" (Thackeray) **213**:327, 330
"The Angler's Farewell" (Hood) **16**:235
"The Angler's Tent" (Wilson) **5**:545, 567
The Anglo-Irish of the Nineteenth Century (Banim) **13**:141
"Angoisse" (Mallarmé) **41**:241; **210**:217
"Angoisse" (Rimbaud) **4**:487; **35**:296, 313, 323; **227**:238-39, 248, 309
"L'Angoisse" (Verlaine) **230**:190, 192, 196-98
"L'Angoisse sincère" (Laforgue) **221**:84-85, 88
"Anguish" (Rimbaud)
See "Angoisse"

"Anguish of Spirit" (Leskov)
See "Tomlenie Dukha"
Anhelli (Slowacki) **15**:348-49, 354-59, 364, 366-69
"Anianpelto" (Kivi) **30**:51
Anima Poetae. From the Unpublished Note-Books of Samuel Taylor Coleridge (Coleridge) **9**:157; **99**:77, 87; **177**:17; **231**:90
"Animal Automatism" (Huxley) **67**:16
"Animal Magnetism" (De Quincey) **198**:85, 88
Animal Magnetism (Inchbald) **62**:143-5, 147-8, 150
"Animal Tranquility and Decay" (Wordsworth)
See "Animal Tranquillity and Decay"
"Animal Tranquillity and Decay" (Wordsworth) **111**:227, 276-77
Animi Figura (Symonds) **34**:323
Die Ankläger (Klopstock) **225**:299
"Anklänge, 3" (Eichendorff) **225**:41
"Ann Lisbeth" (Andersen) **7**:37; **79**:77
"Ann Potter's Lesson" (Cooke) **110**:33
"Ann Withers: The Changeling" (Lamb) **125**:318, 326, 362-63
"Anna" (Hebbel) **43**:253
"Anna Grace" (Ferguson) **33**:293-94
Anna St. Ives (Holcroft) **85**:192-93, 206-07, 228-29, 231, 234, 236-40, 242-44
"Annabel Lee" (Poe) **1**:496, 502-03, 509; **55**:133, 136, 141; **117**:192, 195, 217, 221-22, 224, 237-38, 242-43, 260, 280-82, 297, 299, 309, 334, 336; **211**:321
Annals of a Publishing House: William Blackwood and His Sons, Their Magazine and Friends (Oliphant) **61**:171, 173, 216
Annals of Lacock Abbey (Bowles) **103**:61
Annals of Quodlibet (Kennedy) **2**:429-35
Annals of the Parish; or, The Chronicle of Dalmailing (Galt) **1**:328-37; **110**:76-82, 84-6, 88, 93-4, 96, 98, 101-2
Anne (Woolson) **82**:268-70, 272-73, 277-78, 280-81, 292-93, 308, 314-15, 322, 324-25, 327-28, 330-31, 335
Anne Bäbi Jowäger (Gotthelf)
See *Wie Anne Bäbi Jowäger haushaltet und wie es ihm mit dem Dokterngeht*
Anne Boleyn (Boker) **125**:8, 19-20, 28, 31, 36, 58, 61-62, 64-65, 76
"Anne Hathaway's Cottage" (Blind) **202**:57
Anne Hereford (Wood) **178**:280, 330, 333-34
Anne of Geierstein (Scott) **15**:307; **69**:304, 316, 329, 332, 334
Anne of Geierstein; or, The Maiden in the Mist (Scott) **209**:182, 185
Un année dans le sahel (Fromentin) **10**:226-27, 232, 240, 259; **125**:103-4, 106, 108-12, 114-15, 122, 132, 138, 146
"L'année terrible" (Banville) **9**:16
L'année terrible (Hugo) **3**:256; **161**:175-76, 179
Les Années de Pèlerinage (Liszt) **199**:304, 307, 311
"Annette Delarbre" (Irving) **2**:368, 387, 389
"Annexes" (Whitman) **4**:563; **205**:222-24
"Annie and Rhoda" (Whittier) **8**:505
"Annie of Tharaw" (Pinkney) **31**:273
"The Annihilation of Aesthetics" (Pisarev)
See "Razrushenie estetiki"
"An Anniversary" (Hayne) **94**:159
"Anno 1839" (Heine) **147**:196
"Anno Domini" (Rossetti) **2**:568
"L'annonciateur" (Villiers de l'Isle Adam) **3**:590
Annotated Correspondence (Lampman)
See *An Annotated Edition of the Correspondence between Archibald Lampman and Edward William Thomson, 1890-1898*
An Annotated Edition of the Correspondence between Archibald Lampman and Edward William Thomson, 1890-1898 (Lampman) **194**:129, 132, 140
Annotations to Lavater (Blake) **57**:63-4
"Annotations to Reynold's Discourses" (Blake) **173**:90, 149
Annotations to Swedenborg (Blake) **57**:63
Annouchka (Turgenev)
See *Asya*
"The Annoyer" (Willis) **194**:296, 299-300
"The Annual Execution" (Thackeray) **213**:327
"Annual Message to Congress, December 1, 1862" (Lincoln) **201**:169, 186, 199, 211
"Annual Message to Congress, December 3, 1861" (Lincoln) **201**:169
"The Annuals" (Thackeray) **213**:327
Annus Domini: A Prayer for Every Day in the Year (Rossetti) **50**:271, 273; **66**:305
Annus Mirabilis (Coleridge) **197**:241
"Another Complaint of Lord Pierrot" (Laforgue)
See "Autre complainte de Lord Pierrot"
"Another Defense of Woman's Great Abilities" (Kierkegaard)
See "Ogsaa et Forsvar for Qvindens hoie Anlæg"
"Another Leaf" (Bestuzhev)
See "Eshche listok"
Another Night with the National Guard (Scribe)
See *Encore une nuit de la Garde Nationale; ou, Le poste de la barrière*
Another Philosophy of the History for the Formation of Humanity (Herder)
See *Auch eine Philosophie der Geschichte zur Bildung der Menschheit*
"Another Spring" (Rossetti) **50**:293; **66**:382
"Another View of Hester" (Hawthorne) **10**:289, 297
"Another Way of Love" (Browning) **19**:127; **79**:153
Another's (Dostoevsky) **2**:168
"Anselmo, the Hermit of the Alps" (Robinson) **142**:114, 151
Ansichten der Natur, mit wissenschaftlichen Erläuterungen (Humboldt) **170**:145, 147-48, 150-51, 159-60
An Answer to Reproofs and Replies (Gladstone) **213**:117
Answer to the Bishop of Llandaff (Paine) **62**:314
"Answer to the Letter from My Beloved" (Petofi)
See "Válasz kedvesem levelére"
"A'n't a Woman?" (Neel)
See "Ar'n't I a woman?"
"The Ant Hills" (Cranch) **115**:47
"The Antagonist's Hymn" (Holmes) **81**:98
"The Antchar" (Turgenev) **21**:401
"Ante el retrato de Juana Samary" (Casal) **131**:256-58
L'antéchrist (Renan) **26**:372, 380, 402, 408
"Antéros" (Nerval) **1**:486; **67**:318, 362
Anthologia Germanica—German Anthology (Mangan) **27**:273-75, 277, 314
Anthologia Hibernica (Mangan) **27**:314
Anthologie auf das Jahr 1782 (Schiller) **39**:339, 354, 357, 386-87; **166**:126
Anthology of Classical Poetry (Mörike) **10**:457
Anthony and Cleopatra (Alfieri)
See *Antonio e Cleopatra*
Anthony Trollope: The Complete Short Stories (Trollope) **215**:236, 239
The Anthropological Principle in Philosophy (Chernyshevsky) **1**:159-60, 167
Anthropologie (Kant) **27**:249, 259-60, 262; **67**:215
Anthropology from a Pragmatic Point of View (Kant)
See *Anthropologie*
Anthropology with a Pragmatic Purpose (Kant)
See *Anthropologie*
Antichrist (Renan)
See *L'antéchrist*
"Anticipation: October, 1803" (Wordsworth) **206**:301
"Anticipation of Evil Tidings" (Beddoes) **154**:79
The Antidote (Alfieri)
See *L'antidoto*
L'antidoto (Alfieri) **101**:45, 73
Anti-Dühring (Engels)
See *Herr Eugen Dührings Umwälzung de Wissenschaft: Philosophie; Politische Oekonomie; Sozialismus*
"Antigone" (Arnold) **6**:37
Antigone (Alfieri) **101**:4-5, 11, 12, 32, 42
"The Antigone and Its Moral" (Eliot) **118**:52, 56; **199**:191
"Las antiguedades de Merida" (Larra) **17**:271
"Antike Poesie" (Mörike) **201**:310, 342, 346
"Antiker Form sich nähernd" (Goethe) **4**:193
"The Anti-Marriage League" (Oliphant) **61**:205, 215, 242; **221**:317
Anti-Monarchical Essay (Paine) **62**:271
Anti-Ovid (Wieland) **17**:417-18
"The Antiquarian" (Freneau) **111**:134
The Antiquary (Scott) **15**:259-60, 277, 284, 289, 294-95, 300, 302-03, 309-10, 317; **69**:313, 392; **209**:222, 225, 258
"Antique" (Rimbaud) **35**:322; **82**:232-33; **227**:293, 310
"The Antiquity of Freedom" (Bryant) **6**:168, 189; **46**:7, 47
Anti-Slavery Catechism (Child) **73**:60, 77, 104
The Anti-Slavery Harp: A Collection of Songs for Anti-Slavery Meetings (Brown) **2**:47; **89**:143, 182, 188
"Anti-Slavery in the United States" (Lowell) **90**:213
"The Anti-Slavery Platform" (Garrison) **149**:256
Anti-Slavery Standard (Child) **73**:51-2, 60, 69-70, 77-80, 87, 96, 105-6
"Anti-Thelyphthora" (Cowper) **94**:110
"Antonia" (Galt) **1**:327
Antonia (Sand) **57**:316
"Antonia's Song" (Hoffmann)
See "Rat Krespel"
"Antonie" (Villiers de l'Isle Adam) **3**:590
Antoniella (Lamartine) **11**:279, 286
Antonina; or, The Fall of Rome (Collins) **1**:172-73, 177, 181; **93**:19, 64
Antonio e Cleopatra (Alfieri) **101**:57-8
Antony (Dumas) **11**:42-43, 47-48, 57-58, 63, 66-67, 72, 79, 82-83, 89; **71**:184, 187, 193, 204, 209-10, 229-30, 241
"Antony and Octavius" (Landor) **14**:183
Antrag auf Errichtung der Universität Berlin (Humboldt) **134**:204-5
"Antwerp and Bruges" (Rossetti) **4**:521-22
Antwort an Andres auf seinen letzten Brief (Claudius) **75**:193
Der Anverwandten (Nestroy) **42**:233-34
Die Anweisung zum seligen Leben, oder auch die Religionslehre (Fichte) **62**:35
"Any Wife to Any Husband" (Browning) **19**:90, 127, 131, 155; **79**:163
"Anywhere Out of the World" (Baudelaire)
See "N'importe où hors du monde"
"Anzeige" (Beddoes) **154**:26-27, 32
Ao Correr da Pena (Alencar) **157**:5, 17
"Aozukin" (Ueda Akinari) **131**:13, 24, 26, 28, 34, 38, 41, 48, 71-72, 87
"La aparición" (Casal) **131**:223, 226, 236, 265-68
"Apathy" (Robinson) **142**:109
"The Ape" (Lamb) **10**:405
"Apel podobo na ogled postavi" (Preseren) **127**:312
Apéndice sobre la tragedia española (Martínez de la Rosa) **102**:246
"The Apennines" (Bryant) **46**:21-2
"Aperçus historiques, paraboles, doutes et problèmes" (Schlegel) **142**:308
Aphorismen zur Lebensweisheit (Schopenhauer) **51**:283
"Aphorisms on Man" (Hazlitt) **82**:111

Aphorisms on Man (Lavater) **142**:11, 13-15, 17-19, 24
"Das Aphoristische" (Schumann) **143**:79
"Aphrodite" (Lazarus) **109**:294
"Apocalypse" (Cowper) **8**:127
"Apollo" (Chivers) **49**:47, 53, 56, 74
"Apollo and the Fates" (Browning) **79**:185
"Apollo in Picardy" (Pater) **7**:303; **90**:245, 272, 276, 290
"Der Apollogott" (Heine) **147**:229
"An Apologetic Irenicon" (Huxley) **67**:65
Apologia of a Madman (Chaadaev)
See *Apology of a Madman*
"Apologia Pro Vita Sua" (Coleridge) **231**:72
Apologia pro Vita Sua: Being a Reply to a Pamphlet Entitled "What, Then, Does Dr Newman Mean?" (Newman) **38**:270-71, 281, 283, 285-86, 290, 292, 295-96, 299, 305, 312-14, 318-20, 322-23, 325-27, 332-42, 344, 346, 348; **99**:212, 218, 241, 243-44, 254, 256, 258-61, 266, 271, 274-76, 278, 282, 285-86, 288, 290-93, 297
Apologie d'un fou (Chaadaev)
See *Apology of a Madman*
"Apologue of Critobulus" (Landor) **14**:187
"The Apology" (Hood) **16**:206
"An Apology for Idlers" (Stevenson) **193**:203
"An Apology for the Hellenics" (Landor) **14**:189
"Apology for the Poor" (Clare) **86**:171
Apology of a Madman (Chaadaev) **197**:127, 130-31, 133, 136, 139-41, 145-46, 157-58, 164-65, 167-69
Der Aposte (Ludwig)
See *Der Kandidat*
The Apostles (Renan)
See *Les Apôtres*
"The Apostolical Christian" (Newman) **38**:304
"Apostroph" (Whitman) **205**:162
"L'apostrophe" (Balzac) **5**:78
"Apostrophe" (Mörike) **201**:318
"The Apostrophe to Twilight" (Norton) **47**:239
"Apothéose" (Laforgue) **221**:83, 91
"L'apothéose de Mouça-al-Kébyr" (Leconte de Lisle) **29**:225-26
"Apotheosis" (Alcott) **167**:51, 74
"Apotheosis" (Dickinson)
See "Come Slowly, Eden"
"Apotheosis" (Laforgue)
See "Apothéose"
Les Apôtres (Renan) **26**:378, 402, 408, 421; **145**:351
"Apparent Failure" (Browning) **19**:112
Apparition (Mallarmé) **41**:277, 279
"The Apparition of the Shade of Samuel" (Lamartine) **11**:249, 277
Apparitions (Liszt) **199**:304
An Appeal for the Indians (Child) **73**:84
Appeal in Favor of That Class of Americans Called Africans (Child) **6**:199, 203-04, 209; **73**:51, 55, 59, 68, 72, 76-7, 83-4, 86, 97, 102-07, 109, 118
"An Appeal to the Free" (Moodie) **113**:310
Appeal to the Men of Great Britain in Behalf of Women (Hays) **114**:200, 203, 206-7, 210-13, 216, 219, 223-24, 230-33, 240, 247, 254
An Appeal to the People on Behalf of Their Rights as Authorized Interpreters of the Bible (Beecher) **30**:9, 13
Appeal to the Slavs (Bakunin) **25**:45, 63; 58, 97, 106-7, 133
"Appeal to the Women of the Free States of America on the Present Crisis in Our Country" (Stowe) **195**:161
"Appearance is Against Her" (Opie) **65**:172
Appearance is Against Them (Inchbald) **62**:143, 145-7
The Appearance to Mary Magdalen (N-Town Cycle) (anonymous) **131**:321
Appel au public occidental (Comte) **54**:210
Appel aux conservateurs (Comte) **54**:210
"Appel aux Souverains" (Staël-Holstein) **91**:340, 342
"Appendix" (De Quincey) **4**:87-88
"An Apple Gathering" (Rossetti) **2**:555-6; **50**:295-7, 322; **66**:351-4, 383; **186**:272
"The Apple Orchard" (Webster) **230**:313
"Appledore" (Lowell) **2**:514
"The Apple-Tree Table" (Melville) **3**:380, 382-83
Appreciations: With an Essay on Style (Pater) **7**:299-301, 323, 330; **90**:241-42, 248, 251, 283, 288, 292, 305, 323-26, 334; **159**:257, 313
"An Apprehension" (Barrett Browning) **170**:81
The Apprentice. A Farce in Two Acts. As it is Performed at the Theatre-Royal in Drury-Lane (Murphy) **229**:241-42
The Apprentice Turned Master (More) **141**:190
"Apprenticed" (Ingelow) **39**:264
Apprenticeship (Goethe)
See *Wilhelm Meisters Lehrjahre*
"l'Appressamento della morte" (Leopardi) **129**:241
"The Approach of Summer" (Bowles) **103**:58
"Approaching Spring" (Dyer) **129**:149
Appropriate Stories (Leskov) **25**:228
"Après" (Maupassant) **83**:182
"Après la pluie" (Corbière) **43**:31
"Après le déluge" (Rimbaud) **4**:462, 466, 473, 487; **35**:322; **82**:230, 233; **227**:184, 203, 209-10, 295, 323, 326
"Après ma journée faite" (Nerval) **67**:307
Après une Lecture du Dante (Liszt) **199**:307
"L'Après-midi d'automne" (Laforgue) **221**:89
L'après-midi d'un faune (Mallarmé) **4**:371, 375-76, 380-81, 387, 389, 395-96; **41**:239, 248-50, 277-80, 294; **210**:175, 217, 234-36
Après-midi littéraires (Mallarmé) **210**:167
"April" (Lampman) **25**:165, 183, 188, 198-200; **194**:18, 47, 56, 58, 62, 73-74, 76, 82, 84, 138
"April 27th, 1865" (Lazarus) **109**:293
"April Gossip" (Jefferies) **47**:138
"April in the Hills" (Lampman) **25**:198; **194**:56, 118-19, 139
"April Night" (Lampman) **194**:51
"April Vigil" (Laforgue)
See "Veillée d'avril"
"April Voices" (Lampman) **25**:210
Apuntes biográficos de Emilia Casanova de Villaverde (Villaverde) **121**:335
Apuntes sobre el drama histórico (Martínez de la Rosa) **102**:230
"Aquarelle en cinq minutes" (Laforgue) **221**:91
"Aquarelles" (Verlaine) **51**:369, 381-83
"Aquatics" (Thomson) **18**:411
Aquis Submersus (Storm) **1**:536-37, 540-41, 546; **195**:7, 11, 16, 20, 47-52, 56-57, 67, 72, 76, 78, 80-84, 86, 133, 135-36, 139-40
"The Arab" (Slowacki) **15**:348-50
The Arab (Cumberland) **167**:122, 140, 149, 158, 190
"The Arab Horse" (Gordon) **21**:179
"The Arab Steed" (Very) **9**:372
"The Arab Warrior" (Taylor) **89**:302
"Arabella" (Crabbe) **26**:93, 128, 136
"Arabella Hardy; or, The Sea Voyage" (Lamb) **10**:417
"Arabella Stuart" (Hemans) **71**:292
Arabeski (Gogol) **5**:209, 216, 219, 240, 253; **15**:85, 94; **31**:101; **162**:27, 52, 54, 77, 82, 97
"Arabesque" (Lazarus) **109**:297
Arabesques (Gogol)
See *Arabeski*
"Arabesques de Malheur" (Laforgue) **221**:23
An Arabian Tale (Beckford)
See *Vathek*
"Arakoon" (Kendall) **12**:186, 201
"Aralven" (Kendall) **12**:183, 186, 190-91, 199, 201
Aram (Bulwer-Lytton)
See *Eugene Aram*
Araminta May (Almqvist) **42**:4
Arap Petra Velikogo (Pushkin) **3**:435, 456, 462-63; **27**:376; **83**:322-23
Araspes und Panthea (Wieland) **17**:419
"Arbor vitae" (Patmore) **9**:359, 362
L'arbore dri Diana (Da Ponte) **50**:81, 83-4
"Arbutus and Grass" (Rossetti) **50**:275
"Arc de Civa" (Leconte de Lisle) **29**:221
"Arcades Ambo" (Clarke) **19**:249-50
"Archdeacon Hare and Walter Landor" (Landor) **14**:195
Archeology of the Hebrews (Herder) **8**:306
The Archers; or, Mountaineers in Switzerland (Dunlap) **2**:212-13
Archibald Lampman: Selected Prose (Lampman)
See *Selected Prose of Archibald Lampman*
Archibald Lampman's Letters to Edward William Thomson, 1890-1898 (Lampman) **194**:106-7, 110
"Der Archipelagus" (Hölderlin) **16**:162, 174, 181, 187; **187**:237
"The Arctic Voyager" (Timrod) **25**:374
"'Arcturus' Is His Other Name" (Dickinson) **21**:71
"Ardagh" (Le Fanu)
See "The Fortunes of Sir Robert Ardagh"
"Are God and Nature Then at Strife?" (Tennyson) **30**:243
"Are these wild thoughts" (Timrod) **25**:374
"Are Women to Blame?" (Cooke) **110**:54, 63
"Are You the New Person Drawn Toward Me?" (Whitman) **31**:430; **81**:308
"Argemone" (Gordon) **21**:168, 185
L'Argent (Vallès) **71**:358, 378
L'argent des autres (Gaboriau) **14**:19-20
Argirópolis (Sarmiento) **123**:269-70, 272
Argomenti e abbozzi di poesie (Leopardi) **129**:356
Die Argonauten (Grillparzer) **1**:389; **102**:86-7, 89, 100-03, 163, 186
The Argonauts (Grillparzer)
See *Die Argonauten*
Argow le pirate (Balzac) **5**:58; **53**:23
"Argument" (Wordsworth) **206**:320
Argument of John Quincy Adams Before the Supreme Court of the United States in the Case of the United States, Appellants, vs. Cinque, and Others, Africans, Captures in the Schooner Amistad, by Lieut. Gedney (Adams) **175**:83, 85
"Aria Marcella, Souvenir de Pompei" (Gautier) **1**:344-45, 347, 353-54, 356; **59**:6, 11, 13, 32-5, 40, 42
"Ariadne" (Schlegel) **15**:226; **142**:300
"Ariadne Walking" (Hunt) **1**:415
The Arians of the Fourth Century (Newman) **38**:314, 342
"Ariel and Caliban" (Cranch) **115**:35
Ariel and Caliban, with Other Poems (Cranch) **115**:18, 23, 35, 37, 39, 42, 55
"Ariel in the Cloven Pine" (Taylor) **89**:300-01
Ariels Offenbarungen (Arnim) **159**:34, 43
"Ariettes oubliées" (Verlaine) **2**:630; **51**:351, 355, 360, 369, 381-85; **230**:205, 207
"Arion" (Schlegel) **15**:223; **142**:302
Aristipp und einige seiner Zeitgenossen (Wieland) **17**:395-96, 400-01; **177**:234, 330
"Aristocracy" (Emerson) **98**:7, 134
"The Aristocracy of Letters" (Hazlitt) **29**:148
Aristophanes' Apology (Browning) **19**:118, 131; **79**:156, 159, 174-75, 184
Aristotle: a Chapter from the History of Science (Lewes) **25**:288, 295, 310-11; **215**:86, 122
"Arithmetic" (Emerson) **98**:5
"The Ark and the Dove" (Sigourney) **21**:311
"The Arkansas Traveller" (Haliburton) **149**:289
L'arlésienne (Daudet) **1**:236, 250, 252

"Armadale" (Dumas) **71**:185
Armadale (Collins) **1**:175, 177, 179-80, 182-83, 185-86; **18**:62, 66, 69, 74, 88; **93**:4, 7-9, 36-40, 44, 46-7, 50, 53, 62, 66
"Armageddon" (Tennyson) **65**:258; **115**:247; **202**:186-87, 243
Armance; ou, Quelques scènes d'un salon de Paris en 1827 (Stendhal) **23**:349, 362, 367, 370, 374, 378, 392-98, 419; **46**:262, 296; **178**:143-46, 150, 152-54, 156-57, 165-68, 170-71, 177, 179, 190, 197, 217, 219-20, 222-23, 231
Armand (Mowatt) **74**:216
Der Arme Spielmann (Grillparzer) **1**:385-86, 390-91, 393; **102**:131-32, 139-40, 167-68, 170, 172, 176-79, 184
Der arme Wohltäter (Stifter)
See "Kalkstein"
Armed Neutrality and An Open Letter (Kierkegaard) **125**:265
Das Armenbuch (Arnim) **123**:5, 13-15, 52, 88-89, 92
Die Armennoth (Gotthelf) **117**:4, 32
"Armgart" (Eliot) **4**:107; **13**:334; **183**:64; **199**:285
"Arminius" (Wieland) **17**:396
Arminius. A Tragedy. By Arthur Murphy, Esq. (Murphy) **229**:225, 230, 259
"L'armoire" (Maupassant) **1**:449; **83**:194, 197, 222
The Armorer (Cumberland) **167**:191
Armuth, Reichtum, Schuld und Busse der Gräfin Dolores: Eine Wahre Geschichte zur lehrreichen Unterhaltung (Arnim) **5**:12-13, 16-17, 21, 23
Armuth und Edelsinn (Kotzebue) **25**:144-47
"An Army Corps on the March" (Whitman) **205**:338-39
"The Army Surgeon" (Dobell) **43**:48
Army-Chaplain Schmelzle's Journey to Flaetz (Jean Paul)
See *Des Feldpredigers Schmelzle Reise nach Fätz mit fortgehenden Noten: Nebst der Beichte des Teufels bey einem Staatsmanne*
Arnims Werke (Arnim) **159**:4
"Arnold" (Baillie) **71**:16; **151**:114
"Ar'n't I a woman?" (Truth) **94**:302, 311-12, 328, 340
"Arnulph" (Lampman) **25**:183, 220
Arrah-na-Pogue; or, The Wicklow Wedding (Boucicault) **41**:28-31, 33-4, 39, 41, 43, 49-52
Arrest of Five Members by Charles the First: A Chapter of English History Rewritten (Forster) **11**:115
"Arrival of Birds in the Spring" (Aksakov) **181**:19
"An Arrogant Bagpiper" (Castro)
See "Un arrogante gaitero"
"Un arrogante gaitero" (Castro) **78**:58
"The Arrow and the Song" (Longfellow) **2**:498; **45**:135, 140, 179
"Ars Longa Vita Brevis" (Cranch) **115**:10
"Ars Longa, Vita Brevis" (Gordon) **21**:160, 164, 181
Ars Poética (Martínez de la Rosa) **102**:226, 228-31, 238-39
"The Ars Poetica of Vojtina" (Arany)
See "Vojtina ars poetikájából"
"The Arsenal at Springfield" (Longfellow) **45**:116, 154-55
"Arsène Guillot" (Mérimée) **6**:354, 359, 362, 364, 368-70; **65**:43, 48-50, 58, 60, 62, 87, 102-3, 113
"À Arsène Houssaye" (Banville) **9**:26
"Art" (Emerson) **1**:280; **38**:173; **98**:114
"L'art" (Gautier) **1**:349; **59**:72
"Art" (Thomson) **18**:403, 420
Art (Reade)
See *Nance Oldfield*
"Art and Climate" (Wagner) **119**:249
Art and Revolution (Wagner)
See *Die Kunst und die Revolution*
L'art du dix-huitème siècle (Goncourt and Goncourt) **7**:157, 178-79, 186, 189
Art in Greece (Taine) **15**:419
Art, Literature, and the Drama (Fuller) **211**:92
Art Macguire, or the Broken Pledge (Carleton) **199**:8, 10, 19-20
"L'art moderne" (Gautier) **1**:342
"The Art of Book-Making" (Irving) **2**:368; **19**:328, 347, 350
"The Art of Coquetry" (Lennox) **134**:272, 342
Art of Lying in all its Branches (Opie) **65**:171
"Art of Poetry" (Verlaine)
See "L'Art poètique"
"The Art of Tragedy" (Schiller) **166**:181
"L'Art poètique" (Verlaine) **2**:621, 624, 629-31; **51**:351, 366, 368-70; **230**:151-52, 154, 157, 162-64, 171, 188, 203, 209, 221
"L'art poétique ad hoc" (Verlaine) **230**:164
L'art pour l'art (Dumas) **9**:233
L'art romantique (Baudelaire) **29**:70, 86; **55**:8
Art und Kunst (Herder) **186**:48
"Art under Plutocracy" (Morris) **4**:445
"Artémis" (Nerval) **1**:476, 481-82, 486; **67**:359-63
"Artemis Prologuises" (Browning) **79**:163
Arthur (Sue) **1**:560
"Arthur Gordon Pym" (Poe)
See *The Narrative of Arthur Gordon Pym, of Nantucket*
Arthur Mervyn; or, Memoirs of the Year 1793 (Brown) **22**:3-5, 7, 11-14, 18-22, 24-5, 27-8, 30-3, 40, 42, 48, 50-5, 57; **74**:4, 9, 11, 13, 15, 17, 19, 21, 36, 41, 47-8, 50-1, 54, 56-7, 61-2, 76, 80, 85, 87, 90, 92, 96-8, 101, 104, 111-14, 117-22, 124, 128-30, 133-36, 143, 161-62, 164, 175, 182; **122**:53-54, 85, 90, 116, 150, 153, 157-58
Arthur O'Leary: His Wanderings and Ponderings in Many Lands (Lever) **23**:300-01
Arthur Rimbaud: Oeuvres Complètes (Rimbaud)
See *Oeuvres complètes*
"Arthur Schopenhauer, by H. Zimmern" (Thomson) **18**:400
"The Artic Lover" (Bryant) **6**:169
Articles on the Depreciation of Silver (Bagehot) **10**:26, 31
Artificial Paradises: On Hashish and Wine as a Means of Expanding Individuality (Baudelaire)
See *Les paradis artificiels: Opium et haschisch*
The Artificial Paradises: On Hashish and Wine as a Means of Expanding Individuality (Baudelaire)
See *Les paradis artificiels: Opium et haschisch*
"The Artilleryman's Vision" (Whitman) **81**:322
"The Artist" (Crampton) **115**:40, 67
The Artist (Shevchenko)
See *Xudoznik*
"The Artist of the Beautiful" (Hawthorne) **2**:303, 329, 332; **39**:223; **158**:222; **171**:263; **226**:76
El artista barquero o los cuatro cinco de junio (Gómez de Avellaneda) **111**:14, 20, 25, 33-5
Artistic Visits or Simple Pilgrimages (Fromentin) **10**:226
"The Artists" (Schiller)
See "Die Künstler"
"The Artists" (Thackeray) **213**:243
Artists' Wives (Daudet)
See *Les femmes d'artistes*
"The Artus Exchange" (Hoffmann)
See "Der Artushof"
"Der Artushof" (Hoffmann) **183**:170, 226, 287, 298, 305
The Artwork of the Future (Wagner)
See *Das Kunstwerk der Zukunft*
Arundel (Cumberland) **167**:112, 124, 135, 140, 150
As a Strong Bird on Pinions Free and Other Poems (Whitman) **205**:226
"As Adam Early in the Morning" (Whitman) **31**:430
"As Consequent, Etc." (Whitman) **31**:388
"As duas ilhas" (Castro Alves) **205**:3, 12
"As for me, I sing and sing" (Castro)
See "Yo cantar, cantar, canté"
"As I Ebb'd with the Ocean of Life" (Whitman) **4**:582, 600; **31**:388, 405; **81**:249, 364-66; **205**:203, 207, 260, 309, 331, 336
"As I Lay with My Head on Your Lap Camarado" (Whitman) **81**:315, 331
"As I laye a-thinkynge" (Barham) **77**:17
"As I Ponder'd in Silence" (Whitman) **205**:195, 224
"As I Sat at the Cafe" (Clough) **27**:114
"As I Toilsome Wander'd Virginia Woods" (Whitman) **81**:331
"As I Walkd Forth One May Morning" (Blake) **37**:29
"As If Some Little Arctic Flower" (Dickinson) **21**:8
"As Imperceptibly as Grief" (Dickinson) **21**:67-8; **171**:186
As It Is in Heaven (Larcom) **179**:173
"As kingfishers catch fire" (Hopkins) **189**:23, 35, 37, 44, 47, 55, 86, 106, 125-31, 139-40
As Minas de Prata (Alencar) **157**:8, 16
"As much certainly woman gains" (Verlaine) **230**:176
"As on a Holiday" (Hölderlin)
See "Wie wenn am Feiertage ..."
"As Slow Our Ship" (Moore) **110**:190, 192-93
"As the ocean embraces the earthly sphere" (Tyutchev)
See "Kak okean obemlet shar zemnoi"
"As the Starved Maelstrom laps the Navies" (Dickinson) **77**:151
"As Toilsome I Wander'd Virginia's Woods" (Whitman) **205**:339
"As You Like It" (Lamb) **125**:306
"Asaji ga yado" (Ueda Akinari) **131**:6-8, 13, 24-25, 29, 34, 38-40, 49, 58, 60, 69-70, 76
"Asathor's Vengeance" (Boyesen) **135**:12, 19
Ascanio (Dumas) **71**:203
"Ascención aerostática" (Larra) **130**:233
"The Ascent of Ktaadn" (Thoreau) **207**:257
The Ascent of Man (Blind) **202**:5-7, 9-10, 24, 47-48, 50-52, 57
Aschenbrödel (Grabbe) **2**:271, 278, 287-88
"Ashaverus" (Andersen) **7**:16
"Ashboughs" (Hopkins) **17**:208, 216
Ashby Manor (Allingham) **25**:11
"Ashes denote that Fire was" (Dickinson) **171**:196
"Ashes of Roses" (Osgood) **141**:355
"Ashes of Soldiers" (Whitman) **4**:543
Ashiwake obune (Motoori) **45**:265-66, 275
Ashmat Shomeron (Mapu) **18**:287-88, 290-93, 295, 298-300
Ashtaroth (Gordon) **21**:149, 151-55, 160, 162, 172-73
"Asia" (Blake) **13**:184
Asia (Turgenev)
See *Asya*
"Eine asiatische Vorlesung" (Claudius) **75**:211, 214-15
"Asides of Pierrots" (Laforgue)
See "Pierrots"
Asja (Turgenev)
See *Asya*
Ask Mamma (Surtees) **14**:352-53, 364, 371, 374-75, 377-80
"Ask Me No More" (Tennyson) **30**:239; **202**:180, 197-98, 201
"Askalonskij zlodej" (Leskov) **25**:229, 245

"Asking a Governor to Dine" (Haliburton) **149**:318
Aslauga (Fouqué) **2**:265
Asmodeus at Large (Bulwer-Lytton) **45**:19
Asmus, omnia sua secum portans oder Sämtlich Werke des Wandsbecker Boten (Claudius) **75**:183, 192
Asolando: Fancies and Facts (Browning) **19**:110-11, 152; **79**:112-14, 153, 161, 169
Aspasia (Leopardi) **129**:304
"Aspasia; oder Die Platonische Liebe" (Wieland) **17**:427
"Aspects of the Pines" (Hayne) **94**:149, 168
"Aspiration" (Lampman) **25**:161-62, 189, 206, 209, 212; **194**:38
"Aspirations" (Verlaine) **51**:386; **230**:162, 166-67
Aspirations (Hayne) **94**:134
Aspirations of the World (Child) **6**:203; **73**:54, 72, 84
"The Ass and the Nightingale" (Krylov) **1**:435
"An Assassin" (Adams) **33**:18
"The Assassin of Society" (Cooke) **110**:35-6
"The Assignation" (Poe) **16**:304, 320, 322, 324; **117**:209-10, 281; **211**:246
"Les assis" (Rimbaud) **4**:454, 474; **35**:271, 282, 321; **227**:185
"Assisting at a Negro Night-Meeting" (Harris) **23**:159, 162
"Assommons les pauvres" (Baudelaire) **155**:56-57, 121-29
The Ass's Burial (Smolenskin)
See *Kevurat hamor*
"Assurance" (Lazarus) **109**:292
"Assurances" (Whitman) **205**:158
"Assyrian Bull" (Tennyson) **30**:215
Asthetische Briefe (Schiller) **69**:257, 260
"Asthetische Erziehung" (Schiller) **39**:380-81; **69**:206, 209-10
Ästhetische Versuche I. Über Göthes Hermann und Dorothea (Humboldt) **134**:193
Astoria (Cooper) **1**:221
Astoria (Irving) **2**:376-77; **95**:254-56, 259
Astraea: The Balance of Illusions (Holmes) **14**:102
Astray on the Path of Life (Smolenskin)
See *ha-To'eh be-darke ha-hayim*
"L'astre rouge" (Leconte de Lisle) **29**:221, 225
Asya (Turgenev) **21**:378, 409, 414, 418, 431, 435, 441; **37**:364; **122**:241-42, 245, 259, 267-68, 277, 348
"At a Dinner of Atheists" (Barbey d'Aurevilly)
See "À un dîner d' athées"
"At a Window" (Allingham) **25**:14
"At Belvoir" (Thomson) **18**:417
At Daggers Drawn (Leskov)
See *Na nožax*
"At Dawn" (Levy) **59**:95, 119
"At Dover" (Wordsworth) **206**:304, 306-9
"At Dusk" (Lampman) **25**:185, 210
"At Euroma" (Kendall) **12**:181-82
"At first a thought, embodied" (Baratynsky)
See "Snachala mysl', voploshchena"
"At Half-Past Three a Single Bird" (Dickinson) **21**:33
At His Gates (Oliphant) **61**:173, 206, 211-2, 223
"At Home" (Rossetti) **2**:565; **50**:298; **66**:307; **186**:265, 271, 334
At Home and Abroad (Taylor) **89**:308, 310, 343, 346
At Home and Abroad; or, Things and Thoughts in America (Fuller) **5**:165
At Home and Abroad; or, Things and Thoughts in America and Europe (Fuller) **211**:130
"At Last" (Cooke) **110**:3, 9
"At last, beloved Nature" (Timrod) **25**:366, 374
"At Last, To Be Identified!" (Dickinson) **21**:41
"At Midnight" (Mörike)
See "Um Mitternacht"
"At My Age, I Know . . ." (Verlaine)
See "À mon âge, je sais . . ."
"At Night" (Mörike)
See "Nachts"
"At One O'Clock in the Morning" (Baudelaire)
See "À une heure du matin"
"At Ostend" (Bowles)
See "Written at Ostend. July 22, 1787"
"At Pinney's Ranch" (Bellamy) **86**:75
"At Prato" (Levy) **203**:339
"At Sea" (Lowell) **2**:520
"At Sunset" (Lanier) **6**:238
"At Tarah To-Day" (Mangan) **27**:283
At the Beautiful Gate, and Other Songs of Faith (Larcom) **179**:174
"At the Cabaret-Vert, 5 p.m." (Rimbaud)
See "Au caberet-vert cinq heures du soir"
"At the Caberet-Vert" (Rimbaud)
See "Au caberet-vert cinq heures du soir"
"At the Chateau of Corinne" (Woolson) **82**:276, 308, 310, 341, 345
"At the Door" (Field) **3**:210
"At the Edge of the World" (Leskov)
See "Na kraju sveta"
"At the End of the World" (Leskov)
See "Na kraju sveta"
"At the End of the Year" (Petofi)
See "Az év végén"
"At the Ferry" (Lampman) **25**:169, 188; **194**:19, 23, 81
"At the Foot of the Statue" (Silva)
See "Al pie de la estatua"
"At the Forest" (Mörike)
See "Am Walde"
"At the Grave of Aron Pumnul" (Eminescu) **131**:294
"At the Grave of Burns" (Wordsworth) **38**:371
"At the Height of the Harvest" (Nekrasov) **11**:417
At the Jubilee in Lund (Tegner) **2**:613
At the Long Sault, and Other New Poems (Lampman) **25**:190, 219-20; **194**:11, 16, 71, 99
"At the Long Sault: May, 1660" (Lampman) **25**:184, 186-87, 189, 199, 201, 219; **194**:25, 42, 48
"At the Mermaid Inn" (Lampman) **25**:177, 179, 208, 218
At the Mermaid Inn: Wilfred Campbell, Archibald Lampman, Duncan Campbell Scott in The Globe, 1892-93 (Lampman) **194**:54, 60, 67, 71, 74, 90, 95-97, 105, 107, 109-10, 112, 116-17, 119, 127, 140-41
"At the Mid-Hour of Night When Stars Are Weeping I Fly" (Moore) **6**:391
"At the Pantomime" (Holmes) **14**:109, 128
"At the Polo Ground" (Ferguson) **33**:289
"At the Sun-Rise in 1848" (Rossetti) **77**:292-93, 298
"At the Tea Table" (Pavlova)
See "Za chainym stolom"
"At the Tomb of Leopoldo..." (Isaacs)
See "En la tumba de Leopoldo..."
At the University (Storm)
See *Auf der Universitat*
"At the Water's Edge" (Maupassant)
See "Au bord de l'eau"
"At the West India Docks" (Adams) **33**:16
Atala (Chateaubriand) **134**:3, 15-16, 18-19, 24, 27, 31, 33-36, 39, 46-47, 56-57, 61-63, 70, 78-79, 81, 87, 98, 102-8, 112, 116-23, 127-30, 132, 134, 136-38, 140, 143-49
"Atalanta's Race" (Morris) **4**:416, 427, 447
Atalantis (Simms) **3**:504
"Ataraxia" (Norton) **205**:70
L'Atelier d'un peintre (Desbordes-Valmore) **97**:12
Atheismusstreit (Fichte) **62**:47
The Athelings (Oliphant) **221**:226
Athenaeum Fragment 22 (Schlegel) **226**:205
Athenaeum Fragment 39 (Schlegel) **226**:170
Athenaeum Fragment 46 (Schlegel) **226**:202, 204, 206
Athenaeum Fragment 53 (Schlegel) **226**:160, 203
Athenaeum Fragment 72 (Schlegel) **226**:203
Athenaeum Fragment 91 (Schlegel) **226**:203
Athenaeum Fragment 216 (Schlegel) **226**:173
Athenaeum Fragment 220 (Schlegel) **226**:203
Athenaeum Fragment 297 (Schlegel) **226**:171
Athenaeum Fragment 336 (Schlegel) **226**:204
Athenaeum Fragment 412 (Schlegel) **226**:170, 205, 227
Athenaeum Fragment 422 (Schlegel) **226**:205
Athenaeum Fragment 423 (Schlegel) **226**:205
Athenaeum Fragment 424 (Schlegel) **226**:205
Athenaeum Fragment 425 (Schlegel) **226**:205
Athenaeum Fragment 444 (Schlegel) **226**:243
Athenaeum Fragment 447 (Schlegel) **226**:203
Athenäum Fragments (Schlegel)
See *Athenäums-Fragmente*
Athenaeum-Fragment 51 (Schlegel) **45**:360
Athenaeum-Fragment 77 (Schlegel) **45**:363
Athenaeum-Fragment 116 (Schlegel) **45**:313, 337, 344, 361-62, 366, 369; **226**:203, 245
Athenaeum-Fragment 121 (Schlegel) **45**:381; **226**:171, 247
Athenaeum-Fragment 252 (Schlegel) **45**:364
Athenaeum-Fragment 398 (Schlegel) **45**:382
Athenaeum-Fragment 426 (Schlegel) **45**:366; **226**:205
Athenaeum-Fragment 429 (Schlegel) **45**:315
Athenäums-Fragmente (Schlegel) **45**:313, 343-44, 359, 370; **226**:170-71, 173, 182-83, 199, 203, 206, 236
"Athenais" (Osgood) **141**:357-58
"Athenian Life" (Karamzin)
See "Afinskaia zhizn"
"An Athenian Reverie" (Lampman) **25**:161, 168, 177-78, 200, 206, 216, 220; **194**:4, 20, 23, 33
Athens, Its Rise and Fall (Bulwer-Lytton) **1**:138, 141, 151-52
"Athens Saved by Poetry" (Brontë) **229**:200
Atherton (Mitford) **4**:403
"Atît de frageda" (Eminescu) **33**:249, 251, 265; **131**:339
Atlanta; or, The True Blessed Island of Poesy. A Paul Epic-In Three Lustra (Chivers) **49**:44, 46-7
"The Atlantic Cable" (Ridge) **82**:175
"The Atonement" (Allston) **2**:26
"Atonement" (Taylor) **89**:309
Atrea Tiestes (Heredia) **209**:119
Atta Troll (Heine)
See *Atta Troll: Ein Sommernachtstraum*
Atta Troll: Ein Sommernachtstraum (Heine) **4**:234, 236, 239-41, 244-46, 252, 265-67; **54**:307, 320, 322; 149-50, 177
The Attaché; or, Sam Slick in England (Haliburton) **15**:120, 122, 129, 132, 135-36, 144-46; **149**:267, 270-71, 288, 290, 292-93, 295, 297-98, 318, 336, 340, 345
"Attachments of Kindred" (Beattie)
See *Dissertations Moral and Critical: On Memory and Imagination; On Dreaming; The Theory of Language; On Fable and Romance; On the Attachments of Kindred; Illustrations on Sublimity*
"Attack on Fort Sandusky" (Richardson) **55**:342
The Attack upon 'Christendom' (Kierkegaard)
See *Hvad Christus dömmer om officiel Christendom*
"An Attempt of the Author to Estimate His Own Character" (Hunt) **70**:281
"Attempt to Rebut Some Non-Literary Charges" (Pushkin) **83**:317, 320
"An Attempt to Shew the Folly and Danger of Methodism" (Hunt) **1**:406
L'attente (Maupassant) **42**:174; **83**:221
Attila, König der Hunnen: Eine romantische Tragödie in fünf Akten (Werner) **189**:326, 330-31
"Attis" (Tennyson) **30**:236
"Au bord de l'eau" (Maupassant) **1**:455

Au Bord d'une Source (Liszt) **199**:307
"Au cabaret-vert" (Rimbaud)
See "Au caberet-vert cinq heures du soir"
"Au caberet-vert cinq heures du soir" (Rimbaud) **35**:271, 275, 282
"Au lecteur" (Baudelaire) **6**:83, 108-09, 114, 122; **29**:95-6, 99; **55**:4, 19, 44-6, 49, 53, 56, 62, 67, 73-4, 78; **155**:44, 51, 77, 113
"Au lieu de songer à se créer une position" (Laforgue) **221**:93
"Au loisir" (Sainte-Beuve) **5**:347
"Au rossignol" (Lamartine) **190**:178
"Au seul souci de voyager" (Mallarmé) **210**:218-19
"Au vieux Roscoff" (Corbière) **43**:14, 32, 34
"Au Yung Frau" (Musset) **150**:232
"Aube" (Rimbaud) **4**:482; **35**:299, 322-25; **227**:203, 209, 245-47, 271, 295, 309, 330-32
"L'Aube a l'envers" (Verlaine) **51**:360-61
"L'aube spirituelle" (Baudelaire) **6**:89; **55**:14, 61
L'Auberge rouge (Balzac) **35**:26; **153**:149-50
"Auburn" (Verlaine) **230**:165
"Aucassin and Nicolette" (Pater) **159**:251, 280
"Auch die Griechen hatten ihre Teniers und Ostaden" (Wieland) **177**:261
Auch ein Beitrag über die neue Politik (Claudius) **75**:194
Auch ein Faust (Arnim) **159**:6-8
Auch eine Philosophie der Geschichte zur Bildung der Menschheit (Herder) **186**:11, 15, 18-20, 39, 84-85, 89-91, 93, 98, 101
"Les Audacieux" (Maupassant) **83**:227
Auditor (Murphy) **229**:235, 259
"Audley Court" (Tennyson) **30**:238, 279; **65**:258; **115**:335
"Audley End" (Tennyson) **115**:240
Audubon and His Journals (Audubon) **47**:24
"Auerbachs Keller" (Goethe) **4**:215
"Auf dem Canal Grande" (Meyer) **81**:206, 209
"Auf dem Fluße" (Muller) **73**:391, 394
"Auf dem Rhein" (Brentano) **191**:69
Auf dem Staatshof (Storm) **1**:539, 542; **195**:18, 38, 94
Auf der Höhe (Auerbach) **171**:5-6, 9-10, 16, 19
"Auf der Reise" (Mörike) **201**:301
Auf der Universitat (Storm) **1**:535; **195**:11-12, 18, 40, 72, 94-95
"Auf der Wanderung" (Meyer) **81**:144
"Auf die Ankunft des Grafen von Falkenstein" (Schiller) **39**:387
"Auf die Taufe eines Negers" (Schlegel) **142**:306
"Auf ein altes Bild" (Mörike) **201**:304, 347
"Auf eine Christblume" (Mörike) **10**:454-55; **201**:270-76, 284-85, 347
"Auf eine Lampe" (Mörike) **201**:273-76, 282, 304, 311, 318, 348-49, 354, 356-57, 370
"Auf eine Wanderung" (Mörike) **10**:447
"Auf einen grünen Zweig" (Brentano) **191**:36
"Auf einer Wanderung" (Mörike) **201**:368
"Auf Goldgrund" (Meyer) **81**:140-41, 150-53, 157, 206
Auf meine Freunde (Klopstock)
See *Wingolf*
"Auf Wiedersehen" (Longfellow) **45**:132
"Auf Wiedersehen" (Lowell) **2**:511
"Auferstehen ja auferstehen" (Klopstock) **225**:279
Der Aufruhr in den Cevennen (Tieck) **5**:514; **46**:397
Aufsatz, den sichern Weg des Glücks zu finden (Kleist) **222**:252
"Aufsatz, den sichern Weg des Glücks zu finden, und ungestört, auch unter den größten Drangsalen des Lebens, ihn zu genießen!" (Kleist) **37**:218, 235
"Das Auge des Blinden" (Meyer) **81**:209
L'augellin belverde (Gozzi) **23**:112-14, 118-19, 121, 123, 125
"Augure" (Desbordes-Valmore) **97**:14
"Auguries of Innocence" (Blake) **13**:172, 190, 201, 243; **173**:69; **201**:38, 46
"Augury" (Desbordes-Valmore)
See "Augure"
"August" (Clare) **9**:114
"August" (Taylor) **89**:316
"August 1849" (Prescott) **163**:86
"August Moon" (Lazarus) **109**:292, 294-95, 298
"August Night" (Musset)
See "Nuit d' Août"
"An August Pastoral" (Taylor) **89**:315, 317
"August Wilhelm Schlegel" (Lewes) **25**:285, 300
August Wilhelm von Schlegels sämmtliche Werke (Schlegel) **142**:306-9, 331-32, 334
Auguste Comte and Positivism (Mill) **11**:378; **179**:281, 310, 327
"Augustine de Villebranche ou le stratagéme de l'amour" (Sade) **47**:313
"Aul Bastundzi" (Lermontov) **47**:182
"Aulus Persius Flaccus" (Thoreau) **138**:117, 119, 128-30
"Aumône" (Mallarmé) **41**:241, 250, 291
Aunt Carry's Ballads for Children (Norton) **47**:246
Aunt Fanny (Barham) **77**:9
Aunt Jo's Scrap-Bag (Alcott) **6**:15
Aunt Jo's Scrap-Bag: My Boys (Alcott)
See *Aunt Jo's Scrap-Bag*
"Aunt Tabitha" (Holmes) **81**:104
"Aunt Toothache" (Andersen)
See "Tante Tandpine"
"Auntie Toothache" (Andersen)
See "Tante Tandpine"
"Auras of Delight" (Patmore) **9**:360
"Aurea dicta" (Patmore) **9**:344, 364
Aurélia (Nerval) **1**:476-78, 480-85, 487; **67**:303-07, 309-14, 322-25, 333-35, 338, 342, 356-58, 360-61, 363-64, 371-76
Auriol (Ainsworth)
See *Revelations of London*
Aurora (Herder) **8**:307
Aurora Leigh (Barrett Browning) **1**:118-25, 128-32; **16**:144, 147, 154; **61**:3-4, 11-2, 14-7, 19, 21, 23-4, 37-9, 44, 49, 52-3, 64, 66, 75-6; **66**:1-118; **170**:6, 10, 15-20, 23, 28, 33-35, 37, 42-49, 56, 59-60, 62, 65, 69, 72-74, 78-79, 85-86, 98, 100, 102-4, 106, 108-12, 116, 119
"L'aurore" (Leconte de Lisle) **29**:224, 244
L'Aurore-Promise (Laforgue) **53**:282
Aus dem Bayrischen Walde (Stifter) **198**:286
Aus dem Leben eines bekannten Mannes (Hoffmann) **2**:348
"Aus dem Leben eines Taugenichts" (Eichendorff) **8**:210-16, 224, 230-32
Aus dem Leben eines Taugenichts und Das Marmorbild: Zwei Novellen nebst einem Anhange von Liedern und Romanzen (Eichendorff) **225**:3-4, 8-9, 22, 27, 32, 34, 61-62, 66, 68-74, 77, 79-80, 82-87, 89-90, 92-93, 98-101, 104
Aus dem Regen in die Traufe (Ludwig) **4**:357, 367
Aus den hinterlassenen Papieren (Kotzebue) **25**:133-35
Aus der Chronika eines fahrenden Schülers (Brentano) **1**:96, 100-02, 104-05; **191**:12, 45, 47-49, 66, 70, 94-100, 103, 119, 122
"Aus der Vorzeit" (Klopstock) **11**:236
Aus Goethes Taschenbuch (Goethe) **154**:193
"Aus Groskrähwinkel. Die Beamtentöcher" (Storm) **195**:91-92
Aus meinem Leben: Dichtung und Wahrheit (Goethe) **4**:168-69, 180, 199; **154**:218, 237
Ausgewählte musikalische Werke (Hoffmann) **183**:222
Ausgewählte Schriften (Werner) **189**:328, 346-52, 356-57, 360-61, 365, 367, 369
Ausgewählte Werke (Fouqué) **2**:265
"Auspex" (Lowell) **90**:190
The Auspicious Day (Webster) **230**:235-36
Aussichten in die Ewigkeit (Lavater) **142**:12
"The Austerity of Poverty" (Arnold) **218**:138
"Austin and His Wife" (Opie) **65**:173
Austin Elliott (Kingsley) **107**:188-89, 192, 194, 209, 211, 222-23
"The Austral Months" (Kendall) **12**:200
Australia and New Zealand (Trollope) **215**:218, 309
"Australia Huzza" (Harpur) **114**:144
"The Australian Bell-Bird" (Ingelow) **39**:258
Australian Essays (Adams) **33**:13, 22, 25
Australian Life (Adams) **33**:13
"An Australian Mining Township" (Clarke)
See "Grumbler's Gully"
"Australian Scenery" (Harpur) **114**:125
The Australians (Adams) **33**:2, 13, 25
"The Austrian Influence on the Romanians in the Principalities" (Eminescu) **131**:325
"Auszug aus einem Briefwechsel über Ossian und die Lieder alter Völker" (Herder) **186**:13, 16-18, 20, 108
"Auszug aus einem Schreiben an einen Freund in D ..." (Wieland) **177**:256, 321
Authentic Anecdotes of American Slavery (Child) **73**:60, 77
"The Author of 'Saul'" (Taylor) **89**:341
"The Author's Account of Himself" (Irving) **19**:327, 347; **95**:236
"The Authors Address to his Book" (Clare) **86**:173
"The Author's Chamber" (Irving) **2**:372
"An Author's Confession" (Gogol)
See "Avtorskaya ispoved"
"Author's Introduction" (Lermontov) **5**:304
"Author's Introduction" (Shelley) **170**:206, 258, 299, 301, 364, 367
"An Author's Soliloquy" (Freneau) **111**:161
Authorship, a Tale (Neal) **161**:285, 287, 291, 302-3
"Authorship in America" (Taylor) **89**:342
Auto Mariano para recordar la milagrosa aparición de Nuestra Madre y señora de Guadalupe (Lizardi) **30**:68
Autobiografía (Gómez de Avellaneda) **111**:27, 56, 59, 61-2, 65
Autobiografía (Manzano)
See *Autobiografía, cartas y versos de Juan Fco. Manzano*
Autobiografía, cartas y versos de Juan Fco. Manzano (Manzano) **155**:277-80, 295, 298, 306, 313, 315-16, 323, 325, 332
Autobiographia Literaria, Sketches of My Literary Life and Opinions (Coleridge)
See *Biographia Literaria; or, Biographical Sketches of My Literary Life and Opinions*
Autobiographic Sketches (De Quincey) **87**:3, 14, 52, 55; **198**:6-7, 42-43, 78-80
Autobiographical Essays (De Quincey) **4**:65, 70, 79, 83, 85-86
"Autobiographical Fragment" (Dickens) **206**:39, 131
"Autobiographical Fragment" (Froude) **43**:208, 211
Autobiographical fragments (Clare) **86**:171-72, 174
"Autobiographical Memoir" (Newman) **38**:299, 333
"Autobiographical Preludes" (Laforgue)
See "Préludes autobiographiques"
"Autobiographical Sketch" (James) **53**:233
"Autobiographical Sketches" (Derzhavin) **215**:7
Autobiographical Writings (Clare) **86**:109, 151-53, 156-57, 177, 179
Autobiographical Writings (Newman) **38**:299, 333; **99**:286
"Autobiographie" (Mallarmé) **210**:243, 245, 263
"Autobiographie" (Verlaine) **230**:161
"Autobiography" (Clare) **86**:108
"Autobiography" (Cranch) **115**:23
"Autobiography" (De Quincey) **87**:48

"Autobiography" (Huxley) **67**:16, 48, 51-2
Autobiography (Adams) **106**:4, 26-31
Autobiography (Alfieri)
See *Vita*
Autobiography (Galt)
See *The Autobiography of John Galt*
Autobiography (Gómez de Avellaneda)
See *Autobiografía*
Autobiography (Madison) **126**:235, 312
Autobiography (Manzano)
See *Autobiografía, cartas y versos de Juan Fco. Manzano*
Autobiography (Martineau) **26**:311, 315-16, 318, 322-23, 327-28, 330, 338, 341-47, 349, 352, 357; **137**:236, 242, 245-47, 256, 271-72, 277-79, 281-82, 285, 290, 292-95, 297, 299, 301-3, 315-17, 324-27, 329-36, 356-57, 360
Autobiography (Mill) **11**:351, 353-58, 361, 366-70, 393-94; **58**:319-20, 327, 333, 336-37, 339, 351, 356-59, 361, 375, 378-79; **179**:203, 206, 208, 211, 213, 219-27, 283, 287, 294, 301-4, 316, 327-28, 330-34, 340-41, 346, 354-55, 357-62; **223**:106, 113, 127, 135
Autobiography (Symonds)
See *The Memoirs*
An Autobiography (Trollope) **6**:467, 475, 478, 483-85, 491-92, 495, 497, 506-07, 510, 514, 519; **33**:364-65, 378; **101**:224, 227, 231, 233, 236, 245-46, 249-51, 253, 261-63, 267-68, 271, 273, 287-88, 290-91, 293, 296, 299, 307-08, 318-22, 330, 332, 335-36, 340-45; **215**:208, 210, 218, 221, 225-27, 231, 253-54, 287, 292, 300, 322, 337, 344
The Autobiography and Letters of Mrs. M. O. W. Oliphant (Oliphant) **11**:451-2, 463; **61**:171, 193-4, 196-8, 214-5, 220, 223-4, 234, 237; **221**:237, 239, 247, 261, 281, 296, 318, 325
The Autobiography and Memoirs of Benjamin Robert Haydon (1786-1846) (Haydon) **146**:113-15, 118, 121-22, 132, 135-36, 138-39, 143, 147-50, 152-54
Autobiography, Letters, and Literary Remains of Mrs. Piozzi (Thrale) (Piozzi) **57**:237, 268, 270, 299
Autobiography of a Pocket Handkerchief (Cooper) **203**:73
The Autobiography of a Thief (Reade) **2**:546-47; **74**:272, 292
Autobiography of an Actress; or Eight Years on the Stage (Mowatt) **74**:221, 224, 230, 234-35
"Autobiography of an English Opium-Eater" (De Quincey)
See *Confessions of an English Opium-Eater*
"The Autobiography of Author" (Hogg) **109**:274
The Autobiography of Charles Darwin (Darwin) **57**:123, 168
The Autobiography of Christopher Kirkland (Linton) **41**:165, 172-75
The Autobiography of Goethe: Truth and Poetry from My Own Life (Goethe)
See *Aus meinem Leben: Dichtung und Wahrheit*
The Autobiography of James Clarence Mangan (Mangan) **27**:298, 301, 304
The Autobiography of John Galt (Galt) **1**:334; **110**:86, 88
The Autobiography of Leigh Hunt, with Reminiscences of Friends and Contemporaries (Hunt) **1**:416-18, 424; **70**:259-60, 264, 268, 279-85, 287-88
The Autobiography of Margaret Oliphant: The Complete Text (Oliphant) **61**:238-9
"Autobiography of Mr. Munden" (Lamb) **10**:435
Autobiography of Thomas Jefferson (Jefferson) **11**:173, 196, 199, 205-206; **103**:106, 119, 121, 123, 125, 186-90
The Autobiography of William Carleton (Carleton) **199**:14, 23, 58, 63, 80
"The Autocrat gives a Breakfast to the Public" (Holmes) **81**:98
The Autocrat of the Breakfast-Table (Holmes) **14**:102, 104-06, 110, 112-15, 117, 119-25, 132-33, 139, 143-46; **81**:94-96, 98-99, 104-05
"Autography" (Poe) **55**:170, 188-9; **97**:183-85, 187
"Die Automate" (Hoffmann) **2**:362; **183**:224, 226
"L'Automne" (Lamartine) **11**:264, 269, 282; **190**:222-23, 252
"Automne" (Verlaine) **230**:153-54, 157-58
"Autour d'un livre" (Maupassant) **83**:227
L'Autre (Sand) **42**:310
"Autre complainte de Lord Pierrot" (Laforgue) **53**:265, 279, 287, 290; **221**:50, 67, 69, 77
"Autre complainte de l'orgue de barbarie" (Laforgue) **221**:59
"Autre étude de femme" (Balzac) **153**:54-56, 58, 147, 153
"Autre eventail de Mademoiselle Mallarmé" (Mallarmé) **4**:380; **41**:260, 262, 265, 291; **210**:220, 244
"Autre Explication" (Verlaine) **51**:361-62
Autres chimères (Nerval) **67**:306-07
"Autumn" (Arany)
See "Ősszel"
"Autumn" (Baratynsky)
See "Osen"
"Autumn" (Bloomfield) **145**:141
"Autumn" (Clare) **9**:76, 78, 86, 88, 94, 96, 111, 113-14, 123; **86**:113
"Autumn" (Dickinson)
See "The Morns Are Meeker than They Were"
"Autumn" (Dyer) **129**:149
"Autumn" (Hood)
See "Ode to Autumn"
"Autumn" (Keats)
See "Ode to Autumn"
"The Autumn" (Lamartine)
See "L'automne"
"Autumn" (Moodie) **113**:316
"Autumn" (Pushkin) **3**:443
"Autumn" (Rossetti) **2**:575; **50**:289
"Autumn" (Sigourney) **87**:331, 333
"Autumn" (Smith) **59**:333
"Autumn Afternoons" (Laforgue)
See "L'Après-midi d'automne"
"Autumn Days in Weimar" (Taylor) **89**:325
"Autumn during the Siege of Ochakov" (Derzhavin)
See "Osen' vo vremia osady Ochakova"
"Autumn Flowers" (Very) **9**:378
"Autumn Lament" (Mallarmé)
See "Plainte d'automne"
"Autumn Leaves" (Hugo) **3**:261
"Autumn Leaves" (Very) **9**:388
"Autumn Mood" (Lenau) **16**:275
"An Autumn Morning" (Clare) **9**:111
"Autumn Rivulets" (Whitman) **205**:225-26
"Autumn Sadness" (Lazarus) **109**:292
"Autumn Song" (Gordon)
See "A Song of Autumn"
"Autumn Song" (Verlaine)
See "Chanson d'automne"
"An Autumn Thought" (Taylor) **89**:299
"Autumn. To my brother Arkadii Timofeevich in St. Petersburg" (Aksakov)
See "Osen.' Bratu Arkadiiu Timofeevich v Peterburg"
"Autumn Violets" (Rossetti) **2**:572
"The Autumn Waste" (Lampman) **194**:30, 44, 47, 126, 128-29, 138
"Autumn Woods" (Bryant) **6**:159-60, 172, 176, 183; **46**:46
"Autumnal Leaves" (Harpur) **114**:100
Autumnal Leaves; Tales and Sketches in prose and rhyme (Child) **73**:62
"Autumnal Tints" (Thoreau) **207**:197
"Aux Bourgeois" (Baudelaire) **155**:76
"Aux Chrétiens" (Lamartine) **11**:279
Aux Cyprès de la Villa d'Este (Liszt) **199**:307
"Aux modernes" (Leconte de Lisle) **29**:228, 231, 235
"Aux morts" (Leconte de Lisle) **29**:222, 228
"Aux petits enfants" (Daudet) **1**:248
"Aux rayons consolants . . ." (Laforgue) **221**:87
"Avalon" (Chivers) **49**:49, 71
Avant, pendant, et après (Scribe) **16**:382, 390
"Avant-Propos" (Balzac)
See *Avant-propos de la comédie humaine*
"Avant-propos" (Silva) **114**:263
Avant-propos de la comédie humaine (Balzac) **53**:13; **153**:12, 21, 25-26, 31, 62, 101, 121, 126-28, 151, 153
"Avarice" (Lampman) **25**:194; **194**:24
The Avaricious Knight (Pushkin)
See *Skupoi rytsar*
Avatar (Gautier) **1**:346; **59**:11-14, 33, 37
"Avatarii faraonului Tlá" (Eminescu) **33**:246; **131**:334
"The Avatars of Pharaoh Tlà" (Eminescu)
See "Avatarii faraonului Tlá"
"The Avatars of the Pharaoh Tlà" (Eminescu)
See "Avatarii faraonului Tlá"
"Ave" (Rossetti) **4**:505, 518-22; **77**:303, 348
"El ave muerta" (Villaverde) **121**:333
"Avec ses vêtements ondoyants et nacrés" (Baudelaire)
See "À une madone"
Avellaneda (Echeverria) **18**:148
"Aven om humor och stil däri" (Almqvist) **42**:11, 16
"The Avenger" (De Quincey) **87**:76; **198**:40
"Avenging and Bright" (Moore) **110**:182
L'avenir de la science (Renan) **26**:394-95, 397-98, 412, 415, 418-19, 423-24; **145**:317, 346, 356, 358, 361, 363
Una aventura de Richelieu (Tamayo y Baus) **1**:571
La aventurera (Gómez de Avellaneda) **111**:28, 49, 53
Les aventures d'Arthur Gordon Pym (Baudelaire) **29**:67
Aventures du dernier Abencérages (Chateaubriand)
See *Aben-Hamet, the Last of the Abencerages*
Aventures prodigieuses de Tartarin de Tarascon (Daudet) **1**:231, 235-36, 240-42, 250-51
L'aventurière (Augier) **31**:2-4, 7-12, 14-16, 19, 23-4, 27
Der Averhahn (Arnim) **5**:19, 21
Averroès et l'Averroïsme (Renan) **26**:377, 379, 389, 415; **145**:356
"Avertissement de l'auteur" (Genlis) **166**:60-61
"Les aveugles" (Baudelaire) **29**:101, 113; **55**:16, 19, 22, 35, 40-2; **155**:4-6, 8
Avillion and other Tales (Craik) **38**:119
"Avis" (Holmes) **14**:109
"Avis je vous prie" (Laforgue) **5**:277
"Avolio" (Hayne) **94**:144, 158
Avolio and Other Poems (Hayne) **94**:135, 139-40
"Avtorskaya ispoved" (Gogol) **5**:227, 230, 238, 254; **15**:85, 92; **31**:127-28; **162**:87
Le Avventure di Pinocchio (Collodi) **54**:134-42, 147-63
"Awake Ye Muses Nine, Sing Me a Strain Divine" (Dickinson) **21**:62
The Awakening (Hayne) **94**:166
"The Awakening of the Poetic Faculty" (Boker) **125**:82
"Away from You" (Eminescu) **131**:296
"Away, Haunt Thou Not Me" (Clough)
See "In a Lecture-Room"

"An Axe Lay behind God's Door" (Shevchenko)
See "U Boha za dvermy lezhala sokyra"
Axel (Tegner) **2**:611-14
Axël (Villiers de l'Isle Adam) **3**:582-83, 585-92
Axur, re d' Ormus (Da Ponte) **50**:81
Ayala's Angel (Trollope) **6**:470-71, 507; **33**:363; **101**:237, 264
'Ayit zahvu'a (Mapu) **18**:288, 292-301, 303
"Aylmer's Field" (Kendall) **12**:180
"Aylmer's Field" (Tennyson) **30**:220, 236, 249, 254, 280; **65**:248
"The Aylmers of Bally-Aylmer" (Griffin) **7**:198, 206-07, 211, 217
"Aymerillot" (Hugo) **3**:273
The Ayrshire Legatees; or, The Pringle Family (Galt) **1**:328-29, 335, 337; **110**:78, 80, 84-6, 90, 92, 95-6, 113-16
"The Azalea" (Patmore) **9**:349, 358
Azas de Um Anjo (Alencar) **157**:5
Azemia (Beckford) **16**:29; **214**:146, 163-66
Azeth the Egyptian (Linton) **41**:163
"Azrael" (Longfellow) **45**:145, 188
"Azraël" (Villiers de l'Isle Adam)
See "L'annonciateur"
"Azrael, or Destruction's Eve" (Brontë) **109**:30, 48
"La azucena silvestre" (Zorrilla y Moral) **6**:526
"L'azur" (Mallarmé) **4**:378, 395; **41**:250; **210**:236
"The Azure" (Mallarmé)
See "L'azur"
"Bab Ballads" (Muller) **73**:353
"Baby Bertie's Christmas" (O'Brien) **21**:236
"Baby Bloom" (O'Brien) **21**:236, 243-44
"Baby Eyes" (Webster) **230**:311
"Baby Lies So Fast Asleep" (Rossetti) **186**:237
"The Baby-House" (Barbauld) **185**:59, 93
"Babylon" (Pixérécourt) **39**:284
"The Babylonian Captivity" (Harpur) **114**:144
"Baby's Age" (Timrod) **25**:360
"A baby's cradle with no baby in it" (Rossetti) **186**:237
"Bacchanalia: or, The New Age" (Arnold) **218**:158
"The Bacchanals of Euripides" (Pater) **7**:334; **90**:335
"La bacchante" (Beranger) **34**:28, 30
La Bacchante (Thaïs) (Dumas) **71**:218
Bacchanterna eller Fanatismen (Stagnelius) **61**:248, 253, 260, 264-5, 268, 273
The Bacchantes, or Fanaticism (Stagnelius)
See *Bacchanterna eller Fanatismen*
"Bacchus" (Emerson) **38**:183-84, 187; **98**:177
"Bacchus" (O'Brien) **21**:246
"Bacchus and Ariadne" (Hunt) **1**:410
"Bacchus in Tuscany" (Hunt) **70**:248
"Bacco in Toscana" (Hunt) **1**:415
"The Bachelor" (Stifter)
See "Der Hagestolz"
The Bachelor (Turgenev)
See *Kholostiak*
"Bachelor Housekeeping" (Parton) **86**:348
Bachelor of Music Essays (Liszt)
See *Lettres d'un bachelier ès musique*
"A Bachelor's Complaint of the Behaviour of Married People" (Lamb) **10**:403, 409-10, 430, 436; **113**:235, 245
"A Bachelor's Establishment" (Balzac)
See "La rabouilleuse"
Bachelor's Hall; or, All in a Hobble (Bird) **1**:93
The Bachelor's Wife (Galt) **110**:73, 94
"Baciochis Erzählung vom wilden Jäger" (Brentano) **191**:81
"A Backward Glance" (Whitman) **4**:600, 604; **31**:402, 405; **81**:235, 302
"A Backward Glance o'er Travel'd Roads" (Whitman) **205**:184, 215-16, 222-23, 225, 324
"The Backwater" (Turgenev) **21**:415, 431
The Backwoods of Canada: Being Letters from the Wife of an Emigrant Officer (Traill) **31**:315-17, 321, 323-24, 327-29
"The Back-Woodsman" (Moodie) **113**:346
The Backwoodsman (Paulding) **2**:525, 528, 530
"Bacon to Beethoven" (Lanier) **118**:243
"Bad Blood" (Rimbaud)
See "Mauvais sang"
"Bad Dreams" (Browning) **19**:96; **79**:112-14
"The Bad Glazier" (Baudelaire)
See "Le mauvais vitrier"
Bad Saint Vitalis (Keller)
See *Der Schlimm-heilige Vitalis*
"The Bad Shilling" (Haliburton) **149**:317
"Bad Squire" (Kingsley) **35**:206
"Bad Weather" (Hunt) **1**:417
The Baddington Peerage (Sala) **46**:240-42
Die Bäder von Lucca (Heine) **4**:264; **54**:317-19, 327; **147**:134-35, 165, 178, 202, 205, 226
"Badger" (Clare) **9**:117, 121; **86**:131
Bádnaya nevésta (Ostrovsky)
See *Bednaya nevesta*
"The Bag" (Krylov) **1**:439
The Bag-Pipers (Sand) **57**:338
"La bague d'Annibal" (Barbey d'Aurevilly) **213**:30
"Bahači četvero bolj množnih Slave rodov" (Preseren) **127**:316
"The Bailiff" (Turgenev) **122**:294
Le baiser (Banville) **9**:20
"Le baiser suprême" (Leconte de Lisle) **29**:219
"Bajazeth" (Droste-Hülshoff) **3**:203
"Bajdary" (Mickiewicz) **3**:404
Bajki i przypowieści (Krasicki) **8**:398, 401-02, 404, 406
Bajki nowe (Krasicki) **8**:398, 401-02, 404, 407
"Bajo-Relieve" (Casal) **131**:242
"Bajuški-baju" (Nekrasov) **11**:420
"Bakche-Sarai" (Mickiewicz)
See "Bakczysaraj"
The Bak-Chesarian fountain: A Tale of the Tauride (Pushkin)
See *Bakhchisaraiski Fontan*
"Bakczysaraj" (Mickiewicz) **3**:390, 403
"Baker Farm" (Thoreau) **7**:373, 398
The Bakhchisarai Fontan (Pushkin)
See *Bakhchisaraiski Fontan*
Bakhchisaraiski Fontan (Pushkin) **3**:409, 411, 413-14, 416, 421, 423, 437, 451; **83**:243-44, 248, 299, 332-34, 351, 355, 357, 359
"Bakhchisaray by Night" (Mickiewicz) **101**:190
"Le Bal" (Vigny) **102**:335, 367-68
Bal (Baratynsky) **103**:39-40
"Le bal de Sceaux" (Balzac) **153**:104, 108-9, 111, 149
Un Bal Masqué (Dumas) **71**:205
"The Balance Between the Esthetic and the Ethical in the Development of the Personality" (Kierkegaard) **125**:235
"La balancelle" (Corbière) **43**:33
"Balanide" (Verlaine) **230**:176
Balaustion's Adventure (Browning) **19**:128
"Balcescu and His Followers" (Eminescu) **131**:326
"Le balcon" (Baudelaire) **6**:80, 93, 100, 104; **29**:73, 77, 99; **55**:6-8, 26, 55, 59, 62; **155**:34
"The Balcony" (Baudelaire)
See "Le balcon"
"The Balcony" (Irving) **2**:372
"Balder Dead" (Arnold) **6**:50-51, 67-68, 72; **29**:32; **89**:28, 51, 53; **218**:115, 174, 176-80, 190-91
Balder, Part the First (Dobell) **43**:39-40, 42-5, 49-51, 55, 60-2, 65, 68, 74-5
Baldwin (Barham) **77**:5
"Balin and Balan" (Tennyson) **202**:249, 290, 313
"Balkis et Solomon" (Nerval) **1**:480
"Der Ball" (Gotthelf) **117**:6
"The Ball" (Longstreet) **159**:137-40, 144, 150, 153, 185-86, 192, 201-2
The Ball (Baratynsky)
See *Bal*
"A Ballad" (Turgenev) **21**:376
"Ballad Books" (Child) **173**:224
"Ballad Founded on Fact" (Opie) **65**:160-1
"Ballad in Honor of Louise Michel" (Verlaine)
See "Ballade en l'honneur de Louise Michel"
"Ballad Noticing the Difference of Rich and Poor" (Lamb) **10**:389
The Ballad of Abraham Lincoln (Taylor) **89**:342
"Ballad of an Omnibus" (Levy) **59**:88, 102
"A Ballad of Boding" (Rossetti) **2**:558, 575-6
"Ballad of Carmilhan" (Longfellow) **45**:114
Ballad of Delora, or the Passion of Andrea Como (Horne) **127**:255, 256, 271
"Ballad of Fortunatus" (Schlegel) **15**:223
"Ballad of Human Life" (Beddoes) **3**:34
"Ballad of Oriana" (Tennyson) **30**:223, 245; **202**:337
"A Ballad of Religion and Marriage" (Levy) **59**:99, 114; **203**:351, 359
"The Ballad of Sally Brown and Ben the Carpenter" (Hood)
See "Faithless Sally Brown"
"The Ballad of Sir Brown" (O'Brien) **21**:249
"The Ballad of Sir John Franklin" (Boker) **125**:31
"Ballad of the Barber" (Beardsley) **6**:145-46
"Ballad of the Oysterman" (Holmes) **14**:99, 101
"The Ballad of Trees and the Master" (Lanier) **6**:249, 253-55, 265, 270; **118**:219, 221, 223, 232, 240, 268-9
"Ballad Poetry" (Child) **173**:176, 183, 195-96, 212-13, 218, 220-21, 224, 233, 235
"Ballade" (Laforgue) **53**:278, 290; **221**:58, 70
"Ballade à la lune" (Musset) **7**:254; **150**:232-33
"Ballade de Banville aux enfants perdus" (Banville) **9**:16
"Ballade de ses regrets pour l'an 1830" (Banville) **9**:28
"La ballade des pendus" (Baudelaire) **29**:84
"Ballade en l'honneur de Louise Michel" (Verlaine) **230**:166
"Ballade en rêve" (Verlaine) **230**:169
"Ballade of a Special Edition" (Levy) **203**:343
"Ballade of an Omnibus" (Levy) **203**:343
"Ballade of Summer's Sleep" (Lampman) **25**:164, 204; **194**:30, 123-26
"Ballade Sappho" (Verlaine) **230**:212
Ballades (Hugo) **3**:276
The Ballad-Monger (Banville)
See *Gringoire*
"Ballads" (Kingsley) **35**:218
The Ballads (Banville)
See *Trente-six ballades joyeuses*
Ballads (Child)
See *English and Scottish Ballads*
Ballads (Coleridge)
See *Lyrical Ballads*
Ballads (Stevenson) **5**:410, 428; **193**:211, 215
Ballads (Thackeray) **5**:466
Ballads and Images (Meyer)
See *Romanzen und Bilder*
Ballads and Metrical Tales (Southey) **97**:318
Ballads, and Other Poems (Longfellow) **2**:472; **45**:135, 152, 155, 184, 189
Ballads and Romances (Mickiewicz)
See *Ballady i Romanse*
Ballads and Sonnets (Rossetti) **4**:499, 502; **77**:301
Ballads of New England (Whittier) **8**:506
"Ballads of Wonder" (Baillie) **2**:42
Ballady i Romanse (Mickiewicz) **3**:393, 395-96, 403; **101**:155, 179
Balladyna (Slowacki) **15**:348-50, 352-53, 364-65, 370, 372, 376, 378, 380
Ballantrae (Stevenson)
See *The Master of Ballantrae: A Winter's Tale*
Ballantyne Humbug Handled (Lockhart) **6**:305
"Ballast Island" (Woolson) **82**:331-32
Ballets (Mallarmé) **210**:233
"The Balloon" (Cranch) **115**:47

"The Balloon Hoax" (Poe) **16**:300, 313, 323
Baltasar (Gómez de Avellaneda) **111**:28
Balzac: A Critical Study (Taine) **15**:463
"Balzac and George Sand" (Lewes) **215**:164
Balzac's Contes Drôlatiques: Droll Stories Collected from the Abbeys of Touraine (Balzac) **5**:28, 42, 77-78
"Balzsamcsepp" (Arany) **34**:19
"A bánat? Egy nagy oceán" (Petofi) **21**:279
The Band of Patriots (Baillie) **151**:75
"Bande Mātaram" (Chatterji)
See "Vande Mataram"
"La Bande Noire" (Hugo) **161**:239, 241
"Bandido negro" (Castro Alves) **205**:19, 30, 35
"El bando de Lucifer" (Lizardi) **30**:67
"Bangadesher krishak" (Chatterji) **19**:226
The Banished: A Swabian Historical Tale (Hauff)
See *Lichtenstein: Romantische Sage aus der würtembergischen Geschichte*
"Banished Man" (Baillie) **2**:42
The Banished Man (Smith) **23**:323, 330, 333, 335; **115**:144, 147, 149-50, 158, 166-68, 207, 211
The Banishment of Cicero (Cumberland) **167**:117-18, 131-32, 136-37, 145, 154, 186-87
The Bank Director's Son: A Real and Intensely Interesting Revelation of City Life (Lippard)
See *The Killers: A Narrative of Real Life in Philadelphia, by a Member of the Philadelphia Bar*
"Banker's Dream" (Gordon) **21**:160, 180-81
"The Banker's Secret" (Holmes) **14**:128
The Banker's Wife; or, Court and City (Gore) **65**:20, 38
The Bankrupt (Boker) **125**:25, 28, 38, 58
The Bankrupt (Ostrovsky)
See *Svoi lyudi—sochtemsya!*
The Bankruptcy (Gotthelf) **117**:18, 25
"The Banks of the Jordan" (Trollope)
See "A Ride across Palestine"
The Banks of the Wye; A Poem (Bloomfield) **145**:156-57, 162, 176
"The Banner" (Allingham) **25**:6
"The Banner of England" (Moodie) **113**:308-9
"The Banner of the Jew" (Lazarus) **8**:415-17, 419-21, 424, 428; **109**:293, 314-15, 327, 338, 343
The Banner of the Upright Seven (Keller)
See *The Flag of the Seven Upright Ones*
"Banović Strahinja" (Karadzic) **115**:91-2
"The Banquet" (Kierkegaard) **125**:248
"The Banquet's End" (Meyer)
See "Das Ende des Festes"
Banwell Hill (Bowles) **103**:56, 61
"Le baptëme" (Maupassant) **1**:469
"The Baptism of Fire" (Longfellow) **2**:487
The Baptism on the Savica (Preseren)
See *Krst pri Svici: Povest v verzih*
Baptiste Montauban (Nodier) **19**:383
"Bar Kochba" (Lazarus) **109**:293
"Los barateros" (Larra) **17**:282; **130**:194
"Barbara Frietchie" (Whittier) **8**:496, 501, 508, 510, 513, 516-17, 522-23, 528, 531; **59**:357-61
"Barbara S——" (Lamb) **10**:436
"Barbara's Courtship" (Alger) **8**:16
"Barbare" (Rimbaud) **4**:455, 473; **35**:269, 308-09, 311-13, 322; **82**:233, 238; **227**:203, 210, 244, 247, 271, 292, 294, 297, 309-10, 325, 327
"Barbarian" (Rimbaud)
See "Barbare"
"Barbarians, Philistines, Populace" (Arnold) **218**:197
"La barbe pointue" (Bertrand) **31**:49
"Barber of Bantry" (Griffin) **7**:201, 215, 218
Barberine (Musset) **7**:270, 276; **150**:226
The Barbers at Court (Mayhew) **31**:159
"Barber-Shop Paradox" (Dodgson) **139**:57
"Barbier" (Baudelaire) **29**:70
Barchester Towers (Trollope) **6**:453, 455, 459, 461, 464-66, 468, 470-71, 487, 494, 497, 499-502, 505-06, 510-11, 514, 516-17; **33**:360-426; **101**:232, 235, 253, 265-66, 271, 273-74, 280, 307, 326, 328-30, 332-33, 336-37; **215**:207-8, 231, 261, 307, 338
"Barclay of Ury" (Whittier) **8**:489, 530
"The Barcoo" (Kendall) **12**:195-96
"Bardale" (Klopstock) **11**:220
"Le barde de Temrah" (Leconte de Lisle) **29**:225
"A Bard's Address to his Youngest Daughter" (Hogg) **109**:202
"Bards of Freedom" (Coleridge) **111**:353
"Bards of Passion" (Keats) **8**:360; **73**:202
"Bards of Passion and of Mirth" (Keats) **73**:257; **225**:242
"The Bards of Wales" (Arany)
See "A walesi bárdok"
"Bard's Song" (Blake) **173**:5, 11, 17-18, 59-63, 65, 69, 89-90, 92-95, 98-101, 106, 113, 122, 151
"Bard's Song at the Grave of Victorious Slavs" (Zhukovsky) **35**:378-79
"The Barefoot Boy" (Longfellow) **103**:296
"The Barefoot Boy" (Whittier) **8**:510, 525, 531; **59**:356, 358, 371
Barfüssele (Auerbach) **171**:4, 9, 72
Barham Downs (Bage) **182**:5-7, 10, 12, 17, 20, 23, 25, 27-29, 40-50, 59-60
"Barlow Papers" (Barlow) **223**:9
"Der Barmekiden Untergang" (Droste-Hülshoff) **3**:203
Barnaby Rudge (Dickens) **3**:142, 174; **8**:178, 182; **18**:112, 132; **37**:143, 156; **86**:18, 256-57; **105**:229, 231, 349; **113**:9, 102, 107, 124, 129; **203**:178, 278; **219**:66-67, 70, 83, 91, 108, 110, 112, 117, 119-20, 131, 138, 188, 195, 201, 210-11; **230**:89, 91, 110, 113, 141-42; **231**:174, 182
Barnaby Rudge: A Tale of the Riots of 'Eighty (Dickens) **206**:103, 107, 114, 133
The Barnabys in America; or, Adventures of the Widow Wedded (Trollope) **30**:314, 320-21
"Barnet i Graven" (Andersen) **79**:76-77; **214**:41
Barney Bradley (Carleton) **199**:7
"Barney Brady's Goose" (Carleton) **3**:89
"Barnfloor and Winepress" (Hopkins) **17**:191; **189**:90
"Barnham Water" (Bloomfield) **145**:133
Der Barometermacher auf der Zauberinsel (Raimund) **69**:5-7, 12, 21, 29, 36-7, 43-6, 48-9
The Barometer-maker on the Magic Isle (Raimund)
See *Der Barometermacher auf der Zauberinsel*
"Baron von Raffloff" (Willis) **194**:298
"La Baronne" (Maupassant) **83**:171, 194-95
Barons (Bulwer-Lytton)
See *The Last of the Barons*
"The Baron's Gloves" (Alcott) **58**:47
Barren Genius (Eminescu)
See *Geniu pustiu*
"Barrenness of the Imaginative Faculty in the Productions of Modern Art" (Lamb) **10**:409; **113**:203, 206, 318
Barrington (Lever) **23**:292, 308
Barry Lyndon (Thackeray)
See *The Memoirs of Barry Lyndon, Esq.*
Barsetshire Chronicle (Trollope) **6**:470-71
"Bart Davis's Dance" (Harris) **23**:141, 159, 163; **165**:201, 227, 236, 287
Barth. Kopitars kleinere Schriften (Kopitar) **117**:91
"Barthli der Korber" (Gotthelf) **117**:6
"Bartleby, the Scrivener: A Story of Wall-Street" (Melville) **3**:331, 354, 362, 368, 380-81, 383; **12**:312; **29**:354; **49**:376-426; **93**:197, 224; **123**:186, 261; **157**:70, 159; **181**:295, 327; **193**:49-198; **221**:166, 196
"Baryshnia-krest'ianka" (Pushkin) **83**:272, 275-76, 323, 327, 329-30, 337-38, 354
Bas Blancs (More) **141**:236
The Bas Bleu (More) **141**:232
The Bas Bleu; or, Conversation (More) **27**:325, 335-36
Les Bas-Bleus (Barbey d'Aurevilly) **213**:60
"The Base of All Metaphysics" (Whitman) **81**:332; **205**:253
Bases Del Partido Revolucionario Cubano (Martí) **63**:97, 127-9
"The Basic Forms of Motion" (Engels) **85**:38
Basil: A Story of Modern Life (Collins) **1**:172, 174, 177-78, 181, 184-85, 187; **18**:61; **93**:4, 38, 43-4, 46-8, 50, 52-3, 64
Basil: A Tragedy (Baillie) **151**:6, 8-9, 13, 99-102, 104-5, 114-17
Basil Hymen (Sacher-Masoch) **31**:287, 295
"Basil Lee" (Hogg) **4**:283
"Basile Renaud" (Cooke) **110**:9
The Basis of Morality (Schopenhauer)
See *Die beiden Grundprobleme der Ethik*
Basis of Natural Right (Fichte)
See *Grundlage des Naturrechts nach Prinzipen der Wissenshaftslehre*
Basis of the Entire Theory of Science (Fichte)
See *Grundlage der gesamten Wissenschaftslehre*
"A Basket of Sun-Fruit" (Harpur) **114**:101, 139
"The Bastille, A Vision" (Williams) **135**:255, 297, 314, 333
"La Bataille" (Mérimée) **65**:55
Bataille de dames; ou, Un duel en amour (Scribe) **16**:389, 396-97, 402-03, 405, 407
Le bâtard de Mauléon (Dumas) **11**:51, 68
"bâtard du pape" (Beranger) **34**:38
"Le bateau ivre" (Rimbaud) **4**:453-57, 459, 463, 468, 471-72, 478-79, 485, 487; **35**:266-67, 270-71, 274-75, 279, 283-88, 299, 320-23, 325; **82**:218, 227, 232, 238, 247, 250, 252, 255-56, 262-63; **227**:185-86, 192, 195, 208, 220, 242, 255, 260, 264-66, 316
"The Bath of Aristippus" (Derzhavin) **215**:22
"Bathed in War's Perfume" (Whitman) **81**:318
The Baths of Lucca (Heine)
See *Die Bäder von Lucca*
"Bâtons dans les roves" (Hugo) **10**:357
The Battle of Arminius (Kleist)
See *Die Hermannsschlacht: Ein Drama*
"The Battle Ax" (Leskov)
See "Voitel' nica"
"The Battle of Blenheim" (Southey) **8**:472, 474; **97**:271, 315
"The Battle of Brunanburh" (Tennyson) **30**:236
The Battle of Bunker's Hill (Brackenridge) **7**:43, 47; **227**:48, 72
The Battle of Cheviot (Macaulay) **42**:118
"The Battle of Flowers" (Blind) **202**:9
The Battle of Hastings (Cumberland) **167**:119, 133-34, 138, 142-43, 147, 155, 189
The Battle of Herman (Klopstock)
See *Hermanns Schlacht*
The Battle of Hermann (Kleist)
See *Die Hermannsschlacht*
The Battle of Kings Mountain (Hayne) **94**:167-68
The Battle of Lake Regillus (Macaulay) **42**:111
The Battle of Largs (Galt) **1**:327
The Battle of Life (Dickens) **211**:42
Battle of Love (Daudet)
See *La lutte pour la vie*
The Battle of Marathon: A Poem (Barrett Browning) **61**:41, 48-9, 61; **66**:44, 71; **170**:25
The Battle of New Orleans (Dunlap) **2**:211, 213
"The Battle of Niagara" (Neal) **161**:325
The Battle of Niagara (Neal) **161**:297-98, 301, 308-9
"The Battle of the Baltic" (Campbell) **19**:165, 168-69, 176, 179, 181-82, 185, 188, 190-96

"The Battle of the Bards" (Taylor) **89**:319
"The Battle of the Factions" (Carleton) **3**:89, 92-93, 95; **199**:33, 56, 59, 106, 108
The Battle of the Nile (Bowles) **103**:54, 70
The Battle-Day of Germantown (Lippard)
See *Original Revolutionary Chronicle: The Battle-Day of Germantown*
"The Battlefield" (Bryant) **6**:165, 168-69, 172-73; **46**:7, 15
Battle-Pieces and Aspects of the War (Melville) **3**:331, 333, 352, 363, 378-79; **29**:315, 360; **157**:212; **181**:318
The Battles of Talavera (Croker) **10**:88-89
"Battle-Song" (Petofi)
See "Csatadal"
Les Battuécas (Genlis) **166**:21, 23, 48-52, 54, 68
Der Bauer als Millionär; oder, Das Mädchen aus der Feenwelt (Raimund) **69**:5, 7-10, 12-13, 23, 26, 30-1, 33-4, 38, 43-6, 49-50, 52-3
"Das Bauernlied" (Claudius) **75**:190
Bauernlieder (Claudius) **75**:190
Der Bauern-Spiegel oder Lebensgeschichte des Jeremias Gotthelf: Von ihm selbst beschrieben (Gotthelf) **117**:4, 7, 14, 17-18, 31-2, 38, 51
"Baugmaree" (Dutt) **29**:122, 127
Bausteine (Auerbach) **171**:39
"The Bay of Glasstown" (Brontë) **109**:35
Bazarov (Pisarev) **25**:330-31, 333-34, 338, 348, 352-54
"Bazarov, Once Again" (Herzen) **61**:109
"Be Good!" (Isaacs)
See "Sed buenos!"
"Be of Bronze . . ." (Verlaine)
See "Sois de bronze . . ."
"The Beach of Falesá" (Stevenson) **5**:412, 422, 431, 434; **63**:261; **193**:212, 214, 221-24, 254-55, 274, 277, 279, 281, 298, 334-35, 337-38, 340, 344
"Beachy Head" (Smith) **115**:118, 126, 129-35, 206, 209
Beachy Head, with Other Poems (Smith) **115**:134, 211, 217
The Beacon (Baillie) **2**:37, 39; **71**:6, 18; **151**:115-16
"The Beacons" (Baudelaire)
See "Les phares"
"The Beam in Grenley Church" (Barnes) **75**:75
"Beams" (Verlaine) **51**:381-84
"Beanfield" (Clare) **9**:110
"The Bean-Field" (Thoreau) **7**:388, 399, 403-4
"The Bear Hunt" (Lincoln) **18**:273; **201**:159, 216-17
"The Bear in Charge of the Bees" (Krylov) **1**:435
Bear ye one another's Burthens; or, the Valley of Tears (More) **141**:175
"The Bear-Hunt" (Nekrasov) **11**:409
"The Beast" (Leskov)
See "Zver'"
"The Beasts in the Tower" (Lamb) **125**:376
"Beata" (Patmore) **9**:357
"Beaten Tracks" (Rimbaud) **35**:269
"The Beating of my own Heart" (Milnes) **61**:152
"La Béatrice" (Baudelaire) **6**:109; **55**:70-1, 74, 77-8
"Beatrice" (Dodgson) **139**:30
"Beatrice" (Le Fanu) **58**:276
"Beatrice Cenci" (Landor) **14**:183
Béatrix (Balzac) **5**:84; **153**:62, 69, 77, 81, 152
Beau Austin (Stevenson) **5**:411, 421
Le Beau Laurence (Sand) **57**:316
Le beau Léandre (Banville) **9**:20, 22
Un beau mariage (Augier) **31**:9, 13, 15, 19, 24-5, 27, 31, 34
"Le beau navire" (Baudelaire) **6**:109, 117; **55**:45, 61
Beauchampe; or, The Kentucky Tragedy (Simms) **3**:508-10, 513
"La beauté" (Baudelaire) **6**:123; **29**:97; **55**:58
"Beauté de femmes, leur faiblesse, et ces mains pâles" (Verlaine) **51**:357
"The Beauties of Santa Cruz" (Freneau) **1**:314, 316, 319, 323-24; **111**:80, 82, 100, 140, 143, 146, 148, 151-52, 184
The Beauties of the Court of King Charles II (Jameson)
See *Memoirs of the Beauties of the Court of Charles II*
"A Beautiful Autumn" (Arany)
See "Kies Ősz"
"The Beautiful Aza" (Leskov)
See "Prekrasnaja Aza"
"The Beautiful Beech Tree" (Mörike)
See "Der schöne Buche"
"The Beautiful Beeshareen Boy" (Blind) **202**:53, 55, 57
"The beautiful Cassandra" (Austen) **119**:13
"Beautiful City" (Tennyson) **30**:293
"Beautiful Dreamer" (Foster) **26**:291, 296-97, 299
The Beautiful Fiend (Southworth) **26**:434
"The Beautiful One at Night" (Isaacs)
See "La bella de noche"
"The Beautiful Princess and the Fortunate Dwarf" (Karamzin)
See "Prekrasnaja carevna i ščastlivoj karla"
"Beauty" (Alcott) **167**:51
"Beauty" (Lampman) **25**:209; **194**:71
"The Beauty" (O'Brien) **21**:243, 245, 247
"Beauty" (Shaw) **15**:335
Beauty (Coleridge) **231**:27
"Beauty" (Very) **9**:381
Beauty and the Beast (Lamb) **10**:418
Beauty and the Beast (Planché) **42**:279, 288
Beauty and the Beast; and Tales of Home (Taylor) **89**:314
"Beauty and Truth" (Cranch) **115**:5
"Beauty Cycle" (Baudelaire) **55**:73
"The Beauty of Married Men" (Lewes) **25**:290
"The Beauty—a Fragment" (Pinkney) **31**:277
"Beauty—Be Not Caused—It Is" (Dickinson) **21**:43
Les beaux messieurs de Bois-Doré (Sand) **2**:605; **42**:310; **57**:313
The Beaux' Strategem (Cumberland) **167**:169
"Beaver Brook" (Lowell) **90**:214-15
"Because I Could Not Stop for Death" (Dickinson) **21**:26, 28, 57; **77**:163, 173; **171**:105, 113-14, 183
"Der Becher" (Goethe) **4**:193
Becket (Tennyson) **30**:264-66
"Beclouded" (Dickinson)
See "The Sky Is Low, the Clouds Are Mean"
"Becoming Inured" (Martineau) **137**:283
"A Bed of Forget-Me-Nots" (Rossetti) **186**:270
"Die Bedeutung der Tragödien" (Hölderlin) **187**:241
Bedlam-Comödie (Eminescu) **33**:266
"Bednaia Liza" (Bestuzhev) **131**:168
"Bednaya Liza" (Karamzin) **3**:280, 285-91; **173**:279, 283, 296, 309, 347-48, 350
Bednaya nevesta (Ostrovsky) **30**:99, 102, 105, 107, 109-10, 114-15; **57**:218, 220
Bednost ne porok (Ostrovsky) **30**:97-9, 102, 104, 109-10, 113, 115; **57**:195, 198, 201-2, 208-21
Bednye lyudi (Dostoevsky) **2**:156, 160-61, 163, 170, 177, 199; **7**:80; **33**:176, 200; **119**:90, 132; **167**:247
"The Bedouin Song" (Taylor) **89**:302-03, 343
"The Bee" (Lanier) **6**:236, 238, 253; **118**:203
The Bee (Preseren)
See *Čbelica*
"The Bee and the Flower" (Tennyson) **202**:291
The Bee and the Orange Tree (Planché) **42**:288
"A Bee his burnished Carriage/Drove boldly to a Rose-" (Dickinson) **77**:96
The Bee Hunter; or, The Oak Opening (Cooper)
See *The Oak Openings; or, The Bee Hunter*
"The Beech Tree's Petition" (Campbell) **19**:179, 191, 198
The Bee-Hunter (Cooper)
See *The Oak-Openings; or, the Bee-Hunter*
The Beer Expedition at Schleusingen (Kivi)
See *Olviretki Schleusingenissä*
The Bees. A Poem. From the Fourteenth Book of Vanière's Praedium Rusticum (Murphy) **229**:225
"Bees Are Black, with Gilt Surcingles" (Dickinson) **21**:76
"The Bees in the Lime" (Webster) **230**:310
"Beethoven" (Schumann) **143**:130
"Beethoven, C moll-Sinfonie (No. 5)" (Hoffmann) **183**:178, 180, 188, 313
Beethoven, Zwei Trios (Hoffmann) **183**:180
Beethoven's Brevier (Beethoven) **227**:37
"Beethovens Büste" (Lenau) **16**:281
"Beethoven's Instrumental Music" (Hoffmann)
See "Beethovens Instrumentalmusik"
"Beethovens Instrumentalmusik" (Hoffmann) **183**:170, 180, 224, 297, 308
Beethoven's Letters, 1865 (Beethoven)
See *Briefe Beethovens, 1865*
Beethoven's Letters, 1867 (Beethoven)
See *Neue Briefe Beethovens, 1867*
Beethoven's Letters, 1906-11 (Beethoven)
See *Beethovens sämtliche Briefe, 1906-11*
Beethoven's Letters, 1907-11 (Beethoven)
See *Ludwig van Beethovens sämtliche Briefe und Aufzeichnungen, 1907-11*
Beethoven's Letters, 1910 (Beethoven)
See *Ludwig van Beethovens sämtliche Briefe, 1910*
Beethoven's Letters, 1923 (Beethoven)
See *Ludwig van Beethovens sämtliche Briefe, 1923*
Beethoven's Letters, 1961 (Beethoven)
See *The Letters of Beethoven, 1961*
Beethoven's Letters, 1972 (Beethoven) **227**:4-5, 8
Beethovens sämtliche Briefe, 1906-1911 (Beethoven) **227**:9, 30
The Beetle (Andersen) **79**:32, 89
"Befehlerles" (Auerbach) **171**:68-69
"Befordúltam a konyhára" (Petofi) **21**:260, 283
"Before" (Browning) **79**:153
"Before Breakfast" (Allingham) **25**:6
"Before Breakfast" (Cooke) **110**:35
"Before I got my eye put out" (Dickinson) **171**:157, 200-201
"Before, If I Remember Well . . ." (Rimbaud)
See "Jadis, si je me souviens bien . . ."
"Before Justice" (Goethe)
See "Vor Gericht"
"Before Sleep" (Lampman) **25**:167
"Before the Battle" (Moore) **110**:187
"Before the Curtain" (Thackeray) **5**:494, 499
"Before the Harvest" (Meyer)
See "Vor der Ernte"
"Before the Ice Is in the Pools" (Dickinson) **21**:55
"Before the Robin" (Lampman) **25**:209
Before the Storm (Fontane)
See *Vor dem Sturm*
"Before the Storm: A Conversation on Deck" (Herzen) **10**:336-7
Before the Storm: A Novel of the Winter of 1812-13 (Fontane)
See *Vor dem Sturm: Roman aus dem Winter 1812 auf 13*
"Before Vicksburg" (Boker) **125**:81
"Begegnung" (Grillparzer) **102**:174
"Begeisterung ... die Allerschaffende" (Hölderlin) **16**:185
"The Beggar" (Espronceda)
See "El mendigo"
"The Beggar-Maid" (Tennyson) **202**:334
"The Beggars" (Wordsworth) **12**:395

"Beggars' Ballad" (Meyer)
See "Bettlerballade"
"Begger Woman of Locarno" (Kleist)
See "Das Bettelweib von Locarno"
"Begin by praying for yourself" (Verlaine)
See "Commence par prier pour toi"
"Beginning and End" (Lazarus) **109**:291
"The Beginning and the End" (Very) **9**:376
"Beginning My Studies" (Whitman) **81**:313
"The Beginning of the End" (Hopkins) **189**:142
"Beginning of the End" (Storm) **1**:537
Begrebet Angest (Kierkegaard) **78**:122, 125, 157, 159-60, 169, 182, 191, 228; **125**:199, 209, 255-57, 281
"Behavior" (Emerson) **38**:143
Behind a Mask (Alcott)
See *Behind a Mask: The Unknown Thrillers of Louisa May Alcott*
"Behind a Mask: Or, A Woman's Power" (Alcott) **58**:3, 38, 46, 59, 67, 75-6, 78-80; **83**:6, 33; **218**:84-91
Behind a Mask: The Unknown Thrillers of Louisa May Alcott (Alcott) **58**:3
"Behind me dips Eternity" (Dickinson) **77**:140, 143-44; **171**:143, 158, 183
"Behind the Scenes at a Whist Game" (Barbey d'Aurevilly)
See "Le dessous de cartes d'une partie de whist"
"Behind the Veil" (De Mille) **123**:117-18
"Behold My Homeland" (Aksakov)
See "Vot rodina moia"
"Behold the Man" (Rossetti) **186**:318
"Behold this Swarthy Face" (Whitman) **31**:430
Bei und zu Lande auf dem Lande (Droste-Hülshoff) **3**:200
Die beiden Grundprobleme der Ethik (Schopenhauer) **51**:318
Die beiden Grundprobleme der Ethik, behandelt in zwei akademischen Preisschriften (Schopenhauer) **157**:296, 298-99, 338
Die beiden Herren Söhne (Nestroy) **42**:258
"Die beiden Hunde" (Grillparzer) **102**:174
Die beiden Klingsberg (Kotzebue) **25**:133, 142, 145
Beim Vetter Christian (Storm) **1**:540; **195**:16, 18
"Being Beauteous" (Rimbaud) **4**:455, 487; **35**:294, 296, 308, 311-12, 322; **82**:232-33; **227**:204, 206-7, 243-44, 247, 292, 309-10
"Being the Last Essays of Richard Jefferies, Collected by his Widow" (Jefferies) **47**:133
Beiträge zur Geheimen Geschichte des menschlichen Verstandes und Herzens (Wieland)
See *Beyträge zur geheimen Geschichte des menschlichen Verstandes und Herzens*
Ein Bekenntnis (Storm) **195**:7, 14, 18, 31, 76, 127, 131-32
'Bel of Prairie Eden: A Romance of Mexico (Lippard) **198**:123, 169, 229-30
"Bela" (Lermontov) **5**:291, 295-98, 301-02, 305-06; **126**:147-48, 153-54, 156, 158, 166-67, 169, 173-74, 195-99, 201-2
Bel-Ami (Maupassant) **1**:444, 448, 450, 452-53, 463-64, 467, 469; **42**:169, 189, 201; **83**:171, 173, 186
"Belated" (Webster) **230**:239
A Belated Revenge (Bird) **197**:24, 29-30, 36
Belated Summer (Stifter)
See *Der Nachsommer*
"The Belated Travellers" (Irving) **2**:390
"The Beleaguered City" (Longfellow) **45**:127, 151
A Beleaguered City: Tale of the Seen and Unseen (Oliphant) **11**:439, 445-6, 448-9, 451, 453-4, 459, 463; **61**:174, 216-17; **221**:231, 247, 257-58
Belford Regis; or, Sketches of a Country Town (Mitford) **4**:401, 407
The Belfry of Bruges (Longfellow) **2**:479; **45**:102, 116, 135, 151, 154, 182, 186; **103**:280
The Belgian Essays (Brontë) **217**:154
Belgium and Western Germany in 1833 (Trollope) **30**:307, 313
"Belief and Unbelief" (Freneau) **111**:110
"Belief and Unbelief. An Episode from a Poem" (Baratynsky)
See "Vera i neverie. Stsena iz poemy"
"Belief in One God" (Newman) **99**:300
"Belief, whether Voluntary?" (Hazlitt) **29**:173
"Believe: you, my beloved, are dearer than fame to me; ..." (Baratynsky)
See "O ver: ty, nezhnaya, dorozhe slavy mne;..."
Belinda (Edgeworth) **1**:255-56, 261-63, 265-67, 269, 271-72; **51**:79-81, 83, 85, 87-91, 93, 130-31, 135, 136-38, 140; **158**:7-11, 13-17, 19, 23-24, 34-39, 41, 44
Bélisaire (Genlis) **166**:39-41, 43
Belkin Tales (Pushkin)
See *Povesti Belkina*
"The Bell" (Andersen)
See "Klokken"
"The Bell" (Schiller)
See "Das Lied von der Glocke"
"The Bell of Ivan Veliky" (Schumann) **143**:138
"Bell of the Wreck" (Sigourney) **21**:301
"Bell Songs" (Cooke) **110**:9
"La bella de noche" (Isaacs) **70**:311
"Belladonna" (O'Brien) **21**:236, 242-43
Bellah (Feuillet) **45**:84-5, 87
"Bellambi's Maid" (Kendall) **12**:193
"Bell-Birds" (Kendall) **12**:182, 186, 191, 194, 197-99, 201
Belle au Bois Dormant (Feuillet) **45**:89
"La belle dame sans merci" (Keats) **8**:341, 347-48, 351, 357, 360, 375, 380-81; **73**:154, 188-93, 200, 202, 218, 224, 226-30, 232, 243, 261, 271, 282, 303-04, 307, 329; **121**:144, 205; **225**:126, 162, 164, 166, 168-70
"La belle Dorothée" (Baudelaire) **6**:87; **155**:86, 88-89
La Belle Jenny (Gautier) **1**:346; **59**:12
"La belle Juive" (Timrod) **25**:374, 384
La Belle Rivière (Bird) **197**:29
"La belle Véronique" (Banville) **9**:16
"Bellerophon at Argos" (Morris) **4**:447
"Bellerophon in Lycia" (Morris) **4**:420, 447
"La belleza ideal" (Alarcón) **219**:46
"The Bell-Founder of Breslau" (Muller)
See "Der Glockenguss zu Breslau"
"Bellini" (Wagner) **119**:190
"Bellona" (Gordon) **21**:154, 163, 172, 181
"The Bells" (Poe) **1**:496, 502, 519; **55**:141, 149, 154, 213; **117**:192, 195, 231, 242-43, 280, 283, 287-88, 309; **211**:260-61
"The Bells" (Southey) **8**:472
The Bells (Hayne) **94**:162
Bells and Pomegranates (Browning) **19**:75, 78
Bells and Pomegrantes (Browning) **79**:93, 147, 152, 181
"The Bells of Lynn" (Longfellow) **45**:190
"The Bells of San Blas" (Longfellow) **2**:484; **45**:139, 141, 151, 163-64
Les bells poupées (Banville) **9**:31
"Bell's Trouble" (Cooke) **110**:58
"The Bell-Tower" (Melville) **3**:331, 380, 382
"Beloved Tune" (Child) **6**:201; **73**:90
The Belton Estate (Trollope) **6**:470-71, 499, 501-02, 515-16; **101**:264, 310, 319
Le belvéder; ou, La vallée de l'Etna (Pixérécourt) **39**:274, 277, 279, 282
"Belyi orel" (Leskov)
See "Belyj orel"
"Belyj orel" (Leskov) **25**:240, 242, 244; **174**:37
"Bema pamięci żałobny rapsod" (Norwid) **17**:365, 367, 375-77, 379
Bemerkungen und Ansichten (Chamisso) **82**:25
Ben Jonson (Symonds) **34**:342
Ben, the Luggage Boy; or, Among the Wharves (Alger) **8**:37, 39, 44; **83**:112
"Benbow" (Crabbe) **26**:121
"Bençāo paterna" (Alencar) **157**:30, 35
"Beneath the Cards of a Game of Whist" (Barbey d'Aurevilly)
See "Le dessous de cartes d'une partie de whist"
Beneath the Flood (Storm)
See *Aquis Submersus*
"Benedict Arnold's Departure" (Freneau) **111**:81
"Bénédiction" (Baudelaire) **6**:82, 92, 97, 114, 117, 123; **29**:77, 102; **55**:12, 48-50, 53, 56, 62-5
"Benediction de Dieu dans la solitude" (Lamartine) **11**:265, 270, 279; **190**:225
"The Benevolent Protector, or Bartholomew as Alphonse" (Norwid) **17**:370
"The Benighted Sportsman" (Surtees) **14**:349
Beniowski (Slowacki) **15**:348-49, 354, 358-59, 365, 368, 371, 374-76, 378, 380-81
"Benito Cereno" (Melville) **3**:331, 344, 347, 354, 361-62, 368, 380-84; **29**:362-63; **91**:204; **93**:188-93, 197, 201-7, 210-19, 222-24, 226-27, 229-37, 240-41, 243-45, 248-49; **123**:186, 226, 254-55, 261; **157**:70, 102, 154; **181**:216, 327; **193**:52, 63, 65, 67, 120, 146; **221**:145-46, 182, 184, 187, 196
Benjamin Robert Haydon: Correspondence and Table-Talk. With a Memoir by His Son, Frederic Wordsworth Haydon. With Facsimile Illustrations from His Journals (Haydon) **146**:119
"Benjamin the Waggoner" (Wordsworth) **111**:204, 370
Ben's Nugget (Alger) **8**:44
"Bentham" (Mill) **11**:361, 370; **58**:327, 333, 351; **179**:206, 339
Beobachtungen über das Gefühl des Schönen und Erhabenen (Kant) **67**:214
"Beowulf" (Morris) **4**:441
Beowulfes Beorh (Grundtvig) **158**:171
Beppo (Byron)
See *Beppo: A Venetian Story*
Beppo: A Venetian Story (Byron) **2**:64, 72, 92-94, 97; **12**:70-71, 80, 84, 87, 103, 106, 125, 127; **109**:67; **149**:4, 9, 24, 88, 91, 97, 163-64
"Béranger" (Bagehot) **10**:62
"Berceuse" (Laforgue) **221**:85
"Bereavement" (Bowles) **103**:55
"Bereavement" (Keble) **87**:134
"Berenice" (Poe) **1**:500, 514; **16**:291, 297, 300, 304-05, 308, 314, 331, 334-35; **55**:148, 187, 194, 206; **94**:202; **97**:180, 208-09; **117**:299-300, 322-23; **117**:299-300, 322-23
Berenice, Ein erotischer Spaziergang (Muller) **73**:366
"Berganza" (Hoffmann)
See "Nachricht von den neuesten Schicksalen des Hundes Berganza"
"Bergkristall" (Stifter) **41**:344, 351; **198**:285, 287
Bergmilch (Stifter) **41**:372
"Die Bergwerke zu Falun" (Hoffmann) **2**:360; **183**:194-99, 211-12, 298
"Berkeley the Banker" (Martineau) **26**:314, 330; **137**:267
Berlin Lectures (Schlegel) **142**:332-38
"Berlinischer Damenkalender" (Schlegel) **142**:320
Berlioz and his Harold Symphony (Liszt) **199**:305, 337
Bernard Brooks' Adventures (Alger) **8**:43, 45
"Bernardine du Born" (Sigourney) **21**:298
"Le Bernica" (Leconte de Lisle) **29**:216, 244
Berta (Droste-Hülshoff) **3**:196-97
"Bertha" (Alcott) **83**:5
"Bertha" (Lazarus) **8**:411, 417; **109**:297, 321, 342
"Bertha in the Lane" (Barrett Browning) **1**:112, 115, 117-8; **61**:65-6

Bertha's Christmas Vision: An Autumn Sheaf (Alger) **83**:96
"Berthe" (Maupassant) **83**:219
Berthold Auerbach's Deutscher Volks-Kalender (Auerbach) **171**:72-73, 75, 79-80
Berthold Auerbach's gesammelte Schriften (Auerbach) **171**:55
Bertoldo (Da Ponte) **50**:80
Bertram (Maturin) **169**:10, 13, 18, 37, 93-94, 99-100, 102, 114, 116-17, 119
Bertram; or, The Castle of St. Aldobrand (Maturin) **6**:317-24, 328, 332-33, 339-40, 342-44
"Bertram to Lady Geraldine" (Thomson) **18**:396, 407
The Bertrams: A Novel (Trollope) **6**:463, 470, 484, 499-500, 512, 514-15; **101**:253, 290, 307, 312; **215**:214, 240, 282-83
Bertrand et Raton; ou, L'art de conspirer (Scribe) **16**:388, 414
Beruhigung (Klopstock) **225**:299
"The Beryl Stone" (Barrett Browning) **1**:124
Beschluss, über das Ideal der Sprache (Herder) **8**:317
"Der beschriebene Tännling" (Stifter) **198**:259
De beschriebene Tännling (Stifter) **41**:354
"Besenok" (Baratynsky)
See "Besyonok"
Beshenye dengi (Ostrovsky) **30**:105, 111; **57**:213-4, 220
"El beso" (Bécquer) **106**:98, 108, 121
Bespridannitsa (Ostrovsky) **30**:100, 104, 110, 115; **57**:213, 220
"Der Bessenbinder von Rychiswyl" (Gotthelf) **117**:6
"Bessey of the Glen" (Clare) **86**:89
"Bessonnitsa" (Tyutchev) **34**:389, 391, 393, 395, 399
"Besstydnik" (Leskov) **174**:48
"Bessy's Troubles at Home" (Gaskell) **70**:185
"The Best Man in the Vield" (Barnes) **75**:77
"The Best Thing in the World" (Barrett Browning) **170**:121
"Best Things" (Parton) **86**:352
Die Bestimmung des Menschen (Fichte) **62**:29, 31, 34, 54
"Der Besuch auf dem Lande" (Gotthelf) **117**:6
"Besuch des Eros" (Mörike) **10**:450
*Der Besuch in St. Hiob zu*** (Claudius) **75**:190
"Besuch in Urach" (Mörike) **10**:448; **201**:287, 322-37, 341-42
"Besy" (Pushkin) **83**:279
Besy (Dostoevsky) **2**:158, 161-62, 167-68, 170-72, 175, 179-80, 184-86, 190, 197, 202-04; **7**:80, 102; **21**:88-146; **33**:165, 173, 177-79, 182, 234; **43**:91-92, 99, 122, 130, 134, 143, 148, 151, 155, 160; **119**:81-2, 87-9, 91, 150, 154; **167**:334; **202**:74, 102, 106
"Besyonok" (Baratynsky) **103**:9-10, 16, 22
"Beszel a fákkal..." (Petofi) **21**:285
"La bête à Maître Belhomme" (Maupassant) **1**:463
"Bethesda" (Prescott) **163**:52
"Betrachtungen" (Wieland)
See "Unparteyische Betrachtungen über die dermalige Staats-Revolution in Frankreich"
"Betrachtungen über den Weltlauf" (Kleist) **37**:249
"Betrachtungen über Metrik. An Friedrich Schlegel" (Schlegel) **142**:316, 353-54
Betrachtungen und Gedanken uber verschiedene Gegonstande der Welt und der Litteratur (Klinger) **1**:432
"Betrayal" (Lanier) **118**:202
The Betrothal (Boker) **125**:8, 19-20, 31, 36, 58
The Betrothal (Kivi)
See *Kihlaus*
The Betrothal (Patmore)
See *The Angel in the House, Book I: The Betrothal*
"The Betrothal in Santo Domingo" (Kleist)
See "Die Verlobung in St. Domingo"
The Betrothed (Manzoni)
See *I promessi sposi*
The Betrothed (Scott) **15**:313; **69**:313-14, 319, 331; **209**:182, 185, 222-23
The Betrothed (Tieck) **5**:513
"Das Betrübte Madchen" (Claudius) **75**:191
"Das Bettelweib von Locarno" (Kleist) **2**:448; **37**:246, 248, 254-5
"The Better Day" (Lampman) **25**:217
"The Better Hope" (Jones) **222**:155, 171-72, 175-76
"The Better Land" (Hemans) **29**:207
"Better Late Than Never" (Goncharov)
See "Luchshe pozdno, chem nikogda"
"Better Moments" (Willis) **194**:307
"The Better Part" (Arnold) **218**:121
"A Better Resurrection" (Rossetti) **2**:575; **50**:322; **66**:330
"Better So" (Rossetti) **186**:314
Bettina von Arnims Sätliche Werke (Arnim) **38**:13
Bettinas Briefwechsel mit Goethe (Arnim)
See *Goethes Briefwechsel mit einem Kinde: Seinem Denkmal*
Bettine (Musset) **7**:271; **150**:226, 335, 340
"Bettlerballade" (Meyer) **81**:207
Betty Brown, the St. Giles's Orange Girl (More) **141**:167-68, 172, 188, 190, 270
"Betty Foy" (Wordsworth) **12**:430
Between Heaven and Earth (Ludwig)
See *Zwischen Himmel und Erde*
"Between the Rapids" (Lampman) **25**:160-61, 167-68, 190, 205-06; **194**:37-38, 61
"Between the Showers" (Levy) **203**:343
"Between the Wind and the Rain" (Crawford) **12**:156, 162
"Between Two Stools" (Levy) **59**:95, 107-9, 111, 120; **203**:351
Bevis (Jefferies)
See *Bevis, The Story of a Boy*
Bevis, The Story of a Boy (Jefferies) **47**:91, 93, 101, 111-12, 120, 124, 126-29, 131-32, 142
"Bevis's Zodiac" (Jefferies) **47**:113
"The Bewildered" (Rimbaud)
See "Les effarés"
"Bewitched" (Shevchenko)
See "Prycynna"
Bewitched (Barbey d'Aurevilly)
See *L'ensorcelée*
"A Bewitched Place" (Gogol)
See "Zakoldovannoe mesto"
"The Bewitched Spot" (Gogol)
See "Zakoldovannoe mesto"
"Beyond Kerguelen" (Kendall) **12**:190-91, 199-200
Beyond Recall (Fontane)
See *Unwiederbringlich*
"Beyond the Ravine Another Ravine" (Shevchenko)
See "Za bairakom bairak"
Beytrag zu vielen Beyträgen des Jahrhunderts (Herder) **186**:89
Beyträge zur geheimen Geschichte des menschlichen Verstandes und Herzens (Wieland) **17**:407; **177**:256-57, 286, 363, 365
Beyträge zur Optik (Goethe) **154**:324-26
Bez viný vinovátye (Ostrovsky) **57**:220
Bezdenezh'e (Turgenev) **21**:428, 432
"Bezhin Lea" (Turgenev) **21**:413, 418, 422; **122**:260, 337, 343, 348-49
"Bežin Meadow" (Turgenev)
See "Bezhin Lea"
"Beznadeznost'" (Baratynsky) **103**:26
Bezpridnnitsa (Ostrovsky)
See *Bespridannitsa*
"Beztalanny" (Shevchenko)
See "Tryzna"
"Bezumnykh let vgasshee vesel'e" (Pushkin) **83**:304
B-flat Major String Quartet, op. 130 (Beethoven)
See *String Quartet in B-flat Major, op. 130*
"Bhagavat" (Leconte de Lisle) **29**:221-23, 234, 242, 245
"Bharat kalanka" (Chatterji) **19**:225
"Bharatvarsher swadhinata ebang paradhinata" (Chatterji) **19**:225
Białe kwiaty (Norwid) **17**:371
"Bianca among the Nightingales" (Barrett Browning) **61**:7, 45
Bianca, or The Young Spanish Maiden (Dutt) **29**:129
Bianca Visconti; or The Heart Overtasked (Willis) **194**:292, 304, 309-10
"Bianca's Dream" (Hood) **16**:235
Bibelske Praedikener (Grundtvig) **158**:111
"The Bible as Poetry" (Whitman) **205**:170
Bible de l'humanité (Michelet) **31**:210, 216, 218, 232, 248, 258
The Bible in Spain; or, The Journeys, Adventures, and Imprisonments of an Englishman, in an Attempt to Circulate the Scriptures in the Peninsula (Borrow) **9**:37-40, 42, 47-8, 50-1, 53, 55-6, 59, 65-6
Bible of Hell (Blake) **57**:44, 53, 55, 82, 92-3
The Bible of Humanity (Michelet)
See *Bible de l'humanité*
The Bible of Mankind (Michelet)
See *Bible de l'humanité*
Biblical Dialogues Between a Father and His Family (Rowson) **69**:109, 116-17; **182**:256, 356
Biblical Sermons (Grundtvig)
See *Bibelske Praedikener*
"Bibliographical Notes" (Eminescu) **131**:325
Bibliomanie (Flaubert) **62**:101
"Le bibliophile" (Bertrand) **31**:48
Biblioteca Americana (Bello) **131**:92, 101-2, 107, 109, 116, 118, 129-30
"A bid for an Editorship" (Parton) **86**:318
Die bieden Nachtwandler (Nestroy) **42**:231
"Les bienfaits de la lune" (Baudelaire) **6**:87
"The Bienfilâtre Sisters" (Villiers de l'Isle Adam)
See "Les demoiselles de Bienfilâtre"
"La bienveillance universelle" (Joubert) **9**:292
"Bifurcation" (Browning) **19**:88
"The Big Bear of Arkansas" (Thorpe) **183**:320, 324, 326-27, 333, 338-40, 343-45, 350-51, 354-55, 358-62
"Big Claus and Little Claus" (Andersen)
See "Lille Claus og Store Claus"
The Biglow Papers (Lowell) **2**:504, 508-09, 511, 513-14, 516-17, 519-20, 522-23; **90**:188-90, 193, 198, 210, 215, 217-19, 221, 225
"Les bijoux" (Baudelaire) **29**:73; **55**:7-9, 56, 59, 76
"Les bijoux" (Maupassant) **1**:463
"Das Bild des Bathyllos" (Mörike) **10**:450
Das Bild des Kaisers (Hauff) **185**:351, 353
"Bilder aus Bebenhausen" (Mörike) **201**:349
Bilder aus dem Osten (Schumann) **143**:139
Bilder aus der deutschen Vergangenheit (Freytag) **109**:158, 165-67, 171-72, 177, 180-81
Bilder aus Westphalen (Droste-Hülshoff) **3**:193, 197, 200
"Bilder und Balladen" (Meyer) **81**:150, 152
"Bilder und Sagen aus der Schweiz" (Gotthelf) **117**:33
"Das Bilderbuch" (Eichendorff) **225**:48
"Das Bildnes der Geliebten" (Mörike) **10**:450
"Das Bildnis der Geliebten" (Mörike) **201**:281
"Bill Ainsworth's Quarter Race" (Harris) **23**:140, 142
"Bill Ainsworth's Quarter Race: A Story of Old Times (1833) in East Tennessee" (Harris) **165**:179-80, 210
"The Bill for Divorce" (Gladstone) **213**:112
Bill for Religious Freedom (Jefferson) **103**:157

"Bill Jones on Prayer" (Thomson) **18**:403
"Bill the Bullock-Driver" (Kendall) **12**:190, 192, 195
"Billedbog uden Billeder" (Andersen) **7**:29; **214**:76
"Le Billet" (Desbordes-Valmore) **97**:12
Billet à Lily (Verlaine) **51**:363
"Billet à Whistler" (Mallarmé) **210**:218
"A Billet Doux" (Horton) **87**:96
"Billiards" (Shaw) **15**:335
"Billingsgate Music" (Maginn) **8**:441
The Billiten in the Parsonage (Arnim)
See *Die Einquartierung im Pfarrhause*
"Bills of Mortality" (Cowper) **8**:103
Billy Budd and Other Prose Pieces (Melville) **157**:72, 84, 108, 112, 150, 212; **221**:113, 128, 132-33, 154, 163-66
Billy Budd, Sailor: An Inside Narrative (Melville) **3**:336, 345, 347, 358-59, 363-64, 366-68, 370-73, 375, 384-85; **29**:314-83; **45**:213, 233, 242, 244, 248; **49**:379; **91**:53, 193; **93**:214; **123**:186, 197, 212; **181**:214, 217, 327; **193**:67
"Billy in the Darbies" (Melville) **157**:212
"Billy Vickers" (Kendall) **12**:190-91
"Bimini" (Heine) **4**:238; **54**:330-3, 337; **147**:139, 160, 230, 232
"The Bindweed" (Webster) **230**:311, 313
"Binsey Poplars" (Hopkins) **17**:186, 204, 223, 256; **189**:7, 18, 20-21, 100, 120
Biographia Borealis (Coleridge) **90**:15, 24, 32
Biographia Literaria; or, Biographical Sketches of My Literary Life and Opinions (Coleridge) **9**:136-37, 152, 155, 157, 159-61, 163-65, 169, 173-74, 178-79, 184, 199-200, 205-07; **54**:80, 83, 101, 107, 114-5; **99**:4, 6, 13, 34-5, 38-40, 42, 53-4, 77-9, 86-7, 92, 95, 99, 104, 106, 115; **111**:201, 245, 290-91, 295, 311-13; **177**:36, 42, 103, 107, 140, 150, 154; **197**:179, 187, 210, 228-29, 240-41, 261, 263, 271-72, 275, 277, 281, 284-85, 299, 320; **231**:19, 23, 25, 27, 29, 34, 41, 44, 64, 67, 70, 72, 82, 86-88, 90, 94-95, 98, 100-106, 118, 123, 130, 150-53
Biographical and Critical Miscellanies (Prescott) **163**:346-47
Biographical Essays (De Quincey) **4**:61-62
A Biographical History of Philosophy (Lewes) **25**:274, 276, 287-88, 293, 295-96, 299-300, 304, 307, 320; **215**:84-86, 99, 106, 118, 122-23, 140-43, 148, 162-63, 166
"Biographical Memoir of Mr. Liston" (Lamb) **10**:435
Biographical Memoirs of Extraordinary Painters (Beckford) **16**:15, 17-22, 29, 36-7; **214**:163, 165
Biographical Recreations under the Cranium of a Giantess (Jean Paul) **7**:227
Biographical Sketches (Martineau) **26**:348-49
Biographical Studies (Bagehot) **10**:23, 43
Biographies of Good Wives (Child) **73**:47, 59, 64, 72, 75, 97
The Biographies of Madame de Staël and Madame Roland, Married Women; or, Biographies of Good Wives (Child) **6**:197-98, 203; **73**:59, 72
"Biography and Writings of A. M. Hyde" (Sigourney) **87**:321
"Biography of Females" (Sigourney) **87**:321
"Biography of Pious Persons" (Sigourney) **87**:321
"Biondette in dem Theater" (Brentano) **191**:8
Birāṅganā Kabya (Dutt) **118**:30
"The Birch Grove Near Endermay" (Muller) **73**:352
"Birchington Churchyard" (Rossetti) **186**:333-35
"The Birch-Tree at Loschwitz" (Levy) **59**:90, 119
The Bird (Michelet) **31**:215, 219, 242-44, 247, 259-60, 263
"A Bird and a Flower" (Webster) **230**:239
"The Bird and the Bell" (Cranch) **115**:15, 17, 22, 27, 35
The Bird and the Bell, with Other Poems (Cranch) **115**:17, 22-3, 26, 40, 55
"The Bird and the Hour" (Lampman) **25**:169; **194**:34, 79, 82, 86-88
"The Bird and the Ship" (Muller) **73**:350, 352
"The Bird and the Watch" (Carlyle) **181**:81
"A Bird came down the Walk" (Dickinson) **171**:123, 180
The Bird in the Pear-Tree (Andersen) **79**:11
"Bird Language" (Cranch) **115**:41, 43
"The Bird Mediæval" (Cooper) **129**:71
"Bird of Paradise" (Karamzin)
See "Rayskaya ptichka"
"Bird of Paradise" (Ueda Akinari)
See "Bupposo"
"The Bird Primeval" (Cooper) **129**:71
"Birds Climbing the Air" (Jefferies) **47**:136
"A Bird's Eye View" (Rossetti) **2**:556; **50**:289; **186**:265
"Birds in the High Hall-Garden" (Tennyson) **30**:242
"Birds in the Night" (Verlaine) **2**:632; **51**:381, 383-84; **230**:184-85, 187
"The Bird's Nest" (Hale) **75**:284-85, 289
"The Bird's Nest" (Keble) **87**:134
"Birds' Nests" (Clare) **9**:108, 110-11; **86**:144
Birds of America (Audubon) **47**:3, 11, 13-15, 18, 20, 23, 27-30, 32-3, 36-8, 40, 45-7, 50-3
The Birds of Aristophanes (Planché) **42**:273-75, 277, 281-82, 284-86, 291, 293
"The Birds of Killingworth" (Longfellow) **2**:481; **45**:130, 137, 145, 149, 180, 188, 191
"The Birds of Passage" (Hemans) **71**:263
"Birds of Passage" (Longfellow) **45**:116, 133, 137
"Birds of Passage" (Whitman) **205**:226-27, 260
Birds of Passage: Songs of the Orient and Occident (Blind) **202**:6, 9, 18, 50, 52, 55-58
"The Birds on the Wires" (Cranch) **115**:43
"The Bird's Release" (Hemans) **71**:264
The Birds' Rivalry (Da Ponte)
See *La gara degli uccelli*
"Birds Then and Now" (Cooper) **129**:71
"Birjuk" (Turgenev) **122**:264
Birth (Robertson) **35**:335, 361, 363-65, 369
"The Birth of a Poet" (Neal) **161**:287
"Birth of Criticism" (Murphy) **229**:253
"The Birth of Flattery" (Crabbe) **26**:78-9, 81; **121**:9
"The Birth of Genius" (Rowson) **182**:254
"Birth of the Duke of Bordeaux" (Hugo) **3**:234
"The Birth of the Horse" (Taylor) **89**:302-03
"The Birthday" (Herder) **186**:10
"The Birth-Day" (Robinson) **142**:169, 275-76, 278, 280
"A Birthday" (Rossetti) **2**:559; **50**:289; **66**:311, 342, 344, 382; **186**:264-65, 285, 303, 339
"Birthday of Longfellow" (Sigourney) **87**:326
"The Birthday of the Soul" (Very) **9**:387
"Birthday Song" (Lanier) **6**:237
Birth-Day Song of Liberty (Chivers) **49**:45
"A Birthday Song to S. G." (Lanier) **118**:260
"Birthday Verses" (Willis) **194**:307
"A Birthday Wish" (Lamb) **125**:372
"The Birthmark" (Hawthorne) **2**:311, 319, 322, 324; **17**:145, 151; **23**:218; **79**:308; **95**:105, 110, 207; **171**:243; **191**:199-200; **226**:37-38, 81
"La Bise se rue . . ." (Verlaine) **230**:167
"The Bishop and the Philosopher" (Arnold) **218**:173
"Bishop Berkeley on the Metaphysics of Sensation" (Huxley) **67**:86-7
"Bishop Blougram's Apology" (Browning) **19**:79, 100, 117, 120-23, 131, 136-38; **79**:163, 171
Bishop Bonner's Ghost (More) **141**:234
"The Bishop of Børglurn and his Warriors" (Andersen) **214**:56
"The Bishop Orders His Tomb at San Praxed's" (Browning) **19**:77, 114, 117, 119, 133, 136-37
"The Bishop Orders His Tomb at St. Praxed's" (Browning) **79**:94, 98-99, 103
"Bishop Percy's Folio Manuscript" (Child) **173**:224, 229
Bishop Percy's Folio Manuscript (Percy) **95**:309, 314, 331
"The Bishop: The Philosopher" (Arnold) **126**:89
"Ein bisschen Freude" (Meyer) **81**:145
"A Bit O' Sly Coorten" (Barnes) **75**:78, 82, 93
"A Bit of Injustice" (Parton) **86**:320
The Bit o'Writing (Banim and Banim) **13**:130-31
"Bite deep and wide, O Axe, the tree!" (Crawford) **127**:151
"The Biter Bit" (Collins) **1**:187
Bits of Travel (Jackson) **90**:144, 167
Bitter Drops (Silva)
See *Gotas amargas*
"Bitter for Sweet" (Rossetti) **2**:558, 575
"Bitter Fruits from Chance-Sown Seeds" (Kirkland) **85**:265, 301
"Bitter Potions" (Silva)
See "Gotas Amargas"
Das bittere Leiden unsers Herrn Jesu Christi: Nach den Betrachtungen der gottseligen Anna Katharina Emmerich, Augustinerin des Klosters Agnetenberg zu Dülmen (Brentano) **191**:119
"The Bivouac of the Dead" (Bryant) **6**:172
"Bivouac on a Mountain Side" (Whitman) **205**:159, 338-39
Bjowulfs Drape (Grundtvig) **158**:170
"Blaavin" (Smith) **59**:333
Black (Dumas) **71**:204
"Black and White" (Barnes) **75**:98
"The Black and White Question" (Hood) **16**:239
The Black Arrow: A Tale of Two Roses (Stevenson) **5**:405, 409, 415, 430-31; **63**:222, 228, 255-6, 261; **193**:210, 216-17, 222, 241, 344
"Black Bandit" (Castro Alves)
See "Bandido negro"
The Black Baronet (Carleton) **3**:89-90; **199**:10, 12
"The Black Birds and Yellow Hammers" (Griffin) **7**:218
The Black Cabinet (Sacher-Masoch) **31**:295
"The Black Cat" (Poe) **1**:495, 521; **16**:294-95, 301, 303, 309, 314-15, 325-27, 329-32, 334; **55**:148; **78**:281-87, 298-99; **117**:320, 322-23; **211**:247, 312
"Black Cats" (Coleridge) **90**:9
"The Black Cock" (Baillie) **151**:86, 91
The Black Domino (Scribe)
See *Le domino noir*
The Black Dwarf (Scott) **15**:259-60; **69**:308; **209**:199-201, 250
Black Forest Tales (Auerbach)
See *Schwarzwälder Dorfgeschichten*
"The Black Fox" (Whittier) **8**:526
Black Giles the Poacher (More)
See *Black Giles the Poacher: Containing Some Account of a Family Who Had Rather Live by Their Wits than Their Work*
Black Giles the Poacher: Containing Some Account of a Family Who Had Rather Live by Their Wits than Their Work (More) **27**:346; **141**:167-68, 193, 270, 290
"Black Guitar Blues" (Castro Alves)
See "Cançao do violeio"
"The Black Jack" (Maginn) **8**:438
"A Black Job" (Hood) **16**:238-39
"Black Kate" (Kendall) **12**:192
"Black Lizzie" (Kendall) **12**:192

Black Man (Brown)
See *The Black Man: His Antecedents, His Genius, and His Achievements*
The Black Man: His Antecedents, His Genius, and His Achievements (Brown) **2**:48, 50; **89**:143-44, 163, 178-79
The Black Man's Lament (Opie) **65**:175
The Black Prophet: A Tale of Irish Famine (Carleton) **3**:85-86, 90, 94-96; **199**:8-9, 11, 15, 19, 21-24, 41-44, 46, 48, 74-75, 77-80, 82-84, 91, 95, 97
"Black Regiment" (Boker) **125**:25, 33, 39
The Black Robe (Collins) **1**:184
"The Black Shawl" (Pushkin)
See "Chornaya shal"
"Black Sonnets" (Silva)
See "Sonetos negros"
"The Black Spider" (Gotthelf)
See "Die Schwarze Spinne"
"Black Stories" (Silva)
See "Los cuentos negros"
The Black Tulip (Dumas)
See *La tulipe noire*
"Black, White, and Brown" (Hood) **16**:206
The Blackamoor of Peter the Great (Pushkin)
See *Povesti Belkina*
"Blackballees' Lament" (Laforgue)
See "Complainte des blackboulés"
Blackberries Picked off Many Bushes (Allingham) **25**:22
"Blackbirds" (Ketcham) **118**:242
Black-Eyed Susan; or, All in the Downs (Jerrold) **2**:395, 401, 403-05, 408
Black-Jewel Scroll (Ueda Akinari)
See *Nubatama no Maki*
"Blackmwore Maidens" (Barnes) **75**:4, 101
"Blacksmith" (Rimbaud)
See "Le forgeron"
"Blackstone Edge" (Jones) **222**:142, 156, 176
"Blackwood" (Tennyson) **115**:235
"Blagodarnost' Felitse" (Derzhavin) **215**:26, 57
"Blagodeyaniye" (Karamzin) **173**:284
Blagonamerennyya rechi (Saltykov) **16**:359, 373
Blake (Delany)
See *Blake; or, The Huts of America: A Tale of the Mississippi Valley, the Southern United States, and Cuba*
Blake, Coleridge, Wordsworth, Lamb, Etc.: Being Selections from the Remains of H. C. Robinson (Robinson) **15**:185
Blake: Complete Writings with Variant Readings (Blake) **127**:93-100
Blake; or, The Huts of America: A Tale of the Mississippi Valley, the Southern United States, and Cuba (Delany) **93**:104, 107-09, 112, 153-56, 160-64, 166-67, 169-75
"Blake's Cottage at Felpham" (Blake) **173**:64
"Blakesmoor in H—shire" (Lamb) **10**:435-36
Le blanc et le noir (Grillparzer) **102**:113
Blanche Lisle, and Other Poems (Webster) **230**:245, 255
Blanche of Brandywine; or, September the Eleventh, 1777. A Romance. Combining the Poetry, Legend, and History of the Battle of Brandywine (Lippard) **198**:117-18, 121, 123, 125, 173, 209
"Blanco y negro" (Casal) **131**:256-57
Les Blancs et les bleus (Dumas) **71**:192
Blandina (Hoffmann)
See *Prinzessin Blandina: ein romantisches Spiel in drei Aufzügen*
"Blandois' Song" (Dickens) **113**:131
"Blanduzia's Fountain" (Eminescu)
See "Fântâna Blanduziei"
"Blaney" (Crabbe) **26**:121
"Blank Misgivings of a Creature moving about in Worlds not realised" (Prescott) **163**:43, 45, 47-48
"Blank Misgivings of a Creature Moving about in Worlds Not Realized" (Clough) **27**:106-7, 114
The Blank Paper (Sacher-Masoch) **31**:298
Blank Verse, by Charles Lloyd and Charles Lamb (Lamb) **113**:161, 181, 269, 274, 277-78
Blanka von Kastilien (Grillparzer) **1**:386; **102**:78-9, 148, 189
Blanks and Prizes (Gore) **65**:21
"The Blasphemy of Gasconade and Self-Dependence in a Certain General" (Brackenridge) **7**:44
Blätter für Deutsche Art und Kunst (Herder) **8**:299
"Blätter und Blümchen aus der goldenen Aue" (Schumann) **143**:73, 76, 138
Bleak House (Dickens) **3**:151-52, 159, 166, 169-72, 174, 178, 186-87; **8**:159-205; **18**:100, 127, 132-34; **26**:157, 171, 177, 202, 205; **37**:164, 174, 192, 202, 204; **86**:18, 197, 201, 222, 255-56, 260; **105**:201, 211, 213-14, 228, 244, 256, 288, 290, 292, 294, 311, 317, 320, 330, 334, 336, 354; **113**:29, 34, 42, 48, 51, 63, 69, 91-3, 98, 106-07; **161**:37; **217**:221, 225, 238, 244, 248, 268; **219**:73, 83-84, 108, 111, 138, 142, 144, 158, 160, 163, 186-87, 190, 215; **230**:7, 9, 56, 66-8, 89, 109, 112, 114, 143-44; **231**:176, 179-81, 245
The Bleeding Rock (More) **27**:336
Blenda (Stagnelius) **61**:253-6
"Bless God, He Went as Soldiers" (Dickinson) **21**:55
"Blessed Are They Who Have No Talent:' Emerson's Unwritten Life of Amos Bronson Alcott" (Emerson) **98**:74-5
"The Blessed Damozel" (Rossetti) **4**:491-93, 495, 501-02, 504-05, 508, 510-14, 516-19, 522, 526-27, 529-30; **77**:301-06, 338, 340, 344-46, 348-54
"Blessed Marriage. A Distinctive Omission in the Annals of the History of the Schism" ("Blagosloviennyj brak. KHarakmiernyj propusk v ismorichieskoj limieramurie raskola") (Leskov) **174**:129
"The Blessed Virgin, Compared to the Air We Breathe" (Hopkins) **17**:188, 205, 208, 247; **189**:45, 47
"Blick auf die slavischen Mundarten, ihre Literatur und die Hülfsmittel sie zu studieren" (Kopitar) **117**:73, 115
"The Blind" (Baudelaire)
See "Les aveugles"
"Blind Bartimeus" (Longfellow) **2**:472; **45**:99, 128
"Blind Girl" (Shevchenko)
See "Slepaya"
Blind Love (Collins) **93**:19, 66
"The Blind Man" (Shevchenko)
See "Slipyi"
"Blind One" (Shevchenko)
See "Slepaya"
"The Blind Seer" (Cranch) **115**:9, 40
"A Blind Woman" (Shevchenko)
See "Slepaya"
"Der blinde Sänger" (Hölderlin) **187**:216
"The Blindman's World" (Bellamy) **4**:31; **86**:7, 9, 17, 75, 79
The Blindman's World and Other Stories (Bellamy) **86**:70, 75; **147**:89
"Blindness" (Martineau) **26**:349
"The Blissful" (Kivi)
See "Onnelliset"
The Blithedale Romance (Hawthorne) **2**:300-03, 306, 313-14, 326, 329-30, 332; **10**:295; **17**:108-59; **23**:169, 183, 205, 208-09, 213-14; **39**:177, 180, 186, 188, 224, 227, 229; **79**:295-96, 304; **95**:104, 106, 125, 150, 205; **158**:224, 233, 246, 287-88, 292-93; **171**:237, 262-63, 270, 279, 310, 332, 343, 345-46, 349, 358, 360; **191**:178-79, 242, 253, 302; **226**:1-155
"The Blizzard" (Aksakov)
See "Buran"
"The Blizzard" (Pushkin)
See "Metel"
"Blliz stana yunosha prekrasnyy . . ." (Bestuzhev) **131**:182
"Das Blockhaus" (Lenau) **16**:269, 283
The Blockheads; or, The Affrighted Officers (Warren) **13**:419, 428, 436; **226**:253, 257-61, 271-73
"The Blockhouse" (Traill) **31**:325
Der blonde Eckbert (Tieck) **5**:514, 517, 519, 523-25, 529-31; **46**:332-3, 337-45, 348-52, 355-56, 364-65, 374-75, 377, 381-87, 391-92, 414
"Bloodless Goddess" (Castro Alves)
See "Deusa Incruenta"
"Blood-Money" (Whitman) **205**:171, 312
"The Bloodstained Robe" (Ueda Akinari)
See "Chi katabira"
The Bloody Buoy, Thrown Out as a Warning to the Political Pilots of America (Cobbett) **49**:107, 109
"The Bloody Vestiges of Tyranny" (Brackenridge) **7**:44
"The Blossom" (Blake) **37**:3, 11, 14, 36, 39, 41, 57, 65, 72, 75, 83, 85-7, 92
The Blossom of Happiness (Andersen) **79**:13-14
A Blot in the 'Scutcheon (Browning) **19**:76, 95, 102, 113-14; **79**:147, 188-89
Bloudie Jacke of Shresberrie (Barham) **77**:9
"Blown Up with Soda" (Harris) **23**:140, 143, 153, 159, 163; **165**:200, 225-27, 231, 233, 249, 270
"The Blue and the Gray" (Alcott) **83**:7
"The Blue and the Gray" (Bryant) **6**:172
Blue Beard (Dunlap) **2**:211
Blue Beard (Planché) **42**:279, 288, 292, 299
The Blue Belles of England (Trollope) **30**:327-29
"The Blue Bower" (Morris) **4**:425
"The Blue Closet" (Morris) **4**:411, 419, 421, 423, 425-26, 431
"The Blue Evening" (Isaacs)
See "La tarde azul"
"Blue Flower" (Eminescu)
See "Floare albastra"
"The Blue Hood" (Ueda Akinari)
See "Aozukin"
The Blue Licks (Bird) **197**:29
"A Blue Love Song" (Moore) **110**:172
The Blue Monster (Gozzi)
See *Il mostro turchino*
"The Blue Room" (Mérimée)
See "La chambre bleue"
Bluebeard the Knight (Tieck)
See *Ritter Blaubart*
"Blue-Beard's Closet" (Cooke) **110**:51
"The Bluebell" (Brontë) **71**:165
"Blue-Stocking Reveals" (Hunt) **70**:271
Blumen (Novalis) **178**:15
Blumen-, Frucht-, und Dornenstücke; oder, Ehestand Tod, und Hochzeit des Armena dvocaten Firmian Stanislaus Siebenkäs (Jean Paul) **7**:232, 236, 238-40
Blumensträuße italienischer, spanischer, portugiesischer Poesie (Schlegel) **142**:301, 319
"Blümlein Vergißmein" (Muller) **73**:365, 373-74
Blütenstaub (Novalis) **13**:365, 376, 379
Blüthenstaub (Novalis) **178**:15, 22, 24, 27, 43-44, 60, 126, 128-29
"Der Blutstropfen" (Meyer) **81**:199, 205, 209
Der Blutsuger (Polidori)
See *The Vampyre: A Tale*
Blyzniata (Shevchenko) **54**:392, 396
"Boa Noite" (Castro Alves) **205**:4
"Boädicea" (Tennyson) **30**:230, 233, 236
"Boadicea. An Ode" (Cowper) **8**:107, 111, 120; **94**:32
The Boarder (Turgenev)
See *Nakhlebnik*
Boarding Out; or, Domestic Life (Hale) **75**:341

The Boarding School, or Lessons of a Preceptress to Her Pupils (Foster) **99**:122, 126, 138-42, 144, 167, 197, 199-204
"Boarding Schools" (Hale) **75**:345
"The Boar's Head Tavern, Eastcheap" (Irving) **2**:381; **19**:327, 347
"The Boat on the Serchio" (Shelley) **175**:201
The Boatman Artist (Gómez de Avellaneda)
See *El artista barquero o los cuatro cinco de junio*
"The Boatman of Whitehall" (O'Brien) **21**:248
"Bob Burke's Duel with Ensign Brady" (Maginn) **8**:438-40
Bob Burton; or, The Young Ranchman of the Missouri (Alger) **8**:43
"Bob the Fiddler" (Barnes) **75**:77, 81
"Bobolinks" (Cranch) **115**:41, 43
"Boccaccio and Petrarca" (Landor) **14**:195
"Bocetos antiguos" (Casal) **131**:269
"Bochsa" (Chivers) **49**:73
"Un bock" (Maupassant) **1**:450
La boda y el duelo (Martínez de la Rosa) **102**:253
"The Boding Dreams" (Beddoes) **3**:34; **154**:78
"The Body Snatcher" (Stevenson) **193**:238, 283, 289
"A Body Without a Head" (Haliburton) **149**:307
"Body's Beauty" (Rossetti) **4**:520; **77**:326, 330, 345, 355-56, 358
"Bog" (Derzhavin) **215**:5-7, 10, 26, 30, 32, 39, 52
"The Bog King's Daughter" (Andersen)
See "Dynd-Kongens Datter"
Bogdan Chmielnicki (Mérimée) **65**:85
Bogdan the Blind (Eminescu) **131**:292
Bogdan-Dragoş (Eminescu) **33**:265-66; **131**:291
"Bogdanovicu" (Baratynsky) **103**:25
"The Bogeyman" (Leskov)
See "Pugalo"
Bogle Corbet (Galt) **110**:88-9
"Bog-Wood" (Ichiyō)
See "Umoregi"
"Bohater" (Norwid) **17**:375
La bohème galante (Nerval) **67**:303, 306, 357
"The Bohemian" (O'Brien) **21**:236-37, 239, 243-45, 252
"Bohemian Hymn" (Emerson) **1**:297
La Bohémienne; ou, L'Amérique en 1775 (Scribe) **16**:388
"Bohémiens en voyage" (Baudelaire) **55**:53, 58
Les Bohémiens et leur Musique en Hongrie (Liszt)
See *Des Bohémiens et de leur musique en Hongrie*
"Bohemios" (Casal) **131**:243
Boiarin Orša (Lermontov) **5**:294; **126**:128, 184
Bojarin Orša (Lermontov)
See *Boiarin Orša*
"The bojarynja Plodomasova" (Leskov) **174**:13
"Le Bol de punch" (Gautier) **59**:10, 27
La bola de nieve (Tamayo y Baus) **1**:570
Boland Istók (Arany) **34**:16, 21
"The Bold Dragoon" (Irving) **19**:345
"Bold Words by a Bachelor" (Collins) **93**:61
"Bolond Istók" (Petofi) **21**:264, 267-69
Bolts of Melody: New Poems of Emily Dickinson (Dickinson) **77**:107, 128
"Bolyashchiy dukh vrachuet pesnopenie..." (Baratynsky) **103**:5
"Le bon Dieu" (Beranger) **34**:42
Le Bon Disciple (Verlaine) **51**:363, 367, 372
Un bon enfant (Kock) **16**:247-48
"Bon-Bon" (Poe) **16**:312
Boncourt Castle (Chamisso) **82**:4
"A Bond of Two Generations" (Ueda Akinari)
See "Nise no en"
"Bonden Pavo" (Runeberg) **41**:317
The Bondman (Cumberland) **167**:157
"The Bone Setter" (Le Fanu)
See "The Ghost and the Bone Setter"
"The Bone that has no Marrow" (Dickinson) **171**:200
A Bone to Gnaw, for the Democrats (Cobbett) **49**:109
"The Bones of Columbus" (Freneau) **111**:122
"Le bonheur" (Rimbaud) **4**:484
Bonheur (Verlaine) **2**:618-19; **51**:352, 356; **230**:160-61, 164-66, 169, 171, 178, 211
"Le bonheur dans le crime" (Barbey d'Aurevilly) **1**:74-75; **213**:56-61, 69, 81, 83-84, 100
La bonne chanson (Verlaine) **2**:617, 621-23, 627, 629-30; **51**:350, 356, 359, 361, 363, 376, 382, 384, 387; **230**:152, 154, 160, 164-69, 173, 181, 183, 198-202, 205
"Une bonne fortune" (Musset) **7**:264, 267, 275
"La bonne nourrice" (Banville) **9**:16
"Bonne Pensée du Matin" (Rimbaud) **82**:231-32, 248, 251
"La bonne vieille" (Beranger) **34**:28-9, 39
Bonneybell Vane (Cooke) **5**:126
"Bonnie Dundee" (Scott) **15**:318
"Bonnie Prince Charlie" (Hogg) **4**:284
"The Bonny Brown Hand" (Hayne) **94**:159-60
The Bonny Brown Hand (Hayne) **94**:134, 160
"Bons Bourgeois" (Verlaine) **51**:386
"Les bons chiens" (Baudelaire) **155**:95
"Bonsoir" (Corbière) **43**:25, 27, 33
"A Book" (Mickiewicz) **3**:390
Book for Children (Martínez de la Rosa)
See *El libro de los niños*
"The Book of Ahania" (Blake) **173**:81
The Book of Ahania (Blake) **13**:184, 221-22, 225-26, 252; **127**:111; **190**:3-4, 11-12, 14, 18, 25, 89, 126; **201**:39, 61, 145
"Book of Aphorisms" (Thomson) **18**:429
The Book of Fallacies (Bentham) **38**:37, 90
The Book of Los (Blake) **13**:184, 221-22, 226; **127**:111; **173**:61; **190**:11-12, 14, 39, 90, 100
Book of Memoranda (Dickens) **86**:221-22; **217**:261
The Book of Mormon (Smith) **53**:348, 355-63, 366, 368, 374-8, 380-2, 384-7
The Book of Moses (Smith) **53**:380
The Book of Mothers and Children (Desbordes-Valmore)
See *Le Livre des mères et des enfants*
The Book of My Life (Andersen)
See *Levnedsbogen*
Book of Nonsense (Lear) **3**:295, 297-99, 306
Book of Odds and Ends, or a Manual Encyclopedia (Gogol) **162**:107
"The Book of Odes" (Freneau) **111**:129
"The Book of Revelation" (Engels) **85**:44, 48
A Book of Rhyme (Webster) **230**:239, 303-06, 308
A Book of Romances, Lyrics, and Songs (Taylor) **89**:300, 307, 346
The Book of Roses (Parkman) **12**:347
The Book of Snobs (Thackeray) **5**:445-46, 453, 463, 465-66, 468, 478, 486-87, 500, 502; **14**:395-96, 402, 409, 422, 451; **43**:362, 388, 391; **169**:213; **213**:186-87, 217, 250, 261, 281, 284, 298, 337, 339, 343-44; **213**:250
Book of Songs (Heine)
See *Buch der Lieder*
Book of Sparrows: Collection of Projects, Plots, Ideas, and Plans for Different Things that Might or Might not Be Finished in Accordance with how the Wind Blows (Bécquer)
See *Libro de los gorriones: colección de proyectos, argumentos, ideas y planes de cosas diferentes que se concluirán o no según sople el viento*
The Book of the Church (Southey) **8**:463, 467; **97**:265-66, 268, 283, 330, 337
"Book of the Dead" (Boker) **125**:33
The Book of the Dead (Boker) **125**:18, 41, 78-80, 82
"The Book of the Poets" (Barrett Browning) **61**:58, 66; **66**:44
The Book of the Poets (Barrett Browning) **170**:104-5
The Book of the Wild Rose (Almqvist)
See *Törnrosens bok*
The Book of Thel (Blake) **13**:172, 177, 183-84, 218, 220-21, 234, 250-51; **37**:15, 20, 22, 42, 72, 96; **127**:79-80, 82; **173**:108; **190**:3, 11, 14, 61-62; **201**:29, 54, 64, 77, 83, 126, 140
The Book of Urizen (Blake) **13**:184, 194, 205, 221-29, 243, 252; **37**:53, 56; **57**:44, 91-2; **127**:11, 34, 66, 71, 87, 111; **173**:25, 40, 61, 147; **190**:4-5, 11-12, 14-15, 20, 23, 25, 32, 77-79, 87-89, 94, 97, 100, 111, 145; **201**:61, 64, 70, 75
The Book of Verses (Silva)
See *El libro de versos*
The Book on Adler (Kierkegaard) **78**:247
"Book on Logic" (Bentham) **38**:92
A Book I Value (Coleridge) **231**:151
"The Book to the Reader" (Fuller) **50**:237-8
"Book-Making" (Tennyson)
See "Old Poets Foster'd Under Friendlier Skies"
"Books" (Emerson) **1**:280; **38**:175; **98**:7-8
"The Books" (Eminescu)
See "Carţile"
"Books" (Wordsworth) **166**:217
"Books and Gardens" (Smith) **59**:303, 309
"Books and the World of Readers" (Hauff) **185**:339
"Books of the People" (D'Israeli) **217**:302
The Books of the Polish Nation and the Polish Pilgrimage (Mickiewicz)
See *Księgi narodu polskiego i pielgrzymastwa polskiego*
"Books Which Have Influenced Me" (Stevenson) **63**:239; **193**:259, 263
"The Boon Which I Last Crave" (Eminescu) **33**:267, 273; **131**:294, 297-98
"Booz endormi" (Hugo) **161**:264
"Bor vitéz" (Arany) **34**:15
"Bor'ba za suščestvovanie" (Pisarev) **25**:342, 344
"Bor'ba za žizn" (Pisarev) **25**:344, 346-47, 355-56
The Border Antiquities of England and Scotland (Scott) **209**:196
Border Beagles (Simms) **3**:502, 508-09, 514
The Border States (Kennedy) **2**:432
"A Border Tradition" (Bryant) **6**:180
The Borderers (Cooper) **203**:88
The Borderers (Wordsworth) **38**:421, 425-26; **111**:223, 239, 254, 263, 346-47; **166**:266; **206**:253-55, 258, 260-61
The Borderers; or, The Wept of Wish-ton-Wish (Cooper)
See *The Wept of Wish-ton-Wish*
"Borderland" (Levy) **59**:119; **203**:322
"Boredom" (Kivi)
See "Ikävyys"
"A borigines" (Whitman) **81**:353
Boris Godunov (Pushkin) **27**:379; **83**:246, 248, 250, 256, 264, 303, 305-06, 309, 332-35, 338-40, 342-43, 347, 353, 355, 361-65, 367, 369, 372-73
"A Born Chieftain" (Boyesen) **135**:15
"Borne Along by the Tide" (Eliot) **4**:134
Börne Memorial (Heine) **147**:203
"Bornholm Island" (Karamzin)
See "Ostrov Borngol'm"
"Borodinó" (Lermontov) **5**:295, 300; **126**:144, 223
The Borough (Crabbe) **26**:86, 89, 93, 102, 111, 115-16, 118-19, 122-25, 127, 132-34, 138, 141, 151; **121**:4-5, 10-11, 24, 28-9, 31, 34, 36, 58-9, 62-3, 66, 72, 74, 76-7, 83-6, 88-90
"A borozó" (Petofi) **21**:276
"Borrowed Plumes" (Gordon) **21**:164
"Borrowed Spectacles" (Silva)
See "Lentes ajenos"
"Bos amores" (Castro) **78**:42
Boscobel; or, The Royal Oak: A Tale of the Year 1651 (Ainsworth) **13**:36

"Die böse Farbe" (Muller) **73**:363, 365, 372-73
Der böse Geist Lumpazivagabundus oder Das liederliche Kleeblett (Nestroy) **42**:231-32, 236, 238-40, 254-57, 263
"Böse Stunde" (Grillparzer) **102**:174
"The Bosom Serpent" (Hawthorne) **2**:296, 305, 311; **95**:105
Bosquejo histórico de la política de España (Martínez de la Rosa) **102**:252
"Le bossu Bitord" (Corbière) **43**:3, 5, 7-8, 10, 21, 23, 29, 33
"A Boston Ballad" (Whitman)
See "Poem of Apparitions in Boston in the 73rd Year of These States"
"The Boston Hymn" (Emerson) **1**:279, 284-85, 289, 296; **98**:39, 41, 45, 49-50, 182-83
"Boswell Redivivus, a Dream" (Reynolds) **146**:171
"Boswell's Life of Johnson" (Carlyle) **70**:7, 9
"Boswell's Visit" (Reynolds) **146**:203
The Botanic Garden (Darwin) **106**:181, 186-87, 191-94, 198-200, 203, 207-09, 214, 218-19, 221, 225, 228, 230, 232, 235-37, 241-42, 244-45, 248, 251-52, 259, 261, 265, 273-77
Botany Bay Eclogues (Southey) **97**:260, 314-15
Bötcher Basch (Storm)
See *Bötjer Bosch*
Both Americas (Sarmiento)
See *Ambras Américas*
The Bothie of Tober-na-Vuolich (Prescott) **163**:11, 27-33, 36, 49, 52-53, 55-56, 58, 63-64, 84-86, 107-9, 116-23, 126, 132, 136-37, 149-51
The Bothie of Toper-na-Fuosich: A Long-Vacation Pastoral (Clough) **27**:37-8, 40-1, 43, 45, 49, 52, 56-60, 65-6, 71, 74, 77, 79-80, 82, 91-2, 95-8, 103-04, 111, 113-15
The Bothy System (Miller) **143**:13
Bötjer Basch (Storm) **1**:540, 544
Bötjer Bosch (Storm) **195**:13, 56-57, 73, 127, 131
"The Bottle Imp" (Stevenson) **5**:412, 415, 419; **193**:280-81
"The Bottle in the Sea" (Vigny)
See "La bouteille à la mer"
"The Bottleneck" (Andersen)
See "Flaskehalsen"
"Bottom" (Rimbaud) **4**:484-85; **227**:204-6, 242-43, 309
"Boule de suif" (Maupassant) **1**:442, 447, 449, 454, 459, 462, 465-66; **83**:168, 190, 193-94, 229
Bound to Rise; or, Harry Walton's Motto (Alger) **8**:42; **83**:124, 134
"Bound—a trouble—" (Dickinson) **171**:196
Bouquets and Prayers (Desbordes-Valmore)
See *Bouquets et prières*
Bouquets et prières (Desbordes-Valmore) **97**:13
"Le bourget" (Lamartine) **11**:264
"The Bourne" (Rossetti) **2**:572
"Bournemouth" (Verlaine) **2**:628; **51**:355, 370-71
"La bouteille à la mer" (Vigny) **7**:472, 474, 483-84, 486
"Bouts Rimés in Praise of Old Maids" (Barbauld) **185**:38
Bouvard and Pécuchet (Flaubert)
See *Bouvard et Pécuchet*
Bouvard et Pécuchet (Flaubert) **2**:232-3, 236, 238, 243, 256; **19**:274, 319; **62**:69, 72-3, 79, 82, 91, 98; **66**:256, 263; **179**:16, 30-31, 53; **185**:189, 196, 212, 217
Bouvard et Pécuchet, oeuvre posthume (Flaubert) **135**:93-95, 126, 174, 177
"Bova" (Radishchev) **190**:275, 314, 321-22
Bowden Hill (Bowles) **103**:54
"The Bower by Moonlight" (Harpur) **114**:144
The Box Lobby Challenge (Cumberland) **167**:191
"A Box of Novels" (Thackeray) **43**:350, 383, 385
"The Boy and the Angel" (Browning) **19**:77; **79**:94, 101
The Boy in Grey (Kingsley) **107**:192, 211, 223
A Boy Suffers (Meyer)
See *Das Leiden eines Knaben*
"The Boyar Nikita Yuryevich" (Leskov) **174**:13
The Boyar Orsha (Lermontov)
See *Boiarin Orša*
"Boyarinya Marfa Andreyevna" (Leskov) **25**:246
Boyhood in Norway: Stories of Boylife in the Land of the Midnight Sun (Boyesen)
See *Boyhood in Norway: Stories of Boy-life in the Land of the Midnight Sun*
Boyhood in Norway: Stories of Boy-life in the Land of the Midnight Sun (Boyesen) **135**:8
The Boyne Water (Banim and Banim) **13**:127, 129-32, 134-36, 143-52
The Boy's Froissart (Lanier) **118**:267
The Boy's King Arthur (Lanier) **118**:267
The Boy's Mabinogion (Lanier) **118**:267
Boys of Other Countries (Taylor) **89**:326, 342
"The Boys of Venus" (Landor) **14**:181
The Boy's Percy (Lanier) **118**:267
"A Boy's Poem" (Smith) **59**:318, 321, 329, 332, 336
"Boys' Reading Book" (Sigourney) **87**:321
"Bozedomy" (Leskov) **174**:11, 13-14, 16
Bracebridge Hall (Irving) **2**:368-69, 371, 374, 377-78, 381-82, 384, 387, 390; **19**:331, 333-34, 339, 344; **95**:236-38, 280
Brackenridge Reader 1770-1815 (Brackenridge) **227**:117
Bradamante (Beethoven) **227**:18
"Braga" (Klopstock) **225**:310
Brage-Snak om græske og nordiske Myther og Oldsagn for Damer og Herrer (Grundtvig) **158**:126
"The Braggarts" (Petofi)
See "A szájhösök"
"Brahma" (Emerson) **1**:293-97, 302, 304; **98**:177, 184
"The Brain—is wider than the Sky" (Dickinson) **171**:216
"The Brambles" (Webster) **230**:313
The Bramleighs of Bishop's Folly (Lever) **23**:292
"A Branch from Palestine" (Lermontov) **126**:145
"La branche d'amandier" (Lamartine) **11**:254
"The Branded Hand" (Whittier) **8**:510
"Brandons Both" (Rossetti) **2**:558; **66**:352
"Bransoletka" (Norwid) **17**:369-70
"Brat, stolko let soputstvovavshiy mne" (Tyutchev) **34**:399
Brat'ia Karamazovy (Dostoevsky)
See *Brat'ya Karamazovy*
Brat'ya Karamazovy (Dostoevsky) **2**:161-2, 164, 167, 169-73, 175-8, 180-1, 186, 188, 190-1, 193-5, 204-5; **7**:86, 101-2, 115; **21**:102, 118, 124, 128, 141, 146; **33**:165, 171, 177, 180, 183, 194, 212, 227, 239; **43**:76-173; **119**:71-2, 78, 82, 85, 88, 91, 130-2, 134-6, 153; **167**:217, 221-22, 247, 259, 294, 324, 327-28, 336, 339, 341, 343; **202**:60-170
Bratya Razboiniki (Pushkin) **3**:411, 417, 423, 451; **83**:243, 247, 357
"Die Braut" (Muller) **73**:360
Braut und Bräutigam in einer Person (Kotzebue) **25**:145
"Braut von Korinth" (Goethe) **4**:192
Die Braut von Messina (Schiller) **39**:320-21, 346, 361, 375; **69**:169-71, 181-82, 244-45, 255, 263-64, 267; **166**:159, 190
"Die Brautfahrt" (Eichendorff) **225**:42
Die Brautfahrt oder Kunst von der Rose: Lustspiel in fünf Akten (Freytag) **109**:139
"Bräutigamswahl" (Muller) **73**:360
"Die Brautnacht" (Muller) **73**:366
"Der Brautwahl" (Hoffmann) **183**:170, 175, 186
Brave and Bold; or, The Fortunes of a Factory Boy (Alger) **18**:25, 27, 43; **83**:148
"The Brave Tin Soldier" (Andersen) **214**:59
The Bravo (Cooper) **1**:200, 214, 218-22, 224; **54**:255-6, 263, 278, 288; **203**:7, 72, 77, 144, 152
The Bravo of Venice (Lewis) **11**:297
"The Brazier; or Reciprocal Gratitude" (Genlis) **166**:9
A Breach of Promise (Robertson) **35**:333
"Bread and the Newspaper" (Holmes) **81**:102
"Bread and Wine" (Hölderlin)
See "Brot und Wein"
"The Bread Crust Papers" (Lippard) **198**:133, 163
"Break, Break, Break" (Tennyson) **30**:222, 248, 280
"Breakfast" (Sigourney) **87**:326
"Breakfast ato the Paxes" (Parton) **86**:366
"Breakfast in Sunshine" (Corbière) **43**:15
The Breakfast Table Series (Holmes) **81**:107
The Breath of Childhood (Alcott)
See *Psyche or The Breath of Childhood*
"Breathe Not His Name" (Moore) **110**:185
"Breathings of Spring" (Hemans) **71**:263
"Bredfield Hall" (FitzGerald) **153**:217
"The Breeze on Beachy Head" (Jefferies) **47**:134, 136
"Bref, j'allais" (Laforgue)
See "Dimanches"
"Brennende Liebe" (Droste-Hülshoff) **3**:200-01
Brentano-Runge Briefwechsel (Brentano)
See *Clemens Brentano-Philipp Otto Runge Briefwechsel*
The Brethren of the Cross (Werner)
See *Die Söhne des Thales: Ein dramatisches Gedicht*
"Bretter" (Turgenev) **122**:268
"Brev om den skandinaviska Nordens betydelse för Europas fornhistoria" (Almqvist) **42**:18
"Brevet Brigadier-General Frank Winthrop" (Lazarus) **109**:292
"Brewing of Soma" (Whittier) **8**:516, 520; **59**:360
"Brian the Still Hunter" (Moodie) **14**:231
"The Bridal Ballad" (Poe) **117**:237-38, 280
"Bridal Birth" (Rossetti) **77**:338
The Bridal Journey, or Kunz von der Rosen (Freytag)
See *Die Brautfahrt oder Kunst von der Rose: Lustspiel in fünf Akten*
"The Bridal of Carrigvarah" (Le Fanu) **58**:253
"The Bridal of Malahide" (Griffin) **7**:196
"Bridal of Pennacook" (Whittier) **8**:489, 510, 519, 521; **59**:355
"The Bridal of Polmood" (Hogg) **4**:283
The Bridal of Triermain; or, The Vale of St. John (Scott) **209**:192-93
The Bride (Baillie) **2**:40; **71**:6; **151**:27, 48, 105, 107-9, 111, 115
The Bride in Heaven (Multatuli)
See *De Bruid daarboven*
The Bride of Abydos: A Turkish Tale (Byron) **2**:61, 71-73, 81, 86, 95, 103; **109**:64; **149**:8, 71-72, 161, 163
The Bride of Lammermoor (Scott) **15**:287, 289, 300, 304, 309, 311, 317, 322; **69**:371; **209**:200, 242, 250, 259, 263-64, 266-68, 271-72, 274, 278, 280, 283-86
The Bride of Ludgate (Jerrold) **2**:401, 408
The Bride of Messina (Schiller)
See *Die Braut von Messina*
"The Bride of the Greek Isle" (Hemans) **71**:292, 304, 306
"The Bride of Torrisdale" (Boyesen) **135**:5
"Bride Song" (Rossetti) **50**:264
The Bridegroom (Pushkin) **3**:417
"Bridegroom's Park" (Allingham) **25**:30-1
"The Bride's Chamber" (Rossetti) **4**:528
The Bride's Fate (Southworth) **26**:433
"The Brides of Venice" (Rogers) **69**:80

The Bride's Ordeal (Southworth) **26**:434
"The Bride's Prelude" (Rossetti) **4**:505, 508, 513, 518-20, 523, 527-29, 531-32; **77**:293, 326, 329, 348
The Brides' Tragedy (Beddoes) **3**:24-29, 31-36, 39; **154**:13, 41-42, 44, 48, 50-51, 55, 57, 74, 78-80, 87, 90, 93, 95-98, 100-102
"The Bridge" (Longfellow) **45**:115, 135, 148; **103**:293, 297
"The Bridge of Sighs" (Hood) **16**:205-07, 209, 212, 215, 220-21, 224-26, 228, 231, 233-34, 237-38
"A Brief Appraisal of the Greek Literature" (De Quincey) **87**:77
"Brief Comment on the Songs of the Edda" (Grundtvig) **158**:137
"Brief eines Dichters an einem Andern" (Kleist) **37**:251
Brief eines reisenden Dänen (Schiller) **166**:125
A Brief History of Epidemic and Pestilential Diseases; with the Principal Phenomena of the Physical World, Which Precede and Accompany Them, and Observations Deduced from the Facts Stated . . . (Webster) **30**:406, 426
Brief Outline of Theological Study in the Form of Introductory Lectures (Schleiermacher) **107**:267, 359, 377-78, 399
"Brief über den Durchgang der Venus" (Claudius) **75**:201-03
"Brief über den Roman" (Schlegel) **45**:309, 322, 344, 365, 368, 370-71
"Ein Brief, von C. an D." (Claudius) **75**:202
Briefe (Brentano)
See *Clemens Brentano: Briefe*
"Briefe" (Grillparzer) **102**:118
Briefe (Liszt) **199**:340
Briefe (Mörike) **201**:255
Briefe (Storm) **195**:93
"Briefe an Andres" (Claudius) **75**:210-12, 216-18
Briefe an eine Freundin (Humboldt) **134**:158-59, 162, 167, 209-10
Briefe an Georg Friedlaender (Fontane) **163**:165, 168
Briefe an Lina (La Roche) **121**:271, 279
Briefe an Seinen Freund Jakob Auerbach (Auerbach) **171**:54-55, 73, 76, 79
Briefe aus Berlin (Heine) **54**:306, 316, 336; **147**:207-8, 210
"Briefe aus dem Wuppertal" (Engels) **85**:75, 108
Briefe aus den Bergen (Hoffmann) **183**:174, 176
Briefe aus Paris (Börne) **193**:3, 9, 10, 14-15, 18-19, 23, 31, 35
Briefe Beethovens, 1865 (Beethoven) **227**:9-10
Briefe, das Studium der Theologie betreffend (Herder) **186**:92, 100
Briefe des Dichters Friedrich Ludwig Zacharias Werner: Kritisch durchgesehene und erläuterte Gesamtausgabe (Werner) **189**:346, 350, 366-67
Briefe: Gesamtausgabe (Herder) **186**:89, 91
"Briefe über die ästhetische Erziehung des Menschen" (Schiller) **39**:336, 352, 362, 367, 373, 389; **69**:250, 273
Briefe über die Französische Bühne (Heine) **54**:308
Briefe über Mannheim (La Roche) **121**:242, 250-51
"Briefe über Poesie, Silbenmaß und Sprache" (Schlegel) **142**:331-33, 351, 354, 356
"Briefe über Tempelherrn, Freimäurer und Rosenkreuzer" (Herder) **186**:18
Briefe von Verstorbenen an hinterlassene Freunde (Wieland) **17**:418
Briefe zu Beförderung der Humanität (Herder) **186**:10-13, 18-20, 45, 48, 61-65, 100-101, 103
Briefe zur Beförderung der Humanität (Herder) **8**:313-14
Briefwechsel (Varnhagen von Ense) **130**:340-41, 343
"Briefwechsel über Ossian" (Herder)
See "Auszug aus einem Briefwechsel über Ossian und die Lieder alter Völker"
Briefewechsel zwischen Clemens Brentano und Sophie Mereau (Brentano) **191**:35-36, 63, 68
Die Briefwechsel zwischen Paul Heyse und Theodor Storm (Storm) **195**:11-12
Briery Creek (Martineau) **137**:269, 331
"The Brigadier" (Turgenev)
See "Brigadir"
"Brigadir" (Turgenev) **21**:414-15, 441; **37**:373; **122**:242, 264, 268, 348
The Brigand Brothers (Pushkin)
See *Bratya Razboiniki*
"The Brigand of Askalon" (Leskov)
See "Askalonskij zlodej"
"The Brigands" (Villiers de l'Isle Adam)
See "Les brigands"
"Les brigands" (Villiers de l'Isle Adam) **3**:590
The Brigands (Schiller)
See *Die Raüber*
"Bright Broken Maginn" (Lockhart) **6**:296
"Bright Star! Would I Were Steadfast as Thou Art" (Keats) **73**:154; **121**:123-24; **225**:254
"The Brighton Beauty" (Norton) **205**:130, 138
Brigitta (Auerbach) **171**:20
Brigitta (Stifter) **41**:343, 366, 375, 379; **198**:254, 257, 259-60, 284, 298, 300, 303-4
"Bring Flowers" (Hemans) **71**:264
"Brise marine" (Mallarmé) **4**:395; **41**:250, 289
"A Brisk Wind" (Barnes) **75**:37, 97
The Bristles of the Neck of the Aged Sparrow (Dutt)
See *Buro Sāliker Ghāre Ro*
"Britain's Glory; or, The Blessings of a Good Constitution" (Thelwall) **162**:328
"Britannia" (Jones) **222**:157
"Britannia's Wreath" (Moodie) **113**:309
"British Literature" (Whitman) **205**:252
"British Museum Notes" (Levy) **203**:352
The British Novelists (Barbauld)
See *British Novelists with an Essay and Prefaces Biographical and Critical*
British Novelists with an Essay and Prefaces Biographical and Critical (Barbauld) **50**:16, 17-20; **185**:74-76, 78-80, 117, 121
British Poets (Child) **173**:167, 169, 171-72, 189, 198, 208-9, 225-27, 244
The British Prison-Ship (Freneau) **1**:319; **111**:80, 139-40, 143, 146
"British Senate" (Hazlitt) **29**:161
British Synonymy; or, an Attempt at Regulating the Choice of Words in Familiar Conversation (Piozzi) **57**:242, 252-3, 271, 293, 298, 301
"Britons, Guard Your Own" (Tennyson) **30**:294
Britons, Guard Your Own (Tennyson) **202**:322
"Bro" (Woolson) **82**:303
"Broad, Multiform Love" (Verlaine)
See "L'amour multiforme et large"
"A Broadway Pageant" (Whitman) **31**:393; **81**:313; **205**:226, 260
"Brockes" (Mörike) **201**:344
"Brod und Wein" (Hölderlin)
See "Brot und Wein"
Broke (Turgenev)
See *Bezdenezh'e*
"Broken Crutch" (Bloomfield) **145**:133, 176-79
"The Broken Doll" (Lamb) **125**:330, 337
"The Broken Heart" (Barnes) **75**:7
"The Broken Heart" (Irving) **2**:366, 377; **19**:327, 350; **95**:238, 277
The Broken Jug (Kleist)
See *Der Zerbrochene Krug*
"Broken Love" (Blake) **13**:172
"The Broken Oar" (Longfellow) **45**:146
"The Broken Oath" (Carleton) **3**:92; **199**:20
"Broken Pane" (Corbière) **43**:15
The Broken Ringlet (Eichendorff) **225**:5
"The Broken Toy" (Lazarus) **109**:291
"A Broken-Hearted Lay" (Mangan) **27**:280, 283, 298
The Broker of Bogotá (Bird) **1**:87-90, 93; **197**:6, 12, 16-17, 19, 68, 90, 92-99, 103-5
The Brontës: Their Lives, Friendships, and Correspondence (Brontë) **217**:14-16, 18, 20, 22
The Bronze Horseman (Pushkin)
See *Medny Vsadnik*
"The Bronze Pig" (Andersen)
See "Metalsvinet"
"The Bronze Trumpet" (Kendall) **12**:200, 202
"The Brook" (Krylov) **1**:435
"The Brook" (Tennyson) **30**:215, 223; **115**:358
"The Brook" (Wordsworth) **111**:245
Brooke and Brooke Farm (Martineau) **137**:251-52, 260, 268, 270, 272
"Brooklyniana" (Whitman) **81**:343
"The Brookside" (Milnes) **61**:136
"The Broomstick Train; or, The Return of the Witches" (Holmes) **14**:121, 125, 132
"Brot und Wein" (Hölderlin) **16**:162, 176, 187, 191-92, 194-95; **187**:188, 222-23, 225-26, 283, 289
"Brother and Sister" (Dodgson) **139**:32-33
"Brother and Sister" (Eliot) **4**:107, 115; **13**:334; **183**:120; **199**:117, 234, 255
"Brother and Sister" (Grimm Brothers)
See "Brüderchen und Schwesterchen"
"The Brother and Sister" (Opie) **65**:158, 180
"The Brother and Sister" (Solomos) **15**:389, 396
Brother Jonathan: or, the New Englanders (Neal) **161**:285-87, 291, 300-304, 308-9, 318, 331, 345
"Brother Where Dost Thou Dwell" (Thoreau) **7**:383
"Brother, who accompanied me for so many years" (Tyutchev)
See "Brat, stolko let soputstvovavshiy mne"
"Brotherhood" (Muller)
See "Brüderschaft"
"The Brothers" (Alcott) **58**:47; **83**:7; **218**:11, 23; **218**:11, 23
"The Brothers" (Crabbe) **26**:93, 120, 130-31; **121**:11, 40
"The Brothers" (Runeberg) **41**:312
"The Brothers" (Wordsworth) **12**:396, 402; **111**:212-13, 228-29, 236, 243-44, 254, 294; **166**:317; **206**:224, 311-15
The Brothers (Cumberland) **167**:108, 111, 118-19, 122, 132, 136, 141, 146, 152, 154-55, 161, 166, 187-88, 193
The Brothers (Macha) **46**:201
"Brothers, and a Sermon" (Ingelow) **39**:257, 263
Brothers and Sisters: A Tale of Domestic Life (Bremer)
See *Syskonlif*
"Brothers from Far-Away Lands" (Kendall) **12**:183
The Brothers Highwaymen (Pushkin)
See *Bratya Razboiniki*
The Brothers Karamazov (Dostoevsky)
See *Brat'ya Karamazovy*
The Brothers; or Consequences. A Story of what happens Every day (Hays) **114**:186
"The Brothers, or The Influence of Example" (Child) **73**:131-32, 134
Brothertoft Manor (Winthrop)
See *Edwin Brothertoft*
"Brough Bells" (Southey) **8**:474
"Brougham" (Beddoes) **154**:74-75, 77
Brouillon (Novalis) **13**:405
"Brown and furry" (Rossetti) **186**:237
"Brown Eyes" (Isaacs)
See "Los ojos pardos"
"The Brown Goat" (Carleton) **199**:99

"The Brown Man" (Griffin) **7**:198, 211
"Brown of Ossawatomie" (Whittier) **8**:495
The Brownie of Bodsbeck, and Other Tales (Hogg) **4**:276, 285, 287-88; **109**:190-91, 209, 230-31, 269
"The Brownie of the Black Haggs" (Hogg) **4**:283; **109**:270, 280
The Browning Correspondence (Barrett Browning) **170**:84-87
The Browning's Correspondence (Barrett Browning) **61**:64, 66-7, 70-1, 74-5
Browning's Essay on Chatterton (Browning)
See "Essay on Tasso and Chatterton"
Brownson's Quarterly Review (Brownson) **50**:28, 32-5, 49-55, 61-4, 66, 68
Bruder Moritz der Sonderling, oder Die Colonie für die Pelew-Inseln (Kotzebue) **25**:143, 145-46
"Das Brüderchen und das Schwesterchen" (Grimm Brothers)
See "Brüderchen und Schwesterchen"
"Brüderchen und Schwesterchen" (Grimm Brothers) **3**:228-29, 231
"Brudermord" (Hebbel) **43**:237, 253
"Brüderschaft" (Muller) **73**:352, 379
Bruderzwist (Grillparzer)
See *Ein Bruderzwist in Habsburg*
Ein Bruderzwist im Hause Habsburg (Grillparzer)
See *Ein Bruderzwist in Habsburg*
Ein Bruderzwist in Habsburg (Grillparzer) **1**:385, 389, 395-96; **102**:106, 110, 113, 131, 166, 169, 172, 183, 186-87, 191-92, 195, 203, 205, 214-15
De Bruid daarboven (Multatuli) **165**:320, 343
"A Bruised Reed Shall He Not Break" (Rossetti) **50**:314; **66**:330
"Le Bruit des cabarets . . ." (Verlaine) **230**:173
"Brumes et pluies" (Baudelaire) **6**:79; **29**:101; **55**:23, 61
Brunehilde; or, The Last Act of Norma (Alarcon)
See *El final de Norma*
Bruno and Sylvie (Dodgson)
See *Sylvie and Bruno*
"Bruno Bauer and Early Christianity" (Engels) **85**:44-46, 48
Bruno oder über das göttliche und natürliche Prinzip der Dinge (Schelling) **30**:128, 160-62, 167, 174, 179
Bruno; or, On the Divine and Natural Principle of Things (Schelling)
See *Bruno oder über das göttliche und natürliche Prinzip der Dinge*
"Bruno-Lin, the Irish Outlaw" (Maturin) **169**:16
"Brussels: Merry-Go-Round" (Verlaine) **51**:368, 374
"Brute Neighbours" (Thoreau) **7**:388, 398
Bruto I (Alfieri)
See *Bruto primo*
"Bruto Minore" (Leopardi) **129**:306
Bruto primo (Alfieri) **101**:17-18, 42-3, 50
Bruto secondo (Alfieri) **101**:18-19, 42-3
Brutus (Herder) **186**:94
Brutus the Younger (Alfieri)
See *Bruto secondo*
"Bruxelles" (Rimbaud) **4**:483
"Bruxelles: Simple fesques" (Verlaine) **51**:382; **230**:163, 187
Bryan Perdue (Holcroft)
See *The Memoirs of Bryan Perdue*
Brytan bryś (Fredro) **8**:285
The Bubbles of Canada (Haliburton) **15**:117-19, 128; **149**:272, 346, 349
Bubbles of the Day (Jerrold) **2**:395, 402-03
"The Buccaneer" (Dana) **53**:157, 168-9
The Buccaneer and Other Poems (Dana) **53**:157
Buch der Lieder (Heine) **4**:232, 239, 248-50, 253-54, 259, 261, 268; **54**:308, 335, 348; **147**:127, 148-52, 167-68, 195, 198, 239, 242, 245
"Ein Buch der roten Rose" (Storm) **195**:93
"Ein Buch der weisen Rose" (Storm) **195**:67, 93
Buch des Richters (Kierkegaard) **78**:235
Das Buch Le Grand (Heine) **147**:168
Buch über Shakespeare (Tieck) **5**:520; **46**:359
"La bûche" (Maupassant) **83**:230
"Die Bücher der Zeiten" (Hölderlin) **16**:174, 185
Die Bücher und die Lesewelt (Hauff) **185**:325
Buckstone's Adventures with a Polish Princess (Lewes) **25**:291
The Bucktails; or, Americans in England (Paulding) **2**:527
"Buckthorne" (Irving) **2**:369
"Buckthorne and His Friends" (Irving) **2**:390
"The Buckwheat" (Andersen) **6**:33; **79**:23
Bucolique (Mallarmé) **41**:281
Buda halála (Arany) **34**:5, 8, 10-12, 15, 18-20
Buda's Death (Arany)
See *Buda halála*
Le budget d'un jeune ménage (Scribe) **16**:393
"Budget of a Femme incomprise" (Carlyle) **181**:124, 133, 136
"Budničnye storony žizni" (Pisarev) **25**:344
"Buds and Bird Voices" (Hawthorne) **2**:296, 298
"!Buena pesca¡" (Alarcón) **219**:4, 45, 52
"La buena ventura" (Alarcón) **219**:18
"Buffalo Hunting" (Thorpe) **183**:357
"Le buffet" (Rimbaud) **35**:271; **82**:247-48
Bug-Jargal (Hugo) **3**:234, 236-37, 239, 254; **21**:198, 201; **161**:201-2, 204, 227-32; **189**:267
"The Bugler's First Communion" (Hopkins) **17**:194; **189**:7, 115, 117, 135
Ein Bühnenfestpiel für drei Tage und einen Vorabend (Wagner) **9**:469
"The Builders" (Longfellow) **45**:127, 131
"The Building of the Ship" (Longfellow) **2**:493; **45**:116, 147, 153-54; **101**:92
Bulemanns Haus (Storm) **1**:542; **195**:6, 14, 23-25, 32, 35-36, 41, 66, 70-72, 128
"The Bull" (Allingham) **25**:6
"Bullocktown" (Clarke) **19**:231, 250-51
"Bull-Thomas" (Kivi)
See "Härka-Tuomo"
The Bulwark of Art (Andersen) **79**:16
"Bunch Poem" (Whitman) **81**:360
"Bundeslied" (Hauff) **185**:353
Bunker Hill (Brackenridge)
See *The Battle of Bunkers-Hill. A Dramatic Piece, of Five Acts, in Heroic Measure*
Bunte Steine (Stifter) **41**:337, 351, 359, 362-64, 368-69, 391, 396; **198**:259, 275, 315, 321-22
"Buonaparte" (Hölderlin) **16**:174
"Buonaparte" (Tennyson) **30**:293
De Buonaparte et des Bourbons (Chateaubriand) **134**:5
"Bupposo" (Ueda Akinari) **131**:6, 8-9, 13, 24, 26, 32-33, 38, 40, 57, 65
"Buran" (Aksakov) **2**:13, 15; **181**:18, 21, 62
"The Burden of Egypt" (Milnes) **61**:130
"The Burden of Nineveh" (Rossetti) **4**:491, 502, 511, 517-18, 523-24, 527, 529; **77**:291-97, 299, 340, 348, 352-54
"Burger of St Gall" (Gore) **65**:21
Der Bürgergeneral (Goethe) **4**:222
Les burgraves (Hugo) **3**:256, 268-69, 276; **161**:188, 192, 235-36; **189**:195, 198
"Die Bürgschaft" (Schiller) **39**:388; **166**:105
"The Burial of Arnold" (Willis) **194**:289
"The Burial of King Cormac" (Ferguson) **33**:278, 301, 303
The Burial of the Donkey (Smolenskin)
See *Kevurat hamor*
"Burial of Two Young Sisters" (Sigourney) **87**:337
"A Burial Place" (Allingham) **25**:24
"The Burial-Place of a Favourite Bird" (Collins) **93**:63
"The Buried Life" (Arnold) **29**:27, 31, 34-6; **89**:14, 18, 20-6, 53, 83, 88; **218**:120, 156, 277-79
"A Buried Life" (Ichiyō)
See "Umoregi"
"Burley-bones" (Cranch) **115**:57-8
"Burncombe Hollow" (Barnes) **75**:15
"The Burning of Fairfield" (Dwight) **13**:270, 272, 278
"The Burning of the Caroline" (Moodie) **113**:308
"Burns" (Carlyle) **70**:7, 9
Buro Sāliker Ghāre Ro (Dutt) **118**:5
"Burya" (Baratynsky) **103**:10, 14, 17
"Burza" (Mickiewicz) **3**:390, 403
"Buschlieder" (Ludwig) **4**:353
Die Buschnovelle (Ludwig) **4**:356
Bush Ballads and Galloping Rhymes (Gordon) **21**:149-52, 155, 159, 163-64, 167, 170-71, 173, 175-76, 181, 183-84, 187-88
"A Bush Girl" (Adams) **33**:13
"The Bush Trembles" (Petofi)
See "Reszket a bokor..."
"The Bushfire" (Harpur) **114**:99, 115, 125-26, 158
"The Bushrangers" (Harpur) **114**:94, 114-15
The Bushrangers: A Play in Five Acts and Other Poems (Harpur) **114**:109, 114-15, 120, 122, 127
"The Business Man" (Poe) **16**:312, 324; **211**:284
"Busque Vd. quien cargue el saco, que yo no he de ser el loco" (Lizardi) **30**:67
"The Bustle in a House" (Dickinson) **77**:129, 133
But, However— (Mayhew) **31**:158
"Buttercup, Poppy, Forget-Me-Not" (Field) **3**:206
"The Butterfly" (Andersen)
See "Sommerfuglen"
"The Butterfly" (Brontë) **16**:103; **165**:73, 99-100, 104, 106, 108
"The Butterfly" (Crawford)
See "The Mother's Soul"
"The Butterfly" (Lamb) **125**:347
"A Butterfly" (Pavlova)
See "Motylek"
"The Butterfly" (Sigourney) **87**:330
"Butterfly Collecting" (Aksakov)
See "Sobiranie babochek"
"The Butterfly Obtains" (Dickinson) **21**:29
"Buttoo" (Dutt) **29**:121, 124, 128, 130-31
"Buvaly voiny" (Shevchenko) **54**:390
"Buvard, bavard" (Hugo) **10**:357
"A buzzard has risen from the glade" (Tyutchev)
See "S polyany korshun podnyalsya"
"The Bwoate" (Barnes) **75**:58, 90
"By a River" (Kendall) **12**:183
"By an Autumn Stream" (Lampman) **194**:54, 82, 84-86
"By Blue Ontario's Shore" (Whitman) **4**:579; **31**:388, 444; **81**:293, 313, 350; **205**:158, 160, 162, 196, 205, 225-26, 312
"By Flood and Field" (Gordon) **21**:154, 159
By Order of the King (Hugo)
See *L'homme qui rit*
"By the Alders" (O'Brien) **21**:245
"By the Bivouac's Fitful Flame" (Whitman) **4**:543; **205**:339
"By the Exe" (Jefferies) **47**:136
"By the Fireside" (Browning) **19**:105, 127, 153; **79**:157
By the Fireside (Eminescu) **33**:266
"By the Goddess of Plain Truth A Manifesto and Proclamation" (Paine) **62**:325
"By the Grave of Henry Timrod" (Hayne) **94**:149
"By the Looking-Glass" (Webster) **230**:251-52, 293
"By the Passaic" (O'Brien) **21**:246
"By the River" (Larcom) **179**:170
"By the Roadside" (Whitman) **205**:225-26

"By the Sea" (Lampman) **25**:193
"By the Sea" (Rossetti) **50**:297
"By the Seaside" (Longfellow) **2**:493
By the Waters of Babylon (Lazarus)
See *By the Waters of Babylon: Little Poems in Prose*
"By the Waters of Babylon B.C. 570" (Rossetti) **186**:303
By the Waters of Babylon: Little Poems in Prose (Lazarus) **8**:421-23, 426-28; **109**:296-97, 311, 332
By the Way: Verses, Fragments, and Notes (Allingham) **25**:18, 21
"By Thomas Gage...A Proclamation" (Trumbull) **30**:351, 374
"By Way of Remembrance" (Rossetti) **186**:262, 270, 295
"By Wood and Wold" (Gordon) **21**:159
"Byezhin Prairie" (Turgenev)
See "Bezhin Lea"
"By-Gone Days" (Tonna) **135**:204
Byloe i dumy (Herzen) **61**:83, 88, 90, 93, 95-8, 100, 103-4, 106, 122-3
The By-Passed (Leskov)
See *Obojdennye*
The Bypassed (Leskov)
See *Obojdennye*
"Byron" (Tyutchev) **34**:393
Byron's Letters and Journals (Byron) **149**:149-54, 164
The Byrth, Lyf and Actes of King Arthur (Southey) **97**:263
"Byvalo, otrok, zvonkim klikom..." (Baratynsky) **103**:4, 14, 19-20, 47
By-Ways of Europe (Taylor) **89**:312, 351
C Minor Symphony (Beethoven)
See *Fifth Symphony*
"C moll-Sinfonie" (Hoffmann)
See "Beethoven, C moll-Sinfonie (No. 5)"
"Ça?" (Corbière) **43**:13, 15, 31
"Ça Ira" (Maupassant) **83**:194, 198, 200-01
"À cab, tomorrow . . ." (Verlaine)
See "Un fiacre, demain . . ."
Cabal and Love (Schiller)
See *Kabale und Liebe*
El caballero de las botas azules (Castro) **3**:106-07; **78**:45-47, 52
El Caballo del Rey Don Sancho (Zorrilla y Moral) **6**:525
"Cabbage Soup" (Turgenev)
See "Shchi"
Le Cabinet des antiques (Balzac) **153**:8, 65, 149
The Cabinet Minister (Gore) **65**:20
"El cabo Muñoz" (Isaacs) **70**:305
"Cache-cache" (Tyutchev) **34**:389
"Le Cachet d'Onyx" (Barbey d'Aurevilly) **213**:29-30, 65
"A cachoeira de Paulo Afonso" (Castro Alves) **205**:8
A cachoeira de Paulo Afonso (Castro Alves) **205**:5, 24, 33
"Cäcilie" (Kleist)
See *Die heilige Cäcilie; oder, die Gewalt der Musik*
El cacique de Tumerqué (Gómez de Avellaneda) **111**:28
"Cacka" (Norwid) **17**:374
"Cacoethes Scribendi" (Sedgwick) **98**:302-04
"Cada vez que recuerda tanto oprobio" (Castro) **78**:42
"La cadène" (Hugo) **10**:357
Cadio (Sand) **57**:316
"Le Cadre" (Baudelaire) **55**:10
"Caelicola" (Chivers) **49**:56
Caesar, a Sketch (Froude) **43**:175, 177
Caesar Borgia; or, the King of Crimee: Verses on the Exile of the Prince (Jefferies) **47**:121
"Caesareanism As It Now Exists" (Bagehot) **10**:46
"Caesaris" (Wergeland) **5**:540
"The Caesars" (De Quincey) **4**:61, 74-75
"Caesar's Wife" (Crawford) **12**:155
"El café" (Larra) **17**:267-70, 279
A Café (Ostrovsky) **30**:96
"La Cafetière" (Gautier) **1**:355; **59**:9, 25-6, 29, 32-3, 36, 38
"The Cage at Cranford" (Gaskell) **97**:168
"The Caged Skylark" (Hopkins) **17**:185, 221, 257
Le cahier rouge de Benjamin Constant (Constant) **6**:222-23; **182**:138-41, 187, 219
Cahier staëlien (Staël-Holstein) **91**:359-60
Cahiers de jeunesse (Renan) **26**:413, 415; **145**:354
"Cain" (Coleridge)
See "The Wanderings of Cain"
Cain (Byron) **2**:66-67, 72, 76, 81, 91, 94, 97, 99; **12**:102, 109, 139; **109**:99-106, 123, 126; **149**:46, 73, 91, 95, 149
"Cajuscie dvizenija vody" (Leskov) **174**:10, 12
Cakes and Ale (Jerrold) **2**:397-98, 400-02
"Cal Culver and the Devil" (Cooke) **110**:8-20, 24, 33
Calamities and Quarrels of Authors: A New Edition Edited by His Son the Earl of Beaconsfield (D'Israeli) **217**:322-24
Calamities of Authors: Including some Inquiries Respecting their Moral and Literary Characters (D'Israeli) **217**:278, 284, 292, 295, 297
"Calamus" (Whitman) **4**:546, 554, 557-58, 565, 575, 581-82, 584, 592, 599, 603-04; **81**:249, 258, 268, 271, 299, 301-02, 307-08, 312, 326, 328-33, 364; **205**:161-63, 219-20, 225-27, 242-44, 261-62, 277, 337
"The Calash" (Gogol) **5**:219
Calavar; or, The Knight of the Conquest (Bird) **1**:81-84, 86-87, 90; **197**:5-8, 12-13, 24-29, 68, 75-85
"Los Calaveras, Artículo segundo y conclusión" (Larra) **130**:226
Calaynos (Boker) **125**:8, 18-20, 25, 28, 30-31, 35-36, 58-59, 62, 64-65, 76
"Calculus" (Alcott) **167**:51
"Caldas" (Isaacs) **70**:313
Calderon the Courtier (Bulwer-Lytton) **45**:58
"The Caldron of Kibitsu" (Ueda Akinari)
See "Kibitsu no kama"
Caleb Field: A Tale of the Puritans (Oliphant) **11**:429; **61**:219
Caleb Williams (Godwin)
See *Things As They Are; or, The Adventures of Caleb Williams*
"Calef in Boston" (Whittier) **8**:509
Calendrier positiviste (Comte) **54**:199
Caliban (Renan) **26**:377, 387, 389, 408
"Caliban upon Setebos" (Browning) **19**:130, 153; **79**:150, 164, 185
"Caliban upon Setebos" (Emerson) **1**:289
"Calico Pie" (Lear) **3**:301
"Calidore" (Keats) **73**:151, 214, 311, 321; **121**:162
"Calidore: A Fragment" (Keats) **225**:243
The California and Oregon Trail: Being Sketches of Prairie and Rocky Mountain Life (Parkman)
See *The Oregon Trail*
Caligula (Dumas) **11**:45, 47, 51; **71**:187
"Calin Nebunul" (Eminescu) **33**:260; **131**:299-300, 302-4
"Calin the Fool" (Eminescu)
See "Calin Nebunul"
"Calin the Madcap" (Eminescu)
See "Calin Nebunul"
"Calin—file din poveste" (Eminescu) **33**:247, 249, 262-63; **131**:299-300, 302-3, 305, 332
"Calin—Leaves from a Fairy Tale" (Eminescu)
See "Calin—file din poveste"
"Calin—Leaves from a Folktale" (Eminescu)
See "Calin—file din poveste"
Caliste; or, the Sequel to Letters Written from Lausanne (Charriere)
See *Caliste; ou, Suite des lettres écrites de Lausanne*
Caliste; ou, Suite des lettres écrites de Lausanne (Charriere) **66**:121, 123-6, 128, 135, 138, 142-3, 145-6, 160-1, 163-7, 169
"The Call" (Very) **9**:375, 378
"A Call to Husbands" (Parton) **86**:363, 366-67
"Call to the Ordeal" (Arany) **34**:9
Called to Be Saints (Rossetti) **66**:344
Called to Be Saints: The Minor Festivals Devotionally Studied (Rossetti) **186**:257
Callista: A Sketch of the Third Century (Newman) **38**:290, 292-93, 342; **99**:218, 252-56
"The Callousness Produced by Care" (Brontë) **109**:30
Calm Sea and Prosperous Voyage, op. 112 (Beethoven) **227**:31
La calomnie (Scribe) **16**:388, 412-13
"El calor" (Bécquer) **106**:113
"The Calpe Obessa; or, Siege of Gibraltar" (Bowles) **103**:53, 56
"Calpurnia" (Boyesen) **135**:4
"Le calumet du Sachem" (Leconte de Lisle) **29**:225
Calvary (Cumberland) **167**:123, 135, 140, 193
"Calvary Crossing a Ford" (Whitman) **205**:338
Calypso (Cumberland) **167**:148, 157, 189-90, 199-200, 202
La camaraderie; ou, La courte échelle (Scribe) **16**:384-85, 388-89, 402-03, 407
"The Cambridge Churchyard" (Holmes) **14**:128
"Cambridge Thirty Years Ago" (Lowell) **2**:507, 520
"Cambyses and the Macrobian Bow" (Hayne) **94**:149, 154, 156-59, 169
"The Cameronian Preacher's Tale" (Hogg) **4**:283
Camilla; or, A Picture of Youth (Burney) **12**:18-19, 21-3, 25, 28-30, 32-4, 43, 46, 50-1, 57-9, 62; **54**:18, 25, 27-31, 33-4, 36, 51-63; **107**:12-13, 15-16
Camilla; or, Rome Delivered (Zhukovsky) **35**:377
Camille, ou le nouveau roman (Charriere) **66**:180
Camors; or, Life under the New Empire (Feuillet)
See *Monsieur de Camors*
The Camp (Sheridan) **91**:242
The Camp at the Olympic (Planché) **42**:276, 291, 294
"The Camp of Souls" (Crawford) **12**:156, 162; **127**:202
The Camp of Wallenstein (Schiller)
See *Wallenstein*
Campaign of the Great Army (Sarmiento)
See *Campaña en el Ejército Grande*
Campaña en el Ejército Grande (Sarmiento) **123**:268, 272-73, 346, 351-52
"Campanas de Bastabales" (Castro) **78**:41
Campaner Thal (Jean Paul) **7**:234
"Campaspe" (Kendall) **12**:190, 193
"Camp-Meeting" (Hooper)
See "Simon Suggs Attends a Camp-Meeting"
"El campo americano" (Bello) **131**:109
"Campo Vaccino" (Grillparzer) **102**:175
"Camptown Races" (Foster) **26**:291, 294-95, 298
"Can a Life hide Itself?" (Taylor) **89**:315
Can You Forgive Her? (Trollope) **6**:457, 461-63, 467, 470, 477, 484, 491, 495, 499-500, 504, 508, 515-16; **33**:363, 416; **101**:216, 235, 262, 266-68, 292, 301, 307-08, 319-20, 326-27; **215**:214, 240, 283, 287, 303
"Canada" (Moodie) **113**:349
"Canada to England" (Crawford) **12**:159; **127**:153
"Canadian Boat Song" (Moore) **6**:390

The Canadian Brothers; or, The Prophecy Fulfilled. A Tale of the Late American War (Richardson) **55**:290, 292-3, 299-300, 304, 311, 313, 316, 318-21, 323-4, 326-7, 330-49, 356-7, 362, 364-6, 368
"A Canadian Campaign" (Richardson) **55**:329-31, 333-4, 344
The Canadian Crusoes: A Tale of the Rice Lake Plains (Traill) **31**:316, 324-25, 327-29
"The Canadian Herd Boy" (Moodie) **14**:218
"The Canadian Hunter's Song" (Moodie) **113**:348
"Canadian Life" (Moodie) **113**:325, 332
Canadian Life (Moodie) **113**:326, 333, 370
"A Canadian Scene" (Traill) **31**:324
The Canadian Settler's Guide (Traill)
See *The Female Emigrant's Guide, and Hints on Canadian Housekeeping*
"Canadian Sketches" (Moodie) **14**:231
"A Canadian Song" (Moodie) **14**:227; **113**:344, 348
Canadian Wild Flowers (Traill) **31**:328
"Canadians Will You Join the Band. A Loyal Song" (Moodie) **113**:308-9
"The Canal" (Barlow) **223**:27-29, 36
"Canção do Africano" (Castro Alves) **205**:9
"Cançao do violeio" (Castro Alves) **205**:20-21
"La canción de la morfina" (Casal) **131**:250
"Canción del pirata" (Espronceda) **39**:100, 113-14, 118
"La canción del torero" (Casal) **131**:236
"Canción patriótica" (Espronceda) **39**:105
"Candente esta la atmosfera" (Castro) **78**:41
The Candidate (Crabbe) **26**:76; **121**:10, 18
Candidates for Confirmation (Tegner) **2**:612
"The Candle Indoors" (Hopkins) **17**:195, 245; **189**:7-8, 114, 119
"The Candles" (Andersen) **214**:60
The Candle's Out (Fredro)
See *Świeczka zgasta*
"Cando penso que te fuches" (Castro) **78**:41
The Cannibal's Progress; or, The Dreadful Horrors of French Invasion (Cobbett) **49**:107, 109
"The Canoe" (Crawford) **12**:163-65, 168
The Canoe and the Saddle: or Klalam and Klickitat, to Which Are Now First Added his Western Letters and Journals (Winthrop) **210**:282, 286, 288, 296-98, 300, 302, 304, 312, 322, 327-28, 330-32, 334-35, 337, 339-42
Canolles; or, The Fortunes of a Partisan of '81 (Cooke) **5**:125, 131-32, 135
"Cantan os galos" (Castro) **78**:7
"Cantares 8" (Castro)
See "Un arrogante gaitero"
Cantares gallegos (Castro) **3**:98, 100, 104-05, 107; **78**:2-7, 27-33, 37-38, 54-60
Cantata (Lanier) **118**:203, 208-10, 278
"Cantate pour la première communion" (Mallarmé) **41**:289
"Cantate pour les enfants d'une maison de Charité" (Lamartine) **11**:279
"The Canterbury Pilgrims" (Hawthorne) **79**:296
The Canterbury Tales (Lee) **191**:313, 316, 327
Canti (Leopardi) **129**:245, 304, 310-11, 327-28, 330, 332, 335, 339, 347-49, 351-57, 360
Cantico del gallo silvestre (Leopardi) **129**:230
Cantique de Saint-Jean (Mallarmé) **41**:280
"Cantique des mères" (Desbordes-Valmore) **97**:30
"Cantique sur la mort de la duchesse de Broglie" (Lamartine) **11**:271
"Cantiques des bannis" (Desbordes-Valmore) **97**:30
"Canto a Teresa" (Espronceda) **39**:85, 90-1, 102-04, 117
"Canto al glorioso protomártir San Felipe de Jesús" (Lizardi) **30**:68
"Canto de Maria Clara" (Rizal) **27**:425
"El canto del cosaco" (Espronceda) **39**:100, 120
"Canto del viajero" (Rizal) **27**:425
"Canto notturno di un pastore errante dell'Asia" (Leopardi) **129**:220, 223, 247, 307, 311, 339, 341, 347-48, 350-51, 359
The Cantos (Lautréamont)
See *Les chants de Maldoror: Chants I, II, III, IV, V, VI*
Cantos a Lesbia (Manzano)
See *Poesías líricas *Cantos a Lesbia**
Cantos del trovador (Zorrilla y Moral) **6**:523-24
Canzio (Kivi) **30**:50, 65
Canzone (Liszt) **199**:307
"Canzone per nozze" (Leopardi) **129**:327
Canzonetta del Salvator Rosa (Liszt) **199**:307
Canzoni (Leopardi) **129**:348, 352
"The Cap and Bells" (Keats) **8**:341, 359; **73**:155, 208, 295, 299
Cape Cod (Thoreau) **7**:355-6, 361, 390, 411; **61**:348; **138**:167; **207**:178, 246, 269-75, 299, 330-33, 335
Caper-Sauce: A Volume of Chit-Chat about Men, Women, and Things (Parton) **86**:375
Le Capitaine Pamphile (Dumas) **71**:204
Le capitaine Paul (Dumas) **11**:58
Capital: A Critical Analysis of Capitalist Production (Marx)
See *Das Kapital: Kritik der politischen Ökonomie*
Capital and Labour (Jones)
See *Labour and Capital: A Lecture . . . to Which Are Appended in Full the Leading Articles Thereon from the "Saturday Review," the "Times," and the "Pall Mall Gazette," with Answers Thereto*
"Capital—the Mother of Labor: An Economical Problem Discussed froma Physiological Point of View" (Huxley) **67**:68
El capitán Veneno (Alarcon) **1**:15-16; **219**:4, 19-20
Le capitane Fracasse (Gautier) **1**:344-46, 348; **59**:5-8, 12
Capitola (Southworth)
See *The Hidden Hand*
Un caprice (Musset) **7**:268, 270-72, 275; **150**:251-54, 336, 339-41
"Caprice" (Verlaine) **230**:174
Les caprices de Marianne (Musset) **7**:262, 267, 269, 271-72, 276-78, 281, 283; **150**:226-27, 245, 311, 329, 334-36, 347-50
Caprices et zigzags (Gautier) **1**:341, 344, 352
"Cápsulas" (Silva) **114**:317
Cápsulas (Silva) **114**:263, 273
"Capsules" (Silva)
See "Cápsulas"
"The Captain Attends a Camp-Meeting" (Hooper)
See "Simon Suggs Attends a Camp-Meeting"
Captain Bonneville (Irving)
See "Albert and Emily"
Captain Fracasse (Gautier)
See *Le capitane Fracasse*
"Captain Jackson" (Lamb) **10**:392, 404, 409, 436
"Captain Jones' Invitation" (Freneau) **1**:317
"Captain Jones's Invitation" (Freneau)
See "The Invitation"
"Captain Leka's Sister" (Karadzic) **115**:92
"Captain McSpadden" (Hooper) **177**:175
"Captain Paton's Lament" (Lockhart) **6**:295-96
Captain Rock (Moore)
See *Memoirs of Captain Rock*
Captain Spike; or, The Islets of the Gulf (Cooper)
See *Jack Tier; or, The Florida Reefs*
Captain Spitfire and the Unlucky Treasure (Alarcon)
See *El capitán Veneno*
"Captain Stick and Toney" (Hooper) **177**:215
Captain Sword and Captain Pen (Hunt) **70**:270-71
"Captain Thompson" (Willis) **194**:298
The Captain's Daughter (Pushkin)
See *Kapitanskaya-dochka*
The Captain's Daughter; or, the Generosity of the Russian Usurper Pugatscheff (Pushkin)
See *Kapitanskaya-dochka*
"The Captain's Dream" (Brontë) **4**:44
The Captain's Mistress (Shevchenko)
See *Kapitansha*
"The Captain's Well" (Whittier) **8**:516
"The Captain's Wife" (Dobell) **43**:46
The Captive Ladie (Dutt) **118**:31
"The Captive of Castile; or, The Moorish Maiden's Vow" (Alcott) **83**:4
The Captive of the Caucasus (Pushkin)
See *Kavkazsky plennik*
"The Captive Stork" (Arany)
See "A rab gólya"
The Captive Woman (Echeverria)
See *La cautiva*
"Captivity" (Robinson) **142**:178
"Captivity" (Rogers) **69**:68, 74
Captivity (Robinson) **142**:224
The Capture of Murány (Arany)
See *Murány ostroma*
"The Captured Wild Horse" (Fuller) **5**:169
"Cara-Ali" (Mérimée) **65**:58
The Carabine (Bird) **197**:29
Caractacus (Brontë) **109**:14
"Carácter de mi padre" (Heredia) **209**:160
La caractère estérieur de magistrat (Maistre) **37**:312
"The Caravan" (Hugo) **3**:262
The Caravan (Hauff)
See *Die Karawane*
El carbonero alcalde (Alarcón) **219**:4, 28
"Card Drawing" (Griffin) **7**:197, 201, 211-12, 217
"The Card-Dealer" (Rossetti) **4**:506, 509, 518, 521-22, 524-25, 528
"A Card to the Public" (Willis) **194**:301
"The Carder and the Carrier" (D'Israeli) **217**:305
"Cardinal Newman" (Rossetti) **50**:309
"The Careless Nurse Mayde" (Hood) **16**:237
"Careless Rambles" (Clare) **86**:142
"The Careless Word" (Norton) **205**:48
"The Cares of the World" (Baratynsky)
See "Les Soucis matériels"
"Les Caresses" (Maupassant) **83**:176-77, 223
Les cariatides (Banville) **9**:14, 17-19, 25-26, 28
"Caricatures and Lithography in Paris" (Thackeray) **169**:244; **213**:223, 243
"Caridorf" (Bird) **197**:6
Caridorf (Bird) **1**:87, 89
Carita (Oliphant) **61**:173
Carl Krinken: His Christmas Stocking (Warner) **146**:258
Carl Werner (Simms) **3**:510
"Carlota y Welster" (Lizardi) **30**:71
"Carlsbad" (Field) **3**:206
"Carlyle from American Points of View" (Whitman) **205**:253
Carmagnola (Manzoni)
See *Il conte di Carmagnola*
Carme (Foscolo)
See *Le grazie, carme*
The Carmelite (Cumberland) **167**:122, 134, 140, 142, 144, 149, 157, 189-90
Carmen (Mérimée) **6**:353-7, 360, 362-5, 367, 369, 371-3; **65**:42-3, 48, 52, 54, 56, 58, 62, 64, 66, 79, 82, 85, 87-8, 102, 104, 114, 119-22, 132-3, 137, 140
"Carmen Triumphale" (Timrod) **25**:362, 376
Carmen Triumphale for the Commencement of the Year 1814 (Southey) **97**:262
"Carmilla" (Le Fanu) **9**:312, 318, 321-23; **58**:251, 257-61, 274, 302-3
Carmosine (Musset) **7**:268, 271, 276; **150**:226
"Carnaval" (Banville) **9**:30
Carnaval (Schumann) **143**:69-70, 73, 120, 126

Les carnets de Joseph Joubert (Joubert) **9**:290-92, 295
Carnets de voyage: Notes sur la province, 1863-1865 (Taine) **15**:452
The Carniolan Bee (Preseren)
See *Kranjska čbelica*
Carnioli (Feuillet) **45**:88
"A Carnival Episode" (Blind) **202**:10, 16-18
"Carnival Night" (Laforgue)
See "Soir de carnaval"
Carol (Dickens)
See *A Christmas Carol. In Prose. Being a Ghost Story of Christmas*
"Carolina" (Hayne) **94**:161
"Carolina" (Timrod) **25**:360, 362-63, 367, 372, 375-76, 384, 388
"Caroline" (Brontë) **109**:4-6, 30, 33
"Caroline Vernon" (Brontë) **3**:80; **105**:31
"Caroline's Prayer" (Brontë) **109**:4
"A Carp in a Dream" (Ueda Akinari)
See "Muo no rigyo"
"The Carp that Came to My Dream" (Ueda Akinari)
See "Muo no rigyo"
Carpenter; or, The Dangers of Evil Company (More) **141**:190
"The Carpenter's Son" (Lippard) **198**:139, 229
"The Carpenter's Wife" (Clare) **86**:90
"The Carriage" (Gogol) **5**:235, 254, 257; **15**:94, 97; **162**:16
"A Carrion" (Baudelaire)
See "Une charogne"
"Carrion Comfort" (Hopkins) **17**:204, 243, 249, 256, 261-62; **189**:8-9, 26, 28, 30, 77, 84, 90-91, 93-94, 96, 120, 135, 139, 146-48
"Le carrosse du Saint Sacrement" (Mérimée) **6**:362-3; **65**:59, 79, 81-2
"Carry Carlisle" (Osgood) **141**:322
Carsten Curator (Storm) **1**:540, 546; **195**:7, 11-12, 16, 54, 56-57, 82, 127, 130, 132
"Carta" (Bello) **131**:106
Carta (Bécquer) **106**:119
"Carta ao Dr Jaguaribe" (Alencar) **157**:57
"Carta ás senhoras bahianas" (Castro Alves) **205**:37
Carta desde mi celda (Bécquer)
See *Cartas literarias desde mi celda*
"Carta Escrita de Londres a París por un Americano a Otro" (Bello) **131**:133
"Carta I" (Bécquer) **106**:112-13, 153, 156
"Carta II" (Bécquer) **106**:113-14, 116
Cartas desde mi celda (Bécquer)
See *Cartas literarias desde mi celda*
Cartas inéditas (Gómez de Avellaneda) **111**:57, 62
Cartas literarias a una mujer (Bécquer) **106**:102-03, 105, 109, 112, 114, 116, 118-19, 142, 167-69, 172
Cartas literarias desde mi celda (Bécquer) **106**:93-4, 96, 106, 108-9, 112-13, 118-21, 153, 155, 162
Cartas sôbre a Confederaçao dos tamoios (Alencar) **157**:5, 8, 17, 50
"Carţile" (Eminescu) **33**:251
"The Cartusians" (Meyer)
See "Die Kartäuser"
Carwin, the Biloquist (Brown)
See *Memoirs of Carwin the Biloquist*
"Cary O'Kean'" (Hogg) **109**:250
The Caryatids (Banville)
See *Les cariatides*
"Un cas de divorce" (Maupassant) **83**:176
Casa Guidi Windows: A Poem (Barrett Browning) **1**:118-9, 122, 125, 127, 130; **61**:12, 14-6, 22-4, 37, 43-4; **66**:44-5, 52, 90-1, 95; **170**:6, 32, 56, 67-72, 86, 104, 108-9, 111, 116, 118, 120-21
"La casa paterna" (Isaacs) **70**:303
"Casabianca" (Hemans) **29**:204-06; **71**:270, 272, 279, 283
"Casar Borgias Ohnmacht" (Meyer) **81**:199, 207
"El casarse pronto y mal" (Larra) **17**:275, 278-80; **130**:275
"The Cascade of Melsingah" (Bryant) **6**:180
"A Cascata de Paulo Afonso" (Castro Alves) **205**:3
A Case of Conscience (Inchbald) **62**:144, 147, 149
"The Case of the Officers of the Excise" (Paine) **62**:278
"A Case That Was Dropped" (Leskov)
See "Pogassee delo"
"Casey's Table d'Hôte" (Field) **3**:205, 209
"Cashel of Munster" (Ferguson) **33**:294
"Casino des trépassés" (Corbière) **43**:32
"The Cask of Amontillado" (Poe) **1**:500, 506; **16**:303, 309, 329, 332; **55**:148; **78**:265-66; **97**:180; **117**:260; **211**:312
"Caso de ablativo" (Bécquer) **106**:146
"Cassandra" (Schiller)
See "Kassandra"
"Cassandra" (Webster) **230**:244
"Cassandra Southwick" (Whittier) **8**:489, 505, 509-11, 513, 515, 527, 530; **59**:358
La Casse-Noisette (Dumas) **71**:242
Cassiodor (Eminescu) **33**:266
The Cassique of Accabee (Simms) **3**:504
The Cassique of Kiawah (Simms) **3**:503, 508, 514
"Casta Piana" (Verlaine) **230**:211
"The Castaway" (Cowper) **8**:108, 113, 119, 122, 125, 133, 137-38; **94**:24, 32, 38-9, 123
"A Castaway" (Webster) **230**:231, 233-34, 251, 264, 266, 281-87, 291-94, 297-98, 324
A Castaway (Webster) **230**:242, 256
Caste (Robertson) **35**:330, 332-34, 336, 338, 340-41, 343-47, 349, 351-52, 355-56, 358, 359-60, 362, 364-65, 367, 369-71, 372-73
"El Castellano viejo" (Larra) **17**:278; **130**:230
"Castellanos de Castilla!" (Castro) **78**:40
"Castillo" (Martí) **63**:157-8
El castillo de Balsain (Tamayo y Baus) **1**:571
"El castillo real de Olite" (Bécquer) **106**:106
"The Castle Builder" (Longfellow) **45**:127
"Castle Carnal" (Harpur) **114**:144
Castle Dangerous (Scott) **15**:308; **69**:332, 334; **209**:182, 185
Castle Dismal (Simms) **3**:510
"Castle in the Air" (Paine) **62**:324-5
Castle Nowhere: Lake Country Sketches (Woolson) **82**:269, 272, 277, 283, 286-87, 292-94, 299, 305, 322, 330, 333, 335, 338-40
The Castle of Balsain (Tamayo y Baus)
See *El castillo de Balsain*
The Castle of Loch-Leuven (Pixérécourt)
See *Le chateau de Loch-Leven; ou, L'évasion de Marie Stuart*
"The Castle of Smalholm" (Zhukovsky) **35**:388, 393
Castle Rackrent (Edgeworth) **1**:255, 261-67, 269, 271-73; **51**:75, 77, 79-82, 88-9, 91-3, 95-100, 102, 104-05, 107-08, 113, 135; **158**:3, 6, 12-13, 23-24, 26, 48, 53-68, 77-78, 80-83, 86-91, 93
Castle Richmond: A Novel (Trollope) **6**:470-71, 499, 514; **101**:245-46, 248-53, 262-64, 271, 276, 293-96, 298, 312; **215**:214
The Castle Spectre (Lewis) **11**:294-95, 302, 304-05
Castle Squander (Carleton)
See *The Squanders of Castle Squander*
"A Castle-Builder's World" (Rossetti) **186**:240, 296
Castle-Croquet (Dodgson) **139**:57
Castles in the Air (Gore) **65**:21
The Castles of Athlin and Dunbayne: A Highland Story (Radcliffe) **6**:403, 405, 409, 410, 413, 415, 418, 424, 426, 429, 435, 442; **55**:224-5, 229, 241, 274; **223**:184, 189, 216, 240, 311, 318
"The Castles of the Gleichen" (Taylor) **89**:308, 310
Castruccio Castracani (Landon) **15**:164
"A Casual Observation" (Kleist)
See "Unmaßgebliche Betrachtung"
"Casuisty of Roman Meals" (De Quincey) **4**:69
"Časy" (Turgenev) **122**:242-44, 246, 266
"The Cat" (Brontë) **165**:99
"Cat" (Poe)
See "The Black Cat"
"Cat and Cook" (Krylov) **1**:439
"The Catalogue Raisonné of the British Institution" (Hazlitt) **29**:144
"The Cataract" (Hayne) **94**:134, 153
"The Cataract of Lodore" (Southey) **8**:472, 474
"Catarina to Camoens" (Barrett Browning) **1**:125; **61**:66; **170**:13-14, 56
Catechism of a Revolutionary (Bakunin) **25**:53, 72, 74
Catéchisme Positiviste ou Sommaire exposition de la religion universelle en onze entretiens systématiques entre une femme et un pretre de l'Humanité (Comte) **54**:210
"Catecismo democratico" (Martí) **63**:122
"The Caterpillar" (Barbauld) **185**:132, 149-57
"Catharina" (Cowper) **8**:119
"Catharine" (Austen) **1**:66; **119**:13
Catharine, or the Bower (Austen) **95**:4; **119**:11
"The Cathedral" (Lowell) **90**:190, 193-94, 207-10
The Cathedral Folk (Leskov)
See *Soborjane*
"Cathedral Walk" (Crabbe) **26**:109
"Catherine" (Shevchenko)
See "Kateryna"
Catherine (Arany)
See *Katalin*
Catherine: A Story (Thackeray) **5**:452, 465, 470, 482, 490, 492, 497; **14**:400, 402, 411, 420, 433; **43**:348, 351, 358-59, 364, 375-76, 381, 383, 389-91; **213**:200, 202, 218
Catherine Blum (Dumas) **71**:204
"Catherine Lloyd" (Crabbe) **26**:135; **121**:43, 45, 47-9
"The Catholic Convert" (Hale) **75**:357-61
The Catholic Reaction (Symonds) **34**:331, 346, 360, 368
"Catholicism" (Mallarmé) **41**:254-55
"Catholicisme" (Mallarmé) **210**:251
Catiline (Dumas) **11**:53-54
Catriona, a Sequel to "Kidnapped": Being Memoirs of the Further Adventures of David Balfour at Home and Abroad (Stevenson) **5**:415, 417, 426-27, 437-39; **63**:274; **193**:212, 214, 216-18, 222-23, 238, 242-48, 254, 274, 281
The Catspaw (Jerrold) **2**:402-03
"Catterskill Falls" (Bryant) **6**:172; **46**:19-20, 28, 38
"The Cattle-pen" (Leskov)
See "Zagon"
"El Cauca" (Isaacs) **70**:310
The Caucasian Captive (Pushkin)
See *Kavkazsky plennik*
"The Caucasus" (Shevchenko)
See "Kavkaz"
"Cauchemar" (Banville) **9**:16
"El caudillo de las manos rojas" (Bécquer) **106**:108-10, 113, 130, 133
Cause in the Decline of Taste in Different Nations (Herder) **8**:307
The Cause of Freedom: Which Is Its Champion in America, The North or the South? (Hughes) **207**:125, 128-30
"Causerie" (Baudelaire) **55**:3, 55, 61
Les causeries du lundi (Sainte-Beuve) **5**:325-26, 329-31, 339-40
"The Causes of Methodism" (Hazlitt) **29**:162
La cautiva (Echeverria) **18**:147-54, 156-57
"Cava lixeiro, cava" (Castro) **78**:42
"Cavalry Crossing a Ford" (Whitman) **81**:312; **205**:339
"Cavalry Raids" (Bestuzhev)
See "Nayezdy"

"The Cave" (Taylor)
See "Cave of Trophonius"
"Cave of Trophonius" (Taylor) **89**:311
"The Cave of Vanhest" (Brackenridge) **227**:72, 162-64, 166-67, 170
"The Caves of Dahra" (Patmore) **9**:329
"Cavitri" (Verlaine) **230**:166
Caxtoniana (Bulwer-Lytton) **1**:155; **45**:23
The Caxtons, a Family Picture (Bulwer-Lytton) **1**:144-45, 148, 150, 155; **45**:19, 21-2, 69-70
Čbelica (Preseren) **127**:294
"Ce poème homérique et sans ègal au monde" (Gautier) **59**:18
"Ce qu'aime le gros Fritz" (Laforgue) **221**:39
"Ce que dit la bouche d'ombre" (Hugo) **3**:273
Ce qui est arrivéà la France en 1870 (Gobineau) **17**:95
Ce qui ne meurt pas (Barbey d'Aurevilly) **213**:74, 78, 89, 92
Ce qui se passait aux Feuillantines vers 1813 (Hugo) **189**:178
"Ce qu'on dit au poète à propos de fleurs" (Rimbaud) **4**:472, 475, 486; **35**:282-83, 308, 321; **227**:255
Ce qu'on entend sur la montagne (Liszt) **199**:314
"Ce sont des villes!" (Rimbaud)
See "Villes I"
"Ce te legeni codrule" (Eminescu) **33**:253
Cecil, a Peer (Gore) **65**:22
Cecil Dreeme (Winthrop) **210**:278-83, 285-89, 296-301, 304-5, 312, 314, 319-20, 322-23
Cecil; or, the Adventures of a Coxcomb (Gore) **65**:15, 17, 21, 28, 36
Cécile (Constant) **6**:223-24; **182**:148, 187, 218-19
Cécile (Dumas) **71**:203
Cécile (Fontane) **26**:236, 252, 255, 259, 270-71; **163**:161, 239
Cecilia; or, Memoirs of an Heiress (Burney) **12**:16-18, 21-2, 25, 27-37, 41-6, 48, 50, 57-64; **54**:3, 6-8, 12-14, 17, 29, 36-7, 50, 52-3, 61; **107**:12, 16
Cecilia Valdés (Villaverde) **121**:330-40, 344, 349, 352, 356, 359, 361, 366, 368
Cedarcroft Pastoral (Taylor) **89**:315
Ceinture dorée (Augier) **31**:5, 13, 15, 19, 25, 27, 30, 34
Celebrated Crimes (Dumas)
See *Crimes célèbres*
"The Celebration of Intellect" (Emerson) **98**:48
"Celebration of Peace" (Hölderlin)
See "Friedensfeier"
"Celestial Love" (Emerson) **98**:91, 93
"The Celestial Maidens" (Ueda Akinari)
See "Amatsu otome"
"Celestial Publicity" (Villiers de l'Isle Adam)
See "L'affichage céleste"
"The Celestial Railroad" (Hawthorne) **2**:298, 302-03, 305, 333; **23**:205; **95**:116, 125-26, 137, 156; **171**:345; **191**:204
"The Celestial Surgeon" (Stevenson) **193**:206
Celestina (Smith) **23**:316, 322, 327-29; **115**:123, 146, 157-58, 160, 222-23
"Célestine ou l'Innocence" (Genlis) **166**:55-56, 60-61
Les célibataires (Balzac)
See *Le curé de Tours*
"A celle qui est trop gaie" (Baudelaire) **155**:40-41
"Celle-ci et Celle-là ou la Jeune-France passionnée" (Gautier) **59**:27-8, 31, 63-4
"Celles qui osent" (Maupassant) **83**:228
"The Cell-Theory" (Huxley) **67**:80, 83
Cellulairement (Verlaine) **2**:632; **230**:151-54, 159, 207
"Celovek na casakh" (Leskov)
See "Chelovék na chasákh"
Celtic Bards, Chiefs, and Kings (Borrow) **9**:57
"Celtic Literature" (Arnold) **6**:41
"The Cemetery" (Very) **9**:386
The Cenci (Shelley) **18**:314, 316-17, 320, 336, 341, 344, 360, 362, 365-69, 375, 382; **93**:266-67, 269-72, 275-80, 351-56, 358; **143**:152, 154, 157-69, 173-75, 180, 182-83, 185-90, 193-202, 208-10, 212-26, 228, 230-34, 236-41, 243-50, 256-59, 264, 266, 268, 270-91, 293-95, 298-303, 307-9, 311, 316-17; **175**:202, 236, 238, 246, 318, 324
The Cenci: A Tragedy in Five Acts (Shelley)
See *The Cenci*
"Cenciaja" (Browning) **19**:88
Les 120 journées de Sodome; ou, L'école du libertinage (Sade) **3**:479, 481, 488-89, 492, 494-96; **47**:301, 305-06, 310-12, 315, 318-19, 323, 326-32, 334, 336, 339, 342, 345, 350, 352, 364-65
Le centénaire (Balzac) **5**:58
"The Centenarian's Story" (Whitman) **81**:317, 320
Centenary Edition of the Works of Nathaniel Hawthorne (Hawthorne) **171**:324, 330; **191**:189
"Centennial Cantata" (Lanier) **6**:233-34, 236, 254, 260, 262; **118**:210, 238
The Centennial Edition of the Works of Sidney Lanier (Lanier) **6**:268; **118**:227, 251
"The Centennial Meditation of Columbia" (Lanier) **118**:237, 275
Centennial Meditation of Columbia (Lanier) **6**:232; **118**:261, 278-79
"The Century" (Castro Alves)
See "O Século"
A Century of Dishonor (Jackson) **90**:135, 143-46, 148-50, 153-54, 157, 159, 169
A Century of Sonnets (Lampman) **194**:79, 82, 126
Cenuşotca (Eminescu) **33**:266
"Cerep" (Baratynsky) **103**:6-7, 27
"Certainly, This Is a Great Century . . ." (Laforgue)
See "Certes, ce siècle est grand! . . ."
"Certes, ce siècle est grand! . . ." (Laforgue) **221**:90
"Čertogon" (Leskov) **25**:234
"Certopxanov and Nedopjuskin" (Turgenev)
See "Chertopkhanov and Nedopyuskin"
Cervantes (Oliphant) **11**:439; **221**:233
Ces passions qu'eux seuls nomment encore amours (Verlaine) **51**:363
César Birotteau (Balzac) **53**:11; **153**:7, 9, 65, 74, 79, 152
"César Borgia" (Verlaine) **2**:622, 624; **51**:356
Césarine Dietrich (Sand) **57**:313
"C'est l'automne, l'automne . . ." (Laforgue)
See "Dimanches"
"C'est l'extase langoureuse..." (Verlaine) **51**:355, 381-82, 384
"C'est la fête du blé . . ." (Verlaine) **230**:173
"Cezara" (Eminescu) **131**:297
"The Chace" (Patmore) **9**:351
El Chacho (Sarmiento) **123**:274
"Chactas or the Lament of the Harmonious Voice" (Chivers) **49**:73
"Chacun sa chimère" (Baudelaire) **55**:78; **155**:32, 46
"The Chaffinch" (Jefferies) **47**:139
"Chagrins d'enfance" (Baudelaire) **155**:41
A Chain (Scribe)
See *Une chaîne*
A Chain of Events (Lewes) **25**:291
The Chainbearer; or, The Littlepage Manuscripts (Cooper) **1**:217, 219-21, 224; **54**:258, 280, 288; **203**:75-76
Une chaîne (Scribe) **16**:384, 387-89, 400, 402-03, 405
"La chaîne d'or" (Gautier) **1**:347-48; **59**:32
The Chained Fantasy (Raimund)
See *Die gesfesselte Phantasie*
Chair (Verlaine) **51**:352, 372; **230**:166, 172, 174
"The Chaldee Manuscript" (Hogg) **109**:261, 275
"Chaldee Manuscript" (Wilson) **5**:561
Chaldee Manuscript (Hogg) **109**:258
Chaldee Manuscript (Lockhart) **6**:296
"Châli" (Maupassant) **83**:201-02
"The Challenge" (Longfellow) **45**:161
"The Chamber over the Gate" (Longfellow) **45**:132, 162, 166
"The Chambered Nautilus" (Holmes) **14**:109-10, 118-19, 125-26, 129, 133, 140; **81**:97, 107
"La chambre 11" (Maupassant) **83**:171
"La chambre bleue" (Mérimée) **6**:360, 364, 369, 371; **65**:47-50, 52, 56, 62, 64-5, 85, 96, 98, 104, 140-3
"La chambre double" (Baudelaire) **29**:107; **55**:12; **155**:32, 46
"La chambre gothique" (Bertrand) **31**:46, 51
"Chamouny The Hour before Sunrise A Hymn" (Coleridge)
See "Hymn before Sunrise"
Le Champ d'Oliviers (Maupassant) **1**:459, 464, 468; **42**:170; **83**:175, 179
Champavert, contes immoraux (Borel) **41**:3-6, 8, 10, 12-14, 19
"Champavert le lycanthrope" (Borel)
See "Testament de Champavert"
Champavert: Seven Bitter Tales (Borel)
See *Champavert, contes immoraux*
"The Champion" (Fouqué) **2**:266
The Champion of Virtue (Reeve)
See *The Old English Baron*
Le chandelier (Musset) **7**:262, 264, 267, 270-71, 276; **150**:336
Chandrasekhar (Chatterji) **19**:206, 210, 212, 214-15, 217-21, 224-25
Chandrashekhar (Chatterji)
See *Chandrasekhar*
"The Change" (Smith) **59**:331-2
"Change" (Very) **9**:383
"The Changed Allegiance" (Patmore) **9**:347-48, 351
The Changed Brides (Southworth) **26**:433
"The Changeling" (Lamb) **10**:402
"The Changeling" (Lamb)
See "Ann Withers: The Changeling"
"The Changeling" (Lowell) **90**:214
"The Changes of Home" (Dana) **53**:157-8, 178
"Changing France" (Beddoes) **154**:74
The Channings (Wood) **178**:269-70, 288, 290-91, 335
"Chanson d'automne" (Verlaine) **2**:624; **51**:351, 355; **230**:161, 164, 194, 197
"La chanson de fortunio" (Musset) **7**:275
"Chanson de la plus haute tour" (Rimbaud) **82**:226, 230-31, 233, 247, 249, 259
"La chanson des ingénues" (Verlaine) **2**:629-30; **51**:356, 369
"Le Chanson des morts" (Laforgue) **221**:83
"Chanson du petit hypertrophique" (Laforgue) **5**:275
La Chanson du vitrier (Baudelaire) **155**:75
Chansons bas (Mallarmé) **41**:249; **210**:198
Chansons des rues et des bois (Hugo) **3**:264
"Chansons et légendes du Valois" (Nerval) **1**:485; **67**:371
Chansons inédites (Beranger) **34**:44
Chansons pour elle (Verlaine) **2**:621-22; **51**:352; **230**:160, 166, 168-69, 183
"Chant alterné" (Leconte de Lisle) **29**:223, 239-40
"Chant d'amour" (Lamartine) **11**:283
"Chant d'automne" (Baudelaire) **6**:115; **55**:3, 6, 64
"Chant de guerre parisien" (Rimbaud) **4**:465; **35**:271; **82**:238
Chant du sacre; ou, la Veille des armes (Lamartine) **11**:246; **190**:195
"Chant lyrique du jugement dernier" (Lamartine) **11**:273
Chant premier (Lautréamont)
See *Les chants de Maldoror: Chant premier*

"Chanteuse Nightingale" (Brentano)
See "Sängerin Nachtigall"
"Chanting the Square Deific" (Whitman) **4**:544, 587; **31**:390; **81**:314; **205**:172, 341
Les chants de Maldoror: Chant premier (Lautréamont) **12**:206-09, 211-12, 214-19, 222-44; **194**:218, 221
Les chants de Maldoror: Chants I, II, III, IV, V, VI (Lautréamont) **12**:209-44; **194**:144-48, 150-58, 160-61, 167, 170-71, 173, 175-78, 182-92, 194-95, 197-211, 215, 217-25, 230-40, 242-47, 254-59, 261-69, 271
"Chants Democratic and Native American" (Whitman) **205**:161-62, 164, 166-67, 271, 295-96
Chants Democratic and Native American (Whitman) **81**:349
"Chants Democratic and Native American 1" (Whitman)
See "By Blue Ontario's Shore"
"Chants Democratic and Native American 2" (Whitman)
See "Song of the Broad-Axe"
"Chants Democratic and Native American 3" (Whitman)
See "A Song for Occupations"
"Chants Democratic and Native American 4" (Whitman)
See "Our Old Feuillage"
"Chants Democratic and Native American 5" (Whitman)
See "Transpositions"
"Chants Democratic and Native American 6" (Whitman)
See "Think of the Soul"
"Chants Democratic and Native American 7" (Whitman)
See "With Antecedents"
"Chants Democratic and Native American 8" (Whitman)
See "Song at Sunset"
"Chants Democratic and Native American 9" (Whitman)
See "Thoughts 1"
"Chants Democratic and Native American 10" (Whitman)
See "To a Historian"
"Chants Democratic and Native American 11" (Whitman)
See "Thoughts 2"
"Chants Democratic and Native American 12" (Whitman)
See "Vocalism"
"Chants Democratic and Native American 13" (Whitman)
See "Laws for Creation"
"Chants Democratic and Native American 14" (Whitman)
See "Poets to Come"
"Chants Democratic and Native American 15" (Whitman)
See "Excelsior"
"Chants Democratic and Native American 16" (Whitman)
See "Mediums"
"Chants Democratic and Native American 17" (Whitman) **205**:162, 166
"Chants Democratic and Native American 18" (Whitman)
See "Me imperturbe"
"Chants Democratic and Native American 19" (Whitman)
See "I Was Looking a Long While"
"Chants Democratic and Native American 20" (Whitman)
See "I Hear America Singing"
"Chants Democratic and Native American 21" (Whitman) **205**:166
"Les chants du Crépuscule" (Hugo) **3**:270-71, 273
Chants for Socialists (Morris) **4**:445
"Les chants lyriques de Saül" (Lamartine) **11**:269
The Chapel (Almqvist)
See *Kapellet*
"The Chapel in Lyoness" (Morris) **4**:411, 421, 431
"The Chapel of the Hermits" (Whittier) **8**:492, 495, 500-01; **59**:370
La chapelle des bois; ou, Le témoin invisible (Pixérécourt) **39**:287
"The Chaplet of Cypress" (Chivers) **49**:72
"Chapman's Homer" (Keats)
See "On First Looking into Chapman's Homer"
"A Chapter in the History of a Tyrone Family" (Le Fanu) **58**:253
The Chapter of Accidents: A Comedy, in Five Acts (Lee) **191**:313, 327
A Chapter of Autobiography (Gladstone) **213**:113, 117, 171
"Chapter on Autography" (Poe)
See "Autography"
"A Chapter on Dreams" (Stevenson) **14**:333, 338; **193**:259
"A Chapter on Ears" (Lamb) **10**:409, 411; **113**:200, 235
"A Chapter on Literary Women" (Parton) **86**:348
Chapters on Flowers (Tonna) **135**:203
"Chapters on Ghostcraft" (Mangan) **27**:291, 303
"Chapters on Socialism" (Mill) **179**:282
"A Character" (Barbauld) **185**:154
"Character" (Emerson) **98**:55, 61-2, 75
"A Character" (Tennyson) **30**:280
"Character and Intelligence of the Britons" (Barnes) **75**:64
"The Character and Poetry of Keats" (Lampman) **25**:203, 214-15
"The Character and Scope of the Sonnet" (Timrod) **25**:380
"A Character in the Antithetical Manner" (Wordsworth) **111**:235, 300
"The Character of a Native Georgian" (Longstreet) **159**:117, 136, 142, 144, 161, 182-83
"The Character of Dramatic Poetry" (Wagner) **9**:467
"Character of Lord Chatham" (Hazlitt) **82**:109
"The Character of Milton's Eve" (Hazlitt) **29**:148
"Character of Mr. Burke" (Hazlitt) **82**:110
"The Character of Sir Robert Peel" (Bagehot) **10**:62
"The Character of the Happy Warrior" (Wordsworth) **12**:395; **206**:296
"A Character of the Later Elia. By a Friend" (Lamb) **10**:408; **113**:199, 234
"Characteristics" (Carlyle) **70**:7, 42-44, 57
Characteristics: In the Manner of Rouchefoucauld's Maxims (Hazlitt) **29**:151, 170, 183; **82**:98, 126
"Characteristics of Greek Tragedians" (Schlegel)
See "Charakteristik der griechischen Tragiker"
Characteristics of Shakespeare's Women (Jameson)
See *Characteristics of Women*
Characteristics of the Eighteenth Century (Humboldt) **134**:186, 188
"Characteristics of the Genius of Scott" (Martineau) **26**:350
The Characteristics of the Present Age (Fichte)
See *Die Grundzüge der Gegenwärtigun Zeitalters*
Characteristics of Women (Jameson) **43**:305, 312, 314-17, 319, 323
Characteristiken u Kritiken (Schlegel) **142**:300
"Characters" (Trumbull) **30**:348
"Characters of Dramatic Writers Contemporary with Shakespeare" (Lamb) **10**:387, 412; **113**:256
Characters of Shakespeare's Plays (Hazlitt) **29**:134, 138, 146-48, 163, 174-76, 186-87; **82**:93
"Characters of Worldly Mistresses" (Ueda Akinari)
See "Seken tekake katagi"
"Charakteristik der griechischen Tragiker" (Schlegel) **226**:233
"Charakteristik der Tonleitern und Tonarten" (Schumann) **143**:76
"The Charge of the Heavy Brigade" (Tennyson) **202**:290, 294
"The Charge of the Heavy Brigade at Balaclava" (Tennyson) **30**:295
"The Charge of the Light Brigade" (Tennyson) **30**:223, 280, 286, 294, 296, 298-99; **202**:179, 276, 294
"Charicteristic Descriptive Pastorals in prose on rural life and manners" (Clare) **86**:173
"The Chariot" (Dickinson)
See "Because I Could Not Stop for Death"
"Charity" (Boyesen) **135**:13
"Charity" (Cowper) **94**:27-8, 115, 124, 126
"Charity" (Dodgson) **139**:61
"Charity" (Harpur) **114**:154
Charity (Cowper) **94**:10
"Charity Bowery" (Child) **73**:80
"A Charity Sermon" (Hood) **16**:235
"The Charivari" (Moodie) **14**:231
Le charlatanisme (Scribe) **16**:384
Charlemont; or, The Pride of the Village (Simms) **3**:508-09
"Charleroi" (Verlaine) **51**:370, 382-83; **230**:187
Charles VII. à Naples (Augier) **31**:11
Charles Chesterfield; or, The Adventures of a Youth of Genius (Trollope) **30**:309, 327-29
"Charles Darwin" (Huxley) **67**:48
"Charles Dickens's Readings" (Sarmiento) **123**:383
Charles I (Shelley) **18**:327
"Charles Lamb" (Pater) **7**:306
"Charles Lamb" (De Quincey) **87**:31
Charles O'Malley, the Irish Dragoon (Lever) **23**:270-73, 275, 281, 283-87, 290-92, 294-96, 300, 303-04, 306, 309-10
Charles Stuart (Chivers) **49**:79
Charles the Bold (Pixérécourt)
See *Charles-le-téméraire; ou, Le Siège de Nancy*
Charles VII chez ses grands vassaux (Dumas) **11**:42, 47-48, 57, 71; **71**:241, 243, 244
Charles-le-téméraire; ou, Le Siège de Nancy (Pixérécourt) **39**:274-75, 278, 282, 284, 295-96
"Charles-Quint" (Musset) **150**:309
"Charleston" (Timrod) **25**:362-63, 376, 385-86
Charlotte: A Tale of Truth (Rowson) **5**:309-23; **69**:98-100, 102-06, 108-09, 111-14, 117, 122, 129-36, 140-41, 158; **182**:255-58, 260, 263, 285-86, 288, 290-92, 294-302, 304-7, 313-15, 317-18, 320, 322-33, 336-41, 343, 352, 354, 356, 358, 360-61
"Charlotte Smith" (Scott) **110**:277-78
Charlotte Temple: A Tale of Truth (Rowson)
See *Charlotte: A Tale of Truth*
"Charlotte Wilmot: The Merchant's Daughter" (Lamb) **125**:317
Charlotte's Daughter; or, The Three Orphans (Rowson) **5**:310, 312-13, 315-17; **69**:103, 105-06, 114, 130
Charlotte's Daughter; or, The Three Orphans. A Sequel to Charlotte Temple (Rowson) **182**:259-61, 263, 296, 313, 356, 360
"A Charm" (Dickinson) **171**:189-92
"The Charm of Days Gone By" (Zhukovsky) **35**:403
"Charmed Picture" (Hemans) **29**:206; **71**:303
"The Charmed Sea" (Martineau) **26**:313
"The Charmed Spot" (Gogol)
See "Zakoldovannoe mesto"
"The 'Charming Creature' as a Wife" (Longstreet) **159**:118, 125, 137, 141, 144,

181, 186, 192, 200-201
"Une charogne" (Baudelaire) **6**:93, 115; **29**:83-4, 103; **55**:6, 10, 31-2, 44, 55, 59, 76; **155**:10, 12-15
Charonic Steps (Beddoes) **154**:76
"The Charter; Addressed to My Nephew Athanase C. L. Coquerel, on His Wedding Day, 1819" (Williams) **135**:315, 335
The Charterhouse of Parma (Stendhal)
See *La chartreuse de Parme*
Chartism (Carlyle) **70**:46-47, 53, 71, 73, 93, 105-111
"A Chartist March" (Jones) **222**:157
Chartist Poems (Jones)
See *Chartist Songs*
Chartist Songs (Jones) **222**:131, 154-58, 169, 171, 176
La chartreuse de Parme (Stendhal) **23**:345-56, 358-59, 361-63, 365, 368-71, 374, 376, 378, 383-85, 389, 391, 393, 397, 400-02, 404-05, 408-17, 424-26; **46**:262-63, 279-80, 310, 316, 318, 323, 325; **178**:147-49, 151-52, 154-57, 160-64, 167, 171, 173, 177, 192-93, 198, 200, 203-4, 206, 210-11, 213-14, 223, 226-27, 241, 253, 256-57
Charts de la patrie (Chateaubriand) **3**:126
"Chas voli Bozhiei" (Leskov) **174**:82-83, 86-87, 90
"The Chase" (Scott) **209**:196
"Chasm Lightening" (Laforgue)
See "Eclair de gouffre"
"La chasse" (Bertrand) **31**:49
"Chasse" (Rimbaud) **227**:195
"La chasse au caribou" (Gobineau) **17**:80, 92-3, 103
La Chasse au Chastre (Dumas) **71**:204
"Le chasse de l'aigle" (Leconte de Lisle) **29**:216, 225
"La chasse spirituelle" (Rimbaud) **4**:484
Le Chasseur de Sauvagine (Dumas) **71**:204
"Chasy i zerkalo" (Bestuzhev) **131**:154, 186
"Le Chat" (Baudelaire) **55**:9, 61
"Château" (Woolson)
See "At the Chateau of Corinne"
Le château de Combourg (Chateaubriand) **3**:133
Le château de la misère (Gautier) **1**:346
Le chateau de Loch-Leven; ou, L'évasion de Marie Stuart (Pixérécourt) **39**:277, 279, 285, 294
"Le château de Robert le diable" (Nodier) **19**:378
Le Château des Désertes (Sand) **42**:310-11, 313-14
"The Chateau of Prince Polignac" (Trollope) **215**:208
Chateaubriand (Dumas) **71**:218
Chateaubriand et son groupe littéraire sous l'empire (Sainte-Beuve) **5**:338, 342, 349
"La Châtelaine de Langeville ou la femme vengée" (Sade) **47**:313
De Chatillon (Hemans) **29**:201; **71**:276
"Châtiment de l'orgueil" (Baudelaire) **55**:58
"Le châtiment de Tartuff" (Rimbaud) **4**:471
Les Châtiments (Hugo) **3**:256, 262-64, 271, 273; **21**:214; **161**:231; **189**:267, 273, 275, 300
"Le chat-qui-pelote" (Balzac)
See "La maison du chat-qui-pelote"
Chatterton (Vigny) **7**:471, 473-74, 479; **102**:336, 341-44, 358, 360-65, 378
"Chatterton to His Sister" (Polidori) **51**:242
Chaturdaspadi Kavitāvali (Dutt) **118**:5
"Chaucer" (Longfellow) **45**:161, 186
"Chaucer and Shakspere" (Lanier) **118**:246
"Le Chaudronnier, ou la Reconnaissance Réciproque" (Genlis) **166**:32
"The Chaunt of Cholera" (Banim and Banim) **13**:129
The Chaunt of the Cholera: Songs for Ireland (Banim and Banim) **13**:129
"Che stai?" (Foscolo) **8**:278-79
Cheap Clothes and Nasty (Kingsley) **35**:205, 227-28
Cheap Repository Tracts (More) **27**:350-51; **141**:163-67, 169-77, 179-81, 187-93, 199-200, 216, 218-20, 224, 236, 267-72, 274, 281-82, 285-87, 289-92, 299, 301, 310-11
Checkmate (Le Fanu) **9**:301, 304, 312, 317; **58**:251, 273-5, 295
"Cheerfulness Taught by Reason" (Barrett Browning) **66**:44
The Cheese Factory (Schuecking)
See *Die Käserei in der Vehfreude*
"Le Chef-d'oeuvre inconnu" (Balzac) **5**:53, 67, 79-80; **53**:25; **153**:149-50, 152
Les chefs écossais (Pixérécourt) **39**:284
"Chelovék na chasákh" (Leskov) **174**:7, 37, 40
"The Chemical conviction" (Dickinson) **171**:212
"Le chêne" (Lamartine) **11**:255, 270, 279
"Cher petit oreillet" (Desbordes-Valmore) **97**:16
"Cheramour" (Leskov) **25**:239
"Les chercheuses de poux" (Rimbaud) **35**:271; **4**:454, 458; **227**:185
"Cherep" (Bestuzhev) **131**:150
Chérie (Goncourt) **7**:173-74, 183, 188
"Cherkesy" (Lermontov) **126**:167
"Chernets" (Shevchenko) **54**:387
"The Cherokee Love Song" (Ridge) **82**:175, 181
"The Cherokee's Threat" (Willis) **194**:282
"Cherry Blossoms in a Moonless Night" (Ichiyō)
See "Yamizakura"
"Chertogon" (Leskov) **174**:48
"Chertopkhanov and Nedopyuskin" (Turgenev) **21**:453; **122**:293-94
"The Cherub" (Hogg) **109**:248
"Cherubin" (Grillparzer) **102**:78
"Cherwell" (Bowles)
See "To the River Cherwell, Oxford"
"The Chest and the Ghost" (Stendhal)
See "Le coffre et le revenant"
Chester Rand; or, A New Path to Fortune (Alger) **8**:44, 46; **83**:91
The Chestnut Tree (Tyler) **3**:574
"Chesuncook" (Thoreau) **7**:368; **207**:177-78, 254
The Chevalier (Dumas) **71**:219
Le chevalier de Maison-Rouge (Dumas) **11**:53, 68, 76-7; **71**:193-94, 209, 232
Le chevalier des touches (Barbey d'Aurevilly) **1**:70-73; **213**:5, 23-24, 27, 29, 47-48, 63
Le chevalier d'Harmental (Dumas) **11**:51-52, 60, 63, 68-69, 74; **71**:194, 203-04, 228
"Le Chevalier double" (Gautier) **59**:13, 31, 37
"Chevalier Gluck" (Hoffmann)
See "Ritter Glück"
Les chevaliers (Lamartine) **11**:289
Les Chevaliers du cygne (Genlis) **166**:21-23, 39
"Chevaux de bois" (Verlaine) **51**:383
"La chevelure" (Baudelaire) **6**:79, 117-18, 128; **29**:73, 103, 109; **55**:5-6, 9, 25-6, 50, 55, 64, 67-8; **155**:47
"La Chevelure" (Maupassant) **1**:449; **83**:228
Le Cheveu Blanc (Feuillet) **45**:77, 79-80, 88-90
"Chevlovek na chasakh" (Leskov)
See "Chelovék na chasákh"
"Chevy Chase" (Maginn) **8**:439
"Chez le ministre" (Maupassant) **83**:227-28
"Chi katabira" (Ueda Akinari) **131**:20-22, 52-53
"Chicago Speech" (Lincoln)
See "Speech in Reply to Douglas at Chicago, Illinois"
Chicot the Jester; or, The Lady of Monsareua (Dumas)
See *La dame de Monsoreau*
Chidiock Tichbourne; or, The Catholic Conspiracy (Clarke) **19**:240
"Chiefly About War-Matters" (Hawthorne) **171**:355
Le chien de Montargis; ou, La forêt de Bondy (Pixérécourt) **39**:273, 277, 279, 281, 284, 286, 288-89
"Le chien et le flacon" (Baudelaire) **155**:23, 26, 46, 80
"Chiens" (Verlaine) **51**:363; **230**:174
"The Child" (Kivi)
See "Lapsi"
"Child and Boatman" (Ingelow) **39**:268
"Child and Hind" (Campbell) **19**:190
"The Child and the Profligate" (Whitman) **81**:327
"The Child Angel: A Dream" (Lamb) **10**:404, 435-36; **113**:217
Child from the Sea (Castro)
See *La hija del mar*
"Child Harold" (Clare) **9**:108, 112; **86**:89-90, 99, 102, 114, 117-23, 153, 162
"The Child in the Grave" (Andersen)
See "Barnet i Graven"
"The Child in the House" (Pater)
See "Imaginary Portrait. The Child in the House"
The Child in the House (Pater)
See *An Imaginary Portrait*
"Child Left in a Storm" (Sigourney) **21**:293
Child Life in Prose (Whittier) **59**:349
The Child of Love (Kotzebue)
See *Das Kind der Liebe*
The Child of Nature (Inchbald) **62**:143-3, 147-8
"A Child of the Age" (Boyesen) **135**:13, 20-21, 29
A Child of the Age (Adams) **33**:4, 10, 14, 16-17, 19-20
The Child of the Island (Norton) **47**:246, 254, 260
The Child of the Islands: A Poem (Norton) **205**:49, 67, 138, 144
"The Child that Loved a Grave" (O'Brien) **21**:236
"A Child to His Sick Grandfather" (Baillie) **151**:95
"Child Wife" (Verlaine) **2**:632; **51**:381, 383-84; **230**:152, 166, 169, 187
"Childe Christopher" (Cranch) **115**:13, 38, 54
Childe Harold (Byron)
See *Childe Harold's Pilgrimage: A Romaunt*
"Childe Harold's Last Pilgrimage" (Bowles) **103**:55
Childe Harold's Pilgrimage: A Romaunt (Byron) **2**:59, 62, 69, 71-72, 74-75, 81-82, 85-86, 91-92, 94-95, 103; **12**:73, 76, 88, 92, 95, 102, 103, 104, 109, 112, 113, 114, 122, 128, 129, 138, 143; **109**:62, 66-8, 70, 72, 83, 87-8, 118; **149**:6, 32, 37, 39-40, 46, 53, 72-3, 84, 115, 130, 150-1, 164-5; **149**:53, 55-56, 61, 142, 149-51, 162, 167, 169-70
Childe Harold's Pilgrimage: Canto the Second (Byron) **2**:96, 99, 95
"Childe Roland to the Dark Tower Came" (Browning) **19**:99, 106, 117, 141, 153-54; **79**:106-07, 110-11, 113-15, 164, 174
"Childhood II" (Rimbaud) **35**:269
"Childhood Home" (Lincoln)
See "My Childhood Home I See Again"
Childhood Years (Leskov)
See *Detskie gody*
Childhood Years of a Bagrov Grandson (Aksakov)
See *Detskie gody Bagrova-vnuka*
Childish Recollections (Byron) **149**:162
"The Children" (Very) **9**:383
"Children like Parents" (Keble) **87**:153
"Children of Adam" (Whitman) **4**:551-52, 557, 568-69, 577, 593, 599-601, 603-04; **81**:271, 279, 329-30; **205**:161-64, 219, 225-26, 258, 337
"The Children of Mount Ida" (Child) **6**:201; **73**:77
"Children of Pan" (Lampman) **194**:57
"Children of the Snow" (Bryant) **46**:8

"The Children of Venus" (Landor) **14**:181
Children's and Household Tales (Grimm Brothers)
See *Kinder-und Hausmärchen*
Children's Book (Martínez de la Rosa)
See *El libro de los niños*
Children's Book (Piozzi) **57**:281, 283, 299
"The Children's Crusade" (Longfellow) **45**:128, 137
"The Children's Dance" (Wilson) **5**:567
"The Children's Hour" (Longfellow) **2**:490, 499; **45**:179, 187
"The Children's Joke" (Alcott) **6**:16
"The Child's Answer" (Very) **9**:387
"Child's Book" (Sigourney) **87**:321
"The Child's Champion" (Whitman) **81**:301, 327
"A Child's Dream of a Star" (Dickens) **211**:5
"A Child's Funeral" (Bryant) **46**:3
A Child's Garden of Verses (Stevenson) **5**:395-96, 402, 404, 413, 428; **193**:205, 210, 215, 219, 227
A Child's History of England (Dickens) **18**:117, 134; **187**:172; **230**:141
"The Child's Music Lesson" (Lampman) **194**:44
"Child's Play" (Stevenson) **5**:389, 395
"The Child's Purchase" (Patmore) **9**:352, 357, 360
"A Child's Reminiscence" (Whitman) **205**:336
"A Child's Thought of God" (Barrett Browning) **1**:127
"Chillawassee Mountain" (Woolson) **82**:273
"A Chilly Night" (Rossetti) **186**:271
The Chimeras (Nerval)
See *Les Chimères*
Les Chimères (Nerval) **1**:480, 483-88; **67**:306-07, 311-12, 314-18, 320, 356-57, 359, 363
The Chimes: A Goblin Story of Some Bells That Rang an Old Year Out and a New Year In (Dickens) **3**:145, 149 165; **203**:282; **211**:4, 42; **219**:97; **230**:91-93
"The Chimney Sweeper" (Blake) **13**:219-21, 242; **37**:3, 6, 9, 34, 39, 42, 47, 50, 57, 62-5, 67, 70-2, 76, 79, 91-2, 94; **190**:94
Chinese Miscellanies (Percy)
See *Miscellaneous Pieces Relating to the Chinese*
"Chinese Serenade" (Chivers) **49**:54
"A Chinese Story" (Cranch) **115**:57
Ching-hua yuan (Li Ju-chen) **137**:182, 186-87, 189-97, 200-210, 212-13, 217, 220-21, 225-26
"Chione" (Lampman) **25**:169; **194**:21, 30, 68, 77-78, 132
"A Chippewa Legend" (Lowell) **90**:193
"Chiron" (Hölderlin) **16**:191; **187**:216
"A Chit Chat Letter . . . from Ned Ward, jun. a Fellow in London, to Anthony Wood, Jun. a Fellow at Oxford" (Reynolds) **146**:174
Chitalagai Odes (Derzhavin)
See *Ody perevedennyia i sochinennyia pri gore Chitalagae 1774 goda*
"The Choice" (Allingham) **25**:14
"The Choice" (Lampman) **194**:19
"The Choice" (Lazarus) **8**:421; **109**:304, 335
The Choice (Murphy) **229**:234
"The Choice" (Rossetti) **4**:514, 529
The Choice: A Poem on Shelley's Death (Shelley) **14**:272
"Choice and Chance" (Hayne) **94**:166
"Choice Grain" (Leskov)
See "Otbornoe zerno"
"Choir of the Seven Nixies" (Mörike)
See "Vom Sieben-Nixen-Chor"
Choix de Maximes consolantes sur l'amour (Baudelaire) **155**:108
"Choix entre deux nations" (Hugo) **161**:179
The Choleric Fathers (Holcroft) **85**:216-17
The Choleric Man (Cumberland) **167**:119, 138, 147, 155, 163-67, 170, 188-89
Chopin (Liszt) **199**:298-300, 304, 317, 323, 327, 337, 343, 346
Chopin (Schumann) **143**:69
"Chor der Toten" (Meyer) **81**:205
"Chor' i Kalinyč" (Turgenev) **122**:277
"Choral Song of the Temperance Legions" (Chivers) **49**:49-50
Choral Symphony (Beethoven)
See *Ninth Symphony*
"Chornaya shal" (Pushkin) **83**:247, 350-51, 355
"A Chorus of Ghosts" (Bryant) **46**:21
"Chorus of the Dead" (Meyer)
See "Chor der Toten"
Choses vues (Hugo) **3**:265; **161**:157-58, 263
"Les Chouans" (Balzac) **53**:11, 15, 22; **153**:8-10, 28-29, 31, 62, 69, 75-76, 78, 82, 102, 106-8
Chrestomathia (Bentham) **38**:88
"Le Chretien Mourant" (Lamartine) **11**:245
"Le Christ aux Oliviers" (Nerval) **1**:478, 486; **67**:07, 315, 318, 339, 362
"Christ Crucified" (Emerson) **98**:162
"Christ is not risen" (Prescott) **163**:31
Christ on the Mount of Olives (Beethoven) **227**:33
"Christ Our All in All" (Rossetti) **50**:285
"Christ Stilling the Tempest" (Hemans) **29**:206
"Christ upon the Waters" (Newman) **38**:304, 310
"Christabel" (Coleridge) **9**:133-34, 138-40, 142-44, 146, 148-50, 152, 156, 179-81, 183, 187, 192-94; **54**:79-81, 89, 98, 100, 106, 127-29; **99**:2, 5, 23, 65-66, 101; **111**:201, 232-34, 292, 295-97, 300-1, 303, 308, 322, 332; **177**:1-168; **197**:179, 187, 192-93, 204, 240; **231**:15-16, 26, 56-57, 62, 111-14, 124, 130, 134, 152-59, 161-62
"Christabel" (Rossetti) **4**:510
Den Christelige Bornelærdom (Grundtvig) **158**:112-13
Christenhedens Syvstjerne Et kirkeligt Sagakvad (Grundtvig) **158**:142, 147, 167, 169
Die Christenheit oder Europa (Novalis) **13**:386, 388, 402; **178**:4, 33, 35, 72-73, 77, 81
"Christian" (Prescott) **163**:8
"Christian and Jew: A Dialogue" (Rossetti) **186**:318
"Christian Childhood" (Verlaine)
See "Enfance chrétienne"
"The Christian Church as an Imperial Power" (Newman) **38**:308
Christian Discourses (Kierkegaard) **34**:224, 264; **78**:238
Christian Fundamentals (Grundtvig)
See *Den Christelige Bornelærdom*
Christian Life: Its Course, Its Hindrances, and Its Helps (Arnold) **18**:7, 10, 15
Christian Life: Its Hopes, Its Fears, and Its Close (Arnold) **18**:15
Christian Melville (Oliphant) **61**:219
Christian Morals (More) **27**:334
"The Christian Mysteries" (Newman) **38**:305
The Christian Physiologist: Tales Illustrative of the Five Senses (Griffin) **7**:201, 204, 214, 218
"Christian Politics" (Brownson) **50**:51
"The Christian Slave!" (Whittier) **8**:489, 510
"Christian Sympathy" (Newman) **38**:306
"Christian Worship" (Channing) **17**:47
Christian Writings (Herder)
See *Christliche Schriften*
The Christian Year (Keble) **87**:116-19, 121-23, 126-32, 134-38, 140-41, 149-51, 153-54, 156-57, 159-60, 164, 166-67, 169-78, 181-82, 185-86, 188, 190, 194-95, 198-205
"Christianity and Progress" (Patmore) **9**:342
Christianity or Europe (Novalis)
See *Die Christenheit oder Europa*
Christianity, the Logic of Creation (James) **53**:204, 208-9
Christianity Unveiled (Godwin) **14**:56
Christian's Mistake (Craik) **38**:108-09, 113, 116, 126-27
Christie Johnstone (Reade) **2**:532-34, 536, 539-41, 543, 545, 548; **74**:243, 255, 264-65, 268, 271-72, 278, 281, 293, 319
"Christine" (Leconte de Lisle) **29**:220
Christine; ou, Stockholm, Fontainebleau, et Rome (Dumas) **11**:42, 47, 57, 63; **71**:193, 241, 248, 250
Der christliche Glaube nach den Grundsäzen der evengelischen Kirche im Zusammenhange dargestellt (Schleiermacher) **107**:267-68, 304, 313, 319-21, 323, 325, 347-48, 351-52, 355, 357-59, 361-63, 365, 382, 397, 399-403, 405
Christliche Schriften (Herder) **186**:100
"Ein christliches Sprüchlein" (Meyer) **81**:156
"Christmas" (Irving) **19**:351
"Christmas" (Smith) **59**:303, 309, 315-6, 318-9
"Christmas" (Timrod) **25**:362, 364, 372, 382-83, 386, 388
"Christmas" (Very) **9**:383
"The Christmas Banquet" (Hawthorne) **2**:296; **95**:134, 148; **158**:258, 292-93
Christmas Books (Dickens) **105**:348
Christmas Books (Thackeray) **5**:469
"A Christmas Carol" (Rossetti) **50**:314, 318
A Christmas Carol (Dickens)
See *A Christmas Carol. In Prose. Being a Ghost Story of Christmas*
A Christmas Carol. In Prose. Being a Ghost Story of Christmas (Dickens) **3**:144-45, 152, 165, 173; **26**:222; **37**:144-45; **86**:256; **105**:244, 330, 335; **113**:102-3, 107; **187**:8, 53, 153; **206**:11, 114; **211**:1-84; **217**:228; **219**:114, 190, 193, 227; **231**:177, 229
Christmas Chimes (Dickens)
See *The Chimes*
"Christmas Creek" (Kendall) **12**:194, 199
"Christmas Day" (Irving) **19**:328
"Christmas Day" (Martineau) **26**:313
"The Christmas Dinner" (Irving) **19**:328
"Christmas Eve" (Browning) **19**:132; **79**:152, 184
"Christmas Eve" (Gogol)
See "Noč pered roždestvom"
"Christmas Eve" (Wergeland) **5**:537
Christmas Eve (Runeberg)
See *Julqvällen*
Christmas Eve: A Dialogue on the Celebration of Christmas (Schleiermacher)
See *Die Weihnachtsfeier: Ein Gespräch*
Christmas Eve: Dialogue on the Incarnation (Schleiermacher)
See *Die Weihnachtsfeier: Ein Gespräch*
"Christmas Greeting (From a Fairy to a Child)" (Dodgson) **139**:147
"Christmas Hymm" (Hale) **75**:284
"A Christmas Party" (Woolson) **82**:290
"The Christmas Rose" (Mörike)
See "Auf eine Christblume"
A Christmas Sermon (Stevenson) **193**:219
Christmas Stories (Leskov) **25**:228
"Christmas Storms and Sunshine" (Gaskell) **137**:4, 41
"A Christmas Tree" (Dickens) **211**:37, 51-52
"The Christmas Tree" (Lazarus) **109**:297
Christmas-Eve and Easter Day (Browning) **19**:130, 132; **79**:148, 150
Christophe Colomb; ou, La découverte du nouveau monde (Pixérécourt) **39**:277-79, 282-83, 286
"Christopher at the Lakes" (Wilson) **5**:568
"Christopher Crotchet" (Smith) **187**:319
"Christopher Found" (Levy) **59**:96
"Christopher in His Aviary" (Wilson) **5**:563
Christopher Kirkland (Linton)
See *The Autobiography of Christopher Kirkland*
"Christopher North in His Sporting Jacket" (Wilson) **5**:560
"Christopher on Colonsay" (Wilson) **5**:568

"Christ's Hospital Five and Thirty Years Ago" (Lamb) **10**:407-08, 435-36; **113**:154, 177, 214, 226, 234, 240, 266
"Christ's Idea of Society" (Peabody)
See "A Glimpse of Christ's Idea of Society"
"Christ's Night" (Saltykov) **16**:369
Christus (Hebbel) **43**:234
Christus: A Mystery (Longfellow) **2**:484, 495, 497-98; **45**:113, 124, 127-28, 133, 138-39, 142-44, 150-51, 159, 165
Chronicle in Rhyme for Living School Usage (Grundtvig) **158**:147, 151-52, 155
"The Chronicle of Ladislas Kun" (Petofi)
See "Kun László Krónikája"
The Chronicle of the Cid (Southey) **97**:267, 336
The Chronicle of the Conquest of Granada (Irving) **2**:380, 384, 387; **95**:231, 280
Chronicles of Ballymacruiskeen (Carleton) **199**:20
Chronicles of Carlingford (Oliphant) **11**:429, 432, 438-40, 445, 449, 453-4, 459; **61**:171-2, 187, 195, 198, 216; **221**:226-27, 256, 281, 295, 318
Chronicles of Golden Friars (Le Fanu) **58**:285
Chronicles of the Canongate (Scott) **15**:269, 277, 322; **110**:293; **209**:216, 297
Chronicles of the Clovernook (Jerrold) **2**:400, 402, 404-05
The Chronicle's Retort (Grundtvig) **158**:149
"Chronik von Lutzelflüh" (Gotthelf) **117**:30
Die Chronika des fahrenden Schülers" (Brentano)
See "Aus der Chronika eines fahrenden Schülers"
"Chronique de Paris" (Mallarmé) **210**:170, 223-24
Chronique du temps de Charles IX (Mérimée) **6**:352-3, 356-8, 360, 362-3, 365-6, 369; **65**:46-8, 52, 54-6, 59-62, 79, 86-7, 90-5, 99-101, 103-05, 111
Chroniques (Maupassant) **83**:184-85, 188, 190, 227
Chroniques italiennes (Stendhal)
See *L'abbesse de Castro*
Chroniques, mémoires et recherches pour servir à l'histoire de tous les peuples slaves (Potocki) **229**:295-96
Chronological History of Music (Schumann)
See *Chronologischer Geschichte der Musik*
Chronological History of the United States Arranged with Plates on Bem's Principle (Peabody) **169**:193
Chronologischer Geschichte der Musik (Schumann) **143**:127-28
"Chrysanthemum Tryst" (Ueda Akinari)
See "Kikuka no chigiri"
"Chrysanthos" (Runeberg) **41**:318
"Chrysaor" (Landor) **14**:181, 183-84, 190
"Chrysaor" (Longfellow) **45**:116, 154
Chto delat'? (Chernyshevsky) **1**:159-68
"Chto nuzhno avtoru" (Karamzin) **3**:289; **173**:350
"Chto za zvuki?" (Baratynsky) **103**:16, 22
"Chudny grad" (Baratynsky)
See "Chudnyy grad poroy solyotsya..."
"Chudnyy grad poroy solyotsya..." (Baratynsky) **103**:3, 10, 16, 22
An Chúirt (Merriman)
See *Cúirt an Mheadhon Oidhche*
"The Church" (Runeberg)
See "Kyrkan"
"The Church a Home for the Lonely" (Newman) **38**:306
The Church against No Church (Brownson) **50**:26
Church and State (Coleridge)
See *On the Constitution of Church and State, According to the Idea of Each: with Aids Toward a Right Judgment on the Late Catholic Bill*
Church and State (Gladstone)
See *The State in Its Relations with the Church*
"Church and State" (Moore) **110**:172
"Church Going" (Rogers) **69**:80
"Church Intrigants. Historic Pictures" ("TSierkovnyie inmrigany. Ismorichieskiie karminy") (Leskov) **174**:129
"The Church of Brou" (Arnold) **6**:42, 44, 66-67, 72; **29**:36; **89**:7; **218**:115, 138
"The Church, our Zoar" (Keble) **87**:174
"The Church Porch" (Thackeray) **213**:327
Church Principles Considered in Their Results (Gladstone) **213**:118, 120
"Church Sectarianism" (Coleridge) **90**:9
Church-of-Englandism and its Catechism Examined (Bentham) **38**:34, 92, 96, 98
"The Churchyard among the Mountains" (Wordsworth) **166**:265, 278
La chute d'un ange (Lamartine) **11**:252-53, 255, 268, 271, 273-76, 278, 283-85, 287, 289; **190**:172, 174, 218, 237-41, 258
"Chuvstvitel'nyy i kholodnyy" (Karamzin)
See "Cuvstvitel'nyj i xolodnyj, dva xaraktera"
Chuzzlewit (Dickens)
See *The Life and Adventures of Martin Chuzzlewit*
Cicero (Trollope)
See *The Life of Cicero*
The Cicerone: A Guide to the Enjoyment of the Artworks of Italy (Burckhardt)
See *Der Cicerone: Eine Einleitung zum Genuss der Kunstwerke Italiens*
Der Cicerone: Eine Einleitung zum Genuss der Kunstwerke Italiens (Burckhardt) **49**:10, 27
"The Cid" (Bowles) **103**:61
Der Cid (Herder) **186**:94
"Ciel brouillé" (Baudelaire) **6**:80; **55**:61
"Le ciel est, par-dessus le toit" (Verlaine) **51**:352, 355; **230**:220
"Le ciel et l'enfer" (Mérimée) **6**:351, 362-3; **65**:44, 55, 79, 83
"Ciemność" (Mickiewicz) **101**:159-64
Las ciento y una (Sarmiento) **123**:338, 352
La cifra (Da Ponte) **50**:82
Cigáni (Macha) **46**:201-02, 204, 212-14
"La Cigarette" (Laforgue) **221**:88
Čigiriaski Kobzar' i Gaydamaki (Shevchenko) **54**:379
La ciguë (Augier) **31**:4, 8, 10-11, 14-15, 23, 29, 34
El cinco de Agosto (Tamayo y Baus) **1**:565-66, 571
Cinco Minutos (Alencar) **157**:15, 17-18
Cinderella (Grabbe)
See *Aschenbrödel*
"Cinnamon and Pearls" (Martineau) **137**:251
Cinq Lettres sur l'Éducation Publique en Russie (Maistre) **37**:314
"Le cinq Mai" (Beranger) **34**:28-9
Cinq-Mars: A Conspiracy under Louis XIII (Vigny)
See *Cinq-Mars; ou, Une conspiration sous Louis XIII*
Cinq-Mars; ou, Une conspiration sous Louis XIII (Vigny) **7**:467-71, 473, 477; **102**:335, 337, 345-47, 350, 352-53, 369-70, 378-80, 382-84
The Circassian (Lermontov)
See "Cherkesy"
The Circassian Boy (Lermontov)
See *Mtsyri*
"Circe" (Webster) **230**:232, 234, 254-56, 270, 274-75, 277, 287, 324
"Circe's Palace" (Hawthorne) **226**:135
"Circles" (Emerson) **38**:143, 169-71, 205-06, 224, 229-30; **98**:18-19, 22, 24, 26, 35-6, 58, 65, 89, 101, 109, 116, 145, 147-48, 162, 190-91
"Circumference Thou Bride of Awe" (Dickinson) **21**:82
Circumstances (Staël-Holstein)
See *Des circonstances actuelles qui peuvent terminer la Révolution et des principles qui dolvent fonder la répuldique en France*
The Circumvented (Leskov)
See *Obojdennye*
"Las circunstancias" (Larra) **130**:194
"Cis-Alpine" (Pater) **90**:276
"Cistern Gone Dry" (Laforgue)
See "Citerne tarie"
"Cisza morska" (Mickiewicz) **3**:403-04
Citation and Examination of William Shakespeare (Landor) **14**:165, 173, 178-79
La citerne (Pixérécourt) **39**:272, 274, 277-79, 284
"Citerne tarie" (Laforgue) **221**:82
"La cithare" (Banville) **9**:16
The Citizen. A Farce. As it is Performed at the Theatre-Royal in Covent-Garden. By Arthur Murphy, Esq. (Murphy) **229**:222-23, 234
"The Citizen of the World" (Dyer) **129**:105
"The Citizen's Resolve" (Freneau) **1**:314; **111**:143, 149-51
"Cito Pede Preterit Ætas" (Gordon) **21**:159
"Citronia" (Heine) **147**:173-77, 180, 182-86
"The City" (Lampman) **25**:172, 189, 192, 199-200, 204; **194**:9, 15
"City Burying Places" (Freneau) **111**:81
"The City in the Sea" (Poe) **1**:512; **55**:150; **117**:216-17, 221, 227, 229, 232-34, 236, 244, 264, 274-75, 281-82, 306, 316; **211**:247, 249
The City Looking Glass (Bird) **1**:87-90, 93
The City Looking Glass: A Philadelphia Comedy (Bird) **197**:90-91, 93
"The City of Dreadful Night" (Levy) **59**:91
"The City of Dreadful Night" (Thomson) **18**:388-92, 394-401, 403-12, 415-32
The City of Dreadful Night and Other Poems (Thomson) **18**:390-91
"City of Ships" (Whitman) **205**:159-60
"The City of Sin" (Poe) **117**:274
"The City of the End of Things" (Lampman) **25**:169, 172, 177-78, 180-81, 184, 187, 190, 192-95, 198-99, 204; **194**:9-10, 15, 18, 24, 44, 46, 48, 51-52, 55, 68, 108, 119-20
"The City of the Plague" (Wilson) **5**:546, 550
The City of the Plague, and Other Poems (Wilson) **5**:546, 553, 561
City of the Saints, and Across the Rocky Mountains to California (Burton) **42**:58
The City of the Silent (Simms) **3**:505
City Poems (Smith) **59**:285, 288, 293-4, 297-8, 302, 312, 316, 318-9, 321, 326, 329-33, 336-7
"The City Poet" (Freneau) **111**:132
"City Scenes and City Life" (Parton) **86**:351
"The City Tree" (Crawford) **12**:156, 169
"City Visions" (Lazarus) **109**:294
"Civil and Religious Freedom" (Brownson) **50**:51
"Civil Disobedience" (Thoreau)
See "Resistance to Civil Government"
"Civil Rights" (Lanier) **118**:227-28, 231
The Civil War in France (Marx) **114**:8, 39, 41, 46-7
Le Civilisateur: Histoire de l'humanité par les grands hommes (Lamartine) **11**:259-60, 262; **190**:253
"Civilisation in the United States" (Arnold) **89**:100
Civilización i barbarie: La vida de Juan Facundo Quiroga i aspecto fisico, costumbres, i ábitos de la República Arjentina (Sarmiento) **123**:269-70, 272, 274, 279-82, 291-99, 302, 304-9, 318-20, 322, 329-35, 337-38, 341, 345, 347-52, 357, 360-61, 364-70, 373-81, 383-84

"Civilization" (Emerson) **38**:209
"Civilization" (Mill) **179**:281
Civilization (Burckhardt)
See *Die Kultur der Renaissance in Italien*
Civilization and Barbarism (Sarmiento)
See *Civilización i barbarie: La vida de Juan Facundo Quiroga i aspecto fisico, costumbres, i ábitos de la República Arjentina*
Civilization and Barbarism: the Life on Juan Facundo Quiroga (Sarmiento)
See *Civilización i barbarie: La vida de Juan Facundo Quiroga i aspecto fisico, costumbres, i ábitos de la República Arjentina*
Civilization in the United States: First and Last Impressions of America (Arnold) **218**:250, 257, 259-60
The Civilization of the Renaissance in Italy (Burckhardt)
See *Die Kultur der Renaissance in Italien*
"Civilization—Signs of the Times" (Mill) **58**:329
A civilizátor (Madach) **19**:370-74
"Claims and Positions of the Clergy" (Garrison) **149**:256
The Claims of Labour (Mill) **58**:349
"Claims of the Negro Ethnologically Considered" (Douglass) **7**:124
"Clair de Lune" (Laforgue) **221**:81-82
"Clair de lune" (Verlaine) **2**:628, 631; **51**:352, 373-74, 377, 381; **230**:164, 221
"Claire de Lune" (Maupassant) **83**:168, 182
Claire Lenoir (Villiers de l'Isle Adam) **3**:581, 588
"Clara" (Meyer) **81**:151
Clara Howard (Brown) **22**:7, 12, 14, 18-19, 23, 27, 30, 48-52; **74**:15, 19, 21, 49, 57, 77, 92, 94, 98-9, 102-03, 105, 134, 138-39, 155, 164-66, 176, 179-82, 184; **122**:54-55
"Clara Milich" (Turgenev)
See "Klara Milich"
"Clara's Question" (Cooke) **110**:18
Clarel: A Poem and Pilgrimage in the Holy Land (Melville) **3**:330, 333, 335, 344-45, 352, 363, 366-68, 378, 385; **29**:318, 328-29, 334-35, 361; **45**:228; **91**:9, 184; **93**:205; **123**:252, 256-57, 260; **157**:212; **181**:216, 297; **193**:130; **221**:150
Clarence; or, A Tale of Our Own Times (Sedgwick) **19**:429-33, 443-45, 447-49, 453; **98**:298-99, 321, 334
"Claret and Tokay" (Browning) **19**:77; **79**:94, 101, 103
"Clari" (Kendall) **12**:193
"Claribel" (Tennyson) **30**:211, 223-24, 238; **65**:369; **202**:337
"The Clarionet" (Carleton) **199**:4, 8, 56
"Clary's Trial" (Cooke) **110**:34-6, 51
Class Poem (Lowell) **90**:221-21
"The Class Struggle in France" (Marx) **114**:70
The Class Struggles in France (Engels) **85**:136
The Class Struggles in France, 1848-1850 (Marx) **17**:321, 334-35; **114**:8, 37, 39
"Class War and Class Friendship" (Jones) **222**:140
Classical Dialogues (Landor) **14**:189
"Classical Walpurgis Night" (Verlaine)
See "Nuit du Walpurgis classique"
Claude Duval: A Tale of the Days of Charles the Second (Ainsworth) **13**:28
"Claude Gueux" (Hugo) **10**:367, 369, 381
Claude Gueux (Hugo) **189**:178, 192, 203, 267
Claudie (Sand) **42**:309
Claudine von Villabella (Goethe) **4**:164
The Claverings (Trollope) **6**:457-58, 470, 499-500; **215**:210, 214, 261, 299, 306
Clavigo (Goethe) **4**:164, 174, 211, 219; **34**:69; **154**:229-30
Clavis Fichtiana (Jean Paul) **7**:226
"El clavo" (Alarcon) **1**:14; **219**:18, 42, 44, 47
"The Clay" (Very) **9**:381
Le Clé d'Or (Feuillet) **45**:77, 80, 90
"Cleanliness" (Lamb) **10**:418
"The Clearer Self" (Lampman) **25**:193, 203, 217; **194**:21
"Clef Poem" (Whitman) **81**:367
"Clelia" (Crabbe) **26**:121
Clelia und Sinibald (Wieland) **17**:410
"Clematis Lane" (Jefferies) **47**:136
Clemencia: Novela de costumbres (Caballero) **10**:71, 76, 84-85
Clemens Brentano: Briefe (Brentano) **191**:35-36, 61, 63-65, 68, 70-71, 91
Clemens Brentano: Der Dichter über sein Werk (Brentano) **191**:126
Clemens Brentano-Philipp Otto Runge Briefwechsel (Brentano) **191**:126
Clemens Brentanos Frühlingskranz aus Jugendbriefen ihm geflochten, wie er selbst schriftlich verlangte (Arnim) **38**:15; **123**:5, 31-32, 34-36, 38, 42, 47-49, 52, 59; **191**:35
Clemens Brentanos Romanfragment "Der schiffbrüchige Galeerensklave vom Todten Meer" (Brentano) **191**:18, 63, 120
"Clementina" (Isaacs) **70**:304, 309
Clementina von Poretta (Wieland) **177**:228, 234, 250, 358
Clementina von Porretta (Wieland) **17**:419
"Cleon" (Browning) **19**:79, 117, 130-31, 137, 152; **79**:106-07, 110, 163-64
Cléontine (Sade) **47**:361-62
Cleopatra Prima (Alfieri) **101**:67
Cleopatra Tragedia (Alfieri) **101**:71
Cleopatrassa (Alfieri) **101**:4, 16, 18, 31-32, 36
"The Clergyman's Advice to the Villagers" (Dwight) **13**:270, 272, 278
"The Clergyman's First Tale" (Clough) **27**:60
Clergymen of the Church of England (Trollope) **33**:394; **101**:294; **215**:212
"Clerical Oppressors" (Whittier) **8**:525; **59**:361
"Clever Elsie" (Grimm Brothers) **3**:227
"The Cliff" (Lermontov) **126**:144
Clifford (Bulwer-Lytton)
See *Paul Clifford*
"The Cliffs and Springs" (Thoreau) **7**:384
"Clifton and a Lad's Love" (Symonds) **34**:352
"Clifton Hall" (Yearsley) **174**:299-300, 305
"Climat, faune, et flore de la lune" (Laforgue) **5**:277; **221**:43, 81
"Climbing to Rest" (Larcom) **179**:177
The Clique (Scribe)
See *La camaraderie; ou, La courte échelle*
"Clive" (Browning) **79**:164
Clive (Macaulay) **42**:87
"Clive" (Macaulay)
See "Lord Clive"
"The Cloak" (Gogol)
See "Shinel"
"La Cloche du village" (Lamartine) **190**:225
"La cloche fêlée" (Baudelaire) **6**:129; **29**:94; **55**:43, 51, 61
Les Cloches de Genève (Liszt) **199**:307
"Les Cloches et les larmes" (Desbordes-Valmore) **97**:13
"Clochette" (Maupassant) **83**:174
"The Clock" (Baudelaire)
See "L'horloge"
"The Clock" (Dickinson) **171**:104, 106, 138
Clock (Dickens)
See *Master Humphrey's Clock*
"The Clock and the Mirror" (Bestuzhev)
See "Chasy i zerkalo"
"A Clock stopped, not the mantel's" (Dickinson)
See "The Clock"
"A Clock Striking at Midnight" (Beddoes) **154**:10
"Clock-a-Clay" (Clare) **9**:85, 105, 117
The Clockmaker; or, The Sayings and Doings of Samuel Slick of Slickville (Haliburton) **15**:117, 119, 124-26, 128-33, 135, 137-39, 143-47; **149**:267-70, 272, 287-94, 296-98, 303-4, 313-14, 316-20, 323, 330-37, 339-40, 342-44, 348, 354-58
"The Clockmaker's Opinion of Halifax" (Haliburton) **149**:303
"The Clod and the Pebble" (Blake) **13**:221, 247; **37**:4, 15, 25, 42, 47, 50, 56, 80, 92
"Clod-Hans" (Andersen) **214**:4-5
"Clodpoll" (Andersen) **79**:64
The Cloister and the Hearth: A Tale of the Middle Ages (Reade) **2**:533-35, 537-41, 543-45, 548-52; **74**:243, 245-46, 250, 253-54, 257-59, 261-65, 298-99, 311-15, 323-24, 326-27, 329
"The Cloister Berry. In reminiscence of the Frankfurt Jewish Ghetto" (Arnim)
See "Die Klosterbeere. Zum Andenken an die Frankfurter Judengasse"
"Clopton House" (Gaskell) **137**:4
"The Close of Autumn" (Bryant) **46**:3
The Close of the Eighteenth Century (Prescott) **163**:114
"Close to the Sky" (Meyer)
See "Himmelsnähe"
The Closed Commercial State (Fichte)
See *Der geschlossene Handelsstaat*
"The Closed Industrial State" (Fichte) **62**:17
"Closing In" (Hayne) **94**:166
"The Clote" (Barnes) **75**:23
Clotel; or, The President's Daughter: A Narrative of Slave Life in the United States (Brown) **2**:46-48, 50-52, 54-55; **89**:143, 149, 154-55, 157-61, 170-82, 184-85, 187, 189-91
Clotelle: A Tale of the Southern States (Brown)
See *Clotel; or, The President's Daughter: A Narrative of Slave Life in the United States*
Clotelle; or, The Colored Heroine (Brown)
See *Clotel; or, The President's Daughter: A Narrative of Slave Life in the United States*
"The Cloud" (Lanier) **118**:239, 248, 268
"The Cloud" (Shelley) **18**:329, 355-56; **175**:232, 265
"Cloud and Wind" (Rossetti) **77**:314
"Cloud-Break" (Lampman) **25**:169; **194**:34, 53, 87
"The Cloud Confines" (Rossetti) **4**:499, 509, 518; **77**:314
"The Cloud on the Way" (Bryant) **6**:165
Cloud Pictures (Hayne) **94**:136
"The Clouded Morning" (Very) **9**:383
Cloudesly: A Tale (Godwin) **14**:44-8, 50, 68, 70, 81, 83, 89; **130**:36
"Clouds" (Barnes) **75**:94
Clouds (Petofi)
See *Felhök*
Clouds and Sunshine (Reade) **74**:254, 260, 262-65
"The Cloud's Brother" (Runeberg)
See "Molnets broder"
Clough: Selected Poems (Prescott) **163**:139, 143-44
"Clover" (Lanier) **6**:247-48, 253, 255, 258; **118**:203, 220
The Clover Patch (Bird) **197**:29
"The Clown Chastized" (Mallarmé)
See "Le pitre châtié"
"Le club des hachichins" (Gautier) **1**:355; **59**:22, 32, 36
"A Clump of Daisies" (Dana) **53**:158
"The Clydesdale Yeoman's Return" (Lockhart) **6**:293
"A Clymene" (Verlaine) **51**:379-80, 384, 386
"Clytie" (Lazarus) **109**:294
"Cmyk . . . Cmyk . . . Cmyk!" (Turgenev)
See "Stuk...stuk...stuk"
"Coach" (Barnes) **75**:8
"The Coal-Imp" (Cranch) **115**:58
"The Coast of Fife" (Stevenson) **193**:230
"A Coast View" (Harpur) **114**:105, 126, 142-44, 158, 166-67

Cobbett's Complete Collection of State Trials (Cobbett) **49**:163
Cobbett's Corn (Cobbett)
See *A Treatise on Cobbett's Corn*
Cobbett's Legacy to Parsons; or, Have the Clergy of the Established Church an Equitable Right to the Tithes... (Cobbett) **49**:114
Cobbett's Manchester Lectures (Cobbett) **49**:160
Cobbett's Monthly Religious Tracts (Cobbett)
See *Twelve Sermons*
Cobbett's Monthly Sermons (Cobbett)
See *Twelve Sermons*
Cobbett's Parliamentary History of England (Cobbett) **49**:163
Cobbett's Poor Man's Friend; or, A Defence of the Rights of Those Who Do the Work and Fight the Battles (Cobbett) **49**:148, 154, 156, 160
Cobbett's Tour in Scotland (Cobbett) **49**:133, 160
Cobbett's Twopenny Trash (Cobbett) **49**:94, 111, 120, 135, 160
Cobbett's Weekly Political Register (Cobbett) **49**:87, 89, 94-5, 97-8, 107, 109-11, 113-14, 116, 118-19, 130-32, 134-35, 141-42, 147, 149, 151-52, 153, 155, 160, 162-64, 168, 170, 178, 181
"The Cobbler of Hagenau" (Longfellow) **45**:162, 188
Cobblers on the Heath (Kivi)
See *Nummisuutarit*
"Cobwebs" (Rossetti) **66**:341
"La coccinelle" (Hugo) **3**:263
Le Cocher de Cabriolet (Dumas) **71**:205
"The Cock" (Barnes) **75**:54
The Cock and Anchor, Being a Chronicle of Old Dublin City (Le Fanu) **9**:301, 316-17; **58**:273, 275
"The Cock Is Crowing" (Wordsworth) **12**:447
"Cock-a-Doodle-Doo!" (Melville) **3**:355; **49**:391-92; **157**:72; **193**:130
"Coco" (Maupassant) **83**:181
"Cocoon" (Dickinson)
See "Drab Habitation of Whom?"
"Cocoons" (Silva)
See "Crisálidas"
Le cocu (Kock) **16**:248, 251
"Le Cocu de lui-même ou le raccommodement imprévu" (Sade) **47**:313
Le code des gens honnêtes, ou, l'art de ne pas être dupe des fripons (Balzac) **35**:25; **153**:146-47, 150, 152
Codification Proposal Addressed by Jeremy Bentham to All Nations Professing Liberal Opinions (Bentham) **38**:55, 57
Código Civil (Bello) **131**:116, 124-25
"Codlingsby" (Thackeray) **14**:433, 451
Cœlebs in Search of a Wife: Comprehending Observations on Domestic Habits and Manners, Religion and Morals (More) **27**:325, 328-30, 333-35, 338-39, 349-53, 355; **141**:170, 214-16, 218, 221-23, 225, 281-83
Coelina; ou, L'enfant du mystère (Pixérécourt) **39**:272, 275, 277-79, 289-90
"Un coeur simple" (Flaubert) **2**:227, 232-3, 236, 253, 257-9; **62**:91-2, 97, 105, 107; **66**:281; **135**:83, 109, 145, 169-70; **179**:57, 95-96; **185**:171
"Un cœur sous une soutane" (Rimbaud) **227**:323
"Le coeur supplicié" (Rimbaud) **4**:478; **82**:224, 227; **227**:223
"La coeur volé" (Rimbaud) **4**:485; **35**:275, 279, 281-82; **227**:264
"The Coffer and the Ghost" (Stendhal)
See "Le coffre et le revenant"
"The Coffin-Maker" (Pushkin)
See "Grobovshchik"
The Coffin-Maker (Pushkin)
See "Grobovshchik"
"Le coffre et le revenant" (Stendhal) **46**:307
The Cohee (Bird) **197**:29
"Cohen of Trinity" (Levy) **59**:97-8, 105, 112-3, 115; **203**:309-11, 313, 315, 333
"The Colapeesa" (Bird) **197**:33
"Cold in the Earth" (Brontë)
See "Remembrance"
"The Cold Snap" (Bellamy) **86**:75
The Cold Water Man (Dunlap) **2**:210
"The Cold Wedding" (Allingham) **25**:8
"La colère de Samson" (Vigny) **7**:469, 474, 479, 484-85; **102**:376-77
"Coleridge" (Mill) **11**:361, 370; **179**:206
"Coleridge" (Pater) **7**:321; **90**:241
"Coleridge as a Theologican" (Pater) **90**:276
Coleridge: Poetical Works (Coleridge) **177**:126; **231**:89
Coleridge's Shakespearen Criticism (Coleridge) **231**:68, 73
"Coleridge's Writings" (Pater) **90**:296, 298; **159**:296, 310
"The Coliseum" (Poe) **117**:264, 270-71, 276-71
"The Coliseum" (Shelley) **175**:217
"Coll'alto" (Rogers) **69**:84
"The Collar" (Andersen) **7**:28; **79**:40
Collect, and Other Poems (Whitman) **205**:329
Collected Letters (Dickinson) **21**:46-7
Collected Letters (Robinson) **142**:110, 112, 114-15
The Collected Letters of Samuel Taylor Coleridge (Coleridge) **90**:32; **99**:6, 25-6, 40, 52, 55, 57, 59, 61, 66, 101, 106; **111**:232-33, 243, 290, 293-95, 310-13, 364-66; **177**:98, 103, 105, 109, 124-25, 127, 130, 149-50, 155, 158, 161-62; **197**:215, 282, 284, 310, 318-19, 322, 326; **231**:34, 58, 60-65, 72, 84, 86, 90, 97, 106, 118, 120-21, 141, 150
The Collected Letters of Thomas and Jane Welsh Carlyle (Carlyle) **181**:117-21, 129-36
The Collected Notebooks of Samuel Taylor Coleridge (Coleridge) **54**:107, 109; **99**:3-4, 22, 57, 64, 106
Collected Poems (Arnold) **218**:137
Collected Poems (Dickinson) **21**:46
Collected Poems (Rimbaud) **227**:309-19
The Collected Poems of Isabella Valancy Crawford (Crawford) **12**:155, 175
Collected Works (Aksakov)
See *Sobranie sochinenii*
Collected Works (Baillie) **151**:47
Collected Works (Claudius) **75**:207, 210-11, 215, 218, 220
Collected Works (Herder) **8**:313
Collected Works (Hölderlin)
See *Sämtliche Werke*
Collected Works (Leskov) **174**:14, 17, 34, 60
Collected Works (Liszt) **199**:311
Collected Works (Rossetti) **77**:317
Collected Works (Shelley) **143**:289-90, 294
Collected Works (Stagnelius)
See *Samlade skrifter*
Collected Works (Varnhagen von Ense)
See *Rahel-Bibliothek: Gesammelte Werke*
The Collected Works of Edgar Allan Poe (Poe) **94**:229, 245; **97**:228-9; **117**:209, 225, 235, 260, 262, 268, 271-72, 275-6, 293, 304-5, 309-13, 330-3, 335-6.
The Collected Works of John Galt (Galt) **110**:76-81, 90, 93, 104
Collected Works of John Stuart Mill (Mill) **179**:290-95, 337
The Collected Works of Ralph Waldo Emerson (Emerson) **98**:33-7, 57, 63, 66, 68-73, 75-6, 90, 92, 94-101, 107-17, 129, 132-33, 135, 159, 162, 177
The Collected Works of Samuel Taylor Coleridge (Coleridge) **177**:160
Collected Writings (Liszt) **199**:304
"Collected Writings of Edgar Alan Poe" (Poe) **94**:229-35, 244, 267
The Collected Writings of Thomas De Quincey (De Quincey) **87**:52-7, 61-2, 64-5, 69-70; **198**:38, 105, 107, 110-11
"Collection of Letters" (Austen) **119**:13
A Collection of Papers on Political, Literary, and Moral Subjects (Webster) **30**:408
A Collection of Poems, Chiefly Manuscript, and from Living Authors (Baillie) **71**:2; **151**:10, 86, 114
Collection of Poems on American Affairs (Freneau) **111**:160-61
The Colleen Bawn; or, The Brides of Garryowen (Boucicault) **41**:28-32, 39, 41, 43, 49-50, 53
"College Breakfast Party" (Eliot) **4**:115
"College Lyfe" (Cranch) **115**:3, 6
"A College Magazine" (Stevenson) **193**:211
The Collegians (Griffin) **7**:193-209, 212-19
Le collier de la reine (Dumas) **11**:68-69; **71**:232, 234
"A Colloguy" (Rossetti) **50**:311
"Colloque sentimental" (Verlaine) **2**:628, 631; **51**:355, 374, 377-78, 384, 388; **230**:165
Colloquies on the Progress and Prospects of Society (Southey) **97**:252, 264, 266, 270, 284, 287, 291, 293
"The Colloquy of Monos and Una" (Poe) **1**:519-20; **16**:295, 308, 331; **78**:259; **211**:226
"A Colloquy on the High Road" (Turgenev)
See *Razgovor na bolshoi doroge*
Colomba (Mérimée) **6**:352, 354-5, 357-8, 360, 363, 365-70; **65**:43, 46-7, 50, 54-8, 60-2, 64, 66, 79, 85, 87, 90, 100-05, 123-9, 137
La Colombe (Dumas) **71**:218-19
"Colombine" (Verlaine) **51**:351, 378-80
Colombine (Almqvist) **42**:4, 16, 19
Colon and Spondee (Tyler) **3**:575
Le Colonel Chabert (Balzac) **35**:27; **153**:22-24, 76, 91, 134-42, 149, 151-52
Colored Stones (Stifter)
See *Bunte Steine*
"Colossal Phamtom" (Heredia)
See "Fantasma colosal"
"The Colossi of the Plain" (Blind) **202**:55
"The Coloursense" (Gladstone) **213**:141
"The Colubriad" (Cowper) **94**:34, 122
Columbe's Birthday (Browning) **19**:95, 102; **79**:93-94, 100, 147, 189
"Columbia libre" (Isaacs) **70**:313
The Columbiad (Barlow) **23**:3-8, 10-20, 22-6, 29, 32, 36-9; **223**:4-6, 9-11, 15-19, 22-24, 27, 36, 40, 42-43, 52-53, 58-60, 72-78, 81-86
"Columbian War Hymn" (Isaacs)
See "Himno de guerra columbiano"
"Columbia's Ships" (Sigourney) **21**:299
"Columbine" (Verlaine) **230**:164
"The Columbine" (Very) **9**:372, 376, 380, 385, 391, 396-97
"Columbus" (Baillie) **151**:121
"Columbus" (Herder) **186**:10
"Columbus" (Hölderlin) **187**:224
"Columbus" (Lowell) **90**:219, 221
"Columbus to Ferdinand" (Freneau) **111**:143, 147
Le combe de l'homme mort (Nodier) **19**:379
Combination (Tonna) **135**:208-10, 215-17
"Come Back Again My Olden Heart" (Clough) **27**:105
"Come Down, O Maid" (Tennyson) **30**:280; **202**:174, 177, 198-99
"Come form we round a cheerful ring" (Baillie) **151**:91
Come Hither, Little Girls! (Grundtvig)
See *Kommer hid, I piger smaa!*
"Come Send Round the Wine" (Moore) **110**:185
"Come Slowly, Eden" (Dickinson) **21**:8; **171**:96
"Come Up from the Fields Father" (Whitman) **4**:592; **81**:320-21; **205**:339
"Come Where My Love Lies Dreaming" (Foster) **26**:285, 287, 291, 298

Come, you souls so dearly purchased (Grundtvig)
See *Kommer, Sjæle dyrekiøbte*
La comédie de la mort (Gautier) **1**:340-42; **59**:19, 33-4
"Comédie de la soif" (Rimbaud) **4**:472-73, 487; **35**:321; **227**:313
La Comédie humaine (Balzac) **5**:29-32, 37, 39-42, 44-57, 59-64, 67-73, 76-81, 83-8; **53**:10, 22, 26, 31, 35; **153**:5-6, 8, 10, 12, 15, 18, 21-22, 25-26, 29, 31-32, 34, 49, 53-58, 61-65, 67-80, 82, 88, 92-94, 101-2, 107-8, 111, 117, 119, 121, 125-27, 146-53
"Les comédiens sans le savoir" (Balzac) **153**:147, 153
Comédies (Banville) **9**:22
Comédies et proverbes (Musset) **7**:268, 275-77; **150**:348
"The Comedy of Errors" (Lamb) **125**:305
"Comedy of Thirst" (Rimbaud)
See "Comédie de la soif"
"La comendadora" (Alarcón) **219**:4, 18, 50
"The Comet" (Beddoes) **154**:10, 56
"Comet" (Holmes) **14**:101
"Comfort" (Barrett Browning) **1**:112
"Comfort" (Lampman) **25**:209
"Comfort of the Fields" (Lampman) **25**:189; **194**:21, 79, 87, 93, 101-2, 139
Comic Dramas (Edgeworth) **1**:257
"The Comic in Music" (Schumann) **143**:64
Comic Tales (Wieland)
See *Comische Erzählungen*
Comic Tales and Sketches (Thackeray) **5**:444; **213**:346
Comic Tragedies (Alcott) **83**:4, 9
"The Coming Day" (Jones) **222**:156
"Coming Days" (Crawford) **127**:217-19, 226
"Coming Home" (Webster) **230**:231
"The Coming of Age of The Origin of Species" (Huxley) **67**:4, 61
"The Coming of Arthur" (Tennyson) **202**:208, 247, 325
"The Coming of the Lord" (Very) **9**:378, 385
"The Coming of Winter" (Lampman) **25**:204; **194**:30
The Coming P (Vallès) **71**:372
The Coming Race (Bulwer-Lytton) **1**:150-51, 154; **45**:22, 32, 38-40, 42-6, 71
"The Coming Woman" (Parton) **86**:366
"Cominge" (D'Israeli) **217**:305
Comische Erzählungen (Wieland) **17**:394, 413, 418, 426-28; **177**:251-52, 285, 320, 323, 327-28
"The Command" (Auerbach) **171**:50
"Command of Language to Be Gained in Kindergarten" (Peabody) **169**:204
"Commander-in-Chief" (Lincoln) **201**:154
"Commands" (Preseren)
See "Ukazi"
Comme il vous plaira (Sand) **42**:310, 346-49
Commémoration Générale (Comte) **54**:213
"Commemoration Ode" (Lowell) **2**:509, 514, 516, 519, 522; **90**:188, 193
"Commemorative of the Genius of Shakespeare" (Rowson) **5**:322; **182**:254, 256
Commemorative Song at the Ancestors' Grave (Grundtvig)
See *Mindesang paa Fædres Gravhøi*
"Commemorative Sonnets" (Clough) **27**:104
"Commence par prier pour toi" (Verlaine) **230**:167
Comment je devins auteur dramatique (Dumas) **71**:217
"Comment je suis devenu poète" (Lamartine) **190**:208
Commentaire sur l'ouvrage de Filangieri (Constant) **182**:100
The Commentaries of Caesar (Trollope) **101**:321
Commentaries on the Life and Reign of Charles the First, King of England (D'Israeli) **217**:276, 280, 284-85, 295-98, 302, 324, 339
"Commentaries sur les mœurs de mon temps et document pour l'histoire" (Vigny) **102**:380
"A Commentary in an Easy Chair" (Oliphant) **221**:240
Commentary on Luke (Schleiermacher)
See *Über die Schriften des Lukas: Ein kritischer Versuch*
A Commentary on the Writings of Henrik Ibsen (Boyesen) **135**:46
"Comments and Observations of a Lover of Mushroom Gathering" (Aksakov) **181**:20
"Commerce" (Freneau) **111**:101
A Commercial Crisis (Boker) **125**:28
"Commercial Speculation Offering a Net Profit of 300 Percent in Six Months" (Fourier) **51**:185
"Commes les exilés, ridicule et sublime" (Baudelaire) **155**:5
"The Commissary Driver" (Runeberg) **41**:314
"A Commission of Inquiry on Royalty" (Thomson) **18**:425
"Commodity" (Thoreau) **7**:396
Commodus (Madach) **19**:362, 368, 370
"The Common A-Took In" (Barnes) **75**:43, 48, 57, 93, 101
Common Sense (Paine) **62**:246-8, 251, 257, 263-5, 268, 270-1, 274, 276-7, 279, 281, 285, 293, 295, 298, 309, 312, 319, 322, 334-5, 337-8, 340, 343, 345-50, 352-3, 364-71, 373, 378, 380, 391-3
Common Sense Applied to Religion; or, The Bible and the People (Beecher) **30**:9-10, 12-13
"Common Sense to the Public on Mr Deane's Affairs" (Paine) **62**:249
A Common Story (Goncharov)
See *Obyknovennaya istoriya*
"Commonplace" (Rossetti) **186**:230-31, 234, 243
"The Commonplace" (Whitman) **31**:434
Commonplace, and Other Short Stories (Rossetti) **186**:229-34, 243, 266-67, 269
Commonplace, and Other Short Tales (Rossetti) **2**:557; **50**:271; **66**:328, 330
"Commonplace Book" (Cranch) **115**:68
Commonplace Book (Southey) **8**:472
A Commonplace Book of Thoughts, Memories, and Fancies, Original and Selected (Jameson) **43**:306, 327
"Commonplace Critics" (Hazlitt) **29**:148
La Commune de Paris (Vallès) **71**:332-39
A Communication to My Friends (Wagner) **9**:425, 437, 444; **119**:248
The Communion of Labour (Jameson) **43**:327
Communist Manifesto (Engels)
See *Manifest der kommunistischen Partei*
The Communist Manifesto (Marx)
See *Manifest der Kommunistischen*
Como e Porque Sou Romancista (Alencar) **157**:9, 16, 30, 39
"Cómo llovía, suaviño" (Castro) **78**:59
"Compagne savoureuse . . ." (Verlaine) **230**:166, 170
Le compagnon du tour de France (Sand) **2**:589, 608; **57**:365
"A Companion Fairy" (Pavlova)
See "Sputnica feia"
A Companion to the Heart of the Andes (Winthrop) **210**:296, 300
Companion to the Most Celebrated Private Galleries of Art in London (Jameson) **43**:306, 321
The Companion Tour of France (Sand)
See *Le compagnon du tour de France*
"Comparaison des deux Phèdres" (Schlegel) **142**:320-21
A Comparative Statement of the Two Bills for the Better Government of the British Possessions in India (Sheridan) **91**:273
Comparing Heights (Ichiyō)
See *Takekurabe*
Comparison (Hayne) **94**:138
The Compassionate Beneficence of the Deity (Blair) **75**:116
"Compatriots from an Earlier Age" (Arnim)
See "Altdeutsche Landsleute"
Compatriots from an Earlier Age (Arnim)
See "Altdeutsche Landsleute"
A Compendious Dictionary of the English Language (Webster) **30**:388, 396, 398, 409
Compendium (Schleiermacher) **107**:370, 382
"Compensation" (Emerson) **1**:280; **38**:170-71, 178, 224; **98**:109-14, 131, 190
"Compensation" (Ingelow) **39**:267
"The Complaint" (Wordsworth)
See "The Complaint of the Forsaken Indian Woman"
"The Complaint of a Forsaken Indian Woman" (Wordsworth)
See "The Complaint of the Forsaken Indian Woman"
"Complaint of Consolations" (Laforgue)
See "Complainte des consolations"
"Complaint of Forgetting the Dead" (Laforgue)
See "Complainte de l'oubli des morts"
"Complaint of Monotonous Autumn" (Laforgue)
See "Complainte de l'automne monotone"
"Complaint of the Days' End" (Laforgue)
See "Complainte de la fin des journées"
"The Complaint of the Forsaken Indian Woman" (Wordsworth) **12**:387; **111**:202, 208, 210-11, 314-15
"Complaint of the Great Pines" (Laforgue)
See "Complainte des grands pins dans une villa abandonnée"
"Complaint of the Incurable Angel" (Laforgue)
See "Complainte de l'ange incurable"
"Complaint of the Outraged Husband" (Laforgue)
See "Complainte de l'époux outragé"
"Complaint of the Pianos" (Laforgue)
See "Complainte des pianos qu'on extend dans les quartiers aisés"
"Complaint of the Poor Knight Errant" (Laforgue)
See "Complainte du pauvre chevalier-errant"
"Complaint of the Woman Good and Dead" (Laforgue) **221**:47
"A Complaint on the Decay of Beggars in the Metropolis" (Lamb) **10**:403, 409, 426, 430, 436; **113**:218, 235, 252, 263
"Complainte à Notre-Dame des soirs" (Laforgue) **221**:40
"Complainte de la bonne défunte" (Laforgue) **221**:60
Complainte de la bonne défunte (Laforgue) **53**:283
"Complainte de la fin des journées" (Laforgue) **221**:33, 35
"Complainte de l'ange incurable" (Laforgue) **221**:47, 75, 78-79, 84, 86, 89
"Complainte de l'automne monotone" (Laforgue) **221**:32
"Complainte de l'époux outragé" (Laforgue) **221**:32, 47, 59
"Complainte de Lord Pierrot" (Laforgue) **53**:287; **221**:60, 63, 65-66, 86, 88-89
"Complainte de l'oubli des morts" (Laforgue) **221**:7, 47
"Complainte des blackboulés" (Laforgue) **221**:60, 66, 89
"Complainte des bons ménages" (Laforgue) **221**:91
"Complainte des cloches" (Laforgue) **221**:21
"Complainte des consolations" (Laforgue) **221**:51, 60
"Complainte des complaintes" (Laforgue) **5**:277; **221**:85-86, 91

"Complainte des débats mélancoliques et littéraires" (Laforgue) **221**:82
"Complainte des formalités nuptiales" (Laforgue) **221**:60, 89
"Complainte des grands pins dans une villa abandonnée" (Laforgue) **221**:33-34, 60
"Complainte des Montres" (Laforgue)
See "Complainte des Mounis du Mont-Martre"
"Complainte des Mounis du Mont-Martre" (Laforgue) **221**:43
"Complainte des Noces de Pierrot" (Laforgue) **53**:287
"Complainte des pianos qu'on entend dans les quertiersaisés" (Laforgue) **5**:272; **53**:292; **221**:33, 35, 50, 60, 67
"Complainte des printemps" (Laforgue) **53**:294; **221**:34, 59-60
"Complainte des voix sous le figuier boudhique" (Laforgue) **221**:40, 60, 83-84
"Complainte du pauvre chevalier-errant" (Laforgue) **5**:275; **221**:82, 85, 92
"Complainte du pauvre corps humain" (Laforgue) **221**:59
"Complainte du pauvre jeune homme" (Laforgue) **221**:32, 59, 92
"Complainte du Roi de Thulé" (Laforgue) **221**:25, 60, 76, 78
"Complainte du sage de Paris" (Laforgue) **221**:42, 86-88, 93
"Complainte du soir des comices agricoles" (Laforgue) **221**:87, 92
"Complainte du Temps et de sa commère l'Espace" (Laforgue) **53**:267; **221**:42, 83, 86-88, 92-93
"Complainte du vent qui s'ennuie la nuit" (Laforgue) **53**:294; **221**:81-82, 89
"Complainte d'un autre dimanche" (Laforgue)
See "Complainte d'un certain dimanche"
"Complainte d'un certain dimanche" (Laforgue) **221**:84, 89-90
"Complainte d'une convalescence en mai" (Laforgue) **221**:83, 85
"Complainte propitiatoire à l'inconscient" (Laforgue) **221**:42, 88
"Complainte sous le figuier boudhique" (Laforgue)
See "Complainte des voix sous le figuier boudhique"
"Complainte—épitaphe" (Laforgue) **221**:82
"Complainte-placet de Faust fils" (Laforgue) **221**:7, 84
Les complaintes (Laforgue) **5**:275, 277, 280-2; **53**:278-9, 281, 287-90
Les complaintes de Jules Laforgue (Laforgue) **221**:4, 7, 12, 17, 19, 22, 26, 33-35, 38, 40, 43, 47, 51, 55-56, 58-60, 63-64, 66-67, 70, 81-82, 84-85, 88, 90, 93
"Complaintes des pubertés difficiles" (Laforgue) **221**:59, 84, 89
"Complaintes-litanies de mon sacré-coeur" (Laforgue) **221**:42, 82, 89
The Complaints (Laforgue)
See *Les complaintes de Jules Laforgue*
The Complaints of the Poor People of England (Dyer) **129**:98, 103, 112, 115, 125, 128-29, 136-37, 142, 145
The Complete Andersen (Andersen) **7**:37
Complete Edition (Hayne) **94**:138
Complete Guide to the English Lakes (Martineau) **26**:311
The Complete Nonsense of Edward Lear (Lear) **3**:305
The Complete Novels and Selected Writings of Amy Levy (Levy) **203**:309
Complete Poems (Barrett Browning) **170**:107
The Complete Poems (Dickinson) **21**:71; **171**:98, 194
Complete Poems (Hayne) **94**:134
The Complete Poems of Christina Rossetti: A Variorum Edition (Rossetti) **186**:234, 275-80, 283, 332-40, 342-43, 345-48
Complete Poetic Works (Coleridge) **90**:32-3
The Complete Poetical Works (Baillie) **151**:41, 46
Complete Poetical Works (Byron) **149**:164
The Complete Poetical Works (Coleridge) **197**:215, 284, 312
Complete Poetical Works (Longfellow) **103**:295, 305
The Complete Poetical Works and Letters of John Keats (Keats) **121**:126-27, 192
The Complete Poetical Works of Percy Bysshe Shelley (Shelley) **143**:232; **175**:268
Complete Poetical Works of Samuel Taylor Coleridge (Coleridge) **99**:3, 106; **177**:52-56, 134
Complete Poetry and Collected Prose (Whitman) **205**:318-26, 330
The Complete Poetry and Prose of William Blake (Blake) **127**:32-33, 36, 56-57, 59-60, 63-73, 75, 77-82, 101, 105-7, 112, 123-25, 127-40; **173**:23, 36, 70, 98, 136; **190**:25, 45, 54, 78, 87, 105, 109, 144, 159; **201**:55-56, 60-66, 95-96, 99, 104, 106, 112-13, 116, 118-22, 126-27, 131, 133, 138-45
Complete Prose Works (Milton)
See *The Complete Prose Works of John Milton*
The Complete Prose Works of John Milton (Milton) **175**:319
The Complete Prose Works of Matthew Arnold (Arnold) **89**:31-40, 64-7, 80, 89, 91-3, 98, 100-07, 109-13; **126**:36-38, 42-44, 46, 48-50, 52, 59-60, 87-88, 90-91, 93-95, 100, 102-9, 111-17, 119-22; **218**:196-97, 224-33
Complete Prose Works of Matthew Arnold, Volume I (Arnold) **126**:111-12, 114
Complete Prose Works of Matthew Arnold, Volume II (Arnold) **126**:112-13
Complete Prose Works of Matthew Arnold, Volume III (Arnold) **126**:38, 94, 102-7, 109, 114, 122
Complete Prose Works of Matthew Arnold, Volume IV (Arnold) **126**:88, 115-16
Complete Prose Works of Matthew Arnold, Volume IX (Arnold) **126**:104, 114
Complete Prose Works of Matthew Arnold, Volume V (Arnold) **126**:36-38, 44, 100, 103, 108-9, 119-22
Complete Prose Works of Matthew Arnold, Volume VI (Arnold) **126**:90, 93, 108-9
Complete Prose Works of Matthew Arnold, Volume VIII (Arnold) **126**:37, 91, 104
Complete Prose Works of Matthew Arnold, Volume X (Arnold) **126**:36, 43, 59, 95, 106, 116-17
Complete Prose Works of Matthew Arnold, Volume XI (Arnold) **126**:37, 59-60
The Complete Sermons of Ralph Waldo Emerson (Emerson) **98**:61, 91, 93-5
Complete Short Stories (Trollope)
See *Anthony Trollope: The Complete Short Stories*
The Complete Short Stories of Guy de Maupassant (Maupassant) **83**:189-202
"The Complete Work of Edgar Allan Poe" (Poe) **94**:228-29, 245
Complete Works (Baillie)
See *The Complete Poetical Works*
Complete Works (Bécquer)
See *Obras completas*
Complete Works (Browning) **79**:189-90
Complete Works (Freytag)
See *Gesammelte Werke*
Complete Works (Gómez de Avellaneda)
See *Obras de doña Gertrudis de Avellaneda*
Complete Works (Lampman) **194**:66
Complete Works (Multatuli)
See *Volledige Werken*
Complete Works (Paine) **62**:374-6, 380-1
Complete Works (Rimbaud)
See *Oeuvres complètes*
Complete Works (Tonna)
See *The Works of Charlotte Elizabeth*
Complete Works of Abraham Lincoln (Lincoln) **201**:161, 168
The Complete Works of Edgar Allan Poe (Poe) **211**:238
The Complete Works of Edgar Allen Poe (Poe) **117**:225, 235, 260, 262, 268, 275-76, 304-5, 309-13, 330-33, 335-36
The Complete Works of Elizabeth Barrett Browning (Barrett Browning) **61**:22, 49, 51, 53, 56-8, 66, 76; **170**:27, 84, 105
The Complete Works of Lord Macaulay (Macaulay) **231**:302-9
The Complete Works of Nathaniel Hawthrone (Hawthorne) **95**:91
The Complete Works of Percy Bysshe Shelley (Shelley) **175**:318-19, 321, 324-27, 329-31
The Complete Works of Ralph Waldo Emerson (Emerson) **98**:33, 40-50, 54-63, 66, 68, 72-3, 75-6, 91-2, 96, 101, 109, 113, 127, 130-31, 133-35, 166, 185
The Complete Works of Samuel Taylor Coleridge (Coleridge) **197**:282
The Complete Works of William Hazlitt (Hazlitt) **82**:128
Complete Writings (Whitman) **81**:235, 267
The Complete Writings of William Blake (Blake) **127**:56-57, 59-60, 63-73, 75, 77-82; **190**:25, 36, 45, 54, 78
"Composed by the Sea-side, near Calais, August 1802" (Wordsworth) **206**:301
"Composed during a walk on the Downs, in November 1787" (Smith)
See "Sonnet 42"
"Composed in the Valley, near Dover, On the Day of landing" (Wordsworth) **206**:308
"Composed upon an Evening of Extraordinary Splendour and Beauty" (Wordsworth) **166**:212
"Composed upon Westminster Bridge, Sept. 3, 1802" (Wordsworth) **12**:417
"Compromise" (Tennyson) **30**:295
"Comrades, Fill No Glass for Me" (Foster) **26**:286
Comradeship (Scribe)
See *La camaraderie; ou, La courte échelle*
Le comte de Monte-Cristo (Dumas) **11**:52, 59, 61, 63, 65, 68-9, 71, 74, 76, 83, 86; **71**:184-85, 193, 209
Le comte de Moret (Dumas) **71**:217-220
Le Comte Hermann (Dumas) **71**:193
Comte's Philosophy of the Sciences: Being an Exposition of the Principles of the "Cours de Philosophie Positive" of August Comte (Lewes) **25**:295; **215**:86, 106, 122, 183
La Comtesse de Charney (Dumas) **71**:232, 242
La comtesse de Rudolstadt (Sand) **2**:589, 598; **42**:314, 338, 358; **42**:372; **57**:360; **174**:197
Comtesse de Rudolstadt (Sand) **174**:158
Con Cregan (Lever)
See *Confessions of Con Cregan, the Irish Gil Blas*
"Con motiva de haber abrazado un amigo la carrera militar" (Heredia) **209**:136
"Conaire" (Ferguson)
See "Conary"
"Conary" (Ferguson) **33**:279, 281, 285, 290, 294, 298, 303-04, 306
"Concealed Joy" (Beddoes) **154**:8888
The Concept of Anxiety (Kierkegaard)
See *Begrebet Angest*
"A Concept of Diabolical Possession" (Lamb) **10**:404
The Concept of Dread (Kierkegaard) **34**:200, 204, 223-24, 226-29, 231; **78**:138, 236, 238-39
The Concept of Irony, with Special Reference to Socrates (Kierkegaard)
See *Om Begrebet Ironi med stadigt Hensyn til Socrates*

"Concerning Actors and Singers" (Wagner) **9**:414
"Concerning Geffray, Teste Noire" (Morris) **4**:431, 444
"Concerning Grace and Dignity" (Schiller)
See "Über Anmut und Würde"
"Concerning Illusions and Truth" (Baratynsky)
See "O zabluzhdeniyakh i istine"
Concerning the Aesthetic Education of the Human Being (Schiller)
See "Briefe über die ästhetische Erziehung des Menschen"
"Concerning the Art of Conducting" (Wagner) **9**:414, 475
Concerning the Concept of the Wissenschaftslehre, or, of So-Called Philosophy (Fichte)
See *Über den Begriff der Wissenschaftslehre*
Concerning the Influence of the Passions upon the Happiness of Individuals and of Nations (Staël-Holstein)
See *De l'influence des passions sur le bonheur des individus et des nations*
"Concerning the Procedure of the Poetic Spirit" (Hölderlin) **187**:212
Concerning the Shakespeare Madness (Grabbe) **2**:280
"Concerning the Sublime" (Schiller)
See "Über das Erhabene"
The Conchologist's First Book (Poe) **1**:497; **16**:297
Le concierge de la rue du Bac (Kock) **16**:259
Le concile féerique (Laforgue) **5**:270, 276, 281-82; **221**:4, 7, 24, 60, 84, 92
"Conciliator, Who Had Never Believed" (Hölderlin) **187**:213
"Concluding Address" (Brontë) **109**:35
"Concluding Address, 1808" (Rowson) **182**:257, 261, 345
"Concluding Address, 1810" (Rowson) **182**:259, 261
"Concluding Speech" (Lincoln)
See "Last Speech in Springfield, Illinois, in the Campaign of 1858"
Concluding Unscientific Postscript to the Philosophical Fragments (Kierkegaard)
See *Afsluttende uvidenskabelig Efterskrift*
"Conclusion" (Brackenridge) **227**:104
"Conclusion" (Grillparzer)
See "Schlußwort"
"Conclusion" (Hawthorne) **10**:286-87
"Conclusion" (Pater) **7**:288, 314-15, 327, 332-33, 338-39; **90**:336
"Conclusion" (Tennyson) **65**:368
"Conclusion" (Thoreau) **7**:389, 399
"Conclusion of the Mirror" (Mackenzie) **41**:187
"Conclusion—Autographic Letter from Suggs" (Hooper) **177**:207
Concord and Merrimac Rivers (Thoreau)
See *A Week on the Concord and Merrimack Rivers*
Concord Days (Alcott) **1**:21, 24-26; **167**:72, 85, 89
"Concord Ode" (Emerson) **1**:289, 296, 299, 305
The Concubine (Baratynsky)
See *Nalozhnitsa*
El conde de Moret (Dumas)
See *Le comte de Moret*
El Conde Fernán González (Larra) **17**:279
Condensation of Determinants (Dodgson) **139**:4
Condition (Delany)
See *The Condition, Elevation, Emigration, and Destiny of the Colored People of the United States, Politically Considered*
The Condition (Engels)
See *Die Lage der arbeitenden Klasse in England*
Condition and Elevation (Delany)
See *The Condition, Elevation, Emigration, and Destiny of the Colored People of the United States, Politically Considered*
"The Condition and Prospects of Slavery in America" (Parker) **186**:136
"The Condition, Character and Prospects of America" (Parker) **186**:137
The Condition, Elevation, Emigration, and Destiny of the Colored People of the United States, Politically Considered (Delany) **93**:99, 105, 107, 120, 122, 125, 143, 153-4, 159, 161-63, 166-67, 169
Condition of England (Engels)
See *Die Lage der arbeitenden Klasse in England*
"Condition of the Members of the Christian Empire" (Newman) **38**:308
Condition of the Working Class (Engels)
See *Die Lage der arbeitenden Klasse in England*
The Condition of the Working class in England in 1844 (Engels)
See *Die Lage der arbeitenden Klasse in England*
Condition of Working Class in England (Engels)
See *Die Lage der arbeitenden Klasse in England*
"Condition-of-England" (Norton) **205**:144
"The Conditions and Prospects of Protestantism" (Froude) **43**:213
The Condor (Stifter)
See *Der Condor*
Der Condor (Stifter) **41**:335, 339, 341, 366, 376, 380-81; **198**:259, 275-76
"The Conduct of Life" (Emerson) **98**:8-9
The Conduct of Life (Emerson) **1**:290, 300; **38**:154, 157; **98**:8, 19, 72, 89, 130-33, 151, 186
"Conductor Bradley" (Whittier) **8**:517, 523
"The Confederate Memorial Address" (Lanier) **3**:245; **118**:258
"Confessio Fidei" (Coleridge) **197**:262, 266; **231**:40
"Confession" (Baudelaire) **55**:14, 60
"The Confession" (Lermontov)
See "Ispoved"
"La Confession" (Maupassant) **83**:228
Confession (Bakunin) **25**:40-4, 58, 60, 63, 72, 75; **58**:102, 107-8, 114
The Confession (Cumberland) **167**:154
"La Confession de Théodule Sabot" (Maupassant) **83**:171
La confession d'un enfant du siècle (Musset) **7**:259, 266, 273-74, 280; **150**:226, 233, 240, 243-46, 267, 285, 290, 296-97, 328-33, 334; **150**:225, 339
La confession d'une jeune fille (Sand) **42**:311
"Confession of Faith" (Engels) **85**:127
Confession; or, The Blind Heart (Simms) **3**:506, 509-10, 512, 514
"The Confessional" (Browning) **79**:99, 164
"The Confessional" (Willis) **194**:305
"Confessions" (Barrett Browning) **1**:125; **66**:42
"Confessions" (Browning) **19**:115
Confessions (Bomans) **51**:371
Confessions (Heine)
See *Geständnisse*
Confessions (De Quincey)
See *Confessions of an English Opium-Eater*
Confessions (Verlaine) **51**:371
"Confessions d'une femme" (Maupassant) **83**:213
"Confessions of a Drunkard" (Lamb) **10**:409, 414-15, 435; **113**:261-63
The Confessions of a Justified Sinner (Hogg)
See *The Private Memoirs and Confessions of a Justified Sinner*
"Confessions of a King" (Jones) **222**:158
"The Confessions of a Medium" (Taylor) **89**:308
Confessions of a Murderer (De Quincey)
See *Confessions of an English Opium Eater*
"Confessions of a Reformed Ribbonman" (Carleton) **3**:92
"Confessions of a Second-Rate, Sensitive Mind" (Tennyson) **30**:204
Confessions of a Sinner (Hogg)
See *The Private Memoirs and Confessions of a Justified Sinner*
Confessions of an English Opium Eater (Musset)
See *L'Anglais mangeur d'opium*
Confessions of an English Opium Eater (De Quincey) **198**:3-5, 10-13, 16-19, 21-24, 31, 33, 39, 42, 46-52, 57-58, 61, 65, 75, 78, 83, 87-89, 91, 93, 99, 102-4, 110-11
Confessions of an English Opium-Eater (De Quincey) **87**:3-5, 11, 16, 29, 36, 40-2, 48, 52, 55-6, 60-1, 70, 75, 78
Confessions of an Inquiring Spirit (Coleridge) **197**:266; **231**:59, 68, 72
"The Confessions of an odd-tempered Man" (Opie) **65**:163
"The Confessions of an Office-Holder" (Kennedy) **2**:432
"Confessions of an Opium Eater" (De Quincey) **4**:59-61, 63, 66, 77, 79, 83-85, 87-89
Confessions of Con Cregan, the Irish Gil Blas (Lever) **23**:304, 311
"Confessions of Fitzboodle" (Thackeray) **5**:451; **43**:387
The Confessions of Harry Lorrequer (Lever) **23**:268-73, 281-85, 287, 290-94, 297, 299-300, 302-03, 306, 309
Confessions of the Nun of St. Omer (Dacre) **151**:139-40, 143, 148-50, 152, 155, 162, 171, 190, 199, 212, 215, 224, 226
"The Confessor" (Robinson) **142**:138, 170, 252
"The Confidant" (Crabbe) **26**:93, 102, 130-32, 136; **121**:6, 67, 69
The Confidantes of a King: The Mistresses of Louis XV (Goncourt and Goncourt)
See *Les maîtresses de Louis XV*
La Confidence (Maupassant) **83**:230
"La Confidence des Ruggieri" (Balzac) **153**:149
The Confidence-Man: His Masquerade (Melville) **3**:331, 334, 337, 344, 347, 354-55, 362, 364, 368-70, 372, 384-85; **12**:269, 271, 274, 293; **29**:327-28, 334, 355, 362; **45**:199, 235; **49**:391, 402, 408, 417; **91**:84, 121, 175, 177, 180, 204; **93**:197, 220, 244-45, 249; **123**:179, 201, 204, 219, 241; **157**:64-214; **181**:153, 179, 185, 201, 216, 275; **193**:61-62, 130, 149, 190; **221**:125, 128
Les confidences (Lamartine) **11**:265, 266, 278; **190**:192, 211-12, 215-16, 242-43, 261-62, 264
Confidential Disclosures (Lamartine)
See *Les Confidences*
Confidential Letters on Lucinde (Schleiermacher)
See *Vertraute Briefe über Friedrich Schlegels Lucinde*
Confidential Letters on Schlegel's Lucinda (Schleiermacher)
See *Vertraute Briefe über Friedrich Schlegels Lucinde*
"Confiteor" (Gordon) **21**:150, 164
"Le confitéor de l'artiste" (Baudelaire) **29**:97; **155**:46, 86
"The Conflict" (Schiller)
See "Kampf"
"The Conflict of Convictions" (Melville) **3**:352
"Conflit" (Mallarmé) **210**:260
Conflit (Mallarmé) **41**:280
"Conflits pour rire" (Maupassant) **83**:169, 227-28
The Conformists (Banim and Banim) **13**:121, 129-30, 135-37, 149-50
Confounded Foreigners (Reynolds) **146**:172, 193
"Confrontation" (Mallarmé) **210**:260

Confrontation (Mallarmé) **41**:280
Congal (Ferguson) **33**:283, 285-86, 289-91, 293-94, 296-99, 302-03, 306-09
Congiura de'Pazzi (Alfieri) **101**:32, 42
"Congratulations" (Rizal) **27**:425
Coningsby; or, The New Generation (Disraeli) **2**:139-40, 144-45, 147-54; **39**:2-4, 6-11, 15-17, 19-24, 27-9, 34-5, 40-1, 43-51, 56, 64-6, 69, 73, 75-6, 80; **79**:195, 198-99, 212-14, 216-19, 221-22, 234-35, 239, 245, 248, 250, 257-60, 263, 269-71, 273, 278-79, 281-82
Conjectural Beginning of the Human Race (Kant) **27**:236
Conjugalia (Reade) **2**:549
La conjuración de Venecia (Martínez de la Rosa) **102**:226, 230, 238-47
La Conjuration de Catilina (Mérimée) **65**:85
"Connecticut" (Halleck) **47**:57
"Connecticut River" (Sigourney) **21**:301, 310; **87**:331
"The Connection and the Mutual Assistance of the Arts and Sciences, and the Relation of Poetry to Them All" (Dyer) **129**:110
"The Connection of Mythology and Philosophy" (Hopkins) **189**:92-93
"Connel of Dee" (Hogg) **109**:243-44
El conocido sabio Cornelius (Silva) **114**:263
"The Conqueror" (Schiller)
See "Der Eroberer"
"The Conqueror Worm" (Poe) **1**:512; **97**:181; **117**:192, 242-45, 281, 287, 301; **211**:246-47, 249
"The Conqueror's Grave" (Bryant) **6**:165, 168; **46**:3
The Conquest of Canaän: A Poem in Eleven Books (Dwight) **13**:259, 261-63, 265, 269-71, 273-78
Conquest of Granada (Irving)
See *The Chronicle of the Conquest of Granada*
"Conquest of Mexico" (Prescott) **163**:323, 325-26
Conquête (Constant)
See *De l'esprit de conquête et de l'usurpation dans leurs rapports avec la civilisation européenne*
Conrad and Eudora (Chivers)
See *Conrad and Eudora; or; The Death of Alonzo*
Conrad and Eudora; or; The Death of Alonzo (Chivers) **49**:50, 52, 57, 61-2, 79, 81, 83
Conrad Wallenrod (Mickiewicz)
See *Konrad Wallenrod*
"Conscience" (Patmore) **9**:342
"Conscience l'Innocent" (Dumas) **71**:185, 187, 204
"Conscience-Stricken Daniel" (Leskov)
See "Legenda o sovestnom Danile"
"Conscious Am I in My Chamber" (Dickinson) **21**:53, 74
Consciousness in Concord: The Text of Thoreau's Hitherto "Lost Journal" (Thoreau) **207**:222
"The Conscript" (Balzac) **5**:52-3
The Consecration of Strength (Werner)
See *Martin Luther, oder die Weihe der Kraft: Eine Tragödie vom Verfasser der Söhne des Thales*
The Consecration of Weakness (Werner)
See *Die Weihe der Unkraft: Ein Ergänzungblatt zur deutschen Haustafel*
"Conseil falot" (Verlaine) **230**:167
"Conseils à une Parisienne" (Musset) **150**:309
"The Consequences of an Immoral Principle and False Idea of Life" (Parker) **186**:217
"Consequences of Happy Marriages" (Horton) **87**:110
"The Conservative" (Emerson) **1**:287; **38**:227
"Consider the Lilies of the Field" (Rossetti) **66**:301
A Consideration of Objections against the Retrenchment Association at Oxford during the Irish Famine in 1847 (Clough) **27**:82-3
Considerations (Staël-Holstein)
See *Considérations sur la Révolution française*
"Considerations By the Way" (Emerson) **98**:131
Considerations on France (Maistre)
See *Considérations sur la France*
Considerations on Lord Grenville's and Mr. Pitt's Bill Concerning Treasonable and Seditious Practices, and Unlawful Assemblies (Godwin) **130**:88, 95, 166
Considerations on Religion and Public Education (More) **141**:305-8
Considerations on Representative Government (Mill) **58**:330-1, 350, 376, 379; **179**:210-11, 313-14, 319, 324, 354, 362
Considerations on Spiritual Power (Comte)
See *Considérations sur le pouvoir spirituel*
Considérations philosophiques sur les sciences et les savants (Comte) **54**:210, 237
"Considérations sur la culture en géneral" (Schlegel) **142**:308
Considérations sur la France (Maistre) **37**:278-80, 291-92, 295, 299, 300-06, 313, 315-17, 320, 322-23
Considérations sur la Révolution française (Staël-Holstein) **91**:323, 360
Considérations sur le pouvoir spirituel (Comte) **54**:203, 210, 238
"Considérations sur un chef-d'oeuvre, ou le danger du génie: *Les Misérables* par Victor Hugo" (Lamartine) **190**:203
"Consolatio" (Herzen) **10**:336, 338
Les consolations (Sainte-Beuve) **5**:325, 333, 335, 341, 346, 348, 351
Conspectus of Useful and Harmful Plants that Grow Wild or Cultivated in Northern Germany (Chamisso) **82**:5
"The Conspiracy of Catiline" (Mérimée) **6**:353
The Conspiracy of Fiesco at Genoa (Schiller)
See *Die Verschwörung des Fiesco zu Genua*
The Conspiracy of Kings (Barlow) **23**:14, 27; **223**:7, 25, 48, 57-61
Conspiracy of the Pazzi (Alfieri)
See *Congiura de'Pazzi*
Une Conspiraton sous Louis XIII (Vigny)
See *Cinq-Mars; ou, Une conspiration sous Louis XIII*
"The Conspirators" (Mérimée) **6**:353
The Conspirators (Dumas)
See *Le chevalier d'Harmental*
The Constable of Bourbon (Ainsworth) **13**:41
The Constable of the Tower (Ainsworth) **13**:42
Constance Verrier (Sand) **2**:598; **42**:312; **57**:316
"Constancy to an Ideal Object" (Coleridge) **231**:86-91
"The Constant Tin Solider" (Andersen)
See "Den standhaftige Tinsoldat"
Constantine (Burckhardt)
See *Die Zeit Constantins des Grossen*
Constantine and Valeria (Baillie) **151**:75
Constantine Paleologus; or, The Last of the Caesars (Baillie) **2**:34-35, 37, 39-40; **71**:5, 12-13; **151**:61, 74-5, 114-16, 118-19
Constantinople (Gautier) **1**:344; **59**:5
Constantinople of Today (Gautier)
See *Constantinople*
"The Constellations" (Bryant) **6**:165, 168
Constitución del Colegio de Señoritas de la Advocación de Santa Rosa de América (Sarmiento) **123**:354
"The Constituent Parts of a Drama" (Murphy) **229**:226
Constitution for the School for Young Ladies of the Appellation of Saint Rose of America (Sarmiento)
See *Constitución del Colegio de Señoritas de la Advocación de Santa Rosa de América*
Constitution Lost (Arany)
See *Az elveszett alkomány*
La Constitution républicaine (Constant)
See *Fragments d'un ouvrage abandonné sur la possibilité d'une constitution républicaine dans un grand pays*
Constitutional Code (Bentham) **38**:44-5, 87-8
Constitutionnel (Balzac) **153**:64
"The Constraining Limitation of English Art" ("Smiesniennaya ogranichiennosmsoft anglitskogo iskussmva") (Leskov) **174**:132
Consuelo (Sand) **2**:588-89, 593-96, 603-04; **42**:314, 320, 330-32, 337-38, 343, 372; **57**:310, 313, 316-7, 359-61; **174**:158, 166, 197, 225
Los consuelos (Echeverria) **18**:147-49, 152
Les consultations du Docteur Noir: Stello; ou, les diables bleus, première consultation (Vigny) **7**:467-71, 473-75, 479, 485-86; **102**:335-40, 342-44, 360-61, 378, 380
"Consummatum Est" (Hayne) **94**:165-66
La contagion (Augier) **31**:7-10, 13, 16, 19-24, 27-8, 31
"The Contagiousness of Puerperal Fever" (Holmes) **81**:101-02
"Containing Observations" (Brackenridge) **7**:51, 58, 65
"Containing Reflections" (Brackenridge) **7**:51, 58, 65
Contarini Fleming: The Psychological Romance (Disraeli) **2**:137-38, 143, 145-49, 153; **39**:3, 22, 24, 31, 33, 39-42, 52, 54-6, 66-7, 74; **79**:201-02, 206, 209, 211, 214-15, 217-18, 226-27, 239, 271-73, 282
"Conte" (Rimbaud) **4**:466, 470, 473, 477, 482-83; **35**:290, 294-96, 322, 324-25; **82**:230, 232; **227**:292-93, 297-99, 309
"Un conte" (Verlaine) **51**:368; **230**:165
"Conte de Noël" (Maupassant) **83**:182
Conte di Carmagnola (Manzoni)
See *Il conte di Carmagnola*
Il conte di Carmagnola (Manzoni) **29**:250-51, 254, 261, 275, 300; **98**:201, 204-05, 208-09, 213, 220-21, 223-25, 230, 241
"Contemplation" (Blake) **13**:181
"Contemplation" (Willis) **194**:297, 300, 307
"The Contemplation of God" (Klopstock) **11**:223
Les contemplations (Hugo) **3**:242, 253, 263, 271, 273; **10**:369, 373, 375; **161**:156, 216, 219, 231, 266; **189**:178, 253
"The Contemporary" (Turgenev) **122**:343
"Contemporary" (Tyutchev)
See "Sovremennoe"
"The Contemporary God" (Isaacs)
See "El Dios del siglo"
"Contempt of Court—Almost" (Harris) **23**:159; **165**:201, 206, 244, 254, 260, 276, 280
"A Contented Woman" (Neal) **161**:336
"Contentment" (Field) **3**:208
"Contentment" (Holmes) **14**:109
"Contentment, or If You Please Confession" (Paine) **62**:324
Contes artistes (Balzac) **153**:150
Contes bourgeois (Banville) **9**:31
Contes bruns (Balzac) **153**:150
Contes choisis (Daudet) **1**:243
Contes cruels (Villiers de l'Isle Adam) **3**:581-82, 584, 586, 589-90
Contes de la bécasse (Maupassant) **1**:442
Les contes de la reine de Navarre (Scribe) **16**:412
Contes de la veillée (Nodier) **19**:384
Contes d'Espagne et d'Italie (Musset) **7**:254-56, 259, 263, 265, 278; **150**:224-5, 229-30, 232-4, 299-301, 303, 322, 324, 329
Les contes d'Hoffman (Hoffmann) **2**:341
Contes drolatiques (Balzac) **53**:25; **153**:146, 150-53, 168
Les contes du lundi (Daudet) **1**:231, 234, 239, 243
Contes d'une grand'mère (Sand) **174**:164

Contes en prose (Desbordes-Valmore) **97**:12
Contes en vers (Desbordes-Valmore) **97**:12
Contes et facétites (Nerval) **67**:357
"Contes et nouvelles" (Maupassant) **42**:203; **83**:189-202
Contes et nouvelles (Musset) **7**:259
Contes fantastiques (Banville)
See *Contes féeriques*
Contes fantastiques (Gautier) **59**:33-6, 38, 40
Contes fantastiques (Nodier) **19**:395
Contes féeriques (Banville) **9**:31-32
Contes héroïques (Banville) **9**:31
Contes immoraux (Borel)
See *Champavert, contes immoraux*
Contes philosophiques (Balzac)
See *Romans et contes philosophiques*
Contes pour les femmes (Banville) **9**:31-32
La contesse romani (Dumas) **9**:230
A Contest of Faculties (Kant) **27**:237
"The Contest of the Minstrels" (Hoffmann)
See "Der Kampf der Sänger"
The Continent (Cooke) **110**:39
Continental Journal (Wordsworth)
See *Journal of a Tour on the Continent*
The Continentalist (Hamilton) **49**:295, 325
Continuation and Conclusion of Dead Souls (Gogol) **5**:218
Continuation of Early Tales (Edgeworth) **51**:81, 110
"The Contract" (Patmore) **9**:352, 359
"Contracted Views in Religion" (Newman) **38**:306
"Contradictions" (Levy) **203**:324-25, 351
"Contralto" (Gautier) **59**:19
"The Contrast" (Edgeworth) **51**:82, 88-89
The Contrast (Tyler) **3**:571-79
"Contrasted Songs" (Ingelow) **39**:264
"Le Contrat de mariage" (Balzac) **153**:68-69
Le Contrat de mariage (Balzac)
See "Le Contrat de mariage"
"Contre la peine de mort" (Lamartine) **190**:254
Contribution to Many Contributions of the Century (Herder)
See *Beytrag zu vielen Beyträgen des Jahrhunderts*
Contribution to the Correction of the Public Verdict on the French Revolution (Fichte) **62**:34
"A Contribution to the Critique of Hegel's Philosophy of Right: An Introduction" (Marx) **114**:69, 83
A Contribution to the Critique of Political Economy (Marx)
See *Zur kritik der politischen Ökonomie*
"A Contribution to the History of Early Christianity" (Engels) **85**:44, 48
Contributions Designed to Correct the Judgment of the Public on the French Revolution (Fichte)
See *Contribution to the Correction of the Public Verdict on the French Revolution*
Contributions to the Edinburgh Review (Jeffrey) **33**:314, 322, 332, 348, 354-55
"The Contrite Heart" (Cowper) **8**:130-31; **94**:71-2
The Controversy of the Faculties (Kant) **67**:227
"The Convalescent" (Lamb) **10**:410, 419, 436
"The Convent Threshold" (Rossetti) **2**:562, 564-5, 568, 575-6; **50**:266, 322; **66**:304-5, 308, 311-2, 341; **186**:236, 272, 304
Convention (Barlow)
See *A Letter to the National Convention of France on the Defects in the Constitution of 1791, and the Extent of the Amendments Which Ought to Be Applied*
Convention of Cintra (Wordsworth) **12**:461; **166**:267
"Conversation" (Alcott) **167**:76
"Conversation" (Cowper) **8**:106, 125-26; **94**:14, 23, 26-8, 51, 115
"Conversation" (Mickiewicz)
See "Rozmowa"
"Conversation" (Thoreau) **138**:129
"A Conversation" (Turgenev) **21**:377, 431
Conversation (Schlegel)
See *Gespräch über die Poesie*
"Conversation about Happiness" (Karamzin)
See "Razgover o shchastii"
Conversation entre onze heures et minuit (Balzac) **5**:73; **153**:146
A Conversation in the Kremlin (Pavlova)
See *Razgovor v Kremle*
A Conversation in the Trianon (Pavlova)
See *Razgovor v Trianone*
"The Conversation of Eiros and Charmion" (Poe) **1**:496, 519-20; **16**:297, 331; **97**:179-83; **211**:260
Conversation on Poetry (Schlegel)
See *Gespräch über die Poesie*
"Conversation on the High Road" (Turgenev)
See *Razgovor na bolshoi doroge*
A Conversation on the Highway (Turgenev)
See *Razgovor na bolshoi doroge*
"Conversation with a Genius" (Derzhavin) **215**:16
"Conversations as Good as Real III" (Hazlitt) **82**:98
Conversations for the Use of Children and Young Persons (Smith) **115**:119
Conversations of James Northcote, Esq., R. A. (Hazlitt) **29**:148
Conversations on Liberalism and the Church (Brownson) **50**:63, 65, 67-8
Conversations on Some of the Old Poets (Lowell) **2**:504; **90**:195-97, 212-13
"Conversations on the Transcendental Club and the Dial" (Alcott) **167**:89
Conversations with Children on the Gospels (Alcott) **1**:19-20; **167**:3-4, 6-7, 29-30, 37, 45, 80-82, 97-99
Conversations with Demons (Arnim)
See *Gespräche mit Dämonen. Des Königsbuchs zweiter Band*
"The Conversazióne" (Hale) **75**:347-8
"The Conversazzhyony" (Field) **3**:211
"The Convert" (Crabbe) **26**:93, 129
The Convert (Brownson) **50**:48, 50
"The Convict" (Shevchenko)
See *Varnak*
"The Convict" (Wilson) **5**:547
"The Convict" (Wordsworth) **12**:386, 388; **111**:202, 313, 315, 357
"The Convicts" (Auerbach)
See "Die Sträflinge"
"The Convict's Dream" (Crabbe) **26**:100
"Le convive des dernières fêtes" (Villiers de l'Isle Adam) **3**:590
"Le convive inconnu" (Villiers de l'Isle Adam)
See "Le convive des dernières fêtes"
"Coogee" (Kendall) **12**:181, 199
"The Coolun" (Ferguson) **33**:294
Coombe-Ellen (Bowles) **103**:54-5, 60, 70
"A Coon Hunt in Haunted Hollow" (Harris) **165**:265
Cooper Union Speech (Lincoln) **18**:212, 226, 240, 245-47, 253, 257, 264, 280
"The Cooper's Ward, or the Waif of the New Year" (Alger)
See *Timothy Crump's Ward*
"Cooranbean" (Kendall) **12**:182
"Il Copernico" (Leopardi) **129**:320, 351
"The Copperhead" (Boker) **125**:81
The Copperhead (Frederic) **10**:183-84, 188, 192-94, 203-04
"The Copse" (Mitford) **4**:408
Coquette (Norton) **47**:248
The Coquette, and Other Tales and Sketches, in Prose and Verse (Norton) **205**:130
The Coquette: Or, the History of Eliza Wharton (Foster)
See *The Coquette; or the History of Eliza Wharton. A Novel Founded on Fact, By a Lady of Massachusetts*
The Coquette; or the History of Eliza Wharton. A Novel Founded on Fact, By a Lady of Massachusetts (Foster) **99**:121-22, 126-27, 130-31, 133-35, 137-42, 144, 146-48, 150, 152, 154-57, 161, 163-65, 167-69, 171-72, 176-83, 185-89, 191-92, 197-200, 202-04
The Coquette or, the History of Elizabeth Wharton (Foster)
See *The Coquette; or the History of Eliza Wharton. A Novel Founded on Fact, By a Lady of Massachusetts*
"Les coquillages" (Verlaine) **2**:624; **51**:378-79
"Le cor" (Vigny) **7**:470, 474, 481, 484-85; **102**:335, 366
"Cor Mio" (Rossetti) **186**:295
"The Coral Insect" (Sigourney) **21**:296; **87**:334
Corayda; a Tale of Faith and Chivalry, and Other Poems (Jones) **222**:128, 164
Les corbeaux (Becque) **3**:13-19, 21-22
Cord and Creese (De Mille) **123**:121, 130
"La corde" (Baudelaire) **29**:109-10; **155**:56
La corde au cou (Gaboriau) **14**:18, 20, 22-3, 25
"La corde roide" (Banville) **9**:27
Corilla (Nerval) **1**:485; **67**:363
"Corinna" (Mörike) **201**:273
"Corinne at the Capitol" (Hemans) **71**:297
Corinne ou l'Italie (Staël-Holstein) **91**:291-92, 303, 314-15, 318, 320, 327-31, 337-38, 340-42, 344-56, 359-60, 365
"Coriolanus" (Hazlitt) **82**:164
"Corn" (Lanier) **6**:235-38, 246, 248, 252, 254, 259-60, 269, 278-79, 281; **118**:202-3, 205-6, 215, 218, 230, 233, 235-36, 238, 240, 262, 265, 270
"Corn Shucking Song" (Chivers) **49**:55
Cornaro (Hoffmann) **183**:184
Cornelius O'Dowd upon Men and Women and Other Things in General (Lever) **23**:303
Corner of the Woods (Storm)
See *Waldwinkel*
"The Cornflower" (Krylov) **1**:435
"The Cornflower" (Webster) **230**:310
"Corn-husking" (Arany)
See "Tengerihántás"
"El coro de ángeles" (Alarcón) **219**:47, 49
"Coro dei morti" (Leopardi) **129**:349
"Corona Christi" (Mörike) **201**:275
The Coronal (Child) **6**:198; **73**:42, 59
"The Coronation" (Barham) **77**:19, 26
"Coronation Soliloquy" (Hunt) **1**:423; **70**:258
"Corporal Munoz" (Isaacs)
See "El cabo Muñoz"
"A Corpse Going to a Ball" (Smith) **187**:334
Corpus Inscriptionum Semitacarum (Renan) **26**:399
Correspondance (Baudelaire) **155**:61, 71, 76, 100, 109, 113, 116
Correspondance (Flaubert) **2**:255; **10**:150; **62**:101, 105-6, 114-15, 123; **66**:289; **135**:137; **179**:36, 58-62, 65, 82; **185**:212, 232, 234, 292
Correspondance (Mallarmé) **210**:177, 206, 244
Correspondance (Musset) **150**:316
Correspondance (Sand) **42**:329-31, 370, 372-73; **174**:185, 187, 218, 249
Correspondance (Stendhal) **23**:365; **178**:201
Correspondance avec Hector Malot: 1862-1884 (Vallès) **71**:357-58, 372-73, 376
Correspondance de C. A. Sainte-Beuve, 1822-69 (Sainte-Beuve) **5**:336
Correspondance de George Sand et d'Alfred de Musset (Musset) **7**:266
Correspondance de H. de Balzac, 1819-1850 (Balzac) **5**:44; **153**:21, 147
Correspondance générale (Barbey d'Aurevilly) **213**:41, 56-57
Correspondance intime (Desbordes-Valmore) **97**:32, 35-6
"Correspondances" (Baudelaire) **6**:114-15; **29**:74, 82, 97; **55**:49; **155**:17, 101-2

"A Correspondence" (Turgenev)
See "Peripiska"
Correspondence (Austen)
See *Jane Austen's Letters to Her Sister Cassandra and Others*
Correspondence (Brontë)
See *The Brontës: Their Lives, Friendships, and Correspondence*
Correspondence (Cowper)
See *The Correspondence of William Cowper*
Correspondence (Emerson) **98**:66
Correspondence (Lampman)
See *An Annotated Edition of the Correspondence between Archibald Lampman and Edward William Thomson, 1890-1898*
Correspondence (Melville) **91**:218, 220, 222; **193**:161; **221**:217
Correspondence (Mill) **102**:304, 306, 311-12
Correspondence (Southey) **97**:291
Correspondence (Vigny) **102**:378, 384
Correspondence (Whitman) **81**:308
Correspondence (Williams) **135**:308
The Correspondence and Diaries of the Right Hon. John Wilson Croker (Croker) **10**:96-97
The Correspondence of Arthur Hugh Clough (Prescott) **163**:39, 73, 82, 128, 130
Correspondence of Fräulein Günderode and Bettina von Arnim (Arnim)
See *Die Günderode: Den Studenten*
The Correspondence of Gerard Manley Hopkins and Richard Watson Dixon (Hopkins) **189**:35, 43, 45, 48-49, 68, 112-13, 118, 136, 147
The Correspondence of Henry Crabb Robinson with the Wordsworth Circle, 1808-1866 (Robinson) **15**:189
The Correspondence of Henry David Thoreau (Thoreau) **138**:117, 120-21, 124, 126-28, 130; **207**:300
The Correspondence of Margaret Fuller (Fuller) **211**:113
The Correspondence of Sammuel Richardson (Barbauld) **50**:17, 19
The Correspondence of Samuel Richardson (Barbauld) **185**:74, 79
The Correspondence of Walt Whitman (Whitman) **205**:226
The Correspondence of William Cowper (Cowper) **8**:105, 128; **94**:23-5, 28-9
Correspondence with a Child (Arnim)
See *Goethes Briefwechsel mit einem Kinde: Seinem Denkmal*
Correspondence with John Keble (Newman) **38**:314
"Correspondences" (Cranch) **115**:9, 22, 35-6, 54, 67
"Correspondencia de 'El Duende'" (Larra) **17**:269
"Corridas de torros" (Larra) **17**:269
"Corrupt Youth" (Eminescu) **33**:245
Corruption (Moore) **110**:171
The Corsair (Byron) **2**:61-62, 70, 86, 89-90, 95, 99; **12**:110; **109**:102, 118; **149**:9, 158, 161
"Corsica" (Barbauld) **50**:9; **185**:31-32, 34-35, 38, 119-20, 124, 140-41, 145-46, 149
The Corsican Brothers (Boucicault) **41**:30, 32
Corsino (Balzac) **153**:150, 152
"Cortege" (Verlaine) **51**:378
"La corza blanca" (Bécquer) **106**:88-90, 108, 156
"Corza blanca" (Bécquer)
See "La corza blanca"
Una cosa rara o sia bellezza ed onestá (Da Ponte) **50**:83
Cosas que fueron (Alarcon) **1**:15; **219**:18
Cosette (Hugo) **3**:246
Cosi fan tutte o la scoula delle amanti (Da Ponte) **50**:82, 84-5, 92, 94-6, 98
"Cosi gl'interi giorni" (Foscolo) **8**:278
Cosima (Sand) **42**:309
Cosmo de' Medici, an Historical Tragedy (Horne) **127**:236, 238, 241, 253-54, 256, 258, 270
Cosmos: A Sketch of a Physical Description of the Universe (Humboldt)
See *Kosmos: Entwurf einer physischen Weltbeschreibung*
"Cossack Cradlesong" (Lermontov) **5**:300
"The Cossacks" (Mérimée) **6**:353
"The Cost of Improvement" (Barnes) **75**:103
"Cost of Production" (Bagehot) **10**:20
A Cosy Couple (Lewes) **25**:291
Cot and Cradle Stories (Traill) **31**:323
"The Cottage" (Very) **9**:378
The Cottage Cook; or, Mrs. Jones's Cheap Dishes (More) **141**:189
Cottage Economy: Containing Information Relating to the Brewing of Beer, Making of Bread, Keeping of Cows (Cobbett) **49**:110, 114-15, 130, 138, 140, 146, 152, 156-57, 175-78, 181-82
"The Cottage Girl" (Child) **73**:128, 132-34
"A Cottage in Kolonna" (Pushkin) **83**:272
"The Cottage Maiden" (Runeberg) **41**:312, 321
"The Cottage on the Hill" (Hayne) **94**:161
"A Cottage Scene" (Sigourney) **21**:310
"The Cottager to Her Infant" (Wordsworth) **25**:421; **138**:311
The Cottagers of Glenburnie: A Tale for the Farmer's Ingle-nook (Hamilton) **153**:264-66, 274-75, 277, 295, 301-3, 306-7, 311-12, 319-22, 326, 331, 356
The Cottages of Our Hinds (Miller) **143**:13
"The Cotton Boll" (Timrod) **25**:360, 363, 368, 370, 372, 374-77, 384, 387-88
"Couchant d'hiver" (Laforgue) **221**:19
"Coucher de soleil" (Leconte de Lisle) **29**:216
"Le coucher du soleil romantique" (Baudelaire) **29**:88; **155**:18, 20
"Le Coucher d'un petit garçon" (Desbordes-Valmore) **97**:29, 38
"Could That Sweet Darkness Where They Dwell" (Dickinson) **21**:69
"Councillor Krespel" (Hoffmann)
See "Rat Krespel"
"Counsel to an Unknown Young Man" (Vigny) **7**:483
"The Counsels of Old Men Despised, or, the Revolt and Division of Empire" (Webster) **30**:424
"The Count Arnaldos" (Lockhart) **6**:297
Count Basil (Baillie) **2**:31, 34, 39-40, 43; **71**:4, 6, 12-13, 16, 28-30, 32, 35-38, 43, 45, 47-48, 51, 66; **151**:11, 14, 17, 37, 52, 55, 77, 114
Count Benyowsky; or, The Conspiracy of Kamtschatka (Kotzebue)
See *Graf Benyowsky, oder die Verschwörung auf Kamschatka*
Count Donski (Sacher-Masoch) **31**:289
Count Frontenac and New France under Louis XIV (Parkman) **12**:336, 341, 372, 375
"Count Gismond" (Browning) **19**:129; **79**:164
Count Julian (Landor) **14**:157-58, 161, 176, 182, 192-94
Count Julian (Simms) **3**:507-08
Count Nulin (Pushkin)
See *Graf Nulin*
"The Count of Gleichen" (Taylor) **89**:310
The Count of Monte Cristo (Dumas)
See *Le comte de Monte-Cristo*
The Count of Monte-Cristo (Dumas)
See *Le comte de Monte-Cristo*
The Count of Morian, The Count of Morion, Woman's Revenge (Dumas)
See *Le comte de Moret*
Count Robert of Paris (Scott) **15**:309, 314; **69**:313-14, 319-20, 333-34; **209**:182, 199-200, 219
Count Waldemar (Freytag)
See *Graf Waldemar: Schauspiel in fünf Akten*
"The Counterfeit Coin" (Baudelaire)
See "La fausse monnaie"
"Countess" (Le Fanu)
See "A Passage in the Secret History of an Irish Countess"
"The Countess" (Whittier) **8**:516, 519; **59**:360, 371
"Countess Laura" (Boker) **125**:77
The Countess of Rudolstadt (Sand)
See *La comtesse de Rudolstadt*
"The Counting-House" (Turgenev) **21**:377
"A Country Apothecary" (Mitford) **4**:408
The Country Attorney (Cumberland) **167**:158, 191, 193
"A Country Barber" (Mitford) **4**:408
"Country Boys" (Mitford) **4**:401
"A Country Christmas" (Alcott) **58**:47
"The Country Church" (Irving) **19**:327-28
"The Country Doctor" (Turgenev) **21**:451-52; **37**:435; **122**:293
Country Doctor (Balzac)
See *Le Médecin de Campagne*
A Country Gentleman and His Family (Oliphant) **11**:460, 462; **94**:161; **61**:210-1, 241
"The Country Girl" (Clare) **9**:75
"The Country Girl" (Hogg) **109**:203
"The Country Inn" (Turgenev)
See "The Inn"
The Country Inn (Baillie) **2**:34-35; **71**:2, 13, 64; **151**:36, 115
"The Country Justice" (Crabbe) **26**:133
"The Country Parson" (Balzac)
See *Le Curé de village*
The Country Seat (Barham) **77**:6
Country Stories (Mitford) **4**:401
"The Country Sunday" (Jefferies) **47**:112-13, 138
The Country Waif (Sand)
See *François le Champi*
The Country-House on the Rhine (Auerbach)
See *Das Landhaus am Rhein*
"The Countryman" (Martí)
See "Hombre del campo"
"The Countryside" (Pushkin)
See "Derevnya"
"The County Mayo" (Ferguson) **33**:287
"Un coup de dés" (Baudelaire) **155**:96
Un coup de dés jamais n'abolira le hasard (Mallarmé) **4**:379, 383-86, 392, 395-96; **41**:248-51, 267, 277, 280, 285-88, 301; **210**:156, 163-64, 175, 177, 184-86, 189, 195, 210, 219-20, 241, 244, 257, 264
"Un coup d'etat" (Maupassant) **1**:469
La coupe et les lèvres (Musset) **7**:256, 258, 260, 264, 274; **150**:234, 301, 304, 313-15
"Cour" (Mallarmé) **210**:260
La cour d'Assises (Scribe) **16**:394
"Courage" (Arnold) **29**:23, 27
Courage and Caution (Ueda Akinari)
See *Tandai shoshin roku*
"La Couronne effeuillé" (Desbordes-Valmore) **97**:13
"Cours de 1834-35" (Michelet) **218**:335
Cours de philosophie positive (Comte) **54**:166-88, 190, 205, 209-12, 217-39, 241, 244
Cours de politique (Constant)
See *Principes de politique applicables à tous les gouvernements représentatifs*
Cours familier de littérature: Un entretien par mois (Lamartine) **11**:262, 272-73; **190**:203-5, 207-10, 227, 242-43
A Course of Lectures on Dramatic Art and Literature (Schlegel)
See *Ueber dramatische Kunst und Litteratur*
A Course of Lectures on Dramatic Arts and Literature (Schlegel)
See *Über dramatische Kunst und Litteratur*

Course of Lectures on Positive Philosophy (Comte)
See *Cours de philosophie positive*
"The Courses of Religious Thought" (Gladstone) **213**:112, 160
Court Circular (Dodgson) **139**:57
Court Netherleigh (Wood) **178**:288
"A Courteous Explanation" (Arnold) **6**:62
"The Courtin'" (Lowell) **2**:511, 513-14, 522; **90**:193
Court-intriguing and Love (Schiller)
See *Kabale und Liebe*
The Courtship of Miles Standish (Longfellow) **2**:478-80, 483-84, 487, 495, 498; **45**:103, 106, 109-10, 113-14, 124, 128, 134, 137, 139, 142, 144-45, 147, 149-50, 159, 187; **103**:283
"The Courtship of Susan Bell" (Trollope) **101**:235
"The Courtship of the Yonghy Bonghy Bo" (Lear) **3**:297-98, 301, 309
Cousin Bette (Balzac)
See *La cousine Bette*
Cousin Henry (Trollope) **6**:470; **101**:251, 309, 311
"Cousin Kate" (Rossetti) **2**:575; **50**:270; **66**:329, 331, 350-3, 355
"Cousin Marshall" (Martineau) **26**:305, 351; **137**:264, 267, 315
Cousin Mary (Oliphant) **11**:462
Cousin Phillis (Gaskell)
See *Cousin Phillis: A Tale*
Cousin Phillis: A Tale (Gaskell) **5**:185, 190-92, 197-98, 201-3, 205; **70**:185, 198, 224-25, 227-28, 230, 232; **97**:110; **214**:190
Le cousin Pons (Balzac) **5**:51-52, 55, 76-77, 81-82; **153**:9-10, 46, 64, 66-68, 80, 146, 150, 152-53
"La Cousine" (Nerval) **1**:478; **67**:306
La cousine Bette (Balzac) **53**:35; **153**:35-36, 64, 66, 68-69, 73-76, 82, 125, 146, 152-53
A Cousin's Conspiracy (Alger) **8**:42; **83**:117
"The Covenanters" (Landon) **15**:161
The Covenanters (Galt) **110**:107
The Covetous Knight (Pushkin)
See *Skupoi rytsar*
The Cowled Lover (Bird) **1**:87, 89; **197**:6
"Cowper Hill" (Clare) **9**:78, 108
"Cowper's Grave" (Barrett Browning) **1**:124-6; **66**:44; **170**:106
"Crabbed Age and Youth" (Stevenson) **193**:213
"The Cracked Bell" (Baudelaire)
See "La cloche fêlée"
The Cracked Pot (Kleist)
See *Der Zerbrochene Krug*
"Cradle" (Whitman)
See "Out of the Cradle Endlessly Rocking"
"A Cradle and a Grave" (Lazarus) **109**:291
"A Cradle Song" (Blake) **13**:220; **37**:3, 24, 31, 38, 40, 61, 69, 71-2, 74-5, 92
"The Craft of History" (Bello) **131**:123
"Craintes" (Verlaine) **230**:171
"The Crane" (Lenau) **16**:276
"Cranes" (Radishchev) **190**:314
"The Cranes of Ibycus" (Lazarus) **109**:294
"The Cranes of Ibycus" (Schiller)
See "Die Kraniche des Ibykus"
Cranford (Gaskell) **5**:185-87, 189-91, 193, 197-201, 203, 205; **70**:119, 185, 188, 193, 197, 199, 216-23; **97**:103-76; **137**:41, 167; **214**:220, 222, 234-35, 237, 239-40, 290-92, 294, 296, 332, 334, 336, 338, 340, 343-44
"Le crapaud" (Corbière) **43**:10
Le crapaud (Hugo) **3**:271
The Crater (Cooper)
See *Mark's Reef*
The Crater; or, Vulcan's Peak (Cooper) **1**:220-21; **27**:144; **54**:263, 276
The Crayfish: An Introduction to the Study of Zoology (Huxley) **67**:9, 11, 95
The Crayon Miscellany (Irving) **2**:373; **95**:253
A Crayon Miscellany (Irving)
See *The Crayon Miscellany*
Crayonné au théâtre (Mallarmé) **4**:373; **41**:269-71, 301; **210**:250, 265-66
"La creación" (Bécquer) **106**:97
"Cream Tarts" (Stevenson)
See "Story of the Young Man with the Cream Tarts"
"The Created" (Very) **9**:378, 383-84
"Creation" (Emerson) **1**:282
"Credat Judaeus Apella" (Gordon) **21**:160, 180
"Creed en Dios" (Bécquer) **106**:97, 130, 136
"The Creek of the Four Graves" (Harpur) **114**:92, 96-99, 101, 104-5, 115-17, 121, 123-27, 131, 134, 144, 147, 151-53, 158, 167
"The Cremona Violin" (Hoffmann)
See "Rat Krespel"
"Crépuscule de dimanche d'été" (Laforgue) **53**:270
"Le crépuscule du matin" (Baudelaire) **29**:101, 113; **55**:15, 24, 62
"Le crépuscule du soir" (Baudelaire) **6**:129-30; **29**:101, 109, 113; **55**:15, 22, 24-5
"Crépuscule du soir mystique" (Verlaine) **51**:361; **230**:163, 172
"Crepúsculo" (Silva) **114**:294, 299, 301-2, 313
"The Crescent Moon Shines in the Sky" (Grillparzer)
See "Der Halbmond glänzet am Himmel"
"Crest and Gulf" (Patmore) **9**:358, 362
"The Cretan" (Solomos) **15**:398, 404-05
"Crete" (Lampman) **25**:190
"Le cri de l'âme" (Lamartine) **11**:270
Le Cri du Peuple (Vallès) **71**:377
Crichton (Ainsworth) **13**:17-18, 21-22, 34, 36, 42
"The Cricket on the Hearth" (Dickens) **3**:165; **113**:51
The Cricket on the Hearth: A Fairy Tale of Home (Dickens) **211**:42
"The Crickets Sang" (Dickinson) **21**:67-9
"Cries of the Blindman" (Corbière)
See "Cris d'aveugle"
"Crime and Automatism" (Holmes) **14**:117, 132, 137
Crime and Punishment (Dostoevsky)
See *Prestuplenie i nakazanie*
Le crime d'Orcival (Gaboriau) **14**:16, 19, 21-7, 29, 33
"Crime of Love" (Verlaine)
See *Crimen Amoris*
Crimean Sonnets (Mickiewicz)
See *Sonety Krymskie*
Crimen Amoris (Verlaine) **51**:368-69, 372, 375
Crimes célèbres (Dumas) **11**:46
Les crimes de l'amour (Sade) **3**:468-70, 478, 481; **47**:309, 361
The Crimes of Passion (Sade)
See *Les crimes de l'amour*
Criminal Out of Infamy (Schiller) **69**:275; **166**:140, 147
The Criminal Prisons of London and Scenes of London Life (Mayhew)
See *The Great World of London*
"The Crimson Curtain" (Barbey d'Aurevilly)
See "Le rideau cramoisi"
"The Cripple" (Andersen)
See "Krøblingen"
"Crippled Jane" (Norton) **47**:252
"The cripple's wife" (Lonnrot) **53**:339
"Cris d'aveugle" (Corbière) **43**:11, 13, 17-18, 28-9, 32, 34
"Crisálidas" (Silva) **114**:299
Le Crise (Feuillet) **45**:77, 79, 88, 90
"Crise de vers" (Mallarmé) **41**:240, 267, 273-74, 284-85, 294
"Le crise de vers" (Mallarmé) **210**:158, 171, 184-85, 212, 225, 227, 233, 249, 257-59
"The Crisis" (Mérimée) **6**:353
The Crisis and A Crisis in the Life of an Actress (Kierkegaard) **34**:204, 252
"The Crisis and the Cuban Revolutionary Party" (Martí) **63**:168
Crisis Extraordinary (Paine) **62**:370
"Crisis política de España en el siglo XVI" (Martínez de la Rosa) **102**:252
"Cristina" (Browning) **19**:129
"El Cristo de la calavera" (Bécquer) **106**:99, 120, 130, 135
"El Cristo de la Luz" (Bécquer) **106**:147, 158
The Critic (Cumberland) **167**:200, 202
Critic (Fuller)
See *Margaret Fuller, Critic*
The Critic; or, Tragedy Rehearsed (Sheridan) **5**:357-58, 361-63, 367, 369-73, 378, 383; **91**:242, 244-45, 255-58, 260, 262-64
"Crítica ligera" (Silva) **114**:296
Critical and Historical Essays (Taine)
See *Essais de critique et d'histoire*
Critical and Historical Essays Contributed to the Edinburgh Review (Macaulay) **42**:65, 72, 76, 84, 87-88, 92-3, 103, 124, 152; **231**:294, 299
Critical and Miscellaneous Writings (Parker) **186**:207
A Critical Dissertation on the Poems of Ossian (Blair) **75**:115, 117-18, 125-26, 136
Critical Essay of Political Economy (Engels) **85**:8
Critical Essay on the Gospel of St. Luke (Schleiermacher)
See *Über die Schriften des Lukas: Ein kritischer Versuch*
Critical Essays and Literary Notes (Taylor) **89**:324, 341
Critical Essays on the Performers of the London Theatres, Including General Observations on the Practise (Hunt) **1**:406
"Critical Fancy" (Horne) **127**:257
Critical Fragment 42 (Schlegel) **226**:201
Critical Fragment 94 (Schlegel) **226**:199
Critical Fragment 96 (Schlegel) **226**:199-200
Critical Fragments (Schlegel) **226**:182, 185, 199-200
Critical Groves (Herder)
See *Kritische Wälder*
"The Critical Historians of Jesus" (Renan) **26**:368
"A Critical Letter" (Eminescu) **131**:310
"Critical Notice" (Brown) **74**:37
Critical Remarks on Dr Dorn's Chrestomathy of Pushtu (Burton) **42**:53
Critical Sylvae (Herder)
See *Kritische Wälder*
"Critical Words" (Eminescu) **33**:272
A Criticism of Criticism (Liszt)
See *A Criticism of the Critics Ulibischeff and Séroff*
A Criticism of the Critics Ulibischeff and Séroff (Liszt) **199**:305, 343
Criticisms (Schlegel) **142**:302
"Critics" (Parton) **86**:352
Critique de l'histoire des Girondins (Lamartine) **190**:216
"Critique des *Poèmes saturniens* " (Verlaine) **51**:388; **230**:192, 199
Critique of Hegel's Doctrine of the State (Marx) **114**:69-70
Critique of Judgment (Kant)
See *Kritik der Urtheilskraft*
Critique of Practical Reason (Kant)
See *Kritik der praktischen Vernunft*
Critique of Pure Reason (Kant)
See *Kritik der reinen Vernunft*
"Critique of the Gotha Program" (Marx) **114**:70
Critique of the Power of Judgment (Kant)
See *Kritik der Urtheilskraft*
Critique of the so-called First Epistle of Paul to Timothy (Schleiermacher) **107**:268
"A Critique of Walter Scott's New Novel Kenilworth" (Bestuzhev)
See "Kritika na novyi roman Val'ter Skotta—Kenil'vort"

Critiques and Addresses (Huxley) **67**:44
"Črkarska pravda" (Preseren) **127**:314-15
"A Crocodile" (Beddoes) **154**:42
"The Crocodile" (Dostoevsky)
See "Krokodil"
"The Crofton Boys" (Martineau) **26**:310, 323, 349; **137**:256-59, 262, 277, 281-83, 335
Crohoore of the Bill-Hook (Banim and Banim) **13**:115-17, 122-23, 125-30, 132-34, 139-41
"Croisilles" (Musset) **150**:227
The Croker Papers (Croker)
See *The Correspondence and Diaries of the Right Hon. John Wilson Croker*
Cromwell (Balzac) **5**:51
Cromwell (Hugo) **3**:233, 236, 241, 261, 268-69, 275; **21**:197, 201, 222-23, 226; **161**:186, 201, 228, 234, 236; **189**:249
"Cromwell" (Lamartine) **190**:253
Cromwell (Mérimée) **65**:44, 80, 86-7
Cromwell: A Prize Poem (Arnold) **218**:154-55
Cromwell et Charles 1er (Dumas) **71**:222
"The Crone" (Pavlova) **138**:33
"The Crooked Branch" (Gaskell) **5**:190, 201; **70**:189
"Crooked John" (Boyesen) **135**:13
"Crop Rotation" (Kierkegaard)
See "Rotation Method"
The Croppy (Banim and Banim) **13**:121, 125-27, 129, 134-35, 137-38, 147, 151
"Croquis femenino" (Casal) **131**:258-60, 265
"The Cross of Snow" (Longfellow) **45**:116, 125, 132, 137
The Cross on the Baltic (Werner)
See *Das Kreuz an der Ostsee: Ein Trauerspiel vom Verfasser der Söhne des Thales. Erster Theil: Die Brautnacht*
"Cross-Examination" (Allingham) **25**:4
"Crossing Brooklyn Ferry" (Whitman) **4**:569, 571, 582, 600; **31**:389, 391, 405, 407, 431, 443, 445; **81**:260, 359, 362-68; **205**:202, 207, 226, 228-29, 233, 246, 261, 309, 315, 330-34, 336, 340, 342
"Crossing the Bar" (Tennyson) **30**:223, 280, 282; **115**:239; **202**:180, 290-91
"A Cross-Road Epitaph" (Levy) **59**:98
"Le croup" (Daudet) **1**:248
The Crow (Gozzi)
See *Il corvo*
"Crow and Fox" (Krylov) **1**:439
"The Crowd" (Turgenev) **122**:243, 247
"Crowds" (Baudelaire)
See "Les foules"
"The Crowing of the Red Cock" (Lazarus) **8**:415-17, 419; **109**:293, 304, 327, 337, 343
"Crowland Abbey" (Clare) **86**:108, 110, 112
"Crowley Castle" (Gaskell) **5**:206; **70**:189
Crown Bride (Tegner) **2**:613
The Crown Guardians (Arnim)
See *Die Kronenwächter*
Crowned and Buried (Barrett Browning) **66**:44
"A Crowned King" (Blake) **37**:29
"The Crowning of the Cock" (Lazarus)
See "The Crowing of the Red Cock"
The Crows (Becque)
See *Les corbeaux*
"Le crucifix" (Lamartine) **11**:255, 268, 270-72, 278, 283; **190**:218, 225
"Un Crucifix" (Verlaine) **51**:359
"Cruel Agnes" (Webster) **230**:245
"The Cruel Vengeance" (Gogol)
See "Strašnaja mest"
Cruelty and Despair or the Black Cave and the Wretched Incense Burners (Eminescu) **33**:266
The Cruise of the Betsey; or, A Summer Ramble among the Fossilferous Deposits of the Hebrides (Miller) **143**:6, 13, 29, 48
"Crumbling is not an instant's Act" (Dickinson) **171**:200
"La cruz del diablo" (Bécquer) **106**:97, 110, 121
"Cruzifixus" (Storm) **195**:45
"The Cry at Midnight" (Patmore) **9**:359
"A Cry for Ireland" (Mangan) **27**:311
"The Cry of Hungary" (Chivers) **49**:50
"The Cry of the Children" (Barrett Browning) **1**:115-7, 121, 123-5; **61**:5, 9, 42; **66**:25, 42, 44; **170**:105-7
"The Cry of the Human" (Barrett Browning) **1**:113, 115, 117; **170**:107
"A Cry to Arms" (Timrod) **25**:360, 367, 372, 384
The Cryptogram (De Mille) **123**:119, 121
"The Crystal" (Lanier) **6**:245, 248; **118**:219-21, 234, 239, 268
"The Crystal Bell" (O'Brien) **21**:236, 245-46
"The Crystal Cabinet" (Blake) **13**:172, 243; **173**:109, 111, 117; **190**:27, 89; **201**:64
Csák végnapjai (Madach) **19**:370
"Csaladi kör" (Arany) **34**:16
"A csárda romjai" (Petofi) **21**:285
"Császár Ferenc őnagyságához" (Petofi) **21**:278
"Csatadal" (Petofi) **21**:286
"Csokonai" (Petofi) **21**:283
"C-Stage Reading Text" (Wordsworth) **206**:287
"¿Cuál es el método o sistema preferible para escribir la historia?" (Martínez de la Rosa) **102**:248, 254
"¿Cuál es la influencia del espíritu del siglo actual sobre la literatura?" (Martínez de la Rosa) **102**:254
Cuauhtemoc, The Last Aztec Emperor (Gómez de Avellaneda)
See *Guatimozín, último emperador de México*
The Cuba Journal, 1833-1835 (Hawthorne) **150**:163, 165-66, 173, 180, 185-86, 188, 211
The Cuban Album of the Good and the Beautiful (Gómez de Avellaneda)
See *Album cubano de lo bueno y lo bello*
"The Cuban Soul" (Martí)
See "El alma cubana"
"Cuckoo" (Wordsworth) **12**:431, 436
The Cuckoo in the Nest (Oliphant) **11**:461
"Cudesa i znamenija" (Leskov) **174**:77
"Čudni dihur" (Preseren) **127**:315
Cudzoziemszczyzna; czyli, Nauka zbawlenia (Fredro) **8**:285
Cuento (Espronceda)
See *El estudiante de Salamanca*
Cuentos amartorios (Alarcon)
See *Novelas cortas: Cuentos amartorios*
"Los cuentos negros" (Silva) **114**:300
Cuentos negros (Silva) **114**:267
"Cuerpo y alma" (Casal) **131**:240, 245, 256, 271
"La cueva de la mora" (Bécquer) **106**:99, 130, 133
"La cueva de Taganana" (Villaverde) **121**:333
"Cui Bono?" (Gordon) **21**:154, 156, 160, 164
"Cui Bono?" (Prescott) **163**:347
"The Cuirassier: A Partisan Officer's Story" (Bestuzhev)
See "Latnik: Rasskaz partizanskogo ofitsera"
Cúirt an Mheadhon Oidhche (Merriman) **70**:348-88
"Cúirt an Mheán Oíche" (Merriman)
See *Cúirt an Mheadhon Oidhche*
Cúirt an Mheán Oíche (Merriman)
See *Cúirt an Mheadhon Oidhche*
The Cultural History of Greece (Burckhardt)
See *Griechische Kulturgeschichte*
"Culture" (Emerson) **38**:174, 209; **98**:9, 68
Culture and Anarchy: An Essay in Political and Social Criticism (Arnold) **6**:53, 60, 62; **29**:10, 19-20, 42, 45; **89**:54, 59-66, 81, 84, 101, 104, 110-11, 121-22, 127, 132; **126**:1-125; **218**:111, 119, 121, 137, 142, 172, 174, 178, 184, 194-98, 209, 212-20, 228, 231, 233, 238, 241, 250, 252-53, 256-57, 261-62
"Culture and Its Enemies" (Arnold) **218**:209, 241
Culture and its Enemies (Arnold) **29**:19-21; **126**:7, 16, 23, 40-41, 44
Culture's Garland (Field) **3**:209, 211-12
"Culver Dell and the Squire" (Barnes) **75**:57, 104
"Cumberland" (Longfellow) **45**:189
"The Cummerbund" (Lear) **3**:296, 307
"Çunacépa" (Leconte de Lisle) **29**:219-20, 223, 234
Cunegarde die Heilage, Römisch-Deutsche Kaiserin : Ein romantisches Schauspiel in fünf Akten (Werner) **189**:332, 347, 352, 356-57
The Cup (Tennyson) **30**:265-66
"The Cup of Life" (Lampman) **25**:189, 198, 206, 218; **194**:128
"The Cup of Life" (Lermontov) **5**:299; **126**:223
"Cupid and Psyche" (Morris) **4**:416, 427-28, 445, 447
"The Cupid of Falconet" (Derzhavin) **215**:33
"Cupido" (Taylor) **89**:317
Cupid's Arrow Poisoned (Beddoes) **3**:37-39
The Curate in Charge (Oliphant) **11**:439, 461-62; **221**:275, 277-78
Curator Carsten (Storm)
See *Carsten Curator*
Le curé de Tours (Balzac) **53**:25; **153**:8-9, 117, 131, 149, 151-52
Le Curé de village (Balzac) **153**:71
A Cure for Melancholy (Shewing the Way to Do Much Good with Little Money) (More) **27**:346
A Cure for Melancholy: Showing the Way to Do Much Good with Little Money (More) **141**:191-92, 217, 219-20
The Curé of Tours (Balzac)
See *Le curé de Tours*
"The Cure on the Banks of the Rhone" (Barbauld) **50**:14
"Curfew" (Longfellow) **45**:151; **103**:293
Curiosa Mathematica, Part I: A New Theory of Parallels (Dodgson) **2**:111
Curiosa Mathematica. Part II: Pillow Problems Thought Out during Wakeful Hours (Dodgson) **139**:11
Curiosés estheétiques (Baudelaire) **29**:86
"Curiosités déplacées" (Laforgue) **53**:270; **221**:30, 85
Curiosities: A Second Series (D'Israeli)
See *A Second Series of Curiosities of Literature, Consisting of Researches in Literary, Biographical, and Political History; of Critical and Philosophical Inquiries and of Secret History*
Curiosities of Literature (D'Israeli) **217**:276, 278, 280, 282-85, 287-92, 294-97, 305, 332-35, 338-40
"The Curious Man" (Pushkin) **83**:272
"A Curious Man's Dream" (Baudelaire)
See "Le rêve d'un curieux"
"The Curlew Song" (Kendall) **12**:191
"The Current Has Thickened and Grown Opaque" (Tyutchev) **34**:393
"Curse" (Grillparzer)
See "Verwünschung"
"A Curse for a Nation" (Barrett Browning) **61**:6, 44; **170**:40, 56, 77-78
The Curse of Clifton: A Tale of Expiation and Redemption (Southworth) **26**:432-34, 438, 442
The Curse of Kehama (Southey) **8**:453, 456, 459, 461, 468, 470, 474, 476-77; **97**:261, 278-79, 291, 293-94, 297-98, 307, 322, 329, 336
"The Curse of Love" (Petofi)
See "Szerelem átka"
"The Curse of Mother Flood" (Kendall) **12**:182
"The Curse of the Joyces" (Ferguson) **33**:289
"Curse of the Laureate" (Hogg) **109**:248

"The Cursed Mountain" (Gómez de Avellaneda)
See "La montaña maldita"
"Cursed Place" (Schumann) **143**:140
Cursory Reflections on Political and Commercial Topics (Galt) **110**:76, 92, 94
Cursory Remarks on an Enquiry into the Expediency and Propriety of Public or Social Worship (Hays) **114**:177-78, 185, 194
"Cursory Remarks on Readers, and the Nature of Poetry; on Dreams and Visions" (Dyer) **129**:94
"Cursory Remarks on the Federal Constitution" (Brackenridge) **227**:116
Cursory Strictures on Chief Justice Eyre's Charge to the Grand Jury (Godwin)
See *Cursory Strictures on the Charge delivered by Lord Chief Justice Eyre to the Grand Jury, October 2, 1794*
Cursory Strictures on the Charge delivered by Lord Chief Justice Eyre to the Grand Jury, October 2, 1794 (Godwin) **14**:67; **130**:5, 47, 88
"Curtal Sonnets" (Hopkins) **189**:62
"Curtius" (Crawford) **12**:155
"Curtius rescued from the Gulf" (Cumberland) **167**:134
"The Custom-House" (Hawthorne) **2**:298, 311; **10**:271, 314; **39**:222, 234, 237, 240; **79**:331; **191**:178, 187, 256
"Cuvstvitel'nyj i xolodnyj, dva xaraktera" (Karamzin) **173**:268, 280, 312
The Cyclopaedia of Medieval Costume (Planché) **42**:274
Cyclopaedia of Modern Travel (Taylor) **89**:354
"Cyclopeedy" (Field) **3**:211
Les cydalises (Nerval) **1**:478; **67**:306
Cydippe (Stagnelius) **61**:248, 265
"Cyganskaja pljaska" (Derzhavin) **215**:17-18, 32, 34
"Le cygne" (Baudelaire) **6**:80, 115-16; **29**:81, 100, 107, 115; **55**:3, 16, 19, 26, 29, 36-7, 41-2, 64, 67; **155**:3-7, 21, 101
"Cyhyryne Cyhyryne" (Shevchenko) **54**:364, 378-9, 388
"Cymbeline" (Lamb) **125**:306
Cymon and Iphigenia (Planché) **42**:277
Cynthio and Bugboo (Beddoes) **3**:33
Cyprianus (Storm)
See *Der Spiegel des Cyprianus*
Cyprianusspiegel (Storm)
See *Der Spiegel des Cyprianus*
Cyprus Leaves from the Grave of Dear Ethel (Petofi)
See *Czipruslombok Etelke sírjáról*
"Cythera" (Verlaine)
See "Cythère"
"Cythère" (Verlaine) **51**:378, 380; **230**:173
"Cywilizacja" (Norwid) **17**:378-79, 383
"Czar Alexander the Second (13th of March 1881)" (Rossetti) **77**:298
"Czar Nikita" (Pushkin)
See "Tsar Nikita"
Czarne kwiaty (Norwid) **17**:371, 373
"Czas i prawda" (Norwid) **17**:374
"Czaty" (Mickiewicz) **101**:164
"Czatyr Dagh" (Mickiewicz)
See "Czatyrdah"
"Czatyrdah" (Mickiewicz) **3**:403; **101**:188-90
Czipruslombok Etelke sírjáról (Petofi) **21**:279, 285
"A D. D. D., desde el campo" (Heredia) **209**:162-63, 165
"Da ich ein Knabe war ..." (Hölderlin) **16**:174, 176
"Da, mnogo bylo nas . . ." (Pavlova) **138**:20
"A Dacian's Prayer" (Eminescu) **131**:286-87, 296-98, 346
"Daddy Biggs Scrape at Cockerell's Bend" (Hooper) **177**:210
Daddy Goriot; or, Unrequited Affection (Balzac)
See *Le père Goriot: Histoire Parisienne*
Daddy O'Dowd (Boucicault) **41**:28-9, 34
Daddy's Gogu (Eminescu) **33**:266
Dad's Always Right (Andersen) **79**:25
"Dad's Dog School" (Harris) **23**:140, 159-60, 162-63; **165**:164, 182, 201-2, 207-8, 211, 226, 228, 241-42, 255-57, 259, 275, 277-79
The Daemon of the World (Shelley) **175**:269-70
"Daffodils" (Wordsworth) **12**:420, 427, 431
Dagbøger (Andersen) **214**:66
"Dagestan Theme" (Bestuzhev) **131**:203
"The Dagger" (Pushkin) **83**:253-54
"Un dahlia" (Verlaine) **2**:630; **230**:164
"The Daisy" (Andersen)
See "Gaaseurten"
"The Daisy" (Tennyson) **30**:215, 234, 236
"The Daisy Follows Soft the Sun" (Dickinson) **21**:79; **77**:147-48
"The Daisy's Mistake" (Osgood) **141**:343
"Dalaim" (Petofi) **21**:264, 284
"The Dale" (Lamartine)
See "Le vallon"
"Dalforrás" (Madach) **19**:369
Dalila (Feuillet) **45**:74-5, 78-81, 88
"The Dalliance of the Eagles" (Whitman) **4**:572, 592, 602-03; **205**:309
The Daltons; or, Three Roads in Life (Lever) **23**:289, 292, 297, 304-05
"La dama de Amboto" (Gómez de Avellaneda) **111**:65
"Dama i fefela" (Leskov) **25**:229
La dame aux camélias (Dumas) **9**:219-20, 223-25, 227, 229, 231-32, 234-37, 239-41, 245-47, 250, 252-55
La dame aux perles (Dumas) **9**:219
La dame blanche (Scribe) **16**:401, 408
La dame de Monsoreau (Dumas) **11**:52, 68, 74; **71**:190-91, 193-94, 205, 242
Dames et demoiselles (Banville) **9**:31-32
The Damnation of Theron Ware (Frederic) **10**:184-86, 189-99, 202-06, 208-17, 219-20; **175**:94-183
Damned Album (Verlaine)
See *Album zutique*
"Damned Women" (Baudelaire)
See "Femmes damnées"
"Les damnés" (Leconte de Lisle) **29**:223, 228
Damokles (Klinger) **1**:427
Damon and Pythias (Banim) **13**:128
The Damsel of Darien (Simms) **3**:508
"The Damsel of Peru" (Bryant) **6**:162, 169, 172
Damy i huzary (Fredro) **8**:289-92
Dan, the Newsboy (Alger) **8**:43
"The Dance" (Barrett Browning) **1**:121
"The dance" (Lonnrot) **53**:339
"The Dance" (Schiller)
See "Der Tanz"
"The Dance, A Personal Adventure of the Author" (Longstreet) **159**:117, 133, 137-38, 144-45, 147, 176, 182, 192, 199-202, 204
"Dance of Death" (Beddoes) **3**:34
The Dance of Death (Lazarus)
See *Songs of a Semite: The Dance to Death, and Other Poems*
"The Dance to Death" (Lazarus) **8**:415-17, 420-24, 426, 428; **109**:289, 294, 296, 302, 304, 311-12, 337, 343-44
"The Dance to the Death" (Lazarus)
See "The Dance to Death"
The Dance to the Death (Lazarus)
See *Songs of a Semite: The Dance to Death, and Other Poems*
"The Dancing Bear" (Adams) **175**:29, 31-32
"The Dancing Girl of Shamakha" (Gobineau)
See "La danseuse de Shamakha"
"Dancing on the hill-tops" (Rossetti) **186**:235, 238
The Dandie's Rout (Norton) **47**:246, 248, 250
The Dane (Grundtvig)
See *Danevirke*
Danesbury House (Wood) **178**:314-15, 330
Danevirke (Grundtvig) **158**:143-44, 148-49, 151, 153, 167, 169
"Danger of Praise" (Keble) **87**:119
"Danger of Regulating Our Conduct by the Rules of Romantic Sentiment" (Mackenzie) **41**:190
Dangerous Acquaintances (Laclos)
See *Les liaisons dangereuses; ou, Lettres recueillies dans une société et publiées pour l'instruction de quelques autres*
"The Dangerous Classes" (Parker) **186**:207
Dangerous Connections; or, Letters Collected in a Society, and Published for the Instruction of Other Societies (Laclos)
See *Les liaisons dangereuses; ou, Lettres recueillies dans une société et publiées pour l'instruction de quelques autres*
"A Dangerous Virtue" (Boyesen) **135**:13, 21, 28
"Les dangers de l'inconduite" (Balzac) **35**:26-7
The Dangers of Coquetry (Opie) **65**:174, 178-9
"The Dangers of Immigration" (Boyesen) **135**:16, 30
"The Dangers of Love" (Dacre)
See "The Triumph of Pleasure"
"Dangers Which Threaten the Rights of Man in America" (Parker) **186**:171
"Daniel and the Devil" (Field) **3**:206
Daniel Deronda (Eliot) **4**:108-09, 112-14, 121-26, 128-29, 133, 135-37, 144, 152; **13**:295, 317-18, 320, 322, 344; **23**:49-100; **41**:68, 70, 72, 77, 79, 121, 129, 133-34; **49**:237, 243; **89**:204; **118**:49, 51, 57, 60, 62, 76, 82, 102, 105, 107-10, 136, 164, 173, 182; **183**:33, 35, 45, 51, 55-56, 66, 94, 105, 144, 146, 151; **199**:159, 161, 203, 285-86, 290
Daniel Deronda (Eliot) **209**:25, 42-43
"Daniel Jovard ou la Conversion d'un classique" (Gautier) **59**:10, 27-8
La Daniella (Sand) **2**:592; **42**:311, 338; **57**:316
Danischmend (Wieland)
See *Geschichte des Philosophen Danischmende*
"The Danish Boy" (Wordsworth) **111**:212, 227
Danish Fairy Legends and Tales (Andersen)
See *Eventyr, fortalte for børn*
A Danish Story Book (Andersen)
See *Eventyr, fortalte for børn*
"Danksagung an den Bach" (Muller) **73**:363-64, 370
Dans la fournaise (Banville) **9**:30-31
"Dans la grotte" (Verlaine) **51**:378-80
"Dans la sierra" (Gautier) **59**:19
"Dans le ciel clair" (Leconte de Lisle) **29**:224
"Dans le rue, par un jour funèbre de Lyon" (Desbordes-Valmore) **97**:30
Dans les limbes (Verlaine) **230**:161, 166, 172
"Dans les rues" (Desbordes-Valmore) **97**:30
"Dans l'interminable..." (Verlaine) **51**:382
Danse des Morts (Flaubert) **62**:28
"Danse des Moucherons" (Lanier) **118**:242
"Danse macabre" (Baudelaire) **55**:23; **155**:12
"La danseuse de Shamakha" (Gobineau) **17**:69, 92, 103
Den Danske Statskirke (Grundtvig) **158**:119
"Dante" (Arany) **34**:19
"Dante" (Macaulay) **231**:292
Dante (Macaulay) **42**:116
Dante (Oliphant) **11**:439; **221**:233
"Dante and Beatrice" (Arnold) **126**:42
Dante and His Circle: With the Italian Poets Preceding Him, 1100/1200/1300 (Rossetti) **4**:497
"Dante at Verona" (Rossetti) **4**:493, 497, 518-19, 522, 525, 529-30; **77**:297, 337
"Dante Gabriel Rossetti" (Pater) **7**:306; **159**:257
Dante Symphony (Liszt) **199**:307-8
"Dante und die Göttliche Komödie" (Schlegel) **142**:300, 315

Danton's Death (Büchner)
See *Dantons Tod*
Dantons Tod (Büchner) **26**:3-5, 7-11, 14-17, 20, 23-8, 32-3, 35-48, 49, 51, 56, 62-6, 69-71; **146**:3-4, 6-7, 9-11, 15-16, 18, 20-24, 38, 40, 42-44, 46, 64, 67, 72, 91, 97, 104, 107
Danylo Reva (Shevchenko) **54**:367
"Daphles" (Hayne) **94**:153-58
"Daphne" (Kendall) **12**:181, 192
"Daphne" (Lazarus) **109**:294
Daphné-Deuxième consultation du Docteur Noir (Vigny) **7**:473-74, 485-86; **102**:380
"D'après ce que j'ai vu . . ." (Verlaine) **230**:172
"Darby Anvil" (Longstreet) **159**:125, 193
"Darby, The Politician" (Longstreet) **159**:164
Darby's Return (Dunlap) **2**:208, 210-11, 213, 215, 217
"Dare You See a Soul at the White Heat?" (Dickinson) **21**:21; **77**:67
"Darest Thou Now O Soul" (Whitman) **4**:586; **205**:340
"Dark Ages" (Thoreau) **138**:120
"A Dark Day" (Rossetti) **4**:491
"Dark Days" (Parton) **86**:347
"The Dark Days of Autumn" (Clare) **9**:111
"Dark House By Which Once More I Stand" (Tennyson) **30**:273
"The Dark Interpreter" (De Quincey) **4**:88-89; **87**:9
"The Dark Ladie" (Coleridge) **197**:187
"Dark Night, Clear Night" (Macha) **46**:201
"A Dark Night's Work" (Gaskell) **5**:192, 201-02, 205; **70**:185, 187-90, 198; **137**:40
"Dark Rosaleen" (Mangan) **27**:279, 281-84, 287-90, 293-95, 297-99, 304-11, 313-14, 318-19
"Dark Shadowing Chestnut Tree" (Meyer)
See "Schwarzschattende Kastanie"
"The Dark Stag" (Crawford) **12**:166; **127**:171-73, 223, 228
Darkly (Le Fanu)
See *In a Glass Darkly*
"Darkness" (Byron) **2**:94
"Darkness and the Poet" (Eminescu) **131**:287
"Darling Room" (Tennyson) **30**:210
"The Darning Needle" (Andersen)
See "Stoppenaalen"
Darstellung der Wissenschaftslehre aus dem Jahre 1801 (Fichte) **62**:13
Darstellung meines Systems der Philosophie (Schelling) **30**:127, 167, 174
Dartmoor (Hemans) **29**:202; **71**:261
"Darwin's Critics" (Huxley) **67**:86-7
"Darwin's Thoughts about God" (Symonds) **34**:336
"Dary Tereka" (Lermontov) **5**:287
Dashes at Life with a Free Pencil (Willis) **194**:319
Dastanbuy (Ghalib) **39**:149-51
"Datura suaveolens" (Mörike) **201**:282
"The Daughter" (Webster) **230**:314
Daughter and Mother (Tamayo y Baus)
See *Hija y madre*
"A Daughter of Eve" (Balzac)
See "Une fille d'Eve"
"The Daughter of Herodias" (Osgood) **141**:320
"The Daughter of the Heath" (Mörike)
See "Der Tochter der Heide"
A Daughter of the Philistines (Boyesen) **135**:14, 37, 42-43, 67
"The Daughter, or, A Modern Romance" (D'Israeli) **217**:306-7
Daughters of Fire (Nerval)
See *Les filles du feu*
Davenport Dunn: A Man of Our Day (Lever) **23**:288-89, 292, 296, 301, 305
David (Klopstock) **225**:279
"David and Abigail" (Lampman) **25**
David Balfour (Stevenson)
See *Catriona, a Sequel to "Kidnapped": Being Memoirs of the Further Adventures of David Balfour at Home and Abroad*
David Balfour: Being Memoirs of His Adventures at Home and Abroad (Stevenson)
See *Kidnapped: Being Memoirs of the Adventures of David Balfour in the Year 1751*
David Copperfield (Dickens)
See *The Personal History of David Copperfield*
David Garrick (Robertson) **35**:335, 355
"David Swan" (Hawthorne) **2**:298
"David Whicher" (Neal) **161**:310
Die Davidsbündler (The League of David) (Schumann) **143**:69, 71, 74-76, 123-24, 139
Davila (Adams)
See *Discourses on Davila*
"Dawn" (Isaacs)
See "Albor"
"Dawn" (Rimbaud)
See "Aube"
The Dawn (Krasiński)
See *Przedświt*
"Dawn" (Willis) **194**:307
"Dawn and Sunrise in the Snowy Mountains" (Harpur) **114**:158
Dawn Island (Martineau) **137**:250
"Dawn of Creation" (Gladstone) **213**:121
"A Dawn on the Lievre" (Lampman) **25**:190, 205, 210; **194**:38
"Dawnings of Genius" (Clare) **9**:72, 74, 105, 120; **86**:173
"The Day after To-Morrow" (Patmore) **9**:349, 358
"The Day After Tomorrow" (Stevenson) **63**:239; **193**:206
"Day and Night" (Mörike)
See "Tag und Nacht"
"Day and Night" (Tyutchev)
See "Den i noch"
Day and Night Songs (Allingham) **25**:7, 16, 22
"The Day Before the St. Petersburg Flood of 1824" (Mickiewicz)
See "The Day Preceding the St. Petersburg Flood of 1824"
"The Day Dream" (Coleridge) **99**:104
"A Day! Help! Help! Another Day!" (Dickinson) **77**:161
"A Day in an English Village Tavern" (Bestuzhev)
See "Den' v traktire Angliiskogo gorodka"
"A Day in Surrey with William Morris" (Lazarus) **8**:423
"A Day in the Wilderness" (Frederic) **10**:203
"The Day is Done" (Longfellow) **45**:116, 135, 151-52, 187; **103**:293
"The Day Is Gone" (Keats) **73**:155
"The Day of Dead Soldiers" (Lazarus) **8**:413
"Day of the Dead" (Silva)
See "Día de difuntos"
"The Day of the Lord is at Hand, at Hand!" (Kingsley) **35**:206, 219
"The Day of Tomorrow" (Eminescu)
See "Ziua de mâine"
"The Day of Trial" (Griffin) **7**:214
"The Day Preceding the St. Petersburg Flood of 1824" (Mickiewicz) **3**:401
"A Day with the Surrey" (Surtees) **14**:376
"Daybreak" (Dana) **53**:158, 178
"Day-Dream" (Bryant) **6**:165, 168
"Day-dream" (Coleridge) **231**:62, 65-67, 70-71, 73-74
"The Day-dream" (Tennyson) **65**:232
"a Day-dream at Tintagel" (Poe) **94**:229
"A Daydream in Summer" (Clare) **86**:90
"The Day-Dream: The Revival of the 'Sleeping Beauty'" (Tennyson) **30**:211
"Daydreams" (Lonnrot) **53**:339
"Day-Dreams" (Rossetti) **50**:293
"Daylight and Moonlight" (Longfellow) **45**:160
"Days" (Emerson) **1**:290, 296, 299-300; **98**:177, 184, 191
Days Departed (Bowles) **103**:54
The Days of My Life (Oliphant) **11**:462; **61**:206, 209
The Days of Yore (Cumberland) **167**:192
A Day's Ride: A Life's Romance (Lever) **23**:286, 292, 302, 304
De Brassier: A Democratic Romance (Jones) **222**:139-41, 143-44
"Las de l'amer repos" (Mallarmé) **41**:250; **210**:209
"The Deacon and His Daughter" (Crawford) **12**:151, 172
Deacon Brodie; or, The Double Life: A Melodrama Founded on Facts (Stevenson) **5**:411, 421; **193**:238, 360, 364
"Deacons' Daughters and Ministers' Sons" (Parton) **86**:376
"The Deacon's Masterpiece; or, The Wonderful 'One-Hoss' Shay" (Holmes) **14**:109-10, 115-16, 119, 121, 125-26, 128, 143; **81**:98-99, 107
"The Deacon's Week" (Cooke) **110**:14, 18, 43
"The Dead" (Blind) **202**:31
"The Dead" (Silva)
See "Muertos"
"The Dead" (Very) **9**:373, 378, 397
"Dead Achilles" (Meyer)
See "Der tote Achill"
"The Dead Are in the Silent Graves" (Hood) **16**:222
"The Dead Babe" (Field) **3**:208
"Dead before Death" (Rossetti) **2**:557; **50**:310; **66**:341; **186**:304
"The Dead Boxer" (Carleton) **199**:4-5, 9
"The Dead Bridegroom" (Blind) **202**:13
"Dead Cities" (Lampman) **25**:210
"The Dead City" (Rossetti) **66**:306
"The Dead Drummer Boy" (Barham) **77**:35
"The Dead Eagle" (Campbell) **19**:183
"The Dead Feast of the Kol-Folk" (Whittier) **8**:516; **59**:360
"Dead Friends" (Meyer)
See "Die toten Freunde"
"The Dead Horse" (Bertrand) **31**:54
"Dead Language" (Patmore) **9**:361
"The Dead Leman" (Gautier) **1**:347
"The Dead Man" (Andersen)
See "Dodningen"
"The Dead Man: A Folktale from Funen" (Andersen)
See "Dodningen"
"The Dead Man's Dream" (Darley) **2**:127, 130
"The Dead Man's Grave" (Moodie) **14**:231
"A Dead Man's Love" (Lermontov) **5**:299
"The Dead of Ninety-Two" (Rimbaud)
See "Morts de quatre-vingt-douze et de quatre-vingt-treize"
"The Dead Pan" (Barrett Browning) **1**:123, 124, 128; **66**:44; **170**:89-90, 92-94, 97, 105, 107, 118-19
"The Dead Princess and the Seven Heroes" (Pushkin)
See "Skazka o Mertvoy Tsarevne"
"The Dead Prophet" (Tennyson) **65**:380-1; **202**:294
"A Dead Secret" (O'Brien) **21**:242
The Dead Secret (Collins) **1**:174, 178-79, 182, 184-85; **93**:46-7, 53, 64
"Dead Souls" (Silva)
See "Las almas muertas"
Dead Souls (Gogol)
See *Mertvye dushi*
"The Dead Stone-Breaker" (Crabbe) **26**:103
"The Dead Year" (Thomson) **18**:394, 406, 414
Deaf and Dumb (Holcroft)
See *Deaf and Dumb; or, the Orphan Protected*
Deaf and Dumb; or, the Orphan Protected (Holcroft) **85**:199, 212, 223
"Deákpályám" (Petofi) **21**:279
Dealings with the Firm of Dombey and Son (Dickens) **3**:145, 147, 151, 156, 161, 172-

73, 175, 178-79, 181; **8**:169, 171-72, 175-76, 178, 195, 199; **18**:119; **26**:175; **37**:168, 199; **86**:189, 221; **105**:228, 231, 330; **113**:29, 42, 68, 97, 107, 144; **161**:39, 43, 50; **187**:36; **203**:273, 276; **206**:57; **211**:13, 32, 42; **217**:216, 221, 225, 243; **219**:69, 86, 95, 109-10, 112, 146, 190, 200; **230**:119, 142; **231**:180, 188, 214
Dean Dunham (Alger) **8**:43
The Dean's Doughter; or, The Days We Live In (Gore) **65**:22, 30
"Dear is my little Native Vale" (Rogers) **69**:66
"Dear Lord and Father of Mankind" (Whittier) **8**:520, 525
"Dear Reynolds" (Keats) **225**:166
"Death" (Baratynsky)
See "Poslednyaya smert'"
"Death" (Blind) **202**:31
"Death" (Lampman) **25**:187; **194**:6
"Death" (Turgenev) **21**:413, 454
"Death" (Verlaine)
See "La Mort"
Death (Baudelaire)
See *La mort*
"Death among the Trees" (Sigourney) **87**:337
The Death and Letters of Alice James (James) **206**:195-99
"Death and the Fear of Dying" (Smith) **59**:303, 307, 309, 315, 322
"A Death at Sea" (Adams) **33**:4
"Death in Love" (Rossetti) **77**:313, 339
"A Death in the Bush" (Kendall) **12**:179-80, 186, 189-90, 192, 201-02
"A Death in the Desert" (Browning) **19**:117, 130, 138, 153; **79**:133-34
"Death in the Kitchen" (Hood) **16**:235-36
"Death is the supple Suitor" (Dickinson) **77**:163, 173
"The Death of a Devotee" (Carleton) **3**:92
"The Death of A. G. A." (Brontë) **16**:123
"Death of a Son of the Late Honorable Fisher Ames" (Sigourney) **87**:337
"Death of a Young Lady at the Retreat for the Insane" (Sigourney) **87**:337
"Death of a Young Musician" (Sigourney) **87**:337
"Death of a Young Wife" (Sigourney) **87**:337
"The Death of Adaline" (Chivers) **49**:48
The Death of Adam (Klopstock) **11**:218, 231
The Death of Adam: A Tragedy (Klopstock)
See *Der Tod Adams: Ein Trauerspiel*
"The Death of an Infant" (Sigourney) **21**:299, 310; **87**:326
"The Death of Artemidora" (Landor) **14**:181-82, 190-91
"The Death of Artists" (Baudelaire)
See "La mort des artistes"
Death of Buda (Arany)
See *Buda halála*
"The Death of Byrhtnoth" (Lanier) **118**:216, 218
"The Death of Cicero" (Brown) **122**:119
"The Death of Dermid" (Ferguson) **33**:293
"The Death of Don Pedro" (Lockhart) **6**:297
The Death of Empedokles (Hölderlin)
See *Der Tod des Empedokles*
"Death of General Brock" (Richardson) **55**:342
The Death of General Montgomery at the Siege of Quebec: A Tragedy, with an Ode in Honor of the Pennsylvania Militia, and the Small Band of Regular Continental Troops Who Sustained the Campaign in the Depth of Winter, January, 1777, and Repulsed the British Forces from the Banks of the Delaware (Brackenridge) **227**:72, 105
The Death of General Montgomery in Storming the City of Quebec (Brackenridge) **7**:44, 47, 50
"The Death of Jonathan" (Lamartine) **11**:249
The Death of King Buda (Arany)
See *Buda halála*
"Death of Longfellow" (Whitman) **205**:252
"The Death of Lovers" (Baudelaire)
See "La mort des amants"
The Death of Marlowe: a Tragedy in One Act (Horne) **127**:236, 238, 256-57, 263, 269-71
"Death of Mrs. Harriet W. L. Winslow" (Sigourney) **87**:337
"The Death of Napoleon" (Brontë) **217**:14, 18, 21
"The Death of Oenone" (Tennyson) **30**:233; **115**:337
The Death of Oenone, Akbar's Dream, and Other Poems (Tennyson) **202**:289, 291
"The Death of Pan" (Barrett Browning)
See "The Dead Pan"
"The Death of Paris" (Morris) **4**:447-48
"The Death of Prince Frederick" (Darwin) **106**:181
"The Death of Raschi" (Lazarus) **109**:325, 337, 342
The Death of Richelieu (Dumas) **71**:219
"The Death of Slavery" (Bryant) **6**:169, 174
"Death of Socrates" (Lamartine)
See *La morte de Socrate*
"Death of the Dauphin" (Daudet) **1**:238
"The Death of the Devil" (Chivers) **49**:78
"The Death of the Flowers" (Bryant) **6**:168-69, 171-72, 177, 183; **46**:3, 9, 26
"The Death of the Gentle Usher" (Willis) **194**:298
"Death of the Orphan" (Solomos) **15**:389
"Death of the Poet" (Lermontov)
See "Smert' poeta"
The Death of the Poet (Tieck)
See *Der Tod des Dichters*
"The Death of the Poor" (Baudelaire)
See "La mort des pauvres"
"Death of the Rev. Alfred Mitchell" (Sigourney) **87**:337
"Death of the Rev. Gordon Hall" (Sigourney) **87**:337
"Death of the Rev. W. C. Walton" (Sigourney) **87**:337
"The Death of the Sergeant" (Isaacs)
See "La muerte del sargento"
"Death of the Shepherd" (Solomos) **15**:389
"Death of the Wife of a Clergyman, during the Sickness of Her Husband" (Sigourney) **87**:337
"The Death of the Wolf" (Vigny)
See "La mort du loup"
"The Death of Time" (Chivers) **49**:57
The Death of Wallenstein (Schiller)
See *Wallenstein*
"The Death of Wind-Foot" (Whitman) **81**:343
"Death opens her sweet white arms" (Fuller) **50**:243
"The Death Raven" (Borrow) **9**:54
"Death Ride" (Meyer)
See "Der Ritt in den Tod"
"The Death Song of a Gaelic Warrior of the Sixth Century" (Leconte de Lisle) **29**:236
"The Death Song of the Cherokee Indian" (Freneau) **111**:166
"Death Sweet" (Beddoes) **154**:43
"Death, That Struck when I Was Most Confiding" (Brontë) **16**:87, 122
"Death to the Invalid" (Martineau) **137**:283, 295
"The Death-Bed" (Hood) **16**:216, 219
"The Death-Bed" (Opie) **65**:159, 179
Deathless Golovan: from Tales of Three Righteous Men (Leskov)
See *Nesmertel'nyj Golovan: iz rasskazov o trex pravednikax*
Death's Jest Book; or, The Fool's Tragedy (Beddoes) **6**:26-37, 39-41; **154**:3-6, 8-13, 15-17, 19-22, 26-27, 32, 35-37, 39-41, 43-46, 48, 50-51, 53, 59-60, 62-63, 69, 71, 73, 76-79, 82-83, 86-87, 89-91; **154**:91
"Death's Ramble" (Hood) **16**:224, 237
"The Debate" (Lermontov) **126**:142, 144
"The Debate in the Sennit" (Lowell) **90**:219
"The Debate over the Election of Mr. Maiorescu" (Eminescu) **131**:325
"The Debating Society" (Longstreet) **159**:119, 136, 143-44, 151, 161, 182, 184, 203
"La débauche" (Gautier) **1**:348
Debit and Credit (Freytag)
See *Soll und Haben*
"Deborah's Book" (Ingelow) **107**:162
"Deborah's Parrot, a Village Tale" (Robinson) **142**:135, 170, 253
"The Debtor" (Freneau) **111**:132
"Un début dans la vie" (Balzac) **153**:153
Debutante; or, the London Season (Gore) **65**:21
"Les débuts d'un aventurier" (Mérimée) **6**:353-4, 356; **65**:79-80, 83, 88
"Decay A Ballad" (Clare) **86**:169
A Decayed Family (Leskov)
See *Zaxudalyj rod*
Decebalus (Eminescu) **33**:264
"Deceits" (Heredia)
See "Desengaños"
"Deceived" (Lonnrot) **53**:339
"December Night" (Musset)
See "Nuit de Décembre"
"December XXXI" (Cooke) **110**:3
"Deception" (Leskov)
See "Obman"
Declamatio, qua poetas epopoeiae auctores, recenset Frideric. Gottlieb Klopstock (Klopstock) **225**:291
"The Declaration" (Willis) **194**:297
Declaration of American Independence (Jefferson)
See *In Congress, July 4, 1776: A Declaration by the Representatives of the United States of America, in General Congress Assembled*
"Déclaration foraine" (Mallarmé) **210**:250
Declaration of Independence (Jefferson)
See *In Congress, July 4, 1776: A Declaration by the Representatives of the United States of America, in General Congress Assembled*
A Declaration of Rights (Shelley) **143**:265
"Declaration of Sentiments" (Garrison) **149**:226-29, 231-32, 256
"Déclin" (Corbière) **43**:25, 27
The Decline and Fall of the English System of Finance (Paine) **62**:262, 368
"The Decline of Dramas" (Bird) **197**:16
"The Decline of Faith" (Hayne) **94**:167
The Decline of Heroic Life in the North (Grundtvig)
See *Optrin af Kæmpelivets Undergang i Nord*
Decline of the Heroic Age (Grundtvig) **1**:401
"Décourageux" (Corbière) **43**:11, 31-4
"Découverte" (Maupassant) **42**:174
A Decrepit Clan (Leskov)
See *Zaxudalyj rod*
"Le dedans du désespoir" (Hugo) **10**:357
"Dédicace" (Baudelaire) **155**:39, 104-5
"La Dédicace de la Coupe et les lèvres" (Musset) **150**:322
Dédicaces (Verlaine) **2**:622; **51**:351, 362, 372
"Dedication" (Arnim)
See "Zueignung"
"Dedication" (Crabbe) **121**:85
"A Dedication" (Gordon) **21**:150, 163-64, 167, 175-76, 184-87
"Dedication" (Keble) **87**:199
"Dedication" (Lamartine) **11**:246
"Dedication" (Lamb) **113**:202
"Dedication" (Tennyson) **65**:349
"A Dedication" (Timrod) **25**:361, 372, 375
"Dedication" (Whittier) **8**:520
Dedication (Goethe) **4**:163
"Dedication Hymn" (Willis) **194**:300
"Dedication to Detraction" (Cumberland) **167**:164-66, 168, 170

Dedications (Verlaine)
See *Dédicaces*
"Dedicatory Sonnet: To S. T. Coleridge" (Coleridge) **90**:32
"Dedikation" (Claudius) **75**:207
"Deeds" (Lampman) **25**:199, 210
The Deep, Deep Sea; or, Perseus and Andromeda (Planché) **42**:273, 286, 302
"Deep in Earth" (Poe) **55**:214
Deerbrook (Martineau) **26**:310-11, 315, 317, 319, 322-23, 329-33, 349, 357; **137**:253-55, 259-62, 304, 309-13, 329, 331-32
The Deerslayer (Cooper) **203**:11-15, 39, 71-72, 95, 129-32, 135, 137, 139-40, 162-63
The Deerslayer; or, The First War-Path (Cooper) **1**:205, 207-11, 214, 221-24; **27**:126, 129-30, 132-35, 138-41, 143, 151-54, 158, 186-88; **54**:258-9, 262, 269, 276
The Defeat (Warren) **13**:425-26; **226**:253, 255, 258, 263, 270-71, 290
"Defects in the English Constitution" (Dyer) **129**:110
"Ein defekter locus communis" (Claudius) **75**:213
"The Defence" (Adams)
See "A Defence of the Constitutions of Government of the United States, Against the Attack of Mr Turgot"
"Defence" (Longfellow) **103**:295
"The Defence of Guenevere" (Morris) **4**:412, 420-22, 424, 429-31, 441-44
"The Defence of Lucknow" (Tennyson) **30**:295
"A Defence of Poetry" (Shelley) **93**:258, 295, 310, 312-13; **175**:220, 233-34, 236, 241, 246, 253, 262, 264, 273, 282, 289-91, 309-13, 329, 342, 361, 364, 367-69
A Defence of Poetry. Addressed to Henry James Pye, Esq. To which is added, A Specimen of a New Version of Telemachus (D'Israeli) **217**:283, 292, 295, 304-6
A Defence of Poetry and Other Essays (Shelley) **18**:333, 337, 347, 349-51, 353-55, 357, 363, 371, 384; **93**:266-67, 275, 278, 327, 344-46, 357; **143**:207-10, 212-13, 220, 222, 225, 249, 266, 268, 271, 277, 286, 303
"A Defence of the Constitutions of Government of the United States, Against the Attack of Mr Turgot" (Adams) **106**:11-13, 35-40, 44-7, 54, 66, 79-80
A Defence of the Rockingham Party (Godwin) **130**:49
Défense du Génie du christianisme (Chateaubriand) **134**:24, 26-30
The Defense of Guenevere, and Other Poems (Morris) **4**:412, 418-19, 425-26, 434, 441, 444
Defense of Usury (Bentham) **38**:37, 44
"A Defense of Whigs" (Kennedy) **2**:430, 432
"The Definition of Poetry" (Bestuzhev)
See "Opredelenie poezii"
"Definitively Rotten Sponge" (Laforgue)
See "Eponge définitivenent pourrie"
The Deformed Transformed (Byron) **2**:68, 72, 80; **109**:123; **149**:39
"The Degree to Which Popular Tradition Has Participated in the Development of Russian Literature" (Dobrolyubov) **5**:141
La dégringolade (Gaboriau) **14**:20
Dei Sepolcri (Foscolo)
See *I sepolcri*
Déidamie (Banville) **9**:22
"Deirdre" (Ferguson) **33**:279-80, 285, 290, 298
"Dejaneira" (Arnold) **6**:37
"Dejection" (Baratynsky) **103**:7
"Dejection" (Shelley)
See "Dejection: An Ode"
"Dejection: An Ode" (Coleridge) **54**:66, 70; **99**:5, 19, 81-3; 111;226; **177**:156; **197**:192, 212, 214-15, 231-34, 243, 245, 265, 267; **231**:42-43, 62, 65, 75-82, 86, 88, 98, 110, 114, 123-24, 130, 134
"Dejection: An Ode" (Shelley) **175**:310, 314
"Dekletam" (Preseren) **127**:329
Del dicho al hecho (Tamayo y Baus) **1**:569
Del dramma storico (Manzoni) **98**:216
"Del influjo de la religión cristiana en la literatura" (Martínez de la Rosa) **102**:254
Del principe e delle lettere (Alfieri) **101**:14, 41, 51-2, 58, 62, 69, 76-8, 84, 86
Del romanzo storico (Manzoni) **29**:276, 305, 308-09
"Delay Has Danger" (Crabbe) **26**:100, 110, 130-31; **121**:55, 84-6, 88
"The Delectable Ballad of the Waller Lot" (Field) **3**:211
"Delfica" (Nerval) **1**:478, 486-87; **67**:307, 316, 363
"Delicacy" (Verlaine)
See "Délicatesse"
"Délicatesse" (Verlaine) **230**:167
"Deliciae Sapientiae de Amore" (Patmore) **9**:335, 339, 347, 359, 361
"Delilah" (Gordon) **21**:164, 166
Delineations of American Scenery and Character (Audubon) **47**:14-15, 18
Les Deliquescences (Verlaine) **51**:361-62
"Délires" (Rimbaud) **4**:466; **82**:222, 226, 229, 231, 234, 238-39, 241, 245
"Délires I" (Rimbaud) **4**:481; **35**:291-94, 302, 310, 317-19; **82**:230-31, 241-42, 245-46, 255, 257; **227**:216, 268, 277-78, 280, 303, 306, 315-16
"Délires II" (Rimbaud) **4**:481; **35**:302, 311-12, 317, 319, 324; **82**:232-33, 240-41, 245, 247, 250, 255, 257-58, 260-61
"Delirium" (Rimbaud)
See "Délires I"
"The Dell" (Mitford) **4**:408
"Della poesia moderna" (Foscolo) **97**:89
Della tirannide (Alfieri) **101**:41-2, 45, 51-2, 62, 69, 73, 76, 79, 83-5
"Dell'educare la gioventú italiana" (Leopardi) **129**:329, 332
Dell'indipendenza dell'Italia (Manzoni) **98**:279
Dell'invenzione (Manzoni) **29**:276
"Dell'origine e dell'ufficio della letteratura: Orazione" (Foscolo) **8**:261
Deloraine (Godwin) **14**:68, 70, 81-3
Delphi (Klopstock) **225**:298
Delphine (Staël-Holstein) **3**:517, 523-25, 527, 529-30, 534; **91**:291-92, 297-98, 304-05, 308-10, 312, 3253-55, 359-60, 365
"Delphine et Hippolyte" (Baudelaire)
See "Femmes damnées"
"Delphine, or the Fortunate Cure" (Genlis)
See "Delphine ou l'Heureuse Guérison"
"Delphine ou l'Heureuse Guérison" (Genlis) **166**:9-10, 31
"The Deluge" (Moodie) **113**:317
"The Deluge" (Vigny)
See "Le déluge"
"Le déluge" (Vigny) **7**:472-73, 480-81; **102**:335, 367
"Delusion" (Lenau) **16**:276
"Delusive" (Robinson) **142**:175
"Dely's Cow" (Cooke) **110**:44, 47
"Dem Allgegenwärtigen" (Klopstock) **11**:237
Dem Andenken des k. k. Lyceal-Bibliothekars in Laibach, Mathia Zhop (Preseren) **127**:305
"Dem Erlöser" (Klopstock) **11**:237
"Dem Unendlichen" (Klopstock) **11**:238
"Demagogues" (Kennedy) **2**:432
"The Demeanour of Murderers" (Dickens) **217**:266
"Demerara" (Martineau) **26**:304; **137**:250-51, 260-61, 304, 324-25
"Demeter" (Isaacs) **70**:313
Demeter, and Other Poems (Tennyson) **202**:288-91
"Demeter and Persephone" (Pater) **159**:257
"Demeter and Persephone" (Tennyson) **30**:245; **65**:300
Demetrius (Schiller) **39**:335, 368, 371-72, 375, 380, 385; **69**:169, 243-45, 250; **166**:159, 190
Demetrius: Eine Tragödie (Hebbel) **43**:230, 234, 238, 240, 246, 261-62, 283, 300
Demetrius Zaar von Moscou (Kotzebue) **25**:136, 140
The "Demi-Monde" (Dumas)
See *Le demi-monde*
Le demi-monde (Dumas) **9**:219-24, 227, 229, 231-32, 236-37, 240-41, 245-47, 250
"Democracy" (Arnold) **6**:46; **89**:36-7, 40, 62, 101-02; **126**:77, 88, 112-13; **218**:239, 251-52, 257, 261
"Democracy" (Lowell) **2**:510
"Democracy" (Rimbaud)
See "Démocratie"
"Democracy" (Whitman) **4**:564
Democracy, and Other Addresses (Lowell) **2**:510
Democracy in America (Tocqueville)
See *De la démocratie en Amérique*
"Democracy Vindicated" (Jones) **222**:172, 177
"Democratic Art" (Symonds) **34**:327
"Democratic Catechism" (Martí)
See "Catecismo democratico"
Democratic Legends of the North (Michelet) **31**:258
Democratic Vistas (Whitman) **4**:551, 566, 575, 581, 590, 594-95, 597, 601; **31**:397, 441-42; **81**:255, 295-96, 300, 332; **205**:175, 202-11, 257, 260, 267, 297, 325
"Démocratie" (Rimbaud) **35**:324; **82**:232-33, 238; **227**:247, 323
"Democritus Junior; or, the Laughing Philosopher" (Dyer) **129**:114
La demoiselle à marier; ou, La première entrevue (Scribe) **16**:384, 393
"Les demoiselles de Bienfilâtre" (Villiers de l'Isle Adam) **3**:581
Les demoiselles de Saint-Cyr (Dumas) **71**:209
"Les demoiselles Malfilatre" (Villiers de l'Isle Adam) **3**:588
Demokritus unter den Abderiten (Wieland) **177**:256, 260, 316
"The Demon" (Lermontov) **126**:215, 217, 223-24
"The Demon" (Pushkin) **83**:248, 253, 299
The Demon (Lermontov) **5**:289, 291, 293, 295, 300; **47**:160, 188; **126**:128, 130-32, 138, 140, 144-45
"Le démon de l'analogie" (Mallarmé) **4**:371; **41**:251, 280; **210**:174-83, 185, 187-91, 207, 233
Le démon du foyer (Sand) **42**:314
"The Demon of Perversity" (Poe)
See "The Imp of the Perverse"
Demonio Familiar (Alencar) **157**:5, 9
"Demonism" (Eminescu) **33**:261, 263; **131**:287
"The Demon's Cave" (Darley) **2**:133
"The Demon's Cave" (Whittier) **59**:363
"The Demon-Ship" (Hood) **16**:224, 235
"Demyàn's Fish Soup" (Krylov) **1**:435
"An den Engel in der Wüste" (Brentano) **191**:30, 68
An den erwarteten Sohn (Humboldt) **134**:167
"An den Frühling" (Hölderlin) **16**:181
"Den' v traktire Angliiskogo gorodka" (Bestuzhev) **131**:165
Dene Hollow (Wood) **178**:285
"Deniehy's Grave" (Kendall) **12**:194
Denis Duval (Thackeray) **5**:463, 474, 490; **14**:452; **43**:357; **169**:241; **213**:186
"Denis O'Shaughnessy Going to Maynooth" (Carleton) **3**:88-89, 91, 93, 95; **199**:8-9, 16-17, 28-29, 32, 34, 56, 59-61, 65, 87-88, 102, 108
Denise (Dumas) **9**:228, 231-32, 243, 247, 250
"Denk' es, o Seele" (Mörike) **201**:253, 294, 303, 306-8, 313, 318, 347

Denk- und Dichtbüchlein (Schumann) **143**:127, 130
"Dennis Delany" (Hogg) **109**:201
"Dennis Haggerty's Wife" (Thackeray) **43**:381
The Denounced (Banim and Banim) **13**:121, 147, 149
"Une dentelle s'abolit" (Mallarmé) **4**:393; **41**:274, 281, 294, 297-98, 300-01, 304-05; **210**:241, 244-45, 253
"Denys l'Auxerrois" (Pater) **7**:298, 307, 312; **90**:245, 272, 288, 333, 336; **159**:270
Deontology (Bentham) **38**:40, 44, 48-51, 80, 84, 87
"Départ" (Rimbaud) **35**:322-23; **227**:192, 210
"Depart de Lyon" (Desbordes-Valmore) **97**:23
"Départ pour le sabbat" (Bertrand) **31**:48
"The Departed" (Hemans) **71**:264
"Departure" (Patmore) **9**:343
"Departure" (Rimbaud)
See "Départ"
The Departure from the Theatre (Gogol)
See "Teatral'nyi raz'ezd posle predstavleniia novoi komedii"
"The Departure of Hannah More from Barley Wood, at the Age of Eighty-Three" (Sigourney) **21**:293
The Dependent (Cumberland) **167**:192
"Derevnia" (Turgenev) **122**:308
"Derevnya" (Pushkin) **83**:305
Dermot MacMorrogh, or The Conquest of Ireland (Adams) **175**:14-20, 55, 58, 60, 62-63
Le Dernier amour (Sand) **57**:316; **174**:226, 229
"Le dernier chant de pèlerinage de Childe Harold" (Lamartine) **11**:245-47, 268, 270
Le Dernier Chant du pèlerinage d'Harold (Lamartine) **190**:195
Le Dernier Chouan (Balzac) **153**:151-52
"Le dernier des Maourys" (Leconte de Lisle) **29**:226-27
Le dernier des Mohicans (Cooper)
See *The Last of the Mohicans: A Narrative of 1757*
Le dernier jour d'un condamné (Hugo) **3**:235, 239-40; **10**:367; **21**:192, 225; **161**:202, 230; **189**:160, 178, 192, 202, 236, 267, 286
"Dernier mot" (Amiel) **4**:14
"Le dernier souvenir" (Leconte de Lisle) **29**:228
La Dernière Aldini (Sand) **57**:312, 316
La dernière fée (Balzac) **5**:58
La Derniere Fete galante (Verlaine) **51**:362
Le dernière idole (Daudet) **1**:231, 249
"La dernière incarnation de Vautrien" (Balzac) **5**:46
La Dernière mode (Mallarmé) **41**:249, 294; **210**:167, 169-70, 211-12, 221, 223-24, 226-27, 231, 235, 241
"La Dernière nuit de travail" (Vigny) **102**:361-62
La Dernière Revue de Napoléon (Balzac) **153**:150
"La dernière vision" (Leconte de Lisle) **29**:222, 228
Dernières nouvelles (Mérimée) **6**:355
Derniéres Poésites (de Navarre)
See *Essays*
"Dernières Reflexions" (Pixérécourt) **39**:280-81
Derniers poèmes (Leconte de Lisle) **29**:221, 235
"Derniers soupirs d'un Parnassien" (Laforgue) **221**:40, 92-93
Derniers vers (Rimbaud) **4**:472; **35**:321, 323; **82**:240, 263; **227**:312, 316
Les derniers vers de Jules Laforgue (Laforgue) **5**:270-1, 273, 276-80, 282-3; **53**:258-9, 261-5, 272, 278, 280-2, 289-92, 294-5, 297-300; **221**:4, 12, 15, 22, 25, 34-38, 42, 47-48, 50, 56, 59-62, 64, 66, 70, 77, 83, 93
"Derniers vers III" (Laforgue) **221**:60, 62, 64-65, 68
"Derniers vers IV" (Laforgue) **221**:50, 66, 82
"Derniers vers VI" (Laforgue) **221**:67
"Derniers vers VIII" (Laforgue) **221**:24, 36, 49, 60, 66
"Derniers vers IX" (Laforgue) **221**:60, 65-66, 69-70
"Derniers vers X" (Laforgue) **221**:50, 61-62, 64, 66
"Derniers vers XII" (Laforgue) **221**:61, 70
"La derrochadora" (Casal) **131**:258-60, 264-65
Derry: A Tale of the Revolution in 1688 (Tonna) **135**:203
"Des Arztes Vermächtnis" (Droste-Hülshoff) **3**:196, 199, 201-02
"Des Baches Wiegenlied" (Muller) **73**:363, 365, 374, 376
"Des bells chalonnaises" (Banville) **9**:16
Des Bohémiens et de leur musique en Hongrie (Liszt) **199**:300, 305, 318-19, 325-27, 337, 343, 346
Des circonstances actuelles qui peuvent terminer la Révolution et des principles qui dolvent fonder la république en France (Staël-Holstein) **91**:291
"Dichterin Schwanenlied" (Brentano)
See "Schwanenlied"
Des Dichters Leben (Tieck) **5**:514, 526; **46**:397
Des Feldpredigers Schmelzle Reise nach Fätz mit fortgehenden Noten: Nebst der Beichte des Teufels bey einem Staatsmanne (Jean Paul) **7**:339, 241
Des Fleurs de bonne volonté (Laforgue) **5**:276, 281-2; **53**:256-7, 272, 278, 290, 298-301; **221**:7, 23-24, 35, 60, 64, 77, 82-83, 85, 91, 93
"Des Hallucinations et des songes en matiére criminelle" (Nodier) **19**:400
"Des Kaisers Bildsäule" (Grillparzer) **102**:175
Des Knaben Wunderhorn (Arnim) **5**:12, 19; **159**:34-36, 38, 40-43, 58, 103, 106-8
Des Knaben Wunderhorn: Alte deutsche Lieder (Brentano) **1**:95, 98-99; **191**:5, 18, 25, 47, 87, 92, 117
Des Lebens Überfluss (Tieck) **5**:532
Des Meeres und der Liebe Wellen (Grillparzer) **1**:384-85, 390; **102**:83, 88, 90, 93, 95, 111, 118, 149, 165-66, 170, 187
"Des Morgens" (Hölderlin) **16**:181, 184
"Des Müllers Blumen" (Muller) **73**:363-64
"Des Négociations relatives à la Grèce" (Chateaubriand) **134**:8
Des Oeuvres Complètes de M. Paul de Kock (Kock) **16**:251
Des réactions politiques (Constant) **182**:124, 200, 202-3
"Des Sängers Klage" (Preseren) **127**:315
Des types en littérature (Nodier) **19**:379, 392
Des vers (Maupassant) **1**:455
"Des Vetters Eckfenster" (Hoffmann) **183**:189, 275-76, 278-79, 281-83
El desafío del diablo (Zorrilla y Moral) **6**:523
"El desamor" (Heredia) **209**:135, 162
"Descartes" (Huxley) **67**:87
"The Descent from the Cross" (Rossetti) **186**:301, 318-19
"A Descent into the Maelström" (Poe) **1**:500, 514, 518; **16**:294-96, 301, 303, 306, 315, 331-34; **78**:258; **117**:224, 264, 269, 320; **211**:253
The Descent of Liberty (Hunt) **1**:412, 423; **70**:292
The Descent of Man, and Selection in Relation to Sex (Darwin) **57**:142-3, 147-52, 163, 165, 172, 174
"La descente aux enfers" (Beranger) **34**:41
"Description" (Laforgue)
See "Signalement"
"Description of Bethlehem; in the State of Pennsylvania" (Murray) **63**:181
"Description of My Property" (Radishchev) **190**:320
"Description of New-York one-hundred and fifty years hence" (Freneau) **111**:124
"Description of Recently Founded Communist colonies Still in Existence" (Engels) **85**:124, 180
"A Description of Spinoza's System" (Schleiermacher) **107**:328
A Description of the Ride to Hulne Abbey (Percy) **95**:313, 328
"Description of Various Game in Our Parts" (Aksakov) **181**:22
A Descriptive Catalogue (Blake) **13**:159; **127**:64
A Descriptive Catalogue of Pictures, Poetical and Historical Inventions, Painted by William Blake in Water Colours, being the Ancient Method of Fresco Painting Restored: And Drawing for Public Inspection, etc. (Blake) **173**:48, 52, 70, 143
Descriptive Sketches (Wordsworth) **12**:385-86; **38**:363; **111**:214, 262; **166**:259, 262
Desde mi celda (Bécquer)
See *Cartas literarias desde mi celda*
"El Desdichado" (Nerval) **1**:476, 478, 480-82, 485, 488; **67**:305-07, 316-17, 356, 359-60
"Desengaños" (Heredia) **209**:135
"The Desert" (Blind) **202**:56
"Le désert" (Leconte de Lisle) **29**:223, 225
"The Desert-Born" (Hood) **16**:222, 235-36
The Desert Island. A Dramatic Poem, in Three Acts, As it is Acted at the Theatre-Royal in Drury-Lane (Murphy) **229**:234, 254
"Deserted" (Bellamy) **86**:75
"The Deserted Cottage" (Robinson) **142**:137
The Deserted Daughter (Holcroft) **85**:192, 206, 222-23, 225
"The Deserted Farm-House" (Freneau) **111**:141, 148, 151
"The Deserted Garden" (Barrett Browning) **1**:117
"The Deserted House" (Tennyson) **30**:222
Deserted Village (Dickens) **113**:147
The Deserted Wife (Southworth) **26**:431-32, 437, 443, 445-46
"The Deserter" (Frederic) **10**:203
"The Deserter" (Landon) **15**:161
"Les déserts de l'amour" (Rimbaud) **4**:484, 486; **35**:290-91; **82**:226, 253; **227**:323
"Deserts of Love" (Rimbaud)
See "Les déserts de l'amour"
"Desesperación" (Manzano) **155**:307
"Desespero" (Castro Alves) **205**:18
"Le désespoir" (Lamartine) **11**:245, 254, 264, 272, 279, 282; **190**:237
"Le désespoir de la vieille" (Baudelaire) **155**:46
"The Desire" (Eminescu) **131**:296
"Desire" (Lermontov) **126**:223
"Desire" (Zhukovsky)
See "Zhelanie"
"Desire for Travel" (Grillparzer)
See "Reiselust"
"The Desire to Be a Man" (Zorrilla y Moral) **3**:590
Desmond: A Novel (Smith) **23**:317, 319, 322, 325-29, 333, 335-36, 338, 340; **115**:126, 134, 136, 140, 142, 144-47, 158-64, 167-68, 207, 210-11, 223-26
"Desolation" (Baratynsky)
See "Zapustenie"
"Désolation" (Laforgue) **221**:89
"Despair" (Castro Alves)
See "Desespero"
"Despair" (Lamartine)
See "Le désespoir"
"Despair" (Tennyson) **30**:245, 254
"The Despairing Wanderer" (Opie) **65**:155
"La despedida del patriota griego" (Espronceda) **39**:106, 108
"The Desperado" (Turgenev)
See "Otchayanny"
"A Desperate Character" (Turgenev)
See "Otchayanny"
"Despised and Rejected" (Rossetti) **2**:559; **186**:295

"Despondency" (Arnold) **29**:27
"Despondency" (Lampman) **25**:187, 194, 196-97, 209, 219; **194**:21, 29, 42, 44, 128
"Despondency and Aspiration" (Hemans) **71**:270
"Despondency Corrected" (Wordsworth) **166**:201, 218, 264, 293
"Despondency in Spring" (Willis) **194**:305
Despot Voda (Eminescu) **131**:292
Despotism: or, The Fall of the Jesuits: A Political Romance, Illustrated by Historical Anecdotes (D'Israeli) **217**:292, 304, 311
"Después da la victoria" (Isaacs) **70**:311
"Dessein's" (Thackeray) **213**:306
"Le dessous de cartes d'une partie de whist" (Barbey d'Aurevilly) **1**:74-75; **213**:56, 63, 66-69, 87, 89-90, 96, 100
Les Destinees (Vigny)
See *Les destinées: Poèmes philosophiques*
Les destinées de la poésie (Lamartine) **11**:276; **190**:200, 207-8, 227
Les destinées: Poèmes philosophiques (Vigny) **7**:469-71, 474, 478-86; **102**:336, 353, 378
The Destinies: Philosophical Poems (Vigny)
See *Les destinées: Poèmes philosophiques*
"Destiny" (Byron) **109**:293
"Destiny" (Emerson) **38**:189
"The Destiny of Nations" (Coleridge) **54**:68-9; **99**:105; **177**:117-18, 159; **231**:43, 58, 89, 152
The Destiny of Nations (Coleridge) **197**:320
Destiny; or, The Chief's Daughter (Ferrier) **8**:238, 240, 242-44, 246-52, 255-56
"The Destiny that Spanned Two Lifetimes" (Ueda Akinari)
See "Nise no en"
"La destruction" (Baudelaire) **6**:123; **55**:48, 74-5, 79-80
"The Destruction of Aesthetics" (Pisarev)
See "Razrushenie estetiki"
"The Destruction of Babylon" (Moodie) **113**:317
"The Destruction of Babylon" (Trumbull) **30**:345
"The Destruction of Psara" (Solomos) **15**:386
"The Destruction of Sennacherib" (Byron) **2**:88
"The Destruction of the Pequods" (Dwight) **13**:270, 272, 278
"Desultory Thoughts upon the Utility of Encouraging a Degree of Self-Complacency, Especially in Female Bosoms" (Murray) **63**:184, 206, 210
"Detached Pieces" (Austen) **119**:13
Detached Poems (Schumann)
See *Einzelgedichte*
"Detached Thoughts" (Byron) **149**:20, 112-13
"Detached Thoughts on Books and Reading" (Lamb) **10**:440
"Details of Episcopal Life" (Leskov)
See "Meloči arxierejskoj žizni"
Detective Story (Kingsley) **44**:234-35, 238
Determination of the Concept of a Race of Men (Kant) **67**:215
Detraction Displayed (Opie) **65**:171, 203-4
Detskie gody (Leskov) **25**:253, 258; **174**:16, 65
Detskie gody Bagrova-vnuka (Aksakov) **2**:12-16; **181**:3-10, 14-16, 18, 45, 47, 49-50, 57, 62-63, 65-66
Deukalion (Taylor)
See "The Eye and the Ear"
"Deusa Incruenta" (Castro Alves) **205**:13, 37
Deutsche Abende (Auerbach) **171**:48
Der deutsche Bauernkrieg (Engels) **85**:117, 132, 144, 185
Deutsche Essays: Prosa aux zwei Jahrhunderten (Herder) **186**:13
Die Deutsche Gelehrtenrepublik (Klopstock) **11**:227, 234-36, 238; **225**:291, 323, 326, 335, 337
Deutsche Grammatik (Grimm Brothers) **3**:216-17, 219-20
Die deutsche Hausfrau (Kotzebue) **25**:141
Die deutsche Ideologie (Engels) **85**:44, 93, 97, 109-10, 115-17, 120, 126-28, 157; **114**:52-4, 69-70, 83-6
Der deutsche Mann und die vornehmen Leute (Kotzebue) **25**:145
Deutsche Mythologie (Grimm Brothers) **3**:216-17, 220
Deutsche Philologie im Afris (Herder) **186**:14
Deutsche Rechtsalterthümer (Grimm Brothers) **3**:216-17
Deutsche Sagen (Grimm Brothers) **3**:219
Die deutschen Kleinstädter (Kotzebue) **25**:143
Deutsches Wörterbuch (Grimm Brothers) **3**:216-17
"Deutschland. Ein Fragment" (Heine) **147**:197
Deutschland: Ein Wintermärchen (Heine) **4**:232, 236, 240, 243, 245-46, 252, 265-67; **54**:312, 337-8, 340, 347; **147**:148-50, 170, 185, 189-90, 200, 212, 216-17, 220
"Deutschland und seine Fürsten" (Schiller) **39**:388
"Deux amis" (Maupassant) **83**:181
"Deux augures" (Villiers de l'Isle Adam) **3**:589-90
Les deux aveugles de Chamouny (Nodier) **19**:381, 384
"Les Deux Bonnes Soeurs" (Baudelaire) **55**:74, 77
"Deux chiens" (Desbordes-Valmore) **97**:5
"Les deux héritages" (Mérimée) **6**:362; **65**:79-84
"Les Deux Maîtresses" (Musset) **7**:264; **150**:226-27
"Les Deux mères" (Desbordes-Valmore) **97**:23
Les Deux Musiciens (Balzac) **153**:150
"Les Deux peupliers" (Desbordes-Valmore) **97**:5, 15
"Les deux pigeons" (Laforgue) **5**:278, 281; **221**:7, 14
"Les Deux ramiers" (Desbordes-Valmore) **97**:5
Les Deux Trouvailles de Gallus (Hugo) **161**:234
"Development" (Newman) **99**:297, 300
Development of Christian Doctrine (Newman)
See *An Essay on the Development of Christian Doctrine*
Development of Doctrine (Newman)
See *An Essay on the Development of Christian Doctrine*
"The Development of English Literature" (Clough) **27**:101-2
"The Development of English Literature from Chaucer to Wordsworth" (Prescott) **163**:73
The Development of Socialism from a Utopia to a Science (Engels)
See *Die Entwicklung des Sozialismus von der Uopie zur Wissenschaft*
"The Development of the Kindergarten in the United States" (Peabody) **169**:150
Devereux (Bulwer-Lytton) **1**:145-46, 150, 155; **45**:13, 21, 24, 32, 34, 55, 68-70
"The Devil" (Verlaine)
See "Le Diable"
"The Devil and the Lady" (Tennyson) **30**:282; **65**:248-9
"The Devil and Tom Walker" (Irving) **2**:391; **19**:336
"The Devil in Manuscript" (Hawthorne) **2**:332; **95**:176, 184
"The Devil in the Belfry" (Poe) **16**:301, 323
"The Devil of Jóka" (Arany)
See "Jóka ördöge"
"The Devil-Drive" (Leskov)
See "Čertogon"
"Devilliers Erzählung von den Hexen auf dem Austerfelsen" (Brentano) **191**:81
"The Devils" (Pushkin)
See "Besy"
The Devils (Dostoevsky)
See *Besy*
The Devil's Elixir (Hoffmann)
See *Die Elixiere des Teufels*
"The Devil's Putty and Varnish" (Shaw) **15**:341
"The Devil's Sooty Brother" (Grimm Brothers) **3**:227
Devocionario (Gómez de Avellaneda) **111**:29
"Devon" (Reynolds) **146**:167, 173
"Dévotion" (Rimbaud) **35**:293, 323-24; **82**:233; **227**:235, 237-39, 242, 244, 309
"Devotion: An Epistle" (Brown) **122**:91, 96
Devotional Exercises (Martineau) **26**:310, 312; **137**:326, 329, 335-36
The Dewy Morn (Jefferies) **47**:93, 98, 101-03, 112-13, 117-19, 137
"D'ezesperance d'amour" (Balzac) **153**:168, 171
"Dezvoltarea istorica a României" (Eminescu) **131**:326
Dharmatattwa (Chatterji) **19**:216, 222, 225
"Día de difuntos" (Silva) **114**:262, 272, 294, 301-2, 313
"Día de difuntos de 1836" (Larra) **130**:209, 224, 238, 274
"El día de difuntos de 1836" (Larra) **17**:273, 276, 284-85
"Le diable" (Maupassant) **83**:182
"Le Diable" (Verlaine) **230**:161, 164
Le Diable à Paris (Balzac) **153**:147, 153
Le diable aux champs (Sand) **42**:314, 346-49
El diablo mundo (Espronceda) **39**:84-7, 90-1, 94, 97-8, 101, 108-10, 112-13, 118-21
Les diaboliques (Barbey d'Aurevilly) **1**:70-1, 73-9; **213**:5, 16, 23, 56-57, 59-61, 63, 65, 69-70, 73-74, 78, 81, 87, 89-93
Dialectic (Schleiermacher)
See *Dialektik*
"Dialectics" (Engels) **85**:38
Dialectics of Nature (Engels)
See *Dialektik der Natur*
Dialektik (Schleiermacher) **107**:285, 323, 325, 382
Dialektik der Natur (Engels) **85**:10, 12, 24, 36-44, 95, 105-06
"Dialog om sättet att sluta stycken" (Almqvist) **42**:9, 11, 16
Dialogo della natura e di un islandese (Leopardi) **129**:247, 255, 259
Dialogo di Federico Ruysch e delle sue mummie (Leopardi) **129**:232, 344, 350
"Dialogo di Plotino e di Porfirio" (Leopardi) **129**:250, 257-58
"Dialogo di Torquato Tasso e del suo genio familiare" (Leopardi) **129**:267
"Dialogo di un venditore d'almanacchi e di un passaggero" (Leopardi) **129**:243
"Dialogos" (Solomos) **15**:389, 402, 405
"A Dialogue" (Shelley) **18**:342
"Dialogue" (Solomos)
See "Dialogos"
"Dialogue avant le lever de la Lune" (Laforgue) **221**:86, 91
"Dialogue before Moonrise" (Laforgue)
See "Dialogue avant le lever de la Lune"
"A Dialogue between Cadmus and Hercules" (Montagu) **117**:182
"A Dialogue between the Head and Heart of an Irish Protestant" (Ferguson) **33**:295
"Dialogue entre le drapeau et la girouette" (Hugo) **189**:262
"Dialogue for Three Young Ladies" (Rowson) **69**:117
"A Dialogue in the Reading Room" (Hogg) **109**:262
"Dialogue in the Shades" (Barbauld) **50**:14
"A Dialogue on Different Situations in Life" (Barbauld) **185**:57
"A Dialogue On Happiness" (Karamzin)
See "Razgover o shchastii"
"Dialogue on How to Conclude Pieces" (Almqvist)
See "Dialog om sättet att sluta stycken"
Dialogue on Poetry (Schlegel)
See *Gespräch über die Poesie*

The Dialogue upon the Gardens at Stow (Gilpin) **30**:36, 43
"Dialogues" (Brown) **74**:170, 174
Dialogues between a Pair of Tongues (Wieland) **17**:393
Dialogues et fragments philosophiques (Renan) **26**:374-75, 380, 394-95, 397, 408, 413
Dialogues of the Dead (Montagu) **117**:135, 141, 152, 158, 178-79, 182
"Dialogues of the Living" (Brown) **74**:40
Dialogues philosophiques (Renan) **145**:361
Der Diamant des Geisterkönigs (Raimund) **69**:5, 7, 10, 21, 23, 31-3, 37, 43, 47
Der Diamant: Eine Komödie in fünf Acten (Hebbel) **43**:255, 297
Les diamants de la couronne (Scribe) **16**:384
"Diamantul Nordului" (Eminescu) **131**:348
The Diamond (Hebbel)
See *Der Diamant: Eine Komödie in fünf Acten*
The Diamond and the Pearl (Gore) **65**:32
"The Diamond Lens" (O'Brien) **21**:234-38, 240, 242, 244-51, 253-55
"The Diamond Necklace" (Maupassant)
See "La parure"
The Diamond of the King of Spirits (Raimund)
See *Der Diamant des Geisterkönigs*
"The Diamond of the North" (Eminescu)
See "Diamantul Nordului"
The Diamond of the Spirit-king (Raimund)
See *Der Diamant des Geisterkönigs*
Diana (Warner) **31**:349-51
Diana and Persis (Alcott) **58**:69
Diana Trelawny (Oliphant) **61**:202, 207
Diana's Tree (Da Ponte)
See *L'arbore dri Diana*
Diane (Augier) **31**:4, 8, 11, 14, 23, 34
Diane au Bois (Banville) **9**:18, 20, 22
Diane de Lys (Dumas) **9**:219, 224, 228, 230, 239, 240, 247, 249
"Diaphaneité" (Pater) **7**:304, 312, 333-34; **90**:260, 272-73, 287, 295-90, 298, 305
"Diapsalmata" (Kierkegaard) **125**:230, 248
Diaries (Dodgson) **139**:62, 65
Diario de un testigo de la guerra de Africa (Alarcon) **1**:12, 14; **219**:18
Diario íntimo (Gómez de Avellaneda) **111**:54
Diary (Allingham) **25**:18-21, 23, 26
Diary (Macha) **46**:215
Diary (Mill) **179**:310, 332-33
Diary (De Quincey)
See *A Diary of Thomas De Quincy, 1803*
Diary (Shevchenko) **54**:386-7
Diary and Autobiography of John Adams (Adams) **106**:66
Diary and Letters of Madame d'Arblay (Burney) **12**:26-34, 36-7, 61; **107**:40
A Diary in America, with Remarks on Its Institutions (Marryat) **3**:312-15, 319-20
The Diary of a Cosmopolitan (Sacher-Masoch) **31**:292
The Diary of a Desennuyee (Gore) **65**:26
"Diary of a Madman" (Gogol) **31**:95, 110; **5**:219-20, 227, 232, 236, 241, 252; **162**:8, 20, 52, 54, 56-57, 59, 63-65, 83, 94, 98, 127
"The Diary of a Plain Girl" (Levy) **59**:108
The Diary of a Scoundrel (Ostrovsky)
See *Na vsyakogo mudretsa dovolno prostoty*
"The Diary of a Superfluous Man" (Turgenev)
See "Dnevnik lišnego čeloveka"
The Diary of a Writer (Dostoevsky)
See *Dnevnik pisatelya*
The Diary of Alice James (James) **206**:153-54, 161, 168, 180-92, 197, 201-5
Diary of an Ennuyée (Jameson) **43**:304, 319, 322, 333-38
"The Diary of Anne Rodway" (Collins) **1**:187
The Diary of Benjamin Robert Haydon (Haydon) **146**:132-33, 135, 138-39, 141, 143, 147-48, 150-54
The Diary of C. Jeames de la Pluche, Esq. (Thackeray) **213**:284
The Diary of Dr. John William Polidori (Polidori) **51**:206
Diary of EBB: The Unpublished Diary of Elizabeth Barrett Browning (Barrett Browning) **61**:50
Diary of John Quincy (Adams) **175**:22-23, 25-27
Diary of Marie Bashkirtseff (Bashkirtseff)
See *Le journal de Marie Bashkirtseff*
"A Diary of One Week" (Radishchev)
See "Dnevnik odnoi nedeli"
"Diary of the Seducer" (Kierkegaard) **125**:182, 189-90, 198-200, 202-3, 206-8, 210-12, 214, 229-30, 232, 248, 250, 269, 279
Diary of the Voyage of H.M.S. Beagle (Darwin) **57**:113, 116, 143, 152
A Diary of Thomas De Quincy, 1803 (De Quincey) **87**:60, 75-7, 72
Diary, Reminiscences, and Correspondence of Henry Crabb Robinson (Robinson) **15**:172-73, 176-83, 185-87
"Dichter Firdusi" (Heine) **147**:229
"Der Dichter und der Komponist" (Hoffmann) **2**:347, 350; **183**:180
Dichter und ihre Gesellen (Eichendorff) **8**:222; **225**:8-9, 19, 21-22, 24, 27, 29, 31
Dichter und Kaufmann (Auerbach) **171**:47-48, 54-56, 61
Dichtergarten (Schumann) **143**:144
Dichterliebe (Schumann) **143**:139
"Dichters Blumenstrauss" (Brentano) **1**:95
"Dichters Naturgelfül" (Droste-Hülshoff) **3**:202
"Dichtung and Geschichte" (Arnim) **159**:95
Dichtung und Wahrheit (Goethe) **34**:58, 69, 122
Dichtungen (Schumann) **143**:84
"Dick McCoy's Sketches of His Neighbors" (Hooper) **177**:175
"Dickens in Relation to Criticism" (Lewes) **25**:280, 286, 306, 308, 317, 322; **215**:134, 181, 186
"Dickon the Devil" (Le Fanu) **9**:320
Dictionary of Poetical Quotations (Hale) **75**:284, 341
Dictionary of Received Ideas (Flaubert)
See *Dictionnaire des idées recues*
A Dictionary of the English Language, Compiled for the Use of Common Schools in the United States (Webster) **30**:396
Dictionnaire des étiquettes (Genlis) **166**:26
Dictionnaire des idées recues (Flaubert) **2**:167; **62**:69-70, 72-3, 94; **66**:263, 274; **185**:212, 217
"Did I?" (Cooke) **110**:4
"Did the Harebell Loose Her Girdle" (Dickinson) **21**:41
"Diddling Considered as One of the Exact Sciences" (Poe) **16**:312, 323
"Diderot" (Carlyle) **70**:57
Diderot à Pétersbourg (Sacher-Masoch) **31**:288
Didymus the Clerk (Foscolo) **8**:262-63
"An die aufgelöste Preußische Nationalversammlung" (Arnim) **123**:8
"An die Deutschen" (Hölderlin) **16**:194
"Die drei Nüsse" (Brentano) **191**:50, 119
An die Freiheit (Werner) **189**:355
An die Freude (Schiller)
See *Lied an die Freude*
"An die Geliebte" (Mörike) **10**:449; **201**:280-81
"An die Hofnung" (Hölderlin) **16**:181
"An die jungen Dichter" (Hölderlin) **16**:190
An die Künstler (Liszt) **199**:335
"An Die Natur im Spätsommer" (Meyer) **81**:140-41, 145-48, 151, 151
"An die Sammlung" (Grillparzer) **102**:170
"An die Schriftstellerinnen in Deutschland und Frankreich" (Droste-Hülshoff) **3**:202
An die Slowenen die in deutscher Sprache dichten (Preseren) **127**:306
"An die Sonne" (Schiller) **39**:338, 355
"An die Vollendung" (Hölderlin) **16**:174
"An dienes Kreuzes Stamm o Jesu Christ" (Storm) **195**:95
Dies Buch Gehört dem König (Arnim) **38**:9, 16; **123**:5, 9, 11-12, 31, 42, 47-51, 62, 65, 69-70, 88-89, 92
"Dies Irae" (Leconte de Lisle) **29**:216, 235-36, 242-45
Dies Irae (Macaulay) **42**:116
Dietegen (Keller) **2**:415, 423
"Dieu" (Lamartine) **11**:269; **190**:201-2
Dieu (Hugo) **3**:273; **161**:251, 266
"Le Dieu des bonnes gens" (Beranger) **34**:28
Le Dieu et la bayadère (Scribe) **16**:382, 409-10
Dieu et l'état (Bakunin) **25**:39, 50, 72; **58**:99
"Dieu et ma dame" (Patmore) **9**:341
"Les Dieux" (Verlaine) **230**:167
Les Dieux antiques (Mallarmé) **41**:249, 277
"The Difference between History and Romance" (Brown) **74**:110, 192
Differenz des Fichteschen und Schellingschen Systems der Philosophie, in Beziehung auf Reinholds Beiträge zur leichteren Übersicht des Zustandes der Philosophie zu Anfang des neunzehnten Jahrhunderts (Hegel) **151**:258
Difficulties (Newman)
See *Lectures on Certain Difficulties Felt by Anglicans in submitting to the Catholic Church*
Difficulties of Anglicans (Newman)
See *Lectures on Certain Difficulties Felt by Anglicans in submitting to the Catholic Church*
"Difficulties of the Publishers of Contemporary Memoirs" (D'Israeli) **217**:299
Digging for Gold (Alger) **83**:114
"The Dignity of Woman" (Schiller) **39**:306
The Digression (Mickiewicz) **3**:401
"A Digression" (Willis) **194**:282
"Digressive Letter to the Reader" (Willis) **194**:319
Digte, første ring (Wergeland) **5**:536, 539-40
En Digters Bazar (Andersen) **7**:16-17; **79**:79, 81; **214**:61, 74
Dikter (Runeberg) **41**:313, 317, 325
"The Dilemma" (Holmes) **14**:109
"A Dilettante" (Webster) **230**:231, 233-34
Dilettantism in Science (Herzen) **10**:346; **61**:98
"La diligencia" (Larra) **17**:279
Diligent Dick (More) **141**:193
Dílo (Macha)
See *Dílo Karla Hynka Mácha*
Dílo Karla Hynka Mácha (Macha) **46**:202-3, 212, 218
"Dimanches" (Laforgue) **5**:280; **53**:292, 299; **221**:7, 23-24, 35-36, 42, 47, 50, 64, 68, 82-83, 85, 87, 90-93
Dimitri Roudine (Turgenev)
See *Rudin*
"Dina la belle juive" (Borel) **41**:4, 6-7, 13
"Dining Out" (Haliburton) **149**:297-98
"The Dinkey Bird" (Field) **3**:210
"Dinner Real and Reputed" (De Quincey) **4**:61
Dinorah (Andersen) **79**:9
Diogenes (Wieland)
See *Sokrates Mainomenos; oder, Die Dialogen des Diogenes von Sinope*
"Dion" (Wordsworth) **12**:427; **166**:212
"El Dios del siglo" (Isaacs) **70**:309
"Dios nos asista" (Larra) **17**:282; **130**:223
Dipsychus (Clough) **27**:45, 53, 56, 69, 74, 76-80, 84-6, 97-101, 103, 105, 112-16, 119
Dipsychus (Prescott) **163**:6, 8, 11, 13-14, 18, 27, 29-33, 36, 40, 42, 50-58, 64, 85-87, 90, 114, 126, 128-32, 138-41
"Dipsychus Continued" (Prescott) **163**:53, 89
"Dirce" (Landor) **14**:176, 183, 199
"Directions for Courtship" (Freneau) **111**:132
"Dirge" (Beddoes) **154**:78
"Dirge" (Emerson) **98**:93, 179, 182
"A Dirge" (Levy) **59**:90

"A Dirge" (Rossetti) **2**:557
"A Dirge" (Tennyson) **30**:211, 223
"Dirge for a Soldier" (Boker) **125**:25, 31, 33, 39
"Dirge for Two Veterans" (Whitman) **31**:391
"The Dirty Old Man" (Allingham) **25**:8, 23
"Dîs Aliter Visum" (Browning) **19**:112; **79**:165-66
The Disagreeable Woman: A Social Mystery (Alger) **83**:99, 116, 145
"A Disappointment" (Baillie) **151**:86, 93-96, 123
"Disappointment" (Coleridge) **31**:62
"A Disastrous Partnership" (Boyesen) **135**:14, 20-21, 30
The Discarded Daughter (Southworth) **26**:437
"The Discarded Son" (Alger) **83**:96
"The Discharged Soldier" (Wordsworth) **111**:347-48
"The Disciple" (Very) **9**:383, 393
The Disciples at Saïs (Novalis)
See *Die Lehrlinge zu Saïs*
"The Discontented Poet" (Emerson) **38**:193
Discorso di un italiano intorno alla poesia romantica (Leopardi) **129**:256, 264-65, 314
Discorso sopra alcuni punti della storia longobardica in Italia (Manzoni) **29**:251; **98**:213, 215, 217, 241
"Discorso storico sul testo del 'Decamerone'" (Foscolo) **8**:263
Discorso sul testo e su le opinioni diverse prevalenti intorno alla storio e alla emendazione critica della "Commedia" di Dante (Foscolo) **8**:263
Discours (Constant) **182**:134
"Discours d'Ouverture" (Michelet) **218**:335
Discours Préliminaire (Comte) **54**:210, 214
Discours prononcés à la Chambre (Lamartine) **190**:171
Discours sur la suppression des couvents de religieuses et l'éducation publique des femmes (Genlis) **166**:16
Discours sur la Vertu (Maistre) **37**:302
Discours sur l'ensemble du positivisme (Comte) **54**:203
Discours sur l'esprit positif (Comte) **54**:236
Discours sur l'imortalité de l'âme (Balzac) **153**:150-52
Discours sur Victor Hugo (Leconte de Lisle) **29**:233
"Discourse" (Baillie)
See "Introductory Discourse"
"Discourse for the Congress of Lyons" (Foscolo)
See "Orazione a Bonaparte pel congresso di Lione"
A Discourse of Matters Pertaining to Religion (Parker) **186**:127, 143-45, 148, 201, 204, 206-7, 215, 218
Discourse of Religion (Parker)
See *A Discourse of Matters Pertaining to Religion*
"Discourse of the Wanderer and an Evening Visit to the Lake" (Wordsworth) **166**:265
Discourse on Lyric Poetry or on the Ode (Derzhavin)
See *Rassuzhdenie o liriCeskoj poezii ili ob ode*
"Discourse on Mythology" (Schlegel) **226**:161, 163-67
"Discourse on Poetry" (Harpur) **114**:102, 164
A Discourse on the Constitution and Government of the United States (Calhoun) **15**:22-3, 35, 44, 53, 55, 73
"A Discourse on the Manners of the Antient Greeks" (Shelley) **18**:354
Discourse on the Text of Dante, and on the Various Opinions concerning the History and the Corrections of the "Divina Commedia" (Foscolo)
See *Discorso sul testo e su le opinioni diverse prevalenti intorno alla storio e alla emendazione critica della "Commedia" di Dante*
A Discourse on the Transient and Permanent in Christianity (Parker) **186**:141-42, 157, 162, 180, 185, 187, 200, 212-13
"A Discourse upon Beards" (Freneau) **111**:134
Discourse upon Certain Points of the History of the Longobards (Manzoni)
See *Discorso sopra alcuni punti della storia longobardica in Italia*
Discourses Addressed to Mixed Congregations (Newman) **38**:303, 308-10, 315; **99**:233-34, 266-67
Discourses in America (Arnold) **6**:40-41, 46; **126**:43
Discourses on Davila (Adams) **106**:11-13, 18, 40, 44-5, 51-4
Discourses on Religion (Schleiermacher)
See *Über die Religion: Reden an die Gebildeten unter ihren Verächtern*
Discourses on Religion, addressed to the educated, among those who despise it (Schleiermacher)
See *Über die Religion: Reden an die Gebildeten unter ihren Verächtern*
Discourses on University Education (Newman) **99**:212
Discourses, Reviews, and Miscellanies (Channing) **17**:7, 46
Discourses to Mixed Congregations (Newman)
See *Discourses Addressed to Mixed Congregations*
"The Discoverer of the North Cape" (Longfellow) **45**:160
"Discoveries, Inventions and Improvements" (Lincoln) **201**:166, 183, 185
The Discovery of the Great West (Parkman)
See *La Salle and the Discovery of the Great West*
The Discreet Princess (Planché) **42**:274, 279, 292
Discussion of the Situtation of Artists (Liszt)
See *De la situation des artistes et de leur condition dans la société*
Discussions and Arguments on Various Subjects (Newman) **38**:311-12
"Disestablishment in Wales" (Arnold) **218**:250
"The Dish of Tea" (Freneau) **111**:142
"The Disinherited" (Nerval)
See "El Desdichado"
"The Disinterred Warrior" (Bryant) **6**:172; **46**:3
Disjecta Membra (Barbey d'Aurevilly) **213**:88, 93
The Disowned (Bulwer-Lytton) **1**:138, 145, 150; **45**:10, 13, 21, 24, 34, 68-9
"Dispostions for Faith" (Newman) **38**:305, 310
"Disputation" (Heine) **4**:255; **147**:163
A Disquisition on Government (Calhoun) **15**:22-3, 28, 34, 44, 50-1, 53, 55, 59, 64, 67, 69-71, 73
Dissertation (Kant) **27**:220-21; **67**:214, 219
The Dissertation on Anecdotes (D'Israeli)
See *Miscellanies; or, Literary Recreations*
"Dissertation on Didactic Poetry" (Warton) **118**:338
Dissertation on First Principles of Government (Paine) **62**:261, 267, 271, 300, 302
"Dissertation on Language" (Beattie)
See *Dissertations Moral and Critical: On Memory and Imagination; On Dreaming; The Theory of Language; On Fable and Romance; On the Attachments of Kindred; Illustrations on Sublimity*
"Dissertation on Old and New Styles of the Russian Language" (Karamzin)
See "Rassuzdenie o starom i novom sloge rossijskogo jazyka"
"Dissertation on Pastoral Poetry" (Warton) **118**:338, 342
Dissertation on the Canon and Feudal Law (Adams) **106**:4, 14, 28, 47
A Dissertation on the Theory and Practice of Benevolence (Dyer) **129**:98, 103, 112, 115, 125, 130-31, 136-37, 143
"A Dissertation upon Roast Pig" (Lamb) **10**:392, 404, 415, 435; **113**:159, 162, 200, 238
Dissertations and Discussions, Political, Philosophical, and Historical (Mill) **179**:208, 227; **223**:99
Dissertations Moral and Critical: On Memory and Imagination; On Dreaming; The Theory of Language; On Fable and Romance; On the Attachments of Kindred; Illustrations on Sublimity (Beattie) **25**:98-100, 114-15
Dissertations on Government, the Affairs of the Bank, and Paper Money (Paine) **62**:270, 294, 368
Dissertations on the English Language; with Notes, Historical and Critical (Webster) **30**:403, 408, 410, 413-16
Dissertazione sopra l'anima delle bestie (Leopardi) **129**:324
"The Dissidence of Dissent and the Protestantism of the Protestant Religion" (Arnold) **218**:186
"A Dissolving View" (Cooper) **129**:51, 67, 73-74, 77-80
"Distance" (Lampman) **194**:34, 79
"Distant Correspondents" (Lamb) **10**:436; **113**:245, 249
"Distant View of England from the Sea" (Bowles) **103**:55
Disthyrambic Rhapsody on the Rhapsody of Cabalistic Prose (Herder)
See *Dithyrambische Rhapsodie über Die Rhapsodie Kabbalistischer Prose*
"Distiches" (Taylor) **89**:318
"Distinction" (Patmore) **9**:342, 344
"Disturbed Vigil" (Willis) **194**:282
"Dithyrambe" (Schiller) **166**:96, 115
Dithyrambische Rhapsodie über Die Rhapsodie Kabbalistischer Prose (Herder) **186**:33-34
"La Diva" (Gautier) **59**:18
Diva (Alencar) **157**:9, 16-17, 31, 39, 41
Divagations (Mallarmé) **4**:373, 377, 396; **41**:252; **210**:227, 249, 257, 260, 264
Dīvān (Ghalib)
See *Diwan-E-Ghalib*
"The Divell's Chrystmasse" (Field) **3**:205, 211
"The Diver" (Schiller)
See "Der Taucher"
"Divers Worlds. Time and Eternity" (Rossetti) **50**:285
The Diversions of Purley (Horne Tooke) **195**:288-89, 291, 298, 300-301, 307-8, 310-13, 317-18, 326-27, 331, 335-41, 343-45
The Diversions of Purley, Part One (Horne Tooke)
See *The Diversions of Purley*
The Diversions of Purley, Part Two (Horne Tooke)
See *The Diversions of Purley*
Diversity of Human Language Structure and Its Influence on the Mental Development of Mankind (Humboldt)
See *On Language*
The Diverting History of John Bull and Brother Jonathan (Paulding) **2**:528
"The Diverting History of John Gilpin" (Cowper) **8**:98, 105, 108, 118-19, 122-23, 133, 137; **94**:26, 36-7, 84
"Divided" (Ingelow) **39**:257, 262-63, 268; **107**:119-20, 122-23
"The Divine Image" (Blake) **13**:240-41, 243; **37**:3, 5, 9, 18, 23, 25, 31-3, 38, 40, 44-5, 52-3, 57, 71-2, 79; **127**:31; **173**:16
The Divine Tragedy (Longfellow) **2**:484, 495-98; **45**:113, 127, 129, 150, 159, 164-65
"Divinia Commedia" (Longfellow) **45**:186

"The Divining Cauldron of Kibitsu" (Ueda Akinari)
See "Kibitsu no kama"
"The Divinity School Address" (Emerson) **1**:303, 306-07; **38**:147, 198, 202, 204-05, 207-08; **98**:4, 7, 9, 18-19, 27, 43, 61, 124, 159-65, 176, 181, 190
"The Division" (Krylov) **1**:435
"Division of an Estate" (Horton) **87**:102
"Divorce" (Genlis) **166**:26
"The Divorce Unconsciousness. A Motive of Divorce Proceedings . . ." ("Brakorazvodnoie zabvieniie. Prichina razvodov brachnykh ...") (Leskov) **174**:137
The Divorced Woman (Sacher-Masoch)
See *The Separated Wife*
Diwan-E-Ghalib (Ghalib) **39**:126, 129, 156; **78**:65, 69, 77
Dix années d'exil (Staël-Holstein) **3**:521, 527; **91**:325, 350-1, 360, 363, 365
Dix ans de la vie d'une femme; ou, Les Mauvais Conseils (Scribe) **16**:412
"Les djinns" (Hugo) **3**:261
"Djoûmane" (Mérimée) **6**:369-71; **65**:51-2, 56, 58-9, 63, 98
Dmitri Kalinin (Belinski) **5**:101
Dmitry Samozvanets i Vasily Shuysky (Ostrovsky) **30**:101; **57**:206-7
"Dnevnik lišnego čeloveka" (Turgenev) **21**:388, 401, 414, 418, 433, 439; **37**:438; **122**:247, 258, 266, 342-43
"Dnevnik odnoi nedeli" (Radishchev) **190**:284, 309, 314, 321, 336-38
Dnevnik pisatelia (Dostoevsky)
See *Dnevnik pisatelya*
Dnevnik pisatelya (Dostoevsky) **2**:162, 185-86; **21**:106, 109; **33**:163, 170-71, 175, 179; **43**:87, 92, 157, 159, 167; **119**:74, 90; **167**:241, 336; **202**:93, 99, 102, 105, 109, 114-16, 146
Dnevnik provintsiala v Peterburge (Saltykov) **16**:343, 359, 373-74
Do and Dare; or, A Brave Boy's Fight for Fortune (Alger) **8**:19, 25, 44, 46
"Do czytelnika" (Norwid) **17**:371
"Do I Love Thee?" (Ridge) **82**:182
"Do króla" (Krasicki) **8**:407
"Do no imitate: genius is original..." (Baratynsky)
See "Ne podrazhay: svoeobrazen genity..."
"Do not believe the poet, maiden" (Tyutchev)
See "Ne ver, ne ver poetu, deva"
"Do Not Go Inside" (Storm)
See "Geh nicht hinein"
Do Not Live As You Want To (Ostrovsky)
See *Ne tak zhiví kak khóchetsya*
"Do Osnovjanenka" (Shevchenko) **54**:373-4
"Do przyjaciól Moskali" (Mickiewicz) **3**:401
"Do We Still Have the Public and Fatherland of Yore?" (Herder)
See "Haben wir noch jetzt das Publikum und Vaterland der Alten?"
"Do You Know Why I Love Her?" (Isaacs)
See "Sabéis por qué la amo?"
"Do You Want Me to Settle Down?" (Grillparzer)
See "Willst du, ich soll Hütten bauen?"
"Dobbin Dead" (Barnes) **75**:35
"Döbeln at Juutas" (Runeberg)
See "Döbeln vid Juutas"
"Döbeln vid Juutas" (Runeberg) **41**:312-15, 323
"The Doctor" (Levy) **203**:354
"The Doctor" (Maginn) **8**:435
The Doctor, &c. (Southey) **8**:467-68, 470-73; **97**:264-65, 267, 271, 276, 288-92, 320-24, 329, 331
Doctor Birch and His Young Friends (Thackeray) **5**:459
"Dr. Bullivant" (Hawthorne) **95**:130
"Dr Frühlingsfeier" (Klopstock) **11**:234, 236, 238, 240-41
The Doctor in Spite of Himself (Tyler) **3**:573
Doctor Jekyll and Mr. Hyde (Stevenson)
See *The Strange Case of Dr. Jekyll and Mr. Hyde*
"Doctor Krupov" (Herzen) **61**:108
"Doctor Marigold" (Dickens) **3**:163
"Doctor Parker's Patty" (Cooke) **110**:34
"El Doctor Rafael Núñez" (Silva) **114**:296
"Doctor Tarr and Professor Fether" (Poe)
See "The System of Doctor Tarr and Professor Fether"
"Doctor Theophilus" (Cranch)
See "The Legend of Doctor Theophilus: or, The Enchanted Clothes"
Doctor Thorne: A Novel (Trollope) **6**:453, 459, 463, 470, 480-81, 491, 499-501, 512, 516-17; **101**:235, 251, 253, 264, 272-74, 321, 333; **215**:208, 286, 307, 337-38, 341, 343
"Doctor Tristan's Treatment" (Villiers de l'Isle Adam)
See "Le traitement du docteur Tristan"
Doctor Vandyke (Cooke) **5**:124, 130, 132
"Doctrine" (Heine)
See "Doktrin"
"Doctrine and Discipline of Human Culture" (Alcott) **167**:36, 45-46, 82
"The Doctrine of the Soul" (Emerson) **38**:177
The Dodd Family Abroad (Lever) **23**:288-89, 292, 296-97, 301-02, 305, 307
The Dodge Club (De Mille) **123**:130
"Dodningen" (Andersen) **79**:86
"Det døende Barn" (Andersen) **79**:76
"The Dog" (Turgenev)
See "Sobaka"
Dog and Gun; A Few Loose Chapters on Shooting, Among Which Will Be Found Some Anecdotes and Incidents (Hooper) **177**:182, 214-15
"The Dog and the Water-Lily: No Fable" (Cowper) **8**:119; **94**:122, 124
"Doge und Dogaressa" (Hoffmann)
See "Doge und Dogaresse"
"Doge und Dogaresse" (Hoffmann) **183**:217
Dogma socialista (Echeverria) **18**:150
"The Dogs" (Hunt) **1**:423
"Dogs" (Verlaine)
See "Chiens"
"Dog-Scratcher" (Petofi)
See "Kutyakaparó"
"Doing as One Likes" (Arnold) **218**:197
"Doings of the Sun Beam" (Holmes) **81**:102, 125-26
Dokhodnoye mesto (Ostrovsky) **30**:91, 101, 105, 111, 115; **57**:198, 202, 209-10, 218, 220
Doktor Luther: Eine Schilderung (Freytag) **109**:148
"Doktrin" (Heine) **54**:345-46, 350; **147**:197, 204
Dolce far Niente (Hayne) **94**:136
"Dolefully" (Bestuzhev)
See "Zaunno"
The Dolliver Romance, and Other Pieces (Hawthorne) **2**:324, 326, 335
"Dolly" (Bloomfield) **145**:129, 154
"Dolly's Mistake" (Clare) **9**:74-75; **86**:155-56
Dolores, Pages from a Family Chronicle (Gómez de Avellaneda)
See *Dolores, páginas de una crónica de familia*
Dolores, páginas de una crónica de familia (Gómez de Avellaneda) **111**:13, 24, 30
"Dolorida" (Vigny) **7**:470, 473; **102**:335, 367-68
"Dolorosa" (Casal) **131**:259, 267, 269
"Dolph Heyliger" (Irving) **2**:368, 390; **19**:336-37, 341, 345
Dom Gigadas (Balzac) **5**:58
"The Domain of Arnheim" (Poe) **16**:304, 336; **55**:147; **94**:240; **117**:265, 290, 310
"The Domain or Arnheim" (Poe) **211**:227
"Dombey and Son" (Crawford) **127**:196
Dombey and Son (Dickens)
See *Dealings with the Firm of Dombey and Son*
"The Domestic Affections" (Hemans) **71**:278, 289-91
"The Domestic Affections" and Other Poems (Hemans) **71**:272-73, 278, 289
Domestic Anecdotes of the French Nation During the Last Thirty Years; Indicative of the French Revolution (D'Israeli) **217**:320
"Domestic Asides" (Hood) **16**:235
"Domestic Beverage" (Robinson) **142**:138
"Domestic Economy" (Delany) **93**:162
"Domestic Fame" (Milnes) **61**:136
"Domestic Happiness" (Halleck) **47**:57
"Domestic Life" (Emerson) **1**:280; **38**:212; **98**:82
The Domestic Manners and Private Life of Sir Walter Scott (Hogg) **4**:278
Domestic Manners of the Americans (Trollope) **30**:304, 310, 312, 314-15, 320-24, 326
"Domestic Peace" (Coleridge) **99**:48
A Domestic Picture (Ostrovsky)
See *Semeynaya kartina*
"A Domestic Tale" (Hemans) **71**:289
Domik v Kolomne (Pushkin) **3**:444, 456; **27**:367, 386; **83**:275, 338
"Dominion" (Ingelow) **39**:266
Dominique (Fromentin) **10**:227-28, 230-31, 233, 236-42, 245-46, 248-60, 262; **125**:95-98, 101, 104-15, 121-26, 128-32, 134-36, 138-42, 146-49, 155, 159, 161-63, 165, 167, 169-70
Le domino noir (Scribe) **16**:384, 401
"Don Andréa Vésalius l'anatomiste" (Borel) **41**:4, 6, 13
Don Caesar de Bazan (Boucicault) **41**:30
Don Carlos (Schiller) **39**:312, 314, 324, 330, 334-36, 343, 360, 362, 371, 375-76, 380-81, 389-90; **69**:169, 242-44; **166**:76, 117, 126, 130, 135-36, 159
Don Catrín de la fachenda (Lizardi)
See *Vida y hechos del famoso caballero Don Catrín de la fachenda*
"Don du poème" (Mallarmé) **41**:250, 274-75, 281; **210**:162, 169, 244
Don Garzia (Alfieri) **101**:4, 8, 32, 38, 42
"Don Giovanni" (Kierkegaard) **125**:212
Don Giovanni (Byron) **12**:82-83
Don Giovanni (Da Ponte)
See *Il dissoluto punito o sia il Don Giovanni*
Don John: A Story (Ingelow) **39**:261, 264; **107**:118, 124, 151
"Don Juan" (Clare) **9**:107-08, 124; **86**:90
"Don Juan" (Hoffmann) **2**:345-47; **183**:180-81, 223, 225, 242-44, 246, 248-49, 311
"Don Juan" (Pushkin) **83**:275
Don Juan (Byron) **2**:65, 68-72, 75-7, 80-2, 85-7, 90-4, 97-8; **12**:70-147; **109**:62, 67-8, 73, 85, 93, 99, 102-03, 118, 120, 127; **149**:1-173
Don Juan (Da Ponte)
See *Il dissoluto punito o sia il Don Giovanni*
Don Juan (Lenau) **16**:268-69, 274, 279, 281-82
Don Juan and Faust (Grabbe)
See *Don Juan und Faust*
"Don Juan aux enfers" (Baudelaire) **6**:83, 89; **55**:58
Don Juan de Covadonga (Silva) **114**:262
Don Juan de Marana (Dumas) **11**:45, 47; **71**:211, 214
"Don Juan Duped" (Verlaine) **51**:372
"Don Juan in Hades" (Baudelaire)
See "Don Juan aux enfers"
Don Juan of Kolomea (Sacher-Masoch) **31**:286-87, 290-93
Don Juan Tenorio (Zorrilla y Moral) **6**:523-27
Don Juan und Faust (Grabbe) **2**:272-75, 281, 283-85, 287

"Don Juanito Marques Verdugo do los Leganes" (Chamisso) **82**:6
"Don Paez" (Musset) **7**:256, 265, 267, 277-78; **150**:229-31, 233, 299-305, 311
"Don Pedrillo" (Heine) **147**:152
"Don Pedrillo" (Lazarus) **8**:425; **109**:324
Don Pedro (Cumberland) **167**:152, 190, 192
Don Pedro of Castile (Boker) **125**:58
Don Quixote (Percy) **95**:338
Don Sanche, ou le Château d'amour (Liszt) **199**:320
Don Simplicio Bobadilla (Tamayo y Baus) **1**:571
Don Sylvio de Rosalva (Wieland)
See *Der Sieg der Natur über die Schwärmerei; oder, die Abenteuer des Don Sylvio von Rosalva*
Don Sylvio von Rosalva (Wieland) **17**:390, 397, 404-06, 412, 424
Doña Juana the Magnate (Tamayo y Baus)
See *La ricahembra*
"Donagh, or the Horse-stealers" (Carleton) **199**:9
"Donald Caird" (Scott) **15**:318
"Donald MacDonald" (Hogg) **4**:284
Das Donauweib (Tieck) **5**:519
El doncel de don Enrique el Doliente (Larra) **17**:270, 279; **130**:197-98, 200, 228, 274
"Done For" (Cooke) **110**:9
"Dong, Sounds the Brass in the East" (Thoreau) **7**:384
The Dong with a Luminous Nose (Lear) **3**:299-300, 307-9
"Donkey Cabbages" (Grimm Brothers) **3**:227
"Donna Clara" (Heine) **147**:152
Donna de Solis (Martínez de la Rosa) **102**:228
Donna Florida (Simms) **3**:501
La donna serpente (Gozzi) **23**:108, 119, 121, 123, 125
"Donoso-Cortés, Marqués de Valdegamas, and Julian, Roman Emperor" (Herzen) **10**:339
"Don't Ceäre" (Barnes) **75**:9
Don't Get Into Another's Sleigh (Ostrovsky)
See *Ne v svoi sani ne sadis!*
"Don't propose on a Sunday" (Lonnrot) **53**:339
Don't Sit in Another's Sleigh (Ostrovsky)
See *Ne v svoi sani ne sadis!*
"Doom and Dan" (Cooke) **110**:28
"Doom Is the House without the Door" (Dickinson) **171**:98, 139
"The Doom of a City" (Thomson) **18**:397, 406-07, 409, 412-14, 421, 424-25, 431
"The Doom of English Wills" (Dickens) **217**:255
"The Doom of King Acrisius" (Morris) **4**:442, 447-48
"The Doom of the Griffiths" (Gaskell) **5**:192, 201; **70**:191, 193
"The Doom of the Sirens" (Rossetti) **4**:510
"Doomsday" (Beddoes) **154**:70-72
A Door Must Be Either Open or Shut (Musset)
See *Il faut qu'une porte soit ouvertr ou fermée*
"The Doorkeeper" (Stifter)
See "Tourmaline"
"The Doorkeeper at the Mansion" (Stifter)
See "Tourmaline"
"Doors and Windows" (Corbière)
See "Portes et fenêtres"
Ein Doppelgänger (Storm) **1**:541, 550; **195**:5, 127, 131-32
"Doppelheimweh" (Lenau) **16**:281
"Die Doppeltgänger" (Hoffmann) **2**:360; **183**:166, 193
"Dora" (Ingelow) **39**:258
"Dora" (Kendall) **12**:180
"Dora" (Tennyson) **30**:233, 241
"Dora Dee" (O'Brien) **21**:243, 246-47
"Dora Greenwell" (Whittier) **59**:365
Dora Livingstone, the Adulteress; or, The Quaker City (Lippard)
See *The Quaker City; or, The Monks of Monk-Hall. A Romance of Philadelphia Life, Mystery, and Crime*
El Dorado (Bird) **197**:24
"El Dorado" (Stevenson) **193**:282
"Dorchester Giant" (Holmes) **14**:101
Dorfgeschichten (Auerbach)
See *Schwarzwälder Dorfgeschichten*
Dorfweisthümer (Grimm Brothers) **3**:216
"The Dorian Measure" (Peabody) **169**:176-77, 179, 190, 200, 202-3
"A Dorio ad Phrygium" (Norwid) **17**:368
"Le dormeur du val" (Rimbaud) **4**:465; **35**:271, 321; **82**:230, 233, 247
Dornröschen: Genast's Poem and Raff's Music of the Same Name (Liszt) **199**:305
"Doroga ot stantsii Almaly do posta Mugansy" (Bestuzhev) **131**:160
Dorotheas Blumenkörbchen (Keller) **2**:412, 416
"Dorothée" (Baudelaire)
See "La belle Dorothée"
Dorothy and Other Italian Stories (Woolson) **82**:275, 283, 293, 299, 308, 338, 341, 344
Dorothy Chance (Moodie) **14**:226
"Dorothy Q" (Holmes) **14**:109, 118, 128; **81**:103
"Dorset Folk and Dorset" (Barnes) **75**:57
Dos amores (Villaverde) **121**:333-34
"El dos de mayo" (Espronceda) **39**:120
Dos mujeres (Gómez de Avellaneda) **111**:8, 13-14, 18-22, 25, 28-29, 33-35, 56-57, 61, 64
"Las dos olas" (Bécquer) **106**:126
Le dossier no. 113 (Gaboriau) **14**:14-16, 18-19, 22-4, 26, 29, 32-3
"Dost Thou Not Care?" (Rossetti) **50**:263
Dot (Boucicault) **41**:34
"Doth true Love lonely grow?" (Crawford) **127**:151-52
"Le douanier" (Corbière) **43**:21
"Les douaniers" (Daudet) **1**:252
The Double (Dostoevsky)
See *Dvoynik*
"The Double Chamber" (Baudelaire)
See "La chambre double"
"La double conversion" (Daudet) **1**:249
"Une double famille" (Balzac) **153**:69
"Double Knock" (Hood) **16**:236
The Double Marriage (Reade) **2**:541, 547
La double méprise (Mérimée) **6**:352-4, 357, 360, 366, 368-70; **65**:54-7, 62-4, 100-01, 117, 128
The Double Mistake (Mérimée)
See *La double méprise*
"Double Quatuor" (Hugo) **10**:361
"A Double Thanksgiving" (Cooke) **110**:50
"Double Triangle Serpent and Rays" (Fuller) **50**:247-8
"The Double-Headed Snake" (Whittier) **59**:360
Doublets (Dodgson) **139**:57
"Doubt" (Beddoes) **154**:79
"Doubt" (Cooke) **110**:9
"Doubt and Prayer" (Tennyson) **65**:248, 267
"Doubt Me! My Dim Companion" (Dickinson) **21**:54, 57
"Doubtful Dreams" (Gordon) **21**:155-57, 159-61, 176, 183
"Douces larmes" (Banville) **9**:30
The Dough Face (Brown) **89**:182
"Dover Beach" (Arnold) **6**:37, 44, 48, 64, 66, 73; **29**:33, 35; **89**:14, 20, 22, 25-8, 46, 51-2, 62, 88, 119, 121; **126**:6, 75, 83; **218**:120, 147-48, 152-53, 166, 177-78, 190
"Dover Cliffs" (Bowles)
See "On Dover Cliffs. July 20, 1787"
The Doves (Cowper) **94**:108
"The Doves and the Crows" (Hood) **16**:239
Dovol'no (Turgenev) **37**:443
The Dowager; or, the New School for Scandal (Gore) **65**:20
Dowerless (Ostrovsky)
See *Bespridannitsa*
The Dowerless Girl (Ostrovsky)
See *Bespridannitsa*
"Down Stream" (Rossetti) **4**:511, 518
"Down the Dardanelles" (Darley) **2**:128
"Down Whitechapel Way" (Sala) **46**:246
"Down with the Tide" (Dickens) **105**:217
The Down-Easters (Neal) **161**:303, 309
The Downfall and Death of King Oedipus (FitzGerald) **153**:218
"Downs" (Jefferies) **47**:130
"Downtrodden People" (Dobrolyubov) **5**:147
Dożywocie (Fredro) **8**:285-86, 290, 292
Dr. Bahrdt (Kotzebue) **25**:134, 142
"Dr. Farmer's 'Essay on the Learning of Shakespeare' Considered" (Maginn) **8**:435, 438, 442
"Dr. Francia" (Carlyle) **70**:93
Dr. Grimshawe's Secret (Hawthorne) **2**:315, 324, 333-35; **95**:106; **171**:261
"Dr. Heidegger's Experiment" (Hawthorne) **2**:291-92, 298, 311, 328; **95**:105
Dr. Heidenhoff's Process (Bellamy) **4**:23, 26-27, 29, 31, 34; **86**:6, 10, 17, 29, 64, 66
Dr. Jekyll and Mr. Hyde (Stevenson)
See *The Strange Case of Dr. Jekyll and Mr. Hyde*
Dr Katzenbergers Badereise: Nebst einer Auswahl verbesserter Werkchen (Jean Paul) **7**:239, 241
Dr Luther (Freytag)
See *Doktor Luther: Eine Schilderung*
"Dr. Samuel Parr; or Whiggism in its Relations to Literature" (De Quincey) **198**:13
Dr. Stanley's Lectures on the Irish Church (Arnold) **126**:89
"Dr. Stanley's Lectures on the Jewish Church" (Arnold) **29**:14
"Dr. Tarr and Prof. Fether" (Poe) **78**:278
Dr. Wortle's School (Trollope) **6**:470; **101**:291, 307, 311, 315
"Drab Habitation of Whom?" (Dickinson) **21**:18
"Drachenfels" (Fuller) **50**:248
"Draft of a Communist Confession of Faith" (Engels) **85**:27
Dragées (Laforgue) **221**:40
"The Dragon Fang Possessed by the Conjurer Piou-Lu" (O'Brien) **21**:235-36, 252
Dragoş's Wedding (Eminescu) **33**:265
"Drake-Halleck" (Poe) **211**:232, 235, 241, 247, 249
"The Drama" (Neal) **161**:309
The Drama at Home; or, An Evening with Puff (Planché) **42**:273, 276, 290
"Drama del alma" (Zorrilla y Moral) **6**:524
Drama Indio (Martí) **63**:104
Un drama nuevo (Tamayo y Baus) **1**:565-66, 568-70
"A Drama of Exile" (Barrett Browning) **170**:86, 107-8
The Drama of Exile, and Other Poems (Barrett Browning) **1**:114, 116, 126-7; **61**:43, 45
Dramas (Baillie) **2**:39-40; **71**:2; **151**:55
Dramas in Miniature (Blind) **202**:8, 10, 12, 16, 27, 51
The Drama's Levëe (Planché) **42**:273, 299
The Dramatic and Poetical Works of Joanna Baillie: Complete in One Volume (Baillie) **151**:10, 86
Dramatic Essays (Lewes) **25**:325
"The Dramatic Fragment" (Wordsworth) **12**:387
Dramatic Idylls, Second Series (Browning) **79**:153, 163-64
Dramatic Lyrics (Browning) **19**:109; **79**:93-94, 103, 146, 148, 163, 166, 190
Dramatic Romances and Lyrics (Browning) **79**:93-94, 103, 146, 148, 163
Dramatic Scenes from Real Life (Morgan) **29**:390, 394
Dramatic Studies (Webster) **230**:226, 230, 249, 251, 265
The Dramatic Works of Mary Russell Mitford (Mitford) **4**:404
Dramatic Works of Wycherley, Congreve,

Vanbrugh, and Farquhar (Hunt) **70**:260, 265
Dramatis Personae (Browning) **19**:116, 130; **79**:149, 152, 163, 165, 182
Dramatische Vorlesungen (Schlegel) **142**:321
Dramaturgical Pages (Liszt) **199**:305
Dramaturgische Blätter (Börne) **193**:22
"Un drame au bord de la mer" (Balzac) **5**:53; **153**:152
Drames philosophiques (Renan) **26**:395, 397, 408, 413
"The Draughts" (Mickiewicz) **3**:398
Drausen im Heidedorf (Storm) **195**:119, 121, 126-27, 129, 132
Draussen im Heidedorf (Storm)
See *Drausen im Heidedorf*
Drauszen im Heidedorf (Storm) **1**:540
"A Drawing-Room Drama" (O'Brien) **21**:236, 243, 247
"Dread and Dislike of Science" (Lewes) **215**:87
"The Dread Wild Boar" (Gogol) **162**:15
"The Dreadful Hand" (Gogol) **162**:82
"A Dream" (Allingham) **25**:6, 8, 20, 23-4
"A Dream" (Bertrand)
See "Un rêve"
"A Dream" (Blake) **13**:182; **37**:3, 14, 41, 65, 71-2, 92
"A Dream" (Bryant) **46**:3, 20
"The Dream" (Chivers) **49**:68
"The Dream" (Clare) **9**:84
"Dream" (Laforgue)
See "Rêve"
"Dream" (Lermontov) **126**:227
"The Dream" (Levy) **203**:322
"The Dream" (Mickiewicz)
See "Sen"
"The Dream" (Norton) **47**:236, 238-39, 243, 248, 259; **205**:59, 69-70, 86
"A Dream" (Poe) **117**:214-15, 280
"Dream" (Shevchenko)
See "Son"
"The Dream" (Solomos) **15**:393
"A Dream" (Turgenev)
See "Son"
"The Dream" (Turgenev)
See "Son"
The Dream (Baillie) **2**:36, 39; **71**:12-14, 16; **151**:5-9, 11, 115
Dream (Leopardi) **129**:304
"A Dream, after Reading Dante's Episode of Paolo and Francesca" (Keats) **73**:228, 230
The Dream and Other Poems (Norton) **47**:239-40, 244-46, 248, 253-54, 259-60; **205**:67, 138
"Dream and Waking" (Chamisso) **82**:5
"Dream at Sea" (Tyutchev)
See "Son na more"
"Dream Ballad" (Verlaine)
See "Ballade en rêve"
"The Dream by the Fountain" (Harpur) **114**:92, 94, 97, 106-7, 116, 144
A Dream Is Life (Grillparzer)
See *Der Traum ein Leben*
"The Dream of a Broken Heart" (Carleton) **199**:9
"The Dream of a Queer Fellow" (Dostoevsky)
See "The Dream of a Ridiculous Man"
"The Dream of a Ridiculous Man" (Dostoevsky) **2**:202; **33**:227, 229; **43**:139; **167**:246-47
"A Dream of Antiquity" (Moore) **110**:178
"The Dream of Boccaccio" (Landor) **14**:187
"The Dream of Cesara" (Krasiński)
See "Sen Cezary"
"Dream of Dying" (Beddoes) **154**:51
The Dream of Eugene Aram (Hood) **16**:202, 206-07, 209, 211, 215, 220-21, 225-28, 231, 233-35, 238
"A Dream of Fair Women" (Tennyson) **30**:209, 223-24, 264; **65**:235; **202**:185, 189-90, 333
Dream of Gerontius (Newman) **38**:324, 342, 345-46, 348; **99**:256
"A Dream of John Ball" (Morris) **4**:425, 436-39, 441, 445
"The Dream of John Macdonnell" (Mangan) **27**:308
"A Dream of My Mother" (Foster) **26**:286
"The Dream of Petrarca" (Landor) **14**:187
"Dream of the Universe" (De Quincey) **198**:91
Dream on the Volga (Ostrovsky)
See *Voevoda: Son na Volge*
"A Dream within a Dream" (Poe) **117**:215
"Dream-Children: A Reverie" (Lamb) **10**:404, 407, 410, 415, 421, 430, 435-37; **113**:157, 165, 173, 200, 244
"The Dreamer and the Worker" (Horne) **127**:266
"Dream-Fugue, Founded on the Preceding Theme of Sudden Death" (De Quincey) **4**:82, 86, 89
"Dreaming" (Beattie)
See *Dissertations Moral and Critical: On Memory and Imagination; On Dreaming; The Theory of Language; On Fable and Romance; On the Attachments of Kindred; Illustrations on Sublimity*
"Dream-Land" (Poe) **1**:526-27; **55**:150; **117**:227, 232-35, 242-44, 264, 280-83, 316-18, 330
"Dreamland" (Rossetti) **2**:563
"Dream-Land" (Rossetti) **186**:332, 335, 347
"Dream-Love" (Rossetti) **50**:324; **66**:311
"Dream-Pedlary" (Beddoes) **3**:32, 34, 39; **154**:83
"Dreams" (Brontë) **71**:91
"Dreams" (Cranch) **115**:50
"Dreams" (Heine)
See "Traumbilder"
"Dreams" (Lazarus) **8**:413, 420
"Dreams" (Poe) **1**:514; **117**:214
"Dreams" (Sigourney) **21**:299
"Dreams" (Timrod) **25**:363, 366, 382
Dreams (Robertson) **35**:333, 335, 354, 363, 369
Dreams and Sounds (Nekrasov) **11**:399
"Dreams Awake" (Wieland) **17**:394
Dreams of a Spirit-Seer (Kant) **27**:200; **67**:219
Dreams of Love (Scribe)
See *Rêves d'amour*
Dreams, Waking Thoughts, and Incidents (Beckford) **16**:25, **214**:159
Dreamthorpe (Smith) **59**:295, 299, 302-4, 306, 308-9, 311, 314-17, 319, 322-24, 326, 337
"Dreary Hour" (Arany)
See "Meddőórán"
Dred: A Tale of the Great Dismal Swamp (Stowe) **3**:550-52, 559-61, 567; **195**:235
"The Dred Scott Decision: Speech at Springfield, Illinois" (Lincoln) **201**:163
"Die drei" (Lenau) **16**:265
"Die Drei Brüder" (Gotthelf) **117**:44, 49, 51, 55-8
"Die drei Erznarren" (Arnim) **159**:61
Die drei gerechten Kammacher (Keller) **2**:412, 414-15, 424-25
"Die drei Indianer" (Lenau) **16**:269, 278, 283-84
Drei Märchen (Storm) **195**:14, 24, 33, 35
Drei Novellen (Storm) **195**:95
"Die drei Schmiede ihres Schicksals" (Stifter) **41**:366
Drei Spinnfrauen (Storm)
See *Das Märchen von den drei Spinnfrauen*
Drei Väter auf einmal (Kotzebue) **25**:136
"Die drei Zigeuner" (Lenau) **16**:285
Die drei Zigeuner (Liszt) **199**:308
Dresden Forefathers' Eve Wilno Forefathers' Eve (Mickiewicz)
See *Dziady III*
"The Dresser" (Whitman) **81**:330
The Dressmaker (Martineau) **26**:322
"Drifting Away" (Eliot) **4**:140
Drink (Reade) **2**:544, 551
"Drink of This Cup" (Moore) **110**:190
"Drinking Song" (Smith) **59**:331
Driven from Home (Alger) **8**:43
"Driving Stanhope" (Willis) **194**:282
"Droga nad przepascic w Czufut-Kale" (Mickiewicz) **3**:403; **101**:188-89
"Droll Advice" (Verlaine)
See "Conseil falot"
"A Droll Formulary to Raise Devils" (Coleridge) **231**:151
Droll Stories (Balzac)
See *Contes drolatiques*
Dronningen paa 16 Aar (Andersen) **79**:9
Dronningen Skibet (Andersen) **79**:9
Drood (Dickens)
See *The Mystery of Edwin Drood*
"A Drop of Balm" (Arany)
See "Balzsamcsepp"
"A Drop of Blood" (Meyer)
See "Der Blutstropfen"
"A Drop of Water" (Andersen)
See "Vanddraaben"
Drottningens juvelsmycke (Almqvist) **42**:4, 6, 9-14, 17
The Drowned (Pushkin) **3**:423
"The Drowned Girl" (Gogol)
See "Majskaja noč, ili Vtoplennica"
"The Drowned Girl" (Shevchenko)
See "Utoplena"
"Drowne's Wooden Image" (Hawthorne) **2**:298; **39**:222; **158**:247; **171**:263
Drüben am Markt (Storm) **1**:540, 544; **195**:4, 39, 95
"The Druidical Institution" (D'Israeli) **217**:285
"Drumlanrig" (Hogg) **109**:270
"The Drummer" (Mörike)
See "Der Tambour"
"Drum-Taps" (Whitman) **205**:225-26, 244, 259, 338
Drum-Taps (Whitman) **4**:542-43, 569, 571, 578, 580, 582, 586, 592, 595; **81**:258, 311-21, 326, 330-31; **205**:181-82, 211-12, 225-26, 244, 330, 333, 335, 338-39, 341
"The Drunkard" (Harpur) **114**:141
The Drunkards (Dostoevsky) **167**:250
"The Drunken Boat" (Rimbaud)
See "Le bateau ivre"
"The Drunken Father" (Bloomfield) **145**:158
"The Drunken God" (Meyer)
See "Der trunkene Gott"
"Drunkenness" (Krasicki)
See "Pijaństwo"
"Druses et Maronites" (Nerval) **67**:333
"Dry Be That Tear" (Sheridan) **91**:232
Dry Sticks, Fagoted by W. S. L. (Landor) **14**:170, 177
"The Dryad" (Andersen) **7**:24
The Dryad: A Tale from the Paris Exposition 1867 (Andersen)
See *Dryaden. Et Eventyr fra Udstillingstidin i Paris 1867*
Dryaden. Et Eventyr fra Udstillingstidin i Paris 1867 (Andersen) **214**:62-71
"Le Dryade et Symeta" (Vigny) **102**:335
"La dryade: Idyll in the Manner of Theocritus" (Vigny) **7**:468-69
"Dryden" (Macaulay) **231**:277-78, 292
"Dryden and His Times" (Clough) **27**:103
"Dryden and Pope" (Hazlitt) **29**:166
Du dandysme et de Georges Brummel (Barbey d'Aurevilly) **1**:71; **213**:62-64, 67, 87, 96, 100
Du fantastic dans la littérature (Nodier) **19**:378
Du Pape (Maistre) **37**:288, 290-92, 294, 299-300, 302, 304, 306-09, 314-15
"Du style" (Joubert) **9**:293
"Du vin et du hachisch" (Baudelaire) **155**:41
"The Dual Existence" (Clarke) **19**:231
"Dualisms" (Tennyson) **202**:335-36
Dubrovsky (Pushkin) **3**:429, 435-36, 442, 459; **27**:375; **83**:276, 316
"The Duc De L'Omellette" (Poe) **16**:304, 313
The Duchess of la Vallière (Bulwer-Lytton) **1**:147; **45**:62
La Duchesse de la Vallière (Genlis) **166**:21, 49

The Duchesse de Langeais (Balzac)
See *La Duchesse de Langeais*
La Duchesse de Langeais (Balzac) **5**:45; **35**:2; **153**:23, 151-52, 165-68, 171
"The Duck and the Kangaroo" (Lear) **3**:297, 307, 309
"The Duckling" (Andersen)
See "Den grimme Ælling"
"The Duel" (Kleist)
See *Der Zweikampf*
"The Duel" (Lippard) **198**:133
"The Duel" (O'Brien) **21**:243, 245, 247
"Duel at Midnight" (Arany)
See "Éjféli párbaj"
"Duel aux camélias" (Corbière) **43**:27
"The Duelist" (Turgenev) **21**:417
"The Duellist" (Turgenev)
See "The Duelist"
"Duellum" (Baudelaire) **29**:99; **155**:12
Duels of Honor (Tamayo y Baus)
See *Lances de honor*
El duende satírico del día (Larra) **130**:247
The Duenna; or, The Doubling Elopement (Sheridan) **5**:358-59, 361-62, 365, 369, 380-83; **91**:241-42, 251
"Duets" (Woolson) **82**:322
"Duke Carl of Rosenmold" (Pater) **7**:299; **90**:245, 345-46, 348-49
"Duke Humphrey's Dinner" (O'Brien) **21**:243-44
The Duke of Milan (Cumberland) **167**:157
The Duke of Monmouth (Griffin) **7**:193, 196, 198, 200-01, 204, 216, 219
"Duke of Portland" (Villiers de l'Isle Adam) **3**:590
The Duke of Stockbridge: A Romance of Shay's Rebellion (Bellamy) **4**:26, 30; **86**:11; **147**:116
"Duke Richelieu, Sir Firebrace Cotes, Lady G——, and Mr. Normanby" (Landor) **14**:178
The Duke's Children: A Novel (Trollope) **6**:461, 466-67, 471, 490, 495, 497, 500, 519; **101**:264-65, 268, 288, 291, 311, 318, 324; **215**:212-15, 225, 261, 284, 299, 303
"Duló Zebedeus kalandjai" (Madach) **19**:369, 371
"Duma" (Lermontov) **5**:286, 295; **126**:144, 216
"Duma" (Pavlova) **138**:4, 51
"The Dumb Cake" (Clare) **86**:108
"The Dumb Orators" (Crabbe) **26**:93, 129, 135; **121**:11-12, 61
"Dumka" (Shevchenko) **54**:373
"Dumy moji dumy moji" (Shevchenko) **54**:373
The Dun (Edgeworth) **1**:267; **51**:89-90, 140
"Dunbar" (Smith) **59**:309
"The Duncaid of To-day" (Disraeli) **39**:52-3, 55
"The Dungeon" (Coleridge) **9**:131; **111**:197, 315, 357; **231**:57
"The Dungeon" (Wordsworth) **12**:386-87
"Dungog" (Kendall) **12**:180, 187
"Duns Scotus's Oxford" (Hopkins) **17**:185, 211, 219
Duplicity (Holcroft) **85**:191, 205, 214-16, 218, 225, 234, 239, 246
"Durandarte and Belerma" (Lewis) **11**:297
"Durch die weite, öde Wüste" (Brentano) **191**:63
"Durchwachte Nacht" (Droste-Hülshoff) **3**:196, 200
"Dursli der Brannteweinsäufer" (Gotthelf) **117**:51, 58
"A Dutch Picture" (Longfellow) **45**:144
Dutch Pictures (Sala) **46**:237
"The Dutch Wedding" (Smith) **187**:319
The Dutchman's Fireside (Paulding) **2**:526-30
"Duties and Responsibilities of Unitarian Christians" (Cranch) **115**:47
"The Duties of Man" (Mazzini) **34**:281-282
"Duty" (Clough) **27**:52, 91, 103, 105
"Duty" (Solomos) **15**:399
Duty before All (Herzen) **61**:97
"Duty Ode" (Wordsworth) **166**:266
"The Duty of a Brother" (Lamb) **125**:331
The Duty of American Women to Their Country (Beecher) **30**:15
The Duty of Disobedience to the Fugitive Slave Law (Child) **73**:63
"The Duty of the Free States" (Channing) **17**:25, 32-3
"Duty—that's to say complying" (Prescott) **163**:34-36
"Dva chetverostishiia" (Turgenev) **122**:312
"Dve byli i esche odna" (Zhukovsky) **35**:398
"Dve doli" (Baratynsky) **103**:6-8, 11, 26-7
Dvoinaia zhizn! (Pavlova) **138**:3, 5, 7-10, 13, 20, 22, 31, 36, 38-43, 47, 56-57, 59
Dvoinik (Dostoevsky)
See *Dvoynik*
Dvorianskoe gnezdo (Turgenev)
See *Dvoryanskoe gnezdo*
Dvoryanskoe gnezdo (Turgenev) **21**:393-94, 397, 399-400, 409-10, 413, 417-19, 421-22, 427, 430-31, 434-35, 437-39, 442-44, 446-48, 452; **37**:335, 367, 379, 382, 402, 436, 444; **122**:248-52, 256, 267-68, 270-72, 278-79, 288, 292, 315, 317, 324-26
Dvoynaya zhizn! (Pavlova)
See *Dvoinaia zhizn!*
Dvoynik (Dostoevsky) **2**:157, 177, 179, 199; **33**:167, 171-73, 200, 203-4; **43**:92, 130; **167**:333-34; **202**:104
The Dwarf (Tieck) **5**:517
Dwarf Long-Nose (Hauff)
See *Zwerg Nase*
Dwarf Nose (Hauff)
See *Zwerg Nase*
Dwie blizny (Fredro) **8**:285
"Dying" (Dickinson)
See "I heard a Fly buzz—when I died—"
"The Dying Alchemist" (Willis) **194**:287, 302, 304
"The Dying Alchymist" (Willis)
See "The Dying Alchemist"
"The Dying Beauty" (Chivers) **49**:49, 56
"The Dying Child" (Clare) **9**:85, 102
"The Dying Crow" (Bryant) **46**:13
"The Dying Daughter to her Mother" (Opie) **65**:155, 182
"Dying! Dying in the Night!" (Dickinson) **21**:55
"The Dying Elm" (Freneau) **111**:142-43
"The Dying Enthusiast" (Mangan) **27**:280, 298
Dying Gladiator (Lermontov) **47**:151
"The Dying Indian" (Warton) **118**:335, 356
"The Dying Indian: Tomo-Chequi" (Freneau) **1**:315, 317, 322; **111**:102, 145, 147-50, 152, 166, 190
"The Dying need but little, Dear,/ A Glass of Water's all" (Dickinson) **77**:163
"The Dying Philosopher" (Sigourney) **87**:331-32
"Dying Poet" (Lamartine)
See "La Poète mourant"
"The Dying Raven" (Dana) **53**:158, 168
"The Dying Rosebud's Lament" (Osgood) **141**:319
"The Dying Seneca" (Holmes) **14**:100
"The Dying Soldier" (Runeberg) **41**:312-15, 321, 323
"The Dying Speech of an Old Philosopher" (Landor) **14**:201-02
"The Dying Swan" (Chivers) **49**:71
"The Dying Swan" (Tennyson) **30**:211, 223, 231-32; **202**:337
"A Dying Tiger moaned for Drink" (Dickinson) **77**:162-63
"The Dying Warrior" (Runeberg)
See "The Dying Soldier"
Dym (Turgenev) **21**:389-90, 392-93, 396, 400-01, 406, 409, 411, 413, 419, 421-22, 426-27, 431, 435-39, 441, 444-45; **37**:367-68, 391, 424, 436, 444, 447; **122**:248-49, 261, 269, 271, 279, 282-87, 320, 325-27, 341, 364
The Dynamics of a Particle (Dodgson) **2**:117
The Dynamiter (Stevenson)
See *More New Arabian Nights: The Dynamiter*
"Dynd-Kongens Datter" (Andersen) **7**:28, 30, 32; **79**:7, 28, 58, 70-1; **214**:56, 73, 77
"D'you Want to Know Who I Am" (Radishchev) **190**:314
Dziady III (Mickiewicz) **3**:389, 391-93, 395-97, 399-403; **101**:156-58, 171, 197, 208, 210
"E. B. B." (Thomson) **18**:392
"E. I. Bulgarinoy" (Bestuzhev) **131**:150
E. T. A. Hoffmann Tagebücher (Hoffmann) **183**:268
E. T. A. Hoffmanns Dichtungen und Schriften (Hoffmann) **183**:174-76, 181, 189
E. T. A. Hoffmanns Werke in fünfzehn Teilen (Hoffmann) **183**:192
"Each and All" (Emerson) **1**:285, 296; **38**:184, 190; **98**:177, 179
"The Eagle" (Tennyson) **30**:280
"The Eagle and Fowls" (Krylov) **1**:435
"The Eagle as Maecenas" (Šaltykov) **16**:358
"The Eagle Hunter" (Taylor) **89**:299
"The Eagles" (Very) **9**:383
"Eäriné" (Allingham) **25**:14
"Earl Sigurd's Christmas Eve" (Boyesen) **135**:4
The Earlier Letters, 1812-1848 (Mill) **179**:220
"Early Adieux" (Gordon) **21**:154, 173
"Early American Verse" (Bryant) **46**:32, 51
"Early Death and Fame" (Arnold) **29**:26, 28
The Early Diary of Frances Burney, 1768-1778 (Burney) **12**:33; **54**:18, 24; **107**:12, 14, 38, 40
Early England and the Saxon-English (Barnes) **75**:40, 103
The Early English Church: A Paper Read before the Church of England Institute (De Mille) **123**:120, 125
Early Essays and Miscellanies (Thoreau) **61**:339, 376; **138**:127
Early Essays and Miscellany (Thoreau) **207**:253
"Early Graves" (Klopstock) **11**:220
The Early Italian Poets (Rossetti) **77**:335
The Early Italian Poets from Ciullo to Dante Alighieri, 1100/1200/1300 in the Original Metres, Together with Dante's "Vita Nuova" (Rossetti) **4**:490
The Early Lectures of Ralph Waldo Emerson (Emerson) **98**:66-8, 70, 81, 94-9, 96
Early Lessons (Edgeworth) **51**:81, 85, 89, 102, 110, 114
Early Letters (Wordsworth) **166**:266
The Early Letters of William and Dorothy Wordsworth (Wordsworth) **206**:299, 346
"The Early Life of Sut Lovingood, Written by His Dad" (Harris) **23**:150, 152; **165**:224
Early Notebooks (Darwin) **57**:145-6
Early Poems of John Clare (Clare) **86**:130-31, 160
Early Polemical Writings (Kierkegaard) **125**:271
"Early Remembrances" (Stowe) **195**:180-81
"The Early Spring Book" (Dana) **53**:178
Early Theological Writings (Hegel)
See *Hegels theologische Jungendschriften*
"Early Writers: their Dread of the Press" (D'Israeli) **217**:299, 301
"Earth" (Bryant) **6**:168, 172; **46**:7, 22, 28, 39
"The Earth" (Very) **9**:378, 381
"Earth Has Not Anything to Show More Fair" (Wordsworth) **12**:466
"The Earth Is Too Much with Us" (Wordsworth) **12**:466
"Earth, my Likeness" (Whitman) **31**:430; **81**:258
The Earthly Paradise (Morris) **4**:414-16, 419-22, 424-25, 427-35, 442-43, 446-48
"The Earthquake" (Moodie) **113**:317
The Earthquake (Galt) **1**:328, 335
"The Earthquake in Chile" (Kleist)
See "Das Erdbeben in Chili"

"Earth's Answer" (Blake) **13**:191, 221, 226; **37**:32, 42, 47-9; **190**:61; **201**:63
"Earth's Children Cleave to Earth" (Bryant) **46**:21
"Earth's Holocaust" (Hawthorne) **2**:296, 298, 305; **10**:290, 311; **17**:129; **23**:205; **39**:229; **79**:296; **95**:156; **158**:234; **171**:353; **191**:204
"Earth's Immortalities" (Browning) **79**:94, 101
"Earth—the Stoic" (Lampman) **25**:167; **194**:31-32, 93
"The Easiest Mode of Learning the Greek and Latin Languages" (Dyer) **129**:110
East Angels (Woolson) **82**:268-71, 274-75, 279, 293, 299, 315-19
"East London" (Arnold) **218**:121, 147
East Lynne (Wood) **178**:261-62, 267-69, 272, 276-78, 283, 288-300, 302, 304-10, 313, 315-16, 319, 322-24, 326, 330-31
"East Wind" (Hunt) **1**:417
"Easter Communion" (Hopkins) **189**:113
"Easter Day" (Prescott) **163**:6-7, 30-31, 42, 86-87, 139-40
Easter Day (Browning) **19**:132
"Easter Day I" (Prescott) **163**:58
"Easter Day II" (Prescott) **163**:52, 86-87
"Easter Day: Naples, 1849" (Clough) **27**:55, 76, 87-88, 100
"Easter Day, Naples, 1849" (Prescott) **163**:51, 85-86, 90, 131, 139
"Easter Eve" (Lampman) **25**:160, 167, 199, 201; **194**:53, 55
Easter Gleams (Larcom) **179**:173-74
"An Easter Greeting to Every Child Who Loves Alice" (Dodgson) **139**:12, 52
"Easter Hymn" (Jones) **222**:169
"An Easter Hymn" (Kendall) **12**:192
The Easter Lily (Grundtvig)
See *Paaske-Lilien*
The Easter Recess (Morgan) **29**:390
"Easter Zunday" (Barnes) **75**:77
"An Eastern Legend" (Turgenev)
See "Vostochnaia Legenda"
Eastern Life Past and Present (Martineau) **137**:285, 324, 343
Eastern Life, Present and Past (Martineau) **26**:311, 319, 326, 328-29, 359
Eastern Lyrics (Hugo)
See *Les orientales*
Easy Money (Ostrovsky)
See *Beshenye dengi*
"Eathlina's Lament" (Moore) **110**:194
L'eau de Jouvence (Renan) **26**:386, 389, 408, 417
"L'eau douce" (Desbordes-Valmore) **97**:27
"Eaves-Dropping a Lodge of Free-Masons" (Harris) **23**:139, 161; **165**:163, 240-41, 248, 264, 275
The Ebb-Tide: A Trio and Quartette (Stevenson) **5**:412, 415, 419, 427; **63**:261; **193**:211, 220-21, 223-24, 250, 287, 291, 298-99, 343-47, 349-50
"Les Eboulements" (Lampman)
See "A Sunset at Les Eboulements"
Ecarté; or, The Salons of Paris (Richardson) **55**:293-4, 304, 312-3, 321, 327, 329, 339, 344-6
"Az ecce homo" (Madach) **19**:369
"Eccentricity" (Allston) **2**:19, 21
Ecclesiastical Sketches (Wordsworth) **12**:409, 466; **38**:368, 371; **166**:213; **206**:305
Ecclesiastical Sonnets (Wordsworth)
See *Ecclesiastical Sketches*
"Echa-czasu" (Norwid) **17**:373
Echantillon de causerie française (Balzac) **153**:54-56
"L'echelonnement des hais" (Verlaine) **51**:355, 370
"Echo and the Ferry" (Ingelow) **39**:264
The Echo Club and Other Literary Diversions (Taylor) **89**:319, 337, 339, 343, 351
"An Echo of Antietam" (Bellamy) **86**:10-11, 75, 78
"Echoes" (Lazarus) **8**:423; **109**:294, 301-02, 321
"Echoes in the City of the Angels" (Jackson) **90**:149
"Echoes of the Week" (Sala) **46**:245
"The Echoing Green" (Blake) **13**:181; **37**:3, 14, 25, 35, 37-8, 57, 65-6, 68, 71-2, 80, 92; **127**:81
"Echo-Song" (Osgood) **141**:326
Der Echte und der falsche Waldemar (Arnim) **5**:21
Eckbert (Tieck)
See *Der blonde Eckbert*
Eckbert the Fair (Tieck)
See *Der blonde Eckbert*
"L'eclair" (Rimbaud) **4**:466; **82**:222, 224, 229, 236, 241, 251, 255, 261-62; **227**:234, 278, 305, 315-16
"Eclair de gouffre" (Laforgue) **221**:88
"Les Éclairs" (Desbordes-Valmore) **97**:27
"L'eclatante victoire de Saarebrück" (Rimbaud) **4**:465; **35**:271
"Eclipse in Italy" (Wordsworth) **38**:363
"Eclogue" (Lear) **3**:298
Eclogue (Liszt) **199**:307
"Eclogues" (Barnes) **75**:95
Eco del Occidente (Alarcón) **219**:18
El eco del Torrente (Zorrilla y Moral) **6**:525
Ecole des Femmes (Balzac) **153**:8
L'ecole des ménages (Balzac) **5**:74
"L'ecole païenne" (Baudelaire) **29**:70; **155**:89
"L'Écolier" (Desbordes-Valmore) **97**:38
"L'écolier de Leyde" (Bertrand) **31**:46
Economic and Philosophic Manuscripts of 1844 (Marx) **17**:329-30, 350, 352, 360; **114**:69
Economic Studies (Bagehot) **10**:20-22, 25-26, 32, 34, 48
"Economics" (Thoreau) **7**:389
"Economy" (Thoreau) **7**:387-8, 398-9, 402-3; **138**:78, 125, 129, 192; **207**:254
The Economy of Happiness (Bellamy) **4**:27
"Economy of Moral Error" (Parker) **186**:128
"The Economy of Pain" (Parker) **186**:128
The Economy of Vegetation (Darwin) **106**:187, 189-90, 192-93, 195-97, 203, 205, 208-09, 212, 220, 225, 232, 236-38, 241-42, 245, 248-49, 256, 263-64, 266, 273-77
L'Ecossais (Dumas) **71**:217
"Ecrit en 1846" (Hugo) **189**:253
Ecrits de Jeunesse (Flaubert) **179**:119-20
Ecrits politiques (Constant)
See *De la liberté chez les modernes*
Eda (Baratynsky) **103**:10, 39-40
La Edad de Oro (Martí) **63**:104
"Edax on Appetite" (Lamb) **10**:409, 411; **113**:236-39, 263
Edelweiss (Auerbach) **171**:9
"Eden Bower" (Rossetti) **4**:492, 496, 498, 505, 511, 518, 527, 530; **77**:326, 328-30, 361-62
The Eden of Imagination (Reynolds) **146**:165-66, 187-88, 192
"Edgar and Emma" (Austen) **119**:13, 16
Edgar Huntly; or, Memoirs of a Sleep-Walker (Brown) **22**:3, 5, 7-9, 12-13, 18-22, 24, 27-31, 40-2, 48-9, 52-4, 56-7; **74**:4, 9-12, 15, 19, 24, 36, 41, 49-50, 52-7, 61, 63, 65, 80-2, 84, 86-7, 89, 92-6, 98-9, 101-02, 104-05, 111-12, 117-20, 122, 124-27, 129-30, 133, 135, 139, 141, 143, 147-50, 161, 164; **122**:53-54, 82-84, 90, 93, 95-96, 116
Edgar Poe and His Critics (Whitman) **19**:456-60
"The Edge of the Swamp" (Simms) **3**:507
Edifying Discourses (Kierkegaard) **34**:203, 227, 238; **78**:197, 239
"Edifying Letters of the Rutherford Family" (Stevenson) **193**:327
Edifying Discourses in a Different Vein: Three Godly Discourses (Kierkegaard) **34**:224, 246, 252, 254
Edina (Wood) **178**:288, 321, 324
"Edinburgh" (Smith) **59**:299, 333-4
Edinburgh: Picturesque Notes (Stevenson) **5**:387
Edipo (Martínez de la Rosa) **102**:230, 232, 246
"Edith" (Webster) **230**:245
"Edith and Nora" (Wilson) **5**:550
"Edith Linsey" (Willis) **194**:282, 285, 296, 298
"Edith May; or, The Mistake of a Life-Time" (Parton) **86**:349-50
"The Editor and the Schoolma'am" (Frederic) **10**:193, 212
"Editors" (Parton) **86**:348
"Editor's Table" (Hale) **75**:317
"A Edmond et Jules de Goncourt" (Banville) **9**:26
"Edmund and Anna" (Dacre) **151**:184
"Edmund's Wedding" (Robinson) **142**:137, 249
Edouard (Duras) **154**:108-9, 112-13, 120, 125, 129-30, 143, 157-58, 160-66, 169
Eduard Mörike: Briefe (Mörike)
See *Briefe*
"La educación de entonces" (Larra) **130**:194
The Educated Cat (Hoffmann)
See *Lebens-Ansichten des Katers Murr nebst fragmentarischer Biographie des Kapellmeisters Johannes Kreisler in züfalligen Makulaturblättern*
"Education" (Emerson) **98**:66
Education in the Home, the Kindergarten, and the Primary School (Peabody)
See *Lectures in the Training Schools for Kindergartners*
L'éducation sentimentale: Histoire d'un jeune homme (Flaubert) **2**:225-33, 235-40, 242-3, 245-9, 256; **10**:119, 122, 124-5, 130, 135, 159, 161, 164, 170, 174; **19**:264-322; **62**:69, 74, 76, 83, 88, 90-1, 95-9, 102, 105, 111, 115, 119-21, 123; **66**:256, 270, 293; **135**:78, 89, 93-95, 103, 107-9, 133, 174, 176-77, 180; **179**:1-163; **185**:180, 189, 193-94, 219-20, 227, 229, 231, 238-40
Educational Reminiscences and Suggestions (Beecher) **30**:16, 25
Der Edukationsrat (Kotzebue) **25**:136
Edward Bellamy Speaks Again! (Bellamy) **147**:85
"Edward Fane's Rose-Bud" (Hawthorne) **2**:305; **158**:253, 255; **171**:357
"Edward Gray" (Tennyson) **30**:222
"Edward III" (Blake)
See "King Edward the Third"
"Edward Randolph's Portrait" (Hawthorne) **95**:105; **171**:357; **191**:189
"Edward Shore" (Crabbe) **26**:93, 100
Edwin (Hays) **114**:177
Edwin and Eltruda: A Legendary Tale (Williams) **135**:315, 333
Edwin Brothertoft (Winthrop) **210**:280-89, 296, 299, 305, 314, 316, 319-21, 323
Edwin Drood (Dickens)
See *The Mystery of Edwin Drood*
Edwin of Deira (Smith) **59**:294, 298, 305, 312, 318-21, 326, 333, 337
Edwy and Elgiva (Burney) **12**:17, 46-47; **54**:59
Eekenhof (Storm) **1**:540; **195**:6, 16, 54, 57, 127, 130, 132
De Eerloze (Multatuli) **165**:315
"Les effarés" (Rimbaud) **4**:455, 465, 485; **35**:271; **82**:226, 230, 251; **227**:185
The Effect of Slavery on the American People, a Sermon Preached at the Music Hall, Boston, on Sunday, July 4, 1858 (Parker) **186**:159
"The Effects of Religion on Minds of Sensibility. Story of La Roche" (Mackenzie) **41**:180, 188
"Effects of Rural Objects on the Mind" (Mackenzie) **41**:190-91
Effects of Slavery on Morals and Industry (Webster) **30**:404
"Effet de nuit" (Verlaine) **230**:163
Effi Briest (Fontane) **26**:235-36, 239, 241, 243-

44, 246, 248, 251-52, 258-59, 264-65, 267-72, 276, 278; **163**:158-298
Les éffrontés (Augier) **31**:5, 7, 9-10, 12-13, 15, 19-20, 24-7, 31-2, 34, 38-9
"Effusion on the Death of James Hogg" (Wordsworth) **12**:431
"Effusions" (Thelwall) **162**:303
Egalité (Silva) **114**:263
"L'égalité chrétienne" (Renan) **26**:377
L'Egarement de l'infortune (Sade) **47**:361-62
Egilona (Gómez de Avellaneda) **111**:28
"Eglantine ou l'Indolente Corrigée" (Genlis) **166**:31
L'église chrétienne (Renan) **26**:402
"L'Eglise d'Aroma" (Desbordes-Valmore) **97**:6
Egmont (Goethe) **4**:162-64, 167, 172, 190, 194-96, 204, 211-12, 218-22; **34**:71; **154**:231, 233
"Ego" (Whittier) **59**:364
"The Egoist" (Turgenev) **21**:454
"Egos of the Week" (Sala) **46**:245
"Egotheism, the Atheism of Today" (Peabody) **169**:156, 176-77, 187, 190, 192, 197
"Egotism; or, The Bosom Serpent" (Hawthorne) **158**:341; **171**:345; **191**:209, 261-65, 268, 271
"Egy nyíri temetőn" (Madach) **19**:369
"Egyptian Maid" (Wordsworth) **111**:213
The Egyptian Nights (Pushkin) **3**:435; **83**:273, 275-76
Die Ehenschmiede (Arnim) **5**:22; **159**:35, 96
"Die Ehrenpforte und Triumphbogen für den Theaterpräsidenten von Kotzebue" (Schlegel) **142**:318
Ehrenpforte und Triumphbogen für den Theater-präsidenten von Kotzebue bei seiner gehofften Rückkehr ins Vaterland (Schlegel) **142**:300, 309-10, 342
"Eidólons" (Whitman) **31**:390; **205**:208
"Eifersucht und Stolz" (Muller) **73**:364
The Eight Commandment (Reade) **74**:269, 315
Eight Cousins (Alcott)
See *Eight Cousins; or, The Aunt Hill*
Eight Cousins; or, The Aunt Hill (Alcott) **6**:16-17, 21; **58**:41, 46, 48-50; **83**:44, 47; **218**:92-96, 99, 101-2
815 (Dickinson) **77**:151
892 (Dickinson) **77**:97
801 (Dickinson) **77**:131
875 (Dickinson) **77**:120
872 (Dickinson) **77**:151
864 (Dickinson) **77**:150
838 (Dickinson) **77**:89
822 (Dickinson) **77**:93
Eight Women (Desbordes-Valmore)
See *Huit Femmes*
Eight Years in Canada (Richardson) **55**:294, 298-9, 303, 311, 314, 317, 320, 329, 334-7, 343-4
"1880-85" (Patmore) **9**:339-40, 358, 362
1811 (Barbauld)
See *Eighteen Hundred and Eleven*
1844 Sketch (Darwin)
See *On the Origin of Species by Means of Natural Selection or the Preservation of Favoured Races in the Struggle for Life*
1842 Sketch (Darwin)
See *On the Origin of Species by Means of Natural Selection or the Preservation of Favoured Races in the Struggle for Life*
Eighteen Hundred and Eleven (Barbauld) **50**:5, 17; **185**:4-7, 15, 23-26, 46-47, 54-57, 59-60, 66-67, 69-73, 78, 82, 84-86, 90, 111, 115, 117, 120, 144-46, 150-51, 153-55, 157
"1865-1866" (Tennyson) **202**:278, 280, 282-83
"1867" (Patmore) **9**:334, 337-38, 340, 358, 362
Eighteen Upbuilding Discourses (Kierkegaard)
See *Edifying Discourses*
The Eighteenth Brumaire of Louis Bonaparte (Marx)
See *Der Achtzehnte Brumaire des Louis-Bonaparte*
"The Eighteenth Century" (Radishchev) **190**:275, 314
"Eighty-five Model Farms and Eighty-five Follies" (Fourier) **51**:180
EIIEA IITEPOENTA, or the Diversions of Purley (Horne Tooke)
See *The Diversions of Purley*
"Eileen a Ruin" (Griffin) **7**:204
"Eileen Aroon" (Mangan) **27**:283
"An eine Äolsharfe" (Mörike) **201**:253, 285-86, 309, 311, 313
"An eine Lieblingsbuche meines Gartens" (Mörike) **201**:318-19, 343-44
"An einem Wintermorgen" (Mörike) **201**:253, 271-72, 287-88, 294, 303, 319, 341, 369
"An einem Wintermorgen vor Sonnenaufgang" (Mörike) **10**:448, 453-55
An einen ehemaligen Goetheaner (Heine) **54**:344
"Einer jungen Freundin ins Stammbuch" (Schiller) **166**:118
"Einer Jungfrau bei dem Geschenk der Sakontala" (Brentano) **191**:37
"Einer Toten" (Meyer) **81**:205, 209
Einer Toten (Storm) **195**:21
Einfältiger Hausvater-Bericht uber die christlich Religion (Claudius) **75**:193, 210, 214-16, 220
"Einfluss der Einsamkeit auf die Bildung des Geistes und die Veredelung des Herzens" (Schumann) **143**:73
"Eingelegte Ruder" (Meyer) **81**:199, 201, 203
"Einige vaterländische" (Herder) **186**:18
Einleitung zu Don Quixote (Heine) **54**:329
Einleitung zur Kawi-Sprache, Ueber die Verschiedenheit des menschlichen Sprachbaues und ihren Einfluss auf die geistige Entwicklung des Menschengeschlects (Humboldt) **134**:206
Einnahme von Paris (Werner)
See *Te Deum zur Feyer der Einnahme von Paris durch die zum heiligen Kriege verbündten Heere*
Die Einquartierung im Pfarrhause (Arnim) **5**:21
Eins und Alles (Goethe) **154**:183
"Einsam will ich untergehn" (Brentano) **191**:68
"Einsamkeit" (Lenau) **16**:281
"Einsamkeit" (Muller) **73**:366, 384, 386, 391
"Die Einsiedlerin" (Brentano) **191**:36
Einsiedlerzeitung (Arnim) **159**:43
Einzelgedichte (Schumann) **143**:138
"Der Einzige" (Hölderlin) **16**:166-9, 175-6, 191
"Eiros and Charmion" (Poe)
See "The Conversation of Eiros and Charmion"
"Eisen Castle" (Bestuzhev)
See "Zamok Eyzen"
"Eislauf" (Klopstock) **11**:233; **225**:297, 305-7, 310-11
"Eisode" (Klopstock)
See "Die Kunst Tialfs"
Either/Or: A Fragment of a Life (Kierkegaard)
See *Enten/Eller*
"Éjféli párbaj" (Arany) **34**:5, 15
"Ekalavya" (Dutt) **29**:124
Ekei Ki Bale Sabhyatā (Dutt) **118**:5
"Ekhidna" (Leconte de Lisle) **29**:221-22
"Èksprompt" (Pavlova) **138**:52
"Él y Ella" (Echeverria) **18**:147
"Elaine" (Tennyson)
See "Lancelot and Elaine"
"Elden-Tree" (Baillie) **2**:42
"The Elder Brother" (Crabbe) **26**:111, 129
Elder Edda (Grimm Brothers) **3**:220
"Eldorado" (Poe) **94**:229; **117**:196, 235, 237-38, 242-43, 281, 283
Eldorado (Taylor) **89**:300, 343, 346, 355
"Eldorado at Islington" (Levy) **59**:92; **203**:351-52, 354
"Eleanore" (Tennyson) **30**:207; **202**:332
The Election (Cumberland) **167**:155, 201-2
The Election: A Comedy in Five Acts (Baillie)
See *The Election: A Comedy on Hatred*
The Election: A Comedy on Hatred (Baillie) **2**:31, 33; **71**:12, 64; **151**:114-15, 117-18
"The Elections to the Hebdomadal Council" (Dodgson) **139**:35
Elective Affinities (Goethe)
See *Die Wahlverwandtschaften*
"The Electric Telegraph" (Bryant) **46**:9
"Oi eleftheroi poliorkimenoi" (Solomos) **15**:386, 391-92, 397-401, 405
"Elegant Tom Dillar" (O'Brien) **21**:249
Elegiac Sonnets, and Other Essays (Smith) **23**:314-15; **115**:120, 122-23, 125, 135, 152, 154-56, 165-66, 174-75, 199-204, 207, 209-12, 215, 217, 223
Elegiac Sonnets, and Other Poems (Blake) **115**:180
"Elegiac Stanzas" (Wordsworth) **12**:458-60; **38**:360, 398; **206**:279
"Elegiac Verses" (Longfellow) **45**:129, 161
"Elégie" (Desbordes-Valmore) **97**:7
"Elegie" (Hölderlin) **187**:228, 230, 233
"Elégie" (Lamartine) **11**:254
Elegie (Klopstock) **225**:296
"Elegie auf den Tod eines Jünglings" (Schiller) **39**:339-40, 386
"Elégie sur les ruines de l'abbaye de . . ." (Lamartine) **190**:231
"Elegies" (Tennyson) **115**:236
Elégies (Verlaine) **230**:166, 172
"Elegija" (Pushkin) **83**:259, 304
"An Elegy" (Chivers) **49**:70
"Elegy" (Cowper) **94**:36
"Elegy" (Darwin) **106**:182
"Elegy" (Pushkin)
See "Elegija"
"Elegy" (Thoreau) **7**:355; **138**:116
"Elegy for Sulieman the Magnificent" (Mangan) **27**:285
"Elegy of Rome" (Schlegel) **15**:223
"Elegy on Our Lost Princess" (Hunt) **70**:257
"Elegy on the Death of a British Officer" (Sheridan) **91**:233
"Elegy on the Death of a Young Man" (Schiller)
See "Elegie auf den Tod eines Jünglings"
"Elegy on the Death of Dr. Channing" (Lowell) **2**:507
"An Elegy on the Death of Mr. Buckingham St. John" (Trumbull) **30**:348
"An Elegy on the Times" (Trumbull) **30**:346, 350, 353, 374
"An Elegy on the Tironian and Tirconnellian Princes Buried at Rome" (Mangan)
See "Lament for the Princes of Tyrone and Tyrconnell"
"Elegy to Dr. Small" (Darwin) **106**:182
Elegy to the Memory of the Late Duke of Bedford (Opie) **65**:175-7
"Elegy, written at the Hotwells, Bristol" (Bowles) **103**:79
"An Elegy Written on St. Mark's Eve" (Cumberland) **167**:117
"Elemental Drifts" (Whitman) **4**:544
"Der Elementargeist" (Hoffmann) **183**:198
"Elementargeister" (Heine) **4**:268
"Elementary Education" (Arnold) **89**:110
Elementary History for Children (Grundtvig) **158**:155
Elementary Lessons in Physiology (Huxley) **67**:95
The Elementary Spelling Book (Webster)
See *A Grammatical Institute, of the English Language, Comprising, an Easy, Concise, and Systematic Method of Education, Designed for the Use of English Schools in America*
"The Elementary Spirit" (Hoffmann)
See "Der Elementargeist"
"Elementary Studies" (Newman) **99**:214, 297
"The Elements" (Newman) **38**:345

"Elements of Critical Jurisprudence" (Bentham) **38**:94
The Elements of Mental and Moral Philosophy, Founded upon Reason, Experience, and the Bible (Beecher) **30**:11, 23, 25
Elements of Moral Science (Beattie) **25**:101, 121
The Elements of Rhetoric (De Mille) **123**:161, 163-64
Elën (Villiers de l'Isle Adam) **3**:581, 583-84
"Elena" (Casal) **131**:224-26, 235, 266, 268
"Elena" (Herzen) **10**:347-48; **61**:108
"Elena" (Isaacs) **70**:307-08
"Das Elend soll ich einsam bauen" (Brentano) **191**:68
"Eleonora" (Poe) **1**:497-98; **16**:305-06, 308, 324, 336; **55**:148, 151; **117**:300, 302
"Les eléphants" (Leconte de Lisle) **29**:210, 216-17, 221, 223-24, 230-31
"Elet vagy halál" (Petofi) **21**:286
"The Eleusinian Feast" (Schiller)
See "Das Eleusische Fest"
"The Eleusinian Festival" (Schiller)
See "Das Eleusische Fest"
"Das Eleusische Fest" (Schiller) **39**:305, 337; **166**:105
"Elévation" (Baudelaire) **6**:82-83, 97, 114, 128; **29**:89-90; **55**:27
Elévation sur Paris (Vigny) **7**:469
1126 (Dickinson) **77**:63, 92, 95
Eleven Days In Belgium (Verlaine)
See *Onze jours en Belgique*
Eleven Lectures on the French and Belgian Revolutions (Cobbett) **49**:160
"Eleven Tales of the Arabesque" (Poe) **94**:239
"The Eleventh Hour" (Lazarus) **109**:298, 301, 323
"The Eleventh-Hour Guest" (Villiers de l'Isle Adam)
See "Le convive des dernières fêtes"
"The Elf Hill" (Andersen) **214**:75, 77
"Die Elfen" (Tieck) **46**:350
"Elfenlied" (Mörike) **10**:446, 455; **201**:268, 299
"Les elfes" (Leconte de Lisle) **29**:220
Elfide (Klinger) **1**:429
"The Elfin Mound" (Andersen) **7**:23; **79**:23, 28
"Elfrida" (Lazarus) **8**:411, 417
Elfrida (Eminescu)
See *The King and the Knight*
"Elfrida, a Dramatic Poem" (Osgood) **141**:319, 333, 354
"Elfsong" (Mörike)
See "Elfenlied"
"The Elgin Marbles" (Hazlitt) **82**:160
"Elgin Marbles" (Keats)
See "On Seeing the Elgin Marbles"
Elgskyttarne (Runeberg) **41**:309-10, 313, 317, 331
Elia: Essays Which Have Appeared under That Signature in the "London Magazine" (Lamb) **10**:389, 391, 393, 395, 403, 406-07, 410-11, 414-16, 420-21, 434; **113**:159, 163, 167, 169-70, 202, 221, 228, 230, 234-35, 240-48, 265-67, 281-83
Elia; o, La España de treinta años ha (Caballero) **10**:77
"Elia to Robert Southey" (Lamb) **10**:408
"Elias Wildmanstadius ou l'Homme moyenage" (Gautier) **59**:26-7
"Elijah" (Kendall) **12**:192
"Elijah's Wagon knew no thill" (Dickinson) **77**:68
"Elinor" (Southey) **97**:314
Elinor and Marianne (Austen) **1**:53; **81**:74; **119**:17, 37, 45
"Elinor Forester: The Father's Wedding" (Lamb) **125**:318, 324-25
Elinor Wyllys; or, The Young Folk of Longbridge. A Tale (Cooper) **129**:9-12, 14, 16-18, 20, 49, 57, 61, 65
"Eliot Carson" (Bellamy) **86**:16-17
Eliot, Hampden, and Pym (D'Israeli) **217**:284, 320
Elisa (Goncourt)
See *La fille Élisa*
"Eliveria" (Isaacs) **70**:310
Die Elixiere des Teufels (Hoffmann) **2**:339, 341, 343-44, 348, 358, 360, 362; **183**:165-66, 177, 184-86, 188, 194, 203, 221, 223, 225-26, 228-29, 231-34, 247, 311
L'Elixir de longue vie (Balzac) **53**:25; **153**:149, 151
The Elixir of Long Life (Balzac)
See *L'Elixir de longue vie*
"Elixirs of the Devil" (Hoffmann)
See *Die Elixiere des Teufels*
"Elizabeth" (Longfellow) **45**:128
Elizabeth Barrett Browning: Hitherto Unpublished Poems and Stories with an Inedited Autobiography (Barrett Browning) **61**:48, 50
Elizabeth Barrett Browning: Selected Poems (Barrett Browning) **170**:78
Elizabeth Barrett Browning's Letters to Mrs. David Ogilvy 1849-1861 (Barrett Browning) **170**:85
Elizabeth Barrett to Mr. Boyd: Unpublished Letters of Elizabeth Barrett Browning to Hugh Stuart Boyd (Barrett Browning) **61**:14, 28, 50
Elizabeth Bennet; or, Pride and Prejudice (Austen)
See *Pride and Prejudice*
"Elizabeth Hastings" (Brontë) **109**:42
"Elizabeth Palmer Peabody to William Wordsworth: Eight Letters, 1825-1845" (Peabody) **169**:183
"Elizabeth Peabody Reviews Twice-told Tales" (Peabody) **169**:183
"Elizabeth Villiers: The Sailor Uncle" (Lamb) **125**:312, 317, 324-25, 368-70
"Elizabeth Wilson" (Child) **73**:80
"Elizir d'amor" (Corbière) **43**:13
"The Elk" (Poe) **16**:336
The Elk Hunters (Runeberg)
See *Elgskyttarne*
"Ella duerme!" (Isaacs) **70**:310
"Ella of Garveloch" (Martineau) **26**:304, 306, 351; **137**:243
Elle et lui (Sand) **2**:597, 604; **42**:312; **57**:317; **174**:228
"Ellen Aeyre" (Chivers) **49**:40, 49
"Ellen Bawn" (Mangan) **27**:314
"Ellen Brine ov Allenburn" (Barnes) **75**:8, 46
"Ellen Dare o'Lindenore" (Barnes) **75**:58
Ellen Gray (Bowles) **103**:54
"Ellen Irwin" (Wordsworth)
See "Ellen Irwin, or the Braes of Kirtle"
"Ellen Irwin, or the Braes of Kirtle" (Wordsworth) **111**:323; **206**:312
"Ellen Middleton" (Rossetti) **186**:275-76
"Ellen Orford" (Crabbe) **26**:149; **121**:36, 88-9
Ellernklipp (Fontane) **26**:237, 243-44, 250-53, 255, 272; **163**:161, 169, 197-99, 201-2, 215
Ellie; or, The Human Comedy (Cooke) **5**:121-22, 129
"The Elliotts" (Austen) **1**:53
"The Elm Tree, a Dream in the Woods" (Hood) **16**:210, 220, 222, 224-25, 228-29, 233, 235
"The Elm Trees" (Sigourney) **21**:301
"Eloa" (Vigny)
See "Eloa ou la soeur des anges"
"Eloa ou la soeur des anges" (Vigny) **102**:335-36, 348, 350, 367-68, 379
Eloge de Victor-Amédée III (Maistre) **37**:302, 311
"The Elopement" (Willis) **194**:298
"Eloquence" (Emerson) **1**:280; **98**:7
"Elsi, die seltsame Magd" (Gotthelf) **117**:6
"Elsie in Illinois" (Larcom) **179**:167
Elsie Venner: A Romance of Destiny (Holmes) **14**:103, 105-06, 110, 113-15, 117, 119-20, 123-26, 130-41, 143, 148-49, 151; **81**:102, 107-09, 111, 113
"Az első halott" (Madach) **19**:369
"Elverhøi" (Andersen) **79**:76
"The Elves" (Leconte de Lisle)
See "Les elfes"
Az elveszett alkomány (Arany) **34**:16, 21-2
Elvira and Her Desperate Love for a Ludicrous King (Eminescu) **33**:266
Elvira; o, La novia del Plata (Echeverria) **18**:147-49, 152
"Elvira Silva" (Isaacs) **70**:310, 312
"Elvire" (Lamartine) **190**:225, 246, 251
"Elysium Is as Far as To" (Dickinson) **21**:10; **171**:96, 141
"The Emancipated Slaveholders" (Child) **73**:80
"The Emancipated Woman at last Found" (Fourier) **51**:180
Emancipation (Channing) **17**:25, 32
"Emancipation in the British West Indies" (Emerson)
See "Emancipation of the British West Indies"
"Emancipation of the British West Indies" (Emerson) **98**:43, 45, 48, 167, 171
"Emancipation Proclamation" (Emerson) **98**:43
"Emancipation Proclamation" (Lincoln)
See "Proclamation of Emancipation by the President of the United States, January 1st, 1863"
Emancipation Proclamation (Lincoln) **18**:219, 231-35, 268-71
Die Emanzipation der Domestiken (Ludwig) **4**:367
Emaux et camées (Gautier) **1**:342-43, 347-48, 350; **59**:3, 17-20, 43
"The Embalmer" (Maginn) **8**:438
The Embargo; or, Sketches of the Times (Bryant) **6**:157; **46**:25
"Az ember" (Petofi) **21**:264
Az ember tragédiája (Madach) **19**:354-57, 360-62, 364-74
"Emblem" (Harpur) **114**:116
"Embryon" (Alcott) **167**:51
"Emerald Uthwart" (Pater) **7**:303, 324
"Emerson" (Alcott) **167**:76
"Emerson" (Arnold) **126**:43; **218**:258
Emerson: Collected Poems and Translations (Emerson) **98**:177
Emerson in His Journals (Emerson) **98**:134
"Emerson the Lecturer" (Lowell) **90**:219-21
"Emerson's Limitations as a Poet" (Cranch) **115**:33
"Emerson's Personality" (Lazarus) **109**:305-06
"Emerson's 'Thoreau'" (Emerson) **98**:73-4
"L'Emeute" (Baudelaire) **55**:36
"The Emigrant Mother" (Sigourney) **21**:298
"The Emigrants" (Smith) **115**:121
The Emigrants (Smith) **115**:126, 129, 133-34, 158, 164, 166, 168, 195-97, 199, 204, 206-11, 218
"Emigrant's Farewell" (Allingham) **25**:15
The Emigrant's Guide (Cobbett) **49**:152-53
The Emigrants of Ahadarra (Carleton) **3**:90, 94, 96
The Emigrants of Ahadarra: A Tale of Irish Life (Carleton) **199**:8, 10, 12, 19-20, 23-24, 43, 46-49, 51-52, 80
"The Emigrant's Unhappy Predicament" (Boyesen) **135**:32
L'émigré (Charriere) **66**:136
Les Émigrés (Charriere) **66**:124
"A Emilia" (Heredia) **209**:120, 124, 137
Emilie (Nerval) **1**:485; **67**:304, 363, 365
"Emilie De Coulanges" (Edgeworth) **51**:89; **158**:46
"Emilie de Tourville ou la cruauté fraternelle" (Sade) **47**:313
The Emissary (Sacher-Masoch) **31**:285, 289
Emma (Austen) **1**:30, 32-4, 36-40, 44-6, 48, 50-2, 54-5, 60-1, 63-4; **13**:66, 93-4, 96, 104; **19**:1-70; **33**:39, 57-9, 62-5, 69, 71, 74, 76,

80, 84, 88-90, 92-3, 96-7, 99; **51**:15, 41; **81**:5, 12-3, 18, 35, 68, 78-9, 83; **95**:13, 18, 21, 25, 39, 55-6, 58, 73, 86; **119**:14-18, 21-8, 33, 39-43, 48, 57; **150**:35, 44, 67, 88, 106, 110, 112-13, 138; **222**:26, 28, 30-31, 38, 42-43, 45, 48, 50, 53, 55, 75, 79; **229**:19
Emma (Brontë) **217**:25
"Emma and Ermingard" (Longfellow) **45**:145
Emmeline, the Orphan of the Castle (Smith) **23**:314-15, 319-24, 327-29, 332-33, 335; **115**:136-42, 144-46, 150, 153, 187-90, 192, 210, 221-24
"The Emotional and the Cold, Two Characters" (Karamzin)
See "Cuvstvitel'nyj i xolodnyj, dva xaraktera"
"Emotional Art" (Patmore) **9**:342
Empedocles (Hölderlin)
See *Empedokles*
"Empedocles on Etna" (Arnold) **6**:31, 38, 42, 48, 51-52, 54, 56, 59, 66-67, 70-72; **29**:5-6, 26-7, 29, 31, 36-7, 53; **89**:14, 49-51, 53, 82, 120; **218**:111, 113, 122, 133, 152, 179, 189, 191, 220, 227, 268, 278-79
Empedocles on Etna, and Other Poems (Arnold) **6**:28, 30, 73-74; **29**:27, 35; **89**:88, 91-2; **218**:175, 211
Empedokles (Hölderlin) **16**:159, 164-65, 187-88, 190-91; **187**:189-92, 239-41, 248, 252, 254, 286
Empedokles auf dem Aetna (Hölderlin) **187**:187, 190
"Emperor and Proletarian" (Eminescu)
See "Împarat şi proletar"
"The Emperor of China and Tsing-ti" (Landor) **14**:165, 167, 178
"The Emperor's New Clothes" (Andersen)
See "Keiserens nye Klæder"
"The Emperor's Nightingale" (Andersen) **7**:37
"The Emperor's Son without a Star" (Eminescu) **131**:347
"The Emperor's Statue" (Grillparzer)
See "Des Kaisers Bildsäule"
The Empire City; or, New York by Night and Day (Lippard) **198**:125, 140, 169, 173, 225, 230, 239, 242-47
"L'Empire Knouto-Germanique et la Révolution Sociale" (Bakunin) **25**:46, 48-49, 59; **58**:99, 140
"The Empire of the Chimilas" (Isaacs)
See "El imperio chimila"
Empires of the World (Fouqué) **2**:267
Les employés (Balzac) **35**:3; **153**:8, 56
En 18.. (Goncourt and Goncourt) **7**:161, 167, 186-87, 189
"En balde" (Castro) **78**:40
"En bateau" (Verlaine) **2**:630; **51**:378-79
En Comedie i det Gronne (Andersen) **79**:9
"En el Teocalli de Cholula" (Heredia) **209**:120, 126, 131, 134, 136, 154, 160
"En Historie fra Klitterne" (Andersen) **7**:33; **79**:82, 88
"En la apertura del Instituto Mexicano" (Heredia) **209**:166-68
"En la tortura" (Isaacs) **70**:310
"En la tumba de Leopoldo..." (Isaacs) **70**:306
"En las cumbres de Chisacá" (Isaacs) **70**:310
"En las orillas del Sar" (Castro) **3**:103; **78**:10, 12-13, 16-17, 21, 23, 25, 29-30, 32, 38, 41, 54
"En lisant" (Maupassant) **83**:185
En literair Anmeldelse. To Tidsaldre (Kierkegaard) **34**:200, 239, 269; **78**:176, 238; **125**:203, 231
"En loor de la Reina gobernadora" (Larra) **130**:202
"En los ecos de los organos o en el rumor del viento" (Castro) **78**:41
"En los ecos del Organo o en el rumor del viento" (Castro) **78**:21
"En masse" (Whitman) **4**:564
"En mi cumpleaños" (Heredia) **209**:135
Una en otra (Caballero) **10**:72
"En patinant" (Verlaine) **51**:378-79
"En Route" (Barrett Browning) **61**:15
"En Route" (Rossetti) **186**:266
"En 17 . . ." (Verlaine) **230**:169
"En sourdine" (Verlaine) **2**:624; **51**:351, 378-81; **230**:165
"En Suenos te di un beso, vida mia" (Castro) **78**:23
En Suisse (Dumas) **71**:205
"En un teocalli de Cholula" (Heredia)
See "En el Teocalli de Cholula"
"En una tempestad" (Heredia) **209**:120, 122, 125, 127, 129, 132-33, 149, 152, 162-66
"En voyage" (Maupassant) **83**:158-62, 194, 228
Enamels and Cameos (Gautier)
See *Emaux et camées*
"The Encantadas; or, The Enchanted Isles" (Melville) **3**:331, 344, 347, 354, 361-62, 368, 380-81, 383-84; **45**:233; **123**:254; **157**:71; **181**:327; **193**:52, 108, 116
"The Enchanted Knight" (Taylor) **89**:298
"The Enchanted Lyre" (Darley) **2**:127, 132
"The Enchanted Pilgrim" (Leskov)
See "Očarovannyj strannik"
"The Enchanted Spot" (Gogol)
See "Zakoldovannoe mesto"
"The Enchanted Titan" (O'Brien) **21**:238
"The Enchanted Wanderer" (Leskov)
See "Očarovannyj strannik"
"The Enchantress" (Stevenson) **193**:279-81
Encore une nuit de la Garde Nationale; ou, Le poste de la barrière (Scribe) **16**:391, 393, 400
Encyclopädie der philosophischen Wissenschaften im Grundrisse (Hegel) **151**:238, 241-42, 244, 288, 323, 348-49, 351-53
Encyclopedia of the Philosophical Sciences in Outline. Part 1. The Logic (Hegel)
See *Enzyklopädie der philosophischen Wissenshaften im Grundrisse. Theil 1. Die Logik*
Encyclopedia of the Philosophical Sciences in Outline. Part 2. Philosophy of Nature (Hegel)
See *Enzyklopädie der philosophischen Wissenshaften im Grundrisse. Theil 2. Naturphilosophie*
Der Encyklopädie dritter Teil: Die Philosophie des Geistes (Hegel) **151**:241, 369-72
"The End" (Corbière)
See "La fin"
"An End in Paris" (Wagner)
See "Ein Ende in Paris"
"The End of All" (Brontë) **109**:4, 30
"The End of the World" (Turgenev) **21**:431, 453
"Das Ende des Festes" (Meyer) **81**:143, 169, 200
"Ein Ende in Paris" (Wagner) **9**:475
"Endicott and the Red Cross" (Hawthorne) **2**:329-31; **10**:308; **158**:228; **191**:189; **226**:32
"The Ending of 'The Government Inspector'" (Gogol)
See "Razviazka 'Révizor'"
"Endlessly" (Laforgue)
See "Intarissablement"
"Ends of the Church" (Arnold) **18**:47
"Endymion" (Cranch) **115**:5
"Endymion" (Wieland) **17**:426
Endymion (Disraeli) **2**:145-46, 150; **39**:3-4, 21-4, 31, 36-7, 43-4, 49, 51, 66, 71-81; **79**:212, 222, 234, 257, 269
Endymion (Keats)
See *Endymion: A Poetic Romance*
Endymion: A Poetic Romance (Keats) **8**:323-28, 330-37, 340-42, 344-50, 353-61, 364-66, 368-70, 372, 385-86; **73**:142, 144, 152-53, 158, 170-72, 177, 192, 198, 201-04, 208-09, 211, 233-34, 246, 248, 254, 258, 260, 268-71, 290-91, 310-11, 314, 322-25, 332-36, 338-39, 341-42; **121**:98, 102, 104, 109, 122, 125, 136, 139, 141, 147-48, 151, 162-69, 173, 175, 187, 206, 209, 225, 228-29, 233; **225**:111-13, 115-19, 133-34, 142, 152-55, 163, 169, 174-81, 183, 188, 197, 227, 243, 247, 251, 262
"Enfance" (Rimbaud) **4**:466, 473, 484; **35**:297, 299, 304-07, 322-23; **82**:232-33, 253; **227**:210-11, 309, 334
"Enfance chrétienne" (Verlaine) **230**:168
"Enfans d'Adam" (Whitman)
See "Children of Adam"
"Les enfans de la France" (Beranger) **34**:28
"L'Enfant" (Maupassant) **83**:213-16, 223
"L'enfant aux souliers de pain" (Gautier) **1**:348; **59**:32, 36
"L'Enfant Maudit" (Balzac) **153**:103
"Enfant Perdu" (Heine) **147**:234-35
L'enfant prodigue (Becque) **3**:13, 15-16
L'Enfant prodigue (Mallarmé) **41**:278
"Enfer" (Laforgue) **221**:42
"Enfer et diable" (Beranger) **34**:41
"The Enfranchisement of Women" (Mill) **102**:282-83, 285-87, 297-302, 315-16, 320, 330
The Enfranchisement of Women (Mill) **11**:393
The Engagement (Kivi)
See *Kihlaus*
Der Engel Von Augsburg (Ludwig) **4**:350
"Engelberg" (Meyer) **81**:155
"Den Engelske lods" (Wergeland) **5**:536, 538, 541
"England" (Emerson) **98**:7
England (Cooper) **203**:163
England and France, or a Cure for the Ministerial Gallomania (Disraeli) **79**:269
England and Ireland (Mill) **179**:361
England and Spain; or Valour and Patriotism (Hemans) **71**:271, 278
England and the English (Bulwer-Lytton) **1**:151-53; **45**:32, 36-8, 47-8, 71
England and the Italian Question (Arnold) **218**:250, 253
"England in 1819" (Shelley) **175**:260
"England in Egypt" (Adams) **33**:12
England in Time of War (Dobell) **43**:40, 44, 60, 62
England, the Civilizer (Wright) **74**:375, 377-78
"England's Day" (Dobell) **43**:45
"England's Dead" (Hemans) **71**:278
"England's Forgotten Worthies" (Froude) **43**:184
"England's Glory: A Loyal Song" (Moodie) **113**:310
"England's Mission" (Gladstone) **213**:113
English and Scottish Ballads (Child) **173**:166-70, 172-73, 178-80, 183, 189-91, 193-95, 198-200, 209, 211, 226-29, 232-35, 238, 244
The English and Scottish Popular Ballads (Child) **173**:169-72, 175-79, 186-87, 189, 194, 197-98, 201, 204-6, 209-12, 223-24, 226-28, 232-35, 238, 244
"The English Aristocracy and the Death of Wellington" (Beddoes) **154**:74-75
English Bards (Byron) **149**:14
English Bards and Scotch Reviewers (Byron) **2**:58, 62, 70, 85, 92, 95, 103; **12**:88, 103, 105-06, 129
"The English Boy" (Hemans) **71**:277
The English Constitution (Bagehot) **10**:15, 19, 22-23, 32, 34-35, 40, 45, 48, 50-54, 59, 63-66
English Ecologues (Southey) **97**:315, 318
"The English Factory" (Tonna) **135**:196
The English Gardener (Cobbett) **49**:108, 110, 113-14, 140, 150-51
English Grammar (Cobbett)
See *A Grammar of the English Language*
The English Humourists of the Eighteenth Century: A Series of Lectures Delivered in England, Scotland, and the United

States of America (Thackeray) **5**:457, 466, 490; **43**:376; **213**:200, 203, 223, 268, 305, 317, 319, 341
"English Idylls" (Tennyson) **30**:249
The English in Ireland in the Eighteenth Century (Froude) **43**:193-96
The English in Little (Jerrold) **2**:406-08
The English in the West Indies (Froude) **43**:192
English Laws for Women in the Nineteenth Century (Norton) **205**:67, 74, 81, 85, 110, 123, 129, 143, 145-47
English Laws of Custom and Marriage for Women of the Nineteenth Century (Norton) **47**:248, 254, 261-63
"An English Life" (Jones) **222**:158
"English Literature" (Pater) **90**:333, 337
"The English Mail-Coach" (De Quincey) **87**:22-4, 30, 43-4, 47
The English Mail-coach (De Quincey) **4**:67, 74, 77, 82, 86-89; **87**:3, 15
"The English Mail-Coach, or the Glory of Motion" (De Quincey) **198**:15-16, 19-23, 25-26, 31, 42, 44, 51-52, 54, 72, 74-84, 88-89, 93, 95-99, 103-4, 106-8, 110-11
"English Niggers" (Haliburton) **149**:345
English Notebooks (Hawthorne)
See *Passages from the English Notebooks of Nathaniel Hawthorne*
The English Novel and the Principle of Its Development (Lanier) **6**:245, 252, 265-66; **118**:204, 218, 248, 283
"English Physiology" (De Quincey) **198**:62
"The English Pilot" (Wergeland)
See "Den Engelske lods"
"An English Poet" (Pater) **90**:290, 340
English Poets (Child)
See *British Poets*
"An English Prologue and Epilogue to the Latin Comedy of Ignoramus with a Preface and Notes relative to modern Times and Manners" (Dyer) **129**:105, 116
"The English Revolution of 1848" (Rossetti) **77**:291-92, 294
English Rispetti (Webster) **230**:303, 306-08, 314-15
"English Slavery" (Tonna) **135**:204, 211
English Stornelli (Webster) **230**:303, 306
An English Tragedy (Kemble) **18**:191
English Traits (Emerson) **1**:278, 281, 284, 286, 288, 299; **38**:173, 213-18; **98**:5, 55, 72, 76, 130
"The English View of Internal Crises" (Engels) **85**:121
"English Writers on America" (Irving) **19**:327-28, 347, 350; **95**:293-94
The Englishman from Paris (Murphy) **229**:241
"The Englishman in Italy" (Browning) **19**:98; **79**:94, 97
"Englyn" (Barnes) **75**:54
"Enid and Nimuë" (Tennyson) **30**:249; **65**:378; **202**:218, 221
"An Enigma" (Poe) **117**:242
An Enigmatic Man (Leskov)
See *Zagadocnyj celovék*
L'Enlèvement (Barbey d'Aurevilly) **213**:27
L'Enlèvement (Becque) **3**:13, 16
"L'enlèvement de la rédoute" (Mérimée) **6**:353-4, 358, 363-4, 366-7, 369, 371; **65**:57, 60, 87, 103-4
"L'ennemi" (Baudelaire) **6**:117; **55**:58
Ennui (Edgeworth) **1**:257, 262, 264, 267-68, 270; **51**:86-90, 93, 104, 137; **158**:54, 61, 69-72, 74-75
"L'Ennui de vivre . . ." (Verlaine) **230**:161, 168
Ennuyée (Jameson)
See *Diary of an Ennuyée*
"Enoch" (Very) **9**:378
"Enoch Arden" (Crabbe) **26**:135, 150
Enoch Arden (Tennyson) **202**:331, 333
Enoch Arden, and Other Poems (Tennyson) **30**:218-20, 233, 238, 249, 276, 282
Enoch Arden, Etc. (Tennyson) **202**:279-80
"Enosis" (Cranch) **115**:5, 13-14, 22, 27-9, 32, 35, 54, 67
"Enough" (Turgenev) **21**:420, 435, 440; **122**:241, 243, 247, 337, 343
Enough Silliness in Every Wise Man (Ostrovsky)
See *Na vsyakogo mudretsa dovolno prostoty*
"Enquête sur l'évolution littéraire" (Mallarmé) **210**:171
The Enquirer: Reflections on Education, Manners, and Literature (Godwin) **14**:75, 79-80, 84, 86-7; **130**:7, 40, 113, 115, 125
Enquiry concerning Political Justice and Its Influence on General Virtue and Happiness (Godwin) **14**:37-8, 40-3, 47, 50-1, 54-76, 78, 80-3, 85, 87-8, 90, 92-3; **130**:5, 7-9, 14, 20-21, 23-25, 27, 30, 32-33, 36-37, 47-49, 52-55, 58, 60-62, 64, 70-72, 74-76, 81, 88-98, 100, 107-11, 113-14, 122-23, 129-30, 142-45, 150-52, 154, 156-57, 161, 164, 169-73, 182-83
Enquiry concerning Political Justice and Its Influence on Morals and Happiness (Godwin)
See *Enquiry concerning Political Justice and Its Influence on General Virtue and Happiness*
"An Enquiry Whether the Fine Arts are Promoted by Academies" (Hazlitt) **29**:144
"Enragée" (Maupassant) **83**:223, 230
"Enrica, 1865" (Rossetti) **186**:304
Ensayos (Bécquer) **106**:96
"The Ensign at the Fair" (Runeberg)
See "Fänrikens marknadsminne"
Ensign Stål (Runeberg)
See *Fänrik Ståls sägner*
"The Ensign's Greeting" (Runeberg) **41**:312, 314
"Ensimmäinen lempi" (Kivi)
See "Nuori Karhunampuja"
L'ensorcelée (Barbey d'Aurevilly) **1**:70-73; **213**:5, 8-10, 12, 15, 29-30, 32-37, 39, 46-49, 54
The Entail (Hoffmann)
See "Der Majorat"
The Entail; or, The Lairds of Grippy (Galt) **1**:329, 331-32, 335, 337; **110**:78-9, 82, 93, 96, 98-9, 101-2, 105-7, 114
"Entangled" (Larcom) **179**:177
Enten/Eller (Kierkegaard) **34**:178, 192, 201, 203, 205, 222, 236, 238, 240, 248-54, 258, 268; **78**:166-68, 173-74, 176, 178, 181-82, 187, 198, 215, 227, 238, 242-43, 248, 252; **125**:173-287
Enten/Eller Vol. I (Kierkegaard) **125**:177-79, 182, 191, 198, 200-215, 230, 232-33, 247-57, 278-80
Enten/Eller Vol. II (Kierkegaard) **125**:179-80, 200, 202, 204, 209-10, 213-14, 218-26, 231, 234, 250, 259-64, 282-84
"Entends comme brame" (Rimbaud) **35**:321; **82**:238
"L'enterrement" (Verlaine) **2**:630
Die Entführung (Eichendorff) **225**:9, 19
"L'enthousiasme" (Lamartine) **11**:245
"Enthusiasm" (Moodie) **113**:317-21
Enthusiasm (Baillie) **71**:6
Enthusiasm, and other Poems (Moodie) **113**:313-17, 321, 324, 368
"Enthusiasmus und Schwärmerei" (Wieland) **17**:411
"The Enthusiast: A Daydream in Summer" (Clare) **86**:113
The Enthusiast; or the Lover of Nature (Warton) **118**:297-98, 300-301, 304, 331-33, 335-36, 350, 354, 356
"La entrada del invierno en Londres" (Espronceda) **39**:87, 105
The Entranced; or, the Wanderer of Eighteen Centuries (Lippard) **198**:125, 184, 226-27, 229
Entre quatre murs (Mallarmé) **41**:248-49
"Entre sueños" (Bécquer) **106**:115, 157
Entretiens journaliers avec le très docte et très habile docteur Piffoël (Sand) **57**:380
Entretiens littéraires (Lamartine) **190**:215
"L'entrevue au ruisseau" (Desbordes-Valmore) **97**:27
"Entsagung" (Grillparzer) **102**:117
"Entschluss" (Eichendorff) **225**:52
Die Entwicklung des Sozialismus von der Uopie zur Wissenschaft (Marx) **85**:6, 24, 59, 105, 181; **114**:4, 39, 44
L'Envers de L'Histoire contemporaine (Balzac) **153**:9-10, 71
"L'Envoi" (Taylor) **89**:359
"L'Envoy" (Irving) **95**:265
"The Envoy" (Mangan) **27**:300
Enzyklopädie der philosophischen Wissenshaften im Grundrisse. Theil 1. Die Logik (Hegel) **46**:60-2, 70, 78, 89-91, 108, 112-13, 124-25, 150, 153, 155, 159, 162, 164-65, 181-83, 186, 189
Enzyklopädie der philosophischen Wissenshaften im Grundrisse. Theil 2. Naturphilosophie (Hegel) **46**:70, 89-90, 108, 112, 124-25, 150, 153, 155, 159, 162, 164-65, 181-83, 186, 189
"The Eolian Harp" (Coleridge)
See "The Aeolian Harp"
"Eolova arfa" (Zhukovsky) **35**:398
Eonchs of Ruby (Chivers) **49**:42-3, 47, 49, 52, 70, 72-3
Eonchs of Ruby: A Gift of Love (Chivers)
See *Eonchs of Ruby*
Epea Pteroenta, or the Diversions of Purley (Horne Tooke)
See *The Diversions of Purley*
"L'épée" (Banville) **9**:16
"Epée d'Angantyr" (Leconte de Lisle) **29**:215
Epen Erskine; or, The Traveller (Galt) **1**:334
"The Ephemeral Life" (Ichiyō)
See "Utsusemi"
Ephesus Widow (Eminescu) **33**:266
"The Epic" (Tennyson) **30**:279; **65**:348, 354, 368
The Epic (Tennyson) **202**:308, 320-21
"Epic Fragments" (Thelwall) **162**:303
"Epic Poetry" (Very) **9**:370, 379, 387
"Epic-in three Lustra" (Chivers) **49**:43
The Epicurean (Moore) **6**:384-85; **110**:167-68, 188-89
"The Epicurean's Song" (Brontë) **109**:5
"Epicuréisme" (Laforgue) **221**:39-40, 82
"Epicurius, Leontium, and Ternissa" (Landor) **14**:178
Die Epigonen: Familienmemoiren in neun Büchern (Immermann) **4**:292-97; **49**:365-66, 369, 371-72
"Epigones" (Eminescu) **33**:245, 255; **131**:338
The Epigram (Keller)
See *Das Sinngedicht*
"Epigram on a Long-Nosed Friend" (Paine) **62**:325
Das Epigramm (Kotzebue) **25**:137, 141
"Epigramma na Zhukovskogo" (Bestuzhev) **131**:148
"Epigramme" (Goethe) **4**:193
Epigrammes (Verlaine) **51**:351; **230**:171, 173
"Epilog" (Heine) **4**:257; **147**:184
Epilog zur Lessing-Feier (Auerbach) **171**:39, 55
"Epilogue" (Arany) **34**:5
"Epilogue" (Baudelaire) **155**:18
"Epilogue" (Browning) **79**:169
"Epilogue" (Crawford) **127**:178
"Epilogue" (Lamartine) **11**:286-87, 289
"Epilogue" (Pater) **7**:323
"Epilogue" (Preseren) **127**:293
"Epilogue" (Tennyson) **30**:295

"Epilogue" (Verlaine) **2**:631; **230**:162, 168, 190
"Epilogue à la ville de Paris" (Baudelaire) **29**:79
"Epilogue to Human Woe" (Beddoes) **154**:78
"Epilogue to the Breakfast-Table Series" (Holmes) **14**:109
"Epimetheus; or, The Poet's Afterthought" (Longfellow) **2**:492
"Les epingles" (Maupassant) **1**:458; **83**:194, 201
"Epiphany" (Leconte de Lisle) **29**:218
Epipsychidion (Shelley) **18**:340, 346, 349-51, 354, 362-64, 369-70, 373, 383; **93**:275, 277, 279-81, 343-46, 348; **143**:197, 200; **175**:203, 236, 238, 264
"Les épis" (Leconte de Lisle) **29**:246
"Episcopal Justice" (Leskov)
See "Vladyčnyj sud"
Épisode (Lamartine) **11**:274
"Épisode de l'histoire de la Russie" (Mérimée) **6**:356; **65**:79
Un épisode sous la Terreur (Balzac) **5**:52-53; **153**:28, 31, 149
An Episode under the Terror (Balzac)
See *Un épisode sous la Terreur*
Episodes in a Life of Adventure (Oliphant) **47**:286, 289
The Episodes of Vathek (Beckford) **16**:29, 50; **214**:101-5, 107, 110, 134, 146
"Episteln" (Goethe) **4**:193
"Epistle" (Shevchenko)
See "Poslaniie"
"Epistle IV" (Eminescu) **33**:245, 247, 265; **131**:288, 332
"Epistle from a Father to a Child in her Grave" (Brontë) **109**:6
"Epistle from Henry of Exeter to John of Tehume" (Moore) **6**:388
"An Epistle from Joshua Ibn Vives of Allorqui" (Lazarus) **109**:297
"An Epistle from the Maid of Corinth to Her Lover" (Opie) **65**:174
"Epistle John Hamilton to Reynolds" (Keats) **8**:362, 389; **73**:162, 201, 203, 209, 259, 266
"Epistle of an Indian Brahmin to the Crown Prince Khlor" (Derzhavin)
See "Poslanie indeiskogo bramina k tsarevichu Khloru"
"Epistle of Condolence from a Slave-Lord to a Cotton-Lord" (Moore) **110**:172
"An Epistle of Karshish the Arab Physician" (Browning) **19**:79, 115, 117, 129-30, 137; **79**:140, 142, 164, 185
"Epistle on Miracles" (Very) **9**:395
"Epistle to ..." (Halleck) **47**:77
Epistle to a Friend (Rogers) **69**:73, 78
"An Epistle to a Friend on New-Year's Day" (Opie) **65**:154
Epistle to Anthony Trollope (Lewes) **215**:131
"Epistle to Charles Cowden Clarke" (Keats) **8**:359; **73**:152, 193
"An Epistle to Dr. Moore" (Williams) **135**:255, 333-34
"Epistle to George Felton Mathew" (Keats) **8**:364; **73**:224, 311
"Epistle to M. A. Dmitriev" (Aksakov)
See "Poslanie k M. A. Dmitrievu"
"Epistle to Mr. Hill" (Cowper) **8**:97, 103
"Epistle to My Brother George" (Keats) **73**:152, 257, 323
Epistle to Ovid (Pushkin) **3**:415
"Epistle to Prince Viazemsky" (Aksakov)
See "Poslanie k kn. Viazemskomu"
"Epistle to Schuvaloff" (Derzhavin) **215**:9
"Epistle to Sir Walter Scott" (Brackenridge) **7**:57
"Epistle to the Author of 'Festus'" (Landor) **14**:198
"Epistle to the Duke de Frias" (Martínez de la Rosa) **102**:228-29
"An Epistle to the Hebrews" (Lazarus) **8**:424; **109**:289, 303, 312, 320, 322, 330, 337-39, 346-48
"Epistle to the Recorder by Thomas Castaly Edq" (Halleck) **47**:68, 71-72, 77-78, 81, 86
Epistle to William Wilberforce, Esq., on the Rejection of the Bill for Abolishing the Slave Trade (Barbauld) **185**:65-66, 86, 90, 95, 117, 120-21, 127, 138, 142, 149
"The Epistles" (Eminescu)
See "Scrisorile"
"Epistles" (Keats) **8**:359-60
Epistles (Eminescu) **131**:297
Epistles (Very) **9**:393-96
"Epistles V" (Eminescu) **33**:245, 247, 249
Epistles, Odes, and Other Poems (Moore) **6**:377, 387, 390, 395; **110**:177-78
Epistles of the Fudge Family (Moore) **6**:382
"Epistola a Emilia" (Heredia)
See "A Emilia"
Epistolario Rizalino (Rizal) **27**:417
"Epi-Strauss-Ium" (Clough) **27**:89, 100
"Epitafija" (Radishchev) **190**:329, 331
"Epitalamio" (Lizardi) **30**:68
"Epitaph" (Coleridge) **197**:215
"Epitaph" (Cowper)
See "Epitaph on a Hare"
"Epitaph (On a commonplace person who died in bed)" (Levy) **59**:105, 110
"Epitaph on a Goldfinch" (Barbauld) **185**:133
"Epitaph on a Hare" (Cowper) **94**:32-4, 36
"Epitaph on a Rich Man" (Lampman) **194**:10, 21, 61
"Epitaph on an Infant" (Coleridge) **197**:215
"Epitaph on Brooks" (Sheridan) **91**:233
Epitaph on Henry Martyn (Macaulay) **42**:116
"Epitaph on King John" (Southey) **97**:318
"Épitaphe" (Nerval) **67**:306-07
"Epitaphe pour Tristan Joachim-Edouard Corbière, Philosophe" (Corbière) **43**:11, 17-18, 22, 25-7, 31, 34
"Epithalamion" (Hopkins) **17**:255
"Epithalamium" (Trumbull) **30**:349, 366
"L'Epître au malheur" (Staël-Holstein) **91**:335, 358
"Die Epochen der Dichkunst" (Schlegel) **45**:306, 308, 320, 324, 360, 370
"Epochs" (Lazarus) **8**:413, 418-20; **109**:292, 297-98
"Epochs of Poetry" (Schlegel)
See "Die Epochen der Dichkunst"
"Eponge définitivenent pourrie" (Laforgue) **221**:90
"L'Époux Corrigé" (Sade) **47**:313
"L'Époux infernal" (Rimbaud) **82**:222, 241-42, 245
"Eppich" (Meyer) **81**:200
The Epping Hunt (Hood) **16**:224, 233-35
"Epsom Races" (Reynolds) **146**:177
"Equality" (Arnold) **6**:45, 46; **89**:101, 104; **126**:37, 81
Equality (Bellamy) **4**:25-27, 29-31, 33; **86**:3-4, 12, 22-23, 28, 30, 32, 55, 62, 64-6, 68; **147**:11, 20-21, 24, 26-29, 33, 41, 78-79, 81, 84, 87-89, 93, 96, 116, 118-20
"Equilibrium" (Eminescu) **33**:272
"Equilibrium between the Aesthetic and Ethical" (Kierkegaard) **125**:282
Gli equivoci (Da Ponte) **50**:80
"Det er ganske vist!" (Andersen) **7**:35; **79**:31
Er ist's (Mörike) **201**:268
"Er schuf sie ein Männlein und Fräulein" (Claudius) **75**:192
"Era" (Gaskell) **137**:61-62
"Era apacible el dia" (Castro) **78**:17, 20-22
"Erbauliche Betrachtung" (Mörike) **10**:447
Erbauliche Betrachung (Mörike) **201**:305
Die Erbförster (Ludwig) **4**:347-52, 354, 364-66
"Erbvetter Joggeli" (Gotthelf) **117**:25
"Das Erdbeben in Chili" (Kleist) **2**:445, 452, 456-57; **37**:237, 239, 242-3, 245-9, 253-5; **222**:194, 202-3, 206, 208, 234, 255, 257, 285, 294-96, 299-301
"Das Erdbeeri Mareili" (Gotthelf) **117**:6, 32-3, 43, 51-5, 57-8
Eremit auf Formentera (Kotzebue) **25**:141
The Erie Train Boy (Alger) **8**:30, 44
"Erin, Oh Erin" (Moore) **110**:182
"Erin, the Tear and the Smile in Thine Eye" (Moore) **6**:390
"Erinna" (Landon) **15**:156-57, 166, 168
"Erinna an Sappho" (Mörike) **10**:457, 459; **201**:264
"Erinna to Sappho" (Mörike)
See "Erinna an Sappho"
Der Erinnerer (Lavater) **142**:13
"Die Erinnerung" (Klopstock) **11**:237
"Erinnerung an Horace Benedikt von Saussure. Aus Odoardo's Papieren" (Arnim) **159**:74
Erinnerungen an die letzten Kieler Semester (Storm) **195**:32
Erinnerungen ... an Ferdinand Röse (Storm) **195**:32
Erinnerungen aus meinem Leben (Freytag) **109**:177
Erinnerungen meiner dritten Schweizerreise (La Roche) **121**:242, 251
Erinnerungern aus Rubens (Burckhardt) **49**:14
"Erin's Warning" (Crawford) **127**:217
Erkenne dich selb (Wagner) **9**:475; **119**:291
Erkennen und Empfinden (Herder)
See *Vom Erkennen und Empfinden der meschlichen Seele*
Erklärung (Heine) **4**:248
Die Erlebnisse eines Schuldenbauers (Gotthelf) **117**:6-7, 15, 17-18, 22-3, 25, 32, 38
Erlebtes (Eichendorff) **8**:220-21
"Erl-King" (Goethe)
See *Erlkönig*
Erlkönig (Goethe) **4**:192
"Erlösung" (Muller) **73**:366
"L'Ermite" (Maupassant) **83**:228
"Ermolai and the Miller's Wife" (Turgenev)
See "Ermolaj i mel'ničicha"
"Ermolaj and the Miller's Wife" (Turgenev)
See "Ermolaj i mel'ničicha"
"Ermolaj i mel'ničicha" (Turgenev) **122**:264, 293-94
"Ermunterung" (Hölderlin) **16**:187-9
Ernest Maltravers (Bulwer-Lytton) **1**:138, 140, 148-49, 155; **45**:21, 23, 28-9, 68
Ernestus Berchtold; or, The Modern Oedipus (Polidori) **51**:193-94, 201-02, 206-07, 231-34, 237-39, 241-42
Ernst und Kurzweil, von meinem Vetter an mich (Claudius) **75**:197
"Ernteabend" (Meyer) **81**:152-53, 155-56
"Erntegewitter" (Meyer) **81**:141, 153-57, 206
"Erntelied" (Brentano) **1**:105
"Erntelied" (Meyer) **81**:152-54
"Erntenacht" (Meyer) **81**:152-54, 156
"Der Erntewagen" (Meyer) **81**:140-41, 144, 150-52, 154-55
"Der Eroberer" (Schiller) **39**:338, 355, 386-88; **166**:99-100
Eroica Symphony (Beethoven)
See *Third Symphony*
"Eros and Psyche" (Patmore) **9**:338-39, 365
Errata; or, the Works of Will. Adams (Neal) **161**:290, 299, 318, 348
Les Errinyes (Leconte de Lisle) **29**:222, 225
"The Errors and Abuses of English Criticism" (Lewes) **25**:285, 304
The Errors of Ecstasie (Darley) **2**:124-25, 127, 129, 133-34
Erscheinungen am See Oneida (La Roche) **121**:291, 326
"Erstarrung" (Muller) **73**:385, 394
"Die erste nacht" (Meyer) **201**:155
"Den ersten Tropfen dieser Leidensflut" (Brentano) **191**:38
"Erster Schmerz, letzter Scherz" (Muller) **73**:364, 373
"Erstes Liebeslied eines Mädchens" (Mörike) **10**:448, 455; **201**:303

"Erwin and Linda" (Barnes) **75**:76
Erwin und Elmire (Goethe) **4**:164
Erzählprosa (Gotthelf) **117**:43
Erzählungen (Kleist) **222**:235, 237
Erzählungen (Wieland)
See *Comische Erzählungen*
"Die Erzdes Heckebeutels" (Arnim)
See "Der Heckebeutel"
Es en el siglo XXIV (Silva) **114**:263
"Es ist eine alte Geschichte" (Heine) **4**:249
"Es sang vor langen Jahren" (Brentano)
See "Der Spinnerin Lied"
Esboços Juridicos (Alencar) **157**:5
El escándalo (Alarcon) **1**:12-13, 16-17; **219**:3-4, 11-14, 19-20, 47
The Escape; or, A Leap for Freedom (Brown) **2**:48-52; **89**:143, 153, 163, 182, 187
The Escapes (Holcroft) **85**:199
Escenas norteamericanas (Martí) **63**:74, 81-2, 88, 167
"La esclava ausente" (Manzano) **155**:307-10
Les esclaves de Paris (Gaboriau) **14**:15
"Les esclaves gaulois" (Beranger) **34**:29
"El esclavo Pedro" (Isaacs) **70**:304
Escorial (Symonds) **34**:335
Os escravos (Castro Alves) **205**:5-6, 8, 10, 24-25, 31, 35, 38
"Escuela normal de mujeres" (Sarmiento) **123**:360
Las escuelas, base de la prosperidad y de la república en los Estados Unidas (Sarmiento) **123**:275
"Eshche listok" (Bestuzhev) **131**:165, 171
"La Esmeralda" (Hugo) **3**:261
La Esmeralda; or, The Hunchback of Notre-Dame (Hugo)
See *Notre-Dame de Paris*
"Les Espagnols en Danemark" (Mérimée) **6**:354, 362; **65**:44, 46, 51, 60, 62, 79, 82, 86
España (Gautier) **59**:5, 18
"España libre" (Heredia) **209**:136
El español en Venecia (Martínez de la Rosa) **102**:230
Espatolino (Gómez de Avellaneda) **111**:21, 23
"L'Espérance" (Laforgue) **221**:87
La esperanza de la patria (Tamayo y Baus) **1**:571
El espetón de oro (Villaverde) **121**:333, 361
Espíritu del siglo (Martínez de la Rosa) **102**:228, 248-49, 253
"L'espoir en dieu" (Musset) **150**:309, 315, 318
"L'espoir luit comme un brin de paille . . ." (Verlaine) **230**:209
The Espousals (Patmore)
See *The Angel in the House, Book II: The Espousals*
L'Esprit des religions (Constant)
See *De la religion considérée dans sa source, ses formes, et ses développements*
"L'Esprit pur" (Vigny) **7**:472, 478, 483, 485-86
"L'esprit saint" (Lamartine) **11**:270, 279
Espumas flutuantes (Castro Alves) **205**:4-5, 31
"Esquivez" (Casal) **131**:239
"Essa on the Muel, bi Josh Billings" (Shaw) **15**:339, 341
Essai historique, politique, et moral sur les révolutions anciennes et modernet considérées dans leurs rapports avec la révolution Française (Chateaubriand) **3**:114
Essai politique sur le royaume de la Nouvelle-Espagne (Humboldt) **170**:158-59, 166, 168
Essai politique sur l'île de Cuba (Humboldt) **170**:153, 166, 168-71
Essai psychologique sur Jésus Christ (Renan) **145**:354
Essai sur la Guerre Sociale (Mérimée) **65**:85
Essai sur la littérature Anglaise et considérations sur le génie des hommes, des temps et, des révolutions (Chateaubriand) **3**:119-20, 128, 132; **134**:12-13, 15-17, 19, 43
"Essai sur le drame fantastique: Goethe, Byron, Mickciewicz" (Sand) **42**:314, 369
Essai sur le principe générateur des constitutions politiques et des autres institutions humaines (Maistre) **37**:292, 295, 297, 299, 303-04, 306, 311, 314
Essai sur les fables de La Fontaine (Taine) **15**:410, 430, 463, 468, 472
Essai sur les fictions (Staël-Holstein) **3**:523-4, 532; **91**:299-301, 303-4, 311, 332, 339-40
Essai sur les forces humaines (Balzac) **5**:28
Essai sur les révolutions anciennes et modernes (Chateaubriand) **3**:112; **134**:3, 17, 19, 27, 30, 83, 102-5, 107
Essai sur l'inégalité des races humaines (Gobineau) **17**:60, 62-3, 70-4, 76-7, 79-81, 83-4, 86, 88, 90-2, 94-5, 97-104
Essai sur Tite-Live (Taine) **15**:412, 430-31
Essais de critique et d'histoire (Taine) **15**:410, 438, 468, 473
Essais de morale et de critique (Renan) **26**:364, 379, 414-15, 417; **145**:317, 357
Essay (Staël-Holstein)
See *Essai sur les fictions*
An Essay in Aid of a Grammar of Assent (Newman) **38**:272, 288, 305, 307, 311-12, 314, 317, 321, 324; **99**:217, 237-45, 254, 297-98, 300-01
An Essay in Political and Social Criticism (Arnold) **126**:75
Essay in Refutation of Atheism (Brownson) **50**:53
Essay of 1844 (Darwin) **57**:159
Essay on Aesthetic Poetry (Pater) **90**:326
"Essay on American Literature" (Fuller) **5**:159
"An Essay on an Old Subject" (Smith) **59**:308, 315, 317, 322
Essay on Anglo-Saxon (Jefferson) **11**:199; **103**:106
"An Essay on Anglo-Saxon and Modern Dialects of the English Language" (Jefferson) **103**:106
Essay on Being (Herder) **186**:2, 5, 7
"Essay on Blake" (Robinson) **15**:183
"Essay on Chivalry" (Scott) **69**:329, 341; **209**:248
"Essay on Christianity" (Shelley) **18**:354, 375, 377; **93**:352; **175**:241, 274, 326, 329
"Essay on Commercial Policy" (Galt) **110**:92
"Essay on Critics" (Fuller) **50**:226-7
Essay on Development (Newman)
See *An Essay on the Development of Christian Doctrine*
Essay on Dramatic Compostion (Holcroft) **85**:218
"Essay on Elegiac Poetry" (Dyer) **129**:94
"Essay on English Poetry" (Campbell) **19**:171-73, 175, 184, 191
"Essay on Epitaphs" (Wordsworth) **12**:472; **38**:400; **206**:312
Essay on Faith (Coleridge) **231**:36
Essay on Fiction (Staël-Holstein)
See *Essai sur les fictions*
"An Essay on Human Automatism" (Thelwall) **162**:344
Essay on Human Forces (Balzac)
See *Essai sur les forces humaines*
"Essay on Interpretation" (Arnold) **18**:24
Essay on Irish Bulls (Edgeworth) **1**:267; **51**:97-99; **158**:61-62, 64-65, 67-68, 81, 86-87, 89-93
"An Essay on Irish Swearing" (Carleton) **199**:31-32
"Essay on Landscape" (Clare) **9**:110; **86**:96-7
"Essay on Language" (Bentham) **38**:92
"Essay on Legislation" (Radishchev) **190**:290
"Essay on Life" (Shelley) **93**:338; **175**:258, 260
"Essay on Logic" (Bentham) **38**:56, 92, 94-5, 99
Essay on Logic (Mill)
See *A System of Logic, Ratiocinative and Inductive; Being a Connected View of the Principles of Evidence, and the Methods of Scientific Investigation*
Essay on Love (Stendhal)
See *De l'amour*
"Essay on Machiavelli" (Macaulay) **231**:292
"Essay on Marriage" (Shelley) **143**:244
"Essay on Martial Enthusiasm" (Thelwall) **162**:343
"Essay on Method" (Coleridge) **9**:208
"Essay on Mind" (Barrett Browning) **16**:141; **66**:44
An Essay on Mind, with other Poems (Barrett Browning) **61**:4, 41, 48-50, 61; **170**:25, 67
An Essay on Percy Bysshe Shelley (Browning) **19**:132-33, 155; **79**:107, 111, 167-68, 186
Essay on Political Tactics (Bentham) **38**:91
Essay on Ranke (Macaulay) **42**:80, 96
Essay on Revolutions (Chateaubriand)
See *Essai sur les révolutions anciennes et modernes*
"Essay on Romance" (Scott) **69**:340; **209**:271
"Essay on Self-Justification" (Edgeworth) **1**:262
Essay on Sepulchres; or, A Proposal for Erecting Some Memorial of the Illustrious Dead in All Ages on the Spot Where Their Remains Have Been Interred (Godwin) **14**:40, 53
An Essay on Slavery and Abolitionism with Reference to the Duty of American Females (Beecher) **30**:23-4
"Essay on Tasso and Chatterton" (Browning) **19**:140; **79**:186
"An Essay on the Ancient English Minstrels" (Percy) **95**:323, 327, 329-30, 332, 345, 364-65
An Essay on the Development of Christian Doctrine (Newman) **38**:263, 283, 307, 311, 322, 326; **99**:217, 244
Essay on the Development of Doctrine (Newman)
See *An Essay on the Development of Christian Doctrine*
"Essay on the Different Styles of Goethe's Early and Late Works" (Schlegel)
See "Versuch über den verschiedenen Styl in Goethe's früheren und späteren Werken"
An Essay on the Education of Female Teachers (Beecher) **30**:15
Essay on the Fables of La Fontaine (Taine)
See *Essai sur les fables de La Fontaine*
Essay on the Genius and Writing of Shakespeare (Montagu)
See *An Essay on the Writings and Genius of Shakespeare, Compared with the Greek and French Dramatic Poets: with Some Remarks upon the Misrepresentations of M. de Voltaire*
An Essay on the Genius and Writings of Pope, Vol. 1 (Warton)
See *Essay on the Writings and Genius of Pope*
Essay on the History of Lyric Poetry (Herder)
See *Versuch einer Geschichte der lyrischen Dichtkunst*
Essay on the Inequality of the Human Races (Gobineau)
See *Essai sur l'inégalité des races humaines*
Essay on the Life and Character of William III (Macaulay) **42**:144
"An Essay on the Life and Genius of Henry Fielding" (Murphy) **229**:247, 249
An Essay on the Manners and Genius of the Literary Character (D'Israeli) **217**:278, 280, 283-84, 292, 297, 320, 332, 336, 338

An Essay on the Nature and Immutability of Truth (Beattie) **25**:80-7, 94, 96, 101, 103-05, 112-13, 120-23
"Essay on the nature and moral effect of the work" (Constant)
See *Adolphe: Anecdote trouvée dans les papiers d'un inconnu et publiée par M. B. de Constant*
An Essay on the Principle of Population (Malthus) **145**:184, 193, 197-99, 201-2, 204-5, 207-12, 214-18, 220-23, 226-31, 234, 236, 238, 246-48, 253, 256, 259, 261-63, 265-67
An Essay on the Principles of Human Action (Hazlitt) **29**:133, 159-60, 162, 168-69, 171-72, 183, 185-86; **82**:74, 121, 131-32, 137
"Essay on the Social Progress of States" (Arnold) **18**:53
Essay on the Source of Positive Pleasure (Polidori) **51**:201, 207
"An Essay on the Uses and Advantages of the Fine Arts" (Trumbull) **30**:359
Essay on the Writings and Genius of Pope (Warton) **118**:301, 350, 352-53, 356, 358, 361, 364, 304, 307-14, 322, 324-27, 329, 334-37, 341, 343, 345-48
An Essay on the Writings and Genius of Shakespeare, Compared with the Greek and French Dramatic Poets: with Some Remarks upon the Misrepresentations of M. de Voltaire (Montagu) **7**:250-51; **117**:135, 139-40, 149, 152, 158, 160, 179, 184-87
"Essay on Tragic Influences" (Horne) **127**:258
Essay on Truth (Beattie)
See *An Essay on the Nature and Immutability of Truth*
"Essay on Woman" (Barrett Browning) **61**:40-1
"Essay, Supplementary to the Preface" (Wordsworth) **111**:238-39, 309, 315, 366; **166**:196, 335, 351
Essay Towards a Critique of All Revelation (Fichte)
See *Versuch einer Kritik aller Offenbarung*
"An Essay Towards the Definition of Animal Vitality" (Thelwall) **162**:339
"Essayists Old and New" (Smith) **59**:323
Essays (Coleridge)
See *Essays and Marginalia*
Essays (Eliot) **89**:260; **118**:56, 187, 189, 194
Essays (Emerson) **1**:276, 286, 290, 292; **38**:170, 173, 194, 199, 204 223-24; **98**:4-5, 96, 122, 153, 171
Essays (Huxley) **67**:81-8, 92
Essays (Irving)
See *Salmagundian Essays*
Essays (Smolenskin) **30**:196-98
Essays (Southey) **97**:250-51
Essays (Wordsworth) **12**:436
Essays Addressed to Volunteers (Engels) **85**:83
"Essays and Leaves from a Note-Book" (Eliot) **118**:187
Essays and Lectures (Emerson) **98**:149-55, 163, 176, 181, 186
Essays and Letters on Theory (Hölderlin) **187**:268-72, 274
Essays and Marginalia (Coleridge) **90**:9-10
Essays and Phantasies (Thomson) **18**:393, 395, 415
Essays and Poems (Very) **9**:370, 373, 381
Essays and Reviews (Poe) **94**:269-71, 274, 276
Essays and Reviews (Southey) **8**:461
The Essays and Reviews of Archibald Lampman (Lampman) **194**:115, 127, 132, 134
Essays and Sketches (Newman) **99**:301
Essays Critical and Historical (Newman) **99**:222, 224, 253
Essays Critical and Imaginative (Wilson) **5**:559-60, 562-63
Essays: First Series (Emerson)
See *Essays*
"Essays from "The Guardians"" (Pater) **90**:333, 337
Essays in Criticism (Arnold) **6**:33, 36, 46-48, 53, 56-57, 69, 72; **29**:10, 55-6, 58-60; **89**:30, 36, 112; **126**:3, 6, 19, 22, 42-43, 78-79, 82-83; **218**:111, 165-66, 172, 174, 184, 205, 212, 216, 218
Essays in Modernity: Criticisms and Dialogues (Adams) **33**:9
Essays Moral and Political (Southey) **97**:286
Essays Never Before Published (Godwin) **14**:55
Essays of George Eliot (Eliot) **199**:131, 159, 224, 246
Essays on Bacon (Macaulay) **42**:80, 121-22
Essays on Chivalry (Scott) **69**:338
Essays on His Own Times; Forming a Second Series of The Friend (Coleridge) **177**:116; **231**:57, 60, 154-55, 160-62
Essays on Petrarch (Foscolo) **8**:263, 271
Essays: On Poetry and Music, as They Affect the Mind; On Laughter, and Ludicrous Composition; On the Utility of Classical Learning (Beattie) **25**:97, 114-15, 117-19, 122
Essays on Prints (Gilpin) **30**:36
Essays on Religious History (Renan)
See *Etudes d'histoire religieuse*
Essays on Scandinavian Literature (Boyesen) **135**:8, 22
Essays on Sex Equality (Mill) **179**:324
Essays on Some Controverted Questions (Huxley) **67**:21, 23
"Essays on the Art of Thinking" (Martineau) **26**:309; **137**:350-51
"Essay on the Concept of Republicanism" (Schlegel)
See "Versuch über den Begriff des Republikanismus"
"Essays on the English Stage" (Percy) **95**:323-24
Essays on Various Subjects, Principally Designed for Young Ladies (More) **27**:337; **141**:209-12, 258-59, 271
Essays: Second Series (Emerson) **1**:276, 286, 290, 292; **38**:169, 171; **98**:161
Essays, Speculative and Suggestive (Symonds) **34**:323, 326, 331-32, 336
"Essays, Tales, and Poems" (Freneau) **111**:132
"Essays, upon Epitaphs" (Wordsworth) **111**:238; **166**:221, 227, 267, 306, 308, 310-11, 317, 319
"Essays—Biographical and Literary" (Prescott) **163**:345
The Essence of Christianity (Eliot) **183**:73
The Essence of Christianity (Feuerbach)
See *Das Wesen des Christentums*
Essence of Criticism (Schlegel) **45**:366
The Essence of Religion (Feuerbach)
See *Das Wesen der Religion*
The Essential Margaret Fuller (Fuller) **211**:212-13
Esskünstler am Hoteltisch (Börne) **193**:4
"Essor empirique du républicanisme français" (Comte) **54**:205
"Est, Est" (Muller) **73**:353
"Est! liubimtsy vdokhnovenii" (Pavlova) **138**:14, 20, 50
"Establishment of These United States: An American Account" (Brackenridge) **227**:116
"La estacíon de los nortes" (Heredia) **209**:118, 129
"Les Estampes" (Verlaine) **230**:174
Estatutos secretos (Martí) **63**:128-9
"Este vaise i aquel vaise" (Williams) **78**:40
Ésteticheskie otnosheniia iskusstva k deistvitel'nosti (Chernyshevsky) **1**:158, 161-62
Esther (Grillparzer) **102**:172
"Esthétique" (Laforgue) **221**:89, 91
L'esthétique de la laideur suivi de Diderot à Pétersbourg (Sacher-Masoch) **31**:288
An Estimate of the Religion of the Fashionable World (More) **27**:333, 338; **141**:269, 306
Estimates of Some Englishmen and Scotchmen (Bagehot) **10**:66
"La estrella de Cuba" (Heredia) **209**:124-25, 136, 153
"La estrella de Venus" (Heredia) **209**:119, 135
"Estrellas que entre lo sombrío" (Silva) **114**:296
"Estrofas libres" (Isaacs) **70**:313
"Estrofes do Solitário" (Castro Alves) **205**:12-13, 37
El estudiante de Salamanca (Espronceda) **39**:85-8, 90, 94, 97-9, 101, 108-10
"Estudio sobre Virgilio, por P. F. Tissot" (Bello) **131**:112
"Et ego in Arcadia" (Hoffmann) **2**:356
"Et godt Humeur" (Andersen) **79**:76
"Et la tigresse epouvantable d'Hyrcanie" (Verlaine) **51**:351
Et la-ta'at (Smolenskin) **30**:187, 192-93
Et Nox Facta est (Hugo) **189**:193-94
Étalages (Mallarmé) **210**:210, 212, 214-15, 248, 251, 254, 265
"L'Etat des Esprits en 1849" (Renan) **26**:377
"Etats" (Laforgue) **221**:81, 90
Die Etats Generaux (Klopstock) **225**:298
"Été" (Verlaine) **230**:153-54, 156-59
Un été dans le Sahara (Fromentin) **10**:224-27, 232, 240, 252, 259; **125**:103, 105-7, 110-12, 114-16, 132, 138, 146
"The Eternal Goodness" (Whittier) **8**:517, 524; **59**:361, 365
The Eternal Husband (Dostoevsky)
See *Vechny muzh*
"The Eternal Jew" (Arany)
See "Az örök zsidó"
"Eternal Love" (Bryant) **46**:15
"Eternal Love" (Isaacs)
See "Amor eterno"
The Eternal People (Smolenskin)
See *Am olam*
"L'eternité" (Rimbaud) **4**:456; **35**:321; **82**:230-31, 233, 247, 249-50; **227**:214, 251, 254, 268, 312-13
"Eternity in Time" (Lanier) **118**:224
"The Eternity of Nature" (Clare) **9**:80; **86**:90, 113
"Eth Laasoth" (Smolenskin) **30**:189
"Ethan Brand" (Hawthorne) **2**:318, 322, 327; **95**:110, 116, 137; **158**:228, 243, 247, 256, 337; **171**:243
Ethel Churchill; or, The Two Brides (Landon) **15**:159, 161
Ethelinde; or, The Recluse of the Lake (Smith) **23**:319, 322-24, 327-29, 333; **115**:149
"Etheline" (Kendall) **12**:193
Ethelstan; or, The Battle of Brunanburh (Darley) **2**:125, 128, 130-31, 134
"Ethnogenesis" (Timrod) **25**:360, 363, 367, 372, 374-77, 383-84, 387-88
Ethwald (Baillie) **2**:31-34, 39, 43; **71**:4, 6, 12; **151**:5-9, 11, 15-19, 74-75, 115-17
"Eto bylo blestiashchee more" (Pavlova) **138**:4, 16
"L'étoile a pleuré rose" (Rimbaud) **4**:485
"Les étoiles" (Lamartine) **11**:245, 268, 270
Les Étoiles du monde (Dumas) **71**:247
"L'étranger" (Baudelaire) **155**:46, 78, 80
L'étrangère (Dumas) **9**:222, 224-25, 228, 230-32, 238, 242-43, 245, 249
"Les étrennes des orphelins" (Rimbaud) **4**:465, 484; **35**:282; **82**:226
L'Etruria vendicata (Alfieri) **101**:43
"The Etruscan Vase" (Mérimée)
See "Le vase étrusque"
"Étude de femme" (Balzac) **35**:27; **153**:54, 152
Étude sur la soveraineté (Maistre) **37**:302-04, 312
Etude sur le roman (Maupassant) **1**:467; **42**:163, 169, 179, 183, 188, 198-99, 203

Etuden (Schumann) **143**:120
Études analytiques (Balzac) **5**:28, 32; **153**:10
Etudes anglo-americaines (Mérimée) **65**:90
Études de moeurs au XIXe siècle (Balzac) **5**:28-29; **153**:10, 149, 151-52
Etudes d'histoire religieuse (Renan) **26**:364, 368, 370, 413, 415, 421; **145**:357, 363
Études et Essais (Renan) **145**:276-77
Etudes historiques (Chateaubriand) **3**:114; **134**:16, 19
"Etudes on Caprices of Paganini" (Schumann) **143**:73
Études philosophiques (Balzac) **5**:28-29, 32, 53; **53**:31; **153**:10, 21, 80, 149, 151
Etudes Symphoniques (Schumann) **143**:126
"Etwas über William Shakespeare bei Gelegenheit Wilhelm Meisters" (Schlegel) **15**:227; **142**:302-3, 316, 344
Euclid and His Modern Rivals (Dodgson) **2**:108, 111
"Eugene and Julia" (Karamzin) **3**:290
Eugene Aram (Bulwer-Lytton) **1**:135, 140, 145, 150, 155; **45**:7, 9, 11-13, 19, 24-7, 34, 68-70
Eugene Aram (Hood)
See *The Dream of Eugene Aram*
Eugene Onegin (Pushkin)
See *Yevgeny Onegin*
Eugenia (Keller) **2**:416
Eugénie de Franval (Sade) **3**:470, 492
Eugénie Grandet (Balzac) **5**:29, 32-4, 36, 46, 52, 57, 62-4, 66, 73-5; **35**:2, 6, 7, 13, 55, 60; **53**:1-36; **153**:22-24, 49-50, 52, 68, 71, 79-82, 127, 147, 151-52
"Eulalie—A Song " (Poe) **117**:233, 242-44, 280-82
"Eulogium" (Murray) **63**:179
"Eulogy" (Horton) **87**:95, 100
"Eulogy on Henry Clay Delivered in the State House at Springfield" (Lincoln) **201**:161
Eulogy on King Philip (Apess) **73**:3, 7, 10, 13-14, 16, 27-28
"Eulogy on the Death of Benjamin Ferguson" (Lincoln) **201**:159
Eulogy on Zachary Taylor (Lincoln) **201**:182
"Eulogy to the Memory of George Washington, Esquire" (Rowson) **5**:322
"The Eulogy to the Memory of My Grandfather" (Krylov) **1**:438
Euphemia (Lennox) **23**:229, 233-35, 253
"Euphemia, A Sketch" (Levy) **59**:98
Euphémie de Melun (Sade) **47**:361
"Euphorion" (Taylor) **89**:309-10
Euphranor: A Dialogue on Youth (FitzGerald) **9**:265, 270-71; **153**:222
"Euphrasia" (Shelley) **14**:271
"Euphuism" (Pater) **7**:343
"Eureka" (Larcom) **179**:178
Eureka: A Prose Poem (Poe) **1**:502, 510, 515, 517, 519-20, 522, 526; **16**:300, 330-31, 335; **55**:149, 151-5, 209; **78**:260; **94**:195-200, 212, 217-21, 248; **97**:180-81, 183, 206, 222; **117**:193, 199, 230, 234, 247, 262, 270, 275, 287-91, 304-5, 307-13, 319-24; **211**:226, 243, 246, 249-51, 261, 263, 265-67, 270, 338-42, 344
Euripides unter den Abderiten (Wieland) **177**:256, 260, 316
Ta euriskomena (Solomos) **15**:390
"Euroclydon" (Kendall) **12**:183
Europa (Novalis)
See *Die Christenheit oder Europa*
"Európa csendes, újra csendes" (Petofi) **21**:264, 286
"Europe" (Whitman) **31**:419, 425
Europe: A Prophecy (Blake) **173**:147, 152, 157; **190**:11, 14-15, 25, 33, 76, 92; **201**:15, 20, 29, 35, 61, 64, 76, 93, 114-18, 120, 123, 139
Europe: A Prophecy, 1794 (Blake) **13**:159, 174, 176, 183-85, 214, 216-17, 221-22, 224-25, 232, 251-52; **37**:33, 77, 80; **127**:11, 77, 79-82, 139
"Europe Is Still, Still Again" (Petofi)
See "Európa csendes, újra csendes"
"Europe: The 72nd and 73rd Years of These States" (Whitman) **205**:191-92
"The European Revolution" and Correspondence with Gobineau (Tocqueville) **7**:456-58; **63**:283
Europeiska missnöjets grunder (Almqvist) **42**:19
"Eurycome" (Solomos) **15**:389
"Eurydice" (Lowell) **90**:214
"Eurydice" (Patmore) **9**:343
The Eustace Diamonds (Trollope) **6**:503-04, 511-13; **101**:235, 256, 264, 275, 285, 306, 313, 324-25, 327; **215**:214, 247-48, 253-55, 268-73, 299, 308
Eutaw: A Sequel to The Forayers (Simms) **3**:507-08, 513
"Eutaw Springs" (Freneau) **111**:83, 179
"Euterpe" (Kendall) **12**:199
"Euthanasia" (Mickiewicz) **101**:160
Euthanasia: Drey Gespräche über das Leben nach dem Tode (Wieland) **177**:246
"Az év végén" (Petofi) **21**:286
"A Eva" (Espronceda) **39**:105
"Eva" (Rossetti) **186**:275
Evangele (Alcott) **167**:32
"The Evangelical Movement" (Gladstone) **213**:113
"Evangelical Teaching: Dr. Cumming" (Eliot) **118**:75
Evangeline: A Tale of Acadie (Longfellow) **2**:473-74, 476-78, 480, 483-84, 488, 490, 493, 495; **45**:102-03, 105-06, 109-10, 113, 119, 124, 128, 134, 137, 139, 142, 144-45, 147, 149-50, 157, 159, 163, 166, 179, 180, 187, 190; **101**:92, 149; **103**:270-316
L'évangéliste (Daudet) **1**:233-35, 243-44, 251
Les évangiles (Renan) **26**:402; **145**:350, 361
"Eve" (Rossetti) **66**:330
Eve Effingham; or, Home as Found (Cooper)
See *Home as Found*
L'eve future (Villiers de l'Isle Adam) **3**:581, 583-84, 588
"The Eve of Crecy" (Morris) **4**:423, 426
"The Eve of St. Agnes" (Keats) **8**:328, 333, 340, 347, 351, 355-56, 362, 372-73, 375, 380-81; **73**:142-43, 154-55, 159, 163-65, 170-72, 182, 186, 188-89, 199-200, 228, 233, 255, 259-60, 294-96, 299, 304, 307, 328; **121**:105-6, 110-11, 138, 144, 162, 165
The Eve of St. Agnes (Keats) **225**:112, 139, 174, 177, 263-64, 266-70
"The Eve of St. John" (Scott) **15**:317
"Eve of St. Mark" (Keats)
See "The Eve of St. Mark"
"The Eve of St. Mark" (Keats) **8**:340, 347, 357, 375; **73**:154, 298-99, 307; **121**:162; **225**:174, 263, 265
The Eve of the Fourth (Frederic) **10**:188
The Eve of toldi (Arany)
See *Toldi estéje*
"Evek, ti még jövendőévek" (Arany) **34**:19
"Eveleen's Bower" (Moore) **110**:185
Evelina; or, A Young Lady's Entrance into the World (Burney) **12**:15-17, 19, 21-2, 24-34, 37, 39-40, 42-6, 49-52, 56-7, 60-3; **54**:3, 8, 14-19, 21-4, 26-31, 33-8, 41-52, 61; **107**:1-115
"Evelyn" (Austen) **119**:13
Evelyn (Mowatt) **74**:211, 228
"Evelyn Hope" (Browning) **19**:129
Even a Cat Has Lean Times (Ostrovsky)
See *Ne vse kotu maslenitsa*
"Even beyond Music" (Lampman) **25**:216
Even the Wise Stumble (Ostrovsky)
See *Na vsyakogo mudretsa dovolno prostoty*
"Even when you don't get hard" (Verlaine) **230**:176
"Evenen in the Village" (Barnes) **75**:83, 88-9, 95
"Evenen Twilight" (Barnes) **75**:95
"An Evening" (Allingham) **25**:18
"Evening" (Bowles) **103**:88-9, 92, 95
"Evening" (Chivers) **49**:72
"Evening" (Clare) **9**:111
"Evening" (Grillparzer)
See "Der Abend"
"Evening" (Keble) **87**:169-70, 175, 200
"Evening" (Lampman) **25**:173, 210; **194**:99, 138
"Evening" (Tyutchev) **34**:389
"Evening" (Zhukovsky) **35**:386, 393, 402-05
Evening (Grundtvig)
See *Aftenen*
An Evening: An Epistle in Verse (Wordsworth) **12**:385, 386, 445
"An Evening at a Caucasian Spa in 1824" (Bestuzhev)
See "Vecher na kavkazskikh vodakh v 1824 godu"
"The Evening at Bezděz" (Macha) **46**:205, 208
"An Evening at Home" (Smith) **59**:320, 333, 335-6
"Evening, by a Tailor" (Holmes) **14**:100
"Evening Discourse" (Mickiewicz) **3**:399-400
"Evening Hymn" (Moodie) **113**:317
"Evening Hymn in the Hovels" (Adams) **33**:12
An Evening in Sorrento (Turgenev)
See *Vecher v Sorrente*
"Evening in the Bush" (Kendall) **12**:185
"An Evening Lull" (Whitman) **31**:434
"The Evening of the Holiday" (Leopardi)
See "La sera del dí di festa"
"Evening on a Bivouac" (Bestuzhev)
See "Vecher na bivuake"
"Evening Orison" (Rimbaud)
See "Oraison du soir"
"Evening Prayer at a Girls' School" (Hemans) **71**:290
Evening Readings in History (Sigourney) **87**:321, 339
"An Evening Revery" (Bryant) **6**:168, 183; **46**:38
"Evening sail to Richmond" (Wordsworth)
See "Lines Written near Richmond"
"Evening Song" (Lanier) **6**:249, 254; **118**:238, 240
"The Evening Star" (Eminescu)
See "Luceafarul"
"The Evening Star" (Longfellow) **45**:116; **103**:295
"Evening Star" (Poe) **117**:260, 277
"The Evening Sun Was Sinking Down" (Brontë) **16**:86
An Evening Thought: Salvation by Christ with Penetential Cries (Hammon) **5**:261-65
"Evening Twilight" (Baudelaire)
See "Le crépuscule du soir"
Evening Voluntaries (Wordsworth) **166**:212
An Evening Walk (Wordsworth) **111**:261-64; **166**:230
An Evening Walk: An Epistle in Verse (Wordsworth)
See *An Evening Walk*
"An Evening with Spenser" (Thomson) **18**:402
"Evening—A Close View" (Allingham) **25**:5
"Evenings" (Gogol) **162**:62
Evenings at Home; or, The Juvenile Budget Opened (Barbauld) **185**:57, 128, 131
An Evening's Improvement: Shewing the Necessity of Beholding the Lamb of God (Hammon) **5**:265
"Evenings in Greece" (Moore) **110**:167
Evenings in New England (Child) **73**:123-27
Evenings in the Antilles (Desbordes-Valmore)
See *Veillées des Antilles*
Evenings on a Farm near Dikanka (Gogol)
See *Vechera ná khutore bliz Dikanki*
"The Event Was Directly Behind Him" (Dickinson) **21**:55

"Eventail" (Mallarmé)
See "Autre eventail de Mademoiselle Mallarmé"
"L'éventail de Madame Mallarmé" (Mallarmé) **210**:167, 220
"L'éventail de Méry Laurent" (Mallarmé) **210**:220
Éventails (Mallarmé) **210**:197, 241
The Events of 1848, Especially in Their Relation to Great Britain. A Letter to the Marquis of Lansdowne (Milnes) **61**:138, 145-46
Eventyr, fortalte for børn (Andersen) **7**:16, 18, 20; **79**:3, 7-8, 65, 76, 80; **214**:25, 64, 72, 74-78
"Et Eventyr i syv Historier" (Andersen)
See "Sneedronningen"
Eventyr og historier (Andersen) **7**:28; **79**:23, 25-26, 37, 80
"Ever Let the Fancy Roam" (Keats) **8**:360
"Evergreens" (Pinkney) **31**:276, 281
"The Everlasting Gospel" (Blake) **13**:181, 209, 211; **190**:42, 45; **201**:65
Every Evil Hath Its Good (Tamayo y Baus)
See *No hay mal que por bien no venga*
Every One Has His Fault (Inchbald) **62**:142, 144, 146-9, 184
Every One in His Own Place (Ostrovsky)
See *Ne v svoi sani ne sadis!*
Every Wise Man Can Be a Fool (Ostrovsky)
See *Na vsyakogo mudretsa dovolno prostoty*
"Everybody's Vacation Except Editors" (Parton) **86**:348
"Every-day Aspects of Life" (Pisarev)
See "Budničnye storony žizni"
"Everyone Gets His Name at a Blessed Hour""Gieralsoftdichieskij muman. (Zamiemki o rodovykh prozvaniyakh)" (Leskov) **174**:137, 140
"Everything in its Right Place" (Andersen)
See "Alt paa sin rette Plads"
"Everything in the right Place" (Andersen)
See "Alt paa sin rette Plads"
"Everywhere and Always" (Pavlova)
See "Vezde i vsegda"
Evgeni Onegin (Pushkin)
See *Yevgeny Onegin*
"Evgeniu. Zhizn' Zvanskaya" (Derzhavin) **215**:22, 31-32, 39
"The Evidences of Revealed Religion: Discourse before the University in Cambridge" (Channing) **17**:3
"Evil" (Rimbaud)
See "Le mal"
"The Evil" (Rimbaud)
See "Le mal"
"The Evil Being" (Dacre) **151**:148
The Evil Eye (Carleton) **3**:86; **199**:23, 97
The Evil Genius (Collins) **93**:66
"The Evil Guest" (Le Fanu) **9**:302, 314; **58**:272
"Evil Hour" (Grillparzer)
See "Böse Stunde"
"Evil Landscape" (Corbière)
See "Paysage mauvais"
"The Evil Margaret" (Mörike)
See "Die schlimme Gret"
"Evil May-Day" (Allingham) **25**:11, 30
Evil May-Day, Etc. (Allingham) **25**:18
The Evils of Slavery and the Cure of Slavery (Child) **73**:60, 77
"Eviradnus" (Hugo) **3**:264
"Evolution" (Boyesen) **135**:6, 9, 45-47
"Evolution" (Symonds)
See "Philosophy of Evolution"
"Evolution and Ethics" (Huxley) **67**:10, 29, 62, 64-6, 68-9, 90, 103, 105-08, 111
Evolution and Ethics (Huxley) **67**:44, 90-3, 101, 103-11
Evrei v Rossii (Leskov) **25**:265, 267-69; **174**:105
"Ewig jung ist nur die Sonne" (Meyer) **81**:140, 143-44, 146-48, 155
"Der ewige Jude" (Börne) **193**:22
"Ex Fumo Dare Lucem" (Gordon) **21**:160
Examen critique de l'histoire de la géographie du Nouveau Continent, et des progrès de l'astronomie nautique aux quinzième et seizième siècles (Humboldt) **170**:137
"Examen de conscience philosophique" (Renan) **26**:414, 417
Examen de la philosophie de Bacon (Maistre) **37**:286, 300, 313, 316
"L'Examen du minuit" (Baudelaire) **155**:44
An Examination into the Leading Principles of the Federal Constitution Proposed by the Late Convention Held at Philadelphia (Webster) **30**:408
An Examination of Sir William Hamilton's Philosophy and of the Principal Philosophical Questions Discussed in His Writings (Mill) **11**:358, 390; **58**:337; **179**:290-91, 312
Examination of the Philosophy of Bacon (Maistre)
See *Examen de la philosophie de Bacon*
The Examiner (Hunt) **70**:266
Examples of Questions Calculated to Excite and Exercise the Infant Mind (Hamilton) **153**:310-11
"An Excellent Scotch Parody" (Hunt) **70**:257
"Excelsior" (Longfellow) **2**:473, 493, 498; **45**:100, 102, 111-12, 115-16, 127, 135, 140, 148, 152, 155, 164, 165, 179; **103**:293, 305
"Excelsior" (Whitman) **205**:157, 162, 165
"Exceptional Spleens" (Laforgue)
See "Les Spleens exceptionnels"
"Excerpts from the Biography of Nashchokin" (Pushkin) **83**:273
"Excerpts from the Poem 'Mother'" (Nekrasov)
See "Otryvki iz poèmy 'Mat'"
L'excommunié (Balzac) **5**:58
Excursion (Wordsworth)
See *The Excursion, Being a Portion of "The Recluse"*
Excursión a Vueltabajo (Villaverde) **121**:334, 361-62, 365
The Excursion, Being a Portion of "The Recluse" (Wordsworth) **12**:397-99, 404, 411-12, 414, 416, 420-23, 425-26, 436, 438, 442-45, 447, 450, 458-60, 468, 472; **38**:362, 364, 367, 371, 373, 376-77, 379, 388, 395, 405, 412, 421; **111**:240, 243, 245; **166**:197-354; **206**:281, 287-88, 291-93, 312, 343
Excursion (Futile Enough) to Paris; Autumn 1851 (Carlyle) **70**:91
Excursion on Concord & Merrimack Rivers (Thoreau)
See *A Week on the Concord and Merrimack Rivers*
Excursions (Thoreau) **7**:356; **61**:339; **138**:160
Excursions in Italy (Cooper) **203**:72
"An Excursion in Tsarkoe Selo" (Derzhavin) **215**:12, 16-17
"Excuse macabre" (Laforgue) **53**:272; **221**:82
"Excuse mélancolique" (Laforgue) **221**:89
"The Execution" (Galt) **110**:86
The Execution (Barham) **77**:4
"The Execution Bell" (Bestuzhev)
See "Kolokol kazni"
"The Execution of Troppmann" (Turgenev) **21**:420
"The Executor" (Oliphant) **11**:454, 459; **61**:174
The Executor (Oliphant) **221**:256
"Exegi Monumentum" (Derzhavin) **215**:67
"The Exemplary Key" (Martí) **63**:166
The Exemplary Wife (Rowson)
See *Sarah; or, The Exemplary Wife*
Exercises (Schumann)
See *Etuden*
Exercises in History, Chronology, and Biography (Rowson) **69**:116
Exercises in History, Chronology, and Biography, in Question and Answer (Rowson) **182**:256, 261, 356
Exercises in Religious Knowledge, for the Instruction of Young Persons (Hamilton) **153**:277, 307
"Exhibition Gossip" (Thackeray) **213**:245
Exhibition of My System of Philosophy (Schelling)
See *Darstellung meines Systems der Philosophie*
"Exhilaration—Is Within" (Dickinson) **21**:53
"Exhortation" (Hölderlin)
See "Ermunterung"
"Exil" (Banville) **9**:29
"The Exile" (Dacre) **151**:214
"Exile" (Lewis) **11**:297-98
"The Exile" (Mackenzie) **41**:190
"The Exile" (Robinson) **142**:151
"An Exile from Paradise" (Lermontov) **5**:292
"The Exile of Erin" (Campbell) **19**:179, 181, 190, 194, 198
"The Exiles" (Whittier) **8**:510, 526-28; **59**:358
The Exiles (Banville)
See *Les exilés*
Les exilés (Banville) **9**:17, 19, 27, 30
"An Exile's Farewell" (Gordon) **21**:154, 173
"The Exile's Hymn" (Heredia)
See "Himno de desterrado"
The Exiles; or, Memoirs of the Count de Cronstadt (Reeve) **19**:408, 412
"The Exile's Secret" (Holmes) **14**:128
The Existence of God (Brownson) **50**:27
The Exodiad (Cumberland) **167**:123, 135, 140, 150, 193
"The Exodus (August 3, 1492)" (Lazarus) **109**:332, 335
"Exorcising the Devil" (Leskov)
See "Chertogon"
"Exorcism" (Taylor) **89**:309
"An Exotic" (Timrod) **25**:365-66, 372, 375
"The Expedition of Nadir Shah into Hindostan" (Tennyson) **202**:189
The Expedition of Orsua and the Crimes of Aguirre (Southey) **97**:283
"Experience" (Dacre) **151**:148
"Experience" (Emerson) **1**:301, 307; **38**:143, 169-71, 173-74, 207, 209, 226, 230; **98**:19-24, 27, 55, 59, 61, 63, 89-90, 93, 95-6, 100, 107, 110, 114, 136, 145-46, 153, 180-82, 189
Experience (Blake)
See *Songs of Innocence and of Experience: Shewing the Two Contrary States of the Human Soul*
Experience as a Minister (Parker) **186**:205
"The Experience of the Adolescent" (Hoffmann) **2**:356
Experience, or How to Give a Northern Man a Backbone (Brown) **89**:153-54, 1182
The Experiences of Five Christian Indians of the Pequod Tribe (Apess)
See *The Experiences of Five Christian Indians: Or the Indian's Looking Glass for the White Man*
The Experiences of Five Christian Indians: Or the Indian's Looking Glass for the White Man (Apess) **73**:5-7, 9-11, 15, 29-31
"The Experiences of the A.C." (Taylor) **89**:315
"The Experiments of an Adventurer" (Mérimée)
See "Les débuts d'un aventurier"
"L'Expiation" (Hugo) **3**:270; **10**:373, 375; **189**:249
"Explanation" (Verlaine) **51**:372
"Explanations" (Derzhavin) **215**:37
"Explanatory Notes" (Wright) **74**:348-49
"Explanatory Preface" (Peabody) **169**:165, 172, 200
Explication (Verlaine) **51**:362
"Explication de quelques Mal-entendus" (Schlegel) **142**:302

"Exploit of Ovechkin and Shcherbina in the Caucasus" (Bestuzhev)
See "Podvig Ovechkina i Shcherbiny za Kavkazom"
"The Exposition Ode" (Hayne) **94**:145
Exposition of the False Medium and Barriers excluding Men of Genius from the Public (Horne) **127**:236, 238-40, 251-52, 263, 270, 273
"Expostulation" (Cowper) **8**:106, 110, 112, 120; **94**:28, 30, 52, 58, 111-12, 124
The Expostulation (Murphy) **229**:234
"Expostulation" (Whittier) **8**:512
"Expostulation and Reply" (Wordsworth) **12**:387, 436; **111**:202, 209, 225, 255, 259, 281-83; **206**:312, 317-18
"Expression" (Clare) **9**:121
The Expression of the Emotions in Man and Animals (Darwin) **57**:142
Exspriella (Southey) **97**:289
"Extempore Effusion upon the Death of James Hogg" (Wordsworth) **111**:370
"The Extinguishers" (Moore) **110**:172
An Extract from the Life of Lorenzo Da Ponte (Da Ponte) **50**:97
"Extract of a Letter from Geneva" (Polidori) **51**:218-19
"Extract of a Letter Written by Mr. De Quincey to the American Editor of His Works" (De Quincey) **198**:6
"Extradited" (Crawford) **12**:169-70
"Extra-Hazardous" (Bellamy) **4**:30
El extranjero (Alarcón) **219**:5-6, 16
"An Extraordinary Adventure in the Shades" (Mangan) **27**:291
Extraordinary Tales (Poe) **1**:499
"Extravagantes hijos de mi fantasía" (Bécquer) **106**:118
Extravaganzas (Planché) **42**:273, 299
"Extreme Opinions" (Verlaine)
See "Les Extrêmes Opinions"
"Les Extrêmes Opinions" (Verlaine) **230**:171
"Exultation" (Ingelow) **39**:264
"Exultation is the going" (Dickinson) **77**:75; **171**:97
"The Eye and Ear" (Emerson) **38**:195, 197
"The Eye and the Ear" (Very) **9**:394
An Eye for an Eye (Trollope) **6**:470, 501; **101**:245-47, 251-52, 264, 276, 293-94, 296-97; **215**:253
"The Eye of the Blind" (Meyer)
See "Das Auge des Blinden"
"Eyes" (Ridge) **82**:185
"Eyes and Noses" (Collodi)
See *Occhi e Nasi*
"The Eyes of the Poor" (Baudelaire)
See "Les yeux des pauvres"
"Eyre's March" (Kingsley) **107**:208
"Ez az élet" (Arany) **34**:21
"Ezrivel terem" (Petofi) **21**:283
F. Chopin (Liszt)
See *Chopin*
F Minor String Quartet, op. 95 (Beethoven)
See *String Quartet in F Minor, op. 95*
"F. Smith" (Willis) **194**:282, 298-99
The Fabians (Freytag)
See *Die Fabier: Trauerspiel in fünf Acten*
Die Fabier: Trauerspiel in fünf Acten (Freytag) **109**:139
"A Fable" (Cowper) **94**:121
"Fable" (Emerson) **98**:179
Fable (Lowell)
See *A Fable for Critics: A Glance at a Few of Our Literary Progenies*
"Fable and Romance" (Beattie)
See *Dissertations Moral and Critical: On Memory and Imagination; On Dreaming; The Theory of Language; On Fable and Romance; On the Attachments of Kindred; Illustrations on Sublimity*
"A Fable for Critics" (Willis) **194**:306
A Fable for Critics: A Glance at a Few of Our Literary Progenies (Lowell) **2**:504-07, 510, 513, 516, 519-22; **90**:188, 190, 198, 202, 207, 215-16, 220-22, 225
"Fable of the Maddening Rain" (Coleridge) **231**:84
Fables (Saltykov)
See *Skazki*
Fables and Parables (Krasicki)
See *Bajki i przypowieści*
"Fables choises mises en prose" (Banville) **9**:32
Fables for the Holy Alliance (Moore) **6**:388, 395; **110**:172
"The face I carry with me-last" (Dickinson) **77**:147
The Face of the Deep (Rossetti)
See *The Face of the Deep: A Devotional Commentary on the Apocalypse*
The Face of the Deep: A Devotional Commentary on the Apocalypse (Rossetti) **2**:559, 570, 572; **50**:275, 277-79, 285-87, 321, 342-45; **66**:306-9, 376; **186**:237, 241-42, 255-56, 299-306, 310, 322, 335-37, 339-47
"Face to Face" (Hayne) **94**:149, 153, 167-68, 170
"Faces" (Whitman) **31**:372, 425; **205**:191-94, 301
"Faces in the Fire" (Dodgson) **139**:30
"Faces of the Dead" (Laforgue)
See "Les Têtes de morts"
Facing the World; or, The Haps and Mishaps of Harry Vane (Alger) **8**:40, 43
Facino Cane (Balzac) **35**:44; **153**:23, 80, 152
Fact and Fiction (Child) **6**:201; **73**:61
"Factitious Life" (Dana) **53**:158, 178
The Factory Controversy: A Warning against Meddling Legislation (Martineau) **137**:268
"The Factory Day" (Jones) **222**:158
"The Factory Town" (Jones) **222**:124-25, 127, 139, 154-55
"The Facts in the Case of M. Valdemar" (Poe) **16**:308-09, 314, 331; **117**:300; **211**:316
Facts of Consciousness (Fichte)
See *Tatsachen des Bewusstseins*
El Facundo (Sarmiento)
See *Civilización i barbarie: La vida de Juan Facundo Quiroga i aspecto fisico, costumbres, i ábitos de la República Arjentina*
Facundo (Sarmiento)
See *Civilización i barbarie: La vida de Juan Facundo Quiroga i aspecto fisico, costumbres, i ábitos de la República Arjentina*
Facundo: Civilización y barbarie (Sarmiento)
See *Civilización i barbarie: La vida de Juan Facundo Quiroga i aspecto fisico, costumbres, i ábitos de la República Arjentina*
"Faded" (Webster) **230**:251-52, 293
"The faded joy of heedless years" (Pushkin)
See "Bezumnykh let vgasshee vesel'e"
"Faded Leaves" (Arnold) **89**:14, 49; **218**:122
Fader och dotter: En skildring ur lifvet (Bremer) **11**:34
"Fail Me Not Thou" (Willis) **194**:305
"Failure" (Ingelow) **39**:267; **107**:119
"Faim" (Rimbaud) **82**:231, 247, 249
Faint Heart Never Won Fair Lady (Planché) **42**:292
"Faint yet Pursuing" (Patmore) **9**:358, 365
"Fainting by the Way" (Kendall) **12**:178, 199
"The Fair at Sorochyntsi" (Gogol)
See "Sorochinskaia iarmarka"
"The Fair at Sorotchintsy" (Gogol)
See "Sorochinskaia iarmarka"
"The Fair Azra" (Leskov)
See "Prekrasnaja Aza"
"Fair Charlotte" (Smith) **187**:333-34
The Fair Egbert (Tieck)
See *Der blonde Eckbert*
"Fair Elenor" (Blake) **18**:181
"The Fair Hills of Ireland" (Mangan) **27**:275, 283, 295
"Fair Ines" (Hood) **16**:218, 222, 231, 233
The Fair Maid of Perth (Scott)
See *St. Valentine's Day; or, The Fair Maid of Perth*
"The Fair Morning" (Very) **9**:384
The Fair of May Fair (Gore) **65**:20
The Fair One with the Golden Locks (Planché) **42**:273, 288, 294, 301, 303
Fair Play (Southworth) **26**:434, 446
"Fair Rohtraut" (Mörike)
See "Schön-Rohtraut"
The Fair Syrian (Bage) **182**:6-8, 12, 17, 20, 25, 27, 29, 38, 40, 43-45, 47-49, 59-60, 63
"Fairest, Sweetest, Dearest, A Song" (Opie) **65**:168
Fairfax; or, The Master of Greenway Court: A Chronicle of the Valley of the Shenandoah (Cooke) **5**:124, 126, 128, 132, 134-35
The Fair-Haired Eckbert (Tieck)
See *Der blonde Eckbert*
"The Fairies" (Allingham) **25**:6, 8, 18, 20, 22-3, 25, 30
The Fairies (Wagner)
See *Die Feen*
"Fairies' Chatter" (Webster) **230**:226
"The Fairies of Pesth" (Field) **3**:205
"The Fairy" (Baratynsky)
See "Feya"
"The Fairy" (Lamb) **125**:354
"Fairy" (Rimbaud) **4**:455; **35**:290; **227**:243-44, 247, 295, 298, 334
"A Fairy Companion" (Pavlova)
See "Sputnica feia"
"Fairy Dialogue" (Allingham) **25**:6
Fairy Fingers (Mowatt) **74**:215-16, 218-19
"The Fairy Fountain" (Lampman) **25**:205, 219; **194**:40, 62
"Fairy Hill, or The Poet's Wedding" (Allingham) **25**:30
"The Fairy Island" (Woolson) **82**:272
"Fairy Land" (Poe) **117**:264, 272, 281, 305-6, 316-18
"Fairy of the Lake" (Thelwall) **162**:302
"The Fairy Prince Who Arrived Too Late" (Rossetti) **186**:246, 290
Fairy Tale (Goethe)
See *Märchen*
"Fairy Tale" (Lampman) **194**:59, 61
"Fairy Tale as Almanac" (Hauff) **185**:335-37
The Fairy Tale of My Life (Andersen)
See *Mit Livs Eventyr*
"The Fairy Tale Queen" (Eminescu) **33**:247
"A fairy tale told in seven stories" (Andersen)
See "Sneedronningen"
Fairy Tales (Andersen)
See *Eventyr, fortalte for børn*
Fairy Tales (Pushkin)
See *Skazki*
Fairy Tales (Saltykov) **16**:358-59
Fairy Tales of Isabella Valancy Crawford (Crawford) **12**:172; **127**:181
"Fairy Tales of the Boatsman and the Nixies" (Mörike)
See "Schiffer- und Nixen-Märchen"
Fairy Tales Told for Children (Andersen)
See *Eventyr, fortalte for børn*
"The Fairy Thorn" (Ferguson) **33**:287, 303
"Fairy-Tale Dream" (Petofi)
See "Tündérálom"
"A Fairy-Tale for Children" (Lermontov)
See *Skazka dlya detey*
A Fairytale for Children (Lermontov)
See *Skazka dlya detey*
Le faiseur (Balzac) **5**:52, 74
"Faith" (Lamartine)
See "La foi"
"Faith" (Tennyson) **65**:267; **202**:291
Faith (Robertson) **35**:335

"Faith and Doubt" (Newman) **38**:310
"Faith and Experience" (Newman) **38**:304
"Faith and Knowledge" (Hegel)
See "Glauben und Wissen"
Faith and Love (Novalis)
See *Glauben und Liebe*
"Faith and Private Judgement" (Newman) **38**:310
"Faith and Reason Contrasted as Habits of Mind" (Newman) **38**:307; **99**:298
"Faith and Sight" (Newman) **38**:304
"Faith and Sight" (Very) **9**:385
"Faith and the World" (Newman) **38**:305
"Faith, Hope and Charity" (Crawford) **127**:202
"Faith without Sight" (Newman) **38**:305
Faithful for Ever (Patmore) **9**:332
The Faithful Friend (Cowper) **94**:123
"The Faithful Mountains Stand Guard" (Eichendorff) **8**:210
"A Faithful Servant of His Master" (Grillparzer)
See *Ein Treuer Diener Seines Herrn*
"Faithless Nellie Gray" (Hood) **16**:224, 228, 234
"Faithless Sally Brown" (Hood) **16**:224, 227-28, 234
"The Fakenham Ghost" (Bloomfield) **145**:129-30, 154
"The Falcon" (Patmore) **9**:326
The Falcon (Tennyson) **30**:265
"The Falcon of Ser Federigo" (Longfellow) **2**:492; **45**:145, 149
Falconberg (Boyesen) **135**:7-8, 12, 16, 20-21, 26-27, 51
Falconet (Disraeli) **2**:148; **39**:36, 43-4, 70-2
Falconry in the Valley of the Indus (Burton) **42**:36, 38
"Falkland" (Arnold) **89**:101
Falkland (Bulwer-Lytton) **1**:139, 148, 150; **45**:21, 23, 40, 68-71
Falkner (Shelley) **14**:260-61, 265, 267, 270, 274-75; **59**:155, 189-90, 192-3
"Fall" (Keats)
See *The Fall of Hyperion: A Dream*
The Fall (Keats)
See *The Fall of Hyperion: A Dream*
The Fall of an Angel (Lamartine)
See *La chute d'un ange*
"The Fall of d'Assas" (Hemans) **29**:204
"The Fall of Hebe. A Dithyrambic Ode" (Moore) **110**:178
The Fall of Hyperion: A Dream (Keats) **8**:347, 349, 353, 358-59, 361-62, 365-66, 368, 379, 381; **73**:153, 155, 162-63, 170-71, 198, 202, 207-209, 212-218, 264, 266-67, 294-95, 299, 301, 306, 328-29, 339; **121**:100-113, 116-22, 130-32, 140-49, 154, 160, 169-79, 192, 194-202, 205-6, 208-19, 226, 228-29, 231, 233; **225**:112, 116-17, 119, 162-63, 165-69, 172, 181-82, 217, 227, 230, 236, 239-40, 255
The Fall of Robespierre (Coleridge) **9**:159; **177**:114; **231**:58
The Fall of Robespierre (Southey) **97**:260, 293, 314-16
The Fall of the Angels (Polidori) **51**:201
Fall of the Free City-States of Greece (Humboldt) **134**:186
"The Fall of the House of Usher" (Eminescu) **131**:335
"The Fall of the House of Usher" (Poe) **1**:492-93, 496, 504-05, 513, 522-23; **16**:294-95, 300, 303-07, 309-10, 316-19, 321-22, 324, 326, 332, 334, 336; **55**:133, 148, 151, 153, 155, 169, 194, 198-9, 206; **78**:257, 266; **94**:215; **97**:177-246; **117**:193, 200, 235, 257, 277, 281, 299, 303, 320; **211**:246-48, 253, 262, 264, 283-87, 295, 312, 314-15, 317-19, 342-44
"The Fall of the Leaf" (Mitford) **4**:408
"The Fall of the Leaves" (Brontë) **217**:14, 17
"The Fall of the Pequod" (Sigourney) **87**:339
"The Fall of the Usher" (Chivers) **49**:74
"Fall Time" (Barnes) **75**:32
"The Fallen Elm" (Clare) **9**:86
The Fallen Leaves (Collins) **1**:180, 184; **93**:4
Fallen Pride (Southworth)
See *The Curse of Clifton: A Tale of Expiation and Redemption*
"Das fallende Laub" (Meyer) **81**:141, 145-46, 148-49, 155
"Falling Asleep" (Lampman) **25**:208; **194**:11
Falling in with Fortune (Alger) **83**:119
"Le falot" (Bertrand) **31**:48
Falsche Scham (Kotzebue) **25**:145, 155
"The False and True Idea of a Gentleman" (Parker) **186**:136-37
"False but Beautiful" (Ridge) **82**:182
"The False Collar" (Andersen) **7**:23
"The False Demetrius" (Mérimée) **6**:353
The False Friend (Robinson) **142**:153, 158-59, 184, 201-8, 241
"The False Knights Tragedy" (Clare) **86**:98
False Medium (Horne)
See *Exposition of the False Medium and Barriers excluding Men of Genius from the Public*
False Shame; or, The American Orphan in Germany (Dunlap) **2**:214
False Shame, or The White Hypocrite (Mackenzie) **41**:184, 207, 213-14, 216-17, 226
"A False Step" (Barrett Browning) **170**:121
"Fältmarskalken" (Runeberg) **41**:324
A falu bolondja (Arany) **34**:19
"A faluban utcahosszat" (Petofi) **21**:283
"Fame" (Moodie) **113**:315
Fame and Fortune; or, The Progress of Richard Hunter (Alger) **8**:30, 37; **83**:127, 130-31, 139, 140, 144
La familia de Alvareda: Novela original de costumbres populares (Caballero) **10**:72, 76, 81-84
"The Familiar" (Le Fanu) **9**:302, 317, 319-22; **58**:302
Familiar Anecdotes of Sir Walter Scott (Hogg) **4**:278; **109**:200, 204, 208, 258
Familiar Demon (Alencar)
See *Demonio Familiar*
"A Familiar Epistle" (Sheridan) **91**:231
"Familiar Epistle to a Friend" (Clare) **9**:74
"Familiar Epistle to a Little Boy" (Allingham) **25**:26
Familiar Epistles to Frederick E. Jones, Esq., on the Present State of the Irish Stage (Croker) **10**:88, 91
"A Familiar Letter" (Holmes) **14**:109
"A Familiar Letter to the Reader" (Taylor) **89**:312
The Familiar Letters of John Adams and His wife Abigail during the Revolution (Adams) **106**:4-5
"Familiar Poem to Milo, an Aged Friend, who Wished the Author Riches" (Yearsley) **174**:343
Familiar Portraits (Stevenson)
See *Familiar Studies of Men and Books*
"Familiar Scenes on the Mississippi" (Thorpe) **183**:358
Familiar Studies of Men and Books (Stevenson) **5**:390, 415, 425; **193**:203, 206, 221
Die Familie Schroffenstein (Kleist) **2**:438, 443, 445-46, 449-50, 454-57; **37**:217, 223, 225-26, 229, 236-37, 253, 255, 266-69, 272-74; **222**:206-7, 228-32, 234-35, 254, 266
Die Familien Zwiern, Knieriem und Liem (Nestroy) **42**:231, 251, 255-56
The Families of Plants (Darwin) **106**:226, 232, 274
Familjen H. (Bremer) **11**:17-19, 24, 30, 35
"Famille" (Genlis) **166**:26
La famille de Carvajal (Mérimée) **6**:351, 362; **65**:54, 58, 60, 79, 81, 87
La Famille de Germandre (Sand) **57**:316
Die Famille Ghonorez (Kleist)
See *Die Familie Schroffenstein: Ein Trauerspiel in fünf Aufzügen*
Family Annals, or the Sisters (Hays) **114**:186, 208
A Family Charge (Turgenev)
See *Nakhlebnik*
The Family Chronicle (Aksakov)
See *Semeinaia khronika*
"Family Circle" (Arany)
See "Csaladi kör"
"A Family Court" (Saltykov) **16**:341
Family Distress; or, Self-immolation (Kotzebue)
See *Der Opfertod*
A Family in Decline (Leskov)
See *Zaxudalyj rod*
The Family Legend (Baillie) **2**:35; **71**:5-6, 12-14, 18; **151**:11, 52-57, 60-63, 67-68, 89, 114-15, 119-20
The Family Letters of Christina Georgina Rossetti (Rossetti) **186**:234, 238-39, 252, 311-13, 341
The Family Life of Heinrich Heine (Heine)
See *Heinrich Heines Familienleben*
Family Nurse (Child) **73**:60
The Family of Carvajal (Mérimée)
See *La famille de Carvajal*
The Family of Montorio (Maturin)
See *Fatal Revenge; or, The Family of Montorio*
"The Family Picture" (Longstreet) **159**:125
The Family Picture (Holcroft) **85**:192, 234
A Family Picture (Ostrovsky)
See *Semeynaya kartina*
"Family Portraits" (Sigourney) **21**:290
The Family Robinson Crusoe; or, Journal of a Father Shipwrecked, with His Wife and Children, on an Uninhabitated Island (Wyss)
See *Der Schweizerische Robinson; oder, Der schiffbrüchige Schweizerprediger und seine Familie*
"Family Stories, by Thomas Ingoldsby" (Barham) **77**:4
Family Strife in Habsburg (Grillparzer)
See *Ein Bruderzwist in Habsburg*
Famous Persons and Places (Willis) **194**:320
Fanchon the Cricket (Sand) **57**:338
"A fanciful nickname..." (Baratynsky)
See "Svoenravnoe prozvanie..."
"Le fanciulle nella tempesta" (Leopardi) **129**:340
"The Fancy" (Hazlitt) **82**:128
The Fancy (Reynolds) **146**:168-69, 172-73, 186, 190-91, 202
"The Fancy Ball" (Willis) **194**:298
A Fancy of Hers (Alger) **83**:99, 116, 145
"Fancy's Ramble" (Freneau) **111**:151
"Fancy's Show-Box" (Hawthorne) **2**:291, 298, 305; **95**:91, 128, 134, 136; **171**:245, 335; **191**:276
La Fanfarlo (Baudelaire) **29**:106
Fanferlieschen (Brentano) **1**:102
Fanni ou les effects du désespoir (Sade) **47**:361-62
Fanny (Halleck) **47**:64, 68, 70, 72-73, 76-77, 83, 85, 99
"Fanny Ford" (Parton)
See "Fanny Ford: A Story of Everyday Life"
"Fanny Ford: A Story of Everyday Life" (Parton) **86**:337-39
Fänrik Ståls sägner (Runeberg) **41**:308-21, 323, 325-29, 331
"Fänrikens marknadsminne" (Runeberg) **41**:314, 325
Fanshawe (Hawthorne) **2**:326; **79**:296, 314
"Fantaisie" (Nerval) **1**:486
"Fantaisie" (Laforgue) **221**:88
"Fântâna Blanduziei" (Eminescu) **131**:361

"Fantasia" (Cooke) **110**:51
Fantasia quasi Sonata (Liszt) **199**:307
Fantasie- und Nachtstücke (Hoffmann) **183**:310, 314
Fantasies (Schumann)
See *Kreisleriana*
Fantasies à la manière de Rembrandt et de Callot (Baudelaire)
See *Gaspard de la Nuit*
Fantasiestücke (Schumann) **143**:85, 141
Fantasiestücke in Callots Manier (Hoffmann) **2**:340-41, 348, 361; **183**:164-66, 169, 179-82, 185, 190, 206-7, 221, 225, 228, 269
Fantasiestuecke in Callots Manier (Hoffmann)
See *Fantasiestücke in Callots Manier*
Fantasio (Musset) **7**:258, 260, 262, 264, 269, 272, 276, 282-83; **150**:226, 235, 239, 244, 246-47, 253-54, 263-65, 267, 334-36, 347, 350, 352
"Fantasma colosal" (Heredia) **209**:161
Fantasmagorii (Pavlova) **138**:10-11, 16-17, 22, 34-35, 49, 53
"A Fantastic Simile" (Beddoes) **154**:66
"A Fantasy" (Blind) **202**:15, 18, 53, 58
Fantasy (Schumann) **143**:84, 108, 112, 138
Fantazy (Slowacki) **15**:349, 352, 354, 365, 368, 378, 380-82
"Fantine" (Hugo) **3**:244-46; **10**:355, 361, 364
"Fantoches" (Verlaine) **2**:629; **51**:378-79
"Un fantôme" (Baudelaire) **29**:99; **55**:10
Far Away and Long Ago (Kemble) **18**:191
"Far Edgerley" (Woolson) **82**:273
"Far, Far Away" (Tennyson) **30**:226
"The Far Future" (Kendall) **12**:200
"The Faraway Forest" (Kivi)
See "Kaukametsä"
"Farce éphémère" (Laforgue) **53**:270; **221**:58
Fardorougha the Miser; or, The Convicts of Lisnamona (Carleton) **3**:83, 85, 87, 94; **199**:7, 9, 14, 18-19, 22, 37-40, 44, 56, 66, 80
"A Farewell" (Arnold) **89**:95
"Farewell" (Fuller) **211**:212
"The Farewell" (Lamartine)
See "L'adieu"
"A Farewell" (Levy) **59**:109
"A Farewell" (Patmore) **9**:343, 358
"Farewell" (Pushkin) **83**:259
"Farewell" (Rogers) **69**:82
"Farewell" (Thoreau) **7**:383
"A Farewell" (Wordsworth) **206**:224
Farewell (Eichendorff) **225**:5
"Farewell Address at Springfield" (Lincoln) **18**:213, 254, 259, 264, 280-81
"Farewell Address at Springfield, Illinois" (Lincoln) **18**:225; **201**:154, 156-57, 159, 165, 170, 172, 182
"Farewell Causerie" (Lewes) **215**:117
A Farewell, for Two Years, to England (Williams) **135**:334, 355
"Farewell Life" (Hood) **16**:219, 228, 233
"Farewell of a Missionary to Africa, at the Grave of his Wife and Child" (Sigourney) **87**:337
"The Farewell of a Virginia Slave Mother to Her Daughters Sold into Foreign Bondage" (Whittier) **8**:508-10, 512-13; **59**:354
"Farewell Old Cottage" (Foster) **26**:295
"Farewell, Sweet Mother" (Foster) **26**:286
"Farewell to Deirdre" (Ferguson) **33**:278
"Farewell to Essay-Writing" (Hazlitt) **29**:147-49, 165; **82**:99, 127
"Farewell to Frances" (Horton) **87**:102
"Farewell to Gastein" (Grillparzer)
See "Abschied von Gastein"
"Farewell to Patrick Sarsfield" (Mangan) **27**:297-98, 311, 314
"Farewell to the Caspian" (Bestuzhev)
See "Proshchanie s Kaspiem"
"Farewell to the Market: 'Susannah and Mary Jane'" (Adams) **33**:18
"Farewell to the Muses" (Reynolds) **146**:190
"A Farewell to the South" (Hallam) **110**:119
"Farewell to Tobacco" (Lamb) **10**:389, 404
"A Farewell to Wales" (Hemans) **71**:277
"Farewell to Youth" (Preseren)
See "Slovo od mladosti"
La Farisea (Caballero) **10**:83
"A farkasok dala" (Petofi) **21**:264
The Farm House; or, The Female Duellists (Tyler) **3**:573
The Farm Lease (Almqvist)
See *Ladugårdsarrebnet*
"Farmer Hayden's Thanksgiving-Day" (Alger) **8**:44
"The Farmer of Tilsbury Vale: A Character" (Wordsworth) **111**:235
The Farmer Refuted (Hamilton) **49**:293, 325
"Farmer Stebbin's Opinions" (Crawford) **12**:151, 161
"The Farmer's Advice to the Villagers" (Dwight) **13**:270, 272, 278
The Farmer's Boy (Bloomfield) **145**:126-29, 131, 135-36, 138, 141-43, 145-47, 149-57, 160-64, 166, 169, 174-76, 179
"Farmer's Sons" (Barnes) **75**:101
"The Farmer's Winter Evening" (Freneau)
See "The Citizen's Resolve"
"The Farmer's Woldest Da'ter" (Barnes) **75**:6, 101
"The Farrers of Budge Row" (Martineau) **26**:352
Farys (Mickiewicz) **3**:389, 392, 397
Faschingschwank aus Wien (Schumann) **143**:69, 84
"Fashion" (Madison) **126**:329
"Fashion, a Vision" (Barbauld) **185**:122
Fashion; or Life in New York (Mowatt) **74**:211, 215-15, 219, 221-24, 227-30, 223-33
Fashionable Life; or, Paris and London (Trollope) **30**:332
The Fashionable Lover (Cumberland) **167**:119, 138, 147, 153-54, 160-61, 163, 165-66, 168, 170-71, 175, 178-81, 188-89, 191
"The Fashionable Preacher" (Parton) **86**:352
"The Fashionable Wife" (Krasicki)
See "Żona modna"
"The Fashionable Wife" (Opie) **65**:159
"Fashion's Idol" (Norton) **205**:130, 138
"A Fast Keeper" (Mangan) **27**:301
"Fastnachtsrede von Florestan" (Schumann) **143**:75
"Fata în gradina de aur" (Eminescu) **131**:287, 299
Fata morgana (Fouqué) **2**:267
The Fatal Deception; or, The Progress of Guilt (Dunlap)
See *Leicester*
The Fatal Falsehood: A Tragedy (More) **27**:332, 337; **141**:201, 203-7, 259
Fatal Revenge; or, The Family of Montorio (Maturin) **6**:316-17, 320-24, 328-31, 340-42, 346; **169**:16-18, 20-22, 34-35, 37-39, 41-42, 44, 71-74, 76, 101-2, 114, 116, 120, 122-23
The Fatal Secret (Southworth) **26**:434
"The Fatalist" (Lermontov) **5**:291, 295, 298-99, 301, 303, 306; **126**:151, 153, 195, 201-3, 217
"Fate" (Emerson) **1**:296; **38**:154-55, 157; **98**:19-20, 59, 61, 109, 151-55, 181, 185
"The Fate of Adelaide" (Landon) **15**:165
"The Fate of Cathleen" (Griffin) **7**:194-95
"The Fate of Genius" (Clare) **86**:109
"The Fate of the Explorers" (Kendall) **12**:199
"The Fate of Tyranny and Toryism" (Brackenridge) **7**:44
Fated to be Free (Ingelow) **39**:260-61, 264; **107**:118-19, 124-25
"The Father" (Sigourney) **21**:290, 306, 311-13
"Father Aleksej" (Turgenev)
See "Rasskaz ottsa Aleksaya"
"Father Alexey's Story" (Turgenev)
See "Rasskaz ottsa Aleksaya"
Father and Daughter: A Portraiture from the Life (Bremer)
See *Fader och dotter: En skildring ur lifvet*
The Father and Daughter: A Tale in Prose (Opie) **65**:152-3, 155, 163, 168, 171-2, 174, 178-9, 184-5, 192-5, 197-8
Father Bombo's Pilgrimage to Mecca (Brackenridge) **7**:54, 62-63; **227**:71, 104, 162
"Father Butler: The Lough Dearg Pilgrim" (Carleton) **3**:88, 90, 92
"Father Come Home" (Barnes) **75**:101
Father Connell (Banim and Banim) **13**:122, 128-31
"Father Gerasim's Lion" (Leskov)
See "Lev startsa Gerasimova"
"Father Giles of Ballymoy" (Trollope) **101**:234, 245, 262, 267, 273; **215**:221
Father Goriot (Balzac)
See *Le père Goriot: Histoire Parisienne*
Father Marek (Slowacki)
See *Ksiądz Marek*
"Father Nicholas" (Mackenzie) **41**:189
The Father of an Only Child (Dunlap)
See *The Father; or, American Shandyism*
"The Father of the Deep" (Beddoes) **154**:79
The Father of the Plague-Stricken at El-Arish (Slowacki)
See *Ojciec zadżumionych*
The Father; or, American Shandyism (Dunlap) **2**:207-08, 210-11, 213-15, 217
"A Father to His Motherless Children" (Sigourney) **21**:309
"Fatherhood" (Barnes) **75**:7
"Fatherland" (Grundtvig) **1**:402
Fathers and Children (Turgenev)
See *Ottsy i deti*
Fathers and Sons (Turgenev)
See *Ottsy i deti*
"Father's Letter" (Field) **3**:210
"Father's Return" (Mickiewicz) **3**:398
"The Father's Wedding" (Lamb)
See "Elinor Forester: The Father's Wedding"
"The Father's Wedding-Day" (Lamb) **10**:406
"Fatima" (Tennyson) **202**:185, 189
"Fatima and Urganda: An Eastern Tale" (Rowson) **69**:112, 129
"Fatum" (Norwid) **17**:373-74
"Fauconshawe" (Gordon) **21**:160, 166, 181
"Le Faune" (Verlaine) **51**:378-80, 382
La Fausse Industrie (Fourier) **51**:161, 174
"La fausse maîtresse" (Balzac) **5**:84; **153**:149, 153
"La fausse monnaie" (Baudelaire) **155**:81, 90
Faust (Chamisso) **82**:18
Faust (Goethe)
See *Faust. Die Erster Teil*
Faust (Lenau) **16**:263-64, 266-75, 278-80, 282, 285
Faust (Turgenev) **21**:414, 417-18, 431, 451-52; **122**:243-44, 246-47, 261, 266, 268, 298, 300-304, 324, 337, 348, 364
Faust: A Tragedy (Goethe)
See *Faust. Die Erster Teil*
Faust. Der Tragödie zweiter Teil (Goethe) **4**:181, 191, 222; **34**:48-138; **90**:106; **154**:184-89, 194-95, 197, 199, 201, 204, 217-18, 223, 225, 227, 229, 231-33, 241, 247, 252, 254-57, 259, 264-66, 269-70, 273, 275, 277-79, 288, 295, 297, 300, 307, 311, 313, 316-18, 329, 333, 341
Faust. Die Erster Teil (Goethe) **34**:48-138; **154**:179-347
Faust: Ein Fragment (Goethe) **4**:162, 164, 167-69, 172-77, 179, 181, 183-84, 187-88, 194-95, 199, 201, 205, 210-21; **34**:68, 85-6, 95, 123-24, 127; **154**:191, 195, 223-24, 226, 228-31

Faust: Eine Tragödie (Goethe)
See *Faust. Die Erster Teil*
Faust I (Goethe)
See *Faust. Die Erster Teil*
Faust II (Goethe)
See *Faust. Der Tragödie zweiter Teil*
The Faust of the Orient (Klinger) **1**:433
Faust Overture (Wagner) **119**:189, 279
Faust—Der Tragödie erster Teil (Goethe)
See *Faust. Die Erster Teil*
La faustin (Goncourt) **7**:162-63, 167, 170, 174, 183, 188
"Faustina" (Jacobsen) **34**:168
Faustina (Goncourt)
See *La faustin*
Faust's Leben, Thaten, und Hollenfahrt (Klinger) **1**:430
Faustus: His Life, Death, and Descent into Hell (Klinger)
See *Faust's Leben, Thaten, und Hollenfahrt*
Une faute (Scribe) **16**:394
Les Faux Demetrius (Mérimée) **65**:85
"Favorites of Pan" (Lampman)
See "Favourites of Pan"
"The Favourite Flower" (Norton) **205**:128
"Favourites of Pan" (Lampman) **25**:217; **194**:8, 22, 30, 56, 77-78, 80, 82, 93
The Fawn of Spring Vale (Carleton)
See *Jane Sinclair; or, The Fawn of Spring Vale*
The Fawn of Spring-Vale, The Clarionet, and Other Tales (Carleton) **199**:56
Feadorcha Truaillidhe (Carleton)
See *Fardorougha the Miser; or, The Convicts of Lisnamona*
"Feäir Ellen Dare" (Barnes) **75**:58
"Fear" (Shaw) **15**:335
Fear and Trembling (Kierkegaard)
See *Frygt og Baeven*
"Fears" (Verlaine)
See "Craintes"
"Fears and Scruples" (Browning) **19**:88, 96
"Fears in Solitude" (Coleridge) **197**:211, 311; **231**:57, 71, 112, 155-57, 160-62
Fears in Solitude (Coleridge) **9**:146, 149, 158; **99**:48-9; **111**:310
The Feast during the Plague (Pushkin)
See *Pir vo vremiachumy*
A Feast in Time of the Plague (Pushkin)
See *Pir vo vremiachumy*
"Feast of Brougham Castle" (Wordsworth) **12**:393
"The Feast of Famine" (Stevenson) **5**:410, 428
"The Feast of Lights" (Lazarus) **8**:421; **109**:335, 338
"The Feast of the Poets" (Hunt) **1**:412; **70**:271
The Feast of the Poets, with Notes, and Other Pieces in Verse (Hunt) **1**:407, 412, 414; **70**:253, 292-93
"Feasts" (Baratynsky) **103**:8-9
Feasts of Love (Verlaine)
See *Fêtes galantes*
"Feathertop" (Hawthorne) **171**:357-58, 361-62
"Feats on the Fjord" (Martineau) **26**:317, 323; **137**:255-57, 259, 261
"Features for the Characterization of the Russian Common People" (Dobrolyubov) **5**:140
"February: A Thaw" (Clare) **9**:107, 116; **86**:95, 98, 104, 165
Fedalla, A Tale of Peru (Bird) **197**:24
"Federal Catechism" (Webster) **30**:405
The Federalist (Hamilton) **49**:297-9, 303-04, 306-07, 311-19, 322-25, 327
Federalist "Number 1" (Madison) **126**:265
Federalist "Number 10" (Madison) **126**:234, 252, 254, 260-62, 269-71, 276-87, 297-98, 304, 309, 311, 314
Federalist "Number 14" (Madison) **126**:282-83, 295, 305, 309
Federalist "Number 18" (Madison) **126**:278, 296
Federalist "Number 19" (Madison) **126**:278, 296, 309
Federalist "Number 20" (Madison) **126**:278, 296
Federalist "Number 37" (Madison) **126**:309, 316
Federalist "Number 38" (Madison) **126**:309
Federalist "Number 39" (Madison) **126**:233, 243, 298
Federalist "Number 40" (Madison) **126**:316
Federalist "Number 41" (Madison) **126**:310
Federalist "Number 43" (Madison) **126**:278, 282
Federalist "Number 45" (Madison) **126**:309
Federalist "Number 47" (Madison) **126**:278, 282
Federalist "Number 48" (Madison) **126**:298, 316
Federalist "Number 49" (Madison) **126**:309
Federalist "Number 50" (Madison) **126**:309
Federalist "Number 51" (Madison) **126**:252, 254, 261, 269, 304, 314
Federalist "Number 52" (Madison) **126**:233
Federalist "Number 54" (Madison) **126**:311
Federalist "Number 57" (Madison) **126**:263
Federalist "Number 63" (Madison) **126**:278
"Federigo" (Mérimée) **6**:366; **65**:111-13
"La fédor" (Daudet) **1**:251-52
"Fedor and Abram" (Leskov)
See "Skazanie o Fedore-khristianine i o druge ego Avrame-zhidovine"
"Fedya" (Turgenev) **21**:376
Fée (Feuillet) **45**:88
La fée aux miettes (Nodier) **19**:377, 381, 383-86, 388, 391-92, 396-98, 400
"Fee him, father, fee him" (Baillie) **151**:91, 96
"Feelings of an Enthusiast Upon the Commencement of the French Revolution" (Wordsworth) **38**:424
Die Feen (Wagner) **9**:435-36, 473; **119**:189, 268
"Feet in the Fire" (Meyer)
See "Die Füsse im Feuer"
"Feldblumen" (Stifter) **41**:335, 366, 375-81; **198**:259
Felhök (Petofi) **21**:284
"Félice and Petit Poulain" (Field) **3**:206
"Felicia" (Derzhavin)
See "Felitsa"
"Felicia Hemans" (Barrett Browning) **61**:51; **170**:121
"Felicitations" (Krasicki)
See "Powinszowania"
"Felipa" (Woolson) **82**:273, 299, 307
"Felisa" (Isaacs) **70**:304, 307, 309
"Felitsa" (Derzhavin) **215**:5, 9, 13, 25-28, 30-32, 34, 39-42, 47, 53, 57-59, 61, 68
"Felitza" (Derzhavin)
See "Felitsa"
Felix Holt the Radical (Eliot) **4**:101-03, 111, 114, 121, 123, 127, 133, 137, 144; **13**:318, 325; **23**:51, 55, 57, 63, 80; **41**:68, 72, 82, 84-5, 91, 96-7, 99; **89**:278; **118**:34-194; **183**:4, 16, 28, 94, 143, 146; **199**:203
Felix Holt, the Radical (Eliot) **209**:82
"Felix Randal" (Hopkins) **17**:194, 254; **189**:7, 53, 115, 117
"La Fellah-sur une aquarelle de la Princesse M" (Gautier) **59**:19
"The Fellow Traveller" (Andersen) **7**:32
"Fellowship" (Barnes) **75**:109
"Felo de Se" (Levy) **59**:90, 107-8
The Felons of the Country (Miller) **143**:13
"Female Biography" (Rowson)
See "Sketches of Female Biography"
"The Female Convict" (Landon) **15**:161
"The Female Convict" (Southey) **97**:314
"Female Education" (Beecher) **30**:14
Female Education (Darwin)
See *Plan for the Conduct of Female Education in Boarding Schools*
The Female Emigrant's Guide, and Hints on Canadian Housekeeping (Traill) **31**:316, 327, 329
"Female Fashions for 1799" (Robinson) **142**:169
"Female Fortitude and Filial Duty Rewarded" (Rowson) **182**:253
The Female Patriot; or, Nature's Rights (Rowson) **69**:141; **182**:281, 353
The Female Quixote; or, The Adventures of Arabella (Lennox) **23**:226-30, 232-40, 242-44, 246-56, 261-65; **134**:217-350
Female Quixotism: Exhibited in the Romantic Opinions and Extravagant Adventures of Dorcasina Sheldon (Tenney) **122**:170, 172, 177, 181, 184, 186-87, 193-97, 199-200, 202, 205-10, 212-19, 221-24, 227, 229
"The Female Sovereigns of England When Young" (Hunt) **70**:258
The Female Speaker; or, Miscellaneous Pieces in Prose and Verse, Selected from the Best Writers (Barbauld) **185**:144, 146
"Female Suffrage: A Letter to the Christian Women of America" (Cooper) **129**:70, 87-89
A Female Sultan (Sacher-Masoch) **31**:294
"Female Trials in the Bush" (Traill) **31**:327
"Female Types" (Pisarev) **25**:338
"The Female Vagrant" (Wordsworth) **12**:386-87; **111**:201-2, 234, 253, 265, 268, 306-7, 310-11, 315, 317, 356-57
"The Female Ward" (Willis) **194**:299
"Female Writers on Practical Divinity" (Martineau) **26**:312, 319; **137**:236
"Femme" (Corbière) **43**:9-10, 12, 18, 32, 34
La femme à deux maris (Pixérécourt) **39**:272-73, 277, 279, 282, 284, 286
"La femme abandonnée" (Balzac) **5**:37; **35**:24, 26; **153**:151-52
"La Femme adultere" (Vigny) **102**:335, 367
La femme au 18e siècle (Goncourt and Goncourt) **7**:165, 176
La femme de Claude (Dumas) **9**:225-26, 228-30, 234, 240-43, 245, 248-49
"La femme de Paul" (Maupassant) **83**:182, 194-95, 198-200, 203
"Une femme de Rubens" (Banville) **9**:19
"La femme de trente ans" (Balzac) **5**:37, 49, 83; **35**:2, 26; **153**:74, 147
"Une femme est l'amour" (Nerval) **67**:307
"Une femme est un diable" (Mérimée) **6**:362-3; **65**:50, 54, 57, 79, 82-3
"Femme et chatte" (Verlaine) **2**:630; **51**:356
La femme, la famille, et le prêtre (Michelet) **31**:214, 218, 222, 224-25, 244, 260-62
La femme, le mari, et l'amant (Kock) **16**:245-46
"Femme Passée" (Linton) **41**:164
"La femme sauvage et la petite-maîtresse" (Baudelaire) **155**:23, 86
"Femmes" (Genlis) **166**:26
Femmes (Verlaine) **51**:352, 363; **230**:174-75, 177-78, 181, 212-16
"Femmes damnées" (Baudelaire) **6**:89, 109; **29**:74, 99; **55**:4-6, 26, 32-3, 45, 73-4, 76
Les femmes d'artistes (Daudet) **1**:239, 249
"Les femmes du Caire" (Nerval) **67**:334, 363
"Den femte juli" (Runeberg) **41**:312, 326-27
La Fenêtre (Maupassant) **83**:230
"Les fenêtres" (Baudelaire) **29**:110; **55**:41; **155**:105-7
"Les fenêtres" (Mallarmé) **4**:378, 395; **41**:241-42, 250; **210**:217, 234, 244
Feodore (Kotzebue) **25**:139-40
"Ferdinand and Isabella" (Prescott)
See "History of Ferdinand and Isabella"
"Ferdinand and Ottilie" (Goethe) **4**:197
A férfi és nő (Madach) **19**:362, 370
"Fergus Wry-Mouth" (Ferguson) **33**:285, 301, 304
Ferishtah's Fancies (Browning) **19**:96
"Die Fermate" (Hoffmann) **183**:287
Fermo e Lucia (Manzoni) **29**:307; **98**:213, 217,

219-20, 240, 250, 258, 263-65, 267, 273, 284-88, 290
Fern Leaves (Parton)
See *Fern Leaves, Second Series*
Fern Leaves, Second Series (Parton) **86**:318, 346-52
"The Fern Owls Nest" (Clare) **86**:144
"A Fern Soliloquy" (Parton) **86**:347
A Fernand Longlois (Verlaine) **51**:361-62
Fernande (Dumas) **71**:204, 228
Fernere Darstellungen (Schelling) **30**:128, 174
"Ferragus" (Balzac) **5**:77; **35**:43; **53**:28; **153**:23, 69, 73, 94
Ein Fest auf Haderslevhuus (Storm) **1**:540-41, 547; **195**:67, 127, 130, 132
"The Festal Hour" (Hemans) **29**:207
"A Festival of Life" (Thomson) **18**:409
"Festival of Love" (Lenau) **16**:276, 278
Festklänge (Liszt) **199**:329
"Festus" (Fuller) **50**:227
The Fetches (Banim and Banim) **13**:116, 119, 126, 132, 139-41
"La fête chez Thérèse" (Hugo) **3**:270
"Fêtes de la faim" (Rimbaud) **4**:472-73; **82**:247
"Fêtes de la patience" (Rimbaud) **35**:309, 311; **82**:251; **227**:313
"Fêtes d'hiver" (Rimbaud) **227**:242, 323
Fêtes galantes (Verlaine) **2**:617-18, 623-24, 628-31; **51**:351-2, 355-6, 359, 361, 365, 368-69, 373-74, 376-78, 380-87; **230**:151-52, 160, 164, 168-69, 172-73, 199
"Le feu du ciel" (Hugo) **3**:234, 261
The Feud (Gordon) **21**:160, 173, 183
The Feud of the Schroffensteins (Kleist)
See *Die Familie Schroffenstein*
Feudal Tyrants; or, The Counts of Carlsheim and Sargans (Lewis) **11**:297
Feuerbach (Engels)
See *Ludwig Feuerbach und der Aus gang der klassischen deutschen Philosophie*
"Der Feuerreiter" (Mörike) **10**:451, 453, 455; **201**:252, 268, 292
La Feuille des gens du monde, ou Le Journal imaginaire (Genlis) **166**:60-61
Les feuilles d'automne (Hugo) **3**:236, 261, 266, 270; **21**:196, 214, 222, 225
"Feuilles mortes" (Banville) **9**:30
Le feuilleton d'Aristophane (Banville) **9**:19
The Few (Alfieri)
See *I pochi*
"A Few Biographical and Bibliographical Notes on Pushkin" (Dobrolyubov) **5**:140
A Few Days in Athens (Wright) **74**:363, 372, 376-77
"A Few Words about Pushkin" (Gogol) **162**:97
"A Few Words on Dueling" (Freneau) **111**:135
"A few Words on Ostrovsky's New Play 'The Poor Bride'" (Turgenev) **37**:381
"Feya" (Baratynsky) **103**:10, 16-18, 21-2
Le Fiabe di Carlo Gozzi (Gozzi) **23**:113
"Un fiacre, demain . . ." (Verlaine) **230**:161
"Fiamnak" (Arany) **34**:19
Fiancée (Scribe) **16**:382
Les fiancés (Nodier) **19**:384
"Fiat nox" (Leconte de Lisle) **29**:228, 234-35
"La ficelle" (Maupassant) **1**:447, 457; **83**:188
Fichte Studies (Novalis)
See *Fichte-Studien*
Fichte-Studien (Novalis) **178**:35, 51, 54, 56, 88, 108, 114, 120
"Fiction and Matter of Fact" (Hunt) **1**:421
"The Fiddler" (Melville) **3**:354, 381; **157**:72, 95
"The Fiddler" (O'Brien) **21**:243, 249-50
"Fiddler Bob" (Barnes)
See "Bob the Fiddler"
Fidelio: An Opera in Two Acts (Beethoven) **227**:4-5, 9, 11-12, 18, 25-26, 31-34
"Fidelity" (Wordsworth) **12**:404
"Fidelity Till Death" (Hemans) **71**:291
Field and Hedgerow; Being the last Essays of Richard Jefferies, Collected by his Widow (Jefferies) **47**:102, 111-12, 133, 138-39
"The Field Marshall" (Runeberg)
See "Fältmarskalken"
"Field Notes" (Cranch) **115**:66
"The Field of the Grounded Arms" (Halleck) **47**:57, 62, 74, 79
"Field Play" (Jefferies) **47**:136
"Field Words and Ways" (Jefferies) **47**:138
"Fieldlarks and Blackbirds" (Lanier) **118**:241
"The Fields of Coleraine" (Gordon) **21**:160
The Fields of Fancy (Shelley)
See *Mathilda*
"The Fiends" (Pushkin) **3**:443
Fiesco (Schiller)
See *Die Verschwörung des Fiesco zu Genua*
Fiesques de Lavagna (Dumas) **71**:217, 241, 244
"Fife Player" (Laforgue)
See "Fifre"
Fifine at the Fair (Browning) **19**:121-22, 136; **79**:154, 186
"Fifre" (Laforgue) **221**:91
1572: A Chronicle of the Times of Charles the Ninth (Mérimée)
See *Chronique du temps de Charles IX*
Fifteen Days of Sinai (Dumas) **11**:48
1593 (Dickinson) **77**:97
1528 (Dickinson) **77**:121
1525 (Dickinson) **77**:184
Fifteen Sermons (Newman)
See *Fifteen Sermons Preached before the University of Oxford*
Fifteen Sermons Preached before the University of Oxford (Newman) **99**:219, 224, 297-98, 300-02
Fifteen Years of a Drunkard's Life (Jerrold) **2**:403
"Fifteenth Letter" (Schiller) **166**:104, 110
"Fifth Canto" (Lamartine) **11**:247
"Fifth Epistle" (Eminescu) **131**:331
The Fifth of August (Tamayo y Baus)
See *El cinco de Agosto*
"The Fifth of July" (Cumbaa)
See "Den femte juli"
The Fifth of May (Manzoni)
See *Il cinque maggio*
Fifth Symphony (Beethoven) **227**:4, 6
Fifty Suggestions (Poe) **117**:320
"Fifty Years" (Bryant) **6**:175
Figaro (Baudelaire) **155**:52, 54, 74
Figaro (Holcroft)
See *The Follies of a Day; or, The Marriage of Figaro*
"Fígaro en el cementario" (Larra) **17**:277-78
"The Fight" (Hazlitt) **29**:151, 153, 167, 169; **82**:127
"The Fight" (Longstreet) **159**:117-18, 133-34, 142, 144, 151, 153-54, 161, 164-65, 176, 182-85, 191, 203
"The Fight for Life" (Pisarev)
See "Bor'ba za žizn"
"Fight for Status" (Grillparzer)
See "Rangstreit"
"The Fight for Survival" (Pisarev)
See "Bor'ba za suščestvovanie"
"Fight of Ronscevalles" (Lewis) **11**:298
"The Fight of the Forlorn" (Darley) **2**:133
"A Fight over the Body of Homer" (Rossetti) **186**:267
"The Fight with the Dragon" (Schiller) **39**:330
The Fighting Quaker (Bird) **197**:29
"Figura" (Leskov) **25**:258-60; **174**:7
"Figurez-vous un peu!" (Laforgue) **221**:23
"Filalet k Melodor" (Karamzin) **173**:277, 309, 323
La Filandière (Balzac) **153**:8
File No. 113 (Gaboriau)
See *Le dossier no. 113*
"La Fileuse et l'enfant" (Desbordes-Valmore) **97**:20, 28
Os filhos de Tupã (Alencar) **157**:9, 12, 16
"Filhos de Tupan" (Alencar) **157**:5
"Filial Love" (Brontë) **165**:99-100
El filibusterismo (Rizal) **27**:407-09, 412, 416, 418-25, 427-29
Filippo (Alfieri) **101**:4, 8, 10-11, 15, 18-19, 38, 58-61, 63, 67
"Filisa's Picture" (Isaacs)
See "El retrato de Felisa"
"Fill the Bumper Fair" (Moore) **110**:190
"Une Fille" (Maupassant) **83**:227
La fille aux yeux d'or (Balzac) **5**:46; **35**:22, 24, 26; **53**:29; **153**:23, 62, 64, 68, 149
"La Fille d'Albano" (Sand) **174**:192
The Fille de Chambre (Rowson)
See *Rebecca; or, The Fille de Chambre*
"Fille de Fille" (Maupassant) **83**:227
"La Fille de Jephte" (Vigny) **7**:472, 481; **102**:335, 367
La fille de l'exilé; ou, Huit mois en deux heures (Pixérécourt) **39**:274-75, 278-79, 282, 284, 294
"Une fille d'Eve" (Balzac) **5**:83-84; **35**:26; **153**:62, 64-68, 70, 75, 147, 152-53
Une fille d'Eve (Balzac)
See "Une fille d'Eve"
La fille du marquis (Dumas) **71**:218
Une fille du régent (Dumas) **11**:51
La fille Élisa (Goncourt) **7**:152-53, 155, 161, 170, 182, 188-90
Filles (Verlaine) **2**:632; **51**:363
"Les filles de Milton" (Villiers de l'Isle Adam) **3**:586, 588
Les filles du feu (Nerval) **1**:476-77, 485; 304, 309, 313, 325, 332, 334, 344, 347, 357-58, 360, 363-65, 370
Filles, Lorettes, et Courtisanes (Dumas) **71**:228
"Filles I" (Verlaine) **230**:214
La Filleule (Sand) **57**:316
Filosofia del entendimiento (Bello) **131**:94-97, 131
Filosofia Nova (Stendhal) **178**:216
"Filosofías" (Silva) **114**:262, 264, 319
"Les Filous" (Sade) **47**:314
"Un fils" (Maupassant) **1**:449
Le fils de Cromwell; ou, Une Restauration (Scribe) **16**:388
Le fils de Giboyer (Augier) **31**:3, 5, 7-10, 13, 16, 19-21, 25, 27-8, 31-2, 34, 38-9
"Le fils de Lamartine et de Graziella" (Corbière) **43**:30
Le Fils du Forçat (Dumas) **71**:204
"Le fils du Titien" (Musset) **7**:264; **150**:227, 324, 343, 347
Les fils naturel (Dumas) **9**:224, 232, 236-37, 241-42, 245, 247, 249-51, 253
Le Fils naturel (Sade) **47**:362-63
"La fin" (Corbière) **43**:7, 9, 14, 23, 29-30
La fin de Don Juan (Baudelaire) **6**:119
"El fin de la fiesta" (Larra) **130**:194
"La fin de la fin" (Banville) **9**:32
"La fin de la journée" (Baudelaire) **55**:12, 73
"Fin de l'homme" (Leconte de Lisle) **29**:217
La fin de Satan (Hugo) **3**:273; **10**:377; **21**:201; **161**:205-6, 251, 253; **189**:193-95, 198, 200-201
"A Final Appeal to the Public relative to Pope" (Bowles) **103**:54
The Final Cause of Poetry (Coleridge) **90**:15
"Final Chorus" (Darley) **2**:133
El final de Norma (Alarcon) **1**:13, 15; **219**:3, 18-19
"The Final Death" (Baratynsky)
See "Poslednyaya smert'"
"Final Impenitence" (Verlaine) **51**:372
"Der Findling" (Kleist) **2**:463; **37**:245, 247, 253-55; **222**:190, 194-96, 200, 203, 212, 228, 231, 233, 235-36, 242, 244-48
"The Fine Arts" (Hazlitt) **29**:144
Fine Arts (Symonds) **34**:318-19, 346-48, 357, 368, 370-71, 374-75
"The Fine Arts in America" (Winthrop) **210**:316, 328

"Fine Old English Gentleman" (Dickens) **219**:195
"The Finest Diner in the World" (Villiers de l'Isle Adam)
See "Le plus beau dîner du monde"
"Finis Exoptatus" (Gordon) **21**:159-60
"The Finishing School" (O'Brien) **21**:234, 250
"Finkenlied" (Brentano) **191**:66-67
"Finland" (Baratynsky) **103**:10
Fior d'Aliza (Lamartine) **11**:266, 278, 286, 288
"The Fir-Tree" (Andersen)
See "Grantræet"
"Fire" (Pavlova)
See "Ogon"
"Fire, Famine, and Slaughter" (Coleridge) **9**:146; **177**:113
"The Fire of Drift-Wood" (Longfellow) **2**:475; **45**:154, 162, 166, 187; **101**:92
"Fire Pictures" (Hayne) **94**:149, 161-64
"The Fire That Filled My Heart of Old" (Thomson) **18**:403
"Fire Worship" (Hawthorne) **2**:296, 298; **191**:217-18
"The Fire Worshippers" (Moore) **6**:380, 387-88, 393; **110**:166, 203, 210, 212-14, 216-20, 222-25
"The Fireplace" (Cranch) **115**:42
"The Fire-Rider" (Mörike)
See "Der Feuerreiter"
"The Fires" (Tyutchev) **34**:393
Fireside Travels (Lowell) **2**:507; **90**:202, 206
"The Firmament" (Bryant) **6**:178, 190; **46**:6
"Firmly I Believe and Truly" (Newman) **38**:346
"Firnelicht" (Meyer) **81**:142
"First Attempts in Rhyme" (Hood) **16**:236
First Book of Odes (Brontë) **109**:17
The First Book of Urizen (Blake)
See *The Book of Urizen*
First Brutus (Alfieri)
See *Bruto primo*
The First Communion (Tegner)
See *Nattvardsbarnen*
"First Communions" (Rimbaud)
See "Les premières communions"
"The First Day" (Longfellow) **45**:137-38
"The first Day's Night had come—" (Dickinson) **171**:199
"The First Death in the Clearing" (Traill) **31**:328
"First Edinburgh Reviewers" (Bagehot) **10**:18, 27, 62, 65
"The First English Poet" (Allingham) **25**:11
"The First Epistle" (Eminescu) **33**:245-46, 264; **131**:286, 297, 344
First Essay (Malthus) **145**:230
"The First Extra" (Levy) **59**:92, 120
"The First Fan" (Holmes) **14**:109
"The First Fire" (Barbauld) **185**:15-21
First Footsteps in East Africa (Burton) **42**:40, 42, 58
"The First Founder of a Public Library" (D'Israeli) **217**:300
"First Going to Church" (Lamb) **10**:402, 417
First Impressions (Austen) **1**:52; **13**:97, 107; **119**:17-18, 37; **150**:33-34, 150
First Impressions of England (Miller) **143**:13, 29, 32, 48
"First Impressions—Quebec" (Moodie) **14**:243
"First Inaugual Address" (Lincoln)
See "Address of Abraham Lincoln, on Taking the Oath of Office as President of the United States, March 4, 1861"
First Inaugural Address (Lincoln) **18**:214-15, 235, 242, 254, 257
First Introduction to the Theory of Science (Fichte) **62**:36
"The First Jesuits in England" (D'Israeli) **217**:303
"The First Kiss" (Isaacs)
See "El primer beso"
First Lessons in Grammar on the Plan of Pestalozzi, by a Teacher in Boston (Peabody) **169**:147, 193
"First Letter" (Chaadaev)
See "Philosophic Letter 1"
"The First Love" (Kierkegaard) **125**:203, 207-8, 248, 254, 280
"First Love" (Kivi)
See "Nuori Karhunampuja"
"First Love" (Lazarus) **109**:292
"First Love" (Sedgwick) **98**:302
First Love (Cumberland) **167**:122, 140, 161, 192
First Love (Turgenev)
See *Pervaya lyubov'*
The First Madman (Castro)
See *El primer loco*
"First News from Villafranca" (Barrett Browning) **170**:119
First Nursery Reading Book, Intended to Teach the Alphabet, by Means of English Words, Whose Analysis Shall Give the True Sounds That Were Originally, and Even Now Are Generally, Attached to the Characters in All Languages (Peabody) **169**:141
"First O Songs for a Prelude" (Whitman) **31**:393; **81**:330
"The First of January" (Lermontov) **5**:295
"First Paper" (De Quincey) **87**:77
"The First Part" (Goethe) **154**:223
"First Part" (Wordsworth) **206**:312
"First Philosophical Letter" (Chaadaev)
See "Philosophic Letter 1"
"First Principle and Foundation" (Hopkins) **189**:93
The First Printer (Reade) **74**:331
The First Settlers of New England (Child) **73**:75, 97
"The First Snowfall" (Lowell) **2**:511; **90**:193, 214
"The First Spring Day" (Rossetti) **2**:575
First Steps to the Study of History, Being Part First of a Key to History (Peabody) **169**:147
"The First Sunday after Advent" (Keble) **87**:200
"First Sunday after Christmas" (Keble) **87**:160
"First Sunday after Epiphany" (Keble) **87**:159, 174
"First Sunday after Trinity" (Droste-Hülshoff) **3**:201
The First Temptation of Saint Anthony (Flaubert)
See *La tentation de Saint Antoine*
"First Vision" (Lamartine) **11**:273
"Fischer" (Goethe) **4**:192
"Ein Fischer sass im Kahne" (Brentano) **1**:104
"Fish Soup without Fish" (Leskov)
See "Uxa bez ryby"
"The Fish, the Man, and the Spirit" (Hunt) **1**:415
The Fisher of Souls (Sacher-Masoch) **31**:298, 301
"The Fisherman" (Goethe) **4**:165
"The Fisherman" (Preseren)
See "Ribič"
"The Fisherman" (Whittier) **8**:520
"The Fisherman and the Fish" (Pushkin)
See "Skazka o Rybake i Rybke"
The Fisherman Thorsten (Stagnelius) **61**:260
"The Fisherman's Betrothed" (Webster) **230**:245
"The Fisher's Son" (Thoreau) **7**:408
"A Fisher-Wife" (Rossetti) **50**:288, 313
"Fishing Song" (Cooke) **110**:9
"Fitter to See Him, I May Be" (Dickinson) **21**:57
"Fitz Adam's Story" (Lowell) **2**:520; **90**:190
The Fitzboodle Papers (Thackeray) **5**:507
5 (Dickinson) **77**:120
"The Five Ages" (Freneau) **111**:146
500 (Dickinson) **77**:121
The Five Hundred Dollar Check (Alger)
See "$500; or, Jacob Marlowe's Secret"
"$500; or, Jacob Marlowe's Secret" (Alger) **83**:96, 114
508 (Dickinson) **77**:72, 153
585 (Dickinson) **77**:129
584 (Dickinson) **77**:132
582 (Dickinson) **77**:68, 75
553 (Dickinson) **77**:83
505 (Dickinson) **77**:104-05, 139
540 (Dickinson) **77**:153
547 (Dickinson) **77**:162-64
519 (Cantor) **77**:162-64
593 (Dickinson) **77**:147
579 (Dickinson) **77**:148
577 (Dickinson) **77**:111, 147
506 (Dickinson) **77**:184
564 (Dickinson) **77**:77
566 (Dickinson) **77**:49, 162-63
510 (Dickinson) **77**:88
539 (Dickinson) **77**:94
536 (Dickinson) **77**:88, 163-64
512 (Dickinson) **77**:97
520 (Dickinson) **77**:148
528 (Dickinson) **77**:67, 83
525 (Dickinson) **77**:67
526 (Dickinson) **77**:109-10
"The Five Indispensable Authors" (Lowell) **90**:196
Five Minutes (Alencar)
See *Cinco Minutos*
Five Novelettes: Passing Events. Julia. Mina Laury. Henry Hastings. Caroline Vernon (Brontë) **3**:80
"Five Peas from One Pod" (Andersen) **7**:36
Five Pieces of Runic Poetry Translated from the Islandic Language (Percy) **95**:313, 321, 358, 360-61
"Five Scenes" (Landor) **14**:170
Five Sermons on the Errors of the Roman Catholic Church (Maturin) **169**:46, 114, 117
"A Five-O'Clock Tea" (Crawford) **12**:169-70
The Fixed Period: A Novel (Trollope) **6**:500; **101**:321; **215**:232-34, 260-61, 263-66, 277-81
"Le flacon" (Baudelaire) **6**:80, 129; **55**:61
The Flag of the Seven Upright Ones (Keller) **2**:412
Flamarande (Sand) **2**:596; **57**:316
"Le flambeau vivant" (Baudelaire) **55**:14, 59-60
Flaminio (Sand) **42**:310
"Flaskehalsen" (Andersen) **79**:69
Flaubert's Dictionary of Accepted Ideas: A Dictionary of Platitudes (Flaubert)
See *Dictionnaire des idées recues*
Flavio (Castro) **3**:106-07
"The Flea and the Professor" (Andersen)
See "Loppen og Professoren"
"The Fleece of Gold" (Gautier)
See "La chaîne d'or"
Fleeming Jenkin (Stevenson) **193**:209-10, 223
"The Fleet" (Tennyson) **30**:295; **202**:290
Fleetwood; or, The New Man of Feeling (Godwin) **14**:40, 44, 48, 50, 59-60, 68-71, 73-4, 78, 80-1, 83, 90; **130**:37, 60, 99-101, 105, 115, 122
Flegeljahre: Eine Biographie (Jean Paul) **7**:232, 234, 236, 238, 240, 242
"Flegeljahretraum" (Jean Paul) **7**:239-40
Flesh (Verlaine)
See *Chair*
"Fleur" (Banville) **9**:30
"Fleur d'art" (Corbière) **43**:27
"Les Fleurs" (Mallarmé) **41**:250
"Fleurs" (Rimbaud) **4**:484; **35**:269, 311, 322; **82**:233; **227**:203, 243
Fleurs de bonne volanté (Laforgue)
See *Des fleurs de bonne volonté*
Les fleurs du mal (Baudelaire) **6**:79-87, 89-91, 93, 100-05, 108, 110-11, 114, 116-23, 128; **29**:64-72, 75, 77-84, 86-91, 93, 95-109, 111-12; **55**:1-83; **155**:3, 10, 12, 17, 19-21, 25, 39-45, 47-48, 51-52, 65-68, 71-74, 76, 90,

94-95, 102, 104-6, 109, 113-15
Der fliegende Holländer (Liszt) **199**:298, 325
Der fliegende Holländer (Wagner) **9**:401, 403, 406, 414-17, 421, 437, 440, 446, 448, 461, 463, 469, 473; **119**:176, 189, 192, 198, 240, 274
"The Flight of Genius" (Castro Alves)
See "O Vôo do Gênio"
"The Flight of the Duchess" (Browning) **19**:77, 88, 126, 131; **79**:94, 100-01, 164
"The Flight of the Heather" (Stevenson) **5**:404
"A Flight of Wild Ducks" (Harpur) **114**:125
"The Flight of Youth" (Milnes) **61**:136, 139, 145
Flim-Flams! or, The Life and Errors of my Uncle and his Friends! With Illustrations and Obscurities by Messieurs Tag, Rag, and Bobtail: A Literary Romance (D'Israeli) **217**:292, 297, 304, 309-10
"Fling out the Flag" (Adams) **33**:12
"Flipperne" (Andersen) **79**:23, 34; **214**:59-60
"The Flitting" (Clare) **9**:97, 105; **86**:113, 141-42, 145, 169
"Floare albastra" (Eminescu) **33**:251; **131**:304, 331
"Floating Island at Hawkshead, an Incident in the Schemes of Nature" (Wordsworth) **138**:227-28, 355
"The Flood" (Clare) **9**:122
"The Flood of Years" (Bryant) **6**:168, 172, 175, 179, 182, 189, 193; **46**:21-3, 38-9
The Floods in Emmental (Gotthelf) **117**:22, 25
La flor (Castro) **3**:103-04; **78**:6, 12, 25, 28-29, 32, 37
"Flor entre flores" (Rizal) **27**:425
"Flora" (Smith) **115**:119
Flora Lyndsay; or, Passages in an Eventful Life (Moodie) **14**:217, 226, 237; **113**:295-96, 323, 325, 335, 358, 362
Floral Biography; or Chapters on Flowers (Tonna)
See *Chapters on Flowers*
The Floral Offering; A Token of Friendship (Osgood) **141**:341
Flora's Interpreter; or, The American Book of Flowers and Sentiments (Hale) **75**:349
"Flora's Party" (Sigourney) **21**:311
"Florence Gray" (Willis) **194**:305
Florence Macarthy (Morgan) **29**:389-90, 393
"A Florentine Joke" (Eliot) **4**:111
"Florentinische Nächte" (Heine) **4**:262, 267
Flores pasajeras (Manzano) **155**:277, 297, 332
Florestan (Schumann) **143**:124
"Florian und Creszenz" (Auerbach) **171**:67
Florida: Its Scenery, Climate, and History (Lanier) **6**:264; **118**:212-15, 233, 286
"A Florida Sunday" (Lanier) **118**:275
Florio: A Tale for Fine Gentlemen and Fine Ladies (More) **27**:335, 337; **141**:232
Florise (Banville) **9**:18, 22
Florville et Courval (Sade) **3**:470
"Das flotte Herz" (Muller) **73**:361
"The Flourishing Village" (Dwight) **13**:270, 272, 278-79
The Flower Alphabet in Gold and Colors (Osgood) **141**:341
"The Flower and the Gem; or, The Choice of Grace Gordon" (Osgood) **141**:353
Flower Dust (Novalis)
See *Blütenstaub*
Flower Fables (Alcott) **58**:46; **83**:4
Flower, Fruit, and Thorn Pieces; or, The Married Life, Death, and Wedding of the Advocate of the Poor Firmian Stanislaus Siebankäs (Jean Paul)
See *Blumen-, Frucht-, und Dornenstücke; oder, Ehestand Tod, und Hochzeit des Armena dvocaten Firmian Stanislaus Siebenkäs*
The Flower Garden; or Chapters on Flowers (Tonna)
See *Chapters on Flowers*
"A Flower in a Letter" (Barrett Browning) **1**:117
"Flower in the Crannied Wall" (Tennyson) **30**:222, 280; **202**:276
"A Flower (in Time of War)" (Allingham) **25**:11
"Flower Life" (Timrod) **25**:362, 367
"A Flower of the Snow" (Woolson) **82**:272, 334
Flower Pieces and Other Poems (Allingham) **25**:14
"The Flower Sower" (Cooke) **110**:9
"The Flower That Smiles Today" (Shelley) **93**:303
Flower-De-Luce (Longfellow) **45**:138
"The Flowers" (Crabbe) **26**:138-39
"Flowers" (Longfellow) **45**:129
"Flowers" (Rimbaud)
See "Fleurs"
Flowers (Novalis)
See *Blumen*
"Flowers at Dusk" (Ichiyō)
See "Yamizakura"
Flowers for Children (Child) **73**:61, 66
"Flowers for the Dead" (Adams) **33**:13
"The Flower's Name" (Browning) **79**:94, 99
The Flowers of Evil (Baudelaire)
See *Les fleurs du mal*
Flowers of Exile (Martí) **63**:109
"The Flowers To Come" (Webster) **230**:314
"The Flowery Alchemist" (Beddoes) **154**:78
"The Flowing Tide" (Webster) **230**:310
"Fluctuations" (Brontë) **4**:45, 50; **71**:91
"Die Flüsse" (Schiller) **39**:388
"La flûte" (Vigny) **7**:472-73, 482-83; **102**:336, 339
Flute Player (Augier)
See *Joueur de flûte*
"Flute-Music" (Browning) **19**:153
"FLux et reflux" (Hugo) **161**:179
"The Fly" (Adams) **175**:29, 32
"The Fly" (Blake) **13**:220, 229, 241-42, 247; **37**:4, 12, 43, 50-1, 93
"The Fly and the Bee" (Krylov) **1**:435
"The Fly and the Bullock" (Moore) **110**:172
The Flying Dutchman (Wagner)
See *Der fliegende Holländer*
The Flying Scud (Boucicault) **41**:28
"The Flying Tailor: Being a Further Extract from the Recluse" (Hogg) **4**:282, 284; **109**:247
"The Flying Trunk" (Andersen)
See "Den Flyvende Kuffert"
"Den Flyvende Kuffert" (Andersen) **7**:24; **79**:23, 26, 30, 73, 75-76, 82; **214**:40, 72-73, 77
Fodrejse fra Holmens Canal til Østpynten of Amager (Andersen) **79**:79-80, 86; **214**:39-40, 62, 73
"Fog" (Dacre) **151**:148
"Fog" (Lazarus) **8**:420; **109**:297
"A Foggy Night" (Haliburton) **149**:349
The Foggy Night at Offord (Wood) **178**:291
"La foi" (Lamartine) **11**:245, 269, 282; **190**:264
"Föl a szentháborúra" (Petofi) **21**:286
"Foliage" (Hunt) **1**:411; **70**:263, 283, 293
Folk Songs (Herder)
See *Volkslieder*
The Folk Tribunal (Sacher-Masoch) **31**:287
"The Folk-Mote by the River" (Morris) **4**:423
Follas novas (Castro) **3**:100-01, 104-05, 107; **78**:2-9, 29-30, 32-33, 38, 40-41, 54
Folle (Staël-Holstein) **91**:360
"Follen" (Whittier) **8**:486, 491
The Follies of a Day (Holcroft)
See *The Follies of a Day; or, The Marriage of Figaro*
The Follies of a Day; or, The Marriage of Figaro (Holcroft) **85**:192, 195, 209, 234
The Follies of Marianne (Musset)
See *Les caprices de Marianne*
"The Folly of Atheism" (Darwin) **106**:185-86
"Föltámadott a tenger" (Petofi) **21**:286
"Du fond du grabat . . ." (Verlaine) **230**:167, 171
La Fondateur de la Société positiviste a quiconque désire s'y incorporer (Comte) **54**:210
"La Fontaine and de La Rochefoucault" (Landor) **14**:165
"La fontaine aux lianes" (Leconte de Lisle) **29**:212, 217, 221, 234, 245
"La fontaine de sang" (Baudelaire) **55**:27, 74, 77
"Fontan" (Tyutchev) **34**:397-98, 400
"Fonthill Abbey" (Hazlitt) **82**:154, 159
Foolish Steve (Arany)
See *Boland Istók*
The Fool's Tragedy (Beddoes)
See *Death's Jest Book; or, The Fool's Tragedy*
The Foot Journey to Amager (Andersen)
See *Fodrejse*
A Footnote to History (Stevenson) **193**:250
"Footpaths" (Jefferies) **47**:134
Foot-prints of the Creator; or The Asterolepis of Stromness (Miller) **143**:3, 6, 17, 29, 33, 42, 44
"Footsteps" (Coutinho)
See "Stapfen"
"The Footsteps of Angels" (Longfellow) **2**:479, 493; **45**:132, 155
"For a Venetian Pastoral by Giorgione" (Rossetti) **4**:499
"For an Album" (Clarke) **19**:233
"For an Urn in Thoresby Park" (Landor) **14**:200
"For Annie" (Poe) **1**:509; **117**:211-12, 227, 237-38, 242-43, 281, 283, 309
"For E . . ." (Verlaine)
See "Pour E . . ."
"For Each" (Rossetti) **186**:302
"For Each and For All" (Martineau) **26**:351
"For Exmoor" (Ingelow) **39**:264
For Love and Life (Oliphant) **61**:204
For Love; or, The Two Heroes (Robertson) **35**:333, 335, 356, 369
"For Me" (Lampman)
See "Ambition"
"For our Happiness" (Grillparzer)
See "Für unser Glück"
For Self-Examination (Kierkegaard) **34**:224-25, 261, 266; **78**:238
"For the Book of Love" (Laforgue)
See "Pour le livre d'amour"
"For the Dear Old Flag I'll Die" (Foster) **26**:288
For the Honor of God (Sacher-Masoch) **31**:294
"For the Jews" (Börne)
See "Für die Juden"
For the Major (Woolson) **82**:269-70, 273-74, 278, 293, 297-99, 315-16
"For the Monument of the Rev. W. Mason" (Darwin) **106**:182
"For the Penny-Wise" (Tennyson) **30**:294
"For the Power to whom we bow" (Fuller) **50**:249, 251
For the Term of His Natural Life (Clarke)
See *His Natural Life*
"For Though the Caves Were Rabitted" (Thoreau) **7**:384
"For You O Democracy" (Whitman) **31**:430; **81**:328; **205**:158
The Forayers; or, The Raid of the Dog-Days (Simms) **3**:507-09, 513
"Forbidden Fruit" (Dickinson) **171**:190
Force and Freedom (Burckhardt)
See *Weltgeschichtliche Bertrachtungen*
The Force of Fashion (Mackenzie)
See *False Shame, or The White Hypocrite*
The Force of Ridicule (Holcroft) **85**:198, 223
"The Forces" (Winthrop) **210**:277
"Foreboding" (Pushkin) **83**:257
Forebodings and the Present (Eichendorff)
See *Ahnung und Gegenwart*
Forefathers' Eve (Mickiewicz)
See *Dziady III*
"Foreign Influence" (Madison) **126**:326
"Forerunners" (Emerson) **1**:296

The Forest (Ostrovsky)
See *Les*
Forest (Radcliffe)
See *The Romance of the Forest*
Forest and Game Law Tales (Martineau) **26**:311; **137**:250
"The Forest Hymn" (Bryant) **6**:159, 164-65, 168-72, 177, 187, 192-93; **46**:6, 8, 16, 20, 23, 25, 28, 41, 43, 47, 55
Forest Life (Kirkland) **85**:260-61, 263-65, 270, 282-86, 298, 301
The Forest Minstrel: A Selection of Songs, Adapted to the Most Favourite Scottish Airs (Hogg) **4**:274, 281
"Forest Moods" (Lampman) **194**:56, 79, 82, 84
"Forest, Oh My Forest" (Eminescu) **33**:247
"A Forest Path in Winter" (Lampman) **25**:209; **194**:13
"Forest Pictures" (Hayne) **94**:144, 149, 165
"The Forest Pool" (Eminescu) **131**:293
"Forest Quiet (In the South)" (Hayne) **94**:166
The Forest Rover (Bird) **197**:29
"The Forest Sanctuary" (Hemans) **71**:261, 268-69
The Forest Sanctuary, and Other Poems (Hemans) **29**:196-97, 199, 201-02, 205, 207; **71**:274, 284, 305, 307
Forest Scenes (Schumann)
See *Waldszenen*
The Forest Wanderer (Stifter)
See "Der Waldgänger"
The Forest Warden (Ludwig)
See *Die Erbförster*
"Forest, Why D'You Swing So Low?" (Eminescu)
See "Ce te legeni codrule"
"The Forester" (Bloomfield) **145**:158
"Forester" (Edgeworth) **51**:84-90, 135
The Foresters (Wilson) **5**:549, 558, 561, 567, 569
The Forester's Letters (Paine) **62**:270
The Foresters—Robin Hood and Maid Marian (Tennyson) **30**:265
"La forêt" (Banville) **9**:30
"La forêt vierge" (Leconte de Lisle) **29**:216-17, 231
"Forever at His side to walk-" (Dickinson) **77**:65
"Le forgeron" (Rimbaud) **4**:465; **82**:238; **227**:208
"The Forger's Bride" (Cooke) **110**:36-7
"Forget and Forgive" (Edgeworth) **1**:265
"Forget-me Not" (Rossetti) **186**:270
"Forget-Me-Not Song" (Crawford) **127**:150-52
"The Forging of the Anchor" (Ferguson) **33**:287
"The Forgiven Dead" (Ridge) **82**:182
"A Forgiveness" (Browning) **19**:88; **79**:157
"Forgotten Arietta" (Verlaine)
See "Ariettes oubliées"
"The Forgotten Village" (Nekrasov) **11**:409
"The Forgotten Wedding Day" (Mangan) **27**:275
"The Formation of Coal" (Huxley) **67**:83
"A Former Life" (Baudelaire)
See "La Vie antérieure"
Formerly and Not So Long Ago (Verlaine)
See *Jadis et naguère*
Formosa (Boucicault) **41**:31
"The Forms of Nature and the Unity of Their Origin" (Very) **9**:386-87
Forord (Kierkegaard) **125**:231, 260
"The Forsaken" (Turgenev) **21**:401
"Forsaken" (Webster) **230**:245
"Forsaken Child" (Norton) **47**:246
"The Forsaken Girl" (Mörike) **10**:446
"The Forsaken Home" (Tonna) **135**:194, 198-99, 209, 213-16, 220-22
"The Forsaken Maiden" (Mörike)
See "Das verlassene Mägdlein"
"The Forsaken Merman" (Arnold) **6**:37, 44, 54, 66; **29**:35; **89**:6; **218**:122, 138-39, 188, 190
Fort comme la mort (Maupassant) **1**:446, 450, 459, 464, 467, 470; **42**:169; **83**:175, 180-82
"Fortepjan Szopena" (Norwid) **17**:367, 372
La forteresse du Danube (Pixérécourt) **39**:277, 279, 281, 286
"The Forthcoming Early Life of Sut Lovingood, by His Dad" (Harris) **165**:169
Fortnight in the Wilderness (Tocqueville) **7**:424
Fortunat (Tieck) **5**:514, 525
The Fortunate Beggars (Gozzi)
See *I pitocchi fortunati*
"The Fortunate Fisher-maiden" (Muller)
See "Die Glückliche Fischerin"
"Fortune and the Begger" (Krylov) **1**:435
The Fortune Hunter; or the Adventurers of a Man about Town (Mowatt) **74**:210-11, 228, 230
Fortune; or, The Art of Success (Jefferies) **47**:121
"The Fortune Teller" (Robinson) **142**:138
The Fortunes of Colonel Torlogh O'Brien (Le Fanu) **9**:309
The Fortunes of Glencore (Lever) **23**:286, 292, 301
The Fortunes of Nigel (Scott) **15**:306, 309; **69**:304-05, 308, 313; **110**:264; **209**:216-17, 297-98, 302-3
The Fortunes of Perkin Warbeck (Shelley) **14**:255-56, 262, 265, 267, 270-71; **59**:144, 190, 192; **103**:342, 347
"The Fortunes of Sir Robert Ardagh" (Le Fanu) **9**:322; **58**:253, 263
"Fortunio" (Hayne) **94**:156
Fortunio (Gautier) **1**:346-47, 349-50, 352; **59**:5, 7, 12, 30
Fortunio and his Seven Gifted Servants (Planché) **42**:273, 280, 292, 295
49 (Dickinson) **77**:80, 184
The Forty-Five Guardsmen (Dumas)
See *Les quarante-cinq*
"The Foster Mother's Tale" (Wordsworth) **111**:358
"The Foster-Child: In Imitation of Spenser" (Robinson) **142**:151, 177, 180-81
"The Fostering of Aslaug" (Morris) **4**:447
The Fosterling (Fredro)
See *Wychowanka*
"The Foster-Mother's Tale" (Coleridge) **9**:131
"Le fou" (Bertrand) **31**:46-8
"Un fou" (Maupassant) **1**:449; **83**:176, 181
"Le fou et la Vénus" (Baudelaire) **155**:23-25, 46
Foul Play (Reade) **2**:540-41, 547-48, 551; **74**:248, 258, 263-65, 284, 318
"Les foules" (Baudelaire) **29**:111; **55**:40; **155**:23, 38-40, 56, 105, 107
"Les Foules" (Maupassant) **83**:188
"Found" (Rossetti) **4**:508
The Found Remains (Solomos)
See *Ta euriskomena*
Foundations (Kant) **27**:220, 243; **67**:259-60, 262-63, 265
The Foundations of a Creed (Lewes)
See *The Problems of Life and Mind*
The Foundations of European Discontent (Almqvist)
See *Europeiska missnöjets grunder*
Foundations of Natural Right According to the Principles of Wissenschaftslehre (Fichte)
See *Grundlage des Naturrechts nach Prinzipen der Wissenshaftslehre*
Foundations of the entire Wissenschaftslehre (Fichte)
See *Grundlage der gesamten Wissenschaftslehre*
"The Foundling" (Kleist)
See "Der Findling"
"The Fountain" (Bryant) **6**:168, 188, 191; **46**:26, 39
"The Fountain" (Lowell) **2**:507
"The Fountain" (Tyutchev)
See "Fontan"
"The Fountain" (Wordsworth) **12**:427, 450; **111**:326
The Fountain of Bahchisard (Pushkin)
See *Bakhchisaraiski Fontan*
"The Fountain of Blood" (Baudelaire)
See "La fontaine de sang"
"The Fountain of Oblivion" (Hemans) **71**:304
The Fountain of Youth (Sacher-Masoch) **31**:298, 301
Fountainville Abbey (Dunlap) **2**:212-13
4 (Dickinson) **77**:120
"Four Beasts in One; or, The Homo-Cameleopard" (Poe) **16**:324
"The Four Bridges" (Ingelow) **107**:122
"Four Charades" (Cranch) **115**:58
"Four Charades" (Rossetti) **66**:341
"Four Ducks on a Pond" (Allingham) **25**:20
The Four Georges (Thackeray) **5**:490; **14**:438, 451; **14**:451; **213**:284, 300, 305, 319-20
481 (Dickinson) **77**:173
486 (Dickinson) **77**:131
458 (Dickinson) **77**:139
452 (Dickinson) **77**:152
449 (Dickinson)
See "I died for beauty, but was scarce"
441 (Dickinson) **77**:71, 110, 112
443 (Dickinson) **77**:103
414 (Dickinson) **77**:114
497 (Dickinson) **77**:82
493 (Dickinson) **77**:64
401 (Dickinson) **77**:180
416 (Dickinson) **77**:110, 112
461 (Dickinson) **77**:145
413 (Cantor) **77**:80
430 (Dickinson) **77**:92, 132-34, 139
429 (Dickinson) **77**:93
Four Letters (Paine) **62**:369, 371
Four Letters on the English Constitution (Dyer) **129**:106, 110, 132, 137
Four Old Plays. Three Interludes: Thersytes,Jack Jugler, and Heywood's Pardoner and Frere: and Jocaste, a Tragedy by Gascoigne and Kinwelmarsh (Child) **173**:167, 198, 207-8, 225
"The Four Ox-Cart" (Petofi)
See "A négy ökrös szekér"
Four Stories High (Clarke) **19**:251
"Four to Four" (Hugo) **10**:361
The Four Zoas: The Torments of Love and Jealousy in the Death and Judgement of Albion the Ancient Man (Blake) **13**:173, 177, 183-85, 192-93, 195, 197, 199, 205, 208-10, 213, 220-21, 224-26, 228-29, 231, 233-38, 244; **37**:24-5, 27, 35, 64, 77; **57**:29, 46, 48, 63, 82; **127**:15, 17-18, 24, 29, 50, 53, 57, 67, 87, 89, 93, 97, 124, 132, 134; **173**:10-11, 13-15, 37, 41, 56-58, 61-62, 65, 74, 79-80, 86, 96-97, 111-12, 138; **190**:1-164; **201**:22, 55, 73, 125
Les Fourberies de Nérine (Banville) **9**:20, 22
Les Fourchambault (Augier) **31**:2-3, 8-10, 13, 16, 26, 28, 31, 34
"Fourierism" (Peabody) **169**:146
14 (Dickinson) **77**:149
"1492" (Lazarus) **8**:422, 427; **109**:335-36
1481 (Dickinson) **77**:125
1452 (Dickinson) **77**:92
1445 (Dickinson) **77**:96, 163, 173
1461 (Dickinson) **77**:82
1463 (Dickinson) **77**:95, 118, 121
Fourteen Sonnets, written chiefly on Picturesque Spots during a Journey, 1789 (Bowles) **103**:56, 65, 78, 85-7, 93-4
The Fourteen-Book Prelude (Wordsworth) **206**:283-87, 290-91, 293
"Fourth Epistle" (Eminescu)
See "Epistle IV"
"Fourth Letter" (Schiller) **166**:106
"Fourth of July Ode" (Emerson) **1**:284
"A Fourth of July Oration" (Garrison) **149**:256
"Fourth Sunday after Advent" (Keble) **87**:173

"The Fourth Sunday after Trinity" (Keble) **87**:202
"Fourth Sunday in Advent" (Keble) **87**:160, 173-74
Fourth Symphony (Beethoven) **227**:9
"The Fox and the Bird" (Very) **9**:385
"The Fox and the Marmot" (Krylov) **1**:435
"The Fox and the Wolf" (Krasicki)
See "Lis i wilk"
"The Fox Hunt" (Longstreet) **159**:123, 125, 136, 144, 146-47, 161, 176, 185
"The Fox-Hunters" (Irving) **2**:369
Fra Diavolo; ou, L'hôtellerie de Terraine (Scribe) **16**:401
"Fra Lippo Lippi" (Browning) **19**:79, 132, 152; **79**:163, 171
"Fra Pedro" (Heine) **147**:152
"Fra Pedro" (Lazarus) **8**:425; **109**:324
Fra Rupert (Landor) **14**:165
Fragen zu Denkübungen für Wilhelmine (Kleist) **37**:219
"Fragmen" (Heine) **147**:173
"Fragment" (Allston) **2**:26
"A Fragment" (Baratynsky)
See "Otryvok"
"A Fragment" (Beddoes) **154**:53, 77-78
"A Fragment" (Bryant)
See "Inscription for the Entrance into a Wood"
"Fragment" (Clare) **86**:114-15, 166-67
"A Fragment" (Crawford) **127**:217
"Fragment" (Dickens)
See "Autobiographical Fragment"
"A Fragment" (Gilpin) **30**:40
"A Fragment" (Gogol) **162**:19
"A Fragment" (Pushkin) **83**:320
A Fragment (Keats)
See *Hyperion*
"Fragment 42" (Novalis) **178**:60
"Fragment 48" (Novalis) **178**:60
"Fragment 206" (Novalis) **178**:99
"Fragment 601" (Novalis) **178**:118
"Fragment 603" (Novalis) **178**:117-18
Fragment d'histoire (Hugo) **161**:186
"A Fragment for a System" (Schelling) **30**:155-56
"A Fragment from Fourier on Trade" (Marx) **114**:57
"Fragment: Notes for a Lecture" (Lincoln) **18**:240
"Fragment: Notes for Law Lecture—July 1, 1850" (Lincoln) **18**:240
Fragment of 1790 (Goethe)
See *Faust: Ein Fragment*
"Fragment of a Journal. To G.M. Esq" (Moore) **110**:178
"Fragment of a Mythological Hymn to Love" (Moore) **110**:178-80
"Fragment of an 'Antigone'" (Arnold) **29**:34-5
"Fragment of an Epistle" (Dana) **53**:158
"A fragment of anything you like" (Hopkins) **189**:120
"A Fragment of Bion" (Freneau) **111**:141
A Fragment on Government (Bentham) **38**:37, 44, 49, 58, 84, 88-9, 93
"A Fragment on Ontology" (Bentham) **38**:92-5
"Fragment on Religious Ideas" (Hölderlin) **16**:166-68, 171
Fragment on the Church (Arnold) **18**:24
Fragment von Hyperion (Hölderlin) **187**:198
Fragmentarium (Eminescu) **33**:255-57
Fragmente (Herder)
See *Über die neuere deutsche Litteratur. Fragmente*
Fragmente (Novalis) **178**:73, 81
Fragmente über die neuere deutsche Literatur (Herder) **8**:299, 303, 305-07, 309, 313-15
Fragmente uber Recensenten-Unfug (Kotzebue) **25**:152
Fragmente und Studien 1799-1800 (Novalis) **178**:24, 27
Fragmented einer Abhandlung über die Ode (Herder) **186**:36
Fragmentos (Martí) **63**:124
"Fragmentos descriptivos de un poema mexicano" (Heredia) **209**:160, 167
Fragments (Martí)
See *Fragmentos*
Fragments d'un journal intime (Amiel) **4**:12-15, 17, 19-21
Fragments d'un ouvrage abandonné sur la possibilité d'une constitution républicaine dans un grand pays (Constant) **182**:211, 228, 235
"Fragments from a Writing Desk" (Melville) **123**:175, 251
Fragments historiques et géographiques sur la Scythie, la Sarmatie et les Slaves (Potocki) **229**:274, 295
Fragments of a Roman Tale (Macaulay) **42**:154
"Fragments of an Unfinished Story" (Osgood) **141**:333, 354-55
Fragments of Philosophy (Kierkegaard)
See *Philosophiske Smuler*
Fragments on the New German Literature (Herder)
See *Fragmente über die neuere deutsche Literatur*
"Fragments on Universal Grammar" (Bentham) **38**:92
Fragments Relating to Language and Poetry (Klopstock)
See *Über Sprach und Dichtkunst*
"Fragments Upon the Nymphs" (Hunt) **70**:248
"Le frais matin dorait" (Leconte de Lisle) **29**:224
Framley Parsonage (Trollope) **6**:455, 464, 467, 470, 491, 499-502, 516-17; **33**:363, 365; **101**:234-35, 266, 273, 319, 321, 333; **215**:202-5, 209, 283, 286-87, 307
Les Français peints par euxmêmes (Balzac) **153**:147
"France" (Dutt) **29**:128
"France" (Whitman) **4**:544
France (Morgan) **29**:386
"France: An Ode" (Coleridge)
See "Ode to France"
France and England in North America (Parkman) **12**:336, 351-52, 359, 365, 369, 371-77
"France and Spain" (Browning) **79**:94, 99
France before the Eyes of Europe (Michelet) **31**:219, 258
France depuis vingt-cinq ans (Gautier) **1**:349
Francesca Carrara (Landon) **15**:158-59, 161, 164
Francesca da Rimini (Boker) **125**:20, 22-25, 28-29, 31-34, 36-38, 41-43, 45, 48-50, 52, 55-56, 58, 66-67, 70-72, 75-77
Franchise et trahison (Sade) **47**:361
Francia (Sand) **57**:316
Francillon (Dumas) **9**:228, 231, 235, 243, 246, 249-50
Francis of Assisi (Oliphant) **11**:433, 445; **221**:227, 233
Francis the First (Kemble) **18**:160-62, 164, 167, 178
"Franciscae meae laudes" (Baudelaire) **55**:61
François le Champi (Sand) **42**:309, 323-24, 326-28, 338, 340, 365, 366-68, 374; **57**:317, 338, 358, 365-6, 368
Frank, A Tale (Edgeworth) **1**:262; **51**:78, 81-2
Frank and Fearless; or, The Fortunes of Jasper Kent (Alger) **8**:24, 45
"The Frank Courtship" (Crabbe) **26**:93, 116, 129, 131, 135, 147; **121**:65-7, 69, 71-2, 77
Frankenstein; or, The Modern Prometheus (Shelley) **14**:247-56, 258-72, 274-77, 279-81, 283-90, 292-93, 295-307; **59**:138-251; **103**:322, 329-31, 338, 349, 358, 360, 363-66; **170**:198-378
"Frankfurter Plan" (Hölderlin) **187**:190-92, 241
"Franklin" (Landor) **14**:166
Franklin Evans (Whitman) **4**:582-83; **81**:327, 343, 347
Franklin Evans; or, The Inebriate (Whitman) **205**:236, 321
Frank's Campaign; or, What Boys Can Do on the Farm for the Camp (Alger) **8**:40; **83**:104, 139, 144
"Frank's Sealed Letter" (Morris) **4**:430
Franz Sternbald's Travels (Tieck)
See *Franz Sternbalds Wanderungen*
Franz Sternbalds Wanderungen (Tieck) **5**:521, 525, 527-28, 531; **46**:375-76, 393, 395-98, 401, 405
Französische Maler (Heine) **4**:259, 264; **54**:339; **147**:220
Französische Zustände (Heine) **4**:246; **147**:141, 215, 220, 230, 232
Frascati's; or, Scenes in Paris (Richardson) **55**:329, 350
"Fraser Papers" (Maginn) **8**:435, 437
Fratricide (Macha) **46**:202
"Der Frau Generalin von Varnbüler" (Mörike) **201**:272
Frau Jenny Treibel (Fontane) **26**:235-36, 239-40, 245, 252, 257, 270-72, 278; **163**:197, 218, 225, 230
"Die Frau Pfarrerin" (Gotthelf) **117**:44, 51
"Die Frau Professorin" (Auerbach) **171**:9, 69
"Frau Rebekka mit den Kindern, an einem Maimorgen" (Claudius) **75**:190
Frau Regel Amrain und ihr Jüngster (Keller) **2**:415
"Frau Susanne" (Goethe) **4**:189
Frau von Saverne (Arnim) **159**:95
Frauenliebe und Leben (Chamisso) **82**:3
"Das Fräulein von Scudéri" (Hoffmann) **183**:195-97, 199, 216-17, 219, 225-26, 249
Die Fräulein von Scuderi (Ludwig) **4**:349, 351
"The Freak of a Genius" (Alcott) **218**:54-57, 59
"Frederic" (Southey) **97**:314
"Frederic and Elfrida" (Austen) **1**:67; **119**:13
Frédéric Chopin (Liszt)
See *Chopin*
Frederick (Macaulay) **42**:87
"Frederick and Catherine" (Grimm Brothers) **3**:227
The Frederick Douglass Papers (Douglass) **141**:75
Frederick Engels on Russia (Engels) **85**:9
Fredolfo (Maturin) **6**:322-23, 332, 343-44, 347; **169**:119
"The Free Besieged" (Solomos)
See "Oi eleftheroi poliorkimenoi"
"Free C." (Isaacs)
See "Columbia libre"
Free Labour (Reade) **2**:551
"Free Strophes" (Isaacs)
See "Estrofas libres"
Free Thoughts on Public Affairs (Hazlitt) **29**:169
Freedmen's Book (Child) **73**:63, 71, 84
"Freedom" (Derzhavin) **215**:15-16
"Freedom" (Emerson) **98**:182-83
"Freedom" (Lampman) **25**:182, 188, 192, 198, 217, 219; **194**:8, 18, 31, 33, 58, 62-63, 74, 93
"Freedom" (Lowell) **90**:215
"Freedom" (Radishchev) **190**:313-14
"Freedom" (Tennyson) **65**:285
Freedom Comes to Krähwinkel (Nestroy)
See *Freiheit in Krähwinkel*
"The Freedom of Poland" (Beddoes) **154**:73
"Freedom of the Press" (Whittier) **59**:364
"Freedom Wheeler's Controversy" (Cooke)
See "Freedom Wheeler's Controversy with Providence"
"Freedom Wheeler's Controversy with Providence" (Cooke) **110**:10, 14, 20, 24-5, 28, 34, 44, 46, 48, 50, 57, 65, 68
"Freedon Wheeler's Controversy with God" (Cooke)
See "Freedom Wheeler's Controversy with Providence"

"The Freeholder Ovsyanikov" (Turgenev) **21**:377; **122**:294
Fregat Nadezhda (Bestuzhev) **131**:154-55, 168, 175-76, 187, 210
"La frégate 'La Sérieuse'" (Vigny) **7**:473, 485; **102**:368
Freias Pris (Grundtvig) **158**:138
"Freigeisterei der Leidenschaft" (Schiller) **39**:387
Freiheit in Krähwinkel (Nestroy) **42**:233, 235, 237, 244, 249, 252-53, 263-64, 266
Der Freiheitskrieg (Klopstock) **225**:300
Freis Kærlighed (Grundtvig) **158**:137
"Der Freischütz" (Wagner) **119**:190
"Das Fremde Kind" (Hoffmann) **2**:351; **183**:171, 199
"Fremont's Ride" (Cooke) **110**:9
French Affairs (Heine)
See *Französische Zustände*
French Affairs: Letters from Paris (Heine)
See *Französische Zustände*
"French and English Manners" (De Quincey) **198**:93-95
French and Italian Notebooks (Hawthorne)
See *Passages from the French and Italian Notebooks of Nathaniel Hawthorne*
"A French Critic on Goethe" (Arnold) **6**:45; **218**:225
"A French Critic on Gray" (Arnold) **6**:58
"A French Critic on Heine" (Arnold) **6**:58
"A French Critic on Keats" (Arnold) **6**:58
"A French Critic on Milton" (Arnold) **6**:45, 58; **218**:195, 225
"A French Critic on Shelley" (Arnold) **6**:58
"The French Drama: Racine and Victor Hugo" (Lewes) **25**:285
"A French Eton" (Arnold) **89**:102
A French Eton, or middle-class education and the state (Arnold) **126**:3, 6, 12
A French Grammar (Cobbett) **49**:160
"French Life" (Gaskell) **70**:186, 188-89
"The French Mariner" (Bloomfield) **145**:129-30, 154
"French Novelists of the Day" (Fuller) **211**:137
The French Philosophers of the Nineteenth Century (Taine)
See *Les philosophes Français du XIXme siècle*
The French Revolution (Carlyle) **70**:12, 17, 44-45, 56-61, 70-71, 76-77, 89, 98, 105, 107-108, 111
French Revolution (Michelet)
See *Histoire de la Révolution Française*
The French Revolution: A Poem in Seven Books (Blake) **13**:184, 221, 242, 251-52, 254; **37**:35; **57**:20, 57, 106; **190**:11-12, 14, 86; **201**:93
French XVIII Century Painters (Goncourt and Goncourt)
See *L'art du dix-huitème siècle*
Le frère aîné (Daudet) **1**:249
Frère Ange (Duras) **154**:112
Frère Jacques (Kock) **16**:245, 247-49, 258
Les frères invisibles (Scribe) **16**:412, 414
Les frères Zemganno (Goncourt) **7**:155-57, 162, 166-67, 170, 174-76, 183-84, 188-89
"Fresca, lozana, pura y olorosa" (Espronceda) **39**:94, 102
"Fresh from the Dewy Hill" (Blake) **13**:182; **37**:35
Fresh Leaves (Parton) **86**:337
"Freude" (Hölderlin) **16**:185
"Freude, Töchter aus Elysium" (Beethoven) **227**:36
Der Freund (Hoffmann) **2**:347; **183**:189
"Die Freunde" (Tieck) **5**:523
"Freundeswort" (Grillparzer) **102**:175
"Die Freundschaft" (Schiller) **39**:357
Freyr's Love (Grundtvig)
See *Freis Kærlighed*
"The Friar of Orders Gray" (Percy) **95**:323
"Friede auf Erden" (Meyer) **81**:155
"Der Frieden" (Hölderlin) **16**:181
Friedensblätter (Brentano)
See *Die Schachtel mit der Friedenspuppe*
"Friedensfeier" (Hölderlin) **16**:175, 192, 196; **187**:214, 217, 219, 223, 225, 272
Friedrich der Fünfte (Klopstock) **225**:297
Friedrich der Große von Schwaben (Auerbach) **171**:74-75
"Friedrich Rückert" (Taylor) **89**:325
"The Friend" (Coleridge) **9**:155, 205, 207; **54**:107; **111**:291
"A Friend" (Cranch) **115**:26
The Friend (Coleridge) **177**:101, 160; **197**:240-41, 280, 285, 311; **231**:29, 58, 82, 85, 87, 89, 123, 126, 151, 159
"Friend Brook" (Larcom) **179**:170
"A Friend in Need" (Harpur) **114**:139
"The Friend in Need" (Hood) **16**:221
The Friend of the Family (Dostoevsky) **21**:121; **33**:191, 195; **43**:92
"A Friendly Address to Mrs. Fry" (Hood) **16**:235
A Friendly Letter to the Executive Committee of the American Unitarian Association, Touching Their New Unitarian Creed or General Proclamation of Unitarian Views (Parker) **186**:148
"Friends" (Krasicki)
See "Przyjaciele"
"Friends" (Rossetti) **66**:307
"The Friends" (Tieck)
See "Die Freunde"
"The Friends of Man" (Sigourney) **21**:293
"Friendship" (Cowper) **94**:23, 117
"Friendship" (Emerson) **98**:90, 96-7, 99-101
"Friendship" (Lampman) **25**:196; **194**:36, 39
"Friendship with Nature" (Sigourney) **21**:301
Friendship's Garland: Being the Conversations, Letters, and Opinions of the Late Arminus, Baron von Thunder-Ten-Tronckh (Arnold) **6**:37, 53, 61; **89**:109; **126**:7, 42, 83, 103; **218**:121, 184, 196, 212, 215
The Frigate Hope (Bestuzhev)
See *Fregat Nadezhda*
"Frightful Ivry . . ." (Verlaine)
See "L'Affreux Ivry . . ."
Frinko Balaban (Sacher-Masoch) **31**:303
"Frische Fahrt" (Eichendorff) **225**:25, 52, 54-55, 57
"A frisky lamb" (Rossetti) **186**:235
"Frisson d'hiver" (Mallarmé) **4**:371, 373, 377; **210**:207
Frithiof's Saga (Tegner) **2**:610-14
"Froebel's Principles and Methods in the Nursery" (Peabody) **169**:150
"Frog Lesson" (Lampman)
See "Hans Fingerhut's Frog Lesson"
"The Frogs" (Lampman) **25**:161, 168, 182, 184, 200, 209; **194**:21, 47-48, 58-60, 63, 71, 74, 76, 82-84, 99, 102
"Das frohe Wandersmann" (Eichendorff) **225**:54, 58
"Der Frohsinn" (Klopstock) **225**:319-20
"Frol Silin" (Karamzin) **173**:309
"From All the Jails the Boys and Girls" (Dickinson) **21**:18
"From Bacon to Beethoven" (Lanier) **6**:245
From Canal Boy to President; or, The Boyhood and Manhood of James A. Garfield (Alger) **8**:24, 45
From Farm to Fortune (Alger) **8**:30
"From Goethe" (Lermontov) **126**:223
"From Hand to Mouth" (O'Brien) **21**:248, 250, 252-53
"From Hezekiah Salem's Last Basket" (Freneau) **111**:136
"From House to Home" (Rossetti) **2**:556, 566, 572; **66**:301, 304, 306-9, 312, 320-1, 329, 356, 382; **186**:258, 304
"From Lightning and Tempest" (Gordon) **21**:160, 165, 167, 188
"From Montauk Point" (Whitman) **31**:389
"From Moscow to Leipzig" (Dobrolyubov) **5**:140
"From My Poorman's Bed . . ." (Verlaine)
See "Du fond du grabat . . ."
"From My Window" (Warren) **226**:264
"From Noon to Starry Night" (Whitman) **205**:226
"From One of the Society of Friends to Her Kinswoman" (Haliburton) **15**:129
From Paris to Cadiz (Dumas)
See *Impressions de voyage*
"From Paumanok Starting I Fly like a Bird" (Whitman) **81**:313
"From Pent-Up Aching Rivers" (Whitman) **31**:400, 405; **81**:329; **205**:219
"From Perugia" (Whittier) **8**:493, 512; **59**:373
"From Pindemonte" (Pushkin) **83**:261
"From Roman Scenes" (Herzen) **10**:348
"From Sunset to Star Rise" (Rossetti) **66**:341, 372; **186**:262, 265
From the Annals of the Progress of Concerts and Essays on Chamber Music (Liszt) **199**:305
"From the bosom of ocean I seek thee" (Taylor) **89**:300
"From the Castle in the Air to the Little Corner of the World" (Paine) **62**:324
"From the Flats" (Lanier) **6**:255
"From the German" (Beddoes) **3**:34
"From the High Priest of Apollo" (Moore) **110**:178
"From the Italian" (Halleck) **47**:57
"From the life, that once raged here" (Tyutchev)
See "Ot zhizni toy, chto bushevala zdes"
From the Other Shore (Herzen)
See *Vom andern Ufer*
From the Papers of the Still Living (Kierkegaard)
See *Af en endnu Levendes Papirer*
"From the Sketchbook" (Jacobsen) **34**:170
"From the Upland to the Sea" (Morris) **4**:421
"From the Waves of Time" (Eminescu) **33**:246
"From the Woods" (Hayne) **94**:159-60, 165
"From the Work of Dr. Krupov on Mental Ailments in General and Their Epidemic Development in Particular" (Herzen) **10**:323, 350
"From the Wreck" (Gordon) **21**:149, 155-56, 159, 163-65, 170, 172, 176, 178, 183, 187-88
"From Yule to Yule" (Crawford) **127**:193-96
Fromont jeune et Risler aîné (Daudet) **1**:231-34, 239, 241, 248, 250-51
Fromont the Younger and Risler the Elder (Daudet)
See *Fromont jeune et Risler aîné*
"The Front Yard" (Woolson) **82**:275, 290-91, 293, 296-97, 343
The Front Yard and Other Italian Stories (Woolson) **82**:275, 283, 293, 299, 338, 341, 343
"Frontier Ballads" (Cooke) **110**:3
Die Frösche der Latona (Wieland) **177**:317
"Frost" (Dacre) **151**:148
"Frost and Flirtation" (Willis) **194**:282
"Frost at Midnight" (Coleridge) **9**:150, 158; **54**:69; **99**:2, 5, 19, 61, 73, 104-05; **111**:310; **177**:59, 120; **197**:211, 215, 243; **231**:17, 51, 78, 89, 91, 113, 119, 121, 132, 156
"The Frost Elves" (Lampman) **194**:45
"Frost in the Holidays" (Allingham) **25**:6
"The Frost Spirit" (Whittier) **59**:375
The Frozen Deep (Collins) **1**:183; **93**:38, 40
"The Frozen River" (Webster) **230**:313
"Frozen Tears" (Muller)
See "Gefror'ne Tränen"
"Fru Følss" (Jacobsen) **34**:158, 160, 171
Fru Marie Grubbe: Interieurer fra det syttende Asrhundreded (Jacobsen) **34**:140-44, 151-60, 162, 164, 167, 169

The Frugal Housewife (Child)
See *The American Frugal Housewife*
"Früh im Wagen" (Mörike) **201**:272, 281
"Die frühen Gräber" (Klopstock) **11**:236, 240; **225**:298
"Frühling" (Mörike) **201**:286
"Frühlingseinzug" (Muller) **73**:366
"Die Frühlingsfeyer" (Klopstock) **225**:285-86, 307-9, 330
Der Frühlingskranz (Arnim)
See *Clemens Brentanos Frühlingskranz aus Jugendbriefen ihm geflochten, wie er selbst schriftlich verlangte*
"Frühlingskranz aus dem Plauenschen Grunde bei Dresden" (Muller) **73**:366, 373, 380
"Frühlingslieder aus dem Plauenscen Grunde" (Muller) **73**:366
"Das Frühlingsmahl" (Muller) **73**:366
"Frühlingsschrei eines Knechtes aus der Tiefe" (Brentano) **1**:102, 105; **191**:18, 20-23, 30, 37, 60-61, 63, 65-68, 70-72
"Frühlingstraum" (Muller) **73**:366, 391-92, 397
Le Fruit Défendu (Feuillet) **45**:79, 89
"Fruit of Travel Long Ago" (Melville) **3**:351
Les Fruits secs (Flaubert) **179**:22, 121
"Frustrating a Funeral" (Harris) **23**:156, 159-60; **165**:229, 242-43, 254, 262, 267-68, 277, 279-80, 287, 293-95
Frygt og Baeven (Kierkegaard) **34**:201, 223, 227, 239, 241, 246-47, 259, 260, 262, 263-66; **78**:119, 147, 154, 157-66, 168-69, 173, 178-82, 197, 238, 242, 244, 252; **125**:177, 201, 213, 233, 236, 238
The Fudge Family (Moore) **110**:190
The Fudge Family in England (Moore) **110**:172
The Fudge Family in Paris (Moore) **6**:384, 388, 395; **110**:173, 188
"The Fugitive" (Robinson) **142**:137, 150, 249-50
Fugitive Pieces (Willis)
See *Fugitive Poetry*
Fugitive Poetry (Willis) **194**:300, 304
Fugitive Verses (Baillie) **2**:41-42; **151**:41, 43, 46, 87, 91, 122
The Fugitives (Kivi)
See *Karkurit*
Führer durch die Beethoven Zentenar-Austellung der Stadt Wien (Beethoven) **227**:30
"Fuillet's La Morte" (Pater) **90**:326
"Full of Life Now" (Whitman) **205**:220, 279
A Full Vindication of the Measures of Congress (Hamilton) **49**:293, 296, 325
"Fülle" (Meyer) **81**:155, 169, 208
"Function of Conscience in Relation to the Laws of Men" (Parker) **186**:133
"The Function of Criticism at the Present Time" (Arnold) **6**:34, 47, 57, 69; **29**:9, 38-44, 48, 51, 55-6; 139; **89**:30, 33-4, 38-9, 62, 72, 76, 81-2, 85-6, 101, 109; **126**:6, 38, 52, 73, 78, 83, 88, 94, 114, 122; **218**:111, 171-72, 178, 195, 209, 211, 215, 224, 240
"The Function of the Poet" (Lowell) **2**:521
Fundamental Principles (Kant)
See *Grundlegung*
"Der Fundator" (Droste-Hülshoff) **3**:200
"De fundersamme" (Almqvist) **42**:19
Funérailles (Liszt) **199**:307
"Funeral" (Arnold) **6**:67
"The Funeral" (Nekrasov) **11**:409
"A Funeral" (Rogers) **69**:81
"The Funeral and Party Fight" (Carleton) **3**:92
"The Funeral at Sea" (Sigourney) **21**:293
"Funeral Feast" (Shevchenko)
See "Tryzna"
"Funeral March for the Earth's Death" (Laforgue)
See "Marche funèbre pour la mort de la terre"
"Funeral of Dr. Mason F. Cogswell" (Sigourney) **87**:337
"Funeral of Louis XVII" (Hugo) **3**:234
"Funeral Song for the Princess Charlotte of Wales" (Southey) **8**:474
Fünf Lieder (Schumann) **143**:140
Der funfzehnte November (Tieck) **46**:412-14
"Für die Juden" (Börne) **193**:21-22, 27
"Für die Mouche" (Heine) **4**:247, 269
Für meine Söhne (Storm) **195**:15, 21
"Für unser Glück" (Grillparzer) **102**:175
El Fureidis (Cummins) **139**:165-66, 185, 194-96
"Furlow College Address" (Lanier) **118**:230
Fürst Ganzgott und Sänger Halbgott (Arnim) **159**:35, 96
"Fürst Ganzgott und Sänger Halbogott" (Arnim) **5**:13, 18
Further Exhibitions from the System of Philosophy (Schelling)
See *Fernere Darstellungen*
"Further in Summer Than the Birds" (Dickinson) **21**:19, 59, 67-9; **77**:95
Further Letters of Gerard Manley Hopkins (Hopkins) **189**:45, 47, 50-51, 64, 97-98, 106, 113, 120, 131, 133-36
Further Notes of a Young Man (Herzen) **61**:108
Further Records: 1848-1883 (Kemble) **18**:189-90
"Fusées" (Baudelaire) **29**:71, 98; **55**:8, 11, 40, 43, 45-46; **155**:40
"Die Füsse im Feuer" (Meyer) **81**:207
"Les fussillés" (Hugo) **161**:179
"Fussreise" (Mörike) **10**:448
"The Fust Baby" (Shaw) **15**:335
"Fut-il jamais douceur de coeur pareille" (Musset) **7**:275
"Futura" (Silva) **114**:316
Futura (Silva) **114**:262
"The Future" (Arnold) **218**:120, 158
"Future" (Silva)
See *Futura*
The Future Australian Race (Clarke) **19**:236
"The Future Glory of America" (Trumbull) **30**:349-50
"The Future Home" (Macha) **46**:202
"The Future Life" (Bryant) **6**:168
"The Future of German Philosophy" (Eliot) **199**:131
"The Future of Liberalism" (Arnold) **89**:111
"The Future of Protestantism and Catholicity" (Brownson) **50**:54
The Future of Science (Renan)
See *L'avenir de la science*
"Fyrtøiet" (Andersen) **7**:21, 26, 34; **79**:23, 49-50, 52, 58-59, 64-65, 68, 76, 80-81; **214**:4, 9, 48, 53-54, 59, 61, 76
G Major Violin Sonata, op. 96 (Beethoven)
See *Violin Sonata in G Major, op. 96*
"Gaaseurten" (Andersen) **214**:40, 55
Gabriel (Sand) **2**:587; **42**:359; **57**:312
Gabriel Lambert (Dumas) **71**:194, 204
Gabrièle Mimanso (Almqvist) **42**:5
"The Gabrieliad" (Pushkin) **83**:332
Gabrielle (Augier) **31**:4-5, 7, 9-11, 14, 18-19, 23-4, 29
Gabrielle de Belle-Isle (Dumas)
See *Mademoiselle de Belle-Isle*
"Gadki" (Norwid) **17**:373
"The Gagging Bill" (Kendall) **12**:200, 202
"Gaia, or Willy Rhymer's Address to his London Landladies" (Dyer) **129**:148
"Le galant tireur" (Baudelaire) **155**:107
Galanterie macabre (Mallarmé) **41**:278
"Galatea" (Casal) **131**:223-25, 228, 235, 266, 268
"Galatea" (Kendall) **12**:192
Galician Songs (Castro)
See *Cantares gallegos*
A Galician Tale (Sacher-Masoch) **31**:289, 303
"Galileo" (Landor) **14**:166
Gallant Festivals (Verlaine)
See *Fêtes galantes*
"The Gallant Lads in Green" (Crawford) **127**:220
A Gallery of Illustrious Literary Characters, 1830-1838 (Maginn) **8**:434, 439-40
"A Gallery of Portraits" (Bestuzhev)
See "Portretnaia Gallereia"
Gallician songs (Castro)
See *Cantares gallegos*
Gallophobie de M. Menzel (Börne) **193**:19
"The Gallows" (Whittier) **8**:512, 525; **59**:361
"Gambara" (Balzac) **5**:79; **153**:149
"The Gambler" (Krasicki)
See "Gracz"
"The Gambler" (Pushkin)
See *Skazhi, Kakoi sud'boi*
The Gambler (Dostoevsky)
See *Igrok*
The Gamblers (Gogol)
See *Igroki*
Gambler's Fate (Dumas) **11**:42
"Gambler's Fortune" (Hoffmann)
See "Spielerglück"
"Gambler's Luck" (Hoffmann)
See "Spielerglück"
"The Gambrel-Roofed House and Its Outlook" (Holmes) **81**:103
"The Game of Backgammon" (Mérimée)
See "La partie de tric-trac"
"A Game of Lawn Tennis" (Levy) **59**:92, 119
The Game of Logic (Dodgson) **2**:108; **139**:57
The Game of Speculation (Lewes) **25**:284; **215**:84
The Game-keeper at Home; or, Sketches of Natural History and Rural Life (Jefferies) **47**:88, 90, 97, 103, 107, 111, 114, 121, 133, 137, 141-42
"Games" (Laforgue)
See "Jeux"
"Gamiani ou deux nuits d'excès" (Musset) **150**:234, 322
"The Gaming Table" (Baudelaire)
See "Le jeu"
"Det gamle Egetræes sidste Drøm" (Andersen) **7**:35; **79**:62, 77 **214**:41
Den gamle trädgårdsmästarens brev (Runeberg) **41**:318
"Gamlet i Don Kikhot" (Turgenev) **21**:412, 431, 438, 442; **37**:403; **122**:325, 345-46
"Gamlet ščigrovskogo uezda" (Turgenev) **21**:378; **37**:402; **122**:264, 342
Gammel nok er jeg nu blevet (Grundtvig) **158**:167
Ganar perdiendo (Zorrilla y Moral) **6**:525
"The Gander Pulling" (Longstreet) **159**:118, 134, 142, 144, 146-47, 151-52, 161-64, 166, 176, 185, 191-92, 203
"Der Gang nach dem Eisenhammer" (Schiller) **39**:388; **166**:105
"Der Gang von Wittow nach Jasmund" (Muller) **73**:360
"Gänserich" (Beddoes) **154**:32
"Ganymed" (Hölderlin) **16**:191
"Ganymede" (Chivers) **49**:74
Det går an (Almqvist) **42**:4-8, 14, 18, 20
La gara degli uccelli (Da Ponte) **50**:77
"Garafelia" (Child) **73**:128
"Garcon un bock" (Maupassant) **42**:200; **83**:228
"The Garden" (Alcott) **167**:48
"The Garden" (Cowper) **8**:111, 123, 128; **94**:10, 23, 26-7, 29-30, 120, 128-29
"The Garden" (Cranch) **115**:9-10, 31, 35
"The Garden" (Very) **9**:377, 383-84
"A Garden by the Sea" (Morris) **4**:421
"Garden Fancies" (Browning) **19**:77; **79**:94, 99
"The Garden of Adonis" (Lazarus) **8**:420; **109**:294
"The Garden of Boccaccio" (Coleridge) **231**:59, 62, 67, 70, 73-74
"The Garden of Eden" (Andersen) **79**:23-24, 59, 76, 82
The Garden of Florence and Other Poems (Reynolds) **146**:167-70, 172-73, 190-91, 208, 215
"The Garden of Irem" (Taylor) **89**:304

"Garden of Love" (Blake) **13**:181-82, 220-21; **37**:4, 15-16, 25, 33, 43, 47-8, 52, 57-8, 92
"The Garden of Paradise" (Andersen)
See "Paradisets have"
"The Garden of the World" (Andersen) **7**:29
"The Gardener" (Mörike)
See "Der Gärtner"
"The Gardener and His Master" (Andersen)
See "Gartneren og Herskabet"
The Gardener and the Squire (Andersen) **79**:36
"The Gardener's Daughter" (Tennyson) **30**:213, 267
Les Garibaldiens (Dumas) **71**:205
The Garies and Their Friends (Webb) **143**:324-32, 335-37, 339-40, 342-43, 345-47, 351-52, 355-56, 358-60, 363, 365-66, 369, 372, 374, 376, 378
Garland for Girls (Alcott) **58**:51
"Garland of Sonnets" (Preseren)
See "Sonetni venec"
Garrick Fever (Planché) **42**:294
"The Garrison of Cape Ann" (Whittier) **8**:492; **59**:375
"Der Gärtner" (Mörike) **201**:252, 294
"Gartneren og Herskabet" (Andersen) **7**:37; **79**:55
Garzia (Alfieri)
See *Don Garzia*
Gaslight and Daylight (Sala) **46**:237, 246
"Gaspar Becerra" (Longfellow) **45**:131
Gaspard de la Nuit (Baudelaire) **155**:75
Gaspard de la nuit: fantaisies à la manière de Rembrandt et de Callot (Bertrand) **31**:43-7, 49-55
"Gasparo Bandollo" (Mangan) **27**:301
Der Gastfreund (Grillparzer) **102**:86, 100-03, 163
Gaston de Blondeville; or, The Court of Henry III Keeping Festival in Ardenne, St. Alban's Abbey: A Metrical Tale, with Some Poetical Pieces (Radcliffe) **6**:416-17, 421, 425, 427; **55**:223-25, 274, 281-82; **223**:186, 246, 279, 286
Gaston de Latour (Pater) **7**:308, 323, 340; **90**:242, 288, 290, 338, 340; **159**:282
The Gates of Paradise (Blake) **37**:4; **173**:16
The Gathering of the West (Galt) **110**:79, 114, 116
The Gaucho (Alencar) **157**:9
El gaucho Martín Fierro (Hernández) **17**:162-69, 171-73, 175-79
"Gaudissart" (Balzac)
See "L'illustre Gaudissart"
Gaudissart II (Balzac) **153**:149
Gaule et France (Dumas) **71**:203
La gaviota: Novela de costumbres (Caballero) **10**:72-73, 76-81, 83-84
Gavriiliada (Pushkin) **3**:427-28, 451
The Gavriiliada (Pushkin)
See *Gavriiliada*
"The Gay Day Still Sounded" (Tyutchev) **34**:389
"Gay Grimaces" (Collodi) **54**:137
Gazelle's Hoof (Alencar) **157**:9
Gazette Publications (Brackenridge) **7**:56; **227**:104
Gazzettino del Del Mundo (Foscolo) **97**:88
"Gde sladkiy shyopot..." (Baratynsky) **103**:10
Le géant Yéocis (Sand) **42**:314
"La géante" (Baudelaire) **6**:80, 115, 123; **55**:30, 59
"The Geäte A-Vallen To" (Barnes) **75**:14, 64, 97, 99
Het gebed van den Onwetende (Multatuli) **165**:337-38
"Gebet" (Mörike) **10**:446, 455; **201**:283, 308
Der gebildete Bürger: ein Buch für den denkenden Mittelstand (Auerbach) **171**:40
"Gebir" (Arnold) **6**:54
Gebir (Landor) **14**:155-57, 161, 164, 168, 176, 180-81, 183-84, 188-89, 192-94, 199-200, 203-06
Gebirus (Landor) **14**:203-04
"Geburt und Wiedergeburt" (Claudius) **75**:210, 214, 216
Gedanken über den hohen Wert der Musik (Hoffmann) **183**:180, 183, 310-11
"Gedanken über die Ideale der Alten" (Wieland) **177**:261, 319
"Gedanken über die Natur der Poesie" (Klopstock) **225**:292, 294, 337, 340
Gedanken über Tod und Unsterblichkeit, aus den Papieren eines Denkers, nebst einem Anhang theologischsatyrischer Xenien, herausgegeben von einem seiner Freunde (Feuerbach) **139**:241, 294-95, 297-99, 318, 330, 343-48
"Gedichte" (Grillparzer) **102**:106, 117
Gedichte (Droste-Hülshoff) **3**:200
Gedichte (Eichendorff) **225**:8, 26
Gedichte (Keller) **2**:421
Gedichte (Meyer) **81**:140, 146, 148, 153-57, 199, 208-09
Gedichte (Mörike) **10**:444-45, 447; **201**:247, 252, 298-304, 319, 366, 369
Gedichte, 1853 und 1854 (Heine) **4**:256-57, 260; **147**:184, 229-34
Gedichte aus den hinterlassenen Papieren eines reisenden Waldhornisten, Band II (Muller) **73**:383, 391
"Gedichte vermischten Inhalts" (Droste-Hülshoff) **3**:200
"The 'Gees" (Melville) **93**:201
"Der Gefangene" (Eichendorff) **8**:218; **225**:45
"Der gefesselte Strom" (Hölderlin) **16**:162, 176
"Gefror'ne Tränen" (Muller) **73**:385, 390
Der gefühlvolle Kerkermeister (Nestroy) **42**:224-25
"Die gegeisselte Psyche" (Meyer) **81**:206, 209
Gegen Torheit gebt es kein Mittel (Nestroy) **42**:247, 251
"Das Gegenwärtige" (Klopstock) **11**:237
"Geh nicht hinein" (Storm) **195**:136
"Gehazi" (Kendall) **12**:192
Die Geheime Geschichte des Philosophen Peregrinus Proteus (Wieland) **177**:292, 330-32, 334-38
Geheime Tagebuch eines Beobachter seiner selbst (Lavater) **142**:12
"Das Geheimnis der Reminiszenz" (Schiller) **39**:357; **166**:116, 121
Geheimnisse (Hoffmann) **183**:176
Geist und Vernunft und Verstand (Herder) **8**:306
"Die Geister am Mummelsee" (Mörike) **10**:453; **201**:298
"Das Geisterross" (Meyer) **81**:207
Der Geisterseher (Schiller) **166**:130
"Die Geisterstunde" (Pavlova) **138**:11-12
Das Geistliche Jahr in Liedern auf alle Sonn-und Festtage (Droste-Hülshoff) **3**:196, 199-201, 203
Geistliche Lieder (Novalis) **13**:376-77, 385, 392, 397, 400, 402, 405; **178**:74, 77
"Die geistliche Poesie Deutschlands" (Eichendorff) **225**:46
Geld und Geist oder die Versöhnung (Gotthelf) **117**:5, 8, 20-1, 32-3, 35, 38, 43, 51
Die Gelehrte (Freytag) **109**:138
Gelehrtenrepublik (Klopstock)
See *Die deutsche Gelehrtenrepublik*
"Gellert," op. 48 (Beethoven) **227**:32
Der Gelstag (Gotthelf) **117**:5, 7, 32-3, 35, 38
"Das Gelübde" (Hoffmann) **2**:360; **183**:194-95, 204
"Das Gemälde" (Meyer) **81**:143
Le gendre de Monsieur Poirier (Augier) **31**:3, 5, 8-20, 24-31, 33, 35-6, 38-40
A General Description of Nova Scotia (Haliburton) **15**:144; **149**:274-75, 277, 310-13
"General Gage's Soliloquy" (Freneau) **1**:315
General History and Comparative System of the Semitic Languages (Renan)
See *Histoire général et système comparé des langues Sémitiques*
General Lopez, the Cuban Patriot (Villaverde) **121**:335
General Notebook (Novalis)
See *Das Allgemaine Brouillon*
"General Taylor and the Veto" (Lincoln) **18**:250
"General Toptýgin" (Nekrasov) **11**:407, 421
A General View of Positivism (Comte) **54**:203, 210
"La genèse Polynésienne" (Leconte de Lisle) **29**:228
Die Genesis des Nathan (Auerbach) **171**:55-56
The Genesis of the Spirit (Slowacki)
See *Genezis z ducha*
Genesung (Klopstock) **225**:286
"Geneva's Double Strike" (Bakunin) **58**:131
"Genevieve" (Coleridge) **9**:144, 146
Geneviève de Brabant (Staël-Holstein) **91**:359
Genevieve; or, The Reign of Terror (Boucicault) **41**:32
Genezis z ducha (Slowacki) **15**:360-61, 366, 374
"Gengulphus" (Barham) **77**:19-20, 26-27
"Génie" (Rimbaud) **35**:294-96, 309, 311, 313, 324; **82**:230, 232-33, 251; **227**:210, 239-42, 246-48, 291-94, 297-98, 309-13, 323
Le génie bonhomme (Nodier) **19**:384-85
"Le génie dans l'obsurité" (Lamartine) **11**:289
Génie du christianisme (Staël-Holstein) **91**:332, 359
Le génie du Christianisme; ou, Beautés de la religion Chrétienne (Chateaubriand) **3**:110-17, 124, 126, 128-29, 131-32; **134**:4, 10-19, 24-30, 34, 37, 40, 42-45, 61, 63, 65, 70, 73, 84, 88, 90, 92, 102-7, 118, 120, 132, 140, 143-44
Geniu pustiu (Eminescu) **33**:245, 247, 254, 264; **131**:294
"Genius" (Emerson) **98**:65
"Genius" (Mangan) **27**:298
"Genius" (Rimbaud)
See "Génie"
"Genius Lost" (Harpur) **114**:100, 105, 125, 137, 144-46
"The Genius of America Weeping the Absurd Follies of the Day" (Warren) **13**:431, 433; **226**:261, 267
The Genius of Christianity; or, The Spirit and Beauties of the Christian Religion (Chateaubriand)
See *Le génie du Christianisme; ou, Beautés de la religion Chrétienne*
"The Genius of Harmony. An Irregular Ode" (Moore) **110**:177
The Genius of Judaism (D'Israeli) **217**:285-86, 295
"The Genius of Plato" (Pater) **90**:334
Genoveva (Schumann) **143**:109, 140
Genoveva: Tragödie in fünf Acten (Hebbel) **43**:230, 233-34, 238-39, 243-44, 247, 254-57, 259, 262, 271, 273-74
"Le Genre" (Mallarmé) **41**:239
"Le Genre et les modernes" (Mallarmé) **210**:251
The Genteel Style in Writing (Lamb) **10**:412
Le Gentilhomme de la montagne (Dumas) **71**:194
Gentle and Simple (Martineau) **137**:271
"Gentle Armour" (Hunt) **70**:252-53
"The Gentle Boy" (Hawthorne) **2**:319, 327; **79**:318, 322; **95**:128, 132, 137, 196; **158**:336-37; **171**:356
"The Gentle Giantess" (Lamb) **10**:436
"A Gentle Hint to Writing Women" (Lewes) **25**:290
"The Gentle Look" (Coleridge) **99**:22
"The Gentleman Farmer" (Crabbe) **26**:93; **121**:11-12
A Gentleman from Ireland (O'Brien) **21**:250
Gentleman Jews (Jerrold) **2**:408

The Gentleman of the Blue Boots (Castro) **3**:106-07
"Gentleness" (Lampman) **25**:209-10
"The Genuine Kindergarten versus Ignorant Attempts at it" (Peabody) **169**:150
"Geoffrey Chaucer" (Smith) **59**:309
Geoffrey Hamlyn (Kingsley)
See *The Recollections of Geoffry Hamlyn*
Geoffrey Moncton (Moodie) **113**:295-97, 324-25
"Geoffroy Rudèl und Melisande von Tripoli" (Heine) **147**:232
A Geographical Dictionary of England and Wales (Cobbett) **49**:160
"The Geography of an Irish Oath" (Carleton) **3**:93; **199**:21
"Geologia" (Harpur) **114**:124-25
George and Sarah Green: A Narrative (Wordsworth) **138**:225, 227, 229, 233-37
George Canterbury's Will (Wood) **178**:291
George Crabbe: The Complete Poetical Works (Crabbe) **121**:84-8, 90-1
"George Cruikshank" (Thackeray) **213**:245-46
George Eliot (Blind) **202**:2
George Eliot Letters (Eliot) **89**:266; **118**:88, 90-91, 164-66, 181; **183**:97; **199**:131, 160, 224, 227, 229, 239, 241-42, 245-46, 248-49
The George Eliot Letters (Eliot) **209**:27-30, 76, 82, 105
George Eliot—A Writer's Notebook 1854-1879 (Eliot) **118**:111-13; **199**:247
"George Levison; or, the School Fellows" (Allingham) **25**:7
George Sand in Her Own Words (Sand) **42**:332-33
"George Silverman's Explanation" (Dickens) **3**:164
George the Fourth, A Poem: Dedicated to the Right Honourable the Marquis of Londonderry (Dacre) **151**:148-49
"George the Third's Soliloquy" (Freneau) **111**:140
"George Washington" (Harpur) **114**:140
Georges (Dumas) **71**:204, 229, 242, 244
Georgette; ou, La nièce du tabellion (Kock) **16**:245-46
Georgia Scenes (Longstreet) **159**:116, 123, 126, 128-32, 134-36, 141-45, 147, 149-50, 154, 156-65, 168, 171-72, 174-77, 180-83, 186-89, 191-94, 196-204
Georgia Scenes Completed (Longstreet) **159**:188-89, 191-93
A Georgia Spec; or, Land in the Moon (Tyler) **3**:573-74
"Georgia Theatrics" (Longstreet) **159**:116, 133, 142, 144-45, 147, 151, 153, 157-62, 165, 167, 180, 182, 189, 191, 196-98, 200, 202
"Georgia Waters" (Chivers) **49**:43
"Geraint and Enid" (Tennyson) **202**:210, 334
"Geraldine" (Brontë) **16**:121
"The Geraldine's Daughter" (Mangan) **27**:293
Gerard Manley Hopkins: Selected Prose (Hopkins) **189**:44, 51
Gereimte Psalmen (Lavater) **142**:12
"Ein Gerichtstag auf Huahine" (Chamisso) **82**:21, 27-29
"The German Constitution" (Hegel) **46**:111; **151**:257
German Dictionary (Grimm Brothers) **3**:216
German Evenings (Auerbach)
See *Deutsche Abende*
German Folk Tales (Grimm Brothers) **3**:226
German Grammar (Grimm Brothers)
See *Deutsche Grammatik*
"A German Home" (Taylor) **89**:308
The German Ideology (Engels)
See *Die deutsche Ideologie*
The German Ideology (Marx) **17**:326, 332-34, 349-52, 360; **114**:52-4, 69-70, 83-6
"A German Idyl" (Taylor) **89**:308
"A German Poet" (Mangan) **27**:291
German Popular Stories, Translated from the Kinder und Haus Marchen (Grimm Brothers)
See *Kinder-und Hausmärchen*
German Romance (Carlyle) **70**:94, 108
"Germania" (Hölderlin) **187**:224
"Germanien" (Hölderlin) **16**:174-75, 189, 195
Germany (Staël-Holstein)
See *De l'Allemagne*
"Germany. A Fragment" (Heine)
See "Deutschland. Ein Fragment"
"Germany, France, and England" (Gladstone) **213**:112
Germany: A Winter's Tale (Heine)
See *Deutschland: Ein Wintermärchen*
Germany: Revolution and Counter-Revolution (Engels)
See *Revolution and Counter-revolution in Germany*
Germinie Lacerteux (Goncourt and Goncourt) **7**:155-58, 162-65, 167, 170, 174, 176-80, 182, 184, 187-90
Geroi nashego vremeni (Lermontov) **5**:286-87, 291-92, 294-95, 297-99, 301-02, 304-06; **47**:149-230; **126**:128, 132-33, 139, 145, 147-48, 151, 153-58, 160-62, 164-66, 170, 172, 174, 192, 195-200, 203, 205, 214, 216-17, 223-26
Gerolstein (Sue) **1**:555
Gerontius (Newman)
See *Dream of Gerontius*
"Gertha's Lovers" (Morris) **4**:429
"Gertrude of Wyoming: A Pennsylvanian Tale" (Campbell) **19**:164-66, 168-71, 174-75, 178-79, 181, 183-85, 188-89, 193, 195-96, 198
Gertrude of Wyoming: A Pennsylvanian Tale, and Other Poems (Campbell) **19**:164-65, 176
Gertrude; or, Family Pride (Trollope) **30**:332
Gertrude's Cherries (Jerrold) **2**:403
Gesammelte Gedichte (Keller) **2**:421
Gesammelte Novellen (Tieck) **5**:516
Gesammelte Schriften (Brentano) **191**:31
Gesammelte Schriften (Humboldt) **134**:158, 199-200
Gesammelte Schriften (Liszt) **199**:304, 319
Gesammelte Schriften (Wieland)
See *Wielands Gesammelte Schriften*
Gesammelte Schriften über Musik und Musiker (Schumann) **143**:69, 72, 76, 78, 80, 86
Gesammelte Schriften und Dichtungen (Wagner) **119**:189
Gesammelte Werke (Freytag) **109**:147
Gesammelte Werke (Stifter) **198**:283-84
Gesamtkunstwerk (Goethe) **34**:127
"Der Gesang der Klio" (Meyer) **81**:152
"Gesang der Räuber" (Mörike) **10**:453
"Gesang der Liebe als sie geboren war" (Brentano) **191**:34, 48, 70
"Der Gesang des Meeres" (Meyer) **81**:155, 199
"Gesang Weylas" (Mörike) **10**:446, 448; **201**:272, 291
"Gesang zu Zweien in der Nacht" (Mörike) **10**:448-49; **201**:255-56, 271, 281, 289, 291, 299-302
Die Geschichte der Abderiten (Wieland) **17**:397, 399, 424
Geschichte der Abderiten (Wieland)
See *Die Abderiten, eine sehr wahrscheinliche Geschichte*
Geschichte der alten und neuen Literatur (Schlegel) **45**:294, 299, 305, 317, 323-28
Geschichte der deutschen Sprache (Grimm Brothers) **3**:216-17
Geschichte der europäischen Literatur (Schlegel) **226**:177
"Die Geschichte der Jungfrau von Orleans" (Hebbel) **43**:255
Geschichte der neueren Philosophie von Bacon von Verulam bis Benedict Spinoza (Feuerbach) **139**:283, 303, 344, 347-48
Geschichte der poetischen Literatur Deutschlands (Eichendorff) **8**:219-20, 233; **225**:46, 92-94, 97-100
Die Geschichte der Renaissnce in Italien (Burckhardt)
See *Die Kultur der Renaissance in Italien*
Geschichte des Abfalls der vereinigten Niederlande von der spanischen Regierung (Schiller) **69**:169
Geschichte des Agathon (Wieland) **17**:391, 396-97, 399-400, 405, 408, 413, 420-30; **177**:234, 252, 254, 275, 285, 287-93, 299, 307-8, 311-12, 320, 326-28, 330-32, 339-41, 343-47, 351, 358-59
Geschichte des Dreißigjährigen Kriegs (Schiller) **166**:189, 191-92
Geschichte des Dreissigjährigen Kriegs (Schiller) **69**:188
Geschichte des Fräuleins von Sternheim (La Roche) **121**:242-44, 246-51, 256, 258, 262, 265-66, 268-72, 274-76, 279-85, 291, 298, 302, 304, 308-12, 315, 318-19, 322, 325-26
Geschichte des Philosophen Danischmende (Wieland) **17**:407; **177**:257, 287, 331, 363, 365-66
Geschichte des Romans (Eichendorff) **8**:217
Die Geschichte des weisen Danischmend (Wieland)
See *Geschichte des Philosophen Danischmende*
Geschichte Friedrich des Grossen (Auerbach) **171**:45
Die Geschichte meines Vaters (Kotzebue) **25**:138
"Geschichte vom braven Kasperl und dem schönen Annerl" (Brentano) **1**:95, 99-101, 105
Geschichte vom braven Kasperl und dem schönen Annerl (Brentano) **191**:25, 27, 29, 50, 63, 65, 69-70, 78, 83, 103, 105, 108, 119
Geschichten aus der Tonne (Storm)
See *Drei Märchen*
De Geschiedenis van Wouertje Pieterse (Multatuli) **165**:303, 345, 347-51
Geschischte des Herrn William Lovell (Tieck) **46**:398
Der geschlossene Handelsstaat (Fichte) **62**:34, 48
"Geschwisterblut" (Storm) **195**:93
Die gesfesselte Phantasie (Raimund) **69**:7-8, 12, 24, 35-6, 44-5, 47-9, 52
"Gesicht von einer Welt unschuldiger Menschen" (Wieland) **177**:259
"Die Gespenster" (Beddoes) **154**:25, 29
"Gespräch der Reformatoren im Himmel" (Gotthelf) **117**:30, 35
"Gespräch des Socrates mit Timoclea von der scheinbaren und wahren Schönheit" (Wieland) **17**:418
"Gespräch über die Poesie" (Schlegel) **142**:318
Gespräch über die Poesie (Schlegel) **45**:306-10, 314-16, 320-24, 328, 344, 348, 358-60, 362-65, 367-68, 370, 372, 375, 382; **226**:163-64, 176-77, 197, 222, 226, 240-41
Gespräche, die Freiheit betreffend (Claudius) **75**:194
Gespräche mit Dämonen. Des Königsbuchs zweiter Band (Arnim) **38**:12, 16; **123**:9-10, 12, 15, 60, 62-63, 65-67, 69-70
Geständnisse (Heine) **4**:240-41, 244-45, 248; **147**:143, 163, 167, 200-1, 203-4, 231-33
Der gestiefelte Kater (Tieck) **5**:516-17, 521-24, 529-30, 532; **46**:406-09
"Die Gestirne" (Klopstock) **11**:241
"Gethsemane" (Droste-Hülshoff) **3**:196
"Gethsémani" (Lamartine) **190**:241
"Der Getreue Eckart und der Tannen häuser" (Tieck) **46**:350
"Gettin' On" (Field) **3**:210
"Getting Along" (Larcom) **179**:167

"Getting Up a Pantomime" (Mayhew) **31**:179
"Gettsyburg Address" (Lincoln) **18**:220-21, 227, 235, 238, 241-42, 246-48, 250-51, 254, 257, 264-65, 267, 271, 274, 277, 280-82
"Gettysburg Address" (Lincoln) **201**:155, 157-59, 165, 167, 170-72, 182-84, 186, 191-92, 198, 209, 211, 218-19, 222-25, 228-29
Der Gevattersmann (Auerbach) **171**:72-73
"Ghaselle" (Emerson) **98**:179
"Ghasta; or, The Avenging Demon" (Shelley) **18**:342
"The Ghetto at Florence" (Levy) **59**:111
"The Ghost" (Andersen) **79**:24
"A Ghost" (Barnes) **75**:75
"A Ghost" (Baudelaire)
See "Un fantôme"
The Ghost, a Canterbury Tale (Barham) **77**:5, 36
"The Ghost and the Bone Setter" (Le Fanu) **9**:321, 323
"Ghost Glen" (Kendall) **12**:181, 183
"The Ghost in the Garden Room" (Gaskell)
See "The Crooked Branch"
The Ghost of Abel (Blake) **57**:14
Ghost Stories and Tales of Mystery (Le Fanu) **9**:302-03, 314
"The Ghosts" (Eminescu) **33**:246; **131**:286, 291, 295-96, 335, 347
"Ghosts" (Turgenev) **122**:337
"The Ghost's Moonshine" (Beddoes) **3**:34
"The Ghost's Petition" (Rossetti) **2**:558, 565; **50**:288; **186**:271
Giannettino (Collodi) **54**:140
"Giannettino's Trip through Italy" (Collodi)
See *Minnuzolo; Il Viaggio per l'Italia de Giannettino*
"The Giantess" (Baudelaire)
See "La géante"
"The Giant's Coffin" (Simms) **3**:506
The Giaour (Byron)
See *The Giaour: A Fragment of a Turkish Tale*
The Giaour: A Fragment of a Turkish Tale (Byron) **2**:60, 72-73, 76, 81, 86, 103; **12**:82; **109**:102, 118; **149**:28, 36, 161, 163
Giboyer (Augier)
See *Le fils de Giboyer*
Giboyer's Son (Augier)
See *Le fils de Giboyer*
"The Gift" (Derzhavin) **215**:15
"The Gift of Righteousness" (Newman) **99**:232
A Gift of the Sun (Lampman) **194**:77
"Die Giftmischerin" (Chamisso) **82**:27
"Gifts" (Karamzin) **3**:284
"Gifts" (Lazarus) **8**:420-21; **109**:335-36
"Gifts and Graces" (Rossetti) **50**:285
"The Gifts of the Terek" (Lermontov)
See "Dary Tereka"
Gil Blas (Reynolds) **146**:193
"Gilbert" (Brontë) **105**:54
The Gilded Clique (Gaboriau) **14**:31-2
"Gilded Verse" (Verlaine)
See "Vers dorés"
Giles Corey of the Salem Farms (Longfellow) **2**:496-97; **45**:128, 165
"The Gilliflower of Gold" (Morris) **4**:432
"Gimm gluptsam" (Karamzin) **173**:280
Der Gimpel auf der Messe (Kotzebue) **25**:133
"La ginestra" (Leopardi) **129**:218, 220, 222-23, 225-26, 244, 250, 253, 260, 273, 304, 307-8
"Ginevra" (Shelley) **18**:327
Gin-Shop; or, A Peep into Prison (More) **141**:167, 190
Giovanna of Naples (Landor) **14**:165
The Gipsies (Macha)
See *Cigáni*
Gipsies (Pushkin)
See *Tsygany*
The Gipsy (Runeberg) **41**:309
The Gipsy in Music (Liszt)
See *Des Bohémiens et de leur musique en Hongrie*
"The Gipsy Nurse, or Marked for Life" (Alger) **83**:96
"The Gipsey of Sardis" (Willis) **194**:282
"The Gipsy's Evening Blaze" (Clare) **9**:72
The Gipsy's Prophecy (Southworth) **26**:433-34
"The Girl from Abroad" (Schiller) **39**:306
"The Girl in the Golden Garden" (Eminescu)
See "Fata în gradina de aur"
"The Girl of the Period" (Linton) **41**:160, 163, 169
The Girl of the Period and Other Social Essays (Linton) **41**:163
"The Girl Who Stepped on Bread" (Andersen) **214**:47
"The Girl Who Trod on the Loaf" (Andersen) **7**:31, 32, 37
"The Girl Who Was Danced to Death" (Blind) **202**:13
The Girl Without a Dowry (Ostrovsky)
See *Bespridannitsa*
"The Girl without Hands" (Grimm Brothers) **3**:227
Girlfriends (Verlaine)
See *Les Amies*
The Girl's Book (Child) **6**:198; **73**:41, 50, 59, 75, 96
"The Girl's Lamentation" (Allingham) **25**:7-8, 16-17, 22, 29
"Girls' Reading Book" (Sigourney) **87**:321
"The Girt Woak Tree That's in the Dell" (Barnes) **75**:36, 108
"Girt Wold House o'Mossy Stwone" (Barnes) **75**:6, 103
Gisela (Kotzebue) **25**:136
"Giselle" (Gautier) **59**:34, 39
Gisippus (Griffin) **7**:194-95, 198-99, 202-03, 209, 216
"Gisli the Chieftain" (Crawford) **12**:156, 161, 172; **127**:159-61, 163-64, 174-75, 178, 192, 195-97, 199
"Giulia" (Barnes) **75**:30
Give a Dog a Bad Name (Lewes) **25**:291
"Give All to Love" (Emerson) **1**:296; **98**:92, 179
"Give Me the Splendid Silent Sun" (Whitman) **31**:391, 393-94; **81**:314; **205**:309, 315
"Give me women wine and snuff" (Keats) **73**:322
"Giver of Glowing Light" (Hood) **16**:222
"Gjentagelsen" (Kierkegaard)
See *Gjentagelsen. Et Forsøg i den experimenterende Psychologi*
Gjentagelsen. Et Forsøg i den experimenterende Psychologi (Kierkegaard) **34**:200, 223, 260, 262; **78**:119, 157-66, 168-69, 173, 238; **125**:198, 208, 272, 281
"Gladesmure" (Landon) **15**:161
The Gladiator (Bird) **1**:83, 86-88, 90, 92; **197**:6-8, 12, 16-19, 25, 68, 75, 93-94, 98
"The Gladness of Nature" (Bryant) **6**:161
The Gladstone Diaries (Gladstone) **213**:120
"Gladys and Her Island" (Ingelow) **39**:265; **107**:137-41, 155, 159
Glagolita Clozianus (Kopitar) **117**:64, 68, 117
"A Glance behind the Curtain" (Lowell) **90**:219, 221
"A Glance within the Forest" (Traill) **31**:327
Glanes (Mallarmé) **41**:248
"Glanvil on Witches" (Lamb) **10**:402
"Glasgow" (Smith) **59**:312, 316, 321, 330, 332-4, 336
The Glass of Water (Robertson) **35**:354
The Glass of Water; or, Causes and Effects (Scribe)
See *Le Verre d'eau; ou, Les Effets et les causes*
Glauben und Liebe (Novalis) **178**:4, 10, 15
"Glauben und Wissen" (Hegel) **46**:165
Glaubenslehre (Schleiermacher)
See *Die praktische Theologie nach den Grundsätzen der evangelischen Kirche im Zusammenhang dargestellt*
"Glauben—Wissen—Handeln" (Lenau) **16**:272, 278
"Glaucé" (Leconte de Lisle) **29**:239, 245-46
Glaucus (Boker) **125**:25, 28, 41, 76-78
Glaucus; or, The Wonders of the Shore (Kingsley) **35**:232, 254-55
"The Gleam" (Tyutchev)
See "Problesk"
"A Gleam of Sunshine" (Longfellow) **2**:473; **45**:116
The Gleaner: A Miscellanous Production in Three Volumes (Murray) **63**:174-82, 184-5, 188, 193, 195, 197-201, 203-4, 207-12, 214-5
"The Gleaner Unmasked" (Murray) **63**:201
Gleanings (Sigourney) **87**:326
Gleanings in Europe (Cooper)
See *Recollections of Europe*
Gleanings in Europe. England (Cooper)
See *England*
Gleanings in Europe. Italy (Cooper)
See *Excursions in Italy*
Gleanings of Past Years, 1843-78 (Gladstone) **213**:116
"Glee—The Great Storm Is Over" (Dickinson) **21**:43
Die Gleichen (Arnim) **5**:21
"The Glen of Arrawatta" (Kendall) **12**:180, 186, 190, 192, 201
"The Glen of the Whiteman's Grave" (Harpur) **114**:121, 144, 148, 150, 152
"Glenara" (Campbell) **19**:169, 181
Glenarvon (Duras) **154**:129
Glenarvon (Lamb) **38**:234-46, 248, 250-60
"Gleneden's Dream" (Brontë) **16**:79-80
"Glenfinlas" (Scott) **15**:317
"Glimmerings" (Cranch) **115**:51
"A Glimpse of Christ's Idea of Society" (Peabody) **169**:145-46, 176-77, 190
"The Glimpse of the Coming Day" (Morris) **4**:438
Glimpses Into My Own Life and Literary Character (Barrett Browning) **61**:48
"Glimpses of Psychology" (Peabody) **169**:145
"The Gloamin" (Hogg) **109**:203
"Der Glockenguss zu Breslau" (Muller) **73**:351, 355
"Das Glöcklein" (Meyer) **81**:143-44, 147
"La Gloire" (Baudelaire) **155**:106
"La gloire" (Lamartine) **11**:269
"La gloria de México en María Santísima de Guadalupe" (Lizardi) **30**:68
"Gloria mundi" (Allston) **2**:26
Gloria mundi (Frederic) **10**:189, 192, 194, 201, 205, 211-13, 215-17
"The Glories of Mary for the Sake of Her Son" (Newman) **38**:303, 310
"Glorified Mists" (Hayne) **94**:144
"Gloriola" (Meyer) **81**:156
"The Glory Machine" (Villiers de l'Isle Adam)
See "La machine à gloire"
The Glory of Columbia: Her Yeomanry! (Dunlap) **2**:208, 211-14, 217
"The Glory of Motion" (De Quincey) **4**:82
"The Glory of Poetry" (Ueda Akinari)
See "Uta no homare"
"Glosa" (Preseren) **127**:308
"The Gloss" (Eminescu)
See "Glossa"
"Glossa" (Eminescu) **33**:250; **131**:287, 298
A Glossary of the Dorset Dialect, with a Grammar of its Word Shapening and Wording (Barnes)
See *A Grammar and Glossary of the Dorset Dialect*
"The Glove" (Browning) **19**:126; **79**:94, 102-03, 164
"The Glove" (Schiller)
See "Der Handschuh"

"The Glove and the Lions" (Hunt) **1**:416; **70**:264
"Glowing is her Bonnet" (Dickinson) **77**:121
Das Glück (Schiller) **166**:95
"Das Glück auf der Extrafahrt" (Auerbach) **171**:75
Glück, Mißbrauch und Rückkehr (Nestroy) **42**:250-51, 256
Der glückliche Färber (Arnim) **159**:19
"Der Glücksritter" (Eichendorff) **225**:7, 9
"Die Glückliche Fischerin" (Muller) **73**:353, 361
"Die Glückseligkeit Aller" (Klopstock) **11**:241; **225**:307-9
Die Glücksritter (Eichendorff) **8**:222
"The Gnat and the Shepherd" (Krylov) **1**:435
"El gnomo" (Bécquer) **106**:98, 108, 130, 134-35
"Gnosis" (Cranch) **115**:8
"Go Ahead" (Haliburton) **149**:305
"Go Not, Happy Day" (Tennyson) **30**:242
"Go Slow My Soul, to Feed Thyself" (Dickinson) **21**:66
"Go, Thought!" (Isaacs)
See "Ve, pensamiento!"
"Go Where Glory Waits Thee" (Moore) **110**:182, 185
Goa, and the Blue Mountains; or, Six Months of Sick Leave (Burton) **42**:38
"The Goblet" (Tieck)
See "Der Pokal"
"The Goblet of Life" (Longfellow) **2**:472; **45**:99, 116, 152
"The Goblin and the Huckster" (Andersen)
See "Nissen hos Spekhøkeren"
"The Goblin and the Hukster" (Andersen)
See "Nissen hos Spekhøkeren"
"The Goblin at the Grocer's" (Andersen)
See "Nissen hos Spekhøkeren"
"Goblin Market" (Rossetti) **2**:555, 558, 560, 563, 565-7, 569-73, 575, 577-8; **50**:266, 270, 288, 291-7 , 321-2, 324; **66**:297-390; **186**:231, 246, 250, 253-54, 256-58, 304-5, 316-19, 321-22, 324, 327, 342
Goblin Market, and Other Poems (Rossetti) **2**:555-7, 563, 573-4, 576-7; **66**:312-3; **186**:229, 264-65, 267, 286, 291, 303, 316-17, 332, 335, 347
Gobseck (Balzac) **35**:9, 26-27; **53**:22-23; **153**:152
Gockel, Hinkel und Gackeleia: Märchen, wiedererzählt (Brentano) **1**:95, 100, 102, 105-06, 108; **191**:65-66, 70, 131
"God" (Derzhavin)
See "Bog"
God and the Bible: A Review of Objections to "Literature and Dogma" (Arnold) **6**:40, 48, 53, 66; **29**:15, 50, 52; **126**:63-64, 90
God and the State (Bakunin)
See *Dieu et l'état*
"God and the Universe" (Tennyson) **202**:291
"God Be with You" (Clough) **27**:106-7
"God moves in a mysterious way" (Cowper) **94**:69-70
"God of the Living" (Cowper) **8**:116
"God of the Meridian" (Keats) **73**:269; **225**:184
"God Preserve the King" (Moodie) **113**:310
"God Save the Queen" (Moodie) **113**:371
God: Some Conversations (Herder)
See *Gott! Ein Gespräch*
God: Some Dialogues (Herder)
See *Gott! Ein Gespräch*
"God Spake out of the Skies" (Tennyson) **202**:285
"Godfather's Picture Book" (Andersen)
See "Gudfaders Billedbog"
The Godfather's Treasury (Auerbach) **171**:49-51
"Godiva" (Hunt) **1**:414; **70**:264
"Godiva" (Tennyson) **65**:231
Godolphin (Bulwer-Lytton) **45**:26-7, 29-32, 35-8, 68
"The Gods" (Verlaine)
See "Les Dieux"
"God's Commandments Not Grievous" (Newman) **38**:305
"God's Good Time" (Leskov)
See "Chas voli Bozhiei"
"God's Grandeur" (Hopkins) **17**:191-92, 212, 218-19, 229, 243-44; **189**:5-7, 17, 35, 47-48, 65, 73, 77-78, 81-82, 86, 90, 94, 107, 115, 118-20, 126
Gods in Exile (Heine)
See *Die Verbannten Gotter*
"God's Judgement on a Wicked Bishop" (Southey) **97**:271
"The Gods of Greece" (Schiller)
See "Die Götter Griechenlands"
"Godspeed to the Snow" (Lampman) **194**:139
Godwi oder Das steinerne Bild der Mutter: Ein verwilderter Roman (Brentano) **1**:96, 97-99, 102, 104-07; **191**:6, 11, 18, 38, 40, 56, 58-59, 75, 78, 103, 108, 112, 118-20, 126-33, 139, 141, 143
Godzien litości (Fredro) **8**:286
Godzina myśli (Slowacki) **15**:363-64, 373
"Goethe" (Carlyle) **70**:9, 96
"An Goethe" (Schiller) **39**:389
Goethe (Lewes)
See *The Life and Works of Goethe*
"Goethe and Byron" (Mickiewicz) **101**:175-76
"Goethe and his Time" (Tieck)
See "Goethe und seine Zeit"
Goethe and Schiller (Boyesen) **135**:45, 49
Goethe and Schiller's Xenions (Goethe)
See *Xenien*
"Goethe as a Man of Science" (Lewes) **25**:312; **215**:140, 145, 182
"Goethe und seine Zeit" (Tieck) **46**:356-57, 359, 403
Goethe-Book (Arnim) **123**:42-43
"Goethe's Botany: The Metamorphosis of Plants" (Goethe) **4**:207-08, 210
"Goethes Briefe, Hamburger Ausgabe in 4 Bänden" (Goethe)
See "Werke: Hamburger Ausgabe"
Goethes Briefwechsel mit einem Kinde: Seinem Denkmal (Arnim) **38**:3-4, 8, 10, 13-16; **123**:7, 9, 22, 24-26, 28, 42, 59, 64, 94-95, 98-100
"Goethe's Colour Theory" (Goethe)
See "Theory of Colours"
Goethe's Correspondence with a Child: For His Monument (Arnim)
See *Goethes Briefwechsel mit einem Kinde: Seinem Denkmal*
Goethes Faust in urspünglicher Gestalt nach der Göch hausenschen Abschrift herausgegeben (Goethe) **154**:215, 229-32, 254, 265, 281, 320
Goethe's Roman Elegies (Goethe)
See *Römische Elegien*
Goethes sämmtliche Werke (Goethe) **154**:323
Goethe's Works (Goethe) **4**:173
"Goetz of Berlichingen with the Iron Hand" (Goethe)
See *Götz von Berlichingen mit der eisernen Hand*
"Going to Heaven" (Dickinson) **21**:56
"Going to him! Happy Letter!" (Dickinson) **171**:96
"Going to Maynooth" (Carleton)
See "Denis O'Shaughnessy Going to Maynooth"
Going to See a Man Hanged (Thackeray) **5**:507
Gold (Reade) **2**:551; **74**:244, 277-79, 281, 291-92, 319, 330-31, 342
"The Gold Bug" (Poe) **1**:500, 506, 524; **16**:293, 295-96, 298, 300-01, 303, 312-13, 315, 332, 334; **55**:133, 135, 141, 148-9, 153; **211**:253, 328
The Gold of Chickaree (Warner) **146**:235
"The Gold Pen-A Poem, Inscribed to the Gentleman Who Presented the Gift" (Hale) **75**:284
"Golden Age" (Rimbaud)
See "Age d'or"
The Golden Age (Martí)
See *La Edad de Oro*
The Golden Branch (Planché) **42**:288-89, 293
"Golden Brown" (Jefferies) **47**:143
The Golden Calf (Boyesen) **135**:14, 22, 31, 37, 59, 61-63, 65, 67-68
"Golden Chain" (Moore) **110**:177
"The Golden Cockerel" (Reisman)
See "Skazka o Zolotom Petushke"
"Golden Dreams" (Irving) **2**:390
Golden Dreams (Alencar) **157**:8-9
The Golden Fleece (Grillparzer)
See *Das goldene Vließ*
The Golden Fleece (Planché) **42**:273, 275, 286-87
"The Golden Ingot" (O'Brien) **21**:238-39, 242, 244-45, 248, 252
"The Golden Island" (Clarke) **19**:231
"A Golden Key on the Tongue" (Clough) **27**:107
The Golden Legend (Longfellow) **2**:475-76, 479-80, 484, 486-87, 496, 498; **45**:113-14, 119, 127-28, 130-31, 133, 143, 147, 150, 157, 163-65, 178, 190; **101**:93
The Golden Lion of Granpère (Trollope) **101**:235, 310, 313
"Golden Milestone" (Longfellow) **45**:116, 161
"The Golden Net" (Blake) **13**:243
"The Golden Pot" (Hoffmann)
See "Der goldene Topf"
The Golden Pot: Fairy Tale of Our Times (Hoffmann)
See "Der goldene Topf"
"Golden Rules in Rhyme" (Osgood) **141**:322
The Golden Skull (Slowacki)
See *Złota czaszka*
The Golden Violet with Its Tales of Romance and Chivalry, and Other Poems (Landon) **15**:158, 161, 166, 168
"Golden Wings" (Morris) **4**:411, 419, 425, 432, 444
"The Golden Year" (Tennyson) **65**:285; **115**:240
Der goldene Spiegel (Wieland) **17**:397, 408-09
Der goldene Spiegel; oder, die Könige von Scheschian (Wieland) **177**:256, 284, 287, 331, 363-67
"Der goldene Topf" (Hoffmann) **2**:341, 345, 349-50, 352-56, 361-62; **183**:169-70, 177, 182-83, 186, 188, 193, 195-207, 209, 211, 213-14, 221, 223, 226, 231, 247, 267-70, 272, 287, 297-98
Das goldene Vließ (Grillparzer) **1**:383-85, 387, 389, 397; **102**:86, 95, 100, 107, 117, 149, 163, 165-66, 174, 180, 186-88
"Goldenrod" (Lampman) **25**:210
"Golden-Rod" (Larcom) **179**:175
"Goldilocks and Goldilocks" (Morris) **4**:423, 434
"Der goldne Tag ist heimgegangen" (Brentano) **1**:105
"Der goldne Topf" (Hoffmann)
See "Der goldene Topf"
"Goldoni and Italian Comedy" (Lewes) **25**:285
"Le golfe de Baïa" (Lamartine) **11**:245, 269, 282; **190**:226
"Le Golfe de Baya" (Lamartine)
See "Le golfe de Baïa"
"Golfre, a Gothic Swiss Tale" (Robinson) **142**:95, 249
"The Goloshes of Fortune" (Andersen) **214**:54-57, 59, 77
Golovan (Leskov)
See *Nesmertel'nyj Golovan: iz rasskazov o trex pravednikax*
The Golovlyov Family (Saltykov)
See *Gospoda Golovlyovy*
The Goncourt Journals, 1851-1870 (Goncourt and Goncourt) **7**:160-63
"The Gondola" (Pavlova) **138**:16-17
"Egy gondolat bánt engèmet" (Petofi) **21**:284

"Gondolatok" (Arany) **34**:18
Gondoliera (Liszt) **199**:307
"The Gondolier's Wedding" (Symonds) **34**:364
"Gone" (Gordon) **21**:154, 159, 163-64, 168, 181
"Gone" (Whittier) **8**:491
"Gone Astray" (Dickens) **161**:136
"Gone in the Wind" (Mangan) **27**:298
Gonzaga ou A revolução de Minas (Castro Alves) **205**:3, 12, 14, 30-31
"The Good Aunt" (Edgeworth) **51**:82-4, 87; **158**:7
"The Good Clerk" (Lamb) **113**:199
"The Good Clerk, a Character; With Some Account of 'The Complete English Tradesman'" (Lamb) **10**:436
"Good Deeds" (Karamzin)
See "Blagodeyaniye"
"The Good Disciple" (Verlaine)
See *Le Bon Disciple*
A Good Fight (Reade) **2**:540; **74**:245
"Good for Nothing" (Boyesen) **135**:12, 19, 21, 26
"The Good French Governess" (Edgeworth) **51**:82-3, 85, 87, 89-90
"Good Friday" (Rossetti) **50**:268; **186**:332
The Good Genius That Turned Everything into Gold (Mayhew) **31**:161
"The Good Governess" (Edgeworth) **1**:255
"A Good Knight in Prison" (Morris) **4**:431, 444
"Good Lord, today" (Rossetti) **186**:335
Good Lord! What the Devil Is This! (Fredro)
See *Gwałltu, co sie dzieje*
"Good Measter Collins" (Barnes) **75**:73
Good Militia Men; or, The Man That Is Worth a Host (More) **141**:189
"Good Night" (Barnes) **75**:33
"Good Night" (Castro Alves)
See "Boa Noite"
"Good Night" (Muller)
See "Gute Nacht"
"Good Old Gvadányi" (Petofi)
See "A régi jó Gvadányi"
"The Good Part" (Longfellow) **103**:290
"The Good Part of Mary" (Newman) **38**:306
Good People and Their Adventures (Sacher-Masoch) **31**:295
"A Good Temper" (Andersen) **214**:58
The Good Song (Verlaine)
See *La bonne chanson*
Good Tidings (Bloomfield) **145**:132, 148, 176
"Good Tidings from the Farm" (Bloomfield) **145**:133, 155
"A Good Time Going" (Holmes) **81**:95
Good Wives (Alcott) **6**:16, 21; **83**:34, 79, 82
The Good Woman in the Wood (Planché) **42**:279, 298, 301
"A Good Word for Winter" (Lowell) **2**:510, 517; **90**:196
"Good-bye" (Emerson) **38**:186; **98**:177
"Goodbye, Lyric Mine" (Castro Alves)
See "Adeus, Meu Canto"
"Good-Bye My Fancy!" (Whitman) **4**:563; **31**:434-35
Good-Bye My Fancy (Whitman) **205**:226
"Goodbye, Unwashed Russia" (Lermontov) **5**:295
"Goodbye's the Word" (Crawford) **12**:156
"Good-for-Nothing" (Andersen)
See "Hun duede ikke"
"Good-Nature" (Hazlitt) **29**:150
The Good-Natured Bear (Blake) **127**:264-66
"Goody Blake and Harry Gill" (Wordsworth) **12**:387, 402, 445; **111**:199-200, 202-3, 209, 225, 251, 276, 306, 349-50, 356, 359-60; **206**:234
"Googly-Goo" (Field) **3**:210
"Gora" (Leskov) **25**:229, 239, 245-46
"Góra Kikineis" (Mickiewicz) **3**:403; **101**:188-89
Gordon: A Tale (Lamb) **38**:258-59
Gore ot Uma (Griboedov) **129**:152-54, 161-66, 168-73, 175-81, 186, 192-94, 197-98, 206-10
"Gorodok" (Pushkin) **83**:331
"El gorrión" (Isaacs) **70**:304, 308
"Gospel according to Walt Whitman" (Stevenson) **5**:390
"The Gospel of Love" (Chivers) **49**:72
The Gospel of Suffering (Kierkegaard) **78**:239
The Gospel of the Pentateuch and David (Kingsley) **35**:253
The Gospels (Renan)
See *Les évangiles*
Gospoda Golovlyovy (Saltykov) **16**:342-43, 346-47, 349, 351-57, 359, 361-67, 369-76
Gospoda Tashkentsy (Saltykov) **16**:343, 345, 357, 365, 369, 373
"A Gossip on a Novel of Dumas's" (Stevenson) **5**:430; **63**:240; **193**:208
"A Gossip on Romance" (Stevenson) **63**:239-41, 258, 260, 274; **193**:203, 222, 266, 288
"Gotas Amargas" (Silva) **114**:276, 300
Gotas amargas (Silva) **114**:264, 316-17, 319, 321-22
"The Gothic Room" (Bertrand)
See "La chambre gothique"
Gott! Ein Gespräch (Herder) **186**:18, 100
"Der Gott und die Bajadere" (Goethe) **4**:192
Gott und Welt (Goethe) **154**:183
"Die Götter" (Hölderlin) **16**:181
"Die Götter Griechenlandes" (Schiller)
See "Die Götter Griechenlands"
"Die Götter Griechenlands" (Schiller) **39**:305, 331, 349, 387; **166**:100-1, 118
Die Götter im Exil (Heine)
See *Die Verbannten Gotter*
"Götterdämmerung" (Eichendorff) **225**:36, 43, 45-46
Götterdämmerung (Heine) **4**:252
Die Götterdämmerung (Wagner) **9**:409, 417, 441, 446, 449-51, 454, 460, 463, 467, 469-70; **119**:175, 186, 19 234-35, 277, 283, 310, 318, 322, 346-56
Göttergespräche (Wieland) **177**:243-45, 254
"Götterwink" (Mörike) **201**:274, 282
"Das Gottes-Schwert Stoeckers" (Auerbach) **171**:41
"Gottfried Wolfgang" (Borel) **41**:5, 20-3
Die Göttin Diana (Heine) **4**:267
"Das Göttliche" (Goethe) **4**:193
"Göttliche Reminiszenz" (Mörike) **201**:271-72, 346
Götz von Berlichingen mit der eisernen Hand (Goethe) **4**:162-63, 165, 167, 174, 190, 194-96, 198-99, 211-12, 218-19, 221-22; **34**:69-70, 120-21
"Le Gouffre" (Baudelaire) **155**:44
"Le goût du néant" (Baudelaire) **55**:65, 67
"L'gov" (Turgenev) **122**:294
"Government: Anarchy or Regimentation" (Huxley) **67**:68, 111
"The Government Inspector" (Gogol)
See *Révizor*
"A Government-Man" (Hazlitt) **29**:152
"Government of India" (Macaulay) **231**:301
"Governor Manco" (Irving) **2**:372
"The Gowan Glitters on the Sward" (Baillie) **151**:86
Gr. A. K. Tolstomu (Pavlova) **138**:4
"Das Grab" (Klopstock) **11**:239
"Grabež" (Leskov) **25**:228
"Grabgedanken" (Mörike) **201**:303
"Grabschriften" (Werner) **189**:329
"Grace" (Verlaine) **51**:367, 372
"Grace before Meat" (Lamb) **10**:408-09, 424; **113**:173, 175-76, 219, 243
"Grace Greenwood" (Hale) **75**:353
"The Grace of the Bending Grasses" (Larcom) **179**:178
"Grace O'Malley" (Ferguson)
See "Grana Uaile"
"The Graceful and the Exalted" (Schiller) **39**:367
"Les grâces" (Banville) **9**:30
"The Graces" (Derzhavin) **215**:17
The Graces (Foscolo)
See *Le grazie, carme*
The Graces (Wieland) **17**:399
The Graces: A Classical Allegory, Interspersed with Poetry, and Illustrated with Explanatory Notes: Together with a Poetical Fragment Entitled Psyche among the Graces (Wieland)
See *Die Grazien*
La Graceta de las Mujeres (Gómez de Avellaneda) **111**:7, 27
Graciosa and Percinct (Planché) **42**:280, 288-89
Les Gracques (Dumas) **71**:217
"Gracz" (Krasicki) **8**:407
Graf Benyowsky, oder die Verschwörung auf Kamschatka (Kotzebue) **25**:134, 136-37, 139-40, 145, 147
"Graf Eberhard der Greiner von Wirtemberg" (Schiller) **39**:387
Graf Nulin (Pushkin) **3**:414, 443, 445, 451; **27**:367, 386; **83**:272, 275, 332, 334-38, 357-58
Graf Petöfy (Fontane) **26**:241, 244, 253-54, 258; **163**:161, 197
"Der Graf von Habsburg" (Schiller) **39**:389
"Der Graf von Thal" (Droste-Hülshoff) **3**:195, 200, 202
Graf Waldemar: Schauspiel in fünf Akten (Freytag) **109**:138
Die Gräfin Dolores (Arnim) **159**:4, 18, 69
"An Gräfin Josepha L." (Werner) **189**:351
"Grafven i Perrho" (Runeberg) **41**:309, 313, 317, 325
Graham Hamilton (Lamb) **38**:237, 251
Grains de mil (Amiel) **4**:13, 15
Gramática de la Lengua Castellana destinada al uso de los Americanos (Bello) **131**:94, 116, 120
A Grammar and Glossary of the Dorset Dialect (Barnes) **75**:27, 40, 53, 65, 79
Grammar of Assent (Newman)
See *An Essay in Aid of a Grammar of Assent*
A Grammar of the English Language (Cobbett) **49**:93, 108, 120, 134, 140, 148, 160
Grammar of the Serbian Language (Karadzic)
See *Pismenica serbskoga iezika*
"A Grammarian's Funeral" (Browning) **19**:89, 117; **79**:164
A Grammatical Institute, of the English Language, Comprising, an Easy, Concise, and Systematic Method of Education, Designed for the Use of English Schools in America (Webster) **30**:388, 392-93, 395, 403-04, 414, 417-21
Grammatik der slavischen Sprache in Krain, Kärnten und Steyermark (Kopitar) **117**:65-6, 78, 82-3, 87, 91, 101, 116
"Grammer A-Crippled" (Barnes) **75**:48, 67
"Grammer's Shoes" (Barnes) **75**:77
"Grana Uaile" (Ferguson) **33**:278, 283
"Granada" (Zorrilla y Moral) **6**:523, 525, 527
The Grand Assizes (More) **141**:175
"Grand Caucus at Downingville" (Smith) **187**:329
Grand dictionnaire de cuisine (Dumas) **71**:210, 218
"Un grand homme" (Balzac) **153**:70
"The Grand Inquisitor" (Dostoevsky)
See "The Legend of the Grand Inquisitor"
"Grand March of Intellect" (Keats) **121**:124
Un grand mariage (Balzac) **5**:59
"Grand Master of Alcantara" (Irving) **2**:388
"Grand opéra" (Corbière) **43**:31
"The Grand Signor" (Derzhavin) **215**:7
"Grandad Mazáy" (Nekrasov) **11**:421
"La grande bretèche" (Balzac) **5**:52-53, 78; **153**:149-51

"Grande complainte de la ville de Paris" (Laforgue) **221**:82, 93
"Une grande dame" (Verlaine) **2**:629-30
"Grandeur et Décadence de César Birotteau" (Balzac)
See "Histoire de la grandeur et de la décadence de César Birotteau, parfumeur"
"Grandfather Glen" (Parton) **86**:349
"The Grandfather's Blessing" (Auerbach) **171**:50
Grandfather's Chair (Hawthorne) **95**:140; **158**:234; **226**:99
"Grandfather's Spectacles" (Cranch) **115**:51
"La grand'mère" (Beranger) **34**:28
"The Grandmother and the Granddaughter" (Silva)
See "La abulea y la nieta"
"The Grandmother's Apology" (Tennyson) **202**:284
"The Grandmother's Shoe" (Ingelow) **107**:162
"Grandmother's Story of Bunker-Hill Battle" (Holmes) **14**:116
"The Grandsire" (Field) **3**:210
The Grange Garden (Kingsley) **107**:192
"Granit" (Stifter) **198**:283, 321-22, 325-26
Grannarne (Bremer) **11**:15, 17-20, 25, 27-28, 30, 33-35
"The Granny Grey, a Love Tale" (Robinson) **142**:135, 170
Gran'ther Baldwin's Thanksgiving, with Other Ballads and Poems (Alger) **8**:16
"Grantræet" (Andersen) **7**:22, 28, 34; **79**:23, 32-33, 62, 67, 76; **214**:56, 63, 74-75
"Grasmere and Rydal Water" (Sigourney) **21**:301
Grasmere Journal (Wordsworth) **25**:392, 396, 400, 403, 405-06, 409, 412, 415, 417, 422, 424, 428-30
"Grasmere—A Fragment" (Wordsworth) **138**:230, 284
"The Grass so little has to do" (Dickinson) **171**:100
"The Grasshopper Papers" (Crawford) **12**:169-70
"The Grateful Negro" (Edgeworth) **51**:89; **158**:41-42
"Gratitude" (Horton) **87**:92, 100
"Gratitude to Felitsa" (Derzhavin)
See "Blagodarnost' Felitse"
"Gratulazions-Projekt" (Beddoes) **154**:26-28, 32
"The Grave" (Chivers) **49**:47
"The Grave at Perrho" (Runeberg)
See "Grafven i Perrho"
"Grave Comedy" (Sheridan) **91**:245
"The Grave of a Family" (Hemans) **71**:279
"The Grave of a Poetess" (Hemans) **71**:297
"The Grave of a Suicide" (Campbell) **19**:181
"The Grave of Manuel" (Beranger) **34**:46
"The Grave of Miyagi" (Ueda Akinari) **131**:58, 88
"The Grave of the Countess Potocka" (Mickiewicz)
See "Grób Potockiej"
The Grave of the Last Saxon (Bowles) **103**:54, 61
The Grave of the Reichstal Family (Krasiński)
See *Grób Reichstalów*
"The Gravedigger" (Pushkin) **83**:272, 275
"The Graves of a Household" (Hemans) **29**:198, 204, 206; **71**:279
"Graves of Infants" (Clare) **86**:110
"Graves of the Harem" (Mickiewicz)
See "Mogiły haremu"
"Graves on the Coast" (Storm) **1**:547
"The Graveyard" (Karamzin)
See "Kladbishche"
"The Gray Champion" (Hawthorne) **2**:311, 329-30, 333; **79**:308; **171**:342; **226**:32
The Gray Woman (Gaskell)
See *The Grey Woman*
"Grayling; or, Murder Will Out" (Simms) **3**:502, 506, 508
The Gray's-Inn Journal in Two Volumes (Murphy) **229**:230, 232-39, 242, 244-46, 249-50, 253-56, 264
Grazie (Foscolo)
See *Le grazie, carme*
Le Grazie (Foscolo)
See *Le grazie, carme*
Le grazie, carme (Foscolo) **8**:266-69, 271, 273-74; **97**:51-3, 57, 49-60, 62, 68, 78, 83-4, 87-8, 93
Graziella (Lamartine) **11**:266, 278, 286, 289; **190**:199
"Die Grazien" (Klopstock) **225**:321
Die Grazien (Wieland) **177**:363
"Grażyna" (Mickiewicz) **3**:391-93, 397, 399, 401
"The Great Apostate" (Garrison) **149**:256
"Great Are the Myths" (Whitman) **31**:419, 425; **205**:191-92, 194, 207-8, 301
The Great Battle between Slavery and Freedom (Parker) **186**:130, 173
"The Great Carbuncle" (Hawthorne) **2**:305, 311, 322
The Great Exile (Lermontov) **5**:292
"Great Expectations" (Irving) **2**:390
Great Expectations (Dickens) **3**:156, 170-71, 173, 176, 179, 186; **8**:194-96; **18**:111, 114, 119, 121, 127-28, 132-33; **26**:154-230; **37**:153-54, 164, 172; **86**:186, 189, 207, 222, 256, 258; **105**:227-28, 244, 248, 311, 317, 334, 351; **113**:6, 20, 39, 51, 54, 89, 97, 102-3, 111, 115, 118-19, 127, 137; **161**:41-43, 49, 61, 64, 74-76, 78-79, 98, 109, 116-17; **217**:206, 216-18, 220, 233, 243, 245, 261; **219**:72, 82-85, 96, 111, 138, 186, 221, 232; **230**:56, 88-92, 113, 131; **231**:194, 240, 243
"A Great Grief" (Andersen) **214**:57-58
The Great Hoggarty Diamond (Thackeray) **5**:459, 464-65, 470, 482; **14**:402, 420; **43**:355, 359, 368, 381
"The Great House" (Griffin) **7**:215
"Great Lament of the City of Paris" (Laforgue)
See "Grande complainte de la ville de Paris"
"The Great Lawsuit" (Fuller) **5**:163; **211**:143, 147, 152, 183, 187, 190
"A Great Lord" (Krylov) **1**:439
A Great Man for Little Affairs (Fredro)
See *Wielki cztowiek do matych interesbw*
"Great Men" (Parker) **186**:192
"Great Men Have Been among Us" (Wordsworth) **206**:301
"Great Poets and Small" (Hayne) **94**:160
"The Great Sea Serpent" (Andersen)
See "Den Store Søslange"
"A Great Sorrow" (Andersen) **7**:21, 23
"Great spirits now" (Keats) **73**:147
"The Great Stone Face" (Hawthorne) **2**:322; **95**:105; **158**:243; **171**:240, 286, 345
Great Stuttgart Edition (Hölderlin)
See *Sämtliche Werke*
"The Great Unrepresented" (Oliphant) **61**:238
"The Great Vault" (Shevchenko)
See "Velykyj l'ox"
The Great World of London (Mayhew) **31**:186-87, 189-93
"The Great Wrath of the Tyrant and the Cause of It" (Brackenridge) **7**:44
"The Greatcoat" (Gogol)
See "Shinel"
The Greatest Heiress in England (Oliphant) **221**:230
"The Greatest Love of Don Juan" (Barbey d'Aurevilly)
See "Le plus bel amour de Don Juan"
The Greatest Plague of Life; or, The Adventures of a Lady in Search of a Good Servant (Mayhew) **31**:160-61, 178
"Great-grandfather" (Andersen) **79**:84
"The Greatness and Littleness of Human Life" (Newman) **38**:303
The Grecian Daughter. A Tragedy. As it is Acted at the Theatre-Royal in Drury-Lane (Murphy) **229**:223, 227, 264
"The Grecian Girl's Dream of the Blessed Islands" (Moore) **110**:178
"Grecian Urn" (Keats)
See "Ode on a Grecian Urn"
"Greek Architecture" (Melville) **29**:370
"Greek Boy" (Bryant) **6**:172, 181
Greek Cultural History (Burckhardt)
See *Griechische Kulturgeschichte*
The Greek Drama (Lockhart)
See *Greek Tragedy*
"A Greek Girl" (Levy) **59**:96
"The Greek Minstrel" (Arany) **34**:23
"The Greek Partisan" (Bryant) **6**:172; **46**:7
"A Greek Pastoral" (Hogg) **109**:200
Greek Studies (Pater) **7**:303, 312, 323-24, 330-32; **90**:242, 245-46, 248, 283, 286, 335, 338; **159**:257
Greek Tragedy (Lockhart) **6**:293, 295-96
"Green" (Barnes) **75**:46, 68
"Green" (Verlaine) **51**:381, 383; **230**:152, 207
Green Henry (Keller)
See *Der Grüne Heinrich*
A Green Leaf (Storm) **1**:536
"Green River" (Bryant) **6**:158, 169, 171, 176-77, 182-83; **46**:19, 23, 34, 38-9, 45, 47
"The Green Rustle" (Nekrasov)
See "Zelyóny shum"
"Green Tea" (Le Fanu) **9**:302, 308, 312, 317, 319-22; **58**:251, 254-7, 302
"Green Wood Will Last Longer than Dry" (Webster) **30**:423
Greene Ferne Farm (Jefferies) **47**:93, 113, 116, 142
Greenfield Hill: A Poem in Seven Parts (Dwight) **13**:266, 269-70, 272-73, 276-79
Greenway Court (Cooke) **5**:133
Gregory VII: A Tragedy in One Act (Horne) **127**:236, 238, 241, 257-58, 263, 274-75
"Der greise Kopf" (Muller) **73**:366, 394
Grekh da beda na kogo ne zhivyot (Ostrovsky) **30**:98, 101, 104, 112
"La grenadière" (Balzac) **5**:37; **35**:26; **153**:151-52
"Grenzen der Menschheit" (Goethe) **4**:193; **34**:98
"Gretchens Verkündigung" (Werner) **189**:330
Grete Minde (Fontane) **26**:236-37, 243, 250-51, 258, 272; **163**:161-62, 169, 197, 215, 239
"Gretna Green" (Crabbe) **26**:100
Greville (Bulwer-Lytton) **45**:32, 34-5, 38, 71
Greville; or, a Season in Paris (Gore) **65**:8-9, 20
Grey Dolphin (Barham) **77**:4, 36
"The Grey Woman" (Gaskell) **5**:187, 193, 202; **70**:185, 188; **97**:127; **214**:341
Griechen und Roemer (Schlegel)
See *Poesie der Griechen und Roemer*
Griechenlieder (Muller)
See *Lieder der Griechen*
Die Griechensklavin (Humboldt) **134**:162
Der griechische Kaiser (Tieck) **5**:519
Griechische Kulturgeschichte (Burckhardt) **49**:5, 15-16, 32
"Grief" (Barrett Browning) **16**:133
"Grief" (Lazarus) **8**:419
"Grief an' Gladness" (Barnes) **75**:32
"Grief of the Heart" (Andersen)
See "A Great Sorrow"
"The Grievances of Women" (Oliphant) **61**:240; **221**:260, 303
Griffith Gaunt; or, Jealousy (Reade) **2**:537-39, 541-42, 546, 548-53; **74**:246, 249-50, 253, 255, 257-58, 263-65, 298-300, 309-10
"Grigore Ghicavoevod" (Eminescu) **131**:325
Grillparzers Gespräche und die Charakteristiken seiner Persönlichkeit

durch die (Grillparzer) **102**:106, 108-09, 111
"Grim, King of the Ghosts; or, The Dance of Death" (Lewis) **11**:303
"Grimaldi" (Hood) **16**:200
"Grimm" (Sainte-Beuve) **5**:330
"Den grimme Ælling" (Andersen) **7**:22, 25, 30; **79**:4, 11, 21, 23, 30, 34, 51-52, 62, 64, 70-71, 73-74, 81; **214**:18, 38-40, 55, 57, 74
Grimm's Fairy Tales (Grimm Brothers)
See *Kinder-und Hausmärchen*
Grimms' Fairy Tales (Grimm Brothers)
See *Kinder-und Hausmärchen*
"Grimm's Law" (Grimm Brothers) **3**:220
Grimms' Tales (Grimm Brothers)
See *Kinder-und Hausmärchen*
Grimstahamn's New Settlement (Almqvist)
See *Grimstahamns nybygge*
Grimstahamns nybygge (Almqvist) **42**:4
"Grinding song" (Lonnrot) **53**:339
Gringoire (Banville) **9**:18-19, 21, 24
"Griseld Baillie" (Baillie)
See "The Legend of Lady Griseld Baillie"
"Griselda" (Levy) **59**:112-3; **203**:354
"La Grisette" (Holmes) **14**:100-01
"Grit" (Cooke) **110**:24, 43
Grit, The Young Boatman (Alger) **83**:91, 93
"Grizzly Bear-Hunting" (Thorpe) **183**:357-58
Das Groβartige der Weltverhältnisse, anatomisch-politische Untersuchung, der Luzerner Faschingszeitung gewidmet (Beddoes) **154**:25, 31-32
"The Groans of the Tankard" (Barbauld) **50**:4; **185**:29, 31, 33, 36
Grób Agamemnona (Slowacki) **15**:365, 376
"Grób Potockiej" (Mickiewicz) **3**:390, 403; **101**:188-89
Grób Reichstalów (Krasiński) **4**:312
"Grobovshchik" (Pushkin) **3**:435, 452; **83**:295, 323, 327, 337, 354
"The Grocers Dethroned" (Fourier) **51**:180
Græsk og Nordisk Mythologi for Ungdommen (Grundtvig) **158**:126, 175, 177, 179, 182
Der Groβ-Cophta (Goethe) **4**:222
The Gros Mousqueton Diplomatique, or Diplomatic Blunderbuss (Cobbett) **49**:109
"Die Grösse der Welt" (Schiller) **39**:357
Les grostesques (Gautier) **1**:351
"The Grotto" (Sheridan) **91**:232
The Grounds of an Opinion on the Policy of Restricting the Importation of Foreign Corn (Malthus) **145**:252
Groundwork of the Metaphysics of Morals (Kant)
See *Grundlegung zur Metaphysik der Sitten*
The Group (Warren) **13**:411-14, 416-19, 425-26, 428-29; **226**:253, 255-58, 260, 263, 270-71, 285-87, 290
"Growing Old" (Arnold) **218**:116
Growing Up (Ichiyō)
See *Takekurabe*
"The Growth of Love" (Lampman) **25**:201; **194**:25
"The Growth of Words" (Whitman) **81**:287, 290-91, 293-94
Groza (Ostrovsky) **30**:93, 96, 100, 102, 104, 109-11, 113, 115, 119; **57**:209-10, 212-3, 219, 221-5, 227, 229
"Gruffmoody Grim" (Barnes) **75**:79
Gruie sînger (Eminescu) **33**:265
"A Grumble about the Christmas Books" (Thackeray) **213**:327, 329
"Grumbler's Gully" (Clarke) **19**:250-51
Grumbling and Contradiction (Fredro)
See *Zrzędnosc i przecora*
"Grund zum Empedokles" (Hölderlin) **16**:165, 178; **187**:189-92, 243, 245, 248, 252
Grundlage der gesamten Wissenschaftslehre (Fichte) **62**:11, 13, 34, 39-47
Grundlage des Naturrechts nach Prinzipen der Wissenshaftslehre (Fichte) **62**:34, 48, 58-9
Grundlegung (Kant) **67**:216, 220, 222, 225, 237, 288-94
Grundlegung zur Metaphysik der Sitten (Kant) **27**:194, 217, 259, 261; **67**:214, 216, 222, 260-62, 271, 273-74, 278, 285, 288, 291
Grundlinien der Philosophie des Rechts, order Naturrech und Staatwissenschaft im Grundrisse (Hegel) **46**:111, 113, 140, 147, 151, 157, 171, 175-9, 191-4; **151**:238, 251, 256, 282-3, 285, 288-91, 301-2, 309, 316-7, 322-3, 325-8, 330-1, 370
Grundrisse (Marx) **114**:70, 85-6
Grundsätze der Philosophie der Zukunft (Feuerbach) **139**:283, 290, 293, 343
"Grundsätze seiner Prüfung des Europäischen Verstandes und seine Velledenblätter" (Herder) **186**:19
Die Gründung Prags (Brentano) **1**:101-02; **191**:5, 62, 70-71, 78, 121-22
Die Grundzüge der Gegenwärtigun Zeitalters (Fichte) **62**:35
Der Grüne Heinrich (Keller) **2**:411-12, 414-25
Ein Grünes Blatt (Storm) **1**:539; **195**:13, 20, 89, 93
"Grustno veter voet" (Pavlova) **138**:15
"La gruta del ensueño" (Casal) **131**:256
El guajiro (Villaverde) **121**:334
"The Guardian Angel" (Browning) **19**:116, 127
"Guardian Angel" (Eminescu) **131**:331
The Guardian Angel (Holmes) **14**:104-06, 110, 113, 115, 117, 124, 131, 133-38, 140-43; **81**:102, 107
"The Guardian of the Red Disk" (Lazarus) **109**:338
The Guardians of the Crown (Arnim)
See *Die Kronenwächter*
The Guards in Canada; or, The Point of Honor (Richardson) **55**:303, 358
Guatimozín, último emperador de México (Gómez de Avellaneda) **111**:23-4, 71
Gubernskie ocherki (Saltykov) **16**:342-45, 347, 357, 368, 372, 374-75
"The Gude Greye Katt" (Hogg) **109**:248-49
"Gudfaders Billedbog" (Andersen) **214**:61-62
Gudhataren (Almqvist) **42**:17
"The Guerilla" (Hogg) **4**:282; **109**:246
"The Guerilla Chief" (Landon) **15**:161
"La Guerre" (Maupassant) **83**:189
"Guerre" (Rimbaud) **4**:473; **35**:322; **82**:232; **227**:237-39, 293, 323
Guerre aux Démolisseurs! (Hugo) **189**:181
"La guerre des Turcomans" (Gobineau) **17**:69-70, 103-04
La Guerre Sociale (Mérimée) **65**:85
"The Guests Were Arriving at the Dacha" (Pushkin) **83**:313-17, 319
"Les gueux" (Beranger) **34**:30
"Le gueux" (Maupassant) **1**:448
"Le guignon" (Baudelaire) **29**:103; **55**:58
"Le Guignon" (Mallarmé) **4**:376; **41**:241, 250, 280, 290; **210**:217
"Guilt and Sorrow" (Wordsworth) **206**:341, 344
Guilt and Sorrow (Wordsworth) **38**:426; **111**:201, 253
"'Guilty?'/'Not Guilty?'" (Kierkegaard) **125**:198-99, 201
Guilty Without Guilt (Ostrovsky)
See *Bez viný vinovátye*
"Guinevere" (Tennyson) **30**:279, 292; **65**:228-9, 239, 243-6, 251, 277, 279, 282, 285, 292-3, 296-301, 305, 307, 312, 314, 318-9, 324, 335, 340, 342, 350, 357, 359, 365, 374, 381, 383-6; **202**:206, 221-22, 248, 250, 252-53, 322-23, 334
Guiskard (Kleist)
See *Robert Guiskard, Herzog der Normänner*
"Guitare" (Corbière) **43**:14, 34
"Guitare" (Laforgue) **53**:272; **221**:58-59, 83
"Guizot's Lectures on European Civilization" (Mill) **179**:337
"Gulistan" (Taylor) **89**:302
Gulliver (Dumas) **71**:217
Gulzara; or the Persian Slave (Mowatt) **74**:227
The Günderode (Arnim)
See *Die Günderode: Den Studenten*
Die Günderode: Den Studenten (Arnim) **38**:7, 10, 15; **123**:9, 25-26, 28, 30-31, 38, 42-47, 50, 59, 70, 95
Gunderslev Skov (Grundtvig) **158**:138
Gundersley Forest (Grundtvig)
See *Gunderslev Skov*
Gunlog (Stagnelius) **61**:253, 255-6
Gunnar: A Tale of Norse Life (Boyesen) **135**:3, 5-6, 10-11, 18-19, 24, 30, 32-33, 36-37, 50
"Gunnar's Howe" (Morris) **4**:434
"Gunpowder Treason" (Keble) **87**:204
"Gurresange" (Jacobsen) **34**:163, 165
Gustav Adolfs Page (Meyer) **81**:139, 155, 162-63, 166, 184, 212-13, 217, 220, 227
Gustave; ou, Le mauvais sujet (Kock) **16**:245-46, 260
"Gustavo Moreau" (Casal) **131**:236, 268-69
Gutch Memorandum Book (Coleridge) **231**:56
"Gute Lehre" (Mörike) **10**:453
"Gute Nacht" (Muller) **73**:382, 384-85, 390-93
"An Gutenstein" (Raimund) **69**:10-12, 14-19
Der gutmütig Teufel (Nestroy) **42**:242, 246
"Guy Faux's Night" (Barnes) **75**:77
Guy Fawkes; or, The Gunpowder Treason (Ainsworth) **13**:39-40, 47
Guy Mannering (Scott) **15**:259-60, 272, 280, 289, 300, 302, 309, 324; **69**:303, 391; **110**:299, 325
Guy Mannering; or, The Astrologer (Scott) **209**:216, 225, 258, 343-50, 352
Guy Rivers (Simms) **3**:499-500, 508-10
"Guys" (Baudelaire) **29**:70
La guzla; ou, Choix de poésies illyriques (Mérimée) **6**:350-2, 362; **65**:44, 46, 58, 87, 115
"Guzman's Family" (Maturin) **6**:333, 335
"Gwain Down the Steps vor Water" (Barnes) **75**:6
"Gwain to Brookwell" (Barnes) **75**:4
Gwałltu, co sie dzieje (Fredro) **8**:292
"Gwin, King of Norway" (Blake) **13**:182, 219, 239
"Gyalázatos világ" (Petofi) **21**:278
Gyges and His Ring (Hebbel)
See *Gyges und sein Ring: Eine Tragödie in fünf Acten*
Gyges und sein Ring: Eine Tragödie in fünf Acten (Hebbel) **43**:230, 238-40, 246, 249, 259-62, 278, 283-85, 288-89, 291, 293, 296-300
The Gypsies (Pushkin)
See *Tsygany*
The Gypsies and their Music in Hungary (Liszt)
See *Des Bohémiens et de leur musique en Hongrie*
The Gypsies of Nagy Ida (Arany)
See *A nagyidai czigányok*
"Gypsy Dance" (Derzhavin)
See "Cyganskaja pljaska"
The Gypsy Girl (Baratynsky)
See *Nalozhnitsa*
"The Gypsy King" (Norton) **47**:252
"H" (Rimbaud) **4**:484; **35**:308, 322; **227**:292-93
The H— Family (Bremer)
See *Familjen H.*
H. C. Andersens Eventyr I-VII 1963-1990 (Andersen) **214**:26-27
H. C. Andersens samlede Skrifter (Andersen)
See *Samlede voerker*
H. Taine: Sa vie et sa correspondance (Taine) **15**:453
"Habeas Corpus" (Jackson) **90**:159
"Haben wir noch jetzt das Publikum und Vaterland der Alten?" (Herder) **186**:79-80
"The Habit of Perfection" (Hopkins) **17**:191
"Habits of Grate Men" (Shaw) **15**:335

"Hacen las cosas tan claras que hasta los ciegos ven" (Lizardi) **30**:67
Hackney Coachman (More) **141**:191
"Had a man's fair form" (Keats) **73**:148
"Had we but met in life's delicious spring" (Osgood) **141**:355
Hadlaub (Keller) **2**:414
"Hadst Thou Liv'd in Days of Old" (Keats) **73**:259
"Hafbur and Signy" (Morris) **4**:423
"Hafiz" (Emerson) **98**:179
"The Hag" (Turgenev) **21**:431
"Hagar in the Wilderness" (Willis) **194**:306
ha-Gemul (Smolenskin) **30**:190, 195
"Der Hagestolz" (Stifter) **41**:343, 357, 359-62, 364, 391
Der Hagestolz (Stifter) **198**:261-62, 285
Haidamaky (Shevchenko) **54**:358, 360, 367, 369, 375-6, 379, 381, 386, 388-90
"Das Haidedorf" (Stifter) **41**:335, 341, 366, 376, 380-81, 385
"Hail Briton!" (Tennyson) **30**:293
"Hail Great Republic" (Paine) **62**:324
"Hail, humble Helpstone" (Clare) **86**:93
"Hail Matrimony" (Blake) **37**:29
"Haimatochare" (Hoffmann) **183**:176
"Haine du pauvre" (Mallarmé)
See "Aumône"
"Der Halbmond glänzet am Himmel" (Grillparzer) **102**:174
"Half a Crown's Worth of Cheap Knowledge" (Thackeray) **213**:200
"Half a Lifetime Ago" (Gaskell) **5**:191, 201-02, 205; **70**:185
"The Half of Life Gone" (Morris) **4**:434
The Half-Breed: A Tale of the Western Frontier (Whitman) **81**:344
"The Half-Brothers" (Gaskell) **70**:186
The Half-Brothers; or, The Head and the Hand (Dumas)
See *Le bâtard de Mauléon*
A Half-Century of Conflict (Parkman) **12**:341, 346, 351, 353, 366, 370-72, 377
"Half-Sir" (Griffin) **7**:201, 211-12, 217
"Hälfte des Lebens" (Hölderlin) **16**:174-6, 192; **187**:215, 219
"The Half-way House" (Hopkins) **189**:5-6, 142
"The Hall" (Crabbe) **26**:129
"The Hall and the Wood" (Morris) **4**:434
"The Hall of Cynddylan" (Hemans) **29**:205
"The Hall of Justice" (Crabbe) **26**:78-9, 82, 118; **121**:9, 34
"Hall of the Muses" (Meyer)
See "Der Musensaal"
"Hallam's Constitutional History" (Macaulay) **231**:279
Halle und Jerusalem (Arnim) **5**:19-22, 24; **159**:43
Eine Halligfahrt (Storm) **1**:540, 542, 544; **195**:4, 45
"Hallowed Ground" (Campbell) **19**:179, 183
"Hallowed Pleäces" (Barnes) **75**:7, 59
"Halt" (Muller) **73**:364, 370
"Halte là!—le chant de victoire des Ottomans" (Beranger) **34**:28
The Halton Boys (Crawford) **12**:170, 172-74; **127**:193, 196
"The Hamadryad" (Hayne) **94**:158
"The Hamadryad" (Landor) **14**:168, 190
"Hamalija" (Shevchenko) **54**:358, 367, 377, 379
"Hamatreya" (Emerson) **1**:293, 295-97; **38**:187; **98**:177, 179-80
The Hamiltons; or, Official in Life in 1830 (Gore) **65**:16, 18-19, 28, 31
"Hamlet" (Laforgue) **221**:4, 6, 8, 12-14, 20, 57, 68
"Hamlet" (Lamb) **125**:304
"Hamlet" (Very) **9**:370, 379
"Hamlet and Don Quixote" (Turgenev)
See "Gamlet i Don Kikhot"
"A Hamlet of the Scigry District" (Turgenev)
See "Gamlet ščigrovskogo uezda"
"Hamlet of the Shchigrovsky District" (Turgenev)
See "Gamlet ščigrovskogo uezda"
"Hamlet of the Shchigry District" (Turgenev)
See "Gamlet ščigrovskogo uezda"
"Hamlet; or, The Consequences of Filial Piety" (Laforgue)
See "Hamlet; ou, les suites de piété filiale"
"Hamlet; or, The Results of Filial Devotion" (Laforgue)
See "Hamlet; ou, les suites de piété filiale"
"Hamlet; ou, les suites de piété filiale" (Laforgue) **5**:271, 274, 281-2; **53**:273, 293
"The Hamlets" (Martineau) **137**:251, 271
The Hammer of the Village (Petofi)
See *A helység kalapácsa*
The Hampshire Tragedy (More) **141**:172
Han d'Islande (Hugo) **3**:233-34, 236-37, 239, 254, 258; **21**:195, 198, 201, 205; **161**:201-2, 204-5, 214, 259
"The Hand and Foot" (Very) **9**:382-84, 397
"Hand and Heart" (Gaskell) **70**:185-86
"Hand and Soul" (Rossetti) **4**:504, 510; **77**:331, 333-34, 339, 341
"Hand and Word" (Griffin) **7**:198, 212, 217
"Der Hand der Jezerte" (Mörike) **10**:456-57
"Hand in Hand with Angels" (Larcom) **179**:177
"A Hand Mirror" (Whitman) **81**:364
The Hand of Glory (Barham) **77**:9, 33-34
"The Hand of Jezerte" (Mörike)
See "Der Hand der Jezerte"
The Hand of the Arch-Sinner (Brontë) **109**:52
"The Hand that swept the sounding lyre" (Osgood) **141**:354
Handbook on World History (Grundtvig)
See *Lærebog i Verdenhistorien*
A Handbook to the Courts of Modern Sculpture (Jameson) **43**:327
A Handbook to the Public Galleries of Art in and near London (Jameson) **43**:306, 317, 321-22
Handelsanmassungen (Herder) **186**:11
Handley Cross (Surtees) **14**:343, 346-49, 353-54, 357, 361-63, 366, 369-70, 372-75, 377, 380-81
"Hands All Round!" (Tennyson) **30**:294-95
"Der Handschuh" (Schiller) **39**:337, 388; **166**:106-7
"The Handsome Heart" (Hopkins) **189**:7
The Handy Cook Book (Beecher) **30**:15
"Hanging of the Crane" (Longfellow) **45**:139
"The Hangman" (Espronceda)
See "El verdugo"
The Hangman's Rope (Petofi)
See *A hóhér kötele*
Hangover from Another's Feast (Ostrovsky)
See *V chuzhom piru pokhmelye*
"Hankai" (Ueda Akinari) **131**:21-23, 52-53, 58-60
Hanna (Runeberg) **41**:309-10, 317
"Hannah Binding Shoes" (Larcom) **179**:167, 169, 178, 182
Hannah Thurston (Taylor) **89**:310, 343, 347
"Hannan laulu" (Kivi) **30**:51
"Hanna's Song" (Kivi)
See "Hannan laulu"
Hannibal (Grabbe) **2**:272-73, 276, 282, 284-85, 287-88
Hanns Frei (Ludwig) **4**:349
"An Hans" (Storm) **195**:11, 53
Hans Andersen's Fairy Tales (Andersen)
See *Eventyr, fortalte for børn*
Hans Bär (Storm) **195**:23-24, 35
Hans Christian Andersen's Correspondence (Andersen) **7**:24
Hans Christian Andersen's Fairy Tales (Andersen) **7**:26, 29-33
"Hans Fingerhut's Frog Lesson" (Lampman) **25**:205-06, 219; **194**:6-7, 20, 40, 43, 59, 61-62
"Hans Joggeli der Erbvetter" (Gotthelf) **117**:6, 18
Hans Max Giesbrecht (Kotzebue) **25**:136
Hans of Iceland (Hugo)
See *Han d'Islande*
"Hans ohne Land" (Heine) **147**:229
"Hans Pfaal" (Poe)
See "The Unparalleled Adventure of One Hans Pfaall"
Hans Sachs' Poetische Sendung (Goethe) **154**:183
Hans und Heinz Kirch (Storm) **1**:537, 540, 550; **195**:6, 12, 14, 16, 20, 55-57
Hanswursts Hochzeit (Goethe) **4**:213; **154**:312
Hanz Küchelgarten (Gogol) **162**:29, 61, 129
"Hanz Kuechelgarten" (Gogol) **31**:115
"Hapless Dionis" (Eminescu)
See "Sarmanul Dionis"
"Happier Dead" (Baudelaire)
See "Le mort joyeux"
The Happiest Day of My Life (Scribe) **16**:382
"The Happiest Girl in the World" (Webster) **230**:231-32, 234, 277, 298, 330
"Happiness" (Lampman) **194**:132, 134
"Happiness" (Milnes) **61**:136
Happiness (Verlaine)
See *Bonheur*
"Happiness in Crime" (Barbey d'Aurevilly)
See "Le bonheur dans le crime"
"The Happiness of the Jokers" (Krasicki)
See "Szczęsacliwość filutów"
The Happy Age (Undset)
See *Den lykkelige alder*
"The Happy Daes When I Wer Young" (Barnes) **75**:22, 56
Happy Dodd; Or, "She Hath Done What She Counld" (Cooke) **110**:12, 21, 39, 50, 55, 58
"A Happy Evening" (Wagner) **119**:192, 197
"The Happy Family" (Andersen) **7**:33; **79**:23, 31; **214**:72
"Happy is England" (Keats) **73**:147
"A Happy Poet" (Thomson) **18**:413
"Happy Sundays for Children" (Hale) **75**:282
"Happy: The Leper's Bride" (Tennyson) **202**:292
"The Happy Valley" (Woolson) **82**:272
"Happy Warrior" (Wordsworth) **38**:360; **206**:225
"Happy Women" (Alcott) **83**:34, 36
Hard Cash: A Matter-of-Fact Romance (Reade) **2**:533-37, 539-41, 545, 548-51; **74**:245-48, 250, 253, 255, 257-58, 262-65, 284, 287-89, 298, 318-19
"A Hard Lesson" (Cooke) **110**:39
Hard Times: For These Times (Dickens) **3**:150, 155-56, 158, 166, 172, 174, 184-85, 188; **8**:171, 176; **18**:114, 121-22, 134; **26**:168, 171, 177; **37**:175, 200, 202; **50**:105-215; **86**:249, 260; **105**:231, 244, 254, 256, 258-59, 261, 274, 330-31, 336, 340, 354; **113**:97; **161**:98; **187**:11, 13, 46-47; **203**:181, 253, 284; **206**:19, 140; **217**:206, 221; **219**:82-83, 97, 190; **230**:1-149; **231**:180, 183, 188
"Hard Up" (O'Brien) **21**:249
Hardscrabble; or, The Fall of Chicago. A Tale of Indian Warfare (Richardson) **55**:303-4, 313-4, 321, 344, 346
"The Hardy Tin Soldier" (Andersen)
See "Den standhaftige Tinsoldat"
"The Hare Chase" (Leskov)
See "Zajačij remiz"
"The Hare Park" (Leskov)
See "Zajačij remiz"
"Hareem" (Milnes) **61**:130
"Harem's Graves" (Mickiewicz)
See "Mogiły haremu"
"Hark, My Soul! It Is the Lord" (Cowper) **8**:127; **94**:73
"Hark to the Shouting Wind" (Timrod) **25**:364, 373
"Härka-Tuomo" (Kivi) **30**:64
"Harlem" (Bertrand) **31**:49, 54
"The Harlequin of Dreams" (Lanier) **118**:240

"Harmonie du soir" (Baudelaire) **29**:77; **55**:14, 28
Harmonies poétiques et religieuses (Lamartine) **11**:248, 250, 252-53, 255, 265, 268-74, 278-80, 283, 286; **190**:172, 176, 218-19, 226-28, 232-33, 235, 237, 254, 257, 263
Harmonies poétiques et religieuses (Liszt) **199**:304, 307
Harold (Southey) **97**:312
Harold (Tennyson) **30**:263-64, 293
"Harold and Tosti" (Sigourney) **21**:298-99
Harold the Dauntless (Scott) **209**:182-83, 185, 190-91
Harold, the Last of the Saxon Kings (Bulwer-Lytton) **1**:146, 150-52; **45**:13-15, 21-2, 60-2
"The Harp" (Lonnrot) **53**:327
"The Harp of Broken Strings" (Ridge) **82**:174, 180-81
"The Harp that once" (Moore) **110**:194
"The Harp That Once through Tara's Halls" (Moore) **6**:391, 398
"Harpagus' Ballad" (Beddoes) **3**:34
"The Harper" (Campbell) **19**:188, 190, 198
"The harper, who sat on his low mossy seat" (Baillie) **151**:91
"The Harper Wind" (Jones) **222**:128
The Harper's Daughter (Lewis) **11**:305
"Harriet" (Brontë) **109**:30
"Harriet II" (Brontë) **109**:29
Harriet Martineau's Autobiography (Martineau)
See *Autobiography*
Harriet Martineau's Letters to Fannie Wedgewood (Martineau) **137**:323, 335
Harrington (Edgeworth) **1**:258; **51**:88-90, 117-29
Harriot and Sophia (Lennox)
See *Sophia*
Harry and Lucy Continued, Being the Last Part of Early Lessons (Edgeworth) **51**:81
Harry Clinton; a Tale of Youth (Hays) **114**:186
"Harry Gill" (Wordsworth)
See "Goody Blake and Harry Gill"
Harry Heathcote of Gangoil: A Tale of Australian Bush Life (Trollope) **101**:241; **215**:260-61, 263-64, 266
Harry Joscelyn (Oliphant) **11**:446, 449
Harry Lorrequer (Lever)
See *The Confessions of Harry Lorrequer*
Harry Muir (Oliphant) **11**:432; **221**:226, 244
"Harry Ploughman" (Hopkins) **17**:189, 225, 256
"Hartleap Well" (Wordsworth) **12**:434; **111**:236, 348
"Hart-Leap Well" (Wordsworth)
See "Hartleap Well"
Hartlebury (Disraeli) **79**:269, 274-75
"Hartley Coleridge" (Bagehot) **10**:18, 31, 40-41, 55
"The Hartz Journey" (Heine)
See *Die Harzreise*
The Hartz Journey (Heine)
See *Die Harzreise*
"Harun's Sons" (Meyer)
See "Die Söhne Haruns"
Harusame Monogatari (Ueda Akinari) **131**:20-22, 40-41, 45, 51-53, 55-56, 60, 86, 88
"Harvest Hwome" (Barnes) **75**:78
"The Harvest Moon" (Longfellow) **45**:161
"Harvest Morning" (Clare) **9**:74
"A Harvest of Tares" (Boyesen) **135**:33
"Harvest Song" (Meyer)
See "Schnitterlied"
"Harvest Storm" (Meyer)
See "Erntegewitter"
The Harveys (Kingsley) **107**:192-93
The Harz Journey (Heine)
See *Die Harzreise*
"Harzer Hans" (Gotthelf) **117**:43, 58
Die Harzreise (Heine) **4**:253; **54**:316, 327-8, 336; **147**:150, 168
"Has the Frog a Soul, and of What Nature is That Soul, Supposing It to Exist" (Huxley) **67**:86
Hasara Raba (Sacher-Masoch) **31**:287, 294
"The Haschish" (Whittier) **8**:531
Hastings (Macaulay) **42**:87
"Hastings" (Macaulay)
See "Warren Hastings"
The Hasty-Pudding (Barlow) **23**:14-15, 19, 29, 32-4, 36, 39-44; **223**:27, 65, 67-70
"Hate" (Shelley) **170**:204
ha-To'eh be-darke ha-hayim (Smolenskin) **30**:186, 189-92, 195
"Hatteras" (Freneau) **111**:105
Hau Kiou Choaan (Percy) **95**:313
"Haunted and the Haunters" (Bulwer-Lytton) **1**:151; **45**:71
"The Haunted Baronet" (Le Fanu) **9**:312; **58**:286, 295, 302-4
"The Haunted Beach" (Robinson) **142**:95-96, 99, 110-11, 114-15, 133, 135-36, 140, 149, 180, 225, 249-50, 278-80
Haunted Hearts (Cummins) **139**:166, 185
The Haunted Hotel: A Mystery of Modern Venice (Collins) **1**:180, 183; **93**:36-7, 42-4
"A Haunted House" (Dickens) **187**:172
"The Haunted House" (Hood) **16**:205, 208, 210, 216, 220-22, 224-29, 231-36
"Haunted House" (Whittier) **8**:485
"Haunted Houses" (Longfellow) **45**:116-17
Haunted Lives (Le Fanu) **9**:312; **58**:272-5
The Haunted Man and the Ghost's Bargain: A Fancy for Christmas-time (Dickens) **113**:51; **161**:66, 78; **203**:179, 181; **211**:39, 42
The Haunted Marsh (Sand)
See *La mare au diable*
"The Haunted Mind" (Hawthorne) **2**:305; **39**:224
"The Haunted Palace" (Poe) **1**:508, 512; **16**:295; **55**:169, 181, 212; **97**:181-82, 191-93, 195-96, 199, 204-05, 210; **117**:192, 242-44, 278, 281, 303; **211**:246-48, 263-64, 286-87
The Haunted Pool (Sand)
See *La mare au diable*
"Haunted Tower" (Irving) **2**:372
"The Haunting of the Tiled House" (Le Fanu) **9**:315
"Haunts of the Lapwing" (Jefferies) **47**:137
Häuptlingabendwind (Nestroy) **42**:232
Das Haus der Temperamente (Nestroy) **42**:227, 232, 238, 240, 243
"Häusliche Szene" (Mörike) **10**:453
"Hautot père et fils" (Maupassant) **83**:227
"Have Compassion on Me" (Isaacs)
See "Ten piedad de mi"
"Have Faith" (Harpur) **114**:147
"Have I Not Striven, My God, and Watched and Prayed?" (Rossetti) **50**:317
"Have We Any Men Among Us?" (Parton) **86**:352
"Haverhill" (Whittier) **8**:532
"Having Received Some Favour, a Glance or Salutation, He Turns His Curses Into Blessings" (Liszt) **199**:307
Hawbuck Grange (Surtees) **14**:349, 353, 369, 374, 377, 379
Häwelmann (Storm)
See *Der kleine Häwelmann*
The Hawks of Hawk Hollow: A Tradition of Pennsylvania (Bird) **1**:83-84, 86, 88, 90-91
The Hawks of Hawk-Hollow (Bird) **197**:6, 8, 13-14, 29, 31, 43-44, 68
"Haworth Churchyard" (Arnold) **6**:72; **29**:26, 28, 32-3, 37
"Hawthorne and his Mosses" (Melville) **91**:33-4, 140, 209, 212, 219; **181**:200, 224; **193**:109; **221**:108
"Hay muertos que no hacen ruido" (Lizardi) **30**:67
"Hay-Carren" (Barnes) **75**:77
"Hay-Meaken" (Barnes) **75**:77
"The Haystack in the Floods" (Morris) **4**:422, 425-26, 432, 441, 444
"The Hayswater Boat" (Arnold) **29**:36
Hazelwwod Hall (Bloomfield) **145**:147
"He and I" (Rossetti) **4**:491; **77**:339
"He and She" (Rossetti) **66**:341
"He fumbles at your Soul" (Dickinson) **77**:76-77, 88; **171**:96
"He hath abolished the old drouth" (Hopkins) **189**:142
"He Heard Her Sing" (Thomson) **18**:417, 419
He is not well-born (Andersen) **79**:16
"He is Not Worth the Trouble" (Rowson) **182**:255, 282
He Knew He was Right (Trollope) **6**:459, 477, 491, 493, 497, 504, 513; **33**:363; **101**:241, 289, 291, 321; **215**:201, 212, 214, 240, 242-44
"He put the Belt around my life" (Dickinson) **77**:156; **171**:98
"He Saw My Heart's Woe" (Brontë) **3**:62
"He scanned it—Staggered—" (Dickinson) **77**:162; **171**:197-98
"He strained my faith" (Dickinson) **77**:82
He that Will Not when He May (Oliphant) **221**:226
"He Was Killed" (Bestuzhev)
See "On bly ubit"
"He Was Weak, and I Was Strong—Then" (Dickinson) **21**:79
He Who Hated God (Almqvist)
See *Gudhataren*
He Who Will Not When He May (Oliphant) **11**:446
The Head of the Family (Craik) **38**:110, 120, 126-27
Head of the Family (Oliphant) **11**:428
The Headsman (Cooper) **203**:48-49, 72
The Headsman of Berne (Cooper) **1**:200, 218-19; **54**:256, 262, 288
"The Headstwone" (Barnes) **75**:8
"The Healing of Conall Carnach" (Ferguson) **33**:278-79, 283, 289
"Healing of Jairus' Daughter" (Willis) **194**:288
"A Health" (Pinkney) **31**:269, 272-76, 280
"Health" (Warton)
See "Ode to Health"
Health, Husbandry and Handicraft (Martineau) **26**:346
Hear Both Sides (Holcroft) **85**:199, 218
"Hear what the mournful linnets say" (Rossetti) **186**:237
"The Heare" (Barnes) **75**:35
"The Heart" (Emerson) **38**:211; **98**:94-100
"Heart" (Poe)
See "The Tell-Tale Heart"
Heart and Cross (Oliphant) **61**:203
Heart and Science: A Story of the Present Times (Collins) **1**:176, 180; **93**:12, 66
"The Heart and the Brain" (Lewes) **215**:141
"The Heart asks Pleasure—first" (Dickinson) **77**:163-64; **171**:197
"The Heart Broken" (Lippard) **198**:132, 164
"The Heart Healed and Changed by Mercy" (Cowper) **94**:72
"The Heart of God" (Larcom) **179**:174
The Heart of Gold (Jerrold) **2**:402
"The Heart of John Middleton" (Gaskell) **5**:205; **70**:188-90; **137**:59
The Heart of Mid-Lothian (Scott) **15**:277, 289, 294, 300-01, 304, 317-18, 321-24; **69**:303, 310-13, 368; **209**:173-74, 178, 200-201, 206-7, 209-13, 219, 221, 225, 235, 238, 263-64, 271, 278, 280-83, 285-86, 297-98, 337, 343, 349-50
"The Heart That Lacks Room" (Webster) **230**:311
"Heart, we will forget him" (Dickinson) **171**:97
"Heart's Hope" (Rossetti) **77**:312
Hearts of Oak (Rowson) **69**:140-41
"Heat" (Lampman) **25**:162, 166, 168, 171-72,

180, 182, 184-85, 192-94, 197-200, 202, 210; **194**:7, 28, 31, 34-35, 41-42, 46, 48-50, 52-53, 58-60, 62-64, 72-76, 82, 84, 89, 93, 97-98, 100-103, 139
"Heat Lightning" (Meyer)
See "Wetterleuchten"
The Heath Cobblers (Kivi)
See *Nummisuutarit*
The Heathcock (Arnim)
See *Der Averhahn*
"The Heather" (Webster) **230**:311
The Heather on Fire: A Tale of the Highland Clearances (Blind) **202**:4, 9, 17, 33, 40-44, 46-48, 51
"Heathlands" (Jefferies) **47**:134
"L'héautontimorouménos" (Baudelaire) **6**:115; **55**:24, 61, 71; **155**:17-19, 100
Heaven and Earth (Byron) **2**:67, 80, 91; **12**:139; **109**:102-03, 106; **149**:149
"Heaven Overarches" (Rossetti) **186**:309-10, 312-15
"Heaven-Haven" (Hopkins) **189**:10, 16, 90
"'Heaven'—is what I cannot reach!" (Dickinson) **77**:96
"Heavenly Love" (Horton) **87**:110
"The Heavenly Vision" (Chivers) **49**:50
"Heaven's Mourning" (Lenau) **16**:275
"The Heavy Brigade" (Tennyson)
See "The Charge of the Heavy Brigade"
"A Heavy Heart" (Rossetti) **50**:313
"Hebe" (Adams) **175**:29
"Hebräische Melodien" (Heine) **4**:253-55, 269; **147**:154, 163, 180, 182, 229, 246-47
"Hebraism and Hellenism" (Arnold) **89**:60; **218**:178, 197
"Hebrew Dirge" (Sigourney) **21**:309
"Hebrew Melodies" (Heine)
See "Hebräische Melodien"
Hebrew Melodies (Byron) **2**:63, 90, 103; **149**:45, 149
"The Hebrew Mother" (Hemans) **29**:196; **71**:275
"Der Heckebeutel" (Arnim) **123**:15, 88-92
"Hector in the Garden" (Barrett Browning) **1**:117; **61**:43
Hector's Inheritance; or, The Boys of Smith Institute (Alger) **8**:16, 35, 43-44
Hector-Vadh (Dutt) **118**:5
"Hedge School" (Carleton) **3**:86, 89, 93; **199**:8-9, 16, 107
"The Hedgehog" (Clare) **9**:107
"Hegel" (Marx) **17**:295
"Hegel's Aesthetics: The Philosophy of Art" (Lewes) **25**:288, 299-300; **215**:163
Hegels theologische Jungendschriften (Hegel) **46**:139, 163; **151**:238
Heidebilder (Droste-Hülshoff) **3**:193, 196, 200, 203
Das Heidedorf (Stifter) **198**:259-60, 262, 265-66, 268, 284
"Heidelberg" (Hölderlin) **16**:161
"Die Heidelberger Ruine" (Lenau) **16**:278
"Der Heidemann" (Droste-Hülshoff) **3**:197
The Heidenmauer (Cooper) **1**:218-19, 224; **54**:256, 264, 288; **203**:72
"Heidenröslein" (Goethe) **34**:122
"Die Heideschenke" (Lenau) **16**:285
"Ein heidnisches Sprüchlein" (Meyer) **81**:156
"The Height of the Ridiculous" (Holmes) **14**:98-9, 101
Der Heilige (Meyer) **81**:164, 171-74, 193, 196, 198
"Die heilige Cäcilia" (Herder) **186**:18
Die heilige Cäcilie; oder, die Gewalt der Musik (Kleist) **2**:461; **37**:245, 247, 249, 254-55
Die heilige Familie, oder Kritik der kritischen Kritik: Gegen Bruno Bauer und Consorten (Engels) **85**:6, 8, 13, 57, 109, 114, 120; **114**:69, 83
Die heilige Familie, oder Kritik der kritischen Kritik: Gegen Bruno Bauer und Consorten (Marx) **17**:328, 331-34, 352; **114**:69, 83
"Das heilige Feuer" (Meyer) **81**:208
"Der Heilige Lucas" (Schlegel) **142**:302
"Heiligenstadt Testament" (Beethoven) **227**:18, 22, 35
"Die Heimat" (Eichendorff) **8**:221
"Heimatgefühl" (Brentano) **191**:69
"Heimkehr" (Eichendorff) **225**:46
"Die Heimkehr" (Meyer) **81**:141-45, 147-48, 150-51, 155
Die Heimkehr (Heine) **4**:248-49, 252, 258-59; **54**:326, 348
"Heimkunft" (Hölderlin) **16**:187, 193, 195; **187**:219, 224, 237
"Heimweh, An meinen Bruder" (Eichendorff) **225**:42
Heine on Shakespeare: A Translation of His Notes on Shakespeare's Heroines (Heine)
See *Shakespeares Mädchen und Frauen*
"Heine's Grave" (Arnold) **6**:54, 72; **29**:38; **218**:121, 155, 188
Heinrich der Vogler (Klopstock) **225**:279, 286, 298
"Heinrich Heine" (Arnold) **89**:32, 38, 121; **126**:100, 114, 120
"Heinrich Heine" (Eliot) **41**:65
"Heinrich Heine" (Pisarev) **25**:339
Heinrich Heine's Book of Songs (Heine)
See *Buch der Lieder*
Heinrich Heines Familienleben (Heine) **147**:149
Heinrich von Offerdingen (Novalis) **13**:360, 362-68, 371, 374, 377-78, 381-82, 386, 394-97, 400-02
Heinrich von Ofterdingen (Novalis) **178**:3-5, 7-10, 13-15, 17, 31-36, 38-45, 50, 54-57, 60-62, 67-69, 71-78, 81-82, 86-91, 96, 99-101, 106, 110-11, 130-31
"The Heir of Dremore" (Crawford) **127**:193, 195-96
The Heir of Gaymount (Cooke) **5**:124, 130, 132, 134-35
The Heir of Selwood (Gore) **65**:20
The Heir Presumptive and the Heir Apparent (Oliphant) **61**:204-5
The Heirs in Tail (Arnim)
See *Die Majoratsherren*
Die Heiterethei und ihr Widerspiel (Ludwig) **4**:347-48, 354-57, 362, 367
"Helavalkea" (Kivi) **30**:51
Heldenthum und Christenthum (Wagner) **9**:475
"Heldentod der vierhundert Pforzheimer" (Büchner) **146**:16
Hélé ena (Vigny) **102**:335, 379
"Helen" (Lamb) **125**:374
"Helen" (Lamb) **10**:385
Helen (Edgeworth) **1**:259, 261, 263, 266, 269; **51**:88, 90-1, 93, 95, 113
Helen Fleetwood: A Tale of the Factories (Tonna) **135**:193, 195-201, 203-4, 207-13, 220-21, 236, 238-39, 241, 243, 245-46
Helen Ford (Alger) **8**:42; **83**:139, 142, 145
"Helen Lee" (O'Brien) **21**:246
"Helen of Tyre" (Longfellow) **45**:132
"Helena" (Goethe) **4**:179, 207, 216; **154**:316
"Helena" (Heine) **4**:257
"Helena" (Taylor) **89**:310
"Helena: Zwischenspiel zu Faust" (Goethe)
See "Helena"
Helena's Household: A Tale of Rome in the First Century (De Mille) **123**:117-21, 123-26
"Hélène" (Leconte de Lisle) **29**:222, 224, 238
Hélène Gillet (Nodier) **19**:383-84
"Helen's Rock" (Crawford) **127**:189, 193-94
Hell (Liszt) **199**:308
Hellas (Shelley) **18**:332, 344, 353, 362, 368, 377; **93**:271, 333; **175**:224, 226, 234, 241, 245, 249, 309, 313, 324, 330
"The Hellenic Factor in the Eastern Problem" (Gladstone) **213**:112
The Hellenics (Landor) **14**:168, 177, 181, 189-91, 196-97
"Heloise to Brissot" (Osgood) **141**:353
"The Helot" (Crawford) **12**:153, 155-56, 161, 169, 174; **127**:178, 218
"Help" (Whittier) **8**:509
Helping Himself (Alger) **8**:44
"Helpstone" (Clare) **9**:73, 96, 106, 112-13; **86**:128-29, 155
A helység kalapácsa (Petofi) **21**:265-66, 276-78, 283
"Un hemisferio en una cabellera" (Casal) **131**:264
"Un hemisphère dans une chevelure" (Baudelaire) **6**:87; **155**:47
Hemmen i den nya verlden: En dagbok i bref, skrifna under tvenne års resor i Norra Amerika och på Cuba (Bremer) **11**:26, 30, 32-33
Hemmet; eller, Familje-sorger och fröjder (Bremer) **11**:17-21, 24, 34-36
"Hen Baily's Reformation" (Harris) **23**:159, 162; **165**:184, 226, 254
"The Henchman" (Whittier) **8**:513, 517, 529; **59**:360
"Hendecasyllabics" (Tennyson) **202**:276
"Hendecasyllables" (Coleridge) **9**:143
Henri III et sa cour (Dumas) **71**:184, 193, 209, 231, 241, 248-52
"A Henri Murger" (Banville) **9**:26
Henrietta (Lennox) **23**:228-29, 232-35
Henrietta Temple (Disraeli) **2**:138-39, 143-44, 146-47; **39**:3-4, 20, 22, 24, 26-31, 40, 46, 52, 65, 67-8, 74-6; **79**:205-07, 209-12, 214-15, 218-19, 223-31, 233, 239, 269, 273, 276-77, 279
Henriette et Saint-Clair (Sade) **47**:361-63
Henriette Maréchal (Goncourt and Goncourt) **7**:170-71
"A Henrique. Ora y espera!" (Isaacs) **70**:304, 309
Henriquez (Baillie) **2**:39-41; **71**:4-6; **151**:11, 114
Henry (Cumberland) **167**:112, 124-25, 135, 140, 150
"Henry and Eliza" (Austen) **119**:13
Henry Crabb Robinson on Books and Their Writers (Robinson) **15**:194
Henry Esmond (Thackeray)
See *The History of Henry Esmond, Esq., a Colonel in the Service of Her Majesty Q. Anne, Written by Himself*
"Henry George" (Adams) **33**:25
Henry of Ofterdingen (Novalis)
See *Heinrich von Ofterdingen*
"Henry Purcell" (Hopkins) **17**:225; **189**:8, 60, 62, 126
Henry St. John, Gentleman, of "Flower of Hundreds" in the County of Prince George, Virginia: A Tale of 1774-'75 (Cooke) **5**:122-24, 127-29, 131, 135-36
"Hepzibah's Story" (Woolson) **82**:333
"Her Address to the Moon" (Robinson) **142**:175
"Her cheeks are like roses" (Clare) **86**:119
Her Country's Hope (Tamayo y Baus)
See *La esperanza de la patria*
"Her Ladyship's Private Office" (Turgenev) **21**:441
"Her Little Parasol to Lift" (Dickinson) **21**:56
Her Majesty the Queen (Cooke) **5**:130, 132
Her Majesty's Inspectors' Report (Arnold) **218**:249-50
"Her Memories" (Webster) **230**:239
"Her Name" (Hugo) **3**:234
"Her Seed, It Shall Bruise Thy Head" (Rossetti) **50**:315
"Heraclitean Fire" (Hopkins)
See "That Nature Is a Heraclitean Fire and of the Comfort of the Resurrection"
"Hèraklès au Taureau" (Leconte de Lisle) **29**:217
"Herald of Freedom" (Thoreau) **138**:128-29

"The Heraldic Blazon of Foss the Cat" (Lear) **3**:298
Herbert Carter's Legacy; or, The Inventor's Son (Alger) **8**:46; **83**:92-4, 129
"Herbert Selden, the Poor Lawyer's Son" (Alger) **83**:96
"Herbert Spencer's Psychology" (Lewes) **215**:148
Herbert Tracy, or The Legend of the Black Rangers: A Romance of the Battle-field of Germantown (Lippard) **198**:121, 133-34, 164, 166
"Herbstfeier" (Hölderlin) **16**:162
"Herbstlied" (Brentano) **191**:69
"Herbstmorgen" (Fontane) **163**:161
"Herbsttag" (Meyer) **81**:148
"Hércules ante la Hidra" (Casal) **131**:223, 225-26, 236
"Hércules y las Estinfálides" (Casal) **131**:236
Herders sämmtliche Werke (Herder) **186**:29, 35-38, 87-88, 92
"Here-and-There-ities" (Willis) **194**:319
"Here comes the night" (Fuller) **50**:249
"Here is a faithful list of impressions" (Baratynsky)
See "Vot vernyi spisok vpechatlenii"
"Here the Frailest Leaves of Me" (Whitman) **205**:219
"Here, where the vault of heaven so inertly" (Tyutchev)
See "Zdes, gde tak vyalo svod nebesnyy"
"Hereafter" (Clare) **9**:78
"Hereditary Influence, Animal and Human" (Lewes) **215**:151
"Hérésies artistiques" (Mallarmé) **210**:210
"Hérésies artistiques: L'art pour tous" (Mallarmé) **41**:254, 256, 258, 282
"The Heretic" (Shevchenko)
See "Jeretyk"
"The Heretic's Tragedy" (Browning) **19**:117, 153
Hereward the Wake, "Last of the English" (Kingsley) **35**:208, 220, 226, 230-31, 241, 243-44, 249
"L'héritage" (Maupassant) **83**:229
L'héritière de Birague (Balzac) **5**:58
"Herman and Dorothea" (Goethe)
See *Hermann und Dorothea*
Die Hermann sschlacht (Grabbe) **2**:272, 276, 282-85, 287-88
Hermann und Dorothea (Goethe) **4**:161-62, 167, 172, 191, 193, 205-07, 222; **154**:191, 233
"Hermann und Thusnelde" (Klopstock) **225**:279
Hermann und Thusnelde (Kotzebue) **25**:141
Hermanns Schlacht (Klopstock) **11**:226, 228
Die Hermannsschlacht (Kleist) **2**:440, 442, 446-47, 450; **37**:217, 225, 228, 231-32, 236, 253-55, 267, 269, 270, 272, 274; **222**:236, 256, 258, 273-81
Hermeneutics: The Handwritten Manuscripts (Schleiermacher)
See *Hermeneutik: Nach den Handshriften neu herausgegeben*
Hermeneutik: Nach den Handshriften neu herausgegeben (Schleiermacher) **107**:370, 378-86
Hermes Britannicus (Bowles) **103**:54
"The Hermit" (Beattie) **25**:104, 106-07
"The Hermit and the Bear" (Krylov) **1**:435
"The Hermit of Mont Blanc" (Robinson) **142**:114, 137
"Hermit of Warkworth" (Percy) **95**:343
The Hermit of Warkworth (Percy) **95**:365
"The Hermit Thrush" (Lampman) **194**:87
Hermsprong; or, Man as He Is Not (Bage) **182**:6, 12-13, 15-18, 21-27, 30-32, 34-35, 37-40, 43, 45-47, 50-53, 58, 60-63, 65, 68, 70-71, 74, 76
Hernán Pérez del Pulgar (Martínez de la Rosa) **102**:227-28, 252
Hernani (Hugo) **3**:236-37, 248-49, 261, 264, 268, 273; **10**:362, 373; **21**:194, 197; **161**:149, 230, 234-36, 255, 266
"Hero: A Metamorphosis" (Rossetti) **186**:232-33
"Hero and Leander" (Hood) **16**:200-01, 208, 215, 218, 221, 225, 227, 229-30
"Hero and Leander" (Hunt) **1**:410; **70**:251, 253
Hero and Leander (Grillparzer)
See *Des Meeres und der Liebe Wellen*
"Hero Bor" (Arany)
See "Bor vitéz"
A Hero of Our Time (Lermontov)
See *Geroi nashego vremeni*
Hero of the North (Fouqué) **2**:265-66, 268
Herod (Hebbel)
See *Herodes und Mariamne: Eine Tragödie in fünf Acten*
Herodes und Mariamne: Eine Tragödie in fünf Acten (Hebbel) **43**:230, 234, 238-39, 243, 245, 248, 250, 257-59, 262, 267, 277-79, 282-84, 287, 289, 296-300
Hérodiade (Mallarmé) **4**:371, 375, 377, 380-81, 386-87, 394-96; **41**:233, 236, 239, 245-46, 249-50, 267, 269-72, 274-75, 278-81, 289; **210**:168, 217, 244, 264
"Hérodias" (Flaubert) **2**:227, 233, 236, 246, 256-58; **135**:109, 171
Herodias (Mallarmé)
See *Hérodiade*
"Herod's Work" (Leskov) **174**:34-35
"Heroes" (Lazarus) **8**:411, 413, 420; **109**:293
The Heroes (Kingsley) **35**:220, 232, 249
"A Heroic Death" (Baudelaire)
See "Une mort héroïque"
An Heroic Epistle to Miss Sally Horne (More) **141**:233
Heroic Idylls (Landor) **14**:189-91
The Heroic Slave (Douglass) **7**:130, 146-47; **55**:123-4
Heroic Songs of the Recent Times of the War for Freedom (Karadzic)
See *Pjesme junaĉke srednjijeh vrema*
Héroïde funèbre (Liszt) **199**:318
"Heroism" (Cowper) **8**:139; **94**:41-4, 48
"Heroism" (Emerson) **1**:307; **98**:65, 176
Heroism and Christianity (Wagner)
See *Heldenthum und Christenthum*
"L'Héroisme de l'Esprit" (Michelet) **218**:338
"Der Herr Esau" (Gotthelf) **117**:6, 15, 27, 32
Der Herr Etatsrat (Storm) **1**:540; **195**:7-8, 13, 16, 55, 57, 128
Herr Eugen Dühring's Revolution in Science; or Anti-Dühring (Engels)
See *Herr Eugen Dührings Umwälzung de Wissenschaft: Philosophie; Politische Oekonomie; Sozialismus*
Herr Eugen Dührings Umwälzung de Wissenschaft: Philosophie; Politische Oekonomie; Sozialismus (Engels) **85**:6, 24-25, 31-34, 37-42, 59, 69, 104-06, 121, 128; **114**:41
Herr Rassmussen (Andersen) **79**:16
"El herrador y el zapatero" (Lizardi) **30**:68
"Herrenston" (Barnes) **75**:104-05
Herring Fishery in the Moray Firth (Miller) **143**:8
"Die Herrlichkeit der Schöpfung" (Schiller) **39**:339
"Hershey and the Incarnation" (Brownson) **50**:53
Hertha (Bremer) **11**:30-31, 34-36
Herz und Gemüth (Herder) **8**:306
Herzog Theodor von Gothland (Grabbe) **2**:271-76, 280, 283-84, 286-88
He's Much to Blame (Holcroft) **85**:198, 212, 223
"The Hesperides" (Tennyson) **30**:208, 280; **65**:357-8; **202**:187-88
Hesperus; or, Forty-Five Dog-Post-Days (Jean Paul) **7**:226-27, 230, 232, 238-40
The Hessian Courier (Büchner)
See *Der Hessische Landbote*
The Hessian Messenger (Büchner)
See *Der Hessische Landbote*
Der Hessische Landbote (Büchner) **26**:4-5, 14, 27-8, 64, 68, 70; **146**:14, 17-18, 42, 63-64, 91, 95
"Hester" (Crabbe) **121**:24-6
"Hester" (Lamb) **10**:407
Hester (Oliphant) **11**:441, 446, 461; **61**:187-90, 223, 226, 231-3, 235; **221**:257, 305, 308, 311-12, 314
Hester Wilmot (More) **141**:191
"Hétköznapi történet" (Madach) **19**:369
Hetty (Kingsley) **107**:192
Hetty's Strange History (Jackson) **90**:144, 164-69
Une heure de ma vie (Balzac) **153**:150, 152
"L'heure du sabbat" (Bertrand) **31**:46
"Heures" (Corbière) **43**:34
"L'Heureuse Feinte" (Sade) **47**:313
Heute, nur heute (Storm) **195**:21
Hexameron vom Rosenhain (Wieland) **17**:410
"Hexenküche" (Goethe) **4**:215
Der Hexensabbath (Tieck) **5**:514
"Hiawatha" (Longfellow)
See *The Song of Hiawatha*
Hiawatha (Longfellow)
See *The Song of Hiawatha*
"Hiawatha's Photographing" (Dodgson) **139**:35
The Hibernian Nights' Entertainments (Ferguson) **3**:290
An Hibernian Tale Taken from Facts, and from the Manners of the Irish Squires, before the Year 1782 (Edgeworth) **158**:54
"Les Hiboux" (Baudelaire) **55**:43
The Hidden Hand (Southworth) **26**:433, 438, 441-49
"Hidden Love" (Clough) **27**:55, 77
Hide and Seek (Collins) **1**:178-79, 181, 186-87; **93**:46-47, 53, 64
"Hièronymus" (Leconte de Lisle) **29**:225
"High and Low Life in Italy" (Landor) **14**:165
The High Jumpers (Andersen) **79**:31
High, Low, Jack and the Game (Planché) **42**:295
High Profession and Negligent Practice (More) **27**:342
"The High Tide on the Coast of Lincolnshire, 1571" (Ingelow) **39**:257, 262-63, 266, 268; **107**:119-20, 122-23
High Times and Hard Times (Harris)
See *Sut Lovingood: Yarns Spun by a "Nat'ral Born Durn'd Fool"*
"Higher Laws" (Thoreau) **7**:352, 376, 388, 392, 407
"The Higher Pantheism" (Tennyson) **30**:254, 269-70; **65**:265, 274
Higher Schools and Universities in Germany (Arnold) **218**:144, 195
"A Highland Drover" (Bloomfield)
See "Song for a Highland Drover"
"The Highland Reaper" (Wordsworth) **12**:427
"The Highland Widow" (Scott) **15**:312; **110**:305
The Highlands (Miller) **143**:13
"A Highway for Freedom" (Mangan) **27**:296
Hihon tamakushige (Motoori) **45**:275-76
La hija de las flores (Gómez de Avellaneda) **111**:47
La hija del mar (Castro) **3**:105-06; **78**:45-47, 49, 52
Hija y madre (Tamayo y Baus) **1**:571
El hijo pródigo (Alarcon) **1**:15; **219**:13-14, 18
Hilary St. Ives (Ainsworth) **13**:45
"Hilda Silfverling" (Child) **6**:201
"The Hill and the Valley" (Martineau) **26**:304; **137**:266, 268-70
The Hill by the Sea at Egeløkke (Grundtvig)
See *Strandbakken ved Egeløkke*
"Hill in Kikineis" (Mickiewicz)
See "Góra Kikineis"
"The Hill of Science: A Vision" (Barbauld) **185**:130, 132
"The Hill of Venus" (Lazarus) **109**:290
"The Hill of Venus" (Morris) **4**:447-48

"Hill or Dell" (Barnes) **75**:87
"The Hill Summit" (Rossetti) **4**:515
Hillingdon Hall (Surtees) **14**:343, 345, 349, 353, 362, 364-65, 375, 377, 380
The Hills of the Shatemuc (Warner) **31**:337, 343
Hillyars (Kingsley)
See *The Hillyars and the Burtons*
The Hillyars and the Burtons (Kingsley) **107**:183-86, 188-89, 191-92, 194-95, 206, 209, 211, 213, 216-21, 223-24, 228, 231-32, 250-56
Hilt to Hilt; or, Days and Nights in the Shenandoah in the Autumn of 1864 (Cooke) **5**:127-28, 132, 134
"Himmelsbräute" (Heine) **147**:232
"Himmelsnähe" (Meyer) **81**:206
"Himmelstrauer" (Lenau) **16**:278
"Himno a la divina providencia" (Lizardi) **30**:69
"Himno a Talisay" (Rizal) **27**:425
"Himno al sol" (Espronceda) **39**:100, 106, 109
"Himno al sol" (Heredia) **209**:135, 165
"Himno al trabajo" (Rizal) **27**:425
"Himno de desterrado" (Heredia) **209**:118, 120, 124, 135-37
"Himno de guerra columbiano" (Isaacs) **70**:313
"Himpukuron" (Ueda Akinari) **131**:13, 15, 24, 26, 28, 32, 39, 66
A Hint for Husbands (Cumberland) **167**:198
Hints Addressed to the Patrons and Directors of Schools (Hamilton) **153**:277, 310-11, 322
"Hints for a History of Highwaymen" (Thackeray) **43**:381
Hints from Horace (Byron) **2**:85; **12**:145; **149**:54, 84
"Hints on European Travel" (Jefferson) **103**:114-17
Hints towards Forming the Character of a Young Princess (More) **27**:333, 341; **141**:170
Hints towards the Formation of a More Comprehensive Theory of Life (Coleridge) **9**:197; **177**:56; **197**:286, 310
Hinzelmeier (Storm) **195**:20, 23-29, 31-36, 66-68, 70, 72-73, 89, 127-28
"Hippodromania" (Gordon) **21**:154, 159-60, 164-65, 177, 180
Hippokrates in Abdera (Wieland) **177**:256, 260
"Hiram Powers' Greek Slave" (Barrett Browning) **16**:130; **170**:77-78
"The Hired Man" (Auerbach)
See "Der Lehnhold"
"His Boat Comes on the Sunny Tide" (Baillie) **151**:86, 91
"His Clay" (Crawford) **12**:156, 159, 172
"His Departed Love to Prince Leopold" (Hunt) **70**:257
"His mind alone is kingly ..." (Harpur) **114**:115
His Natural Life (Clarke) **19**:230-46, 248, 251-52, 255-61
"Hisbrien om en Moder" (Andersen) **7**:23, 31-35; **79**:26-27, 76, 81, 89; **214**:41, 75
Histoire critique des origines du Christianisme (Renan)
See *Origines du Christianisme*
Histoire de XIXème siècle (Michelet) **31**:211, 213, 238, 247
Histoire de Don Pédre Ier, roi de Castille (Mérimée) **6**:353, 356; **65**:85
Histoire de France (Michelet) **31**:207, 210-11, 220, 225, 238, 242, 247-48, 253, 257; **218**:307, 309, 316-17, 334-35
"Histoire de Gambèr-Aly" (Gobineau) **17**:69, 103
L'Histoire de Henri le Grand (Genlis) **166**:21
Histoire de Juliette on les Prosperites du vice (Sade)
See *Juliette; ou, Les prospérités du vice*
"Histoire de la grandeur et de la décadence de César Birotteau, parfumeur" (Balzac) **5**:31-33, 47, 57; **35**:26, 34; **153**:12
Histoire de la littérature Anglaise (Taine) **15**:414-15, 418-19, 432, 435, 442-45, 447, 449, 451-52, 454, 456, 459, 462-63, 468, 473
Histoire de la peinture en Italie (Stendhal) **23**:352, 367, 391; **178**:190-91, 221
"L'histoire de la reine du matin et de Soliman, prince Génies" (Nerval) **1**:480, 484; **67**:315
Histoire de la Restauration (Lamartine) **190**:211, 216-17
Histoire de la révolution de 1848 (Lamartine) **11**:258, 260
Histoire de la Révolution Française (Michelet) **31**:211, 213, 217, 231, 234-35, 237, 239, 246-47, 249-51, 255-56, 259; **218**:317, 324, 330, 338
Histoire de la société Française pendant la révolution (Goncourt and Goncourt) **7**:153, 186
Histoire de la Turquie (Lamartine) **11**:260; **190**:211-12
"Histoire de l'Abbé de Bucquoy" (Nerval) **67**:332
"Histoire de ma vie" (Bakunin) **25**:49
Histoire de ma vie (Sand) **2**:604, 607; **42**:311, 324, 328, 331-32, 337, 340, 354, 356-57, 379-81, 385-86; **42**:332, 364-66, 368, 370; **57**:309-10, 312, 326, 333, 336, 359-61, 366-7, 370; **174**:167, 174, 229, 238, 289
Histoire de mes Bêtes (Dumas) **71**:204, 210
Histoire de Napoléon racontée dans une grange (Balzac) **153**:150
Histoire de Pauline (Staël-Holstein) **91**:324, 339-40, 358, 360
Histoire de Sybille (Feuillet) **45**:78-9, 81, 83, 85-7, 91
Histoire des constituents (Lamartine) **11**:257, 261
Histoire des girondins (Lamartine) **11**:256-57, 259-61, 266-67, 274; **190**:191, 196, 211, 213-16, 254
Histoire des origines du christianisme (Renan) **26**:373, 377-79, 381, 390, 393, 395, 398, 400, 407-08, 410-11, 419-21
Histoire des perses (Gobineau) **17**:71, 81
"Histoire des treize" (Balzac) **5**:36; **153**:22-24
L'histoire d'Ottar Jarl, pirate norvégien, conquérant du pays de Bray, en Normandie, et de sa descendance (Gobineau) **17**:81, 88, 101
L'histoire du Calife Hakem (Nerval) **1**:475, 480, 483; **67**:335-36, 365
Histoire du Capitaine Beauvoir (Balzac) **153**:150
Histoire du chien de Brisquet (Nodier) **19**:381, 402
Histoire du peuple d'Israël (Renan) **26**:390, 395, 400, 407-08, 414, 417, 419, 421; **145**:317
"Histoire du rêveur" (Sand) **42**:378; **57**:368; **174**:186
L'histoire du roi de Bohême et de ses sept châteaux (Nodier) **19**:377, 380-82, 387-88, 392, 400-04
L'histoire d'un crime (Hugo) **3**:257, 262; **161**:177; **189**:267
Histoire d'une clarinette (Balzac) **153**:150
Histoire d'une Colombe (Dumas)
See *La Colombe*
"L'histoire d'une fille de ferme" (Maupassant) **1**:448, 466; **83**:208, 210, 212-14, 222-24
Histoire général et système comparé des langues Sémitiques (Renan) **26**:365, 370, 421
Histoire intellectuelle de Louis Lambert (Balzac) **153**:150
Histoire populaire du Christianisme (Leconte de Lisle) **29**:212
Histoire primitive des peuples de la Russie: avec une exposition complete de toutes les nations, locales, nationales et traditionelles, nécessaires a l'intelligence du quartieme livre d'Hérodote (Potocki) **229**:274-75, 295
Une histoire sans nom (Barbey d'Aurevilly) **213**:5, 29, 35-37
Histoires comme ça (Verlaine) **51**:387
Histoires extraordinaires (Baudelaire) **29**:65-7
Histoires extraordinaires (Poe) **16**:298-99
Historia (Bécquer)
See *Historia de los Templos de España*
Historia de los Templos de España (Bécquer) **106**:97, 101, 108, 146, 158
Historia de mis libros (Alarcón) **219**:12, 14, 20-22, 42, 44, 49, 53
"Historia de un salteador italiano" (Heredia) **209**:135
Historia Universal (Heredia) **209**:119
"Historic Evening" (Rimbaud)
See "Soir historique"
"Historic Guidance" (Eliot) **199**:230
"Historic Notes of Life and Letters in New England" (Emerson) **98**:91
Historical and Geographic Fragments on Scythia, Sarmatia, and the Slavs (Potocki)
See *Fragments historiques et géographiques sur la Scythie, la Sarmatie et les Slaves*
An Historical and Statistical Account of Nova Scotia (Haliburton) **15**:116, 125, 127-28, 133, 144; **149**:267-68, 274-75, 277, 279, 281, 311-13, 323
"Historical Anecdotes" (Pushkin) **83**:273
"Historical Character in Fabulous Tales of Recent Composition" (Leskov) **174**:50
"Historical Characters Are False Representations of Nature" (D'Israeli) **217**:322
Historical Childhood Teachings (Grundtvig) **158**:152
"Historical deduction of seats" (Cowper) **94**:120
Historical Dialogues for Young Persons (Hays) **114**:186
"Historical Discourse at Concord" (Emerson) **38**:173
"Historical Discourse on the Text of 'Decamerone'" (Foscolo)
See "Discorso storico sul testo del 'Decamerone'"
"Historical Panegyric to Catherine II" (Karamzin)
See "Istoricheskoye pokhval'noye slovo Yekaterine II"
An Historical, Political and Moral Essay on Revolutions, ancient and modern (Chateaubriand)
See *Essai sur les révolutions anciennes et modernes*
"Historical Romance: Alexandre Dumas" (Lewes) **25**:286
"Historical Sketch" (Bello) **131**:123
Historical Sketches (Newman) **38**:312, 314; **99**:212, 220
Historical Sketches of the Reign of George Second (Oliphant) **11**:433; **221**:229, 237, 263
Historical Sketches of the Reign of Queen Anne (Oliphant) **221**:263
"Historical Song" (Radishchev) **190**:279
"L'Historie d'un merle blanc" (Musset) **150**:324
Historie von der schönen Lau (Mörike) **201**:253
"Historien" (Heine) **4**:254-56; **147**:159, 228-29, 232
Historier (Andersen)
See *Nye Eventyr og Historier*
Historietas nacionales (Alarcón)
See *Novelas cortas: Historietas nacionales*
"History" (Emerson) **38**:176-78; **98**:40, 65-6, 75, 111, 151, 153-55, 185
History (Macaulay)
See *The History of England from the Accession of James II*

History from the Commencement (Martineau) **26**:339-40
History of a Crime (Hugo)
See *L'histoire d'un crime*
The History of a Democratic Movement, Compiled from the Journal of a Democrat, the Confessions of a Demagogue, and the Minutes of a Spy (Jones)
See *De Brassier: A Democratic Romance*
History of a Six Weeks' Tour through a Part of France, Switzerland, Germany, and Holland (Shelley) **14**:251, 276; **59**:234; **103**:358-59; **170**:307, 336
The History of Agathon (Wieland)
See *Geschichte des Agathon*
History of Agrippina (Hamilton) **153**:356
"History of an Italian Highwayman" (Heredia)
See "Historia de un salteador italiano"
History of Ancient and Modern Literature (Schlegel)
See *Geschichte der alten und neuen Literatur*
The History of Arthur Pendennis (Thackeray)
See *The History of Pendennis: His Fortunes and Misfortunes, His Friends and His Greatest Enemy*
History of Brazil (Southey) **8**:452-53, 459, 469; **97**:259, 262, 265, 268-69, 273-75, 283, 303, 305-06, 308-09, 330
History of British Costume (Planché) **42**:273, 281
The History of Caliph Vathek (Beckford) **214**:148
The History of Caroline Evelyn (Burney) **54**:15
The History of Charles the Footman (More) **141**:169
History of Costume (Planché) **42**:274
"History of Don Raymond" (Lewis) **11**:311
The History of Eliza Wharton, A Novel; Founded on Fact (Foster)
See *The Coquette; or the History of Eliza Wharton. A Novel Founded on Fact, By a Lady of Massachusetts*
History of England (Froude) **43**:177-78, 181-82, 185, 187-91, 193, 203, 210-13
History of England (Macaulay)
See *The History of England from the Accession of James II*
The History of England during the Thirty Years' Peace, 1816-46 (Martineau) **26**:311, 323, 338-40, 354, 359
History of England during the Thirty Years' Peace 1816-1846 (Martineau) **137**:236, 262-63, 265, 270, 273-74, 285
The History of England from the Accession of James II (Macaulay) **42**:72, 76, 78, 82-3, 85-8, 92, 94-103, 106-07, 113, 116, 118-20, 122, 124-29, 131-33, 135, 138-43, 149, 151-52, 155-59; **231**:262, 271, 273-77, 281, 285, 294-99, 301-2, 309, 312-15, 319-20
History of English Literature (Taine)
See *Histoire de la littérature Anglaise*
The History of English Philosophy (Hazlitt) **29**:163
The History of European Literature (Schlegel) **226**:234
"History of Ferdinand and Isabella" (Prescott) **163**:322, 324-26
History of France (Michelet)
See *Histoire de France*
History of Friedrich II. of Prussia, Called Frederick the Great (Carlyle) **70**:7, 92-93
History of Greece: From the Earliest Records of that Country to the Time in which it was reduced into a Roman Province (Godwin) **130**:161
The History of Henry Esmond, Esq., a Colonel in the Service of Her Majesty Q. Anne, Written by Himself (Thackeray) **5**:450-51, 453, 459, 461-62, 464, 466-68, 471-72, 474, 478, 480-81, 484, 486, 488-89, 492, 497, 503-04; **14**:397, 406, 412, 434, 451-52; **43**:349-50, 356, 389; **169**:247, 300; **213**:204, 207-8, 211-12, 214, 267, 301, 305, 314-16, 318-19, 323
The History of Hester Wilmot (More) **27**:345; **141**:192
"The History of His Own Time" (Hawthorne) **95**:137
History of Ireland (Allingham) **25**:20-1
History of Lacock Abbey (Bowles) **103**:54
"The History of Lieutenant Ergunov" (Turgenev)
See "Istoriya leytenanta Ergunova"
History of Marcus Aurelius (Sigourney) **87**:321, 339
History of Marie Antoinette (Goncourt and Goncourt) **7**:153
The History of Matthew Wald (Lockhart) **6**:289-90, 292, 294, 296, 302-03, 307, 310-12
History of Mr. Fantom the New-Fashioned Philosopher (More) **27**:342, 344
History of My Acquaintance with Gogol (Aksakov)
See *Istoriia moego znakomstva s Gogolem*
"History of My Botanical Studies" (Goethe) **4**:208
History of My Childhood (Aksakov)
See *Detskie gody Bagrova-vnuka*
History of My Religious Opinions (Newman)
See *Apologia pro Vita Sua: Being a Reply to a Pamphlet Entitled "What, Then, Does Dr Newman Mean?"*
History of Napolean (Blake) **127**:264
A History of New York, for Schools (Dunlap) **2**:210
A History of New York, from the Beginning of the World to the End of the Dutch Dynasty (Irving) **2**:367, 369, 373, 375-81, 385, 388-92; **19**:348-49; **95**:225-26, 230, 274-75, 278
History of Nova Scotia (Haliburton) **149**:269, 327-28
The History of Ottar Jarl, Norwegian Pirate (Gobineau)
See *L'histoire d'Ottar Jarl, pirate norvégien, conquérant du pays de Bray, en Normandie, et de sa descendance*
The History of Our Lord (Jameson) **43**:324, 327
History of Painting (Stendhal)
See *Histoire de la peinture en Italie*
The History of Pendennis: His Fortunes and Misfortunes, His Friends and His Greatest Enemy (Thackeray) **5**:449-50, 453-54, 459-61, 464, 471-72, 474, 477-78, 464, 471, 472, 474, 477, 478, 483-84, 486-90, 492, 497-98, 500, 503-05; **14**:418, 422; **43**:349, 356, 359, 389; **169**:222, 247; **213**:187-95, 198, 204, 207, 210-11, 213-14, 243, 250, 253-55, 264, 281, 283-85, 287, 290-91, 294, 298, 300, 302, 304-7, 309, 323, 327-28, 331, 333, 337, 341
History of Perez del Pilgar (Martínez de la Rosa)
See *Hernán Pérez del Pulgar*
"The History of Perourou; or, The Bellows-Mender; Written by Himself" (Williams) **135**:260, 303, 335
History of Peter the Cruel (Mérimée)
See *Histoire de Don Pédre Ier, roi de Castille*
The History of Philosophy from Thales to Comte (Lewes)
See *A Biographical History of Philosophy*
History of Portugal (Southey) **8**:469; **97**:283, 289
"The History of Primitive Christianity" (Engels) **85**:6
A History of Pugačev (Pushkin) **83**:295
History of Rome (Arnold) **18**:37, 54
The History of Samuel Titmarsh and the Great Hoggarty Diamond (Thackeray)
See *The Great Hoggarty Diamond*
The History of Scotland (Scott) **15**:277; **110**:288, 305
History of South Carolina (Simms) **3**:504
History of the American Revolution (Neal) **161**:321, 323
A History of the American Theatre (Dunlap) **2**:208, 210-11, 213-15, 217-18
The History of the Carrils and Ormes (Brown) **74**:7, 50
History of the Commonwealth of England (Godwin) **14**:48
History of the Condition of Women in Various Ages and Nations (Child) **6**:204; **73**:50, 59, 72, 76, 97
History of the Conquest of Mexico (Prescott) **163**:306, 315-16, 318, 321, 323-28, 333-34, 336, 338, 340, 342-45, 359-60, 364-65
History of the Conquest of Peru (Prescott) **163**:316, 321, 323, 343, 347, 359
History of the Conspiracy of Pontiac, and the War of the North American Tribes against the English Colonies after the Conquest of Canada (Parkman) **12**:330-31, 333, 336, 338-39, 341-42, 348, 351-52, 369
History of the Constituent Assembly (Lamartine)
See *Histoire des constituents*
"History of the English Language" (Whitman) **81**:292
History of the Four Movements (Fourier)
See *Théorie des quatre mouvements*
History of the French Revolution (Michelet)
See *Histoire de la Révolution Française*
History of the French Revolution of 1848 (Lamartine)
See *Histoire de la révolution de 1848*
History of the German Language (Grimm Brothers) **3**:217, 220
History of the Girondists; or, Personal Memoirs of the Patriots of the French Revolution (Lamartine)
See *Histoire des girondins*
History of the Grandeur and Downfall of César Birotteau (Balzac)
See "Histoire de la grandeur et de la décadence de César Birotteau, parfumeur"
History of the Italian Revolution (Fuller) **5**:165
A History of the Life and Voyages of Christopher Columbus (Irving) **2**:371, 387; **95**:223, 225, 228-34, 255, 259
History of the Manor of Goryukhino (Pushkin) **3**:435
History of the Middle Ages (Michelet) **31**:259
History of the Monastic Orders (Southey) **8**:469
History of the Navy of the United States of America (Cooper) **1**:202
History of the Nineteenth Century (Michelet)
See *Histoire de XIXème siècle*
History of the Peace (Martineau)
See *The History of England during the Thirty Years' Peace, 1816-46*
History of the Peninsular War (Southey) **8**:459, 463; **97**:250, 264, 269, 283, 299, 332
History of the People of Israel (Renan)
See *Histoire du peuple d'Israël*
History of the Persians (Gobineau)
See *Histoire des perses*
A History of the Protestant "Reformation" in England and Ireland (Cobbett) **49**:110, 114, 116, 154-55, 157
The History of the Pugachev Rebellion (Pushkin) **3**:436; **83**:275
History of the Reign of Ferdinand and Isabella, the Catholic (Prescott) **163**:301, 312, 315-16, 318, 320, 322, 324-25, 343, 349, 351-52
History of the Reign of Philip the Second, King of Spain (Prescott) **163**:315, 318, 351

History of the Renaissance (Michelet) **31**:211, 245-47
The History of the Restoration of Monarchy in France (Lamartine)
See *Histoire de la Restauration*
The History of the Revolt of the Netherlands (Schiller) **39**:378
A History of the Rise and Progress of the Arts of Design in the United States (Dunlap) **2**:209-10, 214-15
History of the Rise, Progress, and Termination of the American Revolution: Interspersed with Biographical and Moral Observations (Warren) **13**:411-13, 415, 419-20, 422-27, 431-37; **226**:259, 263, 266-67, 272, 276, 282, 289, 293, 310
History of the Russian State (Karamzin)
See *Istoriya gosudarstva Rossiiskogo*
History of the Thirty Years' Peace (Martineau)
See *The History of England during the Thirty Years' Peace, 1816-46*
History of the United States, to Which is Prefixed a Brief Historical Account of Our English Ancestors, from the Dispersion at Babel, to Their Migration to America, and of the Conquest of South America, by the Spaniards (Webster) **30**:421
History of the University and Colleges of Cambridge (Dyer) **129**:115-16
A History of the Village Goryukhino (Pushkin)
See *Istoriia sela Goriukhino*
History of the War (Richardson)
See *War of 1812*
"The History of the Young Men" (Brontë) **109**:34-5, 44, 47
The History of Tom White (More) **141**:288
History of Turkey (Lamartine)
See *Histoire de la Turquie*
"Historyk" (Norwid) **17**:373
"Hit és tudás" (Madach) **19**:369
The Hive of "The Bee-Hunter," A Repository of Sketches (Thorpe) **183**:338-39, 355-56, 358-59
"Hiver" (Verlaine) **230**:153-54, 158-59
"L'Hiver qui vient" (Laforgue) **5**:279; **53**:299-300, 302; **221**:7, 35, 37, 79, 92-93
"Hjertesorg" (Andersen) **79**:76
HMI Report (Arnold)
See *Her Majesty's Inspectors' Report*
Hobart the Hired Boy (Alger) **8**:24
Hobomok: A Tale of Early Times (Child) **6**:196-97, 199-200, 204-05, 207-08; **73**:39, 50, 57-8, 64-5, 74-5, 111-16, 118, 123, 126
Höchst Zerstreute Gedanken (Hoffmann) **183**:179-80
"Der Hochwald" (Stifter) **41**:336, 342, 356, 379, 385
Der Hochwald (Stifter) **198**:262, 266-67, 270, 274-78, 280, 283, 285
Die Hochzeit des Mönchs (Meyer) **81**:164, 181-82, 193-94, 198-99
Hodge and his Masters (Jefferies) **47**:98, 109-12, 121, 133, 137, 142
Hof- und Commerzienräthe (Börne) **193**:4
Hoffmann's Fairy Tales (Hoffmann) **183**:221, 228
"Das hohe Lied" (Brentano) **191**:10
"Hohenlinden" (Campbell) **19**:165, 168-69, 171, 178-79, 181, 185, 187-90, 192-96
Hohenstaufen I: Kaiser Friedrich Barbarossa (Grabbe) **2**:272, 275-76, 281, 284-85
Hohenstaufen II: Kaiser Heinrich der Sechste (Grabbe) **2**:275-76, 281, 284-85
A hóhér kötele (Petofi) **21**:284
"Die Höheren Stufen" (Klopstock) **11**:239
Hojas al viento (Casal) **131**:236
"Hojas Secas" (Bécquer) **106**:129
Hokousaï (Goncourt) **7**:163
Hold Your Tongue (Planché) **42**:293
Hölderlins Lehre vom Wechsel der Töne (Hölderlin) **187**:229
Hölderlins Sämtliche Werke (Hölderlin) **187**:183
Hölderlin's Theory of Tonal Variation (Hölderlin)
See *Hölderlins Lehre vom Wechsel der Töne*
"Holger Danske" (Andersen) **7**:29
"A Holiday at Gwerndovennant" (Wordsworth) **138**:229
A Holiday Dream—Before Dinner (Ostrovsky)
See *Prazdnichny son—do obeda*
Holiday Peak, and Other Tales (Clarke) **19**:236, 249-51
"Holiness" (Emerson) **98**:160
"Holion" (Hebbel) **43**:237, 252
"Holland" (Fromentin) **10**:232
Holländische Liebhabereien (Arnim) **159**:20
Holland-Tide; or, Munster Popular Tales (Griffin) **7**:194, 201, 211-12, 216-17
Höllenangst (Nestroy) **42**:231, 235, 246, 260
Hollins Liebeleben (Arnim) **159**:22-23, 25, 28-31, 45, 73-75, 77, 95
"The Hollow Land" (Morris) **4**:424, 430
"The Hollow of the Three Hills" (Hawthorne) **2**:327; **23**:204; **95**:95; **171**:357
"Hollow-Sounding and Mysterious" (Rossetti) **2**:576
"The Holly Tree" (Southey) **8**:472, 474; **97**:271
"L'holocauste" (Leconte de Lisle) **29**:225
"Holy Baptism" (Keble) **87**:153, 203
The Holy Cross, and Other Tales (Field) **3**:206-08
"Holy Cross Day" (Browning) **19**:79, 98, 116
The Holy Family (Engels)
See *Die heilige Familie, oder Kritik der kritischen Kritik: Gegen Bruno Bauer und Consorten*
The Holy Family (Marx)
See *Die heilige Familie, oder Kritik der kritischen Kritik: Gegen Bruno Bauer und Consorten*
The Holy Genofeva (Tieck)
See *Leben und Tod der heiligen Genoveva*
"The Holy Grail" (Tennyson) **30**:228, 249, 254, 279, 282, 284, 292; **65**:237, 241-2, 245, 247, 250, 256, 270, 280-2, 284, 287, 295-6, 299, 314-5, 317-8, 320, 323, 333, 352, 361-2, 376, 385; **202**:211, 215, 291, 323-25
"Holy Grail" (Verlaine)
See "Saint Graal"
"The Holy Night Has Risen into the Firmament" (Tyutchev)
See "Svyataya noch na nebosklon vzoshla"
"Holy Russia" (Adams) **33**:18
"Holy Thursday" (Blake) **13**:182, 219-21, 241; **37**:3-4, 7, 11, 14, 25, 30-1, 36-7, 40, 42, 46-7, 49-50, 57, 62-4, 66, 69-72, 76, 78, 82, 92, 94
"El hombre de las muletas de níquel" (Casal) **131**:264
"Hombre del campo" (Martí) **63**:88
"El hombre menguado" (Larra) **130**:193-94
"El hombre propone y Dios dispone, o lo que ha de ser el periodista" (Larra) **130**:194, 201
"Un hombre y una musa" (Castro) **3**:106
"El hombre-globo" (Larra) **17**:282
Hombres (Verlaine) **51**:352, 363; **230**:177-78, 180-81
Hombres I (Verlaine) **230**:176-77, 180
Hombres II (Verlaine) **230**:176-77, 180-81
Hombres IV (Verlaine) **230**:176
Hombres VI (Verlaine) **230**:176, 181
Hombres VII (Verlaine) **230**:175-76, 180
Hombres IX (Verlaine) **230**:180
Hombres X (Verlaine) **230**:176, 180-81
Hombres XI (Verlaine) **230**:176-77, 180-81
Hombres XII (Verlaine) **230**:176
Hombres XIV (Verlaine) **230**:176, 181
Los hombres de bien (Tamayo y Baus) **1**:569
"Home" (Nekrasov) **11**:407, 421
Home (Robertson) **35**:335, 369
Home (Sedgwick) **19**:435, 440, 443, 447
Home as Found (Cooper) **1**:216-17, 220; **54**:255-6, 275, 288; **203**:24, 45, 49, 73, 130, 136, 140
Home at Grasmere (Wordsworth) **111**:243, 370; **166**:244, 281, 286
Home Ballads and Poems (Whittier) **8**:492, 495-96; **59**:356, 371
"Home in Grasmere" (Wordsworth) **38**:362
"Home in War Time" (Dobell) **43**:48
"Home of an Early Friend" (Sigourney) **87**:320
The Home; or, Family Cares and Family Joys (Bremer)
See *Hemmet; eller, Familje-sorger och fröjder*
Home Pastorals, Ballads and Lyrics (Taylor) **89**:315
"Home Sweet Home" (Castro)
See "Miña casiña"
"Home They Brought Her Warrior Dead" (Tennyson) **202**:179
"Home Thoughts, From Abroad" (Browning) **79**:94, 98, 163
"Homecoming" (Hölderlin)
See "Heimkunft"
Homecoming (Heine)
See *Die Heimkehr*
Homegoing from the Theatre (Gogol)
See "Teatral'nyi raz'ezd posle predstavleniia novoi komedii"
"Homeland" (Nekrasov)
See "Rodina"
"Homeopathy and Its Kindred Delusions" (Holmes) **81**:101, 108
"Homeopathy vs. Allopathy" (Holmes) **14**:111
"Homer. Ossian. Chaucer." (Thoreau) **138**:121, 126
Homeric Ballads (Maginn) **8**:434-35, 439-40
Homeric Synchronism: An Enquiry into the Time and Place of Homer (Gladstone) **213**:116, 125, 128
Homer's Iliad and Odyssey (Cowper) **8**:119, 121
"Home-Rule Mystery" (Dodgson) **139**:67
Homes Abroad (Martineau) **137**:273
The Homes of England (Hemans) **29**:204-05; **71**:278
The Homes of the New World: Impressions of America (Bremer)
See *Hemmen i den nya verlden: En dagbok i bref, skrifna under tvenne års resor i Norra Amerika och på Cuba*
"Homesick in Heaven" (Holmes) **81**:104
"Homesickness" (Mörike) **10**:446
"The Homestead" (Lanier) **6**:260; **118**:218, 230, 235
"Homeward bound on Easter Eve. . ." (Pushkin) **83**:272
Homeward Bound; or, The Chase (Cooper) **1**:201, 208, 217, 221; **54**:256, 276, 288
Homeward Bound; or, The Chase: A Tale of the Sea (Cooper) **203**:45, 49, 72-73, 130
Homicide (Baillie) **2**:40-41; **151**:55
Hommage à Wagner (Mallarmé) **41**:280
"L'homme" (Lamartine) **11**:245, 264, 269, 273, 282; **190**:168, 237, 241
"L'homme à la cervelle d'or" (Daudet) **1**:249
L'homme à trois visages; ou, Le proscrit de Venise (Pixérécourt) **39**:272-74, 276-77, 279, 284, 286, 293-94
"Un homme d'affaires" (Balzac) **153**:153
L'homme de bien (Augier) **31**:4, 10, 12, 14, 18, 23
L'homme de neige (Sand) **42**:312; **57**:313, 316
"L'Homme et la mer" (Baudelaire) **55**:53, 58, 62, 65
"L'homme juste" (Rimbaud) **4**:465, 485
"L'Homme pauvre d'esprit . . ." (Verlaine) **230**:165
L'homme qui rit (Hugo) **3**:249-50, 252-53, 260, 267; **161**:200-2, 211, 213-20, 230, 264; **189**:211, 240-42

L'homme-femme: Résponse à M. Henri d'Ideville (Dumas) **9**:221, 234, 244
"L'Homme-fille" (Maupassant) **83**:189, 193, 195
Les hommes de lettres (Goncourt and Goncourt) **7**:162, 165-67, 181-82, 186, 188-89
"Homo" (Patmore) **9**:363
"The Honest Man" (Shaw) **15**:335
"Honeysuckle" (Allingham) **25**:14
"The Honeysuckle" (Rossetti) **4**:491
Les honnêtes femmes (Becque) **3**:15-16
Honneur d'Artiste (Feuillet) **45**:92-93
"Honor; or, The Story of the Brave Casper and the Fair Annerl" (Brentano)
See "Geschichte vom braven Kasperl und dem schönen Annerl"
"Honorine" (Balzac) **5**:83-84; **153**:40-46, 55, 80, 153
"Honours" (Ingelow) **39**:255-57
"Honte" (Rimbaud) **227**:198-202
"Hood's Isle and the Hermit Oberlus" (Melville) **3**:362
Hood's Own (Hood) **16**:204, 214, 217, 219, 229, 231
"Hooking Watermelons" (Bellamy) **4**:30; **86**:75
"Hooly and Fairly" (Baillie) **151**:41, 86-87, 92, 123
"Hope" (Clare) **86**:160
"Hope" (Cowper) **8**:105, 115, 120; **94**:26, 29-30, 55-60
"Hope" (Laforgue)
See "L'Espérance"
Hope (Bowles) **103**:56, 69
"Hope against Hope" (Patmore) **9**:328
"Hope A-Left Behind" (Barnes) **75**:7
"Hope Dieth: Love Liveth" (Morris) **4**:421
Hope Leslie; or, Early Times in the Massachusetts (Sedgwick) **19**:427-29, 433, 439, 442-43, 447-53; **98**:296-301, 306-11, 321-22, 326-30, 334, 339=51, 355-57, 359-60, 363-65, 367-72, 374-77, 381
The Hope of a Family (Daudet)
See *Soutien de famille*
The Hope of Albion (Thelwall) **162**:300
"Hope of Liberty" (Horton)
See "The Hope of Liberty. Containing a Number of Poetical Pieces."
"The Hope of Liberty. Containing a Number of Poetical Pieces." (Horton) **87**:83-86, 94, 99-101, 104, 108-11
"A Hopeless Case" (Rossetti) **186**:275
"Hopelessness" (Baratynsky)
See "Beznadeznost'"
"Hop-Frog" (Poe) **16**:312, 324; **117**:300
"Hoping Against Hope" (Rossetti) **50**:288
"Hora tras hora, dia, tras dia" (Castro) **78**:41
Horace (Sand) **2**:589; **57**:361
Horace and Petrarch (Coleridge) **90**:25,
Horace Chase (Woolson) **82**:275, 277, 280, 293, 299, 319-20, 324
Horace Walpole (Macaulay) **42**:87
"Horae Catnachianae" (Thackeray) **213**:200
"Horae Germanicae" (Lockhart) **6**:293
"Horas de invierno" (Larra) **17**:276, 283-84; **130**:209, 238, 278
Horatius (Macaulay) **42**:111, 154
"Horia" (Eminescu) **33**:245
"The Horkey" (Bloomfield) **145**:133, 157, 176
"Le horla" (Maupassant) **1**:449, 453-55, 57, 462-63, 471-72; **83**:218-19, 222
"L'horloge" (Baudelaire) **29**:104; **55**:28, 67
"The Horn" (Vigny)
See "Le cor"
"The Horn of Egremont Castle" (Wordsworth) **12**:395
Horn of Oberon: Jean Paul Richter's School for Aesthetics (Jean Paul)
See *Vorschule der Aesthetik: Nebst einigen Vorlesungen in Leipzig über die Parte ien der Zeit*
Hornby Mills (Kingsley) **107**:192
"Horologe of the Fields, addressed to a Young Lady, on seeing at the house of an acquaintance a magnificent French Time-piece" (Smith) **115**:119
"L'horreur sympathique" (Baudelaire) **29**:85; **55**:13, 65
"A Horse Ride at Dawn" (Eminescu) **131**:330
"The Horse Swap" (Longstreet) **159**:117-18, 133, 142, 144-45, 151, 160-62, 176, 182-83, 199
The Horseman's Manual (Surtees) **14**:350
The Horses of Lysippus (Coleridge) **90**:14
Horse-Shoe Robinson: A Tale of the Tory Ascendancy (Kennedy) **2**:428-33, 435
Horsztyński (Slowacki) **15**:352, 364, 371, 378, 380
"El hortelano" (Manzano) **155**:307
"Hortensia Antomarchi" (Isaacs) **70**:308
"Horton" (Smith) **59**:321, 332, 336
"Horus" (Nerval) **1**:480, 484, 486; **67**:307
"Hospita on Immoderate Indulgence of the Pleasures of the Palate" (Lamb) **10**:409, 411; **113**:236-39
"The Hospital" (Lermontov) **126**:223
"A Hospital Christmas" (Alcott) **83**:7; **218**:23
Hospital Sketches (Alcott) **6**:12-13; **58**:17, 46, 48-9, 67; **83**:8, 34, 78; **218**:15-23, 25
"Das Hospiz auf dem Groszen Sankt Bernhard" (Droste-Hülshoff) **3**:195-96, 199, 201
The Host (Grillparzer)
See *Der Gastfreund*
"Hot and Cold" (Hazlitt) **29**:156
"An Hour" (Alcott) **83**:7
"The Hour and the Ghost" (Rossetti) **2**:557, 563; **186**:318
The Hour and the Man (Martineau) **26**:310-11, 314, 323, 329; **137**:252, 259, 329
"An Hour ere Break of Day" (Mörike)
See "Ein Stündlein wohl vor Tag"
"The Hour of Death" (Le Fanu) **9**:302
"The Hour of Death" (Hemans) **29**:205-06
"The Hour of Feeling" (Bryant) **46**:55
"An Hour of Romance" (Hemans) **29**:194
An Hour of Thought (Slowacki)
See *Godzina myśli*
"Hours Continuing Long" (Whitman) **81**:332
"An Hour's Musings on the Atlantic" (Brontë) **109**:30
Hours of Idleness (Byron) **2**:58, 62, 77, 88, 103; **12**:138; **149**:56
Hours of Life, and Other Poems (Whitman) **19**:455, 457
Hours of Solitude: A Collection of Original Poems, Now First Published (Dacre) **151**:139-40, 143, 148, 170, 179, 199, 212-15
"Hours of Spring" (Jefferies) **47**:102, 138, 143
"An Hour's Talk on Poetry" (Wilson) **5**:552, 558
"House" (Browning) **19**:87, 96, 110
"The House Amidst the Thickets" (Ueda Akinari)
See "Asaji ga yado"
"The House and the Vineyard" (Lamartine)
See "La vigne et la maison"
The House at Kolomna (Pushkin) **83**:277
"The House Beautiful" (Stevenson) **5**:401
The House by the Churchyard (Le Fanu) **9**:300-03, 308-12, 315-17; **58**:251, 256, 266-8, 278, 281, 283, 285
A House Divided against Itself (Oliphant) **11**:460, 462; **61**:204-5, 211
"House Divided" Speech (Lincoln) **18**:208, 238, 280
A House Divided: Speech Delivered at Springfield, Illinois (Lincoln)
See *Speech of Hon. Abraham Lincoln, before the Republican State Convention, June 16, 1858*
"A House in the Blue Ridge" (Cooke) **5**:133
"The House in the Reeds" (Ueda Akinari)
See "Asaji ga yado"
The House Maid (Martineau) **26**:322
"The House of Clouds" (Barrett Browning) **1**:115
A House of Gentlefolk (Turgenev)
See *Dvoryanskoe gnezdo*
"The House of Heine Brothers, in Munich" (Trollope) **101**:235
"The House of Life" (Rossetti) **4**:490, 496-97, 499-503, 507-10, 512, 514-18, 526-29, 531; **77**:308, 312, 326, 329, 333, 337-40, 348, 353, 355, 358, 361
"The House of Night" (Freneau) **1**:314, 316, 318-19, 323; **111**:80, 82, 107, 140, 143, 151-52, 184
The House of the Seven Gables: A Romance (Hawthorne) **2**:298-99, 302-03, 305-06, 309-10, 312, 314-17, 320-21, 324-27, 329, 332; **17**:112, 114, 116-17, 130-32, 147, 149, 150; **23**:168-69, 183, 192, 202, 205, 209, 213; **39**:165-252; **79**:295, 304; **95**:109-10, 116; **158**:194, 233, 287-88, 307; **171**:237, 239, 262-64, 333, 339, 343, 345, 349, 358; **191**:154-310; **226**:7-8, 16, 56, 76, 79-80, 82-83, 96, 103
"The House of the Wolfings" (Morris) **4**:435-38, 440
"The House of Titian" (Jameson) **43**:323
"The House of Usher" (Poe)
See "The Fall of the House of Usher"
The House on the Moor (Oliphant) **11**:432
"The House upon the Hearth" (Lewis) **11**:303
"A House upon the Height" (Dickinson) **171**:120-21
"The House with the Green Blinds" (Stevenson) **5**:393
Household Book of the Earl of Northumberland in 1512 (Percy) **95**:313, 327-28
Household Education (Martineau) **26**:311, 329, 331, 342-43, 346-48; **137**:237, 247, 277, 282, 285, 321, 333, 349-52
Household Tales (Grimm Brothers)
See *Kinder-und Hausmärchen*
Household Words (Dickens) **187**:17, 19, 23, 26, 117, 134-36, 138, 172
"The Household Wreck" (De Quincey) **4**:83; **198**:38, 40, 42-43
"The Householder" (Browning) **19**:96
The Housekeeper (Jerrold) **2**:401
"Housekeeping in Belgravia" (Mayhew) **31**:181
"House-Martins" (Jefferies) **47**:138
"The House-Top" (Melville) **181**:216; **193**:148
"House-Warming" (Thoreau) **7**:398
A Housewife's Opinions (Webster) **230**:237, 238, 240, 242, 244, 298, 303, 330
"The Houstonia" (Very) **9**:372
"The How and the Why" (Tennyson) **30**:204
"How and Why I Am a Novelist" (Alencar)
See *Como e Porque Sou Romancista*
How and Why I Write (Alencar)
See *Como e Porque Sou Romancista*
"How Are You?" (Foscolo)
See "Che stai?"
"How Celia Changed Her Mind" (Cooke) **110**:33-4, 36, 44, 46, 50-1, 65
"How Celia Changed Her Mind" and Other Stories (Cooke) **110**:50-1, 62
"How do I love thee?" (Barrett Browning) **170**:24, 57
"How Far May a Common Tendency Be Traced in All Pre-Socratic Philosophy" (Hopkins) **189**:46
"How gently it rained" (Castro)
See "Cómo llovía, suaviño"
How He Won Her (Southworth) **26**:434, 446
"How Husbands May Rule" (Parton) **86**:349
"How I Learned to Celebrate" (Leskov) **25**:247
"How I Look" (Parton) **86**:376
"How I Overcame My Gravity" (O'Brien) **21**:236, 252-53
"How I Read the Morning Papers" (Parton) **86**:366

"How I Went Out to Service" (Alcott) **58**:11
"How I Wrote Looking Backward" (Bellamy) **147**:85, 96
"How Is It?" (Parton) **86**:351
"How It Happened" (O'Brien) **21**:245
"How It Strikes a Contemporary" (Browning) **19**:79, 132, 139; **79**:175-76
"How Lisa Loved the King" (Eliot) **4**:108; **13**:334
"How Long?" (Lazarus) **8**:413, 417, 420; **109**:295
"How Long?" (Very) **9**:386
"How Love Looked for Hell" (Lanier) **6**:249; **118**:217, 267
"How Many a Time, Beloved . . ." (Eminescu) **131**:332
"How Many Bards" (Keats) **73**:256
"How Many Times Do I Love Thee, Dear" (Beddoes) **154**:10
"How Many Times These Low Feet Staggered" (Dickinson) **21**:9, 38, 41
"How Mr. Storm Met His Destiny" (Boyesen) **135**:12-13, 27
"How Nellie Lee Was Pawned" (O'Brien) **21**:245
"How Oft Has the Banshee Cried" (Moore) **6**:391; **110**:184
"How One Muzhik Fed Two Generals" (Saltykov)
See "Povest' o tom, kak odin muzhik dvukh generalov prokormil"
"How She Found Out" (Cooke) **110**:35
"How Simon Suggs 'Raised Jack'" (Hooper) **177**:190-91
"How Solemn as One by One" (Whitman) **81**:314
"How sweetly slumbers the dark green garden" (Tyutchev)
See "Kak sladko dremlet sad temnozelenyi"
"How the Bell Rang, July 4, 1776" (O'Brien) **21**:247
"How the Change Came" (Morris) **4**:440
"How the Melbourne Cup Was Won" (Kendall) **12**:183
"How the Nightingale and the Parrot Wooed the Rose" (Crawford) **127**:181-84, 186, 188
"How the Old Horse Won the Bet" (Holmes) **14**:109, 115, 128
"How the Women Went from Dover" (Whittier) **8**:529
"How They Brought the Good News from Ghent to Aix" (Browning) **19**:88; **79**:94, 164
"How to be Happy" (Sigourney) **87**:321
"How to Cook Soup upon a Sausage Pin" (Andersen) **7**:28, 37; **214**:56, 58
How to Observe Morals and Manners (Martineau) **26**:322, 333-34; **137**:241, 302, 317, 331, 343, 348-49, 351, 353, 358
"How to Pick Out a Dog" (Shaw) **15**:335
"How to Pick Out a Horse" (Shaw) **15**:335
"How to Read Chaucer" (Lanier) **118**:218
"How to Think in Love of Those Who Passed Away" (Kierkegaard) **34**:198
"How to Write a Blackwood Article" (Poe) **16**:322-23; **55**:134; **117**:322
"How unexpectedly and brightly" (Tyutchev)
See "Kak neozhidanno i yarko"
"How We Beat the Favourite" (Gordon) **21**:149, 151, 154-59, 161, 165, 170, 175-76, 181, 188
"How We Come to Give Ourselves False Testimonials and Believe in Them" (Eliot) **118**:118
"How Weary! How Mournful!" (Lermontov)
See *I skuchno! I grustno!*
"How Willie Coasted by Moonlight" (Cranch) **115**:58
"How Woman Loves" (Parton) **86**:349
"Howarth Churchyard" (Arnold) **218**:188
"Howe's Masquerade" (Hawthorne) **2**:292-93; **191**:189-90
"However heavy the final hour may be" (Tyutchev)
See "Kak ni tyazhel posledniy chas"
"Howling Song of Al-Mohara" (Mangan) **27**:285, 292, 295, 298
Hoze hezyonot (Mapu) **18**:292, 301
The Hubbub; or, the History of Farmer Russel, the Hard-Hearted Overseer (More) **141**:168
Hubert Cauvin (Shelley) **143**:265
Hubert de Sevrac (Robinson) **142**:110, 184
Huckleberries Gathered from New England Hills (Cooke) **110**:19, 33-7, 39, 43-4, 50
The Hue and Cry (Inchbald) **62**:144-6
"Der Hügel und der Hain" (Klopstock) **225**:320
Hugh and Ion (Crawford) **12**:169, 174; **127**:161, 163-67, 169, 218, 222-28
A Hugh Henry Brackenridge Reader (Brackenridge) **227**:166
Hugh Trevor (Holcroft)
See *The Adventures of Hugh Trevor*
"Hugo" (Slowacki) **15**:348-49
Hugo, the Deformed (Alger) **8**:42; **83**:96
Les Huguenots (Scribe) **16**:390, 398, 401, 408-09
Huit Femmes (Desbordes-Valmore) **97**:12
"The Human Abstract" (Blake) **13**:221, 224, 226, 240, 242-43; **37**:4, 25, 33, 44-5, 47, 49, 52-3, 92; **173**:16
"Human Applause" (Hölderlin)
See "Menschenbeifall"
The Human Comedy (Balzac)
See *La Comédie humaine*
"Human Frailty" (Cowper) **94**:102
Human Happiness (Holcroft) **85**:192, 215, 234
"Human Life" (Arnold) **6**:50; **89**:88, 98
Human Life (Rogers) **69**:69-70, 74
"Human Repetends" (Clarke) **19**:251
"Human Responsibility as Independent of Circumstances" (Newman) **38**:307
"Human Sacrifice" (Whittier) **8**:485, 512
"The Human Wheel" (Holmes) **81**:124-30
"Human Work" (Silva)
See "Obra humana"
Humanitätsbriefe (Herder)
See *Briefe zu Beförderung der Humanität*
"L'humanitè" (Lamartine) **11**:255, 270, 279; **190**:257
"Humble Beginnings" (Beddoes) **154**:44
"Humble drame" (Maupassant) **83**:209
"A Humble Remonstrance" (Stevenson) **63**:239, 258, 260; **193**:222, 266, 271, 312
"The Humble-Bee" (Emerson) **1**:289, 296
"The Humboldt Desert" (Ridge) **82**:185
"Humboldt River" (Ridge) **82**:185
"Humboldt's Birthday" (Holmes) **81**:102
Hume, With Helps to the Study of Berkeley (Huxley) **67**:13, 27, 93-5
The Humiliated and the Wronged (Dostoevsky)
See *The Insulted and Injured*
"The Humiliation of the Eternal Son" (Newman) **38**:305
Humilis Domus: Some Thoughts on the Abodes, Life and Social Conditions of the Poor, Especially in Dorsetshire (Barnes) **75**:57-8, 102, 106
"The Humming Bird" (Cranch) **115**:40
"Humphrey and William" (Southey) **97**:314-15
"Hun duede ikke" (Andersen) **79**:72
The Hunchback of Notre-Dame (Hugo)
See *Notre-Dame de Paris*
The Hundred and One (Sarmiento) **123**:268
"The Hungarian Nation" (Petofi)
See "A magyar nemzet"
"The Hungarian Nobleman" (Petofi)
See "A magyar nemes"
Hungarian Rhapsodies (Liszt) **199**:305, 311, 318, 326
Hungary's Decline and Maria of Austria (Sacher-Masoch) **31**:290
"Hunger" (Dickinson) **77**:148; **171**:176
"A Hungry Day" (Crawford) **127**:217
"Hunt after my Captain" (Holmes) **14**:118
The Hunt for Happiness (Adams) **33**:19
"The Hunt of Eildon" (Hogg) **4**:283, 285
Hunt of Eildon (Hogg) **109**:233
"Hunter of Comar" (Hogg) **109**:203
"The Hunter of the Prairies" (Bryant) **6**:169, 172
"The Hunters of Men" (Whittier) **8**:489, 510, 526
"The Hunter's Serenade" (Bryant) **6**:169; **46**:20
Hunter's Sketches (Turgenev)
See *Zapiski okhotnika*
"The Hunter's Twain" (Crawford) **127**:164
The Hunters Twain (Crawford)
See *Hugh and Ion*
"Hunter's Vision" (Bryant) **46**:4, 28
The Hunting of the Snark (Dodgson)
See *The Hunting of the Snark: An Agony in Eight Fits*
The Hunting of the Snark: An Agony in Eight Fits (Dodgson) **2**:106, 117; **53**:40-2, 55-6, 84-5, 107, 109-10, 112, 116; **139**:5-15, 19, 29, 31-32, 35, 38, 40-41, 50, 65, 80, 120, 123-25, 128, 139
Hunting Seat (Almqvist) **42**:17
"Hunting Song" (Bloomfield) **145**:154-55
"Les hurleurs" (Leconte de Lisle) **29**:210, 215, 217, 230
"Hurrahing in Harvest" (Hopkins) **17**:208, 211, 217; **189**:5, 8, 18-20, 29, 46, 53-54, 65, 86-87, 89-90, 92, 94, 107, 110, 126-27, 143, 145
"The Hurricane" (Bryant) **6**:159, 161, 176; **46**:6, 20, 28, 47
"The Hurricane" (Freneau) **1**:323; **111**:105, 147-48, 150, 154, 178-81
Husband and Wife (Fredro)
See *Mąż i żona*
"Husband-Hunting and Match-Making", (Webster) **230**:244
"The Husbandman" (Rossetti) **77**:353
"The Husband's and Wife's Grave" (Dana) **53**:158, 168
"A Hushaby" (Field) **3**:212
"Hussens Kerker" (Meyer) **81**:140-41, 143, 149-50, 155
"The Hut by the Black Swamp" (Kendall) **12**:181-83, 194, 201
"The Hut by the Tanks" (Adams) **33**:13
"Huttens letze Tage" (Meyer) **81**:140-41, 146, 148-49, 152, 156, 164
Hvad Christus dömmer om officiel Christendom (Kierkegaard) **34**:196, 200, 225, 266; **78**:226, 238; **125**:234
"Hvad gamle Johanne fortalte" (Andersen) **79**:74
Hwomely Rhymes. A Second Collection of Poems in the Dorset Dialect (Barnes) **75**:18, 40, 69, 79
"The Hwomestead a-Vell Into Hand" (Barnes) **75**:102
"Hyacinth and Rose Petal" (Novalis)
See "Hyacinth und Rosenblütchen"
"Hyacinth und Rosenblütchen" (Novalis) **178**:54-55, 66, 83
"Hyazinth and Rosenblüte" (Novalis) **13**:393
"Hyazinth und Rosenblütchen" (Novalis)
See "Hyacinth und Rosenblütchen"
"Hy-Brasil" (Kendall) **12**:183, 187, 199
Hydrozoa (Huxley) **67**:4
The Hyena of the Poussta (Sacher-Masoch) **31**:298, 301
Hygiène (Baudelaire) **155**:107
"Hylas" (Taylor) **89**:358
"Hymen and Hirco: A Vision" (Sheridan) **91**:230
"Hymn" (Beddoes) **154**:52
"Hymn" (Emerson) **98**:177, 182
"Hymn" (Lanier) **118**:259

"Hymn" (Willis)
See "Dedication Hymn"
"Hymn before Sunrise in the Vale of Chamouni" (Coleridge) **9**:148; **99**:36, 81; **231**:59, 112, 115, 120
"Hymn by T.P. at school" (Percy) **95**:337
"Hymn for Ascension Day" (Jones) **222**:169
"Hymn for Pentecost" (Mangan) **27**:296
"Hymn I" (Barbauld) **185**:34
"Hymn II" (Barbauld) **50**:8; **185**:11, 50
"Hymn III" (Barbauld) **185**:10, 12
Hymn in Honor of the Plague (Pushkin) **3**:434, 449
"Hymn IV" (Barbauld) **185**:9, 11, 34
"Hymn IX" (Barbauld) **185**:12
Hymn No. VIII (Cowper)
See "O Lord, I Will Praise Thee"
Hymn No. IX (Cowper)
See "The Contrite Heart"
Hymn No. 11 (Cowper)
See "Jehovah Our Righteousness"
Hymn No. V8 (Cowper)
See "The New Convert"
Hymn No. LXVII (Cowper)
See "I will praise the Lord at all times"
"The Hymn of an Exile" (Heredia)
See "Himno de desterrado"
"Hymn of Apollo" (Shelley) **18**:345, 360, 362
"Hymn of Death" (Lamartine)
See "Hymne de la mort"
"Hymn of Evening in the Temples" (Lamartine) **11**:248
"Hymn of Pan" (Shelley) **18**:327
"Hymn of Praise" (Kendall) **12**:183, 192
"Hymn of the Fishermen" (Ferguson) **33**:290
"Hymn of the Morning" (Lamartine)
See "L'hymne du matin"
"A Hymn of the Sea" (Bryant) **6**:168; **46**:6, 9
"Hymn of the Waldenses" (Bryant) **6**:159
"Hymn of Trust" (Holmes) **81**:100
"Hymn on Prosperity" (Darwin) **106**:185
"Hymn to a Child at Waking" (Lamartine)
See "Hymne de l'enfant à son reveil"
"Hymn to Air" (Taylor) **89**:304
"Hymn to Beauty" (Baudelaire)
See "Hymne à la beauté"
"Hymn to Charity" (Hale) **75**:343
"Hymn to Content" (Barbauld) **185**:33, 120
"Hymn to Death" (Bryant) **6**:159-60, 168, 170, 172, 177, 183; **46**:3, 9, 15, 21, 23
"Hymn to Death" (Whitman) **31**:432
"Hymn to Fools" (Karamzin)
See "Gimm gluptsam"
"Hymn to Intellectual Beauty" (Shelley) **18**:331, 341, 361, 364, 376; **93**:262; **175**:235, 301, 303, 310, 315
"Hymn to Intllectual Beauty" (Browning) **79**:113
"Hymn to Liberty" (Solomos)
See "Hymnos eis ten Eleutherian"
"Hymn to Mercury" (Shelley) **18**:363
"Hymn to Mont Blanc" (Coleridge) **9**:144
"Hymn to Pan" (Keats) **8**:344; **73**:198, 204, 218, 280; **121**:141-42, 146-47
"Hymn to the Earth" (Coleridge) **99**:4; **197**:215; **231**:151
"Hymn to the Exile" (Heredia)
See "Himno de desterrado"
"Hymn to the Moon" (Hogg) **109**:248
"Hymn to the Mother of God" (Slowacki) **15**:349
"Hymn to the Night" (Longfellow) **2**:492; **45**:115, 146, 151, 184
Hymn to the Ship of the Muses (Foscolo) **97**:52
"Hymn to the Sun" (Darley) **2**:131
"Hymn to the Sun" (Heredia)
See "Al sol"
"Hymn to the Sun" (Hood) **16**:208, 221
"Hymn V" (Barbauld) **185**:9, 11, 35, 38, 50-51, 53
"Hymn VI" (Barbauld) **185**:11, 34, 51
"Hymn VII" (Barbauld) **185**:52, 103
"Hymn VIII" (Barbauld) **185**:52, 58, 119-20
"Hymn X" (Barbauld) **185**:10-12, 51
"Hymn XI" (Barbauld) **185**:10
"Hymn XII" (Barbauld) **185**:10, 12
"Hymn: Ye are the Salt of the Earth" (Barbauld) **185**:143
"A Hymn Yet Not a Hymn" (Clough) **27**:46
"Hymne à la beauté" (Baudelaire) **6**:123, 128; **29**:97-8; **55**:64-6, 73; **155**:98
"L'hymne à la douleur" (Lamartine) **11**:265, 270, 279
"Hymne an den Genius Griechenlands" (Hölderlin) **16**:174
"Die Hymne an den Unendlichen" (Schiller) **39**:339
"Hymne an die Freiheit" (Hölderlin) **187**:197
"Hymne an die Göttin der Harmonie" (Hölderlin) **16**:173; **187**:194, 196-97
"Hymne an die Schönheit" (Hölderlin) **187**:196
"Hymne an die Unsterblichkeit" (Hölderlin) **187**:195
"Hymne au Christ" (Lamartine) **11**:279
"L'hymne au soleil" (Lamartine) **11**:269; **190**:257
"Hymne de la mort" (Lamartine) **11**:248, 279
"L'hymne de la nuit" (Lamartine) **11**:270
"Hymne de l'ange de la terre après la destruction du globe" (Lamartine) **190**:233
"Hymne de l'enfant" (Lamartine) **11**:279
"Hymne de l'Enfant à Son Reveil" (Lamartine) **190**:177
"L'hymne du matin" (Lamartine) **11**:248, 270, 283
"La hymne du soir dans les temples" (Lamartine) **11**:265, 270, 279
Hymne pour l'inauguration de la colonne de Napoléon à Boulogne (Hugo) **161**:187
"Hymnen an die Menschheit" (Hölderlin) **187**:194, 196
Hymnen an die Nacht (Novalis) **13**:360, 362-63, 365, 367, 374, 376-79, 390-92, 394, 397, 401-02, 405; **178**:23-29, 33, 40, 74, 77, 81
"Hymnos eis ten Eleutherian" (Solomos) **15**:386-90, 392, 403-04
"Hymns for the Kirk" (Baillie) **2**:41
Hymns in Prose for Children (Barbauld) **50**:6-9; **185**:5-6, 8-13, 23, 50-53, 58-59, 102-8, 117-21, 133
"Hymns of the City" (Bryant) **6**:161; **46**:55
"Hymns of the Marshes" (Lanier) **6**:238, 240, 247, 249, 264, 273; **118**:204, 240
Hymns to the Night (Novalis)
See *Hymnen an die Nacht*
Hypatia; or, New Foes with Old Faces (Kingsley) **35**:209, 215-16, 218-20, 222, 224, 226, 228-36, 241-44, 249, 252, 255-56
"Hypatie" (Leconte de Lisle) **29**:213, 223, 238, 240
"Hypatie et Cyrille" (Leconte de Lisle) **29**:240
Hyperboräische Esel (Kotzebue) **25**:138
"Hyperion" (Eminescu)
See "Luceafarul"
Hyperion (Hölderlin) **16**:158, 161, 164-65, 172-74, 176-77, 182-83, 185-87, 190-91
Hyperion (Keats) **8**:328-29, 331, 333-34, 336, 340-41, 345-47, 350, 352-53, 355-56, 358-59, 361-63, 365-68, 381-83, 385-86; **73**:144, 153-54, 159-61, 170-72, 177-78, 181-82, 192, 204, 209, 254-55, 259, 261, 263, 294-95, 328-30, 337-39; **121**:95-239; **225**:112-13, 116-19, 133, 139, 158-59, 162-64, 166-67, 169-70, 172-73, 177-78, 181, 220-21, 226, 236-40, 255
Hyperion (Longfellow) **2**:469-70, 474, 480, 489-90, 494; **45**:103, 181, 183-84; **103**:284-86
Hyperion: A Fragment (Keats)
See *Hyperion*
Hyperion, Empedokles, Aufsätze und Übertragungen (Hölderlin) **187**:253-54
Hyperion oder Der Eremit in Griechenland (Hölderlin) **187**:189-90, 197-98, 211, 214, 216, 228, 233, 236, 267, 291, 299-301, 303-4
Hyperion; or, The Hermit in Greece (Hölderlin)
See *Hyperion oder Der Eremit in Griechenland*
Hyperion: Thalia Fragment, 1794 (Hölderlin)
See *Fragment von Hyperion*
"Hyperions Schicksalslied" (Hölderlin) **16**:173-74, 176, 181, 184
"Hypertrophie" (Laforgue) **221**:87-89
"The Hypnotizers" (Bakunin) **58**:131
Hypochondria (Tegner)
See *Mjältsjukan*
"Hypochondriacus" (Lamb) **10**:389
"Hypocrite lecteur" (Baudelaire)
See "Au lecteur"
"Hyrdinden og Skorsteensfeieren" (Andersen) **79**:70-1
"Hysterical" (Verlaine)
See "L'Hystérique"
"L'Hystérique" (Verlaine) **230**:174
"i a probina qu'esta xorda" (Castro) **78**:2, 7
"I Admire Ambition . . ." (Verlaine)
See "J'admire l'ambition . . ."
"I Am" (Clare) **9**:90, 100, 103, 105; **86**:87, 114, 153, 170
"I Am a Parcel of Vain Strivings Tied" (Thoreau) **7**:383
"I am Almost Afraid . . ." (Verlaine)
See "J'ai presque peur . . ."
"I Am Ashamed—I Hide" (Dickinson) **21**:57
"I Am Here Again under Protection of the Roof" (Pavlova)
See "La snova zdes! pod sen'iu krova"
"I am in Danger—Sir—" (Dickinson) **171**:154
"I Am No Longer . . ." (Verlaine)
See "Je ne suis plus . . ."
"I Am Not the Man I Used to Be" (Foscolo)
See "Non son chi fui"
"I Am Pleading for My People" (Truth) **94**:332
"I Am the Autumnal Sun" (Thoreau) **7**:384
"I Am the Little Irish Boy" (Thoreau) **7**:384
"I Am Weary, Let Me Go" (Gordon) **21**:160-61
"I and My Chimney" (Melville) **3**:354, 380-81, 383; **12**:303; **93**:188; **157**:72, 111
"I and the Dog" (Barnes) **75**:36
"I Andegaarden" (Andersen) **7**:37; **214**:40
"I breathed enough to take the Trick—" (Dickinson) **171**:161
"I Can Wade Grief" (Dickinson) **21**:64
"I Cannot Dance upon My Toes" (Dickinson) **21**:82; **77**:130
"I Cannot Forget with What Fervid Devotion" (Bryant) **6**:177; **46**:38
"I cannot live with You" (Dickinson) **77**:96
"I cannot love thee" (Norton) **47**:238
"I Caught a Little Ladybird" (Rossetti) **186**:238
"I Commend You" (Rossetti) **66**:307
"I Could Not Be up to You" (Eminescu) **33**:265
"I det grø onne" (Wergeland) **5**:541
"I died for beauty, but was scarce" (Dickinson) **21**:43; **77**:119, 129; **171**:86, 88
"I Dream of Bloody Days" (Petofi)
See "Véres napokról álmodom"
"I Dream'd in a Dream" (Whitman) **31**:394; **81**:328, 331
"I Dreamed a Dream" (Clough) **27**:103
"I dreamed a dream" (Prescott) **163**:6, 34
"I Dreamt Last Night" (Brontë) **4**:45
"I drink alone" (Pushkin) **83**:373
"I Dwell in Possibility" (Dickinson) **171**:143, 156, 177, 183
"I felt a Cleaving in my Mind—" (Dickinson) **171**:143, 158, 198
"I Felt a Funeral in My Brain" (Dickinson) **21**:64; **77**:76; **171**:122, 198-99, 216
"I gave myself to him" (Dickinson) **171**:96, 98
"I Give Thee Joy! O Worthy Word" (Clough) **27**:103

"I give thee joy! O worthy word!" (Prescott) **163**:34, 36
"I go, Lord, where Thou sendest me" (Rossetti) **186**:295
"I Got So I Could Take His Name" (Dickinson) **21**:64
"I Got Two Vields" (Barnes) **75**:101
"I Grew up in a Foreign Land" (Shevchenko) See "I vyris ya na chyzhyni"
"I Grieved" (Wordsworth) **206**:300-301
"I gynaika tis Zakynthos" (Solomos) **15**:393, 396-97
"I Had a Dove" (Keats) **8**:360
"I Had a Guinea Golden" (Dickinson) **21**:15
"I had been hungry, all the Years" (Dickinson) See "Hunger"
"I Had No Time to Hate" (Dickinson) **21**:42
"I Had Struggled . . ." (Verlaine) See "J'avais peiné . . ."
"I have a Cottage" (Boker) **125**:7
"I Have a Little Husband" (Rossetti) **186**:238
"I have magnified . . ." (Verlaine) See "J'ai magnifié . . ."
"I Have No Need of the Hoarfrost" (Arany) See "Nem kell dér"
"I Have Said to the Futile Mind . . ." (Verlaine) "J'ai dit à l'esprit vain . . ."
"I Hear America Singing" (Whitman) **205**:166
"I Hear It Was Charged against Me" (Whitman) **31**:430
"I heard a Fly buzz—when I died—" (Dickinson) **77**:49, 156, 163; **171**:104, 110, 113, 183, 210, 216
"I Heard a Thousand Blended Notes" (Wordsworth) **206**:225
"I Heard an Angel Singing" (Blake) **37**:38
"I Held a Jewel in My Fingers" (Dickinson) **21**:64
"I Hide Myself within My Flower" (Dickinson) **21**:8, 69
"I Knew a Man by Sight" (Thoreau) **7**:383
"I know a baby, such a baby" (Rossetti) **186**:236
"I know not why . . ." (Verlaine) See "Je ne sais pourquoi . . ."
"I know not why, but all this weary day" (Timrod) **25**:366
"I know that He exists" (Dickinson) **77**:77; **171**:104, 160, 175, 182
"I know you not" (Rossetti) **186**:258
I Kvæld blev der banket paa Helvedesport (Grundtvig) **158**:167
"I Laid Me Down upon a Bank" (Blake) **13**:181
"I Lay the Lute Down" (Arany) See "Letteszem a lantot"
"I like a look of Agony" (Dickinson) **21**:9, 42; **77**:162
"I like to see it lap the Miles—" (Dickinson) **21**:49; **77**:129
"I live with him, I see his face" (Dickinson) **171**:98
"I Lost the Love of Heaven" (Clare) **9**:101
"I Love, I Love . . ." (Laforgue) See "Dimaches"
"I Love the Jocund Dance" (Blake) **37**:35
"I love you, goddesses of song" (Baratynsky) See "Liubliu ia vas, bogini pen'ia"
"I Love You, My Sweet" (Petofi) See "Szeretlek, kedvesem"
"I love your smile" (Verlaine) See "J'aime ton sourire"
"I Loving Freedom for Herself" (Tennyson) **30**:294
"I make His Crescent fill or lack—" (Dickinson) **171**:159
"I mertvym i zyvym i nenarodzenym zemljakam mojim v Ukrajini i ne v Ukrajini moje druznjeje poslanije" (Shevchenko) See "Poslanie"
"I Never Lost as Much but Twice" (Dickinson) **21**:63; **171**:176
"I Never Told the Buried Gold" (Dickinson) **21**:54
"I Never Will Be Married, I'd Rather Be Excus'd" (Rowson) **182**:282
"Den i noch" (Tyutchev) **34**:396-97
I pitocchi fortunati (Gozzi) **23**:107, 113, 119, 121, 123, 125-26
I pochi (Alfieri) **101**:45, 73
"I Poetic" (Alfieri) **101**:32
I Racconti delle fate (Collodi) **54**:143, 144-7
"I Remember, I Remember" (Hood) **16**:219, 233, 237
"I Rose Because He Sank" (Dickinson) **21**:43, 67
"I Saw A Boy" (Barnes) **75**:70
"I Saw a Monk of Charlemaine" (Blake) **13**:243
"I Saw from the Beach" (Moore) **6**:389, 396
"I Saw Her Once" (Mangan) **27**:298
"I Saw in Louisiana a Live-Oak Growing" (Whitman) **31**:379, 392; **81**:364; **205**:220
"I Saw No Way—The Heavens Were Stitched" (Dickinson) **21**:76, 83
"I Saw Old General at Bay" (Whitman) **81**:319
"I Saw Thee on Thy Bridal Day" (Poe) See "Song"
I Say No (Collins) **1**:188, 191
"I See around Me Tombstones Grey" (Brontë) **16**:98
"I shall know why" (Dickinson) **171**:175
"I should have been to glad, I see-" (Cantor) **77**:84
"I Sing the Body Electric" (Whitman) **4**:571-72; **31**:372, 404, 425, 430; **81**:311, 342, 358-59; **205**:158, 191-94, 218-19, 300, 302
I Sit and Look Out (Whitman) **205**:322
"I sit thoughtful and alone" (Tyutchev) See "Sizhu zadumchiv i odin"
I skuchno! I grustno! (Lermontov) **5**:287
"I Sonnet" (Corbière) **43**:32
"I Started Early—Took My Dog" (Dickinson) **21**:79; **77**:148; **171**:158
"Les i step" (Turgenev) **122**:264
"I Stood on Tiptoe" (Keats) See "I Stood Tip-Toe"
"I Stood Tip-Toe" (Keats) **8**:343, 364; **73**:158, 213, 225-26, 259, 267, 322
"I stood tip-toe upon a little hill" (Keats) **225**:134-35, 165-66
I Sverrige (Andersen) **79**:80
"I Taste a Liquor Never Brewed" (Dickinson) **21**:37, 41, 65; **77**:93, 119; **171**:89, 106, 126, 177
"I thank my God because my hairs are grey!" (Coleridge) **90**:27
"I think the Hemlock likes to stand" (Dickinson) **77**:67
"I Think to Live May Be a Bliss" (Dickinson) **21**:80
"I Thought of Thee, My Partner and My Guide" (Wordsworth) **12**:466
"I Thought That Knowledge Alone Would Suffice" (Whitman) **81**:332
"I tie my Hat" (Dickinson) **77**:103, 105
"I traduttori e le traduzioni" (Collodi) **54**:143
"I travelled among unknown men" (Wordsworth) **111**:323
I troppi (Alfieri) **101**:45, 73
"I Visited Thy Tomb" (Nekrasov) **11**:404
"I vyris ya na chyzhyni" (Shevchenko) **54**:394
"I Wake and Feel the Fell of Dark, Not Day" (Hopkins) **17**:242, 261-62; **189**:54, 77, 84-85, 146
"I Wandered Lonely as a Cloud" (Wordsworth) **12**:456, 463; **111**:323
"I Was Looking a Long While" (Whitman) **205**:166
"I watched the Moon around the House" (Dickinson) **77**:121
"I will praise the Lord at all times" (Cowper) **94**:69, 75
"I wish I were where Helen lies" (Fuller) **50**:243, 245
I Wittenberg i Saksenland (Grundtvig) **158**:112
"I Would I Knew the Lady of Thy Heart" (Kemble) **18**:181
"Iakov Emel'ianovich Shisherin i sovremennye eny teatral'nye znamenitosti" (Aksakov) **181**:68
"Iakov Emel'ianovich Shusherin and Theatrical Celebrities of His Time" (Aksakov) See "Iakov Emel'ianovich Shisherin i sovremennye eny teatral'nye znamenitosti"
"Ib and Christine" (Andersen) See "Ib and Little Christine"
"Ib and Little Christina" (Andersen) See "Ib and Little Christine"
"Ib and Little Christine" (Andersen) **7**:29, 32; **79**:82; **214**:50, 59
"Ibo" (Hugo) **3**:263
"Icarus" (Taylor) **89**:310
"The Ice Island" (Bird) **197**:6
"The Ice Maiden" (Andersen) See "Iisjomfruen"
The Ice-Island (Bird) **1**:87
"Ich bin durch die Wüste gezogen" (Brentano) **191**:36
"Ich kenn ein Haus, ein Freudenhaus" (Brentano) **191**:66, 120
"Ich muß das Elend tragen!" (Brentano) **191**:32
"Ich schnitt' es gern in alle Rinden ein" (Muller) **73**:381
"Ich strafe die Bosheit" (Gotthelf) **117**:58
"Ich träumte hinab in das dunkle" (Brentano) **191**:121
"Ich wandle wieder durch die Waldesspitze" (Meyer) **81**:147
"Ichabod" (Whittier) **8**:490, 495, 500, 509-10, 513, 515, 520-22, 526, 530-31; **59**:357, 360, 368-73
"Ichneumon" (Taylor) **89**:311
"The Icon in its Frame" (Eminescu) **131**:286
Icons Old and New (Eminescu) **131**:313
"Ida Grey" (Levy) **59**:106
"Ida Grey" (Osgood) **141**:354-55, 358
"Ida to Ernest" (Osgood) **141**:354
"Ida's Farewell" (Osgood) **141**:354-58
"Idea for a Rational Catechism for Noble Ladies" (Schleiermacher) **107**:395
Idea for a Universal History with a Cosmopolitan Purpose (Kant) **27**:237; **67**:222
The Idea of a University, Defined and Illustrated (Newman) **38**:286, 294, 296, 302, 307, 323, 342, 344-45; **99**:210-17, 248, 266, 278, 296, 298
"Idea of the Human Soul" (Freneau) See "Robert Slender's Idea of the Human Soul"
"L'idéal" (Baudelaire) **6**:123; **29**:97-8; **55**:31, 58
"The Ideal" (Baudelaire) See "L'idéal"
"Ideal and life" (Schiller) See "Das Ideal und das Leben"
"The Ideal and Life" (Schiller) See "Das Ideal und das Leben"
The Ideal in Art (Taine) **15**:469
"Das Ideal und das Leben" (Schiller) **39**:332, 337, 370; **166**:119-20
"Ideal Women" (Linton) **41**:164
"Ideale" (Schiller) See "Das Ideal und das Leben"
"Ideale der Menschheit" (Hölderlin) **16**:175
"An Idealistic Flounder" (Saltykov) **16**:358
Ideas (Kierkegaard) **78**:122
Ideas (Multatuli) See *Ideeën*
Ideas (Schlegel) See *Ideen*
Ideas, 129a (Schlegel) **45**:343
Ideas, 135 (Schlegel) **45**:343
Ideas for a Philosophy of Nature (Schelling) See *Ideen zu einer Philosophie der Natur*

Ideas of a Philosophy of the History of Humankind (Herder)
See *Ideen zur Philosophie der Geschichte der Menschheit*
Ideas: The Book of Le Grand (Heine)
See *Ideen, Das Buch Le Grand*
L'Idée (Mallarmé) **210**:171
Idée sur les romans (Sade) **3**:468-69; **47**:312, 346
Ideeën (Multatuli) **165**:317-18, 326, 329-31, 337, 344, 346, 348
Ideen (Schlegel) **45**:342-43, 363, 382; **226**:164, 171
Ideen, Das Buch Le Grand (Heine) **4**:250-1, 259, 266, 317; **54**:317, 331, 336, 338-9; **147**:150, 202-3, 226-27, 230
Ideen zu einem Versuch, die Grenzen der Wirksamkeit des Staats zu bestimmen (Humboldt) **134**:164, 170, 177, 184, 192, 202
Ideen zu einer Philosophie der Natur (Schelling) **30**:125, 165, 171-75
Ideen zur Geschichte und Kritik der Poesie und bildenden Künste (Herder) **8**:307, 313
Ideen zur Philosophie der Geschichte der Menschheit (Herder) **8**:299-301, 303, 309-12; **186**:9, 11, 13, 16-20, 39, 45, 48, 52, 59, 61-65, 81, 85, 92, 94, 99-103
Ideen zur Philosophie der Geschichte der Menschheit (Humboldt) **134**:208
Les idées de Madame Aubray (Dumas) **9**:220, 225, 228, 235, 241-43, 249-51
"Les Idées du Colonel" (Maupassant) **83**:181, 194
Idées et sensations (Goncourt and Goncourt) **7**:152
The Identification of the Artisan and the Artist: The Proper Object of American Education. Illustrated by a Lecture of Cardinal Wiseman on the Relation of the Arts of Design with the Arts of Production. Addressed to American W (Peabody) **169**:150, 159
"The Identity of Thought with Nature" (Emerson) **98**:7
"Ideological Analysis of the Tenses of the Spanish Conjugation" (Bello) **131**:120
Ideolus (Baudelaire) **6**:119
"Idilio" (Silva) **114**:263
"Idiosyncrasies" (Neal) **161**:344-45, 348-49
The Idiot (Dostoevsky) **2**:162, 164, 167-69, 171, 175, 180, 187, 199, 202-04; **7**:103; **21**:90, 94, 102, 108-09, 112-13, 115, 121, 140, 142, 144; **33**:165, 179, 199, 212; **43**:91, 98, 134, 167; **119**:64-167; **167**:221, 283, 334, 337; **202**:65, 67, 74, 77, 96
"The Idiot Boy" (Wordsworth) **12**:386-87, 402, 445-46, 451; **111**:200, 202-3, 223, 225-26, 245, 248, 293, 305-7, 313, 316, 348, 367-68; **206**:234, 275, 331-38
"Idiots Again" (Martineau) **26**:349
The Idle Man (Dana) **53**:160, 167, 174, 177
"The Idle Man" (Willis) **194**:298
"The Idle Shepherd-boys" (Wordsworth) **111**:235; **206**:317-18
"Idleness" (Willis) **194**:306, 314
"The Idler" (Very) **9**:383
"L'idole: sonnet du trou du cul" (Rimbaud) **35**:291
Idris: Ein heroisch-comisches Gedicht (Wieland) **17**:410-12; **177**:287
Idris und Zenide (Wieland)
See *Idris: Ein heroisch-comisches Gedicht*
"Idyl from Lake Constance" (Mörike) **10**:456
An Idyl of Lake Constance (Mörike)
See *Idylle vom Bodensee; oder, Fischer Martin und die Glockendiebe*
An Idyl of Work (Larcom) **179**:167, 173-74
Idyll och epigram (Runeberg) **41**:309, 317, 320-21
"Idylle" (Chamisso) **82**:27-29
"Idylle coupée" (Corbière) **43**:33
L'idylle rue Plumet (Hugo) **3**:246
Idylle vom Bodensee; oder, Fischer Martin und die Glockendiebe (Mörike) **201**:252-53, 348-50, 352-55
Idylle von Bodensee; oder, Fischer Martin und die Glockendiebe (Mörike) **10**:447, 449-50, 452
Idylles Prussiennes (Banville) **9**:16, 24, 30
Idyllia heroica (Landor) **14**:181, 190, 204
Idylls of the Hearth (Tennyson)
See *Enoch Arden, and Other Poems*
Idylls of the King (Tennyson) **30**:216-18, 220, 233, 242, 249, 252-54, 258, 265, 267, 269-70, 274, 276, 279-82, 287, 292-93, 295; **65**:223-390; **115**:235, 269, 275, 309, 341; **202**:206-8, 210, 214-15, 218, 220-23, 238-39, 245-46, 248-49, 251, 253-54, 276, 283-84, 290-91, 293, 308, 319-26
"Idylls of the King: Balin and Balan" (Tennyson) **30**:254, 290; **65**:237, 241, 243, 250, 252, 269, 277-8, 281, 290-5, 297-9, 349-51, 374, 376; **115**:335
"Idylls of the King: Gareth and Lynette" (Tennyson) **30**:283, 287-88; **65**:236, 241, 243-5, 278, 281, 284, 287-8, 293, 300-1, 307, 311, 349, 367, 369-76, 382
"Idylls of the King: Geraint and Enid" (Tennyson) **30**:249, 253, 279, 288-90; **65**:226, 237, 241, 278, 324, 328-29, 331, 351, 353, 359, 381
"Idylls of the King: Lancelot and Elaine" (Tennyson) **30**:249, 279, 291-92; **65**:227, 237, 241, 243, 246, 250, 252-4, 278-9, 282, 284, 294-95, 297, 299-301, 307, 310, 312, 315, 318, 335-37, 342, 352, 357-60, 364, 366, 385
"Idylls of the King: Merlin and Vivien" (Tennyson) **30**:254, 279, 290; **65**:226-27, 237, 241, 255, 278, 281-82, 284, 290-93, 297, 99-300, 302, 315-16, 331-33, 335-36, 338, 351, 359, 371-74, 376, 378-81, 383, 386
"Idylls of the King: Pelleas and Ettarre" (Tennyson) **30**:249, 254; **65**:238, 254, 279, 282, 285, 288, 291, 300, 315, 318, 320, 323, 352, 361, 374, 376
"Idylls of the King: The Coming of Arthur" (Tennyson) **30**:249, 253, 279, 287; **65**:236, 239, 243, 249, 252-3, 257, 277-8, 280-1, 288-9, 292, 298, 300-1, 312, 314-5, 319-20, 349, 352, 369, 372
"Idylls of the King: The Last Tournament" (Tennyson) **30**:254; **65**:238-9, 241, 246, 251-3, 269, 279, 282, 285, 291-3, 296-8, 300, 352-3, 363, 369, 372-4, 376, 383
"Idylls of the King: The Marriage of Geraint" (Tennyson) **30**:288; **65**:226, 236, 241, 249, 255, 278, 297, 324, 328-9, 350, 381
"Idylls of the King: To the Queen" (Tennyson) **30**:295; **65**:258, 265, 271, 350, 353, 373
Idyls and Epigrams (Runeberg)
See *Idyll och epigram*
Idyls of Norway and Other Poems (Boyesen) **135**:8-10, 47
"If all were rain and never sun" (Rossetti) **186**:237
"If Ever I See" (Hale) **75**:279, 286
"If I Can Stop One Heart from Breaking" (Dickinson) **21**:37
"If I Drive at Night through the Dark Street" (Nekrasov) **11**:409
"If I Had" (Eminescu) **131**:330-32
"If I shouldn't be alive" (Dickinson) **171**:87
"If I Were Dead" (Patmore) **9**:343, 349, 358
"If Life Be Final" (Cranch) **115**:18
"If Thou Sayest, Behold, We Knew It Not" (Rossetti) **2**:577
"If Thou Wilt Ease Thine Heart" (Beddoes) **3**:34
"If You Come to My Field" (Isaacs)
See "Si vienes a mi campo"
"If You Only Knew Lords" (Shevchenko)
See "Yak by vy znaly panychi"
"If You Speak, I'll Pretend Deafness . . ." (Eminescu) **33**:257
"If You Were Coming in the Fall" (Dickinson) **21**:7, 75
Igitur (Mallarmé) **4**:383, 385-86, 392; **41**:232-34, 237-39, 249, 271, 275, 286, 300
Igitur; ou, la folie d'Elbehnon (Mallarmé) **210**:149-50, 152-54, 156, 264
"Ignaz Denner" (Hoffmann) **183**:192-95, 197
Igrok (Dostoevsky) **2**:188; **43**:92; **119**:147, 156; **167**:278
Igroki (Gogol) **5**:231, 239, 256; **15**:84, 98, 104; **162**:17
Ihr Auge (Hauff) **185**:321
"Ihr hörtet von dem Zwerge argem Sinnen" (Preseren) **127**:313
Ihr Tod (Klopstock) **225**:297-98
"Iisjomfruen" (Andersen) **7**:29, 32; **79**:28, 32, 58, 70-71, 82-84, 88-89; **214**:23, 26-27, 59
"Ikävyys" (Kivi) **30**:51
"Il Bacio" (Verlaine) **230**:172
"Il Balen" (Lanier) **118**:243
Il burbero di buon cuore (Da Ponte) **50**:78
Il Cinque di Maggio (Manzoni)
See *Il cinque maggio*
Il cinque maggio (Manzoni) **29**:263, 299; **98**:201, 204, 211, 213, 220, 223, 245
Il corvo (Gozzi) **23**:107, 112-13, 119, 121, 123, 125
Il dissoluto punito o sia il Don Giovanni (Da Ponte) **50**:76, 80-6, 88-94, 96, 98
Il faut qu'une porte soit ouvertr ou fermée (Musset) **7**:259, 262, 268, 271-72, 275; **150**:251-54
Il filosofo punito (Da Ponte) **50**:80
Il mostro turchino (Gozzi) **23**:108, 119, 121, 123, 125-26
"Il Mystico" (Hopkins) **189**:141
Il ne faut jurer de rien (Musset) **7**:259, 268, 270-72, 275
"Il nome di Maria" (Manzoni) **29**:253
"Il Parini" (Leopardi) **129**:305
"Il Passero Solitario" (Leopardi) **129**:220, 229, 249, 339, 341
Il pasticcio (Da Ponte) **50**:82
Il pastor fido (Da Ponte) **50**:82
Il penseroso (Amiel) **4**:15, 19
Il Pensieroso (Liszt) **199**:307
"Il pleure dans mon coeur" (Verlaine) **2**:631; **51**:351, 355, 384; **230**:161, 205
"Il Ponte del Paradiso" (Symonds) **34**:355
Il re cervo (Gozzi) **23**:107, 112-14, 119, 123, 125-26
Il ricco d' un qiorno (Da Ponte) **50**:77-8
"Il Risorgimento" (Leopardi) **129**:218, 330, 358
"Il Rosseggiar dell' Oriente" (Rossetti) **186**:294
"Il sabato del villaggio" (Leopardi) **129**:219, 229, 243, 339, 341
"Il tramonto della luna" (Leopardi) **129**:220
"Il viccolo di Madama Lucrezia" (Mérimée) **6**:366, 369-70; **65**:47, 52, 57-61, 98, 118, 133, 135
The Ilau (Sacher-Masoch) **31**:295
Ildikó (Arany) **34**:8
The Iliad (Hunt) **1**:411
The Iliad of Homer (Bryant) **6**:166
Ilius Goethes Briefwechsel mit einem Kinde: Seinem Denkmal (Arnim)
See *Goethes Briefwechsel mit einem Kinde: Seinem Denkmal*
Ilius Pamphilius und die Ambrosia (Arnim) **38**:15; **123**:5, 8
Ilka on the Hill-Top (Boyesen) **135**:13
Ilka on the Hill-Top and Other Stories (Boyesen) **135**:13, 27, 30
"I'll Tell Thee All—How Blank It Grew" (Dickinson) **21**:38
"I'll tell you how the Sun rose—" (Dickinson) **171**:196
I'll Tell You What (Inchbald) **62**:143, 146, 148
"Illa Creek" (Kendall) **12**:179, 181, 186

"Ils enseignent" (Laforgue)
See "Dimanches"
The Illuminated Blake (Blake) **201**:71, 83, 139
The Illuminated Books of William Blake (Blake) **201**:140
"The Illuminated City" (Hemans) **71**:277
Illumination (Frederic)
See *The Damnation of Theron Ware*
Les illuminations (Rimbaud) **4**:453-55, 457, 459-63, 465-66, 468, 470-74, 476-77, 479-80, 482-83, 487; **35**:269-72, 275, 278, 291, 293-94, 304, 310-312, 320, 321-26; **82**:218-19, 223-27, 23 0-33, 237, 240-43, 247-48, 250-51, 253, 255, 262-63; **227**:184, 188-90, 192, 197, 202-3, 206, 208-11, 233-44, 246-48, 261, 270-71, 273-74, 276, 279, 281-82, 291-94, 296-99, 308-10, 316, 323-25, 329, 331, 334
Illuminations (Rimbaud)
See *Les illuminations*
"Les illuminés; ou, Les précurseurs de socialisme" (Nerval) **1**:476, 485; **67**:357, 371
The Ill-Used Giant, Being a new and true version of "Jack and the Beanstalk" (Horne) **127**:266
"L'illusion suprême" (Leconte de Lisle) **29**:214, 217-18, 224, 234-36
"Illusion-mad" (Heine)
See "Im tollen Wahn"
"Illusions" (Emerson) **1**:295, 300; **98**:89, 101, 186, 191
Illusions perdues (Balzac) **5**:39, 43, 45, 49, 63, 72, 75, 80; **35**:20, 51, 60; **53**:8; **153**:8-10, 26, 61-62, 66-72, 74-75, 82, 147-49, 153, 158, 161
Illustrated Edition (Tennyson)
See *Moxon's Illustrated Tennyson*
Illustrated Excursions in Italy (Lear) **3**:295
Illustrated Poems (Sigourney) **21**:297; **87**:321
Illustrations of Lying (Opie) **65**:204
Illustrations of Political Economy (Martineau) **26**:303, 309-10, 329-30, 334-35, 337-39, 341, 348, 351, 355; **137**:236, 239-40, 245, 250-51, 256, 259-60, 262-63, 266, 270, 272, 276, 280, 302, 304, 309, 315, 324, 330, 336, 356-58
Illustrations of Taxation (Martineau) **137**:250
Illustrations of the Literary Character (D'Israeli)
See *An Essay on the Manners and Genius of the Literary Character*
"Illustrations on Sublimity" (Beattie)
See *Dissertations Moral and Critical: On Memory and Imagination; On Dreaming; The Theory of Language; On Fable and Romance; On the Attachments of Kindred; Illustrations on Sublimity*
"L'illustre Gaudissart" (Balzac) **35**:11; **153**:152
"L'illustre magicien" (Gobineau) **17**:69, 92, 104
"The Illustrious Gaudissart" (Balzac)
See "L'illustre Gaudissart"
"The Illustrious Magician" (Gobineau)
See "L'illustre magicien"
"Il'ya Muromets" (Karamzin) **173**:283
Im Brauerhaus (Storm) **195**:6
"I'm ceded, I've stopped being theirs" (Dickinson) **77**:143, 153; **171**:153
"Im Dorfe" (Muller) **73**:390-92
"Im Freien" (Mörike) **201**:279, 288-89, 294
"Im Frühling" (Mörike) **201**:253, 268, 273, 341
"Im Grase" (Droste-Hülshoff) **3**:200
"Im Hafen" (Heine) **147**:226
"Im Krug zum grünen Kranze" (Muller) **73**:379-81, 383
"Im Mai" (Heine) **4**:256
"Im Moose" (Droste-Hülshoff) **3**:196
Im Nachbarhaus links (Storm) **195**:6
Im Nachbarhause links (Storm) **1**:540
"I'm Nobody! Who Are You?" (Dickinson) **21**:71
"Im Oktober 1849" (Heine) **147**:229, 231
"Im Park" (Mörike) **201**:283, 285
Im Saal (Storm) **1**:539
Im Schloss (Storm) **1**:540; **195**:5, 15, 39-41, 43, 95-96
Im Sonnenschein (Storm) **1**:539; **195**:94
"Im Spätboot" (Meyer) **81**:199, 201-02
"Im tollen Wahn" (Heine) **147**:195
"I'm Twenty-Two—I'm Twenty-Two" (Willis) **194**:296
"Im Veltlin" (Meyer) **81**:150
"Im Walde" (Eichendorff)
See "Die Zauberin im Walde"
"Im Weinberg" (Mörike) **201**:271, 274, 285, 344, 370
"I'm 'Wife'—I've Finished That" (Dickinson) **21**:64; **171**:154
"L'Image dans l'eau" (Desbordes-Valmore) **97**:27
"The Image in Lava" (Hemans) **71**:276, 304-05, 307
"The Image in the Heart" (Hemans) **71**:303
"Image of Light, Adieu" (Dickinson) **171**:134
Images of travel (Heine)
See *Reisebilder*
L'imagier de Harlem (Nerval) **67**:340
Imaginary Conversations (Landor) **14**:158-59, 162, 165-66, 168, 170-73, 176, 180, 184, 186, 191-95, 201-02, 206-08, 210
An Imaginary Portrait (Pater) **7**:296, 298-99, 303-04, 307, 312, 317, 323-24, 341; **90**:242, 248, 336, 338, 340; **159**:232-33, 268-69, 273
"Imaginary Portrait. The Child in the House" (Pater) **90**:263-4, 272, 276, 290-4, 333, 336-8, 340, 345; **159**:249
Imaginary Portraits (Pater)
See *An Imaginary Portrait*
"Imagination" (Beattie)
See *Dissertations Moral and Critical: On Memory and Imagination; On Dreaming; The Theory of Language; On Fable and Romance; On the Attachments of Kindred; Illustrations on Sublimity*
"Imagination" (Emerson) **1**:282
Imagination and Fancy; or, Selections from the English Poets...and an Essay in Answer to the Question "What Is Poetry?" (Hunt) **1**:417-20
"Imaginative Artists" (Lewes) **215**:135
"Imelda of Bologna" (Sedgwick) **19**:445
L'imitation de Notre-Dame la lune (Laforgue) **5**:275-78, 283; **53**:256-7, 259, 263, 278-79, 287-88, 290-91; **221**:4, 7, 17-18, 43, 55, 59, 63-66, 70, 81, 84, 90-91
Imitation Ermine (Sacher-Masoch) **31**:290
"Imitation of boileau's First Satire" (Bestuzhev)
See "Podrazhaniye pervoy satire Bualo"
"An Imitation of Dr. Watts" (Field) **3**:211
Imitation of Our Lady the Moon (Laforgue)
See *L'Imitation de Notre-Dame la Lune selon Jules Laforgue*
"Imitation of Spenser" (Keats) **8**:342; **73**:151, 158, 328; **225**:263
"Imitations from the German" (Harpur) **114**:144
Imitations of the Koran (Pushkin) **83**:282
"Immalee" (Rossetti) **186**:275
"The Immediate Erotic Stages" (Kierkegaard) **125**:182, 185, 187, 193, 198, 201, 203, 205-8, 210, 212-13, 247-48, 255-56
Immensee (Storm) **1**:535-39, 545-46, 550; **195**:4, 18, 20, 23, 38, 43, 62, 67, 73, 89, 92-93, 104-6, 108
"The Immortal" (Very) **9**:385
"Immortal Beloved Letter" (Beethoven)
See "Letter to the Immortal Beloved"
"The Immortal Golovan" (Leskov)
See "Nesmertel' nyj Golovan"
"Immortal Ode" (Wordsworth)
See "Ode: Intimations of Immortality from Recollections of Early Childhood"
"The Immortal Ones" (Isaacs)
See "Los immortales"
"Immortale jecur" (Hugo) **10**:357
"Los immortales" (Isaacs) **70**:313
"Immortalidad" (Heredia) **209**:129, 131
"L'immortalité" (Lamartine) **11**:269-70, 272, 278, 282; **190**:218, 225
"Immortality" (Allston) **2**:26
"Immortality" (Lamartine)
See "L'immortalité"
"The Immortality Ode" (Wordsworth)
See "Ode: Intimations of Immortality from Recollections of Early Childhood"
"Immortality Ode" (Wordsworth)
See "Ode: Intimations of Immortality from Recollections of Early Childhood"
"The Immortality of the Soul" (Newman) **38**:304-05
L'immortel (Daudet) **1**:237, 239, 244, 249, 251
"The Imp" (Baratynsky)
See "Besyonok"
"The Imp of the Perverse" (Poe) **1**:500-01, 518; **16**:301, 331-32; **78**:260, 278, 281, 284-86, 298-99; **211**:251-52
"Împarat şi proletar" (Eminescu) **33**:245, 250; **131**:288, 295
Impartial Reflections on the Present Situation of the Queen of France (Robinson) **142**:198-99, 281-82, 285-86, 289
An Impartial View of the Danish State Church (Grundtvig) **158**:144
The Impasse (Leskov)
See *Nekuda*
"Impenitent" (Verlaine)
See "L'Impénitent"
"L'Impénitent" (Verlaine) **230**:165
"Imperfect Sympathies" (Lamb) **10**:410-11, 413, 424-25, 435; **113**:164, 199, 202, 217, 219, 235, 243, 247, 250
"Imperfect Thoughts" (Fuller) **5**:169
"El imperio chimila" (Isaacs) **70**:311
The Impertinents (Augier)
See *Les éffrontés*
Impetus philosophicus (Claudius) **75**:190
"Implicit and Explicit Reason" (Newman) **38**:307
"Implora Pace" (Cooke) **110**:9
"Implora Pace" (Taylor) **89**:294
Important Considerations for the People of This Kingdom (Cobbett) **49**:164
"Impossibilité de l'infini en hosties" (Laforgue) **221**:85
"Impossibility of the Infinite in Hosts" (Laforgue)
See "Impossibilité de l'infini en hosties"
"L'Impossible" (Desbordes-Valmore) **97**:5-6, 22
"L'Impossible" (Laforgue) **53**:270, 289; **221**:25, 58
"L'impossible" (Rimbaud) **4**:466; **35**:271, 303-04, 313, 319; **82**:229, 235, 237-38, 241, 250, 253, 260, 262; **227**:269, 278, 315-17
The Impostors (Cumberland) **167**:135, 150, 191
"Impotens" (Levy) **59**:96, 98; **203**:346
"An Impression" (Lampman) **194**:5, 59
Impressions de voyage (Dumas) **11**:48, 52, 62-64, 90; **71**:185
Impressions de voyage: De Paris à Cadix (Dumas)
See *Impressions de voyage*
Impressions de voyage: Suisse (Dumas)
See *Impressions de voyage*
Impressions et Poésies (Liszt) **199**:307
Impressions of Theophrastus Such (Eliot) **4**:110, 152; **23**:73; **183**:64
"Impressions on Reading the Poems of Mr. A. A. de Mendonça" (Castro Alves)
See "Impressões de Leitura das Poesias do Sr. A. A. de Mendonça"
"Impressões de Leitura das Poesias do Sr. A. A. de Mendonça" (Castro Alves) **205**:12
"L'imprévu" (Baudelaire) **6**:109; **55**:2

"The Imprisoned Jesus" (Lippard) **198**:229
"Improbable Veracities" (Kleist) **222**:186
"Impromptu" (Osgood) **141**:325
"Impromptu" (Pavlova)
See "Èksprompt"
"The Impromptu after the Play of Hamlet" (Cumberland) **167**:201
"Impromptu, upon Leaving Some Friends" (Moore) **110**:177
Impromptus sur une Romance de Clara Wieck (Schumann) **143**:120-22
"Improvements Suggested in Female Education" (Hays) **114**:256
"Improvisation" (Taylor) **89**:319
"Improvisation V" (Taylor) **89**:319
"Improvisation VIII" (Taylor) **89**:318
Improvisations (Taylor) **89**:318
"The Improvisatore" (Beddoes) **3**:33; **154**:89
The Improvisatore (Andersen)
See *Improvisatoren*
The Improvisatore, in Three Fyttes, with Other Poems (Beddoes) **3**:28, 32, 36, 38; **154**:8-12, 41, 52-54, 64-69, 78, 87, 89-91, 93-94; **214**:9, 74
The Improvisatore; or, Life in Italy (Andersen)
See *Improvisatoren*
Improvisatoren (Andersen) **7**:14-16, 19, 24; **79**:48, 79-80
The Improvisatrice, and Other Poems (Landon) **15**:154-56, 158, 160-61, 165, 168
"Improvizatory" (Leskov) **174**:38
"The Impulses of Human Nature: Margaret Fuller's Journal from June through October 1844" (Fuller) **211**:183-85, 189-90
"In a Balcony" (Browning) **19**:79, 131
"In a Battle" (Schiller) **39**:336
"In a Bye-Canal" (Melville) **3**:352, 363
In a Dialogue Between Jack Anvil and Tom Hod (More) **141**:216
"In a Drear-Nighted December" (Keats) **8**:360
"In a Garden" (Allingham) **25**:14
In a Glass Darkly (Le Fanu) **9**:302, 308, 312, 315, 317, 320-21, 323; **58**:252, 254-7, 264, 301-2
"In a Gondola" (Browning) **19**:93, 130-31
"In a Lecture-Room" (Clough) **27**:105
"In a Minor Key" (Levy) **59**:96
"In a Neat Cottage" (Crabbe) **26**:139; **121**:12
In a New World; or, Among the Gold-Fields of Australia (Alger) **8**:17, 40, 44-45
In a parallel way (Verlaine)
See *Parallèlement*
"In a Swedish Graveyard" (Lazarus) **109**:294
"In a World of Darkness" (Eminescu) **131**:287
"In a Year" (Browning) **19**:127
"In Absence" (Lanier) **118**:215, 259
"In an Almshouse" (Webster) **230**:233
"In an Artist's Studio" (Rossetti) **66**:350; **186**:327
"In April" (Lampman) **194**:56
"In Beechwood Cemetery" (Lampman) **194**:129, 131
"In Behalf of My Country" (Isaacs)
See "Pro patria"
In Bulemanns Haus (Storm)
See *Bulemanns Haus*
"In Cabin'd Ships at Sea" (Whitman) **31**:387-88
"In Carey's Footsteps" (Ferguson) **33**:289
In Congress, July 4, 1776: A Declaration by the Representatives of the United States of America, in General Congress Assembled (Jefferson) **11**:137, 139-57, 159, 162-66, 169-70, 172-79, 184-85, 189, 193-96, 198-203, 205, 207, 209-10; **103**:103-04, 106, 108, 115, 122, 125-29, 144, 163, 168-72, 183, 189, 193, 201, 206, 209-10, 241, 249-50, 252-53, 255, 259-63
"In Crowds of People, in the Hurly-burly of the Day" (Tyutchev) **34**:389
"In das Femdenbuch de Thalhofes zu Reichenau" (Raimund) **69**:13
"In days of boundless enthusiasms..." (Baratynsky)
See "V dni bezgranichnykh uvlecheniy..."
"In dem Lichte wohnt das Heil" (Brentano) **191**:62
"In der Frühe" (Mörike) **201**:294, 303
"In der Karwoche" (Mörike) **201**:268
In der Nacht (Schumann) **143**:85
"In deserto" (Gautier) **1**:350
"In Ev'ry Dream Thy Lovely Features Rise" (Barnes) **75**:70
"In excelsis" (Leconte de Lisle) **29**:228, 235
"In Exile" (Lazarus) **109**:335, 338
"In Falling Timbers Buried" (Dickinson) **21**:43
"In Gastein again" (Grillparzer)
See "Noch einmal in Gastein"
"In Harbor" (Hayne) **94**:149 167-68
"In Harmony with Nature" (Arnold) **6**:55; **29**:34; **218**:184
"In Him We Live" (Very) **9**:378, 381, 384-85
"In lieblicher Bläue" (Hölderlin) **187**:188
"In Love with a Marble" (Eminescu) **131**:330-31
"In Love with the Devil" (Verlaine)
See "Amoureuse du Diable"
In malayischer Form (Chamisso) **82**:27
"In March" (Lampman) **194**:138
"In May" (Lampman) **25**:172; **194**:81, 92
"In Memoriam" (Lazarus) **8**:413, 417
In Memoriam (Tennyson) **30**:213, 220, 223-24, 226-28, 230, 233, 235-36, 238-43, 245-46, 255-62, 267, 269, 271-77, 279-80, 282-83, 287, 293; **65**:231, 234-5, 240-1, 248-9, 257, 267, 271, 277, 279-80, 282, 334, 348, 358, 375; **115**:231-381; **202**:191, 221, 224-27, 229-30, 238-45, 261-66, 276, 289, 296, 299-307, 331, 334-35
"In Memoriam—William George Ward" (Tennyson) **202**:290
"In Memory of a Happy Day in February" (Brontë) **4**:46; **71**:165-66
"In Memory of A. I. Odoevsky" (Lermontov) **126**:143-44
"In Memory of My Mother" (Opie) **65**:182
"In Memory of Széchenyi" (Arany)
See "Széchenyi emlékezete"
"In Memory of V.A. Zhukovsky" (Tyutchev)
See "Pamyati V.A. Zhukovskogo"
In morte del Carlo Imbonati (Manzoni) **98**:247
In morte del fratello Giovanni (Foscolo) **97**:62, 67
"In My Own Album" (Lamb) **10**:405
"In November" (Lampman) **25**:171, 193-94, 199, 210; **194**:7, 19, 22, 44, 47, 54-55, 58, 70, 72-76, 82, 84, 86, 88-91, 93, 101-2, 139
"In October" (Lampman) **25**:171, 192, 204; **194**:28, 30, 54-55, 73-74, 76, 82, 84, 123-25, 133, 140
"In Our Abode in Arby Wood" (Barnes) **75**:54
"In Our Forest of the Past" (Thomson) **18**:394, 427
In Parallel (Verlaine)
See *Parallèlement*
"In Paths Untrodden" (Whitman) **31**:393; **81**:328; **205**:242
In Praise of Freyja (Grundtvig)
See *Freias Pris*
"In Praise of Poetry" (Ueda Akinari)
See "Uta no homare"
"In Prison" (Morris) **4**:423, 444
"In Progress" (Rossetti) **2**:573; **50**:286, 293
"In School-Days" (Whittier) **8**:513, 517, 522
"In Search of the Earth's Peace" (Eminescu) **33**:264
In Search of Treasure (Alger) **8**:43
"In September" (Levy) **59**:90
"In shades obscure and gloomy warmd to sing" (Clare) **86**:173
In Spain (Andersen) **7**:19; **79**:79
"In Spring" (Mörike)
See "Frühling"
In St. Jürgen (Storm) **1**:536, 540, 543; **195**:43, 127, 129, 132
"In Summer-Time" (Jefferies) **47**:93
In Sweden (Andersen)
See *I Sverrige*
In Switzerland (Slowacki) **15**:348-49, 353-54, 358-59, 364
"In Tenderness To Me Whom Thou Didst Spurn" (Barnes) **75**:70
"In the Air" (Larcom) **179**:171
"In the Bazaar at Smyrna" (Taylor) **89**:357
"In the Beginning of 1812" (Pushkin) **83**:320
"In the Black Forest" (Levy) **59**:93
"In the Bleak Mid-Winter" (Rossetti) **50**:312
"In the Breast of a Maple" (Crawford) **12**:169-70
"In the Canadian Woods" (Traill) **31**:329
"In the cathedral" (Castro)
See "N'a catredal"
"In the Churchyard at Cambridge" (Longfellow) **45**:125
"In the City" (Lampman) **194**:59
"In the Corner of a Small Sqaauare" (Pushkin) **83**:315-18
"In the Cotton Country" (Woolson) **82**:273, 302, 305, 339-40, 343
"In the Desert" (Melville) **29**:375
"In the Duck Yard" (Andersen)
See "I Andegaarden"
"In the Dumps" (Parton) **86**:366
"In the Early Morning" (Mörike)
See "In der Frühe"
"In the Foam" (Lanier) **118**:215
"In the Garden" (Arany)
See "Kertben"
"In the Garden at Swainston" (Tennyson) **115**:341
"In the Garret" (Alcott) **218**:75-76, 78-79, 81
"In the Glooming Light" (Tennyson) **30**:211
"In the Great Metropolis" (Clough) **27**:103, 114
"In the Great Metropolis" (Prescott) **163**:30, 36
"In the Hammock" (Cooke) **110**:51
"In the Hedge I pass a little nest" (Clare) **86**:145
"In the Hospital" (Cooke) **110**:9
"In the Jewish Synagogue at Newport" (Lazarus) **8**:417, 422, 424-25; **109**:296, 302, 324, 332, 336, 342
In the Key of Blue (Symonds) **34**:343, 352-53
"In the manner of Paul Verlaine" (Verlaine)
See "À la manière de Paul Verlaine"
"In the Market" (Arany)
See "Vásárban"
"In the Meadows" (Taylor) **89**:307
"In the Mile End Road" (Levy) **59**:96, 119; **203**:324-26, 339, 344-45, 350
"In the Night" (Levy) **203**:322, 346
"In the Open Air" (Mörike)
See "Im Freien"
"In the Park" (Mörike)
See "Im Park"
"In the Pine Groves" (Lampman) **25**:209; **194**:140
"In the Room" (Thomson) **18**:397, 403, 405, 407, 418, 420, 423
"In the Round Tower at Jhansi, June 8, 1857" (Rossetti) **66**:371, 377
"In the Same Old Lane" (Eminescu) **131**:296
In the Sixties (Frederic) **10**:187-88
In the South Seas (Stevenson) **193**:212, 221, 250, 353, 357, 359
"In the Spring" (Barnes) **75**:21
"In the Springtime" (Mörike)
See "Im Frühling"
"In the Stillness o'Night" (Barnes) **75**:71
In the Sunlight (Storm)
See *Im Sonnenschein*
"In the Temple of Cholula" (Heredia)
See "En el Teocalli de Cholula"
"In the Teutoburger Forest" (Taylor) **89**:313
In the Valley (Frederic) **10**:183-84, 187-88, 190, 192-93, 201, 203-04, 207, 210-11, 213; **175**:149, 152

"In the Valley of Cauteretz" (Tennyson) **30**:280; **115**:341
"In the Valley of Humiliation" (Thomson) **18**:425
"In the Valley of the Elwy" (Hopkins) **17**:220; **189**:18-19, 52
"In the village" (Tyutchev)
See "V derevne"
"In the Vineyard" (Mörike)
See "Im Weinberg"
"In the Wilds" (Lampman) **25**:172, 190, 218
"In the World with You" (Larcom) **179**:171
"In Three Days" (Browning) **19**:127
"In Torture" (Isaacs)
See "En la tortura"
"In Trafalgar Square" (Adams) **33**:4
In Trust (Oliphant) **61**:203; **221**:231
"In Utrumque Paratus" (Arnold) **218**:185, 191
"In Utrumque Paratus" (Gordon) **21**:159, 164
"In Vain Do I . . ." (Verlaine)
See "J'ai beau faire . . ."
"In Vain is the Verdure of Spring" (Rowson) **182**:282
"In Venice" (Woolson) **82**:289-91, 341
"In Vino Veritas" (Kierkegaard) **125**:184, 267
In War Time, and Other Poems (Whittier) **8**:493-94
"In Winter" (Taylor) **89**:309
"In Winter in my Room" (Dickinson) **77**:148
"In winter, when the fields are white" (Dodgson) **139**:39
"Inaugural Address" (Gladstone) **213**:113, 129
"Inaugural Address, March 4, 1865" (Lincoln) **201**:155, 157, 159, 165, 169-70, 172, 182, 186-87, 191, 200, 211, 213-15, 219, 222-25, 228-32, 241
"Inaugural Lecture on the Study of Modern History" (Arnold) **18**:54
"L'incantation du loup" (Leconte de Lisle) **29**:225, 230, 237
"The Incarnate Son, a Sufferer and Sacrifice" (Newman) **38**:305
"The Inca's Daughter" (Whitman) **81**:343, 345
"The Incendiary" (Rowson) **69**:129
"The Inch Cape Rock" (Southey) **8**:474
"An Incident in a Railroad Car" (Lowell) **2**:522; **90**:194
"Incident of the French Camp" (Browning) **79**:164
"Incidents in the Life of a Quiet Man" (Willis) **194**:298
Incidents in the Life of a Slave Girl, Written by Herself (Jacobs) **67**:119-22, 124-27, 130, 135-36, 138-41, 143, 145-48, 150-51, 153, 159, 163-64, 166, 170-76, 178-80, 183, 187-88, 191-93, 196-97; **162**:134-294
"Incidents in the Life of My Uncle Arly" (Lear) **3**:300-1
Incidents of the Insurrection in the Western Parts of Pennsylvania in the Year 1794 (Brackenridge) **7**:48, 55-56; **227**:49, 74, 106, 154
"Incidents on the Hudson" (Willis) **194**:282
"Inclusions" (Barrett Browning) **16**:135-6
"The Incompatibles" (Arnold) **218**:261
"L'Inconnue" (Maupassant) **83**:182, 201
"L'inconnue" (Villiers de l'Isle Adam) **3**:590
"Inconstancy of the Populace" (Webster) **30**:424
Les Inconvénients de la vie de Paris (Staël-Holstein) **91**:358
"Incorrigible, toi . . ." (Verlaine) **230**:172
"The Incredible, Simple Horror . . ." (Verlaine)
See "L'Incroyable, l'unique horreur . . ."
"L'Incroyable, l'unique horreur . . ." (Verlaine) **230**:171
"Incubus" (Grillparzer) **102**:174
"Independence" (Parton) **86**:353
"Independence Bell—July 4, 1776" (O'Brien)
See "How the Bell Rang, July 4, 1776"
"Independence of the Church" (Brownson) **50**:54
India, China, and Japan (Taylor) **89**:302, 355
"The Indian Bride" (Pinkney) **31**:268, 276, 281
"The Indian Burying-Ground" (Freneau)
See "Lines Occasioned by a Visit to an Old Indian Burying Ground"
"The Indian, City" (Hemans) **71**:275, 293
"The Indian Convert" (Freneau) **111**:104
"The Indian Fisherman's Light" (Moodie) **113**:347
"The Indian Girl's Lament" (Bryant) **6**:182; **46**:22
"The Indian Jugglers" (Hazlitt) **29**:167; **82**:90, 95, 97, 101
Indian Library (Schlegel) **142**:302
Indian Nullification of the Unconstitutional Laws of Massachusetts Relative to the Marshpee Tribe; or, the Pretended Riot Explained (Apess) **73**:7, 10, 12-14, 16, 27
"The Indian Spring" (Bryant) **6**:181
"Indian Story" (Bryant) **6**:161, 186; **46**:42
"Indian Student, or, Force of Nature" (Freneau) **1**:315; **111**:103
"Indian Summer" (Lampman) **25**:210; **194**:52, 138
Indian Summer (Stifter)
See *Der Nachsommer*
"An Indian Summer Reverie" (Lowell) **2**:507; **90**:215
"The Indian With His Dead Child" (Hemans) **71**:279
"Indian Woman's Death-Song" (Hemans) **71**:274, 294
Indiana (Sand) **2**:581-85, 589, 598, 603, 605-07; **42**:306-09, 315-17, 320, 324, 328-29, 333, 337-42, 349, 351-54, 356-58, 364, 378-81, 383-89; **57**:308-11, 316, 318-20, 322-5, 327-30, 332-33, 335-39, 344, 348-50, 359, 363-67, 371, 374-81; **174**:147-292
Die Indianer in England (Kotzebue) **25**:145-47
"Der Indianerzug" (Lenau) **16**:269, 278, 284
"Indian's Tale" (Whittier) **8**:485
The Indians: The Ten Lost Tribes (Apess) **73**:15
"Indicaciones sobre la Conveniencia de Simplificar y Uniformar la Ortografía en América" (Bello) **131**:130
"Indications of Immortality" (Channing) **17**:54
The Indicator and the Companion: A Miscellany for the Fields and the Fireside (Hunt) **1**:412
"The Indifferent Shepherdess to Colin" (Yearsley) **174**:343
"Indignation of a High-Minded Spaniard" (Wordsworth) **206**:238
Indira (Chatterji) **19**:209, 213, 217-19, 221-22, 224
"The Indiscretion of an Historian" (D'Israeli) **217**:323
"Individual Duty" (Lampman) **194**:17
"Individuality" (Lanier) **6**:238, 242; **118**:219-20
"The Individuality of the Soul" (Newman) **38**:304
"Indolence" (Keats)
See "Ode on Indolence"
"Indolence" (Thomson) **18**:401
"The Indolence of the Filipinos" (Rizal)
See "Sobre la indolencia de los Filipinos"
"The Indolent Monk" (Baudelaire)
See "Le mauvais moine"
"Les indolents" (Verlaine) **2**:624; **51**:379-80
"Indroducción" (Casal) **131**:269
"Indulgence in Religious Privileges" (Newman) **38**:304
"L'Indulgence qui n'est pas . . ." (Verlaine) **230**:171
"Indulgence That Is Not . . ." (Verlaine)
See "L'Indulgence qui n'est pas . . ."
"The Industrious Family" (Child) **73**:130-31, 134
"Inebriety" (Crabbe) **26**:110-11, 146; **121**:10, 81
"Ines de Castro" (Landor) **14**:161
Inès de las Sierras (Nodier) **19**:377, 384
Ines Mendo (Mérimée) **65**:46-7, 54, 59-60, 63, 79, 83
"The Inevitable Trial" (Holmes) **81**:102
"The Inexpressible" (Zhukovsky)
See "Nevyrazimoe"
The Infamy (Eminescu) **33**:266
"Infancy" (Crabbe) **121**:79
"Infant Joy" (Blake) **13**:182; **37**:6, 9, 13, 39, 41, 44, 57, 65, 71-2, 78, 84, 92, 95-6
"Infant Sorrow" (Blake) **13**:219-20, 242; **37**:11-12, 24, 33, 44, 53, 57, 75, 84, 96; **190**:30
The Infant with the Globe (Alarcon)
See *El niño de la bola*
"The Infant's Prayer" (Sigourney) **21**:299
The Infernal Marriage (Disraeli) **39**:3, 33, 52, 54-5, 75
Infernaliana (Nodier) **19**:378, 383
The Infidel; or, The Fall of Mexico (Bird) **1**:82-84, 86-87, 90
The Infidel; or, The Fall of Mexico. A Romance by the author of "Calavar" (Bird) **197**:6, 8, 13, 24-25, 27-29, 36, 68, 75, 77-86
"The 'Infidelity' of Abolition" (Garrison) **149**:256
"L'infini dans les cieux" (Lamartine) **11**:265, 270
"The Infinite" (Leopardi)
See "L'Infinito"
"L'Infinito" (Leopardi) **129**:217, 228, 232, 246, 263-64, 268-72, 305, 352-55, 357
The Inflexible Captive: A Tragedy (More) **27**:336; **141**:167, 252-55, 258
"Influence of Academies" (Arnold) **6**:47
"The Influence of Authority in Matters of Opinion" (Gladstone) **213**:112
"The Influence of Rationalism" (Eliot) **199**:159
"Influence of Time and Grief" (Bowles) **103**:58
"Information on Martha the Burgomistress from the Life of St Zosima" (Karamzin)
See "Izvestiye o Marfe Posadnitse, vzyatoye iz zhitiya Zosimy"
Les Infortunes de la vertu (Sade)
See *Justine ou les malheurs de la vertu*
"Les ingénus" (Verlaine) **2**:624; **51**:378; **230**:164
The Ingoldsby Legends (Barham) **77**:4, 6, 8-12, 16-23, 25, 28-30, 32-34, 36-37, 39-41, 43-44
The Ingoldsby Lyrics (Barham) **77**:21, 28
The Ingoldsby Penance (Barham) **77**:10
"Ingvi and Alf" (Lampman) **25**:201; **194**:77-78
The Inheritance (Ferrier) **8**:236-40, 242-44, 246-56
The Inheritance (Smolenskin) **30**:189-90
The Inhibited Imaginatin (Raimund)
See *Die gesfesselte Phantasie*
"The Iniquity of the Fathers upon the Children" (Rossetti) **2**:558; **66**:329; **186**:230, 304
"Initium" (Verlaine) **230**:172, 198
"The Injured Tree" (Meyer)
See "Der verwundete Baum"
Injury and Insult (Dostoevsky)
See *The Insulted and Injured*
"An Inkling of Adventure" (Willis) **194**:298
Inklings of Adventure (Willis) **194**:282, 285, 319, 329
"The Inkpot" (Petofi)
See "A tintásüveg"
An Inland Voyage (Stevenson) **5**:386, 388, 390, 405, 410; **193**:203-5, 212-13, 220-21, 290-91, 353-55, 357
"The Inn" (Turgenev) **21**:415, 418, 441, 453; **122**:241
The Inn Album (Browning) **19**:85-6, 106, 112
The Inn in Spessart (Hauff)
See *Das Wirtshaus im Spessart*
"The Inner Life of Art" (Lewes) **25**:294
"Inner Voices" (Hugo) **3**:261
Inni Sacri (Manzoni) **98**:203-04, 220, 228-29
"Inno ai patriarchi" (Leopardi) **129**:347

"Innocence" (Isaacs)
See "Inocencia"
"Innocent Child and Snow-White Flower" (Bryant) **46**:38
"Innocent Prudencij" (Leskov)
See "Nevinnyj Prudencij"
Innocent Prudentius (Leskov)
See *Nevinnyi Prudentsii*
"Inns" (Crabbe) **26**:121
"Inocencia" (Isaacs) **70**:306
Inquiring Spirit (Coleridge)
See *Confessions of an Inquiring Spirit*
Inquiry (Kant) **27**:220-21
An Inquiry into the Literary and Political Character of James the First (D'Israeli) **217**:281, 284, 325-28, 339
An Inquiry into the Nature of Subscription to the Thirty-Nine Articles (Dyer) **129**:100, 102, 106, 112, 115, 125-28, 136
"An Inquiry into those Kinds of Distress which Excite Agreeable Sensations" (Barbauld) **185**:156-57
The Inquisitor (Holcroft) **85**:198
The Inquisitor; or, Invisible Ramble (Rowson) **5**:309-10, 315-16, 321-22; **69**:103, 112, 122-28, 132, 141
The Inquisitor; or Invisible Rambler (Rowson) **182**:254-57, 259, 262, 275
"Insanity: A Fragment" (Brown) **74**:108
"Inschrift auf eine Uhr" (Mörike) **201**:275, 349, 370
The Inscribed Firtree (Stifter)
See *De beschriebene Tännling*
"Inscribed on a Pair of Screens" (Barbauld) **185**:92
"Inscripción para el sepulcro de mi hermano" (Heredia) **209**:131
"Inscription" (Whitman) **4**:589, 603
"Inscription for a Fountain on a Heath" (Coleridge) **197**:215
"Inscription for a Fountain on the Heath" (Coleridge) **99**:104
"Inscription for an Ice-House" (Barbauld) **185**:63-66, 92, 133
"Inscription for the Entrance into a Wood" (Bryant) **6**:158, 168-69, 176, 182-83, 187; **46**:22, 34, 45, 47, 55
"Inscription for the Monument of Dr. Small" (Darwin) **106**:183
Inscription in a beautiful Retreat called the Fairy Bower (More) **141**:232
"Inscription Written at the Request of Sir George Beaumont, Bart., and in His Name, for an Urn, Placed by Him at the Termination of a Newly-Planted Avenue, in the Same Grounds" (Wordsworth) **12**:445
"Inscriptions" (Mackenzie) **41**:184
"Inscriptions" (Whitman) **205**:223-24, 226
Inscriptions (Southey) **8**:468; **97**:318
"The Insect" (Turgenev) **21**:451
The Insect (Michelet) **31**:215, 219, 242, 244-45, 247-48, 260-61, 263-64
"Insects" (Clare) **9**:85
"Insight" (Lampman) **25**:163
"Insolvency" (Turgenev)
See *Bezdenezh'e*
"Insomnia" (Isaacs)
See "Insomnio"
"Insomnia" (Thomson) **18**:394, 397, 400, 403, 405, 407, 409, 415, 417-20
"Insomnia" (Tyutchev)
See "Bessonnitsa"
"Insomnie" (Corbière) **43**:13, 34
"Insomnio" (Isaacs) **70**:313
The Inspector General (Gogol)
See *Révizor*
"Inspiration" (Emerson) **38**:149
"Inspiration" (Thoreau) **7**:383
"Inspiration Has Her Favorites" (Pavlova)
See "Est! liubimtsy vdokhnovenii"
"The Inspiration of Song" (Crawford) **12**:154, 161; **127**:202
The Inspired Version (Smith) **53**:391
"Instans Tyrannus" (Browning) **19**:115
The Instant (Kierkegaard)
See *Hvad Christus dömmer om officiel Christendom*
"Instead of Thinking of Making a Position for Oneself" (Laforgue)
See "Au lieu de songer à se créer une position"
"Instinct and Inspiration" (Emerson) **98**:7-8
"Instinkt" (Droste-Hülshoff) **3**:193, 201
"Instrumental-Musik" (Hoffmann)
See "Beethovens Instrumentalmusik"
The Insulted and Injured (Dostoevsky) **2**:161; **7**:70, 75, 80, 82, 107; **33**:161-62, 165, 195, 203; **43**:92
"The Insurrection of the Working Classes" (Jones) **222**:158
"Intarissablement" (Laforgue) **221**:88
"Intellect" (Emerson) **38**:173; **98**:20, 25, 144-47
"Intellect, the Instrument of Religious Training" (Newman) **38**:305
The Intellectual and Moral Reform of France (Renan)
See *La réforme intellectuelle et morale*
"Intellectual Wants of Greece" (Sigourney) **21**:311
"The Intelligence Office" (Hawthorne) **2**:298; **158**:243, 250
"The Intemperate and the Reformed" (Sigourney) **21**:290
"Inter Vias" (Lampman) **25**:204; **194**:38
"An Intercepted Letter to Dickens" (Kirkland) **85**:270
Intercepted Letters; or, The Two penny Post-Bag (Moore) **6**:382, 384, 388, 392, 395; **110**:171, 190
"L'interdiction" (Balzac) **35**:4; **153**:54, 56-59, 149
"An Interesting Interview" (Longstreet) **159**:125, 144, 163, 175, 184
"Interesting Travels in America" (Adams) **175**:29
"Intérieur" (Laforgue) **221**:90, 92
"Intérieur" (Verlaine) **230**:164
"Interior" (Verlaine)
See "Intérieur"
"The Interior of a Heart" (Hawthorne) **2**:327; **10**:297
"Intermède" (Banville) **9**:32
Intermezzi (Schumann) **143**:129
"Intermezzo" (Heine)
See "Lyrisches Intermezzo"
Das Intermezzo, oder Der Landjunker zum ersten Male in der Residenz (Kotzebue) **25**:147
"Internal Firesides" (Blind) **202**:53
"International Exhibition" (Webb) **143**:357
"The International Working-Men's Movement" (Bakunin) **58**:134
"Interpreting Nature" (Very) **9**:388, 390
"An Interregnum" (Crawford) **127**:159, 163
"L'intersigne" (Villiers de l'Isle Adam) **3**:581
"The Interview" (Hawthorne) **10**:297
"Interviews with German Authors" (Taylor) **89**:308
Intimate Journal (Sand)
See *Le secrétaire intime*
Intimate Journals (Baudelaire)
See *Journaux intimes*
Intimate Liturgies (Verlaine)
See *Liturgies intimes*
"The Intimations Ode" (Wordsworth)
See "Ode: Intimations of Immortality from Recollections of Early Childhood"
"Intimations of Immortality" (Wordsworth)
See "Ode: Intimations of Immortality from Recollections of Early Childhood"
Intimidades (Silva) **114**:310-11, 315-17, 319
"Into the Kitchen Door I Strolled" (Petofi)
See "Befordúltam a konyhára"
Intolerance (Moore) **110**:171
"Intoxication" (Dickinson)
See "I Taste a Liquor Never Brewed"
Intrigue and Love (Schiller)
See *Kabale und Liebe*
An Intrigue in a Hurry (Fredro)
See *Intryga na predce; czyli, Niema złego bez dobrego*
"Introducción a los elementos de física del dr. N. Arnott" (Bello) **131**:109
"Introducción sinfónica" (Bécquer) **106**:109, 113-14, 118, 120, 147-48, 167-69
"Introduction" (Balzac) **153**:31
"Introduction" (Blake) **13**:182, 191, 241-42; **37**:10, 13, 18, 20, 24, 31, 38, 41-2, 45, 47-9, 57, 65, 73, 92; **190**:61, 64
"Introduction" (Shelley)
See "Author's Introduction"
Introduction à l'histoire universelle (Michelet) **31**:227, 246, 258; **218**:321, 332, 335
Introduction to Grammar (Peabody) **169**:147
Introduction to the Dialectics of Nature (Engels) **85**:10
Introduction to the Principles of Morals and Legislation (Bentham) **38**:24-5, 38, 44, 48-56, 81-9
An Introduction to the Study of Dante (Symonds) **34**:351
"Introduction to the Tale of the Dark Ladie" (Coleridge) **177**:113
Introduction to Universal History (Michelet)
See *Introduction à l'histoire universelle*
"Introductions to Wissenschaftslehre" (Fichte) **62**:4, 34
"Introduction—Simon Plays the 'Snatch' Game" (Hooper) **177**:207, 211
"Introductory Address" (Cumberland) **167**:184
"Introductory Discourse" (Baillie) **71**:9, 28-29, 31-32, 65; **151**:8-9, 17-18, 20, 22-23, 37, 52, 71, 73-75, 94, 105-7, 116, 122, 127, 129, 133
"Introductory Discourse on the Nature and Origin of Elocutionary Science" (Thelwall) **162**:339-40
Introductory Lectures Delivered at Queen's College, London (Kingsley) **35**:250
Introductory Lectures on Modern History (Arnold) **18**:12, 14, 29
"Introductory Sonnet" (Rossetti) **77**:359
Intryga na predce; czyli, Niema złego bez dobrego (Fredro) **8**:289
"The Intuitions of the Soul" (Very) **9**:388
"L'inutile beauté" (Maupassant) **1**:448, 459, 464, 468; **83**:177, 179, 223-24
Invariable Principles of Poetry (Bowles) **103**:63-4
The Invasion (Griffin) **7**:194, 197-201, 204, 212, 214, 218
Invectives (Verlaine)
See "Prologue supprimé à un livre d'Invectives"
"An Inventor" (Webster) **230**:231
"An Inventory of the Furniture in Dr. Priestley's Study" (Barbauld) **185**:87, 89, 92-93, 133-34
"Inventory of the Moon" (Zhukovsky)
See "Podrobnyi otchet o lune"
"Inversnaid" (Hopkins) **17**:191, 195; **189**:18, 20-21
An Investigation of the Cause of the Present High Price of Provisions (Malthus) **145**:250
"Investigations" (Bello) **131**:123
The Invisible Brothers (Scribe)
See *Les frères invisibles*
The Invisible Lodge (Jean Paul)
See *Die Unsichtbare Loge*
The Invisible Man (Andersen) **79**:11, 17
The Invisible Prince (Planché) **42**:273, 288, 301

"The Invisible World" (Newman) **38**:282, 303-04
"The Invitation" (Barbauld) **185**:29, 32-33, 37, 120, 129-30, 133, 140, 151
"The Invitation" (Clare) **86**:87
"The Invitation" (Freneau) **111**:105, 154-55
"The Invitation" (Shelley)
See "To Jane: The Invitation"
"Invitation and Reply" (Pinkney) **31**:279, 281
"L'invitation au voyage" (Baudelaire) **6**:87, 115, 118, 128; **29**:109; **55**:29, 61, 69; **155**:47, 56, 66, 86
"Invitation to a Painter" (Allingham) **25**:21, 29
"Invitation to Dinner" (Derzhavin)
See "Priglashenie k obedu"
"An Invitation to Retirement" (Warren) **226**:264
"An Invitation to the Country" (Bryant) **6**:165
"Invite to Eternity" (Clare) **9**:103; **86**:87-91
"Invocation" (Boker) **125**:81
"Invocation" (Hemans) **29**:205
"L'invocation" (Lamartine) **11**:269-70, 273, 277; **190**:176
"Invocation" (Lamartine)
See "L'invocation"
"Invocation, June 1866" (Blind) **202**:41
"Invocation to Misery" (Shelley) **18**:372
"Invokes Reason" (Robinson) **142**:175
"The Inward Morning" (Thoreau) **7**:383
"Inward Morning" (Very) **9**:391
"Inward Pose" (Rossetti) **50**:298
"Inworld" (Cranch) **115**:35
"Ioan Eliad" (Eminescu) **131**:325
"Ion" (Alcott) **1**:25; **167**:72, 76
Ion (Schlegel) **142**:301, 319, 342
The Ipê Trunk (Alencar) **157**:9
Iphigenia in Tauris (Goethe)
See *Iphigenie auf Tauris*
Iphigenie auf Tauris (Goethe) **34**:90-119; **154**:187, 233, 262, 271, 275, 310, 312, 317
"Ippolito di Este" (Landor) **14**:162
Ipsico Poe (Bird)
See *A Belated Revenge*
"¡Qué hace en Portugal su Majestad?" (Larra) **130**:201, 241, 243-44
Iracema (Alencar) **157**:5-9, 11-13, 15, 20-21, 24, 39-40, 42-47, 49-51, 53-57
"Ireland" (Lanier) **118**:218
"Ireland" (Martineau) **26**:305, 307, 309, 352
"Irené" (Lowell) **2**:502, 507
"Irenens Wiederkehr" (Grillparzer) **102**:192
Iridion (Krasiński) **4**:303-05, 307-14, 319
"Iris" (Holmes) **14**:109
Irish Anthology (Mangan) **27**:279
"The Irish Beneficed Clergyman" (Trollope) **101**:293-95
"Irish Catholicism and British Liberalism" (Arnold) **89**:101, 103; **126**:104; **218**:261
Irish Essays, and Others (Arnold) **6**:40
"The Irish Heart" (Child) **73**:80
The Irish Heiress (Boucicault) **41**:28, 40-1, 49
The Irish Melodies (Moore) **6**:383-84, 386-92, 394, 396-400; **110**:166, 168, 171, 181-87, 190-93, 195-96, 198, 203
"Irish National Hymn" (Mangan) **27**:296, 316
The Irish Post (Planché) **42**:278
"The Irish Prophecy Man" (Carleton) **199**:76
"The Irish Schoolmaster" (Hood) **16**:234
"The Irish Senachie" (Carleton) **199**:99
The Irish Sketch Book (Thackeray) **5**:452, 482; **43**:349, 360, 380, 383, 386
Irish Songs and Poems (Allingham) **25**:12, 15, 16
"Irishman and the Lady" (Maginn) **8**:441
The Irishman at Home (Carleton) **199**:54
"The Iron Gate" (Holmes) **14**:116
"An Iron Will" (Leskov)
See "Železnaja volja"
"Iron World" (Smith) **59**:330
"Ironia" (Norwid) **17**:374
"Der irre Spielmann" (Eichendorff) **225**:43
Irregular Stanzas (Wordsworth)
See "Irregular Verses"
"Irregular Verses" (Wordsworth) **25**:421; **138**:226-27, 229, 285
"L'irrémédiable" (Baudelaire) **6**:109, 115; **55**:13, 24, 29, 61, 72
"L'Irréparable" (Baudelaire) **6**:115; **55**:29, 61
"The irresistible" (Lonnrot) **53**:339
"Irrlicht" (Muller) **73**:392
Irrungen (Hoffmann) **183**:176
Irrungen, Wirrungen (Fontane) **26**:235-36, 240, 243-45, 248, 258, 262, 264, 270-71; **163**:166, 188, 197, 215, 220, 237-38
"Irtóztató csalódás" (Petofi) **21**:278
Irving (Oliphant)
See *The Life of Edward Irving, Minister of the National Scotch Church*
Is He Popenjoy? (Trollope) **6**:470, 477, 483; **33**:363; **101**:249, 251, 271-72, 318, 325, 327; **215**:209-10, 215
"Is Housekeeping a Failure?" (Cooke) **110**:63
"Is it not great—this feat of Fate" (Fuller) **50**:249
"Is It True, Ye Gods, Who Treat Us" (Clough)
See "Wen Gott betrügt, ist wohl betrogen"
"Is it true, ye gods, who treat us" (Prescott) **163**:34
"Is Music the Type or Measure of All Art?" (Symonds) **34**:351
Is She His Wife? (Dickens) **37**:153, 210
Is This What You Call Civilization? (Dutt)
See *Ekei Ki Bale Sabhyatā*
"Isaac Laquedem" (Dumas) **71**:185
Isaac T. Hopper: A True Life (Child) **6**:204; **73**:61, 79
"Isabel" (Dobell) **43**:48
"Isabel" (Tennyson) **30**:271; **65**:369; **202**:334, 337
"Isabel" (Whittier) **8**:513
Isabel de Bavière (Dumas) **11**:49, 58
Isabel of Bavaria (Dumas)
See *Isabel de Bavière*
Isabella (Keats) **225**:174, 247
"Isabella" (Keats) **8**:340, 347, 351-52, 355-56, 362; **73**:144-45, 153, 162, 171-72, 174, 183, 189, 208, 233, 255, 259, 323, 328, 336
Isabella of Egypt (Arnim)
See *Isabella von Ägypten, Kaiser Karl des Fünften erste Jugendliebe*
"Isabella; or, The Pot of Basil" (Keats)
See "Isabella"
"Isabella von Ägypten" (Arnim) **159**:66-68
Isabella von Ägypten (Arnim) **159**:4, 19, 44-45, 47, 96-99
Isabella von Ägypten, Kaiser Karl des Fünften erste Jugendliebe (Arnim) **5**:12-13, 17-18, 20-21
"Isabelle" (Hogg) **109**:248
Isabelle de Bavière (Sade) **47**:335
"Isadore" (Chivers) **49**:72
"Isbrand Dying" (Beddoes) **154**:73
Ishmael; or, In the Depths (Southworth) **26**:433-36, 439, 447
"Isidora" (Rossetti) **186**:275, 277
Isidora (Sand) **2**:588-89; **42**:322; **57**:312, 315-6, 368
Isis (Nerval) **1**:485; **67**:363, 371
Isis (Villiers de l'Isle Adam) **3**:581
"An Island" (Barrett Browning) **61**:42
The Island (Byron) **109**:99, 102; **149**:45, 101
An Island in the Moon (Blake) **37**:28-9, 31, 62-3; **57**:80; **190**:45; **201**:116
Island Nights' Entertainments (Stevenson) **5**:412, 422; **193**:211, 216
The Island of Barrataria (Tyler) **3**:572-73
"The Island of Bornholm" (Karamzin)
See "Ostrov Borngol'm"
The Island of Cuba: A Political Essay (Humboldt)
See *Essai politique sur l'île de Cuba*
The Island of Jewels (Planché) **42**:273, 289
"The Island of Maddalena: witha Distant View of Caprera" (Taylor) **89**:313
"The Island of the Fay" (Poe) **16**:331, 335; **117**:273
The Islanders (Leskov)
See *Ostrovitjane*
"L'Isle de Feu" (Dumas) **71**:185
"The Isle of Devils" (Lewis) **11**:300
"The Isle of Palms" (Wilson) **5**:545-46, 550
The Isle of Palms, and Other Poems (Wilson) **5**:544-46, 556, 561, 566
"The Isle of Voices" (Stevenson) **193**:250, 280, 334, 337-38, 340
Ismael: an Oriental Tale: with Other Poems (Bulwer-Lytton) **45**:68
Ismaelillo (Martí) **63**:63, 90, 104-6, 109-10, 126
"Ismaïl Bey" (Lermontov) **5**:289
"Isobel's Child" (Barrett Browning) **1**:112, 126-7; **61**:53, 55-6; **170**:106-7
"Isolation: To Marguerite" (Arnold) **29**:31; **89**:14, 16, 18-19, 22, 48, 88
"Isolation: To Marguerite—Continued" (Arnold) **29**:34-5; **89**:16, 18-19, 48, 88, 95, 119
"L'Isolement" (Lamartine) **190**:219, 232-34, 251-53
"Ispoved" (Lermontov) **126**:128
"Ispytaniye" (Bestuzhev) **131**:154, 175-76, 186-87, 192, 210-13
Israel Potter: His Fifty Years in Exile (Melville) **3**:330, 334, 344, 354-55, 384; **29**:315, 334; **123**:192-93, 261; **157**:84, 89, 109, 169, 199, 202, 209, 211; **193**:190; **221**:155, 217
L'Israëlite (Balzac) **5**:58
"Israfel" (Poe) **1**:527; **16**:330; **117**:221, 227, 232-34, 237, 243-44, 257-62, 281; **211**:249, 260
Isthmiana (Winthrop) **210**:322, 324
"Istina" (Baratynsky) **103**:6-7, 15, 21, 25-6
"Istoricheskoye pokhval'noye slovo Yekaterine II" (Karamzin) **173**:285-86, 288
Istoriia moego znakomstva s Gogolem (Aksakov) **181**:68
Istoriia sela Goriukhino (Pushkin) **3**:447-48, 459; **83**:275, 330
"Istorija lejtenanta Ergunova" (Turgenev)
See "Istoriya leytenanta Ergunova"
Istoriya gosudarstva Rossiiskogo (Karamzin) **3**:279-83, 287, 291-92; **173**:255-60, 262-63, 280, 298, 301, 308, 310, 312, 329-37, 343-46
"Istoriya leytenanta Ergunova" (Turgenev) **21**:399, 415, 440-41; **122**:267
Istoriya moega znakomstva s Gogolem (Aksakov) **2**:13
Istoriya odnogo goroda (Saltykov) **16**:340-41, 343, 345, 357, 359, 361, 364, 368, 372-73, 375-76, 378
"It bloomed and dropt, a Single Noon—" (Dickinson) **77**:121
"It Can't Be 'Summer'" (Dickinson) **21**:55
"It Fortifies My Soul to Know" (Clough)
See "With Whom Is No Variableness, Neither Shadow of Turning"
"It Is Easy to Work When the Soul Is at Play" (Dickinson) **21**:64
It Is Never Too Late to Mend (Reade) **2**:533-34, 539-42, 544-45, 548-49, 551; **74**:244, 246, 251, 255, 262-65, 269, 271-72, 277-79, 281, 284-89, 297-98, 311-12, 315, 318-22, 330-33, 336-37, 339
"It Is Not Always May" (Longfellow) **45**:116, 135; **103**:304
"It Is Not Beauty I Demand" (Darley) **2**:129, 131-33
"It Is Not Time" (Pavlova) **138**:34
"It Is the Evening Hour" (Clare) **9**:103
"It Is the First Mild Day of March" (Wordsworth)
See "Lines on the First Mild Day of March"

"It Is Wrong to Blame Foibles" ("Kak niekhorosho osuzhdamsoft slabosmi") (Leskov) **174**:131
"It Sifts from Leaden Sieves" (Dickinson) **21**:49; **77**:93
"It Snows" (Hale) **75**:279, 283, 285, 293
"It Was a Glittering Sea" (Pavlova)
See "Eto bylo blestiashchee more"
It Was a Lover and His Lass (Oliphant) **11**:439-41
"It Was an April morning" (Wordsworth) **111**:218
"It was not Death, for I stood up" (Dickinson) **77**:88; **171**:161
"It Was Not in the Winter" (Hood) **16**:218, 228
"It was on a morn when we were thrang" (Baillie) **151**:93
"It will be Summer" (Dickinson) **171**:177
"It would have starved a Gnat—" (Dickinson) **77**:131
"Itak, opyat uvidelsya ya s vami" (Tyutchev) **34**:399
Italia (Gautier) **1**:339, 341, 344; **59**:5
"The Italian Banditti" (Irving) **2**:390
Italian By-Ways (Symonds) **34**:323, 364
Italian Chronicles (Stendhal)
See *L'abbesse de Castro*
The Italian Father (Dunlap) **2**:211, 213-15, 217
Italian Letters; or, The History of the Count de St. Julian (Godwin) **130**:102
Italian Literature (Symonds) **34**:321, 340, 346, 348, 357, 368
Italian Notebooks (Hawthorne)
See *Passages from the French and Italian Notebooks of Nathaniel Hawthorne*
The Italian; or, The Confessional of the Black Penitents (Radcliffe) **6**:405-06, 409-21, 425, 427, 429-30, 435, 437, 442-47; **55**:225, 228-31, 233, 249-52, 255-6, 259, 261-5, 267-70, 273-6, 278-81; **106**:295, 300, 341, 343-45, 349, 351, 364; **223**:186, 189-94, 203, 206, 210-13, 224-25, 227, 229, 232-37, 241, 244-46, 285-88, 297, 302-3, 305-7, 311, 315, 318-19, 321-22, 328, 338
Italian Renaissance (Symonds)
See *Renaissance in Italy*
"Italian Villa" (Tyutchev)
See "Italyanskaya villa"
"The Italians" (Pisarev)
See "Italjancy"
"The Italian's Daughter" (Craik) **38**:119
Italienische Reise (Goethe) **154**:238
Italienische Reise (Grillparzer) **102**:189
"Italjancy" (Pisarev) **25**:347
"Italy" (Bryant) **46**:7
"Italy" (Petofi)
See "Olaszország"
"Italy" (Pinkney) **31**:267, 273, 276
Italy (Gautier)
See *Italia*
Italy (Rogers) **69**:70-2, 74, 80-1, 84
"Italy and Her Church" (Gladstone) **213**:112
Italy: Florence and Venice (Taine)
See *Voyage en Italie*
Italy in 1859 (De Mille)
See *The Dodge Club*
"Italy in England" (Browning) **79**:94, 96-97, 104, 164
Italy: With Sketches of Spain and Portugal (Beckford) **16**:18-19, 21, 25; **214**:150-54, 166
"Italyanskaya villa" (Tyutchev) **34**:379, 397
The Itching Parrot (Lizardi)
See *El periquillo sarniento*
"Ite Domum Saturæ, Venit Hesperus" (Clough) **27**:72
"Az ítélet" (Petofi) **21**:286
Itinéraire de Paris à Jérusalem et de Jérusalem à Paris, en allant par la Grèce, et revenant par l'Egypte, a Barbarie, et l'Espagne (Chateaubriand) **3**:110, 113, 118; **134**:4-5, 8, 12, 16, 18-19
It's a Family Affair—We'll Settle It Ourselves (Ostrovsky)
See *Svoi lyudi—sochtemsya!*
"Its Hour with itself" (Dickinson) **77**:75
"It's Jean de Nivelle's Dog" (Verlaine) **51**:368
"It's Perfectly True" (Andersen)
See "Det er ganske vist!"
"It's Wheat Festival Time . . ." (Verlaine)
See "C'est la fête du blé . . ."
"Ivan FederovičŠpon'ka and His Aunt" (Gogol)
See "Ivan FederovičŠpon'ka i ego tetsuška"
"Ivan FederovičŠpon'ka i ego tetsuška" (Gogol) **5**:218, 231, 239, 249, 254, 256; **31**:88, 108; **162**:17, 62, 94, 98, 127
"Ivan Kolosov" (Turgenev) **122**:264, 266
"Ivan Pidkova" (Shevchenko) **54**:373-4, 389
"Ivan Savich Podzhabrin" (Goncharov) **63**:3, 43-4
Ivanhoe (Dumas) **71**:217
Ivanhoe (Scott) **15**:272, 277, 281, 283-84, 288-89, 304, 308, 313, 317-18; **69**:286-394; **209**:181-83, 185, 219, 229, 262, 314-15, 317-18, 320-21, 328-31
"I've dropped my Brain—My Soul is numb" (Dickinson) **77**:163
"I've heard an organ talk sometimes" (Dickinson) **77**:158
"I've Known a Heaven Like a Tent" (Dickinson) **21**:62
"I've seen a Dying Eye" (Dickinson) **77**:162-64
"Ivo, der Hajrle" (Auerbach) **171**:67-68
"The Ivory Carver" (Boker) **125**:7, 31, 38
The Ivory Gate (Beddoes) **154**:32, 73, 76-79
L'ivrogne (Baudelaire) **6**:119-20
"The Ivy" (Barnes) **75**:8
"Ivy" (Meyer)
See "Eppich"
Ixion (Sheridan) **91**:257
Ixion in Heaven (Disraeli) **39**:3, 33, 52, 54-5, 75
"Iz Gafiza, Iz Gete" (Bestuzhev) **131**:150
"Iz Gete" (Bestuzhev) **131**:150
"Iz odnogo doroznogo dnevnika" (Leskov) **25**:259
"Iz pis'ma k S. V. Savitskoy" (Bestuzhev) **131**:148
"Izmail-Bej" (Lermontov) **126**:181
"Izmennik" (Bestuzhev) **131**:156, 171, 182, 185
"Izobrazhenie Felitsy" (Derzhavin) **215**:13, 26, 57, 59-60
"Izvestiye o Marfe Posadnitse, vzyatoye iz zhitiya Zosimy" (Karamzin) **173**:283
J. M. Heredia 1823 (Heredia)
See *Poesías*
J. M. Heredia 1940 (Heredia)
See *Poesías completas*
"A J. Y. Colonna" (Nerval) **67**:307
"Jabberwocky" (Dodgson) **2**:120; **53**:41, 59, 74, 85, 93, 108-9, 113, 124, 144; **139**:13, 29, 33-34, 37-39, 51, 84, 94-95, 137, 153
Jack (Daudet) **1**:231-34, 236, 243-44, 247-50
"Jack and Alice" (Austen) **119**:13; **222**:107-10
Jack and Jill: A Village Story (Alcott) **6**:17-18, 20-21; **58**:41, 49; **83**:68; **218**:7
"Jack Brag in Spain" (Richardson) **55**:301
"Jack Brass, Emperor of England" (Jefferies) **47**:141
"Jack Hall" (Hood) **16**:235
Jack Hatch (Mitford) **4**:404, 406
Jack Hinton, the Guardsman (Lever) **23**:272, 285, 292, 295, 300, 303, 306-07, 309
Jack of All Trades (Reade) **2**:547; **74**:265
Jack Sheppard (Ainsworth) **13**:22-5, 27-31, 33-40
"Jack Tar" (Tennyson) **30**:294
"Jack the Dullard" (Andersen) **214**:58
Jack Tier; or, The Florida Reefs (Cooper) **1**:208, 221, 227; **54**:258, 276-7
"The Jackdaw of Rheims" (Barham) **77**:37
Jack-o'-Lantern (Cooper) **1**:208; **203**:48, 74
Jack's Ward (Alger) **8**:43, 45
"Jackson of Paul's" (Kingsley) **107**:211, 216
Jacob Faithful (Marryat) **3**:315, 318-19, 321-22
Jacob Pasinkov (Turgenev)
See *Yakov Pasynkov*
"Jacob Pasynkov" (Turgenev)
See "Stepnoy Korol 'Lir"
Jacob the Journeyman's Travels through Switzerland (Gotthelf)
See *Jakobs, des Handwerksgesellen Wanderungen durch die Schweiz*
"A Jacobin" (Hazlitt) **29**:152
The Jacobite Relics of Scotland; Being the Songs, Airs, and Legends of the Adherents of the House of Stuart (Hogg) **4**:276
Jacobite's Epitaph (Macaulay) **42**:88
"Jacobo e Irene" (Lizardi) **30**:71
"Jacob's Wives" (Prescott) **163**:52, 58
Jacopo Ortis (Foscolo)
See *Ultime lettere di Jacopo Ortis*
Jacopo Ortis' Last Letters (Foscolo)
See *Ultime lettere di Jacopo Ortis*
Jacqueline (Rogers) **69**:68, 71, 73, 82
"The Jacquerie" (Lanier) **6**:236-37, 244, 269, 276; **118**:202, 206, 217, 230, 236, 257-62
La jacquerie (Mérimée) **6**:351, 360, 362; **65**:47, 49, 54-5, 58-61, 79, 81-3, 86, 90-2, 94
Jacques (Sand) **2**:582, 587-89, 597-98, 603; **42**:316, 320, 335; **57**:313, 316, 318-20; **174**:167, 225, 230, 236, 289
Jacques Ortis (Dumas) **11**:58
Jacques Vingtras (Vallès) **71**:311, 314-17, 320-21, 325, 327, 330-31, 340, 345, 352, 357-58, 362-70, 372, 384-85
Jacques Vingtras IV: Le Proscrit: Correspondance avec Arthur Arnould (Vallès) **71**:358, 365, 372, 375, 377
Jacques Vingtras: Le Bachelier (Vallès) **71**:312, 314-18, 321-23, 326-27, 330, 340-42, 345-46, 350-52, 355, 363, 365, 370, 384-85
Jacques Vingtras: L'Enfant (Vallès)
See *Jacques Vingtras*
Jacques Vingtras: L'Insurgé: 1871 (Vallès) **71**:313-17, 322-23, 330-31, 340-42, 345, 350, 378, 380, 382, 384-86
"Jadis" (Rimbaud)
See "Jadis, si je me souviens bien . . ."
Jadis et naguère (Verlaine) **2**:623, 631-32; **51**:355, 357, 359-61, 366, 369, 371-72, 387-88; **230**:153-54, 160-65, 167, 191, 203, 207-11
"Jadis, si je me souviens bien . . ." (Rimbaud) **82**:245
"J'admire l'ambition . . ." (Verlaine) **230**:164
"Jaffaar" (Hunt) **1**:414
"Die Jagd" (Droste-Hülshoff) **3**:193
"Jagd im Winter" (Grillparzer) **102**:175
"Das Jagdrecht" (Ludwig) **4**:365
"Der Jäger" (Mörike) **10**:451
"Der Jäger" (Muller) **73**:364, 368, 372
Der Jäger (Mörike) **201**:268
"Jägerlied" (Mörike) **201**:294
"Le jaguar" (Leconte de Lisle) **29**:222, 231
Jahrbücher der Medicin (Schelling) **30**:125
Der Jahrmarkt (Tieck) **5**:514
"J'ai beau faire . . ." (Verlaine) **230**:171
"J'ai dit à l'esprit vain . . ." (Verlaine) **230**:164
"J'ai dit à mon coeur, à mon faible coeur" (Musset) **7**:275
"J'ai magnifié . . ." (Verlaine) **230**:168
"J'ai presque peur . . ." (Verlaine) **230**:167
"J'aime, j'aime . . ." (Laforgue)
See "Dimaches"
"J'aime le souvenir de ces époques nues" (Baudelaire) **29**:80, 115; **55**:48, 57-8, 67
"J'aime ton sourire" (Verlaine) **230**:170
Die Jakobiner (Klopstock) **225**:300
Jakobs, des Handwerksgesellen Wanderungen durch die Schweiz (Gotthelf) **117**:6, 14-15, 32, 34, 40

"The Jamaica Funeral" (Freneau) **1**:314, 316; **111**:80, 171
James Clarence Mangan: His Selected Poems (Mangan) **27**:287
"James Lee's Wife" (Browning) **19**:131-32
"James Rigg: Another Extract from the Recluse" (Hogg) **4**:282, 284-85; **109**:192, 247
"James Thompson: A Minor Poet" (Levy) **203**:306, 308
"James Thomson BV A Minor Poet" (Levy) **59**:107
James Wallace (Bage) **182**:6, 12, 17, 20, 23, 25, 27-29, 31, 37, 39, 42, 47, 53, 60-61
Jan Bielecki (Slowacki) **15**:348-49
"Jan Van Hunks" (Rossetti) **4**:532
"Jan van Huysums blomsterstykke" (Wergeland) **5**:536, 538
"Jan van Huysum's Flower-Piece" (Wergeland)
See "Jan van Huysums blomsterstykke"
Jane Austen's Letters (Austen) **210**:130; **222**:76
Jane Austen's Letters to Her Sister Cassandra and Others (Austen) **1**:52; **19**:29; **95**:30; **150**:14, 52, 73, 94, 103; **207**:59, 65; **210**:91-93
Jane Carlyle: Newly Selected Letters (Carlyle) **181**:123
Jane Eyre (Brontë)
See *Jane Eyre: An Autobiography*
Jane Eyre (Dumas) **71**:217
Jane Eyre: An Autobiography (Brontë) **3**:43-7, 49-50, 52-6, 58-80; **8**:51-93; **33**:103, 105, 107, 109, 111-12, 117-22, 131, 140, 144, 148, 151; **58**:155-6, 160, 171-3, 178-9, 184, 187, 189-90, 194-200, 203-4, 210, 213, 219-22, 224; **105**:2, 4, 6-7, 11-21, 45-6, 53, 64, 67, 70, 73, 75; **155**:133-274; **217**:4, 11, 13, 19, 21-22, 26-30, 32-35, 70-73, 76, 80, 82-83, 87-89, 91-92, 96-98, 101-2, 104-7, 110, 118-19, 123, 130, 141-42, 144-46, 149-50, 156, 165-70, 182-83, 185, 187-89, 191-92; **229**:4-5, 15, 23, 26, 31, 34-35, 38-39, 41-42, 46, 56, 66, 72, 85-87, 90, 120-22, 128, 161, 163, 166, 170, 178, 180-81, 187, 201
Jane Gray (Staël-Holstein) **91**:323, 326, 335, 340, 358
Jane la pâle (Balzac) **5**:58, 65
"Jane Redgrave" (Moodie) **14**:238
Jane Sinclair (Carleton) **3**:91
Jane Sinclair; or, The Fawn of Spring Vale (Carleton) **199**:4, 10, 37, 97
Jane Talbot (Brown) **22**:5, 7, 12, 14, 23, 27, 30, 48-52; **74**:11, 15, 19-21, 49, 56, 77-8, 92-6, 98-9, 102-03, 105, 134, 138, 154-55, 164-66, 176, 179, 182-84; **122**:53-54
Jane Welsh Carlyle: Letters to Her Family, 1839-1863 (Carlyle) **181**:101
"Janet's Repentance" (Eliot) **4**:92, 98, 119; **13**:291; **41**:101; **118**:48, 103; **183**:143
János vitéz (Petofi) **21**:258-59, 261, 264, 266-67, 270-71, 273-75, 277, 283-84, 286
"January" (Clare) **9**:107; **86**:102
"January 1795" (Robinson) **142**:152, 276, 278-79
"January in the Sussex Woods" (Jefferies) **47**:136
"A January Morning" (Lampman) **25**:210; **194**:75, 99
Japhet in Search of a Father (Marryat) **3**:318-19
"Jaquez Barraou, le charpentier" (Borel) **41**:4, 6, 13
"Los jardines" (Bello) **131**:112
"Jardines públicos" (Larra) **17**:282
"A Jarifa en una orgía" (Espronceda) **39**:85, 94, 100, 102-04, 108-09, 113, 117-20
"Jasei no in" (Ueda Akinari) **131**:6, 13-14, 23-24, 26-27, 34-35, 38-40, 60, 76-77, 87
"Jasper" (Robinson) **142**:99, 109-11, 115, 180
"Játszik öreg földünk" (Petofi) **21**:279
"J'avais peiné . . ." (Verlaine) **230**:171
"Javert déraillé" (Hugo) **10**:378-80
"The Jay His Castanet Has Struck" (Dickinson) **21**:67
"Jazvitel' nyj" (Leskov) **25**:230; **174**:30, 32, 123
"Je devine..." (Verlaine) **51**:384
"Je n'ai pas oublié voisine de la ville" (Baudelaire) **55**:23, 61, 65
"Je ne sais pourquoi" (Verlaine) **2**:631; **230**:161, 208
"Je ne suis plus . . ." (Verlaine) **230**:170
"Je t'adore a l'égal" (Baudelaire) **55**:60
"Je te donne ces vers" (Baudelaire) **55**:11, 56, 59, 62
The Jealousies (Keats) **73**:299-300; **121**:173, 228; **225**:255
"Jealousy" (Eminescu) **33**:265
"Jeames' Diary" (Thackeray) **169**:213
Jean (Kock) **16**:244
Jean de la Roche (Sand) **42**:312
Jean de Thommeray (Augier) **31**:5, 8, 10, 13, 15-16, 24, 26, 28, 31
Jean de Witt (Staël-Holstein) **91**:358
"A Jean Duseigneur Sculpteur" (Gautier) **59**:19
Jean et Jeannette (Gautier) **1**:348; **59**:12
Jean Louis (Balzac) **5**:58
"Jean Paul Friedrich Richter" (Carlyle) **70**:96
Jean Sbogar (Nodier) **19**:376, 380, 383-84
Jean Valjean (Hugo) **3**:246
"Jeäne" (Barnes) **75**:6, 7, 30, 71
Jean-François les bas-bleus (Nodier) **19**:383, 391
"Jeanie with the Light Brown Hair" (Foster) **26**:291, 293, 297
Jeanne (Sand) **2**:588-89, 594, 601, 605; **42**:322, 340, 365; **57**:338, 365-6; **174**:229
"Jeanne d'Arc" (Musset) **150**:309
Jeanne d'Arc (Pavlova) **138**:13
Jeanne d'Arc at the Stake (Liszt)
See *Jeanne d'Arc au bûcher*
Jeanne d'Arc au bûcher (Liszt) **199**:308
Jeanne d'Arc: Her Life and Death (Oliphant) **221**:233
Jeanne Eyre (Dumas)
See *Jane Eyre*
Jeanne Laisné (Sade) **47**:361
"Jeannette" (Woolson) **82**:284, 305, 307, 333
"Jeannette au cou tortu" (Stevenson) **193**:228
"J'écoute dans la nuit . . ." (Laforgue) **221**:93
Jed, the Poorhouse Boy (Alger) **8**:21, 33-34, 42, 44; **83**:114, 127
"Jefferson: An Intimation of Virgil's Pollio" (Brackenridge) **227**:105
"Jehan Cauvin" (Sand) **174**:186
"Jehovah Our Righteousness" (Cowper) **8**:131; **94**:72
Jehovah-Rophi, I am the Lord That healeth thee (Cowper) **94**:74
"Jehuda ben Halevy" (Heine) **147**:229, 232, 247
Jemmy (Nerval) **1**:485; **67**:363
"Jenny" (Rossetti) **4**:492-93, 495-97, 506-08, 510-12, 514, 517-20, 523-24, 526-27, 529, 531; **77**:308-11, 316-22, 336-37, 339, 348
"Jenny Away from Home" (Barnes) **75**:58
"Jenny Kissed Me" (Hunt) **1**:415; **70**:269
Jenseit des Tweed (Fontane) **26**:233
"Jephthah's Daughter" (Vigny)
See "La Fille de Jephte"
"Jeremiah Desborough" (Richardson) **55**:299
"Jeretyk" (Shevchenko) **54**:381
"Jérôme Chasseboeuf" (Borel) **41**:13
Jerry, the Backwoods Boy (Alger) **8**:44; **83**:119
The Jerseymen Meeting (Martineau) **137**:268
The Jerseymen Parting (Martineau) **137**:264, 268
Jerusalem: The Emanation of the Giant Albion (Blake) **13**:158, 166-67, 172, 177, 179, 183-84, 191-92, 205, 210-14, 220-21, 227, 229, 231, 233-39, 246-49, 252-53; **37**:8, 20, 46, 48, 66, 69, 80, 85; **57**:46, 60, 89, 92-3, 97-8; **127**:1-145; **173**:4, 10-16, 18-19, 36-37, 46, 50, 52, 61, 65-66, 70, 73, 82, 94, 96-98, 108, 152-53, 157; **190**:3, 8, 11, 13-16, 26-27, 39, 41-42, 74, 86, 98, 101, 130, 151, 158, 160-61; **201**:7, 30, 41, 44, 46-47, 49, 52, 64-65, 94, 103, 107, 112-13, 116-17, 121
"Jesse and Colin" (Crabbe) **26**:93, 128
"Jessica" (Brown) **74**:133-34, 138
"Jessie Lee" (Barnes) **75**:58, 89-90
Jest, Satire, Irony and Deeper Significance (Grabbe)
See *Scherz, Satire, Ironie und tiefere Bedeutung*
The Jesuit (Alencar)
See *O Jesuita*
"Die Jesuiterkirche in G." (Hoffmann) **183**:192, 194-97, 212, 226-27, 287
Les Jésuites (Michelet) **31**:225, 241
"Jesuitisme" (Verlaine) **51**:356
"The Jesuits Church in G-" (Hoffmann)
See "Die Jesuiterkirche in G."
The Jesuits in North America in the Seventeenth Century (Parkman) **12**:333, 336, 341, 352, 355, 366, 371
"Jesus and the Poor" (Lippard) **198**:187, 229
"Jesus Christ in Flanders" (Balzac)
See "Jésus-Christ en Flandre"
"Jesus! Thy Crucifix" (Dickinson) **21**:63
Jesus von Nazareth (Wagner) **9**:474
"Jésus-Christ en Flandre" (Balzac) **5**:46; **53**:25
"Le jet d'eau" (Baudelaire) **29**:77
"J'étais naguère . . ." (Verlaine) **230**:168
Jettatura (Gautier) **1**:346; **59**:11-13, 33, 39
"Jetzt rede du" (Meyer) **81**:144, 205
"Le jeu" (Baudelaire) **29**:81, 101; **55**:23; **155**:3
"La Jeune Fille et le ramier" (Desbordes-Valmore) **97**:27
"La Jeune fille et sa mère" (Desbordes-Valmore) **97**:8
Un jeune homme charmant (Kock) **16**:253
Le Jeune Homme Pauvre (Feuillet)
See *Le Roman d'un Jeune Homme Pauvre*
"Jeune ménage" (Rimbaud) **4**:475
Jeunes Têtes et jeunes coeurs (Desbordes-Valmore) **97**:12
Les jeunes-France, romans goguenards (Gautier) **1**:339, 349; **59**:12, 27, 29, 63-5
"Jeunesse" (Rimbaud) **4**:473; **35**:322; **82**:242, 251; **227**:236-40, 248, 293, 309, 323, 333, 335
La jeunesse (Augier) **31**:7-8, 13, 15, 24, 27, 30, 33, 35
La jeunesse à vingt ans (Dumas) **9**:219
Le jeunesse de Louis XIV (Dumas) **71**:210
"Jeux" (Laforgue) **221**:82
Les Jeux d'eau à la Villa d'Este (Liszt) **199**:307
"The Jew" (Turgenev) **21**:399, 414, 417; **122**:243
"The Jew" (Very) **9**:383
The Jew (Cumberland) **167**:111, 122, 140, 150, 152, 160, 171-72, 175, 178, 181, 188, 191-92, 198
"The Jew in Fiction" (Levy) **59**:98, 111, 127; **203**:295-96
"The Jew, Nine Blooming Branches from a Thornbush" (Wergeland) **5**:537-38
The Jew of Mogadore (Cumberland) **167**:180-81, 193, 198
The Jew Suss: A Tale of Stutgard (Hauff)
See *Jud Süss*
The Jew, the Gypsy, and El-Islam (Burton) **42**:61
The Jeweled Comb-Box (Motoori)
See *Tamakushige*
The Jeweled Comb-Box: The Treasured Book (Motoori)
See *Tamakushige*
"The Jewels of the Book" (Reynolds) **146**:181
The Jewess (Planché) **42**:292
The Jewess (Scribe)
See *La Juive*
"The Jewess, Eleven Blooming Branches" (Wergeland) **5**:537-38

The Jewess of Toledo (Grillparzer)
See *Die Jüdin von Toledo*
"The Jewish Cemetery at Newport" (Longfellow) **45**:132, 163, 167, 186
"Jewish Children" (Levy) **203**:302, 320-21, 336
"Jewish Children, By a Maiden Aunt" (Levy) **59**:98, 112, 133
"Jewish Humour" (Levy) **59**:111; **203**:311-12
"The Jewish Lamentation at Euphrates" (Freneau) **111**:110
"The Jewish Problem" (Lazarus) **8**:424; **109**:293, 303, 313, 331, 337-39
"The Jewish Question" (Marx) **114**:69-70, 74, 76
Jewish Tales (Sacher-Masoch) **31**:285
"Jewish Women and Women's Rights" (Levy) **203**:322
"Jewishness in Music" (Wagner)
See "Das Judentum in der Musik"
"The Jews" (Marx) **17**:295
The Jews in Frankfurt" (Börne) **193**:25
The Jews in Russia (Leskov)
See *Evrei v Rossii*
"Język-ojczysty" (Norwid) **17**:373
The Jilt; or, Thundercloud's Year (Boucicault) **41**:27-8
"Jim Is Poetical Rarely" (Kendall) **12**:195
"Jim the Splitter" (Kendall) **12**:190, 192
"Jimmy Rose" (Melville) **3**:354, 380-81; **157**:95
"Jimmy's Cruise in the Pinafore" (Alcott) **58**:49
"The Jinx" (Baudelaire)
See "Le guignon"
Jó név és erény (Madach) **19**:370
"Joachim Du Bellay" (Pater) **7**:338
Joan (Oliphant) **11**:447
"Joan of Arc" (De Quincey) **87**:15
Joan of Arc (Southey) **8**:447, 459, 461, 473-74, 476-79; **97**:260, 268, 273, 278-79, 281, 293, 307, 312-18, 332
Joan of Arc (Tamayo y Baus)
See *Juana de Arco*
"Joan of Arc, in Rheims" (Hemans) **71**:295
Joanna of Montfaucon (Cumberland) **167**:192, 198
Joanna von Montfaucon (Kotzebue) **25**:136, 145
Joaquìn Murieta (Ridge)
See *The Life and Adventures of Joaquìn Murieta, the Celebrated California Bandit*
"Job Warner's Christmas" (Alger) **83**:97
Jocelyn, An Episode: Journal Found in the House of a Village Curate (Lamartine)
See *Jocelyn: Episode; Journal trouvé chez un curé de village*
Jocelyn: Épisode; Journal trouvé chez un curé de village (Lamartine) **11**:251-53, 255, 262, 271-75, 278, 281, 283-89; **190**:172, 174, 196, 201-2, 204, 241, 254, 258
"Jochonan in the City of Demons" (Maginn) **8**:440
"Joe's Courtship" (Cooke) **110**:33
Joe's Luck (Alger) **83**:100, 104-05
"Jogadhya Uma" (Dutt) **29**:120-21, 124, 128, 130
Johanna Gray (Wieland)
See *Lady Johanna Gray*
Johannes Climacus or De Omnibus Dubitandum Est (Kierkegaard) **78**:217
Johannes und Esther (Muller) **73**:365
"John Barbour's Bruce" (Lanier) **118**:218
"John Bloom in Lon'on" (Barnes) **75**:101
John Brent (Winthrop) **210**:280-83, 285-90, 296, 298-305, 313-14, 316, 320-21, 325, 328-30, 332, 337, 339
"John Brown" (Douglass) **7**:126, 129-30
"John Bull" (Irving) **2**:381; **19**:328; **95**:265, 268, 279, 294
John Bull in America; or, The New Munchausen (Paulding) **2**:528
"John Bull on the Guadalquivir" (Trollope) **101**:234; **215**:221
"John Bunyan" (Macaulay) **231**:278, 305
John Caldigate (Trollope) **6**:466, 470; **101**:312
"John Carter's Sin" (Cooke) **110**:18
John Clare: Poems Chiefly from Manuscript (Clare) **9**:86-87, 89-91, 93, 97, 102; **86**:110, 113, 130-32, 179
John de Lancaster (Cumberland) **167**:112, 115, 124, 135, 140, 150, 179, 193
John Doe; or, Peep o'Day (Banim and Banim) **13**:116-17, 119, 122, 126, 129, 131, 133-34, 141
John Endicott (Longfellow) **2**:486, 496-97; **45**:128, 165
"John Ferncliff" (Horne) **127**:260
John Field and his Nocturnes (Liszt) **199**:305
"John Gilpin" (Cowper)
See "The Diverting History of John Gilpin"
John Gilpin (Cowper)
See "The Diverting History of John Gilpin"
John Gilpin's Ghost; or, The Warning Voice of King Chanticleer (Thelwall) **162**:330, 334-36
John Godfrey's Fortunes (Taylor) **89**:310-11, 347, 363
John Halifax, Gentleman (Craik) **38**:106-11, 113, 116-25, 127-28, 131-39
"John Huss" (Shevchenko) **54**:383
"John Inglefield's Thanksgiving" (Hawthorne) **95**:148; **171**:357
John Jerome: His Thoughts and Ways (Ingelow) **39**:264
"John Jones" (Hood) **16**:234
"John Knox and his Relations to Women: Private Life" (Stevenson) **193**:275
John Marr, and Other Sailors (Melville) **3**:363, 379-80; **29**:318, 320, 322, 360; **157**:212
"John Maynard, A Ballad of Lake Erie" (Alger) **8**:16; **83**:138-39
"John Milton" (Emerson) **98**:67
John Riew (Storm) **1**:540; **195**:7-8, 11-12, 57
John Rintoul (Oliphant) **11**:447; **61**:203
"John Samuel and Richard" (Southey) **97**:314
"John Smith's Shanty" (Jefferies) **47**:137, 141
John the Hero (Petofi)
See *János vitéz*
"John to Jonathan" (Hughes) **207**:130-31
"John Trot" (Hood) **16**:234
"John Underhill" (Whittier) **8**:509
John Woodvil: A Tragedy (Lamb) **10**:385, 387-89, 397-98, 400-01, 404, 407, 409, 411; **113**:163, 180-82, 184, 278, 283
Johnny Ludlow (Wood) **178**:288, 290-91
Johnson (Macaulay) **42**:87
"Johnson and Horne Tooke" (Landor) **14**:166
Johnsonian Anecdotes (Piozzi)
See *Anecdotes of the Late Samuel Johnson, LL.D., During the Last Twenty Years of His Life*
"Johnson's Life of Milton" (De Quincey) **198**:13
"La joie de Siva" (Leconte de Lisle) **29**:221
"Jóka ördöge" (Arany) **34**:16
La jolie fille du faubourg (Kock) **16**:254
"Jon of Iceland" (Taylor) **89**:342
"Jonathan to John" (Lowell) **2**:516
"Jones' Private Argument" (Lanier)
See "Jones's Private Argyment"
"Jones's Private Argyment" (Lanier) **118**:227-28
Jorrocks's Jaunts and Jollities (Surtees) **14**:343, 349, 352, 355, 358, 360, 362, 365-66, 369
Jo's Boys (Alcott)
See *Jo's Boys and How They Turned Out*
Jo's Boys and How They Turned Out (Alcott) **6**:20; **58**:3, 31, 35, 41-3, 47, 50-1, 72; **83**:17, 33-34, 39, 42-43, 47, 62; **218**:5, 7, 23, 25
Joseph (Maupassant) **83**:229
Joseph and His Brethren (Tyler) **3**:572-73
Joseph and His Friend (Taylor) **89**:311, 348, 357, 359
Joseph Balsamo (Dumas) **71**:232, 234
"Joseph de Maistre on Russia" (Arnold) **126**:104
Joseph im Schnee (Auerbach) **171**:9
Joseph in the Snow (Auerbach)
See *Joseph im Schnee*
"Joseph Priestley" (Huxley) **67**:48
Joseph Rushbrook; or, The Poacher (Marryat) **3**:320-21
"Josephine" (Mörike) **201**:280
"Josephine de Montmorenci" (Trollope) **101**:235
Josh Billings' Farmer's Allminax (Shaw) **15**:332-33, 338-39
Josh Billings, Hiz Sayings (Shaw) **15**:339
"Josh Billings Insures His Life" (Shaw) **15**:338
Josh Billings' Spice Box (Shaw) **15**:338, 342
Joshua Davidson (Linton)
See *The True History of Joshua Davidson, Christian and Communist*
"Jottings Down in London" (Willis) **194**:289-91
"Joubert" (Arnold) **89**:39, 83; **218**:220
Joueur de flûte (Augier) **31**:4, 11, 14, 23, 27
"Le joueur généreux" (Baudelaire) **155**:107
Jour à jour (Amiel) **4**:13, 15
Le jour des rois (Hugo) **3**:270-71
Journal (Clare) **86**:112
Le Journal (Genlis) **166**:60-61
Journal (Longfellow) **2**:491; **103**:301
Journal (Macaulay) **42**:130; **231**:281-83, 285
Journal (Michelet) **31**:258, 264; **218**:307, 310, 321
Journal (Murphy)
See *The Gray's-Inn Journal in Two Volumes*
Journal (Percy) **95**:315-17
Journal (Scott)
See *The Journal of Sir Walter Scott*
Journal (Thoreau) **7**:369, 372, 376-8, 385-6, 388-91, 397; **21**:321, 328, 331-2, 337-40; **61**:300, 305-6, 311, 316, 331-7, 339, 341-2, 347-8, 352-7, 361-2, 364, 367, 375-7, 382-6; **138**:106, 116-24, 126, 128-29, 134-36, 146-49, 151, 160, 162, 170, 185-89, 192
Journal abrégé (Constant) **6**:223
Journal C (Emerson) **98**:78
Le journal de Mademoiselle d'Arvers (Dutt) **29**:120, 129
Le journal de Marie Bashkirtseff (Bashkirtseff) **27**:1-35
Journal de Stendhal ..., 1801-1814 (Stendhal) **178**:218, 220
Journal des Goncourt: Mémoires de la vie littéraire (Goncourt and Goncourt) **7**:157-59, 165-66, 168, 171-77, 180, 183-86, 189-90
Le journal d'un poète (Vigny) **7**:469, 471-72, 475, 483; **102**:356, 364, 368, 379-80, 383
Le Journal d'une Femme (Feuillet) **45**:91
Journal einer Reise durch Frankreich (La Roche) **121**:242, 298, 301-2, 305
"Journal for 1836" (Alcott) **167**:98-99
"Journal for 1837, Part Two" (Alcott) **167**:100
Journal imaginaire (Genlis) **166**:61
Journal intime de Benjamin Constant et lettres à sa famille et à ses amis (Constant) **6**:214-15, 223
Journal meiner Reise im Jahr (Herder) **186**:48, 80, 84, 86, 93-94
"Journal of a Frenchman" (Brontë) **109**:35
Journal of a Residence in America (Kemble) **18**:164-67, 169-70, 172-74, 179-80, 182, 186, 191, 199, 201-02
Journal of a Residence on a Georgian Plantation in 1838-1839 (Kemble) **18**:185-86, 190-91, 193-99, 202-03
"The Journal of a Superfluous Man" (Turgenev)
See "Dnevnik lišnego čeloveka"
Journal of a tour and residence in Great Britain (Irving) **95**:277
Journal of a Tour in the Isle of Man (Wordsworth) **25**:421

Journal of a Tour on the Continent (Wordsworth) **25**:411, 421; **138**:257, 260, 293
Journal of a Tour through Silesia (Adams) **175**:46
Journal of a Walking Tour in Yorkshire and the Lake District (Mill) **179**:216-17
Journal of a West Indian Proprietor, Kept during a Residence in the Island of Jamaica (Lewis) **11**:299-300
"Journal of an Actress" (Haliburton) **15**:118, 125, 129
The Journal of an Author (Dostoevsky)
See *Dnevnik pisatelya*
Journal of F. A. Butler (Kemble)
See *Journal of a Residence in America*
The Journal of Julius Rodman (Poe) **16**:313; **94**:180-86
The Journal of Marie Bashkirtseff (Bashkirtseff)
See *Le journal de Marie Bashkirtseff*
Journal of My Second Tour in Scotland (Wordsworth) **138**:254, 256, 258
Journal of My Second Tour of Scotland (Wordsworth) **25**:421
Journal of Researches into the Geology and Natural History of the Various Countries Visited by H. M. S. Beagle (Darwin) **57**:113, 117, 119, 123, 125
The Journal of Sir Walter Scott (Scott) **69**:332; **110**:307, 313-14; **209**:230, 259, 281
Journal of the Movements of the British Legion (Richardson) **55**:296-7, 329
Journal of Visit to Hamburgh and of Journey from Hamburgh to Goslar (Wordsworth) **25**:402, 419
The Journal of William Beckford in Portugal and Spain 1787-1788 (Beckford) **214**:149-54, 160
"Journal sans date" (Chateaubriand) **134**:47-49, 51-52
Journal through France and Italy (Hazlitt)
See *Notes of a Journey through France and Italy*
Journal trouvé chez un curé de village (Lamartine) **11**:274
Journalisten (Freytag) **109**:141
The Journalists (Freytag)
See *Journalisten*
Journals (Hazlitt) **82**:100
Journals (Kierkegaard)
See *Papirer*
The Journals and Letters of Fanny Burney-Madame D'Arblay (Burney) **12**:55; **54**:3, 11
The Journals and Miscellaneous Notebooks of Ralph Waldo Emerson (Emerson) **98**:34, 37, 47-8, 55-6, 60-2, 64-8, 72, 74-6, 79-80, 83-4, 86, 89, 92, 94-8, 1089-09, 112, 116-17, 162, 185
The Journals and Papers of Gerard Manley Hopkins (Hopkins) **189**:25, 27, 31, 40, 46-47, 49, 51, 56, 68, 89-93, 97-98, 114, 116, 118, 125-30, 141
Journals of a Residence in Portugal (Southey) **97**:271
The Journals of Bronson Alcott (Alcott) **1**:25; **167**:17-18, 20-22, 27, 30, 37, 45, 71-72, 76, 89-91, 93-94, 97-98
Journals of Dorothy Wordsworth (Wordsworth) **25**:396, 426; **138**:200-4, 205-11, 214-21, 241-48, 251-61, 263, 273-74, 279, 282-84, 290-91, 293, 300-01, 304, 308-9, 311, 315-16, 318-21, 329, 332-34, 340-45, 348-49, 351-52, 354
Journals of Dorothy Wordsworth: The Alfoxden Journal, 1798; The Grasmere Journals, 1800-1803 (Wordsworth)
See *Journals of Dorothy Wordsworth*
The Journals of Francis Parkman (Parkman) **12**:352
The Journals of Henry David Thoreau (Thoreau) **207**:179-81, 186, 188, 203, 219-27, 231-37, 246, 253-54, 256-57, 266-67, 269
The Journals of Mary Shelley (Shelley) **170**:287, 296
The Journals of Ralph Waldo Emerson (Emerson) **1**:292-93, 296; **38**:142
"Journals of Tours" (Robinson) **15**:181
Journaux intimes (Baudelaire) **6**:99-100, 105; **29**:70, 77, 97-9; **55**:14; **155**:44, 107
Journaux intimes (Constant) **6**:223; **182**:84-85, 202-3, 206, 217
Journées de Florbelle (Sade) **47**:365
"Journey" (Irving) **2**:372
"The Journey" (Very) **9**:383-85
"A Journey around Moscow" (Karamzin) **173**:284
A Journey Due North (Sala) **46**:238-40, 244, 246, 249
Journey from Cornhill to Cairo (Thackeray) **5**:452, 482
"A Journey from Philadelphia to New-York" (Freneau) **111**:131
A Journey from Saint Petersburg to Moscow (Radishchev)
See *Puteshestvie iz Peterburga v Moskvu*
Journey into Northern Pennsylvania and the State of New York (Crèvecoeur) **105**:91, 94
"A Journey into Poles'e" (Turgenev)
See *Liebe-Hütten*
A Journey Made in the Summer of 1794 through Holland and the Western Frontier of Germany (Radcliffe) **6**:414, 417; **55**:222, 233
A Journey Made in the Summer of 1794, Through Holland and the Western Frontier of Germany, with a Return down the Rhine; To Which Are Added, Observations During a Tour to the Lakes of Lanchashire, Westmoreland, and Cumberland (Radcliffe) **223**:187-88, 284, 293-95, 297-98, 311, 317, 325
"Journey of Despair" (Eliot) **4**:124
"The Journey of Life" (Bryant) **46**:38, 42
"Journey on foot from Holmens Canal to the east pount of Amager" (Andersen)
See *Fodrejse fra Holmens Canal til Østpynten of Amager*
Journey out of Essex (Clare) **86**:117, 175, 177-78
Journey to America (Tocqueville) **63**:281
A Journey to Central Africa (Taylor) **89**:346
Journey to Germany (Carlyle) **70**:92
A Journey to Moscow (Radishchev)
See *Puteshestvie iz Peterburga v Moskvu*
"The Journey to Panama" (Trollope) **101**:235; **215**:236-37, 239
"Journey to Polessie" (Turgenev) **21**:431
Journey to Reveal (Bestuzhev)
See *Poezdka v Revel'*
"Journey to the Dead" (Arnold) **6**:67
"Journey to the Harz" (Heine)
See *Die Harzreise*
Journey to the Pyrenees (Taine)
See *Voyage aux eaux des Pyrénées*
Journeys in Italy (Gautier)
See *Italia*
"Jours d'été" (Desbordes-Valmore) **97**:20
"Joust First Being the Right Pleasant Joust betwixt Heart and Brain" (Lanier) **118**:238, 259-60
"Joust Second Being the Rare Joust of Love and Hate" (Lanier) **118**:259, 261
La joven de la flecha de oro (Villaverde) **121**:334-35
"Jövendöles" (Petofi) **21**:264
"Joy and Peace in Believing" (Cowper) **94**:75
"The Joy of Saints" (Rossetti) **186**:340
The Joy of the Wicked (Smolenskin)
See *Simhat hanef*
"Joy Passing By" (Barnes) **75**:59
"Joy, Shipmate, Joy" (Whitman) **31**:388-89
Joyce (Oliphant) **61**:202, 206
"Joyeuse vie" (Hugo) **3**:262
"Ju. F. Abaze" (Tyutchev) **34**:413
Juan Dandolo (Zorrilla y Moral) **6**:523
Juana de Arco (Tamayo y Baus) **1**:565, 567, 570-71
"Jubal" (Eliot) **4**:107-08; **13**:334
"Jubal, the Ringer" (O'Brien) **21**:252
"'Jubilate': Lecture for Poetical Persons" (Jean Paul) **7**:234
"Jubilation of Sergeant Major M'Turk in Witnessing The Highland Games" (Smith) **59**:331
Jud Süs (Hauff)
See *Jud Süss*
Jud Süss (Hauff) **185**:326, 345-46, 350-54
Judae Capta (Tonna) **135**:207
Judah's Lion (Tonna) **135**:203, 207, 211
"Judaism" (Newman) **38**:345
Judaism and Modern Literature (Auerbach)
See *Das Judenthum und die neueste Literatur*
"Judaism in Music" (Wagner)
See "Das Judentum in der Musik"
"Judas" (Webster) **230**:226
Judas Iscariot (Horne) **127**:263
Judas Maccabaeus (Longfellow) **2**:496-97; **45**:127-28, 155
"Der Jude, Schauspiel von Cumberland" (Börne) **193**:40
Die Juden in Breslau (Freytag) **109**:167, 180
Die Judenbuche: Ein Sittengemalde aus dem gebirgichten Westfalen (Droste-Hülshoff) **3**:191-92, 196-200
Das Judenthum und die neueste Literatur (Auerbach) **171**:13, 22, 37-39, 41, 54, 57
"Das Judentum in der Musik" (Wagner) **119**:248-49, 253, 291, 305
Judge for Yourselves! (Kierkegaard) **34**:225; **78**:238
"Judge Nothing before the Time" (Rossetti) **50**:309
"Judged" (Cooke) **110**:16, 20
"Judgement" (Petofi)
See "Az ítélet"
The Judgement of Solomon (Tyler) **3**:572-73
"Judgment and Being" (Hölderlin)
See "Urteil und Sein"
"Judgment of God" (Morris) **4**:422, 431, 444
The Judgment of Paris (Beattie) **25**:109-12
"Judicial Special Pleading" (Dickens) **187**:173
Die Jüdin von Toledo (Grillparzer) **102**:85, 87, 110-11, 131, 170-71, 177, 192-93, 195, 203, 205-07, 212
Judith: Eine Tragödie in fünf Acten (Hebbel) **43**:230, 233-34, 239, 242-44, 253-58, 262, 271, 277-80, 283-87, 296-97, 299
The Judith of Bialopol (Sacher-Masoch) **31**:298
Judith und Holofernes (Nestroy) **42**:225, 227-28, 231, 234
"Judol'" (Leskov) **25**:239; **174**:5, 38
"Le jugement de Komor" (Leconte de Lisle) **29**:226
"Jugendandacht, 8" (Eichendorff) **225**:12
Jugenderinnerungen im Grünen (Grillparzer) **102**:175
"Jugendsehnen" (Eichendorff) **8**:213
"The Juggler Pamphalon" (Leskov)
See "Skomorox Pamfalon"
"Jugurtha" (Longfellow) **2**:492; **45**:146
"Jugurtha" (Rimbaud) **4**:465; **227**:208
La Juive (Scribe) **16**:390, 398, 408-10
Jules Michelet: Journal (Michelet)
See *Journal*
Julia (Brontë) **3**:80
Julia (Hebbel) **43**:230, 237, 239, 257
Julia: A Novel; Interspersed with Some Poetical Pieces (Williams) **135**:255-56, 296-99, 301, 333, 343, 346, 349-50, 352
Julia de Roubigné (Mackenzie) **41**:181-82, 184,

203, 209, 212, 222, 224-26, 228
Julia de Trécoeur (Feuillet) **45**:77-9, 85-7, 89, 93
"Julia; or the Convent of St. Clair, a Tale, founded on Fact" (Opie) **65**:160-1
Julian (Eichendorff) **225**:20-21, 98-101
Julian (Mitford) **4**:400, 404
"Julian and Maddalo" (Shelley) **18**:326, 331, 338, 356-57, 359; **93**:277, 315-17, 320, 351; **143**:248, 281; **175**:238, 244
Julian and Maddalo (Shelley)
See "Julian and Maddalo"
"Julian M. and A. G. Rochelle" (Brontë) **16**:73, 75, 86-7
"Julia's Murder" (Dacre) **151**:149
Juliette; ou, Les prospérités du vice (Sade) **3**:495-96; **47**:304, 309, 311, 313, 324-25, 328, 334-36, 341-42, 346, 350, 364-65
Julius (Stifter) **41**:376-77
Julius; or, The Street Boy Out West (Alger) **7**:43; **83**:100
Julqvällen (Runeberg) **41**:309-10, 314, 317-18, 328-32
"July" (Clare) **86**:96-7, 101, 104
"July Fourth 1844" (Fuller) **50**:248
"The Jumblies" (Lear) **3**:309
"June" (Bryant) **6**:165, 168, 172; **46**:3, 19, 22-3
"June" (Clare) **86**:99-101
"June" (Lampman) **25**:172, 183; **194**:81-82, 93
"June" (Levy) **203**:345
"A June Morning" (Ridge) **82**:185
"A June Night" (Lazarus) **109**:294
"A June-Tide Echo (After a Richter Concert)" (Levy) **59**:92, 94
"Jung Tirel" (Meyer) **81**:207
Jung Volker (Mörike) **201**:252, 268
"Jung Volkers Lied" (Mörike) **10**:453
Der junge Tischlermeister (Tieck) **5**:520, 532; **46**:397
"Die Jungen" (Storm) **195**:90
"Die Jungfrau" (Meyer) **81**:206
Die Jungfrau als Ritter (Keller) **2**:416
Die Jungfrau und der Teufel (Keller) **2**:416
Die Jungfrau und die Nonne (Keller) **2**:416
Die Jungfräu von Orleans (Schiller) **39**:319-20, 322, 325, 329-30, 335, 345-46, 350, 360-61, 365, 371-72, 376-80; **69**:175, 181-82, 185, 188, 255, 261, 263-64, 266, 269; **166**:146, 159, 190-94
"Jung-Katerverein für Poesie-Musik" (Heine) **147**:140
"Les jungles" (Leconte de Lisle) **29**:212, 217, 224, 231-32
Die jüngsten Kinder meiner Laune (Kotzebue) **25**:139
"The Juniper-Tree" (Grimm Brothers) **3**:225
Juniusabende und Julitage (Schumann) **143**:73, 138
"Juno and Ganymede" (Wieland) **177**:323
"La junta de Castel-o-Branco" (Larra) **130**:194
Jupiter Lights (Woolson) **82**:275, 280, 293, 299, 318-19, 329, 335
"Júpiter y Europa" (Casal) **131**:236
Jürg Jenatsch (Meyer) **81**:135-36
Juridical Sketches (Alencar)
See *Esboços Juridicos*
Jusan'ya (Ichiyō) **49**:331, 336-37, 341, 345, 348, 353
"Just Lost, When I Was Saved!" (Dickinson) **21**:64
"The Just Man" (Rimbaud)
See "L'homme juste"
"The Just Men" (Leskov)
See "Spravedlivyj čelovek"
"Justice and Expediency" (Whittier) **59**:364
"Justice as a Principle of Divine Governance" (Newman) **99**:298
"Justice for Ireland" (Allingham) **25**:3
"Justice Pettifog" (Haliburton) **149**:304
"Justifiable Homicide in Southern California" (Jackson) **90**:153
A Justified Sinner (Hogg)
See *The Private Memoirs and Confessions of a Justified Sinner*
The Justified Sinner (Hogg)
See *The Private Memoirs and Confessions of a Justified Sinner*
Justin Harley (Cooke) **5**:131, 135
Justine or the misfortunes of virtue (Sade)
See *Justine ou les malheurs de la vertu*
Justine ou les malheurs de la vertu (Sade) **47**:47; 306, 309, 311, 314, 328, 333-36, 340-43, 350, 355, 364-65, 367, 370-72
"Juvat ire jugis" (Arnold) **218**:191
Juvenile Journal (Burney) **54**:16
Juvenile Miscellany (Child) **73**:40, 50, 56, 58, 61, 66, 68, 74-6, 101-02, 121-22, 124-25, 127-32, 134-35
Juvenile Poems (Coleridge) **9**:146
Juvenilia (Austen) **13**:96; **51**:13, 15
Juvenilia 1829-1835 (Brontë) **105**:77
Juvenilia; or, A Collection of Poems Written between the Ages of Twelve and Sixteen (Hunt) **1**:405, 411, 416; **70**:263, 264
Juventus Mundi: The Gods and Men of the Heroic Age (Gladstone) **213**:116, 125-28, 136
"De juventute" (Thackeray) **169**:289; **213**:308
Einen Jux will er sich machen (Nestroy) **42**:239-40, 243, 245, 249, 264
"K ***" (Pavlova) **138**:53
"K chemu nevol'niku" (Baratynsky)
See "K chemu nevolniku mechtania svobody?..."
"K chemu nevolniku mechtania svobody?..." (Baratynsky) **103**:10, 16-17, 21
"K chemy nevol'niku" (Baratynsky)
See "K chemu nevolniku mechtania svobody?..."
"K dobrodeteli" (Karamzin) **173**:280
"K Konsinu" (Baratynsky) **103**:3, 27-9
"K lyre" (Derzhavin) **215**:12-15
"K mesyatsu" (Zhukovsky) **35**:403-04, 407
"K milosti" (Karamzin) **173**:266
"K moriu" (Pushkin) **83**:254-55, 261, 304, 351, 366
"K nekotorym poetam" (Bestuzhev) **131**:148
"K nevernoi" (Aksakov) **181**:60
"K oblaku" (Bestuzhev) **131**:151
K. S. Aksakovu (Pavlova) **138**:5
"K slovesu" (Preseren) **127**:323
"K solov'iu" (Aksakov) **181**:60
"K solov'iu" (Karamzin) **173**:351
"K.A. Sverbeevoy" (Baratynsky)
See "To K.A. Sverbeevaya"
"Kaadt ukrudt" (Wergeland) **5**:541
Kabale und Liebe (Schiller) **39**:310-11, 327, 334, 342, 350, 375, 389-90, 393-94; **69**:169, 171, 196, 242, 277; **166**:79, 125-26, 131, 167
Kadril! (Pavlova) **138**:5, 13-14, 20, 35-36, 47, 49-50, 56-57, 59-62
Kahldorf über den Adel (Heine) **147**:141
"Kaiphas, Kaiphas, Sanchedrin" (Grillparzer) **102**:174
"Kairail Fish" (Brontë) **109**:34
Kaiser Heinrich (Klopstock) **225**:298
"Kaiser Heinrich" (Klopstock) **11**:236
Kaiser Octavianus (Tieck) **5**:514, 519, 521, 525, 529, 532
"Kaizoku" (Ueda Akinari) **131**:20-22, 52, 56
"Kak idyot kuznets da iz kuznitsy . . ." (Bestuzhev) **131**:181
"Kak neozhidanno i yarko" (Tyutchev) **34**:400
"Kak ni tyazhel posledniy chas" (Tyutchev) **34**:399
"Kak okean obemlet shar zemnoi" (Tyutchev) **34**:389, 404-07, 409-10
"Kak ptichka, ranneyu zarey" (Tyutchev) **34**:399
"Kak sladko dremlet sad temnozelenyi" (Tyutchev) **34**:405
Kakaika (Ueda Akinari) **131**:20
"Kakemono" (Casal) **131**:257
Kakizome kigenkai (Ueda Akinari) **131**:19, 51
"Kalamazoo Address against Extending Slavery" (Lincoln)
See "Speech Delivered at Kalamazoo, Michigan"
"Kaleidoscope" (Verlaine) **51**:355, 364, 371
The Kalevala (Lonnrot) **53**:307-10, 312-40
"Kalkstein" (Stifter) **41**:357, 360, 362-64, 373, 375; **198**:275-76, 285
Kallias oder über die Schönheit (Schiller) **166**:133
Kalligone (Herder) **8**:313
"Kallundborg Church" (Whittier) **8**:513, 529
"Kám?" (Preseren) **127**:318, 325
Kamalakanta (Chatterji) **19**:216, 225-26
Kamalakanter daptar (Chatterji) **19**:216, 220, 226
"Kamalakanter jabanbandi" (Chatterji) **19**:226
"Kamalakanter patra" (Chatterji) **19**:226
"Kambaleu" (Longfellow) **45**:145
Kamennyi gost' (Pushkin) **3**:424, 433-34, 447, 452; **83**:263-65, 285-86, 288-90, 327, 338-39, 351-543, 355-36
"Der Kamin" (Klopstock) **225**:310
"Kampf" (Schiller) **39**:331, 387
"Der Kampf der Sänger" (Hoffmann) **183**:189
"Der Kampf mit dem Drachen" (Schiller) **166**:105
Kampl (Nestroy) **42**:221, 249-51
Kan ej (Runeberg) **41**:310
Der Kandidat (Ludwig) **4**:356
"Kane" (O'Brien) **21**:234, 246
Kanervala (Kivi) **30**:51
"The Kangaroo Hunt" (Harpur) **114**:99, 125, 144, 158, 166
"The Kansas Immigrants" (Child) **73**:83, 106
Kantate auf den Tod Ihrer Königlichen Majestät, Louis von Preußen (Brentano) **191**:88
"'Kantate': Lecture on Poetical Poetry" (Jean Paul) **7**:234
Kanteletar (Lonnrot) **53**:321-2, 338-40
Kapalkundala (Chatterji) **19**:204, 206, 208-10, 212, 214-15, 217-19, 222, 224
Kapellet (Almqvist) **42**:4, 16, 19
Das Kapital: Kritik der politischen Ökonomie (Marx) **17**:289, 291, 293, 295-97, 302-03, 308, 310-16, 326-27, 331, 333, 335-39, 344, 354-55, 359; **114**:8, 11, 36-7, 54, 70, 73, 82, 85
Kapitansha (Shevchenko) **54**:363, 392, 395
Kapitanskaya-dochka (Pushkin) **3**:428-29, 436, 442, 452, 460, 464; **83**:268, 275, 291, 293, 295-96, 337, 354-56
"Der Kapwein und der Johannesberger" (Klopstock) **11**:238
"The Karamanian Exile" (Mangan) **27**:278, 286-87, 292, 295, 298
Karamazov (Dostoevsky)
See *Brat'ya Karamazovy*
Karamzin's Memoir on Ancient and Modern Russia: A Translation and Analysis (Karamzin)
See *O drevnei i novoi Rossii v ee politicheskom i grazhdanskom otnosheniiakh*
Die Karawane (Hauff) **185**:318, 334-35, 356
Karkurit (Kivi) **30**:50-1, 53, 64-5
Karl I (Heine) **54**:347
Karl von Berneck (Tieck) **5**:519, 523, 527; **46**:374-75
"Karluv tejn" (Macha) **46**:201
Karsten Kurator (Storm)
See *Carsten Curator*
"Die Kartäuser" (Meyer) **81**:206
Kartofa (Mickiewicz)
See "Kartofel"
"Kartofel" (Mickiewicz) **3**:396-98
Kartofla (Mickiewicz)
See "Kartofel"

Die Käserei in der Vehfreude (Gotthelf) **117**:6, 15, 22-5, 32, 35
Kashoden (Ueda Akinari) **131**:20
The Kasidah (Burton) **42**:42-44, 53
"Kasperl und Annerl" (Brentano)
See "Geschichte vom braven Kasperl und dem schönen Annerl"
"Kassandra" (Schiller) **166**:114-15, 121
"Kastraten und Männer" (Schiller) **39**:356, 386
Katalin (Arany) **34**:16, 23-4
Das Kätchen von Heilbronn; oder, Die Feuerprobe (Kleist) **2**:437, 440, 443, 446, 450, 457-58; **37**:217, 225-28, 230, 233, 237, 253-55, 257, 260, 262, 270, 272, 274; **222**:203, 215, 228, 232-33, 235, 256
"Kate Bouverie" (Norton) **205**:82
Kate Bouverie and Other Tales and Sketches in Prose and Verse (Norton)
See *The Coquette, and Other Tales and Sketches, in Prose and Verse*
"Kate O'Belashanny" (Allingham) **25**:16
Kate of Heilbronn (Kleist)
See *Das Kätchen von Heilbronn; oder, Die Feuerprobe*
"Katechismus der Deutschen abgefasst nach dem Spanischen, zum Gebrauch für Kinder und Alte" (Kleist) **222**:276
Kater Murr (Hoffmann)
See *Lebens-Ansichten des Katers Murr nebst fragmentarischer Biographie des Kapellmeisters Johannes Kreisler in züfalligen Makulaturblättern*
"Kateryna" (Shevchenko) **54**:371, 373-5, 389
"Kathaleen-Ny-Houlahan" (Mangan) **27**:297-98, 310
Katharine Walton; or, The Rebel of Dorchester (Simms) **3**:503, 507-08, 513-14
Käthi die Großmutter (Gotthelf) **117**:5, 18, 25, 32
"Kathleen" (Whittier) **8**:516, 528; **59**:360, 371
"Katie" (Timrod) **25**:361, 367, 372, 375, 384
"Katie Cheyne" (Hogg) **4**:283
Katie Stewart (Oliphant) **11**:439, 446-7; **61**:173; **221**:244
Katzensilber (Stifter) **41**:391
"Kaukametsä" (Kivi) **30**:51-2
"Kaunisnummella" (Kivi) **30**:51
Kaunitz (Sacher-Masoch) **31**:291
Käuzlein (Storm) **195**:17
Kavanagh (Longfellow) **2**:480-81, 489-90, 494; **45**:158, 168, 184; **101**:92
"Kavkaz" (Shevchenko) **54**:383, 389
Kavkazsky plennik (Pushkin) **3**:409-11, 413, 415-16, 421, 423, 437, 445, 451; **27**:392; **83**:242-44, 246-48, 251, 299, 309, 332, 357, 359
The Kawi Language of the Island of Java (Humboldt) **134**:186
"Kdor ne zna napisa brati" (Preseren) **127**:315
Kean, on désordre et genie (Dumas) **11**:46-7; **71**:209-10, 230, 242
"Keats" (Lampman)
See "The Character and Poetry of Keats"
Keep Cool: A Novel (Neal) **161**:288, 290, 296-98, 301, 318-21, 346
"Keepen Up O' Christmas" (Barnes) **75**:77
"Keeping Fast and Festival" (Newman) **38**:304
Keeping House and Housekeeping (Hale) **75**:341
"The Keeping-Room of an Inn" (Haliburton) **149**:319
Kein Wort, auch nicht das kleinste (Storm) **195**:21
"Keinu" (Kivi) **30**:51
"Keiserens nye Klæder" (Andersen) **7**:25, 28, 34; **79**:21, 23, 25-6, 52, 64, 68, 72, 76, 81, 88; **214**:28-33, 39, 41, 55, 61
"Keith of Ravelston" (Dobell) **43**:47-8
"Die Kellnerin von Bacharach und ihre Gäste" (Muller) **73**:366, 380
The Kellys and the O'Kellys; or, Landlords and Tenants (Trollope) **6**:452, 458, 500, 514; **101**:245-51, 253, 263-67, 269, 271, 273, 276, 293, 295, 299, 321
"The Kelp Gatherer" (Griffin) **7**:214
Kenelm Chillingly, His Adventures and Opinions (Bulwer-Lytton) **1**:147, 149, 151, 155; **45**:68-9
Kenilworth (Scott) **15**:277, 289, 309, 313, 317; **69**:303-04, 308, 313; **209**:223, 298
Kensington Gardens in 1830: A Satirical Trifle (Richardson) **55**:329
Kept in the Dark (Trollope) **6**:500-01; **101**:309
"Kéramos" (Longfellow) **45**:130, 139, 147, 157; **103**:295
Kerry (Boucicault) **41**:28
"Kertben" (Arany) **34**:18-19
"Kesäyö" (Kivi) **30**:51-2
"Kettenlied eines Sklaven" (Brentano) **191**:61
Kevurat hamor (Smolenskin) **30**:189-90, 192, 195
"Kew Gardens" (Symonds) **34**:355
"'The Key of the Street" (Sala) **46**:245-46, 248, 250
Key to History, Part II: The Hebrews (Peabody) **169**:147
Key to History, Part III: The Greeks (Peabody) **169**:147
"The Key to My Book" (Rossetti) **50**:274
A Key to the New Testament (Percy) **95**:313, 336, 338
A Key to Uncle Tom's Cabin: Presenting the Original Facts and Documents upon Which the Story Is Founded (Stowe) **3**:543-44, 547, 559; **195**:160, 200-201, 223, 225-26, 229, 260
Keys to Grecian History (Peabody)
See *Key to History, Part III: The Greeks*
"Khadji Abrek" (Lermontov) **47**:182
"Khirôn" (Leconte de Lisle) **29**:222-23, 238, 245-46
Kholostiak (Turgenev) **21**:428, 432
"Khor and Kalinych" (Turgenev)
See "Chor' i Kalinyč"
"Khozyaika" (Dostoevsky) **2**:156, 179; **21**:94; **33**:177; **43**:92
Khudozhnik (Shevchenko)
See *Xudoznik*
"Kiama" (Kendall) **12**:178
"Kibitsu no kama" (Ueda Akinari) **131**:3-4, 6, 13, 24, 26-27, 38-40, 48, 75-76, 87
A Kick for a Bite; or, Review upon Review (Cobbett) **49**:109
Kicklebury's on the Rhine (Thackeray) **5**:459, 506
Kidnapped: Being Memoirs of the Adventures of David Balfour in the Year 1751 (Stevenson) **5**:400, 402-05, 409, 414-15, 417, 424-27, 429, 433-35, 438-39; **63**:257, 261, 269, 274; **193**:204, 210, 212, 214, 216, 218-19, 222-23, 241-46, 248, 250, 274, 282, 294-96, 302-10, 313, 325
The Kidnappers (Bird) **197**:29
Kierkegaard: Letters and Documents (Kierkegaard)
See *Papirer*
Kierkegaard's Attack upon 'Christendom' (Kierkegaard)
See *Hvad Christus dömmer om officiel Christendom*
"Kies Ősz" (Arany) **34**:19
Kihlaus (Kivi) **30**:48, 50, 53, 64
"Kikuka no chigiri" (Ueda Akinari) **131**:5-7, 13-15, 24-25, 27, 32, 34, 38, 40-41, 48, 60, 64-65, 69, 74-75
The Killers: A Narrative of Real Life in Philadelphia, by a Member of the Philadelphia Bar (Lippard) **198**:125, 187, 225
"Kilmeny" (Hogg) **4**:274, 279-80, 282-83, 285; **109**:209, 243, 248, 270-72
"Kin Beyond Sea" (Gladstone) **213**:109
Das Kind der Liebe (Kotzebue) **25**:130, 134, 136, 141, 144-46, 151
"The Kind Master and Dutiful Servant" (Hammon) **5**:262, 264-65
Kinder- und Hausmärchen: 1812 und 1815 (Grimm Brothers)
See *Kinder-und Hausmärchen*
Kinder- und Hausmärchen: 1819 (Grimm Brothers)
See *Kinder-und Hausmärchen*
Kinder- und Hausmärchen: Ausgabe letzier Hand (Grimm Brothers)
See *Kinder-und Hausmärchen*
"Kinderfrühling" (Muller) **73**:366
Kindergeschichten (Stifter)
See *Bunte Steine*
"Kinderlust" (Muller) **73**:366
Kinder-und Hausmärchen (Grimm Brothers) **3**:216, 218-20, 226-27, 230; **77**:189-284
"Die Kindesmörderin" (Ludwig) **4**:353
The King and Queen of Hearts (Lamb) **10**:417
The King and the Knight (Eminescu) **33**:264
King Arthur (Bulwer-Lytton) **1**:143-44; **45**:15-18, 22
"King Arthur's Tomb" (Morris) **4**:426, 431, 444
King Charles, the Young Hero (Tegner) **2**:613
King Charles's Beauties (Jameson)
See *Memoirs of the Beauties of the Court of Charles II*
King Charming (Planché) **42**:300
"King Chaunticlere; or, The Fate of Tyranny" (Thelwall) **162**:330-31, 334, 336
"King Cophetua the First" (Patmore) **9**:335
"King David" (Woolson) **82**:273, 294-95, 300
"King Edward the Third" (Blake) **13**:171, 181, 184, 239; **127**:13; **190**:146-47
"King Etzel's Sword" (Meyer)
See "König Etzels Schwert"
King Fjalar (Runeberg)
See *Kung Fjalar*
"King Harold on the Eve of the Battle of Hastings" (Brontë) **16**:104
"King Lear" (Lamb) **125**:306-7
"A King Lear of the Steppes" (Turgenev)
See "Stepnoy Korol 'Lir"
"The King of Achen's Daughter" (Maginn) **8**:437
"The King of Clubs" (Alcott) **83**:8
"The King of Gnomes" (Gogol)
See "Viy"
"The King of Hukapetapank" (Muller) **73**:353
The King of the Peacocks (Planché) **42**:273, 288, 293-94
King Otakar's Rise and Fall (Grillparzer)
See *König Ottokars Glück und Ende*
King Ottocar: His Rise and Fall (Grillparzer)
See *König Ottokars Glück und Ende*
"King Penguin" (Horne) **127**:263, 266, 268
"King Pest" (Poe) **1**:500; **16**:308, 313
King Philip or the Sagamore (Bird) **197**:9, 29
"King, Queen and Knave" (Andersen) **214**:75
"King Robert of Sicily" (Longfellow) **45**:114, 128, 137, 145, 149, 188
"King Saul at Gilboa" (Kendall) **12**:190-92, 199-202
King Solomon's Mines (Haggard) **63**:257
King Spirit (Slowacki)
See *Król Duch*
King Stephen (Keats) **8**:341, 360; **73**:155, 306
"King Ulysses" (Isaacs)
See "El rey Ulises"
King Victor and King Charles (Browning) **19**:102, 113
"King Volmer and Elsie" (Whittier) **8**:529
"King Wine" (Muller) **73**:353
"King Witlaf's Drinking-Horn" (Longfellow) **45**:116
"The Kingdom of Christ" (Hopkins) **189**:76
"The Kingdom of Darkness" (Dobrolyubov) **5**:140-41, 151
"The Kingdom of the Saints" (Newman) **38**:305
"Kingfishers" (Hopkins)
See "As kingfishers catch fire"

The King's Book (Arnim)
See *Dies Buch Gehört dem König*
"The King's Bride" (Hoffmann)
See "Königsbraut"
"King's College Chapel" (Wordsworth) **166**:213
"The King's Dream" (Andersen) **7**:23; **79**:13, 17
The King's Edict (Hugo)
See *Marion de Lorme*
The King's Fool (Hugo)
See *Le roi s'amuse*
"The King's Garments" (Crawford) **12**:156
Kings in Exile (Daudet)
See *Les rois en exil*
The King's Judgement (Eminescu) **33**:266
"A King's Lesson" (Morris) **4**:439
The Kings on Salamis (Runeberg)
See *Kungarne på Salamis*
The King's Own (Marryat) **3**:317, 319
"The King's Sabbath" (Lampman) **194**:17-18
"The King's Scholar's Story" (Barham) **77**:9
"The King's Tragedy" (Rossetti) **4**:499-500, 502-04, 506, 508, 513, 518, 525-27, 529, 532; **77**:298
"The King's Vow" (Petofi)
See "A király esküje"
The Kingsmen; or, The Black Riders of Congaree (Simms)
See *The Scout*
Kinsa (Ueda Akinari) **131**:20
"A király esküje" (Petofi) **21**:264
Kirjali (Pushkin) **3**:436; **83**:325
Kirsteen: A Story of a Scottish Family Seventy Years Ago (Oliphant) **11**:449-51, 457-8; **61**:173, 195, 202, 216, 223, 226, 233-5, 241; **221**:305, 311-13, 321
"Kismet" (Ingelow) **39**:258
"The Kiss" (Dacre) **151**:170, 172
"The Kiss" (Rossetti) **77**:338-39
"Kitty Tyrrell" (Ferguson) **33**:301
Kjerlighedens Gjerninger (Kierkegaard) **34**:178, 192, 197, 202, 211, 224; **78**:142, 185, 215, 239; **125**:250, 257, 262, 265
"Kladbishche" (Karamzin) **173**:347
Klage und Trost (Tieck) **5**:519
Klalam and Klickitat (Winthrop)
See *The Canoe and the Saddle: or Klalam and Klickitat, to Which Are Now First Added his Western Letters and Journals*
"Klänge aus dem Orient" (Droste-Hülshoff) **3**:195, 203
"Klara Hebert" (Lenau) **16**:286
"Klara Milič" (Turgenev)
See "Klara Milich"
"Klara Milich" (Turgenev) **21**:408, 415, 420, 431, 438, 441, 451-52; **122**:242, 244, 246-47, 265-68, 365, 374-75, 378
"Klára Zách" (Arany) **34**:20
"Klaskaniem mając obrzękłe prawice" (Norwid) **17**:374
Klassische Blumenlese (Mörike) **10**:449, 452, 456
Klaus und Klajus: Ein Roman von einem Schulmeister leben (Ludwig) **4**:356
Kleider machen Leute (Keller) **2**:415, 423
Klein Zaches gennant Zinnober (Hoffmann) **2**:341, 351, 361-62; **183**:170, 173-75, 211, 217, 231
Der kleine Häwelmann (Storm) **195**:20, 23-24, 33
Die kleine Zigeunerin (Kotzebue) **25**:147
Kleinere prosaische Schriften (Schiller) **166**:144
Kleinere prosaische Schriften (Wieland) **177**:227
Kleinere Schriften (Kopitar)
See *Barth. Kopitars kleinere Schriften*
Klelia und Sinibald; oder Die Bevölkerung von Lampeduse (Wieland) **177**:367-68
Kleopatria i Cezar (Norwid) **17**:367, 369, 379
Kling leise, mein Lied (Liszt) **199**:308
"Klingsohr's Fairy Tale" (Novalis)
See "Klingsohrs Märchen"
"Klingsohrs Märchen" (Novalis) **178**:3-4, 7, 15-17, 36, 40-42, 45-46, 61, 63, 72, 77, 89-90, 101, 110
"Kliuch" (Derzhavin) **215**:23
"Klods-Hans" (Andersen) **79**:72, 81
"Klokken" (Andersen) **7**:22-23; **79**:28, 40
Das Kloster bei Sendomir (Grillparzer) **102**:176-77
"Die Klosterbeere. Zum Andenken an die Frankfurter Judengasse" (Arnim) **123**:60, 62-63, 65, 69
Klosterheim; or, The Masque (De Quincey) **4**:65, 81; **87**:76, 79; **198**:88
"Klosterszene" (Grillparzer) **102**:175
"Klytie" (Leconte de Lisle) **29**:239
"Der Knabe im Moor" (Droste-Hülshoff) **3**:193, 200
Knave or Not? (Holcroft) **85**:198-99, 223
"Kniazhna" (Shevchenko) **54**:387, 389, 394
Kniazhna (Shevchenko) **54**:369, 390-4, 397-8
Knickerbocker (Irving)
See *Knickerbocker Stories from the Old Dutch Days of New York*
Knickerbocker Stories from the Old Dutch Days of New York (Irving) **2**:365-66, 368-69, 371, 373, 385-87; **95**:226-27, 317-18
Knickerbocker's History (Irving)
See *A History of New York, from the Beginning of the World to the End of the Dutch Dynasty*
"Knight Aagen and Maiden Else" (Morris) **4**:423
"The Knight and the Dragon" (Hood) **16**:233
The Knight and the Lady (Barham) **77**:10
"The Knight for an Hour" (Nekrasov)
See "Rycar' na čas"
"A Knight of Dannebrog" (Boyesen) **135**:13, 21, 27
The Knight of Guadalquiver (Dunlap) **2**:213, 215
The Knight of Gwynne: A Tale of the Time of the Union (Lever) **23**:292, 305-07, 310-11
"A Knight of Our Time" (Karamzin)
See "Rytsar nashego vremeni"
"A Knight of Our Times" (Karamzin) **3**:281, 287
"Knight Pázmán" (Arany)
See "Pázmán lovag"
"The Knight's Epitaph" (Bryant) **46**:3
The Knights of the Round Table (Planché) **42**:292
Knjaginja (Shevchenko)
See *Kniazhna*
"The Knob Dance" (Harris) **23**:141, 147
"The Knob Dance—A Tennessee Frolic" (Harris) **165**:184, 186-87, 198, 233
"Knocking" (De Quincey) **87**:77
"The Knocking at the Gate in Macbeth" (De Quincey)
See "On the Knocking at the Gate in Macbeth"
"Knock...Knock...Knock" (Turgenev)
See "Stuk...stuk...stuk"
"A Knot of Roses" (Kivi)
See "Ruususolmu"
"The Knouto-Germanic Empire and the Social Revolution" (Bakunin)
See "L'Empire Knouto-Germanique et la Révolution Sociale"
The Knouto-Germanic Empire and the Social Revolution (Bakunin)
See "L'Empire Knouto-Germanique et la Révolution Sociale"
Know Your Own Mind. A Comedy. Performed at the Theatre-Royal in Covent-Garden (Murphy) **229**:234, 242
Know Your Place (Ostrovsky)
See *Ne v svoi sani ne sadis!*
Know Yourself (Wagner)
See *Erkenne dich selb*
"Knoware" (Cooke) **110**:21
"Knowledge" (Lampman) **25**:194, 209; **194**:20
"Knowlwood" (Barnes) **75**:58
"Known in Vain" (Rossetti) **4**:491
"Knyagine Z.A. Volkonskoy" (Baratynsky) **103**:10
Kobboltozo: A Sequel to The Last of the Huggermuggers (Cranch) **115**:16-17, 54-9
"Kobes I" (Heine) **147**:229, 232
Kobzar (Shevchenko) **54**:358-9, 364, 372-5, 379, 384, 386
"Kogda drjaxlejušcie sily" (Tyutchev) **34**:415
"Kogda ischeznet omrachenie" (Baratynsky) **103**:5, 9-10
"Kogda karateliam velikim" (Pavlova) **138**:13
Kohlhaas (Kleist)
See *Michael Kohlhaas*
Kojiki den (Motoori) **45**:268, 274-77
"Kolebka pieśni" (Norwid) **17**:374
"Kółko" (Norwid) **17**:373
"Kolokol kazni" (Bestuzhev) **131**:172
"A Kolozsiak" (Madach) **19**:369
"Kőltőés szabadság" (Madach) **19**:368
"A Kolyvan Husband" (Leskov)
See "Kolyvan'skii muzh"
"Kolyvan'skii muzh" (Leskov) **174**:35-36, 50, 90
Der Komet; oder, Nikolaus Marggraf: Eine komische Geschichte (Jean Paul) **7**:238-39, 242
Komische Erzählungen (Wieland)
See *Comische Erzählungen*
Kommer hid, I piger smaa! (Grundtvig) **158**:139
Kommer, Sjæle dyrekiøbte (Grundtvig) **158**:167
Kompositions-Verzeichnis (Schumann) **143**:120
"Komu na Rusi zhit khorosho" (Nekrasov) **11**:405-09, 413-15, 418-21
"The Kondem Phool" (Shaw) **15**:335
"Konec" (Turgenev) **122**:264-65
König (Arnim)
See *Königsbuch*
"König David" (Heine) **147**:229, 231
"König Etzels Schwert" (Meyer) **81**:207
"Der König in Thule" (Goethe) **34**:122
König Ottokars Glück und Ende (Grillparzer) **1**:383-84, 387, 395, 397; **102**:105, 107-08, 111, 115, 117, 165-66, 168, 180
"Die Königin Luise" (Klopstock) **11**:237; **225**:283, 298
"Die Königsbraut" (Hoffmann)
See "Königsbraut"
"Königsbraut" (Hoffmann) **183**:174-75, 197-99
Königsbuch (Arnim) **123**:9-15
Königsmark, the Legend of the Hounds, and other Poems (Boker) **125**:25, 33, 38, 58, 70, 76-78
"Königsmark the Robber; or, The Terror of Bohemia" (Lewis) **11**:302
Koningsmarke, the Long Finne: A Story of the New World (Paulding) **2**:527, 529-31
Konrad Wallenrod (Mickiewicz) **3**:389-92, 394-95, 398-99, 401; **101**:157, 171, 183-84, 197-201
Konradin (Klinger) **1**:429
"Konyága" (Saltykov) **16**:346, 373-74
"Kooroora" (Kendall) **12**:192, 201
Kopala kundala (Chatterji)
See *Kapalkundala*
Kordian (Slowacki) **15**:348, 352-53, 364-65, 369, 373, 375-76, 378-80
"Körner and His Sister" (Hemans) **71**:275
"Korobeyniki" (Nekrasov) **11**:407, 411, 413, 420-21
"Korrespondent" (Turgenev)
See "Peripiska"
"Eine Korrespondent mit mir selbst" (Claudius) **75**:209
"Korrespondenz zwischen mir und meinem Vetter, die Bibelübersetzungen betreffend" (Claudius) **75**:209-10
Kort Begreb af Verdens Krønike betragtet i Sammenhæng (Grundtvig) **158**:140-41, 147-54

Kort Begreb af Verdens Krønike i Sammenhæng (Grundtvig) **158**:101, 140-41, 147-54
Der Kosak und der Freiwillige (Kotzebue) **25**:140
"Kosme's Busse" (Brentano) **191**:8
"Kosmopolitische Addresse an die Französische Nazionalversammlung" (Wieland) **177**:276
"Kosmos" (Whitman) **205**:202
Kosmos: Entwurf einer physischen Weltbeschreibung (Humboldt) **170**:130, 133-39, 145-50, 152-54, 158, 161, 188
"Kossuth" (Whittier) **59**:371
"Kotin and Platonida" (Leskov)
See "Kotin doilec"
"Kotin doilec" (Leskov) **25**:239
"Kotin doilec i Platonida" (Leskov)
See "Kotin doilets i Platonida"
"Kotin doilets i Platonida" (Leskov) **174**:11-13, 62, 120, 123, 126
"Kotin the He-Cow and Platonida" (Leskov)
See "Kotin doilets i Platonida"
"Koto no Ne" (Ichiyō) **49**:335, 353
"Kotterii" (Baratynsky) **103**:11, 49
"Koxkox und Kikequetzel" (Wieland) **177**:257-58, 286, 363-66
Koz'ma Zakhar'ich Minin Sukoruk (Ostrovsky) **57**:206-7
Kozma Zakharich Minin the One-Armed (Ostrovsky)
See *Koz'ma Zakhar'ich Minin Sukoruk*
"Die Krähe" (Muller) **73**:394
Krak (Slowacki) **15**:353, 371
"The Kraken" (Tennyson) **30**:211, 233; **65**:280
Krakus (Norwid) **17**:366-67, 369, 376, 379
"Die Kraniche des Ibykus" (Schiller) **39**:330, 332, 337, 350; **166**:105
Kranjska čbelica (Preseren) **127**:304, 311-12, 315, 320, 329, 333
"Krasnoe polryvalo" (Bestuzhev) **131**:161
Krates und Hipparchia (Wieland) **17**:400-01
"Kreisleriana" (Hoffmann) **183**:222-23, 225, 236, 297, 310
Kreisleriana (Schumann) **143**:141
Kreisleriana, Kreislers musikalische Leiden (Hoffmann) **2**:346-47, 358-59
"Kreisler's Certificate" (Hoffmann)
See "Kreislers Lehrbrief"
"Kreislers Lehrbrief" (Hoffmann) **2**:346; **183**:226
"Kreislers musikalisch-poetischer Klub" (Hoffmann) **2**:347; **183**:166, 226
"Krempeljnu" (Preseren) **127**:314
"Krestyánskie déti" (Nekrasov) **11**:403, 421
"Das Kreuz" (Lenau) **16**:275, 281
Das Kreuz an der Ostsee: Ein Trauerspiel vom Verfasser der Söhne des Thales. Erster Theil: Die Brautnacht (Werner) **189**:319-20, 322, 331, 347, 360
Die Kreuzesbrüder (Werner)
See *Die Söhne des Thales: Ein dramatisches Gedicht*
Kreuzfahrer (Kotzebue) **25**:136
"Kriegslied" (Claudius) **75**:183, 194
Kriegslied (Klopstock) **225**:298
Kriegslied für die zum heiligen Kriege verbündeten deutschen Heere (Werner) **189**:356, 360
Kriemhilds Rache (Hebbel) **43**:261
Krigssåang för skånska lantvärnet (Tegner) **2**:612
"Krinken" (Field) **3**:211
Krishna charitra (Chatterji) **19**:204-05, 216, 222, 225
Krishna Kumāri (Dutt) **118**:5, 21, 23
Krishnakanter will (Chatterji) **19**:205, 209-10, 213, 215, 217-19, 221-22
Den Kristelige Børnelaerdom (Grundtvig)
See *Den Christelige Bornelærdom*
Kritik der Kantischen Philosophie (Schopenhauer) **157**:312
Kritik der praktischen Vernunft (Kant) **27**:196, 203-05, 208, 224, 229, 231, 246, 248, 251, 255, 257, 264; **67**:214, 216, 219-22, 252, 261, 264, 271, 288, 294-95
Kritik der reinen Vernunft (Kant) **27**:194-201, 203-05, 208-09, 220-26, 229, 231, 233, 246-48, 250-51, 253-57, 259-61, 263-64, 266-68, 270; **67**:212, 214, 216, 218-19, 222, 264, 287, 294
Kritik der Urtheilskraft (Kant) **27**:196, 203, 205, 210, 228, 231, 237, 248, 251, 255, 267; **67**:214
Kritik der Verfassung Deutschlands (Hegel) **46**:150
"Kritika na novyi roman Val'ter Skotta—Kenil'vort" (Bestuzhev) **131**:165
"Kritische Fragments" (Schlegel) **45**:358-59
Kritische Friedrich Schlegel Ausgabe (Schlegel) **45**:355, 357; **226**:158-60, 164-67, 170-73, 176-77, 188-91, 196-97, 236, 240-47
Kritische Schriften und Briefe (Schlegel) **142**:324, 343
Kritische Wälder (Herder) **8**:305, 307-08, 313-14; **186**:14-20, 36, 48, 86-87, 98
"Krivoklad" (Macha) **46**:201, 214
"The Krkonoše Pilgrimage" (Macha) **46**:210-12
"Krøblingen" (Andersen) **7**:28; **79**:77
"Krokodil" (Dostoevsky) **167**:292
Król Duch (Slowacki) **15**:349-50, 354, 356, 360-62, 365-66, 374-77
Die Kronenwächter (Arnim) **5**:13, 16-18, 20, 23; **159**:4-5, 35, 43, 67, 95
"Krónika két pénzdarab sorśaról" (Madach) **19**:369
"Kronos; To Coachman Kronos" (Goethe)
See "An Schwager Kronos"
Krösus (Grillparzer) **102**:105
"Krotkaya" (Dostoevsky) **2**:162; **33**:179-80
Krsnacaritra (Chatterji)
See *Krishna charitra*
Krsnakānter Uil (Chatterji)
See *Krishnakanter will*
Krst pri Svici: Povest v verzih (Preseren) **127**:293, 297, 308-10, 329-32
Kruglyi god (Saltykov) **16**:374
"Das Kruzifix" (Chamisso) **82**:27
"Krytyka" (Norwid) **17**:374
Ksiądz Marek (Slowacki) **15**:348, 352, 360, 365, 371, 378
Księgi narodu polskiego i pielgrzymastwa polskiego (Mickiewicz) **3**:388-89, 395, 397-98, 401; **101**:183-84
"Ktaadn" (Thoreau)
See "The Ascent of Ktaadn"
"Ktaadn, and the Maine Woods" (Thoreau) **138**:72, 115, 128-30, 148
Kto vinovat? (Herzen) **10**:321-3, 326-7, 331, 333-4, 348; **61**:97, 106-9, 113-5
Kuang fang-yen (Li Ju-chen) **137**:206
"Kubla Khan" (Coleridge) **9**:133-34, 140-42, 149, 151, 155, 158, 179-80, 182-83, 192-96, 204; **54**:82, 87, 89, 98-99, 106, 115; **99**:1-118; **111**:250, 258, 308; **177**:7-8, 27, 32, 38, 146, 149, 161; **197**:191, 193-94, 228, 233, 240, 243; **231**:16-18, 21, 56-57, 62, 67-72, 82, 114, 116, 130, 133-35, 154, 156
"Kubla Khan: A Vision" (Coleridge)
See "Kubla Khan"
Kullervo (Kivi) **30**:48, 54-6, 58-62, 64
"Kulneff" (Runeberg) **41**:312, 323
Die Kultur der Renaissance in Italien (Burckhardt) **49**:3, 11, 16-6, 20-1, 23-4, 27, 29-30, 32
Kulturgeschichte (Burckhardt)
See *Griechische Kulturgeschichte*
Kun en spillemand (Andersen) **7**:15-16, 21, 26, 33; **79**:18-19, 21; **214**:33, 74, 79
"Kun László Krónikája" (Petofi) **21**:264
"Kundiman" (Rizal) **27**:425
"Die Künftiege Geliebte" (Klopstock) **11**:236
Die künftige Geliebte (Klopstock) **225**:296
Kung Fjalar (Runeberg) **41**:310, 317-18, 325
Kungarne på Salamis (Runeberg) **41**:310, 318
"Die Kunst Tialfs" (Klopstock) **225**:310
Die Kunst und die Revolution (Wagner) **9**:404, 425-26, 432, 452; **119**:238, 248-53, 256-58
"Die Künstler" (Schiller) **39**:336, 389; **166**:100, 102-3, 119
Das Kunstwerk der Zukunft (Wagner) **9**:405, 425, 432-33, 452; **119**:238, 248-53, 257-60, 274, 294, 323
"Kurze Freude" (Meyer) **81**:147
Kurze Ubersicht der Manufakturen in Russland (Kotzebue) **25**:141
Kuse monogatari (Ueda Akinari) **131**:19, 36, 40, 51
"A kutyák dala" (Petofi) **21**:264
"Kutyakaparó" (Petofi) **21**:260, 277, 285
"Kúza-Náma" (FitzGerald) **153**:213-14
Kuzubana (Motoori) **45**:275-76
"The Kyffhäuser and its Legends" (Taylor) **89**:312
"Kyozukue" (Ichiyō) **49**:352
"Kyrkan" (Runeberg) **41**:318
"L. E. L.'s Last Question" (Barrett Browning) **16**:133; **61**:51; **170**:121
L6T (Leskov)
See *Sobranie sochinenii v shesti tomakh*
L11T (Leskov)
See *Sobranie sochinenii v odinnadtsati tomakh*
"A la Belleza" (Casal) **131**:270-71
"De la bonne doctrine" (Banville) **9**:16
"A la castidad" (Casal) **131**:255, 267
"De la Cause des Hellènes" (Chateaubriand) **134**:8
"De la Clôture de la session de la Chambre des Pairs" (Chateaubriand) **134**:8
"À la Colonne de la Place Vendôme" (Hugo) **161**:186-87
De la démocratie en Amérique (Tocqueville) **7**:417-25, 427, 429, 432-34, 440, 443-46, 448-53, 455-56, 458-59, 461; **63**:279, 281-4, 287-8, 290-3, 297-302, 304, 306, 308, 316-23, 326, 328, 332-3, 336, 342, 352-4, 357-60, 366-8, 371-2, 379, 388, 391
De la educación popular (Sarmiento) **123**:288, 330, 360
A la Feuille de Rose (Maupassant) **83**:199-201, 203
De la Fondation-Goethe à Weimar (Liszt) **199**:298, 305, 326, 337, 343
De la force du gouvernement actuel de la France et de la nécessité de s'y rallier (Constant) **182**:199-201, 203
"A la juventud Filipina" (Rizal) **27**:425
De la liberté chez les modernes (Constant) **182**:134
"De la liberté de la presse" (Constant) **182**:136
"De la liberté des Anciens comparée à celle des Modernes" (Constant) **182**:212, 230, 232, 238-39
"De la liberté religieuse" (Constant) **182**:136
De la littérature considérée dans ses rapports avec les institutions sociales (Staël-Holstein) **3**:519, 524, 527-8, 530-3; **91**:298, 304-6, 310-12, 323-4, 326, 332, 340, 359
"De la littérature dans ses raports avec la liberté" (Constant) **6**:224
"A la luna" (Espronceda) **39**:105-06
"De la misère en Allemagne" (Arnim) **123**:5
"De la monarchie constitutionelle en France" (Renan) **26**:377
De la monarchie selon la charte (Chateaubriand) **3**:110, 112; **134**:5
"A la muerte" (Manzano) **155**:307
"A la muerte de Don Joaquín de Pablo (Chapalangarra)" (Espronceda) **39**:105
"À la musique" (Rimbaud) **4**:485; **35**:289-90
"A la noche" (Heredia) **209**:129
"A la nue accablante tu" (Mallarmé) **41**:250,

294; **210**:163, 241, 244
"A la patria" (Espronceda) **39**:100, 105
"A la paz" (Heredia) **209**:136
"A la poesía" (Gómez de Avellaneda) **111**:28
De la religion considérée dans sa source, ses formes, et ses développements (Constant) **6**:213, 221; **182**:173, 212, 221, 225, 239
La Salle and the Discovery of the Great West (Parkman) **12**:336, 341, 372, 378-79
"La Salle Painted by Himself" (Parkman) **12**:378
"De la sátira y los satíricos" (Larra) **130**:238, 241, 276
De la situation des artistes et de leur condition dans la société (Liszt) **199**:304, 306, 311, 335-37, 343, 345-48
"De la souveraineté du peuple" (Constant) **182**:99-100, 132
"A la Srta. C. O. Y. R." (Rizal) **27**:425
"A la traslación de las cenizas de Napoleón" (Espronceda) **39**:120
El Laberinto (Gómez de Avellaneda) **111**:21
"The Laboratory" (Browning) **19**:77, 96; **79**:94, 99
"The Laboring Classes" (Brownson) **50**:31, 42, 48
"The Laboring Skeleton" (Baudelaire)
See "Le squelette laboureur"
Labour and Capital: A Lecture . . . to Which Are Appended in Full the Leading Articles Thereon from the "Saturday Review," the "Times," and the "Pall Mall Gazette," with Answers Thereto (Jones) **222**:121
"The Labourer's Daily Life" (Jefferies) **47**:141
The Labourers of the Ten Little Hard Parishes to Alexander Baring, Loan-Monger (Cobbett) **49**:113
"Les laboureurs" (Lamartine) **11**:274, 284
"Labour's History" (Jones) **222**:124-25, 157
Labours of Idleness; or, Seven Night's Entertainments (Darley) **2**:127, 129-30
"Le lac" (Lamartine) **11**:245, 248, 263-64, 268-70, 277-78, 280-82; **190**:219, 223-25, 245-49, 252-53
"Le Lac de B . . ." (Lamartine)
See "Le lac"
Le Lac de Wallenstadt (Liszt) **199**:307
Le lac des fées (Scribe) **16**:410
"À l'Académie de Marseille, Gethsémani" (Lamartine) **11**:271
"The Lace Runners" (Tonna) **135**:199-200, 209-10, 213, 216, 220-23
"Lacinularia Socialis" (Huxley) **67**:79-80
Lack of Caution (Turgenev) **21**:428
"Lack of Funds" (Turgenev)
See *Bezdenezh'e*
Lack of Funds (Turgenev)
See *Bezdenezh'e*
"Lacordaire and Catholic Progress" (Brownson) **50**:51
"L'acropole officielle . . ." (Rimbaud)
See "Villes II"
"Lad of Athens, faithful be" (Dickinson) **171**:143
"Ladder of St. Augustine" (Longfellow) **45**:116, 127
Ladies and Hussars (Fredro)
See *Damy i huzary*
The Ladies' Battle (Reade) **74**:331
The Ladies' Battle (Robertson) **35**:354
The Ladies' Battle; or, A Duel of Love (Scribe)
See *Bataille de dames; ou, Un duel en amour*
The Ladies' Family Library (Child) **6**:198; **73**:97, 100
The Ladies Lindores (Oliphant) **11**:439, 441, 445-7; **61**:204, 206, 208-9, 240; **221**:230
The Ladies of Castile (Warren) **13**:412-14, 418-19, 429-30, 436; **226**:253, 259-60, 268-69, 272-74, 278-81, 289, 292, 295-97, 299-300, 302
"The Ladies of the Sacred Heart" (Sedgwick) **19**:446
The Ladies' Wreath (Hale) **75**:337, 341, 349
"Ladislaus the Fifth" (Arany)
See "László V"
"Ladraban contra min" (Castro) **78**:42
Ladugårdsarrebnet (Almqvist) **42**:4
Lady Adelaide's Oath (Wood) **178**:291
"Lady Alice" (Allingham) **25**:18
"The Lady and the Gawk" (Leskov)
See "Dama i fefela"
"The Lady and the Slut" (Leskov)
See "Dama i fefela"
Lady Anna (Trollope) **6**:470, 475; **101**:249, 251, 253, 310, 313; **215**:208
"Lady Anne and Lady Jane" (Opie) **65**:171-2
"Lady Barbara" (Crabbe) **26**:129
"Lady Barbara" (Smith) **59**:320, 331, 333
Lady Byron Vindicated: A History of the Byron Controversy, from Its Beginning in 1816 to the Present Time (Stowe) **3**:556, 562
Lady Car (Oliphant) **61**:208
"Lady Clara Vere de Vere" (Tennyson) **202**:334
"Lady Eleanor's Mantle" (Hawthorne) **191**:189
The Lady from the Provinces (Turgenev)
See *Provintsialka*
"Lady Geraldine's Courtship" (Barrett Browning) **1**:114-8, 125-7; **61**:4, 42, 65-7, 75; **66**:44-5, 56, 71, 74, 87-91, 93, 101; **170**:56
Lady Grace (Wood) **178**:291
"Lady Griseld Baillie" (Baillie)
See "The Legend of Lady Griseld Baillie"
"Lady into Peasant" (Pushkin)
See "Baryshnia-krest'ianka"
"Lady Jane" (Willis) **194**:305
The Lady Jane and Other Humorous Poems (Willis) **194**:306
Lady Johanna Gray (Wieland) **17**:419-20; **177**:229, 234, 250
"The Lady Lisle and Elizabeth Gaunt" (Landor) **14**:185
"Lady Macbeth" (Galt) **1**:327
"Lady Macbeth" (Maginn) **8**:439, 442
"The Lady Macbeth from the Mtsensk District" (Leskov)
See "Ledi Makbet Mcenskogo uezda"
"A Lady Macbeth of the Mtsensk District" (Leskov)
See "Ledi Makbet Mcenskogo uezda"
Lady Mary and Her Nurse; or, A Peep into the Canadian Forest (Traill) **31**:316, 327
"Lady Montrevor" (Rossetti) **186**:275-76
"Lady Moon, Lady Moon" (Milnes) **61**:154
Lady Morgan's Memoirs (Morgan) **29**:394
"The Lady of Amboto" (Gómez de Avellaneda)
See "La dama de Amboto"
The Lady of La Garaye (Norton) **47**:245-46, 248, 252; **205**:53-54, 69, 86
"The Lady of Little Fishing" (Woolson) **82**:272, 286, 293-94, 306, 322, 334
The Lady of Lyons; or, Love and Pride (Bulwer-Lytton) **1**:140; **45**:18, 62, 69
"Lady Ravelgold" (Willis) **194**:298
"The Lady of Shalott" (Tennyson) **30**:206, 211-12, 222-23, 231, 241, 258, 267, 279; **65**:234, 240, 337, 357; **115**:335, 358; **202**:184, 186, 188, 211, 218, 237, 311-12, 314-15, 317
"A Lady of Sorrow" (Thomson) **18**:393, 400-1, 407, 412-13, 421, 424-25, 427
"The Lady of the Black Tower" (Robinson) **142**:180-82
The Lady of the Camelias (Dumas)
See *La dame aux camélias*
"The Lady of the Castle" (Hemans) **29**:198; **71**:288
The Lady of the Ice (De Mille) **123**:119
The Lady of the Lake (Scott) **15**:256, 273, 283, 292-93, 318-19; **69**:304, 361
The Lady of the Lake (Thelwall) **162**:299
The Lady of the Lake: A Poem (Scott) **209**:181, 188-89, 191-93, 253-57
"The Lady of the Land" (Morris) **4**:442, 448
The Lady of the Rock (Holcroft) **85**:199, 212, 218, 224-25
"The Lady of the Sea" (Allingham) **25**:12
"The Lady of Title" (Jones) **222**:146
Lady Susan (Austen) **1**:35-36, 39, 51-52; **33**:86; **119**:17, 26, 30, 44-5; **207**:46
"The Lady Turned Peasant" (Pushkin)
See "Baryshnia-krest'ianka"
Lady und Schnieder (Nestroy) **42**:233-35, 237, 249-50
Lady William (Oliphant) **61**:202
The Ladye Annabel; or, The Doom of the Poisoner: A Romance by an Unknown Author (Lippard) **198**:121, 135, 144, 166, 168-69, 180-81, 208
The Ladye of Albarone; or, The Poison Goblet: A Romance of the Dark Ages (Lippard)
See *The Ladye Annabel; or, The Doom of the Poisoner: A Romance by an Unknown Author*
"The Ladye of Provence" (Reynolds) **146**:191
"The Lady-Peasant" (Pushkin)
See "Baryshnia-krest'ianka"
A Lady's Diary (Jameson)
See *Diary of an Ennuyée*
"The Lady's Dream" (Hood) **16**:209, 220, 235
The Lady's Maid (Martineau) **26**:322
"The Lady's Mistake" (Osgood) **141**:332
"Laeti et errabundi" (Verlaine) **51**:356, 363, 372; **230**:165
"Lafayette en Amérique" (Beranger) **34**:29
Die Lage der arbeitenden Klasse in England (Engels) **85**:3-6, 8, 13, 31, 110-11, 113-15, 121, 125, 165, 171-72, 177, 179-81, 184; **114**:4, 35, 41, 73
Lágrimas: Novela de costumbres contemporáneas (Caballero) **10**:76
"Laida" (Echeverria) **18**:148
The Laird of Norlaw (Oliphant) **11**:432; **221**:226, 244
"The Laird of Peatstacknowe's Tale" (Hogg) **4**:287
Laïs (Eminescu) **33**:267
"Laisser-courre" (Corbière) **43**:31
La laitière de Montfermeil (Kock) **16**:245, 249
"The Lake" (Eminescu) **131**:296
"The Lake" (Lamartine)
See "Le lac"
"The Lake" (Melville) **3**:352
"The Lake in the Forest" (Lampman) **194**:30
"Lake Ontario" (Willis) **194**:282
The Lake Regions of Central Equatorial Africa (Burton) **42**:41, 58
"Lake Zurich" (Klopstock) **11**:220
Lake-Country Sketches (Woolson)
See *Castle Nowhere: Lake Country Sketches*
"The Lake—To—" (Poe) **117**:266, 271-72, 281, 283
Lalla Rookh (Moore) **6**:378-81, 386-88, 391, 393, 396, 399; **110**:165-68, 171, 175-76, 189, 202-3, 211-13, 216, 219-25
De l'Allemagne (Heine)
See *Deutschland: Ein Wintermärchen*
De l'Allemagne (Staël-Holstein) **3**:520, 526-8, 530, 532-4; **91**:338, 340, 350-1, 359-60, 365
"The Lamb" (Blake) **13**:180-82, 221, 241-45; **37**:3, 6, 9, 12, 39, 54, 57, 65, 69, 76, 91-2
"The Lamb" (Krylov) **1**:435
Lambro (Slowacki) **15**:348, 358, 363-64, 376
"O Lambros" (Solomos) **15**:386, 389, 393-94, 396-97, 405
"Lame Jervas" (Edgeworth) **51**:87, 89
"The Lament for Captain Paton" (Lockhart) **6**:293
"A Lament for Kilcash" (Mangan) **27**:315
"Lament for Sarsfield" (Mangan) **27**:279
"A Lament for the Birds" (Cooper) **129**:35, 72
"Lament for the Decline of Chivalry" (Hood) **16**:219

"Lament for the Princes of Tyrone and Tyrconnell" (Mangan) **27**:296-98, 310-12, 319
"Lament of a Birch Tree's Spirit" (Aksakov)
See "Plach dukha berezy"
"The Lament of a Canadian Emigrant" (Moodie) **113**:345
"Lament of Difficult Puberties" (Laforgue)
See "Complaintes des pubertés difficiles"
"Lament of Good Households" (Laforgue)
See "Complainte des bons ménages"
"The Lament of King Cormac" (Mangan) **27**:314
"Lament of Nuptial Formalities" (Laforgue)
See "Complainte des formalités nuptiales"
"The Lament of Swordy Well" (Clare) **9**:108, 110, 118; **86**:131-32, 178
The Lament of Tasso (Byron) **2**:64, 96; **12**:106
"Lament of the Agricultural Show Night" (Laforgue)
See "Complainte du soir des comices agricoles"
"Lament of the Poor Knight Errant" (Laforgue)
See "Complainte du pauvre chevalier-errant"
"Lament of the Springtime" (Laforgue)
See "Complainte des printemps"
"Lament of the Weary Wind at Night" (Laforgue)
See "Complainte du vent qui s'ennuie la nuit"
"Lament of the Winds" (Lampman) **25**:204; **194**:123-25, 128-29
"Lament of Voices beneath the Buddha Tree" (Laforgue)
See "Complainte des voix sous le figuier boudhique"
"The Lament of Youth" (Chivers) **49**:48, 69-70
"Lament on the Death of My Mother" (Chivers) **49**:39
"Lament over the Ruins of the Abbey of Teach Molaga" (Mangan) **27**:319
"A Lamentation" (Baillie) **151**:95
"Lamentation" (Hölderlin)
See "Menons Klagen um Diotima"
"Lamentation for his Daughter's Death" (Thelwall) **162**:303
"Lamentation for the Death of Sir Maurice Fitzgerald" (Mangan) **27**:290, 310-11
"Lamentation of Mac Liag for Kincora" (Mangan) **27**:297, 310-12
"Lamentationen" (Heine) **4**:254-55; **147**:162, 229, 231, 234
"The Lamentations of Round Oak Waters" (Clare) **9**:119
"Lament—Epitaph" (Laforgue)
See "Complainte—épitaphe"
"Lament—My Sacred Heart Litanies" (Laforgue)
See "Complaintes-litanies de mon sacré-coeur"
"Lament—Petition of Faust Son" (Laforgue)
See "Complainte-placet de Faust fils"
"Lamia" (Keats) **8**:333-34, 340-41, 345, 347, 350, 356-57, 360-61, 366, 370, 375, 383, 385-86; **73**:154-55, 171-73, 190, 198, 202, 208-09, 212-13, 218, 228, 232-34, 255, 261-62, 277, 285, 304, 306-07, 322, 325, 328; **225**:162-63, 169, 174, 177, 184, 197, 237, 270
Lamia (Hood) **16**:229
Lamia, Isabella, The Eve of St. Agnes, and Other Poems (Keats) **8**:326-28, 331-32, 340, 350; **73**:155, 197, 233; **121**:108, 112, 154, 165, 173, 162
Lamiel (Stendhal) **23**:384, 395, 397, 409, 418-19; **46**:318; **178**:147, 149, 153-56, 197-202
De l'amour (Stendhal) **23**:347, 368, 374, 423; **46**:262, 273, 276, 323-24, 327-28; **178**:167, 169, 173-79, 190, 201-2, 227-33, 235-37
"La lampe du temple" (Lamartine) **11**:279
The Lamplighter (Cummins) **139**:161-64, 166-68, 170-76, 178, 180-87, 190-94, 198-201, 204-5, 207-9, 213-14, 216, 220, 222, 224, 226-28
The Lamplighter Picture Book, or the Story of Uncle True and Little Gerty, Written for the Little Folks (Cummins) **139**:183
"The Lamp's Shrine" (Rossetti) **77**:339
Lancashire Collier Girl (More) **27**:358; **141**:166-67, 169, 172, 188, 291
The Lancashire Witches: A Romance of Pendle Forest (Ainsworth) **13**:37, 40-1, 47-8
"Lancelot and Elaine" (Tennyson) **202**:206, 208-12, 248-49, 311-13, 317
Lances de honor (Tamayo y Baus) **1**:565, 569
"Land East of the Sun and West of the Moon" (Morris) **4**:416-17, 447
"The Land of Dreams" (Blake) **13**:181, 243
"The Land of Dreams" (Bryant) **46**:39
"The Land of Dreams" (Hemans) **29**:205
Land of Midian Revisited (Burton) **42**:41, 56
"The Land of Pallas" (Lampman) **25**:184, 193-94, 196, 201, 204, 211, 220; **194**:9-11, 18, 22, 24-25, 29, 61-62, 113, 118, 120
The Land of Pallas and Other Poems (Lampman) **194**:79
"The Land of Paoli" (Taylor) **89**:313
"The Land of the Living" (Grundtvig) **158**:122
The Land of Upside Down (Tieck)
See *Die Verkehrte Welt*
Ein Landarzt (Stifter) **198**:282
Landbote (Büchner)
See *Der Hessische Landbote*
Das Landhaus am Rhein (Auerbach) **171**:5, 7, 10-12, 16, 19, 39-40
"The Landing of the Pilgrim Fathers" (Hemans) **71**:271, 283
"The Landlady" (Dostoevsky)
See "Khozyaika"
The Landleaguers (Trollope) **6**:471, 495, 500; **101**:245-46, 250-53, 262, 264, 267, 276, 293-94, 296, 298-99, 319
Ländliche Lieder (Muller) **73**:352, 362, 366-67, 387
"The Landlord" (Thoreau) **138**:121
"Landlord and Tenant" (Carleton) **199**:65
"The Landlord's Visit, a Drama" (Barbauld) **185**:57
Landmarks of Homeric Study (Gladstone) **213**:125-28
Landolin von Reutershöfen (Auerbach) **171**:20
"Landor, English Visiter and Florentine Visiter" (Landor) **14**:195
"Landor's Cottage" (Poe) **16**:304, 336; **55**:147, 153; **97**:184, 187; **117**:310
"The Landowner" (Turgenev) **122**:293
The Lands of the Saracen (Taylor) **89**:346
"The Landscape Garden" (Poe)
See "Landscape Gardening"
"Landscape Gardening" (Poe) **16**:304; **97**:186
"Landscapes" (Baudelaire)
See "Paysages"
"Landscapes" (Crèvecoeur) **105**:102, 125, 177-94
"Landshövdingen" (Runeberg) **41**:325-27
"The Lane" (Barnes)
See "The Leane"
"Lánggal égo" (Petofi) **21**:283
"Language" (Emerson) **38**:178
"Language" (Peabody) **169**:171-72, 200, 202-3
"The Language of Religion" (Patmore) **9**:341
"Langueur" (Verlaine) **51**:360; **230**:215
Lanrick (Dodgson) **139**:57
"The Lantern Out of Doors" (Hopkins) **17**:185, 220, 244; **189**:114, 147
"The Lantern-Bearers" (Stevenson) **5**:410; **63**:239
La lanterne magique (Banville) **9**:21
Lant-virágok (Madach) **19**:368
"Laocoön" (Beddoes) **154**:94
"The Laocoön" (Blake) **127**:53-54, 124; **173**:153, 157; **190**:97
"Laodamia" (Wordsworth) **12**:414, 427, 459; **38**:356; **166**:205, 212; **206**:224, 247
Laon and Cythna (Shelley)
See *Laon and Cythna; or, The Revolution of the Golden City: A Vision of the Nineteenth Century*
Laon and Cythna; or, The Revolution of the Golden City: A Vision of the Nineteenth Century (Shelley) **18**:308, 311, 313-14, 319, 332, 334, 336, 338, 342, 344, 347, 379-81, 384; **93**:267, 270, 292-96, 298, 300, 331-32, 334, 336, 338, 340-41, 355; **143**:188, 196-97, 230, 238, 266; **175**:202-3, 217-18, 220, 231, 237, 239-40, 246, 268, 275, 286, 318-19, 324-25
"Lappen og Professoren" (Andersen)
See "The Professor and the Flea"
"The Lapse of Time" (Bryant) **6**:159-60, 172
"Lapsi" (Kivi) **30**:51
"Laquelle des deux? Histoire perplexe" (Gautier) **59**:29
"Laquelle est la vraie?" (Baudelaire) **29**:110; **155**:28-29
Lara (Byron) **2**:62, 70, 73, 81, 86, 89, 95, 99; **12**:82; **109**:102; **149**:25, 78, 165
"The Largest Life" (Lampman) **25**:163, 190, 217; **194**:15, 34, 71, 129
"A Lark's Flight" (Smith) **59**:303, 309, 311, 315, 317, 319, 323
"Larks in Vacation" (Willis) **194**:282, 298
"The Lark's Nest" (Clare) **9**:108, 110
"Larme" (Rimbaud) **4**:472, 478; **82**:231-33, 247-48; **227**:213
"Une larme du diable" (Gautier) **1**:339, 345
"Les larmes de l'ours" (Leconte de Lisle) **29**:230
"Larmes de Racine" (Sainte-Beuve) **5**:342
"Larry McFarland's Wake" (Carleton) **199**:33
"Larry M'Farland's Wake" (Carleton) **3**:89, 92
Lars: A Pastoral of Norway (Taylor) **89**:315, 349
"A las cubanas" (Gómez de Avellaneda) **111**:30, 65
The Las Essays of Elia. Being a Sequel to Essays Published under that Name (Lamb) **113**:198, 217-218, 221, 228, 247, 252-53, 261, 265, 281, 282-84
"A las flores de Heidelberg" (Rizal) **27**:425
De las Monarchie selon la Charte (Chateaubriand) **134**:5
"The Lascar" (Robinson) **142**:137, 150-51, 249, 251
"Lass die heilgen Parabolen" (Heine) **4**:257
"The Lass of Carrick" (Mangan) **27**:314
"The Lass of the Pamunky" (Child) **173**:210
"Lassitude" (Laforgue) **221**:88
"Lasso a Me!" (Dacre) **151**:148
The Last (Krasiński)
See *Ostatni*
"A Last Adieu" (Hogg) **109**:202
"The Last Banquet of Antony and Cleopatra" (Hemans) **71**:295
The Last Baron of Crana (Banim and Banim) **13**:121, 129-31, 135-37, 147, 149-51
"The Last Buccaneer" (Kingsley) **35**:227
The Last Buccaneer (Macaulay) **42**:88
"Last Canto of Childe Harold" (Lamartine)
See "Le dernier chant de pèlerinage de Childe Harold"
"Last Child" (Lampman) **25**:216
The Last Chronicle of Barset (Trollope) **6**:458, 461, 467, 470-71, 479, 484, 491-92, 494, 497-98, 507, 509, 516-17; **33**:363, 417-18, 422; **101**:235, 265-66, 272-74, 279, 285, 289, 320-21, 326, 333, 342-43; **215**:212, 215, 226, 283-87, 307
"A Last Confession" (Rossetti) **4**:495-97, 500-03, 507-08, 510-12, 518-19, 523-24, 526-27; **77**:286-7, 293, 304, 317, 337
The Last Constantine, with Other Poems (Hemans) **29**:202
The Last Day of a Condemned (Hugo)
See *Le dernier jour d'un condamné*

The Last Day of a Condemned Man (Hugo)
See *Le dernier jour d'un condamné*
"The Last Day of Castle Connor" (Le Fanu) **9**:320
"The Last Days of a Criminal" (Hood) **16**:203
"The Last Days of John Brown" (Thoreau) **7**:406; **207**:283, 335, 340-42
The Last Days of Pompeii (Bulwer-Lytton) **1**:136-38, 140, 146, 149-53; **45**:3, 5, 13, 22, 27, 29, 32-3, 55-7, 62, 68-70
"The Last Death" (Baratynsky)
See "Poslednyaya smert'"
"The Last Dream of the Old Oak" (Andersen)
See "Det gamle Egetæs sidste Drøm"
The Last Essays of Elia (Lamb) **10**:392, 435-37
Last Essays on Church and Religion (Arnold) **6**:53; **29**:21; **89**:65, 131; **126**:90-91; **218**:127-28
Last Evening with Allston, and Other Papers (Peabody) **169**:146, 151, 157, 193, 195
"The Last Fifteen Years of the Bourbons" (Thackeray) **213**:220
Last Foray in Lithuania (Mickiewicz)
See *Pan Tadeusz; czyli, Ostatni zajazd na Litwie*
"The Last Frost of Spring" (Ichiyō)
See "Wakerejimo"
The Last Fruit off an Old Tree (Landor) **14**:169-70
"The Last Generation in England" (Gaskell) **97**:110, 121, 127, 167-68
"The Last Judgement" (Macha)
See "Poslednì soud"
"The Last Judgment" (Levy) **59**:93
"The Last King of Orplid" (Mörike)
See "Der letzte König von Orplid"
"The Last Lamp of the Alley" (Maginn) **8**:441
"The Last Leaf" (Holmes) **14**:100-01, 109, 120-21, 125, 129, 132; **81**:107
"The Last Leap" (Gordon) **21**:159, 181, 186
Last Leaves (Smith) **59**:298-9, 306, 308, 311, 314, 317, 319-23, 333, 337, 340
Last Letters (Foscolo)
See *Ultime lettere di Jacopo Ortis*
The Last Letters of Aubrey Beardsley (Beardsley) **6**:138
The Last Letters of Jacopo Ortis (Foscolo)
See *Ultime lettere di Jacopo Ortis*
Last Letters of Ortis (Foscolo)
See *Ultime lettere di Jacopo Ortis*
"Last Love" (Tyutchev) **34**:403
"The Last Man" (Beddoes) **154**:88
"The Last Man" (Campbell) **19**:176, 179, 181, 187, 190, 192, 196, 198
"The Last Man" (Hood) **16**:202, 231-34
The Last Man (Beddoes) **3**:37-39; **154**:13
The Last Man (Shelley) **14**:253-54, 256, 262, 265, 267, 269-71, 274-76, 290, 292-93, 299; **59**:144, 155, 177, 195; **103**:329, 331-33, 338-40, 348; **170**:226-27, 260, 288, 303
"The Last National Revolt of the Jews" (Lazarus) **8**:424
"The Last Night that She Lived" (Dickinson) **21**:35
"Last Norridgewock" (Whittier) **8**:485
"The Last of His Tribe" (Kendall) **12**:190-92, 196, 201
"The Last of Macquarie Harbour" (Clarke) **19**:257
The Last of the Barons (Bulwer-Lytton) **1**:140-41, 146, 150-52; **45**:14-15, 21, 58-60, 62, 70
The Last of the Family (Cumberland) **167**:192
"The Last of the Flock" (Wordsworth) **12**:386-87; **111**:202-3, 208, 210, 224, 234, 253, 307, 311, 315, 359
The Last of the Foresters; or, Humors on the Border: A Story of the Old Virginia Frontier (Cooke) **5**:122, 128-29, 131, 133-34, 136
The Last of the Huggermuggers (Cranch) **115**:16-17, 54-9
The Last of the Lairds; or, The Life and Opinions of Malachi Mailings, Esq. of Auldbiggings (Galt) **1**:332, 334-35, 337; **110**:76-7, 96
The Last of the Mohicans (Cooper)
See *The Last of the Mohicans: A Narrative of 1757*
The Last of the Mohicans: A Narrative of 1757 (Cooper) **1**:197-200, 202-03, 205, 207, 212, 217, 221, 225; **27**:124, 127-36, 138, 140-44, 147, 150, 153-54, 157, 160-67, 172-73, 175-79, 181, 183-85, 187; **54**:254, 267, 269, 271, 283-4, 286-7, 299, 301; **203**:11, 15-17, 19, 21, 32-36, 38-39, 86-87, 105-9, 111-14, 117, 119, 143-46, 148-53, 156-58, 162-63
The Last of the Mortimers (Oliphant) **11**:446
The Last of the Mușat Kin (Eminescu) **33**:264
"The Last of the War Cases" (Whitman) **4**:554
"The Last of Ulysses" (Landor) **14**:181
Last Poems (Barrett Browning) **1**:121; **61**:44; **170**:67, 82, 115-16, 121-22
Last Poems (Heine) **4**:238
Last Poems (Laforgue)
See *Les derniers vers de Jules Laforgue*
Last Poems (Lowell) **2**:512; **90**:188
Last Poems, 1821-1850 (Wordsworth) **206**:320-21
The Last Poems of Philip Freneau (Freneau) **111**:162, 190
"The Last Poet" (Baratynsky)
See "Posledny poet"
"Last Public Address" (Lincoln)
See "Farewell Address at Springfield, Illinois"
"The Last Reader" (Holmes) **14**:98-100
"The Last Ride Together" (Browning) **19**:127, 131
"The Last Song of Sappho" (Hemans) **71**:296
"Last Songs" (Nekrasov) **11**:407
"Last Speech in Springfield, Illinois, in the Campaign of 1858" (Lincoln) **201**:159, 163
"The Last Sunset" (Isaacs)
See "El último arrebol"
"The Last Tournament" (Tennyson) **202**:212-14
"The Last Walk in Autumn" (Whittier) **8**:517; **59**:360, 366, 368
Last Words (Arnold) **29**:54
"The Last Words of Al-Hassan" (Mangan) **27**:287, 290
"The Last Words of Charles Edwards" (Maginn) **8**:438
"The Last Words of Stonewall Jackson" (Lanier) **6**:237
"László V" (Arany) **34**:15, 20
"Late November" (Lampman) **25**:182; **194**:13
The Late Summer (Stifter)
See *Der Nachsommer*
Later Letters of Edward Lear (Lear) **3**:299
"Later Life" (Rossetti) **2**:563, 566, 570, 575; **50**:272, 284, 292
Later Poems (Whittier) **8**:495
The Later Poems of John Clare 1837-1864 (Clare) **86**:198, 111, 113-15, 117-22, 162, 166, 170, 180
"Laterna Magica" (Pavlova) **138**:51
"The Latest Decalogue" (Clough) **27**:83-4, 91, 103, 114
"The Latest Decalogue" (Prescott) **163**:6, 11, 42, 55
"Latnik: Rasskaz partizanskogo ofitsera" (Bestuzhev) **131**:156-59, 175-76
"The Latter Rain" (Very) **9**:380, 385
Latter-Day Pamphlets (Carlyle) **70**:72, 82, 91
Latter-Day Pamphlets (Froude) **43**:218
"Der Laudachsee" (Lenau) **16**:283
"Laudamus" (Gordon) **21**:160, 164, 175
Laughable Lyrics (Lear)
See *Laughable Lyrics: A Fourth Book of Nonsense Poems, Songs, Botany, Music, Etc.*
Laughable Lyrics: A Fourth Book of Nonsense Poems, Songs, Botany, Music, Etc. (Lear) **3**:296-97, 309
"Laughing Life Cries at the Feast" (Rossetti) **66**:307
"The Laughing Song" (Blake) **37**:3, 9, 13, 40, 61, 65, 71-2, 78-9, 91-2
"Laughter" (Crawford) **12**:156
"Laughter and Grief" (Leskov)
See "Smekh i gore"
"Laughter and Woe" (Leskov)
See "Smekh i gore"
"Die Laune der Verliebten" (Heine) **147**:232
Die Launen des Glückes (Nestroy) **42**:238, 257
"Launfal" (Lowell) **90**:198
Laura (Sand) **42**:359, 363
"Laurance" (Ingelow) **107**:148
"The Laurels of Immortality" (Derzhavin) **215**:15-16
"Laurette; ou, Le cachet rouge" (Vigny) **7**:478
"Laus Deo" (Whittier) **8**:515, 531; **59**:360-1, 385
"Laus Mariae" (Lanier) **118**:215
"Laus Veneris" (Rossetti) **186**:290
"Der Lautenbacher" (Auerbach) **171**:68
Lautréamont's Maldoror (Lautréamont)
See *Les chants de Maldoror: Chants I, II, III, IV, V, VI*
Lautréamont's Preface to His Unwritten Volume of Poems (Lautréamont)
See *Poésies I, II*
Lavengro: The Scholar—The Gypsy—The Priest (Borrow) **9**:40-56, 60-9
The Law and the Lady (Collins) **1**:188, 191
"Law as Suited to Man" (Dana) **53**:180-1
Law Miscellanies (Brackenridge) **227**:64, 105
Lawrence Bloomfield in Ireland (Allingham) **25**:10-11, 13, 16, 18-19, 21-3, 26-7, 29, 31-4
Lawrie Todd; or, The Settlers in the Woods (Galt) **1**:330-31
"The Laws Concerning Women" (Oliphant) **221**:256
"Laws for Creation" (Whitman) **205**:162, 165
"Laws of God and the Statutes of Men" (Parker) **186**:132
The Lawton Girl (Frederic) **10**:183-84, 187-88, 192-93, 201, 203-04, 209, 211, 213-14; **175**:149, 154
The Lawyers (Lewes) **25**:291
"The Lawyer's First Tale" (Clough) **27**:81
"Lawyer's Second Tale" (Prescott) **163**:8
"Lay Morals" (Stevenson) **193**:262
"The Lay of a Golden Goose" (Alcott) **58**:6
The Lay of Maldoror (Lautréamont)
See *Les chants de Maldoror: Chants I, II, III, IV, V, VI*
The lay of St. Cuthbert (Barham) **77**:9
"A Lay of St. Dunstan" (Barham) **77**:41-42
The Lay of St. Gengulphus (Barham) **77**:9, 43
"The Lay of the Bell" (Schiller)
See "Das Lied von der Glocke"
"The Lay of the Brown Rosary" (Barrett Browning) **1**:115, 117, 126; **61**:31-2, 43, 65-7, 74-5; **66**:44
"A Lay of the Early Rose" (Barrett Browning) **1**:117; **61**:43
"The Lay of the Humble" (Milnes) **61**:130, 145
"The Lay of the Laborer" (Hood) **16**:209, 220, 228, 233, 237-38
The Lay of the Last Minstrel (Scott) **15**:249-52, 267, 273, 286, 293, 318-19; **69**:298, 302, 304; **209**:181-82, 187-88, 191-92, 195-96, 198, 254
The Lay of the Laureate: Carmen Nuptiale (Southey) **8**:462; **97**:263
The Lay of the Scottish Fiddle (Paulding) **2**:525
"A Lay Preacher" (Cooke) **110**:37
A Lay Sermon Addressed to the Higher and Middle Classes (Coleridge) **231**:59
Lay Sermons (Coleridge) **197**:240, 317; **231**:58, 83

Lay Sermons (Huxley) **67**:4, 44
"Lay this Laurel on the One" (Dickinson) **77**:118
"Layman's Reply" (Garrison) **149**:237
Lays (Macaulay)
See *Lays of Ancient Rome*
Lays and Legends of the Rhine (Planché) **42**:274
Lays for the Dead (Opie) **65**:182
Lays of Ancient Rome (Macaulay) **42**:84, 86, 88, 111, 113, 151; **231**:290
Lays of Many Lands (Hemans) **29**:202-03; **71**:261, 295
Lays of My Home, and Other Poems (Whittier) **8**:485-86; **59**:353, 370
Lays of the Red Branch (Ferguson) **33**:293-94
Lays of the Western Gael (Ferguson) **33**:279, 281, 285, 287, 289-91, 293-94, 297-99
"Lázaro" (Silva) **114**:301
Lázaro (Silva) **114**:273
"Lazarus" (Heine) **147**:133, 162
"Lazarus" (Silva)
See *Lázaro*
Lazarus (Heine) **4**:248, 254, 257
"The Lazy Crow" (Simms) **3**:509
The Lazy Tour of Two Idle Apprentices (Collins) **1**:185
The Lazy Tour of Two Idle Apprentices (Dickens) **86**:188
Léa (Barbey d'Aurevilly) **213**:74
Lea (Kivi) **30**:48, 50, 53, 65
"Lead, Kindly Light" (Newman) **38**:282, 315, 336
"Lead lunar ray" (Fuller) **50**:249, 250
"The Leaden Echo and the Golden Echo" (Hopkins) **17**:186-87, 193, 200, 205, 210-12, 225; **189**:48, 53-54, 115, 135
"Leady-Day an' Ridden House" (Barnes) **75**:77, 81, 83
"The Leady's Tower" (Barnes) **75**:72-3
"A Leaf from King Alfred's Orosius" (Longfellow) **45**:160
"A Leaf from the Diary of a Guard Officer" (Bestuzhev)
See "Listok iz dnevnika gvardeyskogo ofitsera"
"A Leaf From the Sky" (Andersen) **7**:22
"The Leaf Glancing Boughs" (Harpur) **114**:116
"Leander" (Keats) **8**:361
"The Leane" (Barnes) **75**:15-16, 55, 68, 101, 104
"The Leap Frog" (Andersen) **7**:23, 25
"A Lear of the Steppes" (Turgenev)
See "Stepnoy Korol 'Lir"
"The Learned Boy" (Crabbe) **26**:93, 130; **121**:40
"Learned Lady" (Irving) **95**:239
"The Leather Bottell" (Maginn) **8**:438
Leather Stocking and Silk; or, Hunter John Myers and His Times: A Story of the Valley of Virginia (Cooke) **5**:127-29, 131-32, 136
The Leatherstocking Tales (Cooper) **1**:205-06, 211-12, 215, 217, 221-28; **54**:284
"Leave, O leave Me to My Sorrows" (Blake) **37**:29
"Leaves" (Barnes) **75**:15
"Leaves and Little Flowers from the Golden Meadow" (Schumann)
See "Blätter und Blümchen aus der goldenen Aue"
"The Leaves Are Falling—So Am I" (Landor) **14**:199
"Leaves from a Colleger's Album" (Willis) **194**:296
Leaves from a Notebook (Eliot) **183**:64
Leaves from Australian Forests (Kendall) **12**:180-81, 184, 186, 192-93, 196, 200
Leaves From Margaret Smith's Journal (Whittier) **59**:362, 380-1, 384
"Leaves from My Omnibus Book" (Cranch) **115**:50
Leaves of Grass (Whitman) **4**:535-37, 539-47, 551, 553-55, 558, 561-63, 566-67, 574-76, 579, 581, 583-89, 591-96, 600-01, 603-04; **31**:357-448; **81**:237, 241-42, 244, 254-71, 275, 281, 286-87, 293, 295, 299, 302, 309-10, 312-18, 325-30, 332, 336, 340-43, 345-47, 350-51, 353-54, 361, 363-64, 369; **205**:154-344
"Leaving Fishkill for New York" (Fuller) **50**:249
"Leaving the Theater" (Gogol) **162**:15, 19
"Leaving the Theater after the Performance of a New Comedy" (Gogol)
See "Teatral'nyi raz'ezd posle predstavleniia novoi komedii"
Lebe der Liebe und liebe das Leben. Der Briefwechsel von Clemens Brentano und Sophie Mereau (Brentano) **191**:116-17
"Lebed" (Derzhavin) **215**:61-62
"Lebed" (Tyutchev) **34**:410
Das Leben der Hochgräfin Gritta von Rattenzuhausbeiuns (Arnim) **123**:74, 77, 81-82
"Das Leben des Dichters" (Schumann) **143**:73
"Leben des vergnügten Schulmeisterleins Maria Wuz in Aventhal" (Jean Paul) **7**:235-36, 238, 242
Leben Fibels, des Verfassers der Bienrodischen Fibel (Jean Paul) **7**:235, 239, 241, 242
"Leben und Tod" (Mörike) **201**:301
Leben und Tod der heiligen Genoveva (Tieck) **5**:511, 514, 521, 525, 529, 532
Leben und Tod des kleinen Rothkäppchens (Tieck) **5**:523
Lebens-Ansichten des Katers Murr nebst fragmentarischer Biographie des Kapellmeisters Johannes Kreisler in züfalligen Makulaturblättern (Hoffmann) **2**:340-41, 346-47, 353, 356-58, 360, 362-63; **183**:164-66, 171, 173-76, 185-86, 193, 196, 206, 223, 225-27, 235-36, 238, 240-41, 247, 249, 310-11
Lebenselemente (Tieck) **5**:518
Ein Lebensgemälde aus der Zeit Moses Mendelssohns (Auerbach) **171**:54
"Die Lebenskraft, oder Der Rhodische Genius" (Humboldt) **170**:140-45
Lebens-Lieder und Bilder (Chamisso) **82**:6
"Die Lebensschicksale des Hundes Berganza" (Hoffmann)
See "Nachricht von den neuesten Schicksalen des Hundes Berganza"
Lecoq the Detective (Gaboriau)
See *Monsieur Lecoq*
"A Lecture Delivered before the Female Anti-Slavery Society of Salem" (Brown) **2**:47, 53
"Lecture I" (Keble) **87**:154
Lecture IV (Keble) **87**:151
"Lecture on 'Discoveries; Inventions; and Improvements'" (Lincoln) **18**:240
"Lecture on Fashion" (Willis) **194**:308
"Lecture on Slavery" (Emerson) **98**:169, 171
"Lecture on Spies and Informers" (Thelwall) **162**:322
"Lecture on the Anti-Slavery Movement" (Douglass) **7**:124
"Lecture on the Development of English Literature from Chaucer to Wordsworth" (Prescott) **163**:71
"Lecture on the 'Nature of Poetry'" (Dobell)
See "The Nature of Poetry"
"Lecture on the Poetry of Wordsworth" (Clough) **27**:59, 101-03, 106
"Lecture on the Poetry of Wordsworth" (Prescott) **163**:44, 71-74
"Lecture on the Poets of America" (Poe) **55**:177
"Lecture on the Present War" (Coleridge) **231**:85
"Lecture on the Times" (Emerson) **1**:301; **38**:209
"Lecture on the Use of Words" (Barbauld) **185**:43
Lecture XL (Keble) **87**:151
Lecture XVI (Keble) **87**:154
Lecture XXII (Keble) **87**:150, 154
Lecture XXVIII (Keble) **87**:154
Lecture XXX (Keble) **87**:154
"Lecture XXXIX" (Keble) **87**:153
"The Lectures" (Lippard) **198**:134
Lectures 1795, on Politics and Religion (Coleridge) **197**:310-12, 319, 323; **231**:85, 141-44
Lectures 1795 On Politics and Religion (Coleridge)
Lectures and Biographical Sketches (Emerson) **98**:65
Lectures and Essays on University Subjects (Newman) **38**:324, 327; **99**:212
Lectures and Miscellanies (James) **53**:209, 217
Lectures Chiefly on the Dramatic Literature of the Age of Elizabeth (Hazlitt) **29**:146-47, 163, 174
Lectures for Working Men (Huxley) **67**:85
Lectures in the Training Schools for Kindergartners (Peabody) **169**:150, 166-67
Lectures on Aesthetics (Hegel)
See *Vorlesungen über die Aesthetik*
Lectures on Ancient and Modern Literature (Schlegel)
See *Geschichte der alten und neuen Literatur*
Lectures on Art (Taine) **15**:469
Lectures on Art, and Poems (Allston) **2**:23-25, 27
Lectures on Certain Difficulties Felt by Anglicans in submitting to the Catholic Church (Newman) **38**:291, 310-11, 328; **99**:263
Lectures on Dramatic Arts and Literature (Schlegel)
See *Über dramatische Kunst und Litteratur*
"Lectures on English Philosophy" (Hazlitt) **82**:108
Lectures on Ethics (Kant) **27**:248, 262
Lectures on Justification (Newman)
See *Lectures on the Doctrine of Justification*
"Lectures on Murder Considered as One of the Fine Arts" (De Quincey) **4**:61, 68, 73-74, 78, 85; **87**:76-7, 79; **198**:23, 38-40, 43, 46, 52
Lectures on Painting and Design (Haydon) **146**:129
Lectures on Philosophical Theology (Kant) **27**:244
"Lectures on Poetry" (Bryant) **6**:190; **46**:10, 12, 16, 27, 29, 43, 48, 52
Lectures on Poetry (Keble) **87**:152, 154, 156-57, 161, 175, 183-84, 193, 199
Lectures on Recent Philosophy (Schelling) **30**:163
"Lectures on Revealed Religion" (Coleridge) **99**:41
Lectures on Revealed Religion (Coleridge) **197**:321, 324, 327-28
Lectures on Rhetoric and Belles Lettres (Blair) **75**:115-19, 123, 127, 131, 133, 136-37, 141-44, 146-47, 149-50, 157, 160, 164-65, 177
Lectures on Rhetoric and Oratory (Adams) **175**:6, 51, 64-71, 74-76, 78, 82, 87, 89-90
Lectures on Shakespeare and Milton (Coleridge) **99**:105
Lectures on the Doctrine of Justification (Newman) **38**:315; **99**:223, 229-34, 278
Lectures on the Elevation of the Laboring Portion of the Community (Channing) **17**:26, 41
Lectures on the English Comic Writers (Hazlitt) **29**:145-47, 163, 165, 167, 174
Lectures on the English Humourists (Thackeray)
See *The English Humourists of the Eighteenth Century: A Series of Lectures*

Delivered in England, Scotland, and the United States of America
Lectures on the English Poets (Hazlitt) **29**:134, 138, 145-48, 163-65, 174, 176-77, 183; **82**:123
Lectures on the History of Literature (Schlegel) **45**:288
Lectures on the History of Philosophy (Hegel)
See *Vorlesungen über die Geschichte der Philosophie*
Lectures on the Life of Christ (Schleiermacher) **107**:268
Lectures on the Philosophy of History (Hegel)
See *Vorlesungen über die Philosophie der Geschichte*
Lectures on the Philosophy of History (Schlegel) **45**:300
Lectures on the Philosophy of Religion: Together with a Work on the Proofs of the Existance of God (Hegel)
See *Vorlesungen über die Philosophie der Religion, nebst iener Schrift über die Beweise vom Dasein Gottes*
Lectures on the Present Position of Catholics in England: Addressed to the Brothers of the Oratory (Newman) **38**:294, 310, 328; **99**:211, 264
Lectures on the Prophetical Office of the Church (Newman) **38**:315; **99**:220-21, 225
Led Astray (Feuillet)
See *Tentation*
"Ledi Makbet Mcenskogo uezda" (Leskov) **25**:228, 233-34, 245-48, 264-65; **174**:10, 12, 22-23, 37, 62-63, 120, 123
"De l'Education" (Laclos)
See *De l'Education des femmes*
De l'Education des femmes (Laclos) **4**:325, 340, 342; **87**:239-40, 246, 274
"Ledwina" (Droste-Hülshoff) **3**:196, 203
Lee and His Lieutenants (Cooke) **5**:124
"Lee Shore" (Melville) **49**:414, 416
"The Leech of Folkestone" (Barham) **77**:33, 35
"The Leechgatherer" (Wordsworth)
See "Resolution and Independence"
"The Left-handed Craftsman" (Leskov)
See "Levša"
"The Left-Handed Smith and the Steel Flea" (Leskov)
See "Levša"
"The Lefthander" (Leskov)
See "Levša"
"Lefty, the Tale of the Cross-Eyed Left Handed Craftsman of Tula and the Steel Flea" (Leskov)
See "Levša"
"The Legacy" (Moore) **6**:399; **110**:185
A Legacy for Young Ladies, Consisting of Miscellaneous Pieces, in Prose and Verse (Barbauld) **185**:86, 96, 128, 130
Legacy to Labourers; or, What is the Right Which Lords, Baronets and Squires Have to the Lands of England? (Cobbett) **49**:155
Legacy to Peel (Cobbett) **49**:114
"The Legal Codes of Lycurgus and Solon" (Schiller)
See "The Legislation of Lycurgus and Solon"
"Legem tuam dilexi" (Patmore) **9**:359, 361
"The Legend" (Herzen) **10**:346-47; **61**:108
"A Legend" (Krasiński)
See "Legenda"
Legend (Longfellow)
See *The Golden Legend*
Legend (Pushkin) **3**:445, 448
"The Legend Beautiful" (Longfellow) **45**:188
"The Legend of Bottle Hill" (Maginn) **8**:440
"The Legend of Brittany" (Lowell) **2**:505, 515
"The Legend of Dhruva" (Dutt) **29**:123, 126
"The Legend of Doctor Theophilus: or, The Enchanted Clothes" (Cranch) **115**:54, 57-9
The Legend of Florence (Hunt) **1**:412, 415, 423; **70**:263
Legend of Hamilton Tighe (Barham) **77**:4, 19, 26, 36
"The Legend of Jubal" (Eliot) **183**:64
The Legend of Jubal, and Other Poems (Eliot) **4**:107, 115
"Legend of Khalif Hakem" (Nerval)
See *L'histoire du Calife Hakem*
"The Legend of Knockgrafton" (Maginn) **8**:440
"The Legend of Knocksheogowna" (Maginn) **8**:440
"The Legend of Lady Griseld Baillie" (Baillie) **151**:41-42, 121
"Legend of Lake Switez" (Mickiewicz) **3**:393
"Legend of Maryland" (Kennedy) **2**:431-33
A Legend of Montrose (Scott) **15**:300, 304, 309; **69**:303, 308, 313, 322; **209**:200
"Legend of Oxford" (Sigourney) **21**:290
"Legend of Pennsylvania" (Sigourney) **87**:342
"The Legend of Rabbi Ben Levi" (Longfellow) **45**:137
"The Legend of Saint Julien Hospitaller" (Flaubert)
See "La légende de Saint-Julien l'Hospitalier"
"The Legend of Saint Julien the Hospitator" (Flaubert)
See "La légende de Saint-Julien l'Hospitalier"
"A Legend of Sheppey" (Barham) **77**:44
"The Legend of Sleepy Hollow" (Irving) **2**:367, 376, 379, 381-84, 389-90, 392-93; **19**:327-29, 331-37, 339-41, 343-45, 347-49; **95**:227, 240, 242-44, 249, 265, 268, 283-86, 296
"The Legend of St. Leonor" (Lanier) **118**:218-19
"Legend of St. Lucas" (Schlegel) **15**:223
"A Legend of the Apostle John" (Child) **6**:201
"The Legend of the Brown Rosarie" (Barrett Browning)
See "The Lay of the Brown Rosary"
The Legend of the Centuries (Hugo)
See *La légende des siècles*
"Legend of the Delewares" (Bryant) **46**:4
A Legend of the Devil's Dyke (Boucicault) **41**:40
"The Legend of the Devil's Pulpit" (Bryant) **6**:181
"Legend of the Enchanted Soldier" (Irving) **2**:388
"The Legend of the Grand Inquisitor" (Dostoevsky) **2**:181, 185, 188, 191-92; **21**:112; **33**:177, 230; **43**:92, 95-96, 98, 103, 107, 120, 122-23, 127, 137-38, 149-53, 157, 169-72; **202**:68, 87-88, 91, 130, 161-62
"The Legend of the Hounds" (Boker) **125**:34, 38, 77
"The Legend of the Morning Star" (Eminescu) **131**:288
The Legend of the Rhine (Thackeray) **5**:464
"Legend of the Sheep Fold" (Harpur) **114**:150
"Legenda" (Krasiński) **4**:306, 313
"Legenda o sovestnom Danile" (Leskov) **25**:245
"Lègende" (Laforgue) **5**:280; **53**:294; **221**:24, 36, 49, 60, 66
"La Légende de Saint Julien Hospitalier" (Flaubert)
See "La légende de Saint-Julien l'Hospitalier"
"La légende de Saint-Julien l'Hospitalier" (Flaubert) **2**:227, 232-3, 236, 246, 257-8; **62**:93, 108; **135**:109, 134
La légende de Soeur Béatrix (Nodier) **19**:385
"La légende des Nornes" (Leconte de Lisle) **29**:226-28
La légende des siècles (Hugo) **3**:253, 255, 262, 264, 270-72, 276; **10**:375; **21**:196; **161**:192-93, 195, 264; **189**:156, 193, 200, 235, 249
Legende von der heiligen Marina (Brentano) **191**:68-70
Légendes démocratiques (Michelet) **31**:232
"Légendes rustiques" (Sand) **42**:314
Legends and Lyrics (Hayne) **94**:136, 141-42, 144, 148, 151, 154-57, 159, 164, 169
Legends of Mexico (Lippard) **198**:229
Legends of New England in Prose and Verse (Whittier) **8**:484-85, 526; **59**:363
Legends of the American Revolution, "1776"; or, Washington and His Generals (Lippard)
See *Washington and His Generals; or, Legends of the Revolution, by George Lippard. With a Biographical Sketch of the Author, by Rev. C. Chauncey Burr*
Legends of the Madonna (Jameson) **43**:306, 324, 326
Legends of the Monastic Orders (Jameson) **43**:306, 324-25
"The Legends of the Province House" (Hawthorne) **2**:293, 322; **95**:140; **158**:246, 252; **171**:357
Legends of the Province House (Hawthorne) **191**:189
Legends of Washington and His Generals (Lippard)
See *Washington and His Generals; or, Legends of the Revolution, by George Lippard. With a Biographical Sketch of the Author, by Rev. C. Chauncey Burr*
"The Legislation of Lycurgus and Solon" (Schiller) **39**:363
De l'Église gallicane (Maistre) **37**:295, 299
"Der Lehnhold" (Auerbach) **171**:8
Lehrjahre (Goethe)
See *Wilhelm Meisters Lehrjahre*
Der Lehrling der Griechen (Klopstock) **225**:286-87
Die Lehrlinge zu Saïs (Novalis) **13**:366, 368, 370-71, 374-77, 381, 384-86, 401, 403; **178**:4, 40, 43, 55-56, 65-67, 69, 81, 83-84, 97-98, 101, 106, 109-11, 127, 130-31
"Leib und Seele" (Heine) **4**:257
Leicester (Dunlap) **2**:210-13, 215, 217
Leicester, an Autobiography (Adams)
See *A Child of the Age*
"Leichhardt" (Kendall) **12**:182, 194, 199
"Leiden" (Hölderlin) **16**:185
Die Leiden des jungen Werthers (Goethe) **4**:162-63, 167, 169-71, 173, 176, 178, 188-91, 198-201; **34**:94, 120; **154**:232-33, 237, 266, 277
Das Leiden eines Knaben (Meyer) **81**:175-76, 180, 182, 215
Leiden und Freuden eines Schulmeisters (Gotthelf) **117**:4, 7, 14, 17, 19, 25, 27, 32, 35, 38, 46, 51
Das Leidende Weib (Klinger) **1**:428
Der Leiermann (Muller) **73**:386, 390, 393, 395-97
Leighton Court (Kingsley) **107**:188, 192-93, 197, 209, 228-29
"Leila: A Tale" (Barrett Browning) **61**:36
"Leila and Mejnoun" (D'Israeli)
See "Mejnoun and Leila"
"Leila in the Arabian zone" (Fuller) **50**:247, 250
Leila; or, The Siege of Granada (Bulwer-Lytton) **45**:58
"Leipziger Musikleben" (Schumann) **143**:74
"Leisure" (Lamb) **10**:405
"The Leisure of a Dramatic Critic" (Lewes) **25**:291
"Leitenant Belozor" (Bestuzhev) **131**:154
"A Lejtőn" (Arany) **34**:19
"L.E.L." (Rossetti) **186**:262, 272, 283, 304, 334
Lélia (Sand) **2**:581-85, 587-89, 595-98, 603-04, 606-08; **42**:316, 318, 320, 322, 338, 349-57, 360, 362-6, 379; **57**:313, 318-22, 324-5, 327-37, 339, 360, 367, 370; **174**:186, 225
"Lena Wies" (Storm) **195**:45
"Lenardos Tagebuch" (Goethe) **4**:189
"Lenore" (Osgood) **141**:320
"Lenore" (Poe) **55**:133; **117**:192, 195, 217, 221, 226-27, 236-38, 242, 295-96, 299
Lenore (Storm)
See *Auf der Universitat*

"Lentes ajenos" (Silva) **114**:317

Lenz (Büchner) **26**:4, 18, 20, 27-8, 36, 41-2, 46-8, 50-5, 59, 67; **146**:4, 6, 14, 16, 20-23, 25, 38, 60-63, 65, 75, 79-83, 85-87, 91-93, 95, 101, 107

Leo and Liina (Kivi)
See *Leo ja Liina*

Leo Burckart (Nerval) **1**:475; **67**:303

Leo ja Liina (Kivi) **30**:64

"Leofric and Godiva" (Landor) **14**:185-86

"Leon, dvoretskii syn" (Leskov) **174**:50

"Leon, the Steward's Son" (Leskov)
See "Leon, dvoretskii syn"

"Leonard and Susan" (Coleridge) **90**:7, 25

Leonard and Susan (Coleridge) **90**:16, 20

"Leonardo da Vinci" (Pater) **7**:305, 311; **90**:296, 298, 305; **159**:216, 295, 323

Leonce und Lena (Büchner) **26**:4, 9, 20, 25-8, 30, 32-3, 38-9, 43, 45, 55, 62, 64; **146**:18-23, 27, 29-33, 38-40, 42, 65, 91, 103, 106-7

Leoncia (Gómez de Avellaneda) **111**:12, 15, 55

Leone Leoni (Sand) **2**:587; **57**:312, 316, 341, 360; **174**:186

Leoni or the Orphan of Venice (Chivers) **49**:52, 61-3

Leoni the Orphan of Venice (Chivers)
See *Leoni or the Orphan of Venice*

"Leonine Elegiacs" (Tennyson) **30**:211

Leonor de Guzman (Boker) **125**:8-9, 17, 20-22, 24, 31, 36, 55, 58, 64-66, 76

Leonora (Edgeworth) **1**:256; **51**:87-90

"Leopold" (Beddoes) **3**:33; **154**:9-11, 67-68

"The Leper" (Willis) **194**:287, 304, 306

The Leper of the City of Aoste: A Narrative (Williams) **135**:312, 314

"Leper-House of Janval" (Gore) **65**:21

"Les lépreux" (Bertrand) **31**:47

"Der Lerche" (Droste-Hülshoff) **3**:193, 202

Les (Ostrovsky) **30**:100, 104, 111, 113, 115, 119; **57**:220

The Lesbians (Baudelaire)
See *Les fleurs du mal*

Les Lesbiennes (Baudelaire)
See *Les fleurs du mal*

"Lesbos" (Baudelaire) **29**:66, 72-4; **55**:6-8, 33, 61, 73-4

LesForestiers (Dumas) **71**:193

Leskov o literature (Leskov) **174**:85, 87, 90

"Lesley Castle" (Austen) **13**:72; **119**:13, 15

Lesley's Guardians (Webster) **230**:241, 304

De l'esprit de conquête et de l'usurpation dans leurs rapports avec la civilisation européenne (Constant) **6**:222, 225; **182**:84, 133, 136, 146, 150, 178, 212, 219, 232-33

De l'esprit des traductions (Staël-Holstein) **91**:340

"De l'Essence du rire" (Baudelaire) **55**:68, 72; **155**:15, 59-60

"Lessing" (Lewes) **25**:286

"Lessing" (Lowell) **2**:509

"A Lesson for Kings" (Hunt) **70**:258

The Lesson of Life, and Other Poems (Boker) **125**:18, 30, 35, 57

"The Lesson of the Trees" (Lampman) **194**:74-76, 83, 93

"A Lesson on Sensibility" (Brown) **74**:108

Lessons for Children (Barbauld) **50**:2, 7; **185**:5-6, 23, 102, 117, 119-20, 128

"Lessons in Criticism to William Roscoe, and Farther Lessons to a Quarterly Reviewer" (Bowles) **103**:54

"Let Be!" (Patmore) **9**:339, 358, 365

"Let Down the Bars, O Death" (Dickinson) **21**:20

"Let Erin Remember the Days of Old" (Moore) **6**:397, 399; **110**:185, 194, 198

"Let My Name Survive" (Chivers) **49**:70

Let Off with a Scare (Vigny)
See *Quitte pour la peur*

"Let Pure Hate Still Underprop" (Thoreau) **7**:382

"Let the Brothels of Paris Be Opened" (Blake) **13**:243

"Let them rejoice in their beds" (Rossetti) **186**:314

"Let There Be Light" (Wergeland)
See "Vord lys!"

"Let Us Gather in Congress" (Eminescu) **33**:272

"Leteszem a lantot" (Arany) **34**:13, 19

"Le lethe" (Baudelaire)
See "Léthé"

"Léthé" (Baudelaire) **29**:73

"Lethe" (Meyer) **81**:199, 204, 209

"Letnij vecer" (Tyutchev) **34**:389, 411

"Let's Beat Down the Poor" (Baudelaire)
See "Assommons les pauvres"

"Let's beat up the poor!" (Baudelaire)
See "Assommons les pauvres"

"Let's Put Our Finger on the Wound" (Laforgue)
See "Mettons le doigt sur la plaie"

"A Letter" (Lermontov)
See "Pis'mo"

"Letter" (Martineau) **137**:308

"Letter" (Melville) **93**:210

"Letter" (Whitman) **81**:287

Letter (Crèvecoeur)
See *Lettres d'un Cultivateur Américain*

"Letter 1" (Chaadaev)
See "Philosophic Letter 1"

"Letter 8" (Dickinson) **171**:164

"Letter 10" (Dickinson) **171**:163

"Letter 19" (Dickinson) **171**:163

"Letter 20" (Dickinson) **171**:163

"Letter 22" (Dickinson) **171**:163

"Letter 26" (Dickinson) **171**:164

"Letter 27" (Dickinson) **171**:107

"Letter 29" (Beethoven) **227**:6

"Letter 31" (Dickinson) **171**:163

"Letter 34" (Dickinson) **171**:139

"Letter 35" (Dickinson) **171**:163

"Letter 39" (Beethoven) **227**:5

"Letter 39" (Dickinson) **171**:164

"Letter 44" (Dickinson) **171**:163

"Letter 46" (Dickinson) **171**:163

"Letter 48" (Dickinson) **171**:164

"Letter 50" (Dickinson) **171**:164

"Letter 53" (Beethoven) **227**:5

"Letter 54" (Dickinson) **171**:163

"Letter 58" (Beethoven) **227**:5

"Letter 63" (Dickinson) **171**:164

"Letter 68" (Beethoven) **227**:7

"Letter 69" (Beethoven) **227**:7

"Letter 70" (Dickinson) **171**:163

"Letter 72" (Dickinson) **171**:134, 206

"Letter 73" (Beethoven) **227**:6

"Letter 88" (Dickinson) **171**:164

"Letter 107" (Beethoven) **227**:6

"Letter 107" (Dickinson) **171**:165

"Letter 114" (Herder) **186**:10-11

"Letter 131" (Beethoven) **227**:6

"Letter 133" (Dickinson) **171**:210

"Letter 144" (Dickinson) **171**:205

"Letter 156" (Dickinson) **171**:205

"Letter 158" (Dickinson) **171**:205

"Letter 193" (Dickinson) **171**:166

"Letter 199" (Dickinson) **171**:163

"Letter 200" (Dickinson) **171**:143

"Letter 215" (Dickinson) **171**:163

"Letter 217" (Dickinson) **171**:223

"Letter 245" (Dickinson) **171**:211

"Letter 254" (Beethoven) **227**:5

"Letter 256" (Dickinson) **171**:211

"Letter 261" (Dickinson) **171**:184

"Letter 262" (Beethoven) **227**:6

"Letter 265" (Dickinson) **171**:207, 216

"Letter 268" (Dickinson) **171**:143, 216

"Letter 269" (Dickinson) **171**:222

"Letter 271" (Dickinson) **171**:214

"Letter 275" (Dickinson) **171**:134

"Letter 277" (Dickinson) **171**:163

"Letter 278" (Dickinson) **171**:223

"Letter 280" (Dickinson) **171**:217

"Letter 298" (Dickinson) **171**:223

"Letter 305" (Dickinson) **171**:224

"Letter 316" (Dickinson) **171**:207

"Letter 319" (Dickinson) **171**:212

"Letter 322" (Beethoven) **227**:7

"Letter 330" (Dickinson) **171**:217

"Letter 330a" (Dickinson) **171**:216

"Letter 336" (Dickinson) **171**:211

"Letter 354" (Dickinson) **171**:143

"Letter 357" (Dickinson) **171**:223

"Letter 381" (Beethoven) **227**:6

"Letter 389" (Dickinson) **171**:140

"Letter 405" (Dickinson) **171**:144

"Letter 414" (Dickinson) **171**:205

"Letter 415" (Dickinson) **171**:135

"Letter 418" (Dickinson) **171**:223

"Letter 448" (Dickinson) **171**:168

"Letter 471" (Dickinson) **171**:140

"Letter 484" (Dickinson) **171**:168-69

"Letter 487" (Dickinson) **171**:165

"Letter 560" (Dickinson) **171**:136, 163

"Letter 562" (Dickinson) **171**:136

"Letter 571" (Dickinson) **171**:163

"Letter 575" (Dickinson) **171**:223

"Letter 584" (Dickinson) **171**:143

"Letter 587" (Dickinson) **171**:137

"Letter 641" (Dickinson) **171**:142

"Letter 643" (Dickinson) **171**:226

"Letter 656" (Dickinson) **171**:135

"Letter 669" (Dickinson) **171**:164

"Letter 685" (Dickinson) **171**:140, 163

"Letter 711" (Dickinson) **171**:108

"Letter 750" (Dickinson) **171**:142

"Letter 758" (Dickinson) **171**:163

"Letter 769" (Dickinson) **171**:143

"Letter 781" (Dickinson) **171**:134

"Letter 815" (Dickinson) **171**:136

"Letter 824" (Dickinson) **171**:165

"Letter 830" (Dickinson) **171**:132

"Letter 853" (Dickinson) **171**:140

"Letter 873" (Dickinson) **171**:142

"Letter 910" (Dickinson) **171**:164

"Letter 1000" (Dickinson) **171**:215

"Letter about Censorship in Russia" (Tyutchev) **34**:384

A Letter, Addressed to the People of Piedmont (Barlow) **23**:27-8

A Letter Addressed to the People of Piedmont on the Advantages of the French Revolution and Necessity of Adopting Its Principles in Italy (Barlow)
See *Lettre addressée aux habitans du Piémont sur les avantages de la révolution française et la nécessité d'en adopter les principes en Italie*

Letter and Spirit (Rossetti) **186**:233, 263, 296, 319, 321, 341

Letter and Spirit: Notes on the Commandments (Rossetti) **50**:271, 276-7, 324; **66**:306-7, 342, 375

"Letter: From a Missionary of the Methodist Episcopal Church South in Kansas to a Distinguished Politician" (Whittier) **8**:525, 531; **59**:361, 369-71

"Letter from a Poor Painter to a Great Lord" (Brontë) **217**:19

"Letter from a Traveller Before He Had Travelled" (Haliburton) **149**:269

"Letter from Angus MacMore" (Brackenridge) **227**:116

"Letter from George Henry Boker to Bayard Taylor" (Boker) **125**:87-88

"Letter from George Henry Boker to Elizabeth Stoddard" (Boker) **125**:83

"Letter from George Henry Boker to John Seely Hart" (Boker) **125**:84

"Letter from George Henry Boker to Richard Henry Stoddard" (Boker) **125**:82, 85-87

"A Letter from London to Paris from one American to Another" (Bello)
See "Carta Escrita de Londres a París por un Americano a Otro"

"Letter from Mexico" (Corbière) **43**:14
Letter from Noah Webster, Esq., of New Haven, Connecticut, to a Friend in Explanation and Defense of the Distinguishing Doctrines of the Gospel (Webster) **30**:408
"A Letter from St. Petersburg" (Turgenev) **122**:294
Letter from the Lost Townships (Lincoln) **201**:181
"A Letter from the Pope to the Bishop of Rochester Prior to his Exile" (Bestuzhev)
See "Pis'mo Popa k episkopu Rochester-skomu pered ego izgnaniem"
"The Letter L" (Ingelow) **39**:264
"Letter of a Country Dweller" (Karamzin)
See "Pis'mo sel'skago zitelja"
"Letter of Advice to a Young American" (Godwin) **130**:37
"Letter of Elia to Robert Southey" (Lamb) **113**:178
"Letter of John Bull" (Barbauld) **50**:14
"Letter of the Seer" (Rimbaud)
See "Lettre du voyant"
"Letter of Travel and Romance" (Carlyle) **181**:129, 132
"Letter on Chinese Trade" (Radishchev) **190**:358-59
Letter on Conducting: A Defense (Liszt) **199**:305, 343
"Letter on Julie" (Constant)
See "Lettre sur Julie"
"Letter on Music" (Moore) **110**:192
Letter on the Direction of a Defense (Liszt)
See *Letter on Conducting: A Defense*
Letter on the Novel (Schlegel)
See "Brief über den Roman"
"Letter on travelling, &c." (Cranch) **115**:48
"Letter on Watering-places" (Barbauld) **50**:14
Letter ot Old George Rose (Cobbett) **49**:113
"Letter to a Friend in London" (Shelley) **18**:327
Letter to a Friend of Robert Burns (Wordsworth) **111**:370
"A Letter to a Friend Residing in Tobolsk" (Radishchev) **190**:295, 314
"Letter to a newly elected Young Member of the Lower House" (Freneau) **111**:124
"Letter to a Young Gentleman" (Stevenson) **5**:420
"Letter to a Young Gentleman Commencing His Education" (Webster) **30**:408
"A Letter to An Absent Friend, on seeing Celeste for the first time in the Wept-of-Wish-ton-Wish" (Osgood) **141**:320
"Letter to B—" (Poe) **55**:142, 162, 170; **117**:304; **211**:241, 247
"Letter to B. W. Procter" (Beddoes) **154**:42, 51
"Letter to Balzac" (Stendhal) **46**:325
"Letter to Beethoven" (Fuller) **5**:167
"Letter to Colonel Ellsworth's Parents" (Lincoln) **201**:167
"Letter to Conkling" (Lincoln)
See "Letter to James C. Conkling, August 26, 1863"
"Letter to Doctor Erman" (Bestuzhev)
See "Pis'mo k doktoru Ermanu"
Letter to Dorothea (Schlegel) **45**:363, 365
A Letter to Dr. David Ramsay, Of Charleston, (S. C.) Respecting the Errors in Johnson's Dictionary, and Other Lexicons (Webster) **30**:398
"Letter to Dumas" (Nerval) **67**:357
Letter to Emerson (Landor) **14**:207
"Letter to Erastus Corning and Others" (Lincoln) **201**:168, 211
"Letter to Fanny McCullough" (Lincoln) **201**:167
"A Letter to Francis Jeffrey, Esq. on Certain Calumnies and Misrepresentations in the Edinburgh Review" (Thelwall) **162**:341-42
"Letter to General Joseph Hooker, Janurary 23, 1863" (Lincoln) **201**:168, 224
"Letter to General Rosecrans" (Lincoln) **201**:168
"Letter to George Robertson" (Lincoln) **201**:162
Letter to Governor Hamilton on the Subject of State Interposition (Calhoun) **15**:28, 59
A Letter to Henry Cline (Thelwall) **162**:338, 344-45
A Letter to his Countrymen (Cooper) **54**:256; **203**:91
"Letter to his Son" (Hazlitt) **82**:88
"Letter to Horace Greeley" (Lincoln) **201**:168, 189, 212
"Letter to J. H. Hackett, November 2, 1863" (Lincoln) **201**:172
Letter to Jack Harrow an English Labourer on the New Cheat of Savings Banks (Cobbett) **49**:113
"Letter to James C. Conkling, August 26, 1863" (Lincoln) **201**:168, 211-12
Letter to John Dunning, Esq. (Horne Tooke)
See *Letter to Mr. Dunning*
"Letter to Joshua F. Speed, August 24, 1855" (Lincoln) **201**:162
"Letter to Joshua Speed, June 19, 1841" (Lincoln) **201**:159
Letter to Lafayette (Cooper) **203**:73
"Letter to Lamartine" (Musset)
See "Lettre à M. de Lamartine"
"Letter to Lord Ellenborough" (Shelley) **143**:288
"Letter to Maria Gisborne" (Shelley) **18**:356; **175**:303
"A Letter to Mary Ann" (Cooke) **110**:39, 41-2, 67-8
"Letter to Mathetes" (Wordsworth) **111**:255, 257
"Letter to Mr.—" (Poe) **55**:138; **211**:231
Letter to Mr. Dunning (Horne Tooke) **195**:288, 300, 303, 313
"Letter to Mrs. Bixby" (Lincoln) **18**:257; **201**:167-68, 218
"Letter to R. P. Morgan" (Lincoln) **201**:161
Letter to the Abbé Raynal (Paine) **62**:322, 359
"Letter to the Bishop fo Llandaff" (Wordsworth) **38**:422, 426; **111**:253, 263, 345
A Letter to the Boston Association of Congregational Ministers, touching Certain Matters of their Theology (Parker) **186**:122, 146
"Letter to the Deaf" (Martineau) **26**:349-50
"Letter to the Editor" (Constant) **182**:219
"Letter to the Editor of the Literary Gazette" (Pushkin) **83**:320
"Letter to the Editors of Sovremennik" (Pavlova)
See "Pis'mo v redakcïiu Sovremennika"
A Letter to the French Convention (Barlow)
See *A Letter to the National Convention of France on the Defects in the Constitution of 1791, and the Extent of the Amendments Which Ought to Be Applied*
A Letter to the Governors, Instructors, and Trustees of the Universities, and Other Seminaries of Learning, in the United States, on the Errors of English Grammar (Webster) **30**:414
A Letter to the Hon. Henry Clay, on the Annexation of Texas to the United States (Channing) **17**:22, 32-3, 35
"Letter to the Immortal Beloved" (Beethoven) **227**:21, 24, 26
A Letter to the Marquis of Lansdowne (Milnes)
See *The Events of 1848, Especially in Their Relation to Great Britain. A Letter to the Marquis of Lansdowne*
A Letter to the National Convention of France (Barlow) **23**:18, 27-8
A Letter to the National Convention of France on the Defects in the Constitution of 1791, and the Extent of the Amendments Which Ought to Be Applied (Barlow) **223**:14, 22, 45-46, 48-50, 57-58
A Letter to the People of the United States Touching the Matter of Slavery (Parker) **186**:164-65
"Letter to the People's Party" (Bellamy) **147**:79
"Letter to the Queen on Lord Chancellor Cranworth's Marriage and Divorce Bill" (Norton) **47**:248, 250, 254, 261, 263; **205**:62, 64, 67, 85, 112, 124, 140, 148-50
"Letter to the Women of Bahia" (Castro Alves)
See "Carta ás senhoras bahianas"
Letter to the Women of England, on the Injustice of Mental Subordination (Robinson) **142**:187, 192, 229, 233-34, 281-84, 286-89
"Letter to the Young Women of Malolos" (Rizal) **27**:417
"A Letter to Thomas Campbell" (Bowles) **103**:54
"Letter to Thurlow Weed" (Lincoln) **201**:214-15
Letter to W. Windham (Holcroft)
See *Letter to William Windham, on the Intemperance and Dangerous Tendency of His Conduct*
"Letter to Weed" (Lincoln)
See "Letter to Thurlow Weed"
Letter to William Gifford, Esq. (Hazlitt) **29**:167, 169-70; **82**:98
A Letter to William Smith, Esq. M.P. (Southey) **97**:263, 312
Letter to William Windham, on the Intemperance and Dangerous Tendency of His Conduct (Holcroft) **85**:194-95, 199, 209, 227-28, 235
"Letter XXI" (Schiller) **166**:92
Lettera sul romanticismo (Manzoni) **98**:215
The Letter-Bag of the Great Western; or, Life in a Steamer (Haliburton) **15**:118-19, 125-26, 129, 135, 145; **149**:267, 269
"The Letter-Bell" (Hazlitt) **29**:153
Lettere (Leopardi) **129**:278
Lettere scritte dall'Inghilterra (Foscolo) **97**:88-93
"Letters" (Kirkland) **85**:296, 299, 301
"Letters" (Rossetti) **77**:296, 301
"Letters" (Schiller) **39**:337
Letters (Austen)
See *Jane Austen's Letters to Her Sister Cassandra and Others*
Letters (Baillie) **151**:106
Letters (Byron)
See *Letters and Journals*
Letters (Chaadaev)
See *Philosophical Letters*
Letters (Coleridge)
See *The Collected Letters of Samuel Taylor Coleridge*
Letters (Cowper) **94**:94-5, 119-25
Letters (Dickens) **113**:15, 107, 127, 130; **230**:19, 82
Letters (Dickinson) **21**:21-2, 30
Letters (Dodgson) **139**:63-66
Letters (Eliot)
See *George Eliot Letters*
Letters (Emerson)
See *The Letters of Ralph Waldo Emerson*
Letters (Eminescu) **131**:333
Letters (Freneau)
See *Letters on Various Interesting and Important Subjects*
Letters (Gaskell) **97**:127, 130, 142, 170, 173
Letters (Ghalib) **39**:154-55
Letters (Hayne) **94**:154
Letters (Hegel) **151**:371-72
Letters (Keats) **121**:108, 110-11, 124, 126, 129-30, 132, 172, 174, 177-81, 185-88, 192-94, 197, 202
Letters (Krasicki)
See *Listy*
Letters (Lamb) **113**:182, 202-3, 230

Letters (Longfellow)
See *The Letters of Henry Wadsworth Longfellow*
Letters (Mill) **58**:321
Letters (Moore) **110**:182, 184
Letters (Newman)
See *The Letters and Diaries of John Henry Newman*
Letters (Poe) **117**:321
Letters (Scott) **110**:240, 260-61, 263-64, 313, 315
Letters (Sigourney) **87**:337
Letters (Symonds) **34**:331-32, 336-37
Letters (Trelawny)
See *Letters of Edward John Trelawny*
Letters (Webster) **30**:397
Letters, 1813-1843 (Hawthorne) **191**:257
Letters, 1843-1853 (Hawthorne) **191**:256-57
The Letters, 1857-1864 (Hawthorne) **171**:347
Letters, 1865 (Beethoven)
See *Briefe Beethovens, 1865*
Letters, 1867 (Beethoven)
See *Neue Briefe Beethovens, 1867*
Letters, 1906-11 (Beethoven)
See *Beethovens sämtliche Briefe, 1906-11*
Letters, 1907-11 (Beethoven)
See *Ludwig van Beethovens sämtliche Briefe und Aufzeichnungen, 1907-11*
Letters, 1910 (Beethoven)
See *Ludwig van Beethovens sämtliche Briefe, 1910*
Letters, 1923 (Beethoven)
See *Ludwig van Beethovens sämtliche Briefe, 1923*
Letters, 1961 (Beethoven)
See *The Letters of Beethoven, 1961*
Letters, 1972 (Beethoven)
See *Beethoven's Letters, 1972*
Letters Addressed to the Daughter of a Nobleman, on the Formation of Religious and Moral Principle (Hamilton) **153**:273, 300-301, 316, 326
Letters and Correspondence (Newman) **38**:296, 312-13
The Letters and Diaries of John Henry Newman (Newman) **99**:218-25, 252-53, 283, 285, 291
Letters and Essays, Moral and Miscellaneous (Hays) **114**:177-78, 185, 188, 190, 194, 200, 206-7, 210, 216, 219-20, 229-30
Letters and Journals (Byron) **2**:87; **109**:122, 126
The Letters and Journals of James Fenimore Cooper (Cooper) **203**:39, 50-51, 77
Letters and Journals of Lord Byron, with Notices of His Life (Moore) **6**:385, 393; **110**:175
Letters and Literary Remains of Edward FitzGerald (FitzGerald) **9**:268-70
Letters and Memorials of Jane Welsh Carlyle (Carlyle) **181**:75, 80, 90, 102, 114, 116, 128-29
The Letters and Private Papers of William Makepeace Thackeray (Thackeray) **5**:485; **169**:235, 287, 291, 308-9, 317; **213**:188-89, 242, 275, 289
Letters and Remains (Clough) **27**:53
Letters and Remains (Prescott) **163**:7
Letters and Social Aims (Emerson) **1**:282
Letters Auxiliary to the History of Modern Polite Literature in Germany (Heine) **147**:151
"Letters by Robert Slender, O. S. M." (Freneau) **1**:315
Letters Concerning the Advancement of Humanity (Herder)
See *Briefe zu Beförderung der Humanität*
Letters Concerning the Study of Theology (Herder)
See *Briefe, das Studium der Theologie betreffend*
Letters containing a Sketch of the Politics of France (Williams) **135**:258, 260-61, 268, 282-83, 291-92, 312, 334, 338-41, 343
Letters containing a Sketch of the Scenes which passed in various Departments of France during the Tyranny of Robespierre and of the Events which took place in Paris on the Tenth of Thermidor (Williams) **135**:258, 260-61, 283, 291-92, 312, 338, 341
Letters, etc. dated from June 1836 to July 1841 (Norton) **205**:129
Letters for Literary Ladies (Edgeworth) **1**:267; **51**:81, 83; **158**:83
Letters for the Advancement of Humanity (Herder)
See *Briefe zu Beförderung der Humanität*
Letters for the Furthering of Humanity (Herder)
See *Briefe zu Beförderung der Humanität*
"Letters from Abroad" (Hunt) **1**:416; **70**:279
Letters from Abroad to Kindred at Home (Sedgwick) **19**:441, 445-47
Letters from an American Farmer; describing certain provincial situations, manners and customs (Crèvecoeur)
See *Lettres d'un Cultivateur Américain*
The Letters from Avenue Marigny (Herzen) **61**:86
Letters from Berlin (Heine)
See *Briefe aus Berlin*
"Letters from Dagestan" (Bestuzhev)
See "Pis'ma iz Dagestana"
Letters from England (Southey) **8**:475-76; **97**:266, 268, 270-71, 278-79, 281, 284-87, 291, 322
"Letters from Europe to the Tribune" (Fuller) **211**:91
Letters from France (Williams) **135**:256-58, 261, 267-77, 281-83, 285-93, 296-97, 299, 302, 308, 312, 321-23, 326-28, 333-34, 336-44, 353-55, 358-59
Letters from France, containing a Great Variety of Interesting and Original Information Concerning the most Important Events that have lately occurred in that Country and particularly respecting the Campaign of 1792 (Williams) **135**:258, 267-68, 276, 282-83, 338-39, 341
Letters from France, containing Many New Anecdotes Relative to the French Revolution and the Present State of French Manners (Williams) **135**:257-58, 267, 284, 288-89, 321, 323, 327-28, 334, 342-43
Letters from Hungarian Collections (Liszt) **199**:340
Letters from My Mill (Daudet)
See *Lettres de mon moulin*
Letters from New York (Child) **6**:200-03, 206-07, 209; **73**:51, 56, 59-61, 67, 80-81, 87
Letters from Paris (Barlow) **23**:28
Letters from Paris (Börne)
See *Briefe aus Paris*
Letters from Phocian (Hamilton) **49**:325
"Letters from the Far West" (Thorpe) **183**:328
Letters from the Levant (Galt) **110**:76, 92, 96
Letters from the South (Paulding) **2**:525, 531
Letters from the Underworld (Dostoevsky)
See *Zapiski iz podpol'ya*
Letters from the Wuppertal (Engels)
See "Briefe aus dem Wuppertal"
"Letters from Under a Bridge" (Willis) **194**:308
Letters of a Bachelor of Music (Liszt)
See *Lettres d'un bachelier ès musique*
The Letters of A. Bronson Alcott (Alcott) **1**:27
Letters of a Lifetime (Moodie) **113**:324, 369
Letters of a Russian Traveler (Karamzin)
See *Pis'ma Russkogo puteshestvennika*
Letters of a Russian Traveler, 1789-1790 (Karamzin) **3**:280, 282-83, 286-87
The Letters of a Solitary Wanderer (Smith) **115**:124, 221-22
Letters of a Traveller (Sand)
See *Lettres d'un voyageur*
Letters of a Traveller; or, Notes of Things Seen in Europe and America (Bryant) **6**:171; **46**:5, 25
Letters of a Traveller, second series (Bryant) **6**:171
The Letters of Alexander Pushkin (Pushkin) **3**:457; **83**:247-49
The Letters of Alfred Lord Tennyson (Tennyson) **65**:378; **115**:360; **202**:239, 264, 274, 278-80, 282, 284-85, 287, 321-23
Letters of an American Farmer (Crèvecoeur)
See *Lettres d'un Cultivateur Américain*
"Letters of an Englishman" (Brontë) **109**:44
Letters of an Englishman (Brontë) **109**:27, 37, 50
The Letters of Anthony Trollope (Trollope) **101**:320
The Letters of Beethoven, 1961 (Beethoven) **227**:21-23, 25-26, 29, 32, 34-36
The Letters of Caroline Norton to Lord Melbourne (Norton) **205**:134, 143
The Letters of Charles and Mary Lamb (Lamb) **125**:317, 333-34, 343, 347-48
The Letters of Charles Dickens (Dickens) **187**:116-17, 119, 173; **203**:188-89; **206**:57, 86, 92, 118, 126, 138, 142; **219**:184, 192, 197-98, 202, 228
The Letters of Charlotte Brontë (Brontë) **229**:176, 202
The Letters of Christina Rossetti (Rossetti) **186**:332-35, 340, 344
Letters of Dorothy Wordsworth (Wordsworth) **138**:227, 236
Letters of Dupuis and Cotonet (Musset)
See *Lettres de Dupuis et Cotonet*
The Letters of Edgar Allan Poe (Poe) **211**:285
The Letters of Edgar Allen Poe (Poe) **117**:304
Letters of Edward John Trelawny (Trelawny) **85**:322, 324, 330
The Letters of Elizabeth Barrett Browning (Barrett Browning) **61**:13-17, 29, 48, 51, 61, 67; **66**:50-1, 70; **170**:82, 85-86, 105
Letters of Elizabeth Barrett Browning to Mary Russell Mitford 1836-1854 (Barrett Browning) **61**:29-32, 49, 51-2, 66-7, 73; **66**:74
Letters of Elizabeth Palmer Peabody, American Renaissance Woman (Peabody) **169**:186-87, 189, 193-97, 203
The Letters of Emily Dickinson (Dickinson) **171**:107-8, 132, 135-37, 139-40, 142-44, 163, 166, 184-85, 205
Letters of Emily Dickinson, 2 vols. (Dickinson) **77**:75
The Letters of Francis Parkman (Parkman) **12**:364
The Letters of Franz Liszt (Liszt) **199**:300
The Letters of Gerard Manley Hopkins to Robert Bridges (Hopkins) **17**:214, 223; **189**:45, 47, 49, 51, 55-56, 68, 90, 92, 98, 126-29, 131, 134-36, 146-47
The Letters of Gustave Flaubert (Flaubert)
See *Correspondance*
Letters of Hannah More (More) **27**:338
The Letters of Henry Wadsworth Longfellow (Longfellow) **2**:498
The Letters of Herman Melville (Melville) **91**:30, 32-3; **123**:192, 194-95, 232, 235; **181**:282, 286; **193**:131; **221**:148
"Letters of Horace Fritz, Esq." (Willis) **194**:298
Letters of James Russell Lowell (Lowell) **90**:222
Letters of Jane Austen (Austen) **119**:54
The Letters of Jane Welsh Carlyle (Carlyle) **181**:99, 110, 118-21
Letters of Jane Welsh Carlyle to Joseph Neuberg, 1848-1862 (Carlyle) **181**:129
The Letters of John Clare (Clare) **86**:99, 103, 155-56, 159, 172

The Letters of John Keats (Keats) **225**:134, 151, 162, 165-69, 182, 187-89, 199, 215-16, 218, 224-30, 234, 237, 240, 243-46
Letters of John Keats to Fanny Brawne (Keats) **8**:334, 374
Letters of John Keats to His Family and Friends (Keats) **8**:374, 390-91; **73**:158, 254-58, 264-70, 328-29, 331-32, 335-42
Letters of Julia and Caroline (Edgeworth) **1**:272; **51**:86-7
The Letters of Karl Marx (Marx) **17**:355-56
Letters of Life (Sigourney) **21**:300, 302, 307, 311, 314; **87**:323, 325, 343
The Letters of Lydia Maria Child (Child) **73**:50, 73
The Letters of Macaulay (Macaulay) **231**:294-96, 299, 302, 305-6, 309
Letters of Margaret Fuller (Fuller) **211**:114, 116, 143, 145-47, 149, 151, 174, 176, 185, 187-92, 208-11, 213
The Letters of Mary Wollstonecraft Shelley (Shelley) **170**:286, 289, 335, 337
Letters of Matthew Arnold, 1848-1888 (Arnold) **6**:43-45; **89**:46
The Letters of Matthew Arnold to Arthur Hugh Clough (Arnold) **89**:52; **126**:112
The Letters of Mrs. Elizabeth Montagu (Montagu)
See *The Letters of Mrs. Elizabeth Montagu: With Some of the Letters of Her Correspondents*
The Letters of Mrs. Elizabeth Montagu: With Some of the Letters of Her Correspondents (Montagu) **7**:248-49; **117**:141, 178
Letters of Mrs. Gaskell (Gaskell) **97**:127, 130, 142, 170, 173; **137**:46, 53-54, 64, 90, 95, 99-101, 112, 124, 162-63, 166-67, 169
Letters of Mrs. Henley (Charriere)
See *Lettres de Mistriss Henley publiées par son amie*
"Letters of Parapidemus I" (Prescott) **163**:136
"Letters of Parepidemus II" (Clough) **27**:98
The Letters of Percy Bysshe Shelley (Shelley) **143**:177, 236-37, 247, 265, 288, 293-94; **175**:269, 275, 321, 324-26, 330
The Letters of Ralph Waldo Emerson (Emerson) **1**:296; **98**:81-84, 91-92, 95, 97
The Letters of Robert Browning and Elizabeth Barrett 1845-1846 (Barrett Browning) **61**:27, 32-5, 49, 58, 72; **66**:69, 74, 76-7
The Letters of Robert Louis Stevenson (Stevenson) **5**:422, 430; **63**:234; **193**:289, 296-97
"Letters of Runnymede" (Disraeli) **79**:205, 211, 269, 279-80
The Letters of Sir Walter Scott (Scott) **209**:201, 253-59, 310
The Letters of William and Dorothy Wordsworth (Wordsworth) **138**:214, 227, 236, 251-52, 255, 259, 273-74, 276-79, 291, 329-31, 333, 343-44
The Letters of William and Dorothy Wordsworth: The Early Years (Wordsworth)
See *The Early Letters of William and Dorothy Wordsworth*
The Letters of William and Dorothy Wordsworth: The Early Years 1787-1805 (Wordsworth) **111**:233, 236, 239, 243-44, 294, 315-16; **166**:303, 317
The Letters of William and Dorothy Wordsworth: The Later Years (Wordsworth) **111**:239, 242; **206**:305-6
The Letters of William and Dorothy Wordsworth: The Middle Years (Wordsworth) **111**:243; **206**:269
Letters of William Hazlitt (Hazlitt) **82**:86-7, 90
Letters on Demonology and Witchcraft (Scott) **15**:277
Letters on Don Carlos (Schiller) **69**:241
Letters on Education (Hamilton) **153**:264-65, 272, 277, 294, 296-98, 300, 322, 326
Letters on Lucinda (Schleiermacher)
See *Vertraute Briefe über Friedrich Schlegels Lucinde*
Letters on Old England by a New England Man (Paulding) **2**:525
Letters on Shakespeare (Tieck) **5**:526; **46**:403
Letters on Silesia (Adams) **175**:27-28
"Letters on the Church of the Fathers" (Newman) **99**:260
Letters on the Confederation of the Tamoios (Alencar)
See *Cartas sôbre a Confederaçao dos tamoios*
"Letters on the Coup d'état of 1851" (Bagehot) **10**:25-26, 58, 63
Letters on the Difficulties of Religion (Beecher) **30**:3, 7, 11
Letters on the Elementary Principles of Education (Hamilton)
See *Letters on Education*
Letters on the Epistle of Paul to Philemon or The Connection of Apostolical Christianity with Slavery (Longstreet) **159**:190
Letters on the Events which Have Passed in France since the Restoration in 1815 (Williams) **135**:261, 312, 314, 335
"Letters on the Fine Arts No. 3" (Thackeray) **213**:245
Letters on the Herring Fishing in the Moray Firth (Miller) **143**:37
Letters on the Inspiration of the Scriptures (Coleridge) **231**:35
Letters on the Laws of Man's Nature and Development (Martineau) **26**:311, 327, 329, 336; **137**:236, 327, 332, 335, 360
"Letters on the Oxford Counter-Reformation" (Froude) **43**:178
"Letters on the Significance of the Scandinavian North for Prehistorical Europe" (Almqvist)
See "Brev om den skandinaviska Nordens betydelse för Europas fornhistoria"
Letters on the Spanish Inquisition (Maistre)
See *Lettres à un gentilhomme russe sur l'Inquisition espagnole*
Letters on the Study of Nature (Herzen) **10**:326; **61**:98
Letters on the Works and Character of J. J. Rousseau (Staël-Holstein) **3**:523
Letters on Theron and Aspasio: Addressed to the Author (James) **53**:239
Letters on Various Interesting and Important Subjects (Freneau) **111**:111, 136, 138
Letters Relating to the Study of Theology (Herder) **8**:297, 306
Letters to a Frenchman about the Present Crisis (Bakunin) **25**:48-9, 74; **58**:114
"Letters to a Young Man whose Education has been Neglected" (De Quincey) **87**:33
Letters to Addington on the Peace of Amiens (Cobbett) **49**:113
Letters to an Aunt (Saltykov)
See *Pisma k tyotenke*
Letters to an Englishman (Brontë)
See *Letters of an Englishman*
Letters to an Old Comrade (Herzen) **10**:329
Letters to and from the Late Samuel Johnson, LL.D. (Piozzi) **57**:241-2, 253, 271, 298
Letters to Elizabeth Barrett Browning Addressed to Richard Hengist Horne (Barrett Browning) **61**:34
Letters to Fanny Kemble (FitzGerald) **9**:269
"Letters to Henrietta G." (Brown) **74**:134
Letters to Kindergartners (Peabody) **169**:150
Letters to Kugelmann (Marx) **114**:41
"Letters to Landlords, No. 2" (Kingsley) **35**:255
Letters to Marcie (Sand)
See "Lettres à Marcie"
Letters to Mothers (Sigourney) **87**:321-22, 338
"Letters to My Pupils" (Sigourney) **87**:321-22
Letters to Persons Who are Engaged in Domestic Service (Beecher) **30**:15, 17
Letters to the Chopsticks (Cobbett) **49**:160
Letters to the Mob (Norton) **47**:248, 254
Letters to the People on Health and Happiness (Beecher) **30**:8, 16-17
Letters to William Pitt (Cobbett) **49**:113
Letters to Young Ladies (Sigourney) **21**:295; **87**:321-22, 338
Letters Written During a Short Residence in Spain and Portugal (Southey) **97**:284
Letters written from Lausanne (Charriere)
See *Lettres écrites de Lausanne*
Letters Written in France in the Summer of 1790, to a Friend in England. Containing Various Anecdotes Relative to the French Revolution and the Memoirs of Mons. and Madame du F— (Williams) **135**:256-57, 267-69, 271-77, 282-83, 285-90, 296-97, 321, 323, 327-28, 333, 336-37, 340, 342-43, 353-54
Lettre à Fontanes sur la campagne romaine (Chateaubriand) **134**:18
Lettre à George Sand (Liszt)
See *Lettre d'un voyageur à M. George Sand*
Lettre à Lambert Massart (Liszt) **199**:315
"Lettre à Lord ***" (Vigny) **7**:476
"Lettre à M. Berthelot" (Renan) **26**:380
Lettre à M. Chauvet sur l'unité de temps et de lieu dans la tragédie (Manzoni) **29**:275, 289; **98**:213, 220, 241, 287
Lettre à M. de Fontanes (Chateaubriand) **134**:27, 116, 123
"Lettre à M. de Lamartine" (Musset) **7**:261-62, 266, 273, 275; **150**:280, 307, 315, 318
"Lettre à M. Nisard" (Sand) **174**:290
Lettre à Ronchaud (Liszt) **199**:312
Lettre à un poète voyageur (Liszt)
See *Lettre d'un voyageur à M. George Sand*
Lettre à une Dame Russe (Maistre) **37**:314
Lettre addressée aux habitans du Piémont sur les avantages de la révolution française et la nécessité d'en adopter les principes en Italie (Barlow) **223**:15
Lettre de Cachet (Gore) **65**:20
Une Lettre de femme (Desbordes-Valmore) **97**:2, 10, 22, 26-7
Lettre de Junius (Vallès) **71**:357-58
"Lettre du voyant" (Rimbaud) **4**:457, 471, 473, 475, 481, 486; **35**:274, 282, 295, 297, 302, 307-08, 310-12; **82**:221, 223, 235, 238-40, 246-47, 249
Lettre d'un voyageur à M. George Sand (Liszt) **199**:305, 311-12, 315
"Lettre sur Julie" (Constant) **182**:187, 218, 227
"Lettre sur l'art du dessin dans les paysages" (Chateaubriand) **134**:15
Lettres (Staël-Holstein)
See *Lettres sur les ouvrages et le caractère de Jean-Jacques Rousseau*
Lettres à Madame Hanska (Balzac) **153**:149
"Lettres à Marcie" (Sand) **42**:330, 358-60; **57**:337; **174**:253
Lettres à Trébutien (Barbey d'Aurevilly) **213**:46-47
Lettres à un absent (Daudet) **1**:231
Lettres à un gentilhomme russe sur l'Inquisition espagnole (Maistre) **37**:323, 325
Lettres à une inconnue (Mérimée) **6**:355-6, 356, 359, 361, 364-5; **65**:45
Lettres de Benjamin Constant à Madame de Récamier, 1807-1830 (Constant) **6**:214
Lettres de Dupuis et Cotonet (Musset) **7**:258
Lettres de jeunesse (Fromentin) **125**:100, 139-41
Lettres de Mistriss Henley publiées par son amie (Charriere) **66**:121-3, 125, 128-9, 138-43, 146-54, 156-7, 176
Lettres de mon moulin (Daudet) **1**:231, 234-35,

239, 243, 245, 249-52
"Lettres du voyant" (Rimbaud) **227**:192, 194-97, 208, 222, 242-43, 246, 265, 272, 274-76, 278
Lettres d'un bachelier ès musique (Liszt) **199**:301, 303-6, 311-17, 319, 323-24, 337, 343, 347
Lettres d'un Cultivateur Américain (Crèvecoeur) **105**:90, 93-108, 110-12, 114-28, 130-33, 135-39, 144-47, 149-50, 152-59, 162-65, 168-69, 172-73, 177-83, 185-91, 193-94
Lettres d'un Royaliste Savoisien (Maistre) **37**:312
Lettres d'un voyageraphiques (Sand) **174**:165
Lettres d'un voyageur (Sand) **2**:582, 588, 599; **42**:319, 336-37, 340, 386; **57**:315, 360-1
Lettres écrites de Lausanne (Charriere) **66**:121, 123-5, 135, 138, 142-3, 145, 161, 165, 168-9, 172, 176
Lettres écrites de Vienne en Autriche, sur le célèbre compositeur Jh Haydn, suivies d'une vie de Mozart, et de considérations sur Métastase et l'état present de la musique en France et en Italie (Stendhal) **178**:190, 192
Lettres inedites (Laclos)
See *Lettres inedites de Choderlos de Laclos*
Lettres inedites de Choderlos de Laclos (Laclos) **87**:273
Lettres neuchâteloises (Charriere) **66**:122-6, 136, 138, 160, 165, 168, 176
Lettres philosophiques (Chaadaev)
See *Philosophical Letters*
Lettres sur la littérature (Balzac) **153**:147
Lettres sur les ouvrages et le caractère de Jean-Jacques Rousseau (Staël-Holstein) **91**:339, 358
Lettres sur Rousseau (Staël-Holstein)
See *Lettres sur les ouvrages et le caractère de Jean-Jacques Rousseau*
Lettres trouvées dans des porte-feuilles d'émigrés (Charriere) **66**:125, 136, 172, 174-7
Lettres trouvées dans des porte-feuilles d'émigrés, suite (Charriere) **66**:175-7
"Letzie Heimkehr" (Eichendorff) **225**:57-58
Letzte Gaben (Droste-Hülshoff) **3**:193, 200
Letzte Gedichte und Gedanken (Heine) **4**:248, 250, 252; **147**:174
"Letzte Hoffnung" (Muller) **73**:389
"Der letzte König von Orplid" (Mörike) **201**:267, 273, 289, 299-300, 321, 329-30
Der Letzte König von Orplid (Mörike) **10**:445
"Das letzte Lied" (Kleist) **222**:234
"Das letzte Lied" (Raimund) **69**:10, 18-19
Letzte Mappe (Stifter) **198**:286
"Leucas" (Milnes) **61**:128-9
Die Leute von Seldwyla (Keller) **2**:411, 413-15, 423-24
"Lev starca Gerasima" (Leskov)
See "Lev startsa Gerasimova"
"Lev startsa Gerasimova" (Leskov) **25**:245
Levana; or, The Doctrine of Education (Jean Paul) **7**:226
"Levavi Oculos" (Allingham) **25**:8
"Le lever" (Musset) **7**:267; **150**:232
Levi Blodgett Letter of 1840 (Parker)
See *The Previous Question between Mr. Andrews Norton and His Alumni, Moved and Handled in a Letter to Those Gentlemen*
"An Levin Schücking" (Droste-Hülshoff) **3**:200
Levnedsbogen (Andersen) **214**:6-8
"Le lévrier de Magnus" (Leconte de Lisle) **29**:223, 225
"Levša" (Leskov) **25**:228, 233, 238; **174**:37, 48-50
"The Lew O' the Rick" (Barnes) **75**:79
"Lewti" (Coleridge) **9**:149, 151, 158; **177**:113
"Lex Talionis" (Gordon) **21**:159
Leyendas (Bécquer) **106**:86, 96, 99, 107-10, 118-20, 122, 129-31, 142
"Leyendo a María" (Isaacs) **70**:303
"Liab's First Christmas" (Cooke) **110**:37
Liaisons (Laclos)
See *Les liaisons dangereuses; ou, Lettres recueillies dans une société et publiées pour l'instruction de quelques autres*
Les Liaisons (Laclos)
See *Les liaisons dangereuses; ou, Lettres recueillies dans une société et publiées pour l'instruction de quelques autres*
Les Liaisons dangereuses (Baudelaire)
See *Notes sur Les Liaisons dangereuses*
Liaisons dangereuses (Laclos)
See *Les liaisons dangereuses; ou, Lettres recueillies dans une société et publiées pour l'instruction de quelques autres*
Les liaisons dangereuses; ou, Lettres recueillies dans une société et publiées pour l'instruction de quelques autres (Laclos) **4**:324-38, 340-43; **87**:207-315
"The Lianhan Shee" (Carleton) **3**:96; **199**:9, 18, 31, 33, 35
"The Liar" (Krylov) **1**:438-39
"Libbie Marsh's Three Eras" (Gaskell) **5**:205; **70**:185; **137**:4, 38, 41, 61-62
"Die Libelle" (Heine) **147**:232
Liber Amoris; or The New Pygmalion (Hazlitt) **29**:157, 170; **82**:74-8, 81, 85-91, 97-8, 101-06, 122, 125-26, 141-46
"Liberal" (Saltykov) **16**:374
"Liberal Education and Where to Find It" (Huxley) **67**:10, 26, 28, 40, 53, 56, 85, 92, 97
"Liberal Practitioners" (Arnold)
See "Our Liberal Practitioners"
The Liberal Preacher (Martineau) **137**:315
Liberalism and the Church (Brownson)
See *Conversations on Liberalism and the Church*
Liberia, or Mr. Peyton's Experiments (Hale) **75**:317, 321, 326, 328, 330-1, 339-341
"Libertad" (Heredia) **209**:138
Liberté, Egalité, Fraternité (Silva) **114**:263
"La Liberté, ou une nuit à Rome" (Lamartine) **190**:234
Liberté politique (Constant)
See *La Liberté politique, essentielle à la liberté civile*
La Liberté politique, essentielle à la liberté civile (Constant) **182**:211
The Libertine (Dacre) **151**:152-53, 158, 162, 199, 215-16, 219, 225-27, 229
"Liberty" (Horton)
See "On Liberty and Slavery"
"Liberty" (Lampman) **194**:10
"Liberty" (Pushkin)
See "Vol'nost': Oda"
Liberty (Coleridge) **90**:16
Liberty (Mill)
See *On Liberty*
"Liberty. An Ode" (Pushkin)
See "Vol'nost': Oda"
"Liberty and Love" (Petofi)
See "Szabadság, szerelem"
"Liberty and Necessity" (Thomson) **18**:395
"Liberty and Slavery" (Horton)
See "On Liberty and Slavery"
"Liberty Tree" (Paine) **62**:320, 366, 379
"Liberty's Victim" (Boyesen) **135**:14, 20, 29
"The Library" (Crabbe) **26**:77-79, 81, 110; **121**:18, 26-27, 52, 83-84, 88-89
Library of Poetry and Song (Bryant) **6**:176
Libres méditations d'un solitaire inconnu sur le détachement du monde et sur d'autres objets de la morale religieuse (Senancour) **16**:433, 436
Libro de gorriones (Bécquer)
See *Libro de los gorriones: colección de proyectos, argumentos, ideas y planes de cosas diferentes que se concluirán o no según sople el viento*
Libro de los gorriones: colección de proyectos, argumentos, ideas y planes de cosas diferentes que se concluirán o no según sople el viento (Bécquer) **106**:127, 129, 167, 169
El libro de los niños (Martínez de la Rosa) **102**:229, 254
Libro de versos (Silva) **114**:310-11, 313, 316-18, 321-22
El libro de versos (Silva) **114**:300
Libussa (Grillparzer) **1**:385, 389; **102**:100, 117-18, 131, 170, 192, 196, 198-203, 208, 213
Lichte Stunden eines wahnsinnigen Musikers (Hoffmann) **183**:225
Lichtenstein: Romantische Sage aus der würtembergischen Geschichte (Hauff) **185**:318-25
"An Lida" (Goethe) **4**:193
"Lide" (Bestuzhev) **131**:150
"Lidet om Sangene i Edda" (Grundtvig) **158**:183
Lidet om sangene i Edda (Grundtvig) **158**:175, 179
"Lie A-bed" (Rossetti) **186**:236
"Die Liebe" (Claudius) **75**:193
"Die Liebe" (Hölderlin) **16**:181, 185
"Die liebe Farbe" (Muller) **73**:364, 372-73
Liebe, Mißverständnis und Freundschaft (La Roche) **121**:326
Liebegeschichten und Heiratsachen (Nestroy) **42**:220, 223, 241
Liebe-Hütten (La Roche) **121**:250
"Liebesfrühling" (Lenau) **16**:281
"Die Liebesgeschichte des Kanzlers Schlick und der schonen Sienerin" (Arnim) **159**:60
"Liebesglück" (Mörike) **201**:280
"Liebesjahr" (Meyer) **81**:154
Das Liebesverbot; oder, Die Novize von Palermo (Wagner) **9**:414, 436, 473-74
"Liebesvorzeichen" (Mörike) **201**:279, 281
"Liebeszauber" (Tieck) **46**:350
Das Liebhaber-Theater vor dem Parlament (Kotzebue) **25**:147
"Lieblingsbuche" (Mörike)
See "An eine Lieblingsbuche meines Gartens"
"Lied" (Gautier) **59**:19
Lied an die Freude (Schiller) **39**:331, 336, 358, 388; **166**:115-16, 159
"Lied der Auswanderer nach Amerika" (Ludwig) **4**:353
"Das Lied der Toten" (Novalis) **13**:374, 401-02
"Lied des Lynkeus" (Goethe) **34**:98
"Lied mit Thränen" (Eichendorff) **225**:7
"Lied vom Winde" (Mörike) **201**:253, 268
"Das Lied von der Bernauerin" (Ludwig) **4**:353
"Das Lied von der Glocke" (Schiller) **38**:305, 337, 370; **39**:347; **166**:105, 114
"Lied von der Wüste" (Brentano) **191**:94
"Lieder" (Heine) **147**:148
Lieder aus dem Meerbusen von Salerno (Muller) **73**:352-53, 358, 360, 362, 366-67
Lieder aus Franzensbad bei Eger (Muller) **73**:366
Lieder der Griechen (Muller) **73**:354, 387, 389
Liederbuch dreier Freunde (Storm) **195**:90
Liederkreis (Schumann) **143**:139
"Liederseelen" (Meyer) **81**:149, 201
"Lier der Toten" (Novalis) **178**:74
"Lieutenant Yergunov's Story" (Turgenev)
See "Istoriya leytenanta Ergunova"
"Lieutenant Zidén" (Runeberg) **41**:321-22
"The Lieutenant's Daughter" (Froude) **43**:192
"Life" (Barbauld) **50**:3
"Life" (Bryant) **6**:168
"Life" (Crawford) **127**:202
"Life" (Lampman) **194**:17, 42, 45
"Life" (Rossetti) **50**:311
"Life" (Very) **9**:381

Life (Barham) **77**:21, 28
Life among the Piutes: Their Wrongs and Claims (Winnemucca) **79**:336, 342-52, 354, 358, 361-7
Life and Adventures (Sala) **46**:237
The Life and Adventures of Joaquìn Murieta, the Celebrated California Bandit (Ridge) **82**:176-77, 186, 188, 190-95, 198-209
The Life and Adventures of Jonathan Jefferson Whitlaw; or, Scenes on the Mississippi (Trollope) **30**:314, 319, 322
The Life and Adventures of Martin Chuzzlewit (Dickens) **3**:144-45, 151-52, 161, 163, 172, 178; **8**:165; **18**:100, 112, 116, 132; **26**:157, 184; **37**:145; **86**:189, 256; **105**:227, 229, 311; **113**:29, 98, 106-7; **203**:233, 235, 237; **206**:57; **211**:42, 46; **217**:206, 216, 239; **219**:58-239; **231**:179
The Life and Adventures of Michael Armstrong, the Factory Boy (Trollope) **30**:316-18
The Life and Adventures of Nicholas Nickleby (Dickens) **3**:138-41, 152, 154, 179, 182, 184; **8**:183; **18**:100, 121; **26**:164, 167, 177, 200; **26**:164, 167, 177, 200; **37**:143, 149, 164, 168, 186, 194, 202; **86**:256; **105**:204-05, 214; **113**:88, 92, 103, 106; **161**:98-99; **203**:180, 183, 198, 250; **206**:7-8, 12, 56, 104-5, 129, 131; **217**:204, 217; **219**:70, 96-98, 108, 148, 214; **230**:47, 118; **231**:166-255
The Life and Adventures of Oliver Goldsmith (Forster) **11**:95-96, 99, 101, 115, 128-29
The Life and Adventures of Peter Porcupine (Cobbett) **49**:153
"Life and Art" (Lazarus) **109**:295
The Life and Correspondence of Robert Southey (Southey) **8**:479; **97**:269-70, 282-83, 336
"Life and Death" (Rossetti) **2**:575; **50**:264, 289; **66**:341; **186**:271
The Life and Death of Jason (Morris) **4**:412-16, 418-21, 425-27, 431-36, 442
"Life and Doctrine of Geoffroy St. Hilaire" (Lewes) **215**:145
"Life and Habits of a Literary Antiquary" (D'Israeli) **217**:340
Life and Letters (Huxley) **67**:27, 86-7
The Life and Letters of Charles Darwin (Darwin) **57**:124, 142, 174
"Life and Manners" (De Quincey) **4**:61
"Life and Mind" (Lewes) **215**:149
The Life and Morals of Jesus of Nazareth, extracted textually from the Gospels in Greek, Latin, French, and English (Jefferson) **11**:199; **103**:106, 163
"Life and Nature" (Lampman) **25**:189, 196, 198, 207; **194**:31, 81, 92
The Life and Opinions of Kater Murr: With the Fragmentary Biography of Kapellmeister Johannes Kreisler on Random Sheets of Scrap Paper (Hoffmann)
See *Lebens-Ansichten des Katers Murr nebst fragmentarischer Biographie des Kapellmeisters Johannes Kreisler in züfalligen Makulaturblättern*
The Life and Poems of Theodore Winthrop (Winthrop) **210**:300-301
The Life and Poetical Works of George Crabbe (Crabbe) **26**:113
Life and Recollections (Planché) **42**:274-75, 299
The Life and Reign of Charles the First (D'Israeli)
See *Commentaries on the Life and Reign of Charles the First*
Life and Selected Writings of Thomas Jefferson (Jefferson) **103**:119
"Life and Song" (Lanier) **6**:249, 270; **118**:217, 235, 240
Life and Times of Frederick Douglass, Written by Himself (Douglass) **7**:130-31, 134, 136-37, 145; **55**:107-8, 110-1, 113, 122-3, 128; **141**:55, 64, 74-77, 129-32, 136, 145
The Life and Times of Salvator Rosa (Morgan) **29**:391
"Life and Times of Thomas Becket" (Froude) **43**:178
The Life and Works of Goethe (Lewes) **25**:274-75, 287, 294, 296-98, 301-04, 306, 308, 320-21, 325; **215**:86, 122, 143, 145, 147, 165
"The Life and Works of Leopardi" (Lewes) **25**:286
The Life and Writings of Frederick Douglass (Douglass) **141**:146-48
The Life and Writings of Hugh Henry Brackenridge (Brackenridge) **227**:115
The Life and Writings of Joseph Mazzini (Mazzini) **34**:275
The Life and Writings of Major Jack Downing of Downingville, Away Down East in the State of Maine, Written by Himself (Smith) **187**:312-13, 316, 318-20
Life and Writings of Nancy Maria Hyde (Sigourney) **87**:325
The Life Annuity (Fredro)
See *Dożywocie*
"Life at Zvanka" (Derzhavin)
See "Evgeniu. Zhizn' Zvanskaya"
"Life calls us" (Pavlova) **138**:33-34, 37
Life Book (Andersen)
See *Levnedsbogen*
A Life Drama (Smith) **59**:261-2, 264-5, 267, 269, 272, 288, 291, 296-8, 301, 305, 312-3, 318-21, 326, 328-33, 335-42
A Life for a Life (Craik) **38**:110, 113, 122, 126, 133
"Life for Life" (Boyesen) **135**:15
"A Life Fragment" (Smith) **59**:254, 256-7
Life Here and There (Willis) **194**:294
"Life in a Love" (Browning) **19**:127; **79**:153
"Life in London" (Mayhew) **31**:181
Life in Manchester (Gaskell) **137**:4
Life in the Argentine Republic (Sarmiento)
See *Civilización i barbarie: La vida de Juan Facundo Quiroga i aspecto fisico, costumbres, i ábitos de la República Arjentina*
Life in the Clearings versus the Bush (Moodie) **14**:217, 220-27, 234-36, 239-41; **113**:295, 307-9, 318, 323-26, 331, 333, 353, 355, 358, 361, 373
"Life in the Country" (Haliburton) **149**:297
Life in the Open Air (Winthrop) **210**:281-82, 286, 288, 290, 296, 298-300, 302-3, 319, 328
Life in the Sick-Room (Martineau) **26**:310, 323, 325, 349-50; **137**:277, 283, 334-35
"Life in the Thüringian Forest" (Taylor) **89**:308
"Life in the Wilds" (Martineau) **26**:303; **137**:260
"Life is Growth, and Growth is Change" (Larcom) **179**:177
"Life Is the Desert and the Solitude" (Mangan) **27**:299
The Life, Letters, and Literary Remains of Edward Bulwer, Lord Lytton (Bulwer-Lytton) **1**:148
Life, Letters, and Literary Remains of John Keats (Keats) **8**:374
The Life, Letters, and Literary Remains of John Keats (Milnes) **61**:138, 140, 143-9
Life North and South: Showing the True Character of Both (Hale) **75**:315, 339
Life of a Good-for-Nothing (Eichendorff)
See *Aus dem Leben eines Taugenichts und Das Marmorbild: Zwei Novellen nebst einem Anhange von Liedern und Romanzen*
The Life of a Lover: In a Series of Letters (Lee) **191**:313, 327, 332
"The Life of a Peasant Martyress" (Leskov)
See "Zitie odnoj baby"
The Life of a Peasant Martyress (Leskov)
See *Zitie odnoj baby*
"The Life of a Well-Known Character" (Hoffmann) **2**:342
"The Life of a Woman" ("ZHimiie odnoj baby") (Leskov) **174**:135
"The Life of Alexander Percy" (Brontë) **109**:29
"The Life of an Edinburgh Baillie" (Hogg) **4**:283
Life of Andrew Jackson, President of the United States of America (Cobbett) **49**:160
The Life of Benvenuto Cellini (Symonds) **34**:331, 334, 350
The Life of Bernard Gilpin (Gilpin) **30**:33
Life of Bishop Ken (Bowles) **103**:54
Life of Byrn (Moore) **110**:189
Life of Byron (Galt) **110**:91
Life of Carlyle (Froude)
See *Thomas Carlyle*
The Life of Charles Brockden Brown (Dunlap) **2**:208, 215
The Life of Charles Dickens (Forster) **11**:103-04, 106, 108-12, 115-27, 131-32
The Life of Charlotte Brontë (Gaskell) **5**:183-86, 188-89, 198, 201, 205; **70**:116, 119, 176-77, 182, 196, 199, 205, 213, 234-35, 237-41; **214**:190, 299, 304, 322-28
Life of Charlotte Elizabeth, as Contained in her Personal Recollections (Tonna)
See *Personal Recollections of Charlotte Elizabeth, Continued to the Close of her Life*
Life of Christopher Columbus (Irving)
See *A History of the Life and Voyages of Christopher Columbus*
The Life of Cicero (Trollope) **101**:321, 344; **215**:278
Life of Columbus (Irving)
See *A History of the Life and Voyages of Christopher Columbus*
Life of Cromwell (Southey) **8**:472
The Life of David Garrick, Esq. By Arthur Murphy, Esq. (Murphy) **229**:234, 237-38
The Life of Edward Irving, Minister of the National Scottish Church (Oliphant) **11**:429-30, 433, 439, 446-7; **61**:216; **221**:227, 233-34, 246
The Life of Fedor Ushakov (Radishchev)
See *Zhitie Fedora Vasil'evicha Ushakova, s priobshcheiem nekotorykh ego sochinenii*
Life of Franklin Pierce (Hawthorne) **2**:303, 314; **39**:229; **191**:204
The Life of Friedrich Schiller (Carlyle) **70**:38-39
A Life of General Robert E. Lee (Cooke) **5**:130
Life of Geoffrey Chaucer (Godwin) **14**:53
The Life of George Washington (Irving) **2**:374-75, 377-78
The Life of Goethe (Lewes)
See *The Life and Works of Goethe*
"Life of Goldsmith" (Irving) **2**:376
The Life of Harriot Stuart (Lennox) **23**:226, 231-35, 252-53, 263; **134**:219, 229, 238, 342, 347
The Life of Haydn, in a Series of Letters Written at Vienna, followed by the Life of Mozart, with Observations on Metastasio, and on the Present State of Music in France and Italy (Stendhal)
See *Lettres écrites de Vienne en Autriche, sur le célèbre compositeur Jh Haydn, suivies d'une vie de Mozart, et de considérations sur Métastase et l'état present de la musique en France et en Italie*
The Life of Henri Brulard (Stendhal)
See *Vie de Henri Brulard*
The Life of Hugh Latimer, Bishop of Worcester (Gilpin) **30**:33-4
The Life of Jesus (Renan)
See *La vie de Jésus*
The Life of Jesus (Schleiermacher) **107**:363, 400

Life of John Bunyan (Southey) **8**:465, 472
"The Life of John Smith" (Ingelow)
See "The Life of Mr. John Smith"
The Life of John Sterling (Carlyle) **70**:54
The Life of Jonathan Swift (Forster) **11**:110, 115, 120
"Life of Life" (Shelley) **18**:340, 345; **93**:305-07
Life of Lord George Bentinck (Disraeli) **2**:147; **39**:44; **79**:239, 269
The Life of Ludwig van Beethoven (Beethoven) **227**:10
Life of Madame Roland (Blind)
See *Madame Roland*
The Life of Maximilen Robespierre with Extracts from His Unpublished Correspondence (Lewes) **25**:320
The Life of Michelangelo Buonarroti (Symonds) **34**:328-29, 331, 334, 350-51, 356
"The Life of Mr. John Smith" (Ingelow) **107**:161-64, 175
The Life of Napoleon Bonaparte (Hazlitt) **29**:173; **82**:105, 144, 146, 163, 165
The Life of Napoleon Bonaparte (Scott) **15**:271, 277; **69**:303
The Life of Napoleon Buonaparte (Scott) **209**:346
The Life of Nelson (Southey) **8**:453-54, 459, 463, 467, 471-72, 474; **97**:250, 259, 262, 265-66, 268-71, 283, 290-93, 306, 328, 330
The Life of ... Northangerland (Brontë) **109**:42, 45-6, 52
Life of Perez del Pulgar (Martínez de la Rosa)
See *Hernán Pérez del Pulgar*
Life of Quintus Fixlein (Jean Paul) **7**:223
Life of Robert Burns (Lockhart) **6**:292, 297, 300, 308-10
Life of Robespierre (Lewes) **215**:84
Life of Rossini (Stendhal)
See *Vie de Rossini*
The Life of Samuel Johnson, LL.D., Including a Journal of a Tour to the Hebrides, by James Boswell, Esq. (Croker) **10**:90-93, 95-97
Life of Stonewall Jackson (Cooke) **5**:130
"The Life of Strafford" (Forster) **11**:120
"Life of Sut" (Harris) **165**:224
"Life of the Blessed" (Bryant) **6**:159
The Life of the Countess Gritta von Ratsatourhouse (Arnim)
See *Das Leben der Hochgräfin Gritta von Rattenzuhausbeiuns*
The Life of the Fields (Jefferies) **47**:95-7, 102, 112, 122, 133, 136-37
The Life of Thomas Cranmer, Archbishop of Canterbury (Gilpin) **30**:34
The Life of Ušakov (Radishchev)
See *Zhitie Fedora Vasil'evicha Ushakova, s priobshcheiem nekotorykh ego sochinenii*
"Life of Warner Howard Warner" (Brontë) **109**:34
A Life of Washington (Paulding) **2**:526
The Life of Wesley and the Rise and Progress of Methodism (Southey) **8**:459, 463, 467, 471-72; **97**:259, 263-66, 268, 283, 306
Life of West (Galt) **110**:90, 93
The Life of William Carleton (Carleton) **199**:37, 40, 45, 64
Life of Wolsey (Galt) **110**:76, 96
"Life or Death" (Petofi)
See "Elet vagy halál"
"Life out of Death" (Rossetti) **186**:271
"The Life That Is" (Bryant) **6**:165
Life Without and Life Within; or, Reviews, Narratives, Essays, and Poems (Fuller) **211**:92
"Life Without Principle" (Thoreau) **7**:381, 385, 398; **21**:322, 328, 347-8; **207**:191, 253-54, 256
"Life-in Love" (Rossetti) **77**:339
"Life's Boredom . . ." (Verlaine)
See "L'Ennui de vivre . . ."
"Life's Hebe" (Thomson) **18**:391-92
"A Life's Parallels" (Rossetti) **66**:343
A Life's Secret (Wood) **178**:288, 291, 335
"Life's Uncertainty" (Beddoes) **154**:12
"A Lifetime" (Bryant) **6**:175, 182
"The Lifted Veil" (Eliot) **41**:102-03, 108; **118**:59
The Lifted Veil (Eliot) **199**:234, 237, 241
"Ligeia" (Poe) **1**:504-05, 513-14, 518-19; **16**:295, 303-06, 308, 314, 322, 324, 328, 331, 335; **55**:133, 151, 197, 201; **78**:285; **94**:202; **97**:180, 182, 208-09, 211; **117**:193, 222, 237, 245, 281, 299, 301, 303; **211**:246, 253-55, 257, 312, 341-42, 344
"The Light" (Allingham) **25**:6
"Light" (Hugo) **3**:262
"Light!" (Petofi)
See "Világosságot!"
"The Light and Glory of the Word" (Cowper) **94**:70
"Light and Shade" (Ingelow) **39**:256
"A Light Exists in Spring" (Dickinson) **21**:59, 75
"The Light Has Dawned" (Zhukovsky)
See "Vzoshla zaria..."
"Light Love" (Rossetti) **2**:557; **50**:298; **66**:329, 331, 352; **186**:304
The Light of Her Countenance (Boyesen) **135**:14, 37, 41
"Light of Shadow" (Isaacs)
See "Lumbre de sombra"
"The Light of Stars" (Longfellow) **2**:479, 492; **45**:112, 116, 127, 148, 152; **103**:295
"The Light of the Haram" (Moore) **6**:380-81, 388; **110**:217, 222, 224-25
"Light shining out of darkness" (Cowper) **94**:70
"Light Summer Reading" (Freneau) **111**:33
"Light Up Thy Halls" (Brontë) **16**:80
"A Light Woman" (Browning) **79**:163
"The Lighthouse" (Longfellow) **45**:161; **101**:92
"The Light-House" (Poe) **117**:310
The Lighthouse (Collins) **93**:38, 64
"The Lighthouses" (Baudelaire)
See "Les phares"
"Lightning" (Rimbaud)
See "L'Eclair"
"The Lightning and the Lantern" (Cranch) **115**:49
"The Lightning-Rod Man" (Melville) **3**:331, 354, 381-82
Lights and Shadows of Scottish Life: A Selection from the Papers of the Late Arthur Austin (Wilson) **5**:547-49, 554-55, 558, 567, 569
"Den liile Idas Blomster" (Andersen) **7**:22; **79**:23, 32-3, 50, 65, 76, 87
"Den liile pige med Svovlstikkerne" (Andersen) **79**:76
"Like a little bird at early dawn" (Tyutchev)
See "Kak ptichka, ranneyu zarey"
"Like Clouds Have Passed the Years . . ." (Eminescu) **33**:246
"Like trains of cars on tracks of plush" (Dickinson) **171**:87
Die Likedeeler (Fontane) **26**:244
"Likeness to God: Discourse at the Ordination of the Rev. F. A. Farley" (Channing) **17**:46, 53
"The Lilac" (Barnes) **75**:38
"The Lilac is an ancient shrub" (Dickinson) **171**:181
"Lilacs" (Whitman)
See "When Lilacs Last in the Dooryard Bloom'd"
"Lilian" (Patmore) **9**:326, 328
"Lilian" (Tennyson) **30**:223; **65**:368; **202**:334, 337
"Lilian of the Vale" (Darley) **2**:127, 130
"The Lilies" (Mickiewicz)
See "Lilje"
Lilies in Sharon and The Martyrs (Stagnelius)
See *Liljor i Saron och Martyrerna*
"The Lilies of the Field and the Birds of the Air" (Kierkegaard) **78**:239
"Lilith" (Kendall) **12**:199
"Lilith" (Rossetti) **4**:506
"Lilje" (Mickiewicz) **3**:398
Liljor i Saron och Martyrerna (Stagnelius) **61**:248, 251, 253, 260
Lilla Weneda (Slowacki) **15**:348-49, 352-53, 361, 365, 371, 373, 378, 380
"Lille Claus og Store Claus" (Andersen) **7**:21, 25; **79**:23-4, 50, 59, 64-5, 68, 72, 76; **214**:40, 53-54, 58-59, 75
"Den Lille Havfrue" (Andersen) **7**:23, 26, 28-9, 34, 36; **79**:19, 21, 23, 26, 51, 58, 62-63, 66, 70, 76, 82, 87-88; **214**:10-12, 15, 17-20, 33, 47, 63, 71, 75
"Den lille Idas Blomster" (Andersen) **214**:38-39, 54
"Den Lille Pige med Svovlstikkerne" (Andersen) **7**:33-34; 23, 63, 66; **214**:18, 78
Lilliesleaf: Being a Concluding Series of Passages in the Life of Mrs. Margaret Maitland (Oliphant) **11**:432; **61**:163, 203
"The Lilly" (Blake) **37**:43, 51, 80
"Lily Adair" (Chivers) **49**:38, 42, 49, 72, 74
"A Lily and a Lute" (Ingelow) **39**:264
"The Lily Bed" (Crawford) **12**:162, 166-67, 172; **127**:167-72, 228
"The Lily Confidante" (Timrod) **25**:361, 365-66, 372, 375
"The Lily of Liddesdale" (Wilson) **5**:558, 564
"The Lily of the Valley" (Beddoes) **154**:46, 78
The Lily of the Valley (Balzac)
See *Le lys dans la vallée*
"Lily Song" (Crawford) **127**:151-52
"The Lily's Delusion" (Osgood) **141**:342
"The Lily's Quest" (Hawthorne) **2**:305
Les Limbes (Baudelaire)
See *Les fleurs du mal*
"Limbo" (Coleridge) **231**:67, 94, 115-16
"Limbo" (Verlaine) **51**:371
"The Limerick Gloves" (Edgeworth) **51**:87, 89, 137
Limestone (Stifter)
See "Kalkstein"
"Limits of Knowledge" (Symonds) **34**:336
The Limits of State Action (Humboldt)
See *Ideen zu einem Versuch, die Grenzen der Wirksamkeit des Staats zu bestimmen*
"Lincoln Ode" (Lowell) **2**:511
"Lincoln-Douglas Debates" (Lincoln) **18**:210-11, 234, 243, 245, 247-48, 253, 255, 259, 267, 280
Lincoln's Life (Sarmiento)
See *Vida de Abrán Lincoln*
Linda: Incidents in the Life of a Slave Girl, seven years concealed in Slavery (Jacobs)
See *Incidents in the Life of a Slave Girl, Written by Herself*
Linda Tressel (Trollope) **101**:334
"Linden Lea" (Barnes) **75**:33
"Der Lindenbaum" (Muller)
See "Am Brunnen vor dem Tore"
"Lindenborg Fool" (Morris) **4**:430, 440
"Lines" (Cowper)
See "Lines Written during a Period of Insanity"
"Lines" (Fuller) **211**:92
"Lines" (Horton)
See "Lines to My —"
"Lines Above Tintern Abbey" (Wordsworth)
See "Lines Composed a Few Miles above Tintern Abbey, on Revisiting the Banks of the Wye during a Tour, July 13, 1798"
"Lines Addressed to Mr. Jefferson, On his retirement from the presidency of the United States.—1809" (Freneau) **111**:160
"Lines Attributed to Alexander Selkirk" (Cowper) **8**:107
"Lines by A. G. A. to A. S." (Brontë) **16**:79

"Lines By a Lady on the Loss of Her Trunk" (Sheridan) **91**:233
"Lines by Claudia" (Brontë) **16**:80
"Lines Composed a Few Miles above Tintern Abbey, on Revisiting the Banks of the Wye during a Tour, July 13, 1798" (Wordsworth) **12**:386, 388, 407, 431, 436, 441, 449, 455, 464, 467-70; **38**:360, 366-67; **111**:198-200, 202, 225, 236, 243, 248, 251, 256-59, 284, 286-87, 294, 307, 310-11, 314-15; **166**:241; **206**:225, 235, 242, 244, 246-48, 250, 270, 275, 283-85, 316, 318-19, 322, 331-32, 336
"Lines Composed in a Wood on a Windy Day" (Brontë) **4**:49; **71**:85
"Lines Extempore by Thomas Paine July 1803" (Paine) **62**:325
"Lines from an Unpublished Drama" (Osgood) **141**:355
"Lines from the Port-Folio of H——" (Pinkney) **31**:276, 279
"Lines in Memory of Kutusoff" (Derzhavin) **215**:8
"Lines in Memory of Schiller's 'Der Pilgrim'" (Rossetti) **186**:268
"Lines Intended for Edith Southey's Album" (Wordsworth) **138**:285
"Lines Intended for My Niece's Album" (Wordsworth) **138**:226
"Lines Left upon a Seat in a Yew-tree" (Wordsworth) **12**:386-87, 345, 464; **111**:200, 202, 306, 313-14, 316, 349, 359; **166**:264, 266; **206**:225
"Lines Left upon a Seat in a Yew-Tree, Which Stands near the Lake of Esthwaite, on a Desolate Part of the Shore, Commanding a Beautiful Prospect" (Wordsworth)
See "Lines Left upon a Seat in a Yew-tree"
"Lines Occasioned by a Visit to an Old Indian Burying Ground" (Freneau) **1**:315, 317, 319, 323; **111**:81, 140, 164-71, 173-74, 190
"Lines, Occasioned by a Visit to Whittlebury Forest" (Bloomfield) **145**:154
"Lines Occasioned by reading Mr. Paine's Rights of Man" (Freneau) **111**:108, 124
"Lines Occasioned by the Death of an Infant" (Murray) **63**:208
"Lines on a Friend" (Coleridge) **99**:22; **231**:119
"Lines on a Humming Bird Seen at a Lady's Window" (Ridge) **82**:181
"Lines on Alexandria" (Campbell) **19**:181
"Lines on an Autumnal Evening" (Coleridge) **99**:17
"Lines on Constantinople" (Opie) **65**:160
"Lines on Leaving Europe" (Willis) **194**:287, 307
"Lines on Poland" (Campbell) **19**:183
"Lines on Revisiting the Country" (Bryant) **46**:39
"Lines on Seeing the Duchess of Devonshire in Her New and Splendid Carriage" (Robinson) **142**:167
"Lines on the Birth of Her Majesty's Third Child" (Hunt) **70**:260
"Lines on the Death of an Aged Relative" (Cranch) **115**:8
"The Lines on the Death of Joseph Rodman Drake" (Halleck) **47**:57, 65
"Lines on the Death of Lucy Hooper" (Whittier) **8**:486, 520
"Lines on the First Mild Day of March" (Wordsworth) **12**:387; **111**:200, 281
"Lines on the Loss of the Royal George" (Cowper) **8**:111, 116, 118, 120; **94**:32-3, 38
"Lines on the Opening of a Spring Campaign" (Opie) **65**:160
"Lines on the Place de Concorde, at Paris" (Opie) **65**:160
"Lines on the Portrait of a Celebrated Publisher" (Whittier) **8**:525; **59**:361
"Lines on the Receipt of My Mother's Picture" (Cowper) **8**:108, 112, 135-37; **94**:20, 33-4
"Lines Placed over a Chimney-Piece" (Barbauld) **185**:92-93
"Lines Suggested by Reading a State Poper" (Whittier) **59**:371
"Lines Suggested by the Last Words of Berengarius" (Coleridge) **231**:87
"Lines Tangled about the Round Table" (Lanier) **118**:260
"Lines: The Soft Unclouded Blue of Air" (Brontë) **16**:111
"Lines to a Friend on His Marriage" (Bryant) **6**:177
"Lines to a Friend on the Death of His Sister" (Whittier) **8**:491
"Lines to a Lady on the Death of her Lover" (Rogers) **69**:67
"Lines to a Reviewer" (Shelley) **18**:327
"Lines to a Teapot" (Baillie) **151**:123
"Lines to a Young Ass" (Coleridge) **9**:149
Lines to Agnes Ballie on Her Birthday (Baillie) **71**:2-3; **151**:95, 123
"Lines to Dora H." (Wordsworth) **138**:284
"Lines to Hartley Coleridge" (Wordsworth) **12**:431
"Lines to Him Who Will Understand Them" (Robinson) **142**:140
"Lines to Louisa" (Poe) **1**:514
"Lines to Melrose Abbey" (Wilson) **5**:545
"Lines to Miss F. Kemble" (Reynolds) **146**:176
Lines to Mr. Hodson Written on Board the Lisbon Packet (Byron) **149**:4
"Lines to My ——" (Horton) **87**:109-110
"Lines to —— On the Death of His Friend" (Very) **9**:376
"Lines to the Planet Mars" (Longfellow) **2**:473; **45**:116
"Lines to Tooke" (Coleridge) **231**:83
"Lines upon the Late Proceedings of the College Government" (Adams) **175**:40, 45
"The Lines upon the Yew-Tree Seat" (Coleridge) **9**:131
"Lines: When the Lamp is Shattered" (Shelley) **18**:362, 371
"Lines with a Wedding Present" (Barbauld) **185**:92
"Lines written a few miles above Tintern Abbey" (Wordsworth)
See "Lines Composed a Few Miles above Tintern Abbey, on Revisiting the Banks of the Wye during a Tour, July 13, 1798"
"Lines Written among the Euganean Hills" (Shelley) **18**:329, 371-73; **143**:248; **175**:281, 342
"Lines Written at a Small Distance from My House" (Wordsworth)
See "Lines Written at a Small Distance from My House, and Sent by My Little Boy to the Person to Whom They Are Addressed"
"Lines Written at a Small Distance from My House, and Sent by My Little Boy to the Person to Whom They Are Addressed" (Wordsworth) **12**:445; **111**:202
"Lines Written at Geneva" (Beddoes) **154**:51
"Lines written at Norwich on the First News of Peace" (Opie) **65**:175
"Lines, Written at Seventeen" (Mangan) **27**:298
Lines Written at Shurton Bars (Coleridge) **197**:190
"Lines Written at the Foot of Brother's Bridge" (Wordsworth) **12**:393
"Lines written at the Pallisades, near Port-Royal, in the Island of Jamaica—September 1784" (Freneau) **111**:148
"Lines Written at Thorp Green" (Brontë) **71**:165
"Lines Written during a Period of Insanity" (Cowper) **8**:137; **94**:24, 32, 38
"Lines Written in 1799" (Opie) **65**:160
"Lines Written in a Burial-Ground" (Wilson) **5**:567
"Lines Written in a Young Lady's Album of Different-coloured Paper" (Barbauld) **185**:92
"Lines Written in Bridgewater" (Thelwall) **162**:317, 324
"Lines Written in Early Spring" (Wordsworth) **12**:387, 436, 450, 466; **111**:200, 202, 224, 281-82, 284, 317
"Lines Written in Kensington Gardens" (Arnold) **29**:34; **218**:156-57, 189
"Lines written in Switzerland" (Beddoes) **154**:75, 81-82
"Lines Written in the Bay of Lerici" (Shelley) **18**:362, 369, 373
"Lines written in the Highlands" (Keats) **73**:176, 201, 209, 226
"Lines written into the album of a young lady" (Schiller)
See "Einer jungen Freundin ins Stammbuch"
"Lines Written near Richmond" (Wordsworth) **12**:387; **111**:202, 350
"Lines Written on 29 May, the Anniversary of Charles's Restoration" (Keats) **73**:331
"Lines Written on a Sickbed" (Robinson) **142**:179
"Lines Written on a Summer Evening" (Clare) **9**:75, 117, 122
"Lines Written on Hearing the News of the Death of Napoleon" (Shelley) **18**:362; **175**:321
"Lines Written on Leaving a Scene in Bavaria" (Campbell) **19**:179, 193
"Lines, Written on Reading Several Pamphlets Published by Clergymen Against the Abolition of the Gallows" (Whittier)
See "The Gallows"
"Lines Written on Revisiting a Scene in Argyleshire" (Campbell) **19**:181, 193
"Lines—Now heavily in clouds" (Brontë) **109**:30
De l'influence des femmes sur la littérature française comme proctectrices des lettres et comme auteurs; ou Précis de l'histoire des femmes françaises les plus célèbres (Genlis) **166**:43-44, 53
De l'influence des passions sur le bonheur des individus et des nations (Staël-Holstein) **3**:524; **91**:298-305, 311, 332-6, 340
"Les linges, le cygne" (Laforgue) **5**:277
"The Linnet and the Lark" (Webster) **230**:309
"The Linnet in the Rocky Dells" (Brontë) **109**:27
De l'intelligence (Taine) **15**:465, 467
"Lintukoto" (Kivi) **30**:51-2
The Linwoods; or, "Sixty Years Since" in America (Sedgwick) **19**:433-34, 436, 439, 442, 445, 447-49, 453; **98**:296, 299-301, 334, 351
"Liodor" (Karamzin) **173**:290
"Le lion du cirque" (Gautier) **1**:342
"The Lion Huntress of Belgravia" (Thackeray) **213**:302
The Lion of the West (Paulding) **2**:527
"The Lion, the Chamois, and the Fox" (Krylov) **1**:435
Lionel Lincoln (Cooper) **203**:46
Lionel Lincoln; or, The Leagues of Boston (Cooper) **1**:197, 200, 221; **54**:254, 299, 301
"Lionizing" (Poe) **16**:295, 313, 321-22
Les lionnes pauvres (Augier) **31**:2, 5-7, 9-10, 12-13, 15, 19, 24, 27, 30
Lions and Foxes (Augier)
See *Lions et renards*
Lions et renards (Augier) **31**:8-9, 13, 16, 19, 25-8, 31, 34, 38
"The Lions in Trafalgar Square" (Jefferies) **47**:141
"Lis i wilk" (Krasicki) **8**:403

"Lise" (Hugo) **3**:263
"Lisjomfruen" (Andersen)
See "Iisjomfruen"
"Lissy" (Barbauld) **185**:29, 34, 37
"Listening" (Rossetti) **50**:310; **66**:307
"Listok iz dnevnika gvardeyskogo ofitsera" (Bestuzhev) **131**:148, 165, 182
Listy (Krasicki) **8**:398
"Le lit 29" (Maupassant) **83**:169
De l'Italie (Stendhal) **178**:171
"La litanie du sommeil" (Corbière) **43**:17, 24, 31, 34
"Litanies de misère" (Laforgue) **53**:270; **221**:58
"Les litanies de satan" (Baudelaire) **6**:80, 83, 89, 94, 116
"Litanies des derniers quartiers de la Lune" (Laforgue) **221**:84
"Litanies from the Moon's Last Quarters" (Laforgue)
See "Litanies des derniers quartiers de la Lune"
"Litanies nocturnes" (Laforgue) **221**:85, 88
"The Litanies of Satan" (Baudelaire)
See "Les litanies de satan"
"Litany of Sleep" (Corbière)
See "La litanie du sommeil"
"Literärische Scherze" (Preseren) **127**:315
"Literarischer Reichsanzeiger" (Schlegel) **142**:341
"Literarischer Reichsanzeiger; oder, Archiv der Zeit und ihres Geschmacks" (Schlegel) **15**:229
"Literarischer Sansculottismus" (Goethe) **154**:270
Literary and General Lectures and Essays (Kingsley) **35**:250
Literary and Social Silhouettes (Boyesen) **135**:23, 38, 51
Literary and Theatrical Reminiscences (Aksakov)
See *Literaturnye i teatralnya vospominaniya*
"Literary Aspects of the Romantic School" (Boyesen) **135**:6
The Literary Character, illustrated by the History of Men of Genius, Drawn from their Own Feelings and Confessions (D'Israeli)
See *An Essay on the Manners and Genius of the Literary Character*
Literary Commonplace Book (Jefferson) **103**:241
Literary Essays (Mill) **179**:345, 347-48, 355
"Literary Ethics" (Emerson) **38**:209; **98**:176
The Literary History of England in the End of the Eighteenth and Beginning of the Nineteenth Century (Oliphant) **61**:171; **221**:236-39
"Literary Importation" (Freneau) **111**:111
"The Literary Influence of Academies" (Arnold) **6**:57, 69; **29**:55, 57; **89**:35-6; **218**:172, 200, 231, 233
Literary Letters to a Woman (Bécquer)
See *Cartas literarias a una mujer*
The Literary Life and Miscellanies of John Galt (Galt) **1**:330, 334-35; **110**:115
Literary Memoranda (Prescott) **163**:349
Literary Miscellanies: including a Dissertation on Anecdotes (D'Israeli)
See *Miscellanies; or, Literary Recreations*
Literary Note-Book (Thoreau) **21**:338, 340
Literary Recollections (D'Israeli)
See *Miscellanies; or, Literary Recreations*
Literary Recreations (Whittier) **59**:365
The Literary Remains of Samuel Taylor Coleridge (Coleridge) **9**:157; **177**:106, 114-15; **231**:9, 34-36
The Literary Remains of the Late Henry James (James) **53**:193, 199, 201-2, 204, 209-13, 215, 219-21, 223, 225, 227, 232-3, 235, 242, 250
"Literary Reminiscences" (Hood) **16**:206, 229, 240
"Literary Reminiscences" (De Quincey) **4**:61-62
Literary Reminiscences (De Quincey) **87**:62
Literary Reminiscences (Turgenev) **122**:256, 262
The Literary Republic of the Germans (Klopstock)
See *Die Deutsche Gelehrtenrepublik*
"Literary Reveries" (Belinski) **5**:96, 102, 108
Literary Studies (Bagehot) **10**:18-19, 25, 31, 43
"Literary Work" (Smith) **59**:306
Literary Works (Gómez de Avellaneda) **111**:57
The Literati (Poe) **211**:225
The Literati: Some Honest Opinions about Authorial Merits and Demerits, with Occasional Words of Personality (Poe) **55**:133, 138, 164, 182, 189
"Literatura. Rápida ojeada sobre la historia e índole de la nuestra" (Larra) **17**:280-84; **130**:217-18, 278
"Literature" (Emerson) **1**:278
"Literature" (Newman) **38**:296, 327
"Literature and Dogma" (Arnold)
See *Literature and Dogma: An Essay towards a Better Apprehension of the Bible*
Literature and Dogma: An Essay towards a Better Apprehension of the Bible (Arnold) **6**:39-40, 48, 53-54, 61, 66; **29**:11, 15, 18, 20-21, 45, 50-2; **89**:66-67, 82, 112; **126**:3, 28, 90, 93, 108; **218**:111-12, 115, 120, 125, 127, 131, 184, 196, 206-7, 256, 275
"Literature and Science" (Arnold) **6**:46, 72; **29**:46, 49; **126**:36, 114-17; **218**:228
"Literature at the South: The Fungous School" (Hayne) **94**:143
"Literature from Botoşani" (Eminescu) **131**:311
"Literature in the South" (Timrod) **25**:384
Literaturnye i teatralnya vospominaniya (Aksakov) **2**:13, 15
"The Litigation" (Gogol) **5**:224
"Litość" (Norwid) **17**:373
"Litterarischer Briefwechsel" (Herder) **186**:18
"Littérature" (Verlaine) **230**:174
Littérature et philosophie mêlées (Hugo) **3**:247, 273; **21**:203
"Little Annie's Ramble" (Hawthorne) **2**:291
A Little Bacchante (Crawford) **127**:192
Little Barefoot (Auerbach)
See *Barfüssele*
"The Little Beach-Bird" (Dana) **53**:158
The Little Bee from Kranj (Preseren)
See *Kranjska čbelica*
"Little Ben" (Longstreet) **159**:123, 125
"Little Benny" (Parton) **86**:377
A Little Bible Chronicle for Children and the General Reader (Grundtvig) **158**:148, 155
The Little Bird Fair Green (Gozzi)
See *L'augellin belverde*
"The Little Black Boy" (Blake) **13**:220; **37**:3, 6, 39, 67-8, 71-2, 78, 82-3, 91-2, 94; **201**:21, 24, 74, 123
A Little Boat Breaking a Path Through the Reeds (Motoori)
See *Ashiwake obune*
"Little Book, in Green and Gold" (Southey) **8**:474
A Little Book of Profitable Tales (Field) **3**:205, 208
A Little Book of Western Verse (Field) **3**:205-06, 211
"The Little Boy Blue" (Chivers) **49**:41, 54-5
"Little Boy Blue" (Field) **3**:205, 208, 210, 212
"The Little Boy Found" (Blake) **37**:3, 31, 67, 72, 77, 92
"A Little Boy Lost" (Blake) **13**:220-21, 242; **37**:3-4, 31, 40, 44, 57, 65, 67, 72, 92
"Little Britain" (Irving) **19**:327-28, 351
"Little Brother and Little Sister" (Grimm Brothers)
See "Brüderchen und Schwesterchen"
"A Little Bunker Hill" (Parton) **86**:350
"The Little Chap" (Boyesen) **135**:15
The Little Children of the Snow (Bryant)
See "The Little People of the Snow"
"Little Claus and Big Claus" (Andersen)
See "Lille Claus og Store Claus"
"Little Death for a Laugh" (Corbière) **43**:18
Little Dorrit (Dickens) **3**:151, 159, 166, 169, 173-74, 186-87; **8**:195; **18**:100, 116, 121-22, 127, 132, 134, 139; **26**:157, 168, 171, 177-78, 228; **37**:164, 174, 177, 192, 204-06; **86**:197, 201, 233, 265; **105**:201, 214, 228, 244, 248, 258, 261, 311, 318, 330; **113**:3-149; **161**:78, 99; **187**:153; **203**:176, 246, 251; **206**:35; **217**:220, 225, 243-44; **219**:73, 83, 97, 108-9, 158, 200; **230**:66, 84, 141, 144; **231**:179, 181, 229
"A Little East of Jordan" (Dickinson) **21**:63; **77**:161
"The Little Elder-Tree Mother" (Andersen) **214**:60
"Little Ella" (Lanier) **118**:243
Little Fadette (Sand)
See *La petite Fadette*
"The Little Fir Tree" (Andersen)
See "Grantræet"
Little Foxes (Cooke) **110**:21
"The Little Girl Found" (Blake) **37**:4, 40, 42, 55, 57, 71-3, 77, 92; **190**:61
"The Little Girl Lost" (Blake)
See "A Little Girl Lost"
"A Little Girl Lost" (Blake) **13**:220; **37**:4, 11, 13, 19, 44, 49, 55, 57, 71-3, 77, 92; **127**:82; **190**:61; **201**:18, 89
The Little Girl's Own Book (Child)
See *The Girl's Book*
"The Little Girl's Song" (Dobell) **43**:48
Little Green Bird (Gozzi)
See *L'augellin belverde*
"The Little Green Duck" (Andersen)
See "Den grimme Ælling"
"The Little Handmaiden" (Lampman) **25**:199
"Little Homer's Slate" (Field) **3**:210
The Little House of Kolomna (Pushkin)
See *Domik v Kolomne*
Little Hunting Stories (Aksakov)
See *Melkie okhotnich'i rasskazy*
"Little Ida's Flowers" (Andersen)
See "Den liile Idas Blomster"
Little Kirsten (Andersen) **79**:17
"Little Klaus and Big Criticism" (Andersen)
See "Lille Claus og Store Claus"
The Little Lame Prince (Craik) **38**:122
"The Little Land of Appenzell" (Taylor) **89**:312
Little Long-Nose (Hauff)
See *Zwerg Nase*
"The Little Lost Sister" (Barnes) **75**:58
"The Little Mahometan" (Lamb)
See *The Works of Charles and Mary Lamb*
"The Little Maid I Lost Long Ago" (O'Brien) **21**:246
"The Little Match Girl" (Andersen)
See "Den Lille Pige med Svovlstikkerne"
"The Little Match Seller" (Andersen)
See "Den Lille Pige med Svovlstikkerne"
Little Men (Alcott)
See *Little Men: Life at Plumfield with Jo's Boys*
Little Men: Life at Plumfield with Jo's Boys (Alcott) **6**:15, 20; **58**:41, 43, 47, 69; **83**:31, 34-35, 39, 44, 47, 61; **218**:4-12, 25
"The Little Mermaid" (Andersen)
See "Den Lille Havfrue"
"A Little More about Irish Snobs" (Thackeray) **43**:388
"The Little Old Women" (Baudelaire)
See "Les petites vielles"
The Little Parish Church (Daudet)
See *La petite paroisse*
"The Little Peach" (Field) **3**:211
"The Little People of the Snow" (Bryant) **6**:165, 169, 171; **46**:4, 21

A Little Pilgrim in the Unseen (Oliphant) **11**:448, 452; **221**:232
"The Little Pin Headers" (Tonna) **135**:199-200, 209, 213, 215-16, 220-22
"Little Plays For Children" (Edgeworth) **51**:81
Little Poems in Prose (Baudelaire)
See *Le spleen de Paris, petits poèmes en prose*
"The Little Post-Boy" (Taylor) **89**:342
The Little Reader's Assistant (Webster) **30**:418
"Little Rie and the Rosebuds" (Ingelow) **107**:150
"The Little Sailor Boy" (Rowson) **182**:282
"The Little Sea-Maid" (Andersen)
See "Den Lille Havfrue"
A Little Slaveno-Serbian Songbook (Karadzic)
See *Mala prostonarodnja slaveno-serbska pjesnarica*
Little Slaveno-Serbian Songbook for the Common Folk (Karadzic)
See *Mala prostonarodnja slaveno-serbska pjesnarica*
Little Snowdrop (Ostrovsky)
See *Snegurochka*
"Little Soul" (Meyer)
See "Das Seelchen"
The Little Stepmother (Storm)
See *Viola tricolor*
"Little Tiny" (Andersen)
See "Tommelise"
"The Little Tower" (Morris) **4**:423, 444
Little Tragedies (Pushkin) **3**:433-34, 446-47, 454-55, 461
"Little Travels and Roadside Sketches" (Thackeray) **14**:452
"Little Trotty Wigtail" (Clare) **9**:85
"Little Tuck" (Andersen) **214**:49-50
"Little Tuk" (Andersen) **7**:29
"The Little Vagabond" (Blake) **13**:182, 219-21, 242; **37**:15, 34, 43, 46-7, 52
"A Little While" (Rossetti) **4**:492
"A Little While, a Little While" (Brontë) **16**:87
The Little Widow (Alencar)
See *A Viovinha*
Little Women and Good Wives (Alcott)
See *Little Women; or, Meg, Jo, Beth and Amy*
Little Women: Four Funny Sisters (Alcott)
See *Little Women; or, Meg, Jo, Beth and Amy*
Little Women Married (Alcott)
See *Little Women; or, Meg, Jo, Beth and Amy*
Little Women; or, Meg, Jo, Beth, and Amy (Alcott) **6**:15-25; **58**:3-9, 17-23, 25, 31-2, 35, 39-41, 46-7, 49-53, 55-7, 59, 61, 64-73, 75, 78-9, 88; **83**:1-87; **218**:4, 7-9, 11, 15, 23-24, 28-34, 39, 52, 54, 56-57, 61-71, 73-77, 79-81, 84-85, 91
Little Women Wedded (Alcott)
See *Little Women; or, Meg, Jo, Beth and Amy*
"The Little Yaller Baby" (Field) **3**:208, 211
Little Zach (Hoffmann)
See *Klein Zaches gennant Zinnober*
Little Zaches, Surnamed Zinnober (Hoffmann)
See *Klein Zaches gennant Zinnober*
Little Zack (Hoffmann)
See *Klein Zaches gennant Zinnober*
"Little-Oh-Dear" (Field) **3**:210
Liturgies intimes (Verlaine) **230**:160, 167, 171-72
"Liubliu ia vas, bogini pen'ia" (Baratynsky) **103**:48
Live and Let Live; or, Domestic Service Illustrated (Sedgwick) **19**:438, 447, 449; **98**:330, 334
"Live Oak With Moss" (Whitman) **81**:328, 364
"Live Poetry" (Silva)
See "Poesía viva"
A Lively Spot (Ostrovsky)
See *Na bóikom méste*
"Lives" (Rimbaud)
See "Vies"
Lives (Coleridge)
See *Lives of the Northern Worthies*
Lives and Deeds of Our Self Made Men (Stowe) **195**:222
Lives of Celebrated Female Sovereigns (Jameson)
See *Memoirs of Celebrated Female Sovereigns*
Lives of E. and J. Philips, Nephews and Pupils of Milton (Godwin) **14**:53
Lives of the British Admirals (Southey) **97**:265, 269, 283
"Lives of the Great Composers" (Fuller) **50**:227; **211**:92
Lives of the Most Eminent Literary and Scientific Men of Italy, Spain, and Portugal (Shelley) **14**:263, 271
Lives of the Necromancers; or, An Account of the Most Eminent Persons Who Have Claimed or to Whom Has Been Imputed the Exercise of Magical Power (Godwin) **14**:50-1
Lives of the Northern Worthies (Coleridge) **90**:8, 21, 23-4
Lives of the Saints (Froude) **43**:177
"Living Alone" (Ichiyō) **49**:348
"A Living and a Dead Faith" (Cowper) **94**:72
"Living Authors: A Dream" (Reynolds) **146**:171, 192
"The Living Lost" (Bryant) **6**:162
"A Living Relic" (Turgenev) **21**:416, 441; **122**:244, 294, 337, 343
"Living Relics" (Turgenev)
See "A Living Relic"
"The Living Temple" (Holmes) **14**:109-10; **81**:98
"Living Without God in the World" (Lamb) **113**:268-75
"Livre Antique" (Vigny) **102**:335
Livre d'amour (Sainte-Beuve) **5**:331, 351-52
Le Livre des mères et des enfants (Desbordes-Valmore) **97**:12
"Le Livre, instrument spirituel" (Mallarmé) **210**:248
"Livre Moderne" (Vigny) **102**:335
"Livre Mystique" (Vigny) **102**:335
Le livre posthume (Boulter) **51**:356, 364
Le livre posthume (Verlaine) **51**:356, 364; **230**:168
"Lizzie" (Field) **3**:210
"Lizzie Griswold's Thanksgiving" (Cooke) **110**:33
"Lizzie Leigh" (Gaskell) **5**:187, 201-02, 205; **70**:150, 171-72, 176-78, 182-186, 190, 193; **97**:127
Lizzie Lorton of Gregrigg (Linton) **41**:159, 166, 167
"The Lloyds" (Hale) **75**:298
"Lo, Here Is God, and There Is God!" (Clough)
See "The New Sinai"
"Lo, Victress on the Peaks" (Whitman) **81**:318; **205**:309
The Loan of a Lover (Planché) **42**:272
"A Lobster: Or, the Study of Zoology" (Huxley) **67**:16, 82-3
"Lochiel's Warning" (Campbell) **19**:165, 168-69, 179, 181, 193, 196
"Lochinvar" (Scott) **209**:196
"Lochleven Castle" (Sigourney) **21**:309
"Lock the Door, Lariston" (Hogg) **4**:284
"Locksley Hall" (Tennyson) **30**:213, 221, 223, 233, 236, 243, 245, 260, 280, 283, 296; **65**:232, 363; **115**:252, 263, 359
"Locksley Hall Sixty Years After" (Tennyson) **30**:233, 254, 269, 296; **65**:241, 285, 381; **202**:187, 229, 292, 331
Locksley Hall Sixty Years After, Etc. (Tennyson) **202**:288, 290, 326
"El loco y la Venus" (Casal) **131**:263
La locura de amor (Tamayo y Baus) **1**:565, 570-71
"Locutions de Pierrot" (Laforgue) **5**:277; **53**:287-88; **221**:60, 66, 78, 88
"The Lodge House" (Clare) **86**:172
"The Lodge in the Wilderness" (Traill) **31**:325
"A Lodging amidst Shallow Reeds" (Ueda Akinari)
See "Asaji ga yado"
"A Lodging for the Night: A Story of François Villon" (Stevenson) **5**:391, 394, 407, 415, 431; **193**:218, 250, 256
Lodore (Shelley) **14**:259-60, 265, 267, 269-71, 275; **59**:192, 195; **103**:329, 347
Lærebog i Verdenhistorien (Grundtvig) **158**:147-48, 150-55
"A Lofty Beauty from her Poor Kinsman" (Coleridge)
See "To a Lofty Beauty Edith Southey, from her Poor Kinsman"
"A Log in the Archipelago" (Willis) **194**:282
Logan, a Family History (Neal) **161**:285-86, 288-91, 297, 299, 318, 321-24, 326
Logic (Hegel)
See *Wissenschaft der Logik*
Logic (Mill)
See *A System of Logic, Ratiocinative and Inductive: Being a Connected View of the Principles of Evidence and the Methods of Scientific Investigation*
"Logic of Political Economy" (De Quincey) **4**:78
"Logical Arrangements or Instruments of Inventions and Discovery Employed by Jeremy Bentham" (Bentham) **38**:92
Logological Fragments (Novalis)
See *Logologische Fragmente*
Logologische Fragmente (Novalis) **178**:24, 28, 106
Logosophia (Coleridge) **231**:95, 106, 150
"Lohengrin" (Laforgue) **221**:4, 7, 9-10, 14, 16, 25
"Lohengrin" (Lazarus) **8**:413-14; **109**:292, 294, 319
"Lohengrin" (Levy) **59**:92, 120
Lohengrin (Nestroy) **42**:225
Lohengrin (Wagner) **9**:403, 406, 410, 415-16, 418-19, 421, 437, 441-42, 444, 446, 448-50, 452, 462-63, 469, 473-74; **119**:171, 180, 192, 198, 241, 248, 259, 268-72, 274, 328
Lohengrin et Tannhaüser de Richard Wagner (Liszt) **199**:298, 334-35
"Lohengrin, fils de Parsifal" (Laforgue) **5**:269, 271, 274, 278, 281; **53**:294
"Lohengrin, Son of Parsifal" (Laforgue)
See "Lohengrin, fils de Parsifal"
Lohn der Wahrheit (Kotzebue) **25**:141, 147
"Lois the Witch" (Gaskell) **5**:202-3, 205; **70**:176, 182-83, 188, 189, 194, 200, 213; **214**:283-88, 333
Les Loisirs de la poste (Mallarmé)
See *Vers de circonstance*
Loiterings of Travel (Willis)
See *The Romance of Travel*
"Lokis" (Mérimée) **6**:355-6, 360, 364, 366, 369-71; **65**:48, 52, 54, 56-9, 61, 63, 98, 101-03, 114, 117, 140
"Lola Montez" (Grillparzer) **102**:171
Lombard Street: A Description of the Money Market (Bagehot) **10**:19-22, 26, 30-31, 34-35, 40, 45, 48, 50, 58, 64
"London" (Adams) **33**:17
"London" (Baillie) **151**:122
London (Blake) **13**:240, 242; **37**:17, 26, 33-35, 43, 49, 52, 57-58, 82, 84-86, 89, 92; **127**:30
"London, 1802" (Wordsworth) **206**:276, 301
"London: A National Song" (Moodie) **113**:310
London Assurance (Boucicault) **41**:26-9, 32, 40-1, 44-6, 48-9
London Characters (Mayhew) **31**:181
"London in July" (Levy) **59**:89, 102; **203**:339-45, 350-51

London Labour and the London Poor (Mayhew) **31**:156, 161-62, 165, 167-69, 173, 176-82, 186-87, 189, 193-98, 200-03
"A London Plane-Tree" (Levy) **59**:88, 119; **203**:343-44
A London Plane-Tree and Other Verse (Levy) **59**:86, 88-9, 93-4, 99, 102-3, 114, 118, 120; **203**:315, 322, 339, 343
"London Poets" (Levy) **59**:119; **203**:339, 344
"The London Road" (Jefferies) **47**:95
"A London Sabbath Morn" (Stevenson) **193**:205
"A London Trout" (Jefferies) **47**:134
London up to Date (Sala) **46**:247-48
"London's Summer Morning" (Robinson) **142**:103-4, 107-9, 181, 277-78
Lone Genius (Eminescu)
See *Geniu pustiu*
"Lone I Walk at Night" (Lermontov) **5**:301
"Loneliness" (Lampman) **194**:21
"Loneliness" (Lazarus) **8**:419
"Loneliness" (Lenau) **16**:277
"Loneliness" (Muller)
See "Einsamkeit"
"Lonely lady tell me why" (Fuller) **50**:249
Long Ago and A Short While Ago (Verlaine)
See *Jadis et naguère*
Long Ago and Not So Long Ago (Verlaine)
See *Jadis et naguère*
"Long Branch, Saratoga, and Lake George" (Shaw) **15**:338
"Long, Long Hence" (Whitman) **31**:434
Long Odds (Clarke) **19**:234
"The Long Path" (Holmes) **81**:97
"The Long Sigh of the frog" (Dickinson) **171**:91
The Long Strike (Boucicault) **41**:31
"A Long Talk" (Prescott) **163**:47
"The Long-Ago" (Milnes) **61**:130, 136, 145
"Longbow's Horse" (Cooke) **5**:130
"The Longest Hour of My Life" (Hood) **16**:217
"Longfellow and Other Plagiarists" (Poe) **1**:507
"Longing" (Eminescu) **131**:293
"Longing" (Lanier) **118**:242
"Longing" (Schiller)
See "Sehnsucht"
Longnose the Dwarf (Hauff)
See *Zwerg Nase*
"A Look at Old and New Literature in Russia" (Bestuzhev) **131**:178-79
"A Look at Russian Literature during 1823" (Bestuzhev) **131**:178
"Look at Russian Literature during 1824 and the Beginning of 1825" (Bestuzhev) **131**:179
"Look at the Clock" (Barham) **77**:34
Look before you Leap (More) **141**:270
"Look Down Fair Moon" (Whitman) **31**:392
"Look, how on the river expanse" (Tyutchev)
See "Smotri kak na rechnom prostore"
"Look on This Picture and on This" (Rossetti) **186**:304
"Look You, My Simple Friend, 'Tis One of Those" (Clough) **27**:103, 107
"Look you, my simple friend, 'tis one of those" (Prescott) **163**:34, 36
"The Looker-on" (Oliphant) **221**:240, 242, 320
"Looking at a Bust" (Meyer)
See "Vor einer Büste"
Looking at Life (Sala) **46**:237
"Looking Back" (Arany)
See "Visszatekintés"
"Looking Back" (Muller) **73**:385-86
"Looking Backward" (Eliot) **118**:36
Looking Backward, 2000-1887 (Bellamy) **4**:23-29, 31-34; **86**:3-4, 6-7, 9-14, 17-20, 22, 25, 27, 30, 32, 36, 38, 43-55, 58, 60-71, 75, 77, 79-82; **147**:1-123
"Looking Forward" (Bellamy) **147**:108
Looking Glass (Dodgson)
See *Through the Looking-Glass and What Alice Found There*
Looking towards sunset (Child) **73**:63, 71
"Looking Westward" (Keble) **87**:134
The Loom and the Lugger (Martineau) **137**:267
"The Loons" (Lampman) **194**:38
Loose Pages from the diary of an Old Man (Multatuli)
See *Losse bladen uit het dagboek van een oud man*
"Loppen og Professoren" (Andersen) **214**:41
"Lord Alcohol" (Beddoes) **3**:32, 34
Lord Byron and Some of His Contemporaries: With Recollections of the Author's Life and of His Visit to Italy (Hunt) **1**:412, 424; **70**:261, 279-88, 2
"Lord Clive" (Macaulay) **231**:302-6, 308-9
"Lord Coleraine, Rev. Mr. Bloombury, and Rev. Mr. Swan" (Landor) **14**:178
"'Lord Erlistoun'" (Craik) **38**:113
"Lord Ivan and His Daughter" (Willis) **194**:287, 309, 319
"Lord Ivon and His Daughter" (Willis)
See "Lord Ivan and His Daughter"
"Lord John of the East" (Baillie) **2**:42
Lord Kilgobbin: A Tale of Ireland in Our Own Time (Lever) **23**:291-92, 297, 299, 306, 308, 311-12
"Lord Lindsay" (Jones) **222**:155, 157-58, 160, 164
Lord Oakburn's Daughters (Wood) **178**:273, 291, 325
"The Lord of Burleigh" (Tennyson) **202**:334
"The Lord of the Castle of Indolence" (Thomson) **18**:391-92, 397, 402
The Lord of the Isles (Scott) **15**:273, 283, 319-20
The Lord of the Isles: A Poem (Scott) **209**:189, 191-92
The Lord of Thoulouse (Barham) **77**:9
Lord Ruthwen; ou, Les Vampires (Nodier) **19**:378
Lord Ruthwen ou les Vampires (Polidori)
See *The Vampyre: A Tale*
"Lord Ullin's Daughter" (Campbell) **19**:169, 179, 181, 186, 188, 190, 193, 195-96
"Lord Walter's Wife" (Barrett Browning) **61**:8, 45, 76; **66**:90; **170**:56, 121
"Die Lorelei" (Heine) **147**:127, 135, 150, 160, 195
"Loreley" (Brentano) **1**:95, 104
Lorely: Souvenirs d'Allemagne (Nerval) **1**:475; **67**:303, 357
Lorenzaccio (Musset) **7**:258-59, 261-62, 264-65, 268-69, 271, 274, 276; **150**:227, 231, 234, 243-46, 255-56, 258, 262-63, 272-75, 285, 287, 290, 292-96, 304-5, 319-20, 322-23, 329-30, 342-44, 347, 353
La lorette (Goncourt and Goncourt) **7**:153
De l'origine des Hindous (Schlegel) **15**:224
De l'origine du langage (Renan) **26**:377
The Los Pleiad and Other Poems (Chivers) **49**:38-40, 42-4, 47
"A los terremotos occurridos en España en el presente año de 1829" (Larra) **17**:270
"Lose Ware" (Mörike) **10**:450
"The Losing of the Child" (Tennyson) **65**:373, 376
Loss and Gain: The Story of a Convert (Newman) **38**:290-93, 324, 326, 342; **99**:250-54, 262, 286, 296-98, 300
"Loss of Breath" (Poe) **16**:312; **117**:322; **211**:292
"The Loss of Conscience" (Saltykov) **16**:352
"The Loss of the Eurydice" (Hopkins) **17**:183-85, 194, 203-04, 220, 255; **189**:52, 55, 135
Losse bladen uit het dagboek van een oud man (Multatuli) **165**:315, 317
"Lost" (Bellamy) **4**:31
"Lost" (Silva)
See "Perdida"
"The Lost" (Very) **9**:378, 384-85, 391, 393-94
"Lost Adventurer" (Freneau) **111**:149, 153
Lost and Saved (Norton) **47**:248, 256, 258; **205**:60-61, 67-68, 71, 82-83, 85-87, 90-93, 95-96, 101-4, 109-12, 115-16
"The Lost and the Living" (Parton) **86**:349
"The Lost Bird" (Bryant) **6**:165
"The Lost Bower" (Barrett Browning) **1**:115, 117; **61**:43
"The Lost Charter" (Gogol) **5**:231
Lost Constitution (Arany)
See *Az elveszett alkomány*
"Lost Days" (Rossetti) **4**:491, 498-99
"The Lost Diamond of St. Dalmas" (Crawford) **127**:193-94
The Lost Eden (Rizal)
See *Noli me tangere*
"A Lost Evening" (Musset) **7**:256
"Lost Faith" (Preseren)
See "Zgubljena vera"
"Lost for Me, Smiling You Walk By" (Eminescu) **33**:265
"Lost for Me, You Move Smilingly in the World" (Eminescu) **131**:297
"The Lost Friend" (Levy) **203**:345-46
"A Lost Halo" (Baudelaire)
See "Perte d'auréole"
"The Lost Heir" (Hood) **16**:207
The Lost Heiress (Southworth) **26**:434, 440
The Lost Husband (Reade) **74**:263
Lost Illusions (Balzac)
See *Illusions perdues*
Lost in the Backwoods (Traill) **31**:314
"Lost in the Bush" (Harpur) **114**:99, 102
"The Lost Leader" (Browning) **19**:78; **79**:94, 97
"The Lost Leader" (Wordsworth) **206**:236
"The Lost Letter" (Gogol)
See "Propavšaja gramotax"
Lost Love—Lost Life (Eminescu) **33**:264
"The Lost Mistress" (Browning) **19**:115; **79**:94, 97-98
A Lost Name (Le Fanu) **9**:302; **58**:272, 301-2
"Lost Notes" (Silva)
See "Notas perdidas"
"The Lost Occasion" (Whittier) **8**:509-10
"Lost on the Color" (Allingham) **25**:6
"Lost on the Prairie" (Cooke) **110**:9
"The Lost Pleiad" (Hemans) **71**:264
"The Lost Pleiad" (Simms) **3**:507
The Lost Pleiad and Other Poems (Chivers) **49**:38-40, 42-4, 47
"The Lost Reflection" (Hoffmann)
See "Das Verlorene Spiegelbild"
"The Lost Room" (O'Brien) **21**:234, 236-37, 239, 245, 248-50, 252-53
Lost Sheep (Ostrovsky) **30**:96
The Lost Smile (Keller)
See *Das Verlorene Lachen*
"Lost Speech" (Lincoln) **201**:162
"The Lost Sword" (Meyer)
See "Das verlorene Schwert"
"The Lost Titian" (Rossetti) **66**:328; **186**:232, 264
"A Lot o' Maidens A-Runnèn the Vields" (Barnes) **75**:67
"Lota" (Allingham) **25**:6
"Lota" (Webster) **230**:226, 228
Lothair (Disraeli) **2**:141-47, 149-50; **39**:4-5, 19-20, 23-5, 29-31, 36-7, 39-44, 46, 51-2, 71, 75-80; **79**:212, 222, 269, 276
"The 'Lotments" (Barnes) **75**:18, 43-4, 93, 101, 104
"The Lotos-Eaters" (Tennyson) **30**:209, 211, 222-24, 241, 258, 279-80, 283, 298; **65**:357; **115**:235-36, 275, 305; **202**:187-89, 336
"Lotta Schmidt" (Trollope) **215**:282
Lotta Schmidt and Other Stories (Trollope) **215**:212, 221, 236
"Lotta Svärd" (Runeberg) **41**:326, 328
"The Lottery" (Edgeworth) **51**:87, 89
"The Lottery Ticket" (Hale) **75**:298
"The Lotus" (Dutt) **29**:127
"The Lotus Garland of Antinous" (Symonds) **34**:342
"De l'oubli des morts" (Laforgue)
See "Complainte de l'oubli des morts"

"The Lough Derg Pilgrim" (Carleton) **199**:14, 34, 53, 63, 66
"Louis XI" (Beranger) **34**:28
Louis Lambert (Balzac) **5**:49, 67, 77, 79-81; **53**:22, 28; **153**:22, 24, 102-5, 108, 119, 122, 151-52
Louis XI (Boucicault) **41**:30, 32
"Louisa" (Wordsworth) **12**:395; **111**:323
"Louisa Preston" (Child) **73**:131-32, 134
"Louisa Venoni" (Mackenzie) **41**:189
Louison (Musset) **7**:260; **150**:340
"Le loup criait" (Rimbaud) **82**:231, 247, 249
Les Louves de Machecoul (Dumas) **71**:219
"Love" (Alger) **8**:44
"Love" (Coleridge) **9**:140, 149, 151; **54**:81; **177**:16, 33-34
"Love" (Cooke) **110**:33
"Love" (Emerson) **98**:90, 96-101
"Love" (Halleck) **47**:57
"Love" (Heine) **147**:242
"Love" (Horton) **87**:89
"Love" (Shaw) **15**:335
"Love" (Tennyson) **65**:248
"Love" (Very) **9**:381
Love (Michelet)
See *L'amour*
Love (Sacher-Masoch) **31**:287, 291, 295
Love (Verlaine)
See *Amour*
"The Love a Life can show Below" (Dickinson) **171**:140, 183
Love Abused: The Thought Suggested by 'Thelyphthora' (Cowper) **94**:109
Love Affairs and Wedding Bells (Nestroy)
See *Liebegeschichten und Heiratsachen*
Love Affairs of a Bibliomaniac (Field) **3**:207, 210-12
"Love Affairs of Soledad" (Isaacs)
See "Amores de Soledad"
"Love among the Ruins" (Browning) **19**:105, 127, 153; **79**:161-62
"Love and Death" (Leopardi)
See "Amore e Morte"
"Love and Death: A Symphony" (Symonds) **34**:354
"Love and Diplomacy" (Willis) **194**:282
"Love and Duty" (Opie) **65**:181
"Love and Duty" (Tennyson) **65**:248
Love and Fortune (Planché) **42**:277, 285, 291, 293, 295
Love and Freindship (Austen) **51**:7, 24-25, 30, 59; **119**:13, 16, 30-1
"Love and Friendship" (Austen) **1**:41-42, 46, 58-59, 65-66; **13**:74, 107; **95**:30
Love and Friendship (Austen)
See *Love and Freindship*
"Love and Harmony Combine" (Blake) **13**:182; **37**:35
"Love and Humility. A Roman Romance" (D'Israeli) **217**:275, 306-7
Love and Intrigue (Schiller)
See *Kabale und Liebe*
Love and Money (Reade) **2**:551
"Love and Reason" (Prescott) **163**:57
"Love and Self-Love" (Alcott) **83**:6
"Love and Skates" (Winthrop) **210**:280, 283, 287-89, 297, 301-2, 314, 323
"Love and Speculation" (Willis) **194**:282
"Love Can Do All but Raise the Dead" (Dickinson) **21**:55
"The Love Child" (Barnes) **75**:7, 57
"Love Dreams and Death" (Levy) **59**:119; **203**:322, 324
"Love Enthroned" (Rossetti) **4**:507
"Love from the North" (Rossetti) **2**:555; **66**:328
"Love, Hope, and Patience Supporting Education" (Coleridge) **9**:159
"Love, Hope, Desire, and Fear" (Shelley) **18**:373
"Love in a Dairy" (Crawford) **127**:170
"Love in a Life" (Browning) **19**:127; **79**:153
"Love in Idleness" (Beddoes) **3**:34
"Love in the Drama" (Eliot) **183**:120
Love in the Phalanstery (James) **53**:245-7, 249
Love Is Enough; or, The Feeling of Pharamond (Morris) **4**:420-22, 424, 433-34, 442-43
"Love Is Strong as Death" (Rossetti) **50**:317
"Love Letter" (Hogg) **109**:200
Love Letters (Multatuli) **165**:319, 337, 362-63, 365-68
Love Letters of Mrs. Piozzi written when she was eighty to William Augustus Conway (Piozzi) **57**:243
"Love, Love" (Petofi)
See "A szerelem, a szerelem"
"Love me,—I love you" (Rossetti) **186**:234, 236
Love Me Little, Love Me Long (Reade) **2**:534, 537, 539, 542, 548-49; **74**:245, 251, 253-54, 258, 262, 264-65
"Love, Mystery and Superstition" (Opie) **65**:172
"The Love of a Marble" (Eminescu) **33**:267; **131**:286
"The Love of Alcestis" (Lazarus) **109**:290
"The Love of Alcestis" (Morris) **4**:447-48
"The Love of Christ which Passeth Knowledge" (Rossetti) **50**:268; **66**:330
"Love of Flowers" (Traill) **31**:327
"The Love of Plato" (Sacher-Masoch)
See "Platonic Love"
"Love of the Country" (Bloomfield) **145**:133
"Love of the Fatherland" (Smolenskin) **30**:198
"The Love of the Lie" (Baudelaire)
See "L'amour de mensonge"
"The Love of the World Reproved; or, Hypocrisy Detected" (Cowper) **94**:117
The Love of Three Oranges (Gozzi)
See *L'amore delle tre melarance*
The Love of Toldi (Arany)
See *Toldi szerelme*
Love on St. Nicholas Tower, or What Says the Pit (Andersen) **79**:10
Love Poems (Coleridge) **9**:146
"The Love Poet" (Dyer) **129**:94
"Love Song" (Beddoes) **3**:34
"The Love Song of the Conquering Lovers" (Turgenev)
See "Pesn' torzhestvuyushchey lyubvi"
Love Stories (Alarcón)
See *Novelas cortas: Cuentos amatorios*
Love Stories from Several Centuries (Sacher-Masoch) **31**:295
"The Love Story of Chancellor Schlick and the Beautiful Sienese" (Arnim)
See "Die Liebesgeschichte des Kanzlers Schlick und der schonen Sienerin"
"A Love Story Reversed" (Bellamy) **4**:30; **86**:70, 74-5; **147**:90, 95, 97
"Love Thou Thy Land, with Love Far-Brought" (Tennyson) **30**:293
"The Love-Charm" (Tieck) **5**:511
"Loved Once" (Barrett Browning) **1**:117, 125
"Love-Doubt" (Lampman) **25**:209
Lovel the Widower (Thackeray) **14**:411; **169**:247; **213**:285, 322-25
"Lovelessness" (Heredia)
See "El desamor"
Love-Letters of Margaret Fuller (Fuller) **211**:113-16, 118, 120
"Love-Lily" (Rossetti) **4**:512; **77**:310
"Lovely Mary Donnelly" (Allingham) **25**:8, 13, 16-17, 20, 22-3
"The Lovely Sisters" (Sigourney) **87**:321
"The Lover and Birds" (Allingham) **25**:8
A Lover by Proxy (Boucicault) **41**:40, 44
The Lover of Nature (Warton)
See *The Enthusiast; or the Lover of Nature*
"The Lovers" (Andersen) **7**:23
"The Lovers" (Webster) **230**:311
"Lovers' Death" (Baudelaire)
See "La mort des amants"
"The Lover's Farewell" (Horton) **87**:110
"Lovers' Farewels" (Baillie) **2**:42
"The Lover's Journey" (Crabbe) **26**:93, 122, 129-30, 139; **121**:11, 54, 78
"The Lovers of Gudrun" (Morris) **4**:416-17, 420, 427, 442-43, 447
"The Lovers of Kandahar" (Gobineau)
See "Les amants de Kandahar"
"The Lovers, or the Birth of the Pleasing Arts, An Arcadian Romance" (D'Israeli) **217**:275, 306-7
"A Lovers' Quarrel" (Browning) **19**:127
"The Lover's Resolutions" (Coleridge) **231**:38
Lovers' Resolutions (Cumberland) **167**:198
"The Lover's Secret" (Holmes) **14**:128
"The Lovers' Tale" (Maturin) **6**:333, 335
The Lover's Tale (Tennyson) **202**:331-33
Lover's Vows (Dunlap) **2**:211
Lovers' Vows (Inchbald) **62**:142, 144, 146-8, 150, 154, 183, 185
Lovers' Vows (Kotzebue)
See *Das Kind der Liebe*
"Lovers' Wine" (Baudelaire)
See "Le vin des amants"
Loves (Darwin)
See *The Loves of the Plants*
"Love's Apparition and Evanishment" (Coleridge) **231**:62, 73
"Love's Counterfeit" (Webster) **230**:329
"Love's Delay" (Crabbe) **26**:129
"Love's Farewell" (Brontë) **16**:86
"Love's Forget-Me-Not" (Crawford) **12**:155
Love's Frailties (Holcroft) **85**:198, 212, 221-23, 235
"Love's Gleaning Tide" (Morris) **4**:434
"Love's like a Dizziness" (Hogg) **109**:201
"Love's Logic" (Timrod) **25**:372
"Love's Mourner" (Webster) **230**:329-30
"Love's Natural Death" (Crabbe)
See "The Natural Death of Love"
"Love's Nocturn" (Rossetti) **4**:492, 501, 510-13, 518; **77**:358-59, 361
"The Loves of Mejnoun and Leila" (D'Israeli)
See "Mejnoun and Leila"
Loves of Plants (Darwin)
See *The Loves of the Plants*
The Loves of the Angels (Moore) **6**:382-83, 387-88, 393; **110**:167-68
"The Loves of the Plants" (Crabbe) **26**:103
The Loves of the Plants (Darwin) **106**:183, 187-92, 194-95, 197, 199, 205, 209, 216, 225-27, 230, 232, 234, 236, 238-39, 241-42, 245, 247-48, 251-52, 259-60, 266, 269, 273-76
Loves of the Plants (Darwin)
See *The Loves of the Plants*
The Loves of the Poets (Jameson)
See *Memoirs of the Loves of the Poets*
"Love's Philosophy" (Shelley) **18**:345, 358
"Love's Rebuke" (Brontë) **16**:80
"Love's Reply" (Osgood) **141**:324-25
"Love-Sight" (Rossetti) **4**:498
Love-Songs of Childhood (Field) **3**:209
"Love-Sweetness" (Rossetti) **4**:491, 496, 498
"Love-Wonder" (Lampman) **25**:208
"A Loving Epistle to Mr William Cobbett of North Hempstead Long Island" (Halleck) **47**:76
"Low Life" (Thomson) **18**:411-12
Low Wages: Their Causes, Consequences and Remedies (Mayhew) **31**:176
"Lower Bohemia Series" (Clarke) **19**:234, 256-58
"The Lower World" (Heine)
See "Unterwelt"
"The Lowest Place" (Rossetti) **2**:563, 566; **50**:272; **66**:330-31, 352; **186**:267, 271, 303, 330
"The Lowest Room" (Rossetti)
See "The Lowest Place"
The Loyal Sailor; Or, No Mutineering (More) **141**:171
"Loyal Woman's No" (Larcom) **179**:169
"Luca della Robbia" (Pater) **159**:238

"Lucca della Robbia" (Pater) **7**:338
"Luceafarul" (Eminescu) **33**:245-47, 249-50, 252, 259; **131**:286-88, 290, 293, 297, 332, 348
"Luchshe pozdno, chem nikogda" (Goncharov) **1**:367, 375; **63**:3-4, 32, 47, 53
"Lucia to Edgardo" (Lazarus) **109**:294
"Lucian and Timotheus" (Landor) **14**:165, 167
Lucianic Comediettas (Maginn) **8**:439
Lucie Gelmeroth (Mörike) **201**:252, 254
"Lucien Létinois" (Verlaine) **51**:367
Lucien Leuwen (Stendhal) **23**:370, 374, 376, 378, 384, 392-93, 395-97, 404-06, 410, 412-13, 416; **46**:263, 275, 285, 294, 310, 316, 318, 325; **178**:147, 151, 153-54, 156-57, 197, 200, 221, 254-55, 257-58
"Lucifer" (Auerbach) **171**:67, 69
"Lucifer" (Brontë) **109**:30
"Lucifer" (Eminescu) **131**:332
Lucinde (Schlegel) **45**:283, 287, 289-92, 302-03, 305, 321-22, 339-48, 350-56, 358-59, 365, 373, 375, 380-81; **226**:183, 188-94, 196-97, 208-14, 216-17
Lucinde (Schleiermacher)
See *Vertraute Briefe über Friedrich Schlegels Lucinde*
Lucíola (Alencar) **157**:3, 5, 9, 16-18, 20, 30-32, 34, 36-37, 39-40
Lucius (Eichendorff) **225**:22
Luck and Pluck Series (Alger) **8**:43-44; **83**:140
The Luck of Barry Lyndon (Thackeray)
See *The Memoirs of Barry Lyndon, Esq.*
The Lucky Beggars (Gozzi)
See *I pitocchi fortunati*
Lucky Peer (Andersen)
See *Lykke-Peer*
A Lucrative Job (Ostrovsky)
See *Dokhodnoye mesto*
Lucrèce Borgia (Hugo) **3**:236, 239, 248, 261, 264, 269; **161**:236
Lucretia Borgia (Hugo)
See *Lucrèce Borgia*
Lucretia; or, The Children of the Night (Bulwer-Lytton) **1**:153, 155; **45**:19, 69
"Lucretius" (Tennyson) **30**:222, 254, 280; **115**:335; **202**:278, 280, 284-87, 290
Lucrezia Floriani (Sand) **2**:597, 599; **57**:311, 314, 316-7
"Lucy" (Bloomfield) **145**:154
Lucy Crofton (Oliphant) **11**:445
"Lucy Gray" (Wordsworth) **12**:426, 446; **111**:218, 226-27, 324, 326
Lucy Temple (Rowson)
See *Charlotte's Daughter; or, The Three Orphans. A Sequel to Charlotte Temple*
Lucy Temple; or, The Three Orphans (Rowson)
See *Charlotte's Daughter; or, The Three Orphans*
"Lucy's Birthday" (Thackeray) **213**:327
Ludwig Börne: Recollections of a Revolutionist (Heine) **4**:260-61, 264, 266; **54**:322
Ludwig Feuerbach (Engels)
See *Ludwig Feuerbach und der Aus gang der klassischen deutschen Philosophie*
Ludwig Feuerbach und der Aus gang der klassischen deutschen Philosophie (Engels) **85**:6, 9, 24, 37, 40, 105-06, 109
Ludwig Marcus. Words in his Memory (Heine) **54**:321
Ludwig Tieck's Schriften (Tieck) **5**:524
Ludwig van Beethovens sämtliche Briefe, 1910 (Beethoven) **227**:10
Ludwig van Beethovens sämtliche Briefe, 1923 (Beethoven) **227**:10, 12-13
Ludwig van Beethovens sämtliche Briefe und Aufzeichnungen, 1907-11 (Beethoven) **227**:10
"A Lufs" (Castro Alves) **205**:11
"Lui?" (Maupassant) **1**:457
Luigia Pallavicini, Thrown from her Horse (Foscolo) **97**:50
Luise Millerin (Schiller)
See *Kabale und Liebe*
"An Luise Nast" (Hölderlin) **16**:174
Luke Walton or The Chicago Newsboy (Alger) **83**:112-13
"Lullabies" (Lonnrot) **53**:339
Lullabies (Nekrasov) **11**:411
"Lullaby" (Laforgue)
See "Berceuse"
"Lullaby" (Mangan) **27**:292
"Lullaby" (Nekrasov)
See "Bajuški-baju"
Lullaby-Land: Songs of Childhood (Field) **3**:209
"Lulling D. to Sleep" (Isaacs)
See "Adormeciendo a David"
Lulu's Library (Alcott) **58**:51
"Lumbre de sombra" (Isaacs) **70**:313
"The Lumley Autograph" (Cooper) **129**:66
Lumpazivagabundus (Nestroy)
See *Der böse Geist Lumpazivagabundus oder Das liederliche Kleeblett*
"Luna Through a Lorgnette" (Cranch) **115**:41
"Lunatic's Skate" (Willis) **194**:282
Lunch with the Marshal of the Nobility (Turgenev) **21**:428
Les lundis (Sainte-Beuve) **5**:342-43
"La lune blanche" (Verlaine) **2**:631; **51**:352, 355
"La Lune est stérile" (Laforgue) **221**:89-91
"Lunes en Détresse" (Laforgue) **221**:47
"Lurelay" (Mangan) **27**:282
Luria (Browning) **19**:103, 113; **79**:159-60
"The Lusiad" (Chivers) **49**:71
"The Lust of the Serpent's Spirit" (Ueda Akinari)
See "Jasei no in"
"The Lust of the White Serpent" (Ueda Akinari)
See "Jasei no in"
Die lustigen Musikanten: Singspiel (Brentano) **191**:35
"Eine Lustreise ins Elysium" (Wieland) **177**:277-79, 336-38
"Lusts" (Verlaine)
See "Luxures"
"Das Lustspiel" (Meyer) **81**:154
Lutetia (Heine) **147**:150, 207, 210, 232
Lutezia (Heine) **4**:265, 268; **54**:309
La lutte pour la vie (Daudet) **1**:236
Luttrell of Arran (Lever) **23**:292, 295, 305
"Luxures" (Verlaine) **51**:372
"La luz" (Bello) **131**:112
"Luz de la luna" (Silva) **114**:301-2
Luz de luna (Silva) **114**:262, 271
Lyceum 26 (Schlegel) **45**:364
Lyceum 42 (Schlegel) **45**:363
"Lyceum Address" (Lincoln)
See "Address before the Young Men's Lyceum of Springfield, Illinois"
Lyceum Fragment 57 (Schlegel) **45**:312
Lyceum Fragment 48 (Schlegel) **226**:170, 173
Lyceum Fragment 60 (Schlegel) **45**:314
Lyceum Fragment 108 (Schlegel) **226**:167, 170, 172-74, 176
Lyceum Fragment 115 (Schlegel) **226**:159
Lyceum Fragments (Schlegel) **45**:343, 359; **226**:170-72
"Lycus the Centaur" (Hood) **16**:199-201, 208, 210, 218, 221, 225-27, 229-32, 236
"Lydia and Marian" (Rowson) **69**:128
"Lyell and Owen on Development" (Lewes) **215**:144
Den lykkelige alder (Undset) **3**:516, 522
Lykke-Peer (Andersen) **214**:5-6, 9
Lyon (Liszt) **199**:307
Lyra Apostolica (Keble) **87**:131-32, 160
Lyra Apostolica (Newman) **38**:282, 336, 343-44
—Lyra Innocentium (Keble)
See *Lyra Innocentium: Thoughts in Verse on Christian Children, Their Ways, and Their Privileges*
Lyra Innocentium: Thoughts in Verse on Christian Children, Their Ways, and Their Privileges (Keble) **87**:119, 134, 152-53, 159-60, 195
The Lyre (Sand)
See *Les sept cordes de la lyre*
"Lyric Intermezzo" (Heine)
See *Lyrisches Intermezzo*
"The Lyric Muse" (Allingham) **25**:6
*Lyric Poetry *Songs to Lesbia** (Manzano)
See *Poesías líricas *Cantos a Lesbia**
Lyrical and Other Poems Selected from the Writings of Jean Ingelow (Ingelow) **39**:264
Lyrical Ballads (Coleridge) **9**:130-31, 137, 163, 165; **54**:80, 99-100, 103, 114, 120-1, 127; **99**:22; **111**:195-374; **197**:181-82, 187-88, 191, 204, 228, 235, 240-41, 263, 271, 313, 319
Lyrical Ballads (Wordsworth) **38**:359, 364, 420; **111**:195-374; **166**:214, 265, 317, 319-20; **206**:233-35, 258, 274, 285, 298, 311-12, 316, 318-20, 322, 332, 334-37
Lyrical Ballads, with a Few Other Poems (Coleridge) **177**:38, 102, 105, 133, 136, 149, 161; **231**:21, 24, 52, 122, 125, 137, 156
Lyrical Ballads, with a Few Other Poems (Wordsworth) **12**:386, 390, 394, 398, 400, 410-11, 413, 444, 450, 463
"Lyrical Dedication for the Year 1834" (Gogol) **162**:82
"Lyrical intermezzo" (Heine)
See "Lyrisches Intermezzo"
"Lyrical Poem on the Death of Lord Byron" (Solomos)
See "Poiema lyriko eis ton thanato tou Lord Byron"
Lyrical Tales (Robinson) **142**:95, 102, 112, 114, 131-33, 135-38, 148-49, 154, 170, 174, 202, 226, 240-45, 247-54, 278-79
Lyrics of Earth (Lampman) **25**:162, 169, 178, 183, 199, 212, 220; **194**:17, 19, 22-23, 48, 51-54, 56, 67-72, 74-88, 90-93, 95, 103, 113, 139
Lyrics of Earth: Sonnets and Ballads (Lampman) **25**:170, 174, 194-96; **194**:20, 92
"Lyrisches Intermezzo" (Heine) **147**:152, 239
Lyrisches Intermezzo (Heine) **4**:248-49, 252, 254, 258-59
Le lys dans la vallée (Balzac) **35**:2, 34; **53**:28; **153**:45-46, 117, 149
"Lysene" (Andersen) **79**:76
"Lyudmila" (Zhukovsky) **35**:378-79, 388-89, 398-99, 400-01
M. Dupont; ou, La jeune fille et sa bonne (Kock) **16**:245
"M. Renan and the Jews" (Lazarus) **109**:337
"Ma bohème" (Rimbaud) **4**:484; **35**:266, 271-72, 275, 282, 289; **82**:226
"Ma Candidature" (Verlaine) **230**:161, 167
"Ma Fille" (Verlaine) **51**:386; **230**:174
"Ma Gouge!" (Verlaine) **230**:166
Ma soeur Jeanne (Sand) **57**:322, 325-6
Ma Vie (Constant)
See *Le cahier rouge de Benjamin Constant*
"Ma vocation" (Beranger) **34**:28
"Mabel Martin" (Whittier) **8**:516; **59**:351, 360
Mabel Parker: or The Hidden Treasure. A Tale of the Frontier Settlements (Alger) **83**:98, 119, 145
Mabel Vaughan (Cummins) **139**:164-66, 185-86
"Mabel's May Day" (Alcott) **83**:5
"Macabre Excuse" (Laforgue)
See "Excuse macabre"
An Macalla (Merriman) **70**:372
"Macbeth" (Lamb) **125**:304
The Maccabees (Ludwig)
See *Die Makkabäer*
The Macdermots of Ballycloran (Trollope) **6**:452, 500, 509, 514; **33**:364; **101**:222-29,

245-48, 251-53, 262-64, 271, 293-94, 296-300, 312; **215**:215
"La machine à gloire" (Villiers de l'Isle Adam) **3**:581
"Die Macht des Gesanges" (Schiller) **39**:388
"Macht des Weibes" (Schiller) **39**:388
Macías (Larra) **17**:277, 279; **130**:217, 228, 251, 253, 274
"Mackery End, in Hertfordshire" (Lamb) **10**:408, 435-36; **113**:155-56, 235
Mackintosh (Macaulay)
See *Sir James Mackintosh*
"Le maçon" (Bertrand) **31**:47-8
"The Macrobian Bow" (Hayne)
See "Cambyses and the Macrobian Bow"
"MacSwiggen" (Freneau) **1**:315
"The Mad Banker of Amsterdam" (Lockhart) **6**:293, 295
"The Mad Convalescent at Fort Rattonneau" (Arnim)
See "Der Tolle Invalide auf dem Fort Ratonneau"
Mad Monkton (Collins) **1**:185
"The Mad Mother" (Coleridge) **9**:131
"The Mad Mother" (Solomos) **15**:389, 396
"The Mad Mother" (Wordsworth) **12**:387, 402; **111**:200, 202-3, 208, 211, 248, 261, 314-15; **206**:309, 331, 336
"Mad Senior" (Willis) **194**:282
"Mad Song" (Blake) **13**:181-82; **37**:72
Mad Song (Blake) **127**:27
"The Mad Wanderer, a Ballad" (Opie) **65**:160
Madam (Oliphant) **11**:450; **61**:216
"A Madame A. Tastu" (Desbordes-Valmore) **97**:5
"Madame Ackermann" (Barbey d'Aurevilly) **213**:42
Madame Bovary: A Tale of Provincial Life (Flaubert)
See *Madame Bovary; moeurs de province*
Madame Bovary; moeurs de province (Flaubert) **2**:220-44, 246-54, 256-7; **10**:115-78; **19**:271, 273, 276-8, 280-1, 286, 290, 294, 296, 300-2, 304, 306-9, 313, 315; **62**:69, 82, 91-3, 96-8, 103, 109-12, 121; **66**:233-96; **135**:78, 80-81, 83, 85, 89, 93, 95, 102-3, 107-8, 115, 125, 133-34, 139, 167, 170-72, 174, 183; **179**:11-12, 15, 17, 31, 34, 53, 66, 72, 74, 78, 81, 91, 96, 121-22, 146
Madame Caverlet (Augier) **31**:8, 10, 13, 16, 26, 28, 31, 34-5
"Madame Crowl's Ghost" (Le Fanu) **9**:317
Madame Crowl's Ghost, and Other Tales of Mystery (Le Fanu) **9**:301
Madame de Chamblay (Dumas) **71**:194
"Madame de Fleury" (Edgeworth) **51**:87, 89; **158**:46
Madame de Maintenon (Genlis) **166**:37, 39-45
"Madame de Soubise" (Vigny) **7**:473; **102**:366-67
"Madame Emile de Girardin" (Desbordes-Valmore) **97**:30
Madame Firmiani (Balzac) **153**:152
Madame Gervaisais (Goncourt and Goncourt) **7**:157, 159-60, 166-67, 174, 182, 188-89
"Madame Hermet" (Maupassant) **83**:176, 216, 218-19
"A Madame Ida Dumas" (Nerval) **67**:307, 316
"Madame la marquise" (Musset) **7**:267; **150**:232
Madame Putiphar (Borel) **41**:3, 5, 8-10, 12, 14-20
Madame Robert (Banville) **9**:31
Madame Roland (Blind) **202**:4
"Madame Sand and the New Apocalypse" (Thackeray) **213**:221
"Madame Tellier's Girls" (Maupassant) **1**:461
Madame Valentine (Freytag)
See *Die Valentine: Schauspiel in fünf Aufzügen*
"Madamoiselle Agathe" (Banville) **9**:32
"Das Mädchen aus der Fremde" (Schiller) **166**:110
"Das Mädchen von Orleans" (Schiller) **39**:376
Madeleine (Kock) **16**:246
"Madeline: A Domestic Tale" (Hemans) **71**:288, 303, 307
Madeline: A Tale (Opie) **65**:172, 174, 178, 180, 182-3, 198
"Madeline, the Temptress" (Alger) **83**:96
"Mademoiselle" (Oliphant) **61**:204
"Mademoiselle Bistouri" (Baudelaire) **29**:79; **155**:105-10
Mademoiselle de Belle-Isle (Dumas) **11**:57, 71; **71**:193, 209-10, 242
Mademoiselle de Clermont (Genlis) **166**:21, 49, 63-68
Mademoiselle de La Fayette (Genlis) **166**:26
Mademoiselle de Marsan (Nodier) **19**:384-85
Mademoiselle de Maupin (Gautier) **1**:339, 342-43, 346, 348-56; **59**:3, 5-6, 12, 21-2, 25, 28, 30, 41-5, 59, 63-8
"Mademoiselle de Scuderi" (Hoffmann)
See "Das Fräulein von Scudéri"
Mademoiselle de Scudéry (Hoffmann) **2**:342, 344-45, 356, 360
Mademoiselle Irnois (Gobineau) **17**:91-2, 103
Mademoiselle La Quintinie (Sand) **57**:313
Mademoiselle Mathilde (Kingsley) **107**:187-88, 190, 192, 224-28
Mademoiselle Merquem (Sand) **57**:316
"Mademoisselle Fifi" (Maupassant) **1**:442; **83**:190, 200
"Los maderos de San Juan" (Silva) **114**:299, 301-3, 310, 313
Los maderos de San Juan (Silva) **114**:269-70
"The Madhouse of Palermo" (Willis) **194**:282, 329
"Madhouses Prisons Wh-re shops" (Clare) **86**:118
Das Mädl aus der Vorstadt (Nestroy) **42**:248-49
"The Madman" (Petofi)
See "Az örült"
"The Madman" (Whitman) **205**:297
"A Madman's Diary" (Gogol)
See "Diary of a Madman"
"Madness" (Dacre) **151**:148
The Madness of Love (Tamayo y Baus)
See *La locura de amor*
"Madness of Orestes" (Landor) **14**:168
Madoc (Southey) **8**:450-51, 453, 456, 459, 461, 469-70, 474, 476, 478-79; **97**:260-62, 268, 273, 278-79, 293-94, 296-97, 322
"The Madonna" (Baratynsky) **103**:8
"Madonna" (Pushkin) **83**:259
"The Madonna" (Tennyson) **30**:209
Madonna Mary (Oliphant) **11**:447-8, 450; **61**:173, 206, 209, 239
"Mador of the Moor" (Hogg) **4**:275, 280, 282
Mador of the Moor (Hogg) **109**:204-07, 240-41, 244, 250
"Madrid" (Musset) **150**:232
De Madrid à Nápoles (Alarcon) **1**:12
"The Madrigal" (Beddoes) **154**:55
"Madrigal" (Silva) **114**:263
"Madrigal" (Verlaine) **51**:360-61
Madrigals and Chronicles: Being Newly Founded Poems Written by John Clare (Clare) **9**:91, 93-94
"Maelzel's Chess-Player" (Poe) **211**:253
Maerchenalmanach für Söhne und Töchter gebildeter Stände auf das Jahr 1827 (Hauff) **185**:318
Maerchenalmanach für Söhne und Töchter gebildeter Stände auf das Jahr 1828 (Hauff) **185**:318
"Det mærkværdige Aar, da Kjøbenhavn fik Gas istedtfor de Garnle Tranlygter" (Andersen)
See "Gudfaders Billedbog"
"Maese Pérez el organista" (Bécquer) **106**:95-7, 120, 161
"Magdalen" (Halleck) **47**:57, 69
"Magdalen" (Levy) **59**:98, 110; **203**:311, 313-15, 321, 350
Magdalen Hepburn: The Story of the Reformation (Oliphant) **11**:448; **61**:163, 219
"A Magdalena" (Gómez de Avellaneda) **111**:30
"Mägdlein" (Mörike)
See "Das verlassene Mägdlein"
Magelone (Tieck) **5**:525
"Les mages" (Hugo) **3**:273
"Maggie, a Lady" (Rossetti) **66**:302, 331
"The Magic Mirror" (Wilson) **5**:567
The Magic of Kindness (Mayhew) **31**:161
The Magic Ring (Fouqué)
See *Der Zauberring*
The Magic Skin (Balzac)
See *La peau de chagrin*
"The Magic Slippers" (Allston) **2**:26
"The Magician" (Emerson) **1**:307-09
"Magistrale" (Preseren) **127**:295-96
"The Magistrate" (Petofi)
See "A táblabíro"
"Magna est veritas" (Patmore) **9**:358
"Magna moralia" (Patmore) **9**:344
"The Magnate" (Derzhavin) **215**:29-30, 32
"The Magnetic Lady to her Patient" (Shelley) **18**:369
"Der Magnetiseur" (Hoffmann) **2**:345, 360; **183**:166, 183-84, 186, 204, 223, 266-69, 271-72
"Magnetism" (Lazarus) **109**:294
"Magnit" (Bestuzhev) **131**:150
"Magnolia Cemetery Ode" (Timrod)
See "Ode Sung on the Occasion of Decorating the Graves of the Confederate Dead at Magnolia Cemetery"
"Magnolia Gardens (Near Charleston, S.C.)" (Hayne) **94**:138
"Magus Wandering among the Stars" (Eminescu) **131**:348
"A magyar ifjakhoz" (Petofi) **21**:280
"A magyar nemes" (Petofi) **21**:264
"A magyar nemzet" (Petofi) **21**:279
"Mahmoud" (Hunt) **1**:416
"Mahomets Gesang" (Goethe) **4**:212
"Mahommed and the Assassin" (Milnes) **61**:130
"Mahommedanism" (Milnes) **61**:130
Mai (Alencar) **157**:5, 9
Maid Marian (Planché) **42**:273
"The Maid Martyr" (Ingelow) **39**:258
"The Maid o' Newton" (Barnes) **75**:58, 89
The Maid of All Work (Martineau) **26**:322
"Maid of Astolat" (Tennyson) **65**:227
The Maid of Orleans (Schiller)
See *Die Jungfräu von Orleans*
The Maid of Warsaw, or the Tyrant Czar: A Tale of the Last Polish Insurrection (Jones) **222**:139-40
"The Maid Vor My Bride" (Barnes) **75**:71
The Maiden from the Fairy-world or the Peasant as Millionaire (Raimund)
See *Der Bauer als Millionär; oder, Das Mädchen aus der Feenwelt*
"Maiden Song" (Rossetti) **2**:563, 571; **50**:264; **66**:302, 328
"Maidenhood" (Longfellow) **2**:493; **45**:100, 135, 140, 155
"Maiden-Tsar" (Derzhavin)
See "Tsar'-Devitsa"
"The Maiden's Complaint" (Schiller) **39**:306
"Maiden's Sorrow" (Bryant) **46**:20
Maidens' Vows; or, The Magnetism of the Heart (Fredro)
See *Śluby panieńskie; czyli, Magnetyzm serca*
"The Maids of Elfin-Mere" (Allingham) **25**:18, 20, 23
"The Maid's Story" (Crabbe) **26**:129
"Maid's Tragedy" (Tennyson) **65**:228
"Mail from Tunis" (Dickinson) **77**:118

"Mail-Coach" (De Quincey)
See "The English Mail-Coach, or the Glory of Motion"
"La Main du Major Muller" (Verlaine) **51**:387
"La main enchantée" (Nerval) **1**:483; **67**:332
"Main Street" (Hawthorne) **2**:329-30; **10**:315; **17**:152; **39**:212; **95**:95, 128, 139; **158**:242-44, 246, 263; **171**:357
"The Main-Chance" (Hazlitt) **82**:126
The Maine Woods (Thoreau) **7**:361, 368, 378, 390; **21**:372; **61**:348; **138**:124, 134, 148, 155, 159, 167; **207**:199, 267, 269, 299
"Mais ve que o meu corazon" (Castro) **78**:42
La maison blanche (Kock) **16**:245
La maison claes (Balzac) **5**:33
"La Maison de ma mère" (Desbordes-Valmore) **97**:23, 28
"La maison du Berger" (Vigny) **7**:469, 472, 478-79, 481-82, 484-86; **102**:354-55, 357-58
"La maison du chat-qui-pelote" (Balzac) **5**:74, 83; **153**:149
La maison d'un artiste (Goncourt) **7**:175
La maison nucingen (Balzac) **5**:46; **35**:43; **153**:12, 105-9, 111, 152
"La maison Tellier" (Maupassant) **1**:459, 463, 466; **83**:169, 171, 190, 193, 200
Maison Turque (Maupassant) **83**:199-201, 203
Maître Cornélius (Balzac) **53**:23; **153**:152
Maître Guérin (Augier) **31**:2, 8-10, 13, 15-16, 25, 28, 31, 34
"Maitre Pied" (Villiers de l'Isle Adam) **3**:588
Les maîtres d'autrefois: Belgigue, Hollande (Fromentin) **10**:226-35, 251; **125**:97, 103-16, 124, 134-35, 148, 169
Les maîtres mosaïstes (Sand) **42**:319
"Les maitres sonneurs" (Maupassant) **1**:448
Les maîtres sonneurs (Sand) **2**:601, 603, 606; **42**:240, 370; **57**:313, 317, 338; **174**:226
Les maîtresses de Louis XV (Goncourt and Goncourt) **7**:164-65
Máj (Macha) **46**:198-207, 213-26, 228-30
The Majolo (Galt) **1**:327-28
"Der Majorat" (Hoffmann) **2**:340, 346, 361; **183**:185, 193, 195, 213
Die Majoratsherren (Arnim) **5**:13, 18, 20, 23; **159**:22-29, 31, 44-45, 96-97
"Majskaja noč, ili Vtoplennica" (Gogol) **5**:218, 224, 231, 251; **162**:93, 95
"Maker" (Lampman) **194**:34
The Maker of His Fortune (Keller)
See *Der Schmied seines Glückes*
"The Maker to Posterity" (Stevenson) **5**:401
The Makers of Florence (Oliphant) **11**:439, 445
Makers of Florence, Dante, Giotto, Savonarola (Oliphant) **221**:229
The Makers of Modern Rome (Oliphant) **61**:215
"The Make-Up Artist" (Leskov)
See "Tupejnyi xudožnik"
Making His Way (Alger) **8**:25
"The Making of Man" (Tennyson) **30**:274
Die Makkabäer (Ludwig) **4**:347-48, 350
"Maksim Maksimovich" (Lermontov) **5**:291, 295-96, 298, 301-02, 304-05; **126**:148-49, 153, 156-57, 195-96, 199
"Le mal" (Rimbaud) **35**:271, 321
Mal' chik v shtanakh i mal' chik bez shtanov (Saltykov) **16**:375
"Le Mal d'André" (Maupassant) **83**:221
"El mal del siglo" (Silva) **114**:316
El mal del siglo (Silva) **114**:272
"Le Mal du pays" (Desbordes-Valmore) **97**:29
Le Mal du Pays (Liszt) **199**:307
"Mal du siécle" (Silva) **114**:316
Mala prostonarodnja slaveno-serbska pjesnarica (Karadzic) **115**:77, 82, 100-1, 105, 110
"Målaren" (Almqvist) **42**:16
"Mal'aria" (Tyutchev) **34**:397
"Mal'aria" (Verlaine) **230**:174
"Malavolti" (Chivers) **49**:47
"The Malay—took the Pearl" (Dickinson) **77**:152
"Malcolm's Katie" (Crawford) **12**:151, 153, 155-59, 161-62, 166, 168-69, 171-72; **127**:148-53, 155-56, 158-59, 161, 163-67, 169-76, 178, 181-82, 192, 194-95, 197-201, 203-4, 212, 217-18, 223-24, 228
"The Maldive Shark" (Melville) **3**:352
Maldoror (Lautréamont)
See *Les chants de Maldoror: Chants I, II, III, IV, V, VI*
"Male Fashions for 1799" (Robinson) **142**:169
"Malédiction de Cypris" (Banville) **9**:20
"La malédiction de Vénus" (Banville) **9**:14
"Malen' kaja ošibka" (Leskov) **25**:234
"Le Malencontreux" (Genlis) **166**:21
Maler Nolten (Mörike) **10**:444-47, 450-51, 454-55
Maler Nolten: Novelle in zwei Theilen (Mörike) **201**:252-54, 256-57, 262-68, 289-91, 299, 302, 309, 321
Eine Malerarbeit (Storm) **195**:18, 44
"Malheureux! Tous les dons . . ." (Verlaine) **230**:161
"Le maline" (Rimbaud) **35**:271
"Malines" (Verlaine) **51**:383; **230**:163
Mallarmé's Prose Poems (Mallarmé) **210**:174-75
Die Maltheser (Schiller)
See *Demetrius*
Maltravers (Bulwer-Lytton)
See *Ernest Maltravers*
Malvino; ou, Le mariage d'inclination (Scribe) **16**:382, 393
The Mammon of Unrighteousness (Boyesen) **135**:14, 22-23, 31-32, 37, 48, 54-57, 59, 61, 63, 67-68
"Man" (Allston) **2**:26
"The Man" (Kivi)
See "Mies"
"Man" (Lamartine)
See "L'homme"
"A Man and a Muse" (Castro)
See "Un hombre y una musa"
"The Man and His Shadow" (Krylov) **1**:435
"Man and Nature" (Lampman) **25**:217; **194**:8, 71, 74
Man and Wife (Collins) **1**:180, 182; **18**:63-4, 66; **93**:5, 12, 19, 34
Man as He Is (Bage) **182**:4-6, 12-14, 16-19, 25, 27, 29-31, 39, 42-43, 46, 48, 50-52, 59-61
Man as He Is Not (Bage)
See *Hermsprong; or, Man as He Is Not*
"The Man at Home" (Brown) **74**:47, 173, 196; **122**:60, 119
"Man Born to Be King" (Morris) **4**:417, 420, 427
A Man Full of Nothing (Nestroy)
See *Der Zerrissene*
"The Man in Business" (Freneau) **111**:132
"Man in Harmony with Nature" (Very) **9**:387, 389-90
"Man in the Bell" (Maginn) **8**:436, 438, 440
"The Man in the Cloak" (Mangan) **27**:302
The Man in the Iron Mask (Dumas) **71**:242-43
"A Man Like Many Others" (Turgenev) **21**:376
"A Man Made of Money" (Jerrold) **2**:396-99, 401-06
"Man not a Free Agent" (Neal) **161**:329
"The Man of Adamant" (Hawthorne) **79**:316; **95**:131; **158**:235; **171**:243; **191**:262
The Man of Feeling (Mackenzie) **41**:180-86, 188-89, 194-96, 198-204, 207, 214, 217-220, 222-28
"The Man of Feeling and the Cold-Blooded Man" (Karamzin)
See "Cuvstvitel'nyj i xolodnyj, dva xaraktera"
The Man of Fortitude; or, The Knights Adventure (Dunlap) **2**:213
"The Man of Ninety" (Freneau) **1**:320; **111**:101
"The Man of Snow" (Horne) **127**:264
The Man of Surrenders (Sacher-Masoch) **31**:291
The Man of Taste, or Love too Late (D'Israeli) **217**:304
The Man of Ten Thousand (Holcroft) **85**:198, 222-23
Man of the Backlands (Alencar) **157**:9
"The Man of the Crowd" (Poe) **1**:500, 518; **16**:295, 297, 303, 316, 331, 336; **78**:281; **211**:253-57, 283-86, 288
The Man of the World (Mackenzie) **41**:181, 184, 195-96, 199, 200, 202-03, 208-09, 214, 222-26, 228
The Man out of Business (Freneau) **111**:132
"The Man That Was Used Up" (Poe) **16**:292, 308, 312; **211**:225, 245, 316-17
"Man the Reformer" (Emerson) **98**:26, 110, 112-13, 116
"Man Thinking" (Emerson) **98**:18
"Man to April" (Freneau) **1**:317
The Man Who Laughs (Hugo)
See *L'homme qui rit*
"The Man Who Lost His Name" (Boyesen) **135**:12, 20, 25-26
"The Man Who Never Laughed Again" (Morris) **4**:417, 447-48
The Man with the Double Mind (Prescott) **163**:40
The Man with Three Faces (Pixérécourt)
See *L'homme à trois visages; ou, Le proscrit de Venise*
"A Man Without Shame" (Leskov)
See "Besstydnik"
"Manasseh" (Kendall) **12**:192
"The Manchester Marriage" (Gaskell) **5**:202; **70**:185; **214**:332, 340
"A Manchester Strike" (Martineau) **26**:305; **137**:250-51, 265-66, 304
"Le manchy" (Leconte de Lisle) **29**:210, 212, 214, 217-18, 224
Mandeville: A Tale of the Seventeenth Century in England (Godwin) **14**:40-2, 44, 49-51, 57, 68-71, 81, 83; **130**:52
"Mandoline" (Verlaine) **2**:628; **51**:351, 374, 378, 380
Mandrivka z pryemnistiu ta y ne bez morali (Shevchenko)
See *Matros*
Mands Minde (Grundtvig) **158**:142, 147, 166, 168, 171
Manette Salomon (Goncourt and Goncourt) **7**:155, 157-58, 162, 167, 175-76, 180, 182, 187
Manfred (Byron) **2**:64, 66, 70, 72, 79-81, 84, 87, 90, 93, 97, 99-101, 103; **12**:88, 100, 102; **109**:55-134; **149**:54, 71, 73, 142
Un mangeur d'opium (Baudelaire) **155**:41
The Manhaters and the Poet (Fredro)
See *Odluki i poeta*
"Manhood" (Thoreau) **7**:383
The Mania for Things Foreign (Fredro)
See *Cudzoziemszczyzna; czyli, Nauka zbawlenia*
"The Maniac" (Robinson) **142**:140, 226
"Maniacal" (Laforgue)
See "Maniaque"
"Maniaque" (Laforgue) **221**:49, 90
Manifest der Kommunistischen (Marx) **17**:293-94, 296, 303, 309-10, 314, 316, 319, 321-23, 333-34, 336, 357, 359; **114**:3, 8-24, 28-41, 43-57, 59-80, 82-7
Manifest der kommunistischen Partei (Engels) **85**:6, 8, 13, 21, 32, 53, 65, 68, 105, 117, 120, 127-28, 132, 136-38, 140-41, 147-49, 151, 157, 161-62, 170, 181-82; **114**:3, 8-24, 28-41, 43-57, 59-80, 82-7
"Manifest Destiny" (Shaw) **15**:341
"Manifeste du Comité central des 20 arrondissements" (Vallès) **71**:330
Manifesto (Engels)
See *Manifest der kommunistischen Partei*
Manifesto of the Communist Party (Engels)
See *Manifest der kommunistischen Partei*

"The manifold Hills forsaken by the sun" (Harpur) **114**:115-16
The Manikins (Cooper) **1**:216, 220, 223
The Manliness of Christ (Hughes) **207**:113, 140-41, 146, 155
"Manly Amusement" (Pater) **7**:342
Der Mann im Mond oder Der Zug des Herzens ist des Schicksals Stimme (Hauff) **185**:318
"Der Mann von fünfzig Jahren" (Goethe) **4**:193, 197
"The Manna Gatherers" (Keble) **87**:134
"Mannahatta" (Whitman) **31**:393-94
Le Mannequin (Staël-Holstein) **91**:326, 360
The Mannequin (Staël-Holstein)
See *Le Mannequin*
Mannering (Scott)
See *Guy Mannering*
"Manners" (Emerson) **38**:211; **98**:101
Manners; or, Happy Homes and Good Society All the Year Round (Hale) **75**:283
Männerwürde (Schiller) **39**:331, 339
Människosläkets saga (Almqvist) **42**:18
"Manoeuvering" (Edgeworth) **1**:267; **51**:89-90
"The Man-of-War Bird" (Whitman) **31**:363
Manon Lescaut (Daudet) **1**:237
Manor Sackville (Morgan) **29**:390, 394-95
"Man's Future" (Lampman) **25**:217
A Man's Life (Trelawny) **85**:347
Man's Place in Nature (Huxley) **67**:4, 9-10, 46, 72, 81-2, 96, 98, 105-06
"A Man's Requirements" (Barrett Browning) **61**:43
"Man's Three Guests" (Sigourney) **21**:299
"The Manse" (Stevenson) **193**:207
Mansfield Park (Austen) **1**:32-34, 36, 38-40, 44-45, 47, 49-54, 59-62, 64; **13**:54, 60-1, 84, 93, 97, 101, 106; **19**:2, 5-6, 14, 32, 39, 42, 55, 64; **33**:35, 37, 41, 55, 57, 63-4, 66, 69-70, 74-5, 85-6, 88-93, 96, 99; **51**:8, 25-6; **81**:5, 18, 52, 61, 69, 77; **95**:2-7, 9-18, 20-6, 28-36, 38-40, 42-6, 48-50, 52-6, 58-60, 62, 65, 67-80, 83-4; **119**:12, 14, 18, 20-1; **222**:36, 38-39, 48, 75, 79, 100, 109
"Mansion of Many Apartments" (Keats) **121**:207
Manson the Miser, or Life and Its Vicissitudes (Alger) **8**:42; **83**:96
Manthorn (Holcroft)
See *Manthorn the Enthusiast*
Manthorn the Enthusiast (Holcroft) **85**:228, 230, 236-39, 243
A Manual of Parliamentary Practice (Jefferson) **11**:148, 199
A Manual of Political Economy (Bentham) **38**:45, 92
A Manual of Useful Studies: For the Instruction of Young Persons of Both Sexes, in Families and Schools (Webster) **30**:420
Manuel (Maturin) **6**:320, 322, 328, 331-32; **169**:119
"The Manufacturers" (Edgeworth) **51**:87, 89-90
The Manuscript Found in Saragossa (Potocki)
See *Manuscrit trouvé à Saragosse*
Manuscript Journals (Alcott)
See *The Journals of Bronson Alcott*
"The Manuscript of St Alexius" (Webster) **230**:233
Manuscript Remains (Schopenhauer) **157**:333
Manuscripts (Whitman) **81**:364
Le Manuscrit de l'Évêque (Hugo) **189**:178
Le manuscrit de ma mère (Lamartine) **11**:265; **190**:261-65
Manuscrit trouvé à Saragosse (Potocki) **229**:275-77, 279-81, 283-88, 290, 294-95
Man-Woman; or, The Temple, the Hearth, the Street (Dumas)
See *L'homme-femme: Résponse à M. Henri d'Ideville*
"Many a pilgrim goes to Rome, to Compostella" (Preseren) **127**:293
Many Moods (Symonds) **34**:323, 325
"The Maple Tree" (Clare) **86**:180
"The Maple Tree" (Moodie) **113**:348-49, 371
"Die Mappe meines Urgrossvaters" (Stifter) **41**:335-37, 343-44, 358, 380
"Die Mappe meines Urgrosvaters" (Stifter) **198**:259-60, 283-84, 286, 320-21, 326
Die Mappe meines Urgrosvaters. Schilderungen. Briefe (Stifter) **198**:284, 286-87
Les marana (Balzac) **35**:25
La marâtre (Balzac) **5**:52; **153**:62, 81
The Marble Faun (Hawthorne)
See *The Marble Faun; or, The Romance of Monte Beni*
The Marble Faun; or, The Romance of Monte Beni (Hawthorne) **2**:305-07, 310, 313-14, 317, 320-21, 324-25, 328, 333; **10**:296; **17**:116, 124; **23**:168-221; **39**:170, 177, 222, 224, 231; **79**:302, 304, 314; **95**:205; **158**:194, 231; **171**:234-366; **191**:178-79; **226**:17, 55, 76, 137
"The Marble Statue" (Eichendorff)
See "Das Marmorbild"
The Marble Statue (Eichendorff)
See *Aus dem Leben eines Taugenichts und Das Marmorbild: Zwei Novellen nebst einem Anhange von Liedern und Romanzen*
"A Marble Woman; or, The Mysterious Model" (Alcott) **58**:46, 75-6; **83**:6; **218**:84
"The Marble Youth" (Meyer)
See "Der Marmorknabe"
"The Marbles of Aegina" (Pater) **7**:330
"Marbre de Paros" (Gautier) **59**:19
Marc-Aurèle et la fin du monde antique (Renan) **26**:402, 408, 410, 420-21
"Marceline Desbordes-Valmore" (Verlaine) **230**:166
Marcelle Rabe (Banville) **9**:31
"Marcellus and Hannibal" (Landor) **14**:189
"March" (Bryant) **46**:9, 38
"March" (Clare) **9**:106; **86**:94, 102, 104, 165-67
"March" (Crawford) **12**:155
"March" (Lampman) **25**:160
"March" (Taylor) **89**:300
"A March Day in London" (Levy) **59**:89; **203**:339, 344
"The March Hare" (Leskov)
See "Zajačij remiz"
March Hares (Frederic) **10**:186, 188, 192, 194, 201-02, 208, 212
"A March in the Ranks Hard-Prest, and the Road Unknown" (Whitman) **81**:321-23, 331
"The March into Virginia" (Melville) **3**:352
"March of the Seventh Regiment. Our March to Washington" (Winthrop) **210**:273, 280-82, 296, 298, 303
"The March of Winter" (Lampman) **25**:210; **194**:30
"The March to Moscow" (Southey) **8**:474
"Le marchand de tulipes" (Bertrand) **31**:48
"Marche de funèbre pour la mort de la terre" (Laforgue) **5**:275; **221**:42-43, 86, 90
Märchen (Goethe) **34**:122; **90**:107
Märchen vom Müller Radlauf (Brentano) **191**:70
"Märchen vom Murmeltier" (Brentano) **1**:100
"Märchen vom Schneider Siebentot auf einen Schlag" (Brentano) **1**:100, 104
Märchen vom sichern Mann (Mörike) **201**:252
Das Märchen von blonden Eckbert (Tieck)
See *Der blonde Eckbert*
"Das Märchen von dem Hause Starenberg" (Brentano) **1**:104
Das Märchen von den drei Spinnfrauen (Storm) **195**:23, 31, 33, 35
Märchenbilder (Schumann) **143**:114
Märchenerzählungen (Schumann) **143**:114
Marchmont (Smith) **23**:323, 335; **115**:148
"Marco" (Verlaine) **230**:166, 172
"Marco Bozzaris" (Halleck) **47**:56, 66-67, 69-70, 78-, 81, 83-84
"Marcus Aurelius" (Arnold) **89**:36; **218**:111
Marcus Aurelius and the End of the Ancient World (Renan)
See *Marc-Aurèle et la fin du monde antique*
Mardi: And a Voyage Thither (Melville) **3**:327, 332-33, 335, 337-39, 341-42, 348-49, 352, 355-56, 359-60, 363-65, 367, 370, 380, 383; **12**:252, 262, 274, 317; **29**:317, 324, 329, 354; **45**:197, 210, 229, 247, 251-54; **49**:376, 391, 407; **91**:4, 7, 10, 18, 30-2, 42-3, 45-6, 55, 88, 121, 204, 212; **93**:188, 193, 205; **123**:193-94, 203-4, 211, 231, 241, 243, 251-52; **157**:64; **193**:130, 146; **221**:104, 106, 108-11, 118, 134, 148-49, 155, 157, 170
"Mardoche" (Musset) **7**:254, 267, 275, 278-79; **150**:229, 231-34, 299, 311
La mare au diable (Sand) **2**:599-601, 603-06, 608; **42**:314, 327, 338, 340, 363, 367; **57**:317, 338, 359, 361, 366; **174**:226, 229
"Mare Rubrum" (Holmes) **81**:98
La maréchale d'ancre (Vigny) **7**:473; **102**:336
"The Maremma" (Hemans) **71**:291
"Marenghi" (Shelley) **18**:345
"Marfa posadnica" (Karamzin) **3**:285-86
"Marfa the Mayoress" (Karamzin)
See "Marfa posadnica"
"Marfa-posadnitsa" (Karamzin) **173**:280, 283, 296, 312, 333
"Marfeast" (Arany)
See "Ünneprontók"
"Marfiles viejos" (Casal) **131**:267-68
La marfisa bizzarra (Gozzi) **23**:110
"Margaret" (Wordsworth) **12**:429; **206**:243
"Margaret: A Pearl" (Field) **3**:205
"Margaret Fuller and Mary Wollstonecraft" (Eliot) **118**:134; **183**:68, 86
Margaret Fuller, Critic (Fuller) **211**:211-12
"Margaret Green: The Young Mahometan" (Lamb) **125**:302, 312, 319, 323, 343, 349
"Margaret has a milking-pail" (Rossetti) **186**:238
"Margaret in the Xebec" (Ingelow) **39**:264
Margaret Maitland (Oliphant)
See *Passages in the Life of Mrs. Margaret Maitland of Sunnyside, Written by Herself*
Margaret of Navarre; or, The Massacre of Saint Bartholome's Eve (Dumas)
See *La reine Margot*
Margaret Smith's Journal (Whittier) **8**:509, 512
"Margareta" (Ludwig) **4**:353
"Margareta" (Mörike) **201**:271, 281
Margareta (Kivi) **30**:65
"Margarita" (Castro) **3**:102
Margarita (Hugo) **3**:264
"Marginalia" (Poe) **55**:134, 136, 138, 160, 171, 182; **94**:178; **117**:202, 285, 320, 330, 337
Marginalia (Coleridge) **99**:113; **231**:138, 152
Marginalia (Poe) **211**:226, 250, 268, 288
Marginalia (Stendhal) **46**:324
"Margret" (Barrett Browning) **1**:126
"Marguerite" (Arnold)
See "To Marguerite"
"Marguerite" (Whittier) **8**:509, 519; **59**:371
Marguerite d'Anjou (Pixérécourt) **39**:276, 284
Marguerite de Valois (Dumas) **71**:205-06
"Marguerite Schneider" (Banville) **9**:16
Mari Magno (Prescott) **163**:8, 52-53, 114
Mari Magno; or, Tales on Board (Clough) **27**:52-3, 57, 59-60, 62, 65, 69, 74, 77-81, 90, 114-19
María (Isaacs) **70**:302-04, 311-12, 317-29, 331-45
Maria (Ludwig) **4**:356, 367
"Maria, A Fiction" (Rowson) **182**:255
"Maria: A Fragment" (Thelwall) **162**:317, 321-23
"Maria, A Highland Legend" (Hogg) **109**:203
"Maria Antoinette" (Heine) **147**:232
Maria Antoinette (Heine) **54**:347
"Maria Howe" (Lamb) **10**:417
Mária királynő (Madach) **19**:370

Maria Magdalen: Ein bürgerliches Trauerspiel in drei Acten, nebst einem Vorwort (Hebbel) **43**:230, 234, 237, 239, 242-43, 248, 251, 255, 257-59, 261-62, 266-67, 269-71, 277, 279-80, 283, 286-87, 296-97, 299-301
Maria Stuarda (Alfieri) **101**:8, 18, 21, 32
Maria Stuart (Schiller) **39**:318-19, 330, 345-46, 368, 372, 375-76, 378-80, 383-84; **69**:169, 175, 194, 239, 244, 246, 277; **166**:95, 140-44, 146-47, 159, 190-94
"Maria Szécsi" (Petofi)
See "Szécsi Mária"
Un Mariage dans le Monde (Feuillet) **45**:83, 85
Le mariage d'argent (Scribe) **16**:382, 384, 386-88, 393
Le mariage de raison (Scribe) **16**:382, 393
Le mariage de Victorine (Sand) **42**:310
Le mariage d'Olympe (Augier) **31**:2-3, 5-8, 12, 15, 19, 23-5, 27, 29-31, 35
"Le Mariage du lieutenant Laré" (Maupassant) **83**:172, 181, 195
Le Mariage du siècle (Sade) **47**:361-62
Un mariage sous Louis XV (Dumas) **11**:71; **71**:209
Marian and Lydia (Rowson) **5**:312
"Marian Hume" (Brontë) **109**:42
"Mariana" (Tennyson) **30**:211, 223, 237, 276, 279, 286; **115**:358; **202**:184-85, 189, 330, 336-37
"Mariana and Oenone" (Tennyson) **30**:245
"Mariana in the South" (Tennyson) **30**:207
"Mariana's Grove" (Zhukovsky)
See "Mar'ina roshcha"
Marianna (Dumas) **71**:205
Marianne (Sand) **42**:370
"Marianne's Dream" (Shelley) **18**:326
"Maria's Tale" (Hogg) **109**:203
Marie Antoinette; or, The Chevalier of the Red House: A Tale of the French Revolution (Dumas)
See *Le chevalier de Maison-Rouge*
"Marie Antoinette's Lamentation, in Her Prison of the Temple" (Robinson) **142**:199-200
"Marie Bertrand, or the Felon's Daughter" (Alger) **83**:96, 143
Marie Grubbe: Interiors from the Seventeenth Century (Jacobsen)
See *Fru Marie Grubbe: Interieurer fra det syttende Asrhundreded*
"Marie Rogêt" (Poe)
See "The Mystery of Marie Rogêt"
Marie Tudor (Hugo) **3**:240, 256, 268-69; **161**:235-36
Marienbader Elegie (Goethe) **4**:193
"Mariia" (Shevchenko) **54**:389
Marina (Brentano)
See *Legende von der heiligen Marina*
"Mar'ina roshcha" (Zhukovsky) **35**:379, 384, 398
"Marine" (Rimbaud) **35**:269, 309; **4**:475
Mariner (Coleridge)
See *The Rime of the Ancient Mariner: A Poet's Reverie*
Marinere (Coleridge)
See *The Rime of the Ancient Mariner*
"The Mariner's Cave" (Ingelow) **39**:267
"The Mariner's Compass" (Jones) **222**:169
"Marinka" (Macha) **46**:198, 204, 208-09, 214-15
Marino Caboga (Arnim) **5**:21
Marino Faliero: Doge of Venice (Byron) **2**:65-66, 70, 79-80, 90, 99; **149**:73
Marion de Lorme (Hugo) **3**:236, 238-39, 261, 268-69; **10**:369; **21**:197; **161**:236
"Marion Delorme" (Dumas) **71**:189
Marion Fay (Trollope) **6**:470, 475, 484; **101**:311-13, 315, 322, 325
"Marionettentheater" (Kleist)
See "Über das Marionettentheater"
Marius (Hugo) **3**:246; **10**:359, 375
Marius the Epicurean (Pater)
See *Marius the Epicurean: His Sensations and Ideas*
Marius the Epicurean: His Sensations and Ideas (Pater) **7**:293-96, 298, 301, 306-12, 314-15, 317-19, 322-23, 325, 327, 329, 335-36, 340-42; **90**:239-42, 248, 251-54, 257-58, 264, 268-69, 272-76, 280-81, 283-91, 314, 318, 325-32, 340-41; **159**:222, 232-33, 236, 242, 248, 250-53, 263, 270, 273, 279, 282, 285-86, 319, 324
Marius und Sulla (Grabbe) **2**:272, 274-75, 280-82, 284, 287-88
Marja Stuart (Slowacki) **15**:348-50, 353, 362-63, 369, 373, 378
Marjam (Almqvist) **42**:19
"The Mark Bachelder Tragedy" (Smith) **187**:334
Mark Hurdlestone (Moodie) **113**:295, 297, 324, 334, 370, 372-73
Mark Hurdlestone, the Gold Worshipper (Moodie) **14**:217, 226, 237
Mark, the Match Boy; or, Richard Hunter's Ward (Alger) **8**:37, 39; **83**:105, 131
"Mark the Nihilist" (Goncharov) **63**:3
"The Market Man" (Freneau) **111**:132
"Market Night" (Bloomfield) **145**:129-30, 153
The Market-Place (Frederic) **10**:189-92, 194, 202, 206-08, 213, 215, 217; **175**:160
Markgraf Carl Philipp von Brandenburg (Arnim) **5**:21
"Markheim" (Stevenson) **5**:415, 418, 424, 429; **193**:209, 216, 222, 226, 283, 360, 364
"Marko Kraljević and Demo of the Mountain" (Karadzic) **115**:91
"Marko Kraljević and Lujutica Bogdan" (Karadzic) **115**:91
"Marko Kraljević and Musa Kesedžij" (Karadzic) **115**:91
"Marko Kraljević and the Daughter of the Arab King" (Karadzic) **115**:91
"Marko Kraljević Knows His Father's Sword" (Karadzic) **115**:91
Mark's Peak; or The Crater (Cooper)
See *The Crater; or, Vulcan's Peak*
Mark's Reef (Cooper) **203**:49-50, 77, 84-85, 87-89
Marmion (Scott) **15**:252, 254-56, 267, 273, 283, 285, 292-93, 318-20; **69**:304
Marmion: A Tale of Flodden Field (Scott) **209**:187-88, 191, 196, 253, 255-56
Das Marmorbild (Eichendorff)
See *Aus dem Leben eines Taugenichts und Das Marmorbild: Zwei Novellen nebst einem Anhange von Liedern und Romanzen*
"Das Marmorbild" (Eichendorff) **8**:216, 225, 233
"Der Marmorknabe" (Meyer) **81**:207
"Le Marquis de Carabas" (Beranger) **34**:29
"Le Marquis de Fumerol" (Maupassant) **83**:171
Marquis de Grandvin (Melville) **3**:379-80
Le marquis de Villemer (Sand) **2**:604-05; **42**:310, 312-13; **57**:317
Le marquis du Ier Houzards (Baudelaire) **6**:119-20
The Marquis of Villemer (Sand)
See *Le marquis de Villemer*
La marquise (Sand) **2**:594, 598-99
La Marquise de Ganges (Sade) **47**:314, 326
"Die Marquise von O..." (Kleist) **37**:217, 230, 237, 245-9, 253-5; **222**:185-92, 203, 206-7, 221-23, 225, 232, 236, 238-39, 256-57, 272, 292, 295
La Marraine (Sand) **57**:367; **174**:186
"Marriage" (Genlis) **166**:26
Marriage (Ferrier) **8**:236-56
The Marriage (Gogol)
See *Zhenit'ba; Sovershenno neveroyatnoye sobitye*
Marriage (Liszt)
See *Sponsalizio*
The Marriage: An Utterly Incredible Occurence (Gogol)
See *Zhenit'ba; Sovershenno neveroyatnoye sobitye*
"Marriage Bells" (Lazarus) **109**:292
The Marriage of Elinor (Oliphant) **61**:202-3, 205, 210-1, 242
The Marriage of Figaro (Da Ponte)
See *Le nozze di Figaro*
"The Marriage of Geraint" (Tennyson) **202**:207
The Marriage of Heaven and Hell (Blake) **13**:167, 170, 174, 176, 178-79, 184, 187, 192-93, 195, 200, 208, 210-11, 218, 222, 229-30, 246; **37**:18, 40, 42, 44-5, 48-9, 56, 59, 79; **57**:1-110; **127**:17, 23, 25, 33, 39, 46, 73, 77, 82-83, 88, 90, 112, 123-25, 128-29; **173**:8, 10, 39, 44, 52, 56-57, 66, 73, 78-79, 84, 112, 116; **190**:6, 14, 26, 36, 45-46, 49, 58, 88-89, 96, 112, 150, 162; **201**:5, 16, 20, 34, 38-40, 43, 46, 60-61, 73, 75, 79, 82, 84, 94-96, 99
The Marriage of the Monk (Meyer)
See *Die Hochzeit des Mönchs*
"Marriage Service" (Dodgson) **139**:65
"Marriages" (Crabbe) **121**:89
The Married Man (Inchbald) **62**:143, 146
Married or Single? (Sedgwick) **19**:445-47, 453; **98**:300, 334
"Married Peäir's Love Walk" (Barnes) **75**:7
"Married with an Opal" (Crawford) **127**:193, 195
"Marroca" (Maupassant) **83**:201
"Les marrons du feu" (Musset) **7**:254, 256, 264, 277-79; **150**:229-31, 299-300, 303-5
"Marrying in haste" (Lonnrot) **53**:339
"Mars of Florence" (Meyer)
See "Der Mars von Florenz"
"Der Mars von Florenz" (Meyer) **81**:199
"Marseillaise" (Whittier) **8**:504
"La marseillaise de la paix" (Lamartine) **11**:271, 276
Marsena, and Other Stories of Wartime (Frederic) **10**:188, 192, 203-04
"The Marsh King's Daughter" (Andersen)
See "Dynd-Kongens Datter"
The Marsh King's Daughter (Andersen)
See "Dynd-Kongens Datter"
"Marsh Song at Sunset" (Lanier) **6**:246, 249, 258; **118**:240
"The Marshes of Glynn" (Lanier) **6**:236-38, 240, 243, 246-47, 253-54, 256, 265, 268-73, 280-81; **118**:204, 223-24, 232, 238-40, 260, 263, 265, 267-71, 274-75, 287
"Martha" (Karamzin)
See "Marfa-posadnitsa"
"Martha Wyatt's Life" (Cooke) **110**:35
Marthe und ihre Uhr (Storm) **1**:537, 546; **195**:19, 92
"Marthy's Younkit" (Field) **3**:211
The Martian (Du Maurier) **86**:278-82, 286-87
Martin Chuzzlewit (Dickens)
See *The Life and Adventures of Martin Chuzzlewit*
Martin Faber (Simms) **3**:499, 502, 504, 510, 514
Martin Fierro (Hernández)
See *El gaucho Martín Fierro*
"Martin Luther" (Emerson) **98**:67
Martin Luther, oder die Weihe der Kraft: Eine Tragödie vom Verfasser der Söhne des Thales (Werner) **189**:320-22, 324, 326, 330-31, 352
Martin Luther, or the Consecration of Strength (Werner)
See *Martin Luther, oder die Weihe der Kraft: Eine Tragödie vom Verfasser der Söhne des Thales*
"Martin Relph" (Browning) **79**:163
Martin Salander (Keller) **2**:413, 415-16, 419-20, 423
"Martina y Jacinto" (Isaacs) **70**:306
"La Martine" (Maupassant) **83**:223

The Martins of Cro' Martin (Lever) **23**:292, 297, 306, 308
The Martyr (Baillie) **2**:39, 41; **151**:48, 115
The Martyr Age of the United States (Martineau) **137**:317, 327-28, 331
The Martyr of the Catacombs: A Tale of Ancient Rome (De Mille) **123**:117, 123
"Martyrdom of John Brown" (Thoreau) **207**:342
"Martyrdom of Saint Maura" (Kingsley) **35**:206, 211, 222
"Une martyre" (Baudelaire) **6**:87; **29**:104; **55**:5, 74-5, 79
"The Martyrs" (Lampman) **25**:160, 199; **194**:55
Les martyrs; ou, Le triomphe de la religion Chrétienne (Chateaubriand) **3**:110-12, 117, 124-26, 128-29, 132; **134**:4, 15-16, 18-20, 37, 70, 73, 80, 87
"Marvel and Parker" (Landor) **14**:165, 167
"Marvel of Marvels" (Rossetti) **2**:570
The Marvellous Adventures of Pinocchio (Collodi)
See *Le Avventure di Pinocchio*
The Marvellous Tale of Peter Schlemihl (Chamisso)
See *Peter Schlemihls Wundersame Geschichte*
Marvin Hayle (Webb) **143**:325, 337, 351, 357
Marx and his Book: The Music of the Nineteenth Century and Its Development (Liszt) **199**:305
"Mary" (Blake) **13**:243; **201**:27-28, 32, 114
"Mary and Her Little Lamb" (Hale)
See "Mary's Lamb"
"Mary Ann" (Cooke)
See "A Letter to Mary Ann"
"Mary Ann's Mind" (Cooke) **110**:35, 51
"Mary Ann's New Year" (Cooke) **110**:56
Mary Barton: A Tale of Manchester Life (Gaskell) **5**:177-80, 182-85, 187, 189-92, 196-200, 203-06; **70**:119-24, 126, 129-33, 135-36, 140, 144, 146, 149-50, 152-58, 161-65, 170-71, 173, 175-78, 185-87, 189, 190, 193, 196, 198, 200, 206-07, 214, 218, 221; **97**:110, 112, 173; **137**:3-180; **214**:183-84, 195-202, 205-11, 221, 235, 237, 242, 253-57, 273, 275-81, 284-85, 314-15, 321, 323, 332, 335, 342, 344
"Mary Burnie of the Mill" (O'Brien) **21**:243, 245-46
"Mary Garvin" (Whittier) **8**:509; **59**:371
"Mary Gresley" (Trollope) **101**:233, 265
"Mary Had a Little Lamb" (Hale)
See "Mary's Lamb"
"Mary Lee" (Parton) **86**:337, 349-50
"Mary Magdalene" (Bryant) **6**:159, 161
"Mary Magdalene" (Rossetti) **4**:498
Mary; or The Test of Honor (Rowson) **5**:321; **69**:112, 114, 122, 125-28, 134, 141-42
Mary; or, The Test of Honour, A Novel. By a Young Lady (Rowson) **182**:252-53, 255, 260, 263, 274, 276-77, 352
"Mary Rivers" (Kendall) **12**:183, 199
"Mary Scott" (Hogg) **4**:284
Mary Shelley Reader (Shelley) **170**:290
Mary Stewart (Alfieri)
See *Maria Stuarda*
Mary Stuart (Schiller)
See *Maria Stuart*
Mary Stuart (Slowacki)
See *Marja Stuart*
"Maryelle" (Villiers de l'Isle Adam) **3**:589-90
"Mary's Dream" (Hood) **16**:203
"Mary's Ghost" (Hood) **16**:237
"Mary's Lamb" (Hale) **75**:279, 284-294, 323, 349
"Mary's Little Lamb" (Hale)
See "Mary's Lamb"
Marzella; or, The Fairy Tale of Love (Sacher-Masoch) **31**:287, 292
Marzo 1821 (Manzoni) **98**:213, 219-20, 279
Masaniello; or, The Dumb Girl of Portici (Scribe)
See *La muette de Portici*
"Masha" (Turgenev) **21**:454
"The Mask" (Barrett Browning) **1**:125
"The Mask" (Baudelaire)
See "Le masque"
The Mask of Anarchy (Shelley)
See *The Masque of Anarchy*
Mask of Anarchy (Shelley)
See *The Masque of Anarchy*
Maskarad (Lermontov) **5**:294; **47**:160; **126**:154, 192, 216-17
Maskaradeballet i Dannemark (Grundtvig) **158**:138, 184-85
The Masked Ball in Denmark (Grundtvig)
See *Maskaradeballet i Dannemark*
Die Masken (Kotzebue) **25**:147
"Der Maskenball" (Lenau) **16**:278
Masks and Faces (Reade) **2**:534, 544; **74**:243, 277-78, 319, 331
"Le masque" (Baudelaire) **6**:79, 123; **55**:67, 73
"Le masque" (Maupassant) **1**:469
The Masque of 1818 (Goethe) **154**:262
The Masque of Anarchy (Shelley) **18**:328, 336, 338, 362, 368; **93**:272, 334; **143**:206, 216, 232, 272, 288; **175**:220, 274, 325, 330
The Masque of Pandora (Longfellow) **2**:497; **45**:113
The Masque of the Devils; or, The Canterbury Clock (Bird) **1**:93
The Masque of the Gods (Taylor) **89**:313-14
"The Masque of the Red Death" (Poe) **1**:500, 513, 521; **16**:306, 324, 331, 335; **55**:151; **211**:247-48
"A Masque of Venice" (Lazarus) **8**:411, 420
"Masquerade" (Lermontov)
See *Maskarad*
Mass in C (Beethoven) **227**:6
Mass in D (Beethoven) **227**:17, 20
"The Mass of Christ" (Adams) **33**:18
"Massachusetts to Virginia" (Whittier) **8**:486, 526, 530-31; **59**:349, 364, 368
The Massacre (Inchbald) **62**:144
"The Massacre at Scio" (Bryant) **46**:3, 7
"Le massacre de Mona" (Leconte de Lisle) **29**:226, 228
"Massa's in de Cold Ground" (Foster) **26**:283, 285, 291, 295, 298
"Massimilla doni" (Balzac) **5**:65, 67; **153**:149, 151
"The Master and the Dog" (Krasicki)
See "Pan i pies"
Master Flea (Hoffmann)
See *Meister Floh: Ein Mährchen in seiben Abenteuern zweier Freunde*
"Master Hugues of Saxe-Gotha" (Browning) **19**:97, 153; **79**:106, 108, 164
Master Humphrey's Clock (Dickens) **187**:26; **206**:3, 6, 8, 26, 29, 36-37, 39-41, 55, 82, 104, 108-9, 111-14, 119, 131
"Master letters" (Dickinson) **171**:149
"Master Martin and His Workmen" (Hoffmann)
See "Meister Martin der Küfner und seine Gesellen"
The Master of Ballantrae: A Winter's Tale (Stevenson) **5**:405-09, 415, 418, 422, 425, 429-37; **63**:243, 261, 274; **193**:212, 216-18, 221, 223-24, 238, 250, 287, 289, 294, 296-99, 304, 325, 334, 338, 358
The Master of Greylands (Wood) **178**:322, 324
"The Master of Masters" (Mickiewicz) **3**:399-400
"'Master of St. Bede's'" (Craik) **38**:113
"Master Pinty" (Petofi)
See "Pinty úrfi"
Master Thaddeus; or, The Last Foray in Lithuania (Mickiewicz)
See *Pan Tadeusz; czyli, Ostatni zajazd na Litwie*
"Master Theme" (Preseren)
See "Magistrale"
Master William Mitten (Longstreet) **159**:131
Masterman Ready; or, The Wreck of the Pacific (Marryat) **3**:316, 320, 322-23
The Master's House; A Tale of Southern Life (Thorpe) **183**:330-36
The Mastersingers of Nuremberg (Wagner)
See *Die Meistersinger von Nürnberg*
Masurao monogatari (Ueda Akinari) **131**:57
"Mat" (Nekrasov) **11**:419
"El matadero" (Echeverria) **18**:148-54
The Match (Baillie) **71**:6, 64
"Match-Making" (Cooke) **110**:35
"Matelots" (Corbière) **43**:7, 30-1, 33
"Mater Dolorosa: A Slave-Mother's Lullaby" (Castro Alves) **205**:18
"Mater Pulchrae Delectionis" (Rossetti) **77**:301, 344
"Mater Tenebrarum" (Thomson) **18**:403, 418
"Materialen zu einem Lebenslauf" (Schumann) **143**:73
Materiali estetici (Manzoni) **98**:215
Mathews (Reynolds)
See *The Youthful Days of Mr. Mathews*
Mathilda (Shelley) **59**:154, 190, 192; **103**:320-85; **170**:260, 288, 370
Mathilde Möhring (Fontane) **26**:240, 244, 258, 271
Matiju Čopu (Preseren) **127**:330
Matilda Montgomerie (Richardson)
See *The Canadian Brothers; or, The Prophecy Fulfilled. A Tale of the Late American War*
"Matilda Muffin" (Cooke)
See "The Memorial of A.B., or Matilda Muffin"
"Matin" (Rimbaud) **4**:466; **35**:292, 304; **82**:222, 225, 229, 236-37, 240-41, 243, 251-53, 255, 261-62; **227**:278, 305, 314, 316, 318
"Matinée d'ivresse" (Rimbaud) **4**:474; **35**:269, 272, 295-96, 311-12, 322; **82**:233, 235; **227**:235-40, 242, 244, 247, 294, 309-10, 314
"Matins" (Lazarus) **8**:418
Matrimonial Speculations (Moodie) **14**:226, 236; **113**:295, 297
The Matrons (Percy) **95**:313, 336, 338
"The Matron's Tale" (Wordsworth) **111**:233, 237
Matros (Shevchenko) **54**:391-3, 397-8
"Matt Hyland" (Griffin) **7**:194, 198, 201-02
Matteo Falcone (Mérimée) **6**:354, 358-60, 362-6, 368-70; **65**:54-5, 57, 66, 100, 102, 106-7, 109-10, 113, 124
Matthew Arnold: Selected Prose (Arnold) **218**:209-12, 215, 217, 219
"Mátyás anyja" (Arany) **34**:20
"Mátyás's Mother" (Arany)
See "Mátyás anyja"
"Maud" (Tennyson) **115**:237
Maud (Tennyson) **202**:331-33
Maud, and Other Poems (Tennyson) **30**:213-14, 218-19, 221, 231-33, 236, 241-42, 245, 254, 258, 266-67, 276-85, 287, 294-95, 297-99; **65**:234, 267-9, 285, 348, 369, 372, 380, 384, 386; **115**:252, 269, 275, 341, 359; **202**:263
"Maud Miller" (Whittier) **8**:496, 501, 509-11, 513, 515, 521-24; **59**:358, 361, 371
Maude (Rossetti)
See *Maude: Prose and Verse*
"Maude Clare" (Rossetti) **2**:555, 575; **66**:330-1, 352-3, 355; **186**:269, 272
Maude: Prose and Verse (Rossetti) **50**:301; **66**:317, 320-21, 331; **186**:229-30, 263-64, 281-83, 306
Mauprat (Sand) **2**:586, 588-89, 599-600, 603, 605, 608; **42**:310, 319-20, 324, 327-28, 332, 338, 340, 363-64, 366; **57**:316-7, 320-1, 341, 360, 366, 375, 381; **174**:167, 226, 229
Les maures d'espagne; ou, Le pouvoir de l'enfance (Pixérécourt) **39**:273-74, 277-79, 281, 293
"Maurice de Guerin" (Arnold) **89**:81-2

The Maurice Mystery (Cooke) **5**:132
Maurice Tiernay, the Soldier of Fortune (Lever) **23**:292, 294, 304
"Mausfallen-Sprüchlein" (Mörike) **10**:455
"Mausolée" (Lamartine) **190**:222
"Le mauvais moine" (Baudelaire) **6**:120, 130; **55**:49, 58
"Mauvais sang" (Rimbaud) **4**:476, 481; **35**:290-91, 302, 313-15, 319, 325; **82**:218, 222, 224, 229, 234-35, 237-38, 240-45, 251, 255, 257, 262; **227**:210, 271, 277-78, 280, 306-7, 315
"Le mauvais vitrier" (Baudelaire) **155**:46, 57, 87, 113
Max Havelaar, of de Koffijveilingen der Nederlandsche Handelmaatschappij (Multatuli) **165**:303-5, 307-14, 317-18, 323, 334-36, 339-41, 343-45, 349, 351, 353-57, 360-69
"Maxim Maximych" (Lermontov)
See "Maksim Maksimovich"
Maximen und Reflexionen (Goethe) **154**:241, 271, 277-78
"Maximes" (Pushkin) **83**:270
Maxims and Reflections (Goethe)
See *Maximen und Reflexionen*
"Maxims for Republics" (Brackenridge) **227**:105, 108, 110
Maxims of Sir Morgan O'Doherty, Bart. (Maginn) **8**:436, 438, 440-42
"May" (Barnes) **75**:6
"May" (Clare) **86**:100-02
May (Macha)
See *Máj*
May (Oliphant) **11**:434, 446; **61**:173; **221**:230
"May Day 1837" (Norton) **47**:238, 241
May Day in Town; or, New York in an Uproar (Tyler) **3**:573-74
"May Evening" (Bryant) **6**:176
"The May Flower" (Very) **9**:372
"May Gambols" (Thackeray) **213**:247
"The May Magnificat" (Hopkins) **17**:202, 216
"A May Night" (Gogol)
See "Majskaja noč, ili Vtoplennica"
"May Night" (Musset)
See "Nuit de Mai"
"A May Night; or, The Drowned Maiden" (Gogol)
See "Majskaja noč, ili Vtoplennica"
"The May Queen" (Tennyson) **202**:334
The May Queen (Tennyson) **30**:223
"May Your Soul Be . . ." (Verlaine)
See "Que ton âme soit . . ."
Māyā Kānan (Dutt) **118**:5
"Maya, the Princess" (Cooke) **110**:3, 45-6
"May-Day" (Emerson) **1**:279, 284, 296, 299-300; **38**:184; **98**:182-84
May-Day and Other Pieces (Emerson) **1**:279; **38**:192-93; **98**:177, 179, 182-84
May-day with the Muses (Bloomfield) **145**:135-36, 148, 157-60, 162, 176, 178-79
The Mayfair Set (Frederic)
See *Mrs. Albert Grundy: Observations in Philistia*
The Mayflower; or, Sketches of Scenes and Characters among the Descendants of the Puritans (Stowe) **3**:549, 564
"Mayo" (Isaacs) **70**:303-04
The Mayor of Wind Gap (Banim and Banim) **13**:129-30
Mayor of Zalamca (FitzGerald) **9**:258-59
"The Maypole of Merry Mount" (Hawthorne) **2**:329-31; **10**:300, 302, 307; **17**:157; **79**:296; **95**:131, 137, 213; **158**:197, 327, 336; **171**:343; **191**:215; **226**:32
"May-Time" (Taylor) **89**:316
"The May-Tree" (Barnes) **75**:32
Mąż i żona (Fredro) **8**:285, 289-92
Mazépa (Pushkin) **3**:422
Mazepa (Slowacki) **15**:348-49, 351-53, 364, 371, 378
Mazeppa (Byron) **2**:65, 96; **12**:110, 139; **109**:103; **149**:21, 87-88
"Mazzini on Music" (Lanier) **118**:243
"Mcyri" (Lermontov)
See *Mtsyri*
"Me, Change! Me, Alter!" (Dickinson) **21**:65
"Me hitotsu no kami" (Ueda Akinari) **131**:21-22, 57
"Me imperturbe" (Whitman) **4**:568, 569; **205**:162, 166
"Me piden versos" (Rizal) **27**:425
"Me prove it now—Whoever doubt" (Dickinson) **171**:159
"Mea Culpa" (Allingham) **25**:7
"The Meadow" (Lampman) **194**:31, 56, 93
"The Meadow Lake" (Clare) **9**:117
Meadow Saffron (Arany)
See *Őszikék*
"Meadow Thoughts" (Jefferies) **47**:101, 136
"The Meadows in Spring" (FitzGerald) **153**:217
The Meadows in Spring (FitzGerald) **9**:275
"The Meal-Mongers; or, Food Riots in Ireland" (Jones) **222**:158
"Meaning of Swedish Poverty" (Almqvist)
See "Svenska fattigdomens betydelse"
Means and Ends; or, Self-Training (Sedgwick) **19**:441, 446; **98**:330, 333, 335-38
"Meäry Wedded" (Barnes) **75**:58, 71
"Measure for Measure" (Lamb) **125**:304, 306
Mechanism in Thought and Morals (Holmes) **14**:130, 132, 135-37, 150
"Les mécontents" (Mérimée) **6**:362; **65**:58, 63, 79, 81-3
"Le médaillon" (Villiers de l'Isle Adam)
See "Antonie"
Médaillons et portraits (Mallarmé)
See *Quelques médaillons et portraits en pied*
Médallions et Portraits (Mallarmé) **210**:250
"Meddőórán" (Arany) **34**:21
Medea (Grillparzer) **1**:387; **102**:86-8, 90-1, 93-104, 110, 164, 186-87
Medea (Webster) **230**:241
"Medea, a Fragment of Drama after Euripides" (Levy) **59**:91, 102, 109-10
Medea auf dem Kaukasos (Klinger) **1**:426-27
"Medea in Athens" (Webster) **230**:232, 270, 287, 323-24
Medea in Korinth (Klinger) **4**:426-27
Le Médecin de Campagne (Balzac) **5**:31, 33; **35**:25; **53**:9, 28; **153**:91, 147, 150, 152
"Medfield" (Bryant) **6**:178, 181
"The Median Supper" (Beddoes) **3**:33
"The Mediatorial Life of Jesus" (Brownson) **50**:48
Medical Essays (Holmes) **81**:108
"El médico y su mula" (Lizardi) **30**:67
"Médiocrité" (Laforgue) **221**:42, 77, 85
"Meditation" (Barbauld)
See "A Summer's Evening Meditation"
"Meditation" (Baudelaire)
See "Recueillement"
"Meditation" (Lermontov)
See "Duma"
"A Meditation" (Pavlova)
See "Duma"
"A Meditation in Tuscany" (Barrett Browning) **170**:69
"Meditation of a Thirsty Man" (Petofi)
See "Szomjas ember tünödése"
"Meditations" (Pavlova) **138**:33-34
"Meditations in Verse" (Emerson) **1**:285
"Meditations on Divine Liturgy" (Gogol) **162**:31
"Meditations on Rhode Island Coal" (Bryant) **6**:161
Méditations poétiques (Lamartine) **11**:244-46, 248-50, 252-55, 263, 265, 268-69, 271-73, 275-77, 279, 281-82, 284; **190**:167, 172, 200, 211, 214, 218-19, 221, 226-27, 230, 232, 234, 237, 250-53, 257
Meditative Poems (Coleridge) **9**:146
The Medium; or Happy Tea Party (Murray)
See *The Medium; or Virtue Triumphant*
The Medium; or Virtue Triumphant (Murray) **63**:184-5, 189, 193, 195, 199, 201, 214
"Mediums" (Whitman) **205**:162, 165
"A Medley" (Coleridge) **90**:27
Medny Vsadnik (Pushkin) **27**:386; **83**:251, 312-13, 350, 352-53, 358
"Medusa Dying" (Meyer)
See "Die sterbende Meduse"
"A Meek One" (Dostoevsky)
See "Krotkaya"
"Meeresstille" (Lenau) **16**:283; **225**:45
Eine Meerfahrt (Eichendorff) **8**:215, 217; **225**:19-21
"Meeting" (Arnold) **89**:15-16, 19, 95
"The Meeting" (Clare) **9**:74
"Meeting" (Grillparzer)
See "Begegnung"
"Meeting" (Rossetti) **66**:311
"The Meeting" (Turgenev)
See "Svidanie"
"The Meeting of the Dryads" (Holmes) **14**:109, 128
"A Meeting with Martinists" (Aksakov)
See "Vstrecha s Martinistami"
"Még ez egyszer" (Arany) **34**:21
"Meg Merrilies" (Keats) **8**:360
Meghanād (Dutt)
See *Meghnādbadh Kābya*
Meghnādbadh Kābya (Dutt) **118**:2, 5-9, 11-15, 25-31
"Mehr Unterricht" (Klopstock) **11**:238
Die Mehreren Wehmüller und die ungarischen Nationalgesichter (Brentano) **1**:100-01; **191**:75, 77-81, 118, 120-22, 144, 148-49
Mehri-Nimroze (Ghalib) **39**:152
"Le meilleur amour" (Villiers de l'Isle Adam) **3**:588
"Mein!" (Muller) **73**:351, 364, 368, 370-72
"Mein Beruf" (Droste-Hülshoff) **3**:193
"Mein Eigentum" (Hölderlin) **16**:173
"Mein Fluss" (Mörike) **10**:448; **201**:286-87
Mein Freund (Nestroy) **42**:221, 243, 248, 250
"Mein Jahr" (Meyer) **81**:141, 153, 155-56
Mein Leben (Stifter) **41**:375
Mein Leben (Wagner) **119**:187, 189, 192-94, 288
"Mein Stern" (Lenau) **16**:269
"Mein Stern" (Meyer) **81**:146
"Mein Vaterland" (Klopstock) **11**:236
"Mein Wäldchen" (Klopstock) **225**:314-15, 319-21
"Mein Wort über das Drama" (Hebbel) **43**:264, 267, 280, 283
"Meine Erklärung" (Wieland) **177**:320
"Meine Göttin" (Goethe) **4**:193
Meine Kinderjahre (Fontane) **26**:234, 247, 258-64, 271-72; **163**:238
"An Meinen Sohn Johannes 1799" (Claudius) **75**:210
"Eine Meinung über die vorige Meinung" (Herder) **186**:19
Meister Floh (Hoffmann)
See *Meister Floh: Ein Mährchen in seiben Abenteuern zweier Freunde*
Meister Floh: Ein Mährchen in seiben Abenteuern zweier Freunde (Hoffmann) **2**:359, 362; **183**:171, 188, 213, 219, 231
"Meister Johannes Wacht" (Hoffmann) **183**:189
"Meister Martin der Küfner und seine Gesellen" (Hoffmann) **183**:217
*Meister Martin der Ku****fner und seine Gesellen: ErzaUMLhlung* (Hoffmann) **2**:340
Meisters Wanderjahre (Goethe)
See *Wilhelm Meisters Wanderjahre; oder, Die Entsagenden*
Die Meistersinger von Nürnberg (Wagner) **9**:408-10, 412-13, 415-16, 419, 421, 425, 443, 446-47, 452-56, 465, 468; **119**:176,

180, 182, 198, 210, 228, 241, 268-69, 290-91, 293, 349
"Mejnoun and Leila" (D'Israeli) **217**:275, 277, 279, 283, 292, 304, 306-7
"The Melamed of Osterreich" (Leskov)
See "Rakušanskij melamed"
"Melancholia" (Gautier) **1**:350
"Melancholia" (Hugo) **189**:178
"Melancholy" (Coleridge) **90**:9
"Melancholy" (Eminescu) **33**:264; **131**:332, 334-35
"Melancholy" (Karamzin)
See "Melankholiya"
"Melancholy" (Lenau) **16**:276
"Melancholy" (Macha)
See "Tezkomyslnot"
"Melancholy: A Fragment" (Coleridge) **231**:130-33
"Melancholy at Evening" (Schumann) **143**:138
"A Melancholy Moon" (Baudelaire)
See "Les tristesses de la lune"
"Melancholy Ode" (Hood)
See "Ode to Melancholy"
"Melancholy Ode" (Keats)
See "Ode on Melancholy"
"Melancthon and Calvin" (Landor) **14**:165, 167
Mélanges de littérature et de politique (Constant) **6**:224; **182**:211, 227
Mélanges posthumes (Laforgue) **53**:291, 294; **221**:29, 52-53, 66
"Melanie" (Willis) **194**:292
Melanie and Other Poems (Willis) **194**:286, 304-5
"Melankholiya" (Karamzin) **173**:280
The Melbournians (Adams) **33**:15, 18
"Melhill Feast" (Barnes) **75**:20, 26, 30, 68, 94
"Meliore und Apone" (Brentano) **191**:7
Melkie okhotnich'i rasskazy (Aksakov) **181**:65
Mellichampe (Simms) **3**:503, 507-08
"Mellonta Tauta" (Poe) **55**:152; **94**:212, 215, 217; **211**:224, 226
Melmoth the Wanderer (Maturin) **6**:323-30, 332-42, 344-47
Melmoth the Wanderer: A Tale (Maturin) **169**:3, 14, 16, 18, 23, 26-30, 34, 37, 39-40, 44-45, 51, 56-59, 62, 64-67, 70-71, 74-75, 77-78, 80-81, 83, 85-86, 90-91, 101-3, 105-6, 111, 114, 116-18, 120-23, 126, 129, 131-32
Melochi zhizni (Saltykov) **16**:369, 375
"Meloci archierejskoj zizni" (Leskov) **174**:38
Meloci archierejskoj zizni (Leskov) **174**:30
"Meloči arxierejskoj žizni" (Leskov) **25**:228
Melodies (Moore)
See *The Irish Melodies*
Mélodies hongroises (Liszt)
See *Des Bohémiens et de leur musique en Hongrie*
"Melodor k Filalet" (Karamzin) **173**:277, 323, 352
Melück Maria Blainville (Arnim) **159**:95
Melusina (Grillparzer) **102**:113, 149, 189-90
"Melusine" (Fontane) **163**:169
Melville's Marquesas (Melville) **45**:194
The Member (Galt) **110**:76, 79, 94
"Member of the Haouse" (Holmes) **81**:103
Même histoire (Balzac) **153**:147, 149-50
"Memento" (Eichendorff) **225**:41, 43
"Memento mori" (Eminescu) **33**:250, 259, 261; **131**:286, 288, 290
"Memento Sonnet triste" (Laforgue) **221**:40
"Memoir" (Radcliffe) **223**:187
"Memoir" (Thelwall) **162**:329
Memoir (Jefferson)
See *Autobiography of Thomas Jefferson*
Memoir (Southey) **97**:288
Memoir (Tennyson) **65**:249
Memoir and Correspondence of Susan Ferrier, 1782-1854 (Ferrier) **8**:245
Memoir, Letters, and Remains Alexis de Tocqueville (Tocqueville) **7**:424; **63**:282
Memoir of Count de Montalembert (Oliphant) **11**:434; **221**:227, 233-34
Memoir of Fleeming Jenkin (Stevenson)
See *Fleeming Jenkin*
A Memoir of Maria Edgeworth (Edgeworth) **51**:108, 114, 117
"Memoir of the Cats of Greta Hall" (Southey) **97**:274
Memoir of the Early Life of William Cowper, Esq. (Cowper) **8**:124, 129, 133-35; **94**:19-20, 27, 57-8
Memoir of the Life of John Tullach (Oliphant) **221**:233-34
Memoir of the Life of Laurence Oliphant and of Alice Oliphant, His Wife (Oliphant) **221**:233
"Memoir of the Philosophical Society" (Brackenridge) **227**:73
"Memoir of the Rev. R. Barbauld" (Barbauld) **185**:122
Memoir on Ancient and Modern Russia (Karamzin)
See *O drevnei i novoi Rossii v ee politicheskom i grazhdanskom otnosheniiakh*
"A Memoir on the Discovery of Certain Bones of a Quadruped of the Clawed Kind in the Western Parts of Virginia" (Jefferson) **103**:106
"Mémoire" (Rimbaud) **4**:475, 478-79, 484, 486; **35**:297, 299, 301-02, 304, 307; **82**:218, 255; **227**:211-14, 236, 271
"Mémoire apologétique" (Constant) **182**:191
Memoire de Lorenzo Da Ponte da Ceneda (Da Ponte) **50**:76-82, 84-7, 96, 99-101
"La mémoire d'une chatte naine que j'avais" (Laforgue) **221**:83
Mémoires inédits de Lamartine, 1790-1815 (Lamartine) **190**:197, 242
Mémoire sur la captivitéde madame la duchesse de Berry (Chateaubriand) **134**:97
"Mémoire sur le système nerveux de barbeau" (Büchner) **146**:67
"Mémoire sur l'état de l'Allemagne et sur les moyens d'y former former une insurrection nationale" (Schlegel) **142**:322
Mémoire sur l'Orient (Chateaubriand) **134**:8
Memoiren (Heine) **54**:329; **147**:174, 180
"Die Memoiren des Herren von Schnabelewopski" (Heine) **4**:262, 268
Memoires (Flaubert)
See *Les mémoires d'un fou*
Mémoires (Genlis) **166**:15, 21-22, 38
Mémoires de deux jeunes mariées (Balzac) **5**:40, 83-84; **153**:80
Mémoires de Marquis de Calvière (Goncourt and Goncourt) **7**:164
Mémoires de Sophie (Duras) **154**:112-13, 158, 163
Mémoires de Sophie Arnoud (Goncourt and Goncourt) **7**:164
Mémoires d'outre-tombe (Chateaubriand) **3**:118-21, 127, 129, 134-35; **134**:7, 12, 14-20, 25, 51, 63-64, 66-69, 77, 80, 86-87, 91, 93-95, 102-7, 109-10, 112-14, 129, 147
Les mémoires d'un fou (Flaubert) **2**:249, 255-6; **10**:170; **19**:288, 299, 304; **62**:83-91, 95; **66**:269-72; **179**:13, 24
Mémoires d'un médecin: Joseph Balsamo (Dumas) **11**:51, 76
Mémoires d'un touriste (Stendhal) **23**:355, 359, 409-10; **46**:269, 325; **178**:199
Les Mémoires d'un veuf (Verlaine) **230**:174
Mémoires inédites (Lamartine) **11**:265
Memoires of a Physician (Dumas)
See *Mémoires d'un médecin: Joseph Balsamo*
Mémoires sur le Duc de Berry (Chateaubriand) **134**:84
Mémoires sur les Cent-Jours en forme de letters (Constant) **182**:191, 219
"Memoirs" (Hogg) **109**:268
"Memoirs" (Scott) **209**:253
Memoirs (Aksakov)
See *Vospominaniia prezhei zhizni*
Memoirs (Alfieri)
See *Vita*
Memoirs (Bashkirtseff)
See *Le journal de Marie Bashkirtseff*
Memoirs (Holcroft)
See *Memoirs of the Late Thomas Holcroft, Written by Himself and Continued by William Hazlitt to the Time of His Death from His Diary, Notes and Other Papers*
Memoirs (Huxley) **67**:79-80
Memoirs (Moore) **110**:202
The Memoirs (Symonds) **34**:331-32, 335-37, 374-75
Memoirs and Essays Illustrative of Art, Literature, and Social Morals (Jameson) **43**:323
Les Memoirs d'un veuf (Verlaine) **51**:363, 386
Memoirs from Underground (Dostoevsky)
See *Zapiski iz podpol'ya*
Memoirs of a Former Life (Aksakov)
See *Vospominaniia prezhei zhizni*
"Memoirs of a Good-for-Nothing" (Eichendorff)
See "Aus dem Leben eines Taugenichts"
The Memoirs of a Madman (Flaubert)
See *Les mémoires d'un fou*
The Memoirs of a Nihilist (Turgenev)
See *Ottsy i deti*
The Memoirs of a Preacher, a Revelation of the Church and the Home (Lippard) **198**:125, 167, 225
The Memoirs of a Sportsman (Turgenev)
See *Zapiski okhotnika*
Memoirs of a Tourist (Stendhal)
See *Mémoires d'un touriste*
Memoirs of Alexander Herzen (Herzen)
See *Byloe i dumy*
Memoirs of an Egotist (Stendhal)
See *Souvenirs dégotisme*
The Memoirs of Barry Lyndon, Esq. (Thackeray) **5**:452, 459-60, 465, 470-71, 482, 490, 492, 497; **14**:400, 402, 451; **43**:346-97; **169**:243; **213**:186-87, 189, 263-64, 270-72, 275-77, 281
Memoirs of Beelzebub (Hauff)
See *Mittheilungen aus den Memoiren des Satan*
The Memoirs of Bryan Perdue (Holcroft) **85**:193, 199-200, 207, 228, 231, 236, 238, 244-46
Memoirs of Captain Rock (Moore) **6**:395; **110**:193
Memoirs of Carwin the Biloquist (Brown) **74**:5, 17-18, 48, 54, 76, 133, 142-43, 161-62, 164, 199-200, 202-03; **122**:30, 33, 36, 53, 91, 94, 157-58, 163
Memoirs of Celebrated Characters (Lamartine)
See *Le Civilisateur: Histoire de l'humanité par les grands hommes*
Memoirs of Celebrated Female Sovereigns (Jameson) **43**:305-06, 309, 319
Memoirs of Chateaubriand, written by himself (Chateaubriand)
See *Mémoires d'outre-tombe*
Memoirs of Dr. Burney: Arranged from His Own Manuscripts, from Family Papers, and from Personal Recollections (Burney) **12**:23-6, 28, 32-3, 47-8; **54**:15-16, 18
Memoirs of Dr. Richard Gilpin, of Scaleby Castle in Cumberland; and of His Posterity in the Two Succeeding Generations (Gilpin) **30**:35
The Memoirs of Emma Courtney (Hays) **114**:172, 175, 178-80, 182-83, 185-86, 188-89, 191-92, 194, 197, 200, 207-8, 210-16, 219, 223, 229-30, 232, 240-44, 247-49, 251

Memoirs of François René, Vicomte de Chateaubriand, Sometime Ambassador to England (Chateaubriand)
See *Mémoires d'outre-tombe*
Memoirs of Himself (Stevenson) **193**:229
Memoirs of John Quincy Adams (Adams) **175**:21-22, 36-37, 45, 82-86, 88-89
Memoirs of Josias Rogers, Esq., Commander of His Majesty's Ship Quebec (Gilpin) **30**:35
"Memoirs of Literature and Life" (Turgenev) **122**:242
Memoirs of Lorenzo Da Ponte (Da Ponte)
See *Memoire de Lorenzo Da Ponte da Ceneda*
Memoirs of Margaret Fuller Ossoli (Fuller) **5**:162, 170; **50**:223, 236, 253; **211**:87, 89-92, 114, 119-20, 132, 134, 159, 174-77, 210, 212
Memoirs of Mary Wollstonecraft (Godwin) **130**:37, 115
Memoirs of Mme. de Stael and Mme. Roland (Child)
See *The Biographies of Madame de Staël and Madame Roland, Married Women; or, Biographies of Good Wives*
Memoirs of Modern Philosophers (Hamilton) **153**:268, 270, 272, 274, 283-87, 289, 291-94, 297, 306, 312, 315-16, 319, 322, 325-35, 339-40, 348, 356, 2395
Memoirs of Morgan O'Doherty (Maginn) **8**:438
"Memoirs of Phoebe Hammond" (Sigourney) **87**:321
Memoirs of Queens Illustrious and Celebrated (Hays) **114**:187, 200
Memoirs of Richard Cumberland (Cumberland) **167**:106, 114, 117, 122-23, 125-26, 136-37, 140, 144, 151-52, 154-55, 158, 166, 169-71, 174-80, 183, 186, 193
Memoirs of Richard Lovell Edgeworth (Edgeworth) **51**:81
Memoirs of Richard Lovell Edgeworth, Esq. Begun by Himself and Concluded by His Daughter, Maria Edgeworth (Edgeworth) **158**:25-26, 54, 56, 80
Memoirs of Rossini (Stendhal)
See *Vie de Rossini*
Memoirs of Sir Roger de Clarendon, the Natural Son of Edward Prince of Wales, Commonly Called the Black Prince (Reeve) **19**:408, 412
Memoirs of Stephen Calvert (Brown) **74**:15, 51, 133-34, 161, 164; **122**:53
Memoirs of the Aksakov Family (Aksakov)
See *Semeinaia khronika*
Memoirs of the Author of "A Vindication of the Rights of Women" (Godwin) **14**:53, 88-91
Memoirs of the Author's Life (Hogg) **109**:200, 258-63, 267
Memoirs of the Beauties of the Court of Charles II (Jameson) **43**:308-09
Memoirs of the Duke of Sully (Lennox) **134**:219
Memoirs of the Early Italian Painters (Jameson) **43**:323, 333, 335-38
Memoirs of the Late Mrs. Robinson, Written by Herself. With Some Posthumous Pieces (Robinson) **142**:94, 97-98, 102-3, 110, 119-20, 125, 128, 140-45, 148, 153-59, 178, 181, 195-99, 219, 222-27, 231, 241, 247, 251, 279
Memoirs of the Late Thomas Holcroft, Written by Himself and Continued by William Hazlitt to the Time of His Death from His Diary, Notes and Other Papers (Holcroft) **85**:190, 192, 195, 199-200, 205, 209-10, 212, 221, 237
Memoirs of the Life and Correspondence of Hannah More (More) **141**:210, 294-95, 299, 307-11
Memoirs of the Life and Writings of Robert Robinson (Dyer) **129**:97, 104, 112, 115, 126, 145
Memoirs of the Life of Agrippina, the Wife of Germanicus (Hamilton) **153**:272-73, 294, 297, 299
Memoirs of the Life of George Frederick Cooke (Dunlap) **2**:208
Memoirs of the Life of Sir Walter Scott, Bart. (Lockhart) **6**:290-95, 297-98, 300, 305, 307, 309-10
Memoirs of the Life of William Collins, Esq., R.A. (Collins) **1**:184-85; **93**:46
Memoirs of the Life of William Wirt, Attorney General of the United States (Kennedy) **2**:429, 432, 435
Memoirs of the London Doll (Blake) **127**:262-69
Memoirs of the Loves of the Poets (Jameson) **43**:305-09, 315, 319
Memoirs of the Modern Philosophers (Hamilton) **153**:264-65
"Memoirs of the Right Honourable James Wilson" (Bagehot) **10**:31
Memoirs of Two Young Married Women (Balzac)
See *Mémoires de deux jeunes mariées*
Memoirs on the Hundred Days (Constant)
See *Mémoires sur les Cent-Jours en forme de letters*
Memorabilien (Immermann) **49**:368
"The Memorable Victory of Paul Jones" (Freneau)
See "Poem on the memorable victory obtained by the gallant capt. Paul Jones, or the Good Man Richard, over the Seraphis, etc. under the command of capt. Pearson"
Memoralia; or Phials of Amber Full of the Tears of Love: A Gift for the Beautiful (Chivers) **49**:40, 42-4, 73
Memoranda (Barbey d'Aurevilly) **213**:91
Memoranda (Prescott) **163**:349-52
"Memoranda during the War" (Whitman) **4**:551
"Memorandum" (De Quincey) **198**:13
"Memorandum about the Cenci Case" (Shelley) **143**:176-77
"A Memorandum at a Venture" (Whitman) **81**:276
"Memorandum of Probable Failure of Re-Election" (Lincoln) **201**:215
Memorandum of the Improvements in the Administration of India and Petition of the East-India Company to Parliament (Mill) **179**:354
Memorandum on Old and New Russia (Karamzin)
See *O drevnei i novoi Rossii v ee politicheskom i grazhdanskom otnosheniiakh*
Memoria sobre ortografía americana (Sarmiento) **123**:325, 377
"Memorial and Remonstrance" (Madison) **126**:312-13, 315
A Memorial and Remonstrance against Religious Assessments (Madison) **126**:291-92, 296
Memorial Edition of Jefferson's Works (Jefferson) **103**:106
"The Memorial of A.B., or Matilda Muffin" (Cooke) **110**:51, 67
"Memorial Thresholds" (Rossetti) **77**:359-61
"Memorial to Robert Browning" (Cranch) **115**:22
"Memorial Verses" (Arnold) **29**:4, 31; **89**:22-3, 47; **218**:114, 117, 119, 147, 156-57, 183, 189, 274
Memorialia (Chivers)
See *Memoralia; or Phials of Amber Full of the Tears of Love: A Gift for the Beautiful*
The Memorials of a Residence on the Continent, and Historical Poems (Milnes) **61**:137, 144
"Memorials of a Tour in Italy, 1837" (Wordsworth) **12**:465
Memorials of a Tour in Some Parts of Greece (Milnes) **61**:137, 145
Memorials of a Tour on the Continent (Wordsworth) **12**:409
"Memorials of Gormandizing" (Thackeray) **213**:192
Memorials of Many Scenes (Milnes) **61**:145
Memorias de un estudiante de Manila (Rizal) **27**:424
Memorie inutili della vita di Carlo Gozzi (Gozzi) **23**:115, 123
"Memories" (Whittier) **8**:486, 505, 511, 513
Memories (Renan)
See *Souvenirs d'enfance et de jeunesse*
Memories and Portraits (Sheridan) **5**:416, 421, 530
Memories and Portraits (Stevenson) **193**:206, 208, 211, 219
Memories of a Tourist (Stendhal)
See *Mémoires d'un touriste*
"Memories of Leconte de Lisle" (Verlaine) **230**:162
"Memories of President Lincoln" (Whitman) **205**:225-26
"Memories of Youth in the Countryside" (Grillparzer)
See *Jugenderinnerungen im Grünen*
"Memory" (Brontë) **109**:27
"Memory" (Lamb) **125**:371
"Memory" (Rimbaud)
See "Mémoire"
"Memory" (Rossetti) **2**:575; **186**:262, 270
"Memory and Imagination" (Beattie)
See *Dissertations Moral and Critical: On Memory and Imagination; On Dreaming; The Theory of Language; On Fable and Romance; On the Attachments of Kindred; Illustrations on Sublimity*
"Memory and Want of Memory" (Hunt) **70**:257
"Memory of Dwarf Cat I Had" (Laforgue)
See "La mémoire d'une chatte naine que j'avais"
"A Memory Picture" (Arnold) **29**:35; **89**:20
Men (Verlaine)
See *Hombres*
Men and Women (Browning) **19**:79, 89, 110, 116, 118, 126-27, 130, 133, 154-56; **79**:140-42, 148-49, 151-52, 163-64, 175, 182, 184
Men of Capital (Gore) **65**:36
Men of Character (Jerrold) **2**:395, 397-98, 401-03
Men of Color, to Arms! (Douglass) **7**:132
"Men of England" (Campbell) **19**:176, 183, 191
"Men of Letters" (Smith) **59**:322
Men of Letters (Goncourt and Goncourt)
See *Les hommes de lettres*
"The Men of Old" (Milnes) **61**:136
Men of the Hills (Bird)
See *The Hawks of Hawk-Hollow*
Un ménage de garçon en province (Balzac) **5**:32-33
Menander und Glycerion (Wieland) **17**:400
"El mendigo" (Espronceda) **39**:85, 100, 108, 113-14, 118
"Menego" (Norwid) **17**:370, 381-83
Le Meneur de Loups (Dumas) **71**:204
Mennesket (Wergeland)
See *Skabelsen, mennesket, og messias*
"Menons Klagen um Diotima" (Hölderlin) **16**:187; **187**:228, 230, 233, 236-37
"Meno's Lamentation for Diotima" (Hölderlin)
See "Menons Klagen um Diotima"
Men's Wives (Thackeray) **43**:381
"Der Mensch" (Hölderlin) **16**:181, 185-86
"Der Mensch und das Leben" (Ludwig) **4**:353
"Menschenbeifall" (Hölderlin) **16**:190
Der Menschenfeind (Schiller) **166**:130, 132
Menschenhass und Reue (Kotzebue) **25**:129-31, 133-34, 136-37, 140-41, 144-46, 148-51
"The Mental Condition of Babies" (Lewes) **25**:287

"Mental Disorder" (Silva)
See "Psicopatía"
"The Mental Sufferings of Our Lord in His Passion" (Newman) **38**:303, 309
"The Mental Traveller" (Blake) **13**:172, 244; **37**:71, 96; **190**:20, 30, 33, 36-37, 40, 86, 89-90
The Mental Traveller (Blake) **201**:76
Mentoria; or, The Young Lady's Friend (Rowson) **3**:310, 312-13, 315-16; **69**:103, 105, 112, 114, 128-30, 134-35, 141; **182**:254, 333, 352
"Menzel, Critic of Gogol" (Belinski) **5**:96, 115
Menzel der Franzosenfresser (Börne) **193**:19, 33
Menzel, the Eater of the French (Börne)
See *Menzel der Franzosenfresser*
La mer (Michelet) **31**:215, 242, 245-47, 260, 262-63; **218**:312-13
Mercadet (Balzac)
See *Le faiseur*
Mercedes of Castile; or, The Voyage to Cathay (Cooper) **1**:220; **54**:258, 262, 264
"The Merchant" (Krylov) **1**:435
"Merchant and his Wife" (Froude) **43**:178
"The Merchant of Venice" (Lamb) **125**:304
"Merchant Sailor Nikitin" (Bestuzhev)
See "Morekhod Nikitin"
The Merchant's Crime (Alger) **8**:41, 43-44; **83**:96, 148
"The Merchant's Daughter" (Lamb)
See "Charlotte Wilmot: The Merchant's Daughter"
The Merchant's Wedding (Planché) **42**:273
"Mercury and a Modern Fine Lady" (Montagu) **117**:182
Mercy Philbrick's Choice (Jackson) **90**:144, 164-65, 168
"La Mère aux monstres" (Maupassant) **83**:181, 208, 223
"La Mère qui pleure" (Desbordes-Valmore) **97**:8
"La mère sauvage" (Maupassant) **83**:181, 210-11, 219, 222
Merkland: A Story of Scottish Life (Oliphant) **11**:428-9, 432, 454; **61**:238; **221**:244
"Merkwürdiger Scheintod" (Schlegel) **142**:307
Das merkwürdigste Jahr meines Lebens (Kotzebue) **25**:138
"Merlin" (Emerson) **1**:296; **38**:170, 184; **98**:179-81
Merlin (Immermann) **4**:292; **49**:358
"Merlin and the Gleam" (Tennyson) **30**:254, 282
"Merlin and Vivien" (Tennyson) **202**:208, 221, 291-93
"The Mermaid" (Hogg) **4**:284
"The Mermaid" (Lermontov) **126**:144-45
Mermaid Inn (Lampman)
See *At the Mermaid Inn: Wilfred Campbell, Archibald Lampman, Duncan Campbell Scott in The Globe, 1892-93*
"Mermaid of Margate" (Hood) **16**:224
"The Mermaidens Vesper Hymn" (Darley) **2**:131
"Merope" (Kendall) **12**:183, 192
Merope (Alfieri) **101**:18-19, 42
Merope (Arnold) **6**:33, 37, 44, 49-51; **29**:2, 54; **89**:14, 28, 51, 53; **218**:111, 113, 123, 176, 180, 190-91, 274
"Merriment and Grief" (Baratynsky)
See "Veselie i gore"
"The Merry Bachelor" (Baillie) **151**:91
"Merry England" (Hazlitt) **29**:148, 153
"The Merry Men" (Stevenson) **193**:210, 212, 214, 221, 238, 254
The Merry Men and Other Tales and Fables (Stevenson) **5**:403, 415, 418, 429, 431; **193**:209, 216, 254-55
The Merry Tales of the Three Wise Men of Gotham (Paulding) **2**:528
The Merry-Go-Round (Becque)
See *La navette*
Mertvye dushi (Gogol) **5**:210-11, 213-14, 218-20, 222-24, 226-27, 229-31, 234, 239-40, 243-44, 247-48, 250, 253-57; **15**:80, 88-9, 98-100, 105; **31**:72-148; **162**:5-19, 21-25, 27-30, 32, 35, 39, 44, 47-48, 50-51, 58, 61, 63-65, 68, 70, 72-73, 75-79, 84, 87-89
Mervyn Clitheroe (Ainsworth) **13**:40, 45
"Mes bouquets refermés" (Mallarmé) **210**:245
Mes hôpitaux (Verlaine) **2**:625
"Mes Memoirs" (Dumas) **71**:186, 188, 204-05, 211, 214, 217, 228, 237-38, 240-41
"Mes petites amoureuses" (Rimbaud) **4**:455; **35**:282, 290-91, 294, 321
Mes prisons (Verlaine) **51**:372; **230**:160, 167-68, 171
Mes souvenirs (Banville) **9**:18, 20-21
"Meses do inverno frios" (Castro) **78**:41
"Mesgedra" (Ferguson) **33**:279-80, 285, 304
"Mesmeric Revelation" (Poe) **1**:496; **16**:295, 297, 335; **78**:258; **117**:310; **211**:247, 338, 344
"Mesmerism" (Browning) **19**:131
"The Message" (Blind) **202**:16
"The Message" (Very) **9**:375
"Message of a Friend" (Grillparzer)
See "Freundeswort"
"A Message of Remembrance to My Home Town" (Rizal) **27**:425
"The Message of the March Wind" (Morris) **4**:434, 443
"The Message of Victory" (Webster) **230**:240
"Message to Congress in Special Session, July 4, 1861" (Lincoln) **201**:169, 208-10, 223
"Message to Congress of 1862" (Lincoln)
See "Annual Message to Congress, December 1, 1862"
"Message to Siberia" (Pushkin) **83**:256
The Messalinas of Vienna (Sacher-Masoch) **31**:294
"La messe de l'athée" (Balzac) **153**:149, 152-53
The Messenger of Europe (Pushkin) **3**:414
The Messiah (Klopstock)
See *Der Messias*
Der Messias (Klopstock) **225**:279, 283, 285-86, 288, 291, 295, 301, 305, 307, 309, 323, 326-27, 329-30
Mesyats v derevne (Turgenev) **21**:428-29, 432-33; **122**:257, 261, 275
"Metacom" (Whittier) **8**:485
"The Metallic Pig" (Andersen)
See "Metalsvinet"
"Metalsvinet" (Andersen) **7**:37; **79**:89; **214**:49
"Les métamorphoses du vampire" (Baudelaire) **29**:73, 99; **55**:10, 29-30, 33-4, 70, 73, 76
"The Metamorphoses of the Vampire" (Baudelaire)
See "Les métamorphoses du vampire"
"Metamorphosis of Animals" (Goethe) **4**:172
"Metamorphosis of Plants" (Goethe) **34**:70
Metaphysical Elements of Justice (Kant) **67**:267
Metaphysical Principles of Doctrine of Virtue (Kant)
See *Grundlegung zur Metaphysik der Sitten*
Metaphysical Principles of Right (Kant)
See *Grundlegung zur Metaphysik der Sitten*
Metaphysics of Morals (Kant)
See *Grundlegung zur Metaphysik der Sitten*
"La métaphysique et son avenir" (Renan) **26**:380, 426
"Metel" (Pushkin) **3**:452; **83**:272, 276, 323, 326-27, 329, 337, 354; **3**:435
"Metellus and Marius" (Landor) **14**:189
"Metempsychosis" (Cooke) **110**:3, 10
"The Metempsychosis" (Mangan) **27**:301
"Method" (Coleridge) **231**:123, 126
"The Method of Nature" (Emerson) **38**:158, 169; **98**:65-6, 72, 108, 113-14, 176, 191
"Methuselah" (Field) **3**:206
Metn Vaterland (Klopstock) **225**:297
Metrical Legends of Exalted Characters (Baillie) **2**:37-38; **71**:2; **151**:41-42, 86, 89, 120-22
"Metrical Romances" (Percy)
See "On the Ancient Metrical Romances"
"Métropolitain" (Rimbaud) **35**:322-24; **82**:233; **227**:209-10, 244-45, 247-48, 271, 309
"The Metropolitan Museum of Art" (Martí) **63**:112
"Mettons le doigt sur la plaie" (Laforgue) **221**:83
"Metzengerstein" (Poe) **1**:514; **16**:320-21, 324, 335; **55**:185; **117**:193, 300
Le meunier d'Angibault (Sand) **2**:589, 601; **42**:322-23, 340, 378
"Die Mewe" (Muller) **73**:358-59
"Mexican Sketches" (Horne) **127**:256
The Mexican Thinker (Lizardi)
See *El pensador Mexicano*
"Mezzo Cammin" (Longfellow) **45**:131, 142, 181-82, 186
M'Fingal: A Modern Epic Poem in Four Cantos (Trumbull) **30**:339-44, 346-47, 349, 351-58, 360, 362-65, 373-79, 382-82
"A mi" (Rizal) **27**:425
Mi defensa (Sarmiento) **123**:283, 309, 312, 321-22, 324-25, 351, 373
"Mi ensueño" (Casal) **131**:240
"A mi hija Clementina" (Isaacs) **70**:311
"Mi lárma ez megént?" (Petofi) **21**:278
"A mi madre" (Casal) **131**:255
A mi madre (Castro) **3**:104; **78**:23-25, 37
"Mi museo ideal" (Casal) **131**:219-20, 222-23, 227-29, 235-37, 244, 252, 265-70, 281
"Mi nombre y mis propósitos" (Larra) **130**:248
"A mi padre, en sus días" (Heredia) **209**:160
"A mi padre encanecido" (Heredia) **209**:131
"Mi raza" (Martí) **63**:91
"Mi retiro" (Rizal) **27**:425
"Mi ultimo adios" (Rizal) **27**:425
"The Mice in Council" (Krylov) **1**:435
"Michael" (Coleridge) **177**:149, 161
"Michael" (Wordsworth) **12**:396, 402, 427, 429, 436, 444, 447, 451; **38**:389; **111**:212, 219-20, 226, 228-29, 232-34, 236, 241, 243-45, 254, 294-301, 303, 322, 350, 367; **166**:244, 304-5, 308, 314, 317; **206**:244, 247, 250, 281, 317
Michael Angelo (Longfellow) **2**:486; **45**:113, 127, 130-32, 138-39, 150, 162
Michael Bonham; or, The Fall of Bexar (Simms) **3**:505, 514
Michael Kohlhaas (Kleist) **2**:438, 442, 446-48, 450, 455, 458, 463; **37**:217, 230, 241, 243, 245, 247-49, 253-55; **222**:186, 194, 203, 236-38, 241, 255, 257-59, 287
Michael O'Dowd (Boucicault)
See *Daddy O'Dowd*
"Michael Scott's Wooing" (Rossetti) **4**:510
Michel Angelo: Ein Drama in zwei Akten (Hebbel) **43**:230, 234, 239, 259
"Michel et Christine" (Rimbaud) **4**:475; **82**:232, 255
Michel Pauper (Becque) **3**:13, 15-16
"Michelangelo and His Statues" (Meyer)
See "Michelangelo und seine Statuen"
"Michelangelo und seine Statuen" (Meyer) **81**:204
"Michelangelo's Kiss" (Rossetti) **77**:314
"Michels Brautschau" (Gotthelf) **117**:6, 18, 25
Midas (Shelley) **14**:268, 272
"Middle of Life" (Hölderlin)
See "Hälfte des Lebens"
"Middle-Class Jewish Women of To-Day" (Levy) **59**:111; **203**:319-20
Middlemarch: A Study of Provincial Life (Eliot) **4**:106-07, 109-12, 114, 116-18, 120-23, 125, 127, 129-31, 133-39, 144, 147, 152-54, 154; **13**:282-355; **23**:49-51, 53-4, 57, 60, 64-5, 67-8, 75, 80; **41**:68, 72, 76, 80, 82-3, 85, 91, 93, 96-7, 99, 103-04, 107-09, 126, 133-34; **49**:188, 215, 222, 227, 265; **89**:221, 261; **118**:36, 41, 48, 51-4, 62, 70, 78, 80, 102-10, 121, 125, 130-31, 134, 136, 1

Middlemarch: A Study of Provincial Life (Eliot) **209**:25, 54, 56, 60, 65-66, 72
Middlemarch Notebooks (Eliot) **183**:118
"Middleton Sonnet" (Smith)
See "Sonnet 44"
"Midi" (Leconte de Lisle) **29**:213, 222-24, 236, 242-43
Midlothian (Scott)
See *The Heart of Mid-Lothian*
"Midnight" (Cooke) **110**:3
"Midnight" (Crabbe) **26**:139, 143, 146; **121**:10
"Midnight" (Lampman) **25**:168, 180, 194, 204; **194**:23-24, 61
"Midnight" (Mörike) **10**:445-46
"Midnight Attack" (Whittier) **8**:485
The Midnight Court (Merriman)
See *Cúirt an Mheadhon Oidhche*
"A Mid-Night Drama" (Bellamy) **4**:30
"Midnight Duel" (Arany)
See "Éjféli párbaj"
The Midnight Hour (Inchbald) **62**:142-3, 145-7, 150
"A Midnight Landscape" (Lampman) **25**:217; **194**:44
"The Midnight Mass" (Carleton) **3**:89, 96; **199**:17, 32
"Midnight Mass for the Dying Year" (Longfellow) **2**:471, 474, 479
The Midnight Queen; or, Leaves from New-York Life (Lippard) **198**:140
"A Midnight Storm in the Gulph Stream" (Freneau) **111**:105
"Midsummer" (Bryant) **46**:48
The Midsummer Cushion (Clare) **86**:94-5, 132-33, 160, 166-69
"Midsummer in the South" (Hayne) **94**:149
"Midsummer Night" (Lampman) **194**:52
"A Midsummer Night's Dream" (Lamb) **125**:303, 305, 353, 355-58
"A Midsummer Noon in the Australian Forest" (Harpur) **114**:101, 103-4, 110-11, 125, 144, 156, 158, 164
"Midsummer was it when they died" (Dickinson) **171**:98
"A Midwinter Phantasy" (Lampman) **194**:77-80
"A Mien to Move a Queen" (Dickinson) **21**:61-2, 65; **77**:66
"Mies" (Kivi) **30**:51
"Might versus Right" (Sedgwick) **19**:446
"The Mighty Dead" (Chivers) **49**:71
The Mighty Magician (FitzGerald) **9**:264; **153**:186
"Mighty Maker" (Moodie) **113**:348
Mignons (Goethe) **4**:173
"Mike Fink, the Keel-Boatman" (Thorpe) **183**:358
"Mikhail Tverskoy" (Bestuzhev) **131**:147-48, 182
Mikkel's Parisian Love Stories (Andersen) **79**:11
Mikołaja Doświadczyńskiego przypadki (Krasicki) **8**:398-99, 404
"Milczenie" (Norwid) **17**:371
"Mildew" (Dacre) **151**:148
"Mile End" (Levy)
See "In the Mile End Road"
Miles Standish (Longfellow)
See *The Courtship of Miles Standish*
Miles Wallingford (Cooper)
See *Afloat and Ashore; or, The Adventures of Miles Wallingford*
The Milesian Chief (Maturin) **6**:322, 328, 331-32, 335, 342-43, 346-47
The Milesian Chief: A Romance (Maturin) **169**:18, 20-24, 43, 71-74, 101, 114, 116-20, 122-24, 126, 128-29
The Military Necessity (Vigny)
See *Servitude et grandeur militaires*
"The Militia Drill" (Longstreet) **159**:144
"Militona" (Gautier) **1**:345, 347-48; **59**:12
"The Milkmaid" (Allingham) **25**:8, 16
"The Milk-maid o' the Farm" (Barnes) **75**:58, 77
"The Mill of the Rapids: A Canadian Sketch" (Traill) **31**:324
The Mill on the Floss (Eliot) **4**:95-102, 107, 109-12, 114-17, 119, 121, 123, 126-27, 131-33, 135, 137, 139-40, 145, 148, 150, 152; **13**:282, 291, 293, 305, 322, 335, 444; **23**:51, 57, 59; **41**:58-9, 61, 68, 72, 76, 80-2, 91, 99-103, 106, 108-09, 116, 118, 134, 136, 138-40, 143-45, 147; **49**:184-277; **89**:234, 239, 278, 283; **118**:40, 43, 49, 57, 59, 104, 108, 164; **183**
The Mill on the Floss (Eliot) **209**:15, 18, 22, 25-26, 43
"Mille ans après" (Leconte de Lisle) **29**:228, 235
"Mille e tre" (Verlaine) **230**:176
"La Mille et deuxieme nuit" (Gautier) **59**:31
Mille Francs de récompense (Hugo) **161**:235-36
"The Millennium" (Freneau) **111**:112
The Miller of Angibault (Sand)
See *Le meunier d'Angibault*
"The Miller of Mohill" (Carleton) **199**:41
"The Miller's Daughter" (Tennyson) **30**:207, 279; **65**:248
"The Miller's Maid" (Bloomfield) **145**:128, 130, 152
"Milliners and Dressmakers" (Tonna) **135**:199, 208-9, 212-17, 220-23
Millioenen-Studiën (Multatuli) **165**:331
"Milly Dove" (O'Brien) **21**:235, 239, 243
"Milly; ou, La terre natale" (Lamartine) **11**:248, 270, 289; **190**:225, 233, 235
Miłość czysta u kąpieli morskich (Norwid) **17**:379
"Milton" (Lamartine) **190**:253
"Milton" (Landor) **14**:166
"Milton" (Longfellow) **45**:186
Milton (Blake) **13**:174, 176, 183-84, 186, 192-93, 195, 205-07, 211-13, 221, 231, 234-35, 245, 247-48, 251-54; **37**:20, 66, 88; **57**:56-64, 89-90, 93; **127**:15-16, 20, 22-24, 28-29, 50-51, 65-67, 78, 80, 87-88, 90, 96-97, 124-27, 132, 134; **173**:1-163; **190**:3, 11, 13-16, 23, 26, 33, 35, 41, 74, 93, 95, 98, 101-2, 109, 112, 123, 130, 138, 151; **201**:30, 32, 41-42, 44, 46, 64-65, 73, 96, 113
Milton (Macaulay) **42**:116
"Milton" (Macaulay) **231**:277-78, 290, 305
"Mimi Pinson" (Musset) **7**:264, 275; **150**:309
Mimic Life; or Before and Behind the Curtain (Mowatt) **74**:219, 221, 233-38
"Mimie's Grass Net" (Ingelow) **107**:161
"Miña casiña" (Castro) **78**:2
"Mind and Motive" (Hazlitt) **82**:75, 103
Mind as the Function of the Organism (Lewes) **215**:88
"The Mind the Greatest Mystery" (Very) **9**:396
"Mind under Water" (Jefferies) **47**:136
"Minden House" (Barnes) **75**:78
Mindesang paa Fædres Gravhøi (Grundtvig) **158**:144
Mindowe (Slowacki) **15**:348-49, 353, 369, 373
"The Mind-Reader's Curse" (Clarke) **19**:240
"Mindvégig" (Arany) **34**:21
"Mine!" (Muller)
See "Mein!"
"Mine by the Right of the White Election" (Dickinson) **21**:57; **77**:67-68; **171**:96, 109, 183
"Minek nevezzelek" (Petofi) **21**:285
Mineralogische Betrachtungen über einige Basalte am Rhein: Mit vorangeschickten, zerstreuten Bemerkungen über den Basalt der ältern und neuern Schriftsteller (Humboldt) **170**:130, 140
"Mines and Miners" (Hugo) **10**:377
"The Mines at Falun" (Hoffmann)
See "Die Bergwerke zu Falun"
Les mines de Pologne (Pixérécourt) **39**:277-79, 292
"The Mines of Falun" (Hoffmann)
See "Die Bergwerke zu Falun"
Minin (Ostrovsky)
See *Koz'ma Zakhar'ich Minin Sukoruk*
"The Minister in a Maze" (Hawthorne) **10**:269
"El ministerial" (Larra) **130**:194, 197, 201, 204
"The Minister-Painter" (Smith) **59**:316-7
"The Minister's Black Veil" (Hawthorne) **2**:291-92, 317, 320, 322, 324, 331; **79**:288-90, 294-96, 299, 301-04, 307-11, 313, 315-18, 322, 324, 327, 330, 332-33; **95**:105, 140, 148, 187; **158**:228, 307; **191**:189, 215
"The Minister's Vigil" (Hawthorne) **10**:269, 297
The Minister's Wife (Oliphant) **11**:432, 446, 448-9; **61**:162-4, 166, 173, 205, 209, 211, 238
The Minister's Wooing (Stowe) **3**:553, 555, 558-59, 563, 567
Minnebrieven (Multatuli) **165**:318-19, 323-25, 328, 349
Minnesota; or, The Far West (Oliphant) **47**:288
"Minnie and Mattie" (Rossetti) **186**:235, 237-38
"Minnie Bakes Oaten Cakes" (Rossetti) **186**:238
Minnuzolo; Il Viaggio per l'Italia de Giannettino (Collodi) **54**:140
"The Minor Festivals Devotionally Studied" (Rossetti) **2**:568, 572; **50**:271, 274-5, 285, 294, 321
Minor Morals, interspersed with sketchs of natural history, historical anecdotes, and original stories (Smith) **115**:129
"The Minor Peace of the Church" (Pater) **7**:337
"A Minor Poet" (Levy) **59**:90, 94, 108, 110, 119; **203**:328-30, 332-33, 335, 351
A Minor Poet and Other Verse (Levy) **59**:81, 86, 91, 93, 98, 102, 107-9; **203**:308, 321, 339
"A Minor Prophet" (Eliot) **4**:107; **41**:65
Minor Works (Austen) **51**:59; **95**:77-8; **119**:55; **150**:17; **222**:107-8, 110
"The Minotaur" (Hawthorne) **79**:309
"The Minstrel" (Lampman) **25**:201, 216; **194**:40
The Minstrel (Shevchenko)
See *Kobzar*
"The minstrel boy" (Moore) **110**:198
Minstrel Love (Fouqué) **2**:263
The Minstrel; or, the Progress of Genius (Beattie) **25**:81-2, 103, 105-09, 111-12, 117-20, 122-23, 126
"Minstrel's Song, on the Restoration of Lord Clifford the Shepherd" (Wordsworth) **12**:395
"The Minstrel's Valedictory" (Chivers) **49**:69
The Minstrelsy of the Scottish Border (Scott) **15**:273-74, 318, 320, 322; **69**:377; **209**:195-96, 198, 226
"M'introduire dans ton histoire" (Mallarmé) **41**:243-44, 250, 280; **210**:218
"Minute on Indian Education" (Macaulay) **231**:301-2, 323-24, 329-30
"Minute Philosophies" (Willis) **194**:282, 298
Miorita (Eminescu) **33**:252, 267
Mira (Eminescu) **33**:254, 264; **131**:289, 333
"Le Miracle des roses" (Laforgue) **5**:271, 281; **53**:256-7, 294; **221**:4, 6, 10, 12, 14
"The Miracle of Our Being" (Emerson) **38**:148
"The Miracle of the Roses" (Laforgue)
See "Le Miracle des roses"
"Miracles" (Emerson) **38**:148
"Miradoniz" (Eminescu) **33**:261, 263; **131**:290
"Mirage" (Rossetti) **186**:348
Miralda; or, The Beautiful Quadroon (Brown)
See *Clotel; or, The President's Daughter: A Narrative of Slave Life in the United States*
"Mirandola" (Hebbel) **43**:237
Mirgorod (Gogol) **5**:209, 216, 218, 231, 235, 242, 248-49, 256-57; **15**:94-5; **31**:106, 118; **162**:27, 52, 54, 62, 95, 99, 121-22
Miriam, and Other Poems (Whittier) **8**:501
"Le miroir" (Baudelaire) **155**:79-80

"Miron and the Beautiful Girl without a Body" (Eminescu)
See "Miron şi frumoasa fara corp"
"Miron şi frumoasa fara corp" (Eminescu) **131**:299
Mirra (Alfieri)
See *Myrrha*
"The Mirror" (Rossetti) **77**:358, 360
"The Mirror" (Whittier) **59**:361
"The Mirror of Diana" (Blind) **202**:6, 55-56
The Mirror of Peasants (Gotthelf)
See *Der Bauern-Spiegel oder Lebensgeschichte des Jeremias Gotthelf: Von ihm selbst beschrieben*
"Mirrors of Life and Death" (Rossetti) **186**:303
Mirza, ou lettre d'un voyageur (Staël-Holstein) **91**:339-42, 358, 360
"A Mirza's Vision" (Derzhavin)
See "Videnie Murzy"
"Mis treinta años" (Manzano)
See "Treinta años"
"The Misadventures of John Nicholson" (Stevenson) **193**:274, 281
Le Misanthrope par amour (Sade) **47**:361-63
"Misanthropic Musings" (Willis) **194**:305
"Misanthropy" (Heredia)
See "Misantropía"
Misanthropy and Repentance (Kotzebue)
See *Menschenhass und Reue*
"Misantropía" (Heredia) **209**:135
Misc C (Coleridge) **99**:63
Misc. Essays (Lamb) **113**:230
Miscellaneous and Uncollected Writings of Charlotte and Patrick Branwell Brontë (Brontë) **109**:26, 51
Miscellaneous and Unpublished (Brontë)
See *Miscellaneous and Uncollected Writings of Charlotte and Patrick Branwell Brontë*
Miscellaneous Criticism (Coleridge) **197**:281
"Miscellaneous Papers" (Willis) **194**:282
Miscellaneous Pieces in Prose (Barbauld) **50**:3
Miscellaneous Pieces Relating to the Chinese (Percy) **95**:313, 315, 336
Miscellaneous Plays (Baillie) **2**:34-35; **71**:6, 64; **151**:36, 52, 72, 115
Miscellaneous Poems (Lampman) **194**:78-79
Miscellaneous Poems (Mitford) **4**:400
Miscellaneous Poems (Paine) **62**:322, 325
Miscellaneous Poems (Rowson) **69**:129; **182**:254-57, 260-61
Miscellaneous Poems (Silva)
See *Poesías varias*
Miscellaneous Prose Works (Scott) **110**:277
Miscellaneous Studies (Pater) **7**:303; **90**:248, 250, 261, 276, 287, 289-90, 333, 335-37
The Miscellaneous Works of Mr. Philip Freneau, Containing His Essays and Additional Poems (Freneau) **111**:130-32, 134, 139, 149, 159, 161
Miscellanies (Martineau) **137**:316, 335
Miscellanies (De Quincey) **198**:31
Miscellanies (Thackeray) **43**:367, 373, 378, 381, 387
Miscellanies; or, Literary Recreations (D'Israeli) **217**:276, 283-84, 292, 295, 308, 320-22, 325, 335-39
Miscellanies: Prose and Verse (Maginn) **8**:436-37, 442
Miscellany (Schumann)
See *Allerley*
The Mischief-Making Crown (Raimund)
See *Die unheilbringende Zauberkrone*
"Mischka" (Lenau) **16**:265
Mischmasch (Dodgson) **139**:32-33, 57
"Misconceptions" (Browning) **19**:127
"The Miser" (Krylov) **1**:435, 439
The Miser (Carleton)
See *Fardorougha the Miser; or, The Convicts of Lisnamona*
The Miser or The Convicts of Lisnamona (Carleton)
See *Fardorougha the Miser; or, The Convicts of Lisnamona*
Les misérables (Hugo) **3**:243-50, 252-53, 255, 259, 263-65, 267, 270, 272, 274; **10**:354-83; **21**:195; **161**:167, 170, 172, 180-83, 189-90, 193-94, 202, 206, 208-9, 211, 219, 228, 235-36, 243-46, 248, 251-53, 255, 264, 266; **189**:153-312
Misere (Bécquer) **106**:162-63
Misère de la philosophie: Réponse à la philosophie de la misère de M. Proudhon (Marx) **17**:332-34, 336, 339, 357; **114**:3, 43, 69, 86
"Miserere" (Bécquer)
See *Cartas literarias desde mi celda*
"El miserere" (Bécquer)
See *Cartas literarias desde mi celda*
"Miserere" (Heine) **4**:257
Les Misères (Hugo)
See *Les misérables*
"Miserie" (Rossetti) **186**:302
"The Miseries of the First English Commentator" (D'Israeli) **217**:323
"'Miserikordia': Lecture for Stylists" (Jean Paul) **7**:234
The Miser's Daughter (Ainsworth) **13**:28, 35, 40
"Misery" (Brontë) **109**:36
"Misery I" (Brontë)
See "Misery, Part I"
"Misery II" (Brontë)
See "Misery, Part II"
"Misery Landing" (Woolson) **82**:272, 285, 333
"Misery, Part I" (Brontë) **109**:30, 33
"Misery, Part II" (Brontë) **109**:30, 33
"A Misfortunate Girl" (Turgenev)
See "Neschastnaya"
"The Misfortunes of Barney Branagan" (Carleton) **199**:5, 9
"The Misfortunes of Frederick Pickering" (Trollope)
See "The Adventures of Frederick Pickering"
Misogallo (Alfieri) **101**:79
"Miss Austen and Miss Mitford" (Oliphant) **61**:234
"Miss B ****" (Barbauld) **185**:29
"Miss B—" (Clare) **86**:89
Miss Beecher's Housekeeper and Healthkeeper (Beecher) **30**:15, 22
"Miss Beulah's Bonnet" (Cooke) **110**:33, 40, 47, 51
"Miss Brooke" (Eliot) **4**:133; **13**:282; **183**:97
"Miss C's Secretary" (Levy) **203**:354
Miss Eden's Letters (Eden) **10**:104
"The Miss Greens" (Moodie) **14**:237
"Miss Grief" (Woolson) **82**:275, 295-96, 308, 310, 324
"Miss Harriet" (Maupassant) **83**:228
Miss Kelly's New Entertainment Entitled Dramatic Recollections (Reynolds) **146**:193
Miss Kilmansegg and Her Precious Leg: The Golden Legend (Hood) **16**:207, 217, 219-20, 222, 225-27, 229, 231, 233-36, 238
"Miss Lucinda" (Cooke) **110**:20, 35, 43, 47, 51, 57
Miss Ludington's Sister: A Romance of Immortality (Bellamy) **4**:23, 26-27, 31, 34; **86**:6, 9, 11, 17
Miss Mackenzie (Trollope) **6**:457, 470-71, 499, 515-16; **101**:237-38, 241, 274, 307, 309, 313; **215**:282
Miss Marjoribanks (Oliphant) **11**:442, 446, 449, 452, 454, 456-61, 463; **61**:174-5, 180-1, 188, 196, 198, 201, 212, 221-2, 226-9, 239; **221**:231, 267, 277-78, 295-300, 323-33
Miss Meredith (Levy) **59**:86-7, 98, 112, 115-6; **203**:353-54
Miss Oona McQuarrie (Smith) **59**:314, 319
"Miss Ophelia Gledd" (Trollope) **101**:234
"Miss R—" (Barbauld) **185**:29, 35
"Miss Scalpel" (Baudelaire) **155**:106
Missa Solemnis in D, op. 123 (Beethoven) **227**:6, 35
Die Missbrauchten Liebesbriefe (Keller) **2**:415, 423
"Mission Endeavor" (Woolson) **82**:333-34
"The Mission of America" (Brownson) **50**:50
"The Mission of Moses" (Schiller) **166**:113
"The Mission of St. Philip" (Newman) **38**:310
"The Mission of the War" (Douglass) **7**:126
The Missionary of the Andes (Bowles) **103**:54-5, 71
"Les missionnaires" (Beranger) **34**:29
"Missions to the Oneidas" (Cooper) **129**:72
"Mist" (Lenau) **16**:277
"The Mistletoe, a Christmas Tale" (Robinson) **142**:138, 252
"Mistress Agnes" (Arany)
See "Agnes asszony"
Mistress and Maid (Craik) **38**:109, 113
"Mistress and Maid on Dress and Undress" (Linton) **41**:164
"Mistress Gurton's Cat" (Robinson) **142**:170
"Mistress into Maid" (Pushkin)
See "Baryshnia-krest'ianka"
Mistress Lee (Arnim) **5**:13, 18, 21
"The Mistress to the Spirit of Her Lover" (Dacre) **151**:179, 182
"Mistris Lee" (Arnim) **159**:62-63, 84-85, 92
Mistriss Henley (Charriere)
See *Lettres de Mistriss Henley publiées par son amie*
"Mists and Fogs" (Hunt) **1**:417
"Mists and Rain" (Baudelaire)
See "Brumes et pluies"
"Mit dem grünen Lautenbande" (Muller) **73**:368, 372
Mit Livs Eventyr (Andersen) **79**:4, 18-19, 21-22, 26, 48, 59, 64; **214**:7-8
"Mit zwei Worten" (Meyer) **81**:199
"Mithridates" (Emerson) **1**:299
Die Mitschuldigen (Goethe) **4**:211
"Um Mitternacht" (Mörike) **201**:253, 271, 289, 300-301, 304
Mittheilungen aus den Memoiren des Satan (Hauff) **185**:318
"Mixed Days of May and December" (Jefferies) **47**:138
Mixed Essays (Arnold) **6**:58; **89**:101, 103, 113
"The Mixed School Question" (Webb) **143**:357
"Miyagi ga tsuka" (Ueda Akinari) **131**:21-22, 58
"Mizpah" (Bryant) **46**:3
Mjältsjukan (Tegner) **2**:614
"M'Kinnon" (Hogg) **4**:275
"M.L." (Alcott) **83**:7
"Mlle. Luther and the Art of Acting" (Lewes) **25**:291
"Mnemosyne" (Hölderlin) **16**:192; **187**:215-16, 218
"Mneniye russkogo grazhdanina" (Karamzin) **173**:286
"Mnich" (Slowacki) **15**:348-49
Mnich (Macha) **46**:200, 202-03, 206
Moby-Dick; or, The Whale (Melville) **3**:329, 332-55, 357, 359-64, 366-71, 373-8, 380-5; **12**:249-322; **29**:315-17, 324-27, 329, 331-32, 334, 337-38, 340, 343, 349, 354-57, 362, 364-65, 367, 369, 371-72, 378-79; **45**:197, 204, 206, 210, 212-13, 228-9, 231, 235, 243-7, 251-2, 254; **49**:376-8, 391, 402, 407, 409-10, 414, 416, 421; **91**:3-6, 9-10, 18, 21, 24, 28-34, 41-7, 50-1, 53-6, 68, 74, 81, 88-90, 93, 111, 113, 115, 121, 134, 180-81, 193, 198, 204, 206, 212-13, 217-20; **93**:187-88, 203, 222; **123**:186-87, 190, 192, 196, 200, 204, 211-12, 230, 232, 241, 251-52, 256; **157**:65, 69, 72, 75, 79, 84-85, 89, 100 , 106, 108, 110-12, 145-46, 149-53, 159, 161, 209; **181**:140-358; **193**:64-65, 67,

70, 76, 126-27, 130, 136, 143, 147, 195; **221**:103, 105, 108, 111, 116-21, 125-26, 128-29, 132, 150, 155-56, 160, 163, 165-66, 168, 181, 184, 195-99, 208, 218
The Moccasin Girl (Bird) **197**:29
"The Mocker" (Leskov)
See "Jazvitel' nyj"
"The Mocking Bird" (Lanier) **6**:236, 238-39, 248
"The Mocking-Bird" (Hayne) **94**:149, 166
"La Mode" (Mallarmé) **210**:223
"The Model Husband" (Parton) **86**:376
"A Model Husband" (Parton) **86**:351
"The Model Man" (Shaw) **15**:335
"The Model Minister" (Parton) **86**:376
"The Model Step-Mother" (Parton) **86**:349
"The Model Wife" (Parton) **86**:376
"Modern" (Wagner) **119**:291
The Modern Abraham (Polidori) **51**:233
"Modern Antiques" (Mitford) **4**:401
The Modern Aria (Klinger)
See *Die neue Arria*
"The Modern Chevalier" (Brackenridge) **7**:54; **227**:73-74, 107, 115, 118
Modern Chivalry: Containing the Adventures of Captain John Farrago and Teague O'Regan, His Servant (Brackenridge) **7**:42-61, 63-65; **227**:43, 47-49, 52, 60-69, 71-81, 83-86, 91-92, 94, 98-99, 106-11, 113, 115, 117-18, 120-21, 125, 127-30, 133-37, 139-43, 147-48, 154-57, 165, 167-74
"A Modern Cinderella" (Alcott) **83**:8-9
"A Modern Classic" (Patmore) **9**:345
"The Modern Element in Literature" (Arnold)
See "On the Modern Element in Literature"
"Modern Gallantry" (Lamb) **10**:404, 408, 420-21, 436
Modern Greece (Hemans) **29**:202; **71**:261, 274
The Modern Griselda (Edgeworth) **1**:262, 272; **51**:90
The Modern Job (Sacher-Masoch)
See *Der neue Hiob*
"Modern Literature—Bayle's Critical Dictionary" (D'Israeli) **217**:338
A Modern Man's Confession (Musset)
See *La confession d'un enfant du siècle*
A Modern Mephistopheles (Alcott) **6**:20-21
"A Modern Mephistopheles or The Fatal Love Chase" (Alcott) **58**:46, 66, 69; **83**:35
"Modern Metaphysics and Moral Philosophy in France" (Lewes) **25**:314
"The Modern Migration of Nations" (Boyesen) **135**:31
"Modern Mothers" (Linton) **41**:164
Modern Novel Writing; or, The Elegant Enthusiast, and Interesting Emotions of Arabella Bloomville (Beckford) **16**:29, 36-7, 41; **214**:146, 163-66
The Modern Oedipus (Polidori)
See *Ernestus Berchtold; or, The Modern Oedipus*
"Modern Painters" (Lewes) **215**:135
Modern Painters (Scott) **209**:187
"The Modern Philosophy of France" (Lewes) **25**:288
"The Modern Politician" (Lampman) **25**:194, 209; **194**:10, 54
"Modern Romance" (D'Israeli)
See "The Daughter, or, A Modern Romance"
"A Modern Sappho" (Arnold) **6**:44; **218**:122
"The Modern School of Poetry in England" (Lampman) **25**:203, 211-13, 215; **194**:32, 57, 63, 127
"The Modern Thames" (Jefferies) **47**:143
The Modern Vikings: Stories of Life and Sport in the Norseland (Boyesen) **135**:8, 13
"Modern Women" (Linton) **41**:160
Modern Women and What is Said of Them (Linton) **41**:163, 170
"A Modern Workshop" (Silva)
See "Taller moderno"
The Modest Soldier; or, Love in New York (Dunlap) **2**:211, 213
Modeste Mignon (Balzac)
See *Les trois amoureux*
"Modjesky as Cameel" (Field) **3**:206
"Modos de vivir que no dan de vivir" (Larra) **17**:282
Moeurs de Province (Flaubert)
See *Madame Bovary; moeurs de province*
Mogens (Jacobsen) **34**:152, 155-56, 159-60, 163, 165-68
Mogg Megone (Whittier) **8**:489, 492, 501, 510, 517; **59**:353, 355
"Mogiły haremu" (Mickiewicz) **3**:403-04; **101**:188-89
The Mogul Tale (Inchbald) **62**:142, 145-6, 148
Les Mohicans de Paris (Dumas) **71**:192-94
Mohun; or, The Last Days of Lee and His Paladins: Final Memoirs of a Staff-Officer in Virginia (Cooke) **5**:128, 130, 132-35
"Moi Istukan" (Derzhavin) **215**:7, 39, 66-67, 72-73
"Moia napast.! Moe bogatstvo, moe sviatoe remeslo" (Pavlova) **138**:11
Le Moine ou l'Abbé du Mont Saint-Bernard (Duras) **154**:112-13
"Moiron" (Maupassant) **1**:449; **83**:176
Moisasur's Magic Curse (Raimund)
See *Moisasur's Zauberfluch*
Moisasur's Zauberfluch (Raimund) **69**:8, 15, 18-19, 24, 27, 45, 47-8, 52
"Moïse" (Vigny) **7**:469, 479, 481, 484; **102**:335, 340, 372
Moïse (Chateaubriand) **134**:15, 97
"Moja ispoved" (Karamzin) **3**:290; **173**:268, 280, 285, 312, 322-26
"Moja piosnka" (Norwid) **17**:365, 367
Molière (Oliphant) **11**:439; **221**:233
Moll Pitcher and The Minstrel Girl (Whittier) **59**:353
"Molly Astore" (Ferguson) **33**:301
"Molnets broder" (Runeberg) **41**:311-13, 315, 318, 321
"Moloch" (Crawford) **127**:213-14
Moloch (Hebbel) **43**:234, 240, 258, 262
Molodye suprugi (Griboedov) **129**:162-63, 172
"Mon ami, ma plus belle amitié . . ." (Verlaine) **230**:169
"Mon Ange!" (Verlaine) **230**:166
"Mon Apologie" (Verlaine) **230**:170
"Mon coeur mis à nu" (Baudelaire) **6**:100, 112; **29**:70-1, 97; **55**:68; **155**:39
"Mon Dieu m'a dit" (Verlaine) **51**:351-2
"Mon files, après l'avoir conduit au collège" (Desbordes-Valmore) **97**:29
"À mon fils, avant le collège" (Desbordes-Valmore) **97**:9, 29
"Mon rêve familier" (Verlaine) **51**:351-52, 355-56; **230**:165
Mon voisin Raymond (Kock) **16**:245
"Monadnoc" (Emerson) **1**:299; **38**:169
"Monadnock from Wachuset" (Whittier) **8**:531
Monakh (Pavlova) **138**:4
Monaldi (Allston) **2**:20-22, 24-28
The Monarchy according to the Charter (Chateaubriand)
See *De la monarchie selon la charte*
Le monastère abandonné; ou, La malédiction paternelle (Pixérécourt) **39**:278, 289-90
The Monastery (Scott) **15**:263, 289; **69**:313; **110**:233; **209**:182, 184, 229-37
The Monastery of Sendomir (Grillparzer)
See *Das Kloster bei Sendomir*
"Monastery Scene" (Grillparzer)
See "Klosterszene"
Die Monate (Muller) **73**:366
"Der Mönch und die Nonne auf dem Mittelstein" (Wieland) **177**:263-65
"Der Mönch von Bonifazio" (Meyer) **81**:143
"Monday in Holy Week" (Droste-Hülshoff) **3**:202
Monday Tales (Daudet)
See *Les contes du lundi*
"Mondesaufgang" (Droste-Hülshoff) **3**:200
"Mondesnacht" (Droste-Hülshoff) **3**:193
"Mondnacht" (Eichendorff) **8**:230; **225**:56-57
Der Mondsüchtige (Tieck) **5**:519
"Moneta" (Keats) **225**:169
"Money!" (Verlaine) **230**:169
Money and Spirit (Gotthelf)
See *Geld und Geist oder die Versöhnung*
"The Money Diggers" (Irving) **2**:390; **95**:227
"The Money Diggers and Old Nick" (Smith) **187**:319-20
The Money Question (Dumas)
See *La question d'argent*
The Money-Lender (Gore) **65**:37-8
"Moneyless" (Turgenev)
See *Bezdenezh'e*
De Monfort (Baillie) **2**:31, 34, 38-40, 43; **71**:4, 6-7, 9-12, 16-17, 19, 26-27, 31-32, 35-36, 38, 44-45, 48, 51, 53, 66; **151**:6-18, 20, 22-24, 26-27, 37, 52, 55, 67, 73-77, 114-15, 118-19, 128-29, 133-34
Monikins (Cooper) **54**:256; **203**:11, 47
"The Monitions of the Unseen" (Ingelow) **39**:267
"The Monitors" (Hogg) **109**:202
"The Monk" (Lampman) **25**:168, 176, 192, 199, 206, 220
"The Monk" (Shevchenko)
See "Chernets"
"The Monk" (Slowacki)
See "Mnich"
The Monk (Duras) **154**:158
The Monk (Macha)
See *Mnich*
The Monk, a Romance (Lewis) **11**:292-303, 306-15, 317-25
"Monk and the Face" (Eminescu) **33**:264
The Monk Knight of St. John: A Tale of the Crusades (Richardson) **55**:304, 313, 319, 322-7, 350-3, 366
"Monk Tellenbach's Exile" (Boyesen) **135**:13, 29
"The Monks of Casal-Maggiore" (Longfellow) **45**:138, 149, 162, 180, 188, 191
The Monks of Monk-Hall (Lippard)
See *The Quaker City; or, The Monks of Monk-Hall. A Romance of Philadelphia Life, Mystery, and Crime*
The Monk's Wedding (Meyer) **81**:136
"Monna Innominata" (Rossetti) **2**:561, 563, 565, 571, 575, 577; **50**:272, 282, 284, 288, 290, 299, 321-4; **186**:295, 303
"The Monochord" (Rossetti) **4**:491; **77**:314
"Monodies II" (Harpur) **114**:144
Monody at Matlock (Bowles)
See *Monody Written at Matlock*
"Monody on Prince Mestchasky" (Derzhavin) **215**:8
"Monody on the Death of a Friend" (Dyer) **129**:137
"Monody on the Death of Chatterton" (Coleridge) **99**:58; **231**:62
Monody on the Death of Chatterton (Coleridge) **197**:184
"Monody on the Death of Dr. Warton" (Bowles) **103**:53, 78-9, 83
"Monody on the Death of Robert Robinson A celebrated Dissenting Preacher, formerly of Cambridge" (Dyer) **129**:149
"Monody to the Memory of Chatterton" (Robinson) **142**:112
"Monody to the Memory of Marie Antoinette, Queen of France" (Robinson) **142**:189, 199
Monody Written at Matlock (Bowles) **103**:55, 60, 72, 87
Monographs: Personal and Social (Milnes) **61**:136, 138
"Monolog" (Novalis) **178**:55, 102, 114-21

Monologen: Eine Neujahrsgabe (Schleiermacher) **107**:266-68, 335-36, 376, 378, 384, 397-98, 407
Monologues (Schleiermacher)
See *Monologen: Eine Neujahrsgabe*
"Monos and Daimonos" (Bulwer-Lytton) **45**:19
"À Monsieur A.L." (Desbordes-Valmore)
See "À Monsieur Alphonse de Lamartine"
Monsieur Alphonse (Dumas) **9**:224-25, 228, 230, 232, 242, 247, 250
"À Monsieur Alphonse de Lamartine" (Desbordes-Valmore) **97**:3, 17, 26
M. Antoine (Sand)
See *Le péché de M. Antoine*
"M. Augustin Thierry" (Renan) **26**:417
M. Cazotte (Nodier) **19**:384
Monsieur de Camors (Feuillet) **45**:75, 77-80, 85-6, 90
"M. de Lamennais" (Renan) **26**:417
"Monsieur de l'Argentière, l'accusateur" (Borel) **41**:4, 6, 12
"Monsieur de Miroir" (Hawthorne) **2**:298; **95**:105
Monsieur Jean (Sainte-Beuve) **5**:341
Monsieur Lecoq (Gaboriau) **14**:17-20, 23-9, 31-2
M. P.; or, The Blue-Stocking (Moore) **6**:378, 392, 395
"Monsieur Parent" (Maupassant) **83**:201
"Monsieur Phoebus" (Crawford) **127**:193, 216
Monsieur Sylvestre (Sand) **57**:313
"Monsort est orphelin . . ." (Laforgue)
See "Dimanches"
"The Monster with Three Names" (Lippard) **198**:165
"The Monstre Balloon" (Barham) **77**:19, 26
"Monstrous World" (Petofi)
See "Gyalázatos világ"
"Mont Blanc" (Shelley) **18**:327, 338, 361, 363-64, 378; **93**:256-60, 264, 333; **175**:216, 239, 301-4, 306, 308-10, 312, 316
"Le mont des Oliviers" (Vigny) **7**:469, 472-74, 479, 481-82, 484; **102**:372-73
La Montagne"and Mr. Coullery" (Bakunin) **58**:131
"Montaigne; or, the Skeptic" (Emerson) **38**:169, 171, 227; **98**:22, 25-6, 33, 68, 76
Montalbert (Smith) **23**:323, 330, 336; **115**:145
Montalembert (Oliphant)
See *Memoir of Count de Montalembert: A Chapter of Recent French History*
"La montaña maldita" (Gómez de Avellaneda) **111**:28, 65
"La montañero" (Isaacs) **70**:305
Montcalm and Wolfe (Parkman) **12**:335-36, 341, 343, 345, 348, 359-60, 370-71, 375, 377-79
"El monte de las ánimas" (Bécquer) **106**:99, 108, 112, 120
"Les monténégrins" (Nerval) **67**:340
"A Month at the Achensee" (Blind) **202**:13, 31-32
A Month in the Country (Turgenev)
See *Mesyats v derevne*
"The Months: A Pageant" (Rossetti) **186**:238, 317
"The Months of Apprenticeship" (Hoffmann) **2**:356
"Months of Youth" (Hoffmann) **2**:356
Montjoie (Feuillet) **45**:75, 79, 89
Montmorency (Staël-Holstein) **91**:358
Montorio (Maturin)
See *Fatal Revenge; or, The Family of Montorio*
Mont-Oriol (Maupassant) **1**:450, 467-69; **42**:167, 169, 174, 189; **83**:173-75, 186, 200
"Montreurs" (Leconte de Lisle) **29**:214
"The Monument" (Derzhavin)
See "Pamiatnik"
"Monument" (Pushkin)
See "Pamjatnik"
"The Monument and the Bridge" (Lowell) **2**:516
"Monument für Beethoven" (Schumann) **143**:75
"A Monument I Reared" (Pushkin) **3**:451
"Monument miloserdiiu" (Derzhavin) **215**:72
"Monument Moors des Räubers" (Schiller) **39**:386
"Monument Mountain" (Bryant) **6**:183, 186-87; **46**:6, 19, 28
"The Monument of Phaon" (Freneau) **111**:148, 150
"Monument Petra Velikogo" (Derzhavin) **215**:71
"Monument to a Dactylotrochaic Knight" (Radishchev) **190**:321-22
"The Monument to I. Heliade Radulescu" (Eminescu) **131**:311
"The Monument to Peter the Great" (Derzhavin)
See "Monument Petra Velikogo"
"The Monument to Peter the Great" (Mickiewicz) **3**:401
"Moods" (Longfellow) **45**:139
Moods (Alcott) **6**:12-14; **58**:24-5, 28-33, 37, 47-9, 69, 75; **83**:9, 52
"Moods and Thoughts" (Levy) **59**:119
"Moods of My Own Mind" (Wordsworth) **12**:393
"The Moon and the Comet, a Fable" (Opie) **65**:160
"The Moon is distant from the Sea" (Dickinson) **77**:93
"The Moon Is Sterile" (Laforgue)
See "La Lune est stérile"
"The Moon of Mobile" (Chivers) **49**:49
"The Moon of Ramadân" (Blind) **202**:56
"The Moon Path" (Lampman) **25**:204; **194**:82
"Moon Solo" (Laforgue)
See "Derniers vers VII"
"The Moon upon her fluent Route" (Dickinson) **77**:121
"The Moon was a-Waning" (Hogg) **109**:268
"Mooni" (Kendall) **12**:182-83, 187, 190, 197, 199
"Moonlight" (Eichendorff)
See "Mondnacht"
"Moonlight" (Laforgue)
See "Clair de Lune"
"Moonlight" (Silva)
See "Luz de la luna"
"Moonlight" (Thoreau) **207**:264
"Moonlight" (Verlaine)
See "Clair de lune"
A Moonlight Adventure (Mitford) **4**:406
A Moonlight Night (Sacher-Masoch) **31**:287, 291, 302
"Moonlight" Sonata (Beethoven)
See *Sonata, op. 27*
"The Moon's Climate, Fauna and Flora" (Laforgue)
See "Climat, faune et flore de la Lune"
"Moonshiners" (Cooke) **5**:133
The Moonstone: A Romance (Collins) **1**:175, 177, 180-84, 187-91; **18**:60-93; **93**:7, 12, 19, 42, 44, 46-7, 50, 53, 61-2, 66-74, 76-83
The Moor of Peter the Great (Pushkin)
See *Arap Petra Velikogo*
The Moorish Girl (Andersen) **79**:12-13
"Moorish Melodies" (Maginn) **8**:441
The Moorland Cottage (Gaskell) **5**:183, 198, 202, 205; **70**:185, 188, 190
"The Moors" (Wilson) **5**:560-61
"Moors and Christians" (Alarcon)
See "Moros y cristianos"
"The Moor's Legacy" (Irving) **2**:372
"A Moosehead Journal" (Lowell) **2**:520; **90**:202-06
Mopsa the Fairy (Ingelow) **39**:259, 264, 266-68; **107**:118, 129, 134-37, 143, 151, 164-77
"The Morai" (Williams) **135**:315
"The Moral Argument against Calvinism" (Channing) **17**:9, 52-3
"The Moral Bully" (Holmes) **14**:126
Moral Culture of Infancy, and Kindergarten Guide, with Music for the Plays (Peabody) **169**:150, 202
"La moral del juguete" (Casal) **131**:263
"The Moral Effect of Works of Satire" (Clough) **27**:104
"The Moral Effect of Works of Satire" (Prescott) **163**:33
Moral Epistle, Respectfully Submitted to Earl Stanhope (Landor) **14**:175
"Moral Independence" (Martineau) **137**:316
The Moral of Many Fables (Martineau) **137**:250, 265, 270
Moral Pieces (Sigourney)
See *Moral Pieces, in Prose and Verse*
Moral Pieces, in Prose and Verse (Sigourney) **21**:289; **87**:320-21, 325, 337
"A Moral Poem" (Lermontov) **126**:133
"Moral Poetry of England in Education" (Peabody) **169**:187
"Moral Reflection on the Cross of Saint Paul's" (Hood) **16**:235
"The Moral Satires" (Cowper) **8**:113
Moral Sketches of Prevailing Opinions and Manners, Foreign and Domestic: With Reflections on Prayer (More) **27**:334
Moral Tales (Edgeworth) **158**:7, 10
Moral Tales (Laforgue)
See *Moralités légendaires*
Moral Tales for Young People (Edgeworth) **1**:255-56, 267; **51**:81-7, 89, 102, 119
The Moral Teaching of Jesus Christ (Shelley) **93**:352
"A Moral Thought" (Freneau) **111**:144-45, 150, 154
"The Moral View of Plato as Unfolded in the Gorgias" (Child) **173**:207
"Morale du joujou" (Baudelaire) **155**:39, 41
Moralism and Christianity; or, Man's Experience and Destiny (James) **53**:216, 236
"Moralitas" (Hogg) **109**:203
Moralités légendaires (Laforgue) **5**:268-69, 271, 274, 276, 278, 280-82; **53**:256-57, 272, 287, 290-91, 293-5, 298-99; **221**:3, 7, 11-16, 52-54, 56-57, 64, 66-68, 93
"Morality" (Arnold) **6**:56; **218**:121
"The Morality of Wilhelm Meister" (Eliot) **89**:227; **183**:94
"Morals" (Emerson) **1**:282
Morayma (Martínez de la Rosa) **102**:245-46
"Morbid Appetite for Money" (Whitman) **81**:238
"De Morbo Oneirodynia" (Polidori) **51**:223
"Morcia Funebre" (Chivers) **49**:75
Le more de Venise (Vigny) **7**:476
More Letters of Charles Darwin (Darwin) **57**:147, 151
More Letters of Edward FitzGerald (FitzGerald) **9**:269
"More Life" (Larcom) **179**:178
"The More Mature Months" (Hoffmann) **2**:356
More New Arabian Nights: The Dynamiter (Stevenson) **5**:391, 393-94, 397, 399, 402-04, 407-08, 415, 430-31, 433; **193**:222, 254
More Nonsense, Pictures, Rhymes, Botany, Etc. (Lear) **3**:295, 297
More Sinned Against Than Sinning (Ostrovsky)
See *Bez viný vinovátye*
More Than Pearls and Gold (Andersen) **79**:14
"The Morehens Nest" (Clare) **86**:141
"Morekhod Nikitin" (Bestuzhev) **131**:154-55, 159
"Morella" (Eminescu) **131**:334
"Morella" (Poe) **1**:492, 514; **16**:304, 316, 331, 335-36; **55**:151, 197, 201; **97**:180, 208-09; **117**:299-301, 303; **211**:319-21
"The Mores" (Clare) **9**:114; **86**:140-41, 145
Morgane (Villiers de l'Isle Adam) **3**:581, 583-84
"Morgengesang am Schöpfungsfeste" (Klopstock) **11**:238

Morgengespräch zwischen A. und dem Kandidaten Bertram (Claudius) **75**:197, 210-11, 217
"Morgengruß" (Muller) **73**:364
"Morgenlied" (Meyer) **81**:141, 151, 155
"Morgenlied" (Muller) **73**:366
"Moria el sol, y las marchitas hojas" (Castro) **78**:41
Mörikes Werke (Mörike)
See *Werke*
Morituri salutamus (Longfellow) **2**:486; **45**:130-31, 146
Morley Court (Le Fanu)
See *The Cock and Anchor, Being a Chronicle of Old Dublin City*
"The Mormon's Wife" (Cooke) **110**:4, 9, 33, 36
"A Morn of May" (Ingelow) **39**:264
"Morning" (Browning) **79**:94, 101, 153
"Morning" (Cranch) **115**:5
"Morning" (Harpur) **114**:115
"Morning" (Keble) **87**:169, 174, 200
"Morning" (Lazarus) **8**:420
"Morning" (Rimbaud)
See "Matin"
"Morning" (Very) **9**:383
"A Morning After Storm" (Hayne) **94**:166
"The Morning Air Plays on my Face" (Baillie) **151**:86, 91
"Morning and Evening" (Arany)
See "Reg és Est"
"The Morning Angelus" (Verlaine)
See "L'Angelus du matin"
"Morning Bells" (Bowles) **103**:55
"Morning Hymn" (Keble) **87**:153
"Morning Hymn" (Moodie) **113**:317
"Morning in the Bush" (Kendall) **12**:185
"A Morning in the Library" (Willis) **194**:298
"Morning in the Mountains" (Tyutchev) **34**:389
"Morning Midday and Evening Sacrifice" (Hopkins) **189**:126, 135
"The Morning Moon" (Barnes) **75**:72
The Morning of a Man of Business (Gogol) **15**:94
"Morning of Intoxication" (Rimbaud)
See "Matinée d'ivresse"
"Morning on the Lievre" (Lampman) **25**:172, 190; **194**:38, 75, 88
"Morning on the Wissahiccon" (Poe) **211**:226
"Morning Prayer" (Verlaine)
See "Prière du matin"
"The Morning Star" (Eminescu)
See "Luceafarul"
"The Morning Star" (Hogg) **109**:249
"Morning Twilight" (Baudelaire)
See "Le crépuscule du matin"
"Morning Walk" (Clare) **9**:122
"The Morning Watch" (Very) **9**:378, 383
"The Morning Wind" (Clare) **9**:104
Morning-Glories and Other Stories (Alcott) **58**:50
"'Morning'—means 'Milking'—to the Farmer" (Dickinson) **171**:135, 142
"The Morning's Hinges" (Ferguson) **33**:290
"The Morns Are Meeker than They Were" (Dickinson) **21**:7; **171**:99
"The Moro River" (Isaacs)
See "Río Moro"
"Moros y cristianos" (Alarcon) **1**:14; **219**:4
Moroz krasni nos (Nekrasov) **11**:402, 404-05, 407-09, 412-14, 416, 420-21
"Mort!" (Verlaine) **51**:266
La mort (Baudelaire) **6**:116, 122; **55**:5, 53, 62-3, 66, 73-4; **155**:113
"La Mort" (Verlaine) **230**:160
"La mort de l'exilé" (Nerval) **67**:307
"La mort de Philippe II" (Verlaine) **2**:622, 624; **51**:356
"La Mort de S.M. le Roi Louis II de Bavière" (Verlaine) **51**:359
La Mort de Socrate (Lamartine) **190**:195, 200
"La mort de Valmiki" (Leconte de Lisle) **29**:215, 223, 234, 241
"La mort des amants" (Baudelaire) **6**:116; **29**:105; **55**:12, 73
"La mort des artistes" (Baudelaire) **55**:12, 29, 62, 66, 73
"La mort des pauvres" (Baudelaire) **29**:80, 112-13; **55**:73
"La mort des petits poux" (Rimbaud) **35**:266
"La mort du diable" (Beranger) **34**:42
"La mort du loup" (Vigny) **7**:469, 472-73, 478-79, 481-82; **102**:336, 373-75
"Une mort héroïque" (Baudelaire) **155**:8, 56-63
"Le mort joyeux" (Baudelaire) **55**:12, 44
"Une mort trop travaillée" (Corbière) **43**:31
"Mortal, Angel AND Demon" (Verlaine) **51**:372
A Mortal Antipathy: First Opening of the New Portfolio (Holmes) **14**:113, 115, 131, 133-34, 136-39, 143; **81**:107, 118
"The Mortal Immortal" (Shelley) **14**:264, 267, 272, 299; **59**:155
La Morte (Feuillet) **45**:90-1
"La morte amoureuse" (Gautier) **1**:341, 346, 348, 350, 353, 355; **59**:8-13, 29, 33-6, 39-40
"Morte d'Arthur" (Tennyson) **30**:212-13, 222, 224, 230, 242, 249, 253, 269, 279-80; **65**:240, 245-7, 278-82, 285, 297-8, 300-1, 305, 311, 315, 318-20, 324, 339, 349, 368, 376; **115**:235; **202**:206, 208, 218, 220-21, 223, 253, 291, 308, 320-21, 323, 326, 330
La morte de Socrate (Lamartine) **11**:245, 268-70, 289
"Morton Hall" (Gaskell) **5**:201, 205; **70**:188-89
"Morts de quatre-vingt-douze" (Rimbaud)
See "Morts de quatre-vingt-douze et de quatre-vingt-treize"
"Morts de quatre-vingt-douze et de quatre-vingt-treize" (Rimbaud) **4**:465
"Mortua est" (Eminescu) **33**:249, 257, 264; **131**:294, 297, 331
Mosaïque (Mérimée) **65**:79, 113
"Moscow" (Pavlova)
See "Moskva"
"Moses" (Vigny) **7**:474
"Moses on the Mountain" (Wergeland) **5**:537
"Moskaleva Krynycja" (Shevchenko) **54**:368, 389
"Moskva" (Pavlova) **138**:50, 54
"Mosque" (Milnes) **61**:130
"Moss on a Wall" (Kendall) **12**:179-80, 186, 194, 199, 201
"The Moss Supplicateth for the Poet" (Dana) **53**:178
"Mosses" (Melville)
See "Hawthorne and his Mosses"
Mosses from an Old Manse (Hawthorne) **2**:294, 298; **39**:233; **95**:104, 110; **158**:194, 242-44, 246, 262, 327; **171**:342-43, 345, 361; **191**:178
"Most Deaf" (Laforgue)
See "Très-sourd"
"Un Mot au Soleil pour commencer" (Laforgue) **221**:43, 81
"Un mot sur la littérature russe" (Karamzin) **173**:267
"Un mot sur la rime" (Verlaine) **230**:164
"Motes in the Sun-Beans" (Lamb) **125**:348
"The Moth" (Pavlova)
See "Motylek"
"The Moth and the Flowers" (Zhukovsky)
See "Motylyok i tsvety"
"The Mother" (Andersen) **79**:66
"The Mother" (Crabbe) **26**:93, 128-30; **121**:11, 36
"Mother" (Nekrasov)
See "Mat"
Mother (Alencar)
See *Mai*
"Mother and Eliza" (Child) **73**:129
"The Mother and Her Child" (Longstreet) **159**:119, 137, 140, 144, 186, 201-2
"Mother and Poet" (Barrett Browning) **61**:10, 14, 44-5, 66; **170**:67, 118, 122
"Mother and Son" (Morris) **4**:434
"The Mother and the Child" (Kivi)
See "Äiti ja lapsi"
"Mother Earth" (Isaacs)
See "La tierra madre"
Mother Elder (Andersen) **79**:15
The Mother of God (Sacher-Masoch) **31**:295, 298, 302
"Mother of God I Shall Pray in Humility" (Lermontov) **126**:143
"Mother of Pearl" (O'Brien) **21**:239-40, 244-45, 252
The Mother of the Maccabees (Werner)
See *Die Mutter der Makkabäer: Tragödie in fünf Akten*
"The Mother Perishing in the Snow Storm" (Smith) **187**:333-34
"Mother, Thou'rt Faithful to Me" (Foster) **26**:295
"A Mother to Her Waking Infant" (Baillie) **151**:46, 86, 95, 123
"Motherhood" (Blind) **202**:10
The Mother-in-Law (Southworth) **26**:431-32, 446-47
"Motherland" (Lermontov)
See "Rodina"
"The Motherless Child" (Barnes) **75**:58
"A motherless soft lambkin" (Rossetti) **186**:237, 242
Mothers and Daughters (Gore) **65**:16, 20, 30-1
The Mother's Book (Child) **6**:198-99; **73**:41, 50, 59, 67, 73, 75, 96, 101, 130
"Mother's Cry" (Webster) **230**:227
"The Mother's Dream" (Barnes) **75**:17
"The Mother's Heart" (Norton) **47**:241-42
"The Mother's Hymn" (Bryant) **6**:165
"Mother's Name" (Grundtvig) **1**:402
"Mother's Name is a Heavenly Sound" (Grundtvig) **158**:102
"The Mother's Prayer" (Lazarus) **109**:293
"A Mother's Prayer in Illness" (Osgood) **141**:321
"Mother's Revenge" (Whittier) **8**:485
"The Mother's Secret" (Holmes) **14**:128
"The Mother's Soul" (Crawford) **12**:156, 171; **127**:160
"A Mother's Wail" (Timrod) **25**:372, 382, 384
The Motley Assembly (Warren) **13**:419, 428-29, 436; **226**:253, 258-59, 261, 272-73
Les Mots Anglais (Mallarmé) **210**:251
Les Mots anglaise (Mallarmé) **41**:249
Motsart i Sal'eri (Pushkin) **3**:424, 433-34, 444, 447, 452; **83**:263-64, 275, 285-88, 324, 338-39, 351, 353
"Motylek" (Pavlova) **138**:3-4, 14, 48
"Motylyok i tsvety" (Zhukovsky) **35**:393, 403
"Mouche" (Maupassant) **1**:464, 468-69; **83**:194, 198
"Le mouchoir rouge" (Gobineau) **17**:80, 92-3, 103
Mount Henneth (Bage) **182**:6-7, 12, 17, 19-20, 23, 25-29, 38, 40-43, 45-49, 52, 59
"Mount Kikineis" (Mickiewicz)
See "Góra Kikineis"
"Mount me like a woman" (Verlaine) **230**:176
"The Mount of Olives" (Vigny)
See "Le mont des Oliviers"
"Mount Orient" (Griffin) **7**:215
"Mount Shasta, Seen from a Distance" (Ridge) **82**:174, 184, 195, 197, 210
Mount Vernon, a Letter to the Children of America (Cooper) **129**:4
"The Mountain" (Leskov)
See "Gora"
The Mountain (Michelet) **31**:215, 242, 247-48, 257-58, 260, 262-63
The Mountain Bard: Consisting of Ballads and Songs, Founded on Facts and Legendary Tales (Hogg) **4**:277, 281-82; **109**:268-69, 276
"The Mountain Cot" (Dacre) **151**:149
"The Mountain Fires" (Hemans) **71**:277

"The Mountain Forest" (Stifter)
See "Der Hochwald"
"The Mountain Girl" (Isaacs)
See "La montañero"
The Mountain King and the Misanthrope (Raimund)
See *Der Alpenkönig und der Menschenfeind*
"Mountain Lyre" (Hogg) **109**:270
"Mountain Moss" (Kendall) **12**:179, 186
The Mountain of the Lovers: With Poems of Nature and Tradition (Hayne) **94**:137-38, 141, 148, 151, 168-69
"A Mountain Spring" (Kendall) **12**:183
"The Mountain Village of Bastundzhi" (Lermontov)
See "Aul Bastundzi"
"The Mountain Violet" (Dacre) **151**:148, 169-71
"Mountaineer and Poet" (Barrett Browning) **170**:118
"The Mountain's Face" (Boyesen) **135**:13
"Le mourant" (Banville) **9**:16
"The Mourner" (Opie) **65**:155
"The Mourner" (Shelley) **14**:264, 272; **59**:155; **103**:343, 345-47
"The Mourning Daughter" (Sigourney) **21**:299
"Mourning Women" (Blind) **202**:58
"The Mouse" (Shaw) **15**:335
"The Mouse's Nest" (Clare) **9**:101
"The Mouse's Petition" (Barbauld) **185**:33, 92, 126-27, 130-34, 152, 156
Le Mousqetaire (Dumas) **71**:204
"Le mousse" (Corbière) **43**:28
"Mouvement" (Rimbaud) **4**:475; **35**:269; **82**:232; **227**:246-47, 298
"Movables Credit" (Eminescu) **33**:273
Movements of the British Legion with Strictures on the Course of Conduct (Richardson)
See *Journal of the Movements of the British Legion*
"Möwenflug" (Meyer) **81**:199-200, 208
Moxon's Illustrated Tennyson (Tennyson) **202**:283
"Moy dar ubog, i golos moy ne gromok..." (Baratynsky) **103**:9
"Moy Eliziy" (Baratynsky) **103**:8
"Moya ispoved" (Karamzin)
See "Moja ispoved"
Moya Rodoslovnaya (Pushkin) **83**:317
Mozart and Salieri (Pushkin)
See *Motsart i Sal'eri*
Mozart auf der Reise nach Prag (Mörike) **10**:445, 448-49, 458; **201**:252-54, 257, 264, 267, 271, 301, 303, 306, 313
Mozart on the Occasion of the Hundredth Celebration of his Birth (Liszt) **199**:305
Mozart on the Way to Prague (Mörike)
See *Mozart auf der Reise nach Prag*
Mozart's Journey from Vienna to Prague: A Romance of His Private Life; Mozart on the Way to Prague (Mörike)
See *Mozart auf der Reise nach Prag*
Mózes (Madach) **19**:362, 368, 371
The M.P. (Robertson) **35**:333-34, 336, 340, 351, 357, 360-62, 364-65, 369
"Mr. Alcott's Book and School" (Peabody) **169**:166
Mr. Ambrose's Letters on the Rebellion (Kennedy) **2**:432
"Mr. and Mrs. Discobbolos" (Lear) **3**:308
Mr. Benet (Fredro)
See *Pan Benet*
"Mr. Brown's Letters to a Young Man About Town" (Thackeray) **213**:341-42, 347
Mr. Buckstone's Ascent of Mount Parnassus (Planché) **42**:273, 276, 291
Mr. Buckstone's Voyage Round the World (Planché) **42**:273, 291
"Mr. Clifford" (Austen) **119**:13
"Mr. Dana, of the New York Sun" (Field) **3**:211
"Mr. Darwin's Hypothesis" (Lewes) **25**:287, 311; **215**:146-47
"Mr. Deucease at Paris" (Thackeray) **43**:367
"Mr. Emerson's New Course of Lectures" (Lowell) **90**:220
Mr. Facey Romford's Hounds (Surtees) **14**:347, 349-50, 353, 355, 364, 366, 369-72, 374-75, 380-81
Mr. Fantom, the New-Fashioned Philosopher and Mr. Bragwell, or, the Two Wealthy Farmers (More) **141**:190, 199, 311
"Mr. Fox" (Dacre) **151**:198
"Mr. Gilfil's Love Story" (Eliot) **4**:92-93, 98; **41**:101; **118**:103; **183**:31
Mr. H. or Beware A Bad Name (Lamb) **10**:401; **113**:158, 202, 256, 278, 280, 286
"Mr. Harley" (Austen) **119**:13
"Mr. Harrison's Confessions" (Gaskell) **5**:187, 190, 193, 201-03, 205; **97**:127, 168, 171; **137**:54
"Mr. Higginbotham's Catastrophe" (Hawthorne) **2**:292, 298, 305, 324, 333; **171**:356, 362
"Mr. Hosea Biglow to the Editor of the Atlantic Monthly" (Lowell) **2**:516
Mr. Joviality (Fredro)
See *Pan Jowialski*
"Mr. Justice Harbottle" (Le Fanu) **9**:302, 317, 320-22; **58**:272, 301-2; **58**:256
"Mr. Kean's Iago" (Hazlitt) **82**:75
"Mr. Lowe as Chancellor of the Exchequer" (Bagehot) **10**:31
Mr. Midshipman Easy (Marryat) **3**:316-19, 322
Mr. Moneyful (Fredro)
See *Pan Geldhab*
"Mr. Morgan at His Ease" (Thackeray) **213**:252
"Mr. Paul Pató" (Petofi)
See "Pató Pál úr"
Mr. Scarborough's Family (Trollope) **6**:471, 501, 503; **101**:249, 267, 292, 318, 321; **215**:283, 331, 333
"Mr Shuffleton's Allegorical Survey" (Hogg) **109**:248
"Mr. Sludge, 'The Medium'" (Browning) **19**:98, 131; **79**:150, 163-64, 171
Mr. Sponge's Sporting Tour (Surtees) **14**:345-47, 349-50, 353, 355-56, 358, 361, 363, 365, 369-72, 374, 377-78, 380-83
"Mr Thelwall's Plans and Terms of Tuition" (Thelwall) **162**:342
Mr. Waddy's Return (Winthrop) **210**:296, 301
"Mr. Wordsworth's Poetry" (Reynolds) **146**:204
Mrinalini (Chatterji) **19**:204, 209-10, 212-13, 215, 217-21, 224
Mrnālinī (Chatterji)
See *Mrinalini*
"Mrs. Adolphus Smith Sporting the 'Blue Stocking'" (Parton) **86**:352
Mrs. Albert Grundy: Observations in Philistia (Frederic) **10**:194, 201-02, 214
Mrs Armytage; or, Female Domination (Gore) **65**:19-20, 30
Mrs. Arthur (Oliphant) **61**:203-4, 209-10
"Mrs. Battle's Opinions on Whist!" (Lamb) **10**:390, 428, 436; **113**:155-56, 200, 227, 244
"Mrs. Brumby" (Trollope) **101**:234
"Mrs. Bullfrog" (Hawthorne) **171**:357
"Mrs. Captain Thompson" (Willis) **194**:282
"Mrs. Caudle's Breakfast Talk" (Jerrold) **2**:407
Mrs. Caudle's Curtain Lectures (Jerrold) **2**:395-96, 398, 402-03, 405-08
"Mrs. Caudle's Papers" (Jerrold) **2**:407
"Mrs. Flint's Married Experience" (Cooke) **110**:19-20, 24, 33-4, 37, 44, 46, 50, 56, 58, 66
"Mrs. Følnss" (Jacobsen)
See "Fru Følnss"
"Mrs. General Talboys" (Trollope) **101**:234-35
Mrs. Halliburton's Troubles (Wood) **178**:288, 290-91, 324
"Mrs. Hutchinson" (Hawthorne) **158**:340; **171**:356-57
"Mrs. Jaypher" (Lear) **3**:301
Mrs. Leicester's School (Lamb) **10**:402-03, 406, 417; **113**:278, 286
Mrs. Leicester's School (Lamb) **125**:302, 312, 314, 316-17, 320, 322-23, 325-26, 332, 349, 360, 362-63, 365, 368-71, 375
"Mrs. Macsimmum's Bill" (O'Brien) **21**:243
Mrs. Mathews; or, Family Mysteries (Trollope) **30**:331-32
"Mrs. P—" (Barbauld)
See "On Mrs. Priestley's Leaving Warrington"
Mrs. Perkins' Ball (Thackeray) **5**:445
"Mrs. Philip Schuyler" (Cooper) **129**:71
"Mrs Pierrepoint" (Levy) **59**:106
"Mrs. Rowe" (Barbauld) **185**:36
"Mrs. Rozgonye" (Arany)
See "Roz goniné"
"Mrs. Throckmorton's Bulfinch" (Cowper)
See "On the Death of Mrs. Throckmorton's Bulfinch"
"Mrs. Twardowski" (Mickiewicz) **3**:398
"Mrs. Weasel's Husband" (Parton) **86**:350
"Mrs. Yardley's Quilting" (Harris) **23**:140, 159; **165**:177, 191, 201, 242, 244, 254, 270
"MS. Found in a Bottle" (Poe) **1**:492, 514; **16**:292, 299, 301, 315, 330-34; **55**:185, 202, 205-6; **94**:223-25
MS I (An Enquiry Concerning Political Justice and Its Influence on General Virtue and Happiness) (Godwin)
See *Enquiry concerning Political Justice and Its Influence on General Virtue and Happiness*
MS II (An Enquiry Concerning Political Justice and Its Influence on General Virtue and Happiness) (Godwin)
See *Enquiry concerning Political Justice and Its Influence on General Virtue and Happiness*
MS III (An Enquiry Concerning Political Justice and Its Influence on General Virtue and Happiness) (Godwin)
See *Enquiry concerning Political Justice and Its Influence on General Virtue and Happiness*
MS IV (An Enquiry Concerning Political Justice and Its Influence on General Virtue and Happiness) (Godwin)
See *Enquiry concerning Political Justice and Its Influence on General Virtue and Happiness*
MS V (An Enquiry Concerning Political Justice and Its Influence on General Virtue and Happiness) (Godwin)
See *Enquiry concerning Political Justice and Its Influence on General Virtue and Happiness*
"Mtsiri" (Lermontov)
See *Mtsyri*
"Mtsyri" (Lermontov)
See *Mtsyri*
Mtsyri (Lermontov) **5**:289, 293, 295; **126**:128-29, 131, 145, 181-83, 185-87, 217, 224
"Much ado about Nothing" (Carlyle) **181**:119, 131-32, 136
"Much Ado about Nothing" (Lamb) **125**:304, 306
The Muddy Bay (Ichiyō)
See *Nigorie*
"Mudfog Papers" (Dickens) **203**:191
"Mudrecu" (Baratynsky) **103**:27
"La muerte del sargento" (Isaacs) **70**:306
"Muertos" (Silva) **114**:301, 303
Los muertos (Silva) **114**:269-70
La muette de Portici (Scribe) **16**:382, 386, 398, 401, 408-11
Muhganni Nama (Ghalib) **39**:153
"Das Mühlenleben" (Muller) **73**:364, 370
"La mujer" (Gómez de Avellaneda) **111**:30, 33, 56-7, 64-7
"La mujer alta" (Alarcon) **1**:14

"La mujer de piedra" (Bécquer) **106**:146, 149, 167-69
"La mula y el macho" (Lizardi) **30**:68
The Mulatto (Andersen) **79**:12-13, 17
Mulla Nur (Bestuzhev) **131**:152, 161, 186, 200
Müller Kohlenbrenner und Sesseltrager (Nestroy) **42**:240, 256
"Müller Radlauf" (Brentano) **1**:104
"Der Müller und der Bach" (Muller) **73**:365, 373
The Multiple Wehmüllers and Hungarian National Faces (Brentano)
See *Die mehreren Wehmüller und ungarischen Nationalgesichter*
The Mummy's Tale (Gautier)
See *Le Roman de la momie*
"Mumu" (Turgenev) **21**:399, 415, 418, 457, 459; **122**:241, 244, 265, 294-97, 344, 348-49
Münchhausen: Eine Geschichte in arabesken (Immermann) **4**:290-95, 297; **49**:358, 361-62, 366-67
De mundi sensibilis et intelligibilis forma ac principiis (Kant) **67**:210
"Un mundo por un soneto" (Isaacs) **70**:306
"El mundo todo es máscaras, todo el año es carnaval" (Larra) **130**:230-31
Munio Alfonso (Gómez de Avellaneda) **111**:4, 12, 24, 28
"Munter" (Runeberg) **41**:312, 314, 327
"Muo no rigyo" (Ueda Akinari) **131**:9, 13-14, 16, 24-25, 28, 32, 34, 38, 40-41, 48, 60, 70-72
"Murad the Unlucky" (Edgeworth) **51**:88-9
"La muralla de México en la protección de María Santísima Nuestra Señora" (Lizardi) **30**:68
Murány ostroma (Arany) **34**:4, 16
"Murder" (De Quincey)
See "Lectures on Murder Considered as One of the Fine Arts"
"Murder Considered" (De Quincey)
See "Lectures on Murder Considered as One of the Fine Arts"
"The Murder of the Lamb" (Harpur) **114**:148, 150
"Murder Will Out" (Opie) **65**:159
"The Murdered Cousin" (Le Fanu)
See "A Passage in the Secret History of an Irish Countess"
"Murdered Lady" (Whittier) **8**:485
"The Murdered Maid" (Robinson) **142**:114
"The Murdered Traveller" (Bryant) **46**:3, 42
"The Murdered Trooper" (Jones) **222**:158
"The Murderer" (Dacre) **151**:148
"The Murderer's Haunted Couch" (Beddoes) **154**:63
"The Murders in the Rue Morgue" (Poe) **1**:506, 521, 530-31; **16**:293, 295-96, 298, 300-01, 303, 306, 312, 315, 332; **55**:135, 141, 149; **78**:281-82; **94**:245; **97**:208, 211-12; **211**:253-57, 267-68
Murders. True examples of the interposition of Providence, on the discovery and punishment of murder (More) **141**:179
"Mureşanu" (Eminescu) **131**:287
"The Murmuring of Bees Has Ceased" (Dickinson) **21**:68-9
Murnis (Almqvist) **42**:10
"A Murza's Vision" (Derzhavin)
See "Videnie Murzy"
"Musa" (Holmes) **14**:133
Musarion (Wieland) **17**:394, 396, 398-400, 411-16, 426-27, 429
Musarion; oder, die Philosophie der Grazien (Wieland) **177**:252, 254, 320, 323, 327
"Muşat and the Weirds" (Eminescu) **33**:269
"Muscadine Story" (Hooper) **177**:191
"Muscadines" (Hayne) **94**:149, 167, 169
"Muscheln" (Muller) **73**:360, 371
Muscheln von der Insel Rügen (Muller) **73**:352, 356, 358-60, 367, 371
"The Muse" (Baratynsky)
See "Muza"
The Muse (Pushkin) **3**:423
La muse du département (Balzac) **5**:84; **153**:54-59, 66, 80, 153
"La Muse malade" (Baudelaire) **55**:48, 58
"The Muse of Australia" (Kendall) **12**:184, 195-96
"The Muse of the Coming Age" (Andersen) **7**:23; **79**:84
"The Muse of the New Century" (Andersen) **214**:57
"Muse, un nommé ségur" (Hugo) **3**:256
"La Muse vénale" (Baudelaire) **55**:46-7, 58, 62
"Musée secret" (Gautier) **1**:348
"Der Musensaal" (Meyer) **81**:140, 154-56, 199, 209
"Music" (Emerson) **38**:193
"Music" (Halleck) **47**:57
"Music" (Lampman) **25**:167, 187, 208, 210, 216
"Music" (Thoreau) **7**:384
"The Music Grinders" (Holmes) **14**:99
"The Music Master" (Allingham) **25**:3, 5, 7, 9, 12, 16, 18, 23, 25, 27
"The Music of Nature" (Cranch) **115**:67
"Music of the Future" (Wagner)
See "Zukunftsmusik"
"Music, when soft voices die" (Shelley) **18**:373
"A Musical Instrument" (Barrett Browning) **1**:124; **66**:85; **170**:115, 118-22
"A Musical Reminiscence" (Harpur) **114**:144
The Musician (Shevchenko)
See *Muzykant*
"Musician's Tale" (Longfellow) **45**:148
"Musik zu Goethes "Egmont" (Hoffmann) **183**:181
"Musikalishce Haus- und Lebensregeln" (Schumann) **143**:76
Der Musikfeind (Hoffmann) **183**:169
"The Musing Maniac" (Dacre) **151**:148
"Musings" (Dana) **53**:173-5
"Musings" (Thoreau) **138**:106
"Musings of a Recluse" (Cranch) **115**:32, 51
"La Musique" (Baudelaire) **55**:29, 61; **155**:114
La musique and les lettres (Mallarmé) **210**:167, 169, 171, 188, 201, 206, 208, 215, 231, 255, 264-66
La Musique et les lettres (Mallarmé) **41**:277, 280-81, 298
"The Musk Ox" (Leskov)
See "Ovcebyk"
The Musk-Ox, and Other Tales (Leskov) **25**:230-31
"The Musk-Ox" ("Ovtsiebyk") (Leskov)
See "Ovcebyk"
Musterkarte (Muller) **73**:366
"Mut" (Muller) **73**:390
"Mutability" (Shelley) **18**:340, 344
"Mutability" (Wordsworth) **166**:205, 213
"The Mutability of Literature" (Irving) **19**:328, 347
"Mutation" (Bryant) **46**:46
The Mute from Portici (Scribe)
See *La muette de Portici*
"Mute Thy Coronation" (Dickinson) **21**:56
"Muted" (Verlaine)
See "En sourdine"
"Muth" (Muller) **73**:366
The Mutiny at the Nore (Jerrold) **2**:401
Die Mutter der Makkabäer: Tragödie in fünf Akten (Werner) **189**:323, 327, 330, 332, 363, 367-70
"Der Mutter Erde" (Hölderlin) **16**:174
"Die Mutter und die Tochter" (Klopstock) **11**:238
Mutter und Kind (Hebbel) **43**:238
"The Mutual Interdependence of Things" (Hoffmann) **2**:342
"Művészeti értekezés" (Madach) **19**:370
"Muza" (Baratynsky) **103**:9, 11
Muzykant (Shevchenko) **54**:387, 390, 392, 394
"My Acquaintance with Derzhavin" (Aksakov)
See "Znakomstvo s Derzhavinym"
"My Aged Uncle Arly" (Lear)
See "Incidents in the Life of My Uncle Arly"
"My ain Fireside" (Hamilton) **153**:317
"My Ancient Ship upon My Ancient Sea" (Brontë) **109**:28
"My Angel!" (Verlaine)
See "Mon Ange!"
"My Aunt" (Holmes) **14**:109, 128
"My Aunt Margaret's Adventure" (Le Fanu) **9**:323
My Aunt Margaret's Mirror (Galt) **1**:334
My Aunt Susan (Frederic) **10**:188
"My Baby Has a Father and a Mother" (Rossetti) **186**:234, 236
"My baby has a mottled fist" (Rossetti) **186**:236
"My Beth" (Alcott) **218**:75-77, 79-81
"My Biography" (Beranger) **34**:37
"My Birth-day" (Lamb) **125**:364
"My Birthplace" (Nekrasov) **11**:403
"My Bohemian Life" (Rimbaud)
See "Ma bohème"
My Bondage and My Freedom (Douglass) **7**:124-25, 128-29, 131, 134, 143; **55**:106-7, 113, 117, 120-8; **141**:33, 45, 55, 62, 72-73, 75-76, 98, 110, 126, 128-29, 131-32, 136, 139, 145-46, 149-50, 157
"My Books" (Longfellow) **45**:121
"My Boots" (Thoreau) **7**:384
My Boys (Alcott)
See *Aunt Jo's Scrap-Bag*
My Brother Jack; or, The Story of What-D'ye-Call'em (Daudet)
See *Le petit chose*
"My Bugle and How I Blow It" (Mangan) **27**:302
"My Bust" (Derzhavin)
See "Moi Istukan"
"My Candidacy" (Verlaine)
See "Ma Candidature"
"My Castle" (Alger) **8**:16
"My Childhood Home I See Again" (Lincoln) **201**:159, 181, 216, 218
"My Childhood's Home I See Again" (Lincoln) **18**:240, 272
"My Children" (Larcom) **179**:170
My Cid (Southey) **8**:459
"My Coat" (Beranger) **34**:46
"My Companions" (Holmes) **14**:100
"My Confession" (Karamzin)
See "Moja ispoved"
"My Conscience" (Stevenson) **193**:205
"My Contraband" (Alcott)
See "The Brothers"
"My Country" (Hale) **75**:286
"My Countrymen" (Arnold) **89**:102; **126**:7, 15; **218**:215-16, 241
My Cousin Nicholas (Barham) **77**:6
"My Cricket" (Dickinson)
See "Further in Summer Than the Birds"
"My Darling Julia" (Barnes)
See "My Dearest Julia"
"My Daughter" (Verlaine)
See "Ma Fille"
"My Days among the Dead Are Passed" (Southey) **8**:474
"My Dearest Julia" (Barnes) **75**:72-3
"My Depature" (Whitman) **81**:237
My Desire (Warner) **146**:233
"My Elysium" (Baratynsky)
See "Moy Eliziy"
"My Emma, my darling" (Hogg) **109**:250
"My Fairy" (Dodgson) **139**:61
"My Familiar Dream" (Verlaine)
See "Mon Rêve familier"
"My Fate Is Orphaned . . ." (Laforgue)
See "Dimanches"
"My Fate is Sealed: I Am Getting Married" (Pushkin) **83**:320

"My First Acquaintance with Poets" (Hazlitt) **29**:148-49, 165-66; **82**:107, 123, 126, 144
"My First Book" (Stevenson) **63**:229, 240, 243, 269; **193**:324, 332
"My First Play" (Lamb) **113**:153-54, 177, 200, 202, 218
"My French Master" (Gaskell) **5**:190, 201
"My Friend, My Guardian Angel" (Zhukovsky) **35**:376, 403
"My Friend, My Loveliest Friendship . . ." (Verlaine)
See "Mon ami, ma plus belle amitié . . ."
"My Friends in the Madhouse" (Bird) **197**:44, 49
"My Garden" (Very) **9**:388
"My Garden Acquaintance" (Lowell) **2**:517
My Geneology (Pushkin)
See *Moya Rodoslovnaya*
"My gift is mean and my voice is low..." (Baratynsky)
See "Moy dar ubog, i golos moy ne gromok..."
"My Gouge!" (Verlaine)
See "Ma Gouge!"
"My Great-Grandfather's Papers" (Stifter)
See "Die Mappe meines Urgrossvaters"
"My Great-Grandfather's Portfolio" (Stifter)
See "Die Mappe meines Urgrossvaters"
"My harvest is done" (Rossetti) **186**:302
"My Heart and I" (Barrett Browning) **170**:121
"My Heart Laid Bare" (Baudelaire)
See "Mon coeur mis à nu"
"My Heart Leaps Up" (Wordsworth) **12**:431; **206**:266-67, 271
My Heart's Idol (Planché) **42**:293
"My Hope" (Arany)
See "Reménvem"
"My Hopes Have Departed Forever" (Foster) **26**:295
"My Hunt After 'The Captain'" (Holmes) **81**:102
"My Ideal Museum" (Casal)
See "Mi museo ideal"
"My Idol" (Derzhavin)
See "Moi Istukan"
"My Kingdom" (Alcott) **58**:37
"My Kinsman, Major Molineux" (Hawthorne) **2**:329-31; **17**:137; **23**:201, 217; **39**:180; **79**:299, 304; **95**:105, 112, 114-16, 125, 196; **158**:288; **171**:245, 279, 327, 343, 345, 356
My Lady Ludlow (Gaskell) **5**:191, 201-03, 205; **70**:185-86; **214**:284, 298-99, 302, 304-6
My Lady Pokahontas (Cooke) **5**:126, 132, 135
My Lady's Money (Collins) **1**:188
"My Landlady and Her Lodgers" (Galt) **110**:79
"My Last Duchess" (Browning) **19**:114, 117, 119, 126, 133, 135-37; **79**:95-96, 100, 164, 169-70, 185
My Life (Constant)
See *Le cahier rouge de Benjamin Constant*
My Life (Sand)
See *Histoire de ma vie*
My Life (Wagner)
See *Mein Leben*
"My Life Closed Twice before Its Close" (Dickinson) **21**:19, 23; **171**:107
"My Life Had Stood—A Loaded Gun" (Dickinson) **21**:48, 71; **77**:88, 143, 161; **171**:148, 153
My Life; or, Our Social State: A Poem (Jones) **222**:116, 152, 155, 160
"My Life Is like a Stroll upon the Beach" (Thoreau) **7**:355
My Literary Life (Linton) **41**:165
"My Little Lovers" (Rimbaud)
See "Mes petites amoureuses"
"My Little Rabbit" (Wergeland) **5**:539
My Little Song Book (Hale)
See *School Song Book*
"My Lost Self" (Boyesen) **135**:20, 32
"My Lost Youth" (Longfellow) **45**:116, 131, 137, 142, 160, 186-87, 189
"My Love is Good" (Barnes) **75**:6, 8, 58
"My Love's Guardian Angel" (Barnes) **75**:17, 21
"My Mary" (Clare) **9**:74-75
"My Mary of the Curling Hair" (Griffin) **7**:198, 201
My Miscellanies (Collins) **1**:185
"My Misfortune. My Riches, My Holy Craft" (Pavlova)
See "Moia napast.! Moe bogatstvo, moe sviatoe remeslo"
My Mother's Manuscript: Being a True Picture of the Private Life a French Family during Many of the Most Eventful Periods of the Nineteenth Century (Lamartine)
See *Le Manuscrit de ma mère*
"My Mountain" (Larcom) **179**:175
"My Nanny O" (Baillie) **151**:91-92
"My Native Land" (Lermontov)
See "Rodina"
My Novel; or, Varieties in English Life (Bulwer-Lytton) **1**:145-46, 148-51, 155; **45**:22, 69-70
"My Old Kentucky Home, Good Night" (Foster) **26**:283-87, 289-91, 297-98
"My Old Oak Table" (Bloomfield) **145**:176
"My Old Village" (Jefferies) **47**:102, 138-39, 143
"My Orcha'd in Linden Lea" (Barnes) **75**:20, 29, 46, 60, 69, 87-8, 96, 101
"My Own Heart Let Me More Have Pity On" (Hopkins) **17**:245, 261; **189**:28, 77, 146
My Past and Thoughts (Herzen)
See *Byloe i dumy*
"My period had come for Prayer" (Dickinson) **77**:564
"My Playmate" (Whittier) **8**:505-06, 508-09, 520; **59**:349, 356, 371
"My Pretty Rose Tree" (Blake) **37**:43, 45, 48, 51, 92
My Prisons (Verlaine)
See *Mes prisons*
"My Psalm" (Whittier) **8**:496
"My Race" (Martí)
See "Mi raza"
"My Relations" (Lamb) **10**:436; **113**:236, 248
My Relations with Carlyle (Froude) **43**:191, 202, 210, 220
"My Remarks on the Russian Theater" (Pushkin) **83**:331
"My River" (Mörike)
See "Mein Fluss"
"My River Runs to Thee" (Dickinson) **21**:8; **171**:96
"My School Career" (Petofi)
See "Deákpályám"
My Schools and Schoolmasters; or The Story of My Education (Miller) **143**:3, 6, 27-30, 36, 48, 54-55
"My seal ring" (Fuller) **50**:247-8
"My 71st Year" (Whitman) **31**:434
"My Sister's Sleep" (Rossetti) **4**:517-19, 521-22, 525-26; **77**:303, 306, 344
"My Son, Sir" (O'Brien) **21**:237, 243, 247
"My Song" (Norwid)
See "Moja piosnka"
"My Songs" (Petofi)
See "Dalaim"
"My Soul and I" (Whittier) **8**:491; **59**:348, 361, 375, 377
"My Soul Is Dark" (Byron) **2**:103
My Southern Home; or, The South and Its People (Brown) **2**:48-51, 53; **89**:144, 160
"My Springs" (Lanier) **6**:238, 242; **118**:202, 215
"My Star" (Browning) **19**:96; **79**:140-41
"My Story of an Affinity" (Lampman)
See "The Story of an Affinity"
"My stranno soshlis! . . ." (Pavlova) **138**:4
"My Strip of Blue" (Larcom) **179**:176
"My Study Windows" (Lowell) **2**:510
My Study Windows (Lowell) **90**:197, 220
"My Stuffed Owl" (Sigourney) **87**:326
"My Style of Drawing Birds" (Audubon) **47**:24
"My sweet Ann Foot, my bonny Ann" (Clare) **86**:89
"My Tale" (Clough) **27**:115-16, 118
"My Tenants" (Cooke) **110**:4
"My Testament" (Slowacki) **15**:365
"My Thirty Years" (Manzano)
See "Treinta años"
My Thirty Years Out of the Senate (Smith) **187**:313, 322
"My Thoughts" (Cranch) **115**:15
"My Thoughts on Shakhovskoy" (Pushkin) **83**:332
"My Tract" (Hood) **16**:216
"My Triumph" (Whittier) **59**:361
"My Two Springs" (Lanier) **118**:231, 235
"My Valentine" (O'Brien) **21**:246
"My Visitation" (Cooke) **110**:36, 45
"My Vocation" (Dutt) **29**:127
"My Wheel Is in the Dark" (Dickinson) **21**:63; **171**:196
My Wife and I (Stowe) **3**:561-62, 567
"My Wife's Tempter" (O'Brien) **21**:234, 239, 243, 245, 247
My Years of Childhood (Fontane)
See *Meine Kinderjahre*
"Mycerinus" (Arnold) **6**:34, 44; **29**:32, 34; **218**:114, 188, 192
Mykyta Hajday (Shevchenko)
See *Nikita Hayday*
Myrrha (Alfieri) **101**:13, 19, 22, 39, 41, 50, 59
"Myrtho" (Nerval) **1**:476, 480, 486; **67**:307, 363
Myrtis, with Other Etchings and Sketchings (Sigourney) **21**:301; **87**:321
"Mysli iz raznykh avtorov" (Bestuzhev) **131**:168
"Mysli ob istinnoy svobode" (Karamzin) **173**:286
"Le mystère dans le lettres" (Mallarmé) **210**:175, 211, 228, 231, 234, 251-52, 264, 266
Le Mystère dans les lettres (Mallarmé) **41**:272, 282
"Le mystère des trois cors" (Laforgue) **5**:279-80; **221**:92
Les mystères de Paris (Sue) **1**:553-55, 557-63
Les mystères du peuple (Sue) **1**:558-59
Les mystères du théâtre (Goncourt and Goncourt) **7**:153
The Mysteries of Florence (Lippard)
See *The Ladye Annabel; or, The Doom of the Poisoner: A Romance by an Unknown Author*
"The Mysteries of Nature and of Grace" (Newman) **38**:304, 310
The Mysteries of Paris (Sue)
See *Les mystères de Paris*
The Mysteries of the Backwoods; or, Sketches of the Southwest: Including Character, Scenery, and Rural Sports (Thorpe) **183**:342, 356
Mysteries of the Pulpit; or, a Revelation of the Church and the Home (Lippard)
See *The Memoirs of a Preacher, a Revelation of the Church and the Home*
The Mysteries of Udolpho (Radcliffe) **6**:404-06, 408-11, 413-23, 425, 427, 429-31, 433-39, 441-44, 446-47; **55**:216-22, 224, 226-31, 235-41, 252-4, 256-7, 259-60, 263, 265-6, 270-8; **106**:281-373; **223**:181-83, 186, 188-95, 206, 209-13, 215, 220, 224-25, 232, 235, 241, 243-44, 248-49, 254, 256, 258, 262-63, 270-78, 285-86, 288, 293, 311, 315-20, 322, 324-26, 328, 331-38
"The Mysterious Bride" (Hogg) **109**:233, 281
The Mysterious Husband (Cumberland) **167**:140, 143, 148, 157, 189-90
"The Mysterious Lodger" (Le Fanu) **9**:319
The Mysterious Monk (Dunlap) **2**:214

"The Mysterious Stanger" (Opie) **65**:172-3
"The Mysterious Visitor" (Holmes) **14**:99, 121, 128
"The Mystery" (Austen) **119**:13
The Mystery of Edwin Drood (Dickens) **3**:160, 177; **18**:96-143; **26**:228; **37**:164, 172-73; **86**:257; **105**:244, 290; **161**:89; **203**:234-35, 237; **217**:201-71; **219**:201, 209
"The Mystery of Major Molineux" (Clarke) **19**:251
The Mystery of Major Molineux, and Human Repetends (Clarke) **19**:251
"The Mystery of Marie Rogêt" (Poe) **1**:530-31; **16**:293, 295-96, 300, 303, 306, 315; **97**:208, 211-12; **211**:253, 255
The Mystery of Mrs. Blencarrow (Oliphant) **61**:208
The Mystery of Orcival (Gaboriau)
See *Le crime d'Orcival*
"The Mystery of Pain" (Dickinson)
See "Pain Has an Element of Blank"
"The Mystery of Reminiscence" (Schiller) **39**:339
The Mystery of the Fall (Clough)
See *Adam and Eve*
The Mystery of the Fall (Prescott) **163**:27, 75
"Mystery of the Three Horns" (Laforgue)
See "Mystère des trois cors"
"The Mystic" (Tennyson) **30**:283
"Mystic Trumpeter" (Whitman) **4**:579, 586; **205**:208
"Mystical Evening Dusk" (Verlaine)
See "Crépuscule du soir mystique"
"Mystification" (Poe) **16**:322
"Mystification of the Sirens of Progress" (Fourier) **51**:185
"Mystique" (Rimbaud) **4**:487; **35**:269, 309; **82**:232-33, 243; **227**:203-4, 206, 243, 334
"The Myth of Demeter and Persephone" (Pater) **90**:245, 247, 263
"Mythological Hymn" (Moore)
See "Fragment of a Mythological Hymn to Love"
Mythology for Youth (Grundtvig)
See *Græsk og Nordisk Mythologi for Ungdommen*
"The Mythology of the Greeks and Its Expression in Art" (Fuller) **211**:145
Mythology of the North (Grundtvig)
See *Nordens mytologi*
N. F. S. Grundtvig's Selected Writings (Grundtvig)
See *Udvalgte Skrifter*
N. M. Yazykovu: Otvet na otvet (Pavlova) **138**:4
"N. M. Yzykovu" (Baratynsky)
See "To N. M. Yazykov"
"N:o femton, Stolt" (Runeberg) **41**:325
N. S. Leskov o literature i iskusstve (Leskov) **174**:77
Na bóikom méste (Ostrovsky) **57**:220
"N'a catredal" (Castro) **3**:101; **78**:5
"Na chto vy, dni" (Baratynsky) **103**:22
"Na kraiu sveta (Iz vospominanii arkhiereia)" (Leskov)
See "Na kraju sveta"
"Na kraju sveta" (Leskov) **25**:228, 231, 239, 255, 259; **174**:5, 32, 44, 46, 110
Na nozakh (Leskov)
See *Na nožax*
Na nožax (Leskov) **25**:225, 237, 248, 252-53; **174**:9, 11, 16, 20, 58-65, 90
"Na pokoj grecki w eomu księżnej Zeneidy Wøkońskiej w Moskwie" (Mickiewicz) **101**:204-06, 208-09
"Na pokorenie Derbenta" (Derzhavin) **215**:56
"Na posev lesa" (Baratynsky) **103**:45, 48
"Na puti k Troitse" (Karamzin) **173**:342
"Na rodine" (Goncharov) **63**:18
"Na rozhdenie v Severe porfironosnogo ostroka" (Derzhavin)
See "Stikhi na rozhdenie v Severe porfirorodnago otroka"
"Na sčast'e" (Derzhavin) **215**:38, 42-43
"Na smert Generala-Enshefa Bibikov" (Derzhavin) **215**:10, 22
"Na smert Gyote" (Baratynsky) **103**:8, 10
"Na smert ' kniazia Meshcherskogo" (Derzhavin) **215**:23, 29-30, 34, 52
"Na śmierćś.p. Jana Gajewskiego" (Norwid) **17**:368
"Na vicnu pamjat' Kotljarevs' komu" (Shevchenko) **54**:371-2
"Na vozvrashchenie Grafa Zubova iz Persii" (Derzhavin) **215**:55
Na vsyakogo mudretsa dovolno prostoty (Ostrovsky) **30**:100, 105, 112-13, 116, 118; **57**:219
"Na vzyatie Izmaila" (Derzhavin) **215**:27, 38-39, 55
"Na znatnost" (Derzhavin) **215**:44, 52
Le nabab (Daudet) **1**:232-35, 237, 240-41, 243-48, 250
"Nabby" (Freneau) **111**:124
The Nabob (Daudet)
See *Le nabab*
"Nach der Lese" (Meyer) **81**:146
"Nach einem Niederländer" (Meyer) **81**:206
Nachgelassene Predigten gehalten in den Jahren 1814-1816 (Werner) **189**:348-51, 356, 359
Nachgelassene Schriften (Büchner) **146**:20, 23
"Nachgelassene Werke" (Fichte) **62**:7
"Nachklänge Beethovenscher Musik" (Brentano) **1**:102
"Nachkommenschaften" (Stifter) **41**:375, 377
Nachkommenschaften (Stifter) **198**:274-76
Nachlaß (Schopenhauer) **157**:315
Nachlass (Fichte) **62**:39
"Nachlese zu Aristoteles' Poetick" (Goethe) **154**:220
"Nachricht aus dem Leben eines bekannten Mannes" (Hoffmann) **183**:197
"Nachricht von den neuesten Schicksalen des Hundes Berganza" (Hoffmann) **183**:169, 181, 245
Nachricht von einem gebildeten jungen Mann (Hoffmann) **183**:171
"Nachricht von Fossilen Colossalen Knochen eines Raubthieres in Virginien Gefunden" (Jefferson)
See "A Memoir on the Discovery of Certain Bones of a Quadruped of the Clawed Kind in the Western Parts of Virginia"
Nachricht von meiner Aidienz beim Kaiser von Japan (Claudius) **75**:183, 194
"Nachruf an meinen Bruder" (Eichendorff) **225**:43
Der Nachsommer (Stifter) **41**:334, 337-39, 343-46, 348, 351, 354, 357-60, 363, 369, 374-75, 378, 380, 384-85, 387-400; **198**:260, 262, 269, 276-77, 282-83, 285, 298, 303
"Ein Nachspiel aus der jüngsten Zeit, oder Peter wird ein Stück Weltgeschichte" (Auerbach) **171**:75
"Nacht in der Ernte" (Meyer) **81**:151
"Nacht, 2" (Eichendorff) **225**:43
"Nacht, 3" (Eichendorff) **225**:12
"Nachtgedanken" (Heine) **147**:193-98
"Nachtgeräusche" (Meyer) **81**:201, 203
Nachtgesänge (Hölderlin) **16**:191
Nachtgeschichten (Hoffmann)
See *Nachtstücke*
"Nachtgesichte" (Mörike) **201**:299
"Die nächtliche Fahrt" (Lenau) **16**:286
"Nächtliche Fahrt" (Mörike) **201**:301
"Nachträge Zu den Reisebildern" (Heine) **4**:231
"Nachträgliche Bemerkungen über Spontinis Oper "Olympia"" (Hoffmann) **183**:188
"Nachts" (Eichendorff) **225**:46, 56-57
"Nachts" (Mörike) **201**:273, 289, 299-303
"Nachts, Im Walde" (Eichendorff) **8**:213
Nachtstücke (Hoffmann) **2**:341-42, 348; **183**:165-66, 185, 192-95
Nachtstücke (Schumann) **143**:84, 141
Nachtwachen (Bonaventura) **35**:77-106
Die Nachtwachen des Bonaventura (Tieck) **46**:384
"Nachtzauber" (Eichendorff) **225**:6, 42-43, 46
"Nachwort" (Heine) **147**:173-76, 181, 185, 228
Nacoochee (Chivers) **49**:42-5, 47-8, 52, 57
Nadeschda (Runeberg) **41**:310, 317, 328
"Nadie pase sin hablar al portero o los viajeros en Vitoria" (Larra) **130**:193, 221
"Nadorvannye" (Saltykov) **16**:372
"Nadpis' nad mogiloy Mikhalevykh v Yakutskom monastyre" (Bestuzhev) **131**:150
Nagerl und Handschuh (Nestroy) **42**:225, 242
Några ord om nejderna, folklynnet och levnadssättet i Saarijärvi socken (Runeberg) **41**:316
A nagyidai czigányok (Arany) **34**:5, 16, 23
The Naiad: A Tale, WIth Other Poems (Reynolds) **146**:166, 172-73, 189-90
"The Nail" (Alarcon)
See "El clavo"
Naimychka (Shevchenko) **54**:383, 387, 392
"Le Nain de Beauvoisine" (Desbordes-Valmore) **97**:14
"The Naive" (Verlaine)
See "Les Ingénus"
Nakanune (Turgenev) **21**:382-83, 385-86, 393-94, 396-97, 399-400, 409-10, 413, 418-19, 426, 432, 434-39, 442-45, 448-49, 452-54; **37**:372, 379, 382, 384-85, 402-03, 407, 411, 428, 442, 444; **122**:249, 251-52, 256, 261, 267, 270-72, 276-77, 288, 292, 315, 320, 343
"Nakanune godovščiny avgusta 1864 g." (Tyutchev) **34**:412
Naked Genius (Horton) **87**:86, 101-02
"The Naked Goddess" (Thomson) **18**:391-92
Nakhlebnik (Turgenev) **21**:428
"Nala and Damayanti" (Zhukovsky) **35**:379
Nalozhnitsa (Baratynsky) **103**:8, 10, 39-44, 46
"Nameless Grave" (Landon) **15**:166
"A Nameless Grave" (Longfellow) **45**:121
"The Nameless Grave" (Moodie) **113**:316
"The Nameless One" (Mangan) **27**:276, 280-81, 287-89, 292, 297-98, 305
"Names upon a Stone" (Kendall) **12**:187, 189
"The Naming of Cuchullin" (Ferguson) **33**:279, 285
"Namouna" (Musset) **7**:255, 259, 264, 267, 275; **150**:268-71, 311, 322, 349
Nance Oldfield (Reade) **74**:265
"Nancy" (Bloomfield) **145**:154
"Nancy Chisholm" (Hogg) **109**:203
"Nancy Collins" (Mackenzie) **41**:189
"Nänie" (Schiller) **166**:95, 98-99
Nannette und Maria (Grabbe) **2**:275-76, 287
"Nanny" (Freneau) **111**:124
"Nanny's Sailor Lad" (Allingham) **25**:8, 17
"Nannys Traum" (Mörike) **201**:270-71
Naobi no mitama (Motoori) **45**:275-76
"Naomi" (Moodie) **14**:231
"Naples" (Pavlova)
See "Neapol"
"Napoleon and his System" (Thackeray) **213**:215
"Napolean's Grave" (Tyutchev) **34**:389
"Napolean's Midnight Review" (Hood) **16**:235
"Napoleón" (Gómez de Avellaneda) **111**:6
"Napoleon" (Lockhart) **6**:309
"Napoléon" (Musset) **150**:309
"Napoleon" (Wergeland) **5**:539
"Napoleon and the British Sailor" (Campbell) **19**:187, 190
"Napoleon at Gotha" (Taylor) **89**:319
"Napoleon at Helena" (Sigourney) **21**:299
Napoléon Bonaparte; ou, Trente ans de l'histoire de France (Dumas) **11**:42, 57, 71; **71**:193
"Napoleon III in Italy" (Barrett Browning) **61**:12

Napoleon III in Italy, and Other Poems (Barrett Browning)
See *Poems before Congress*
Napoléon le petit (Hugo) **3**:262; **161**:189-90
Napoleon oder die hundert Tage (Grabbe) **2**:276-77, 281-82, 284-85, 287-88
Napoléon the Little (Hugo) **189**:267, 273
Nápolyi Endre (Madach) **19**:370
Narbonne (Schiller) **69**:169
Narcisse (Sand) **42**:311
Narcissus (Stagnelius) **61**:248, 265
"The Nard" (Meyer)
See "Die Narde"
"Die Narde" (Meyer) **81**:206
"Narobe Katon" (Preseren) **127**:316
Narodna srbska pjesnarica (Karadzic) **115**:77, 110-11
"Narodnyye knizhki" (Pisarev) **25**:348
Der Narr auf Manegg (Keller) **2**:414
Narraciones inverosimiles (Alarcón)
See *Novelas cortas: Narraciones inverosimiles*
"Narrara Creek" (Kendall) **12**:187, 199
"Narrative" (Yearsley) **174**:331, 334-36
Narrative (Truth)
See *The Narrative of Sojourner Truth*
Narrative (Wordsworth)
See *George and Sarah Green: A Narrative*
"A Narrative of American Slavery" (Brown) **2**:52
The Narrative of Arthur Gordon Pym (Poe)
See *The Narrative of Arthur Gordon Pym, of Nantucket*
The Narrative of Arthur Gordon Pym, of Nantucket (Poe) **1**:499-501, 518, 526, 529; **16**:300, 302, 312-13, 315, 324, 334; **55**:133, 149, 202; **78**:258; **94**:174, 176-88, 192, 195-206, 209-21, 225-28, 230-35, 239-49, 251-53, 255-58, 260-63, 266-76; **117**:197, 205, 224, 335; **211**:326-27, 329-32
Narrative of Events in Vienna, from Latour to Windischgrätz (Auerbach)
See *Tagebuch aus Wien. Von Latour bis auf Windischgrätz*
Narrative of Events Which Have Taken Place in France from the Landing of Napoleon Bonaparte, on the 1st of March, 1815, till the Restoration of Louis XVIII, with an account of the Present State of Society & Public Opinion (Williams) **135**:261, 310-13, 335
A Narrative of Facts (Holcroft)
See *A Narrative of Facts relating to a Prosecution for High Treason*
A Narrative of Facts relating to a Prosecution for High Treason (Holcroft) **85**:194-95, 199, 209, 227, 235
The Narrative of Sojourner Truth (Truth) **94**:288-90, 292, 297-305, 308, 310, 312, 314, 316-24, 330, 333, 337
The Narrative of Sojourner Truth, A Northern Slave Emancipated Frodily Servitude By The State of New York in 1828 (Truth) **94**:301
Narrative of the Earl of Elgin's Mission to China and Japan . . . (Oliphant) **47**:287
Narrative of the Life and Escape of William Wells Brown (Brown)
See *Narrative of William W. Brown, a Fugitive Slave, Written by Himself*
A Narrative of the Life of David Crockett of the State of Tennessee (Crockett) **8**:144-49, 151-55
Narrative of the Life of Frederick Douglass, an American Slave, Written by Himself (Douglass) **7**:120-21, 125, 128-31, 133-39, 141-42; 144-45; **55**:87, 95-119, 121-6, 128; **141**:1-160
Narrative of the Operations of the Right Division of the Army in Upper Canada (Richardson) **55**:344
Narrative of William W. Brown, a Fugitive Slave, Written by Himself (Brown) **2**:46-9, 55; **89**:156, 160-68, 184
Narrative Poems (D'Israeli) **217**:275, 284, 304-6
"Narrative Two" (Crawford) **127**:164
"Die Narrenburg" (Stifter) **41**:335, 366, 279; **198**:261-62, 276
"A narrow Fellow in the Grass" (Dickinson) **77**:129; **171**:101, 174, 207
"A Narrow Girdle of Rough Stones and Crags" (Wordsworth) **111**:348
"The Narrow Way" (Brontë) **4**:46
"Nashi poslali" (Turgenev) **122**:256-57
"Naslazhdaytes: vsyo pokhodit!..." (Baratynsky) **103**:11
"Natal'ya, boyarskaya doch" (Karamzin) **173**:279, 283, 295-96, 313-14, 333, 350-51
Les Natchez (Chateaubriand) **134**:12, 16, 19, 23-25, 27, 47, 76, 81-83, 95, 102, 112, 143
"Nathalie, the Boyar's Daughter" (Karamzin)
See "Natal'ya, boyarskaya doch"
"Nation of London" (De Quincey) **198**:22
National Airs (Moore) **110**:186
National Anti-Slavery Standard (Child)
See *Anti-Slavery Standard*
"National Apostasy" (Keble) **87**:131, 199
"The National Capital, Abraham Lincoln" (Douglass) **7**:126
"National Literature" (Paulding) **2**:531
"National Ode" (Taylor) **89**:296, 326
"National Penitence" (Barbauld)
See "Reasons for National Penitence"
"National Song" (Petofi)
See "Nemzeti dal—Talpra magyar"
"A National Song. The Wind That Sweeps Our Native Sea" (Moodie) **113**:308, 311
Nationalausgabe (Schiller) **166**:170
"Nationalism" (Bellamy) **147**:72-73
"Nationality in Drinks" (Browning) **19**:96
A Nation's Duty in a War for Freedrom (Schleiermacher) **107**:364
"The Nation's First Number" (Mangan) **27**:315
"A Native Georgian" (Longstreet) **159**:151
"Native Moments" (Whitman) **31**:430; **81**:329
"The Nativity" (Manzoni) **29**:253
"Nattergalen" (Andersen) **7**:37; **79**:23, 35, 40, 42, 51-52, 59, 62, 65, 73-74, 76; **214**:39, 55, 57
Nattvardsbarnen (Tegner) **2**:611-14
Die Natur der Dinge (Wieland) **17**:416-18
"Natur und Kunst oder Saturn und Jupiter" (Hölderlin) **16**:162, 173
"De Natura Deorum" (Patmore) **9**:338-39, 360, 365
"Natura Naturans" (Clough) **27**:106-7, 113
"Natura Naturans" (Prescott) **163**:55, 84, 136
The Natural Daughter (Dunlap) **2**:213
Natural Daughter (Goethe)
See *Die Natürliche Tochter*
The Natural Daughter (Robinson) **142**:95, 184-87, 190-92, 226, 241
"The Natural Death of Love" (Crabbe) **26**:100, 109, 111, 147
"The Natural History" (Thoreau) **7**:396
"Natural History Letters" (Clare) **9**:116
The Natural History of Birds (Smith) **115**:126, 211
"The Natural History of German Life" (Eliot) **89**:212, 234, 260, 266; **118**:53-4, 189; **183**:133
Natural History of Intellect and Other Papers (Emerson) **38**:172; **98**:55-60
"Natural History of Massachusetts" (Thoreau) **138**:83, 119, 127, 154; **207**:194-96, 199, 248, 264
"Natural History of the Intellect" (Emerson) **1**:302; **38**:142, 147, 180; **98**:7-8, 190
"The Natural History of the Vale of Belvoir" (Crabbe) **121**:44
The Natural History Prose Writings of John Clare (Clare) **86**:129, 172
Natural Law (Hegel) **151**:317
"Natural Science and Spirit World" (Engels) **85**:40
Natural Selection (Darwin)
See *On the Origin of Species by Means of Natural Selection or the Preservation of Favoured Races in the Struggle for Life*
The Natural Son (Cumberland) **167**:140, 149-50, 157, 180, 191
"Naturam furca expellas" (Arany) **34**:21
"Nature" (Alcott) **1**:23
"Nature" (Emerson) **98**:109, 143-46
"Nature" (Longfellow) **2**:488
"Nature" (Mill) **11**:359, 379; **179**:210-11, 287, 292, 295, 327-34, 338
"Nature" (Turgenev) **21**:431
"Nature" (Very) **9**:376, 380, 387
Nature (Emerson) **1**:275, 285, 287, 293, 300-01, 305-06, 309; **38**:143, 146, 169, 171, 173-74, 176-78, 180-81, 183, 186, 194-200, 202, 208-10; **98**:3, 7, 9, 17, 21, 24-7, 32, 35, 47, 57-9, 63, 65, 99, 107, 109, 111-12, 115-16, 126, 131-33, 160, 189
"Nature II" (Emerson) **38**:184
"Nature and Art" (Newman) **38**:343
Nature and Art (Inchbald) **62**:132-6, 139-40, 144, 161, 180
"The Nature and Artifice of Toryism" (Brackenridge) **7**:44
"Nature and Books" (Jefferies) **47**:143
Nature and Eternity (Jefferies) **47**:114
Nature and Human Nature (Haliburton) **15**:124-27, 131, 136, 145; **149**:318, 344-49
"Nature as Discipline" (Emerson) **1**:295, 309
La Nature et l'art (Charriere) **66**:126
"Nature in the Louvre" (Jefferies) **47**:94, 101, 138
"Nature Intelligible" (Very) **9**:390
"Nature is not what you think" (Tyutchev)
See "Ne to, chto mnite vy, priroda"
"Nature morte" (Corbière) **43**:28
"Nature Myths" (Symonds) **34**:336
Nature near London (Jefferies) **47**:112, 133-36, 138
The Nature of Evil, Considered in a Letter to the Reverend Edward Beecher, D.D., Author of "The Conflict of the Ages" (James) **53**:184, 235
"The Nature of Faith in Relation to Reason" (Newman) **38**:307; **99**:300
"The Nature of Poetry" (Dobell) **43**:60-1, 66-7
"The Nature of Slavery" (Douglass) **141**:157
"Nature on the Roof" (Jefferies) **47**:137
"Nature Teaches Us of Time and Its Duration" (Very) **9**:388
Nature, the Utility of Religion, and Theism (Mill) **11**:358, 365; **58**:338
"Nature-Notes 1877-'81" (Whitman) **81**:369-70
"Nature's Beauty" (Sigourney) **21**:293
"Nature's Help for the Soul" (Very) **9**:387
Naturgeschichte der Philisters (Brentano) **191**:90
Die Natürliche Tochter (Goethe) **4**:167, 222
Natur-Philosophie (Schelling) **30**:122, 124
"The Naughty Boy" (Andersen) **79**:25, 88; **214**:45, 48, 52
"The Naughty Child" (Andersen)
See "The Naughty Boy"
Naval History of the United States (Cooper) **54**:256
La navette (Becque) **3**:15-16
"La navicella Greca" (Solomos) **15**:405
"Navigation" (Mickiewicz)
See "Żegluga"
"Nay Tell Me Not Today the Publish'd Shame" (Whitman) **31**:435
"Nayezdy" (Bestuzhev) **131**:167, 176, 208
Nazar Stodolja (Shevchenko) **54**:365, 367-8, 381, 391
"Le Nazaréen" (Leconte de Lisle) **29**:231
The Nazarene; or, The Last of the Washingtons: A Revelation of

Philadelphia, New York, and Washington, in the Year 1844 (Lippard) **198**:184, 187, 229
"Ne bod'mo šalobarde! Moskvičanov" (Preseren) **127**:314
"N'e de morte" (Castro) **78**:8
"Ne Plus Ultra" (Coleridge) **231**:94
"Ne podrazhay: svoeobrazen genity..." (Baratynsky) **103**:3
"Ne raz seba ia voproshaiu strogo" (Pavlova) **138**:15
Ne tak zhiví kak khóchetsya (Ostrovsky) **30**:102; **57**:197-8, 201-2, 220
"Ne to, chto mnite vy, priroda" (Tyutchev) **34**:398
Ne v svoi sani ne sadis! (Ostrovsky) **30**:96, 101, 110, 113; **57**:198, 201, 208-9
"Ne ver, ne ver poetu, deva" (Tyutchev) **34**:400, 404
Ne vse kotu maslenitsa (Ostrovsky) **30**:104, 112
"Neal Malone" (Carleton) **3**:89, 93
Neal Malone (Carleton) **199**:10, 16
"Neapol" (Pavlova) **138**:53-54
"Near Hastings" (Dutt) **29**:122
"Near the camp stood a handsome youth" (Bestuzhev)
See "Blliz stana yunosha prekrasnyy . . ."
"A Nearness to Tremendousness" (Dickinson) **21**:77
"Die Nebensonnen" (Muller) **73**:366, 393, 396
!Nebo bleshchet biryuzoyu! (Pavlova) **138**:4
The Nebraska Question. Some Thoughts on the New Assault upon Freedom in America, and The General State of the Country in Relation Thereunto, Set Forth in a Discourse Preached at the Music Hall, in Boston, on Monday, Feb. 12, 1 (Parker) **186**:169
"Nebuchadnezzar's Dream" (Keats) **73**:333
"Necedad yanqui" (Silva) **114**:263-64
The Necessity of Atheism (Shelley) **18**:374; **175**:277, 325
"The Necessity of Kindergarten Culture in our Systems of Public Instruction" (Peabody) **169**:150
"Necessity of Religion, Especially in Adversity" (Murray) **63**:207
"Nechto o gluptsakh" (Bestuzhev) **131**:168
"Nechto o naukakh, isskustvakh i prosveshchenii" (Karamzin) **173**:309, 323-25
"The Neckan" (Arnold) **6**:66
"The Necklace" (Maupassant)
See "La parure"
"Necrologia. Exequias del Conde de Campo Alange" (Larra) **130**:238, 278
Necrology (Liszt) **199**:303-4
"Nečto o naukax, iskusstvax, i prosveščenii" (Karamzin) **3**:284, 289
"Ned Bratts" (Browning) **19**:117
"Ned Connor" (Harpur) **114**:102, 150
"Ned Mc'eown" (Carleton) **199**:59
"Ned M'Keown" (Carleton) **3**:92
Ned Myers (Cooper) **54**:274
"Nedonosok" (Baratynsky) **103**:16, 21
"Needlework" (Tonna) **135**:217
"Néférou-Ra" (Leconte de Lisle) **29**:215
Die Negersklaven (Kotzebue) **25**:141, 143, 145
"Neglect of Divine Calls and Warnings" (Newman) **38**:304, 309
"Negra Sombra" (Castro) **78**:24
"Une négresse par le démon secouée" (Mallarmé) **41**:241, 250, 280
"The Negro Boy's Lament" (Opie) **65**:175
The Negro Boy's Petition (More) **141**:268
"The Negro Boy's Tale" (Opie) **65**:156
The Negro in the American Rebellion: His Heroism and His Fidelity (Brown) **2**:48, 51-53; **89**:143
The Negro in the Rebellion (Brown)
See *The Negro in the American Rebellion: His Heroism and His Fidelity*
The Negro of Peter the Great (Pushkin)
See *Arap Petra Velikogo*
Negro Slavery Described By a Negro: Being the Narrative of Ashton Warner, a Native of St. Vincent's (Moodie) **113**:310
The Negro Slaves (Kotzebue)
See *Die Negersklaven*
"Negro Speculation" (Horton) **87**:102
"The Negroe Girl" (Robinson) **142**:136-37, 249
"A négy ökrös szekér" (Petofi) **21**:264
"La neige" (Vigny) **7**:474; **102**:335, 366-67
"The Neighbour-in-Law" (Child) **6**:201
The Neighbours: A Story of Every-Day Life (Bremer)
See *Grannarne*
"Neighbours on the Green" (Oliphant) **61**:217
"Neihausen Castle" (Bestuzhev)
See "Zamok Neigauzen"
"Neiztrohnjeno srce" (Preseren) **127**:298
Nekam berit (Smolenskin) **30**:192, 195
"Nekrescenyj pop" (Leskov) **174**:5, 40, 46
Nekuda (Leskov) **25**:225, 237, 250-53; **174**:9-11, 20, 52, 58, 60-63, 65, 90, 123
"Nell and I" (Foster) **26**:285
Nell Cook (Barham) **77**:9, 36
Nell Gwynne (Jerrold) **2**:401
"Nelle nozze della sorella Paolina" (Leopardi) **129**:219, 327-32, 334-35
"Nelly Bly" (Foster) **26**:287, 291
"Nelly Was a Lady" (Foster) **26**:286, 291
"Nem kell dér" (Arany) **34**:21
Nemesis of Faith (Froude) **43**:177, 192-93, 195, 202, 204, 208-09, 217
"A nemzetgyüléshez" (Petofi) **21**:279
"A nemzethez" (Petofi) **21**:280
"Nemzeti dal—Talpra magyar" (Petofi) **21**:280, 286
"Le nénuphar blanc" (Mallarmé) **4**:376; **41**:279-80; **210**:163, 203-4
"Nénuphar blanc" (Mallarmé)
See "Le nénuphar blanc"
"Neobyknovennaya istoriya" (Goncharov) **1**:367
"The Neophytes" (Shevchenko) **54**:390, 397
"Neostorožnost" (Turgenev) **122**:268
Nepenthe (Darley) **2**:125-29, 131-34
"Neptune's Shore" (Woolson) **82**:276, 291
Nerina (Leopardi) **129**:304
"The Nervous Man" (Whittier) **59**:367
"Nerwy" (Norwid) **17**:372, 374
"Nesčastnaja" (Turgenev)
See "Neschastnaya"
"Neschastnaia" (Turgenev)
See "Neschastnaya"
"Neschastnaya" (Turgenev) **21**:415, 437, 440-41, 451; **122**:243, 245, 265, 267, 279, 364
"Nesmertel' nyj Golovan" (Leskov) **25**:239
Nesmertel'nyj Golovan: iz rasskazov o trex pravednikax (Leskov) **174**:37, 72, 74, 76-79
A Nest of Gentlefolk (Turgenev)
See *Dvoryanskoe gnezdo*
The Nest of Gentlefolk (Turgenev)
See *Dvoryanskoe gnezdo*
"The Nest of Nightingales" (Gautier) **1**:347
"A Nest of Nightingales" (O'Brien) **21**:236
Nest of Noblemen (Turgenev)
See *Dvoryanskoe gnezdo*
Nest of the Gentry (Turgenev)
See *Dvoryanskoe gnezdo*
"Nesting Time" (Lampman) **25**:210; **194**:140
"Nests" (Silva)
See "Nidos"
"Nesžastnye" (Nekrasov) **11**:418
"Nesžataja polosa" (Nekrasov) **11**:412-13
Netherlands (Schiller)
See *The History of the Revolt of the Netherlands*
Netley Abbey (Barham) **77**:9, 37
Das Neue (Klopstock) **225**:299
Der neue Amadis (Wieland) **17**:396, 399, 424
Die neue Arria (Klinger) **1**:429
Neue Briefe Beethovens, 1867 (Beethoven) **227**:9-10
Der Neue Don Quixote (Ludwig) **4**:356
Neue Erfindung (Claudius) **75**:193
Neue Gedichte (Heine) **4**:249; **54**:345; **147**:149, 193-94, 196-98
Der neue Hiob (Sacher-Masoch) **31**:287
"Das neue Jahrhundert" (Klopstock) **225**:324
Das neue Jahrhundert (Kotzebue) **25**:147
"Neue Liebe" (Mörike) **10**:455; **201**:281
Die neue romantische Poesie in Deutschland (Eichendorff) **225**:8
Die Neue Undine (Ludwig) **4**:356
Neuer Frühling (Heine) **4**:259
Neues Leben (Auerbach) **171**:17, 19
"Der Neugierige" (Muller) **73**:364, 370-71, 374
"Neurosis" (Casal) **131**:274
La neuvaine de la chandeleur (Nodier) **19**:378, 380, 384
"Die Neve Melusine" (Goethe) **4**:194
"Never Bet the Devil Your Head" (Poe) **16**:323-24
"Never Mind" (Harpur) **114**:101
"Never Return" (Milnes) **61**:136
"Nevermore" (Verlaine) **230**:173, 190, 193-95, 197, 200
"The 'Nevers' of Poetry" (Harpur) **114**:105, 117, 144
Nevinnye razskazy (Saltykov) **16**:343, 368
"Nevinnyi Prudentsii" (Leskov)
See "Nevinnyj Prudencij"
Nevinnyi Prudentsii (Leskov) **174**:88
"Nevinnyj Prudencij" (Leskov) **25**:245
"Nevskij Avenue" (Gogol) **5**:209, 219, 227, 232, 241, 250, 252, 255; **31**:122
"Nevsky Prospect" (Gogol)
See "Nevsky Prospekt"
"Nevsky Prospekt" (Gogol) **5**:209, 219, 227, 232, 241, 250, 252, 255; **31**:122; **162**:7, 18, 52-53, 55, 61, 82-83, 86, 96, 128, 130
"Nevyrazimoe" (Zhukovsky) **35**:403
"The New Adam and Eve" (Hawthorne) **2**:325; **10**:290
"The New Age" (Arnold) **6**:51
"The New Age; or, Truth Triumphant" (Freneau) **1**:320; **111**:110
New and Old (Symonds) **34**:323
"The New and the Old" (Bryant) **6**:165; **46**:48
The New Arabian Nights (Stevenson) **14**:312, 335; **193**:203-4, 210, 215, 221-22, 250-51, 254-58, 294, 313-14, 317-18, 321
The New Belfry of Christ Church, Oxford (Dodgson) **139**:35
"The New Birth" (Very) **9**:375, 378, 390
"The New Body" (Very) **9**:394
A New Canto (Lamb) **38**:258-60
New Churches Considered with Respect to the Opportunities They Afford for the Encouragement of Painting (Haydon) **146**:143
"The New Colossus" (Lazarus) **8**:416, 420, 427; **109**:289, 300, 306-07, 310, 318, 334-35, 337-40, 345, 347, 349
New Connecticut (Alcott) **167**:56, 72
"The New Convert" (Cowper) **8**:132; **94**:72-3
"The New Covenant" (Paine) **62**:324
The New Crime against Humanity. A Sermon, Preached at the Music Hall, in Boston, on Sunday, June 4, 1854 (Parker) **186**:130, 170
"The New Dodo" (Beddoes) **154**:12
A New Drama (Tamayo y Baus)
See *Un drama nuevo*
The New Egypt (Adams) **33**:8, 18
New Elements of Geometry (Smith) **187**:335
A New England Girlhood, Outlined from Memory (Larcom) **179**:171, 177-82, 185-87, 189-91, 193-95
"A New England Legend" (Whittier) **59**:360
The New England Primer, Amended and Improved . . . (Webster) **30**:409

"New England Reformers" (Emerson) **38**:157; **98**:112, 115, 117
"A New England Sketch" (Stowe) **3**:562
New England Tragedies (Longfellow) **2**:484, 487, 496-98; **45**:113, 142, 149-50, 159, 165
"New England Two Centuries Ago" (Lowell) **2**:509; **90**:195
"New Enigmas" (Rossetti) **66**:341
"The New Ezekiel" (Lazarus) **8**:428; **109**:312, 338, 343
"New Fables" (Krasicki)
See *Bajki nowe*
New Fairy Tales and Stories (Andersen)
See *Nye Eventyr og Historier*
"New feet within by garden go" (Dickinson) **171**:87
"A New Forest Ballad" (Kingsley) **35**:218
A New French and English Dictionary (Cobbett) **49**:160
The New Gown (More) **141**:192
"New Guinea Converts" (Adams) **33**:18
The New Haymarket Spring Meeting (Planché) **42**:291
A New Home (Kirkland)
See *A New Home—Who'll Follow?*
A New Home—Who'll Follow? (Kirkland) **85**:251, 255-56, 259-61, 263, 265, 267-70, 274-89, 291, 293, 295-301
The New Housekeeper's Manual (Beecher) **30**:15
The New Industrial World (Fourier)
See *Le Nouveau Monde industriel et sociétaire*
"New Jerusalem and Its Citizens" (Rossetti) **50**:285
The New Justine (Sade)
See *La nouvelle Justine*
"The New Kite" (Horne) **127**:264
"The New Laocoon" (Arnold) **6**:51
New Leaves (Castro)
See *Follas novas*
A New Lesson for the Day (Parker) **186**:174
New Letters (Southey) **97**:270, 276, 278-79, 290
New Letters and Memorials of Jane Welsh Carlyle (Carlyle) **181**:97, 99, 124-25, 137
New Letters of James Russell Lowell (Lowell) **90**:222
"The New Locksley Hall: 'Forty Years After'" (Adams) **33**:18
"New Love New Life" (Levy) **59**:96
The New Magdalen (Collins) **1**:176, 180, 182-83; **93**:5, 38
"The New Man" (Very) **9**:378, 382, 397
The New Maternity Ward (Andersen) **79**:15-17
"A New Method of Evaluation of p" (Dodgson) **139**:6
"New Moon" (Cooke) **110**:9
"New Morality" (Coleridge) **111**:353
"New Morality" (Keats) **73**:316
The New Nation (Bellamy) **147**:22
"New Philosophy Scrapbook" (Cranch) **115**:54
New Pilgrim's Progress; or, A Christian's Painful Passage from theTown of Middle Class to the Golden City (Jefferies) **47**:93
The New Planet; or, Harlequin out of Place (Planché) **42**:290
The New Pleasing Instructor; or, Young Lady's Guide to Virtue and Happiness (Tenney) **122**:210
New Poems (Arnold) **6**:37; **29**:26; **89**:46, 51
New Poems (Coleridge) **90**:32
New Poems (Heine)
See *Neue Gedichte*
New Poems (Rossetti) **2**:563-64; **186**:267, 294, 309
New Poems and Variant Readings (Stevenson) **5**:427
New Poems by George Crabbe (Crabbe) **26**:139; **121**:13
New Poetical Meditations (Lamartine) **11**:245, 283
"The New Poor Laws" (Barnes) **75**:43-4, 101, 103
"The New Proserpine" (Blind) **202**:57
"New Readings" (Hopkins) **189**:142
"New School" (Cranch) **115**:40
"The New School of American Fiction" (Levy) **59**:110; **203**:356
The New Schoolma'am; or, A Summer in North Sparta (Alger) **83**:116, 142
"A New Sin" (Webster) **230**:238
"The New Sinai" (Clough) **27**:41, 77, 106
"The New Sinai" (Prescott) **163**:6
"The New Sirens" (Arnold) **6**:71; **126**:111; **218**:162, 274
"The New South" (Lanier) **6**:245, 256, 260, 263; **118**:206, 218, 230
A New Spirit of the Age (Horne) **127**:238, 263, 285, 287
New Stories (Andersen)
See *Eventyr, fortalte for bøorn*
New Tales (Opie) **65**:171, 174, 179, 197-8
"New Testament Jews" (Leskov)
See "Novozavetnye evrei"
The New Timon (Bulwer-Lytton) **1**:141-42
"New Variations on an Old Theme" (Herzen) **61**:102
New Views of Christianity Socity and the Church (Brownson) **50**:47
"New Wife and the Old" (Whittier) **8**:487, 508-09, 528; **59**:350
The New World: A Democratic Poem (Jones) **222**:126, 130-36, 142
The New Woman: In Haste and at Leisure (Linton) **41**:161, 164
"The New World" (Very) **9**:378, 397
"The New Writing" (Preseren)
See "Nova pisarija"
"The New Year" (Whittier) **8**:524
"The New Year—Rosh Hashanah, 5643" (Lazarus) **8**:420, 427; **109**:338
"A New Year's Blessing" (Alcott) **83**:5
"A New Year's Burden" (Rossetti) **4**:491
"New Year's Day" (Sedgwick) **19**:428, 444-45
"New Year's Eve" (Lamb) **10**:415; **113**:217, 235-36, 248-49, 251-52
"New Year's Eve" (Lampman) **25**:199, 201, 209; **194**:24
"New Year's Eve" (Landon) **15**:166
New Year's Eve or A Brief Glance at Christianity and History (Grundtvig)
See *Nytaarsnat eller Blik paa Kristendom og Historie*
"A New Year's Lay" (Mangan) **27**:296
New Year's Morn (Grundtvig)
See *Nyaars-Morgen*
New York: Its Upper Ten and Lower Million (Lippard) **198**:125, 140, 169, 197-203, 230, 239, 242, 245-48
The New Zealander (Trollope) **215**:264, 344
"The New Zealot to the Sun" (Melville) **29**:380
"Newborn Death" (Rossetti) **4**:491
"The New-Born Star" (Beddoes) **154**:53
The Newcomes: Memoirs of a Most Respectable Family (Thackeray) **5**:454-57, 459-61, 465-66, 472, 476, 478, 484, 488, 497-505; **14**:397, 406, 434; **43**:356, 389; **213**:187, 194, 196-98, 204, 207-10, 214, 267, 285, 288, 300-301, 306-7, 328-29, 333
The Newcomes: Memoirs of Most Respectable Family (Thackeray) **169**:222, 231, 247
A New-England Tale; or, Sketches of New-England Character and Manners (Sedgwick) **19**:424-25, 427, 430, 439, 442, 447, 450; **98**:296, 307, 321, 326, 334, 342
"News from Nowhere" (Morris) **4**:425, 436, 439-41, 445-46
"News from Pannonia" (Allingham) **25**:11
News from Parnassus (Murphy) **229**:234
"News from the Farm" (Bloomfield) **145**:134-35
News of the Night; or, A Trip to Niagara (Bird) **1**:89, 90, 92-93
"Newscarrier's Address" (Trumbull) **30**:375
The News-paper (Crabbe) **26**:78-9, 81, 110, 132; **121**:15, 18, 21, 23, 26, 83, 89
Newstead Abbey (Irving) **2**:373
Newton Forster (Marryat) **3**:317
Next Door Neighbours (Inchbald) **62**:144-6, 149
"Nezakonska mati" (Preseren) **127**:292, 298
"Nezhnost' druzhby v nizkom sostoianii" (Karamzin) **173**:309
"N'hay peor meiga qu'un-ha gran pena" (Castro) **78**:7
Ni jamais ni toujours (Kock) **16**:246-47
"Niágara" (Heredia) **209**:118-20, 122, 125-27, 129, 131-35, 138, 140-44, 149-54, 161, 164
"Niagara" (Lenau) **16**:269, 283
"Niagara" (Neal) **161**:297
"Niagara" (Sigourney) **21**:296, 299; **87**:326, 333-34
"Niagara" (Willis) **194**:282, 285
"A Niagara Landscape" (Lampman) **25**:210
Die Nibelungen (Hebbel) **43**:230, 234-35, 240, 242-44, 246, 261, 276, 278, 297, 300
Nibelungen-Lied (Fouqué) **2**:265
The Nibelungs (Hebbel)
See *Die Nibelungen*
The Nibelung's Ring (Wagner)
See *Der Ring des Nibelungen*
Nice Wives (Alcott)
See *Little Women; or, Meg, Jo, Beth and Amy*
Nicholas Nickleby (Dickens)
See *The Life and Adventures of Nicholas Nickleby*
"Nick" (Rossetti) **186**:232-33, 264-65
Nick of the Woods; or, The Jibbenainosay (Bird) **197**:3-4, 6-9, 11-12, 14, 19-24, 29, 31-38, 43, 45-46, 48-49, 51, 53-59, 61, 64-71, 73-75, 109, 111, 113-14, 117-18
Nick of the Woods; or, The Jobbenainosay (Bird) **1**:85-86, 88-89, 91-92
Nickleby (Dickens)
See *The Life and Adventures of Nicholas Nickleby*
"Nicolas Flamel" (Nerval) **1**:484
"Le Nid d'hirondelles" (Desbordes-Valmore) **97**:12
"Le Nid solitaire" (Desbordes-Valmore) **97**:28
"Nidos" (Silva) **114**:316
Nieboska komedyia (Krasiński) **4**:301
Niels Lyhne (Jacobsen) **34**:142-47, 150-58, 160-62, 166-68
Niera Baranoff (Sacher-Masoch) **31**:302
Nieve (Casal) **131**:235-36, 255-58, 264-65, 268-70
Niewola (Norwid) **17**:369, 377
Nigel (Scott)
See *The Fortunes of Nigel*
"Nigger Book" (Rimbaud) **4**:456
The Nigger of Peter the Great (Pushkin)
See *Arap Petra Velikogo*
"Night" (Blake) **13**:181, 220-21; **37**:3, 6, 9, 13-14, 37, 40, 54, 62, 64, 66, 69, 82, 84, 92
"Night" (Brontë) **71**:106
"Night" (Browning) **79**:94, 101, 153
"Night" (Hugo) **3**:262
"Night" (Lampman) **25**:175, 209, 217; **194**:43, 52
"Night" (Lanier) **6**:237
"Night" (Thomson) **18**:418
"Night" (Very) **9**:393
"Night and Day" (Lanier) **6**:237; **118**:234, 240
Night and Day (Kivi)
See *Yö ja päivä*
"Night and Morning" (Browning) **79**:94, 101
Night and Morning (Bulwer-Lytton) **1**:140, 145, 150; **45**:19, 22, 69
"Night and the Merry Man" (Barrett Browning) **1**:126
"Night and the Soul" (Cranch) **115**:5
"A Night at Sea" (Griffin) **7**:215

"A Night at the Ugly Man's" (Hooper) **177**:175
"Night Effect" (Verlaine)
See "Effet de nuit"
A Night in Roskilde (Andersen) **79**:14
"The Night Journey of a River" (Bryant) **6**:165; **46**:38-9
"The Night Mare or Superstitions Dream" (Clare) **86**:113
"A Night of Don Juan" (Flaubert) **179**:10
"Night of Hell" (Rimbaud)
See "Nuit de l'enfer"
"A Night of Storm" (Lampman) **25**:188, 209-10; **194**:9
"The Night of Taras" (Shevchenko)
See "Tarasova nic"
"A Night of Terror" (Maginn) **8**:440
"Night on Board Ship" (Bestuzhev)
See "Noch' na korable"
"A Night on Salisbury Plain" (Wordsworth) **111**:265-68
"A Night on Terrapin Rocks" (Bird) **197**:45, 49
"Night on the Prairies" (Whitman) **4**:577
"Night Owls" (Leskov)
See "Polunoščniki"
Night Pieces (Hoffmann)
See *Nachtstücke*
Night Pieces (Schumann)
See *Nachtstücke*
Night Pieces after the Manner of Callot (Hoffmann)
See *Fantasiestücke in Callots Manier*
"A Night Scene" (Ridge) **82**:182, 184
"Night Sketches" (Hawthorne) **23**:204; **39**:229
"Night Sounds" (Meyer)
See "Nachtgeräusche"
"Night Thoughts" (Heine)
See "Nachtgedanken"
"Night. To Stella" (Yearsley) **174**:296, 299, 305
The Night Watches (Bonaventura)
See *Nachtwachen*
A Night with the National Guard (Scribe)
See *Encore une nuit de la Garde Nationale; ou, Le poste de la barrière*
"The Nightingale" (Andersen)
See "Nattergalen"
"The Nightingale" (Coleridge) **9**:131, 132, 150; **99**:2, 66; **111**:200, 307, 317, 358; **197**:211, 215; **231**:71, 76-77, 113, 130, 132, 134, 156
"Nightingale" (Keats)
See "Ode to a Nightingale"
"The Nightingale" (Verlaine)
See "Le Rossignol"
"The Nightingale" (Wordsworth) **12**:387
The Nightingale (Robertson) **35**:333, 335, 354, 356, 361, 363, 369
"The Nightingale and Glow-worm" (Cowper) **94**:121
The Nightingale and Other Tales (Andersen)
See *Eventyr, fortalte for børn*
"The nightingale and the cuckoo" (Pushkin)
See "Solovei i Kukushka"
"The Nightingale and the Rose" (Crawford) **127**:187-88
"The Nightingale in a Dream" (Derzhavin) **215**:19, 35
"Nightingale Ode" (Keats)
See "Ode to a Nightingale"
"The Nightingales" (Krylov) **1**:435
"The Nightingales Nest" (Clare) **9**:105; **86**:144
"A Nightmare" (Rossetti) **186**:296-97
"A Night-Piece" (Wordsworth) **12**:446, 451; **166**:257, 259-61
"The Nights" (Musset)
See "Les nuits"
A Night's Adventure (Robertson) **35**:354
"Nights at Home" (Silva)
See "Las noches del hogar"
"The Nights in the Mountains" (Isaacs)
See "Las noches en la montaña"
"A Night's Lodging" (Hugo) **3**:262
"Nights of Jealousy" (Runeberg)
See "Svartsjukans nätter"
"The Nights of Ramazan" (Nerval)
See "Les nuits de Ramazan"
"A Night's Work" (Gaskell)
See "A Dark Night's Work"
Nigorie (Ichiyō) **49**:331, 336-37, 345-48, 351, 353-54
"Nihilismo" (Casal) **131**:274
Nikita Gaidai (Shevchenko)
See *Nikita Hayday*
Nikita Hayday (Shevchenko) **54**:367, 386, 391
"The Nile" (Hunt) **70**:263
The Nile Basin (Burton) **42**:41
"Nima" (Isaacs) **70**:304, 308
"Nimmersatte Liebe" (Mörike) **201**:279
"N'importe où hors du monde" (Baudelaire) **155**:66
"Nimuë" (Tennyson)
See "Enid and Nimuë"
Nina (Bremer) **11**:20, 34-35
Nina Balatka: The Story of a Maiden of Prague (Trollope) **101**:313, 334; **215**:282, 299
La Nina de Guatemala (Martí) **63**:104
"Nina Replies" (Rimbaud)
See "Les reparties de Nina"
"Nina's Replies" (Rimbaud)
See "Les reparties de Nina"
"9 from 8" (Lanier) **118**:227-28
986 (Dickinson) **77**:129, 173
978 (Dickinson) **77**:121
960 (Dickinson) **77**:118
930 (Dickinson) **77**:122-24
922 (Dickinson) **77**:68
1994 (Hölderlin)
See *Hyperion, Empedokles, Aufsätze und Übertragungen*
1962 (Dickinson) **77**:162
"Nineteenth Century Scholastics" (Pisarev)
See "Sxolastiki xix veka"
"19th March 1823" (Zhukovsky) **35**:381
"A XIX század koltöi" (Petofi) **21**:264
"Nineteenth-Century Poets" (Petofi)
See "A XIX század koltöi"
98 (Dickinson) **77**:120, 163
Ninety-Three (Hugo)
See *Quatre-vingt treize*
"Ninguna diga queén es, que sus obras lo dirán" (Lizardi) **30**:67
El niño de la bola (Alarcon) **1**:12-15; **219**:3, 12, 19-20
"Ninth Letter" (Schiller) **166**:98
Ninth Symphony (Beethoven) **227**:4, 17, 20, 33
"Niobé" (Barbey d'Aurevilly) **213**:41-42
"Niobé" (Leconte de Lisle) **29**:222, 224-25, 238, 245-46
"Nirvâna" (Lanier) **6**:236, 238, 270; **118**:235
"Nise no en" (Ueda Akinari) **131**:20-22, 52-53, 56
"Nissen hos Spekhøkeren" (Andersen) **79**:28, 55, 63, 73; **214**:57-60, 77
"Die Nixe" (Pavlova) **138**:12
"Nixe Binsefus" (Mörike) **201**:298
"Nixe Binsefuss" (Mörike) **10**:455
"The Nixy's Chord" (Boyesen) **135**:15, 33-34
No (Cooke) **110**:50, 66
"No Compromise With Slavery" (Garrison) **149**:256
"No Coward Soul Is Mine" (Brontë) **16**:70, 74, 86, 88; **35**:147
"No doubt 'twere Heresy, or something worse" (Coleridge) **90**:33
No Entr'acte Music (Liszt) **199**:305
No hay mal que por bien no venga (Tamayo y Baus) **1**:569
"No Man Saw Awe, Nor to His House" (Dickinson) **21**:83
No más mostrador (Larra) **17**:267, 273-74, 279; **130**:228
No más mostrator (Larra)
See *No más mostrador*
"No Name" (Gordon) **21**:161, 164, 166, 176
No Name (Collins) **1**:174-75, 180, 182, 185, 187; **18**:63-6; **93**:5, 7, 11-12, 19-23, 34, 36-8, 44, 46, 50-3, 61-3, 65-6
"No Novyi god" (Derzhavin) **215**:53
No One's Enemy but His Own. A Comedy in Three Acts. As it Was Intended to be Acted at the Theatre-Royal in Covent-Garden (Murphy) **229**:234
"No Poet Is Bill" (Kendall) **12**:194
"A nő teremtése" (Madach) **19**:369
"No, Thank You, John!" (Rossetti) **66**:331; **186**:262
No Thoroughfare (Collins) **1**:185
No Trifling with Love (Musset)
See *On ne badine pas avec l'amour*
No Way Out (Leskov)
See *Nekuda*
"No Worst, There Is None" (Hopkins) **17**:261; **189**:28, 35, 48, 77, 84, 90, 146
"Noah's Ark" (Muller) **73**:353
Noah's Warning over Methuselah's Grave (Brontë) **109**:4, 14
Le Noble (Charriere) **66**:121-2, 172-6, 178
"Noble and Touching Ramblings beneath the Moon" (Laforgue)
See "Nobles et touchantes divagations sous la Lune"
The Noble Heart: A Tragedy, in Three Acts (Lewes) **25**:284, 298-99; **215**:84
The Noble Jilt (Trollope) **101**:266
A Noble Life (Craik) **38**:107, 116
The Noble Peasant (Holcroft) **85**:192
"The Noble Savage" (Dickens) **217**:245
"Noble Sisters" (Rossetti) **2**:575; **66**:302, 312, 352
The Nobleman (Charriere)
See *Le Noble*
"The Nobleman" (Derzhavin)
See "Vel'mozh"
A Nobleman's Nest (Turgenev)
See *Dvoryanskoe gnezdo*
"The Nobleman's Wedding" (Allingham) **25**:7-8, 17
Noblemen's Home (Turgenev)
See *Dvoryanskoe gnezdo*
"The Nobler Lover" (Lowell) **2**:512
"Nobles et touchantes divagations sous la Lune" (Laforgue) **221**:86, 89
Nobody (Warner) **31**:338
"Noč pered roždestvom" (Gogol) **5**:217, 231; **162**:17, 26, 62, 70, 92, 95, 121, 128
Noc tysiączna druga (Norwid) **17**:367
Les Noces d'Hérodiade (Mallarmé)
See *Hérodiade*
"Noch einmal" (Meyer) **81**:206
"Noch einmal in Gastein" (Grillparzer) **102**:175
"Noch' na korable" (Bestuzhev) **131**:185
"La Noche de difuntos" (Bécquer) **106**:96
"La Nochebuena de 1836" (Larra) **17**:276-78, 285; **130**:209, 211, 213, 237-38, 257-65, 274-75, 278-79, 281-86
"Las noches del hogar" (Silva) **114**:316
"Las noches en la montaña" (Isaacs) **70**:309
Noches tristes y día alegre (Lizardi) **30**:67, 70-73
"Nochnoi smotr" (Zhukovsky) **35**:398
"Noctes" (Willis) **194**:298
Noctes Ambrosianae (Wilson) **5**:553-57, 559-60, 562-63, 565-69
Noctes Ambrosiannae (Lockhart) **6**:305
"Nocturnal Boat" (Meyer)
See "Im Spätboot"
"Nocturnal Litanies" (Laforgue)
See "Litanies nocturnes"
"Nocturnal Sketch" (Hood) **16**:236
"Nocturnal Song of a Wandering Shepherd in Asia" (Leopardi)
See "Canto notturno di un pastore errante dell'Asia"
"Nocturne" (Blind) **202**:10, 14-15, 17, 29-30
"Nocturne" (Silva)
See "Nocturno III"
"Nocturne II" (Desbordes-Valmore) **97**:5

"Nocturne of a Wandering Shepherd in Asia" (Leopardi)
See "Canto notturno di un pastore errante dell'Asia"
"Nocturne parisien" (Verlaine) **2**:624; **230**:171-72, 195
"Nocturne vulgaire" (Rimbaud) **4**:487; **35**:323; **82**:232-33, 248; **227**:243, 309
"Nocturno III" (Silva) **114**:261-62, 267, 270, 294-97, 299-304
"Noël résigné" (Laforgue) **221**:87
"Noël sceptique" (Laforgue) **221**:87
"Noget" (Andersen) **79**:75, 77; **214**:42
"The Noise of Bars . . ." (Verlaine)
See "Le Bruit des cabarets . . ."
"A Noiseless Patient Spider" (Whitman) **31**:379, 442; **81**:309; **205**:341
"Nola" (Isaacs) **70**:310
Noli me tangere (Rizal) **27**:407-09, 411, 415-16, 419-29, 431-32
Nolten the Painter (Mörike)
See *Maler Nolten: Novelle in zwei Theilen*
"Nominalist" (Emerson) **98**:143-45
"Nominalist and Realist" (Emerson) **38**:173, 208; **98**:65, 69, 71, 151
"Nomography" (Bentham) **38**:92
"Non son chi fui" (Foscolo) **8**:278
"Nondum" (Hopkins) **189**:5-6, 37, 142
"None Spoke a Single Word to Me" (Webb) **143**:357
The Nonesuch Dickens (Dickens) **206**:51
Nonsense Songs, Stories, Botany, and Alphabets (Lear) **3**:295, 297, 304
"Noon" (Tyutchev)
See "Polden"
"Noonday Rest" (Blind) **202**:58
"Nora of the Amber Hair" (Ferguson) **33**:301
"Nora or Records of a Poet's Love" (Harpur) **114**:138
Nordens Mythologi (Grundtvig) **158**:124-26, 145, 149, 153, 155, 175-76, 178-81
Nordens mytologi (Grundtvig) **1**:403; **158**:101, 103, 107, 123-27, 138-39, 157, 175-76, 178-80, 183, 185
Das Nordlicht: Proben er neuen russichen Literatur (Pavlova) **138**:11-12, 30
"Die Nordsee" (Heine) **4**:248-49, 254-55, 289-59, 266, 269; **54**:318; **147**:178
Nordsee III (Heine) **147**:227
"The Normal Dean of the Present Day" (Trollope) **215**:212
"Normal School for Women" (Sarmiento)
See "Escuela normal de mujeres"
Norman Maurice: The Man of the People (Simms) **3**:502, 505, 514
"Un normand" (Maupassant) **83**:171-72
"Norna; or, The Witch's Curse" (Alcott) **83**:4
"A Norse Atlantis" (Boyesen) **135**:15, 20, 33
"The Norse Emigrant" (Boyesen) **135**:5, 25
"A Norse Stev" (Boyesen) **135**:5, 10, 18, 36
Norseland Tales (Boyesen) **135**:8, 15
A Norseman's Pilgrimage (Boyesen) **135**:6, 11, 24-25
"The Norseman's Ride" (Taylor) **89**:306
"Norsemen" (Whittier) **8**:486
North America (Trollope) **215**:211-12, 218-24
"The North American Indian" (Richardson) **55**:313
North American Men (Martí) **63**:74
North American Scenes (Martí)
See *Escenas norteamericanas*
North and South (Gaskell) **5**:183, 187, 189-92, 196-97, 201, 204-05; **70**:119-20, 123, 129, 133, 152, 154, 187, 189, 193, 196, 198-99, 205-06, 219-20; **97**:110, 127, 134; **137**:9, 17, 20, 33, 40, 42, 64, 101, 104, 124, 129, 146-47, 163, 167, 170-71, 173-77; **214**:178-81, 183, 195-96, 199-202, 208, 242, 249, 260-69, 278, 280-81, 284-85, 308, 310-13, 332, 335, 338-39, 342, 344
"The North and the South" (Barrett Browning) **61**:24; **170**:122
The North Sea (Heine)
See "Die Nordsee"
"The North Wind" (Brontë) **4**:44
"The North Wind Rushes In . . ." (Verlaine)
See "La Bise se rue . . ."
Northanger Abbey (Austen) **1**:30-1, 33-4, 36-41, 44, 49-51, 53, 58-61, 64; **13**:68, 73, 76, 104; **19**:8, 14, 17, 38, 44, 62; **33**:68, 75-6, 79-80, 96; **51**:1-73; **81**:3-5, 12, 18, 70, 77-78; **95**:12, 30, 49; **119**:14, 17-18, 25-6, 28, 31-5, 37-8, 47, 51-3; **150**:33, 36-37, 49, 71-74, 89, 103, 110, 149, 151, 153; **207**:10, 46, 92; **210**:3, 5, 84; **222**:25, 36, 52, 58, 66, 96-100, 109-10
"Northangerland's Name" (Brontë) **109**:30
Northern Antiquities (Percy) **95**:313, 321, 364
"The Northern Farmer" (Tennyson) **30**:222, 226, 233
"The Northern Farmer—New Style" (Tennyson) **30**:280
"The Northern Farmer—Old Style" (Tennyson) **30**:280
Northern Lights (Pavlova)
See *Das Nordlicht: Proben er neuen russichen Literatur*
"Northern Tour" (Cobbett) **49**:159
Northern Travel (Taylor) **89**:346
Northern Worthies (Coleridge)
See *Lives of the Northern Worthies*
The Northern Worthies (Coleridge)
See *Lives of the Northern Worthies*
Northumberland Houshold Book (Percy)
See *Household Book of the Earl of Northumberland in 1512*
Northwood: A Tale of New England (Hale) **75**:280, 295, 301, 311-315, 317-319, 321, 326, 328-330, 336-7, 339, 341, 343-4, 349, 357
"Norway and the Norwegians" (Boyesen) **135**:15
"Norwegian Painters" (Boyesen) **135**:32
"Nos Anglais" (Maupassant) **83**:176
Nos fils (Michelet) **31**:214, 218, 226, 248, 260
"The Nose" (Gogol) **5**:219, 226-29, 232, 234, 254-56; **31**:103, 111, 117, 144; **162**:8, 16, 18-19, 27, 54-57, 64, 67, 82, 96-97
"Nostalgias" (Casal) **131**:248
"Not as These" (Rossetti) **77**:353
"Not at Home" (Coleridge) **177**:160
Not Paul but Jesus (Bentham) **38**:92, 98-9
"Not Sing at Night" (Barnes) **75**:22
Not So Bad As We Seem (Bulwer-Lytton) **45**:22
"Not That From Life, and All Its Woes" (Bryant) **46**:21
"Not to Be" (Webster) **230**:239
"Not Yet" (Bryant) **46**:7
"Not Youth Pertains to Me" (Whitman) **81**:316
"Notas perdidas" (Silva) **114**:300
The Note of Hand, or a Trip to Newmarket (Cumberland) **167**:133, 143, 147, 155, 188
"Note on George Meredith" (Thomson) **18**:402
"A Note on Realism" (Stevenson) **63**:229, 234; **193**:266, 288
"Note on the Projected Gathering at Stephen the Great's Tomb at Putna" (Eminescu) **33**:272
"Note sur la Grèce" (Chateaubriand) **134**:7
The Note-Book of William Blake (Blake) **13**:240, 242-43
Notebook (Lewes) **215**:157, 160
Notebooks (Whitman) **81**:358-60
Notebooks and Journals of Dorothy and Mary Wordsworth (Wordsworth) **138**:252, 254, 257-58
Notebooks and Unpublished Prose Manuscripts (Whitman) **205**:228, 253, 265-67
Notebooks for "The Idiot" (Dostoevsky) **119**:71, 81-84, 86-89, 98-99, 130, 140, 143, 146, 159-60
Notebooks of Percy Bysshe Shelley (Shelley) **143**:177
The Notebooks of Samuel Taylor Coleridge (Coleridge) **177**:32-34, 108, 156-57, 160; **197**:215, 244, 279, 283, 311, 317-18; **231**:56, 60, 62-64, 67, 73, 85, 87-88, 94, 98, 101, 103, 106, 121-22, 142, 151-52
Notebooks on Transmutations of Species (Darwin) **57**:141, 144-6, 153
"Notes" (Gogol) **5**:224
Notes (Dickens)
See *American Notes for General Circulation*
Notes and Fragments (Whitman) **205**:251-53, 255
Notes and Journal of Travel in Europe, 1804-05 (Irving) **2**:385
Notes de voyage (Flaubert)
See *Voyages*
Notes de Voyage (Mérimée) **65**:87
"Notes for the Biography of a Distinguée" (Kirkland) **85**:270-72
Notes from the House of the Dead (Dostoevsky) **167**:311, 319, 336
Notes from the Underground (Dostoevsky)
See *Zapiski iz podpol'ya*
Notes from Underground (Dostoevsky)
See *Zapiski iz podpol'ya*
Notes in England and Italy (Hawthorne) **150**:168, 202, 208-11, 213-15
Notes inédites de Flaubert (Flaubert) **179**:23
Notes littéraires (Sade) **47**:333
Notes of a Hunter (Turgenev)
See *Zapiski okhotnika*
Notes of a Journey through France and Italy (Hazlitt) **29**:153; **82**:154, 161
"Notes of a Madman" (Gogol)
See "Diary of a Madman"
"Notes of a Sitter-still" (Carlyle) **181**:129
"Notes of a Still-sitter" (Carlyle) **181**:129
"Notes of a Three-Days' Tour to the Netherlands, August, 1842" (Carlyle) **70**:89-90, 93
The Notes of a Young Man (Herzen) **10**:348; **61**:108
Notes of an Old Man (Fredro)
See *Zapiski starucha*
Notes of an Orenburg Province Rifle Hunter (Aksakov)
See *Zapiski ruzheynago okhotnika*
Notes of an Orenburg-Province Hunter (Aksakov)
See *Zapiski ruzheynago okhotnika*
"Notes of Archeological Rambles" (Mérimée) **6**:352
Notes of the Unknown (Leskov)
See *Zametki neizvestnogo*
Notes of Travel (Hugo) **189**:180
Notes on a Journey (Petofi)
See *Úti jegyzetek*
"Notes on Ancient and Modern Confederacies" (Madison) **126**:297
Notes on Ancient Britain and the Britons (Barnes) **75**:40, 46, 107
Notes on Angling (Aksakov)
See *Zapiski ob uzhenyi ryby*
"Notes on Eighteenth-Century Russian History" (Pushkin) **83**:309
Notes on England (Taine)
See *Notes sur l'Angleterre*
Notes on Fishing (Aksakov)
See *Zapiski ob uzhenyi ryby*
"Notes on Form in Art" (Eliot) **4**:153; **13**:334-35, 342; **183**:30, 32, 38, 94; **199**:131
Notes on Paris (Taine)
See *Notes sur Paris: Vie et opinions de M. Frédéric-Thomas Graindorge*
"Notes on Reynolds" (Blake) **13**:179
"Notes on Sculptures in Rome and Florence" (Shelley) **175**:345
"Notes on Style" (Symonds) **34**:336

"Notes on the Advisability of Simplifying and Standardizing Orthography in America" (Bello)
See "Indicaciones sobre la Conveniencia de Simplificar y Uniformar la Ortografía en América"
"Notes on the Religious Tradition" (Clough) **27**:85
Notes on the State of Virginia (Jefferson) **11**:148, 166, 172-73, 192, 199, 203, 205-10; **103**:105, 110-11 121, 124, 128-36, 144-6, 157, 159, 186, 194, 203, 207, 221, 227-29, 231-36, 240-47, 250-51
"Notes on Theism" (Symonds) **34**:336
Notes on Virginia (Jefferson)
See *Notes on the State of Virginia*
Notes sur l'Angleterre (Taine) **15**:427-28, 431, 437, 441, 452, 462-63
Notes sur Les Liaisons dangereuses (Baudelaire) **155**:18
Notes sur Paris: Vie et opinions de M. Frédéric-Thomas Graindorge (Taine) **15**:424, 436-37, 440, 449-50, 452
"Notes upon a Ramble" (Willis) **194**:298
Notes upon Some of Shakespeare's Plays (Kemble) **18**:192
"Der Nothpfennig" (Auerbach) **171**:75
Notice (Gautier) **1**:351
"Notice historique" (Genlis) **166**:39, 41
Notions élémentaires de linguistique (Nodier) **19**:401
Notions of the Americans (Cooper) **1**:218; **27**:153; **54**:254-6, 283; **203**:49-50
Notions of the Americans: Picked up by a Travelling Bachelor (Cooper)
See *Notions of the Americans*
"Notizia intorno a Didimo Chierico" (Foscolo) **97**:90-1
Notre coeur (Maupassant) **1**:447-48, 450, 452, 459, 464, 468, 470; **42**:169, 201; **83**:180-81
Notre Dame des Soirs (Laforgue) **53**:281
Notre-Dame: A Tale of the Ancient Regime (Hugo)
See *Notre-Dame de Paris*
Notre-Dame de Paris (Hugo) **3**:236-40, 245, 251, 253-55, 257-59, 261, 263, 267, 274, 276; **10**:367, 369, 371, 373, 377; **21**:190-231; **161**:145-53, 192, 202, 236, 252, 255-57, 259, 261, 264, 267-72; **189**:157, 177, 179, 183, 190, 193, 198, 200, 221, 223, 237, 240, 295, 305
Notre-Dame; or, The Bellringer of Paris (Hugo)
See *Notre-Dame de Paris*
"Notus Ignoto" (Taylor) **89**:317-18
Nous ne sommes pas le troupeau (Verlaine) **51**:363
Nous n'irons plus au bois (Banville) **9**:18
Nous tour (Banville) **9**:20, 30
"Le nouveau Diogène" (Beranger) **34**:30
Le nouveau monde (Villiers de l'Isle Adam) **3**:582
Le Nouveau Monde industriel et sociétaire (Fourier) **51**:156, 161
Le nouveau Pourceaugnac (Scribe) **16**:388
"Un nouveau-né" (Desbordes-Valmore) **97**:6, 9, 13, 22, 24
Nouveaux contes cruels (Villiers de l'Isle Adam) **3**:582, 586
Les nouveaux jeux de l'amour et du hasard (Scribe) **16**:388
Nouveaux lundis (Sainte-Beuve) **5**:328, 331, 339, 341
Nouvelles Confidences: Avec une partie entièrement inédite (Lamartine) **11**:265; **190**:213, 242-43
La Nouvelle Justine (Leopardi) **129**:304
La nouvelle Justine (Sade) **3**:480; **47**:309-12, 334, 336, 350, 365
Nouvelles asiatiques (Gobineau) **17**:68-9, 92-3, 96, 103
Nouvelles histoires extraordinaires (Baudelaire) **29**:67, 92
Nouvelles lettres d'un voyageur (Sand) **57**:366, 368
Nouvelles méditations poétiques (Lamartine) **11**:245, 248, 254, 269-70, 273, 275-77, 283; **190**:200, 202, 218, 225-26, 232, 234, 236-37
"Nouvelles Variations sur le Point-du-Jour" (Verlaine) **51**:361
Nov' (Turgenev) **21**:402, 412, 414, 419, 421, 432, 435, 437-39, 441, 445; **37**:394, 404, 417, 443; **122**:249, 257, 286-89, 292, 337, 341, 376
"Nova pisarija" (Preseren) **127**:293, 298, 312-13
"Novalis and the Blue Flower" (Boyesen) **135**:6
"Novel" (Rimbaud)
See "Roman"
A Novel in Letters (Pushkin)
See *Roman v pismakh*
A Novel in Seven Letters (Bestuzhev)
See *Roman v semi pis'makh*
Novel of the War of 1808 (Runeberg) **41**:314
"La novela natural" (Alarcón) **219**:49-50
Novelas cortas: Cuentos amartorios (Alarcon) **1**:14-15; **219**:4, 42, 47, 53
Novelas cortas: Historietas nacionales (Alarcon) **1**:14-15; **219**:4, 18
Novelas cortas: Narraciones inverosimiles (Alarcon) **1**:14-15; **219**:4
Novellas and Sketches (Jacobsen)
See *Noveller of Skitser*
Novelle (Arnim) **159**:84, 92
"Novelle Mistris Lee" (Arnim) **159**:84
Novellen (Tieck) **5**:514
Novellensammlung (Arnim) **159**:47, 49
Noveller of Skitser (Jacobsen) **34**:171
Novelletten (Schumann) **143**:144
"Novels" (Oliphant) **221**:236
Novels and Selected Works of Mary Shelley (Shelley) **170**:334
The Novels and Tales of Robert Louis Stevenson (Stevenson) **193**:259, 261
"Novels by Eminent Hands, or Punch's Prize Novelists" (Thackeray) **169**:330; **213**:263
The Novels of Charles Brockden Brown (Brown) **22**:8
"The Novels of Jane Austen" (Lewes) **215**:132
The Novels, Travels, Essays, and Poems of Robert Louis Stevenson (Stevenson) **193**:220
"November" (Clare) **9**:114; **86**:97, 103-04, 110, 168
"November" (Coleridge) **90**:26
"November" (Taylor) **89**:316
November Boughs (Whitman) **4**:551, 576
"Novembersonne" (Meyer) **81**:146-48, 155
Novembre (Flaubert)
See *Novembre: Fragments de style quelconque*
Novembre: Fragments de style quelconque (Flaubert) **2**:249, 255-6; **10**:139, 160, 170; **19**:282, 288-91, 299, 304, 309; **62**:83, 85-91, 95; **66**:269-72; **135**:107; **179**:10, 24, 77-78, 84, 120-21
The Novice (Lermontov)
See *Mtsyri*
The Novice of St. Dominick (Morgan) **29**:389-90
The Novices of Saïs (Novalis)
See *Die Lehrlinge zu Saïs*
"El novillo y el toro viejo" (Lizardi) **30**:68
"Novissima verba" (Lamartine) **11**:270, 278-79; **190**:241
"Novozavetnye evrei" (Leskov) **174**:105-6, 115-16
"Now" (Browning) **79**:161
"Now Finalè to the Shore" (Whitman) **31**:389
"Now Precedent Songs, Farewell" (Whitman) **31**:434
"Now Sleeps the Crimson Petal" (Tennyson) **30**:279-80; **202**:174, 177, 198-99, 330
"Now You Shall Speak" (Meyer)
See "Jetzt rede du"
Nowa dejanira (Slowacki)
See *Fantazy*
"Now—But One Moment, Let Me Stay" (Brontë) **109**:31
The Nowlans (Banim and Banim) **13**:117, 119-22, 124, 128-31, 133-35, 141-43
"Nox" (Leconte de Lisle) **29**:243
Le nozze di Figaro (Da Ponte) **50**:76, 79-82, 85, 92-3, 96, 98
Le nuage rose (Sand) **42**:314
Nubatama no Maki (Ueda Akinari) **131**:63, 68
"Nuesta America" (Martí) **63**:131, 153
"Nuestro pecado de los folletines" (Sarmiento) **123**:378
"La nuit" (Banville) **9**:30
"La Nuit" (Musset) **150**:229, 309
"Nuit d'Août" (Laforgue) **221**:25
"Nuit d'Août" (Musset) **7**:255, 261-2, 274; **150**:223-4, 285, 316-7, 323, 326-7, 346
"Une nuit de Clèopâtre" (Gautier) **1**:341, 344-45, 348, 350; **59**:10-11, 13-14, 30, 33, 42
"Nuit de Décembre" (Musset) **7**:255, 262, 274, 280; **150**:245, 315-7, 325-6, 346
"Une nuit de Don Juan" (Flaubert) **10**:176
"La Nuit de Juin" (Musset) **150**:317
"Nuit de l'enfer" (Rimbaud) **4**:452, 474, 481-82; **35**:289, 292, 302-03, 310, 317; **82**:218, 222-23, 225, 229, 235-36, 238, 240-45, 249, 252, 255, 257, 262; **227**:200, 210, 276, 278-80, 305, 315-16
"Nuit de Mai" (Musset) **7**:255, 261-62, 274, 280; **81**:150;223, 246-7, 308, 315-7, 319, 323, 325, 346
"Une nuit de mon âme" (Desbordes-Valmore) **97**:13, 23-4
"Nuit de Noël" (Maupassant) **83**:172, 194, 197, 223
La nuit de Noël (Sand) **42**:313
"Nuit d'hiver" (Sand) **57**:368
"Nuit d'Octobre" (Musset) **7**:255, 261; **150**:224, 316-8, 327, 345-6
"Nuit du Walpurgis classique" (Verlaine) **230**:161, 163
"La nuit irrésistible établit son empire" (Baudelaire) **155**:18
"Une Nuit que j'étais" (Baudelaire) **55**:6
La nuit Vénitienne; ou, Les noces de laurette (Musset) **7**:259-60, 267, 275-76, 280-81; **150**:226, 303, 313, 335, 343, 347-8
"Les nuits" (Musset) **7**:255-58, 262-63, 266, 272, 274-75
Les Nuits (Musset) **150**:227-28, 234, 315-18, 323-25, 327-28, 345, 347, 349
"Nuits de juin" (Hugo) **3**:273
"Les nuits de Ramazan" (Nerval) **1**:475; **67**:311, 333
Les nuits d'Octobre (Nerval) **1**:482; **67**:313, 324, 332-33, 336, 357
"Nul" (Mallarmé) **210**:250
Numa Roumsetan (Daudet) **1**:233-35, 237, 239, 241, 243, 246, 250-51
Number 91; or, The Adventures of a New York Telegraph Boy (Alger) **8**:43; **83**:112
"Number Fifteen, Stolt" (Runeberg)
See "N:o femton, Stolt"
Number Seventeen (Kingsley) **107**:192
"Number Two" (Cooke) **110**:35-6
"Numbers; on the Majority and the Remnant" (Arnold) **6**:41, 46; **126**:106; **218**:257, 260
"Numbness" (Muller)
See "Erstarrung"
Nummisuutarit (Kivi) **30**:48, 50-1, 53, 55, 64
"Numpholeptos" (Browning) **19**:88, 153
"The Nun" (Rogers) **69**:80
Nun of St. Omer's (Dacre)
See *Confessions of the Nun of St. Omer*
"Nuori Karhunampuja" (Kivi) **30**:51
"Nuptial Sleep" (Rossetti) **4**:494, 496-97; **77**:326, 338-41
"Nur zu" (Mörike) **201**:280

"Nuremberg" (Longfellow) **2**:473, 479; **45**:116
"Nurse Green" (Lamb) **125**:362
"Nurse Miller" (Crawford) **127**:220
The Nursery "Alice" (Dodgson) **139**:120, 147
Nursery and Household Tales (Grimm Brothers)
See *Kinder-und Hausmärchen*
Nursery Reminiscences (Barham) **77**:6, 9
"Nurse's Song" (Blake) **13**:220; **37**:3, 9, 24, 31, 41-2, 50, 57, 61, 66, 71-2, 92
"Nurse's Stories" (Dickens) **217**:267
"The Nurse's Story" (Barham) **77**:33
"Nursing" (Lamb) **125**:332
"Nussknacker und Mausekönig" (Hoffmann) **2**:351-52; **183**:226, 298
"Nutcracker and Mouse-King" (Hoffmann)
See "Nussknacker und Mausekönig"
"Nutting" (Wordsworth) **38**:370; **111**:227, 250; **206**:306, 309
Nyaars-Morgen (Grundtvig) **158**:122, 139-40, 142
"Nydia" (Rossetti) **186**:275
Nydia (Boker) **125**:25-26, 28, 41, 58, 76-78
Nye Eventyr og Historier (Andersen) **214**:25-26
"The Nymphs" (Hunt) **70**:291
The Nymphs (Hunt) **1**:412, 415, 421
Nytaarsnat eller Blik paa Kristendom og Historie (Grundtvig) **158**:150
"O Blest Unfabled Incense Tree" (Darley) **2**:133
"O Bogdanoviche i yego sochineniyakh" (Karamzin) **173**:281
"O Breathe Not His Name" (Moore) **6**:391, 398-99
"O bylom, o pogibshem . . ." (Pavlova) **138**:20
"O Captain! My Captain!" (Whitman) **4**:602; **31**:438; **81**:319, 321; **205**:185, 187-88
"O cheloveke, o ego smertnosti i bessmertii" (Radishchev) **190**:275, 309, 320-21, 326, 328-32, 337
"O chem ty voesh, vetr nochnoy?" (Tyutchev) **34**:398
"O Dearest Friend! Now Thou Art Joyful" (Zhukovsky) **35**:403
"O Deutschland, Deutschland" (Hauff) **185**:353
"O Diaphanous Geraniums" (Laforgue)
See "Ô géraniums diaphanes"
"O don't blaspheme, poet, and remember" (Verlaine) **230**:176
O drevnei i novoi Rossii v ee politicheskom i grazhdanskom otnosheniiakh (Karamzin) **3**:283; **173**:254, 258, 269, 286, 300-2, 304, 310
O Garicho (Alencar) **157**:5
O Gaúcho (Alencar) **157**:39
"Ô géraniums diaphanes" (Laforgue) **221**:83
"O gerojax i pravednikax" (Leskov) **174**:76
"O God! While I in Pleasure's Wiles" (Brontë) **109**:37
"Ô gouffre, aspire-moi!" (Laforgue) **221**:84
O Guarani (Alencar) **157**:3, 5-7, 9, 12, 15, 19-24, 39, 42, 50
"O Jeannie There's Naethin tae Fear Ye" (Hogg) **4**:284
O Jesuita (Alencar) **157**:5
"O Krytykach i Recenzentach" (Mickiewicz) **101**:191-92
"O kühler Wald" (Brentano) **1**:105
"O Laco de fito" (Castro Alves) **205**:4
"O Land of Empire, Art and Love!" (Clough) **27**:103
"O Let the Solid Ground" (Tennyson) **30**:242
"O light canoe, where dost thou glide?" (Crawford) **127**:151, 155
"O Living Always, Always Dying" (Whitman) **81**:308-09
"O Lord, I Will Praise Thee" (Cowper) **8**:131
"O Love builds on the azure sea" (Crawford) **127**:151
"O lvubvi k otechestvu i narodnoy gordosti" (Karamzin) **173**:282
"O lyogkoy odezhde modnykh drasavits XIX veka" (Karamzin) **173**:288
"O Magnet-South" (Whitman) **205**:311
"O May, Thou Art a Merry Time" (Darley) **2**:133
"O Me! O Life!" (Whitman) **81**:315
"O mes amants" (Verlaine) **230**:177
"O, Mother" (Eminescu) **131**:297
"O Mutter halte dein Kindlein warm" (Brentano)
See "Gesang der Liebe als sie geboren war"
"O my lovers" (Verlaine) **230**:176
"O my prophetic soul!" (Tyutchev)
See "O veschaya dusha moya!"
"O My Thoughts My Thoughts" (Shevchenko)
See "Dumy moji dumy moji"
"O mysl! tebe udel tsvetka:..." (Baratynsky) **103**:11
"O nadador" (Castro Alves) **205**:21
"O Navio Negreiro" (Castro Alves) **205**:5-6, 14, 16, 23-25, 27-28, 33, 35-36
"O Nightingale!" (Wordsworth) **111**:323
"O Qui Me" (Clough) **27**:103
"O qui me—" (Prescott) **163**:34, 36
"O rozne. Uvet synam protivlenija" (Leskov) **174**:6-7, 85, 90
"O saisons, ô châteaux!" (Rimbaud) **82**:231, 233, 247
"O Schweig nur Herz!" (Brentano) **191**:37
"O Século" (Castro Alves) **205**:6, 14, 22, 34
O Sertanejo (Alencar) **157**:39
"O si chère de loin" (Mallarmé) **210**:211
"O Sibarita Romano" (Castro Alves) **205**:26
"O sluchayakh i kharaterakh v rossiyskoy istorii, kotoryye mogut byt' predmetom khudozhestv" (Karamzin) **173**:283
"O Solitude" (Keats) **225**:208, 224, 244
"O stanowisku Polski z Bożych i ludzkich względów" (Krasiński) **4**:313
"O Star of France" (Whitman) **205**:309
"O Stern und Blume, Geist und Kleid" (Brentano) **1**:105
"O Strength and Stay, Upholding All Creation" (Cowper) **8**:116
"O Swallow, Swallow" (Tennyson) **202**:177, 196, 198-99, 272-73
O. T. (Andersen) **7**:16; **79**:18; **214**:74
"O Tell Me, Friends" (Clough) **27**:52
"O tend my flowers" (Dickinson) **77**:148
"O Thou Whose Image" (Clough) **27**:53
"O thought! the flower's fate is yours:..." (Baratynsky)
See "O mysl! tebe udel tsvetka:..."
"Ô toi triomphante . . ." (Verlaine) **230**:164
"Ô triste, triste était mon âme . . ." (Verlaine) **51**:384; **230**:161
"O ver: ty, nezhnaya, dorozhe slavy mne;..." (Baratynsky) **103**:11
"O veschaya dusha moya!" (Tyutchev) **34**:397
"O Vôo do Gênio" (Castro Alves) **205**:11
"O, Wand'ring is the Miller's Joy" (Muller)
See "Das Wandern ist des Müllers Lust"
"O Welcome Bat and Owlet Gray" (Baillie) **151**:86, 90-91
"O Welt, du schöne Welt, du" (Eichendorff) **8**:233
"O World, O Life, O Time" (Shelley) **93**:303-04
"O! would that Fortune might bestow on me" (Boker) **125**:82
"O zabluzhdeniyakh i istine" (Baratynsky) **103**:19
"O zemście" (Norwid)
See "Z pamiętnika"
"The Oak" (Tennyson) **202**:290
"The Oak and the Broom" (Wordsworth)
See "The Oak and the Broom, A Pastoral"
"The Oak and the Broom, A Pastoral" (Wordsworth) **111**:242
"The Oak and the Poplar" (Very) **9**:372
"Oak in Autumn" (Sigourney) **87**:332
The Oak Openings (Cooper)
See *The Oak-Openings; or, the Bee-Hunter*
The Oak Openings; or, The Bee Hunter (Cooper) **1**:221; **27**:139, 141-42, 145; **54**:259, 263
"The Oak Tree and the Ivy" (Field) **3**:208
The Oak-Openings; or, the Bee-Hunter (Cooper) **203**:88
"Oaks" (Castro)
See "Los robles"
Oakshott Castle, Being the Memoir of an Eccentric Nobleman (Kingsley) **107**:192-93, 195, 209
"Oars at Rest" (Meyer)
See "Eingelegte Ruder"
Oasis (Child) **73**:60, 77
The Oath (Macha) **46**:212
"The Oath of the Canadian Volunteers. A Loyal Song for Canada" (Moodie) **14**:222; **113**:308
"Ob inosmrannom priedikanmie" (Leskov) **174**:139
"Ob okhote" (Aksakov) **181**:61
"Ob slovesu" (Preseren) **127**:292, 298
"Ob ungehemmte Ausbildung der menschlichen Gattung nachteilig sei?" (Wieland) **177**:258
"Der Oberamtmann und der Amtsrichter" (Gotthelf) **117**:6
Der Oberhof (Immermann) **4**:291, 293, 295, 297
Der Oberhof: A Tale of Westphalian Life (Immermann)
See *Der Oberhof*
"Obermann" (Arnold)
See "Stanzas in Memory of the Author of 'Obermann'"
Obermann (Liszt)
See *Vallée d'Obermann*
Obermann (Senancour) **16**:423, 425, 427-28, 431-38, 441-50, 454-55
"Obermann Once More" (Arnold) **6**:51, 72; **29**:11; **89**:82, 132; **218**:119, 132
"Die Obermedicinalräthin" (Hebbel) **43**:238
Oberon (Adams) **175**:27-30
Oberon (Planché) **42**:273, 292
Oberon (Wieland) **17**:392-93, 396-98, 400, 402-04, 410-11; **177**:223, 238, 247, 251-52, 254, 320, 361-62, 366-68
Oblomov (Goncharov) **1**:359, 361-66, 368-69, 371-80; **63**:3-5, 10, 17, 20-4, 26-30, 35-6, 41, 46
"Oblomov's Dream" (Goncharov) **1**:369, 372, 377-78; **63**:45-6
"The Oblong Box" (Poe) **55**:148; **211**:253, 255-57
"Obman" (Leskov) **25**:265-67
Obojdennye (Leskov) **25**:232, 251-52; **174**:6, 10, 60
"Obra humana" (Silva) **114**:303
Obras (Manzano) **155**:306, 323, 334
Obras completas (Alarcón) **219**:18, 20
Obras completas (Bécquer) **106**:126, 168-69
Obras completas (Bello) **131**:102, 107, 109-10
Obras completas (Martí) **63**:122, 167
Obras Completas (Sarmiento) **123**:319-23, 325, 346
Obras Completas (Silva) **114**:296
Obras completas (Williams) **78**:23, 29, 58-59
Obras completas de Castro Alves (Castro Alves) **205**:12, 14
Obras completas de D. Esteban Echeverría (Echeverria) **18**:154
Obras de doña Gertrudis de Avellaneda (Gómez de Avellaneda) **111**:3-4, 6, 9, 17, 19-25, 27-9, 75
Obras de Mariano José de Larra (Larra) **130**:193-99, 201, 203-6, 209-16, 218-20, 226, 228-29, 231, 233, 241-46, 269-76
Obras de Mariano José de Larra, Vol. 1 (Larra)
See *Obras de Mariano José de Larra*

Obras de Mariano José de Larra, Vol. 127 (Larra)
See *Obras de Mariano José de Larra*
Obras de Mariano José de Larra, Vol. 128 (Larra)
See *Obras de Mariano José de Larra*
Obras de Mariano José de Larra, Vol. I (Larra)
See *Obras de Mariano José de Larra*
Obras de Mariano José de Larra, Vol. II (Larra)
See *Obras de Mariano José de Larra*
Obras de Mariano José de Larra, Vol. III (Larra)
See *Obras de Mariano José de Larra*
Obras de Mariano José de Larra, Vol. IV (Larra)
See *Obras de Mariano José de Larra*
Obras de Martínex de la Rosa (Martínez de la Rosa) **102**:248-51, 252-54
Obras literatias (Martínez de la Rosa) **102**:231-32, 246
The O'Briens and the O'Flahertys (Morgan) **29**:389-90, 393
Obryv (Goncharov) **1**:362-66, 368-69, 371, 373-75, 378-79; **63**:3-4, 15-6, 26, 29-30, 32, 50
"Observation on the Tragedies of Mrs. Warren" (Murray) **63**:180, 196
"Observations" (Bowles) **103**:64
Observations and Reflections Made in the Course of a Journey through France, Italy, and Germany (Piozzi) **57**:242, 251, 253-4, 257, 259, 266, 271, 298
"Observations on An Infant" (Alcott) **167**:32
"Observations on Female Abilities" (Murray) **63**:184, 211-12
"Observations on the Country at the Head of the Ohio River" (Brackenridge) **227**:114-16
Observations on the Feeling of the Beautiful and the Sublime (Kant) **27**:200, 262
"Observations on the Language of Chaucer" (Child) **173**:168-69, 171, 189, 209, 226
Observations on the Language of Gower's Confessio Amantis (Child) **173**:168-69, 171-72, 189, 209
Observations on the New Constitution and on the Federal Convention by a Columbian Patriot, Sic Transit Gloria Americana (Warren) **13**:420, 422, 436; **226**:292
"Observations on the Principles and Methods of Infant Instruction" (Alcott) **167**:36, 46
Observations on the River Wye (Gilpin) **30**:41
Observations, Relative Chiefly to Picturesque Beauty, Made in the Year 1772 (Gilpin) **30**:31-2, 42
Observations sur la langue et la littérature provencale (Schlegel) **142**:323
The Observer (Cumberland) **167**:114, 121-22, 134, 140, 148, 169, 172-73, 179-80, 191
"Obsession" (Baudelaire) **55**:46, 55, 65, 68; **155**:101
"The Obstructions of Genius" (Horton) **87**:102
Obyknovennaya istoriya (Goncharov) **1**:359, 361-62, 364-69, 367, 373-74, 377-79; **63**:3-5, 9, 17-8, 20-22, 24, 26-7, 29, 32, 34-5, 42-3, 45-53
"Očarovannyj strannik" (Leskov) **25**:227-28, 233, 238-39; **174**:9, 12, 20, 38-43, 52, 63, 78, 120-21, 123-26
L'occasion (Mérimée) **6**:362-63; **65**:47, 49-50, 55, 58, 60, 63-4, 79, 82-3
An Occasional Attempt (Cumberland) **167**:201
"Occasional Discourse on the Nigger Question" (Carlyle) **70**:72, 91
Occasional Papers (Keble) **87**:188-91, 195
Occasional Sermons (Newman)
See *Sermons Preached on Various Occasions*
Occasional Services (Keble) **87**:116
"Occasioned by a Legislation Bill proposing a Taxation upon Newspapers" (Freneau) **111**:124
Occhi e Nasi (Collodi) **54**:137, 140
"L'Occident" (Lamartine) **11**:270, 279; **190**:228
Les occidentales (Banville) **9**:19, 22
"Occult Memories" (Villiers de l'Isle Adam)
See "Souvenirs occulte"
"The Occultation of Orion" (Longfellow) **45**:154-55
"Occupations" (Whitman)
See "A Song for Occupations"
"The Ocean" (Cranch) **115**:5, 67
Océan (Hugo) **161**:264
Oceana (Froude) **43**:186
"Oceane von Parceval" (Fontane) **163**:166, 169
"Oceano" (Foscolo) **8**:266
"Oceano nox" (Herzen) **10**:327
"Ocharovannyi strannik" (Leskov)
See "Očarovannyj strannik"
"O'Connor's Child" (Campbell) **19**:169, 181, 193
"O'Connorville" (Jones) **222**:125, 127, 156
"The O'Conors of Castle Conor, County Mayo" (Trollope) **101**:234, 245, 262, 264, 271
"Octave" (Musset) **150**:310-11
Octavia (Kotzebue)
See *Oktavia*
"Octavie" (Beranger) **34**:28
Octavie: L'illusion (Nerval) **1**:477-78, 485-86; **67**:357-58, 363-64
"October" (Bryant) **6**:183; **46**:4
"October" (Clare) **86**:93, 98, 101, 168
"October Evening" (Verlaine)
See "Un soir d'octobre"
"October 10!" (Martí) **63**:130
"October 17. For Apollon Nikolaevich Maikov" (Aksakov)
See "17 oktiabra A. N. Maikovu"
"October Hills" (Ridge) **82**:185
"October Night" (Musset)
See "Nuit d'Octobre"
October Nights (Nerval)
See *Les nuits d'Octobre*
"October Sunset" (Lampman) **25**:204; **194**:56, 58, 138
"Octogenary Reflections" (Barbauld) **50**:5
The Octoroon; or, Life in Louisiana (Boucicault) **41**:29, 31-3, 35-6, 49
"Oda a la exposición de la industria española del año 1827" (Larra) **17**:266
"Oda a los habitantes de Anáhuac" (Heredia) **209**:131, 136, 154
"Oda Bog" (Derzhavin)
See "Bog"
"Oda în metru antic" (Eminescu) **33**:250
"Oda o Mlodości" (Mickiewicz) **3**:392-93, 398; **101**:155
"Oda. Prelozhenie 81-go psalma" (Derzhavin) **215**:24, 61
"Odd Characters" (Hogg) **109**:281
"Odd Miss Todd" (Cooke) **110**:35, 37, 44
The Odd Number: Thirteen Tales (Maupassant) **1**:447
"Odds and Ends" (Levy) **59**:119-20
"An Odd-tempered Man" (Opie) **65**:172
"Ode" (Boyesen) **135**:47
"Ode" (Coleridge)
See "Dejection, an Ode"
"Ode" (Emerson) **38**:189
"Ode" (Freneau) **111**:140
"Ode" (Lamartine) **11**:264
"An Ode" (Lowell) **2**:507
"An Ode" (Reynolds) **146**:165, 188
"Ode" (Taylor) **89**:349
"Ode" (Tennyson) **30**:215
Ode (Klopstock) **225**:296
"Ode: 1815" (Wordsworth) **38**:427
"Ode à Bonaparte" (Lamartine) **11**:245, 268, 270
"Ode against Capital Punishment" (Lamartine)
See "Ode contre la peine de mort"
Ode all'amica risanata (Foscolo) **97**:50, 72
"Ode au lac de Bourget" (Lamartine)
See "Le Lac"
"Ode auf die glückliche Wiederkunft unseres gnädigsten Fürsten" (Schiller) **39**:338, 387
"Ode Concerning Revolutions" (Lamartine)
See "Ode sur les révolutions"
"Ode contre la peine de mort" (Lamartine) **11**:276, 283
"Ode for a Celebration" (Bryant) **6**:172
"Ode for a Social Meeting/With slight alterations by a teet.taler" (Holmes) **81**:97-98
"Ode for Saint Cecilia's Eve" (Hood) **16**:234
"An Ode for the Celebration of St. Andrew's Day" (Brackenridge) **227**:73
"Ode for the Charleston Centennial Celebration" (Hayne) **94**:145
"Ode Fourth / For New Year's Day" (Robinson) **142**:167
"Das öde Haus" (Hoffmann) **183**:193-94, 206
"Ode III" (Moore) **6**:392
"Ode in Ancient Metre" (Eminescu)
See "Oda în metru antic"
"Ode in Saphic Metre" (Eminescu)
See "Ode (In Sapphic Metre)"
"Ode (In Sapphic Metre)" (Eminescu) **33**:262; **131**:298
"Ode Inscribed to the Infant Son of S. T. Coleridge" (Robinson) **142**:96, 111, 114
"Ode Inscribed to W. H. Channing" (Emerson) **38**:184, 191; **98**:179-80, 183
"Ode: Intimations of Immortality from Recollections of Early Childhood" (Wordsworth) **12**:395, 416, 423, 425, 427, 429-31, 436, 440-49, 451-52, 460, 462, 467, 471, 473; **38**:359-60, 367-68, 396, 398; **111**:219, 226, 235; **166**:212, 226, 271, 278, 293, 309; **206**:245, 247, 262, 266-72, 277, 298, 325, 329, 336
"Ode on a Distant Prospect of Clapham Academy" (Hood) **16**:234
"Ode on a Grecian Urn" (Keats) **8**:351-52, 355, 365, 368, 382, 386-90; **73**:154, 158-60, 165, 198-99, 202-04, 209, 230, 246, 258, 262, 268, 270, 282, 309; **121**:106, 144; **225**:111, 122, 130, 132, 136-37, 148, 169, 184-85, 187-88, 195-97, 199, 217, 225, 231, 233, 235, 245, 248, 251-53
"Ode on a Jar of Pickles" (Taylor) **89**:338
"Ode on Dejection" (Coleridge) **9**:147-49, 158, 181, 193
"Ode on Immortality" (Wordsworth)
See "Ode: Intimations of Immortality from Recollections of Early Childhood"
"Ode on Indolence" (Keats) **8**:387, 391; **73**:154, 158, 198, 211, 289, 328; **225**:149
"Ode on Liberty" (Dyer) **129**:103, 107, 112, 137, 140
"Ode on Lord Hay's Birth-day" (Beattie) **25**:106
"Ode on Melancholy" (Keats) **8**:351, 361, 375, 378-79; **73**:159-60, 165, 198, 201, 206, 244, 259-60, 271, 308-09; **121**:111, 144; **225**:121-22, 124-26, 140, 145-46, 148-49, 168, 245
"Ode on Nobility" (Derzhavin)
See "Na znatnost"
"Ode on Occasion of the Meeting of the Southern Congress" (Timrod) **25**:387
"Ode on Peace, written in Jesus College Garden" (Dyer) **129**:103, 112
"Ode on Pity" (Dyer) **129**:137
"Ode on the Death of General Bibikov" (Derzhavin)
See "Na smert Generala-Enshefa Bibikov"
Ode on the Death of Napoleon (Manzoni)
See *Il cinque maggio*
"Ode on the Death of Prince Meshchersky" (Derzhavin)
See "Na smert ' kniazia Meshcherskogo"
"Ode on the Death of the Duchess de Frias" (Martínez de la Rosa) **102**:226

"Ode on the Death of the Duke of Wellington" (Tennyson) **30**:294
Ode on the Death of the Duke of Wellington (Tennyson) **202**:260-61, 263-66, 276, 307
"Ode on the Departing Year" (Coleridge) **231**:71, 83
An Ode on the Peace (Williams) **135**:305, 333
"Ode on the Recollections of Early Childhood" (Wordsworth)
See "Ode: Intimations of Immortality from Recollections of Early Childhood"
"Ode on the Spring" (Dyer) **129**:137
"Ode prima: Accenna le cagioni della guerra" (Alfieri) **101**:48
"Ode quarta: Commenda il Generale Washington" (Alfieri) **101**:48
"Ode Recited at the Harvard Commemoration" (Lowell) **90**:190
"Ode seconda: Annovera i popoli belligeranti" (Alfieri) **101**:48
"Ode Sung at the Opening of the International Exhibition" (Tennyson) **30**:295
"Ode Sung in the Town Hall, Concord, July 4, 1857" (Emerson) **98**:182-83
"Ode Sung on the Occasion of Decorating the Graves of the Confederate Dead at Magnolia Cemetery" (Timrod) **25**:368-69, 372, 376, 382, 386, 388-89
"Ode sur les Révolutions" (Lamartine) **11**:271, 279, 283; **190**:205, 254
"Ode terza: Parla del Sig. de La Fayette" (Alfieri) **101**:48
"An Ode. The Poet to his Favourite Critic" (D'Israeli) **217**:305
"Ode to a Child" (Blind) **202**:41
"Ode to a Mountain Oak" (Boker) **125**:78
"Ode to a Nightingale" (Keats) **8**:328, 332, 351, 355, 365, 368-69, 376-78, 380, 386-88, 390-91; **73**:143, 154, 159, 165-66, 174, 184, 198-201, 203, 209, 212-13, 244, 261-62, 294, 309, 312; **121**:110-12, 123, 144; **225**:122, 124-25, 130, 132, 136, 140, 142, 148, 162, 168-69, 187, 196, 242-45, 263
"Ode to America" (Boker) **125**:39
"Ode to Apathy" (Robinson) **142**:98
"Ode to Apollo" (Cowper) **94**:34
"Ode to Apollo" (Keats) **73**:151, 257, 328
"Ode to Autumn" (Hood) **16**:225, 227-28, 231, 233
"Ode to Autumn" (Keats) **8**:348-49, 368, 379-83; **73**:155, 158, 163, 165, 193, 198, 213-14, 218, 233-37, 248, 285, 308-09, 327, 329, 339-42; **121**:113, 145-46, 149, 211; **225**:112, 122, 126, 130, 134, 136-37, 149, 162, 165, 167-70, 214, 217-21, 226, 251-53, 263
"Ode to Beauty" (Emerson) **1**:296-97; **38**:192
"Ode to Corinth" (Landor) **14**:161, 187, 196
"Ode to David the Sculptor" (Sainte-Beuve) **5**:340
"Ode to Diana" (Mill) **58**:319
Ode to Dragon, Mr. Garrick's House-Dog at Hampton (More) **141**:256
"Ode to Duty" (Wordsworth) **12**:395, 444, 451, 458, 459, 460; **38**:360, 368, 398; **111**:228; **206**:225, 266, 288
"Ode to Evening" (Warton) **118**:298
"The Ode to Fancy" (Freneau) **1**:314; **111**:151
"Ode to Fancy" (Warton) **118**:298, 349-51, 353-57, 359
"Ode to Felitsa" (Derzhavin)
See "Felitsa"
"Ode to Fortune" (Derzhavin)
See "Na sčast'e"
"Ode to Fortune" (Halleck) **47**:76
"Ode to France" (Coleridge) **9**:149; **54**:85; **111**:310; **177**:113, 116; **197**:211; **231**:51, 57, 60, 155
"Ode to Freedom" (Pushkin)
See "Vol'nost': Oda"
"Ode to Freedom" (Slowacki) **15**:349
"Ode to Friendship, Inscribed to J. F. M. Dovaston of West Felton" (Reynolds) **146**:187
"Ode to Genius" (Hunt) **1**:406
"Ode to God" (Derzhavin)
See "Bog"
"Ode to Health" (Warton) **118**:298
"Ode to Heaven" (Shelley) **18**:332; **175**:239
Ode to His Lady on Her Recovery (Foscolo)
See *Ode all'amica risanata*
"Ode to Hope" (Beattie) **25**:106
"Ode to Ingratitude" (Robinson) **142**:109
"Ode to Joy" (Beethoven) **227**:32
Ode to Joy (Schiller)
See *Lied an die Freude*
"Ode to Liberty" (Horton) **87**:101
"Ode to Liberty" (Pushkin)
See "Vol'nost': Oda"
"Ode to Liberty" (Radishchev) **190**:277-78, 280, 287, 289, 293, 315, 320
"Ode to Liberty" (Shelley) **18**:319, 327, 361-62; **93**:271, 359; **143**:196; **175**:196, 220, 272, 281, 324
"Ode to Maia" (Keats) **8**:348
"Ode to Meditation" (Robinson) **142**:150
"Ode to Melancholy" (Hood) **16**:206, 219, 224, 236
"Ode to Memory" (Tennyson) **30**:204, 211, 223, 233; **65**:358; **115**:358
"Ode, to Miss Shiells" (Yearsley) **174**:339
"Ode to Naples" (Shelley) **18**:338; **93**:359, 367; **175**:221, 268
"Ode to Napoleon Buonaparte" (Byron) **2**:62
"Ode to Peace" (Beattie) **25**:112
"Ode to Peace" (Williams) **135**:300, 305-7, 314, 334
"Ode to Pity" (Austen) **119**:13
"Ode to Psyche" (Keats) **8**:363, 368-71, 376, 379, 389, 391; **73**:154, 158-59, 165, 198-200, 211, 215, 231, 233, 243, 270; **121**:100, 102-3, 106, 123, 128; **225**:122, 127, 129-30, 132, 135, 148, 166, 168
"Ode to Rae Wilson, Esquire" (Hood) **16**:205, 216, 219, 226, 229, 233, 235
Ode to Sappho (Grillparzer)
See *Sappho*
"Ode to Sir Andrew Agnew, Bart." (Hood) **16**:235
"Ode to Sleep" (Trumbull) **30**:348-49, 352
"Ode to Solitude" (Warton) **118**:298, 350
"Ode to Sorrow" (Keats) **8**:348; **73**:198
"Ode to Spring" (Barbauld) **185**:7
"Ode to Spring" (Robinson) **142**:178
"Ode to Spring" (Timrod) **25**:362
"Ode to Superstition" (Warton) **118**:356
Ode to Superstition (Rogers) **69**:66-7, 73
"Ode to the Confederate Dead" (Timrod)
See "Ode Sung on the Occasion of Decorating the Graves of the Confederate Dead at Magnolia Cemetery"
"Ode to the Departing Year" (Coleridge) **99**:66; **197**:310
"Ode to the Great Unknown" (Hood) **16**:200
"Ode to The Happy Life" (Warton) **118**:349, 359
"An Ode to the Hills" (Lampman) **25**:186, 189, 193, 204, 219; **194**:38, 43, 77-80, 93
"Ode to the Moon" (Hood) **16**:219, 221
"Ode to the Nightingale" (Keats)
See "Ode to a Nightingale"
"Ode to the Nightingale" (Robinson) **142**:150
"Ode to the Polar Star" (Brontë) **109**:27
"Ode to the River Derwent" (Darwin) **106**:182
"Ode to the Sun" (Heredia)
See "Al sol"
"Ode to the Surveyor-General" (Halleck) **47**:76
"The Ode to the West Wind" (Morris) **4**:431
"Ode to the West Wind" (Shelley) **18**:319, 345, 361, 372; **93**:305; **143**:197; **175**:224, 264, 273, 336
"Ode to Twilight" (Opie) **65**:156
"Ode to West" (Warton) **118**:298
"Ode to Winter" (Campbell) **19**:188
"Ode to Youth" (Mickiewicz)
See "Oda o Mlodości"
"An Odelet to Master Izaak Walton" (Reynolds) **146**:172
"Ode. Transposition of Psalm 82" (Derzhavin)
See "Oda. Prelozhenie 81-go psalma"
Les odelettes (Banville) **9**:19, 26
Odelettes (Nerval) **1**:486; **67**:303, 306
Oden (Klopstock) **225**:290, 305-8, 310-11
Oden an den Herrn Ebert (Klopstock) **225**:298
"Oden an Laura" (Schiller) **39**:339
"Odes" (Patmore) **9**:345
Odes (Cumberland) **167**:186
Odes (Foscolo) **97**:62
Odes and Addresses to Great People (Hood) **16**:200, 202, 219, 223, 233
Odes and Addresses to Great People (Reynolds) **146**:170, 173, 175, 188, 193
Odes en son honneur (Verlaine) **230**:160, 164, 166, 170, 183
Odes et ballades (Hugo) **3**:234, 236; **21**:202, 214; **161**:241, 264
Odes et poésies diverses (Hugo) **3**:236
Odes et poesies sacrées (Hugo) **3**:233, 236
Odes funambulesques (Banville) **9**:16-17, 19, 23-25, 27, 30
Odes in Her Honor (Verlaine)
See *Odes en son honneur*
Odes of Anacreon (Moore) **6**:376-77, 382, 392, 399; **110**:183-84, 189
The Odes of John Keats (Keats) **225**:251-53
Odes of Klopstock from 1747 to 1780 (Klopstock) **11**:228
Odes on Various Subjects (Warton) **118**:300, 304, 308, 335-37, 349-51, 358-60
Odes to Free America (Alfieri)
See *Odi per l'America libera*
Odes to His Royal Highness the Prince Regent, and His Imperial Majesty the Emperor of Russia (Southey) **97**:262
Odes Translated and Composed at Chitalagay Hill in 1774 (Derzhavin)
See *Ody perevedennyia i sochinennyia pri gore Chitalagae 1774 goda*
Odi per l'America libera (Alfieri) **101**:41, 51-2
"Odin" (Boker) **125**:35
Odluki i poeta (Fredro) **8**:284
"Odnodum" (Leskov) **174**:6, 54, 57
O'Donnel (Morgan) **29**:387, 389, 393
The O'Donoghue: A Tale of Ireland Fifty Years Ago (Lever) **23**:292, 294, 300, 305, 307
The O'Dowd (Boucicault)
See *Daddy O'Dowd*
Ody perevedennyia i sochinennyia pri gore Chitalagae 1774 goda (Derzhavin) **215**:22, 51
"Odyn and the Poet" (Eminescu) **131**:287
"L'Odyssée d'une fille" (Maupassant) **83**:194, 197, 200
Odyssey (Zhukovsky) **35**:379-81, 391-93
The Odyssey of Homer (Morris) **4**:420-21, 441
Oedipus Tyrannus; Or Swellfoot the Tyrant (Shelley) **93**:271, 359-61, 363-65, 367; **175**:325
L'oeillet blanc (Daudet) **1**:231, 249
"Oenone" (Tennyson) **30**:212, 223, 245, 258, 280; **65**:227, 267; **115**:235, 258; **202**:184
Oenone (Tennyson)
See *The Death of Oenone, Akbar's Dream, and Other Poems*
"O'er the Tree Tops" (Eminescu) **33**:265
"Ó-és újkor" (Madach) **19**:369
Oeuvre (Rimbaud) **4**:476
L'oeuvre de Watteau (Goncourt and Goncourt) **7**:165
Oeuvres (Leopardi) **129**:247
Oeuvres (Renan) **145**:346
Oeuvres (Sand) **2**:586
Oeuvres (Schlegel) **142**:308
Oeuvres autobiographiques (Sand) **42**:332
Oeuvres complémentaires (Nerval) **67**:315

Oeuvres complètes (Charriere) **66**:134-5, 137, 141-2, 146, 161, 172
Oeuvres complètes (Chateaubriand) **3**:114; **134**:37
Œuvres complètes (Flaubert) **135**:104; **185**:302
Oeuvres complètes (Lautréamont) **194**:190-93, 261-64
Oeuvres complètes (Mallarmé) **210**:167-69, 175, 206-7, 209-15, 231-34, 249-55, 257
Oeuvres complètes (Maupassant) **83**:163
Oeuvres complètes (Michelet) **218**:332-36, 338
Oeuvres complètes (Rimbaud) **227**:191, 199, 201, 250, 273-81, 292-99, 309-18, 323, 330
Oeuvres complètes (Sade) **47**:349
Oeuvres complètes (Staël-Holstein) **91**:332-36
Oeuvres complètes (Verlaine) **51**:365
Oeuvres Completes d'Alexis de Tocqueville (Tocqueville) **63**:280
Oeuvres complètes de Charles Baudelaire (Baudelaire) **155**:16-18, 20-21, 66-79, 82, 87-91, 98-101, 104-8, 112-14
Oeuvres complètes de George Sand (Sand) **42**:323, 357; **57**:337
Oeuvres complètes de Honoré de Balzac (Balzac) **153**:148-49, 153
Œuvres complètes de Jules Laforgue (Laforgue) **53**:277; **221**:21, 52
Oeuvres complètes de Lamartine publiées et inédites (Lamartine) **190**:254
Oeuvres complètes de Victor Hugo (Hugo) **189**:203
Oeuvres de jeunesse (Balzac) **5**:58
Oeuvres de jeunesse inédites (Flaubert) **2**:255; **135**:93
Oeuvres diverses (Balzac) **153**:150-51
Oeuvres dramatiques du comte Alfieri (Alfieri) **101**:75
Les oeuvres et les hommes (Barbey d'Aurevilly) **213**:39, 41-44, 93
Oeuvres intimes (Stendhal) **178**:219-21
Oeuvres philosophiques (Balzac)
See *Études philosophiques*
Oeuvres poétiques (Hugo) **161**:241
Oeuvres poétiques (Verlaine) **230**:185
Oeuvres poétiques complètes (Lamartine) **190**:219, 225-26
Oeuvres poétiques complètes (Verlaine) **230**:160-75, 178
Oeuvres poétiques: La volupté et pièces diverses (Bertrand) **31**:54-5
Oeuvres posthumes (Verlaine) **51**:365
Oeuvres posthurnes (Maupassant) **83**:178-79, 181
Œuvres romanesques complètes (Barbey d'Aurevilly) **213**:40-42, 62-69, 98-101
"Of All the Souls That Stand Create" (Dickinson) **21**:74; **171**:96
"Of Bronze—and Blaze" (Dickinson) **21**:64-5; **171**:118, 185-86
"Of Choice in Reading" (Godwin) **130**:115
"Of Course—I prayed—" (Dickinson) **171**:101
Of Dandyism and of George Brummel (Barbey d'Aurevilly)
See *Du dandysme et de Georges Brummel*
"Of Difference of Opinion" (Godwin) **130**:113
"Of History and Romance" (Godwin) **130**:170
"Of Increasing Wealth, as it Affects the Condition of the Poor" (Malthus) **145**:209
Of Laws in Gerneral (Bentham) **38**:94
"Of Literary Genius" (D'Israeli) **217**:315-16
"Of Love and Friendship" (Godwin) **130**:136
"Of Many a Smutch'd Deed Reminiscent" (Whitman) **31**:435
"Of Miscellanies" (D'Israeli) **217**:321, 339
"Of Old Sat Freedom on the Heights" (Tennyson) **30**:294
"Of Pacchiarotto, and How He Worked in Distemper" (Browning)
See "Pacchiarotto"
"Of Paradise' Existence" (Dickinson) **21**:65
Of Population (Godwin) **14**:50
"Of That Blithe Throat of Mine..." (Whitman) **31**:434
"Of That Blithe Throat of Thine" (Whitman) **205**:159
Of The Difference Between a Genius and an Apostle (Kierkegaard) **78**:197
"Of the disease of the woe in dreams" (Polidori)
See "De Morbo Oneirodynia"
Of the Force of the Present Government of France and of the Necessity of Rallying behind it (Constant)
See *De la force du gouvernement actuel de la France et de la nécessité de s'y rallier*
Of the Goethe Foundation at Weimar (Liszt)
See *De la Fondation-Goethe à Weimar*
"Of the Terrible Doublt of Appearances" (Whitman) **81**:314, 363
"Of the Terrible Doubt of Appearances" (Whitman) **205**:314
"Of the Weakness of Feelings and the Intensity of Theirs (The Double Assiduity of Epistemology and Observation)""O slabosmi chuvsmv i o napryazhiennosmi onykh. (Dvoyakij priklad om poznanij i nablyudieniya)" (Leskov) **174**:136
Of Tombs (Foscolo)
See *I sepolcri*
"Of Tradition" (Sainte-Beuve) **5**:350
"Of Tribulation These Are They" (Dickinson) **21**:31, 38, 55
"Of Truth" (Hölderlin)
See "Von der Wahrheit"
Of Tyranny (Alfieri)
See *Della tirannide*
"Of what do you wail, wind of the night?" (Tyutchev)
See "O chem ty voesh, vetr nochnoy?"
"Of what use are the dreams of freedom to a slave?..." (Baratynsky)
See "K chemu nevolniku mechtania svobody?..."
"Of Yore" (Hugo) **3**:253
"Off Rough Point" (Lazarus) **8**:426
Off the Skelligs (Ingelow) **39**:259-60, 264; **107**:118, 124-25
Offenbarungen (Arnim) **159**:35
"The Offering of the New Law, the One Oblation Once Offered" (Rossetti) **186**:258
"Offices" (Mallarmé) **210**:254
Offices (Mallarmé) **41**:254, 259
"Official Piety" (Whittier) **8**:525-26; **59**:361
Official Report of the Niger Valley Exploring Party (Delany) **93**:158-61, 167, 170, 173
"An Official's Morning" (Gogol) **162**:16, 20
"Oft in the Stilly Night" (Moore) **6**:389; **110**:194, 196
Ofterdingen (Novalis)
See *Heinrich von Ofterdingen*
"Ogier the Dane" (Morris) **4**:417, 442, 447
The Ogilvies (Craik) **38**:109, 120, 122
Ogilvies (Oliphant) **11**:428
"Ogon" (Pavlova) **138**:4, 12
"Ogorodnik" (Nekrasov) **11**:412
"Ogres" (Thackeray) **213**:235
"Ogsaa et Forsvar for Qvindens hoie Anlæg" (Kierkegaard) **125**:265
"Ogyges" (Kendall) **12**:190-92, 201
"Oh! Blame Not the Bard" (Moore) **6**:390; **110**:185
"Oh! Can You Leave Your Native Land?" (Moodie) **113**:344
"Oh Canada! Thy Gloomy Woods" (Moodie) **113**:345-46
"Oh Chasm, Suck Me in!" (Laforgue)
See "Ô gouffre, aspire-moi!"
"Oh, Clear Up Cold Dark . . ." (Eminescu) **33**:263
"Oh, Do Not Look at Me" (Arany)
See "Oh! ne rézz rám"
"Oh Fairest of the Rural Maids" (Bryant) **6**:171-72, 179, 182, 186
"Oh! For a Closer Walk with God" (Cowper) **8**:127
"Oh! Had We Some Bright Little Isle of Our Own" (Moore) **6**:396
"Oh, knell of a passing time" (Rossetti) **186**:343, 346
"Oh love, art thou a silver deer?" (Crawford) **127**:202
"Oh Mother of a Mighty Race" (Bryant) **46**:7
"Oh! ne rézz rám" (Arany) **34**:19
"Oh seasons, oh castles" (Rimbaud)
See "O saisons, ô châteaux!"
"Oh, Stay with Me" (Eminescu) **131**:296, 340
"Oh! Susanna" (Foster) **26**:282, 285, 291-92, 294, 298
"Oh, to be in England" (Browning) **79**:98
"Oh, to the Dead Be Faithful" (Storm) **1**:537
"Oh Triumphant You . . ." (Verlaine)
See "Ô toi triomphante . . ."
"O'Hussey's Ode to the Maguire" (Mangan) **27**:283, 289, 292, 296-98, 311, 313-14
"Oinea" (O'Brien) **21**:244
"L'oiseau bleu" (Daudet) **1**:249
Ojciec zadżumionych (Slowacki) **15**:348-50, 354, 358, 364
"Los ojos negros" (Alarcón) **219**:45, 52
"Los ojos pardos" (Isaacs) **70**:307
"Los ojos verdes" (Bécquer) **106**:86-8, 97-8, 108, 120-21, 124, 130, 132, 134
"Okatootáia" (Petofi) **21**:280
Oktavia (Kotzebue) **25**:134, 141
"Oktober 1849" (Heine) **147**:234
Oktoberlied (Storm) **195**:21
"Olalla" (Stevenson) **5**:429, 431; **14**:334, 339; **193**:209, 215, 279
"Olaszország" (Petofi) **21**:286
The Old Adam (Boyesen) **135**:13
"Old Adam, the Carrion Crow" (Beddoes) **3**:32
"Old Age" (Emerson) **1**:280
Old Age Echoes (Whitman) **205**:226
Old age of Toldi (Arany)
See *Toldi estéje*
"The Old Agency" (Woolson) **82**:272, 284
Old and Modern Poems (Vigny)
See *Poèmes antiques et modernes*
"Old and New Art" (Rossetti) **4**:529; **77**:348
"Old and New Year Ditties" (Rossetti) **50**:272
"The Old and the New Schoolmaster" (Lamb) **10**:408, 410, 436; **113**:162, 190, 192-93, 217, 236
"The Old and the Young" (Eminescu) **131**:325
"The Old Apple Dealer" (Hawthorne) **2**:296; **226**:76
"The Old Ash Tree" (Moodie) **113**:316-17
"The Old Bachelor" (Crabbe) **26**:110
"An Old Bachelor" (Mitford) **4**:408
"Old Bachelors at Auction" (Smith) **187**:333
"The Old Bachelor's Nightcap" (Andersen) **214**:57-58
"Old Ballads" (Reynolds) **146**:186
"The Old Bardic Poetry" (Barnes) **75**:46, 53-4
"Old Barnard, a Monkish Tale" (Robinson) **142**:136, 170, 249
"The Old Benchers of the Inner Temple" (Lamb) **10**:407, 416, 435-36; **113**:162, 177, 218, 236
"Old Billowy Hawksb'ry" (Harpur) **114**:144
"Old Black Joe" (Foster) **26**:285-86, 289, 291, 295, 298-99
"Old Burns's Bull-Ride" (Harris) **23**:159, 163; **165**:182, 200, 210, 224, 228, 230, 242, 244, 254-55
The Old Castellan (Sacher-Masoch) **31**:295
"Old China" (Lamb) **10**:407-08, 410, 428, 435-37; **113**:157, 163, 173, 200, 252, 265-66
Old Christmas (Irving) **19**:351
The Old Church: What Shall We Do with It? (Hughes) **207**:131
The Old Clothesman (Holcroft) **85**:198

The Old Continental; or, The Price of Liberty (Paulding) **2**:527-28, 530
"Old Coppees" (Verlaine) **51**:372
Old Court (Ainsworth) **13**:42
"The Old Cumberland Beggar" (Wordsworth) **12**:470; **111**:228, 236, 279, 347-48
The Old Curiosity Shop (Dickens) **3**:141, 142, 152, 156, 166, 167, 173, 181, 182, 183, 184; **8**:174, 182; **18**:100, 112, 121; **26**:167; **86**:256; **105**:227, 231; **113**:91, 107, 110, 124, 127, 129; **161**:19; **203**:246; **206**:1-151; **217**:245; **219**:67, 70, 109, 143, 210, 227, 229; **230**:89, 91, 113; **231**:176, 225
Old Days in Plodomasovo (Leskov)
See *Starye gody v sele Plodomasove*
"Old Dog Tray" (Foster) **26**:283, 291
The Old English Baron (Reeve) **19**:407-13, 415-16, 418-21
Old English Theatre (Tieck) **5**:511
Old enough have I become now (Grundtvig)
See *Gammel nok er jeg nu blevet*
"Old Esther Dudley" (Hawthorne) **158**:228
"Old Familiar Faces" (Lamb) **10**:404, 407; **113**:161
"An Old Foe with a New Face" (Webb) **143**:357
"Old Folks at Home" (Foster) **26**:281-87, 289-91, 294, 297-99
"The Old Folks' Party" (Bellamy) **4**:31; **86**:75
"Old Gardiston" (Woolson) **82**:273, 294-95, 297, 300-03, 322, 339
The Old Gardner's Letters (Runeberg)
See *Den gamle trädgårdsmästarens brev*
"Old General de Berir—Untitled story about" (Crawford) **127**:193
"The Old Ghost" (Beddoes) **154**:50
Old Goriot (Balzac)
See *Le père Goriot: Histoire Parisienne*
"Old Hannah; or, The Charm" (Moodie) **14**:231
Old Heads and Young Hearts (Boucicault) **41**:28
"The Old House" (Andersen) **79**:89; **214**:72
"The Old House" (Lampman) **194**:74-76, 82-83, 91-92
"The Old House" (Levy) **59**:80, 93, 119
The Old House at Coate (Jefferies) **47**:129
Old Humphrey's Clock (Dickens)
See *Master Humphrey's Clock*
"Old Icons and New Icons" (Eminescu) **131**:326
"Old Ironsides" (Holmes) **14**:98, 109, 125, 128
The Old Judge; or, Life in a Colony (Haliburton) **15**:125-26, 129, 132, 145, 147-48, 151; **149**:267, 269, 286, 309-10, 313-14, 318-20
"The Old Lady in Threadneedle Street" (Dickens) **187**:135-36, 138
"Old Lady Mary" (Oliphant) **221**:232, 260
Old Lady Mary (Oliphant) **11**:446
"The Old Landowner" (Turgenev) **21**:376-77
"Old Leaven" (Gordon) **21**:160
"An Old Lesson from the Fields" (Lampman) **25**:194; **194**:21, 74, 102
"Old Love" (Morris) **4**:431, 444
The Old Maid. A Comedy in Two Acts. As it is Performed at the Theatre-Royal in Drury-Lane. By Mr. Murphy (Murphy) **229**:254
"Old Maids" (Sedgwick) **19**:440
"The Old Man" (Derzhavin) **215**:19
"The Old Man Dreams" (Holmes) **81**:96
The Old Man of the Mountain, The Love-Charm, and Pietro of Abano (Tieck) **5**:512
"The Old Man Travelling" (Wordsworth) **12**:387; **111**:202, 273-77, 279-83, 286-87, 306, 310, 315, 348, 357, 367
The Old Manor House (Smith) **23**:318, 320, 322-31, 333, 336; **115**:133, 145, 147-50, 166, 174, 207, 211, 222-24
"The Old Man's Comforts" (Southey) **97**:291
"The Old Man's Counsel" (Bryant) **6**:187; **46**:25, 49
"The Old Man's Funeral" (Bryant) **6**:159, 162; **46**:3
An Old Man's Love (Trollope) **6**:467, 500, 518
"The Old Manse" (Hawthorne) **39**:181; **79**:311; **95**:106, 137; **158**:243, 329
Old Margaret (Kingsley) **107**:192, 211
"The Old Margate Hoy" (Lamb) **10**:411, 435-36; **113**:217, 219, 251
The Old Masters of Belguim and Holland (Fromentin)
See *Les maîtres d'autrefois: Belgigue, Hollande*
"Old Mat and His Man" (Krylov) **1**:439
"Old Memories" (Foster) **26**:295
"Old Mortality" (Stevenson) **5**:416
Old Mortality (Scott) **15**:260-61, 272, 283, 285, 289, 292, 300, 303-04, 309, 313-15, 321-22; **69**:304-05, 308, 366, 371; **110**:233, 313-14; **209**:199-203, 230, 235, 242, 250, 263-64, 272, 302, 316, 318
"The Old Mountebank" (Baudelaire) **155**:113
Old Mr. Tredgold (Oliphant) **11**:449; **61**:215
"Old Myers" (Smith) **187**:319
"Old News" (Hawthorne) **2**:329
"The Old Nurse's Story" (Gaskell) **5**:206; **70**:186, 189, 193, 196-97; **97**:127; **214**:333, 341
"Old Oak of Summer Chace" (Tennyson) **30**:215
"Old Oak Tree's Last Dream" (Andersen)
See "The Last Dream of the Old Oak"
"The Old Oak Tree's Last Dream" (Andersen)
See "Det gamle Egetæs sidste Drøm"
"The Old Oak Tree's Last Thoughts" (Andersen)
See "Det gamle Egetæs sidste Drøm"
"Old Pictures in Florence" (Browning) **19**:131-32, 154; **79**:161
"The Old Poet" (Levy) **59**:89
"Old Poets Foster'd Under Friendlier Skies" (Tennyson) **202**:290
"Old Portraits" (Turgenev)
See "Starye portrety"
Old Portraits and Modern Sketches (Whittier) **59**:365
The Old Red Sandstone; or, New Walks in an Old Field, to Which Is Appended a Series of Geological Papers Read before the Royal Physical Society of Edinburgh (Miller) **143**:3, 6, 16-20, 22, 24, 29-30, 33, 39, 41-44, 58
The Old Regime and the Revolution (Tocqueville)
See *L'ancien régime et la révolution*
The Old Régime in Canada (Parkman) **12**:333-34, 336, 341-44, 348, 351, 370-71, 374
Old Saint Paul's: A Tale of the Plague and the Fire (Ainsworth) **13**:28, 31-4, 36-7, 39-40, 43, 45, 47
"The Old Saloon" (Oliphant) **221**:240, 242, 320-21
"Old Sári" (Petofi)
See "Sári néni"
"The Old Seer" (Tennyson)
See "The Ancient Sage"
Old Sir Douglas (Norton) **47**:248, 257-58; **205**:67, 69, 71, 81-82, 86
"Old Skissim's Middle Boy" (Harris) **23**:156-57, 159; **165**:184, 252, 254, 264, 291-92
"An Old Song" (Stevenson) **193**:281
"An Old Song Ended" (Rossetti) **77**:337
"Old Spense" (Crawford) **12**:151-52, 172
"Old Spookses' Pass" (Crawford) **12**:151-54, 156-58, 160-63, 171-72; **127**:178, 195, 197, 199-200, 203, 224-25
Old Spookses' Pass, Malcolm's Katie, and Other Poems (Crawford) **12**:151-53, 158; **127**:148, 161, 203, 218
"Old St. David's at Radnor" (Longfellow) **45**:130
"The Old Stoic" (Brontë) **16**:70
The Old Stone House (Woolson) **82**:272, 325
Old Tales of a Young Country (Clarke) **19**:256-59
"Old Things" (Silva)
See "Vejeces"
"Old things need not be therefore true" (Prescott) **163**:6
"Old Times" (Dana) **53**:178
Old Times in Poshekhouie (Saltykov)
See *Poshekhonskaya starina*
"Old Times in the Village of Plodomasovo" (Leskov)
See "Starye gody v sele Plodomasove"
"Old Uncle Ned" (Foster) **26**:281-82, 285-86, 289, 291
"Old War-Dreams" (Whitman) **31**:392
"The Old Washerwoman" (Chamisso) **82**:6
The Old Weathercock on the Tower (Mörike)
See *Der alte Turmhahn: Idyll*
"The Old Woman" (Pavlova)
See "Starukha"
"The Old Woman" (Turgenev) **21**:452
"The Old Woman Clothed in Grey" (Barham) **77**:36
"The Old Woman of Berkeley" (Southey) **8**:472, 474
"The Old Woman's Despair" (Baudelaire)
See "Le désespoir de la vieille"
"Old Woman's Gossip" (Kemble)
See *Record of a Girlhood: An Autobiography*
The Old World and Russia (Herzen) **10**:329
The Old World and the New (Trollope) **30**:315
"An Old World Thicket" (Rossetti) **50**:293; **66**:342; **186**:235, 306
"Old Years in Plodomasova" (Leskov)
See "Starye gody v sele Plodomasove"
Old Years in Plodomasovo (Leskov)
See *Starye gody v sele Plodomasove*
"Olden Times in the Village of Plodomasovo" (Leskov)
See "Starye gody v sele Plodomasove"
"The Olden Warrior" (Harpur) **114**:144
The Oldest Document of the Human Race (Herder)
See *Älteste Urkunde des Menschengeschlechts*
Oldest Heroic Songs (Karadzic)
See *Pjesme junaĉke najstarije*
"The Oldest Inhabitant" (Webster) **230**:239
An Old-Fashioned Girl (Alcott) **6**:14-16, 20-21; **58**:48, 69; **83**:30, 47
"Old-Fashioned Landowners" (Gogol)
See "Starosvetskie Pomešciki"
"Old-Testament Gospel" (Cowper) **94**:74
Oldtown Fireside Stories (Stowe) **3**:563
Oldtown Folks (Stowe) **3**:553-56, 561-63, 568
"Old-World Landowners" (Gogol)
See "Starosvetskie Pomešciki"
"Ole luck-oin" (Andersen) **7**:16
"Ole Luköie" (Andersen) **79**: **79**:15, 17, 23, 28, 34; **214**:55, 76-77
"Ole Shut-Eye" (Andersen)
See "Ole luck-oin"
"Ole the Tower-Keeper" (Andersen) **214**:58
"Oleszkiewicz" (Mickiewicz) **3**:401
Olive (Craik) **38**:110, 119, 120, 130
"Olive Buds" (Sigourney) **87**:321
Oliver Twist (Dickens) **3**:138-41, 153-54, 168-69, 175-77, 182, 184; **8**:182, 199; **18**:122-23, 132, 139; **26**:156, 159, 167, 172; **37**:133-214; **86**:255-56; **105**:214, 226, 337; **113**:28, 89, 96, 98, 102-3, 106, 118, 120, 124; **161**:42-43, 50, 76, 124; **203**:169-291; **211**:25, 32; **217**:225, 244-45; **219**:66, 83-84, 86, 98, 101, 110, 118, 184, 186, 191, 193, 210, 235
"Oliver Twist, or, The Parish Boy's Progress" (Dickens)
See *Oliver Twist*
Oliver Twist; or, The Parish Boy's Progress (Dickens) **187**:84-85, 90-91; **206**:7, 12, 16, 27, 47, 51, 56, 88, 90, 104-5, 129, 131,

140; **231**:174-76, 180, 187, 194, 205, 212, 214, 220, 240, 250
Olivier, ou le secret (Duras) **154**:108, 112-15, 117-21, 130, 157, 160-62, 164-66
Olney Hymns (Cowper) **8**:140; **94**:68-9, 72, 102, 116
Olviretki Schleusingenissä (Kivi) **30**:50, 65
"Olympe et Théophile" (Genlis) **166**:11
Olympic Devils (Planché) **42**:286, 298, 300
Olympic Revels; or, Prometheus and Pandora (Planché) **42**:272, 285-86, 295, 297, 299
Om Asalæren (Grundtvig) **158**:175, 179
"Om Bacchanterna" (Stagnelius) **61**:266
Om Begrebet Ironi med stadigt Hensyn til Socrates (Kierkegaard) **34**:222-23, 236, 268; **78**:250; **125**:184, 186, 189-90, 192-93, 202-3, 209, 232,
Om brottsliges behandling (Almqvist) **42**:17
"Om poesi i sak" (Almqvist) **42**:18-19
O'Malley (Lever)
See *Charles O'Malley, the Irish Dragoon*
"Ombra adorata" (Hoffmann) **2**:346-47
"L'ombre des arbres" (Verlaine) **51**:384
The Omen (Galt) **1**:330, 334
"Omens" (Baratynsky)
See "Primety"
Omne animal (Silva) **114**:263
Omniana (Southey) **8**:468, 472; **97**:271, 288, 330
"Omnibuses" (Dickens) **187**:26
"Omnipotence in Bonds" (Newman) **38**:305, 310
"Omnipresence" (Grillparzer)
See "Allgegenwart"
Omoo (Melville)
See *Omoo: A Narrative of Adventures in the South Seas*
Omoo: A Narrative of Adventures in the South Seas (Melville) **3**:326-28, 330, 333-34, 337, 339-41, 347, 355-56, 360, 363-64, 370; **12**:255, 257; **29**:331, 354; **45**:194-95, 206, 210, 212, 244, 248-49, 251, 253; **91**:10, 42, 45, 55, 212; **123**:187, 192, 211, 231-32, 236-39, 251-52; **157**:65, 68, 109; **181**:154, 164, 204, 212, 230, 263, 327-28; **221**:104, 116, 118, 122, 128, 140, 157
"Omphale ou la Tapisserie amoureuse, histoire rococo" (Gautier) **1**:355; **59**:10, 29, 32, 37-8, 42
"On a Cattle Track" (Kendall) **12**:181, 191
"On a Certain Condescension in Foreigners" (Lowell) **2**:517
"On a Chalk-Mark on the Door" (Thackeray) **213**:286
"On a Christmas Rose" (Mörike)
See "Auf eine Christblume"
"On a Dead Woman" (Laforgue) **221**:50
"On a Dream" (Keats) **73**:191-94
"On a Dutch Landscape" (Lenau) **16**:276
"On a Forsaken Lark's Nest" (Blind) **202**:48
"On a Future State" (Shelley) **175**:240
"On a Goldfinch Starved to Death in His Cage" (Cowper) **94**:123
"On a Lady's Singing Bird" (Freneau) **111**:145
"On a Lady's Writing" (Barbauld) **185**:91
"On a Landscape of Nicholas Poussin" (Hazlitt) **82**:157
"On a Lock of My Mother's Hair" (Lazarus) **8**:417; **109**:290
"On a Lost Greyhound" (Clare) **9**:105
"On a Panegyric of Theocracy and Mortmain" (Fourier) **51**:184
"On a Peal of Bells" (Thackeray) **213**:308
"On a Picture of a Girl Leading Her Blind Mother" (Willis) **194**:288, 297
"On a Picture of the Corpse of Napoleon lying in State" (Coleridge) **90**:27
"On a Piece of Chalk" (Huxley) **67**:16, 48, 58, 80, 83, 90
"On a Piece of Music" (Hopkins) **17**:194; **189**:56
"On a Prayer-Book: With Its Frontispiece, Ary Scheffer's 'Christus Consolator,' Americanized by the Omission of the Black Man" (Whittier) **8**:525, 531; **59**:361
"On a Rock" (O'Brien) **21**:249
"On a Spiteful Letter" (Tennyson)
See "The Spiteful Letter"
"On a Street" (Kendall) **12**:198
"On a Sunday" (Meyer)
See "Sonntags"
"On a Sun-Dial" (Hazlitt) **82**:95-6
"On a Survey of the Heavens" (Warren) **226**:261
"On a Target at Drakelow" (Darwin) **106**:182
"On a Tear" (Rogers) **69**:73
"On a Text Heard in the Street" (Crawford) **127**:220
"On a Torso of Cupid" (Blind) **202**:57
"On a Tuft of Grass" (Lazarus) **8**:413
"On a Winter's Morning" (Mörike)
See "An einem Wintermorgen"
On Actors and the Art of Acting (Lewes) **25**:284-85, 290, 308, 315-17, 319, 325; **215**:86, 131
"On Amanda's Singing Bird" (Freneau) **111**:133
On an Ancient Hymn to the Graces (Foscolo) **97**:53
"On an Infant Dying as Soon as Born" (Lamb) **10**:405
"On an Infant: Which Died Before Baptism" (Coleridge) **197**:215
"On an Infant's Grave" (Clare) **9**:74
"On Another's Sorrow" (Blake) **13**:220; **37**:3, 5, 23, 41, 72, 92
"On Application to Study" (Hazlitt) **29**:147
"On Art in Fiction" (Bulwer-Lytton) **45**:23, 69
On Authority and Revelation: The Book on Adler (Kierkegaard) **34**:238; **78**:152, 154, 197
"On Awakening the Mind" (Godwin) **14**:75
"On Becoming Sober" (Kierkegaard) **34**:225
On Beethoven's Music to Egmont (Liszt) **199**:305
"On Being a Good Hater" (Hazlitt) **82**:90
"On being cautioned against walking on an headland overlooking the sea, because it was frequented by a lunatic" (Smith)
See "Sonnet 70"
"On Being Presented with a Silver Pen" (Yearsley) **174**:317, 339
"On Blending Spirit with Matter" (Murray) **63**:207
"On bly ubit" (Bestuzhev) **131**:161
On Board "The Emma" (Dumas)
See *Les Garibaldiens*
"On Bogdanovich and his Works" (Karamzin)
See "O Bogdanoviche i yego sochineniyakh"
"On Burial Societies and the Character of the Undertaker" (Lamb) **10**:436
"On Burlesque" (Murphy) **229**:251
"On Calais Sands" (Wordsworth) **38**:413
"On Caroline" (Brontë) **109**:4
"On Catullus" (Landor) **14**:199
"On Certain Political Measures Proposed to Their Consideration" (Barlow) **23**:28
"On Chapman's Homer" (Keats) **73**:342
On Church Music of the Future (Liszt) **199**:305
"On City Burying Places" (Freneau) **111**:134
"On Classical Learning" (Brown) **74**:192
"On Comedy" (Murphy) **229**:250-51
"On Consistency of Opinion" (Hazlitt) **82**:108, 110
"On Courting" (Shaw) **15**:335
"On Cranial Nerves" (Büchner)
See "Über Schädelnerven"
"On Criticism" (Hazlitt) **29**:148, 167
"On Death" (Clare) **86**:160
"On Death" (Horton) **87**:110
"On Democracy" (Arnold) **218**:215
"On Depth and Superficiality" (Hazlitt) **82**:108, 123-24
"On Descartes' 'Discourse on Method'" (Huxley) **67**:86
"On Descartes' 'Discourse Touching the Method of Using One's Reason Rightly and of Seeking Scientific Truth'" (Huxley) **67**:65
"On Diligence in the Study of Several Learned Languages" (Herder)
See "Über den Fleis in mehreren gelehrten Sprachen"
"On Diotima" (Schlegel)
See "Über die Diotima"
"On Dover Cliffs. July 20, 1787" (Bowles) **103**:68, 72
"On Dreams" (Hazlitt) **82**:142
"On Dreams and Dreaming" (Smith) **59**:315
"On Dress" (Willis) **194**:297
"On Duelling" (Mackenzie) **41**:190
"On Education" (Barbauld) **185**:95
"On Effeminacy of Character" (Hazlitt) **29**:148
"On Elgin Marbles" (Keats) **73**:152
"On English Prose Fiction as a Rational Amusement" (Trollope) **6**:508; **33**:364; **101**:333
"On Envy" (Hazlitt) **29**:147, 156
"On Epic Poetry" (Freneau) **111**:160
"On Epic Poetry" (Murphy) **229**:252
"On Erudition and Philosophy" (D'Israeli) **217**:335
"On Falling in Love" (Stevenson) **193**:274
"On Fame" (Keats) **73**:194-95, 197
"On Familiar Style" (Hazlitt) **29**:148, 167; **82**:97-101, 115, 125
"On Female Education" (Martineau) **26**:320; **137**:237
"On Female Studies" (Barbauld) **185**:112, 122
"On First Looking into Chapman's Homer" (Keats) **8**:343, 349, 354, 361; **73**:152, 173, 258, 278, 279, 323, 339-40; **225**:137, 205, 207-8, 210-11, 223
"On Folk Songs" (Arnim)
See "Von Volksliedern"
"On Genius" (Mill) **58**:326
"On Genius and Common Sense" (Hazlitt) **29**:147, 162, 179
"On Genius. On taking leave of Dr. Priestley, when preparing to go to America" (Dyer) **129**:149
"On Gentleness" (Blair) **75**:154
"On German Opera" (Wagner) **119**:190
On Germany (Staël-Holstein) **91**:326-27
"On Goethe's *Wilhelm Meister* " (Schlegel)
See "Uber Goethes *Meister* "
"On Going a Journey" (Hazlitt) **29**:153, 166; **82**:95
"On Going a Walk" (Hazlitt) **82**:90
"On Golden Ground" (Meyer)
See "Auf Goldgrund"
"On Good-Nature" (Hazlitt) **82**:115
"On Grace and Dignity" (Schiller)
See "Über Anmut und Würde"
"On Great and Little Things" (Hazlitt) **82**:76, 89, 97
"On Greatness" (Irving) **2**:391
"On Growing Old" (Arnold) **6**:52
"On Gusto" (Hazlitt) **82**:117
"On hearing of the intention of a gentleman to purchase the Poet's freedom" (Horton) **87**:101, 109
"On Hearing the 'Messiah'" (Bowles) **103**:55
On Heroes, Hero-Worship, and the Heroic in History (Carlyle) **70**:20, 23, 26, 43, 46-55, 71
"On Himself" (Beddoes) **154**:82, 86
"On History" (Carlyle) **70**:39, 73
"On Homer's Poetry" (Blake) **173**:157
"On Howells' Work" (Boyesen) **135**:39
"On Humour" (Murphy) **229**:251
"On Idleness" (Musset) **7**:256
"On Imitation in Writing" (Murphy) **229**:252
"On Imprisonment for Debt" (Freneau) **111**:129

"On Improving Natural Knowledge" (Huxley) **67**:20
"On Incomprehensibility" (Schlegel)
See "Über die Ünverständlichkeit"
"On Jephthah's Vow" (Yearsley) **174**:316
"On Kaunisnummi" (Kivi)
See "Kaunisnummella"
"On Lake Temiscamingue" (Lampman) **25**:186, 210
"On Landing at Ostend" (Bowles) **103**:85
On Language (Humboldt) **134**:198-200
"On Latmos" (Clough) **27**:107
"On Leaving California" (Taylor) **89**:357
"On Leaving the Bottoms of Gloucestershire" (Thelwall) **162**:317, 320
On Liberty (Mill) **11**:343, 352, 360, 363, 368, 374-75, 377, 383-84, 389; **58**:327, 330-1, 342, 349-51, 359, 375-80; **179**:202, 204-6, 209-10, 227, 281, 283-84, 287, 301-5, 308-11, 316-20, 324, 329, 337, 340-41, 344, 354, 362; **223**:89-177
"On Liberty and Necessity" (Hazlitt) **82**:108, 112
"On Liberty and Slavery" (Horton) **87**:99, 101-102, 105, 109
"On Life" (Shelley) **93**:294-95, 311, 326; **175**:236
"On Literary Industry" (D'Israeli) **217**:316
"On Little Russian Songs" (Gogol) **162**:77
"On Living to One's-self" (Hazlitt) **29**:142
"On Love" (Shelley) **18**:354; **93**:286, 289, 295
On Love (Stendhal)
See *De l'amour*
"On Love of One's Country and National Pride" (Karamzin)
See "O lvubvi k otechestvu i narodnoy gordosti"
"On Luculle's Recovery" (Pushkin) **83**:272
"On Madan's Answer to Newton's Comments on Thelyohthora" (Cowper) **94**:110
"On Man, His Mortality and Immortality" (Radishchev)
See "O cheloveke, o ego smertnosti i bessmertii"
"On Manufactures" (Barbauld) **185**:57
"On Men and Pictures" (Thackeray) **213**:247-48, 329
On Mendelssohn's Music to A Midsummer Night's Dream (Liszt) **199**:305
"On Milton's Lycidas" (Hazlitt) **82**:117-18
"On Milton's Sonnets" (Hazlitt) **29**:148
"On Mme. de Staël and her works" (Constant) **182**:227
"On Modern Revolutions" (Carlyle) **70**:47
"On Monastic Institutions" (Barbauld) **50**:3
"On Mrs. Kemble's Readings from Shakespeare" (Longfellow) **45**:125
"On Mrs. Montagu" (Yearsley) **174**:300-301, 304, 318
"On Mrs. Priestley's Leaving Warrington" (Barbauld) **185**:29, 31, 36, 130
"On Murder Considered as a Fine Art" (De Quincey)
See "Lectures on Murder Considered as One of the Fine Arts"
"On Murder Considered as One of the Fine Arts" (De Quincey)
See "Lectures on Murder Considered as One of the Fine Arts"
"On Music" (Brown) **74**:174
"On Music" (Moore) **6**:399
"On My Bad Poems" (Petofi)
See "Rosz verseimröl"
"On My Birthday" (Heredia)
See "En mi cumpleaños"
"On My Volcano Grows the Grass" (Dickinson) **21**:80
On My Work as an Author (Kierkegaard) **34**:205
"On Naive and Sentimental Poetry" (Schiller)
See "Über naïve und sentimentalische Dichtung"
On Natural Acting (Lewes) **215**:131
On ne badine pas avec l'amour (Musset) **7**:258-60, 267-72, 276-78, 282-83; **150**:226-27, 234, 239, 243, 245, 282-85, 304-5, 336-37, 347, 352
On ne saurait penser à tout (Musset) **150**:251, 253-54
"On Needle-Work" (Lamb) **125**:290, 293-95, 297-98, 313, 325, 327, 361, 371
"On Nobility" (Derzhavin)
See "Na znatnost"
"On Novel Writing" (Hays) **114**:217-18
"On Novelty and Familiarity" (Hazlitt) **82**:97, 99, 101, 110
"On November 10th, 1840" (Pavlova) **138**:18
"On Observing Some Names of Little Note in the Biographia Britannica" (Cowper) **94**:121
On Oehlenschläger's Balder the Good (Grundtvig) **158**:144
"On, on the Same Ye Jocund Twain" (Whitman) **4**:586
"On Originality and Imitation" (Bryant) **46**:11, 32, 34, 53
"On Our European Literature" (Mazzini) **34**:277
"On Our Knowledge of the Causes of the Phenomena of Organic Nature" (Huxley) **67**:60
On Our Own Ground: The Complete Writings of William Apess, A Pequot (Apess) **73**:14-16
"On Oysters and the Oyster Question" (Huxley) **67**:87
"On Painting" (Brown) **74**:174
"On Paradox and Commonplace" (Hazlitt) **29**:147; **82**:99
"On Parliamentary Reform" (Southey) **97**:263
"On Pathos" (Schiller) **39**:349, 367
"On Peace" (Keats) **73**:145, 332
"On Pedantry" (Hazlitt)
See "Pedantry"
"On Personal Character" (Hazlitt) **29**:184
"On Personal Identity" (Hazlitt) **82**:81, 101
"On Philosophy" (Schlegel)
See "Uber die Philosophie"
"Das Pickenick des Katers Mores" (Brentano) **191**:81, 120
On Picket Duty, and Other Tales (Alcott) **58**:49
"The Picnic of Mores the Cat" (Brentano)
See "Das Pickenick des Katers Mores"
"On Picturesque Beauty" (Gilpin) **30**:36
"Pietro" (Brentano) **191**:8
"On Planting a Forest" (Baratynsky)
See "Na posev lesa"
"On Poesy or Art" (Coleridge) **99**:6, 87; **197**:285
"Les Poètes" (Barbey d'Aurevilly) **213**:93
"Poetess Swan Song" (Brentano)
See "Schwanenlied"
"On Poetry and Its Relation of Our Age and Country" (Bryant) **46**:33
"On Poetry and Music" (Horton)
See "On Poetry and Musick"
"On Poetry and Musick" (Horton) **87**:91, 99
"On Poetry and Painting" (Murphy) **229**:253
"On Poetry in General" (Hazlitt) **29**:160-61, 165, 174, 176, 179; **82**:93
"On Ponkawtasset, Since We Took Our Way" (Thoreau) **7**:383
"On Ponkawtasset, since, with such delay" (Thoreau)
See "On Ponkawtasset, Since We Took Our Way"
On Popular Editions of Important Works (Liszt) **199**:305
On Popular Education (Sarmiento)
See *De la educación popular*
"On Present-Day Architecture" (Gogol) **162**:97, 108
"On Pressing Some Flowers" (Timrod) **25**:372
"On Rationalism" (Coleridge) **31**:63
"On Reading" (D'Israeli) **217**:335
"On Reading New Books" (Hazlitt) **29**:148
"On Reading Old Books" (Hazlitt) **29**:147
"On Reading the Proclamation Delivered by William Lyon Mackenzie, On Navy Island" (Moodie) **113**:308, 310-11
"On Reading the 'Rubaiyat' of Omar Khayyam in a Kentish Rose Garden" (Blind) **202**:53
"On Reason and Imagination" (Hazlitt) **29**:185
"On receiving a curious Shell" (Keats) **73**:311
"On Receiving a Laurel Crown from Leigh Hunt" (Keats) **73**:332
"On Receiving an Account that His Only Sister's Death Was Inevitable" (Coleridge) **177**:161
"On Reflection" (Kleist)
See "Von der Überlegung"
On Religion (Constant)
See *De la religion considérée dans sa source, ses formes, et ses développements*
On Religion (Schleiermacher)
See *Über die Religion: Reden an die Gebildeten unter ihren Verächtern*
On Religion (Schopenhauer) **51**:271, 340
On Religion and Liturgy (Grundtvig) **158**:101, 138
On Religion and Psychology (Coleridge) **231**:153
On Religion and Public Education (More) **141**:267
On Religion: Speeches to its Cultured Despisers (Schleiermacher)
See *Über die Religion: Reden an die Gebildeten unter ihren Verächtern*
"On Retirement" (Freneau) **111**:100
On Revelation, Art and Knowledge (Grundtvig) **158**:144
"On Russian History" (Radishchev) **190**:295
"On Satirical Productions" (Trumbull) **30**:365
On Scholarship and its Encouragement (Grundtvig) **158**:138
"On Science and Art in Relation to Education" (Huxley) **67**:33, 72
"On Seeing a Lock of Milton's Hair" (Keats) **73**:257; **225**:184
"On Seeing a Skull on Cowper Green" (Clare) **9**:76, 80, 108, 119
"On Seeing the Countess of Yarmouth at Her Window in Piccadilly, On Sunday Last" (Robinson) **142**:167
"On Seeing the Elgin Marbles" (Keats) **225**:139-40, 142, 186, 248, 253, 255
"On Self-Delusion" (Adams) **106**:4
"On Sensation and the Unity of Structure of Sensiferous Organs" (Huxley) **67**:95
"On Sensibility" (Blair) **75**:155
"On Shakespeare and Milton" (Hazlitt) **29**:146, 161
"On Sitting Down to Read King Lear Once Again" (Keats) **8**:344; **73**:259, 323
"On Social Freedom" (Mill) **58**:378
"On Some Carp at Sans Souci" (Thackeray) **213**:308
"On Some Fossil Remains of Man" (Huxley) **67**:83
"On Some French Fashionable Novels" (Thackeray) **213**:220
"On Some of the Characteristics of Modern Poetry, and on the Lyrical Poems of Alfred Tennyson" (Hallam) **110**:128, 158
"On Some of the Old Actors" (Lamb) **10**:423; **113**:206
"On Some Political Snobs" (Thackeray) **213**:250, 286
"On Spring" (Horton) **87**:110
"On Steppes and Deserts" (Humboldt) **170**:159
"On Strike" (Dickens) **230**:143, 145
"On Sublimity" (Tennyson) **202**:185-86
"On Suicide" (Schopenhauer) **157**:331
"On Summer" (Horton) **87**:110
"On Superstition" (Freneau) **1**:320; **111**:110
"On Superstition" (Warton)
See "Ode to Superstition"
"On Taste" (Hazlitt) **29**:148

"On Teaching the Children of the Poor to Read" (Cobbett) **49**:97
"On the Abuse of Satire" (D'Israeli) **217**:305
"On the Advisableness of Improving Natural Knowledge" (Huxley) **67**:16, 26, 48, 56, 83-4, 87
"On the Aesthetic Education of Man" (Schiller)
See "Briefe über die ästhetische Erziehung des Menschen"
"On the Agency" (Martineau) **137**:350
"On the Alliterative Metre of Pierce Plowman's Visions" (Percy) **95**:313, 324
"On the Altar-Piece by Tiepolo" (Symonds) **34**:352
"On the Anatomy and the Affinities of the Family of the Medusae" (Huxley) **67**:79
"On the Ancient Metrical Romances" (Percy) **95**:323-24
"On the Application of Evolutionary Principles to Art and Literature" (Symonds) **34**:326
"On the Approaching Revolution in Great Britain" (De Quincey) **87**:40
"On the Art of the Classic Poets to Excite Compassion" (Murphy) **229**:252
"On the Artificial Comedy of the Last Century" (Lamb) **10**:392, 409, 411, 413, 419, 422-24, 427, 432; **113**:167, 202, 286
On the Athenian Orators (Macaulay) **42**:118, 120
"On the Backwardness of the Spring 1771" (Barbauld) **185**:32
"On the Banks of the Torrent" (Isaacs)
See "A orillas del torrente"
On the Basis of Aesthetics (Schlegel) **45**:332
"On the Beach" (Larcom) **179**:174
"On the Beach at Midnight" (Whitman) **4**:592
"On the Beach at Night" (Whitman) **31**:391, 431; **205**:309
"On the Birth of a Royal Son in the North" (Derzhavin)
See "Stikhi na rozhdenie v Severe porfirorodnago otroka"
"On the boundless plain careering" (Fuller) **50**:246-7
On the Brink (Feuillet) **45**:88
"On the British Constitution" (Paine) **62**:325
"On the Canal Grande" (Meyer)
See "Auf dem Canal Grande"
"On the Capture of Fugitive Slaves Near Washington" (Lowell) **90**:215, 219
"On the Capture of Izmail" (Derzhavin)
See "Na vzyatie Izmaila"
"On the Catholic Claims" (Dyer) **129**:110
"On the Character of Hamlet" (Reynolds) **146**:165, 172
"On the Character of Rousseau" (Hazlitt) **82**:164
On the Church, the State and the School (Grundtvig) **158**:153
"On the Civilization of the Western Aboriginal Country" (Freneau) **111**:190
"On the Classics" (Barbauld) **185**:96
"On the Clerical Character" (Hazlitt) **29**:152
On the Cognition and Sensation of the Human Soul (Herder)
See *Vom Erkennen und Empfinden der meschlichen Seele*
"On the Companionship with Nature" (Lampman) **194**:90, 140
On the Concept of Irony, with Special Reference to Socrates (Kierkegaard)
See *Om Begrebet Ironi med stadigt Hensyn til Socrates*
"On the Conduct of Life" (Hazlitt) **29**:150, 156; **82**:75, 122
"On the connection between man's animal nature and his spiritual nature" (Schiller)
See *Über den Zusammenhang der tierischen Natur des Menschen mit seiner geistigen*
On the Connection between the Animal and the Spiritual Nature of Man (Schiller)
See *Über den Zusammenhang der tierischen Natur des Menschen mit seiner geistigen*
"On the Connexion between Mythology and Philosophy" (Hopkins and Hugo) **17**:229
"On the Conquest of Derbent" (Derzhavin)
See "Na pokorenie Derbenta"
On the Constitution of the Church and State (Coleridge)
On the Constitution of Church and State, According to the Idea of Each: with Aids Toward a Right Judgment on the Late Catholic Bill (Coleridge) **99**:115; **231**:7, 58, 82-84, 118
"On the Conversation of Authors" (Hazlitt) **29**:147
"On the Conversation of Poets" (Hazlitt) **29**:165
On the Cracow-Vienna Line (Fredro) **8**:286
"On the Cranial Nerves" (Büchner) **26**:50, 68
"On the Custom of Hissing at the Theatres" (Lamb) **10**:409-11
"On the Death of Adaline" (Chivers) **49**:68
"On the Death of an Infant" (Horton) **87**:110
"On the Death of Captain Biddle" (Freneau) **1**:317; **111**:143
"On the Death of Dr. Adam Clarke" (Sigourney) **21**:309
"On the Death of Elizabeth Linley" (Sheridan) **91**:232
"On the Death of General Wolf" (Darwin) **106**:182
"On the Death of Goethe" (Baratynsky)
See "Na smert Gyote"
"On the Death of Katerina Iakovlevna [Bastidon], Occurring on the 15th Day of July, 1794" (Derzhavin) **215**:30, 32
"On the Death of Lieut William Howard Allen" (Halleck) **47**:57
"On the Death of Mrs. Jennings" (Barbauld) **185**:29
"On the Death of Mrs. Throckmorton's Bulfinch" (Cowper) **94**:33-8, 120, 123-24
"On the Death of My Parents" (Petofi)
See "Szüleim halálára"
"On the Death of Prince Meshchersky" (Derzhavin)
See "Na smert ' kniazia Meshcherskogo"
On the Death of Pushkin (Lermontov)
See "Smert' poeta"
"On the Death of Rebecca" (Horton) **87**:94, 101, 110
"On the Death of Sir W. Russell" (Cowper) **94**:24
"On the Death of Tennyson I" (Lampman) **194**:126-29
"On the Death of Tennyson II" (Lampman) **194**:126-27, 129
"On the Death of the Right Honorable William Pitt" (Dacre) **151**:198
"On the Death of the Young Girl" (Willis) **194**:306
"On the Defects and Abuses in Public Institutions" (Dyer) **129**:110
"On the Definition of Political Economy" (Mill) **58**:338
On the Development of Revolutionary Ideas in Russia (Herzen) **10**:324; **61**:109
"On the Development of the Teeth" (Huxley) **67**:52-3, 81-3
"On the Devil, and Devils" (Shelley) **18**:367, 375; **143**:196, 212
"On the Difference of the Poetic Genres" (Hölderlin)
See "Über den Unterschied der Dichtarten"
"On the Disadvantages of Intellectual Superiority" (Hazlitt) **29**:150
"On the Discoveries of Captain Lewis" (Adams) **175**:44-45
"On the Doctrine of the Indestructibility of Our True Nature by Death" (Schopenhauer) **157**:332
"On the Domestic Education of Children" (Murray) **63**:181
"On the Dove's Leaving the Ark" (Sigourney) **21**:289
"On the Dread and Dislike of Science" (Lewes) **25**:314
"On the Dual Form" (Humboldt)
See "Über den Dualis"
"On the Duties of Children" (Channing) **17**:4
On the Duty of Carrying Religion into our Amusements (More) **141**:175
"On the Early English Dramatists" (Reynolds) **146**:201
"On the Edge of the World" (Leskov)
See "Na kraju sveta"
"On the Educational Value of the Natural History Sciences" (Huxley) **67**:52-3, 81-3
On the Ego (Schelling) **30**:152-53
"On the Emigration to America" (Freneau) **111**:166
"On the Equality of the Sexes" (Murray) **63**:180, 184, 188, 193, 206, 208-9, 212
"On the Essence of Religion" (Schleiermacher) **107**:340
On the Eve (Turgenev)
See *Nakanune*
"On the Eve of the First Anniversary of August 4, 1864" (Tyutchev)
See "Nakanune godovščiny avgusta 1864 g."
"On the Evening and Morning" (Horton) **87**:92
"On the Evening, Meditated on the Welsh Coast" (Dyer) **129**:148
"On the Evils of Human Life" (Freneau) **111**:111
"On the Extinction of the Venetian Republic" (Wordsworth) **12**:395, 431; **206**:300
"On the Fear of Death" (Hazlitt) **29**:152, 170-71; **82**:96, 106
"On the Feeling of Immortality in Youth" (Hazlitt) **29**:152; **82**:96
"On the Feminine Characters in Greek Poetry" (Schlegel) **226**:197
"On the Field of Waterloo" (Rossetti) **77**:296, 363, 365
"On the Formation of Coal" (Huxley) **67**:27
"On the Foundation of Our Belief in a Divine Government of the Universe" (Fichte) **62**:62
On the Fourfold Root of the Law of Sufficient Reason (Schopenhauer)
See *Über die vierfache Wurzel des Satzes vom zureichenden Grunde*
On the Fourfold Root of the Thesis of Adequate Ground (Schopenhauer)
See *Über die vierfache Wurzel des Satzes vom zureichenden Grunde*
"On the French School of Painting" (Thackeray) **213**:223, 243-44, 248
"On the Functions of Laymen in the Church" (Gladstone) **213**:112
"On the Future Extinction of Blue Eyes" (Lewes) **25**:310
"On the Genius and Character of Hogarth" (Lamb) **10**:387, 408, 411, 420; **113**:203
On the Gods of Samothrace (Schelling) **30**:143
On the Goethe Foundation in Weimar (Liszt)
See *De la Fondation-Goethe à Weimar*
"On the Gradual Formation of Thought during Speech" (Kleist)
See "Über die allmähliche Verfertigung der Gedanken beim Reden"
"On the Gradual Production of Thoughts While Speaking" (Kleist)
See "Über die allmähliche Verfertigung der Gedanken beim Reden"
"On the Grasshopper and the Cricket" (Keats) **73**:218, 324
"On the grassy banks" (Rossetti) **186**:235

"On the Grecian Room in Princess Zeneida Volkonskaia's House in Moscow" (Mickiewicz)
See "Na pokoj grecki w eomu księżnej Zeneidy Wøkońskiej w Moskwie"
On the Ground of our Belief in a Divine World-Order (Fichte)
See *Ueber den Grund unseres Glaubens an eine göttliche Weltregierung*
"On the Headland" (Taylor) **89**:309
On the Heights (Auerbach)
See *Auf der Höhe*
On the Historical (Manzoni)
See *Del romanzo storico*
"On the Historical Progress of Free Thought in Russia" (Bestuzhev) **131**:178, 184
"On the Honourable Emanuel Swedenborg's Universal Theology" (Freneau) **111**:110
"On the Hypothesis that Animals Are Automata and Its History" (Huxley) **67**:86-7, 95, 100
"On the Ideal in Art" (Cranch) **115**:68
"On the Ignorance of the Learned" (Hazlitt) **29**:150
"On the Importance of a Man to Himself" (Smith) **59**:303, 309, 316, 322-3
"On the Importance of Educating Hindu Females" (Dutt) **118**:30
"On the Importance of Religion" (More) **141**:259
"On the Incidents and Characters in Russian History, Which May Provide Subjects for the Arts" (Karamzin)
See "O sluchayakh i kharaterakh v rossiyskoy istorii, kotoryye mogut byt' predmetom khudozhestv"
"On the Inconveniency of Being Hanged" (Lamb) **10**:387
"On the Independence of Judges" (Dyer) **129**:110
"On the Indestructibility of Our True Being through Death" (Schopenhauer) **51**:333
"On the Inevitable Crisis" (Holmes) **14**:111
"On the Influence of Authority and Custom on the Female Mind and Manners" (Hays) **114**:206
"On the Ingratitude of Republics" (Freneau) **111**:160, 162
On the Inhumanity of the Slave Trade (Yearsley) **174**:318
"On the Intimate Relationship between Poetry and Music" (Schumann) **143**:138
"On the Introduction of Rationalistic Principles into Revealed Religion" (Newman) **99**:266
"On the Judgement of Connnoisseurs being preferred to that of Professional Men" (Haydon) **146**:142
"On the Judging of Pictures" (Hazlitt) **29**:144
"On the Knocking at the Gate in 'Macbeth'" (De Quincey) **4**:78, 85; **87**:74
"On the Knocking at the Gate in Macbeth" (De Quincey) **198**:38, 53
"On the Knocking on the Door in Macbeth" (De Quincey)
See "On the Knocking at the Gate in 'Macbeth'"
"On the Knowledge of Character" (Hazlitt) **29**:186; **82**:76
"On the Last Day of the Year" (Ichiyō)
See "Otsugomori"
On the Late Persecution of the Protestants in the South of France (Williams) **135**:311, 335
"On the Light Dress of Fashionable Beauties" (Karamzin)
See "O lyogkoy odezhde modnykh drasavits XIX veka"
"On the Literary Character" (Hazlitt) **29**:148
"On the Literary Criticism and Views of the 'Moscow Observer'" (Belinski) **5**:96
"On the Living Poets" (Hazlitt) **29**:161, 166
"On the Loss of the Royal George" (Cowper)
See "Lines on the Loss of the Royal George"
"On the Love of Life" (Hazlitt) **82**:115
"On the Marionette Theater" (Kleist)
See "Über das Marionettentheater"
"On the Memorable Victory" (Freneau)
See "Poem on the memorable victory obtained by the gallant capt. Paul Jones, or the Good Man Richard, over the Seraphis, etc. under the command of capt. Pearson"
"On the Method of Zadig" (Huxley) **67**:48, 63
"On the Methods and Results of Ethnology" (Huxley) **67**:97
"On the Metre of Pierce Plowman's Visions" (Percy)
See "On the Alliterative Metre of Pierce Plowman's Visions"
"On the Mode of Operation of the Poetic Spirit" (Hölderlin)
See "Über die Verfahrungsweise des poetischen Geistes"
"On the Modern Element in Literature" (Arnold) **29**:11, 53; **89**:32, 38, 40, 42, 44, 118, 121; **218**:212, 227
On the Modern Spirit in Literature (Arnold) **29**:23
"On the Monument of Dante to be erected in Florence" (Leopardi)
See "Sopra il monumento di Dante"
"On the Morphology of the Cephalous Mollusca" (Huxley) **67**:53
"On the Moscow Earthquake of 1802" (Karamzin) **173**:284
"On the Moscow Revolt in the Reign of Aleksey Mikhaylovich" (Karamzin) **173**:284
"On the Mysticism Attributed to the Early Fathers of the Church" (Keble) **87**:191
"On the Natural History of the Man-like Apes" (Huxley) **67**:83
"On the Natural Inequality of Men" (Huxley) **67**:67
"On the Nature and Means of Early Intellectual Education, as Deduced from Experience" (Alcott) **167**:46
"On the Nature of Poetry" (Bryant) **6**:182; **46**:31, 33, 33
On the Nature of the Scholar (Fichte)
See *Ueber das Wesen des Gelehrten*
On the New Dramatic School in Italy (Foscolo) **8**:270
"On the New Year, 1816" (Tyutchev) **34**:387
On the Night after His Recitation of a Poem on the Growth of An Individual Mind (Coleridge) **231**:49
"On the Oldest Myths" (Schelling) **30**:150, 152
"On the Origin and Progress of Novel-Writing" (Barbauld) **50**:17; **185**:75-76, 78
"On the Origin of Beauty" (Hopkins) **189**:10, 89
On the Origin of Species by Means of Natural Selection or the Preservation of Favoured Races in the Struggle for Life (Darwin) **57**:113-25, 127, 131, 133-7, 139-40, 142, 145, 149-52, 154-5, 158-9, 161-2, 164-70, 173-5, 181-2, 189, 192
"On the Paroo" (Kendall) **12**:192
"On the Passions" (Coleridge) **177**:156
"On the Past and Future" (Hazlitt) **29**:142; **82**:157
"On the Periodical Essayists" (Hazlitt) **82**:93
"On the Physical Basis of Life" (Huxley) **67**:37, 40-2, 58, 78, 80, 84-6, 95
"On the Place of Man in Nature" (Herzen) **10**:347-8
"On the Pleasure of Hating" (Hazlitt) **29**:147, 152, 182; **82**:98, 106, 129
"On the Pleasure of Painting" (Hazlitt) **29**:182, 184; **82**:154-55, 161, 165
"On The Pleasures of College Life" (Horton) **87**:95
"On the Poet and His Contemporary Significance" (Zhukovsky) **35**:397
"On the Poetic Muse" (Horton) **87**:94, 111
"On the Poetry of Essence" (Almqvist)
See "Om poesi i sak"
"On the Portrait of Two Beautiful Young People" (Hopkins) **189**:135
"On the Position and Incomes of the Cathedral Clergy" (Bowles) **103**:54
On the Position of Artists (Liszt)
See *De la situation des artistes et de leur condition dans la société*
On the Possibility of a Form for Philosophy in General (Schelling) **30**:151-52
"On the Power of Sound" (Wordsworth) **206**:286-90, 292, 306-7, 320-21, 334-35
On the Power of the Spirit to Control Its Morbid Feelings by Mere Resolution (Kant) **27**:227
"On the Present State of Literature" (Mill) **11**:384; **58**:332
"On the Principles of Genial Criticism" (Coleridge) **197**:285; **231**:118
"On the probable formation of a School of Art at Plymouth" (Haydon) **146**:141
"On the Process of the Poetic Mind" (Hölderlin)
See "Über die Verfahrungsweise des poetischen Geistes"
"On the Proposal to Erect a Monument in England to Lord Byron" (Lazarus) **109**:294
"On the Proposed System of State Consolidation" (Freneau) **111**:191
"On the Prose Style of Poets" (Hazlitt) **29**:147, 167; **82**:123-24
"On the Prospect of Establishing a Pantisocracy in America" (Coleridge) **99**:48
"On the Punishment of Death" (Shelley) **93**:324; **143**:194
"On the Punishment of Death" (Wilson) **5**:568
"On the Puppet Theater" (Kleist)
See "Über das Marionettentheater"
"On the Qualifications Necessary to Success in Life" (Hazlitt) **29**:147
"On the Realities of the Imagination" (Hunt) **1**:421
"On the Receipt of My Mother's Picture out of Norfolk" (Cowper)
See "Lines on the Receipt of My Mother's Picture"
"On the Receipt of My Mothers's Picture from Norfolk" (Cowper)
See "Lines on the Receipt of My Mother's Picture"
On the Relative Social Position of Mothers and Governesses (Jameson) **43**:323
"On the Religion of Nature" (Freneau) **1**:321; **111**:141
"On the Religious Tradition" (Prescott) **163**:42
"On the Remembrance of a Mother" (Yearsley) **174**:317
"On the Removal of an Ancient Mansion" (Sigourney) **87**:320
On the Report of a Monument to Be Erected in Westminster Abbey, to the Memory of a Late Author (Beattie)
See *Verses on the Death of the Revd Mr Charles Churchill*
"On the Return of Count Zubov from Persia" (Derzhavin)
See "Na vozvrashchenie Grafa Zubova iz Persii"
"On the Rise and Progress of Popular Disaffection" (Southey) **97**:263
"On the Rising Glory of America" (Freneau)
See *A Poem, on the Rising Glory of America*

"On the Road" (Nekrasov)
See "V doroge"
"On the running away of the nineteen members of assembly from the house, when it was proposed to call a convention to consider the new system of congressional government; and on the apology made by them in their address" (Brackenridge) **227**:104-5
"On the Ryne" (Bowles)
See "Sonnet on the Ryne"
"On the Sanity of True Genius" (Lamb) **10**:410
"On the Sea" (Keats) **73**:259; **225**:152-55, 220
"On the Secret Chancellery" (Karamzin) **173**:284
"On the Sending of 'The Ball' to S.E." (Baratynsky) **103**:5
"On the Separate Existence of the Soul" (Hogg) **109**:231
"On the Signs of Health and Decay in the Arts" (Hopkins) **189**:89, 92
On the Situtation of Artists and their Status in Society (Liszt)
See *De la situation des artistes et de leur condition dans la société*
"On the Sleep of Plants" (Freneau) **1**:320; **111**:101
"On the Slops" (Arany)
See "A Lejtőn"
On the Spirit of Conquest and Usurpation (Constant)
See *De l'esprit de conquête et de l'usurpation dans leurs rapports avec la civilisation européenne*
On the Spirit of Hebrew Poetry (Herder)
See *Vom Geist der ebräischen Poesie*
"On the Spirit of Monarchy" (Hazlitt) **82**:103
"On the Spirit of Obligations" (Hazlitt) **82**:74
"On the Stage" (Kemble) **18**:192
"On the Standard of Taste" (Brown) **74**:192, 194
"On the Standards of Modern Criticism" (Murphy) **229**:252
On the State of the Poor (Southey) **97**:250
"On the State of Women in the French Republic" (Williams) **135**:304, 335
"On the Study of Biology" (Huxley) **67**:83, 87
On the Study of Celtic Literature (Arnold) **6**:42, 46-47, 69; **29**:11, 58; **126**:44, 101-8; **218**:203, 206, 225-29, 234, 249-50, 252-53, 257-58, 262
"On the Study of Greek Poetry" (Schlegel)
See "Über das Studium der griechischen Poesie"
"On the Style and Imitation of Models" (Lewes) **25**:325
On the Subjection of Women (Mill)
See *The Subjection of Women*
"On the Sublime" (Schiller)
See "Über das Erhabene"
"On the Summits of Chisacá" (Isaacs)
See "En las cumbres de Chisacá"
"On the Supernatural in Poetry" (Radcliffe) **55**:223-4; **223**:305
"On the System of Policy Hitherto Pursued by Their Government" (Barlow) **23**:28
"On the Taking of Izmail" (Derzhavin)
See "Na vzyatie Izmaila"
"On the Teaching of Universal History" (Gogol) **162**:73, 77, 97
"On the Teocalli of Cholula" (Heredia)
See "En el Teocalli de Cholula"
On the Thirteenth Night (Ichiyō)
See *Jusan'ya*
"On the Threshold" (Levy) **59**:96, 105, 119; **203**:322, 346
"On the Too Remote Extension of American Commerce" (Freneau) **111**:101
"On the Tragedies of Shakespeare Considered with Reference to Their Fitness for Stage Representation" (Lamb) **10**:387, 409, 411-13, 420, 427, 432; **113**:202, 204, 206, 218, 280
"On the Translation of the Odyssey" (Zhukovsky) **35**:391
On the Treatment of the Criminal (Almqvist)
See *Om brottsliges behandling*
"On The True Religion" (Brownson) **50**:39
"On the Truth of the Saviour" (Horton) **87**:110
"On the Uniformity and Perfection of Nature" (Freneau) **1**:324; **111**:109, 141
"On the Unity of Epism and Dramatism: A Conception of the Poetic Fugue" (Almqvist) **42**:10
"On the Universality and Other Attributes of the God of Nature" (Freneau) **111**:109, 141
"On the Vanity of Youthful Expectations" (Trumbull) **30**:348
On the Variation of Taste and Mentality among Peoples (Herder)
See *Von der Verschiedenheit des Geschmacks und der Denkart unter den Menschen*
On the Various Races of Mankind (Kant) **27**:215
"On the Vicissitudes of Things" (Freneau) **111**:107, 113
"On the Volga" (Nekrasov) **11**:400, 420
"On the Want of Money" (Hazlitt) **29**:183
"On the Way to Trinity Monastery" (Karamzin)
See "Na puti k Troitse"
"On the Wing" (Rossetti) **2**:561
On the World Soul (Schelling) **30**:171
"On the Writing of Essays" (Smith) **59**:314, 322
"On the Wye in May" (Levy) **59**:89
"On the Zoological Relations of Man with the Lower Animals" (Huxley) **67**:81-2
On Translating Homer (Arnold) **6**:46-47, 59; **29**:9, 41, 54; **89**:82; **126**:28, 46, 114; **218**:201, 206
On Transmigration of Souls: Three Dialogues (Herder)
See *Ueber die Seelenwandrung. Drei Gespräche*
On Tyranny (Alfieri)
See *Della tirannide*
"On Vagabonds" (Smith) **59**:303, 309, 315-6
"On Violet's Wafers, Sent Me When I Was Ill" (Lanier) **118**:219
"On Virgil" (Blake) **173**:157
"On Visiting a Favourite Place" (Clare) **9**:120, 124; **190**:45
"On Visiting the Graves of Hawthorne and Thoreau" (Very) **9**:397
"On Visiting the Tomb of David Hume" (Dyer) **129**:105
"On Vulgarity and Affectation" (Hazlitt) **82**:99-100
"On War" (De Quincey) **198**:76
"On Warsaw Critics and Reviewers" (Mickiewicz)
See "O Krytykach i Recenzentach"
"On Wine and Hashish" (Baudelaire)
See "Du vin et du hachisch"
"On Winter" (Horton) **87**:110
"On Winter" (Warren) **226**:264
"On Women Who Cultivate Letters" (Staël-Holstein) **91**:311
"On Wordsworth" (Pater) **90**:323
"Ona" (Baratynsky) **103**:28
"Once Again" (Meyer)
See "Noch einmal"
"Once, as a lad, with a ringing call" (Baratynsky)
See "Byvalo, otrok, zvonkim klikom..."
"Once I Pass'd through a Populous City" (Whitman) **205**:321
"Once I Passed through a Populous City" (Whitman) **31**:378
"Once More This Time" (Arany)
See "Még ez egyszer"
Once Upon a Time There Were Two Kings (Planché) **42**:288-89, 295, 298
"L'onde et l'ombre" (Hugo) **10**:357
"Den onde Fryste" (Andersen) **79**:77
"Ondine à l'école" (Desbordes-Valmore) **97**:29
"L'Ondine et le pêcheur" (Gautier) **59**:34
1 (Dickinson) **77**:120
The One (Alfieri)
See *L'uno*
"One Among So Many" (Adams) **33**:4
One and All (Goethe)
See *Eins und Alles*
"One Bumper at Parting" (Moore) **110**:190
"The One Called Dead" (Muller) **73**:352
"One Certainty" (Rossetti) **186**:277-78
"One Crucifixion is recorded only" (Dickinson) **77**:83
"One Day" (Rossetti) **66**:307
"One Dignity Delays for All" (Dickinson) **21**:62; **77**:163
"One Foot in Sea and One on Shore" (Rossetti) **66**:341
"The One Hope" (Rossetti) **4**:491, 518
188 (Dickinson) **77**:113
140 (Dickinson) **77**:84
144 (Dickinson) **77**:162-63
196 (Dickinson) **77**:93
106 (Dickinson) **77**:147
164 (Dickinson) **77**:83
130 (Dickinson) **77**:122-24
The 120 Days of Sodom; or, The Romance of the School for Libertinage (Sade)
See *Les 120 journées de Sodome; ou, L'école du libertinage*
124 (Dickinson) **77**:173
102 (Dickinson) **77**:173
"One Identity" (Whitman) **4**:564
"One Life" (Shelley) **93**:327-28
"One More Letter to Mary Ann" (Cooke) **110**:39, 67-8
One More Philosophy of the History of Humankind (Herder)
See *Auch eine Philosophie der Geschichte zur Bildung der Menschheit*
"The One Mystery" (Mangan) **27**:280-81, 298
"One Need Not Be a Chamber to Be Haunted" (Dickinson) **77**:97; **171**:101
"One of Cleopatra's Nights" (Gautier)
See "Une nuit de Clèopâtre"
One of the Forty (Daudet)
See *L'immortel*
"One of the New Voters" (Jefferies) **47**:112, 137, 139, 143
"One of Them" (Cooke) **110**:35, 56
One of Them (Lever) **23**:289, 292-93
"One Thought Keeps Tormenting Me" (Petofi)
See "Egy gondolat bánt engémet"
1084 (Dickinson) **77**:50
1082 (Dickinson) **77**:94
1058 (Dickinson) **77**:94
1053 (Dickinson) **77**:183
1046 (Dickinson) **77**:130, 163
1099 (Dickinson) **77**:84
1078 (Dickinson) **77**:129
1071 (Dickinson) **77**:89
1076 (Dickinson) **77**:80
1032 (Dickinson) **77**:49
1026 (Dickinson) **77**:163
The One Too Many (Linton) **41**:164
One Tract More (Milnes) **61**:129, 137-8
One, Two, Three, Four, Five; By Advertisement (Reynolds) **146**:168-69, 191
"One Versus Two" (Woolson) **82**:272
"One Way of Love" (Browning) **19**:127; **79**:153
"The One who could repeat the Summer day" (Dickinson) **171**:118, 178
"One Word More" (Browning) **19**:110, 127, 131; **79**:163
One Word More (Barrett Browning) **66**:52
"One Year Ago—Jots What?" (Dickinson) **21**:64; **77**:63, 147

"The One-Eyed God" (Ueda Akinari)
See "Me hitotsu no kami"
The Ones Passed-By (Leskov)
See *Obojdennye*
"One's-Self I Sing" (Whitman)
See "Song of Myself"
Onestá (Feuillet) **45**:87
"The One-Track Mind" (Leskov)
See "Odnodum"
"Only a Curl" (Barrett Browning) **61**:9; **170**:122
Only a Fiddler (Andersen)
See *Kun en spillemand*
Only a Girl (Jefferies) **47**:92-93, 121
Only an Irish Boy (Alger) **8**:40; **83**:143
"Only Friendship" (Isaacs)
See "Solo amistad?"
"The Only One" (Hölderlin)
See "Der Einzige"
"Onnelliset" (Kivi) **30**:51
"Onuphrius ou les Vexations fantastiques d'un admirateur d'Hoffmann" (Gautier) **1**:356; **59**:9, 26-7
"Onward and Upward" (Jones) **222**:156, 158, 170
"Onward to the Holy War" (Petofi)
See "Föl a szenthábórúra"
Onze jours en Belgique (Verlaine) **230**:166
The Open Air (Jefferies) **47**:95, 102, 107, 122, 130, 133, 137
The Open Door (Oliphant) **11**:454; **221**:257-60
"Open Letter to a French Friend (Frederic Villot)" (Wagner) **119**:198
"The Open Question" (Hood) **16**:235
"Open Secret Societies" (Thomson) **18**:401
"Open Thy Lattice Love" (Foster) **26**:285
"Open Vields" (Barnes) **75**:101
"Opening Discourse" (Sainte-Beuve) **5**:349
"Opening of the Indian and Colonial Exhibition by the Queen" (Tennyson) **202**:290
"The Opening of the Piano" (Holmes) **81**:99
Oper und Drama (Wagner) **9**:405-06, 414, 426, 452-56, 467, 475; **119**:202, 248, 250, 253, 256, 258-63, 274-75, 291, 294
Opera and Drama (Wagner)
See *Oper und Drama*
L'Opéra italien: Notes d'un dilettante (Stendhal) **178**:231, 234
The Opera of "The Prophet" (Scribe)
See *Le prophète*
Opere (Leopardi) **129**:246-53
Opere inedite o rare (Manzoni) **98**:214
Operette morali (Leopardi) **129**:222, 226, 241-44, 255, 257, 259, 265, 267, 276, 302, 304, 307, 339, 343-44, 350-51, 353
Der Opfertod (Kotzebue) **25**:144, 154-55
"Ophélie" (Rimbaud) **4**:458, 484, 486; **82**:247
"Opinion of a Russian Citizen" (Karamzin)
See "Mneniye russkogo grazhdanina"
"Opinion on American Affairs" (Hughes) **207**:125-26
"Opinions of Mansfield Park" (Austen) **95**:18
Opium Confessions (De Quincey)
See *Confessions of an English Opium-Eater*
Opium-Eater (De Quincey)
See *Confessions of an English Opium-Eater*
"The Opossum Hunters" (Kendall) **12**:191
"Opossum Hunting" (Thorpe) **183**:357
"The Opposite Neighbour" (Opie) **65**:168, 172
"The Opposite Page" (Eminescu) **33**:254
"Opposition" (Lanier) **6**:254; **118**:239, 265
"Opravdanie" (Baratynsky) **103**:28
"Opredelenie poezii" (Bestuzhev) **131**:165
"The Optimist" (Bestuzhev)
See "Otryvok iz Komedii 'Optimist'"
Optrin af Kæmpelivets Undergang i Nord (Grundtvig) **158**:101, 139
Opus 2 (Schumann)
See *Papillons*
Opus 3 (Schumann)
See "Etudes on Caprices of Paganini"
Opus 5 (Schumann)
See *Impromptus sur une Romance de Clara Wieck*
Opus 7 (Schumann)
See "Toccata"
Opus 9 (Schumann)
See *Carnaval*
Opus 10 (Schumann)
See "Etudes on Caprices of Paganini"
Opus 11 (Schumann)
See "Piano Sonata in F# minor"
Opus 12 (Schumann)
See *Fantasiestücke*
Opus 16 (Schumann)
See *Kreisleriana*
Opus 17 (Schumann)
See *Fantasy*
Opus 21 (Schumann)
See *Novelletten*
Opus 22 (Schumann)
See "Piano Sonata in G minor"
Opus 23 (Schumann)
See *Nachtstücke*
Opus 24 (Schumann)
See *Liederkreis*
Opus 26 (Schumann)
See *Faschingschwank aus Wien*
Opus 35 (Schumann)
See *Zwölf Gedichte*
Opus 37 (Schumann)
See *The Springtime of Love*
Opus 39 (Schumann)
See *Liederkreis*
Opus 40 (Schumann)
See *Fünf Lieder*
Opus 48 (Schumann)
See *Dichterliebe*
Opus 66 (Schumann)
See *Bilder aus dem Osten*
Opus 68 (Schumann)
See *Album für die Jugend*
Opus 82 (Schumann)
See *Waldszenen*
Opus 90 (Schumann)
See *Sechs Gedichte und Requiem*
Opus 113 (Schumann)
See *Märchenbilder*
Opus 121 (Schumann)
See "Violin Sonata in D minor"
Opus 132 (Schumann)
See *Märchenerzählungen*
Opus Maximum (Coleridge) **54**:109; **177**:155-56, 162; **231**:153
Opus Postumum (Kant) **27**:239, 245, 248
"Oración" (Casal) **131**:243
"La oración" (Isaacs) **70**:303-04
"Les oracles" (Vigny) **7**:480
Oráculos de Talía (Gómez de Avellaneda) **111**:51, 53
Orage (Liszt) **199**:307
"Oraison du soir" (Rimbaud) **4**:454, 484; **35**:282
Oralloossa, Son of the Incas (Bird) **1**:87, 90; **197**:6-7, 16, 19, 24-26, 33, 68
"The Orange and Green" (Griffin) **7**:195-96
"Orara" (Kendall) **12**:182, 186-87, 190-92, 195, 198-99, 201
Oration at Cincinnati (Adams) **175**:35
Oration Delivered at Plymouth, at the Anniversary Commemoration of the First Landing of our Ancestors (Adams) **175**:72
An Oration Delivered before the Phi Beta Kappa Society at Cambridge, August 31, 1837 (Emerson)
See "The American Scholar"
"Oration on the Celebration of the Anniversary of Independence, July 4th 1793" (Brackenridge) **227**:118
An Oration, Pronounced before the Knox and Warren Branches of the Washington Benevolent Society, at Amherst . . . (Webster) **30**:414-16
"Oration upon Rum" (Freneau) **111**:81
Orations and Addresses (Bryant) **46**:5
"Orator" (Bestuzhev) **131**:165, 183
"Orazione a Bonaparte pel congresso di Lione" (Foscolo) **8**:261
"The Orchard Harvest" (Mitford) **4**:401
"The Orchard Pit" (Rossetti) **4**:504, 510, 516; **77**:355-56
"The Orchestra of Today" (Lanier) **6**:276; **118**:243
"Ordeal of the Bier" (Arany)
See "Tetemrehívás"
The Order of Nature (Bryant) **46**:16, 25
The Order of St. Vladimir (Gogol) **15**:84-5; **78**:258; **162**:18, 20
The Oregon Trail (Parkman) **12**:328, 336, 338, 341, 346, 351-52, 354, 358, 377
"L'Oreiller de ma Maitresse" (Dacre) **151**:149
"L'Oreiller d'une petite fille" (Desbordes-Valmore) **97**:29, 38
Orenburg-Province Hunter (Aksakov)
See *Zapiski ruzheynago okhotnika*
Oreste (Alfieri) **101**:4, 8, 32, 42
"The Organic Development of Man in Connection with His Mental and Spiritual Activities" (Dobrolyubov) **5**:140
"The Organist" (Lampman) **25**:160, 192, 199, 216
"The Organization of the International" (Bakunin) **58**:136
"L'Orgie parisienne" (Rimbaud)
See "Paris se repeuple"
"L'orgie Parisienne; ou, Paris se Repeuple" (Rimbaud) **4**:458, 466; **35**:271; **82**:238
"Oriana" (Sigourney) **21**:290
"Oriana and Vesperella, or The City of Pearls" (Reynolds) **146**:172
Les orientales (Hugo) **3**:234, 236, 261-62, 265, 270; **10**:362; **21**:194, 202
Origin and Objects of Ancient Freemasonry (Delany) **93**:159, 163
The Origin and Principles of the American Revolution, compared with the Origin and Principles of that of France (Adams) **175**:29
"The Origin and Progress of the Art of Writing" (Bello) **131**:120, 130
"Origin and the Duties of Literature" (Foscolo)
See "Dell'origine e dell'ufficio della letteratura: Orazione"
Origin of Masonry (Paine) **62**:314
"Origin of Poe's 'Raven'" (Chivers) **49**:38
"The Origin of Poetry, Eloquence, and Argument" (Murphy) **229**:252
"The Origin of Species" (Huxley) **67**:83
The Origin of Species (Darwin)
See *On the Origin of Species by Means of Natural Selection or the Preservation of Favoured Races in the Struggle for Life*
"Origin of the English Language" (D'Israeli) **217**:302
"The Origin of the English Stage" (Percy) **95**:313, 323-24, 327
Origin of the Family, Private Property and the State (Engels)
See *Der Ursprung der Familie, des Privateigenthums und des Staats*
The Origin of the Feast of Purim; or, The Destinies of Haman and Mordecai (Tyler) **3**:572-73
The Origin of the Hindoos (Schlegel)
See *De l'origine des Hindous*
"Origin of the Mexican Civilization—Analogies with the Old World" (Prescott) **163**:364
"The Origin of the Sail" (Opie) **65**:160
Original Letters, etc., of Sir John Falstaff and his Friends (Lamb) **113**:277
Original Panoramic Views (Brown) **89**:184, 188
Original Poetry by Victor and Cazire (Shelley) **18**:307, 342

Original Revolutionary Chronicle: The Battle-Day of Germantown (Lippard) **198**:121
"Originality" (Alcott) **167**:75
Les origines de la France contemporaine (Taine) **15**:424-25, 429, 432, 437, 440-42, 445-46, 453-56, 466, 471, 473-77
Origines du Christianisme (Renan) **145**:311, 315, 317, 331, 346, 350-52, 354
Origines du droit française cherchées dans les symboles et formules du droit universel (Michelet) **31**:228-29; **218**:320, 324, 335
The Origins of Christianity (Renan)
See *Histoire des origines du christianisme*
The Origins of Contemporary France (Taine)
See *Les origines de la France contemporaine*
Origins of the Family, Private Property and the State (Engels)
See *Der Ursprung der Familie, des Privateigenthums und des Staats*
"A orillas del torrente" (Isaacs) **70**:310
"Orina, the Soldier's Mother" (Nekrasov) **11**:404-05, 421
Orion (Horne) **127**:236, 238, 242, 245-48, 259, 263, 268-69, 277-81
"Oriska" (Sigourney) **21**:299
Orlandino (Edgeworth) **158**:24
"Orlando Innamorato" (Bello) **131**:92
Orley Farm: A Novel (Trollope) **6**:455-56, 463, 470, 492-94, 499, 514-15; **33**:363; **101**:269, 279, 285, 301-02, 306, 308, 310, 319; **215**:195-96, 347
Ormond (Edgeworth) **1**:258, 262-64, 266-68, 270-71; **51**:77, 79-80, 88, 90-1, 104-05; **158**:61
Ormond Grosvenor (Hale) **75**:320
Ormond; or, The Secret Witness (Brown) **22**:3-4, 7-8, 12, 14, 17-18, 20-1, 25, 27, 30, 45, 47-52, 54-5; **74**:4, 9-10, 15, 17, 19, 21, 36, 47-8, 51, 54, 56, 61, 68, 73, 76, 80, 82-3, 92-4, 96-7, 101, 103-04, 109-12, 117-21, 124, 126, 129-30, 133-35, 137-39, 142-43, 153, 156, 159-61, 164; **122**:53-54, 118-19, 150, 153, 159
Ormus och Ariman (Almqvist) **42**:15-16
"Ormuzd and Ahriman" (Cranch) **115**:23
"Orn Aartusinder" (Andersen) **214**:61
"Ornières" (Rimbaud) **4**:473; **227**:204, 242, 271, 294
Ornithological Biography (Audubon) **47**:11, 13-14, 24, 32-3, 38, 40, 42, 44, 51
"Az örök zsidó" (Arany) **34**:18-19
"The Orphan" (Opie) **65**:158
"The Orphan Boy's Tale" (Opie) **65**:156, 175
The Orphan of China. A Tragedy. As it is Perform'd at the Theatre-Royal, in Drury-Lane (Murphy) **229**:219, 221, 223, 227, 234, 257-58, 260-62, 264-67
The Orphan of the Castle (Smith)
See *Emmeline, the Orphan of the Castle*
"Orphans' New Year's Gifts" (Rimbaud)
See "Les étrennes des orphelins"
"Orpheus" (Coleridge) **231**:152
"Orpheus" (Lazarus) **8**:412-14, 418, 420, 425; **109**:292, 294, 319
Orpheus (Liszt) **199**:329
Orpheus in der Unterwelt (Nestroy) **42**:232
Orpheus in the Haymarket (Planché) **42**:275, 287, 294
"Orphic Saying XXVI" (Alcott) **167**:71
"Orphic Sayings" (Alcott) **1**:21-22, 24-26; **167**:9, 38-41, 49-51, 57, 59, 74, 82, 84-86
"Orphisch" (Hölderlin) **16**:176
"Orplid" (Mörike)
See "Der letzte König von Orplid"
Orra (Baillie) **71**:6-7, 12; **151**:6, 8-9, 13, 27, 115
Orra: A Lapland Tale (Barnes) **75**:14-15, 18, 22, 26, 69-70, 92
"Orthography and Orthoepy" (D'Israeli) **217**:303
Ortis (Foscolo)
See *Ultime lettere di Jacopo Ortis*
"Az örült" (Petofi) **21**:264
Orville College (Wood) **178**:291
The Orville College Boys: A Story of School Life (Wood) **178**:304-6, 308
Oscar; ou, Le mari qui trompe sa femme (Scribe) **16**:389, 412
"Oscar y Malvina" (Espronceda) **39**:106
"Oséculo" (Castro Alves)
See "O Século"
"Osen" (Baratynsky) **103**:25, 28, 39
"Osen.' Bratu Arkadiiu Timofeevich v Peterburg" (Aksakov) **181**:61
"Osen' vo vremia osady Ochakova" (Derzhavin) **215**:11, 27, 33
Osorio (Coleridge)
See *Remorse*
Ossa arida (Liszt) **199**:348
Osservazioni sulla morale cattolica (Manzoni) **29**:269, 289, 294-95, 299, 301-03; **98**:238
"Ossian" (Herder)
See "Auszug aus einem Briefwechsel über Ossian und die Lieder alter Völker"
"Ősszel" (Arany) **34**:19, 24
Ostatni (Krasiński) **4**:307, 311
"Der Ostermorgen" (Ludwig) **4**:353
"Ostrov Borngol'm" (Karamzin) **3**:285-89, 291; **173**:342, 348, 350-54
Ostrovitjane (Leskov) **25**:232, 252; **174**:1, 10, 47, 65, 77
Oswald Cray (Wood) **178**:276-77, 335
Őszikék (Arany) **34**:16
"Ot chego v Rossii malo avtorskikh talantov" (Karamzin) **173**:282
"Ot zhizni toy, chto bushevala zdes" (Tyutchev) **34**:398, 409
"Otbornoe zerno" (Leskov) **174**:53-54, 57
"Otbornoje zerno" (Leskov)
See "Otbornoe zerno"
"Otchayanny" (Turgenev) **21**:441; **122**:242
Otcy i deti (Turgenev)
See *Ottsy i deti*
Other People's Money (Gaboriau)
See *L'argent des autres*
The Other Side of the Tweed (Fontane)
See *Jenseit des Tweed*
Otho: A Tragedy (Neal) **161**:297, 321
Otho the Great (Keats) **8**:341, 348, 360; **73**:154, 173, 208, 234, 306; **121**:108, 177-78; **225**:217
"The Otonabee" (Moodie) **113**:347
"Otryvki iz poèmy 'Mat'" (Nekrasov) **11**:419-20
"Otryvki iz vospominanij svoich i čužich" (Turgenev) **122**:267
"Otryvok" (Baratynsky) **103**:8-9
"Otryvok iz Komedii 'Optimist'" (Bestuzhev) **131**:181
"Otsego Leaves" (Cooper) **129**:71-72
"Otsugomori" (Ichiyō) **49**:336-37, 343-44, 353
Ottavia (Alfieri) **101**:8, 38, 50
"Ottawa" (Lampman) **194**:20
"Otter-Bag" (Neal) **161**:310, 344
Otto (Klinger) **1**:428
Otto of Wittelsbach (Mitford) **4**:404
"Otto von Fieandt" (Runeberg) **41**:314
Ottokar (Grillparzer)
See *König Ottokars Glück und Ende*
Ottsy i deti (Turgenev) **21**:388-89, 391-92, 394, 396, 400-01, 405, 409-10, 413, 418-20, 422-23, 425-26, 432, 434, 436-37, 439, 442-49, 452; **37**:353-452; **122**:248-49, 251-52, 254, 256-57, 262, 265, 268, 275, 277-80, 282-83, 287, 292, 306, 315-17, 320, 325, 336
"Oui, tu m'inspires . . ." (Verlaine) **230**:166
"Our America" (Martí)
See "Nuesta America"
"Our Anecdotage" (D'Israeli) **217**:337
"Our Aunt" (Andersen) **214**:58
"Our Be'th Place" (Barnes) **75**:59
"Our Casuarina Tree" (Dutt) **29**:121-22, 125, 127, 129
"Our Christ" (Larcom) **179**:174
"Our Countrymen in Chains!" (Whittier) **8**:489, 510
"Our Country's Call" (Bryant) **46**:7
"Our Dead Singer" (Holmes) **14**:129
"Our Destiny" (Jones) **222**:124, 156
"Our Dramatic Repertoire" (Eminescu)
See "Our Theatrical Repertory"
"Our Father in Heaven" (Hale) **75**:279, 286
"Our Father's Works" (Barnes) **75**:79
"Our Granite Hills" (Hale) **75**:284
"Our Hatty" (Parton) **86**:348
"Our Heroic Themes" (Boker) **125**:33, 39
Our Hundred Days in Europe (Holmes) **81**:107
"Our Jack" (Kendall) **12**:192
"Our Land" (Runeberg) **41**:312, 315-16, 319-20, 326-27
"Our Language and Literature" (Whitman) **81**:287, 289, 292
"Our Liberal Practitioners" (Arnold) **126**:10, 29, 61, 81; **218**:197-98, 216
"Our little Kinsmen" (Dickinson) **171**:126
"Our Love Is Gone" (Eminescu) **131**:287
"Our March to Washington" (Winthrop)
See "March of the Seventh Regiment. Our March to Washington"
"Our Master" (Whittier) **8**:524; **59**:361
"Our Mothers, lovely women pitiful" (Rossetti) **186**:347
Our Mutual Friend (Dickens) **3**:159, 163, 166, 169-70, 173-74, 181, 188; **8**:194; **18**:111-12, 114, 116, 119-22, 132-34; **26**:170, 174, 184, 225; **37**:164, 173-4, 192, 206; **86**:198, 201, 204, 207, 214, 222, 224; **105**:199-357; **113**:20, 39, 42, 97, 118-19, 124, 127, 135, 142-44; **161**:38, 116, 119; **187**:71, 80; **203**:179-81, 183, 187, 278; **217**:206, 220-21, 225, 238-39, 243, 248, 266, 268; **219**:73, 83, 85, 109-10, 159, 167, 190, 200, 202, 229; **230**:32-3, 113, 118, 144; **231**:179-81, 245
"Our Native Land" (Grundtvig) **158**:103
"Our Nelly" (Parton) **86**:351
Our Nig; or, Sketches from the Life of a Free Black (Wilson) **78**:311-13, 315-20, 322-25, 327-31, 334-35, 338-41, 343, 345, 348-58, 360-63; **219**:242-51, 256-58, 260-61, 263, 265-66, 268, 273-91, 294-98, 301-4, 306, 308-18, 320-28, 330-32, 334-35, 341-44, 348
"Our Old Earth Is Playing" (Petofi)
See "Játszik öreg földünk"
"Our Old Feuillage" (Whitman) **31**:387, 392; **81**:312; **205**:157, 162, 164, 226
Our Old Home (Hawthorne) **2**:306-07, 314; **39**:179, 245
"Our Own" (Lowell) **90**:198
Our Own Folks—We'll Settle It Among Ourselves (Ostrovsky)
See *Svoi lyudi—sochtemsya!*
"Our Parish" (Dickens) **105**:353; **203**:250
"Our People Sent Me" (Turgenev)
See "Nashi poslali"
"Our Rally" (Jones) **222**:124, 157, 172
"Our Slave" (Cooke) **110**:57-8
"Our Society at Cranford" (Gaskell) **5**:205; **70**:216
Our Sons (Michelet)
See *Nos fils*
"Our Summons" (Jones) **222**:124, 156, 170
"Our Talisman" (Lippard) **198**:133, 181, 208
"Our Theatrical Repertory" (Eminescu) **33**:272; **131**:310-11
"Our Tsar is a Russian (Prussian) German" (Bestuzhev)
See "Tsar, nash, nemets russkiy . . ."
"Our Village Post Office" (Sedgwick) **19**:444
Our Village: Sketches of Rural Character and Scenery (Mitford) **4**:400-01, 403-05, 407-08

"Our Village—By a Villager" (Hood) **16**:235-36
"Our Warning" (Jones) **222**:125, 174
"Our Willie" (Timrod) **25**:372
Ourika (Duras) **154**:108-10, 112-14, 123-30, 133-35, 137, 139, 143-44, 146, 149, 153, 157-70
Ours (Robertson) **35**:330, 333-34, 336, 338, 340-41, 345, 349, 351-56, 358, 360, 362, 363-65, 369-72
L'ours et le pacha (Scribe) **16**:382, 400
Out for Business or Robert Frost's Strange Career (Alger) **83**:118, 119
"Out little baby fell asleep" (Rossetti) **186**:234
"Out of Debt, Out of Danger" (Edgeworth) **51**:89
"Out of Doors in February" (Jefferies) **47**:137, 143
"Out of Place Inquisitiveness" (Laforgue)
See "Curiosités déplacées"
"Out of Prison" (Lampman)
See "Freedom"
"Out of the Cradle Endlessly Rocking" (Whitman) **4**:544, 551, 561, 567, 571, 579, 582, 592, 594-96, 602; **31**:368, 370, 379, 388-92, 403-04, 418, 421-22, 431, 437; **81**:249, 255, 257-58, 264, 271, 281-83, 366-70; **205**:157-59, 172, 194, 203, 237, 308-9, 336-38, 340-41
"Out of the Depths I Cried to Thee" (Baudelaire)
See "De Profundis clamavi"
Out of the Foam (Cooke) **5**:130, 132
Out of the Frying Pan (Tamayo y Baus) **1**:571
Out of the Life of a Good-for-Nothing (Eichendorff)
See *Aus dem Leben eines Taugenichts und Das Marmorbild: Zwei Novellen nebst einem Anhange von Liedern und Romanzen*
"Out of the Rolling Ocean, the Crowd" (Whitman) **4**:544, 601
"Out of the World" (Levy) **203**:340, 342, 345
"Out of Town" (Levy) **59**:89, 119; **203**:339, 344
"Out Walking" (Verlaine)
See "À la promenade"
Outamaro (Goncourt) **7**:163
"The Outer from the Inner" (Dickinson) **21**:65
"The Outlaw" (Kingsley) **35**:219
"The Outlet" (Dickinson)
See "My River Runs to Thee"
"Outline" (Bello) **131**:105
An Outline of English Speech-Craft (Barnes) **75**:27, 40, 65
An Outline of Rede-Craft (Barnes) **75**:27, 40
"Outline of Universal History" (Rowson) **69**:115-16; **182**:257
"Outlines for a Tomb" (Whitman) **31**:432; **81**:290
"Outlines of a Critique of Political Economy" (Engels) **85**:110, 114, 125, 167
Outlines of a Philosophy of the History of Man (Herder)
See *Ideen zur Philosophie der Geschichte der Menschheit*
"Outlook" (Lampman) **25**:209; **194**:4, 20, 102
"Outoplena" (Shevchenko)
See "Utoplena"
"Outre-Mer" (Kendall) **12**:183, 189
Outre-Mer: A Pilgrimage beyond the Sea (Longfellow) **2**:469, 475, 478, 489, 494; **45**:181, 183
"Outside London" (Jefferies) **47**:137
"Outside the Church" (Lazarus) **109**:298, 322
"Outsiders of Society and Their Homes in London" (Mayhew) **31**:181
"Outworld" (Cranch) **115**:35
"Ouverture ancienne d'Hérodiade" (Mallarmé) **41**:242, 277
"Ouvriers" (Rimbaud) **4**:465, 485; **35**:323; **227**:209, 236-37, 239, 244, 247, 271
"The Oval Portrait" (Poe) **1**:500; **16**:331, 336; **117**:293-94
"Ovcebyk" (Leskov) **25**:230, 239; **174**:21, 37, 52, 90, 109, 123, 135
"Over the Carnage Rose Prophetic a Voice" (Whitman) **81**:313, 331
Over the Teacups (Holmes) **14**:115, 124, 133, 143, 146; **81**:118
"Over Vryen Arbeid in Nederlands Indië en de tegenwoordige Koloniale Agitatie" (Multatuli) **165**:323, 329
"The Overcoat" (Gogol)
See "Shinel"
"Over-Soul" (Emerson) **1**:295, 298, 300, 307; **38**:154, 168-71, 176-77; **98**:92, 100, 190
"An Ovid" (Grillparzer) **102**:174
Ovingdean Grange: A Tale of the South Downs (Ainsworth) **13**:36, 41-3
"Ovsianko the Freeholder" (Turgenev)
See "The Freeholder Ovsyanikov"
"Ovskyanikov the Freeholder" (Turgenev)
See "The Freeholder Ovsyanikov"
Owen Tudor (Arnim) **5**:22; **159**:18
"The Owl and the Pussycat" (Lear) **3**:297, 307-09
"The Owl and the Sparrow" (Trumbull) **30**:345, 349
"Owlet" (Cooke) **5**:133
The Owners of the Entail (Arnim)
See *Die Majoratsherren*
"Owney and Owney Napeak" (Griffin) **7**:198
"Oxford" (Verlaine) **230**:168
"Oxford in the Vacation" (Lamb) **10**:407, 436-37; **113**:192, 194, 199, 225, 236, 248, 253
"The Oxford Malignants and Dr Hampden" (Arnold) **18**:53
The Oxford Thackeray (Thackeray) **213**:192, 200, 202-3, 215
Oxford University Sermons (Newman) **38**:289, 304, 307, 309, 312
Oxtiern (Sade) **47**:361
"Ozero Valen" (Pavlova) **138**:54
"Ozorniki" (Saltykov) **16**:372
"P. Calamus, Esq." (Willis) **194**:298
"The P. R. B." (Rossetti) **186**:262
"Paa den yderste Dag" (Andersen) **214**:55
"Paa Sygeleiet" (Wergeland) **5**:541
Paaske-Lilien (Grundtvig) **158**:139
"Pacchiarotto" (Browning) **19**:86-88, 98
Pacchiarotto, and Other Poems (Browning) **19**:86
Pacific Series (Alger) **8**:43
"Pacsirtaszót hallok megint" (Petofi) **21**:286
Paddy-go-Easy (Carleton)
See *Parra Sastha, or the History of Paddy-go-Easy and his wife Nancy*
"The Padlocked Lady" (Dyer) **129**:94, 105
Padmā vati (Dutt) **118**:5
"A Paean" (Poe) **117**:238
"Pagan and Mediaeval Religious Sentiment" (Arnold) **29**:55; **89**:34, 39
"Paganini" (Hunt) **1**:415
"Page and the Lady" (Smith) **59**:257
"Une Page d'histoire" (Barbey d'Aurevilly) **213**:72-74, 76-79
"A Page from A Woman's Heart" (Parton) **86**:347
"Page from the Diary of a Guards Officer" (Bestuzhev)
See "Listok iz dnevnika gvardeyskogo ofitsera"
The Page of Gustavus Adolphus (Meyer)
See *Gustav Adolfs Page*
"The Page, the Baron, and the Minstrel" (D'Israeli) **217**:302
"A Pageant" (Rossetti) **2**:558-9, 571, 576
A Pageant, and Other Poems (Rossetti) **2**:558, 563, 575; **50**:271; **186**:238, 266, 317, 334
"The Pageant of Summer" (Jefferies) **47**:97, 101, 114, 136-37
Pages (Mallarmé) **4**:376-77; **210**:264
"The Pah-Utes" (Winnemucca) **79**:340
"Paimentyttö" (Kivi) **30**:51
"Pain" (Coleridge) **99**:22
"Pain" (Patmore) **9**:347, 360, 363, 365
"Pain and Time Strive Not" (Morris) **4**:434
"Pain Has an Element of Blank" (Dickinson) **21**:8, 77
"The Pains of Sleep" (Coleridge) **9**:133-34, 155, 177, 194; **54**:87; **99**:67, 74, 91, 93; **177**:43-44, 60, 78, 149, 161; **197**:215, 265; **231**:73, 89
"The Paint King" (Allston) **2**:20
"The Painted Columbine" (Very) **9**:380
"The Painted Cup" (Bryant) **46**:7
"The Painter" (Adams) **175**:29-32
"The Painter" (Almqvist)
See "Målaren"
"The Painter" (Crabbe) **26**:102
"A Painter" (Webster) **230**:249
"The Painter of Modern Life" (Baudelaire)
See "Le Peintre de la vie moderne"
A Painter's Atelier (Desbordes-Valmore)
See *L'Atelier d'un peintre*
"The Painter's Bargain" (Thackeray) **213**:243
"The Painter's Scarecrow" (Cranch) **115**:57
A Painter's Work (Storm)
See *Eine Malerarbeit*
"Pairing Time Anticipated" (Cowper) **94**:121
"Paisaje espiritual" (Casal) **131**:239, 242, 267
"Paisaje tropical" (Silva) **114**:301
"La paix des dieux" (Leconte de Lisle) **29**:221, 229, 231, 234
"La paix du ménage" (Balzac) **153**:149
"Las palabras" (Larra) **17**:275; **130**:204-5
The Palace (Almqvist)
See *Palatset*
"The Palace of Art" (Tennyson) **30**:209, 211, 223-24, 233, 258, 266-67; **65**:248, 258, 261, 270, 357-8; **115**:237, 274, 335; **202**:185-86, 188, 190, 232, 234, 236-37, 337
"The Palace of Death" (Brontë) **165**:99
"The Palace of Humbug" (Dodgson) **139**:33
"Palace of Pleasure" (Hunt) **1**:406
"The Palace of Ruin" (Darley) **2**:128
"The Palace Peasant's Vesele" (Auerbach) **171**:50
"Le Palais de la Mort" (Brontë) **217**:154
"Palais-Promontoire" (Rimbaud) **227**:204
Palatset (Almqvist) **42**:20
"Palinodia al marchese Gino Capponi" (Leopardi) **129**:248
"Palladium" (Arnold) **218**:120, 149
The Palliser Novels (Trollope) **6**:506
"The Palm and the Pine" (Taylor) **89**:310
Palm Leaves (Milnes) **61**:130, 137
"Palm Sunday" (Keble) **87**:177, 201
Palma, ou la nuit du Vendredi-Saint (Feuillet) **45**:89
"La paloma celosa" (Lizardi) **30**:68
"The Palsy of the Heart" (Milnes) **61**:136
Paméla Giraud (Balzac) **5**:51-52
"Pamela ou l'Heureuse Adoption" (Genlis) **166**:32
"Pamfalon the Clown" (Leskov)
See "Skomorox Pamfalon"
"Pamiati Iu. P. Vrevskoi" (Turgenev) **122**:313
"Pamiatnik" (Derzhavin) **215**:30, 61-62, 66-67
"Pamiatnik" (Pushkin)
See "Pamjatnik"
"Pamiatnik Geroiu" (Derzhavin) **215**:72
"Pamjatnik" (Pushkin) **83**:261
"Pamphalon the Clown" (Leskov)
See "Skomorokh Pamfalon"
A Pamphlet to the Journeymen and Labourers of England, Wales, Scotland, and Ireland (Cobbett) **49**:110
"Pamyati V.A. Zhukovskogo" (Tyutchev) **34**:398
"Pan" (Emerson) **1**:297
"Pan" (Leconte de Lisle) **29**:224
"Pan and Luna" (Browning) **19**:153; **79**:153
"Pan and the Syrinx" (Laforgue)
See "Pan et la Syrinx"

Pan Benet (Fredro) **8**:285
"Pan et la Syrinx" (Laforgue) **5**:271, 274, 278, 281; **53**:293; **221**:4, 6-7, 10, 14, 16, 26
Pan Geldhab (Fredro) **8**:285-86, 289-90, 292
"Pan i pies" (Krasicki) **8**:403, 407
"Pan is Dead" (Barrett Browning)
See "The Dead Pan"
Pan Jowialski (Fredro) **8**:285-87, 290, 292-93
Pan Podstoli (Krasicki) **8**:398-401, 405-06
Pan Tadeusz; czyli, Ostatni zajazd na Litwie (Mickiewicz) **3**:389-92, 394-95, 397, 400-03; **101**:158, 167, 169, 171, 183-86, 193-94, 196-97, 210
Pandora (Nerval) **67**:312-13, 363-64
Panegirico do Plinio a Traiano (Alfieri) **101**:41-2
Panegyric of Pliny to Trahan (Alfieri)
See *Panegirico do Plinio a Traiano*
"Panegyric on the Drama" (Murray) **63**:184
Panegyric. ... to Trajan (Alfieri)
See *Panegirico do Plinio a Traiano*
"The Panjandrum" (Trollope) **101**:234-35
Pankraz, der Schmoller (Keller) **2**:415
"Panni Panyó" (Petofi) **21**:285
"Panorama" (Whittier) **8**:496, 531
The Panorama, and Other Poems (Whittier) **8**:495; **59**:371
"Panorama matritense. Cuadros de costumbres de la capital observados y descritos por un Curioso Parlante" (Larra) **130**:228, 255
"The Panorama of Lausanne" (Jameson) **43**:337
"The Panorama of Vanities" (Eminescu) **131**:287, 343
"Pan's Pipes" (Stevenson) **5**:388
"A Pansy from the Grave of Keats" (Whitman) **19**:457
"Panthère noire" (Leconte de Lisle) **29**:216-17, 224
"Pantisocracy" (Coleridge) **99**:48; **231**:108
"Pantomime" (Verlaine) **2**:629; **51**:378-80; **230**:164
"Papa above!" (Dickinson) **171**:99
"Le papa de Simon" (Maupassant) **1**:462
Papa Gobseck (Balzac)
See *Gobseck*
"The Papacy and the Roman Question" (Tyutchev) **34**:383
Der Papagei (Kotzebue) **25**:146-47
"Papal Benediction" (Milnes) **61**:129
Paper Against Gold and Glory Against Prosperity (Cobbett) **49**:110
The Papers of James Madison (Madison) **126**:247, 278
The Papers of Thomas Jefferson (Jefferson) **103**:127
Papers on Literature and Art (Fuller) **5**:159-60, 164; **211**:209-11
The Paphian Bower (Planché) **42**:286, 299
Die Papiere des Teufels (Nestroy) **42**:260
Papillons (Schumann) **143**:69-70, 73, 83-85, 101, 129
Papirer (Kierkegaard) **34**:200, 207, 222, 238-40; **78**:136, 158, 160, 162-63, 166, 189, 197-98, 21 7, 225-29, 238-39, 242-43, 251; **125**:184, 193, 207, 260, 262, 265-67
Pappenheim Cuirassier (Fouqué) **2**:267
La pâques dramatique (Nerval) **67**:324
Par les champs et les grèves (Flaubert) **185**:219
Par les champs et par les grèves (Flaubert) **62**:73
"The Parable" (Pushkin) **83**:272
"Les paraboles de Dom Guy" (Leconte de Lisle) **29**:225
Paracelsus (Browning) **19**:74-5, 78, 99, 103, 105, 109, 116, 120, 139-40; **79**:98, 140, 146, 149, 159, 168, 181, 185, 190
"Parade" (Rimbaud) **35**:308, 312, 322; **82**:232; **227**:203, 247, 270, 297-98, 310
Das Paradies und die Peri (Schumann) **143**:111, 115
Les paradis artificiels: Opium et haschisch (Baudelaire) **6**:80, 84, 119, 124; **29**:67, 71, 96; **55**:68-9; **155**:13, 33, 73
"Paradise" (Rossetti) **2**:563; **50**:272; **186**:279
Paradise (Liszt) **199**:308
"The Paradise and the Peri" (Moore) **6**:380-81, 387-88; **110**:213, 217, 221
"Paradise Lost" (Barrett Browning) **1**:128
"The Paradise of Bachelors and the Tartarus of Maids" (Melville) **3**:354, 380; **157**:111; **181**:341; **193**:151, 191; **221**:196
Paradise on the Dniester (Sacher-Masoch) **31**:287, 295, 310
"Paradise (to Be) Regained" (Thoreau) **21**:347
"Paradisets have" (Andersen) **7**:24; **214**:55
"Paradox of Achilles and the Tortoise" (Dodgson) **139**:57
"Parallel between the Phædra of Euripides and the Phédre of Racine" (Schlegel) **142**:301
Parallèlement (Verlaine) **2**:618, 620-21, 625, 632; **51**:352, 359, 361-63, 366, 368, 371-72, 388; **230**:160-61, 164-66, 169-70, 178, 207-8, 210-12
Parasha (Turgenev) **21**:376; **122**:247, 276
The Parasite (Turgenev)
See *Nakhlebnik*
"Pardon of Sainte-Anne" (Corbière)
See "La rapsode foraine et le pardon de Saint-Anne"
"Parental Indulgence" (Webster) **30**:424
Parentation uber Anselmo (Claudius) **75**:191
The Parent's Assistant (Edgeworth) **1**:261-63, 266-67; **51**:78-9, 81, 87, 89, 102, 110; **158**:56
Les parents pauvres (Balzac) **5**:35, 37, 63; **153**:153
Parere sulle tragedie (Alfieri) **101**:73
Parerga and Paralipomena (Schopenhauer)
See *Parerga und Paralipomena*
Parerga und Paralipomena (Schopenhauer) **51**:246, 271, 275, 278, 296-97, 326-27, 333-34, 336, 345-47; **157**:224, 226, 262, 316, 331-32, 338
"Un parfum à sentir" (Flaubert) **2**:256; **179**:120-21
"Parfum de Hélios-Apollon" (Leconte de Lisle) **29**:246
"Parfum exotique" (Baudelaire) **6**:79, 128; **29**:103; **55**:9, 26, 69-70
"Le parfum impérissable" (Leconte de Lisle) **29**:218
"Paria" (Corbière) **43**:26-7, 31, 34
"Paris" (Vigny) **102**:368
De Paris à Cadix (Dumas)
See *Impressions de voyage*
"Paris at Daybreak" (Baudelaire)
See "Le crépuscule du matin"
"Paris at Nightfall" (Baudelaire)
See "Le crépuscule du soir"
"Paris diurne" (Corbière) **43**:31
"Paris Manuscripts" (Marx) **114**:69
"Paris nocturne" (Corbière) **43**:15, 31, 34
"Paris se repeuple" (Rimbaud) **227**:208
The Paris Sketch Book (Thackeray) **5**:444, 507; **43**:359, 392; **169**:327; **213**:200, 215, 221, 223
Paris Spleen (Baudelaire)
See *Le spleen de Paris, petits poèmes en prose*
Paris under Siege, 1870-1871: From the Goncourt Journal (Goncourt and Goncourt) **7**:185
Paris-Guide (Hugo) **189**:256
"The Parish" (Clare) **9**:96-97
The Parish (Dickens)
See *Oliver Twist*
The Parish (Martineau) **137**:269-72
"Parish Boy's Progress" (Dickens)
See *Oliver Twist*
"The Parish Register" (Crabbe) **26**:78, 81-2, 86, 111, 118-19, 122, 124, 127, 132-33, 141; **121**:9-11, 26-7, 31, 48-9, 59-60, 66, 73-7, 83-5, 88-90
"The Parish Register: Burials" (Crabbe) **121**:43, 49
"The Parish-Clerk" (Crabbe) **26**:79, 134, 136
"A Parisian Dream" (Baudelaire)
See "Rêve parisien"
"Parisian Nocturne" (Verlaine)
See "Nocturne parisien"
Parisian Paintings (Baudelaire)
See *Tableaux parisiens*
The Parisian Prowler (Baudelaire)
See *Le spleen de Paris, petits poèmes en prose*
The Parisians (Bulwer-Lytton) **1**:150
La Parisienne (Becque) **3**:12-18
"Parisina" (Byron) **2**:63, 72, 96, 99
Parkman Reader (Parkman) **12**:368
"Parleying with Charles Avison" (Browning) **19**:149
"Parleying with Francis Furini" (Browning) **19**:126, 128-29
"Parleying with Gerard de Lairesse" (Browning) **19**:104, 108; **79**:174
Parleyings (Browning)
See *Parleyings with Certain People of Importance in Their Day*
Parleyings with Certain People of Importance in Their Day (Browning) **19**:99
"Parmenides" (Hopkins) **189**:89
"A Parnassian's Last Sighs" (Laforgue)
See "Derniers soupirs d'un Parnassien"
Parnassus (Rowson)
See *A Trip to Parnassus; or, The Judgment of Apollo on Dramatic Authors and Performers*
Parochial and Plain Sermons (Newman) **38**:282, 302-06, 309-10, 314, 336; **99**:219, 221-25
The Parochial History of Bremhill (Bowles) **103**:54
Parochial Sermons (Newman)
See *Parochial and Plain Sermons*
Le parole dopo la musica (Da Ponte) **50**:79
Parra Sastha, or the History of Paddy-go-Easy and his wife Nancy (Carleton) **199**:8-9, 19, 21, 97, 100
"Parrhasius" (Willis) **194**:302, 304
El parricida (Martínez de la Rosa) **102**:247
"The Parrock" (Barnes) **75**:70
"Parrot" (Baillie) **2**:42
"The Parrot of Mull: A Domestic Anecdote" (Campbell) **19**:186-87, 190
"Parsifal" (Verlaine) **230**:210
Parsifal (Wagner) **9**:414-15, 418-19, 421, 423, 433-35, 440, 443, 446-47, 450-51, 454, 456, 461, 465, 470-71; **119**:171-78, 183, 185, 188, 193, 195, 228, 241, 243-44, 264-73, 291, 293, 300-07, 311, 328-45
"Parson Avery" (Whittier) **8**:509
"Parson Field's Experience" (Cooke) **110**:33, 36
"Parson John Bullen's Lizards" (Harris) **23**:159, 161, 163; **165**:230, 237-38, 242-43, 254, 270, 291
"Parson Turell's Legacy; or, The President's Old Arm-Chair" (Holmes) **14**:109, 115, 126, 128
"The Parsonage" (Wordsworth) **166**:265
"The Parson's Daughter of Oxney Colne" (Trollope) **101**:235
La part du rêve (Amiel) **4**:13
"Part One of the Tragedy" (Goethe) **154**:223
"The Part Played by Labor in the Transition from Ape to Man" (Engels)
See "The Role Played by Labor in the Transition from Ape to Man"
"A Parthian Peep at Life, an Epistle to R—d A—n" (Reynolds) **146**:186
"A Particular Providence as Revealed in the Gospel" (Newman) **38**:306
"Une partie de campagne" (Maupassant) **83**:228
"La partie de tric-trac" (Mérimée) **6**:353-54, 366-71; **65**:49, 52, 54, 56-7, 61, 63, 66, 102

"Parting" (Arnold) **89**:17-19, 48, 95
"The Parting" (Brontë) **4**:44, 46
"Parting" (Dickinson)
See "My Life Closed Twice before Its Close"
"Parting" (Rossetti) **66**:311
"Parting after parting" (Rossetti) **186**:348
Parting and Meeting (Andersen) **79**:10-11, 16-17
"The Parting Hour" (Crabbe) **26**:93, 100, 124, 126, 135, 149; **121**:11, 56
"Parting Lovers" (Barrett Browning) **61**:44-5; **170**:122
"The Parting of Friends" (Keble) **87**:125
"The Parting of Friends" (Newman) **38**:306, 308-09
"The Parting of the Ways" (Ichiyō)
See "Wakare-Michi"
"The Parting of the Ways" (Lowell) **90**:214
"Parting Words" (Preseren)
See "Ob slovesu"
The Partisan (Simms) **3**:500-02, 506-10, 513
"The Partition of the Earth" (Schiller) **39**:333, 337
"The Partridges" (Turgenev) **122**:293
"The Party Fight and Funeral" (Carleton) **199**:9, 16, 32, 34, 56, 104, 108-9
"The Party of Cats" (Craik) **38**:119
"A Party of Travellers" (Oliphant) **61**:217-8
"Party Politics" (Froude) **43**:187, 215
"La parure" (Maupassant) **1**:447, 463
"Parus" (Lermontov) **47**:215
"The Parvenue" (Shelley) **14**:264
Les Parvenus (Genlis) **166**:21, 24
"Pas d'Extase" (Chivers) **49**:74-5
"Pascal" (Pater) **7**:308
Pascal Bruno (Dumas) **71**:204
"Paseo" (Silva) **114**:263
The Pasha of Many Tales (Marryat) **3**:319
"The Pasha's Son" (Taylor) **89**:342
"La pasionaria" (Zorrilla y Moral) **6**:526
"Pasquali" (Willis) **194**:298
Passage Birds (Tegner) **2**:612
"A Passage in the Secret History of an Irish Countess" (Le Fanu) **9**:304, 314, 316; **58**:253-4, 261, 307, 313
"Passage to India" (Whitman) **4**:551, 567-68, 579, 582, 586-87, 590; **31**:388, 404, 432-33, 442; **81**:310; **205**:167, 197, 203-4, 206-8, 226, 335, 341-42
Passage to India (Whitman) **205**:208, 225
"A Passage upon Oxford Studies" (Clough) **27**:70
Passages from the American Notebooks of Nathaniel Hawthorne (Hawthorne) **2**:307, 310, 314; **17**:153; 95; 105-8, 110-11; **158**:288, 291; **171**:275; **191**:257, 271, 275-76, 280, 302
Passages from the English Notebooks of Nathaniel Hawthorne (Hawthorne) **2**:306-07, 310, 314; **39**:245; **226**:26
Passages from the French and Italian Notebooks of Nathaniel Hawthorne (Hawthorne) **2**:310, 314; **23**:196-97; **171**:238, 240-42, 262, 346-47
Passages in the Life of Mrs. Margaret Maitland of Sunnyside (Oliphant) **11**:427-8, 431-2, 445-6, 448-9; **61**:163, 216; **221**:224, 244, 247
"Le passé" (Lamartine) **11**:281
"Passereau l'élier" (Borel) **41**:4, 6-7, 13
"Passe-Temps" (Claudius) **75**:212, 218
"Passing Away, Saith the World, Passing Away" (Rossetti) **2**:559, 567, 570, 572
"Passing by the Odd Number of Poplars" (Eminescu) **33**:246
"Passing Clouds" (Ichiyō)
See "Yuku Kumo"
"The Passing of Arthur" (Tennyson)
See "Morte d'Arthur"
"The Passing of Spring" (Lampman) **25**:185, 210
"Passing of the Sires" (Taylor) **89**:310
"The Passing of the Spirit" (Lampman) **25**:207, 210; **194**:35
"Passion" (Lampman) **25**:184
"The Passion" (Manzoni) **29**:253
"Une passion" (Maupassant) **83**:173
"Une passion dans le désert" (Balzac) **5**:46
"Passion et vertu" (Flaubert) **62**:102; **179**:120
Passion Flower (Robertson) **35**:335
"A Passion for Questions" (Bestuzhev)
See "Strast' sprosit"
"A Passion in the Desert" (Balzac)
See "Une passion dans le désert"
The Passion of Our Lord Jesus Christ According to the Revelations of Anne Catharina Emmerich (Brentano)
See *Das bittere Leiden unsers Herrn Jesu Christi: Nach den Betrachtungen der gottseligen Anna Katharina Emmerich, Augustinerin des Klosters Agnetenberg zu Dülmen*
"Passion Uninspired by Sentiment" (Dacre) **151**:148
"The Passionate Father" (Parton) **86**:349
The Passions (Dacre) **151**:148, 153, 163, 182, 198, 203-7, 219, 224-25, 227, 230
Passions (Staël-Holstein)
See *De l'influence des passions sur le bonheur des individus et des nations*
The Passions of the Human Soul (Fourier) **51**:161
The Passive Husband (Cumberland) **167**:193-97
"Passive Imagination and Insanity" (Coleridge) **90**:9
"The Past" (Bryant) **6**:168-69, 172, 174, 182, 189; **46**:38
"The Past" (Timrod) **25**:366-68
Past and Present (Carlyle) **70**:16-20, 46, 71, 90-91, 93
"The Past Condition of Organic Nature" (Huxley) **67**:59
Past Meridian (Sigourney) **21**:301; **87**:326
"Pasticcio" (Wagner) **119**:190
Paston Carew, Millionaire and Miser (Linton) **41**:165
"The Pastor" (Wordsworth) **166**:264
"El Pastor Clasiquino" (Espronceda) **39**:101
"Pastor Cum" (Gordon) **21**:181
"A Pastoral Ballad, by John Bull" (Moore) **110**:172
"Pastoral Fancies" (Clare) **9**:123
"The Pastoral of Bowman" (Wordsworth) **111**:236
"Pastoral Poesy" (Clare) **9**:100, 120-21; **86**:132
Pastoral Symphony (Beethoven)
See *Sixth Symphony*
"La pastorale de Conlie" (Corbière) **43**:28
"Pastoral-Erfahrung" (Mörike) **10**:453
Pastorals (Hogg)
See *Scottish Pastorals*
"Pastorals in Prose" (Clare) **86**:173
A Pata da Gazela (Alencar) **157**:39
Pater Brey (Goethe) **4**:213
"The Paternal Home" (Isaacs)
See "La casa paterna"
"A Paternal Ode to My Son" (Hood) **16**:235
"Paternity" (Lampman) **194**:118-19, 129
"The Path" (Bryant) **46**:49
"Path of Perseverance" (Wordsworth) **166**:313
The Path of Sorrow (Chivers)
See *The Path of Sorrow; or the Lament of Youth: A Poem*
The Path of Sorrow; or the Lament of Youth: A Poem (Chivers) **49**:43-4, 46-8, 51-2, 57, 68-70
The Path through the Woods (Stifter)
See *Der Waldsteig*
The Pathfinder (Cooper) **203**:11-15, 39, 73, 98-102, 111, 130, 158
The Pathfinder; or, The Inland Sea (Cooper) **27**:127, 129-35, 138, 140, 150-51, 153-54, 156, 158-59, 185-88; **1**:202, 204-07, 211; **54**:258-59, 265
"Patience" (Hopkins) **189**:77, 90
"Patience, Hard Thing!" (Hopkins) **17**:261
"Patmos" (Hölderlin) **16**:166-72, 174-76, 180-81, 189, 191-92; **187**:192, 194, 218, 223, 283, 298, 304
"Pató Pál úr" (Petofi) **21**:264
"The Patriarch" (Sigourney) **21**:290
The Patriarchal Institution (Child) **73**:63
Patrice (Renan) **145**:357
Patricia Kemball (Linton) **41**:166
"The Patriot" (Browning) **19**:96
Patriotic Sketches of Ireland, Written in Connaught (Morgan) **29**:391
Patriotic Songs (Moodie) **113**:309
"Patriotische Phantasien eines Slaven" (Kopitar) **117**:107, 117-18
"The Patriot's Test" (Jones) **222**:157, 169
"The Patron" (Crabbe) **26**:93; **121**:11, 61, 78, 83-5
"Patronage" (Edgeworth) **1**:268; **51**:81, 87-90, 93, 104, 136
Patronage (Edgeworth) **158**:22, 65
"La patronne" (Maupassant) **1**:469
"Pauca meae" (Hugo) **10**:373
"Paucity of Original Writers. Passages which Pope has borrowed pointed out" (Warton) **118**:337
Paul and Virginia (Williams) **135**:334
Paul and Virginia (Zhukovsky) **35**:377
Paul Ardenheim: The Monk of Wissahikon (Lippard) **198**:120, 122, 132, 135, 165, 169, 225
Paul Clifford (Bulwer-Lytton) **1**:140, 145, 148, 150; **45**:7, 11-13, 19, 23-4, 27, 30, 34, 69-70
Paul Erdmanns Fest (Claudius) **75**:182-83, 186-87
Paul Fane, or, Parts of a Life Else Untold (Willis) **194**:319
"Paul Felton" (Dana) **53**:160, 174, 176, 178-9
Paul Forestier (Augier) **31**:7-8, 10, 13, 16, 23, 28, 31, 35
"Paul H. Hayne's Poetry" (Lanier) **6**:252
Paul; ou, La ressemblance (Nodier) **19**:384
Paul Prescott's Charge (Alger) **8**:43; **83**:139, 142, 144-45
"Paul Revere's Ride" (Longfellow) **2**:490, 498; **45**:114, 124, 137, 139, 179-80, 188, 191
Paul, the Peddler; or, The Adventures of a Young Street Merchant (Alger) **8**:44; **83**:112, 133
"Pauline" (Hemans) **71**:292
Pauline (Browning)
See *Pauline: A Fragment of a Confession*
Pauline (Dumas) **11**:49; **71**:204
Pauline (Sand) **42**:373; **57**:316
Pauline (Staël-Holstein)
See *Histoire de Pauline*
Pauline: A Fragment of a Confession (Browning) **19**:73, 102, 105, 110, 116, 120, 126, 133; **79**:107, 146-47, 151, 166, 174, 176, 188, 190
"Pauline's Passion and Punishment" (Alcott) **58**:39, 46, 59; **83**:6; **218**:85
The Paulo Afonso Falls (Castro Alves)
See *A cachoeira de Paulo Afonso*
"Paumanok" (Whitman)
See "Starting from Paumanok"
"A Paumanok Picture" (Whitman) **81**:319
Pauper Labour (Miller) **143**:13
"The Pauper's Christmas Carol" (Hood) **16**:235
Pausanias the Spartan (Bulwer-Lytton) **1**:151-52; **45**:61-2
"Pause" (Muller) **73**:351, 368, 372
"A Pause" (Rossetti) **2**:574; **50**:289
"A Pause of Thought" (Rossetti) **186**:268, 294, 343
Pauvre Belgique! (Baudelaire) **155**:56-57, 62
"Le pauvre énfant pâle" (Mallarmé) **4**:371
"Pauvre garçon" (Corbière) **43**:25, 27, 34

"Les pauvres à l'église" (Rimbaud) **4**:454-55, 458, 466; **82**:230
Pauvres fleurs (Desbordes-Valmore) **97**:12, 18, 28, 30
"Les pauvres gens" (Hugo) **3**:273
Les pauvres Saltimbanques (Banville) **9**:19
"The Pavilion on the Links" (Stevenson) **5**:391, 394, 397, 403, 408, 413, 426, 431, 434; **63**:243, 274; **193**:212, 221, 250, 254-56, 279
"Le Pavillon sur l'eau" (Gautier) **59**:32
"Pavlin" (Leskov) **174**:12
"The Pawnbroker's Shop" (Dickens) **187**:26; **219**:151
"Pax animae" (Casal) **131**:267
"Pay Day in the Theatre" (Lippard) **198**:133
"Paysage" (Baudelaire) **155**:8
"Paysage mauvais" (Corbière) **43**:15, 28, 31
"Paysage polaire" (Leconte de Lisle) **29**:230
"Paysages" (Baudelaire) **29**:100; **55**:24, 35-6, 65
"Paysages belges" (Verlaine) **51**:381-82
"Paysages tristes" (Verlaine) **51**:355
Les paysans (Balzac) **5**:40, 66-69, 73; **153**:8-10, 46
Les Paysans (Barbey d'Aurevilly) **213**:5
"Pázmán lovag" (Arany) **34**:5
Pazukhin's Death (Saltykov) **16**:368
"Peace" (Bloomfield) **145**:128
"Peace" (Clare) **9**:78; **86**:160
"Peace" (Crawford) **127**:221
"Peace" (Hopkins) **17**:255; **189**:62
"Peace" (Lampman) **25**:219
"Peace" (Patmore) **9**:334, 358
"Peace in Believing" (Newman) **38**:305
"Peace in Life and Art" (Patmore) **9**:342, 346
"Peaceful Death and Painful Life" (Brontë) **109**:31, 38
"The Peacock" (Derzhavin) **215**:32
"The Peacock" (Leskov)
See "Pavlin"
"The Peal of Another Trumpet" (Mangan) **27**:296
"A Peal of Bells" (Rossetti) **66**:307
"Pearl" (Tennyson) **202**:291
"The Pearl Divers" (Krylov) **1**:438
"The Pearl of Good Fortune" (Andersen) **7**:23
Pearl of Great Price (Smith) **53**:381
The Pearl of Orr's Island: A Story of the Coast of Maine (Stowe) **3**:555-56, 559, 561, 563, 567
Pearls and Pebbles; or, The Notes of an Old Naturalist (Traill) **31**:314-15, 317, 323, 328-29
The Pearls of Love (Petofi)
See *Szerelem Gyöngyei*
"The Peasant and the Prince" (Martineau) **26**:323; **137**:256-57
"The Peasant and the Sheep" (Krylov) **1**:435, 439
"The Peasant and the Workman" (Krylov) **1**:435
The Peasant as Millionaire, or The Maiden from the Fairy World (Raimund)
See *Der Bauer als Millionär; oder, Das Mädchen aus der Feenwelt*
"The Peasant Children" (Nekrasov)
See "Krestyánskie déti"
"The Peasant Gentlewoman" (Pushkin) **3**:435
The Peasant in Debt (Gotthelf)
See *Die Erlebnisse eines Schuldenbauers*
"The Peasant in Distress" (Krylov) **1**:435
Peasant Justice (Sacher-Masoch) **31**:294
"The Peasant Pavo" (Runeberg)
See "Bonden Pavo"
Peasant Properties (Miller) **143**:13
The Peasant War (Engels)
See *Der deutsche Bauernkrieg*
The Peasant War in Germany (Engels)
See *Der deutsche Bauernkrieg*
"A Peasant Woman" (Nekrasov) **11**:416
The Peasantry (Balzac)
See *Les paysans*
"The Peasants and the River" (Krylov) **1**:435
The Peasants' Mirror (Gotthelf)
See *Der Bauern-Spiegel oder Lebensgeschichte des Jeremias Gotthelf: Von ihm selbst beschrieben*
Peasants' War (Engels)
See *Der deutsche Bauernkrieg*
La peau de chagrin (Balzac) **5**:29, 32, 49, 58, 79-80; **53**:8, 22, 25, 35; **153**:5, 21, 116, 119-23, 126, 131, 147, 149, 151-52, 161
"Peccavi, Domine" (Lampman) **25**:193; **194**:33, 43, 69
"Pečerskie antiki" (Leskov) **25**:258-59
Le péché de M. Antoine (Sand) **2**:589; **42**:322; **57**:375
Le Péché de Monsieur Antoine (Sand) **174**:229
"Le péché véniel" (Balzac) **5**:78
Pechorin's Journal (Lermontov) **5**:295-98, 301-02, 304
"Der Pechvogel" (Lenau) **16**:265
A Peculiar Position (Scribe) **16**:405
"Pedantry" (Hazlitt) **29**:148; **82**:115
"Pedantry" (Mackenzie) **41**:188
"The Pedlar" (Hogg) **4**:282; **109**:280
"The Pedlar" (Wordsworth) **166**:241
"Pedlar Karl" (Willis) **194**:282, 298
"The Pedlars" (Nekrasov)
See "Korobeyniki"
"Pedro Ivo" (Castro Alves) **205**:5-6, 12
"Pedro Ladron; or, The Shepherd of Toppledown Hill" (Darley) **2**:129
"Pedro the Slave" (Isaacs)
See "El esclavo Pedro"
"Peele Castle" (Wordsworth)
See "Stanzas on Peele Castle"
Peers and Parvenus (Gore) **65**:21
Peg Woffington (Reade) **2**:533-34, 536, 539-40, 544-45, 548, 552; **74**:243-44, 253, 255-56, 262-65, 268, 277, 281, 299, 319
"Pegasus in Harness" (Schiller) **39**:337
"Pegasus in Pound" (Longfellow) **103**:284
"Le Peintre de la vie moderne" (Baudelaire) **55**:8, 33-34; **155**:40, 94
Le peintre de Salztbourg (Nodier) **19**:378-79, 384-85
Pelayo (Espronceda) **39**:84, 100
Pelayo: A Story of the Goth (Simms) **3**:507-08
Le pèlerin blanc; ou, Les orphelins du hameau (Pixérécourt) **39**:277, 284, 289, 291
Pélérinage a Ermenonville (Pilgrimage to Ermenonville) (Dumas) **71**:241
Pelham; or, The Adventures of a Gentleman (Bulwer-Lytton) **1**:135, 140, 145, 148-50, 153-55; **45**:11, 18-19, 21, 23, 32-5, 37-8, 68-71
"The Pelican Chorus" (Lear) **3**:307
"Le Pélican ou les deaux mères" (Desbordes-Valmore) **97**:5
Pelopidas (Bird) **1**:88, 90; **197**:6, 16
Pembroke (Lee) **191**:316
The Pen and the Album (Thackeray) **5**:485
"La peña blanca" (Villaverde) **121**:333
Pencillings by the Way (Willis) **194**:285, 290, 302, 316, 319
"Pencillings by the Way" (Willis) **194**:298, 301-2, 308
Pendennis (Thackeray)
See *The History of Pendennis: His Fortunes and Misfortunes, His Friends and His Greatest Enemy*
Pénélope (Charriere) **66**:127
"Penelope's Choice" (Lazarus) **109**:294
The Peninsular War (Southey) **97**:265
"Pénitence" (Verlaine) **230**:171
El penitente (Villaverde) **121**:333-34
"Penitentiary Systems" (Neal) **161**:329
"Penmaen Pool" (Hopkins) **189**:53
"Penn and Peterborough" (Landor) **14**:178
Penniless (Turgenev)
See *Bezdenezh'e*
"Pennilessness" (Turgenev)
See *Bezdenezh'e*
"A Pennsylvania Legend" (Bryant) **6**:180
"The Pennsylvania Pilgrim" (Whittier) **8**:511, 521-23
The Pennsylvania Pilgrim, and Other Poems (Whittier) **8**:501, 516; **59**:366
"A Penny Plain and Two-pence Colored" (Stevenson) **5**:421; **63**:237-8, 242; **193**:207
El pensador Mexicano (Lizardi) **30**:67, 77, 85
"Pensar, dudar" (Hugo) **3**:271
"Pensée de Byron" (Nerval) **67**:307
"Pensée des morts" (Lamartine) **190**:235, 263
Pensée des Morts (Liszt) **199**:304
"Pensées" (Amiel) **4**:14-15
Pensées (Stendhal) **178**:156
Pensées d'aôut (Sainte-Beuve) **5**:331, 335, 341
Pensées de Joseph Joubert (Joubert) **9**:290
"Pensées de minuit" (Gautier) **59**:18
"Pensées des morts" (Lamartine) **11**:255, 265, 279
Pensées detachées (Barbey d'Aurevilly) **213**:88-89, 92
Pensées, essais, maxmimes, et correspondance de Joseph Joubert (Joubert) **9**:281, 283-86
"Pensées et paradoxes" (Laforgue) **221**:41
Pensées, réflexions et maximes (Chateaubriand) **134**:116
Pensieri (Leopardi) **129**:276-77, 302
"Pensiero dominante" (Leopardi) **129**:341
Pensiero XVIII (Manzoni) **98**:214
La pension bourgeoise (Scribe) **16**:394
"Pensive on Her Dead Gazing" (Whitman) **31**:370
The Pensive One (Liszt)
See *Il Pensieroso*
La Pentacoste (Manzoni) **29**:253; **98**:213, 220
The Pentameron and Pentalogia (Landor) **14**:164-65, 175, 178, 191, 193-95, 202, 207
"La pente de la rêverie" (Hugo) **21**:223
"The Pentecost" (Manzoni)
See *La Pentacoste*
Penthesilea (Kleist) **2**:437-38, 440-42, 444, 446-47, 450, 452, 454-57, 461, 463; **37**:217, 219, 223, 225-26, 228, 230-34, 237, 253, 255, 263, 266-72, 274; **222**:205, 207-8, 227-34, 255-56, 273-74, 277-81
"Pentheus" (Meyer) **81**:207
"The Pentland Uprising" (Stevenson) **193**:229
"Pentridge by the River" (Barnes) **75**:59
"Pentucket" (Whittier) **8**:520
"Penumbra" (Rossetti) **4**:491
The People (Michelet)
See *Le peuple*
The People of Seldwyla (Keller)
See *Die Leute von Seldwyla*
"The People of Stargorod" (Leskov) **174**:12
"People of the House of God" (Leskov)
See "Bozedomy"
The People's Cause or Pugachov, Romanov, or Pestel (Bakunin) **25**:64
"The People's Hands Were Swollen with Applause" (Norwid) **17**:364
"Peoria Speech" (Lincoln) **201**:156-57, 161-62, 186, 197, 204-5
"The peperman's nightcap" (Andersen) **79**:83-84
"Per amica silentia" (Verlaine) **230**:169
"Per Contra: The Poet, High Art, Genius" (Thomson) **18**:412, 421
"Per prima Messa" (Solomos) **15**:385-86
"Perambulatory Musings, from Blenheim House, at Woodstock, in Oxfordshire, the Seat of the Duke of Marlborough, to Titley House, in Herefordshire, the Seat of William Greenly" (Dyer) **129**:138-39
"Perchatka" (Zhukovsky) **35**:398
"Perchè Pensa? Pensando S'Invecchia" (Clough) **27**:72
Percival Keene (Marryat) **3**:319-20
Percy: A Tragedy (More) **27**:324-25, 332, 337; **141**:167, 202-3, 205, 207, 247, 256-59
"Percy Hall" (Brontë) **109**:4-5, 30

"Percy's Musings upon the Battle of Edwardston" (Brontë) **109**:30
"Perdida" (Silva) **114**:311
Perdita (Robinson) **142**:178-79, 181
Perdu (Droste-Hülshoff) **3**:197
"Le père amable" (Maupassant) **1**:448, 469; **83**:171
"Le Père Canet" (Balzac)
See *Facino Cane*
Le père Goriot: Histoire Parisienne (Balzac) **5**:29, 32, 34, 43-46, 52-53, 67, 76, 85-87; **35**:1-76; **53**:9, 13, 21-22, 28-29; **153**:21, 65, 67-69, 71, 74, 76-77, 79-81, 116-17, 125, 127-29, 131, 149, 152-53, 158-61, 163
"Le Père Judas" (Maupassant) **83**:176
Le Père la Ruine (Dumas) **71**:204
Un père prodigue (Dumas) **9**:224, 229, 231, 237, 241, 245-46, 248-50, 253
"Perebendja" (Shevchenko) **54**:373
"Peregrina" (Mörike) **10**:449, 451, 454-55
Peregrina (Mörike) **201**:252, 268, 270-71, 285, 301-2
Peregrinus Proteus (Wieland)
See *Die Geheime Geschichte des Philosophen Peregrinus Proteus*
"Père-la-Chaise" (Adams) **33**:17
"Perepiska" (Turgenev)
See "Peripiska"
"La pereza" (Bécquer) **106**:93, 96
The Perfect Life (Channing) **17**:46
"Perfect Love" (Lampman) **25**:209
The Perfumed Garden of the Cheikh Nefzaoui, A Manual of Arabian Erotology (Burton) **42**:29
"Una peri" (Casal) **131**:226, 236, 267
"La Péri" (Gautier) **59**:34-6
"Perichole" (Mérimée) **6**:353
Pericles (Lamb) **125**:304
Pericles and Aspasia (Landor) **14**:165, 176, 178, 187, 189, 194
"Périer" (Beddoes) **154**:31-32
"A Perilous Incognito" (Boyesen) **135**:13, 29
A Perilous Secret (Reade) **74**:257, 263-64, 289
"The Perils of Certain English Prisoners" (Dickens) **217**:247; **219**:99
The Perils of the Nation: An Appeal to the Legislature, the Clergy, and the Higher and Middle Classes (Tonna) **135**:193, 200, 205, 207-9, 211-13, 215-17
"The Periodical Essayists" (Hazlitt) **29**:165, 167
The Peripatetic (Thelwall) **162**:304-6, 308, 325
"Das Peripatetiker" (Muller) **73**:366
"Peripiska" (Turgenev) **21**:397, 401, 414, 418; **122**:243-45, 247, 266, 268, 312
El periquillo sarniento (Lizardi) **30**:67, 69-80, 82-3, 85-8
"The Perishing Classes" (Parker) **186**:207
"El perjurio" (Villaverde) **121**:333
"Perkin Warbeck" (Schiller) **39**:368
Perkin Warbeck (Shelley)
See *The Fortunes of Perkin Warbeck*
Perourou, the Bellows-Mender (Williams)
See "The History of Perourou; or, The Bellows-Mender; Written by Himself"
The Perpetual Curate (Oliphant) **11**:439, 446-9, 454-7, 459-60; **61**:166, 174, 177-8, 180, 198, 202, 206-8, 218, 220, 222, 226-7; **221**:230-31, 244, 246
"Perpetual Forces" (Emerson) **98**:61
Perpetual Peace: A Philosophical Sketch (Kant)
See *Zum ewigen Frieden: Ein philosophischer Entwurf*
"The Perpetuation of Our Political Institutions" (Lincoln) **18**:240, 248, 278-79
"Perplexed Music" (Barrett Browning) **16**:133
"Perplexities" (Clare) **86**:166-67
"El perro en barrio ageno" (Lizardi) **30**:68
The Persecuted (Fouqué)
See *Der Verfolgte*
"Persée et Andromède" (Laforgue) **5**:269, 271, 281; **53**:294, 298-9, 301; **221**:4, 10, 12, 14-15
"Persephone" (Ingelow) **39**:263
"Perseus and Andromeda" (Laforgue)
See "Persée et Andromède"
"Persia" (Kendall) **12**:198
"Persia" (Tennyson) **202**:188
"A Persian Lesson" (Whitman) **205**:159
"Persian Poetry" (Emerson) **1**:295
The Personal History of David Copperfield (Dickens) **3**:146-47, 149, 151, 156-57, 162, 171-72, 180, 172, 186; **8**:165, 173, 176, 182; **18**:99, 111, 121; **26**:156-57, 163, 168-69, 171, 174-75, 177, 201; **37**:145, 164, 168, 171, 197; **86**:186, 201, 256, 258; **105**:231, 311, 338; **113**:29, 41, 56, 70, 80-1, 88, 97, 102-3, 110, 113-14, 118-19, 124, 127; **161**:1-142; **187**:46, 53, 71; **217**:217, 245; **219**:69, 73-74, 84-85, 91, 99, 138, 159; **230**:7; **231**:176, 222, 245
"Personal Influence: the Means of Propagating the Truth" (Newman) **99**:301
Personal Memoirs of Major Richardson; As Connected with the Singular Oppression of that Officer While in Spain (Richardson) **55**:297, 299, 336
Personal Narrative of a Pilgrimage to El-Medinah and Meccah (Burton) **42**:35, 40, 42, 52-54, 57-59, 61
A Personal Narrative of Travels to the Equinoctial Regions of the New Continent, During the Years 1799-1804, by Alexander de Humboldt and Aimé Bonpland; with maps, plans, etc. (Williams) **135**:309
Personal Recollections (Tonna) **135**:194-95, 207, 228
Personal Recollections of Charlotte Elizabeth, Continued to the Close of her Life (Tonna) **135**:194
"Personal Reminiscences" (Cranch) **115**:27
"Personal Talk" (Wordsworth) **12**:431; **111**:286
"The Persons of the Tale" (Stevenson) **193**:326
"Persten'" (Baratynsky) **103**:2, 30-3, 47
Persuasion (Austen) **1**:30-31, 33-35, 37-41, 44-46, 50, 53, 60-64; **13**:61, 84, 93-94; **19**:8, 52, 55; **33**:27-101; **51**:33, 41; **81**:48, 52; **95**:11, 15, 84, 86; **119**:12, 14, 17-18, 20-21, 23-28, 36-41, 48, 55, 57; **150**:33, 110, 138, 148-49; **207**:14, 37, 39-40, 46, 57, 65; **210**:9, 130; **222**:1-112
"La Perte" (Baudelaire) **155**:95
"Perte d'auréole" (Baudelaire) **155**:56, 95, 107
Peru, A Poem. In Six Cantos (Williams) **135**:286, 300, 314-15, 333, 341
Pervaia liubov (Turgenev)
See *Pervaya lyubov'*
Pervaja ljubov (Turgenev)
See *Pervaya lyubov'*
Pervaya lyubov' (Turgenev) **21**:393, 415, 418-20, 422, 431, 435, 439, 441, 449-51; **37**:382; **122**:241, 243, 245, 247, 259-60, 265, 267-68, 280, 306, 333-36, 342, 346, 348, 358, 360-62
"Pervoe filosoficheskoe pis'mo" (Chaadaev)
See "Philosophic Letter 1"
"Pervonte oder die Wünsche" (Wieland) **177**:265
Pescara's Temptation (Meyer)
See *Die Versuchung des Pescara*
"Peschiera" (Clough) **27**:79
"Pesn skandinavskix voinov" (Tyutchev) **34**:412
"Pesn' toržestvujuščej liubvi" (Turgenev)
See "Pesn' torzhestvuyushchey lyubvi"
"Pesn' torzhestvennoi liubvi" (Turgenev)
See "Pesn' torzhestvuyushchey lyubvi"
"Pesn' torzhestvuyushchey lyubvi" (Turgenev) **21**:408, 415, 420, 441, 452; **37**:449; **122**:241, 267, 306, 337, 350, 365, 371, 373-74, 376, 378
Pesnja pro kuptsa Kalashinikova (Lermontov)
See *Pesnya pro tsarya Ivana Vasilievicha, molodogo oprichnika i undalogo kuptsa Kalashnikova*
Pesnya pro tsarya Ivana Vasilievicha, molodogo oprichnika i undalogo kuptsa Kalashnikova (Lermontov) **5**:288, 294, 300; **126**:136-38, 215, 224
"Pessimism" (Symonds) **34**:337
"Pessimisme" (Banville) **9**:31
"The Pessimist" (Crawford) **12**:174-75; **127**:222-23
"Pest-Nests" (Mayhew) **31**:179
"The Pet Name" (Barrett Browning) **1**:117
Peter Bell (Wordsworth)
See *Peter Bell: A Tale in Verse*
Peter Bell: A Tale in Verse (Wordsworth) **12**:408-09, 421-22, 445; **111**:202-3, 222, 226, 245, 267; **166**:282; **206**:333-36
Peter Bell. Lyrical Ballad (Reynolds) **146**:166, 168-69, 172-73
Peter Bell the Third (Shelley) **18**:351, 358, 368; **175**:325
"Peter Connell" (Carleton) **3**:85
"Peter Goldthwaite's Treasure" (Hawthorne) **39**:190; **171**:243
"Peter Grimes" (Crabbe) **26**:111, 113, 116, 119, 124-26, 128, 134-35, 141, 147; **121**:5, 10, 24-5, 52, 56, 62, 83, 87
Peter Ibbetson (Du Maurier) **86**:278-80, 285, 287-88, 290, 292
Peter Leberecht, eine Geschichte ohne Abeuteuerlichheiten (Tieck) **5**:515, 519-21
Peter Leberechts Volks mährchen (Tieck) **5**:515
"Peter of Barnet" (Hogg) **109**:248
Peter of the Castle (Banim and Banim) **13**:117-18, 129, 131
"Peter Pendulum" (Poe)
See "The Business Man"
Peter Pilgrim (Bird) **1**:86
Peter Pilgrim: or, A rambler's recollections. By the author of "Calavar," "Nick of the woods," &c. (Bird) **197**:29, 44, 68
Peter Schlemihls Wundersame Geschichte (Chamisso) **82**:6, 9-12, 15-16, 18, 20-22, 27, 30, 32, 35, 38, 40-41, 48-49, 51, 53, 56-57, 60, 62-65, 67-69
Peter Simple (Marryat) **3**:315, 317-19, 321-22
Peter the Great (Dunlap) **2**:215
"Peter the Hermit" (Brontë) **217**:18
"Peter the Parson" (Woolson) **82**:284, 286, 293, 330, 333, 3367
"Peter the Piccaninny" (Kendall) **12**:192
Peter's Letters to His Kinsfolk (Lockhart) **6**:285, 293, 295-97, 300, 305, 308
"The Petersburg Stage" (Gogol) **31**:94
"Le Petit Bègue" (Desbordes-Valmore) **97**:14
Le petit chose (Daudet) **1**:231, 234-36, 243, 249-51
"Petit Gervais" (Hugo) **10**:357
"Le Petit Incendiaire" (Desbordes-Valmore) **97**:14
"Le Petit Peureux" (Desbordes-Valmore) **97**:38
Le petit Picpus (Hugo) **10**:373-74
Petit traité de poésie Françause (Banville) **9**:20-21, 23-25, 27-28
Le petit vieux des Batignolles (Gaboriau) **14**:17-18, 22, 29
La Petite Comtesse (Feuillet) **45**:85-7
"La petite Fadette" (Maupassant) **1**:448
La petite Fadette (Sand) **2**:599, 601, 603, 605; **42**:323, 340, 363-65, 367, 373-75, 377; **57**:317, 338
La petite paroisse (Daudet) **1**:237, 251
Petite prière sans prétentions (Laforgue) **53**:265
"La petite rogue" (Maupassant) **1**:454; **83**:197, 199, 201
"Petites misères d'automne" (Laforgue) **221**:85
"Petites misères de juillet" (Laforgue) **221**:24
Petites Misères de la vie conjugale (Balzac) **153**:147
"Petites misères d'octobre" (Laforgue) **221**:91

Petites moralités légendaires (Laforgue)
See *Moralités légendaires*
"Petites prière sans prétention" (Laforgue) **221**:88
"Les petites vieilles" (Baudelaire) **155**:3-4, 6
"Les petites vielles" (Baudelaire) **6**:79, 85, 91-2, 109, 116; **29**:80, 100, 114; **55**:2-4, 16, 19, 21-2, 28, 35, 39-42, 67, 73
"Petition" (Barbauld)
See "The Mouse's Petition"
"Pétition" (Laforgue) **5**:280; **221**:7, 36, 48-49, 60, 62, 64, 83, 90
Les Petits Bourgeois (Balzac) **153**:7-10
Petits châteaux de bohème (Nerval) **67**:305, 331
"Les petits coups" (Beranger) **34**:29
Petits poèmes lycanthropes (Baudelaire)
See *Le spleen de Paris, petits poèmes en prose*
"Les Petits Sauvages" (Desbordes-Valmore) **97**:14
"The Pet-Lamb: A Pastoral" (Wordsworth) **111**:235
"Petöfi dem Sonnengott" (Arnim) **123**:8
Petrarka und Laura (Klopstock) **225**:285, 295-96, 300
"Petr Petrovič Karataev" (Turgenev) **122**:264
"Der Petrefaktensammler" (Mörike) **201**:346
Petru rareş (Eminescu) **33**:264-65; **131**:292
"Petru Velikomu" (Derzhavin) **215**:71
"Pettichap's Nest" (Clare) **9**:85; **86**:144-45
Petticoat Government (Trollope) **30**:331
Le peuple (Michelet) **31**:207, 214, 217-18, 229-32, 234, 239-42, 248, 250-51, 257, 260-61; **218**:306, 316-19, 323-24, 330, 336-38
Le peuple russe et le Socialisme (Herzen) **10**:332, 335-6
"Pevcu" (Preseren) **127**:298
Peveril of the Peak (Scott) **15**:313; **209**:298, 300
"Pevuchest est v morskikh volnakh" (Tyutchev) **34**:398
"Pewit's Nest" (Clare) **9**:85; **86**:133
"The Pewter Quart" (Maginn) **8**:438, 441
La Peyrouse (Kotzebue) **25**:141, 145, 147
"Pfalzgräfin Jutta" (Heine) **147**:229, 232
Die Pfarrose (Ludwig) **4**:349, 351
"Pfeifferbund" (Beddoes) **154**:26
"Pferd und Esel" (Heine) **147**:231
Pfingstbetrachtung (Freytag) **109**:180
"Der Pförtner im Herrenhause" (Stifter)
See "Tourmaline"
"Phadrig's Dilemma" (Griffin) **7**:198
"Phaeton" (Cranch) **115**:58
Phaeton: Loose Thoughts for Loose Thinkers (Kingsley) **35**:249
Die Phänomenologie des Geistes (Hegel) **151**:237-40, 259-63, 267, 276, 282-83, 286-88, 293, 295-98, 300-301, 303, 306, 313, 316-18, 331, 335, 337, 341-47, 360-72
Phantasie (Schumann)
See *Fantasy*
"Phantasie an Laura" (Schiller) **39**:338; **166**:117
"Phantasies" (Lazarus) **8**:418-19; **109**:291
Phantasiestücke in Callot's Manier (Hoffmann)
See *Fantasiestücke in Callots Manier*
Phantasiestüeke in Callots Manier (Hoffmann)
See *Fantasiestücke in Callots Manier*
Phantasmagoria (Dodgson) **139**:29, 35, 124, 127, 129
Phantasmagoria (Pavlova)
See *Fantasmagorii*
Phantasmion (Coleridge) **31**:58-63
"Phantasms" (Turgenev)
See "Prizraki. Fantaziya"
Phantasus (Tieck) **5**:515, 517, 527; **46**:332-33, 348-50
"A Phantasy" (Taylor) **89**:307
"The Phantom" (Taylor) **89**:307
The Phantom (Baillie) **2**:40-41; **71**:6
"The Phantom-Head upon the Table. A Singular Story from Real Life. Showing the Humiliations of the Barriers of High-Life" (Willis) **194**:319
"The Phantom Horse" (Meyer)
See "Das Geisterross"
"The Phantom Hour" (Pavlova) **138**:31
"Phantom or Fact" (Coleridge) **231**:62, 73
"Phantom Players" (Bird) **197**:6
The Phantom Ship (Marryat) **3**:317, 320
The Phantom Wedding; or, The Fall of the House of Flint (Southworth) **26**:434
"The Phantom Wooer" (Beddoes) **154**:57-58
"Phantoms" (Turgenev)
See "Prizraki. Fantaziya"
Le phare des Sanguinaires (Daudet) **1**:247
"Les phares" (Baudelaire) **6**:98, 114, 123; **29**:97; **55**:4, 58; **155**:12, 54-55
"The Pharisees" (Parker) **186**:204, 206
"Pharoah Tla's Avatars" (Eminescu)
See "Avatarii faraonului Tlá"
"Phaudhrig Crohoore" (Le Fanu) **9**:299
"Phebe" (Larcom) **179**:174
"Phelim O'Toole's Courtship" (Carleton) **3**:86, 91; **199**:9, 16, 33, 35, 59-60, 87-88, 103
Phenix-Fuglen (Grundtvig) **158**:167, 177-79
"Phenomena" (Hoffmann) **2**:342
"Le phénomène futur" (Mallarmé) **4**:371; **41**:281; **210**:167, 169
The Phenomenology of Mind (Hegel) **46**:114-15, 126, 133-34, 136, 138-39
The Phenomenology of Spirit (Hegel)
See *Die Phänomenologie des Geistes*
The Phenomenology of the Spirit (Hegel)
See *System der Wissenschaft: 1. Theil. Der Phänomenologies des Geistes*
"Phidylé" (Leconte de Lisle) **29**:224
Phil Fogarty: A Tale of the Fighting Onety-Oneth (Thackeray) **14**:450; **43**:384
"Phil Fogarty—A Tale of the Fighting Onety-Oneth By Harry Rollicker" (Thackeray) **169**:330-31, 333
"Phil Purcel, the Pig-Driver" (Carleton) **3**:86; **199**:15
Phil, the Fiddler; or, The Story of a Young Street Musician (Alger) **8**:21, 24, 33-34, 43; **83**:127
"Philalet to Melodor" (Karamzin)
See "Filalet k Melodor"
"Philander" (Arnim) **5**:13
"Der Philanthrop" (Heine) **147**:140
"The Philanthropist" (Griffin) **7**:215
"Philanthropy" (Thoreau) **7**:351
Philiberte (Augier) **31**:2, 4, 10, 12, 14, 23-4, 27
Philip (Alfieri)
See *Filippo*
Philip II (Alfieri) **101**:18
"Philip, my King" (Craik) **38**:120
"Philip of Pokanoket" (Irving) **19**:328; **95**:265-66, 268-69
Philip Stanley; or, the Enthusiasm of Love (Brown)
See *Clara Howard*
Der Philister vor, in und nach der Geschichte: Scherzhafte Abhandlung (Brentano) **191**:88, 90-92
"The Philistine and the Rascal King" (Schumann) **143**:139
"Phillippe de Agramont" (Lippard) **198**:121, 133
Philological Grammar (Barnes) **75**:19, 26, 40, 64-5
"Philomela" (Arnold) **89**:7, 19; **218**:153
"The Philosopher" (Brontë) **16**:68, 74
"The Philosophers" (Schiller)
See "Die Weltweisen"
"The Philosopher's Conclusion" (Brontë) **35**:147
"Philosophers, Drunken and Sober" (Derzhavin) **215**:14
"The Philosopher's Stone" (Andersen) **214**:55
Les philosophes Français du XIXme siècle (Taine) **15**:409, 412, 431, 458
"Philosophic Humbugs" (Clarke) **19**:234
"Philosophic Letter 1" (Chaadaev) **197**:125-31, 133, 137, 141, 144-45, 147-50, 152, 155-57, 163, 165, 167-68
"Philosophic Letter 3" (Chaadaev) **197**:126, 137
"Philosophic Letter 6" (Chaadaev) **197**:137
"Philosophic Letter 8" (Chaadaev) **197**:137
Philosophic Studies (Balzac)
See *Études philosophiques*
A Philosophical and Practical Grammar of the English Language (Webster) **30**:413
"Philosophical Considerations on the General Science of Mathematics" (Comte) **54**:180-3
Philosophical Considerations on the Physical Sciences (Comte) **54**:172, 180-3
Philosophical Dialogues and Fragments (Renan)
See *Dialogues et fragments philosophiques*
Philosophical Fragment 228 (Schlegel) **226**:158
Philosophical Fragment 668 (Schlegel) **226**:159, 166
Philosophical Fragments (Kierkegaard)
See *Philosophiske Smuler*
Philosophical Fragments (Schlegel) **226**:171, 244
Philosophical Fragments; or, A Fragment of Philosophy (Kierkegaard)
See *Philosophiske Smuler*
Philosophical Lectures (Coleridge) **9**:208; **231**:88
Philosophical Letters (Chaadaev) **197**:125, 136-40, 142-43, 146, 152-54, 157, 163-64, 167-69
Philosophical Letters (Schelling)
See *Philosophische Briefe über Dogmatismus und Kriticismus*
Philosophical Letters (Schiller)
See *Philosophische Briefe*
Philosophical Notebooks (Newman) **99**:244
"Philosophical Reflections" (Freneau) **111**:146
"A Philosophical Satire" (Moore) **110**:171
A Philosophical View of Reform (Shelley) **18**:338; **143**:169, 231-32, 247, 266, 268; **175**:224, 318-19, 325, 329
La philosophie dans le boudoir (Sade) **3**:492-93, 495; **47**:304, 310, 318, 327, 334-35, 339, 341, 346, 350-53, 355-59, 364
Philosophie de l'art (Taine) **15**:452
Philosophie der Geschichte (Heine) **147**:227
Philosophie der Mythologie (Schelling) **30**:142, 144
Philosophie der Mythologie und Offenbarung (Schelling) **30**:138
Philosophie des Lebens (Schlegel) **45**:294, 298
Philosophische Briefe (Schiller) **166**:117, 154, 164
Philosophische Briefe über Dogmatismus und Kriticismus (Schelling) **30**:128, 153-55
Philosophische Untersuchungen über das Wesen der menschlichen Freiheit und die damit zusammenhängende Gegenstände (Schelling) **30**:135, 168
Philosophiske Smuler (Kierkegaard) **34**:200-01, 204, 223-224, 237; **78**:119, 131, 134, 144, 148, 152, 154, 161-62, 189, 199, 201, 204, 211, 214-18, 227, 237-38, 240-41; **125**:250
"Philosophy" (Levy) **59**:102, 120
"Philosophy" (Silva)
See "Filosofías"
"Philosophy" (Thomson) **18**:390, 418
Philosophy and Common Sense (Brownson) **50**:27
"Philosophy and Religion" (Very) **9**:386
"Philosophy as an Element of Culture" (Lewes) **25**:288
Philosophy in the Bedroom (Sade)
See *La philosophie dans le boudoir*
Philosophy in the Boudoir (Sade)
See *La philosophie dans le boudoir*
Philosophy of Art (Schelling) **30**:175-77, 181
"The Philosophy of Composition" (Poe) **1**:512, 516-18, 523, 526, 528; **55**:138-9, 141,

147-8, 161, 208-9, 211-2; **97**:213; **117**:203, 205, 241, 245, 275-76, 282, 286-88, 290, 294, 296, 312, 315-16, 318, 327, 333-38; **211**:234-35, 239, 242, 247, 259, 262
"Philosophy of Evolution" (Symonds) **34**:336
"Philosophy of Ferries" (Whitman) **205**:321
"The Philosophy of Furniture" (Poe) **16**:304; **55**:147
"The Philosophy of History" (Lanier) **118**:283
The Philosophy of History (Emerson) **98**:66
Philosophy of History (Hegel)
See *Vorlesungen über die Philosophie der Weltgeschichte*
"The Philosophy of History in the Education of Republican Men and Women" (Peabody) **169**:177
Philosophy of Mythology (Schelling)
See *Philosophie der Mythologie*
Philosophy of Nature (Hegel) **46**:171
Philosophy of Nature (Schelling)
See *Natur-Philosophie*
Philosophy of Physiology (Schiller) **166**:140
Philosophy of Revelation (Schelling) **30**:157, 159
"The Philosophy of the Obvious" (Pisarev) **25**:332
"The Philosophy of the Supernatural" (Brownson) **50**:52
"Philosophy of War" (Horne) **127**:253
Philothea: A Grecian Romance (Child) **6**:199-201, 203-05, 208-09; **73**:51, 60, 68, 77-8
"A Philoxène Boyer" (Banville) **9**:26
"The Philter" (Stendhal)
See "Le Phitre"
"The Philtre" (Rossetti) **4**:510
Phineas Finn, the Irish Member (Trollope) **6**:461, 463, 466, 470, 472, 495; **33**:364; **101**:253, 262, 267-70, 276, 307, 312-13; **215**:210, 214-15, 240, 301, 304-6, 308, 315-16
Phineas Redux (Trollope) **6**:463, 466, 472-73, 495, 513, 519; **33**:424; **101**:251, 253, 267-68, 271, 274, 302, 306-08; **215**:210, 212-15, 253, 304-6, 308, 315-16, 323, 349-50
"Le Phitre" (Stendhal) **46**:294, 307
"The Phocaeans" (Landor) **14**:164, 181, 184
"Phoebe Dawson" (Crabbe) **26**:100, 102, 116, 133
Phoebe, Junior: A Last Chronicle of Carlingford (Oliphant) **11**:446-8, 454, 456-7, 459, 462; **61**:162-3, 165-8, 174, 182, 198, 216, 229-30; **221**:229, 273, 275-77, 302, 304-5, 307-8, 312
Phoebe Junior: A Last Chronicle of Carlingford (Trollope) **215**:283-84
Phoebus (Kleist) **2**:437
"The Phoenix" (Andersen) **79**:84
"Phokaia" (Lampman) **25**:203
"Phosphorous and Civilization" (Lewes) **25**:310
"Photography Extraordinary" (Dodgson) **139**:125
"Phrases" (Rimbaud) **35**:297; **82**:232-33; **227**:210, 309-10, 334
The Physical Basis of Mind, Being the Second Series of Problems of Life and Mind (Lewes)
See *The Problems of Life and Mind*
The Physician, the Dying, and the Dead (Herzen) **10**:329
Physics and Politics; or, Thoughts on the Application of the Principles of "Natural Selection" and "Inheritance" to Political Society (Bagehot) **10**:16, 19, 24-26, 34-36, 39, 44-46, 48, 65-66
"The Physics of Music" (Lanier) **118**:215, 242
Physiognomischen Fragmente zur Beförderung der Menschenkenntnis und Menschenliebe (Lavater) **142**:4-8, 13-15, 23-31, 38, 40, 42-46, 49, 53-54, 56-61, 65-68, 76-78, 85-88
"Physiognomy of Fortress Monroe" (Winthrop) **210**:275
"Physiognomy of the Country" (Winthrop) **210**:276
"Physiognomy of Water" (Winthrop) **210**:276
Physiography (Huxley) **67**:11
Physiologie du mariage; ou, Méditations de philosophie éclectique sur le bonheur et le malheur conjugal (Balzac) **5**:28, 32, 42, 78, 83; **53**:22; **153**:147, 150-52
Physiology and Calisthenics (Beecher) **30**:16
The Physiology of Common Life (Lewes) **25**:288, 296, 310-11, 317-18; **215**:86, 99, 122, 164-65, 183-84
The Physiology of Marriage (Balzac)
See *Physiologie du mariage; ou, Méditations de philosophie éclectique sur le bonheur et le malheur conjugal*
"The Physiology of Versification" (Holmes) **14**:111, 127
The Phytologia; or, Philosophy of Agriculture and Gardening (Darwin) **106**:183, 218, 234, 241, 245, 274
"The Piano of Chopin" (Norwid)
See "Fortepjan Szopena"
"Le piano que baise une main frê" (Verlaine) **51**:383
"Piano Sonata in F# minor" (Schumann) **143**:120
"Piano Sonata in G minor" (Schumann) **143**:120
Piano Sonata, no. 2 (Beethoven) **227**:15
Piano Sonata, op. 32 (Beethoven) **227**:15
Piano Sonata, op. 57 (Beethoven) **227**:15
"The Piano-Organ" (Levy) **59**:92; **203**:339, 344
Piast Dantyszek's Poem on Hell (Slowacki)
See *Poema Piasta Dantyszka o piekle*
"The Piazza" (Melville) **3**:380, 383; **49**:392; **221**:196
The Piazza Tales (Melville) **157**:70-71, 109, 131; **221**:196
The Piazza Tales and Other Prose Pieces, 1839-1860 (Melville) **3**:331, 361, 384; **29**:315; **93**:205, 242-44, 246-49; **123**:255, 260
Piccadilly: A Fragment of Contemporary Biography (Oliphant) **47**:266, 271, 274-76, 278-79, 284-85, 296-98
Le Piccinino (Sand) **57**:316
Die Piccolomini (Schiller)
See *Wallenstein*
Pickwick (Dickens)
See *The Posthumous Papers of the Pickwick Club*
The Pickwick Papers (Dickens)
See *The Posthumous Papers of the Pickwick Club*
Pickwick Papers (Dickens)
See *The Posthumous Papers of the Pickwick Club*
"Pico della Mirandola" (Pater) **7**:313; **159**:215, 258, 265, 302, 323, 256255
"Pictor Ignotus" (Browning) **19**:132; **79**:94-96
"A Pictorial Rhapsody" (Thackeray) **169**:244; **213**:242-43, 245-48
The Pictorial Ukraine (Shevchenko)
See *Zivopisnaja Ukraina*
"The Picture" (Coleridge) **99**:3, 5, 81, 83-4; **231**:69-70
The Picture (Bowles) **103**:54
"A Picture at Rustrum" (Arnold) **29**:23
"A Picture Book without Pictures" (Andersen)
See "Billedbog uden Billeder"
"The Picture Gallery" (Freneau) **111**:134
"Picture Gossip" (Thackeray) **213**:244, 246-48
"The Picture of a Blind Man" (Wilson) **5**:545
"Picture of an Old Man" (Bowles) **103**:88-9, 91, 93, 95
The Picture of Palermo (Robinson) **142**:96
"The Picture of Sappho" (Norton) **205**:119-21, 123-25
"The Picture of St. John" (Taylor) **89**:311-12, 346
"A Picture of the Times" (Freneau) **111**:140-41
The Picture; or, the Lover's Resolution (Coleridge) **99**:88-93
"Picture Song" (Pinkney) **31**:268, 273-74, 276-77, 279
A Picture-Book without Pictures (Andersen) **7**:21, 27, 36
"Pictures" (Whitman) **81**:342
The Pictures (Tieck) **5**:513
Pictures and Meditations (Lampman) **194**:77, 79-80, 90
"Pictures at Wilton" (Hazlitt) **29**:144
Pictures from Italy (Dickens) **3**:146; **18**:120; **113**:69; **219**:218
Pictures from My Life (Macha) **46**:201, 208-10, 212
Pictures from the East (Schumann)
See *Bilder aus dem Osten*
"The Pictures of Columbus, the Genoese" (Freneau) **1**:319, 322; **111**:101, 119, 141
Pictures of Sweden (Andersen) **7**:17-18
Pictures of Travel (Heine)
See *Reisebilder*
"The Picturesque and the Ideal" (Hazlitt) **29**:156
"Picturesque Travel" (Gilpin) **30**:38, 43
"A Piece of String" (Maupassant)
See "La ficelle"
Pieces, in Prose and Verse (Sigourney)
See *Moral Pieces, in Prose and Verse*
"Pied Beauty" (Hopkins) **17**:208, 215-16, 238, 244, 255-56; **189**:29, 47, 62, 65, 82, 85, 89, 94, 107, 126, 148
"Le Pied de la momie" (Gautier) **1**:355; **59**:31, 35-6, 38
"The Pied Piper of Hamelin" (Browning) **19**:98
"Pielgrzym" (Mickiewicz) **3**:404
"Pielgrzym" (Norwid) **17**:367
La pierre de touche (Augier) **31**:5, 12, 14-15, 24-5, 35
"Pierre Dupont" (Baudelaire) **29**:70
Pierre et Jean (Maupassant) **1**:446-47, 450, 452, 461, 463-64, 467, 469-71; **42**:162-217; **83**:172, 181, 188
Pierre; or, The Ambiguities (Melville) **3**:330, 333, 335-38, 341, 343-44, 347-48, 351, 354, 361, 363-64, 366-70, 372, 374-75, 380, 384-85; **12**:281, 293; **29**:315-18, 323-24, 326-27, 329-32, 334-35, 338, 344, 368; **45**:195, 210, 235, 247, 251; **49**:376, 391-92, 399, 402-03, 407, 416, 420-21; **91**:1-228; **93**:240; **123**:179, 192, 194, 204, 207-8, 241, 252, 260; **157**:66, 73, 75, 84-85, 97, 106, 108, 111, 140, 143, 152, 159-61, 167, 198, 202, 211; **181**:153, 164, 213, 216, 221, 286, 289, 295; **193**:52, 61, 64, 77, 89, 111, 113, 125-26, 129, 136, 147, 190; **221**:110, 128, 155, 181, 198-99, 217
Pierre qui roule (Sand) **42**:311; **57**:316
"Pierrette" (Balzac) **53**:8; **153**:69, 71, 81-82, 94-95, 98-100
Pierrot fumiste (Laforgue) **5**:281-2; **53**:291; **221**:25, 60, 67
"Pierrots" (Laforgue) **53**:279, 286-8, 290-1; **221**:51, 63, 65-66, 86-87, 89
"Pierrots' Expressions" (Laforgue)
See "Locutions des Pierrots"
"Pierrots II" (Laforgue) **53**:288
"Pierrots III" (Laforgue) **53**:288
"Pierrots, I-V" (Laforgue) **5**:277; **53**:288
"Piers Plowman" (Morris) **4**:441
Pierścień wielkiej damy (Norwid) **17**:379
"Pietro Aretino" (Büchner) **146**:38-40, 63
Pietro of Abano (Tieck)
See *Pietro von Abano oder Petrus Apone, Zaubergeschichte*
Pietro Tasca (Dumas) **71**:217, 221-22
Pietro von Abano oder Petrus Apone, Zaubergeschichte (Tieck) **5**:525
"Pig under the Oak" (Krylov) **1**:439
"Pigen, som traadte paa Brødet" (Andersen) **79**:77
"The Pigeons at the British Museum" (Jefferies) **47**:95

"Pijaństwo" (Krasicki) **8**:403, 407
"The Pike" (Krylov) **1**:435, 439
Pikovaya dama (Pushkin) **3**:429-30, 435-37, 442, 447-48, 452, 456, 459, 464; **83**:274-77, 279, 323, 332, 350, 354-55
"Pilate" (Webster) **230**:226, 247
"Eine Pilgerfahrt zu Beethoven" (Wagner) **9**:414, 455-56, 475; **119**:190, 192
"Pilgrim" (Mickiewicz)
See "Pielgrzym"
"The Pilgrim" (Newman) **38**:344
"The Pilgrim" (Norwid)
See "Pielgrzym"
"Der Pilgrim" (Schiller) **166**:108-10
"The Pilgrim" (Schiller)
See "Der Pilgrim"
The Pilgrim Edition of the Letters of Charles Dickens (Dickens)
See *The Letters of Charles Dickens*
Pilgrim Fathers (Hemans) **29**:205
"The Pilgrim of Glencoe" (Campbell) **19**:179, 181, 184, 193
The Pilgrim of Glencoe, and Other Poems (Campbell) **19**:184
Pilgrimage (Boyesen)
See *A Norseman's Pilgrimage*
Pilgrimage (Southey) **97**:269
"The Pilgrimage of Living Poets to the Stream of Castaly" (Reynolds) **146**:166, 190, 192, 202
Pilgrimage to Al-Madinah and Meccah (Burton)
See *Personal Narrative of a Pilgrimage to El-Medinah and Meccah*
"A Pilgrimage to Beethoven" (Wagner)
See "Eine Pilgerfahrt zu Beethoven"
"A Pilgrimage to Patrick's Purgatory" (Carleton) **3**:92; **199**:63
The Pilgrimage to the Giants' Mountain (Macha) **46**:201, 204
A Pilgrimage to the Holy Land (Lamartine)
See *Souvenirs, impressions, pensées, et paysages pendant un voyage en Orient, 1832-1833; ou, Notes d'un voyageur*
The Pilgrims (More) **141**:175
The Pilgrims of Hope (Morris) **4**:438, 441, 443
The Pilgrims of the Sun (Hogg) **4**:275-76, 279-80, 282; **109**:200, 204, 209, 242-44, 272
The Pilgrim's Progress (Wordsworth) **166**:287
"A Pillar at Sebzevar" (Browning) **79**:157
"The Pillar of the Cloud" (Newman) **38**:343, 345-46
"Pillows of Stone" (Crawford) **12**:174; **127**:192-93, 195-97
"El pilluelo de París" (Larra) **130**:269
The Pilot (Cooper) **1**:197, 199-202, 207-08, 221-22; **54**:252-4, 265-6, 275; **203**:7-9, 11, 45-47, 50-51, 86
"The Pilot's Daughter" (Allingham) **25**:6-7, 24
"The Pilot's Song" (Allingham) **25**:18
"A pin has a head" (Rossetti) **186**:268
Pin Money (Gore) **65**:2-5, 28
Pinakidia (Poe) **94**:229, 233
The Pine Apple and the Bee (Cowper) **94**:104
"The Pine Tree" (Andersen) **79**:62-63
"The Pines and the Sea" (Cranch) **115**:18
"The Pine's Mystery" (Hayne) **94**:149
The Pink and the Green (Stendhal)
See *Le rose et le vert*
Pink and White Tyranny (Stowe) **3**:558, 562
"A Pink Villa" (Woolson) **82**:276, 290, 343, 345
Pinocchio (Collodi)
See *Le Avventure di Pinocchio*
Pinocchio: The Story of a Puppet (Collodi)
See *Le Avventure di Pinocchio*
Pinocchio's Adventures (Collodi)
See *Le Avventure di Pinocchio*
"Pins" (Coleridge) **90**:9
"Pinty úrfi" (Petofi) **21**:283
"The Pioneer" (Lowell) **90**:215, 219
The Pioneers (Cooper) **203**:8-9, 11, 23-24, 35, 38, 48-49, 53-54, 56, 60, 64, 66-70, 74-75, 78, 80-82, 87, 118, 135, 144, 152, 156-58, 162-63
"Pioneers! O Pioneers!" (Whitman) **4**:571-72, 580; **81**:316, 319, 339
Pioneers of France in the New World (Parkman) **12**:333, 336, 339, 341, 355, 371, 374, 376
The Pioneers; or, The Sources of the Susquehanna (Cooper) **1**:197-202, 205, 207, 221, 223; **27**:123-25, 127-29, 131-37, 139-44, 146-47, 149, 151, 153, 165, 167-69, 171-72, 178, 182-85, 187; **54**:250, 252-4, 266, 277, 280, 283, 291, 297, 301
"The Pious Aspirations of Solomon M'Slime" (Carleton) **199**:9
"La Pipe" (Baudelaire) **55**:3
"La pipe" (Mallarmé) **4**:371, 373, 376
"La pipe au poète" (Corbière) **43**:13, 31
"La Pipe d'opium" (Gautier) **59**:36
"The Piper" (Blake) **13**:190-91; **37**:6
"Piping Down the Valleys Wild" (Blake) **13**:180
"Pippa Passes" (Blake) **37**:5
Pippa Passes (Browning) **19**:75, 82, 96, 103, 110, 113; **79**:140, 146, 148, 156, 161, 166, 181, 190
Pique Dame (Pushkin) **27**:379
Piquillo Alliaga (Scribe) **16**:385
Pir vo vremiachumy (Pushkin) **3**:426, 433-34, 448, 450, 452; **83**:263, 265-66, 285, 338, 351
"La pirámide" (Sarmiento) **123**:351
"Piranése, contes psychologiques, à propos de la monomanie réflective" (Nodier) **19**:384, 400
"The Pirate" (Brontë) **109**:47
"The Pirate" (Ueda Akinari)
See "Kaizoku"
The Pirate (Marryat) **3**:317, 320
The Pirate (Scott) **209**:242, 250
"Pirates' Prize" (Jones) **222**:158
"Piroskaf" (Baratynsky) **103**:17, 23-4
"Pis-aller" (Arnold) **218**:121
"Pisa's Leaning Tower" (Melville) **3**:363
"Pisemski, Turgenev and Goncharov" (Pisarev)
See "Pisemskij, Turgenev, i Goncarov"
"Pisemskij, Turgenev, i Goncarov" (Pisarev) **25**:338, 346, 352
"Pis'ma iz Dagestana" (Bestuzhev) **131**:160
Pisma k tyotenke (Saltykov) **16**:343, 345, 358, 374
Pisma o provintsii (Saltykov) **16**:343, 374
Pis'ma Russkogo puteshestvennika (Karamzin) **3**:279; **173**:251, 254, 267, 272-76, 278-79, 308, 325-26, 333, 348, 353-54
Pis'ma v chetyrekh tomakh (Dostoevsky) **119**:90; **167**:256, 259
Pisma wszystkie (Fredro) **8**:291
Pismenica serbskoga iezika (Karadzic) **115**:83, 105
"Pis'mo" (Lermontov) **126**:217
"Pis'mo k doktoru Ermanu" (Bestuzhev) **131**:161
"Pis'mo Popa k episkopu Rochester-skomu pered ego izgnaniem" (Bestuzhev) **131**:165
"Pis'mo sel'skago zitelja" (Karamzin) **173**:268, 286
"Pis'mo v redakcïiu Sovremennika" (Pavlova) **138**:47, 51
"The Pit and the Pendulum" (Poe) **1**:500, 502, 530; **16**:308-10, 332-34; **55**:136; **78**:257-58, 264; **94**:225; **211**:267, 316
"Le pitre châtié" (Mallarmé) **41**:250, 291; **210**:170, 244, 251
"Pitt" (Bagehot) **10**:31
"Pity for Poor Africans" (Cowper) **94**:32
"Pity's Gift" (Lamb) **10**:398
"The Pixy and the Grocer" (Andersen)
See "Nissen hos Spekhøkeren"
Pizarre; ou, La conquête de Pérou (Pixérécourt) **39**:279, 286
Pizarro (Kotzebue)
See *Die Spanier in Peru, oder Rollas Tod*
Pizarro (Sheridan) **5**:362, 369, 371; **91**:274, 279-87
Pjesme junačke najstarije (Karadzic) **115**:112
Pjesme junačke srednjijeh vrema (Karadzic) **115**:112
"Place de la Bastille" (Rossetti) **77**:297
"A Place in Thy Memory, Dearest" (Griffin) **7**:201
"Place of Ancient Greece" (Gladstone) **213**:113
"The Place Where I Was Born" (Chivers) **49**:49
"Placeres de la melancolía" (Heredia) **209**:130, 135
"Placet" (Mallarmé)
See "Placet futile"
"Placet futile" (Mallarmé) **4**:376; **41**:291
"Plach dukha berezy" (Aksakov) **181**:61
"Plagiarism" (Murray) **63**:179
"Plagiarism" (Poe) **55**:177
"The Plague" (Schiller) **39**:340
"The Plague in Bergamo" (Jacobsen) **34**:157, 168-70, 172
A Plain Letter to the Lord Chancellor on the Infant Custody Bill (Norton) **205**:75-76, 85, 102, 124, 134-38, 143, 146-47
Plain or Ringlets? (Surtees) **14**:349, 353, 365-67, 371, 374-75, 377-80
Plain Sermons (Newman)
See *Parochial and Plain Sermons*
The Plain Speaker: Opinions on Books, Men, and Things (Hazlitt) **29**:147, 162, 175, 185
"La plaine" (Sainte-Beuve) **5**:347
"The Plainest City in Europe" (Jefferies) **47**:136
"The Plains" (Petofi)
See "Az alföld"
"Plaint of the Missouri 'Coon in the Berlin Zoological Gardens" (Field) **3**:208
"Plainte d'automne" (Mallarmé) **4**:371, 373
"Plainte de cyclope" (Leconte de Lisle) **29**:217
"Le Plaisant" (Baudelaire) **155**:46
"Plaisir sacré" (Mallarmé) **210**:251
"Plan" (Austen)
See "Plan of a Novel"
Plan de travaux scientifiques nécessaires pour reorganiser la société (Comte) **54**:210
Plan for an Army (Cobbett) **49**:113
"A Plan for an Universal Peace" (Bentham) **38**:67
"A Plan for My Maturity" (Verlaine)
See "Un projet de mon âge mûr"
Plan for the Conduct of Female Education in Boarding Schools (Darwin) **106**:193-94, 242, 245
"Plan of a Novel" (Austen) **95**:78-8,
"Plan of the West Roxbury Community" (Peabody) **169**:145
Plan of Theological Study (Schleiermacher) **107**:268, 279
"Planches et Feuillets" (Mallarmé) **210**:251
Plane-Tree (Levy)
See *A London Plane-Tree and Other Verse*
"A plank of flesh" (Lonnrot) **53**:339
Plans of Education (Reeve) **19**:415
"La planta nueva, o el faccioso" (Larra) **130**:194, 201, 221
"The Planting of the Apple Tree" (Bryant) **6**:165, 169, 171, 182
Plastik (Herder) **8**:314; **186**:13, 16, 19, 86, 92
Plato (Sacher-Masoch)
See "Platonic Love"
Plato and Platonism (Pater)
See *Plato and Platonism: A Series of Lectures*
Plato and Platonism: A Series of Lectures (Pater) **7**:301-03, 308-10, 323; **90**:243-44, 257, 261, 273, 284, 288, 295, 301, 325, 333-34; **159**:218, 273, 282, 316
"Plato: New Readings" (Emerson) **98**:68
"Plato, or the Philosopher" (Emerson) **1**:294; **98**:93, 143-44, 147

"Plato the Philosopher to his friend Theon" (Freneau) **111**:144-45, 154-55
"Platonic Love" (Sacher-Masoch) **31**:287, 292, 297, 310
"Platonisme" (Verlaine) **51**:361
"Plato's Aesthetics" (Pater) **90**:325
Plato's Love (Sacher-Masoch)
See "Platonic Love"
Plautus im Nonnenkloster (Meyer) **81**:139
Play (Robertson) **35**:334, 336, 340, 351-52, 357, 362, 365, 369, 371
"Players" (Crabbe) **121**:83, 91
The Playfellow (Martineau) **26**:310-11, 323; **137**:255-57, 262
"Playing Old Sledge for the Presidency" (Harris) **23**:150
"Playing Old Sledge for the Presidency—A Dream of Sut Lovingood's" (Harris) **165**:165
Plays and Poems (Boker) **125**:28, 33, 38, 58, 76, 81-82, 84, 86
The Plays of Clara Gazul (Mérimée)
See *Théâtre de Clara Gazul*
Plays on the Passions (Baillie) **71**:3-5, 8-9, 12-13
A Plea for a Miserable World . . . (Webster) **30**:413
"A Plea for Captain John Brown" (Thoreau) **7**:385-6, 406; **21**:329, 331, 347, 350, 370; **207**:281-83, 319, 323, 335, 339-41
"A Plea for Froebel's Kindergarten as the First Grade of Primary Education" (Peabody) **169**:150, 159, 201, 204
"A Plea for Gas Lamps" (Stevenson) **5**:388-89
"The Plea of the Midsummer Fairies" (Hood) **16**:201, 205, 208, 210, 215, 218, 221, 225-27, 229-33
The Plea of the Midsummer Fairies, Hero and Leander, Lycus the Centaur, and Other Poems (Hood) **16**:200-02, 233, 240
"Pleasant Days of My Childhood" (Traill) **31**:328
Pleasant Memories of Pleasant Lands (Sigourney) **21**:296, 299; **87**:321
"Pleasing Prospects, Hopes and Desires of the Present Time" (Karamzin)
See "Priyatnyye vidy, nadezhdy i zhelaniya nyneshego vremeni"
"Pleasure" (Dacre)
See "The Triumph of Pleasure"
"The Pleasure-Boat" (Dana) **53**:158
"The Pleasures of Hope" (Campbell) **19**:162-63, 165, 169, 171, 174-75, 178-81, 184-85, 189, 191-93, 195-99
The Pleasures of Hope, with Other Poems (Campbell) **19**:176-77
"The Pleasures of Love" (Dacre)
See "The Triumph of Pleasure"
"Pleasures of melancholy" (Heredia)
See "Placeres de la melancolía"
"The Pleasures of Melancholy" (Warton) **118**:351
The Pleasures of Memory (Rogers) **69**:68-9, 74-5, 77-8, 80-3, 85-92
"Pleasures of Spring" (Clare) **9**:98-99
"A Pledge to Hafiz" (Taylor) **89**:305
Les pléiades (Gobineau) **17**:65-9, 91-3, 96, 98, 100, 103-04
The Pleiades of Christendom (Grundtvig)
See *Christenhedens Syvstjerne Et kirkeligt Sagakvad*
Les Pleurs (Desbordes-Valmore) **97**:12, 26, 29, 39
"Pleurs dans la nuit" (Hugo) **3**:263
Plighted Troth (Darley) **2**:128
"The Plodomasov Dwarfs" (Leskov) **174**:13-14
"Plorata Veris Lachrymis" (Barnes) **75**:72
The Plot Discovered (Coleridge) **231**:57
"Plots and Counterplots" (Alcott)
See "V.V.: or Plots and Counterplots"
Plots and Counterplots: More Unknown Thrillers of Louisa May Alcott (Alcott) **58**:3
"The Ploughboy Is Whooping Anon Anon" (Wordsworth) **12**:393
"Plovec" (Pavlova) **138**:50
"Plovets" (Pavlova) **138**:4, 16
La Plume (Verlaine) **230**:168
"Le plus beau dîner du monde" (Villiers de l'Isle Adam) **3**:581
"Le plus bel amour de Don Juan" (Barbey d'Aurevilly) **1**:74-75; **213**:60, 64, 90, 92
"Plus de chants" (Desbordes-Valmore) **97**:6, 10
"Plus de politique" (Beranger) **34**:28
"Plutarch, Charon and a Modern Bookseller" (Montagu) **117**:182
"Pluviôse irrité contre la ville entière" (Baudelaire) **55**:70
Po und Rhein (Engels) **85**:83
"The Poacher" (Hood) **16**:234
"The Pobble Who Has No Toes" (Lear) **3**:308-09
"Pocahontas" (Sigourney) **21**:298, 303; **87**:342
Pocahontas, and Other Poems (Sigourney) **87**:321, 326, 330, 332, 342
Pochi versi inediti (Manzoni) **98**:276
"A Pocket Handkerchief to Hem" (Rossetti) **186**:238
"Początek broszury politycznej" (Norwid) **17**:372
"Pod oknom" (Preseren) **127**:298
"Podas Okus" (Gordon) **21**:156, 160, 163, 166, 173, 181
The Podesta's Daughter (Boker) **125**:7, 21, 82
"podrazhaniye" (Bestuzhev) **131**:150
"podrazhaniye Gete" (Bestuzhev) **131**:150
"Podrazhaniye pervoy satire Bualo" (Bestuzhev) **131**:181
"Podrazhatelyam" (Baratynsky) **103**:3
"Podrobnyi otchet o lune" (Zhukovsky) **35**:406
Podrostok (Dostoevsky) **2**:167, 170, 175, 204; **7**:80, 103; **21**:101-02, 118; **33**:165, 170, 178-79, 182; **43**:92, 95; **167**:286, 334; **202**:90
Podróż na Wschód—Podróż do Ziemi Swietej z Neopolu (Slowacki) **15**:374
"Podvig Ovechkina i Shcherbiny za Kavkazom" (Bestuzhev) **131**:182
"Poem" (Ridge) **82**:199
"Poem 13" (Dickinson) **171**:137
"Poem 19" (Barbauld) **185**:126
"Poem 21" (Dickinson) **171**:134
"Poem 37" (Dickinson) **171**:136
"Poem 43" (Dickinson) **171**:168
"Poem 45" (Dickinson) **171**:170
"Poem 49" (Dickinson)
See "I Never Lost as Much but Twice"
"Poem 59" (Dickinson) **171**:220
"Poem 61" (Dickinson)
See "My Wheel Is in the Dark"
"Poem 65" (Dickinson) **171**:143
"Poem 70" (Dickinson) **171**:181
"Poem 76" (Dickinson) **171**:158
"Poem 79" (Dickinson) **171**:223
"Poem 119" (Dickinson) **171**:160
"Poem 122" (Dickinson) **171**:144
"Poem 125" (Dickinson) **171**:100
"Poem 130" (Dickinson)
See "These are the days when birds come back"
"Poem 133" (Dickinson)
See "The Grass so little has to do"
"Poem 135" (Dickinson) **171**:112
"Poem 139" (Dickinson) **171**:109
"Poem 140" (Dickinson) **171**:135
"Poem 159" (Dickinson) **171**:168
"Poem 160" (Dickinson) **171**:106, 109
"Poem 165" (Dickinson)
See "A Wounded Deer—leaps highest—"
"Poem 168" (Dickinson) **171**:181
"Poem 180" (Dickinson) **171**:120
"Poem 182" (Dickinson) **171**:194
"Poem 184" (Dickinson) **171**:160
"Poem 185" (Dickinson) **171**:107, 182
"Poem 191" (Dickinson) **171**:140
"Poem 193" (Dickinson)
See "I shall know why"
"Poem 199" (Dickinson) **171**:110
"Poem 204" (Dickinson)
See "I'll tell you how the Sun rose—"
"Poem 210" (Dickinson) **171**:119, 140
"Poem 214" (Dickinson)
See "I Taste a Liquor Never Brewed"
"Poem 216" (Dickinson)
See "Safe in their Alabaster Chambers"
"Poem 232" (Dickinson) **171**:133
"Poem 239" (Dickinson) **171**:160
"Poem 240" (Dickinson)
See "Bound—a trouble—"
"Poem 241" (Dickinson) **171**:112, 161
"Poem 243" (Dickinson) **171**:160
"Poem 250" (Dickinson) **171**:125
"Poem 256" (Dickinson) **171**:107
"Poem 257" (Dickinson) **171**:134
"Poem 258" (Dickinson)
See "There's a Certain Slant of Light"
"Poem 262" (Dickinson) **171**:137
"Poem 263" (Dickinson) **171**:226
"Poem 272" (Dickinson)
See "I breathed enough to take the Trick—"
"Poem 275" (Dickinson) **171**:115
"Poem 277" (Dickinson) **171**:208
"Poem 280" (Dickinson) **171**:110
"Poem 281" (Dickinson) **171**:112
"Poem 284" (Dickinson) **171**:158
"Poem 287" (Dickinson)
See "The Clock"
"Poem 289" (Dickinson) **171**:106
"Poem 290" (Dickinson)
See "Of Bronze—and Blaze"
"Poem 291" (Dickinson) **171**:181
"Poem 293" (Dickinson) **171**:140
"Poem 295" (Dickinson) **171**:106
"Poem 300" (Dickinson)
See "'Morning'—means 'Milking'—to the Farmer"
"Poem 301" (Dickinson) **171**:221
"Poem 303" (Dickinson)
See "The Soul Selects Her Own Society"
"Poem 304" (Dickinson) **171**:135
"Poem 306" (Dickinson)
See "The Soul's Superior instants"
"Poem 307" (Dickinson)
See "The One who could repeat the Summer day"
"Poem 308" (Dickinson) **171**:118
"Poem 311" (Dickinson) **171**:135
"Poem 313" (Dickinson) **171**:112
"Poem 315" (Dickinson) **171**:226-27
"Poem 320" (Dickinson) **171**:139
"Poem 322" (Dickinson) **171**:110
"Poem 324" (Dickinson) **171**:108
"Poem 327" (Dickinson) **171**:156
"Poem 328" (Dickinson)
See "A Bird came down the Walk"
"Poem 332" (Dickinson) **171**:121
"Poem 335" (Dickinson)
See "Tis not that Dying hurts us so"
"Poem 336" (Dickinson)
See "Before I got my eye put out"
"Poem 338" (Dickinson)
See "I know that He exists"
"Poem 340" (Dickinson)
See "I Felt a Funeral in My Brain"
"Poem 342" (Dickinson)
See "It will be Summer"
"Poem 345" (Dickinson) **171**:101
"Poem 348" (Dickinson) **171**:170, 214
"Poem 357" (Dickinson) **171**:108
"Poem 369" (Dickinson)
See "She Lay as If at Play"
"Poem 372" (Dickinson)
See "After Great Pain, a Formal Feeling Comes"
"Poem 376" (Dickinson) **171**:108

"Poem 377" (Dickinson) **171**:108
"Poem 379" (Dickinson) **171**:134
"Poem 383" (Dickinson) **171**:196, 206
"Poem 384" (Dickinson) **171**:112, 227
"Poem 399" (Dickinson)
See "A House upon the Height"
"Poem 405" (Dickinson) **171**:104
"Poem 407" (Dickinson) **171**:136
"Poem 412" (Dickinson) **171**:100
"Poem 415" (Dickinson) **171**:166
"Poem 420" (Dickinson) **171**:118, 141
"Poem 421" (Dickinson) **171**:189
"Poem 423" (Dickinson) **171**:199
"Poem 426" (Dickinson) **171**:170
"Poem 428" (Dickinson) **171**:161
"Poem 439" (Dickinson)
See "Undue Significance"
"Poem 441" (Dickinson) **171**:118, 140
"Poem 448" (Dickinson) **171**:118
"Poem 451" (Dickinson) **171**:119
"Poem 452" (Dickinson) **171**:121
"Poem 453" (Dickinson) **171**:140
"Poem 459" (Dickinson) **171**:118
"Poem 465" (Dickinson)
See "I heard a Fly buzz—when I died—"
"Poem 466" (Dickinson) **171**:217
"Poem 473" (Dickinson) **171**:110
"Poem 490" (Dickinson) **171**:160
"Poem 491" (Dickinson) **171**:222
"Poem 500" (Dickinson)
See "Within my Garden, rides a Bird"
"Poem 501" (Dickinson) **171**:222
"Poem 510" (Dickinson)
See "It was not Death, for I stood up"
"Poem 512" (Dickinson)
See "The Soul Has Bandaged Moments"
"Poem 519" (Dickinson)
See "This Is My Letter to the World"
"Poem 520" (Dickinson) **171**:159
"Poem 528" (Dickinson)
See "Mine by the Right of the White Election"
"Poem 532" (Dickinson) **171**:160
"Poem 536" (Dickinson) **171**:107
"Poem 537" (Dickinson)
See "Me prove it now—Whoever doubt"
"Poem 546" (Dickinson) **171**:168
"Poem 547" (Dickinson) **171**:119
"Poem 554" (Dickinson) **171**:167
"Poem 555" (Dickinson) **171**:140, 142
"Poem 562" (Dickinson) **171**:160
"Poem 564" (Dickinson) **171**:108
"Poem 566" (Dickinson) **171**:116
"Poem 569" (Dickinson) **171**:118, 179
"Poem 577" (Dickinson) **171**:177
"Poem 578" (Dickinson) **171**:144
"Poem 579" (Dickinson)
See "Hunger"
"Poem 580" (Dickinson) **171**:143
"Poem 586" (Dickinson) **171**:142
"Poem 588" (Dickinson)
See "The Heart asks Pleasure—first"
"Poem 595" (Dickinson) **171**:210, 214
"Poem 598" (Dickinson)
See "The Brain—is wider than the Sky"
"Poem 605" (Dickinson) **171**:136
"Poem 611" (Dickinson) **171**:141, 156
"Poem 613" (Dickinson) **171**:143
"Poem 615" (Dickinson) **171**:143
"Poem 627" (Dickinson) **171**:157, 181
"Poem 628" (Dickinson) **171**:135
"Poem 632" (Dickinson) **171**:108, 112, 159
"Poem 633" (Dickinson) **171**:112
"Poem 638" (Dickinson) **171**:210
"Poem 639" (Dickinson) **171**:177
"Poem 640" (Dickinson) **171**:109, 115
"Poem 657" (Dickinson)
See "I Dwell in Possibility"
"Poem 662" (Dickinson) **171**:119
"Poem 669" (Dickinson) **171**:197
"Poem 670" (Dickinson) **171**:116, 226
"Poem 673" (Dickinson)
See "The Love a Life can show Below"
"Poem 674" (Dickinson) **171**:107, 180
"Poem 675" (Dickinson) **171**:108
"Poem 683" (Dickinson) **171**:226
"Poem 686" (Dickinson) **171**:166
"Poem 696" (Dickinson) **171**:140
"Poem 700" (Dickinson)
See "You've seen Balloons set"
"Poem 702" (Dickinson) **171**:140
"Poem 705" (Dickinson) **171**:143
"Poem 708" (Dickinson) **171**:168, 206, 216
"Poem 712" (Dickinson)
See "Because I Could Not Stop for Death"
"Poem 721" (Dickinson)
See "Behind me dips Eternity"
"Poem 723" (Dickinson) **171**:158
"Poem 739" (Dickinson) **171**:156
"Poem 740" (Dickinson) **171**:139
"Poem 745" (Dickinson) **171**:156
"Poem 754" (Dickinson) **171**:108
"Poem 761" (Dickinson) **171**:156
"Poem 775" (Dickinson) **171**:209
"Poem 782" (Dickinson)
See "Renunciation—is a piercing Virtue—"
"Poem 786" (Dickinson) **171**:112
"Poem 797" (Dickinson) **171**:12
"Poem 798" (Dickinson) **171**:180
"Poem 800" (Dickinson) **171**:109
"Poem 803" (Dickinson) **171**:167
"Poem 812" (Dickinson) **171**:136
"Poem 817" (Dickinson) **171**:107
"Poem 820" (Dickinson) **171**:210
"Poem 827" (Dickinson) **171**:140
"Poem 838" (Dickinson) **171**:112
"Poem 861" (Dickinson)
See "Split the Lark—and you'll find the Music"
"Poem 867" (Dickinson)
See "I felt a Cleaving in my Mind—"
"Poem 870" (Dickinson) **171**:143
"Poem 883" (Dickinson) **171**:121, 139-40
"Poem 885" (Dickinson) **171**:125
"Poem 887" (Dickinson)
See "Severer Service of myself"
"Poem 889" (Dickinson) **171**:135
"Poem 904" (Dickinson) **171**:141
"Poem 906" (Dickinson) **171**:106, 139
"Poem 909" (Dickinson)
See "I make His Crescent fill or lack—"
"Poem 910" (Dickinson) **171**:135
"Poem 912" (Dickinson) **171**:140
"Poem 915" (Dickinson) **171**:143
"Poem 922" (Dickinson) **171**:183
"Poem 937" (Dickinson) **171**:116
"Poem 939" (Dickinson) **171**:156
"Poem 952" (Dickinson) **171**:168
"Poem 962" (Dickinson) **171**:186
"Poem 963" (Dickinson) **171**:112
"Poem 964" (Dickinson) **171**:107
"Poem 979" (Dickinson) **171**:168
"Poem 983" (Dickinson) **171**:141
"Poem 985" (Dickinson) **171**:111
"Poem 986" (Dickinson)
See "A narrow Fellow in the Grass"
"Poem 988" (Dickinson) **171**:141
"Poem 1010" (Dickinson)
See "Crumbling is not an instant's Act"
"Poem 1012" (Dickinson) **171**:166
"Poem 1035" (Dickinson) **171**:102
"Poem 1049" (Dickinson) **171**:210
"Poem 1068" (Dickinson) **171**:118
"Poem 1070" (Dickinson)
See "The Chemical conviction"
"Poem 1071" (Dickinson) **171**:112, 134, 181
"Poem 1072" (Dickinson) **171**:110
"Poem 1075" (Dickinson) **171**:102
"Poem 1090" (Dickinson) **171**:226
"Poem 1093" (Dickinson) **171**:168
"Poem 1097" (Dickinson)
See "Ashes denote that Fire was"
"Poem 1099" (Dickinson) **171**:140, 181
"Poem 1100" (Dickinson) **171**:104
"Poem 1113" (Dickinson) **171**:112, 168
"Poem 1129" (Dickinson) **171**:99, 170
"Poem 1135" (Dickinson) **171**:120
"Poem 1144" (Dickinson) **171**:108
"Poem 1165" (Dickinson) **171**:202
"Poem 1170" (Dickinson) **171**:143
"Poem 1177" (Dickinson) **171**:102
"Poem 1181" (Dickinson) **171**:111, 202
"Poem 1200" (Dickinson) **171**:141
"Poem 1218" (Dickinson)
See "The Bone that has no Marrow"
"Poem 1219" (Dickinson)
See "Who goes to dine must take his Feast"
"Poem 1223" (Dickinson) **171**:167
"Poem 1238" (Dickinson) **171**:198
"Poem 1241" (Dickinson)
See "The Lilac is an ancient shrub"
"Poem 1245" (Dickinson) **171**:143
"Poem 1247" (Dickinson) **171**:119, 135, 138
"Poem 1261" (Dickinson) **171**:117, 185
"Poem 1262" (Dickinson) **171**:106
"Poem 1264" (Dickinson) **171**:115
"Poem 1283" (Dickinson) **171**:161
"Poem 1285" (Dickinson) **171**:184
"Poem 1304" (Dickinson) **171**:121
"Poem 1317" (Dickinson) **171**:168
"Poem 1331" (Dickinson) **171**:143
"Poem 1333" (Dickinson) **171**:169, 181
"Poem 1335" (Dickinson) **171**:134
"Poem 1337" (Dickinson) **171**:177
"Poem 1343" (Dickinson) **171**:103
"Poem 1383" (Dickinson) **171**:117
"Poem 1393" (Dickinson) **171**:137
"Poem 1398" (Dickinson) **171**:200
"Poem 1400" (Dickinson)
See "What mystery pervades a well"
"Poem 1411" (Dickinson) **171**:143
"Poem 1429" (Dickinson) **171**:116
"Poem 1430" (Dickinson) **171**:190
"Poem 1431" (Dickinson) **171**:227
"Poem 1434" (Dickinson) **171**:161
"Poem 1439" (Dickinson) **171**:166
"Poem 1441" (Dickinson) **171**:106
"Poem 1445" (Dickinson) **171**:113
"Poem 1448" (Dickinson) **171**:214
"Poem 1452" (Dickinson) **171**:126
"Poem 1454" (Dickinson) **171**:137, 142
"Poem 1458" (Dickinson) **171**:115
"Poem 1461" (Dickinson) **171**:108
"Poem 1463" (Dickinson)
See "A Route of Evanescence"
"Poem 1468" (Dickinson) **171**:134
"Poem 1470" (Dickinson) **171**:167
"Poem 1485" (Dickinson) **171**:166
"Poem 1492" (Dickinson) **171**:225, 227
"Poem 1518" (Dickinson) **171**:113
"Poem 1540" (Dickinson) **171**:105, 186
"Poem 1543" (Dickinson) **171**:227
"Poem 1545" (Dickinson) **171**:108
"Poem 1550" (Dickinson) **171**:200
"Poem 1551" (Dickinson) **171**:108, 140, 160
"Poem 1556" (Dickinson)
See "Image of Light, Adieu"
"Poem 1576" (Dickinson) **171**:227
"Poem 1577" (Dickinson) **171**:118
"Poem 1584" (Dickinson) **171**:227
"Poem 1588" (Dickinson) **171**:227
"Poem 1600" (Dickinson)
See "Upon his Saddle sprung a Bird"
"Poem 1601" (Dickinson) **171**:181
"Poem 1602" (Dickinson) **171**:144
"Poem 1604" (Dickinson) **171**:168
"Poem 1616" (Dickinson) **171**:119, 138
"Poem 1620" (Dickinson) **171**:112, 121
"Poem 1624" (Dickinson) **171**:166
"Poem 1634" (Dickinson) **171**:144
"Poem 1638" (Dickinson) **171**:119, 137
"Poem 1645" (Dickinson) **171**:167
"Poem 1646" (Dickinson) **171**:143
"Poem 1656" (Dickinson) **171**:165

"Poem 1668" (Dickinson) **171**:141
"Poem 1677" (Dickinson) **171**:135
"Poem 1687" (Dickinson) **171**:143
"Poem 1694" (Dickinson) **171**:168
"Poem 1695" (Dickinson) **171**:139
"Poem 1700" (Dickinson) **171**:141
"Poem 1713" (Dickinson) **171**:142
"Poem 1732" (Dickinson)
See "My Life Closed Twice before Its Close"
"Poem 1738" (Dickinson) **171**:123
"Poem 1754" (Dickinson) **171**:139
"Poem 1768" (Dickinson)
See "Lad of Athens, faithful be"
"Poem 1769" (Dickinson) **171**:166
"A Poem for Children, with Thoughts on Death" (Hammon) **5**:262, 264-65
"Poem of Apparitions in Boston in the 73rd Year of These States" (Whitman) **31**:419, 425; **81**:329; **205**:191-92
"Poem of the Road" (Whitman) **81**:329
"Poem of The Singers and of The Words of Poems" (Whitman) **205**:204
A Poem on Divine Revelation (Brackenridge) **227**:105
A Poem on the Bill Lately Passed for Regulating the Slave Trade (Williams) **135**:333
A Poem on the Inhumanity of the Slave-Trade (Yearsley) **174**:339
"Poem on the memorable victory obtained by the gallant capt. Paul Jones, or the Good Man Richard, over the Seraphis, etc. under the command of capt. Pearson" (Freneau) **1**:314, 317, 319; **111**:143
A Poem, on the Rising Glory of America (Freneau) **1**:314, 316, 319, 324; **111**:101, 113, 139, 156-58
A Poem on the Rising Glory of America: Being an Exercise Delivered on the Public Commencement at Nassau-Hall (Brackenridge) **227**:48, 72, 105
"Poem Read at the Dinner Given to the Author by the Medical Profession" (Holmes) **14**:128
"Un poema" (Silva) **114**:262, 270, 294
Poema Piasta Dantyszka o piekle (Slowacki) **15**:355, 358-59
Los poemas de la carne (Silva) **114**:267, 300
"Poème de la femme" (Gautier) **59**:19
Poëmes (Vigny) **7**:484
"Poëmes antiques" (Vigny) **102**:379
Poèmes antiques (Baudelaire) **6**:102
Poèmes antiques (Leconte de Lisle) **29**:212-17, 221-25, 231, 233, 235-43
Poèmes antiques et modernes (Vigny) **7**:480-81, 483-84; **102**:366, 368, 373
Poèmes barbares (Baudelaire) **6**:102
Poèmes barbares (Leconte de Lisle) **29**:212, 215-17, 221-25, 235
Poèmes d'Edgar Poe (Mallarmé) **41**:269
Poëmes en prose (Baudelaire)
See *Le spleen de Paris, petits poèmes en prose*
Poèmes en prose (Mallarmé) **4**:377
Poèmes et légendes (Nerval) **1**:484
Poèmes et poésies (Leconte de Lisle) **29**:226, 230-31, 237
"Poëmes judaïques" (Vigny) **102**:379
"Poëmes modernes" (Vigny) **102**:379
Poèmes nocturnes (Baudelaire)
See *Le spleen de Paris, petits poèmes en prose*
Poemes Philosophiques (Vigny)
See *Les destinées: Poèmes philosophiques*
Les Poèmes saturniens (Verlaine) **2**:617, 619, 622-24, 628-31; **51**:352, 354-56, 359, 361-62, 365, 368, 372, 386-87; **230**:151, 160, 162-64, 168-69, 172-73, 183, 190-92, 194-203, 205-7, 211-12
Poèmes tragiques (Leconte de Lisle) **29**:221-25, 235
"Poems" (Cooke) **5**:132
Poems (Allingham) **25**:24, 26
Poems (Arnold) **6**:32, 44; **29**:12, 27, 53; **89**:43, 85-6, 92; **126**:46, 111; **218**:165, 233
Poems (Barbauld) **50**:9; **185**:26-29, 32, 35-36, 38, 44, 46-47, 86-93, 95-96, 116, 124, 126, 134, 140
Poems (Barrett Browning) **1**:112, 117, 129; **170**:25, 84, 86, 90, 107, 119
Poems (Bécquer)
See *Rimas*
Poems (Brontë) **71**:165-66; **102**:24
Poems (Clare)
See *The Poems of John Clare*
Poems (Coleridge)
See *The Poems of Samuel Taylor Coleridge*
Poems (Cooke) **110**:12
Poems (Cowper) **8**:102, 113; **94**:77
Poems (Crabbe) **26**:78, 102; **121**:8-9, 11, 23, 34, 72, 83
Poems (Cranch) **115**:15, 22, 26, 28, 34, 40, 42, 55
Poems (Desbordes-Valmore)
See *Pósies*
Poems (Dyer) **129**:113, 116
Poems (Emerson) **1**:285, 295; **38**:185; **98**:177, 179-82, 184
Poems (Ferguson) **33**:279, 285, 287, 290, 299
Poems (Hayne) **94**:137, 139, 141, 148, 151, 167
Poems (Hemans) **71**:271-72
Poems (Hogg)
See *The Works of the Ettrick Shepherd*
Poems (Holmes) **14**:98, 100-01, 127
Poems (Ingelow)
See *Poems by Jean Ingelow*
Poems (Keats) **8**:321-22, 324-25, 331-32, 340; **73**:152, 182, 186, 192, 208, 290, 311-12, 314; **121**:141, 215-16; **225**:165, 262
Poems (Lanier) **6**:236
Poems (Larcom) **179**:167, 177
Poems (Longfellow) **2**:472-73
Poems (Lowell) **2**:502-03, 511, 515; **90**:215, 220
Poems (Meyer)
See *Gedichte*
Poems (Opie) **65**:175, 182
Poems (Osgood) **141**:320, 332, 335, 341-43, 353-54
Poems (Patmore) **9**:326-28, 336, 348
Poems (Pavlova)
See *Stikhotvoreniia*
Poems (Pinkney) **31**:267, 270, 273
Poems (Poe) **55**:162; **97**:184; **117**:195, 235, 280
Poems (Ridge) **82**:174, 185, 199, 201
Poems (Rimbaud)
See *Poésies*
Poems (Robinson) **142**:102, 142, 170, 173, 224
Poems (Rogers) **69**:77
Poems (Rossetti) **4**:490, 492-93, 495, 497-98, 500, 502, 511; **77**:294, 302, 336-37, 340-41, 346
Poems (Rossetti) **2**:557-58; **186**:264, 310
Poems (Runeberg)
See *Dikter*
Poems (Shelley) **18**:331
Poems (Sigourney) **21**:291, 308; **87**:321, 326, 331, 334, 337
Poems (Slowacki) **15**:363
Poems (Smith) **59**:259, 264, 312, 319, 326, 328-33
Poems (Southey) **8**:447; **97**:260, 314
Poems (Tennyson) **30**:211, 275-76; **115**:246; **202**:312, 333
Poems (Timrod) **25**:359, 366, 382
Poems (Very) **9**:371-72, 379
Poems (Webster) **230**:252
Poems (Whittier) **8**:488; **59**:354
Poems (Williams) **135**:333-34
Poems (Wordsworth) **12**:393-94, 401, 416, 463, 468
Poems, 1792 (Dyer) **129**:112, 132, 140
Poems, 1800 (Dyer) **129**:95, 122-23, 146
Poems, 1801 (Dyer) **129**:93, 96, 120-21, 132, 136-37
Poems, 1802 (Dyer) **129**:99, 105, 107, 114, 121-23
Poems and Ballads (Heine) **147**:152
Poems and Ballads of Heinrich Heine (Lazarus) **8**:418, 425
Poems and Essays (Very) **9**:370
Poems and Plays (Lamb) **113**:230
"Poems and Prose Pieces 1855-58" (Harpur) **114**:123
The Poems and Prose Remains of Arthur Hugh Clough (Prescott) **163**:42, 54, 71-74, 131
Poems and Prose Remains of Arthur Hugh Clough, with a Selection from His Letters, and a Memoir (Clough) **27**:60, 64, 70
Poems and Prose Writings (Dana) **53**:170
Poems and Songs (Kendall) **12**:179, 184-86, 190, 192
The Poems and Stories of Fitz-James O'Brien (O'Brien) **21**:234-35, 244
Poems and Translations, Written between the Ages of Fourteen and Sixteen (Lazarus) **109**:289, 304-05
Poems before Congress (Barrett Browning) **1**:120, 130; **61**:6, 11-2, 15, 24, 44; **170**:86, 112, 116, 118, 120-21
Poems by a Slave (Horton) **87**:86, 101
Poems by a Slave in the Island of Cuba, Recently Liberated; translated from the Spanish by R. R. Madden, M.D. with the History of the Early Life of the Negro Poet, written by Himself; To which are prefixed... (Manzano) **155**:306
Poems by Currer, Ellis, and Acton Bell (Brontë) **16**:63, 67, 87
Poems by Currer, Ellis, and Acton Bell (Brontë) **4**:38
Poems by Currer, Ellis, and Acton Bell (Brontë) **3**:43, 62
Poems by Herman Melville (Melville) **157**:212
Poems by James Clarence Mangan (Mangan) **27**:276, 301, 315, 318
Poems by Jean Ingelow (Ingelow) **39**:257, 263-64; **107**:118, 134, 146
Poems by Robert Lovell and Robert Southey (Southey) **97**:260
Poems by Robert Southey (Southey) **97**:260
Poems by the Way (Morris) **4**:421-23, 425, 443
Poems by Two Brothers (Tennyson) **30**:223; **202**:312
Poems by William Cowper, of the Inner Temple, Esq. (Cowper) **94**:92, 112, 117
Poems by William Cullen Bryant, an American (Bryant) **6**:157-60, 162
"Poems by William Morris" (Pater) **90**:296, 305-06, 308, 326; **159**:284, 295-96, 322, 325
Poems, Chiefly Lyrical (Tennyson) **30**:203, 211, 275; **65**:280; **202**:183-84
Poems Chiefly Written in Retirement (Thelwall) **162**:302, 341
Poems Descriptive of Rural Life and Scenery (Clare) **9**:72-73, 76, 78, 112; **86**:92, 110, 125, 128, 151, 153-55, 159-60, 173-74
Poems, Dialogues in Verse, and Epigrams (Landor) **14**:177
Poems Dramatic and Miscellaneous (Warren) **13**:411-13; **226**:259-60, 264-65, 267-69, 272, 274, 277-78, 289, 291-92
Poems, Essays, and Fragments (Thomson) **18**:394
Poems for Our Children (Hale) **75**:284-86, 288-89, 341, 349
"Poems for the Sea" (Sigourney) **87**:321
Poems for the Times (Heine)
See *Zeitgedichte*
"Poems Founded on the Affections" (Wordsworth) **111**:323
Poems in Early Life (Harpur) **114**:144

Poems in Prose (Turgenev)
See *Stikhotvoreniya v proze*
Poems in Prose from Charles Baudelaire (Baudelaire)
See *Le spleen de Paris, petits poèmes en prose*
Poems, in Two Volumes (Wordsworth) **206**:266, 296
Poems: Legendary and Historical (Milnes) **61**:137
Poems: New Edition (Barrett Browning) **170**:112
Poems of 1820 (Keats)
See *Poems*
Poems of 1833 (Barrett Browning) **61**:48
Poems of 1844 (Barrett Browning) **61**:2, 4-5, 42-3, 61, 64-5, 71-2; **66**:88
Poems of 1850 (Barrett Browning) **61**:43, 49, 69
The Poems of 1850 (Barrett Browning)
See *Poems: New Edition*
The Poems of Anna Letitia Barbauld (Barbauld) **185**:138-41, 143-45, 150-52, 154, 156-57
The Poems of Archibald Lampman (Lampman) **25**:217; **194**:16, 48-59, 62-65, 71, 75-76, 92, 99-103, 108, 112-13, 118-21, 123, 126, 128, 130-31, 133, 138-40
The Poems of Arthur Hugh Clough (Clough) **27**:44
The Poems of Arthur Hugh Clough (Prescott) **163**:78-82, 128-29, 136
The Poems of Charlotte and Patrick Branwell Brontë (Brontë) **109**:26
Poems of Charlotte Smith (Smith) **115**:172, 176-78, 180, 182
Poems of Early and After Years (Willis) **194**:294, 304
The Poems of Edgar Allan Poe (Poe) **117**:231
The Poems of Elizabeth Barrett Browning (Barrett Browning)
See *Poems: New Edition*
The Poems of Emily Dickinson (Dickinson) **21**:7, 9, 11-12, 43; **77**:48, 66-67, 75, 165, 169; **171**:86-89, 99, 114, 131-44, 179
The Poems of Emma Lazarus (Lazarus) **8**:419-20, 424
The Poems of Eugene Field (Field) **3**:209
The Poems of Francè Prešeren (Preseren)
See *Poezíje Dóktorja Francèta Presérna*
The Poems of Geoffrey Chaucer, Modernized (Horne) **127**:285
Poems of Gerard Manley Hopkins (Hopkins) **17**:196; **189**:23, 25-30, 32, 41, 51-56, 62, 68, 127-28
Poems of Henry Kendall (Kendall) **12**:198
The Poems of Henry Timrod (Timrod) **25**:361, 378, 386
Poems of Home and Travel (Taylor) **89**:307, 309
"Poems of Imagination" (Wordsworth)
See "Poems of the Imagination"
The Poems of John Clare (Clare) **9**:96-97; **86**:103-04
The Poems of John Keats (Keats) **225**:217-18, 220
The Poems of Joseph Sheridan Le Fanu (Le Fanu) **58**:251-2
Poems of Many Years (Milnes) **61**:137, 144-5
Poems of Passion (Willis) **194**:304
The Poems of Patrick Branwell Brontë (Brontë) **109**:25-6, 51
Poems of Philip Freneau (Freneau) **111**:139, 148-51, 153, 157, 159, 166
Poems of Religion and Society (Adams) **175**:35
Poems of Religious Sorrow, Comfort, Counsel and Aspiration (Child) **173**:167
Poems of Rural Life in Common English (Barnes) **75**:18, 40, 69
Poems of Rural Life in the Dorset Dialect (Barnes) **75**:18, 40, 52-3, 67-81, 83, 85, 92
Poems of Rural Life in the Dorset Dialect; Third Collection (Barnes) **75**:18, 40, 69
The Poems of Samuel Taylor Coleridge (Coleridge) **54**:73; **90**:7, 15, 19-21, 26, 29; **99**:17, 22; **111**:233, 245; **177**:160; **231**:120-21
"Poems of Sentiment and Reflection" (Milnes) **61**:135
Poems of Sidney Lanier (Lanier) **6**:236
Poems of Sorrow and Comfort (Child)
See *Poems of Religious Sorrow, Comfort, Counsel and Aspiration*
"Poems of the Imagination" (Wordsworth) **111**:323; **166**:212
Poems of the Lake George Darley (Darley) **2**:125
Poems of the Orient (Taylor) **89**:302, 304-07, 343, 346, 355, 357, 359
"Poems of the War" (Cranch) **115**:23
Poems of the War (Boker) **125**:25, 28, 33-34, 39, 42, 80-81
The Poems of Walter Savage Landor (Landor) **14**:157, 175
The Poems of William Allingham (Allingham) **25**:20
"The Poems of William Blake" (Thomson) **18**:404
The Poems of William Wordsworth (Wordsworth) **166**:251
Poems on American Affairs (Freneau) **111**:141
Poems, On American Affairs, and a Variety of Other Subjects, Chiefly Moral and Political (Freneau) **111**:183
"Poems on rural life etc." (Clare) **86**:174
Poems on Several Occasions (Lennox) **134**:219
Poems, on Several Occasions (Yearsley) **174**:310, 316, 318, 321, 331, 333-35, 337
Poems on Slavery (Longfellow) **45**:132, 140, 155; **103**:290
"Poems on the Naming of Places" (Wordsworth) **12**:452; **111**:233; **166**:222
Poems on Various Subjects (Coleridge) **231**:60
Poems on Various Subjects (Lamb) **113**:186
Poems on Various Subjects (Rowson) **69**:141; **182**:276
Poems, on Various Subjects (Yearsley) **174**:316-17, 331, 334, 336, 338, 343
Poems on Various Subjects, with Introductory Remarks on the Present State of Science and Literature in France (Williams) **135**:286, 314-15, 335-36
Poems Partly of Rural Life in National English (Barnes) **75**:15, 40, 69, 85
Poems Relating to the American Revolution by Philip Freneau (Freneau) **111**:157
The Poems, Sacred, Passionate, and Humorous, of Nathaniel Parker Willis (Willis) **194**:304
Poems, second series (Arnold) **6**:32
Poems, second series (Dickinson) **21**:22-3
Poems, third series (Dickinson) **21**:15
"Poems to Caroline" (Brontë) **109**:10
Poems: Wherein It Is Attempted to Describe Certain News of Nature and of Rustic Manners (Baillie) **71**:1-2, 51-53; **151**:86-7, 89, 91, 93, 96, 113-14, 116
Poems Written between the Years 1768 and 1794 (Freneau) **111**:123, 147
Poems, Written in the Leisure Hours of a Journeyman Mason (Miller) **143**:4, 10, 25, 33, 37, 40
Poe's Helen Remembers (Whitman) **19**:459
"Poesi och politik" (Almqvist) **42**:19
"Poesía" (Heredia) **209**:118, 134, 138-40, 142, 144
"Poesia e Mendicidade" (Castro Alves) **205**:11
"Poesía viva" (Silva) **114**:301
Poesías (Casal) **131**:255-57
Poesías (Gómez de Avellaneda) **111**:3, 6, 9, 18, 27-8, 30, 43
Poesías (Heredia) **209**:131-32, 134, 160, 162, 168
Poesías (Martínez de la Rosa) **102**:238
Poesías (Silva) **114**:261, 294-98
Poesías completas (Heredia) **209**:160-68
"Poesías de don Francisco de la Rosa" (Larra) **130**:254
*Poesías líricas *Cantos a Lesbia** (Manzano) **155**:276, 297, 305
Poesías varias (Silva) **114**:315, 318
Poesie (Foscolo) **8**:267, 278
Poesie (Leopardi) **129**:218
Poesie der Griechen und Roemer (Schlegel) **45**:283, 320, 359
"Poesie des Lebens" (Schiller) **166**:113
"Poésie; ou, Le paysage dans le Golfe de Glafenes" (Lamartine) **11**:270, 280
"Poésie ou paysage dans le Golfe de Gênes" (Lamartine) **190**:233
"Poésie sacrée" (Lamartine) **11**:269
Poesier (Wergeland) **5**:538
Poèsies (Gautier) **1**:350
Poésies (Laforgue) **53**:277
Poésies (Mallarmé) **41**:240-44, 249, 280; **210**:171, 241, 245, 264, 266
Poésies (Rimbaud) **82**:240
Poésies allemandes (Nerval) **1**:484
Poésies and Complete Miscellanea (Lautréamont) **194**:198, 207, 209
Poésies complètes (Gautier) **59**:18, 34-5, 72
Poésies Complètes (Laforgue) **221**:73-79, 81-93
Poèsies complètes (Rimbaud) **4**:472-74
Poésies de Choderlos de Laclos (Laclos) **4**:325
Les poésies de Joseph Delorme (Sainte-Beuve) **5**:333, 340-41
Poésies I, II (Lautréamont) **12**:210, 212, 215-16, 220-21, 237-41, 243-44; **194**:144, 147, 153-56, 185, 190-91, 193-94, 211-18, 223, 226, 239, 246-49, 251-52, 255-57, 259, 261-69
Poésies inédites (Desbordes-Valmore) **97**:13, 18, 20, 25-7, 29-30
Poésies novelles, 1836-1852 (Musset) **7**:256, 272, 279
"Poesy or Art" (Coleridge) **231**:29-30
"The Poet" (Bryant) **6**:182; **46**:6
"The Poet" (Cranch) **115**:5, 40-1
"The Poet" (Emerson) **1**:295, 307; **38**:173-74, 180-81, 184, 187, 189, 190; **98**:25-6, 47, 65, 114-16, 176, 181-82, 189
"The Poet" (Lampman) **25**:216
"The Poet" (O'Brien) **21**:249
"The Poet" (Pavlova) **138**:33
"The Poet" (Pushkin) **83**:249, 257
"The Poet" (Thoreau) **7**:396
"The Poet: A Fragment" (Keats) **225**:183
"Poet and Crowd" (Pushkin) **83**:249, 257
"The Poet and His Muse" (Thomson) **18**:415, 419
"The Poet and His Songs" (Longfellow) **2**:491
Poet and Merchant (Auerbach)
See *Dichter und Kaufmann*
The Poet and the Composer (Hoffmann)
See "Der Dichter und der Komponist"
"The Poet and the Throng" (Pushkin)
See "Poet and Crowd"
The Poet at the Breakfast-Table (Holmes) **14**:106, 110, 113-15, 124, 126, 132-33, 143-44, 146; **81**:102-04
"The Poet Boy's Love Wishes" (Harpur) **114**:107
"Poet-Heart" (Lampman) **194**:34
"The Poet Heine" (Lazarus) **8**:426; **109**:326
"The Poet in the East" (Taylor) **89**:305
"The Poet of Love" (Chivers) **49**:44-6, 53, 55
"Poet of Poets" (Lanier) **118**:268
"The Poet of the Spring" (Crawford) **127**:202
"The Poet, the Oyster and Sensitive Plant" (Cowper) **94**:121
"El poeta y la sirena" (Casal) **131**:255
"Le poète contumace" (Corbière) **43**:6, 10-11, 18, 24, 27, 30, 32, 33
"Le poëte dans les révolutions" (Hugo) **21**:214
"Le poète décho" (Musset) **7**:274

Le Poète déchu (Musset) **150**:233, 296-97, 299, 324, 347, 349
"La poéte Mourant" (Lamartine) **11**:245, 248, 270, 280; **190**:193, 200-1
Le poète sifflé (Grillparzer) **102**:104
"Les Poètes" (Verlaine) **230**:210
"Les poètes de sept ans" (Rimbaud) **4**:466, 471-72, 474, 479, 486; **35**:271; **82**:226, 247; **227**:195, 208, 242, 264-65
"Les poëtes du XVIe siècle" (Nerval) **67**:303
Les poètes maudits (Verlaine) **51**:354; **230**:163, 178
Poetic and Religious Harmonies (Lamartine) **11**:283
"Poetic Art" (Verlaine)
See "Art poétique"
Poetic Contemplations (Lamartine)
See *Les recueillements poétiques*
"Poetic Diction" (Hopkins) **189**:90, 92
"Poetic Diction" (Wordsworth) **38**:416
"Poetic Discriptions of Violent Death" (Harpur) **114**:131
A Poetic Epistle to Mr. Samuel Johnson, A.M. By Arthur Murphy (Murphy) **229**:234
"Poetic Interpretation" (Lampman) **25**:203, 214-15; **194**:72, 85, 96, 100
The Poetic Mirror; or, The Living Bards of Britain (Hogg) **4**:282, 284; **109**:192, 209, 240, 246-50, 258, 260, 262
"Poetic Possessions" (Lampman) **194**:95
"The Poetic Principle" (Poe) **1**:510-11, 526; **16**:307; **55**:132, 138, 159, 164, 170-1; **94**:220; **117**:194, 257, 04, 312-13, 335; **211**:232-33, 235, 238, 240-42, 246, 248-49, 262
"Poetic Sympathies" (Dyer) **129**:95, 118, 120
Poetic Works (Horton)
See *Poetical Works*
"Poetical Essay on Romance" (D'Israeli) **217**:306
The Poetical Meditations (Lamartine)
See *Méditations poétiques*
The Poetical Meditations of M. Alphonse de La Martine (Lamartine)
See *Méditations poétiques*
Poetical Pieces (Barnes) **75**:14, 69
Poetical Recreations of the Champion (Thelwall) **162**:345
"A Poetical Reverie" (Warren) **13**:412
Poetical Sketches (Blake) **13**:159, 171, 181-82, 184-85, 219, 239-40; **37**:3-4, 8-9, 13-14, 20, 35, 38, 40, 72; **190**:15, 29; **201**:113, 140
"Poetical Studies" (Harpur) **114**:144
"Poetical Versatility" (Hazlitt) **29**:148
Poetical Works (Adams) **33**:5, 7, 11, 16
Poetical Works (Barrett Browning) **61**:12, 14-5, 24
Poetical Works (Browning) **79**:149, 152, 189-90
Poetical Works (Coleridge)
See *The Complete Poetical Works*
Poetical Works (Crabbe) **121**:29, 78
Poetical Works (Hemans) **71**:271-72, 274-77
Poetical Works (Horton) **87**:101-102, 104
Poetical Works (Moore) **110**:177-80
Poetical Works (Rossetti) **77**:291-98, 303, 343, 349, 356-63
Poetical Works (Schlegel)
See *Poetische Werke*
The Poetical Works (Taylor) **89**:325
Poetical Works (Whittier) **59**:371
The Poetical Works of Christina Georgina Rossetti (Rossetti) **2**:566, 572, 576; **50**:279; **66**:304, 310; **186**:246, 262, 310, 313
The Poetical Works of Edmund Spenser (Child) **173**:167, 169, 171, 189, 208, 225
The Poetical Works of James Thomson (B. V.) (Thomson) **18**:395
The Poetical Works of John Trumbull, LL.D. (Trumbull) **30**:346, 351, 376
The Poetical Works of Leigh Hunt (Hunt) **70**:257
The Poetical Works of Mathilde Blind (Blind) **202**:9, 24
The Poetical Works of Robert Southey, Collected by Himself (Southey) **97**:268-69, 277-80, 315, 317
The Poetical Works of Samuel Taylor Coleridge (Coleridge) **177**:149-50; **231**:56-60, 105, 150-53, 155
The Poetical Works of Shelley (Shelley) **93**:343-46
The Poetical Works of Sydney Dobell (Dobell) **43**:45
The Poetical Works of the Late Mrs. Mary Robinson (Robinson) **142**:103, 105, 109-15, 143, 148, 169-70, 173, 177, 182, 199, 214
The Poetical Works of the Late Thomas Little, Esq. (Moore) **6**:388; **110**:190
The Poetical Works of William Wordsworth (Wordsworth) **111**:234, 237, 239-43, 293, 301, 315, 338; **166**:267, 299, 308-9, 314, 318-20; **206**:298
Poetics, or a Series of Poems and Disquisitions on Poetry (Dyer) **129**:96-97, 132, 138
Poetische Werke (Schlegel) **142**:203, 300
"Poetischer Realismus" (Ludwig) **4**:360
Poetry (Karamzin) **3**:284
Poetry (Mickiewicz) **101**:174-75
"Poetry: A Metrical Essay" (Holmes) **14**:98, 127
"Poetry and Imagination" (Emerson) **1**:295; **38**:175, 187-88; **98**:55, 58-60, 62
"Poetry and Mendicancy" (Castro Alves)
See "Poesia e Mendicidade"
"Poetry and Politics" (Almqvist)
See "Poesi och politik"
Poetry and Prose (Shelley) **93**:294-95
The Poetry and Prose of William Blake (Blake)
See *The Complete Poetry and Prose of William Blake*
Poetry and Tales (Poe) **211**:284
Poetry and Tales of Edgar Allan Poe (Poe) **117**:321
Poetry and Truth (Goethe)
See *Dichtung und Wahrheit*
Poetry and Truth out of My Life (Goethe)
See *Dichtung und Wahrheit*
"Poetry and Verse" (Hopkins) **17**:250
"Poetry and Verse" (Hugo) **17**:250
"Poetry for Children" (Sigourney) **87**:321
Poetry for Children (Lamb) **125**:329-30, 332-35, 345-46, 354, 360, 371, 373
Poetry for Children (Lamb) **10**:418; **113**:230, 286
Poetry for the People (Milnes) **61**:129, 137
"Poetry heals an ailing spirit" (Baratynsky)
See "Bolyashchiy dukh vrachuet pesnopenie..."
Poetry Notebooks (Emerson) **98**:177
"The Poetry of Byron" (Lampman) **25**:212; **194**:38
"The Poetry of Christina Rossetti" (Levy) **59**:86; **203**:352
The Poetry of Dorothy Wordsworth (Wordsworth) **25**:408, 420, 422
The Poetry of Flowers, and Flowers of Poetry (Osgood) **141**:338-39, 341-42, 347
The Poetry of Julián del Casal (Casal) **131**:267-69, 271
"The poetry of life" (Schiller)
See "Poesie des Lebens"
"The Poetry of Michelangelo" (Pater) **159**:257-58
"The Poetry of Pope" (De Quincey) **198**:9
The Poetry of Sacred and Legendary Art (Jameson) **43**:323-25, 327-28, 333-34, 337-8
"Poetry of the Celtic Races" (Renan) **26**:364
Poetry of the Pacific (Ridge) **82**:185
"Poets" (Hayne) **94**:160, 164
"The Poets" (Lampman) **25**:160, 173, 194, 209, 212; **194**:38, 57
The Poets (Alfieri) **101**:36
"Poets and Personal Pronouns" (Webster) **230**:266-67
"Poets and Poetry of America" (Poe) **55**:177
The Poets and Poetry of Munster (Mangan) **27**:280, 307-08, 314, 318
A Poet's Bazaar (Andersen)
See *En Digters Bazar*
"The Poet's Consolation" (Mangan) **27**:276
"A Poet's Daughter" (Halleck) **47**:57, 79, 81
"The Poet's Death" (Lermontov)
See "Smert' poeta"
"The Poet's Delay" (Thoreau) **207**:179
"The Poet's Epitaph" (Wordsworth) **111**:242; **206**:225, 312
The Poet's Fate. A Poetical Dialogue (Dyer) **129**:95, 104-5, 113-15, 118, 132
"The Poet's Feeble Petition" (Horton) **87**:102
A Poet's Garden (Schumann) **143**:144
"The Poet's Garret" (Robinson) **142**:98, 105
"A Poet's Home" (Harpur) **114**:115
The Poet's Journal (Taylor) **89**:309, 346
Poet's Life (Tieck)
See *Des Dichters Leben*
A Poet's Love (Schumann)
See *Dichterliebe*
"The Poet's Mind" (Tennyson) **65**:357-8
"The Poet's Mission" (Jones) **222**:160
"The Poets of Seven Years" (Rimbaud)
See "Les poètes de sept ans"
The Poet's Pilgrimage to Waterloo (Southey) **8**:466; **97**:263, 269, 291
"The Poet's Possession" (Lampman) **194**:81
"The Poet's Soliloquy" (Cranch) **115**:43
"The Poet's Song" (Lampman) **25**:184, 192, 204, 216; **194**:36, 50, 120
"The Poet's Tale" (Longfellow) **45**:124
"Poets to Come" (Whitman) **205**:162, 165
"The Poet's Vow" (Barrett Browning) **61**:53, 56, 58, 64-5, 67-70; **66**:56; **170**:5
"Poezdka v Poles'e" (Turgenev) **122**:264, 343-44, 348-49
Poezdka v Revel' (Bestuzhev) **131**:165-66, 183
Poezíje Dóktorja Francèta Presérna (Preseren) **127**:296, 300, 304, 323, 327, 333
Poganuc People (Stowe) **3**:562-63, 568
Poganuc People: Their Loves and Lives (Stowe) **195**:222, 228
"Pogasšee delo" (Leskov) **25**:247; **174**:24-26
The Poggenpuhl Family (Fontane)
See *Die Poggenpuhls*
Die Poggenpuhls (Fontane) **26**:236, 244, 256-57, 270-71, 278; **163**:161-62, 168-69, 203, 217, 255
"Pogibšie i pogibajuščie" (Pisarev) **25**:344
"Poiema lyriko eis ton thanato tou Lord Byron" (Solomos) **15**:386, 388, 390, 395, 397
"Poietes Apoietes" (Coleridge) **90**:15, 28
"point d'adieux" (Desbordes-Valmore) **97**:5
"Le point noir" (Nerval) **1**:486
The Point of View for My Work as an Author (Kierkegaard)
See *Synspunktet for min Forfatter-Virksomhed*
The Point of View for My Work as an Author: A Report to History (Kierkegaard)
See *Synspunktet for min Forfatter-Virksomhed*
"Point Rash-Judgment" (Wordsworth) **111**:367
"Le poison" (Baudelaire) **6**:80, 129; **55**:29, 61, 69
"A Poison Tree" (Blake) **13**:180; **37**:4, 44, 49, 53, 92; **173**:90
The Poison Tree (Chatterji)
See *Vishavriksha*
"The Poisoned Girl" (Solomos) **15**:393
"Der Pokal" (Tieck) **46**:350
Poland and Russia: A Legend on Kosciusko (Michelet) **218**:287

"Polden" (Tyutchev) **34**:400
Pole Poppenspäler (Storm) **195**:5-6, 14, 18, 20, 83-86
Polemic with the Catholic Review regarding the Work of Aimé Martin (Sarmiento)
See *Polémica con la Revista Católica sobre la obra de Aimé Martin*
Polémica con la Revista Católica sobre la obra de Aimé Martin (Sarmiento) **123**:360
"Polemica cu România libera" (Eminescu) **131**:326
"The Polemics with the România libera" (Eminescu)
See "Polemica cu România libera"
"Der Polenflüchtling" (Lenau) **16**:264, 286
Les polichinelles (Becque) **3**:16
Polinice (Alfieri) **101**:4, 11, 42, 67, 69
Polinices and Virginia (Alfieri) **101**:32
The Polish Faust (Sacher-Masoch) **31**:295
"A Polish Insurgent" (Thomson) **18**:391
The Polish Mines (Pixérécourt)
See *Les mines de Pologne*
"Polish Pilgrims" (Mickiewicz)
See "Pielgrzym"
The Polish-American System of Chronology, Reproduced with Some Modifications, from General Bem's Franco-Polish Method (Peabody) **169**:149
Politian (Poe) **1**:504; **55**:180-1, 209
The Political and Confidential Correspondence of Lewis the Sixteenth; with Observations on Each Letter (Williams) **135**:260, 307, 335
"Political Aspect of the Colored People of the United States" (Delany) **93**:166
"Political Biography, Hugh Gaine's Life" (Freneau) **111**:111
"The Political Destination of America" (Parker) **186**:192
"Political Destiny" (Delany)
See "The Political Destiny of the Colored Race on the American Continent"
"The Political Destiny of the Colored Race on the American Continent" (Delany) **93**:100, 105, 129-30, 156, 169, 172
Political Economy (Mill)
See *Principles of Political Economy, with Some of Their Applications to Social Philosophy*
Political Essay on the Island of Cuba (Humboldt)
See *Essai politique sur l'île de Cuba*
Political Essay on the Kingdom of New Spain: With Physical Sections and Maps Founded on Astronomical Observations and Trigonometrical and Barometrical Measurements (Humboldt)
See *Essai politique sur le royaume de la Nouvelle-Espagne*
Political Essays (Hazlitt) **82**:105, 129
Political Essays (Lowell) **2**:515
"A Political Molecule" (Eliot) **118**:38
"Political Poems" (Heine) **147**:193, 196-97
"Political Reflections" (Madison) **126**:326
"A Political Reverie" (Warren) **226**:261
Political Tales (Saltykov) **16**:351
The Political Theology of Mazzini and the International (Bakunin) **25**:49
Political Work (Eminescu) **131**:289
Political Works (Cobbett) **49**:107, 112
"Politiciennes" (Maupassant) **83**:189
"Politics" (Emerson) **98**:116-17
"Politics" (Tennyson) **30**:295
"Politics" (Tonna) **135**:204, 210
"Politics as a Profession" (Bagehot) **10**:31
"Politique (1831)" (Nerval) **67**:331
Politisk camara optica (Almqvist) **42**:19
Die Polizei (Schiller) **69**:169, 250
"The Poll Cat" (Shaw) **15**:335
"Poll Jenning's Hair" (Cooke) **110**:35
Pollen (Novalis)
See *Blüthenstaub*
"Pollice Verso" (Martí) **63**:102
"Pollion's Supper" (Pavlova)
See "Uzhin Polliona"
"Polly Be-en Upzides Wi' Tom" (Barnes) **75**:78
"Polly Mariner, Tailoress" (Cooke) **110**:20, 25, 33, 36, 44
Polnoe sobranie sochinenii (Dostoevsky) **202**:112-20
Polnoe sobranie socinenij (Radishchev) **190**:318, 320-21
Polnoe sobranie sochinenii (Gogol) **162**:104, 128
Polnoe sobranie sochinenii (Zhukovsky) **35**:396
Polnoe sobranie sochinenij v tridcati tomakh (Dostoevsky) **167**:309-15
Polnoe sobranie socinenij (Leskov) **174**:60
Polnoe sobranie stikhotvorenii (Baratynsky) **103**:47-9
Polnoe sobranie stikhotvoreniia (Pavlova) **138**:31-36
Polnoye sobraniye sochineniy (Bestuzhev) **131**:186
Polonius: A Collection of Wise Saws and Modern Instances (FitzGerald) **153**:219, 228
Poltava (Pushkin) **3**:413-14, 416, 422-23, 445, 452, 460-62; **27**:369; **83**:243, 246, 250, 257, 312-14, 335, 357
"Polunoščniki" (Leskov) **25**:234-36; **174**:38, 40, 53
"Polunoshchniki" (Leskov)
See "Polunoščniki"
"Polycrates" (Thomson) **18**:411
"Pomare" (Heine) **4**:252
Pomeroy Abbey (Wood) **178**:288
Pomona für Teutschlands Töchter (La Roche) **121**:250, 263, 271, 297, 305-6, 325
Pompeii (Bulwer-Lytton)
See *The Last Days of Pompeii*
Pompeo in Egitto (Leopardi) **129**:347
"Pompey's Ghost" (Hood) **16**:234, 239
Ponce de Leon (Brentano) **1**:101-02; **191**:38, 103
"The Ponds" (Thoreau) **7**:388; **138**:75
"Les ponts" (Rimbaud) **35**:323; **227**:203, 209-10, 242, 247, 271, 296, 309-10
"The Poor and Their Dwellings" (Crabbe) **121**:58, 62, 90
"The Poor Artist: or, Seven Eyesights and one Object" (Horne) **127**:269
"The Poor at Church" (Rimbaud)
See "Les pauvres à l'église"
The Poor Benefactor (Stifter)
See "Kalkstein"
"The Poor Bird" (Andersen) **7**:21
The Poor Book (Arnim)
See *Das Armenbuch*
The Poor Bride (Ostrovsky)
See *Bednaya nevesta*
"The Poor Clare" (Gaskell) **5**:202; **70**:182, 189, 191, 193, 196-98
The Poor Clare (Gaskell) **137**:99
"Poor Dionis" (Eminescu)
See "Sarmanul Dionis"
"The Poor Fiddler" (Grillparzer)
See *Der Arme Spielmann*
Poor Flowers (Desbordes-Valmore)
See *Pauvres fleurs*
Poor Folk (Dostoevsky)
See *Bednye lyudi*
The Poor Gentleman (Oliphant) **11**:446-7
A Poor Gentleman (Turgenev)
See *Nakhlebnik*
"The Poor Ghost" (Rossetti) **2**:558, 565; **186**:271
"The Poor in Church" (Rimbaud)
See "Les pauvres à l'église"
"The Poor in Spirit . . ." (Verlaine)
See "L'Homme pauvre d'esprit . . ."
Poor Jack (Marryat) **3**:317-18, 320
"Poor John" (Andersen) **7**:21
Poor Laws and Paupers Illustrated (Martineau) **137**:302
"Poor Little Heart" (Dickinson) **21**:55
"Poor Liza" (Bestuzhev)
See "Bednaia Liza"
"Poor Liza" (Karamzin)
See "Bednaya Liza"
"Poor Lorraine" (Kingsley) **35**:212
The Poor Man's Friend (Cobbett)
See *Cobbett's Poor Man's Friend; or, A Defence of the Rights of Those Who Do the Work and Fight the Battles*
"Poor Man's Pudding and Rich Man's Crumbs" (Melville) **193**:148
"Poor Marguerite" (Robinson) **142**:137, 251
"Poor Mathew" (Lincoln) **18**:272-73
Poor Miss Finch (Collins) **1**:184; **18**:65
The Poor Musician (Grillparzer)
See *Der Arme Spielmann*
The Poor of New York (Boucicault) **41**:31, 34
"The Poor of the Borough" (Crabbe) **121**:62
"The Poor of the Land" (Martí) **63**:165
"Poor Relations" (Lamb) **10**:411, 436-37; **113**:210
Poor Relations (Balzac)
See *Les parents pauvres*
The Poor Rich Man, and the Rich Poor Man (Sedgwick) **19**:437-38, 440, 444
"Poor Scholar" (Carleton) **3**:83, 85, 87, 90, 92; **199**:5, 7-9, 13, 16-17, 23, 55-56
"The Poor Scholar" (Hale) **75**:298
"The Poor, Singing Dame" (Robinson) **142**:136-37
"Poor Susan" (Wordsworth) **111**:281
"Poor Thumbling" (Andersen) **7**:21, 24
"A Poor Young Shepherd" (Verlaine) **51**:381, 383-84; **230**:152, 207
"The Poor-Rate Unfolds a Tale" (Robertson) **35**:370
Popanilla (Disraeli)
See *The Voyage of Captain Popanilla*
"The Pope" (Browning) **79**:111
"The Poplar" (Shevchenko)
See "Topolja"
"The Poplar-Field" (Cowper) **8**:139; **94**:33, 38
"Poppies" (Coleridge) **31**:71
The Popular Ballads of the English Race by Professor F. J. Child (Child)
See *The English and Scottish Popular Ballads*
"Popular Discontent" (Webster) **30**:424
The Popular Education of France (Arnold) **89**:101-02; **126**:3, 6, 77, 82, 112; **218**:239, 251-52
"Popular Fallacies" (Lamb) **10**:411, 415
"Popular Fallacies—XIV" (Lamb) **113**:198
Popular Geology: A Series of Lectures Read before the Philosophical Institution of Edinburgh, with Descriptive Sketches from a Geologist's Portfolio (Miller) **143**:24
"Popular Poetry—Periodical Criticism, &c." (Reynolds) **146**:205
Popular Songs (Herder) **8**:305
Popular Stories (Grimm Brothers)
See *Kinder-und Hausmärchen*
Popular Tales (Edgeworth) **1**:256, 267; **51**:81, 89, 135, 137; **158**:41, 66
Popular Tales (Tieck) **5**:515
"The Popular Theology of Christendom regarded as a principle of Ethics" (Parker) **186**:126, 216
"Popularity in Authorship" (Clare) **9**:115, 121
"Por ahora" (Larra) **130**:204, 241
"¿Por qué era rubia?" (Alarcón) **219**:44-45, 47, 52
"Por que tan terca...?" (Castro) **78**:42
Porcupine's Gazette (Cobbett) **49**:113
Porcupine's Works (Cobbett) **49**:87, 107, 109
"Porog" (Turgenev) **21**:455; **122**:307-8
"O pórphyras" (Solomos) **15**:390, 399
"Porphyria's Lover" (Browning) **19**:131

"Porro Unum Est Necessarium" (Arnold) **89**:101, 103; **218**:178, 197
"Le port" (Baudelaire) **29**:110
"Le port" (Maupassant) **1**:460
"Port Marsel'sky" (Pavlova) **138**:4, 16
Port Salvation (Daudet)
See *L'évangéliste*
"Portent" (Grillparzer)
See "Vorzeichen"
"The Portent" (Melville) **3**:378
"The Porter's Son" (Andersen) **214**:58
"Portes et fenêtres" (Corbière) **43**:14, 31
"Portia" (Musset) **7**:265, 267, 278-79; **150**:229, 231-33, 299-305, 311
"Le Portrait" (Baudelaire) **55**:10
"The Portrait" (Gogol)
See "Portret"
"The Portrait" (Hood) **16**:206
"Un Portrait" (Maupassant) **83**:181
"The Portrait" (Rossetti) **4**:492, 506, 508, 511, 518, 521-22; **77**:311, 314, 317, 348, 353-54, 358-59, 363
"A Portrait" (Rossetti) **186**:304
"A Portrait" (Willis) **194**:301
"Portrait by Vandyck" (Hazlitt) **29**:144
"Portrait de Lord Byron" (Flaubert) **179**:119
"A Portrait for Amoret" (Sheridan) **91**:233-34
"A Portrait in Six Sonnets" (Lampman) **25**:219; **194**:16, 21-22, 25, 112
"Portrait: King Harold before the Battle of Hastings" (Brontë) **165**:99
"Portrait of Felitsa" (Derzhavin)
See "Izobrazhenie Felitsy"
Portraits (Pater)
See *An Imaginary Portrait*
Portraits (Webster) **230**:230-32, 234, 248-51, 253, 255-56, 270, 281, 297-98, 304, 323-24
Portraits contemporains (Sainte-Beuve) **5**:346
"Portraits des maîtresses" (Baudelaire) **155**:107
Portraits Intimes of the Eighteenth Century (Goncourt and Goncourt) **7**:153
Portraiture of Judaism (D'Israeli) **217**:277
"A Portrayal of Felitsa" (Derzhavin)
See "Izobrazhenie Felitsy"
"Portret" (Gogol) **5**:219, 240-42, 248, 252-54, 256-58; **31**:103; **162**:17-18, 27, 32, 56, 70, 86, 88, 107-8, 128-29
"Portretnaia Gallereia" (Bestuzhev) **131**:165
Port-Royal (Sainte-Beuve) **5**:333-34, 336, 338-40, 349
Port-Tarascon (Daudet) **1**:236-37, 242
"Posąg i obuwie" (Norwid) **17**:373
Poshekhonskaya starina (Saltykov) **16**:343, 345-49, 351-52, 357, 359, 369, 373, 375
"Posielenie" (Slowacki) **15**:355
Pósies (Desbordes-Valmore) **97**:12, 26-7
"The Position of Poland with Respect to God and Man" (Krasiński)
See "O stanowisku Polski z Bożych i ludzkich wzgledów"
A Positive Philosophy of Auguste Comte (Martineau) **26**:323; **137**:236
Positive Politics (Comte)
See *Système de Politique Positive ou Traité de Sociologie instituant la Religion de l'Humanité*
Positive Polity (Comte)
See *Système de Politique Positive ou Traité de Sociologie instituant la Religion de l'Humanité*
"A Positive Romance" (Bellamy) **4**:30; **86**:75
Positivist Calendar (Comte)
See *Calendrier positiviste*
"Positivity of the Christian Religion" (Hegel) **151**:313
Lo positivo (Tamayo y Baus) **1**:565, 569
"Poslanie indeiskogo bramina k tsarevichu Khloru" (Derzhavin) **215**:57
"Poslanie k Baronu Del'vigu" (Baratynsky) **103**:28
"Poslanie k kn. Viazemskomu" (Aksakov) **181**:61
"Poslanie k M. A. Dmitrievu" (Aksakov) **181**:26
"Poslaniie" (Shevchenko) **54**:383, 389
"Poslednì soud" (Macha) **46**:202
"Posledniaia smert" (Baratynsky)
See "Poslednyaya smert'"
"Poslednii poet" (Baratynsky)
See "Posledny poet"
"Poslednjaja smert" (Baratynsky)
See "Poslednyaya smert'"
"Posledny poet" (Baratynsky) **103**:13-20, 22, 36, 38-9, 46
"Poslednyaya smert'" (Baratynsky) **103**:3, 6-7, 9, 11, 13-20, 22-3, 25, 27, 35, 38-9, 46
"Le Possédé" (Baudelaire) **55**:66
The Possessed (Dostoevsky)
See *Besy*
"Possibilities" (Longfellow) **2**:492
"Die Post" (Muller) **73**:366, 383, 385, 393, 396-97
"The Post Office" (Sedgwick) **19**:446
Post-Bag (Moore)
See *Intercepted Letters; or, The Two penny Post-Bag*
"Das Posthorn" (Lenau) **16**:282
The Posthumous Book (Verlaine)
See *Le Livre posthume*
The Posthumous Dramatic Works of Richard Cumberland (Cumberland) **167**:154, 158, 193, 197
The Posthumous Papers of the Pickwick Club (Dickens) **3**:138-40, 144, 151-52, 154, 171, 176-77, 180-82; **8**:197; **18**:97, 113, 121, 133; **26**:156, 158, 167; **37**:142-5, 147-50, 153-54, 156, 164, 169, 177, 182, 184, 193-96, 198, 204-05, 208-09, 211; **86**:186, 255-56; **105**:227, 229-30, 249; **113**:9, 28, 81, 84, 91, 97, 103, 108, 118, 123-24, 127; **161**:15, 30, 32, 100; **187**:8; **217**:225; **219**:72, 74, 90, 109, 117-20, 124, 138, 160, 184, 192; **231**:170-72, 174, 176, 179-80, 182, 205, 238
Posthumous Poems of Percy Bysshe Shelley (Shelley) **18**:325
Posthumous Remains (Hazlitt) **82**:88
Posthumous Tales (Crabbe) **26**:103, 105, 110
Posthumous Works (De Quincey) **87**:36
Posthumous Works (Radcliffe) **223**:187
The Posthumous Works of Thomas De Quincey (De Quincey) **198**:41
Postille (Manzoni) **98**:214
"Der Postillion" (Lenau) **16**:266, 270, 282
"The Postmaster" (Pushkin)
See "Stantsionnyi smotritel"
"Postscript" (Pater) **7**:330-31; **90**:292, 323
"Postscript" (De Quincey) **87**:76-7, 79; **198**:39-43, 52-53
Postscript (Kierkegaard) **125**:176-77, 209
"Postscript, Found in the Handwriting of Mr. Knickerbocker" (Irving) **19**:343
The Post-Script to Gebir (Landor) **14**:203
Le postscriptum (Augier) **31**:8, 16, 34
Post-Stage Master (Pushkin) **3**:447-48
"Postulates of Political Economy" (Bagehot) **10**:20, 30-31
"Pot de fleurs" (Gautier) **1**:344
"The Pot of Tulips" (O'Brien) **21**:239, 242-45, 249-50, 252
"The Potato" (Mickiewicz)
See "Kartofel"
"Potter's Clay" (Gordon) **21**:159, 166
"Pott's Painless Cure" (Bellamy) **4**:30-31
"Poulain the Prisoner" (Webster) **230**:239
"Pounds, Shillings and Pence" (Clare) **86**:172
"Pour avoir peché" (Verlaine) **51**:361
"Pour E . . ." (Verlaine) **230**:170
Le Pour et le Contre (Feuillet) **45**:89-90
"Pour la Mort de la terre" (Laforgue) **53**:268, 271
"Pour le livre d'amour" (Laforgue) **53**:268; **221**:41, 59, 81, 89
"Pour les pauvres" (Hugo) **21**:214
"Pour Rita" (Verlaine) **230**:214
Pour un tombeau d'Anatole (Mallarmé) **210**:155-56, 158, 161-62, 164, 264
"Pourquoi mon âme est-elle triste?" (Lamartine) **11**:270
"Pourquoi seuls?" (Banville) **9**:29
"Pourtant!—S'il y avait . . ." (Laforgue) **221**:88
"Poverty" (Thoreau) **7**:383
Poverty and Nobleness of Mind (Kotzebue)
See *Armuth und Edelsinn*
Poverty Is No Crime (Ostrovsky)
See *Bednost ne porok*
The Poverty of Philosophy (Marx)
See *Misère de la philosophie: Réponse à la philosophie de la misère de M. Proudhon*
Poverty, Wealth, Sin, and Penance of Countess Dolores: A True Story, Recorded for the Instruction and Amusement of Poor Young Ladies (Arnim)
See *Armuth, Reichtum, Schuld und Busse der Gräfin Dolores: Eine Wahre Geschichte zur lehrreichen Unterhaltung*
"Povest' o bogougodnom drovokole" (Leskov) **25**:245
"Povest' o tom, kak odin muzhik dvukh generalov prokormil" (Saltykov) **16**:342, 358, 373
Povesti Belkina (Pushkin) **3**:428, 435-3, 447; **83**:272-73, 275-76, 279, 308-16, 319, 323, 337-38, 354-55
Povisty o besrodnom Petrush (Shevchenko) **54**:391
"Povodni mož" (Preseren) **127**:308
"Power" (Emerson) **98**:9, 134-35, 151, 153-55, 185
"Power" (Lampman) **194**:34
"The Power of an Injured Look" (Willis) **194**:297
"The Power of Fancy" (Freneau) **1**:316; **111**:100, 140, 151
The Power of Her Sympathy (Sedgwick) **98**:364
"The Power of Love" (Brontë) **71**:91
"The Power of Memory" (Preseren)
See "Sila spomina"
"Power of Music" (Wordsworth) **111**:235
"The Power of Novelty" (Freneau) **111**:134
"The Power of Prayer" (Lanier) **118**:227, 235
"The Power of Prayer" (Newman) **38**:345
The Power of Prayer in Relation to Outward Circumstances (Schleiermacher) **107**:362
"The Power of Russia" (Campbell) **19**:183, 194
"The Power of Sound" (Wordsworth)
See "On the Power of Sound"
"The Power of Words" (Poe) **1**:519-20; **117**:258, 267, 269; **211**:260
"Power of Youth" (Arnold) **29**:27
"The Powers of Nature" (Newman) **38**:305
Powhatan: A Metrical Romance in Seven Cantos (Smith) **187**:331-33
"Powieść" (Norwid) **17**:374
"Powinszowania" (Krasicki) **8**:404
"The Powldoodies of Burran" (Maginn) **8**:441
"Powwaw" (Whittier) **8**:485
Poyezdka v Poles'ye (Turgenev) **37**:443
Poyezdka v Revel' (Bestuzhev) **131**:178-80
"Practical Atheism, regarded as a Principle of Ethics" (Parker) **186**:126
"A Practical Blue Stocking" (Parton) **86**:373
"The Practical Blue-Stocking" (Parton) **86**:348
Practical Education (Edgeworth) **1**:267; **51**:78-9, 82, 84, 86, 114, 138; **158**:7, 35, 37, 44, 56
Practical Piety; or, The Influence of the Religion of the Heart on the Conduct of the Life (More) **27**:334, 338
"Praeceptor Amat" (Timrod) **25**:360, 362, 375, 384
—Praelectiones (Keble)
See *Praelectiones Academicae Oxonii Habitae, Annis MDCCCXXXII...MDCCCXLI*

Praelectiones Academicae (Keble)
See *Praelectiones Academicae Oxonii Habitae, Annis MDCCCXXXII...MDCCCXLI*
Praelectiones Academicae Oxonii Habitae, Annis MDCCCXXXII...MDCCCXLI (Keble) **87**:142, 152, 156, 183
"Præections on Poetry" (Keble) **87**:135
"Prahlad" (Dutt) **29**:120, 125, 128, 130
The Prairie (Cooper) **1**:199-200, 202, 205-07, 217, 221, 223, 228; **27**:125, 127, 130-36, 138-43, 148-50, 153-55, 172, 177, 179, 183-86; **54**:254, 265, 274, 277, 288, 291; **203**:11, 48, 62, 71-73, 86, 120, 139, 157-58, 162-63
"The Prairie States" (Whitman) **31**:432
"A Prairie Sunset" (Whitman) **81**:370-71
"The Prairie-Grass Dividing" (Whitman) **31**:430
"The Prairies" (Bryant) **6**:162, 168, 170, 172, 183, 185-86, 189, 191-92; **46**:3, 6, 19, 28, 34, 43, 47, 52, 55-6
"Praise and Prayer" (Lampman) **25**:183
"Praise for the fountain open'd" (Cowper) **94**:74
"Praise It—'tis Dead" (Dickinson) **21**:69
"Praise My Lady" (Morris) **4**:426, 444
"Praise o' Do'set" (Barnes) **75**:8, 101, 108
"The Praise of Chimney-Sweepers" (Lamb) **10**:398, 402-03, 407, 409-10, 415, 423, 426, 436; **113**:169, 235, 263
"Praise of Creation" (Horton) **87**:110
Die praktische Theologie (Schleiermacher)
See *Die praktische Theologie nach den Grundsätzen der evangelischen Kirche im Zusammenhang dargestellt*
Die praktische Theologie nach den Grundsätzen der evangelischen Kirche im Zusammenhang dargestellt (Schleiermacher) **107**:268, 284, 407
"Präludium" (Heine) **147**:160
"Prayer" (Cooke) **110**:9
"Prayer" (Hale) **75**:284, 285
"The Prayer" (Isaacs)
See "La oración"
"A Prayer" (Lampman) **25**:201; **194**:33, 74, 102
"Prayer" (Lermontov) **5**:288
"A prayer" (Levy) **59**:107
"Prayer" (Mörike)
See "Gebet"
"The Prayer" (Very) **9**:376, 385
"Prayer for Conformity to God's Will" (Rossetti) **50**:275
"The Prayer of a Lonely Heart" (Kemble) **18**:181
"The Prayer of Agassiz" (Whittier) **8**:524
"A Prayer of Columbus" (Whitman) **4**:582, 586; **31**:371, 435; **205**:172, 208, 226
The Prayer of the Ignorant (Multatuli)
See *Het gebed van den Onwetende*
Prayer on the Acropolis (Renan)
See *Prière sur l'acropole*
"Prayer Without Ceasing" (Cranch) **115**:50
"Praying Always" (Rossetti) **50**:316
Prazdnichny son—do obeda (Ostrovsky) **30**:104, 113
"Prazdnik Rima" (Pavlova) **138**:4, 13
"Le pré du déshonneur" (Maupassant) **83**:190
"A Preacher" (Webster) **230**:249, 291
"The Preacher" (Whittier) **59**:356, 360
"Preambolo alla ristampa delle 'Annotazioni' nel 'Nuovo Ricoglitore' di Milano" (Leopardi) **129**:327-30
Préambule (Schumann)
See *Carnaval*
"Préambule aux *Nouvelles confidences* " (Lamartine) **190**:214
Precaution (Cooper) **1**:196; **27**:129, 171; **54**:251, 273; **203**:4, 6, 45, 91
The Precipice (Goncharov)
See *Obryv*
Précis de ma conduite (Genlis) **166**:20, 22
Précis de l'histoire de France jusqu'à la Révolution (Michelet) **218**:317, 335
Précis d'histoire modern (Michelet) **31**:235
"The Precursor" (Patmore) **9**:341
"A Predicament" (Poe) **16**:322-23; **117**:231, 235
"Prediction" (Lermontov) **126**:228
Predigt eines Laienbruders zu Neujahr 1814 (Claudius) **75**:213, 215, 218
"Pre-eminence of the Man of Letters" (Boker) **125**:35
"Preface" (Baillie) **151**:87
"Preface" (Crabbe) **121**:83, 85
"Preface" (Dickens) **206**:14, 19, 37, 72, 88, 97
"Préface" (Genlis) **166**:61
"Preface" (Harris) **165**:245
"Preface" (Humboldt) **170**:159
"Preface" (Kierkegaard) **125**:204
"Preface" (Manzoni) **29**:275
"Preface" (Peabody) **169**:167
"Preface" (Poe) **117**:305
"Preface" (Wordsworth) **166**:335, 349; **206**:233-34, 255-56, 258, 274, 285, 298-99, 301, 320, 322, 332, 334-35, 337-38
Preface (Laclos)
See *Preface du Redacteur*
"Préface aux *Recueillements poétiques* " (Lamartine) **190**:214
"La préface de Cromwell" (Hugo) **3**:268-69, 273; **21**:196, 202-03, 212, 228; **161**:193-94, 196, 200-203, 209, 247, 270
"Préface de la Première Edition" (Balzac) **153**:12
"Préface des *Méditations* " (Lamartine) **190**:213
Préface du livre mystique (Balzac) **153**:125
Preface du Redacteur (Laclos) **87**:217, 221-22
The Preface of Cromwell (Hugo) **189**:284
"Préface Personnelle" (Comte) **54**:209-12, 239
"Préface pour la tradution d'un ouvrage de M. Wilberforce" (Staël-Holstein) **91**:340
"Preface to Cromwell" (Hugo)
See "La préface de Cromwell"
"Preface to Maria Magdalene" (Hebbel) **43**:239-40, 256, 267
"Preface to Poems" (Arnold) **6**:46-47, 69; **29**:5-7, 23, 25, 27, 36, 53
"Preface to 'Studies in the History of the Renaissance'" (Pater) **7**:338-39; **90**:324
Preface to the Edition of 1815 (Wordsworth) **166**:281
"Preface to the Fables" (Krasicki)
See "Wstęp do bajek"
"Preface to *The Hasty-Pudding* " (Barlow) **223**:65, 67
"Preface to the Lyrical Ballads" (Wordsworth) **38**:400, 408, 416; **111**:211, 213, 230, 232-33, 237, 239-40, 243-44, 272, 291-95, 298, 307-9, 311-14, 322-23, 331, 335-45, 357, 363-64, 367-70
"Preface to The Poetical Works of William Wordsworth" (Wordsworth) **111**:237-38
"Preface to 'The School of Giorgione'" (Pater) **7**:338
Prefaces (Kierkegaard)
See *Forord*
Prefaces (Wordsworth) **12**:436
"Prefatory Essay on Lyric Poetry" (Dyer) **129**:93
"Prefatory Letter" (FitzGerald) **153**:218
"Prefatory Letter on Irish Music" (Moore) **110**:181, 186-87
"Prefatory Note" (Pater) **7**:323
Preferment; or, My Uncle the Earl (Gore) **65**:20
Prehistory of the Peoples of Russia (Potocki)
See *Histoire primitive des peuples de la Russie: avec une exposition complete de toutes les nations, locales, nationales et traditionelles, nécessaires a l'intelligence du quartieme livre d'Hérodote*
Der Preis (Hoffmann) **183**:185
"Prekop" (Preseren) **127**:297
"Prekrasnaja Aza" (Leskov) **25**:229, 239, 245
"Prekrasnaja carevna i ščastlivoj karla" (Karamzin) **3**:287
"Preliminary Confessions" (De Quincey) **4**:85
Preliminary Emancipation Proclamation (Lincoln) **18**:216-19, 268-70
"Preliminary Observations" (Bentham) **38**:90
"Preliminary Theses for the Reform of Philosophy" (Feuerbach)
See "Vorläufige Thesen zur Reform der Philosophie"
Preliminary Treatise on Method (Coleridge) **231**:27
Preliminary Word (Dickens) **187**:19; **230**:143
"Prelude" (Allingham) **25**:14
"Prelude" (Blind) **202**:50, 52, 55
"Prelude" (Longfellow) **2**:492; **45**:115, 131, 183
The Prelude (Coleridge) **197**:238
Prelude (Crabbe) **121**:12
Prelude (Cumberland) **167**:200
The Prelude (Wordsworth)
See *The Prelude; or, Growth of a Poets Mind: Autobiographical Poem*
"Prelude in the Theater" (Goethe)
See "Vorspiel auf dem Theater"
The Prelude; or, Growth of a Poet's Mind, An Autobiographical Poem (Wordsworth) **206**:235-36, 240, 242-43, 253-56, 260, 268, 270-71, 275, 277-80, 283, 285, 287, 290-91, 293, 297, 300, 306, 312, 315-17, 319, 321-22, 324-29, 336-37, 341-42
The Prelude; or, Growth of a Poets Mind: Autobiographical Poem (Wordsworth) **12**:415, 419-20, 425, 429, 431, 433, 435-37, 442, 444-49, 453, 458-61, 465-66, 468, 471-73; **38**:355-71, 373-83, 385, 387-88, 390-96, 398-408, 411-13, 415-18, 420-24, 426; **111**:213, 233, 237, 245, 251, 254, 257-61, 263, 266, 273, 290, 314, 322, 332, 345-47, 350; **166**:205-6, 215-17, 230, 241, 248, 253, 255, 258-63, 267-68, 270-71, 280, 285-87, 290-93, 296, 298, 307-0
"Prelude to the Voices of the Night" (Longfellow) **2**:472
"Les préludes" (Lamartine) **11**:245, 248, 270
Préludes (Liszt) **199**:320, 329
Preludes (Pavlova)
See *Les préludes*
Les préludes (Pavlova) **138**:30
"Préludes autobiographiques" (Laforgue) **53**:289; **221**:40, 58, 83-85, 88-90, 93
"Preludes to a Penny Reading" (Ingelow) **39**:258, 264
"The Premature Burial" (Poe) **16**:308-09; **117**:322; **211**:251, 315-16
"Le Premier Chagrin d'un enfant" (Desbordes-Valmore) **97**:29
"Le premier rayon de mai" (Gautier) **1**:348
"Le premier regret" (Lamartine) **11**:255, 270, 278, 280
"Première soirèe" (Rimbaud) **4**:471, 485; **35**:289
Les premières amours; ou, Les souvenirs d'enfance (Scribe) **16**:387
"Les premières communions" (Rimbaud) **4**:454-55, 474
Les Premières Communions (Laforgue) **53**:256
Premières poésies (Leconte de Lisle) **29**:234
"Premoère consultation" (Vigny) **7**:475
"Premonition" (Whitman) **4**:603
"Premudryi piskar" (Saltykov) **16**:374
Pre-Revolutionary France (Taine)
See *L'ancien régime*
Presage and Presence (Eichendorff)
See *Ahnung und Gegenwart*
"The Presence" (Very) **9**:381, 384
"The Present Age" (Emerson) **98**:65
The Present Age (Kierkegaard)
See *En literair Anmeldelse. To Tidsaldre*
"The Present Aspect of the Anti-Slavery Enterprise" (Parker) **186**:173
"The Present Aspect of the Church" (Gladstone) **213**:112, 120
"The Present Condition of Organic Nature" (Huxley) **67**:59

"The Present Crisis" (Lowell) **2**:506; **90**:215, 219, 221
"The Present Crisis in American Affairs" (Parker) **186**:173
"The Present Day" (Krasiński) **4**:305
A Present for Young Ladies (Rowson) **69**:115-17, 150; **182**:252, 254, 256-57, 259, 261, 355
Present Position (Newman)
See *Lectures on the Present Position of Catholics in England: Addressed to the Brothers of the Oratory*
Present Position of Catholics (Newman)
See *Lectures on the Present Position of Catholics in England: Addressed to the Brothers of the Oratory*
Present Positions of Catholics (Newman)
See *Lectures on the Present Position of Catholics in England: Addressed to the Brothers of the Oratory*
"The present revolution in Spain" (Martínez de la Rosa)
See "La revolución actual en España"
"A Presentiment" (Bryant) **46**:47
"Presentiment—is that long Shadow" (Dickinson) **171**:139
"Presentiment—Is That Long Shadow—On the Lawn" (Dickinson) **21**:59
"President is President" (Lincoln) **201**:154
"Le Président mystifié" (Sade) **47**:313
Presidentens döttar (Bremer) **11**:17-18, 20, 30, 34-35
"The Presidential Question: Speech in the United States House of Representatives, July 27, 1848" (Lincoln) **201**:160
The President's Daughter: A Narrative of a Governess (Bremer)
See *Presidentens döttar*
El presidio político en Cuba (Martí) **63**:87, 102, 157-8
Le Pressoir (Sand) **42**:309
Prestuplenie i nakazanie (Dostoevsky) **2**:157, 159, 161-62, 167, 172, 175, 180-81, 184, 186, 188, 195-96, 203; **7**:69-116; **21**:90, 94, 100, 109, 113, 140, 144, 146; **33**:161, 165, 176-77, 194-94, 203, 207, 212, 227, 233; **43**:92, 122, 130, 144, 149, 162, 167; **119**:73, 76-7, 82, 85, 98, 132, 135, 147, 150, 154-55; **167**:211-358; **202**:74, 111-12, 118
Prestupleniye i nakazaniye (Dostoevsky)
See *Prestuplenie i nakazanie*
Pretended Infidelity (Griboedov)
See *Svoia sem'ia, ili Zamuzhniaia nevesta*
The Pretender Dmitry and Vasily Shuysky (Ostrovsky)
See *Dmitry Samozvanets i Vasily Shuysky*
"Pretensions of Commerce" (Herder) **186**:11
"Preternatural Beings" (Montagu) **7**:251
Le Prêtre de Némi (Renan) **26**:388, 408
Un prêtre marié (Barbey d'Aurevilly) **1**:70, 72, 77; **213**:5, 22, 29, 33-37, 48, 56, 66-67, 91
"Pretty Dick" (Clarke) **19**:231, 233, 235
Pretty Green Bird (Gozzi)
See *L'augellin belverde*
Pretty Lessons in Verse for Good Children (Coleridge) **31**:61-2, 70-1
The Pretty Maid of the Mill (Muller)
See *Die schöne Müllerin*
Pretty Mrs. Gaston (Cooke) **5**:130
Preussen und die Konstitutionen (Eichendorff) **8**:220
Preussens ältere Geschichte (Kotzebue) **25**:140
Die preussische Militärfrage und die deutsche Arbeiterpartei (Engels) **85**:83
Le Prévaricateur (Sade) **47**:361-62
The Previous Question between Mr. Andrews Norton and His Alumni, Moved and Handled in a Letter to Those Gentlemen (Parker) **186**:139, 164
"The Price of Blood" (Jones) **222**:158
"Pride" (Coleridge) **90**:9
Pride and Overthrow (Smolenskin) **30**:189-90
"Pride and Prejudice" (Jones) **222**:160
Pride and Prejudice (Austen) **1**:30, 32-4, 36-8, 40, 44-7, 50-2, 56-61, 63-4, 66; **13**:51-112; **19**:2, 4-8, 14, 17, 32, 42, 55-6, 58, 66-7; **33**:28, 44, 58, 62, 64, 66, 69, 72, 76, 78, 86, 89-90, 92, 96; **51**:12, 15, 33, 35, 55; **81**:18, 48, 69, 77-9, 81-5; **95**:4, 9-11, 14, 16-8, 21, 25, 39, 45, 55-6, 58, 63, 73, 80, 83-4, 86; **119**:11, 14, 16-18, 21, 24-5, 27-8, 35-40; **222**:26, 30, 38, 47, 50, 52, 83, 108
"The Pride of the Village" (Irving) **19**:327, 332, 334, 345-47
"La prière" (Lamartine) **11**:245, 269
Prière du Matin (Comte) **54**:213
"Prière du matin" (Verlaine) **230**:167
Prière du Soir (Comte) **54**:213
"La Prière d'une mère" (Mallarmé) **41**:290
"La Prière pour Tous" (Bello) **131**:93
"La prière pour tous" (Hugo) **21**:224
"Prière suprême" (Laforgue) **221**:83
Prière sur l'acropole (Renan) **26**:408, 414, 419
Prières (Comte) **54**:213
The Priest (Michelet) **31**:241
"Die Priesterinnen der Sonne" (Schiller) **39**:388
The Priestly Consecration (Tegner) **2**:613
"The Priest's Funeral" (Carleton) **3**:88, 92
Priests of Parnassus (Pushkin) **3**:423
"Priest's Reshuffle and Parish Whims. Morals and Pictures from the History of the Church" ("Popovskaya chiekharda i prikhodskaya prikhomso ft. TSierkovno-ismorichieskiie nravy i karminy") (Leskov) **174**:129
"Priglashenie k obedu" (Derzhavin) **215**:6, 30-32
"Prigover" (Dostoevsky) **33**:179-80
The Prime Minister (Trollope) **6**:461, 463, 466, 471, 473, 495, 500, 504, 507-08, 510; **33**:417, 421-22, 424; **101**:253, 268, 274, 290, 307, 310; **215**:212, 290-91, 293, 295, 302-4, 306, 319-22, 327
Primechaniia (Derzhavin) **215**:71
"El primer beso" (Isaacs) **70**:305
El primer loco (Castro) **3**:107
Primer of Words (Whitman) **81**:287
"Primera representación de la comedia refundida y puesta en cuatro actos titulada Juez y reo de su causa o Don Jaime el Justiciero" (Larra) **130**:195
"Primety" (Baratynsky) **103**:13, 16-22
"Primeval Man" (Peabody) **169**:157
"The Primose" (Allingham) **25**:14
"The Primrose" (Clare) **9**:72
"The Primrose" (Webster) **230**:309
"Primrose Gold" (Jefferies)
See "Primrose Gold in Our Villages"
"Primrose Gold in Our Villages" (Jefferies) **47**:143
Prince (Alfieri)
See *Del principe e delle lettere*
"Prince Adeb" (Boker) **125**:34
"Prince Ahmed; or, The Pilgrim of Love" (Irving) **2**:372
"Prince Aldfrid's Itinerary through Ireland" (Mangan) **27**:283
The Prince and Letters (Alfieri)
See *Del principe e delle lettere*
"The Prince and the Detective" (Stevenson)
See "The Adventure of Prince Florizel and a Detective"
"Prince Athanase" (Shelley) **18**:327, 340, 344
"Prince Charming of the Lime Tree" (Eminescu)
See "Prince Charming of the Linden Tree"
"Prince Charming of the Linden Tree" (Eminescu) **33**:249
"Prince Charming the Tear-Born" (Eminescu) **33**:247
Prince Csaba (Arany) **34**:8, 11
"Un Prince de la Bohème" (Balzac) **153**:55, 149, 153
Une prince de la Bohème (Balzac) **5**:75
"Le prince de Sots" (Nerval) **1**:482-83; **67**:322, 324
Prince Deukalion (Taylor) **89**:320-24, 343, 349
Prince Dorus; or, Flattery Put out of Countenance (Lamb) **10**:418
Prince Frederick of Homburg (Kleist)
See *Prinz Friedrich von Homburg: Ein Schauspiel*
"Prince Hamlet of Shehrigov Province" (Turgenev)
See "Gamlet ščigrovskogo uezda"
Prince Hohenstiel-Schwangau (Browning) **19**:136
Prince Michael Twerski (Slowacki) **15**:378
"Prince mort en soldat" (Verlaine) **2**:632
"A Prince of Court-Painters: Extracts from an Old French Journal" (Pater) **7**:298, 324; **90**:264, 288, 340-41, 344
The Prince of Darkness (Southworth) **26**:434
The Prince of Happy Land (Planché) **42**:292, 302
The Prince of Homburg (Kleist)
See *Prinz Friedrich von Homburg*
The Prince of Tunis (Mackenzie) **41**:184, 208-10, 212, 217
The Prince of Viana (Gómez de Avellaneda) **111**:12
Prince Otto (Stevenson) **5**:397-99, 402-03, 408-09, 433; **193**:210, 212, 216, 218, 222, 250, 274, 279, 281-82, 313, 318, 320-21
"Prince Papillon" (Crawford) **127**:181-84, 186, 189
"The Prince Shalikov" (Pushkin) **83**:272
"The Prince Who Arrived Too Late" (Rossetti) **186**:265
Prince Zerbino in Search of Good Taste (Tieck)
See *Prinz Zerbino; oder, Die Reise nach dem guten Geschmack*
"The Prince's Day" (Moore) **110**:184
The Prince's Justice (Eminescu) **33**:266
"The Prince's Progress" (Rossetti) **2**:558, 560, 562-3, 565-6, 568, 570-1, 573, 575; **50**:264, 266, 288, 291-3, 321, 324; **66**:304, 328, 356; **186**:246, 248, 250, 265, 288, 304, 326-30, 332
The Prince's Progress, and Other Poems (Rossetti) **2**:556, 563, 574; **50**:271, 287; **66**:349; **186**:229, 265-67, 286-91, 303
"The Princess" (Shevchenko)
See "Kniazhna"
The Princess (Shevchenko)
See *Kniazhna*
The Princess: A Medley (Tennyson) **30**:213, 219, 233, 237-38, 242, 268, 275-77, 279-80, 282-84; **65**:230-31, 234, 248, 263, 274, 324, 359-60, 362, 367-70, 373-5; **115**:237, 240, 255; **202**:174-75, 178, 181, 191, 193-202, 268-69, 271-76, 330-31, 333, 335
"The Princess and the Pea" (Andersen)
See "Prindsessen paa Ærten"
Princess Brambilla (Hoffmann)
See *Prinzessin Brambilla: Ein Capriccio nach Jakob Callot*
Princess Ligovskaya (Lermontov) **47**:162-63, 225-26; **126**:156-57
"The Princess Marie" (Barrett Browning) **61**:75
"Princess Mary" (Lermontov) **5**:291, 293, 295, 297-98, 301-03; **126**:153-54, 174, 195-99, 202-3, 216
Princess of Bagdad (Dumas)
See *La princesse de Bagdad*
The Princess of Parma (Cumberland) **167**:155, 201
"The Princess on the Pea" (Andersen)
See "The Princess and the Pea"
The Princess; or, The Beguine (Morgan) **29**:396
"Princess Sabbath" (Heine) **4**:253
La princesse de Bagdad (Dumas) **9**:223, 230, 232, 243, 245
La Princesse de Clermont (Genlis) **166**:65

La princesse Georges (Dumas) **9**:225, 228, 230, 241-42, 246, 250
Principes de politique applicables à tous les gouvernements représentatifs (Constant) **182**:99-100, 132, 134-36, 147, 189, 191, 210-12, 217, 219, 232
Principios del derecho de gentes (Bello) **131**:93-94, 96-97, 116, 124
Principle in Art (Patmore) **9**:349
"Principles and Methods of Intellectual Instruction Exhibited in the Exercises of Young Children" (Alcott) **167**:46-47
Principles of Church Reform (Arnold) **18**:8, 19, 46, 51, 55
"Principles of Communism" (Engels) **85**:127-28
Principles of Communism (Engels) **85**:32-34, 157
"Principles of Criticism" (Symonds) **34**:336
"Principles of General Criticism" (Coleridge) **231**:27
Principles of International Law (Bello)
See *Principios del derecho de gentes*
Principles of International Law (Bentham) **38**:67
The Principles of Morals and Legislation (Bentham)
See *Introduction to the Principles of Morals and Legislation*
Principles of Political Economy, with Some of Their Applications to Social Philosophy (Mill) **11**:334-37, 350-51, 366, 375, 383; **58**:330, 351, 375, 378; **179**:209, 211, 227, 295, 354; **223**:93, 124
Principles of Politics (Constant)
See *Principes de politique applicables à tous les gouvernements représentatifs*
Principles of Revolution (Bakunin) **25**:56
The Principles of Success in Literature (Lewes) **25**:289, 293, 296-97, 299-301, 304, 308, 316, 323, 325; **215**:107, 118, 164, 167-69
Principles of the Philosophy of Law (Hegel) **46**:119, 124, 130, 186
Principles of the Philosophy of the Future (Feuerbach)
See *Grundsätze der Philosophie der Zukunft*
"Prindsessen paa Ærten" (Andersen) **7**:23, 28, 34; **79**:23-24, 50, 64-65, 80-81; **214**:54, 74
"The Pringle Family" (Galt) **110**:84
"Printemps" (Verlaine) **230**:153-59
"The Printing Press" (Cranch) **115**:42
"Prints" (Verlaine)
See "Les Estampes"
Prinz Friedrich von Homburg (Kleist) **2**:437-42, 444, 447, 450, 453-54, 458-59, 463-66; **37**:217, 220, 225, 227-28, 231-33, 237-38, 241, 243-44, 254-55, 263, 267, 272-74; **222**:204, 233-34, 256-57, 285, 287, 291
"Prinz Louis Ferdinand" (Fontane) **26**:243
Prinz Zerbino; oder, Die Reise nach dem guten Geschmack (Tieck) **5**:517, 521, 524, 529-30
Prinzessin Blandina: ein romantisches Spiel in drei Aufzügen (Hoffmann) **183**:176, 185, 188
Prinzessin Brambilla (Hoffmann)
See *Prinzessin Brambilla: Ein Capriccio nach Jakob Callot*
Prinzessin Brambilla: Ein Capriccio nach Jakob Callot (Hoffmann) **2**:357, 359, 361-62; **183**:170, 173-75, 187-88, 201, 209, 211-12, 214, 231
"Prinzessin Sabbat" (Heine) **147**:229, 231
"Prišla je jesenka noč" (Preseren) **127**:319
"The Prison" (Very) **9**:378
"La Prison" (Vigny) **102**:335, 340, 367
"Prison Amusements" (Clare) **86**:162
Prison and Exile (Herzen) **61**:88
"Prison Bars" (Jones) **222**:176
"The Prison Door" (Hawthorne) **2**:331
"Prison Fancies" (Jones) **222**:175
"The Prisoner" (Barrett Browning) **1**:115; **61**:5
"The Prisoner" (Brontë)
See "Julian M. and A. G. Rochelle"
"The Prisoner" (Pushkin)
See "Uznik"
The Prisoner of Chillon, and Other Poems (Byron) **2**:64, 76, 99; **12**:139; **109**:69, 82
"The Prisoner of the Caucasus" (Lermontov) **126**:167
The Prisoner of the Caucasus (Pushkin)
See *Kavkazsky plennik*
"Prisoner of War" (Jerrold) **2**:395, 402-03
"The Prisoner to the Slaves" (Jones) **222**:173-74
"Le Prisonnier de guerre" (Desbordes-Valmore) **97**:5
"La prisonnière et le chevalier" (Beranger) **34**:28
"Prisons" (Crabbe) **121**:87-8, 91
"Les Prisons et les prières" (Desbordes-Valmore) **97**:29
Private Galleries (Jameson)
See *Companion to the Most Celebrated Private Galleries of Art in London*
Private History of Peregrinus Proteus, the Philosopher (Wieland)
See *Die Geheime Geschichte des Philosophen Peregrinus Proteus*
The Private Memoirs and Confessions of a Justified Sinner (Hogg) **4**:278, 280-81, 283-87; **109**:188-94, 197-98, 200, 204, 206, 209-10, 217-19, 221, 223, 229-34, 236-39, 242, 252, 255-56, 258-60, 262, 264, 270-72, 274-76, 278-82
The Private Schoolmasters (Grundtvig) **158**:135
Private Thoughts (Silva)
See *Intimidades*
The Privateer (Cumberland) **167**:193
The Privateersman (Marryat) **3**:320
Le prix Martin (Augier) **31**:8, 26
"Priyatnyye vidy, nadezhdy i zhelaniya nyneshego vremeni" (Karamzin) **173**:285
Priznaki vremeni (Saltykov) **16**:351
Prizraki (Turgenev) **37**:443
"Prizraki. Fantaziya" (Turgenev) **21**:399, 415, 420, 431, 441, 451, 453; **122**:241, 243, 266, 364-66, 375
"Pro patria" (Isaacs) **70**:310
"Probability as a Guide of Conduct" (Gladstone) **213**:113
"The Probable Future of Metaphysics" (Hopkins) **189**:89
"The Problem" (Emerson) **1**:285, 296; **38**:187; **98**:180-82
"The Problem" (Timrod) **25**:362, 374
"The Problem" (Whittier) **59**:366
A Problem in Greek Ethics (Symonds) **34**:343, 353
A Problem in Modern Ethics (Symonds) **34**:343, 353, 374
The Problems of Life and Mind (Lewes) **25**:282-83, 288-89, 293, 295-97, 304, 312-15, 318-19; **215**:86, 88, 93, 99, 106, 122, 124, 140, 147-48, 150-51, 159, 165-68, 181, 184
"Problesk" (Tyutchev) **34**:389, 395, 398-99
"Le Procès à la Révolution" (Hugo) **161**:180
"The Procession of Life" (Hawthorne) **2**:305, 309
"Processional of Creation" (Rossetti) **2**:566
"Proclamation" (Trumbull)
See "By Thomas Gage...A Proclamation"
"Proclamation of a National Fast Day" (Lincoln) **201**:168
"Proclamation of Emancipation by the President of the United States, January 1st, 1863" (Lincoln) **201**:168, 211, 213, 228
"Procrastination" (Crabbe) **26**:93, 109, 120, 122, 131-32, 135-36, 151; **121**:43
La pródiga (Alarcon) **1**:12-13; **219**:3-4, 19-20
"The Prodigal Son" (Hogg) **109**:281
The Prodigal Son (Becque)
See *L'enfant prodigue*
The Prodigious Adventures of Tartarin of Tarascon (Daudet)
See *Aventures prodigieuses de Tartarin de Tarascon*
"A Product of Nature" (Leskov)
See "Produkt prirody"
"Produkt prirody" (Leskov) **174**:37, 53
"Proem" (Patmore) **9**:334
"Proem" (Thomson) **18**:403, 415, 417, 429
"Proem" (Whittier) **8**:515, 519-21, 525; **59**:351, 354, 364-5
"Proem Dedicatory, An Epistle from Mount Tmolus to Richard Henry Stoddard" (Taylor) **89**:305, 307, 359
"Proem to Genesis" (Gladstone) **213**:121
Professional Education (Edgeworth) **1**:267; **51**:93
"Professions" (Thackeray) **43**:381
The Professor (Thackeray) **5**:470
The Professor: A Tale (Brontë) **3**:49-51, 54, 56, 60, 64, 68-72, 74-76, 78-79; **8**:54, 72, 75; **33**:117-19; **58**:187-89, 191, 194-97, 199, 208, 222, 224, 227; **105**:1-87; **155**:158, 163-64, 166, 177-78, 217, 225, 227; **217**:21, 25, 118, 125, 129-31, 136-38; **229**:28-29, 31, 34, 157, 161, 174, 180, 183
"The Professor and the Flea" (Andersen) **79**:73-75
The Professor at the Breakfast-Table (Holmes) **14**:102, 105-06, 110, 113-15, 120, 123-24, 132-33, 137, 144, 146; **81**:98-104
"Professor Child's Appeal" (Child) **173**:233
"The Professor's Wife" (Auerbach)
See "Die Frau Professorin"
A Profitable Position (Ostrovsky)
See *Dokhodnoye mesto*
"De profundis" (Barrett Browning) **16**:135; **170**:119
"De Profundis" (Tennyson) **30**:254, 270-72; **65**:235, 265, 272; **115**:341
"De Profundis clamavi" (Baudelaire) **6**:105; **55**:10
"DE PROFUNDIS CLAMAVI" (Coleridge) **197**:215
"Progress" (Arnold) **218**:121
Progress (Robertson) **35**:335, 352, 362-66, 369
Progress and Prejudice (Gore) **65**:29, 32
"The Progress and Prospects of Society" (Jones) **222**:158
"Progress in Maine" (Neal) **161**:337
"Progress in the World of Plants and Animals" (Pisarev) **25**:330
"The Progress of Art" (Hazlitt) **29**:162
"Progress of Culture" (Emerson) **98**:171
The Progress of Dulness (Trumbull) **30**:338, 340, 345, 347, 349-50, 352-53, 360-61, 363, 373-78, 381-82
The Progress of Dulness, Part First: or, The Rare Adventures of Tom Brainless (Trumbull) **30**:368, 370, 376
The Progress of Dulness, Part Second: or, An Essay on the Life and Character of Dick Hairbrain of Finical Memory (Trumbull) **30**:371, 373
The Progress of Dulness, Part Third, and Last: Sometimes Called The Progress of Coquetry; or The Adventures of Miss Harriet Simper (Trumbull) **30**:373
"The Progress of Error" (Cowper) **8**:110; **94**:9, 11-12, 14, 16, 29, 51, 110-12, 117
The Progress of Liberty (Robinson) **142**:170
"The Progress of Mankind" (Parker) **186**:136-37
"Progress of Painting" (Hunt) **1**:406
Progress of Religious Ideas (Child) **6**:202-03; **73**:51, 56, 62, 70, 82, 87
"The Progress of Rhyme" (Clare) **9**:100; **86**:94, 112
The Progress of Romance, through Times, Countries, and Manners (Reeve) **19**:411-12, 415, 418
"The Progress of Science 1837-1887" (Huxley) **67**:64, 103, 105

"Progress of Social Reform on the Continent" (Engels) **85**:122
"Progress of Thought in Our Time" (Symonds) **34**:371
"Progress of Unbelief" (Newman) **38**:343
"The Progressive Realism of American Fiction" (Boyesen) **135**:22
"Un projet de mon âge mûr" (Verlaine) **230**:161
Projet d'une école rurale pour l'education des filles (Genlis) **166**:31
Projets inédits (Flaubert)
See *Notes inédites de Flaubert*
"Der Prokurator" (Goethe) **4**:197
"Prolegomena" (Huxley) **67**:29, 62, 90, 92, 99, 102-03, 108, 110-11
Prolegomena (Kant) **27**:201, 225
"Prolog" (Heine) **54**:331, 336
"Prolog an deutsche Söhne und Töchter" (Werner) **189**:346-49, 351-52
"Prolog im Himmel" (Goethe) **4**:186, 202, 205; **154**:228-29, 232, 241-42, 247-48, 259, 261, 263-64, 301, 307, 312, 319, 325-26, 328, 339-40
"Prólogo" (Bécquer) **106**:85
"Prólogo al poema intitulado 'Bienaventurados los que lloran' de Rivas Frade" (Silva) **114**:317
"Prologue" (Browning) **79**:112-14
"Prologue" (Cooke) **5**:123
"Prologue" (Hugo) **161**:175
"Prologue" (Lamartine) **11**:287, 289
"Prologue" (Sheridan) **5**:371, 378
"Prologue" (Tennyson) **65**:368
"Prologue" (Verlaine) **2**:631; **230**:162, 192, 197
"Prologue" (Werner)
See "Prolog an deutsche Söhne und Töchter"
Prologue (Rimbaud) **227**:208, 211
"Prologue in Heaven" (Goethe)
See "Prolog im Himmel"
"Prologue Intended for a Dramatic Piece of King Edward the Fourth" (Blake) **13**:239
"Prologue supprimé à un livre d'Invectives" (Verlaine) **2**:621; **51**:351; **230**:166, 174
"Prologue to Controverted Questions" (Huxley) **67**:62, 64, 66, 70-1, 96
"Prologue to King John" (Blake) **13**:181
"Prologue to Science and Christian Tradition" (Huxley) **67**:28
"Prologue to the Play of Henry the Eighth, Spoken by a Warrington Student in hs Morning Gown" (Barbauld) **185**:32
"Prologue—Delivered at a Greek Benefit, in Baltimore,—1823" (Pinkney) **31**:276
"Prologues to the Poem Entitled 'Blessed Are Those Who Cry' by Rivas Frade" (Silva)
See "Prólogo al poema intitulado 'Bienaventurados los que lloran' de Rivas Frade"
"Promenade" (Maupassant) **83**:228
Promenade autour d'un village (Sand) **42**:312
"Promenade sentimentale" (Verlaine) **230**:163
Promenades dans Rome (Stendhal) **23**:352, 410; **46**:269; **178**:221
"La promesa" (Bécquer) **106**:97, 99, 130, 135-36
"Les promesses d'un visage" (Baudelaire) **29**:77
I promessi sposi (Manzoni) **29**:253-54, 261, 263-70, 272, 275-87, 289-94, 296, 298-300, 302-11; **98**:197-98, 201, 204, 213, 216, 218-20, 228, 234-40, 249-51, 256, 258-59, 265, 267, 269-77, 283-87, 289-90
"Prometeo" (Casal) **131**:223, 228, 236
"Prometheus" (Goethe) **4**:163, 199; **34**:98
"Prometheus" (Lowell) **2**:503; **90**:195, 219, 221
"Prometheus" (Schlegel) **15**:223
Prometheus (Liszt) **199**:330
Prometheus Bound (Webster) **230**:225, 241
Prometheus Bound, and Miscellaneous Poems (Barrett Browning) **66**:44, 47
Prometheus, the Fire-Bringer: A Drama in Verse (Horne) **127**:260, 268-69
Prometheus Unbound (Shelley) **18**:317, 319, 331-32, 334-38, 340, 343-45, 349, 352, 355, 361-65, 367-69, 374, 376-77, 380-83; **93**:256, 260-64, 267, 269-71, 278, 294, 305-06, 310-11, 313, 315, 327, 330, 343-44, 351-52; **143**:169, 174, 182-83, 196-98, 200-202, 206, 208-9, 212, 215-16, 221-26, 238-41, 247, 265-66, 270-71, 286-87, 293, 316; **175**:184-370
Prometheus Unbound: A Lyrical Drama in Four Acts, with Other Poems (Shelley)
See *Prometheus Unbound*
Promethidion (Norwid) **17**:367-69, 371-72, 375, 378, 380, 384-86
"The Promise" (Darley) **2**:133
The Promise of May (Tennyson) **30**:265-66; **202**:290
"The Promise of Sleep" (Levy) **59**:94
"Promontoire" (Rimbaud) **35**:269, 322; **227**:204, 206, 210, 242-43, 271, 296, 309-10
"Promontory" (Rimbaud)
See "Promontoire"
The Prompter; or, A Commentary on Common Sayings and Subjects, Which Are Full of Common Sense, the Best Sense in the World . . . (Webster) **30**:421-24
"Pronunciation" (De Quincey) **198**:93, 96-97
"Propagation of the Species, Christianity wants to bar the way" (Kierkegaard) **78**:225
"Propavšaja gramotax" (Gogol) **5**:224-25; **162**:62, 92, 104
"A Proper Trewe Idyll of Camelot" (Field) **3**:210-11
"Property" (Madison) **126**:311, 327-29
Property (Alencar)
See *A Propriedade*
Property (Sacher-Masoch) **31**:287, 291, 294-95
"Properzia Rossi" (Hemans) **71**:296
"Prophecy" (Petofi)
See "Jövendöles"
Prophecy from the Past. Benjamin Constant on Conquest and Usurpation (Constant)
See *De l'esprit de conquête et de l'usurpation dans leurs rapports avec la civilisation européenne*
The Prophecy of Capys (Macaulay) **42**:112
Prophecy of Dante (Byron) **12**:106
"The Prophecy of King Tammany" (Freneau) **111**:166
"The Prophecy of Samuel Sewall" (Whittier) **59**:375
"The Prophecy of St. Oran" (Blind) **202**:13, 16, 26, 30, 51
"The Prophecy—To the Memory of the Brave Americans under General Greene, Who Fell in the Action of September 8, 1781" (Freneau) **1**:315, 323; **111**:140-41
"The Prophet" (Pushkin)
See "Prorok"
"The Prophet" (Shevchenko)
See "Prorok"
The Prophet (Taylor) **89**:315, 349
"The Prophet Unveiled" (Cranch) **115**:39, 41
Le prophète (Scribe) **16**:390, 401, 408
"The Prophetic Pictures" (Hawthorne) **2**:291, 305; **39**:186; **95**:105, 110
Prophetical Office (Newman)
See *Lectures on the Prophetical Office of the Church*
"The Prophet's Chamber" (Parton) **86**:347, 372
"The Prophet's Dream" (Chivers) **49**:47, 69
"Prophets Who Cannot Sing" (Patmore) **9**:360
"Propitiatory Lament to the Unconscious" (Laforgue)
See "Complainte propitiatoire à l'inconscient"
A Proposal for Putting Reform to the Vote Throughout the Kingdom (Shelley) **175**:325-26
Proposals (Cowper) **94**:80-5
"Proposals for the Speedy Extinction of Evil and Misery" (Thomson) **18**:393, 405, 425-27
Propria Quae Maribus (Reade) **74**:256
A Propriedade (Alencar) **157**:5
"Proprietors of the Olden Time" (Gogol)
See "Starosvetskie Pomeščiki"
"Prorok" (Pushkin) **3**:438, 442-43; **83**:255
"Prorok" (Shevchenko) **54**:389
"Pros and Cons" (Rossetti) **186**:233
Prosas (Casal) **131**:239-45, 247-53, 256, 258-59, 262-66
"Prosas breves" (Silva) **114**:300
"Proščaj, nemytaja Rossija" (Lermontov) **126**:190-91, 193
"Proscenia" (Shevchenko)
See "Prycynna"
Prose (Mallarmé) **210**:195
"Prose Fragments" (Dickinson) **171**:167
The Prose of John Clare (Clare) **86**:96, 104, 129
The Prose of Philip Freneau (Freneau) **111**:160, 162
Prose Poems (Baudelaire)
See *Le spleen de Paris, petits poèmes en prose*
Prose Poems (Turgenev)
See *Stikhotvoreniya v proze*
Prose Poems from Les illuminations of Arthur Rimbaud (Rimbaud)
See *Les illuminations*
"Prose pour des esseintes" (Mallarmé) **4**:376-77, 389-90; **41**:259, 279, 289, 294; **210**:170, 218-20
Prose Tales (Desbordes-Valmore)
See *Contes en prose*
Prose Works (Wordsworth)
See *The Prose Works of William Wordsworth*
Prose Works 1892 (Whitman) **205**:206, 255, 257-58, 260, 266-67
The Prose Works of William Wordsworth (Wordsworth) **38**:425; **111**:311, 315, 336-42, 363-64, 366-70; **166**:305-6, 309-10, 319-20, 335, 349, 351
The Prose Writings of James Clarence Mangan (Mangan) **27**:291-92
Prose Writings of William Cullen Bryant (Bryant) **46**:10-12, 38
"Proserpina" (Stagnelius) **61**:248
Proserpine (Pushkin) **3**:423
Proserpine (Shelley) **14**:268-69, 272
"Proses évangéliques" (Rimbaud) **227**:323
"Proshchanie s Kaspiem" (Bestuzhev) **131**:160
"Proshlo spolna . . ." (Pavlova) **138**:20
"Prošnja" (Preseren) **127**:298
"The Prospect" (Dwight) **13**:270, 272, 276, 278
"The Prospect of Efficient Patronage to the Arts from Princess Charlotte" (Haydon) **146**:141
The Prospect of Peace (Barlow) **223**:59-60
"A Prospective Meeting" (Rossetti) **50**:295
Prospecto de un establecimiento de educación para señoritas (Sarmiento) **123**:354
"Prospects" (Thoreau) **7**:396
Prospects on the Rubicon (Paine) **62**:266, 334
"Prospectus" (Wordsworth) **166**:215, 281-82, 286
Prospectus (Grundtvig) **158**:167
Prospectus for an Educational Establishment for Young Ladies (Sarmiento)
See *Prospecto de un establecimiento de educación para señoritas*
"Prospectus of a History of English Philosophy" (Hazlitt) **82**:108
Prospectus to the Excursion (Wordsworth)
See *The Excursion, Being a Portion of "The Recluse"*
Prosper Mérimée's Letters to an Incognita (Mérimée)
See *Lettres à une inconnue*

Les Prosperites du vice (Sade)
See *Juliette; ou, Les prospérités du vice*
"Prospice" (Browning) **19**:89, 110
A Protégée of the Mistress (Ostrovsky)
See *Vospitannitsa*
"Protest against the Ballot" (Wordsworth) **12**:413
"The Protestant" (Tonna) **135**:204, 211
"Protestantism" (Newman) **38**:343
Protivorechiya (Saltykov) **16**:368
"Proto-Leaf" (Whitman) **205**:161, 200, 204, 225, 256
"Protus" (Browning) **19**:117
"Proud King" (Morris) **4**:417, 442
"Proud Maisie" (Scott) **15**:294, 318
"Proud Music of the Storm" (Whitman) **4**:579, 582; **205**:196, 204, 208, 226
"The Proud Pedestrian" (Holmes) **14**:100
Proverb Stories (Alcott) **58**:47
Proverbes (Musset) **7**:258, 260
"Proverbs of Hell" (Blake) **37**:27, 55; **201**:34, 39
"Providence" (Parker) **186**:128
"La providence à l'homme" (Lamartine) **11**:278
"Providence and the Guitar" (Stevenson) **5**:394; **193**:218, 274, 276-77, 280, 282
"Providential Design" (Harpur) **114**:148
"Provinces and Relations of the Arts" (Symonds) **34**:336
"The Provincial Governor" (Runeberg)
See "Landshövdingen"
A Provincial Lady (Turgenev)
See *Provintsialka*
"Provincial Tales" (Hawthorne) **158**:246-47, 251
Provintsialka (Turgenev) **21**:428
The Provost (Galt) **1**:329, 331-35, 337; **110**:79, 81, 84-6, 93-4, 98, 101
"Proyecto" (Heredia) **209**:130
Der Prozes um des Esels Schatten (Wieland)
See *Der Prozess um des Esels Schatten*
Der Prozess um des Esels Schatten (Wieland) **177**:261, 317
"Prudence" (Emerson) **38**:152
"Prudence" (Larcom) **179**:167
"Les prunes" (Daudet) **1**:246
"Prussian Vase" (Edgeworth) **1**:255; **51**:87, 89
Prvi srpski bukvar (Karadzic) **115**:106
"Prycynna" (Shevchenko) **54**:371, 375
Przedświt (Krasiński) **4**:301-08, 310-11, 313, 318-19
"Przyjaciele" (Krasicki) **8**:403
"Psalm cxxxvii" (Halleck) **47**:57
"A Psalm for the Conventicle" (Kendall) **12**:200
"Psalm of Faith" (Krasiński) **4**:303
"Psalm of Good Will" (Krasiński) **4**:303-04, 307, 311
"Psalm of Grief" (Krasiński) **4**:307
"Psalm of Hope" (Krasiński) **4**:303
"A Psalm of Life" (Hayne) **94**:144
"A Psalm of Life" (Longfellow) **2**:471, 483, 493, 498; **45**:112, 115-16, 124-25, 127, 134, 139, 140-41, 144, 148, 152, 156-58, 164-65, 179, 184; **103**:285, 292-93, 295-96, 305-06
"The Psalm of Life" (Whittier) **8**:525
"Psalm of Love" (Krasiński) **4**:303, 307
"Psalm of the West" (Lanier) **6**:238, 248-49, 254, 256-60, 269; **118**:210-11, 215, 237-38, 275
"The Psalmist's Repenting" (Keble) **87**:177
"The Psalms of David" (Shevchenko)
See "Psalmy Davydovi"
"Psalmy Davydovi" (Shevchenko) **54**:383-4
"Psaumes de l'ame" (Lamartine) **11**:272
"Psicopatía" (Silva) **114**:300, 302-3, 316
Psicopatía (Silva) **114**:274
"Psicoterapéutica" (Silva) **114**:263
"Psovaja oxota" (Nekrasov) **11**:412
"Psyche" (Andersen)
See "Psychen"
"Psyche" (Keats)
See "Ode to Psyche"
Psyche (Alcott) **167**:27, 32, 48, 52-53, 97-100
Psyche (Storm) **1**:542
Psyche an Evangele (Alcott) **167**:52-53
"Psyche at School" (Larcom) **179**:178
"Psyche before the Tribunal of Venus" (Willis) **194**:297
"Psyche Flagellated" (Meyer)
See "Die gegeisselte Psyche"
"Psyche Odes" (Patmore) **9**:349, 352, 357, 360, 362-66
Psyche or The Breath of Childhood (Alcott) **167**:32, 52
"Psychen" (Andersen) **7**:37; **79**:58, 60, 84, 89
"Psyche's Discontent" (Patmore) **9**:339, 360, 364
Psychology (Schleiermacher) **107**:285
"Der Psychometer" (Schumann) **143**:120, 128
Public Address (Blake) **57**:79
"A Public Dinner" (Hood) **16**:236
Public Galleries (Jameson)
See *A Handbook to the Public Galleries of Art in and near London*
"The Public Life of Mr. Tulrumble, Mayor of Mudfog" (Dickens) **203**:189-90
"Public Opinion" (D'Israeli) **217**:299, 301
"Public Opinion" (Madison) **126**:325
"Publication Is the Auction" (Dickinson) **21**:56; **77**:71
"Publication is the Auction of the Mind" (Dickinson) **171**:139
"Publications pour le piano (Kroll, Reinecke)" (Liszt) **199**:343
"Publius to Pollia" (Freneau) **111**:105
La pucelle de Belleville (Kock) **16**:251
Pudding (Barlow)
See *The Hasty-Pudding*
Le puff; ou, Mensonge et vérité (Scribe) **16**:388
Puffery; or, Lie and Truth (Scribe)
See *Le puff; ou, Mensonge et vérité*
"Pugalo" (Leskov) **174**:7
"The Pugsley Papers" (Hood) **16**:206-07
"Puisque l'aube grandit . . ." (Verlaine) **230**:168
Pulcherie (Sand) **2**:589
"Pulvis et Umbra" (Stevenson) **5**:410, 425; **193**:210, 213, 219, 259, 262
"The Pumpkin Freshest" (Smith) **187**:319
El puñal del godo (Zorrilla y Moral) **6**:523, 525
Punch's Complete Letter Writer (Jerrold) **2**:403, 408
Punch's Letters to His Son (Jerrold) **2**:395-96, 399, 402, 408
"Punch's Prize Novelists" (Thackeray) **213**:216
"Punctuality" (Dodgson) **139**:61
"Punin and Baburin" (Turgenev)
See "Punin i Baburin"
"Punin i Baburin" (Turgenev) **21**:416, 437, 441; **122**:241, 243, 245, 264, 266, 342
The Puppet Show: A Tale (More) **141**:233
The Purcell Papers (Le Fanu) **58**:251-3, 255, 302-4
"The Pure Spirit" (Vigny)
See "L'Esprit pur"
Purgatory (Liszt) **199**:308
"Purgłitz" (Macha)
See "Krivoklad"
Les puritaines d'Ecosse (Dumas) **71**:217
The Puritan and His Daughter (Paulding) **2**:527-30
"Puritanism and Drunkenness" (Sarmiento) **123**:276
Puritanism and the Church of England (Arnold) **126**:89-90
"The Puritan's Vision" (Holmes) **14**:101
"Purity and Love" (Newman) **38**:310
"The Purloined Letter" (Poe) **1**:518, 528, 530-31; **16**:293, 295-96, 298, 300-01, 303, 306, 315, 332; **55**:148, 155; **78**:281; **94**:188; **97**:208, 213, 238; **117**:235, 252, 254, 256, 290; **211**:253, 256, 268, 270, 280, 291-96
"The Purple Flower of the Heather" (Thomson) **18**:407
"The Purple Jar" (Edgeworth) **1**:267; **51**:110-11, 116
"Purport" (Whitman) **31**:435
"The Pursuits of Happiness" (Mackenzie) **41**:184
"Pushkin and Belinsky" (Pisarev) **25**:332, 335, 348, 354
Puss in Boots (Planché) **42**:273, 279, 280, 288, 302
Puss in Boots (Tieck)
See *Der gestiefelte Kater*
"Pustka" (Shevchenko) **54**:364
"Pustopljasy" (Leskov) **174**:7
"Put' do goroda Kuby" (Bestuzhev) **131**:160
Put Yourself in His Place (Reade) **2**:540, 542, 547-49; **74**:248-49, 251, 253-55, 258, 263-64, 284, 318
Puteshestvie iz Peterburga v Moskvu (Radishchev) **190**:270, 274-80, 283-87, 289, 291-92, 294, 296-97, 300-309, 313-20, 322, 326, 331, 334-43, 349-58
"The Puzzle of Spring" (Larcom) **179**:176
"PVs Correspondence" (Hawthorne) **2**:303
"Pyetushkov" (Turgenev) **21**:414
"Pygmalion" (Beddoes) **154**:44, 76-77
"Pygmalion" (Schlegel) **15**:223; **142**:302
"Pygmalion and the Image" (Morris) **4**:416, 447
Pym (Poe)
See *The Narrative of Arthur Gordon Pym, of Nantucket*
"The Pyramids of Egypt" (Freneau) **1**:314
"Die Pythagoräer" (Meyer) **81**:147-48
"Pytheas" (Kendall) **12**:199
"Pythona: or the Prophetess of En-Dor" (Freneau) **111**:110
"Pytor Petrovich Karataev" (Turgenev) **21**:377
"Qaïn" (Leconte de Lisle) **29**:215, 217, 221-24, 226, 229, 231, 234-36
"Qasida in praise of Ali" (Ghalib) **39**:147
"Qua Cursum Ventus" (Clough) **27**:44, 77, 79, 90, 108
"Qua Cursum Ventus" (Prescott) **163**:33
Die Quackerstadt und ihre Geheimnisse (Lippard)
See *The Quaker City; or, The Monks of Monk-Hall. A Romance of Philadelphia Life, Mystery, and Crime*
Quadrille (Pavlova)
See *Kadril!*
"The Quadroon Girl" (Longfellow) **2**:483; **45**:123, 155; **103**:290
"Quae Nocent Docent" (Coleridge) **99**:22
"The Quail" (Turgenev) **122**:289
"The Quaker City" (Lippard) **198**:242
The Quaker City and its Mysteries (Lippard)
See *The Quaker City; or, The Monks of Monk-Hall. A Romance of Philadelphia Life, Mystery, and Crime*
The Quaker City; or, The Monks of Monk-Hall. A Romance of Philadelphia Life, Mystery, and Crime (Lippard) **198**:117-18, 120-22, 124-25, 129-33, 135-40, 143, 145-46, 148, 150-53, 155-57, 160, 164, 168-73, 176, 178, 181, 185-86, 197-204, 206-10, 212-21, 225, 227, 229-31, 239-43, 245
The Quaker City play (Lippard) **198**:176-79
"The Quaker of the Olden Time" (Whittier) **8**:491
"A Quakers Meeting" (Lamb) **10**:408; **113**:250
"Quand l'hombre menaca de la fatale loi" (Mallarmé) **210**:244
"Quand l'ombre menaça" (Mallarmé) **4**:388; **41**:242
"Quand tu me racontes . . ." (Verlaine) **230**:166
"The Quangle Wangle's Hat" (Lear) **3**:309
Quant au livre (Mallarmé)
See *L'Action restreinte*
Les quarante-cinq (Dumas) **11**:68, 74
"Quare Fatigasti" (Gordon) **21**:150, 154, 160, 164

"The Quarrel of Two Ivans" (Gogol)
See "The Tale of How Ivan Ivanovich Quarrelled with Ivan Nikiforovich"
Quarrels of Authors: or, Some Memoirs for our Literary History, Including Specimens of Controversy to the Reign of Elizabeth (D'Israeli) **217**:278, 284, 292, 295, 297
"Quarter Racing in Tennessee" (Harris) **165**:179
"Quarterly" (Tennyson) **115**:235
"The Quartette" (Gautier) **1**:347
Quatre Chapitres sur la Russie (Maistre) **37**:288
Les quatre talismans (Nodier) **19**:384-85
Les quatre vents de l'esprit (Hugo) **3**:256, 258, 264; **21**:214
Quatre-vingt treize (Hugo) **3**:250-51, 253, 260, 267, 276; **10**:367; **21**:195; **161**:157, 192-98, 202-5, 207-8, 214-17, 222, 224-25; **189**:177, 179, 211, 251, 253
"Que diras-tu ce soir" (Baudelaire) **55**:59
"Que pasa o redor de min?" (Castro) **78**:41
"Que ton âme soit . . ." (Verlaine) **230**:170
"Quebec" (Moodie) **113**:344, 347
Queechy (Warner) **31**:333, 337, 341-43; **146**:221-22, 228-29, 233, 235-36, 258, 261, 346
"The Queen" (Hunt) **70**:258
"The Queen and the Working Classes" (Hunt) **70**:259
"Queen Eleanor and Fair Rosamond" (Oliphant) **61**:210, 241
"Queen Hynde" (Hogg) **4**:282-83; **109**:205-8, 244-45, 250, 271
Queen Hynde: A Poem (Hogg)
See "Queen Hynde"
"Queen Mab" (Hood) **16**:224
Queen Mab (Shelley) **18**:330-32, 334, 336, 338, 342, 344, 346, 368, 374, 379; **93**:272, 294-95, 371-72; **143**:193, 265, 267, 288; **175**:204-5, 215, 217, 222, 226, 231, 233-37, 247, 270, 282-83, 293, 321, 326-27, 330
Queen Mab: A Philosophical Poem, with Notes (Shelley)
See *Queen Mab*
The Queen Mary (Tennyson) **30**:219, 262-64
"The Queen Must Dance" (Boker) **125**:81
"The Queen of Hearts" (Rossetti) **186**:240
The Queen of Hearts (Collins) **93**:46
The Queen of Spades (Pushkin)
See *Pikovaya dama*
"The Queen of the Army Camp" (Isaacs)
See "La reina del campamento"
The Queen of the Frogs (Planché) **42**:288, 293
"The Queen of the Highlands" (Oliphant) **221**:262
"Queen of the Isles" (Tennyson) **30**:295
"Queen Oriana's Dream" (Lamb) **10**:418
"Queen Orraca and the Five Martyrs of Morocco" (Southey) **8**:474
"The Queen, the Opening of Parliament" (Hunt) **70**:259
"Queen Titania" (Boyesen) **135**:13
Queen Titania (Boyesen) **135**:13, 21, 28
Queen Victoria: A Personal Sketch (Oliphant) **221**:233, 261
"Queen Ysabeau" (Villiers de l'Isle Adam)
See "La reine Ysabeau"
Queeney Letters (Piozzi) **57**:245
The Queen's Jewelpiece (Almqvist)
See *Drottningens juvelsmycke*
The Queen's Necklace (Dumas)
See *Le collier de la reine*
The Queen's Wake (Hogg) **4**:274-76, 279, 284; **109**:204, 240, 246, 249, 270, 272
A Queer Book (Hogg) **109**:272
"Quelle soie aux baumes de temps" (Mallarmé) **210**:211
"Quelques caricaturistes français" (Baudelaire) **155**:14
Quelques Détails sur les Mœurs des Grecs, des Arabes et des Turcs (Chateaubriand) **134**:4
Quelques médaillons et portraits en pied (Mallarmé) **41**:249, 269
"De quelques phénomènes du sommeil" (Nodier) **19**:400
"Qu'en avez-vous fait?" (Desbordes-Valmore) **97**:6
La Quenouille de Barbérine (Musset) **150**:339-41
Quentin Durward (Scott) **15**:283, 308, 312-14; **69**:303-04, 308, 313, 316, 318, 328, 330, 332-34, 366; **209**:174, 181-82, 184, 216, 240, 242, 247-50
"Queries to My Seventieth Year" (Whitman) **31**:433
The Quest of the Absolute (Balzac)
See *La recherche de l'absolu*
"Qu'est-ce pour nous" (Rimbaud) **82**:232
"Qu'est-ce pour nous, mon coeur . . ." (Rimbaud)
See "Qu'est-ce pour nous"
"Qu'est-ce que la poésie?" (Lamartine) **190**:208
"The Question" (Shelley) **18**:340, 345
"Question and Answer" (Barrett Browning) **16**:135
La question d'argent (Dumas) **9**:220-21, 224, 239-42, 246, 250-51
La question du divorce (Dumas) **9**:225-26, 244-45
"The Questioning Spirit" (Clough) **27**:41, 52, 80, 104
Questions contemporaines (Renan) **26**:377, 414
"Questions of Life" (Whittier) **8**:491, 510, 524; **59**:371
"Questions of Varying Import" (Almqvist) **42**:12
Questions politiques et sociales (Sand) **5**:318
"A qui la faute?" (Hugo) **161**:179
"Qui Laborat, Orat" (Clough) **27**:55, 77, 89, 105
"Qui laborat, orat" (Prescott) **163**:6, 33
"Qui sait?" (Maupassant) **1**:457, 464, 468
"Quicksand Years" (Whitman) **31**:433; **81**:311
Quidam (Norwid) **17**:369, 378-79
"Quidquid volueris" (Flaubert) **62**:101
"The Quiet After the Storm" (Leopardi)
See "La quiete dopo la tempesta"
A Quiet Gentlewoman (Mitford) **4**:406
The Quiet Heart (Oliphant) **61**:209; **221**:226
"The Quiet Home" (Jones) **222**:173
"A Quiet Spot" (Turgenev) **21**:409, 418-20, 451; **122**:247, 280, 350
"Quiet Work" (Arnold) **6**:44; **29**:34; **218**:191
"La quiete dopo la tempesta" (Leopardi) **129**:219, 229, 338-41, 344, 348
The Quill (Verlaine)
See *La Plume*
De Quincey's Writings (De Quincey) **198**:4, 6
Quitt (Fontane) **26**:234, 243-44, 260, 272; **163**:161-62, 215
La Quittance du diable (Musset) **150**:301
Quitte pour la peur (Vigny) **7**:473
La Quixotita y su prima (Lizardi) **30**:67-73, 78-9
"Quotation and Originality" (Emerson) **38**:203; **98**:185
"A rab gólya" (Arany) **34**:9, 16
"Rabbi Ben Ezra" (Browning) **19**:89, 103, 130, 152
"Rabbi Ishmael" (Whittier) **59**:361
"Der Rabbi von Bacherach" (Heine) **4**:268-69
"The Rabbit Carriage" (Leskov)
See "Zajačij remiz"
"The Rabbit Refuge" (Leskov)
See "Zajačij remiz"
"The Rabbit Warren" (Leskov)
See "Zajačij remiz"
"La rabouilleuse" (Balzac) **5**:32, 53, 75; **153**:149
"A Race for a Sweetheart" (Smith) **187**:320
"Die Rache" (Klopstock) **11**:238
Die Rache (Klopstock) **225**:298
Rachel Dyer (Neal) **161**:285, 287, 291-93, 295-97, 299, 302, 312-13, 315-17
Rachel Ray (Trollope) **6**:456, 470-71, 492, 499, 501, 515-16; **101**:235, 238-41, 309, 335
Rachel Wilde; or, Trifles from the Burthen of a Life (Moodie) **14**:241-44
"Rachel's Refusal" (Cooke) **110**:53, 58
Racine et Shakespeare (Stendhal) **23**:352, 391; **46**:307, 325; **178**:173-74, 204, 218, 250, 258
"Racing Ethics" (Gordon) **21**:179
Radharani (Chatterji) **19**:217-19, 221
The Radical (Galt) **110**:94
A Radical War Song (Macaulay) **42**:154
"Radlauf erzählt seine reise nach dem Starenberg" (Brentano) **1**:100, 104
"Raeburn's Portraits" (Stevenson) **5**:389
Rage et impuissance (Flaubert) **2**:256
"Rages de césars" (Rimbaud) **4**:465; **35**:271
Ragged Dick; or, Street Life in New York with the Boot-Blacks (Alger) **8**:15, 27, 30, 34, 37; **83**:95, 98, 104-6, 125, 127, 130-31, 135, 138-40, 142, 144, 146
"Ragged Mountains" (Poe)
See "A Tale of the Ragged Mountains"
"The Ragged Schools of London" (Barrett Browning)
See "A Song for the Ragged Schools of London"
Ragionamenti (Gozzi) **23**:110
Ragna-rok (Grundtvig) **158**:167, 169
Rahel, ein Buch des Andenkens fü4 ihre Freunde, Vol. II (Varnhagen von Ense)
See *Rahel, ein Buch des Andenkens für ihre Freunde*
Rahel, ein Buch des Andenkens für ihre Freunde (Varnhagen von Ense) **130**:292-94, 299-301, 303, 305, 310, 327, 329, 340-41, 344, 359, 367, 371
Rahel, ein Buch des Andenkens für ihre Freunde, Vol. I (Varnhagen von Ense)
See *Rahel, ein Buch des Andenkens für ihre Freunde*
Rahel, ein Buch des Andenkens für ihre Freunde, Vol. III (Varnhagen von Ense)
See *Rahel, ein Buch des Andenkens für ihre Freunde*
Rahel-Bibliothek: Gesammelte Werke (Varnhagen von Ense) **130**:367, 369
"Raids" (Bestuzhev)
See "Nayezdy"
"The Railroad" (Barnes) **75**:73
"The Railroad" (Nekrasov) **11**:416-17
"Railroad Song" (Chivers) **49**:41, 43
The Railway Man and His Children (Oliphant) **11**:449, 461; **61**:203-5, 242
"The Railway Station" (Lampman) **25**:172, 198, 204, 208-09; **194**:9, 46, 118-19
"A Rain Dream" (Bryant) **6**:165, 168, 175
"The Rainbow" (Sigourney) **21**:299
"The Rainbow" (Wordsworth) **206**:262, 272
"A Rainy Day" (Hunt) **1**:417
"The Rainy Day" (Longfellow) **45**:147
"The Rainy Season in California" (Ridge) **82**:185
"Raisa" (Karamzin) **173**:266
"The Rajah's Diamond" (Stevenson) **5**:393, 403; **193**:250-52, 254-57, 279-80, 316
"The Rajah's Diamond: The Adventure of Prince Florizel and a Detective" (Stevenson)
See "The Adventure of Prince Florizel and a Detective"
"The Rajah's Diamond: The Bandbox" (Stevenson)
See "Story of the Bandbox"
"The Rajah's Diamond: The House with the Green Blinds" (Stevenson)
See "Story of the House with the Green Blinds"
Rajani (Chatterji) **19**:210, 215, 217-19, 221-22, 224
Rajmohan's Wife (Chatterji) **19**:215
Rajsingha (Chatterji) **19**:210-13, 215, 217-21, 223-25

"Rakušanskij melamed" (Leskov) **25**:265-67; **174**:105
"Rakushanskii melamed" (Leskov)
See "Rakušanskij melamed"
"Ralph Farnham's Romance" (Alger) **83**:98
"Ralph Raymond's Heir" (Alger)
See *The Merchant's Crime*
Ralph the Heir (Trollope) **101**:239, 249, 251, 272, 292, 309, 311, 320; **215**:208, 331-33
"Ralph Waldo Emerson" (Cranch) **115**:33, 39
Ralph Waldo Emerson (Alcott) **1**:25; **167**:72, 76
Ralph Waldo Emerson (Holmes) **14**:107; **81**:115, 117
Ralph Waldo Emerson: Essays and Lectures (Emerson)
See *Essays and Lectures*
Die Ramanzen vom Rosenkranz (Brentano) **1**:95, 102, 104
"Ramble" (Wordsworth)
See "A Winter's Ramble in Grasmere's Vale"
Rambles (Allingham) **25**:15
Rambles Among Words (Whitman) **81**:286-87, 291-96, 348-50
Rambles beyond Railways (Collins) **1**:184-85; **93**:46, 64
Rambles by Patricius Walker (Allingham)
See *Rambles*
Rambles in Germany and Italy (Shelley) **14**:260
Rambles (Incursions)—Critical, Polemical, and Contemporary Essays (Liszt) **199**:305
Rambles of a Geologist (Miller) **143**:3, 6
Ramido Marinesco (Almqvist) **42**:4
Ramona (Jackson) **90**:125-26, 129-32, 134-42, 145-46, 150-55, 157, 159-60, 164, 166, 169, 171-78
"Ramsumowsky" Quartets (Beethoven) **227**:7, 32-33
Randbemerkungen zu Friedrich Schlegels 'Ideen' (Novalis) **178**:23-24, 60
Randolph (Neal) **161**:279, 290, 293, 296, 299, 318, 320, 344
"Randolph of Roanoke" (Whittier) **8**:501, 505, 508; **59**:353
Ranelagh House (Warton) **118**:308, 336, 350
"The Ranger" (Whittier) **8**:509, 518
"Rangstreit" (Grillparzer) **102**:174
"The Ransacked Grave" (Shevchenko)
See "Rozryta mohyla"
Ranthorpe (Lewes) **25**:273, 286, 293, 298, 307, 309; **215**:84, 182
"Raphael" (Pater) **7**:308
"Raphael" (Whittier) **8**:486, 489
Raphael; or, Pages of the Book of Life at Twenty (Lamartine)
See *Raphaël: pages de la vingtième année*
Raphaël: pages de la vingtième année (Lamartine) **11**:257, 266, 278-79, 285-86, 288-89; **190**:202, 216
Raphael Sanzio von Urbino (Werner) **189**:350
Raphael und seine Nachbarinnen (Arnim) **159**:31, 96
"Raphael's deposition from the cross" (Fuller) **50**:249, 250
A Rapid Thaw (Robertson) **35**:333, 335-36
"Rappaccini's Daughter" (Hawthorne) **2**:294, 311, 319, 322, 331; **10**:308; **17**:137, 145; **23**:201, 218; **39**:198, 237; **79**:299; **95**:92, 109, 132, 136-37, 150; **158**:243-44, 250, 257; **171**:243, 327, 343, 345, 357
The Rapparee (Boucicault) **41**:28, 49, 51
"Rappelle-toi" (Musset) **150**:309
"La rapsode foraine et le pardon de Saint-Anne" (Corbière) **43**:2-3, 7, 11, 13, 15, 18, 23-4, 28-30
"Rapsodie du sourd" (Corbière) **43**:13, 19, 21, 25, 27, 32-4
Raptularz (Slowacki) **15**:372
"Rapture—To Laura" (Schiller) **39**:339
"Rapunzel" (Morris) **4**:421, 423, 426, 431, 444
"Rare Ripe Garden-Seed" (Harris) **23**:159; **165**:182, 193, 196, 201, 221, 232, 242, 249, 271-72, 280, 287
Rasch und wild (Schumann) **143**:144
"Raschi in Prague" (Lazarus) **8**:422; **109**:326, 337, 342
"The Rash Conjurer" (Coleridge) **231**:151
"Rasskaz ofitsera, byvshego v plenu u gorcev" (Bestuzhev) **131**:160-61, 187
"Rasskaz otca Alekseja" (Turgenev)
See "Rasskaz ottsa Aleksaya"
"Rasskaz ottsa Aleksaya" (Turgenev) **21**:420, 441; **122**:242, 265, 267, 348, 365, 367, 370, 376-78
Rasskazy i vospominaniia okhotnika o raznykh okhotakh (Aksakov) **181**:20, 22, 45-47, 65
"Rasskazy kstati" (Leskov) **174**:24, 90
"Rasskazy neizvestnogo" (Leskov) **174**:24
"Rassuzdenie o starom i novom sloge rossijskogo jazyka" (Karamzin) **173**:269
Rassuzhdenie o liri Ceskoj poezii ili ob ode (Derzhavin) **215**:53
"Rast" (Muller) **73**:366, 391
Rastočitel (Leskov) **25**:248; **174**:10
"Rat Krespel" (Hoffmann) **2**:346, 356; **183**:298-99, 301, 303, 307-8, 311
"Le rat qui s'est retiré du monde" (Banville) **9**:32
"Ratbert" (Hugo) **3**:264
Ratcliff (Heine) **4**:253
"Rath Krespel" (Hoffmann)
See "Rat Krespel"
The Rationale of Reward (Bentham) **38**:90, 92
"The Rationale of Verse" (Poe) **117**:335; **211**:243
"Rationale of Verse" (Timrod) **25**:373
De ratione, una, universali, infinita (Feuerbach) **139**:302-5, 308-9, 311-12
Ratos entretenidos (Lizardi) **30**:67
"Les rats" (Banville) **9**:16
"Rattle-Snake Hunter" (Whittier) **8**:484
Die Raüber (Schiller) **39**:299, 304, 306-11, 323-24, 326-27, 331, 334, 336, 338, 342-43, 348, 350, 354, 358, 365, 368-71, 375-76, 385, 390-94; **69**:169, 239, 275; **166**:79, 115-17, 140, 147, 150-56, 158-59
"Die Räuberbraut" (Hebbel) **43**:253
"The Ravaged Villa" (Melville) **3**:363
"The Raven" (Poe) **1**:493, 496, 502, 512, 516-18, 522-25; **16**:305; **55**:132-3, 135, 138-9, 141, 147-8, 154, 176, 178, 208, 212-3; **97**:238, 240; **117**:192, 195, 197, 200, 203, 208, 215, 217, 226-27, 231, 236-37, 240-44, 252, 257, 264, 275-76, 278, 280-82, 287-90, 296-98, 301, 303, 309, 315, 327-29, 333-36; **211**:242, 247-48
The Raven (Gozzi)
See *Il corvo*
The Raven, and Other Poems (Poe) **55**:174; **117**:333
"The Raven and the King's Daughter" (Morris) **4**:423
"The Raven Days" (Lanier) **118**:234, 240, 287
"A Raven in a White Chine" (Ingelow) **39**:264
The Ravens (Becque)
See *Les corbeaux*
"The Ravens of Odin" (Boyesen) **135**:5
Ravenshoe (Kingsley) **107**:186, 188-89, 192, 194-204, 206-11, 215-16, 219-21, 223-24, 226, 228-29
Ravensnest (Cooper)
See *The Redskins; or, Indian and Injin: Being the Conclusion of the Littlepage Manuscripts*
"The Ravenswing" (Thackeray) **14**:402; **213**:305
The Ravine (Goncharov) **63**:21-6
"La ravine Sainte-Gilles" (Leconte de Lisle) **29**:212, 216
Ravnikar (Preseren) **127**:314
The Raw Youth (Dostoevsky)
See *Podrostok*
A Raw Youth (Dostoevsky)
See *Podrostok*
"A Ray of Light in the Realm of Darkness" (Dobrolyubov) **5**:140-42, 151
Raymond and Agnes (Lewis) **11**:305
Rayner (Baillie) **2**:34-35, 39; **71**:5-6, 12-13; **151**:11, 27, 72-76, 115
"Un rayo de luna" (Bécquer)
See "El rayo de luna"
"El rayo de luna" (Bécquer) **106**:92, 103, 108, 112-13, 115, 121, 130, 132-33
Les rayons et les ombres (Hugo) **3**:271, 273; **189**:178
"Rayons jaunes" (Sainte-Beuve) **5**:340, 342, 347
"Rayskaya ptichka" (Karamzin) **173**:283
"Razbojnik" (Leskov) **174**:24-28, 37
"Razgover o shchastii" (Karamzin) **173**:309, 323-25
Razgovor na bolshoi doroge (Turgenev) **21**:428, 432; **122**:247
Razgovor v Kremle (Pavlova) **138**:3-4, 13, 31, 51
Razgovor v Trianone (Pavlova) **138**:3-4, 13, 52
"A Razor-Grinder in a Thunder-Storm" (Harris) **23**:159, 163; **165**:254
"Razrushenie estetiki" (Pisarev) **25**:334, 338, 340
"Razskaz" (Pavlova) **138**:49
"Razviazka 'Révizor'" (Gogol) **15**:85, 106, 110
RC (Parton)
See *Rose Clark*
Re Teodoro a Venezia (Da Ponte) **50**:78
"Le Rê ve intermittent d'une nuit triste" (Desbordes-Valmore) **97**:17-19, 23, 29
"Reaction in Germany" (Bakunin) **25**:40, 58, 62; **58**:105, 120, 130, 135
"Readen ov a Headstone" (Barnes) **75**:8
Reader (Shelley)
See *Mary Shelley Reader*
"Readers against the Grain" (Lamb) **10**:411; **113**:202
"Readers at the British Museum" (Levy) **203**:352-53
Readiana (Reade) **74**:281
"Reading" (Thoreau) **7**:402
A Reading Diary (Rossetti)
See *Time Flies: A Reading Diary*
"Reading María" (Isaacs)
See "Leyendo a María"
Readings in Crabbe: Tales of the Hall (FitzGerald) **153**:218
Real Life in Verdopolis (Brontë) **109**:45, 49-50, 52
"Real Rest" (Brontë) **109**:31
"A Real Vision of Sin" (Thomson) **18**:403, 407, 414
"Realism" (Stevenson)
See "A Note on Realism"
"Realism in Art" (Lewes) **215**:136, 164
The Realists (Pisarev)
See *Realisty*
Realisty (Pisarev) **25**:332-34, 337, 341, 344-48, 353
"Realities" (Lazarus) **8**:420
Realities (Linton) **41**:167
"Reality" (Lampman) **25**:204; **194**:11-12, 42
"Reality" (Reade) **2**:549
Reallexikon der deutschen Literaturgeschichte (Herder) **186**:14
"The realm of shadows" (Schiller)
See "Das Reich der Schatten"
"A Reaper and the Flowers" (Longfellow) **2**:473, 479; **45**:116, 121
"Rearrange a 'Wife's' Affection" (Dickinson) **21**:58
"Reason" (Coleridge) **231**:83-87
"Reason and Faith" (Mickiewicz) **3**:399-400
Reason and Heart (Eminescu) **33**:266

Reason Triumphant over Fancy, Exemplified in the Singular Adventures of Don Sylvio de Rosalva (Wieland)
See *Der Sieg der Natur über die Schwärmerei; oder, die Abenteuer des Don Sylvio von Rosalva*
"Reasons for National Penitence" (Barbauld) **185**:94-95
"Reasons Why the English Should Not Be Our Standard, Either in Language or Manners" (Webster) **30**:406
"Rebecca Letter" (Lincoln) **201**:159-61
Rebecca; or, The Fille de Chambre (Rowson) **5**:310-12, 316; **69**:99, 102, 105, 113, 133-35, 141; **182**:255, 258-60, 313, 350-52, 354
The Rebel of the Family (Linton) **41**:164, 174
"Le rebelle" (Baudelaire) **29**:80; **55**:13
The Rebellion in Ghent under the Emperor Charles V (Sacher-Masoch) **31**:289
The Rebellion in the Cévennes (Tieck)
See *Der Aufruhr in den Cevennen*
"The Rebellion of the Waters" (Darley) **2**:131
The Rebels; or, Boston before the Revolution (Child) **6**:197-98, 200, 204, 208; **73**:39-40, 50, 58, 66, 74, 115
"Reburial" (Preseren)
See "Prekop"
"De Rebus Scenicis (Et Quibusdam Aliis)" (Lewes) **25**:291
"Rec, proiznesënnaja na torzestvennom sobranii imperatorskoj Rossijskoj akademii" (Karamzin) **173**:294
"The Recantation: An Ode" (Coleridge) **177**:116
"Recent English Poetry" (Clough) **27**:102-03
"Recent English Poetry" (Prescott) **163**:43-44, 71
"Recent Social Theories" (Clough) **27**:82
"The Recent Telepathic Occurrence at the British Museum" (Levy) **59**:112; **203**:352
The Recess; or, A Tale of Other Times (Lee) **191**:313-22, 324, 327-35, 337-43, 346-50, 354-55
La recherche de l'absolu (Balzac) **5**:32-34, 36, 62, 73, 79; **53**:12; **153**:117, 119, 123-24, 131
Die Rechte des Herzens (Ludwig) **4**:349, 351
Rechtslehre (Fichte)
See *Grundlage des Naturrechts nach Prinzipen der Wissenshaftslehre*
"The Recluse" (Stifter)
See "Der Hagestolz"
The Recluse (Wordsworth)
See *The Recluse; or Views on Man, Nature, and on Human Life*
The Recluse of the Lake (Smith)
See *Ethelinde; or, The Recluse of the Lake*
The Recluse; or Views on Man, Nature, and on Human Life (Wordsworth) **12**:442, 445-46, 451, 459, 466, 468; **38**:362, 364-65, 368, 370, 373, 376-77, 380, 387, 399-400, 405, 411-12, 415; **111**:233, 243, 332, 347; **206**:231, 296
"El recluta" (Silva) **114**:263, 270, 300, 315
"Recollection" (Musset) **7**:256
"The Recollection" (Shelley)
See "To Jane: The Recollection"
Recollection (Storm) **195**:32
Recollection of Aleksandr Semenovich Shishkov (Aksakov)
See *Vospominanie ob Aleksandre Semenoviche Shishkove*
"Recollections" (Coleridge)
See "Recollections of Love"
"The Recollections" (Leopardi)
See "Le ricordanze"
"Recollections" (Norton) **47**:235
Recollections (Renan) **145**:346
Recollections (Sedgwick) **19**:445
Recollections (Tonna)
See *Personal Recollections*
Recollections (Trelawny)
See *Recollections of the Last Days of Shelley and Byron*
"Recollections After a Ramble" (Clare) **9**:78, 123
"Recollections After an Evening Walk" (Clare) **9**:123
Recollections and Reflections (Planché)
See *Life and Recollections*
Recollections of a Literary Man (Daudet)
See *Souvenirs d'un homme de lettres*
Recollections of a Tour Made in Scotland (Wordsworth) **25**:391, 393-94, 398, 407, 411-12, 415, 419, 423-24, 428
Recollections of a Tour Made in Scotland, A.D. 1803 (Wordsworth) **138**:199, 252-53, 255, 259, 263, 283, 289-91, 293, 310-11
The Recollections of Alexis de Tocqueville (Tocqueville)
See *Souvenirs de Alexis de Tocqueville*
Recollections of an Excursion to the Monasteries of Alcobaça and Batalha (Beckford) **16**:26; **214**:166
"Recollections of Arthur Hallam" (Gladstone) **213**:121
"Recollections of Belinsky" (Turgenev) **122**:276
"Recollections of Christ's Hospital" (Lamb) **113**:234
Recollections of Europe (Cooper) **1**:201; **54**:256; **203**:72
The Recollections of Geoffry Hamlyn (Kingsley) **107**:186, 189, 191-95, 205-21, 223, 229, 231-50
Recollections of Gógol (Aksakov)
See *Istoriya moega znakomstva s Gogolem*
Recollections of Literary Life; or, Books, Places, and People (Mitford) **4**:401-03
"Recollections of Love" (Coleridge) **99**:103-04; **231**:62, 67, 70, 73-74
Recollections of My Youth (Renan)
See *Souvenirs d'enfance et de jeunesse*
"Recollections of Nova Scotia" (Haliburton) **149**:330-32, 337
"Recollections of Past Times and Events" (Freneau) **111**:138
"Recollections of Shakespeare" (Lazarus) **109**:294
"Recollections of Sully" (Cooke) **5**:132
"Recollections of the Antislavery Contest" (Douglass) **7**:126
"Recollections of the Arabian Nights" (Tennyson) **30**:204, 211, 223; **202**:190, 203
"Recollections of the Lakes" (De Quincey) **4**:70-71
Recollections of the Lakes and the Lake Poets (De Quincey) **87**:60-1, 63
Recollections of the Last Days of Shelley and Byron (Trelawny) **85**:315, 317-18, 320, 322-24, 332-38
"Recollections of the West Indies" (Richardson) **55**:301
"Recollections of the Year 1848" (Grillparzer) **102**:77
Recollections of Tsarskoe-Selo (Pushkin)
See "Vospominanie v Tsarskom Sele"
Recollections Written at the Request of Miss Berry (Baillie) **151**:88
"Reconciliation" (Hayne) **94**:144
"Reconciliation" (Whitman) **205**:309
Reconnaissance (Schumann) **143**:69
Record of a Girlhood: An Autobiography (Kemble) **18**:187-90
Record of a School: Exemplifying the General Principles of Spiritual Culture (Peabody) **169**:147, 154, 164-65, 167, 172-73, 188-89, 193, 200-201
Record of Conversations on the Gospels (Alcott)
See *Conversations with Children on the Gospels*
A Record of Courage and Cowardice (Ueda Akinari)
See *Tandai shoshin roku*
"A Record of Observations on the Phenomena of Life as Developed in the History of an Infant During the First Year of its Existence" (Alcott) **167**:52
"Recorders Ages Hence" (Whitman) **81**:260
Records (Trelawny)
See *Records of Shelley, Byron and the Author*
Records of Later Life (Kemble) **18**:188-90
Records of Shelley, Byron and the Author (Trelawny) **85**:307, 309, 312, 314, 335
"The Records of Woman" (Hemans) **71**:261, 271, 274
Records of Woman, with Other Poems (Hemans) **29**:197, 202-03; **71**:274-79, 288-89, 291-94, 296-98, 302-04, 307
"Recovery" (Karamzin)
See "Vyzdorovlenie"
The Recreations of Christopher North (Wilson) **5**:551-52, 558, 560-62
"The Recruit" (Silva)
See "El recluta"
The Rector, and the Doctor's Family (Oliphant) **11**:454-5, 457, 459; **61**:174-5, 198, 226, 239; **221**:245
"Rectoral Address at St. Andrews" (Mill) **58**:327
The Rectory Umbrella (Dodgson) **53**:51, 104
Recueil de morceaux détachés (Staël-Holstein) **91**:339, 358
"Recueillement" (Baudelaire) **6**:97-102; **29**:108; **55**:5, 26; **155**:44
Les recueillements poétiques (Lamartine) **11**:265, 271, 283; **190**:196, 200
"Recuerdos de colegial" (Isaacs) **70**:311
Recuerdos de provincia (Sarmiento) **123**:273, 278, 291, 304, 308-9, 312, 318-25, 328-40, 344, 347, 352, 361
"A Recusant" (Thomson) **18**:414
The Red and the Black (Stendhal)
See *Le rouge et le noir, chronique du XIXe siècle*
The Red Book (Kennedy) **2**:432
"The Red Cape" (Bestuzhev)
See "Krasnoe polryvalo"
Red Cotton Night-Cap Country; or, Turf and Towers (Browning) **19**:106, 140; **79**:153
The Red Court Farm (Wood) **178**:335
"The Red Cross Corps" (Crawford) **127**:220
"Red Death" (Poe)
See "The Masque of the Red Death"
Red Deer (Jefferies) **47**:136
"The Red Fisherman" (Hood) **16**:221-22
The Red Hall, or the Baronet's Daughter (Carleton)
See *The Black Baronet*
"Red Hoss Mountain" (Field) **3**:208
"The Red Inn" (Balzac)
See *L'Auberge rouge*
"Red Jacket (from Aloft)" (Whitman) **81**:345
The Red Mask (Planché) **42**:275, 292
The Red Note-Book (Constant)
See *Le cahier rouge de Benjamin Constant*
"Red Rébék" (Arany)
See "Vörös Rébék"
"Red River Voyager" (Whittier) **59**:356
"Red Roofs of London" (Jefferies) **47**:95, 132
The Red Rover (Cooper) **1**:199-200, 202, 207-08, 221; **54**:254, 275; **203**:7, 11, 87-88
"The Red Shoes" (Andersen)
See "De røde Skoe"
"The Red Snake" (Adams) **33**:13
"The Redbreast and the Butterfly" (Wordsworth) **12**:395
Redburn: His First Voyage (Melville) **3**:328, 333, 337, 344-45, 360-61, 366-67, 381; **29**:324-25, 328, 340, 354, 358, 367; **45**:196; **49**:391; **91**:42, 45, 54-5, 218; **123**:166-265; **157**:109, 131; **181**:154, 156-57, 160, 164,

186, 193, 204, 212, 231-32, 263, 283, 300; **193**:130, 146, 148; **221**:101-4, 106-8, 113, 116-17, 122-23, 132, 144, 147-48, 155, 157-60, 163, 166-70, 172
"Reddition" (Verlaine) **230**:213-15, 220
Rede des toten Christus (Jean Paul) **7**:238, 240
"Die Rede über Mythologie und symbolische Anschauung" (Schlegel) **45**:308, 316, 333, 337, 356
Rede zum Schäkespears Tag (Goethe) **34**:121
Redémption (Feuillet) **45**:75, 77, 82, 88
Reden an die deutsche Nation (Fichte) **62**:16, 19, 35, 38
Redgauntlet (Scott) **15**:300-01, 304, 312, 315; **69**:304, 308, 318, 331; **110**:233, 305, 316
Redgauntlet: A Tale of the Eighteenth Century (Scott) **209**:193, 216, 230, 235, 242, 250, 280, 286, 335-38, 343-44, 346, 349-52
"Red-Jacket" (Halleck) **47**:57, 67, 69, 71, 73, 79
Redmond Count O'Hanlon, the Irish Rapparee: An Historical Tale (Carleton) **199**:97-100
Red-Nosed Frost (Nekrasov)
See *Moroz krasni nos*
"The Redress: To a Young Poet" (Dyer) **129**:121, 149
The Redskins; or, Indian and Injin: Being the Conclusion of the Littlepage Manuscripts (Cooper) **1**:216-17, 219-20, 224, 226; **54**:258, 283; **203**:24, 75-76
Redwood (Sedgwick) **19**:425-27, 429-30, 433, 439, 445, 447, 453; **98**:299, 301, 307, 321, 326, 334
"Redwood-Tree" (Whitman)
See "Song of the Redwood Tree"
"The Reed" (Barrett Browning) **170**:117-18
"A Reed" (Barrett Browning) **61**:44
"Re-enlisted" (Larcom) **179**:169
Refections (Paine) **62**:353-4
"The Reflection" (Grillparzer)
See "Das Spiegelbild"
"A Reflection in Autumn" (Clare) **9**:72
"Reflections" (Robinson) **142**:152
Reflections and Prayers (Duras)
See *Réflexions et prières*
"Reflections and Remarks on Human Life" (Stevenson) **14**:335
"Reflections in the Pillory" (Lamb) **10**:420; **113**:285
"Reflections on Didactic Poetry" (Warton) **118**:353
"Reflections on Having Left a Place of Retirement" (Coleridge) **99**:5-6, 48; **231**:110, 120
"Reflections on Marriage" (Kierkegaard) **125**:261
"Reflections on the Constitution, or Frame of Nature" (Freneau) **111**:109
"Reflections on the General Debased Condition of Mankind" (Freneau) **111**:105
Reflections on the High Value of Music (Hoffmann)
See *Gedanken über den hohen Wert der Musik*
Reflections on the Novel (Sade)
See *Idée sur les romans*
"Reflections on the Printing, etc., of my Histories" (Prescott) **163**:324
"Reflections on the Resurrection of Bodies" (Dobrolyubov) **5**:140
Reflections on World History (Burckhardt)
See *Weltgeschichtliche Bertrachtungen*
Reflections upon the Study of Asiatic Languages (Schlegel)
See *Réflexions sur l'étude des langues Asiatiques*
Reflector (Hunt) **70**:266
Reflex (Lewes) **215**:98
Reflexion sur l'Etude des Langues Asiatiques (Schlegel) **142**:302
Reflexions (Maistre) **37**:314
Réflexions et prières (Duras) **154**:153, 158, 163
"Réflexions sur la paix" (Staël-Holstein) **91**:340
"Réflexions sur la tragédie" (Constant) **6**:224-25
"Réflexions sur la vérité dans l'art" (Vigny) **7**:470; **102**:346-47, 378-79, 383
"Réflexions sur le procès de la reine" (Staël-Holstein) **91**:340
Réflexions sur le suicide (Staël-Holstein) **91**:360
Réflexions sur les constitutions, la distribution, et les garanties dans une monarchie constitutionelle (Constant) **182**:99-100, 211
Réflexions sur l'étude des langues Asiatiques (Schlegel) **15**:224
"Reform and the Reformers" (Thoreau) **207**:257
Reform Papers (Thoreau) **207**:254
La réforme intellectuelle et morale (Renan) **26**:377, 414, 421
"A Reformer" (Hazlitt) **29**:152
"The Reformer" (Whittier) **8**:520, 530
"Reforms" (Emerson) **98**:81, 167
"Reforms of the Constitution" (Bello) **131**:124
Les Réfractaires (Vallès) **71**:315-16, 327-28
"Refreshing Retrospections" (Willis) **194**:307
"Refuge" (Desbordes-Valmore) **97**:29
"Refuge" (Lampman) **25**:207; **194**:79
The Refuge of Monrepo (Saltykov)
See *Ubezhishche Monrepo*
The Refugee in America (Trollope) **30**:314, 319
"The Refusal of Aid between Nations" (Rossetti) **4**:499; **77**:293-94
A Refutation of Deism (Shelley) **18**:374; **175**:307
"Reg és Est" (Arany) **34**:19
Regency Cantos of Don Juan (Byron) **149**:165
Die Regentrude (Storm) **1**:536, 548-50; **195**:14, 20, 23-25, 32, 35, 66, 68-70, 127, 129, 131-32
The Regent's Daughter (Dumas)
See *Une fille du régent*
"A régi jó Gvadányi" (Petofi) **21**:277
Regina (Keller) **2**:412-13
Reginald Dalton (Lockhart) **6**:288-89, 292-96, 302-03, 310-12
Reginald Glanshaw, or the Man, who Commanded Success (Crabbe) **121**:24, 33
Reginald Hetherege (Kingsley) **107**:192, 195, 210, 218
Register (Cobbett)
See *Cobbett's Weekly Political Register*
"Regret" (Lazarus) **8**:419
"Les regrets" (Sainte-Beuve) **5**:350
Das Reh (Tieck) **5**:519
Der Rehbock (Kotzebue) **25**:133, 136, 142-43
"Das Reich der Schatten" (Schiller) **166**:120
"Reife" (Meyer) **81**:146, 149-50
The Reign of Greed (Rizal)
See *El filibusterismo*
The Reign of King George the Second (Oliphant)
See *Historical Sketches of the Reign of George Second*
The Reign of Moderation and Order (Saltykov)
See *V srede umerennosti i akkuratnosti*
Reign of Terror (Gore) **65**:20
"La reina de la sombra" (Casal) **131**:257
"La reina del campamento" (Isaacs) **70**:306
La Reine Coax (Sand) **42**:314
"La reine des poissons" (Nerval) **1**:480
"La Reine Hortense" (Maupassant) **83**:168, 171
La reine Margot (Dumas) **11**:51-52, 68, 70; **71**:184-86, 189-90, 193
"La reine Ysabeau" (Villiers de l'Isle Adam) **3**:590
Reineke Fuchs (Goethe) **4**:163, 207
Reinhart Fuchs (Grimm Brothers) **3**:217, 228
Reise auf dem Río Magdalena, durch die Anden und Mexico (Humboldt) **170**:194
"Die Reise des Priesters Abulfauaris" (Wieland) **177**:257
"Reise nach Frankreich" (Schlegel) **45**:336
"Reise um die Welt" (Chamisso) **82**:24, 28-30
Reise von München nach Genua (Heine) **147**:177-79, 186, 189, 209, 230
Die Reise von Munchen nech Genua (Heine) **54**:336
Reisebilder (Heine) **4**:231, 233, 235-36, 239-40, 252, 259; **54**:320, 322, 330, 339; **147**:134, 147, 149-51, 177-79, 185, 189, 226-28, 233, 243
Reisebilder I (Heine) **147**:177
Reisebilder II (Heine) **147**:177
Reiseblätter (Lenau) **16**:270
Reisejournal (Herder)
See *Journal meiner Reise im Jahr*
"Reisekammeraten" (Andersen) **214**:38, 49, 54, 74-75
Reiselieder (Muller) **73**:362, 387
"Reiselust" (Grillparzer) **102**:174
Reisen (Bartram)
See *Travels*
"Reisephantasie" (Meyer) **81**:142
"Rejects the Influence of Reason" (Robinson) **142**:174
Rejsen i Sommeren 1807 (Grundtvig) **158**:138
Relation historique du voyage aux régions équinoxiales du nouveau continent, fait en 1799, 1800, 1801, 1802, 1803 et 1804 (Humboldt) **170**:148, 150, 157-62, 166-67, 169, 171, 178-88
The Relation of Jesus to His Age and the Ages. A Sermon Preached at the Thursday Lecture in Boston, December 26, 1844 (Parker) **186**:145
"The Relation of the Death of the Family of the Cenci" (Shelley) **143**:158, 175-78, 189, 191-92, 228-29, 232, 248-49, 290
"The Relation of the Individual to the State" (Thoreau) **138**:128
"The Relations of Poetry and Science" (Lanier) **118**:218
"The Relics of General Chassé" (Trollope) **101**:234
Religio poetae (Patmore) **9**:340-42, 344, 349
"Religion" (Emerson) **38**:177; **98**:79, 160
Religion (Constant)
See *De la religion considérée dans sa source, ses formes, et ses développements*
"Religion a Weariness to the Natural Man" (Newman) **38**:302
Religion and Art (Wagner)
See *Die Religion und die Kunst*
"Religion and Philosophy in Germany" (Heine)
See "Zur Geschichte der Religion und Philosophie in Deutschland"
"The Religion and Superstitions of the North American Indians" (Smith) **187**:332
La Religion considérée comme l'unique base du bonheur et de la véritable philosophie (Genlis) **166**:64
"The Religion of Numa" (Pater) **7**:317
"Religion of Socrates" (Martineau) **26**:309
"The Religion of Solidarity" (Bellamy) **147**:88-89, 107
The Religion of Solidarity (Bellamy) **4**:27-28, 30-31; **86**:4, 6, 8-9, 47, 70, 74, 78
"The Religion of the Day" (Newman) **38**:304-05
The Religion of the Heart (Hunt) **70**:287-88
Die Religion und die Kunst (Wagner) **9**:475
Religion within the Limits of Pure Reason (Kant)
See *Religion within the Limits of Reason Alone*
Religion within the Limits of Reason Alone (Kant) **27**:148, 208, 249
"Les religions de l'antiquité" (Renan) **26**:415
Religious Discourses by a Layman (Scott) **69**:365-66
"Religious Musings" (Coleridge) **9**:149; **54**:68-9, 71; **99**:58; **111**:264; **231**:43, 68, 71, 83-84, 86-89, 91, 109, 151
Religious Musings (Coleridge) **197**:184, 310, 316-17, 325, 327
"Religious Orders" (Brownson) **50**:53

Religious Songs (Fouqué) **2**:267
Religious Training of Children in the School, the Family, and the Church (Beecher) **30**:9, 13
Reliquat (Hugo) **189**:203
"La Relique" (Maupassant) **83**:168
"Reliques" (Percy) **95**:309, 340
Reliques (Percy)
See *Reliques of Ancient English Poetry: Consisting of Old Heroic Ballads, Songs, and Other Pieces of Our Earlier Poets, (Chiefly of the Lyric Kind.) Together with Some Few of Later Date*
Reliques of Ancient English Poetry: Consisting of Old Heroic Ballads, Songs, and Other Pieces of Our Earlier Poets, (Chiefly of the Lyric Kind.) Together with Some Few of Later Date (Percy) **95**:307-13, 316, 318-32, 334-40, 342-51, 354-58, 360-62, 364-65
The Remains (Bloomfield) **145**:160
Remains in Verse and Prose (Hallam) **110**:120-22, 141, 145
Remains of Henry Kirke White (Southey) **97**:268
"Remarkable Case" (Lincoln) **201**:159
Remarks on a Speech of M. Dupont (More) **141**:267, 272, 305-6, 308, 310
"Remarks on Associations" (Channing) **17**:6
Remarks on Forest Scenery, and Other Woodland Views (Gilpin) **30**:36
Remarks on Mr. Gilbert Wakefield's Enquiry into the Expediency and Propriety of Public or Social Worship (Barbauld) **185**:52, 118, 120-21
"Remarks on National Literature" (Channing) **17**:31-2, 38, 50
"Remarks on the Biographical Accounts of the late Samuel Johnson, LL.D, with an Attempt to vindicate his Character from late Misrepresentations" (D'Israeli) **217**:282
"Remarks on the Character and Writings of Fenelon" (Channing) **17**:8, 31
"Remarks on the Character and Writings of John Milton" (Channing) **17**:4, 7-8, 12, 25, 31, 38, 41, 49
"Remarks on the 'Jagiellonid' by Dyzma Boncza Tomaszewski" (Mickiewicz) **101**:174
"Remarks on the Life and Character of Napoleon" (Channing) **17**:4, 6, 25, 31, 38
"Remarks on the Royal Supremacy" (Gladstone) **213**:112
Remarks on the Slavery Question, in a Letter to Jonathan Phillips , Esq. (Channing) **17**:32
"Rember thee" (Moore) **110**:195
"Remember" (Lazarus) **109**:298
"Remember" (Rossetti) **2**:572, 574; **186**:270-71
"Remember, oh Soul" (Mörike)
See "Denk' es, o Seele"
"Remember the Glories of Brien the Brave" (Moore) **110**:182, 185
"Rememberance" (Hölderlin)
See "Andenken"
"Remembered Grace" (Patmore) **9**:359, 365
"Remembrance" (Brontë) **16**:70, 75, 80, 86-7, 122; **35**:111
"Remembrance" (Darwin) **106**:184
"Remembrance" (Hölderlin)
See "Andenken"
"Remembrance" (Opie) **65**:160
"A Remembrance" (Osgood) **141**:323
"Remembrance in Tsarskoe Selo" (Pushkin)
See "Vospominanie v Tsarskom Sele"
"Remembrance of a Summer's Night" (Ridge) **82**:174, 183
"Remembrance of Spain" (Martínez de la Rosa) **102**:228
"Remembrances" (Clare) **9**:97; **86**:168-69
"Remembrances" (Leopardi)
See "Le ricordanze"
"Remembrances du viellard idiot" (Rimbaud) **227**:201
"Remembrances of a High School Student" (Isaacs)
See "Recuerdos de colegial"
"Reménvem" (Arany) **34**:18
"A Reminiscence" (Levy) **59**:119
Reminiscence of Aleksandr Semenovich Shishkov (Aksakov)
See *Vospominanie ob Aleksandre Semenoviche Shishkove*
"A Reminiscence of Federalism" (Sedgwick) **98**:315
Reminiscences (Aksakov)
See *Vospominaniia prezhei zhizni*
Reminiscences (Carlyle) **70**:25, 72, 76
"Reminiscences at Tsarskoe Selo" (Pushkin)
See "Vospominanie v Tsarskom Sele"
Reminiscences of Dr. Channing (Peabody)
See *Reminiscences of Rev. Wm. Ellery Channing, D.D.*
"Reminiscences of Edgar A. Poe" (Osgood) **141**:355
Reminiscences of His Youth (Renan)
See *Souvenirs d'enfance et de jeunesse*
Reminiscences of My Childhood (Fontane)
See *Meine Kinderjahre*
Reminiscences of My Irish Journey (Carlyle) **70**:90-91, 93
"Reminiscences of New York" (Bryant) **6**:181
Reminiscences of Rev. Wm. Ellery Channing, D.D. (Peabody) **169**:145, 147, 151, 164, 166, 185-91, 193, 197
"Remonstrance" (Ingelow) **107**:159
"Remonstrance" (Lanier) **6**:246, 259; **118**:217, 273
"Remonstrance in the Platonic Shade, Flourishing on an Height" (Yearsley) **174**:306, 343
"Remonstratory Ode from the Elephant at Exeter Change" (Hood) **16**:233
"Remords posthume" (Baudelaire) **6**:80; **55**:59
Remorse (Coleridge) **9**:138, 142-43, 146; **111**:197; **177**:12, 133
"La rempailleuse" (Maupassant) **83**:157, 159, 161, 194, 229
"Le remplacant" (Maupassant) **83**:232
La renaissance (Gobineau) **17**:75, 79-80, 88, 96, 98
The Renaissance (Gobineau)
See *La renaissance*
Renaissance in Italy (Symonds) **34**:316, 319, 321, 331, 334-35, 337, 340, 342, 344-51, 356-60, 362-65, 368, 374
The Renaissance: Studies in Art and Poetry (Pater) **7**:288-92, 294-99, 305, 308-10, 312-17, 323-24, 327, 332-34, 336-40, 342; **90**:239, 241-42, 244-45, 247-52, 254, 260-64, 269, 273-74, 276-80, 284, 286-91, 293, 298, 300, 304-06, 308-11, 315-17, 321-26, 328, 333-40; **159**:208-330
"Renan and the Jews" (Lazarus) **8**:423-24
Renate (Storm) **1**:540, 544, 546; **195**:6, 19, 82
"Rencontre" (Maupassant) **83**:181, 209
"The Rendezvous" (Lermontov) **5**:300
"Le Rendez-vous" (Maupassant) **83**:173
"Rendez-vous" (Verlaine) **230**:176, 214
"The Rendition" (Whittier) **8**:530
René (Chateaubriand) **3**:112, 117, 121-26, 128, 130, 133-34; **134**:11-13, 16, 18, 24-30, 61, 63, 70-73, 77-83, 86-88, 90-92, 94-95, 112, 116-17, 119, 121, 130, 134, 143-44
Renée Mauperin (Goncourt and Goncourt) **7**:151, 153, 155, 157, 161, 164, 166-67, 181, 187-88
"Le reniement de Saint-Pierre" (Baudelaire) **6**:94, 121; **29**:104
"Renoncement" (Desbordes-Valmore) **97**:17
"Renouveau" (Mallarmé) **41**:277
The Renovation of Society, or an Essay on the Propriety of a Revolution in the Governments of Europe (Barlow)
See *Advice to the Privileged Orders in the Several States of Europe, Resulting from the Necessity and Propriety of a General Revolution in the Principle of Government*
The Rent Day (Jerrold) **2**:395, 401, 403
A Rent in a Cloud (Lever) **23**:292
"Renunciation" (Eminescu) **33**:265
"Renunciation—is a piercing Virtue—" (Dickinson) **171**:156-57, 168, 201
"El reo de muerte" (Espronceda) **39**:100, 107
"A Reorganization of Society to Extirpate Sorrow" (Bellamy) **86**:65
"Les reparties de Nina" (Rimbaud) **4**:471; **35**:289-90; **82**:224; **227**:208
"The Repeal of the Differential Duties on Foreign and Colonial Wood" (Haliburton) **15**:128
"The Repeal of the Missouri Compromise and the Propriety of Its Restoration: Speech at Peoria Illinois, in Reply to Senator Douglas" (Lincoln)
See "Peoria Speech"
"Repentance: A Pastoral Ballad" (Wordsworth) **111**:234, 236
Repertorio Americano (Bello) **131**:108-9, 112, 116, 118-19, 129-31
Repetition (Kierkegaard)
See *Gjentagelsen. Et Forsøg i den experimenterende Psychologi*
"Repetition: An Essay in Experimental Psychology" (Kierkegaard)
See *Gjentagelsen. Et Forsøg i den experimenterende Psychologi*
"Repining" (Rossetti) **2**:566; **50**:288, 293; **66**:386
"Reply" (Coleridge) **90**:27
"Reply" (Constant) **182**:219
Reply (Coleridge) **90**:20
A Reply to an Answer to Cursory Strictures (Godwin) **130**:88
Reply to 'Mathetes' (Wordsworth) **166**:298
"Reply to my Friend, who Wanted Me to Write an Ode to Catherine the Great" (Karamzin) **173**:309
Reply to the Charges in the Quarterly (Bowles) **103**:64
"A Reply to the Essay on Population" (Hazlitt) **82**:99
A Reply to the Report of the Earl of Durham (Haliburton) **149**:272, 341, 346
"Reply to the Spanish Regency" (Bello) **131**:97-98
"Reply to the Strictures of Three Gentlemen upon Carlyle" (Coleridge) **31**:64
"Reply to the Warsaw Critics" (Mickiewicz)
See "O Krytykach i Recenzentach"
A Reply to 'Z' (Hazlitt) **29**:169
"Réponse a un acte d'accusation" (Verlaine) **51**:352
"Report" (Jackson)
See "Report on the Condition and Needs of the Mission Indians of California"
Report (Delany)
See *Report of the Select Committee on Emancipation and Colonization*
"Report of the Committee on the Question of Inheritance" (Bakunin) **58**:132
Report of the Select Committee on Emancipation and Colonization (Delany) **93**:97, 172
Report on Manufactures (Hamilton) **49**:298, 302, 324
Report on Public Credit (Hamilton) **49**:298
"Report on the Condition and Needs of the Mission Indians of California" (Jackson) **90**:136-42, 150, 169
Report on Weights and Measures (Adams) **175**:35-37, 57, 69

Report to Court of Proprietors on India Bills (Mill) **179**:356
The Report to Fothergill (Bartram)
See *Travels in Georgia and Florida, 1773-74: A Report to Dr. John Fothergill*
Reporting Editing and Authorship: Practical Hints for Beginners (Jefferies) **47**:139, 141
"The Repose on the Flight" (Fouqué) **2**:266
"The Repository" (Murray) **63**:181, 209
"Representación de La mojiigata" (Larra) **130**:195
"Representación de La niña en casa y la madre en la máscara de Don Francisco Martínez de la Rosa" (Larra) **130**:201
Representative Government (Mill)
See *Considerations on Representative Government*
"Representative Man" (Emerson) **98**:176
Representative Men: Seven Lectures (Emerson) **1**:281, 286, 288, 292-93, 299; **38**:172, 180, 206, 209, 211, 227; **98**:25, 65-6, 68-72, 155
Representative System (Alencar)
See *Systema Representative*
"Representatives of the Synod. The Period of Struggle for Predominance""Sinodalsoftnyie piersony. Pieriod borsoftby za prieobladaniie (1820-1840 gg.)" (Leskov) **174**:129
"The Reprieve" (Norton) **205**:128, 138
"Reproach to Laura" (Schiller) **39**:358
The Republic of Fools: Being the History of the State and People of Abdera in Thrace (Wieland)
See *Die Abderiten, eine sehr wahrscheinliche Geschichte*
"The Republic of the Pyrenees" (Taylor) **89**:312
Die Republik des Diogenes (Wieland)
See *Sokrates Mainomenos; oder, Die Dialogen des Diogenes von Sinope*
"La république" (Beranger) **34**:29
"A Request" (Preseren)
See "Prošnja"
"Requiem" (Meyer) **81**:146
"Requiem" (Stevenson) **5**:427
"Requies" (Leconte de Lisle) **29**:235
"Requiescat" (Arnold) **6**:44
"Requiescat in Pace" (Ingelow) **39**:263; **107**:119
"Requiescat in Pace" (Milnes) **61**:136
"Requirement" (Whittier) **8**:509
"Le réquisitionnaire" (Balzac) **5**:78; **153**:151
"The Res Gestae of a Poor Joke" (Hooper) **177**:175
Research on Sarmatia (Potocki) **229**:274
Researches, Concerning the Institutions & Monuments of the Ancient Inhabitants of America, with Descriptions & Views of Some of the Most Striking Scenes in the Cordilleras! (Williams) **135**:309
"Rešemyslu" (Derzhavin)
See "To Reshemysl"
"Resentment" (Crabbe) **26**:93, 129-30; **121**:5, 36
"Reshemysl" (Derzhavin)
See "To Reshemysl"
Residence in Europe (Cooper) **54**:255
Resident Women-Students (Dodgson) **139**:56
"Resignation" (Arnold) **6**:56, 74; **29**:29, 34-6; **89**:47, 88, 93; **126**:111; **218**:116, 145-48, 161, 183, 188, 275-76
"Résignation" (Laforgue) **221**:85
"Resignation" (Longfellow) **2**:475, 483; **45**:132, 140; **101**:92
"Resignation" (Schiller) **39**:331, 387; **166**:100-1, 118
"Résignation" (Verlaine) **230**:190, 193-96, 200
"Resignation—To Faustus" (Prescott) **163**:112
"Resigned Christmas" (Laforgue)
See "Noël résigné"
"Resistance to Civil Government" (Thoreau) **7**:375, 381, 385-6, 400, 406; **21**:318-72; **61**:368, 370, 373; **138**:130-31; **207**:191-93, 212-13, 228, 232-33, 236, 257, 276-77, 280, 282, 284, 286, 315-16, 318-27, 335-41
"Resolucióne tomadas por le emigracion cubana de Tampa" (Martí) **63**:127-9, 137
"Resolution and Independence" (Wordsworth) **12**:418, 427, 435-36, 445, 447, 450, 455, 459, 470; **111**:218, 226; **206**:245, 271, 275
"Resolutions Taken by the Cuban Emigrants of Tampa" (Martí)
See "Resolucióne tomadas por le emigracion cubana de Tampa"
"Resolutions to the United States House of Representatives, December 22, 1847" (Lincoln) **201**:160
"Respectability" (Browning) **19**:131
"The Respectable Folks" (Thoreau) **138**:67
"Respondez!" (Whitman) **81**:263-65; **205**:158
"The Response" (Whittier) **8**:489
"Respublica" (Petofi) **21**:286
La respuesta de la tierra (Silva) **114**:274
Les ressources de Quinola (Balzac) **5**:51
Ressouvenir du lac Léman (Lamartine) **190**:213-14
"The Rest" (Barnes) **75**:69
"Rest" (Hopkins) **189**:10-12
"Rest" (Kendall) **12**:183
"Rest" (Rossetti) **2**:563; **50**:271, 282, 289-90; **66**:301; **186**:304
"Rest at Last" (Lazarus) **109**:291
"Rest Only in the Grave" (Mangan) **27**:298
Restless Human Hearts (Jefferies) **47**:92-93, 116
The Restoration of the Works of Art to Italy (Hemans) **29**:192; **71**:261
Results of Experience (Thelwall) **162**:344
"Resurgemus" (Whitman) **205**:312
"Resurrección" (Isaacs) **70**:310-11
"Resurrection" (Lanier) **6**:236, 238
"The Resurrection" (Manzoni) **29**:253
Resurrecturis (Krasiński) **4**:304, 307
"Resurrexit" (Silva) **114**:263-64
"Reszket a bokor..." (Petofi) **21**:285
"The Retaliation of the Individual to the State" (Thoreau)
See "Resistance to Civil Government"
"The Reticent Volcano Keeps" (Dickinson) **21**:82
"The Retired Cat" (Cowper) **8**:119
Retired from Business (Jerrold) **2**:403
"Retirement" (Beattie) **25**:106, 108, 111
"Retirement" (Cowper) **8**:113, 139-40; **94**:23, 27, 51, 115
"Retirement" (Timrod) **25**:372, 381
Retirement (Cowper) **94**:14, 59-65, 92
"Le retour" (Lamartine) **11**:289
"Retour dans une église" (Desbordes-Valmore) **97**:29
"La retraite" (Lamartine) **11**:245, 264
"El retrato de Felisa" (Isaacs) **70**:307
The Retreat (Warren) **13**:414
"Retribution" (Chamisso) **82**:6
Retribution; or, The Vale of Shadows: A Tale of Passion (Southworth) **26**:430-32, 435-37, 439, 442, 446-47
"Retro Me, Sathana!" (Rossetti) **4**:529
"The Retrospect" (Chivers) **49**:70
Retrospect of Western Travel (Martineau) **26**:311, 315, 318, 322, 334, 336; **137**:302, 316-18, 322, 328, 331-34, 336, 357-58, 360
The Retrospect; or, The American Revolution (Dunlap) **2**:218
Retrospection (Cumberland) **167**:125, 135
Retrospection; or, a Review of the Most Striking and Important Events, Characters, Situations, and Their Consequences, Which the Last Eighteen Hundred Years Have Presented to the View of Mankind (Piozzi) **57**:233, 243, 252-3, 267, 271, 302
"The Retrospective Review" (Hood) **16**:201, 219, 233
"Retrospects and Prospects" (Lanier) **6**:245, 257, 277; **118**:218, 220, 260, 272-75
"The Return" (Macha) **46**:203
"Return at Evening" (Lenau) **16**:276
"The Return of Claneboy" (Ferguson) **33**:287, 299
The Return of Martin Fierro (Hernández)
See *La vuelta de Martín Fierro*
"The Return of Peace" (Hayne) **94**:145-46, 149
The Return of the Druses (Browning) **19**:102, 113
The Return of the O'Mahony (Frederic) **10**:183, 192-94; **175**:124
"The Return of the Recruit" (Isaacs)
See "La vuelta del recluta"
"The Return of the Year" (Lampman) **194**:30, 81-82, 139
"A Return To Barbarism" (Frederic) **175**:151
"Return to Spain" (Martínez de la Rosa) **102**:228
"Return to the South" (Heredia)
See "Vuelta al sur"
Reuben and Rachel; or, Tales of Old Times (Rowson) **5**:310-12, 314, 316-17, 320-21; **69**:103, 105-06, 113, 148-55; **182**:256, 259-60, 262, 313, 356
Reuben Sachs (Levy) **59**:77, 84-7, 91, 95-7, 101-5, 111-3, 115-9, 127-8, 130-5
Reuben Sachs: A Sketch (Levy) **203**:294-302, 304, 309-10, 320, 336, 349
"Reullura" (Campbell) **19**:176, 181
"Re-union" (Taylor) **89**:298
"Un rêve" (Bertrand) **31**:47, 54
"Rêve" (Laforgue) **221**:82
"Un Rêve" (Musset) **150**:229, 309
"Le rêve du jaguar" (Leconte de Lisle) **29**:216, 224
"Le rêve d'un curieux" (Baudelaire) **29**:77, 105; **55**:12, 52, 66, 73
Le rêve et la vie (Nerval) **1**:476, 478; **67**:335
"Rêve familier" (Verlaine) **2**:617, 622
"Rêve parisien" (Baudelaire) **6**:84; **29**:92, 101; **55**:12, 23-4, 31; **155**:3
"Rêve pour l'hiver" (Rimbaud) **35**:271-72, 321; **227**:255
"Révélation" (Desbordes-Valmore) **97**:15
"The Revelation" (Patmore) **9**:347
"The Revelation of all Posey" (Fuller) **50**:245
"The Revelation of the Spirit through the Material World" (Very) **9**:390
Revelations of London (Ainsworth) **13**:45
"Revel'skii turnir" (Bestuzhev) **131**:165, 172, 183, 185, 209-10
"Revenge" (Balzac)
See "La vendetta revenge"
"Revenge" (Shelley) **18**:342
"Revenge of America" (Warton) **118**:356
The Revenge of Etruria (Alfieri)
See *L'Etruria vendicata*
"The Revenge of Hamish" (Lanier) **6**:236, 249, 254, 265, 269-70, 279-80; **118**:203, 238
"Revenge of the Signor Basil" (Willis) **194**:282
Revenue and Public Expenditure (Barlow)
See *Advice to the Privileged Orders in the Several States of Europe, Resulting from the Necessity and Propriety of a General Revolution in the Principle of Government*
"Les révérend pères" (Beranger) **34**:28
"A Reverie" (Baillie) **151**:86, 93-95, 123
"Reverie at Glenmary" (Willis) **194**:307
"Rêverie d'un passant" (Hugo) **21**:214
"Reversals" (Whitman) **205**:157
"Reversibilité" (Baudelaire) **55**:14, 45, 60
"Reversibilities" (Verlaine) **51**:368
"Revery" (Mallarmé) **41**:258
Rêves d'amour (Scribe) **16**:412
"Les rêves morts" (Leconte de Lisle) **29**:228, 235
"Review of Aenesidemus" (Fichte) **62**:8
"Review of Lockhart's Life of Scott" (Keble) **87**:135
"Review of Some Poems by Alexander Smith and Matthew Arnold" (Prescott) **163**:71

"The Review of the Army" (Mickiewicz) **3**:401
"Review of the Causes of the Late War" (Brontë) **109**:35
Review of the Decision of the Supreme Court of the United States in the Case of McCulloch vs. the State of Maryland (Longstreet) **159**:173
A Review of the Speeches of Pope Pius IX (Gladstone) **213**:117
"The Revival of Antiquity" (Pater) **159**:255
The Revival of Learning (Symonds) **34**:318-19, 346-48, 357, 363, 368, 370
"The Revival of Romanism" (Froude) **43**:214-15
Révizor (Gogol) **5**:210, 213-14, 216, 219-23, 213-34, 239, 250, 255, 257; **15**:78-114; **31**:82-4, 92, 94, 97, 99-100, 102, 106, 111-13, 116-19, 135, 139, 141, 144; **162**:8, 11-13, 17, 19, 25, 27-30, 44, 46, 49-51, 62-64, 67-68, 87-88, 97, 117
The Revolt (Villiers de l'Isle Adam)
See *La révolte*
The Revolt of Hindostan; or, the New World: A Poem (Jones)
See *The New World: A Democratic Poem*
"The Revolt of Islam" (Lampman) **25**:211; **194**:26-27, 36
The Revolt of Islam (Shelley)
See *Laon and Cythna; or, The Revolution of the Golden City: A Vision of the Nineteenth Century*
The Revolt of Islam; A Poem, in Twelve Cantos (Shelley)
See *Laon and Cythna; or, The Revolution of the Golden City: A Vision of the Nineteenth Century*
"The Revolt of the Tartars" (De Quincey) **87**:3
"Révolte" (Baudelaire) **6**:91, 113, 116, 122, 124; **55**:66, 73-4
Révolte (Baudelaire) **155**:44, 113
La révolte (Villiers de l'Isle Adam) **3**:584-85
La revolte des Maures sous Philip II (Martínez de la Rosa) **102**:243-44
"La revolución actual en España" (Martínez de la Rosa) **102**:245, 248, 250
La revolución de Cuba vista desde Nueva York (Villaverde) **121**:335
La Révolution (Hugo) **161**:155-60, 163
La révolution (Taine) **15**:428-29, 433, 447-48, 455, 474-76
Revolution and Counter-Revolution (Engels)
See *Revolution and Counter-revolution in Germany*
Revolution and Counter-Revolution (Marx) **114**:8
Revolution and Counter-revolution in Germany (Engels) **85**:117, 132, 138-39, 141, 145-46, 150
"Revolution at Athens" (Landor) **14**:187
The Revolution in France, Considered in Respect to Its Progress and Effects (Webster) **30**:415
The Revolution of the World (Paine) **62**:254
"Revolutionary Catechism" (Bakunin) **58**:109, 135
Revolutionary Epic (Disraeli) **2**:148; **39**:67; **79**:215-16, 220, 233, 269, 275, 277
The Revolutionary Government (Taine)
See *La révolution*
The Revolutionary Question: Federalism, Socialism, and Anti-Theologism (Bakunin) **25**:48; **58**:110, 135, 140
"Revolutions" (Arnold) **29**:36
"Les Révolutions" (Lamartine)
See "Ode sur les Révolutions"
The Revolver (Fredro)
See *Rewolwer*
Revue de Paris (Balzac)
See *Revue parisienne*
Revue du Salon (Goncourt and Goncourt) **7**:153
Revue parisienne (Balzac) **153**:147, 153
Reward (Bentham)
See *The Rationale of Reward*
Reward (Norton)
See *The Woman's Reward*
The Reward of the Virtuous (Smolenskin)
See *ha-Gemul*
Rewolwer (Fredro) **8**:293
"El rey Ulises" (Isaacs) **70**:311
Reynard the Fox (Goethe)
See *Reineke Fuchs*
Reynard the Fox (Grimm Brothers)
See *Reinhart Fuchs*
Rhapsodies (Borel) **41**:3, 5, 10, 19
The Rhapsodist: And Other Uncollected Writings (Brown) **74**:54, 67, 109-10, 115, 170, 172-74, 201
"A Rhapsody" (Clare) **9**:107; **86**:111
"Rhapsody of a Southern Winter Night" (Timrod) **25**:373
"The Rhapsody of Life's Progress" (Barrett Browning) **1**:115, 129; **170**:108
"Der Rhein" (Hölderlin) **16**:162, 175-6, 180, 192, 195-6; **187**:218, 225, 232, 282, 284
Rhein Fairytales (Brentano)
See *Rheinmärchen*
Das Rheingold (Wagner) **9**:408-09, 441, 445, 448, 454, 456, 459, 463, 466, 469; **119**:177, 186-87, 193, 197, 202-08, 212, 221-25, 228-32, 268, 277, 282, 318-20, 346, 350, 354
"Rheinische Thalia" (Schiller) **39**:338
Rheinmärchen (Brentano) **191**:68, 70, 136
"The Rhenish Apprentice" (Muller) **73**:350
"Rhetoric" (De Quincey) **4**:61, 81
Le Rhin (Hugo) **3**:276; **21**:201; **161**:187-88
"The Rhine" (Bowles) **103**:80
"The Rhine" (Hölderlin)
See "Der Rhein"
"Rhine" (Schlegel) **142**:302
"Der rhodische Genius" (Humboldt)
See "Die Lebenskraft, oder Der Rhodische Genius"
"The Rhodora" (Emerson) **1**:289, 296; **98**:177, 179
"Rhoecus" (Lowell) **2**:503, 522
"Rhoecus and the Dryad" (Hayne) **94**:158
"Rhyme" (Baratynsky)
See "Rifma"
Rhyme? And Reason? (Dodgson) **139**:9, 124, 127, 129
The Rhyme and Reason of Country Life (Cooper) **129**:4, 9-10, 12, 46-47, 68-69
"The Rhyme of Joyous Garde" (Gordon) **21**:153-55, 157, 160, 163, 166-68, 170, 173-75, 183, 187-88
"Rhyme of Sir Christopher" (Longfellow) **45**:149
"The Rhyme of Sir Lancelot Bogle" (Barrett Browning) **1**:126
"The Rhyme of the Duchess May" (Barrett Browning) **1**:115, 117, 121-2, 124, 126; **61**:6, 43, 65, 67, 75
"Rhymed Criticisms" (Harpur) **114**:97, 126
Rhymes of Travel, Ballads and Poems (Taylor) **89**:297, 299, 307
A Rhyming Chronicle of Incidents and Feelings (Ingelow) **39**:263; **107**:118
Ribbemont; or, The Feudal Baron (Dunlap) **2**:212-15
"Ribblesdale" (Hopkins) **17**:250; **189**:7, 43, 47
"Ribič" (Preseren) **127**:298
La ricahembra (Tamayo y Baus) **1**:570-71
"Ricaurte" (Isaacs) **70**:313
Ricciarda (Foscolo) **8**:262, 270
"The Rice Lake Plains" (Traill) **31**:327
"Rich and Rare" (Maginn) **8**:441
A Rich Man (Galt) **110**:78-9, 95
"Rich Man and Cobbler" (Krylov) **1**:439
"A Rich Scene in Bank on Tuesday" (Lippard) **198**:133
"Richard and Kate" (Bloomfield) **145**:128, 130, 147, 149-55, 177
Richard Darlington (Dumas) **11**:42-43, 47-48, 67, 71; **71**:184, 192-93
Richard Hurdis; or, The Avenger of Blood (Simms) **3**:507-09, 512-14
Richard II (Cumberland) **167**:191
"Richard Redpath" (Moodie) **14**:237-38
Richard Wagner's Prose Works (Wagner) **119**:189
Richardson's War of 1812 (Richardson)
See *War of 1812*
"Un riche en Bretagne" (Corbière) **43**:3, 29
Richelieu; or, The Conspiracy (Bulwer-Lytton) **1**:139; **45**:62-4, 67, 69
The Richest Heiress in England (Oliphant) **11**:454
"Richmond Hill" (Arnold) **29**:27
Richochets de conversation (Barbey d'Aurevilly) **213**:61, 66, 90-91, 96
Die Richterin (Meyer) **81**:163-65, 194, 196, 217
"Le ricordanze" (Leopardi) **129**:219, 228, 250, 339, 341, 356-57, 360
Riddertornet (Stagnelius) **61**:248
"The Riddle" (Auden) **79**:274-75
"Riddle" (Lampman) **194**:34
"Riddles: Anne and Joey A-Ta'ken" (Barnes) **75**:78
"A Ride across Palestine" (Trollope) **101**:233
"The Ride of Paul Revere" (Longfellow)
See "Paul Revere's Ride"
"A Ride over the Mountains" (Cranch) **115**:48
"The Ride Round the Parapet" (Mangan) **27**:296, 298
"Ride to Aix" (Browning) **79**:274-75
"A Ride with Old Kit Knucker" (Hooper) **177**:175
A Ride with Old Kit Knucker, and Other Sketches, and Scenes of Alabama (Hooper) **177**:172, 175, 215
"Le rideau cramoisi" (Barbey d'Aurevilly) **1**:74, 78; **213**:21, 68
"Le Rideau de ma voisine" (Musset) **150**:309
The Rider on the White Horse (Storm)
See *Der Schimmelreiter*
"Ridiculous Distress of a Country Weekly News Printer" (Freneau) **111**:129
"Riding Together" (Morris) **4**:444
"The Ridotto" (Sheridan)
See "The Ridotto of Bath, a Panegyrick, Being an Epistle from Timothy Screw, Under Server to Messrs. Kuhf and Fitzwater, to his brother Heny, Waiter at Almack's"
"Ridotto of Bath" (Sheridan)
See "The Ridotto of Bath, a Panegyrick, Being an Epistle from Timothy Screw, Under Server to Messrs. Kuhf and Fitzwater, to his brother Heny, Waiter at Almack's"
"The Ridotto of Bath" (Sheridan)
See "The Ridotto of Bath, a Panegyrick, Being an Epistle from Timothy Screw, Under Server to Messrs. Kuhf and Fitzwater, to his brother Heny, Waiter at Almack's"
"The Ridotto of Bath, a Panegyrick, Being an Epistle from Timothy Screw, Under Server to Messrs. Kuhf and Fitzwater, to his brother Heny, Waiter at Almack's" (Sheridan) **91**:230-31, 239
Rienzi (Mitford) **4**:403
Rienzi (Wagner) **9**:401, 406, 414-16, 419, 433, 436-37, 444, 473, 475; **119**:189, 191-92, 241
Rienzi, the Last of the Tribunes (Bulwer-Lytton) **1**:138, 140, 150-51; **45**:13-15, 22, 27, 55, 57-8, 69
"Rienzi's Downfall" (Wagner) **9**:475
Rienzi's Fall (Wagner)
See "Rienzi's Downfall"
"Rifle Clubs!!!" (Tennyson) **30**:294
"Riflemen Form" (Tennyson) **30**:294; **202**:291
"Rifma" (Baratynsky) **103**:16, 22, 36

"Right at Last" (Gaskell) **5**:201; **70**:190
The Right Way the Safe Way, proved by Emancipation in the British West Indies and Elsewhere (Child) **73**:63
"The Rights and Duties of the Individual in Relation to the Government" (Thoreau)
See "Resistance to Civil Government"
The Rights of Man (Paine) **62**:247, 252-5, 257, 259, 261, 266, 270, 274-5, 277-9, 281, 285, 295-302, 312, 327-9, 331-2, 334-9, 341-3, 345-9, 351-5, 357, 359-63, 365, 369, 373-80, 385, 390-1, 393
"Rights of Man in America" (Parker) **186**:193
The Rights of Nature Against the Usurpations of Establishments (Thelwall) **162**:310, 312-13
"Rights of the Temporal" (Brownson) **50**:51
"The Rights of Woman" (Barbauld) **50**:14; **185**:15, 111, 113-14, 122, 154-55
"Rights of Woman" (Rowson) **5**:313, 322; **182**:257, 261
"Rights of Women" (Neal) **161**:348
"The Rill from the Town-Pump" (Hawthorne) **2**:291; **191**:215
"Rim" (Gogol) **5**:227, 256; **31**:137; **162**:17-18, 64, 108, 130
"Rim" (Pavlova) **138**:53
"Rima 60/xv" (Bécquer) **106**:102
"Rima I" (Bécquer) **106**:148, 161
"Rima II" (Bécquer) **106**:106, 126-27
"Rima III" (Bécquer) **106**:105, 114, 116, 126-27, 160
"Rima IV" (Bécquer) **106**:101, 103, 125, 150
"Rima IX" (Bécquer) **106**:150
"Rima L" (Bécquer) **106**:161
"Rima LI" (Bécquer) **106**:170
"Rima LII" (Bécquer) **106**:127, 170
"Rima LVI" (Bécquer) **106**:126
"Rima LXII" (Bécquer) **106**:126
"Rima LXIX" (Bécquer) **106**:126
"Rima LXXI" (Bécquer) **106**:112, 124, 155-56
"Rima LXXII" (Bécquer) **106**:127, 150
"Rima LXXIII" (Bécquer) **106**:125
"Rima LXXIV" (Bécquer) **106**:103, 114, 159
"Rima LXXIX" (Bécquer) **106**:170
"Rima LXXV" (Bécquer) **106**:123-25, 129
"Rima LXXVI" (Bécquer) **106**:127
"Rima LXXXVI" (Bécquer) **106**:114, 124
"Rima V" (Bécquer) **106**:104, 124, 127
"Rima VI" (Bécquer) **106**:150
"Rima VII" (Bécquer) **106**:104, 160
"Rima VIII" (Bécquer) **106**:105, 116, 124, 126, 137
"Rima X" (Bécquer) **106**:110, 149-50
"Rima XI" (Bécquer) **106**:102, 108, 134
"Rima XII" (Bécquer) **106**:127, 169
"Rima XIV" (Bécquer) **106**:115, 124, 126
"Rima XVI" (Bécquer) **106**:124, 161
"Rima XXI" (Bécquer) **106**:102
"Rima XXIII" (Bécquer) **106**:151
"Rima XXIV" (Bécquer) **106**:127, 150
"Rima XXIX" (Bécquer) **106**:150, 169
"Rima XXVI" (Bécquer) **106**:106
"Rima XXVII" (Bécquer) **106**:128
"Rima XXX" (Bécquer) **106**:170
"Rima XXXIV" (Bécquer) **106**:150
"Rima XXXVII" (Bécquer) **106**:126-27
Rimas (Bécquer) **106**:92, 96, 99, 101, 109-10, 112, 118, 123, 125, 130, 137, 142, 167-75
Las rimas (Bécquer)
See *Rimas*
Rimas (Casal) **131**:255, 269-71
Rimas (Echeverria) **18**:147-49, 152-54
"Rimas II" (Bécquer)
See "Rima II"
"Rimas III" (Bécquer)
See "Rima III"
Rimbaud: Oeuvres Complètes (Rimbaud)
See *Oeuvres complètes*
Rimbaud's Illuminations: A Study in Angelism (Rimbaud)
See *Les illuminations*
"The Rime" (Coleridge)
See *The Rime of the Ancient Mariner: A Poet's Reverie*
"The Rime of the Ancient Mariner" (Coleridge)
See *The Rime of the Ancient Mariner: A Poet's Reverie*
The Rime of the Ancient Mariner (Coleridge) **197**:176-333
The Rime of the Ancient Mariner: A Poet's Reverie (Coleridge) **9**:130-32, 138-44, 146, 148-53, 156, 158-59, 164-67, 175-77, 179-89, 191, 194, 204, 210-12; **54**:65-132; **99**:2, 4-7, 19, 25, 41, 56, 65-6, 89, 94, 101, 104; **111**:197, 199-200, 239, 248-51, 256, 259, 289-95, 305-9, 311-16, 322, 332; **177**:13-14, 17, 21, 27, 32, 36, 59, 104, 146, 149, 155-56, 158, 160-62; **231**:14, 16, 18, 21, 26, 53-57, 62, 82-83, 86-87, 91, 94, 104, 111, 113-14, 124-25, 130, 133-34, 137-38, 140-45
"The Rime of the Ancient Waggoner" (Maginn) **8**:438
The Rime of the Ancyent Marinere (Coleridge)
See *The Rime of the Ancient Mariner: A Poet's Reverie*
Rime of the Merrie Devil of Edmonton (Horne) **127**:255
Rimes dorées (Banville) **9**:18
Rinaldo Rinaldini (Dunlap) **2**:211
"The Ring" (Baratynsky)
See "Persten'"
"The Ring" (Tennyson) **30**:226; **115**:247
The Ring and the Book (Browning) **19**:80-3, 88, 90, 92, 94-6, 98, 102, 110-11, 114, 118-19, 126-28, 133, 135, 142, 148, 152, 154-58; **79**:111, 116-21, 123, 125-27, 129-34, 149-53, 156, 161, 163-66, 180, 182, 184, 187, 189-90
"The Ring and the Books" (Gordon) **21**:179
The Ring Cycle (Wagner)
See *Der Ring des Nibelungen*
Der Ring des Nibelungen (Wagner) **9**:409-10, 412-14, 416-17, 419, 421-22, 424-29, 433, 435, 437-38, 440-42, 444-50, 452, 458-60, 462-65, 469-71, 473-74; **119**:175, 182-83, 185-88, 190, 195-98, 203-17, 219-31, 233-38, 241-43, 248, 259, 264, 274-83, 289-93, 295, 300, 305, 308-11, 316-23, 329, 346-56
"Der Ring des Polykrates" (Schiller) **39**:330, 337, 388; **166**:105
"The Ring Fetter" (Cooke) **110**:34, 41, 46, 51, 56, 58, 65
"The Ring Given to Venus" (Morris) **4**:448
Ring of Gyges (Hebbel)
See *Gyges und sein Ring: Eine Tragödie in fünf Acten*
"The Ring of Polycrates" (Schiller)
See "Der Ring des Polykrates"
The Ring of the Nibelung (Wagner)
See *Der Ring des Nibelungen*
"Ringan and May" (Hogg) **4**:282-83
Ringan Gilhaize (Galt) **1**:333-34; **110**:107-12
"Rings" (Barnes) **75**:46
"Río Moro" (Isaacs) **70**:309
The Riot; or, Half a Loaf Is Better than No Bread (More) **27**:358-59; **141**:167, 171, 189, 216, 311
"The Rioters" (Martineau) **26**:309; **137**:264-65, 267
"Rip Van Winkle" (Irving) **2**:366-68, 376-79, 381-83, 386, 389-92; **19**:327-29, 331-39, 341, 345, 347-48, 350; **95**:227, 235-36, 240, 243, 245, 247, 249-50, 265, 283, 286, 300
Rip Van Winkle (Boucicault) **41**:31
"Rippling Water" (Gordon) **21**:160, 181
Riquet with the Tuft (Planché) **42**:278-80, 287, 298
"The Rise and Fall of the European Drama" (Lewes) **25**:302
Rise and Fall of the Free City-States of Greece (Humboldt) **134**:186
"Rise and Progress of Navigation" (Rowson) **69**:115
"Rise O Days" (Whitman) **205**:158, 338
"Rise O Days from Your Fathomless Deeps" (Whitman) **81**:313, 330
The Rise of Iskander (Disraeli) **39**:24, 40, 46; **79**:214-14, 228, 274-75
The Rise, Progress and Termination of the American Revolution (Warren)
See *History of the Rise, Progress, and Termination of the American Revolution: Interspersed with Biographical and Moral Observations*
Risen from the Ranks; or, Harry Walton's Success (Alger) **8**:24; **83**:104, 131
"The Rising Glory of America" (Brackenridge) **7**:54, 57
The Rising Glory of America (Brackenridge)
See *A Poem on the Rising Glory of America: Being an Exercise Delivered on the Public Commencement at Nassau-Hall*
"The Rising Glory of America" (Freneau)
See *A Poem, on the Rising Glory of America*
"The Rising of the Nations" (Chivers) **49**:75
The Rising Son; or, The Antecedents and Advancements of the Colored Race (Brown) **2**:48-51, 53; **89**:161, 163-64
"Rispah" (Bryant) **6**:162
Rispetti (Webster) **230**:303, 307-08, 310
Rite of the Graces (Foscolo) **97**:53
"Der Ritt in den Tod" (Meyer) **81**:142, 207-09
"The Ritter Bann" (Campbell) **19**:176, 190
Ritter Blaubart (Tieck) **5**:513, 515, 517, 521-23
"Ritter Glück" (Hoffmann) **2**:345, 361; **183**:197, 214, 223, 228, 314
"Ritter Kurts Brautfahrt" (Goethe) **4**:192
"The Rival Painters. A Tale of Rome" (Alcott) **83**:5
The Rival Races; or, The Sons of Joel (Sue)
See *Les mystères du peuple*
"The Rival Roses" (Crawford) **12**:172; **127**:182, 184
The Rival Sisters. A Tragedy. Adapted for Theatrical Representation, as Performed at the Theatre-Royal, Drury-Lane. Regulated from the Prompt-Book (Murphy) **229**:229, 234
The Rivals (Griffin) **7**:195, 201, 213-14, 218
The Rivals (Sheridan) **5**:354-55, 357-63, 365, 369-73, 375-76, 378-83; **91**:236-37, 239-41, 245-48, 251-54, 256-64, 266-70
"Rivals, A Shadow of Saint Dorothea" (Rossetti) **66**:307
"The River" (Bryant) **6**:175
"The River" (Hayne) **94**:159, 161-62
"The River" (Patmore) **9**:326-27, 348
"The River and the Hill" (Kendall) **12**:178
"The River, By Night" (Bryant) **46**:22
"The River Cherwell" (Bowles)
See "To the River Cherwell, Oxford"
The River Duddon (Wordsworth) **166**:213
"The River Gwash" (Clare) **9**:72
"The River Itchin" (Bowles)
See "To the River Itchin, Near Winton"
"River of beauty flowing through the life" (Fuller) **50**:250
"The River of Death" (Cranch) **115**:49
The River of Time (Grundtvig) **158**:155
"The River Path" (Whittier) **8**:531
"The River Rhone" (Longfellow) **45**:121
"The River Swelleth More and More" (Thoreau) **7**:383
"Rivers Don't Gi'e Out" (Barnes) **75**:88
La rivoluzione francese del 1789 e la rivoluzione italiana del 1859: Osservazioni comparative (Manzoni) **98**:216, 276-78
"The Rivulet" (Bryant) **6**:159, 169; **46**:8, 13, 15, 39, 48
"The Rivulet" (Webster) **230**:308-13

"Rivulet" (Whitman) **4**:551
"The Rivulet's Dream" (Osgood) **141**:323-24, 326
"Rizpah" (Bryant) **46**:43
"Rizpah" (Kendall) **12**:192
"Rizpah" (Tennyson) **30**:245
Rjeĉnik (Karadzic) **115**:77, 104
"Road along the Precipice in Czufut-Kale" (Mickiewicz)
See "Droga nad przepascic w Czufut-Kale"
"The Road from Station almala to the Post at Mugansa" (Bestuzhev)
See "Doroga ot stantsii Almaly do posta Mugansy"
"The Road to a Woman's Heart" (Haliburton) **149**:288
"The Road to Avernus" (Gordon) **21**:155, 160, 163, 167-68, 187-88
The Road to Ruin (Holcroft) **85**:192-93, 195, 204-07, 209, 221-23, 225, 234, 239
"The Road to Russia" (Mickiewicz) **3**:401
"A Road-side Post-office" (Cooper) **129**:71
"Roaring Brook" (Willis) **194**:307
Rob of the Bowl: A Legend of St. Inigoe's (Kennedy) **2**:429-33
Rob Roy (Scott) **15**:300, 303-04; **69**:310, 313; **110**:305; **209**:215-16, 230, 235, 238, 242, 250, 252, 271, 281-82, 285-86, 297, 305-7, 309, 319, 350
"The Robber" (Clare) **86**:103
"The Robber" (Leskov) **174**:123
"The Robber" (Opie) **65**:159
The Robber Brothers (Pushkin)
See *Bratya Razboiniki*
The Robbers (Schiller)
See *Die Raüber*
"The Robber's Song to His Mistress" (Ridge) **82**:180
"A Robbery" (Leskov)
See "Grabež"
The Robbery (Dunlap) **2**:214
"Robert Ardagh" (Le Fanu)
See "The Fortunes of Sir Robert Ardagh"
"Robert Burns" (Halleck) **47**:56, 65, 69, 71, 78, 83
"Robert Burns" (Thomson) **18**:414
Robert der Teufel (Nestroy) **42**:225-26
Robert Elsmere (Gladstone) **213**:117
"Robert Franz" (Liszt) **199**:298
Robert Guiskard, Herzog der Normänner (Kleist) **2**:437-38, 440-43, 445; **37**:217, 219, 223, 229, 255, 267, 272; **222**:203-4, 206, 227-29, 232, 254
Robert le Diable (Scribe) **16**:390, 408, 411
"Robert of Lincoln" (Bryant) **6**:165, 169, 182
"Robert Slender's Idea of a Visit to a Modern Great Man" (Freneau) **111**:134
"Robert Slender's Idea of the Human Soul" (Freneau) **111**:132
Robert the Devil (Scribe)
See *Robert le Diable*
"The Robin" (Lampman) **194**:140
"The Robin" (Very) **9**:380
"The Robin and the Violet" (Field) **3**:205
"Robin Redbreast" (Allingham) **25**:7
Robinson Crusoë (Pixérécourt) **39**:278-79, 281-82
"Los robles" (Castro) **3**:103
"La Roche" (Mackenzie)
See "The Effects of Religion on Minds of Sensibility. Story of La Roche"
"The Rock and the Sea" (Tyutchev)
See "The Sea and the Cliff"
"Rock Crystal" (Stifter)
See "Bergkristall"
"The Rock of Cader-Idris" (Hemans) **71**:277, 306
"Rock of the Candle" (Griffin) **7**:198
"The Rock-a-by-Lady" (Field) **3**:210
The Rockite, an Irish Story (Tonna) **135**:203
The Rocky Mountains; Or, Scenes, Incidents, and Adventures in the Far West (Irving) **95**:258
The Rod, the Root, and the Flower (Patmore) **9**:344, 354, 363-64
"De røde Skoe" (Andersen) **7**:21, 23, 31, 34-35; **79**:23, 51, 53, 59-60, 67, 76; **214**:41, 47, 50
Roderick: The Last of the Goths (Southey) **8**:454-56, 459, 461, 469-71, 474, 476, 478-79; **97**:261-62, 268-69, 278-79, 291, 293-94, 297-300, 330-338
"Rodina" (Lermontov) **5**:295; **126**:144, 190-91, 213
"Rodina" (Nekrasov) **11**:412, 418, 420
"Rodman the Keeper" (Woolson) **82**:294-95, 297, 300-02
Rodman the Keeper: Southern Sketches (Woolson) **82**:268-69, 272-73, 283, 292-94, 299, 303-04, 306-07, 338-39
"Rodolph" (Beddoes) **154**:9-12, 68
"Rodolph" (Pinkney) **31**:267, 269-70, 273, 275-77, 279, 281
"Rodolph the Wild" (Beddoes) **154**:9, 67
Rody the Rover; or, the Ribbonman (Carleton) **199**:8-9, 19-20, 97
"Roger Bontemps" (Beranger) **34**:34
"Roger Malvin's Burial" (Hawthorne) **2**:298; **23**:201; **39**:197, 200; **79**:311; **95**:115, 147; **171**:342
"Rogêt" (Poe)
See "The Mystery of Marie Rogêt"
A Rogue's Life (Collins) **93**:38
"Rohtraut" (Mörike)
See "Schön-Rohtraut"
"Le Roi candaule" (Gautier) **1**:344-45; **59**:10-11, 13-14, 31-3
"Le roi de Bicêtre" (Nerval) **1**:483, 485; **67**:335
Le roi de Ladawa (Slowacki) **15**:368
"Roi d'Yvetot" (Beranger) **34**:39
Le roi Pépin (Dumas) **71**:219
Le roi s'amuse (Hugo) **3**:236, 239, 241, 261-62, 269; **161**:236; **161**:235
Les rois en exil (Daudet) **1**:233-37, 239-41, 243-44, 247, 250-51
"Roisin Dubh" (Mangan) **27**:307, 318
Rokeby: A Poem (Scott) **209**:189-91, 258
Roland Cashel (Lever) **23**:292, 295, 301, 311
Roland Yorke (Wood) **178**:283, 288, 291
"The Role of the National Literature in the Public Spirit" (Eminescu) **33**:257
"The Role of the Semitic Peoples in the History of Civilization" (Renan) **26**:421
"The Role Played by Labor in the Transition from Ape to Man" (Engels) **85**:38-42, 95
"The Roll of Fame" (Chivers) **49**:51
"The Roll of the Kettledrum; or, The Lay of the Last Charger" (Gordon) **21**:154, 156, 159, 177, 181
"Rolla" (Musset) **7**:255, 258-64, 274; **150**:231, 234, 241, 244, 246, 250, 311-12, 322
Rolla (Musset) **150**:225-26, 314
"Le roman" (Maupassant)
See *Etude sur le roman*
"Roman" (Rimbaud) **35**:290; **82**:224
Roman (Dobell) **43**:40, 42, 44, 49-51, 53-6, 59-60, 62, 74
"Roman and Olga" (Bestuzhev)
See "Starinnaia povest'—Roman i Ol'ga"
The Roman and the Teuton (Kingsley) **35**:246, 253
"Roman Anemones" (Blind) **202**:57
Le Roman de Charles Cecil (Charriere) **66**:126
Le Roman de la momie (Gautier) **1**:340, 342, 344-45, 347; **59**:6, 12, 56, 58-59, 61
Le Roman d'un Jeune Homme Pauvre (Feuillet) **45**:74-5, 78-9, 84-5, 87-9
Roman Elegies (Goethe)
See *Römische Elegien*
"The Roman Fountain" (Meyer)
See "Der römische Brunnen"
"Roman Journal" (Hawthorne) **150**:201-5, 207
A Roman Journal (Stendhal)
See *Promenades dans Rome*
The Roman Matron (Tieck)
See *Vittoria Accorombona*
"Roman Rose-Seller" (Crawford) **12**:161
Roman tragique (Nerval) **1**:486; **67**:325, 328-31
Roman v pismakh (Pushkin) **3**:447; **83**:319-20, 323, 331
Roman v semi pis'makh (Bestuzhev) **131**:172, 210-11
"Romance" (Poe) **117**:195, 227, 231-32, 240, 244, 260
"Romance" (Scott) **110**:285-6
Romance and Reality (Landon) **15**:156-58, 164
"Le romance de Doña Blanca" (Leconte de Lisle) **29**:225
A Romance in Letters (Pushkin)
See *Roman v pismakh*
"The Romance in Real Life" (Sedgwick) **98**:304
The Romance of a Mummy (Gautier)
See *Le Roman de la momie*
"The Romance of a People" (Jones) **222**:140, 158
Romance of a Poor Young Man (Feuillet)
See *Le Roman d'un Jeune Homme Pauvre*
The Romance of a Shop (Levy) **59**:76-7, 86-7, 90, 92, 95, 98, 102-5, 108, 113-5, 119; **203**:294-95, 339, 349-59
"The Romance of Britomarte" (Gordon) **21**:149, 154-56, 160, 163, 175, 183, 188
"Romance of Immortality" (Hawthorne) **2**:335
Romance of Ladybank (Oliphant) **11**:447
"A Romance of the Age" (Barrett Browning)
See "Lady Geraldine's Courtship"
The Romance of the Forest (Radcliffe) **6**:403-06, 409, 411, 413-16, 419-20, 423-27, 429-31, 435, 443-45; **55**:226, 228-35, 244-5, 250, 252-8, 261; **106**:283, 341-45, 349; **223**:184, 186, 189, 193, 210-13, 218, 224, 240-41, 243, 248, 256, 262-63, 265-68, 285, 289, 311-13, 318, 320, 322-24, 327-28
"A Romance of the Ganges" (Barrett Browning) **61**:30-1, 64-5, 67, 70
"Romance of the Lily" (Beddoes) **3**:34; **154**:20
Romance of the Republic (Child) **6**:203-05, 209; **73**:54, 63, 72, 84
"The Romance of the Swan's Nest" (Barrett Browning) **1**:113, 125; **61**:43, 65, 73; **66**:44
The Romance of Travel (Willis) **194**:319
"The Romance of Travelling" (Hale) **75**:356, 359
A Romance of Vienna (Trollope) **30**:319
"The Romance of Youth" (Reynolds) **146**:167, 173, 191, 196-98
Romancero (Heine)
See *Romanzero*
Romances (D'Israeli) **217**:275, 292, 295, 304-8, 311
Romances sans paroles (Verlaine) **2**:617, 620-21, 623, 629-32; **51**:350, 352-53, 355, 357, 359, 361-63, 365-66, 368, 370, 376-77, 379-85, 387; **230**:152-55, 160-61, 163, 169-70, 172, 177, 182-83, 185-88, 199, 201-4, 206-8, 210, 212
Romanees and Ballads (Mickiewicz)
See *Ballady i Romanse*
"Romanes Lecture" (Huxley) **67**:4
"Romania's Historical Development" (Eminescu)
See "Dezvoltarea istorica a Românei"
Romano Lavo-Lil: Word Book of the Romany; or, English Gypsy Language (Borrow) **9**:46-47
Romans et Contes (Gautier) **59**:36-7
Romans et contes philosophiques (Balzac) **153**:150, 152
Romanstudien (Ludwig) **4**:357, 359-60
Romantic Ballads (Borrow) **9**:54
The Romantic Expression and the Ranz-des-Vaches (Liszt) **199**:307
A Romantic Idea (Planché) **42**:294
"The Romantic School" (Heine)
See "Die Romantische Schule"

The Romantic School (Heine)
See "Die Romantische Schule"
"Romantic Sunset" (Baudelaire)
See "Le coucher du soleil romantique"
"Romanticism" (Pater) **90**:292, 294, 322-23, 325
Romanticism (Mickiewicz)
See *Romantycznoś*
"Die Romantik" (Heine) **147**:243
"Die romantische Poesie" (Goethe) **154**:316
"Die Romantische Schule" (Heine) **4**:233-34, 252, 259, 264; **54**:337, 344
Romantycznoś (Mickiewicz) **3**:393, 399
"Romantyczność" (Mickiewicz) **3**:405
"The Romany Girl" (Emerson) **1**:279; **38**:193
The Romany Rye: A Sequel to "Lavengro" (Borrow) **9**:45-6, 48, 51-6, 60-3, 65, 66-9
"Romanzen" (Heine) **147**:196
Romanzen (Heine) **4**:248, 250
Romanzen und Bilder (Meyer) **81**:146, 152, 199, 208
Romanzen vom Rosenkranz (Brentano) **191**:4-6, 9, 11-12, 17, 22-23, 63, 65, 68, 70-71, 119, 122-23
Romanzero (Heine) **4**:238-39, 240-41, 247, 252-56, 268; **147**:133, 163, 180, 184, 228-32, 234-35, 246
"The Romaunt of Margret" (Barrett Browning) **61**:53, 56, 58, 64-5, 70-1, 74; **170**:106
"The Romaunt of the Page" (Barrett Browning) **1**:115, 117, 124; **61**:43, 64-7, 70-5; **66**:56
"Rome" (Gogol)
See "Rim"
"Rome" (Pavlova)
See "Rim"
"Rome and the World" (Brownson) **50**:54
"The Rome Egg Affair" (Harris) **23**:151
Rome, Naples, et Florence (Stendhal) **23**:352, 410
Romeo et Juliette (Dumas) **71**:218
Romeo und Julia auf dem Dorfe (Keller) **2**:411-17, 424
"Rome's Holiday" (Pavlova)
See "Prazdnik Rima"
Romiero (Baillie) **2**:39-40; **71**:3; **151**:11
"Romilly and Wilberforce" (Landor) **14**:166
"Der römische Brunnen" (Meyer) **81**:200-01
Römische Elegien (Goethe) **4**:165, 176, 193, 207
Romola (Eliot) **118**:49, 58-60, 62, 105, 129, 136
Romola (Eliot) **209**:1-114
Romulus (Dumas) **71**:210
"Ronald and Helen" (Thomson) **18**:405-06
"Roncesvalles" (Bécquer) **106**:158
"Ronda" (Silva) **114**:294
"La ronde sous la cloche" (Bertrand) **31**:49
"Rondeau" (Hunt) **1**:423; **70**:264
"Rondeau" (Musset) **7**:267
Rondo in G, op. 51, no. 2 (Beethoven) **227**:22
"The Rooks" (Barnes) **75**:34, 40
Rookwood (Ainsworth) **13**:15-18, 20-1, 29, 31-2, 34-7, 40
"The Room in the Dragon Volant" (Le Fanu) **9**:317; **58**:251, 264, 266, 302
"Root Bound" (Cooke) **110**:16
Rootbound (Cooke)
See *Root-Bound and Other Sketches*
Root-Bound and Other Sketches (Cooke) **110**:18, 21, 39, 43
"The Roots of the Mountains" (Morris) **4**:435, 437
"The Rope" (Baudelaire)
See "La corde"
"The Ropewalk" (Longfellow) **2**:492; **45**:162, 167, 187
"Rory and Darborgilla" (Mangan) **27**:275
"Ros Gheal Dubh" (Mangan) **27**:307-08
"Rosa" (Harpur) **114**:138
"La Rosa Blanca" (Martí) **63**:84
"La rosa de pasión" (Bécquer) **106**:90
"Rosa Mystica" (Hopkins) **17**:191; **189**:141-42
Rosa; or, The Black Tulip (Dumas)
See *La tulipe noire*
Rosa; ou, L'ermitage du torrent (Pixérécourt) **39**:291, 295
"Rosabelle" (Scott) **15**:318
"Rosablanka und Biondette" (Brentano) **191**:8
"Rosenblankens Traum" (Brentano) **191**:7
"Rosace en vitrail" (Laforgue) **221**:82
"Rosalie" (Allston) **2**:21
"Rosalie Lee" (Chivers) **49**:46, 49, 52-3, 74
"Rosalie Prudent" (Maupassant) **83**:215-16
Rosaliens Briefe (La Roche) **121**:242, 250, 265-66, 269-71, 276, 279, 325-26
Rosalind and Helen (Shelley) **18**:313, 329, 336, 343-44
"Rosamond's Song of Hope" (Bloomfield) **145**:159
"Rosamund" (Ingelow) **39**:258, 264
Rosamund, A Sequel To Early Lessons (Edgeworth) **51**:78, 81, 108, 110
Rosamund Gray (Lamb) **10**:397, 400, 404-05, 409, 411; **113**:230, 281, 284
"Rosanna" (Edgeworth) **1**:265; **51**:87
"Roscoe" (Irving) **2**:392; **19**:350; **95**:265
"The Rose" (Cowper) **8**:119
"Rose" (Sainte-Beuve) **5**:333
Rose and Ninette (Daudet)
See *Rose et Ninette*
The Rose and the Key (Le Fanu) **58**:273
"The Rose and the Rainbow" (Crawford) **12**:172; **127**:182
Rose and the Ring (Thackeray) **5**:454, 469
"Rose Aylmer" (Landor) **14**:176, 183, 193, 199
Rose, Blanche, and Violet (Lewes) **25**:273-74, 286, 293, 298; **215**:84
Rose Clark (Parton) **86**:324, 333-35, 337, 339-44, 366-67
"La rose de l'infant" (Hugo) **3**:273
"The Rose Did Caper on Her Cheek" (Dickinson) **21**:63
"The Rose Elf" (Andersen) **7**:34
"The Rose Enthroned" (Larcom) **179**:169-70, 175, 177
Rose et Blanche (Sand) **2**:606; **42**:316-17, 352-53, 355; **174**:185-87, 189, 192, 194
Le rose et le vert (Stendhal) **23**:410, 419
Rose et Ninette (Daudet) **1**:237, 239, 244, 251
The Rose Family. A Fairy Tale (Alcott) **58**:48
Rose in Bloom (Alcott) **6**:18; **58**:4, 69; **83**:28, 47; **218**:93, 95, 100-101
"A Rose in His Grace" (Crawford) **127**:181, 188
A Rose in June (Oliphant) **11**:439, 447; **61**:173, 206-7
"Rose Knows Those Bows' Woes" (Hood) **16**:222
"Rose Lorraine" (Kendall) **12**:193, 201
"Rose Mary" (Rossetti) **4**:499-501, 505-07, 512-13, 518-19, 526-27, 531-32; **77**:326, 328-30
"The Rose of a Nation's Thanks" (Crawford) **127**:153, 221
"The Rose of Newport" (Meyer)
See "Die Rose von Newport"
The Rose of Wissahikon; or, The Fourth of July (Lippard) **198**:169
"Rose on the Heath" (Goethe)
See "Heidenröslein"
"Die Rose von Newport" (Meyer) **81**:207, 209
"Rose Wreath" (Klopstock) **11**:230
"Les Roseaux" (Desbordes-Valmore) **97**:15
"The Rosebud" (Keble) **87**:176
"Rose-Morals" (Lanier) **118**:215
Rosemunde (Wieland) **177**:256, 317
"Rosenzeit" (Mörike) **10**:451
Roses de Noël (Banville) **9**:29-30
"Les Roses de Saadi" (Desbordes-Valmore) **97**:13, 20, 27
"Les roses d'Ispahan" (Leconte de Lisle) **29**:224
Roskilde Rhyme (Grundtvig)
See *Roskilde-Riim*
Roskilde-Riim (Grundtvig) **158**:140, 147, 149
Roskilde-Saga (Grundtvig) **158**:140
Roslavlev (Pushkin) **3**:435
"Rosmowa wieczorna" (Mickiewicz) **3**:405
Rosmunda (Alfieri) **101**:8, 38
"Le rossignol" (Lamartine) **11**:255
"Le Rossignol" (Verlaine) **51**:361; **230**:164
"Rosy Hannah" (Bloomfield) **145**:154
"The Rosy Hour" (Beddoes) **154**:78
"Rosy maiden Winifred" (Rossetti) **186**:238
"Rosy O'Ryan" (Child) **73**:132-34
"Rosz verseimröl" (Petofi) **21**:278
"Rotation Method" (Kierkegaard) **125**:178, 193, 207-8, 280
"Die Rotentaler Herren" (Gotthelf) **117**:44, 48, 58
Rothelan (Galt) **1**:334
Rothschilds Gräber (Klopstock) **225**:298
"Rotkäppchen und Wolf" (Mörike) **201**:273
"A Rotting Corpse" (Baudelaire)
See "Une charogne"
Les Roués innocents (Gautier) **1**:350; **59**:12
Le rouge et le noir, chronique du XIXe siècle (Stendhal) **23**:348-49, 352-54, 356-64, 369-70, 373-74, 376-77, 383-89, 392-93, 395-98, 400, 404-05, 408-09, 411-12, 415-18, 420-24, 426; **46**:251-330; **178**:137-38, 140-41, 145-47, 150, 153-57, 173-74, 177, 179, 183, 187, 193-96, 198-201, 203, 213, 216, 221, 223-24, 227, 231, 234, 240-47, 250, 252-53, 255-56
Rough and Ready; or, Life among the New York Newsboys (Alger) **8**:15, 37
"A Rough Rhyme on a Rough Matter" (Kingsley) **35**:228
Roughing It in the Bush (Moodie) **113**:292-93, 295-304, 306-8, 311, 318, 323-38, 344-54, 358-49, 361, 364, 367-74
Roughing It in the Bush; or, Life in Canada (Moodie) **14**:215-41, 243-44
"La rouille" (Maupassant) **83**:231-32
Round about a Great Estate (Jefferies) **47**:103, 111-12, 133, 137, 142
"The Round Table" (Tennyson) **65**:241
Round the Sofa (Gaskell) **214**:299, 304
Roundabout Papers (Thackeray) **5**:466, 473, 485, 490, 506-07; **43**:350; **169**:310; **213**:235, 265, 305, 308
"The Rounded Catalogue Divine Complete" (Whitman) **31**:435
"Rousseau" (Hölderlin) **16**:194
"Rousseau" (Mörike) **201**:274
"Rousseau" (Schiller) **166**:126
"Rousseau and the Sentimentalists" (Lowell) **2**:509
La route de Thèbes (Dumas) **9**:231, 246
"A Route of Evanescence" (Dickinson) **21**:31, 49; **77**:95, 121; **171**:131, 134, 169, 180
"The Route to the Town of Kuba" (Bestuzhev)
See "Put' do goroda Kuby"
A Rover on Life's Path (Smolenskin)
See *ha-To'eh be-darke ha-hayim*
"The Royal Ascetic and the Hind" (Dutt) **29**:123, 126, 130
The Royal Captives: A Fragment of Secret History (Yearsley) **174**:319-27, 329
"The Royal Jubilee" (Hogg) **109**:200
"A Royal Poet" (Irving)
See "The Royal Poet"
"The Royal Poet" (Irving) **19**:347, 350; **95**:266
"A Royal Princess" (Rossetti) **66**:331; **186**:303-4, 326, 330
The Royal Suitors (Horne) **127**:256
"Royalists of Peru" (Gore) **65**:21
"Royauté" (Rimbaud) **4**:484; **35**:322, 324-25; **227**:210, 244-45, 247-48
"Roz goniné" (Arany) **34**:24
"Rozmowa" (Mickiewicz) **101**:185
"Rozryta mohyla" (Shevchenko) **54**:378
Rubáiyát of Omar Khayyám (FitzGerald) **153**:176-247

Rubáiyát of Omar Khayyám, Astronomer Poet of Persia (FitzGerald)
See *Rubáiyát of Omar Khayyám*
Der Rubin: Ein Märchen-Lustspiel in drei Acten (Hebbel) **43**:258, 289
"Rückblick" (Muller) **73**:392, 394
"Rückblick in die Jahre der Kindheit" (Brentano) **1**:105
"Rückkehr" (Eichendorff) **225**:46
Rudin (Turgenev) **21**:388, 397-98, 400, 412-13, 418-19, 426, 432, 436-38, 442, 444-46, 448, 455, 457; **37**:364, 379, 382, 402, 444; **122**:249, 251-52, 254, 256, 261, 265, 271-72, 288, 292, 298, 303, 315
"Rudokop" (Pavlova) **138**:3-4, 12, 21, 33
Rudolf von Hapsburg und Ottokar von Bohmen (Kotzebue) **25**:137
Rudolph (Beddoes) **3**:33
"Rudolph and Elisabetha" (Auerbach) **171**:48
Rudolph Prinz von Korsika (Nestroy) **42**:224
La Rue (Vallès) **71**:377
La Rue à Londres (Vallès) **71**:372-73, 375-76, 378
"Rue de l'eperon" (Banville) **9**:32
Une rue de Paris et son habitant (Balzac) **5**:51
"Rue Morgue" (Poe)
See "The Murders in the Rue Morgue"
"Une Ruelle de Flandres" (Desbordes-Valmore) **97**:14
"A Ruffian" (Beddoes) **154**:88
"The Ruffian Boy" (Opie) **65**:162, 171
Rufus and Rose; or, The Fortunes of Rough and Ready (Alger) **8**:37
Rugantino (Lewis) **11**:305
"Rugby Chapel" (Arnold) **218**:118, 188
"Rugby, Tennessee" (Hughes) **207**:134
Rugby, Tennessee: Being Some Account of the Settlement Founded on the Cumberland Plateau by the Board of Aid to Land Ownership (Hughes) **207**:131-35
"Ruhelechzend" (Heine) **4**:256
"The Ruin of the Year" (Lampman) **25**:210; **194**:30
Ruine (Schumann) **143**:84
"The Ruined Chapel" (Allingham) **25**:24
"The Ruined Cottage" (Wordsworth) **12**:397; **38**:362, 364, 390; **111**:241, 260-61, 263-68, 282; **166**:206-7, 233, 241, 243, 253, 271, 299, 341
The Ruined Cottage and The Pedlar (Wordsworth) **206**:312, 316-17, 322
"The Ruined Inn" (Petofi)
See "A csárda romjai"
"The Ruined Laird" (Norton) **205**:81
Les ruines de Babylone; ou, Le massacre des barmécides (Pixérécourt) **39**:276-77, 279, 290
"Ruins" (Derzhavin) **215**:16-17
"The Ruins of Ithaca" (Bryant) **6**:165
"Les ruisseau" (Banville) **9**:29
Rule and Misrule of the English in America (Haliburton) **15**:122, 128; **149**:310, 313-15, 318, 320, 340, 345-47
"Rules and Directions how to Avoid Creditors, Sheriffs, Constables, etc" (Freneau) **111**:132
"Rules and Regulations" (Dodgson) **139**:32, 61
"Rules how to get through a crowd" (Freneau) **111**:135
"The Rumble of Wheels" (Turgenev) **122**:293
"Rumors from an Aeolian Harp" (Thoreau) **7**:382
"Run to Death" (Levy) **59**:106-7
"The Runaway Slave at Pilgrim's Point" (Barrett Browning) **1**:118; **61**:9, 33-4, 43, 66-8; **170**:74-79, 108
"The Rune Mountain" (Tieck)
See "Der Runenberg"
"Der Runenberg" (Tieck) **5**:514, 517, 519, 524-25, 529; **46**:339-45, 347-50, 360, 363, 365, 374-75, 377, 387-88, 390-92, 414
"The Runenberg" (Tieck)
See "Der Runenberg"
Runic Poetry (Percy)
See *Five Pieces of Runic Poetry Translated from the Islandic Language*
Runic Poetry translated from the Islandic Language (Percy)
See *Five Pieces of Runic Poetry Translated from the Islandic Language*
"Le Runoïa" (Leconte de Lisle) **29**:223, 225-26
Rupert's Ambition (Alger) **83**:114
"Rural Architecture" (Wordsworth) **111**:234
"Rural Felicity" (Hood) **16**:235
"Rural Funerals" (Irving) **2**:381; **19**:334
Rural Hours. By a Lady (Cooper) **129**:3-6, 9-10, 12-17, 19-22, 24-26, 28, 34-35, 37-39, 41-54, 57-59, 62, 65-68, 72-75, 77-78, 82-89
Rural Letters (Willis) **194**:305
"Rural Life in England" (Irving) **19**:328, 334
The Rural Lyre (Yearsley) **174**:316, 318, 343
"Rural Morning" (Clare) **9**:113
The Rural Muse (Clare) **9**:79-80, 85; **86**:125, 160
"A Rural Picture" (Harpur) **114**:144
Rural Rambles. By a Lady (Cooper) **129**:4, 68-69
Rural Rides (Cobbett) **49**:97, 99, 101, 105-08, 110, 114, 116, 118, 120, 122, 130-34, 140, 142, 145, 147, 150, 153-55, 159-60, 163-65, 168, 171
Rural Tales, Ballads and Songs (Bloomfield) **145**:132, 135, 147, 149-50, 160, 176
Rural Walks (Smith) **115**:173, 210
"Rusalka" (Lermontov) **5**:287
Rusalka (Pushkin) **3**:415, 434; **83**:333, 339
Une Ruse (Maupassant) **83**:229
"The Ruse" (Willis) **194**:297
La Ruse de l'amour (Sade) **47**:360-61
"Rushing Headlong into Marriage" (Wood) **178**:312
The Rush-Light (Cobbett) **49**:109
Ruslan and Lyudmila (Pushkin)
See *Ruslan i Lyudmila*
Ruslan i Lyudmila (Pushkin) **3**:409-11, 413, 415, 417, 421, 423, 443, 445, 450; **27**:379; **83**:242-43, 245, 247, 250, 332, 349
Der Russe in Deutschland (Kotzebue) **25**:133, 138-40, 145, 147
Russia (Gautier) **59**:5
"Russia and Revolution" (Tyutchev)
See "La Russie et la Révolution"
The Russiade (Hogg) **109**:271
"The Russiade; a Fragment of an Ancient Epic Poem" (Hogg) **4**:280; **109**:250
"Russian and Germany" (Tyutchev) **34**:382
"The Russian at a Rendez-Vous" (Chernyshevsky) **1**:162
"Russian Christianity versus Modern Judaism" (Lazarus) **8**:419, 421-22, 428; **109**:303, 306, 310, 319, 329, 336, 344
"Russian Civilization As Concocted by Mr. Zherebtsov" (Dobrolyubov) **5**:140
A Russian Gentleman (Aksakov)
See *Semeinaia khronika*
"Russian Geography" (Tyutchev) **34**:381
"A Russian Hamlet" (Turgenev)
See "Gamlet ščigrovskogo uezda"
"The Russian Historical Novel" (Dobrolyubov) **5**:140
"The Russian Language" (Turgenev)
See "Russkii iazyk"
Russian Life in the Interior (Turgenev)
See *Zapiski okhotnika*
"Russian Maidens" (Derzhavin)
See "Russkie devuski"
A Russian Pelham (Pushkin) **3**:435, 447; **83**:273
The Russian People and Socialism (Herzen)
See *Le peuple russe et le Socialisme*
A Russian Schoolboy (Aksakov)
See *Vospominaniia prezhei zhizni*
"Russian Statesmen in the Ostsee Region" (Leskov) **174**:34-35
"The Russian Student's Tale" (Blind) **202**:10, 16
"The Russian Tale and the Tales of Gogol" (Belinski) **5**:97
Russian Women (Nekrasov) **11**:400, 404-05, 409, 414-18
"La Russie et la Révolution" (Tyutchev) **34**:382-83, 404
"Russkie devuski" (Derzhavin) **215**:12, 17-18
"Russkie obshchestvennye zametki" (Leskov) **174**:86
"Russkie vtorostepennye poety" (Nekrasov) **11**:422-24
"Russkii iazyk" (Turgenev) **21**:420; **122**:308, 313
"Rustem and Zorav" (Zhukovsky) **35**:378
"Rustic Childhood" (Barnes) **75**:15, 85
Rustic Songs (Muller)
See *Ländliche Lieder*
"Rustic Venus" (Maupassant)
See "La venus rustique"
"Rusticus Dolens; or, Inclosures of Common" (Barnes)
See "The Common A-Took In"
"Rusticus Emigrans or Over Sea to Settle" (Barnes) **75**:43-4, 101
"Rusticus gaudens" (Barnes)
See "The 'Lotments"
"Rusticus Res Politicas Animadvertens" (Barnes)
See "The New Poor Laws"
"Ruszaj z Bogiem" (Norwid) **17**:373
"Ruth" (Crabbe) **26**:124
"Ruth" (Hood) **16**:219, 225-27, 234
"Ruth" (Wordsworth) **12**:402; **111**:213, 245, 294; **166**:259; **206**:224
Ruth (Gaskell) **5**:180-83, 185, 187-89, 191, 196-97, 204; **70**:119, 123, 146, 149-51, 185, 188, 190, 196, 198, 200, 219; **97**:127, 134; **137**:40, 167; **214**:205, 209-11, 214-22, 227, 233, 235, 321-23, 332, 334, 338-40, 343-44
Ruth, A Short Drama From the Bible (Barnes) **75**:70, 73-4
Ruth Hall and Other Writings (Parton) **86**:312, 316, 318, 320, 323-26, 328-35, 337, 339, 341-44, 346-47, 352-57, 359-62, 366-69, 373-74, 376-77
"Ruth's Secret" (Alcott) **83**:5
"Ruts" (Rimbaud)
See "Ornières"
"Ruusuolmu" (Kivi) **30**:51
Ruy Blas (Hugo) **3**:254, 257, 261, 269; **161**:231, 235-36, 255
"Rybak" (Zhukovsky) **35**:397, 407
"Rycar' na čas" (Nekrasov) **11**:400, 416, 418-20
"Ryghte Conceyted Verse toe Master Hoode on his new Boke of Jestis" (Reynolds) **146**:176
Rythmes oubliés (Barbey d'Aurevilly) **213**:92
"Rytsar nashego vremeni" (Karamzin) **173**:280, 295, 311-13, 316-20
Rzecz o wolności słowa (Norwid) **17**:369
"s persidskogo" (Bestuzhev) **131**:150
"S polyany korshun podnyalsya" (Tyutchev) **34**:398, 400
S togo berega (Herzen)
See *Vom andern Ufer*
"Sa fosse est creuse" (Mallarmé) **210**:160
A Sa Majesté le tzar Nicolas (Comte) **54**:211
"Sa Majesté Très Chrétienne" (Clough) **27**:103
"Sa Majesté très Chrétienne" (Prescott) **163**:34, 37
"Saadi" (Emerson) **1**:296; **98**:179
"Saatyr" (Bestuzhev) **131**:151
Sab (Gómez de Avellaneda) **111**:8-9, 12, 14-18, 20-2, 29, 33-6, 38-9, 42-6, 54-62, 64, 69-72, 74-5
"The Sabbath Bell" (Sigourney) **21**:310
"Sabbath Bells" (Clare) **9**:105
"Sabbath Lays" (Barnes) **75**:70, 74
"A Sabbath Scene" (Whittier) **59**:364, 366
"Sabbath Sonnet" (Hemans) **71**:270

"The Sabbath's-Day Child" (Coleridge) **90**:33
"The Sabbatia" (Very) **9**:372
"Sabéis por qué la amo?" (Isaacs) **70**:307
Sachwörterbuch der Literatur (Herder) **186**:14
The Sack of Rome (Warren) **13**:412-14, 418-19, 424, 429-30, 436; **226**:253, 259-60, 268, 272-73, 278-79, 281, 292, 295-300, 302
"Sacra fames" (Leconte de Lisle) **29**:222, 230
Sacred and Legendary Art (Jameson)
See *The Poetry of Sacred and Legendary Art*
Sacred Dramas (More)
See *Sacred Dramas: Chiefly Intended for Young Persons, the Subjects Taken from the Bible*
Sacred Dramas: Chiefly Intended for Young Persons, the Subjects Taken from the Bible (More) **27**:332; **141**:232, 235
"The Sacred Fire" (Meyer)
See "Das heilige Feuer"
Sacred Hymns (Manzoni)
See *Inni Sacri*
"The sacred marriage" (Fuller) **50**:249, 251
Sacred Melodies (Moore) **6**:382
"Sacred Memories" (Lanier) **118**:241
"Sacred Pleasure" (Mallarmé) **41**:254, 259
The Sacred Poems of N. P. Willis (Willis) **194**:304, 308
"Sacred Poetry" (Keble) **87**:153
Sacred Songs of Novalis (Novalis)
See *Geistliche Lieder*
"Sacred to the Memory of Lord Nelson" (Hemans) **71**:272
"Sacrifice" (Emerson) **1**:290
"Sacrifice" (Whittier)
See "Human Sacrifice"
"The Sacrifice of Abraham" (Willis) **194**:304, 306
Sacrificial Death (Kotzebue)
See *Der Opfertod*
"The Sad Coronation" (Mörike)
See "Der traurige Krönung"
"The Sad Fortunes of the Rev. Amos Barton" (Eliot) **4**:92, 98, 117, 120, 125; **23**:57; **41**:101, 106-09; **89**:228; **118**:103
"Sad Occurrence That Took Place in the Year 1809" (Zhukovsky) **35**:384
"Sad, oh Sad, was my Soul" (Verlaine)
See "Ô triste, triste était mon âme . . ."
"Sad, Sad" (Laforgue)
See "Triste, triste"
"The Sad Wind of Autumn Speaks to the Trees..." (Petofi)
See "Beszel a fákkal..."
"Sadly Wails the Wind" (Pavlova)
See "Grustno veter voet"
"Säerspruch" (Meyer) **81**:140-41, 148-49, 155-56
"Safe in their Alabaster Chambers" (Dickinson) **77**:71; **171**:106, 181-82
"A Safe Investment" (Rossetti) **186**:233
"Safe where I cannot lie yet" (Rossetti) **186**:347
Safie: An Eastern Tale (Reynolds) **146**:159, 165-66, 173, 188
Saga (Grundtvig) **158**:140
"The Saga of Ahab Doolittle" (Taylor) **89**:338
"The Saga of King Olaf" (Longfellow) **45**:115, 132, 137, 145, 148-49, 155
The Saga of Mankind (Almqvist)
See *Människosläkets saga*
The Sagamore (Bird)
See *King Philip or the Sagamore*
"sāgare tari" (Dutt) **118**:30
Un Sage (Maupassant) **83**:831
"A Sage Conversation" (Longstreet) **159**:123, 133, 136-37, 141, 143-44, 161, 186, 201-2
"Sages" (Mickiewicz) **3**:399
"La sagesse" (Lamartine) **11**:254
Sagesse (Verlaine) **2**:617-21, 624-25, 627-28, 632; **51**:351-53, 355-59, 364-65, 368, 370, 372, 376, 382, 384, 388; **230**:155, 160-61, 164-65, 167-71, 173, 178, 199, 207-9, 211, 221
Saggio sopra gli errori popolari degli antichi (Leopardi) **129**:230-31
Sägner (Runeberg)
See *Fänrik Ståls sägner*
"Said the Canoe" (Crawford) **12**:156, 167, 171; **127**:171-73, 179-81, 200-02
"Said the Daisy" (Crawford) **12**:156
"Said the Skylark" (Crawford) **12**:161, 171
"Said the Thistle-Down" (Crawford) **127**:170
"Said the West Wind" (Crawford) **12**:156
"Said the Wind" (Crawford) **12**:161
"The Sail" (Lermontov) **126**:129, 144, 223
"The Sailer" (Dyer) **129**:96
"Sailing Beyond Seas" (Ingelow) **39**:264; **107**:123-24
"The Sailing of the Sword" (Morris) **4**:431
"The Sailor" (Allingham) **25**:7-8
"Sailor" (Crabbe) **26**:100
"The Sailor" (Mickiewicz) **3**:392
"The Sailor" (Pavlova)
See "Plovec"
"A Sailor" (Rogers) **69**:67
The Sailor (Shevchenko)
See *Matros*
"The Sailor Boy" (Tennyson) **65**:373, 376
"The Sailor Uncle" (Lamb)
See "Elizabeth Villiers: The Sailor Uncle"
The Sailor's Daughter (Cumberland) **167**:198
"The Sailor's Funeral" (Sigourney) **21**:304
"The Sailor's Mother" (Wordsworth) **12**:426; **111**:273-74
"The Sailor's Relief" (Freneau) **111**:134
The Saint (Meyer)
See *Der Heilige*
"Saint Agnes of Intercession" (Rossetti) **4**:504, 510; **77**:241, 331-34, 336
Saint-Anne (Charriere) **66**:125, 172, 178
"Saint Benoit Joseph Labre" (Verlaine) **51**:359
"Saint Cecilia" (Kleist)
See *Die heilige Cäcilie; oder, die Gewalt der Musik*
"Saint Graal" (Verlaine) **230**:167
"Saint Guido" (Jefferies) **47**:137
"Saint Julien" (Flaubert)
See "La légende de Saint-Julien l'Hospitalier"
"Saint Monica" (Smith) **23**:321, 323; **115**:119, 121
"Saint Olaf's Fountain" (Boyesen) **135**:5
"Saint Opportune" (Webster) **230**:330
Saint Patrick's Eve (Lever) **23**:275-76, 307
Saint Paul (Renan) **26**:372, 402, 408, 420-21
Saint Paul and Protestantism (Arnold)
See *St. Paul and Protestantism, with an Essay on Puritanism and the Church of England*
"St. Petersburg Notes of 1836" (Gogol) **31**:137
"Saint Romualdo" (Lazarus) **109**:294
"Saint the First" (Cooke) **110**:18, 35
"Saint the Second" (Cooke) **110**:18
"The Saint, Your Patron . . ." (Verlaine)
See "La Sainte, ta patronne . . ."
"Sainte" (Mallarmé) **4**:378; **210**:169, 234-35, 244
"La sainte alliance des peuples" (Beranger) **34**:29
"A Sainte-Beuve" (Banville) **9**:26
"Sainte Cécile jouant sur l'aile d'un chérubin" (Mallarmé) **41**:289-90
"Sainte-Pélagie en 1832" (Nerval) **67**:332, 336
"La Sainte, ta patronne . . ." (Verlaine) **230**:170
"Saintliness the Standard of Christian Principle" (Newman) **38**:305
"The Saints' Rest" (Dickinson)
See "Of Tribulation These Are They"
The Saint's Tragedy (Kingsley) **35**:204, 209, 211-13, 218-19, 222, 226, 249
"Saint-Tupetu de Tu-pe-tu" (Corbière) **43**:28
La Saisiaz (Browning) **19**:106, 110-12, 134
Une saison en enfer (Rimbaud) **4**:453-54, 456-66, 468-74, 476-83, 486; **35**:266, 270-71, 275-78, 282-83, 289, 291, 294, 297-98, 302, 304-05, 307, 309-13, 314-15, 317, 320-21; **82**:218-30, 232-34, 236-38, 240-45, 247-48, 250, 252-55, 257, 259-60, 262-63; **227**:188-90, 192, 196-97, 199-200, 202, 210-12, 233-37, 239-41, 253, 266-67, 269-71, 274, 276-81, 293, 302-7, 309, 312-17, 332
"Sakontalá" (Tyutchev) **34**:412
Die Salamandrin und die Bildsäule (Wieland) **17**:410-11
Salambo (Flaubert)
See *Salammbô*
Salammbô (Flaubert) **2**:226-28, 230-34, 236-39, 242-44, 246-47, 249, 251-52, 255-56; **10**:125, 145; **19**:268, 273, 276-78, 299-300, 302, 304, 307-8, 313, 317; **62**:80, 92, 98, 109-20, 123; **66**:293; **135**:77-86, 88-103, 109, 111-15, 117-19, 121-29, 131, 133-38, 141-43, 145-53, 155-57, 166-67, 169-78, 180-84; **179**:146; **185**:219
"Salas y Gomez" (Chamisso) **82**:6, 21, 27, 30
"A Sale" (Maupassant) **1**:457
"Sale" (Rimbaud)
See "Solde"
"The Sale of the Pet Lamb" (Collins) **93**:63
Salem (Klopstock) **225**:285, 296
Salem Chapel (Oliphant) **11**:429-31, 445, 447-9, 454-7, 459, 463; **61**:162-9, 172, 174-7, 180, 183, 197-8, 202, 216, 226-7; **221**:244-46, 281-84, 287, 290-91, 293
"Salida del señor Nicanor Puchol en Pelayo" (Larra) **130**:250
"Salisbury Plain" (Wordsworth) **206**:315, 340-46
Salisbury Plain (Wordsworth) **111**:253, 261, 263-65, 267-68, 273, 311
The Salisbury Plain Poems of William Wordsworth (Wordsworth) **206**:341, 344, 346
La salle d'armes (Dumas) **11**:58
"Sally Parson's Duty" (Cooke) **110**:35
Salmagundi (Irving) **95**:219, 221-23, 225-27, 275, 291-93, 295-96
Salmagundi; or, The Whim-Whams and Opinions of Launcelot Langstaff, Esq., and Others (Irving and Paulding) **2**:525
Salmagundian Essays (Irving) **95**:219-21
"Salomé" (Casal) **131**:223, 225-26, 235, 265-66, 268
"Salomé" (Laforgue) **5**:269-71, 274, 278, 280-1; **53**:292, 293-4; **221**:4-5, 10, 12, 14-16
"Salome" (Lamb) **125**:375-76
Salome (Cumberland) **167**:158
Salomo, ein Trauerspiel (Klopstock) **225**:279
Salomon: A Sacred Drama in Five Acts (Klopstock)
See *Salomo, ein Trauerspiel*
Der Salon (Heine) **4**:235, 262, 264, 268-69
Le salon de 1845 (Baudelaire) **29**:79-80
Le salon de 1846 (Baudelaire) **6**:81; **29**:100; **55**:8, 36
Salon de 1846 (Baudelaire) **155**:76-77
Salon de 1859 (Baudelaire) **155**:13, 108
Le salon de 1859 (Baudelaire) **29**:79; **55**:43
The Salon; or, Letters on Art, Music, Popular Life, and Politics (Heine)
See *Der Salon*
"Les Salons . . ." (Verlaine) **230**:173
"Salut" (Mallarmé) **41**:294; **210**:172, 218-20
"Salut au Monde!" (Whitman) **4**:571, 578, 594; **31**:390, 398-99, 431; **81**:312, 319-20; **205**:157-58, 160, 226, 311
"Salutation to Palmares" (Castro Alves)
See "Saudaçao a Palmares"
"Salvation" (Lampman) **194**:45
"Salvator" (Dumas) **71**:185
Salvator Rosa (Hoffmann) **2**:340
"Sam Patch" (Smith) **187**:333
Sam Slick's Wise Saws and Modern Instances (Haliburton) **149**:318

Sam Slick's Wise Saws and Modern Instances; or, What He Said, Did, or Invented (Haliburton) **15**:126-27, 132, 135-36, 145
The Same Old Story (Goncharov)
See *Obyknovennaya istoriya*
Samlade skrifter (Stagnelius) **61**:248
Samlede digte (Andersen) **7**:19
Samlede Skrifter (Andersen)
See *Samlede voerker*
Samlede Vaerker (Kierkegaard)
See *Soren Kierkegaards Samlede Vaerker*
Samlede voerker (Andersen) **214**:26
Sämtliche Werke (Brentano) **191**:39
Sämliche Werke (Heine) **147**:174
Sämtliche Werke und Briefe (Brentano) **191**:126, 130
Sämltliche Romane and Erzählungen (Arnim) **159**:4-6
Sämmtlich Werke (Schlegel) **45**:361
Sämmtliche Werke (Herder)
See *Herders sämmtliche Werke*
Sämmtliche Werke (Hoffmann) **183**:223, 287-95
Sämmtliche Werke (Klopstock) **225**:308
Sämmtliche Werke (Wieland) **17**:392-93; **177**:267
Sam's Chance; and How He Improved It (Alger) **83**:132-33, 139
"Samson" (Blake) **13**:182
Samson (Dumas) **71**:217
"Samson Agonistes" (Cooke) **110**:9
Samson Agonistes (Wordsworth) **166**:308
Samson's Anger (Vigny)
See "La colère de Samson"
Sämtliche Werke (Claudius) **75**:182-84, 201
Sämtliche Werke (Fontane) **163**:161-62, 166, 169-70
Sämtliche Werke (Grillparzer) **102**:101, 106, 118, 170, 172, 187-88
Sämtliche Werke (Hoffmann)
See *Sämmtliche Werke*
Sämtliche Werke (Hölderlin) **187**:209-10, 214-19, 230-32, 237, 239-48, 267-79
Sämtliche Werke (Mörike) **201**:310, 357
Sämtliche Werke (Schopenhauer) **157**:275, 278-81
Sämtliche Werke (Storm) **195**:11-13, 16, 89-90, 92-95
Sämtliche Werke in drei Bänden (Hauff) **185**:326, 336-37, 340-41, 351-53
Sämtliche Werke Kritische Textausgabe (Hölderlin) **187**:241
Sämtliche Werke und Briefe (Hölderlin) **187**:281-88, 293, 297
Sämtliche Werke und Briefe (Kleist) **222**:222-23, 238-39, 252-57, 259-60, 285
Samuel Zborowski (Slowacki) **15**:360, 365, 371-72, 375-77
"San Antonio bendito" (Castro) **78**:40
"San Antonio de Bexar" (Lanier) **6**:245
San Francesco a Ripa (Stendhal) **23**:349
"San Juan de los Reyes" (Bécquer) **106**:146
Sancho García (Zorrilla y Moral) **6**:525
Sancho Saldaña (Espronceda) **39**:100, 110
"Sanct Joseph der Zweite" (Goethe) **4**:194, 197
"Sanctity the Token of the Christian Empire" (Newman) **38**:308
"Sanctuary" (Lenau) **16**:263, 277
"Das Sanctus" (Hoffmann) **2**:346; **183**:192, 194
"Sandalphon" (Longfellow) **45**:116, 146
"Sandels" (Runeberg) **41**:314, 324-25
Sanditon (Austen) **207**:46; **222**:34, 42, 109
Sanditon—Fragments of a Novel (Austen) **1**:41-42, 46-47, 51-52, 54, 60-61; **33**:70, 72, 75, 77, 93; **95**:49; **119**:12, 18, 42-3, 46-7; **150**:36
"The Sandman" (Andersen)
See "Ole Luköie"
"The Sandman" (Hoffmann)
See "Der Sandmann"
"Der Sandmann" (Hoffmann) **183**:170, 192-96, 223, 225-26, 253, 258-60, 262, 287, 297
"Sandro Botticelli" (Pater) **90**:334
"Sands at Seventy" (Whitman) **4**:563
Sands at Seventy (Whitman) **205**:226
"The Sands of Dee" (Kingsley) **35**:218-19, 226, 232
Le sang de la coupe (Banville) **9**:18-19
"Der Sänger" (Brentano) **191**:117
"Sängerfahrt" (Eichendorff) **225**:10, 42
"Sängerin Nachtigall" (Brentano) **191**:136
Le sanglot de la terre (Laforgue) **5**:275, 282-3; **53**:258-9, 269, 277, 279, 287, 289-90, 293; **221**:17, 19, 31, 55, 58, 60
"Sanglot perdu" (Laforgue) **221**:76
"Les Sanglots" (Desbordes-Valmore) **97**:8, 18, 20, 24
"Sangre de africano" (Castro Alves) **205**:19
"The Sanguine Poetaster" (Lippard) **198**:133, 163, 181, 208
Sang-Værk til den danske Kirke (Grundtvig) **158**:161, 179
"Sanity of True Genius" (Lamb) **10**:432; **113**:218, 252
"Santa Cruz" (Freneau)
See "The Beauties of Santa Cruz"
"Santa Filomena" (Longfellow) **45**:116
"Santa Leocadia" (Bécquer) **106**:158
"Santa Maura" (Kingsley)
See "Martyrdom of Saint Maura"
"Santo Domingo" (Douglass) **7**:126
Sapho (Daudet) **1**:237, 239, 242-44, 248-49, 251
Sapho (Staël-Holstein)
See *Sappho*
"Sapphic Strokes" (Radishchev) **190**:314
"Sapphics" (Lampman) **25**:202; **194**:21, 93, 122, 132-34
"Sappho" (Rossetti) **186**:270
Sappho (Daudet)
See *Sapho*
Sappho (Grillparzer) **1**:382-85, 387, 389, 397; **102**:81, 85, 91, 104, 108, 116-17, 147, 154-56, 180, 187
Sappho (Staël-Holstein) **91**:326, 359
Sappho and Phaon (Robinson) **142**:113, 115, 132, 141-43, 173-74, 176, 210-11, 213-15, 218, 225, 241-43, 245, 275, 285
"Sappho Discovers Her Passion" (Robinson) **142**:175
Sappho's Slipper (Sacher-Masoch) **31**:298
"Sappho's Song" (Landon) **15**:165
"Sara la Baigneuse" (Hugo) **3**:261
Sara Videbeck (Almqvist)
See *Det går an*
Saragossa (Potocki)
See *Manuscrit trouvé à Saragosse*
Sarah de Berenger (Ingelow) **39**:261, 264; **107**:112-19, 124
Sarah; or, The Exemplary Wife (Rowson) **5**:311-13, 316, 319; **69**:103, 105, 113-14, 137; **182**:255, 258, 261-62, 352
"Sarah Winnemucca's Practial Solutions of the Indian Problem" (Peabody) **169**:193
"Saratoga Springs" (Willis) **194**:282
"Saratoga Trunk" (Stevenson)
See "Story of the Physician and the Saratoga Trunk"
Sardanapale (Becque) **3**:16
Sardanapalus (Byron) **2**:66, 70, 79-81, 99; **12**:139; **109**:65, 102; **149**:20
Sardonic Tales (Villiers de l'Isle Adam)
See *Contes cruels*
"Sári néni" (Petofi) **21**:285
"Sarmanul Dionis" (Eminescu) **33**:245-47; **131**:315-17, 319, 334
"Sarmis" (Eminescu) **131**:290
Sarmisthā (Dutt) **118**:5, 20
Sarrasine (Balzac) **5**:46; **35**:22, 68-9-70; **153**:42, 44, 73, 152
Sartor Resartus (Carlyle) **70**:7, 9, 22-24, 26-27, 31, 36-47, 49, 53, 56-58, 62-76, 87-88, 93, 95, 97-102, 108
"Sasha" (Nekrasov) **11**:404, 407
"Sashka" (Lermontov)
See *Sashka*
Sashka (Lermontov) **126**:133-34, 138, 154
Satan: A Libretto (Cranch) **115**:17-18, 23, 26, 35-6, 55
Satansoe; or, The Littlepage Manuscripts (Cooper) **203**:75, 144, 152
Satanstoe; or, The Littlepage Manuscripts (Cooper) **1**:219-21; **54**:258, 279
"Satire III" (Eminescu) **131**:328-29
Satires (Krasicki)
See *Satyry*
"Satires against the Tories" (Brackenridge) **227**:71, 104
Satiry v proze (Saltykov) **16**:368, 374
"The Satrap-Bear" (Saltykov) **16**:358
"Saturday Afternoon" (Willis) **194**:288-89, 297, 300, 307
"Saturday in Holy Week" (Droste-Hülshoff) **3**:203
"Saturnian Poem" (Verlaine) **51**:368, 372
Saturnine Poems (Verlaine)
See *Les Poèmes saturniens*
"Le satyre" (Hugo) **3**:273; **21**:226
Satyry (Krasicki) **8**:398, 401, 403-07
"Saudaçao a Palmares" (Castro Alves) **205**:18, 20, 36-37
"Saul" (Browning) **19**:111, 119, 129-32, 139; **79**:94, 102, 111
Saul (Alfieri) **101**:18-19, 22, 32, 41, 50, 54, 56, 79, 83, 87-8
"Saul" (Willis) **194**:306
"Saul Spradlin's Ghost" (Harris) **165**:266
"Le saule" (Musset) **7**:256, 273; **150**:311
Saulo (Isaacs) **70**:311-12
"Saul's Last Day" (Bird) **197**:6
"The Sausage Skewer" (Andersen)
See "How to Cook Soup upon a Sausage Pin"
"Le Saut du berger" (Maupassant) **83**:169
"Le saut du Tremplin" (Banville) **9**:16, 25
"De Sauty" (Holmes) **14**:129
"La sauvage" (Vigny) **7**:472-73, 479-80; **102**:336
Sauvée (Maupassant) **83**:230
"Sauvegarde" (Mallarmé) **41**:294-98, 300, 304-05
"The Savage Landowner" (Saltykov) **16**:358
"The Savage of Aveyron" (Robinson) **142**:149-50, 279-80
"Savannah Sesqui-Centennial Ode" (Hayne) **94**:145, 152
"The Savings Book" (Auerbach) **171**:50
"Savitri" (Dutt) **29**:120-21, 124, 126, 128, 131
Savonarola (Lenau) **16**:263, 266, 268-70, 272-75, 279-81, 285
"Savory Companion" (Verlaine)
See "Compagne savoureuse . . ."
Savoyen, Nizza und der Rhein (Engels) **85**:83
Say and Seal (Warner) **146**:258
"Say, by What Chance" (Pushkin)
See *Skazhi, Kakoi sud'boi*
"Say Not the Struggle Naught Availeth" (Clough) **27**:75, 77, 79
"Say not, the struggle nought availeth" (Prescott) **163**:6, 31-33, 41
"Say, Tell Me . . ." (Bestuzhev)
See "Ty skazhi, govori . . ."
"Saying X" (Alcott)
See "Apotheosis"
"Saying XIV" (Alcott) **167**:75
"Saying XLVII" (Alcott)
See "Actual and Ideal"
"Saying XVIII" (Alcott) **167**:75
"Saying XXI" (Alcott)
See "Originality"
"Says" (Whitman) **205**:271
"The Scamper of Life" (Harpur) **114**:144
The Scandal (Alarcon)
See *El escándalo*
"The Scandinavian in the United States" (Boyesen) **135**:33

"Scar" (Woolson) **82**:273
"Scarabaeus Sisyphus" (Blind) **202**:58
"The Scarecrow" (Leskov)
See "Pugalo"
Scarlet and Black (Stendhal)
See *Le rouge et le noir, chronique du XIXe siècle*
The Scarlet Letter: A Romance (Hawthorne) **2**:295-96, 298, 305, 307, 309-12, 314-18, 320-32; **10**:269-317; **17**:110-12, 114, 116, 120, 122, 124, 128-29, 132, 146-147, 151-53, 156-57; **23**:168-69, 177-78, 183-84, 194-97, 205, 213-14, 220; **39**:167-68, 176-77, 180, 185, 187, 189-90, 195-97, 200, 220-22, 225, 227, 236-37, 239-40, 247, 249; **79**:290-92, 299, 308-11, 313, 327, 332; **95**:91, 109, 120, 123, 151, 170, 176, 178, 213; **158**:189-369; **171**:237, 245, 275, 277, 279, 299, 317, 327, 332, 342-43, 349, 3; **191**:179-80, 187, 189, 193, 207, 211, 242, 263, 271, 298; **226**:8, 16, 37, 55-56, 75, 80, 82-83, 95-96, 98-99, 118, 138
The Scarlet Shawl (Jefferies) **47**:91-92, 97, 116
"Scaroni" (Beddoes) **154**:52-53, 55
Scaroni (Beddoes) **3**:38
"Sčast' e v dvux ètažax" (Leskov) **25**:258-59
Scattered Leaves (Herder)
See *Zerstreute Blätter*
Scattered Pages (Renan) **26**:422
Scattered Waifs of Fifty Years (Smith) **187**:335
"A Scene" (Clare) **9**:72
"A Scene" (Pavlova) **138**:35-36
"A Scene along the Rio de Las Plumas" (Ridge) **82**:184
"Scène courte mais typique" (Laforgue)
See "Pierrots"
Scene from Faust (Pushkin) **3**:446
"A Scene in a Workhouse" (Tonna) **135**:217
Scene in an Armchair (Musset)
See *Un spectacle dans un fauteuil*
"A Scene on the Banks of the Hudson" (Bryant) **46**:19-20, 38-41, 43
"Scenery and a Scene" (Willis) **194**:282
"Scènes" (Rimbaud) **82**:233; **227**:204-6, 242
"Scenes and Hymns of Life" (Hemans) **71**:270
Scenes and Hymns of Life, with Other Religious Poems (Hemans) **29**:201
Scenes and Legends of the North of Scotland; or, The Traditional History of Cromarty (Miller) **143**:3, 5, 9, 27-28, 37-40, 43, 48, 50, 54-58
Scenes and Shadows of Days Departed, a Narrative (Bowles) **103**:54
"Scenes at a Target-Shooting" (Taylor) **89**:308
Scènes de la vie de province (Balzac) **5**:28-9, 31-2, 36; **53**:10, 31
Scènes de la vie militaire (Balzac) **5**:31-2
Scènes de la vie orientale (Nerval)
See *Voyage en Orient*
Scènes de la vie Parisienne (Balzac) **5**:28-29, 31, 36; **153**:21
Scènes de la vie politique (Balzac) **5**:31
Scènes de la vie privée (Balzac) **153**:21, 148-49, 151-52
Scènes et Comédies (Feuillet) **45**:88-9
Scènes et Proverbes (Feuillet) **45**:88
"Scenes from Life in Town" (Sedgwick) **19**:444
"Scenes from Politian" (Poe) **117**:227
Scenes from Russian Life (Turgenev)
See *Zapiski okhotnika*
Scenes from the Battle of Norns and Aesir (Grundtvig) **158**:139
Scenes from the Downfall of the Heroic Life in the North (Grundtvig)
See *Optrin af Kæmpelivets Undergang i Nord*
"Scenes in Buffalo Hunting" (Thorpe) **183**:357
"Scenes in Canada" (Moodie) **14**:243
"Scenes in My Native Land" (Sigourney) **87**:321
"Scenes in the Wood" (Lazarus) **109**:291
Scenes musicales sur un thême connu (Schumann) **143**:120
Scenes of Clerical Life (Eliot) **4**:92-93, 95, 97-98, 102, 109-10, 114, 116-17, 120-21, 123, 126-27, 142, 152, 154; **13**:290; **23**:80; **41**:99, 103; **49**:216, 237; **89**:228; **118**:60, 103-4; **183**:30-31, 143
Scenes of Clerical Life (Eliot) **209**:76, 79
"Scenes of Fear" (Willis) **194**:282, 298
Scenes of Military Life (Balzac)
See *Scènes de la vie militaire*
Scenes of Parisian Life (Balzac)
See *Scènes de la vie Parisienne*
Scenes of Political Life (Balzac)
See *Scènes de la vie politique*
Scenes of Private Life (Balzac)
See *Scènes de la vie privée*
Scenes of Provincial Life (Balzac)
See *Scènes de la vie de province*
"Scented Herbage of My Breast" (Whitman) **4**:575; **31**:387, 402, 416; **205**:242
The Sceptic (Moore) **6**:395; **110**:171
The Sceptic, a Poem (Hemans) **29**:192-93, 195, 202; **71**:261
Schach von Wuthenow (Fontane) **26**:236, 240, 243, 245-46, 254, 259, 270-71; **163**:197
Die Schachtel mit der Friedenspuppe (Brentano) **191**:49-50, 103
"Schalken the Painter" (Le Fanu)
See "A Strange Event in the Life of Schalken the Painter"
"Schastlivaiia oshibka" (Goncharov) **63**:48
"Der Schatten" (Mörike) **201**:252, 298
Schattenreise abgeschiedener Stunden von Offenbach nach Weimar und Schönebeck im Jahre (La Roche) **121**:242
Der Schatz (Mörike) **10**:456
"Schatzgräber" (Goethe) **4**:192
Die Schauspielerin (Hebbel) **43**:230
"Der Scheidende" (Heine) **147**:184-86
Der Scheik von Alessandria und seine Sklaven (Hauff) **185**:318, 334-36, 356
"Schelm von Bergen" (Heine) **4**:256
"Die Schenke am See" (Droste-Hülshoff) **3**:200
"Scherz" (Werner) **189**:329
Scherz, Satire, Ironie und tiefere Bedeutung (Grabbe) **2**:271-81, 283-84, 286-88
"Scherz und Satire" (Droste-Hülshoff) **3**:200
Der schiffbrüchige Galeerensklave vom todten Meer (Brentano)
See *Clemens Brentanos Romanfragment "Der schiffbrüchige Galeerensklave vom Todten Meer"*
"Der Schiffer im Kahne" (Brentano) **191**:68-69
"Schiffer- und Nixen-Märchen" (Mörike) **201**:272, 292, 298
"Der Schiffsjunge" (Lenau) **16**:278
"An Schillers Nachruhm" (Raimund) **69**:16
Schillers Sämtliche Werke (Schiller) **166**:140-43
Schillers Werke (Schiller) **166**:140-47, 172
Schillers Werke, Nationalausgabe (Schiller) **69**:225, 237-39, 257, 271-77
Der Schimmelreiter (Storm) **1**:541-42, 544, 549-51; **195**:11, 13, 20, 49, 56-57, 63-64, 71, 73, 76, 83, 97, 109, 112-13, 131
Schism in High Society (Leskov)
See *Velikosvetskii raskol*
"Schlacht" (Hölderlin) **16**:174
"Die Schlacht im Loener Bruch" (Droste-Hülshoff) **3**:195-97, 199, 201
Schlacht von Vittoria (Beethoven) **227**:18
"Schlachtfeld bei Hastings" (Heine) **147**:229
Schlachtgesang für die zum neuen Kreuzzuge gegen den Erzfeind der ganzen Menschheit verbündeten deutschen christlichen Strafheere (Werner) **189**:358-59
Schleiermacher's Soliloquies (Schleiermacher)
See *Monologen: Eine Neujahrsgabe*
"Die schlesischen Weber" (Heine) **147**:139, 150
"Die schlimme Gret" (Mörike) **201**:252, 291
"Schlimme Wahl" (Eichendorff) **225**:43
"Die schlimmen Monarchen" (Schiller) **39**:338, 356, 386-88
Der Schlimm-heilige Vitalis (Keller) **2**:416
"Das SchloBß Boncourt" (Chamisso) **82**:30
"Das Schloss Dürande" (Eichendorff) **8**:222; **225**:9
"Schlosslegende" (Heine) **147**:231
"Schlüssel zur Abderiten-Geschichte" (Wieland) **177**:256
"Schluswort über die Schule" (Stifter) **198**:283
"Schlußwort" (Boyd) **102**:175
Der Schmied seines Glückes (Keller) **2**:414-15, 424
Schmucker's Psychology (Brownson) **50**:27
"Schnapphahn und Schnapphenne" (Heine) **147**:232
"Die Schnecke und der Hisch" (Beddoes) **154**:25
Schneewittchen (Storm) **195**:23
"The Schnellest Zug" (Field) **3**:208
"Schnitterlied" (Meyer) **81**:140, 142, 148, 152-57, 206
"Scholar and Carpenter" (Ingelow) **39**:255-56; **107**:122
"The Scholar Gypsy" (Arnold)
See "The Scholar-Gipsy"
"The Scholar-Gipsy" (Arnold) **6**:42, 44, 50-52, 65-66, 72; **29**:6-7, 32-3, 37; **89**:7, 9, 46, 49, 53, 88-99; **126**:52, 75, 83, 111; **218**:114, 117-18, 122, 134, 139, 154, 159-61, 177, 188-89, 192, 203, 277
The Scholars of Arneside (Martineau) **137**:250
"The Scholar of Thebet Ben Chorat" (Willis) **194**:302, 304
"The Scholasticism of the Nineteenth Century" (Pisarev)
See "Sxolastiki xix veka"
"Die Schöne Buche" (Mörike) **10**:454
"Der schöne Buche" (Mörike) **201**:273, 284-85, 315-16, 319-20, 346
Der schöne Bund (La Roche) **121**:326
Die schöne Kellnerin von Bacharach (Muller) **73**:361
Die schöne Müllerin (Muller) **73**:350, 355, 360, 363, 365-68, 373, 380, 382, 389, 396
Schönes Bild der Resignation (La Roche) **121**:249
"Schönheit" (Hölderlin) **16**:185
"Schön-Rohtraut" (Mörike) **10**:453; **201**:252-54, 256, 258, 292-93
School (Robertson) **35**:333-34, 336, 340, 345-46, 351-52, 357, 362, 364-66, 369, 371-72
"The School Boards: What They Can Do, and What They May Do" (Huxley) **67**:92
"School Days" (Whittier) **59**:360, 371
The School for Arrogance (Holcroft) **85**:192-93, 206-7, 218-21, 225, 234, 237
The School for Guardians. A Comedy. As it is Performing at the Theatre-Royal in Covent-Garden (Murphy) **229**:254
The School for Husbands (Carlyle) **181**:134-35
The School for Scandal (Sheridan) **5**:355-72, 374-78, 380, 382-83; **91**:233-34, 242-43, 251, 253-54, 256, 258, 260-64, 266-70, 272
The School for Widows (Cumberland) **167**:191, 193
The School for Widows (Reeve) **19**:412, 415
A School History of Germany (Taylor) **89**:342
"The School of Giorgione" (Pater) **7**:326; **90**:242, 323, 335; **159**:215-16, 235, 237, 240, 245, 295, 321
"The School Question" (Brownson) **50**:54
School Song Book (Hale) **75**:286, 349
"The School-Boy" (Blake) **13**:182; **37**:14, 33, 45, 72
"The Schoolboy" (Nekrasov) **11**:404
Schooldays at Rugby (Hughes)
See *Tom Brown's School Days*
The Schoolfellows (Jerrold) **2**:395, 401
The Schoolmaster (Gotthelf)
See *Leiden und Freuden eines Schulmeisters*

"The Schoolmaster's Progress" (Kirkland) **85**:265
"The Schoolmistress Abroad" (Hood) **16**:209
Schools and Universities on the Continent (Arnold) **126**:6, 115-16; **218**:245
The Schools: Basis for the Prosperity and for the Republic in the United States (Sarmiento)
See *Las escuelas, base de la prosperidad y de la república en los Estados Unidas*
"Der Schosshund" (Klopstock) **11**:238
"Der Schrecken im Bade" (Kleist) **37**:237
Das Schreibepult, oder Die Gefahren der Jugend (Kotzebue) **25**:147
Die Schreibfeder (Grillparzer) **102**:188-89
Schrift und Volk (Auerbach) **171**:36-38, 49, 51, 73-74, 77
Schriften (Goethe) **34**:123
Schriften (Novalis) **13**:359-60, 362
Schriften (Tieck)
See *Ludwig Tieck's Schriften*
Schriften I (Novalis) **178**:61-64
Schriften Novalis: Die Werke Friedrich von Hardenbergs (Novalis) **178**:88-91, 106-11
The Schroffenstein Family (Kleist)
See *Die Familie Schroffenstein*
"Der Schuß von der Kanzel" (Meyer) **81**:184
"Schulmeister Klopfstock und seine fünf Söhne" (Brentano) **1**:100
Der Schutzgeist (Kotzebue) **25**:134, 136
Der Schützling (Nestroy) **42**:232, 243, 254
"An Schwager Kronos" (Goethe) **4**:192
"Schwärmbriefe" (Schumann) **143**:75
"Schwanenlied" (Brentano) **191**:136
"Der Schwarze in der Zuckerplantage" (Claudius) **75**:183
"Der schwarze See" (Lenau) **16**:283
"Die Schwarze Spinne" (Gotthelf) **117**:6-11, 13, 15, 32, 36, 43-6, 48-9, 52
"Schwarzschattende Kastanie" (Meyer) **81**:209
Schwarzwälder Dorfgeschichten (Auerbach) **171**:12, 21, 23-24, 27, 35, 37, 40, 45, 49-51, 54-55, 61, 64, 66-68, 70-72
"Schweig Herz! kein Schrei!" (Brentano) **191**:30-33
Das Schweigen (Klopstock) **225**:297
Schweigen (Storm) **195**:4
Der Schweizerische Robinson; oder, Der schiffbrüchige Schweizerprediger und seine Familie (Wyss) **10**:466-73
"Das schwerste Scheiden" (Werner) **189**:367
"Die Schwestern" (Mörike) **201**:293
"Schwüle" (Meyer) **81**:199, 201-02
"Science and Culture" (Huxley) **67**:28, 44, 61, 63-4, 69-72, 83, 87
"Science and Morals" (Huxley) **67**:60, 62, 97
Science Lectures for the People (Huxley) **67**:85
The Science of English Verse (Lanier) **6**:237, 240, 245, 247, 250, 252, 256, 263-65, 269-70, 279; **118**:200, 203, 205, 216-17, 219, 239, 263-66, 286-87, 294
The Science of Ethics as Based on the Scienc of Knowledge (Fichte)
See *Das System der Sittenlehre nach den prinzipen der Wissenschaftslehre*
"The Science of History" (Froude) **43**:184, 191
The Science of Knowledge (Wissenschaftslehre) (Fichte) **62**:40-1, 43, 52, 56
The Science of Legislation (Constant)
See *Commentaire sur l'ouvrage de Filangieri*
The Science of Rights (Fichte)
See *Grundlage des Naturrechts nach Prinzipen der Wissenshaftslehre*
"Scientific and Pseudo-Scientific Realism" (Huxley) **67**:69, 73
"Scientific Education" (Huxley)
See "Scientific Education: Notes of an After-Dinner Speech"
"Scientific Education: Notes of an After-Dinner Speech" (Huxley) **67**:64; 85-86
Scientific Memoirs (Huxley) **67**:33
"The Scientific Poltroons" (Fourier) **51**:185
Scientific Religion (Oliphant) **47**:288-89, 291, 293-94
"A Scientific Vagabond" (Boyesen) **135**:11-12, 19
"The Scientific Ways of Treating Natural Law" (Hegel)
See "Über die wissenschaftlichen Behandlungsarten des Naturrechts"
"Scientifique" (Banville) **9**:31
Scinde; or the Unhappy Valley (Burton) **42**:37-8
The Scorpion Brethren (Hoffmann)
See *Die Serapions Brüder*
The Scotch Parents (Hays) **114**:175
The Scotch Poor Law (Miller) **143**:13
Scotch Recollections (Wordsworth)
See *Recollections of a Tour Made in Scotland*
"Scotch Songs" (Baillie) **2**:41
"A Scot's Mummy" (Hogg) **109**:258, 260
"Scottish Ballads" (Smith) **59**:309
Scottish Pastorals (Hogg) **109**:268
"Scottish Weaver" (Sigourney) **87**:326
The Scouring of the White Horse; or, the Long Vacation Ramble of a London Clerk (Hughes) **207**:138, 141, 154, 170
The Scout (Simms) **3**:508
Scrap-Bag (Alcott)
See *Aunt Jo's Scrap-Bag*
"The Scrap Book" (Willis) **194**:298, 309
"A Scrap, from a Keg, of Hezekiah Salem's Sermons" (Freneau) **111**:135
"Scraps" (Austen) **119**:13
"Scrap-stall of Paris" (Gore) **65**:21
"A Screw Loose" (O'Brien) **21**:236, 247
"Scribblings" (Willis) **194**:298
"Scrisoarea a treia" (Eminescu) **33**:248, 252, 271; **131**:290, 293, 338
"Scrisorile" (Eminescu) **33**:245, 250
"A Scruple Seeming Daft to Me . . ." (Verlaine)
See "Un scrupule qui m'a l'air sot . . ."
"Un scrupule qui m'a l'air sot . . ." (Verlaine) **230**:164
"Scuderi" (Hoffmann)
See "Das Fräulein von Scudéri"
"The Sculptor" (Baratynsky)
See "Skul'ptor"
Sculpture (Herder)
See *Plastik*
"Sculpture, Painting, and Music" (Gogol) **162**:77, 82
"Scutari" (Milnes) **61**:138
The Scuttled Ship (Reade) **2**:544
Se Gefylsta (Barnes) **75**:40
"A se stesso" (Leopardi) **129**:219-20, 251, 308, 350, 355-56
"Sea" (Boyesen) **135**:47
"The Sea" (Bryant) **6**:175
"The Sea" (Taylor) **89**:314
The Sea (Michelet)
See *La mer*
"Sea and Sky" (Larcom) **179**:171
"Sea and Sky" (Muller) **73**:352
"The Sea and the Cliff" (Tyutchev) **34**:383, 404
"The Sea and the Skylark" (Hopkins) **17**:212, 220, 225, 257
"A Sea Dialogue" (Holmes) **14**:129; **79**:23, 35, 40, 42, 51-52, 59, 62, 65, 73-74, 76
"A Sea Dream" (Darley) **2**:133
"A Sea Dream" (Whittier) **8**:513
"Sea Dreams" (Tennyson) **30**:233; **202**:284
The Sea Gull (Caballero)
See *La gaviota: Novela de costumbres*
"Sea Gulls in Flight" (Meyer)
See "Möwenflug"
"A Sea Has Wakened Up" (Petofi)
See "Föltámadott a tenger"
The Sea Lions (Cooper) **203**:50, 77, 85, 87
The Sea Lions; or, The Lost Sealers (Cooper) **1**:208, 221-22; **27**:142; **54**:275-7
"The Sea of Death" (Hood) **16**:208, 234
"The Sea said 'come' to the Brook" (Dickinson) **77**:93
"The Sea Shell on the Desert" (Jones) **222**:128
Sea Spray and Smoke Drift (Gordon) **21**:150, 163, 170, 173, 179, 181
"The Sea View" (Smith)
See "Sonnet 83"
"The Sea-Bride" (Darley) **2**:134
"Sea-Drift" (Whitman) **4**:563, 606; **205**:225-26, 262
"The Sea-Fairies" (Tennyson) **30**:204, 223, 241
"The Sealed Angel" (Leskov)
See "Zapechatlennyi angel"
"The Sea-Limits" (Rossetti) **4**:491-92, 512; **77**:310
"The Seamstress" (Galt) **110**:114
The Search After Happiness (More)
See *The Search after Happiness: A Pastoral Drama*
The Search after Happiness: A Pastoral Drama (More) **27**:332; **141**:167, 232, 249, 254, 258, 279-83
Seashells from the island of Rugen (Muller)
See *Muscheln von der Insel Rügen*
"Sea-Shore" (Emerson) **1**:296
"A Seashore Drama" (Balzac)
See "Un drame au bord de la mer"
The Seaside and the Fireside (Longfellow) **2**:475, 492-93, 495; **45**:116, 153; **101**:92
Sea-side Studies at Ilfracombe, Tenby, the Scilly Isles, and Jersey (Lewes) **25**:280, 288, 296, 308, 310-12; **215**:86, 122, 183
A Season in Hell (Rimbaud)
See *Une saison en enfer*
"The Season of the Northers" (Heredia)
See "La estacíon de los nortes"
"Season Tokens" (Barnes) **75**:70
The Seasons (Hogg) **109**:268
"The Seasons Moralized" (Freneau) **1**:317
The Season's Ticket (Haliburton) **149**:267, 269, 300
The Season-Ticket (Haliburton) **15**:126, 136, 145
"The Sea-Spell" (Hood) **16**:234
"Seating the Parish" (Smith) **187**:319
"Seaweed" (Longfellow) **2**:492; **45**:116, 146, 148, 154; **103**:298
"Seaweed" (Lowell) **2**:509
Sebastian of Portugal (Hemans) **29**:201
"Sebastian van Storck" (Pater) **7**:298, 307, 312; **159**:269
"Sebe lyubeznogo ishchu" (Bestuzhev) **131**:148
Sechs Gedichte und Requiem (Schumann) **143**:141
"Seclusion" (Mörike) **10**:446
"Second" (De Quincey) **87**:77
"The Second Best" (Arnold) **218**:121, 275
"The Second Birth-Day" (Sigourney) **21**:310
A Second Book of Verse (Field) **3**:205-06, 208
The Second Brother (Beddoes) **3**:26, 29, 33, 35-36, 38-39; **154**:14, 45-46, 51, 71
Second Brutus (Alfieri)
See *Bruto secondo*
"The Second Day" (Longfellow) **45**:138
"Second Dialogue for Three Young Ladies" (Rowson) **69**:115
"Second Epistle" (Eminescu) **131**:332
The Second Funeral of Napoleon, in Three Letters to Miss Smith of London; and The Chronicle of the Drum (Thackeray) **169**:330; **213**:312, 320
"Second Inaugural Address" (Lincoln)
See "Inaugural Address, March 4, 1865"
Second Inaugural Address (Lincoln) **18**:222-23, 235, 238, 246-48, 250-54, 257, 266-67
"A Second Lecture on the Fine Arts" (Thackeray) **213**:245-46, 327
"Second Love" (Timrod) **25**:375
Second Love; or, Beauty and Intellect (Trollope) **30**:331
The Second Marriage: A Comedy on Ambition (Baillie) **2**:31, 34; **71**:64; **151**:6, 115

The Second Part of Tom White the Postboy; or, The Way to Plenty (More) **27**:347
"A Second Psalm of Life" (Longfellow)
See "The Light of Stars"
Second Rhapsody (Liszt) **199**:305
A Second Series of Curiosities of Literature, Consisting of Researches in Literary, Biographical, and Political History; of Critical and Philosophical Inquiries and of Secret History (D'Israeli) **217**:333
"Second Sight" (Hemans) **71**:277
The Second Son (Oliphant) **61**:216-7
"The Second Spring" (Newman) **38**:310
"Second Sunday after Easter" (Keble) **87**:177
"Second Sunday after Trinity" (Keble) **87**:118, 159
"Second Sunday in Advent" (Droste-Hülshoff) **3**:202
"Second Sunday in Lent" (Keble) **87**:177
"Second Thoughts" (Pater) **7**:295, 336
Second Tour (Wordsworth)
See *Journal of My Second Tour in Scotland*
The Second Youth of Theodora Desanges (Linton) **41**:168, 175-76
seconda minutia (Manzoni) **98**:263, 267
La seconde année; ou, À qui la faute? (Scribe) **16**:394
La Seconde boussole (Fourier) **51**:171
"The Secret" (Brontë) **105**:54
"The Secret" (Dickinson) **171**:87
"The Secret Drawer, or the Story of a Missing Will" (Alger) **83**:96
"Secret Faults" (Newman) **38**:304
"Secret Love" (Clare) **9**:89, 95
"Secret Love" (Opie) **65**:160
"The Secret of Lord Singleworth" (Norwid)
See "Tajemnica Lorda Singleworth"
"The Secret of reminiscence" (Schiller)
See "Das Geheimnis der Reminiszenz"
The Secret of Swedenborg: Being an Elucidation of His Doctrine of the Divine Natural Humanity (James) **53**:192-3, 204-9, 214, 225, 229-30, 232, 234
"The Secret of the Sea" (Longfellow) **2**:493; **45**:116, 144, 153; **101**:92
"The Secret of the Stars" (Holmes) **14**:128
"Secret Parting" (Rossetti) **4**:498
The Secret Records (Bird) **197**:15-17
Secret Service (Planché) **42**:292
Le secrétaire intime (Sand) **2**:599; **42**:358
"Les Secrètes Pensées de Rafaël, gentilhomme français" (Musset) **150**:233-34, 322
"Les secrets de la Princesse de Cadignan" (Balzac) **5**:59; **153**:149, 152-53
Secrets of the Magazine Prison-House (Poe) **55**:136
"Sectionalism" (Lincoln) **201**:163
"Sed buenos!" (Isaacs) **70**:313
"Sed non satiata" (Baudelaire) **29**:99; **55**:33, 44
"The Seducer's Diary" (Kierkegaard)
See "Diary of the Seducer"
Seduction (Holcroft) **85**:205-06, 216-18, 234, 237
"Seein' Things at Night" (Field) **3**:208
"Seeing the World" (O'Brien) **21**:236, 247
"Seek and Find" (Rossetti) **2**:568, 572; **50**:271, 273-6, 289, 318, 320; **66**:331, 362
Seek and Find (Rossetti) **186**:230, 266, 337, 339
"Seeking Rest" (Rossetti) **50**:311-2
"Das Seelchen" (Meyer) **81**:201, 206
"Der Seelenkranke" (Lenau) **16**:281-82
Seelenwanderung (Kotzebue) **25**:136
"Seemorgen" (Lenau) **16**:283
"The Seer on Death" (Hayne) **94**:153
"Segen und Unsegen" (Gotthelf) **117**:43, 58
Segunda parte (Lizardi) **30**:68
"Sehnsucht" (Beethoven) **227**:32, 34
"Sehnsucht" (Schiller) **166**:108-10, 119
Sehnsucht (Hauff) **185**:321
Sehnsucht (Mörike) **201**:268
The Seige of Murány (Arany)
See *Murány ostroma*
"Die Seitenwunde" (Meyer) **81**:207
Seitsemän veljestä (Kivi) **30**:46-51, 53, 55, 62-5
"Seken tekake katagi" (Ueda Akinari) **131**:18, 45-46, 58, 67
"Selbstbiographie" (Raimund) **69**:12
Selbstbiographie (Grillparzer) **102**:101, 103, 105, 107, 143, 148, 167, 180
Selbstbiographie (Kopitar) **117**:91, 122
The Select Letters (Smith) **187**:313
"A Select Party" (Hawthorne) **2**:297-98; **226**:96
Select Poems (Sigourney) **87**:321, 326, 331, 337
Select Poems of Rural Life in the Dorset Dialect (Barnes) **75**:40
Select Poems of William Barnes (Barnes) **75**:10, 23, 40, 95
Selected Correspondence (Marx) **114**:22
Selected Letters (Liszt) **199**:340
Selected Letters and Journals of George Crabbe (Crabbe) **121**:88
Selected Letters of Charles Baudelaire (Baudelaire) **155**:113, 116
Selected Letters of Mary Wollstonecraft Shelley (Shelley)
See *The Letters of Mary Wollstonecraft Shelley*
Selected Letters of Matthew Arnold (Arnold) **218**:210-11
Selected Passages from Correspondence with Friends (Gogol)
See *Vybrannye mesta iz perepiski s druzyami*
Selected Passages from Correspondence with My Friends (Gogol)
See *Vybrannye mesta iz perepiski s druzyami*
"Selected Poems" (Browning) **79**:142, 189
Selected Poems (Barrett Browning)
See *Elizabeth Barrett Browning: Selected Poems*
Selected Poems (Emerson) **98**:177
Selected Poems (Lampman) **194**:92
Selected Poems (Tennyson) **202**:295
Selected Poems (Verlaine) **230**:220
Selected Poems of Joanna Baillie (Baillie) **151**:86
Selected Poems of William Barnes (Barnes) **75**:40, 52, 54
Selected Poetry and Prose (Barbauld) **185**:149, 156
Selected Poetry and Prose (Coleridge) **197**:239
Selected Prose of Archibald Lampman (Lampman) **194**:52, 55-57, 59-63, 95-96, 115
Selected Prose of Christina Rossetti (Rossetti) **186**:335-37, 339, 341
Selected Satirical Writings (Saltykov) **16**:376
Selected Stories of Isabella Valancy Crawford (Crawford) **12**:170
Selection (Hemans) **71**:277
Selection from the Papers of the Devil (Jean Paul) **7**:227
A Selection from the Poems of Mathilde Blind (Blind) **202**:9, 28
A Selection from Unpublished Poems (Barnes) **75**:18, 40
The Selection of a Tutor (Fonvizin)
See *Lavengro: The Scholar—The Gypsy—The Priest*
Selections (Browning) **79**:149
Selections from George Eliot's Letters (Eliot) **199**:255
Selections from Jonson (Symonds) **34**:342
Selections from the Correspondence of Mrs. Hannah More and Observations on Several Subjects (More) **141**:170
Selections from the Poems of William Wordsworth, Esq. Chiefly for the Use of Schools or Young Persons (Wordsworth) **206**:335
Selections from the Spectator (Barbauld) **185**:6, 23
Selections from the Verse of Augusta Webster (Webster) **230**:242
Selene (Schumann) **143**:73, 102, 138
"Self-Apology" (Verlaine)
See "Mon Apologie"
"Self-Communion" (Brontë) **4**:44-45, 56; **71**:91; **102**:24
"Self-Conquest" (Parton) **86**:347
"The Self-Consumed" (Griffin) **7**:214
"Self-Culture" (Channing) **17**:21
"Self-Deception" (Arnold) **29**:34; **218**:114
"Self-Dependence" (Arnold) **29**:34; **218**:120, 150
Self-Education; or, The Means and Art of Moral Progress (Peabody) **169**:187
"Selfia" (Isaacs) **70**:304, 307
"The Selfish Crotaire" (Griffin) **7**:214
"Self-Knowledge" (Coleridge) **177**:160; **231**:105
"Self-Love and Benevolence" (Hazlitt) **29**:169, 172-73
Self-Made (Southworth) **26**:436, 439-40
"Self-Made Men" (Douglass) **7**:126; **55**:108, 123; **141**:55, 74
"Self-Portrait" (Foscolo) **8**:279
Self-Raised; or, From the Depths (Southworth) **26**:434, 439, 447
"Self-Reliance" (Emerson) **1**:305, 307; **38**:169, 173-75, 204-05, 208-09, 224-27; **98**:9, 18-19, 27, 31-7, 61, 65, 72, 82, 89, 93, 98, 107, 109, 111-14, 116, 136, 151, 186, 191
"Selige Sehnsucht" (Goethe) **34**:98
"Selim" (Wieland) **17**:418
"Sella" (Bryant) **6**:165, 169, 171, 187; **46**:4, 21, 47
Selmar und Selma (Klopstock) **225**:285, 296
"Sel'skii prazdnik i svad'ba" (Karamzin) **173**:309
Seltsame Leiden eines Theaterdirektors (Hoffmann) **183**:174, 176, 187
Seltsames Begegnen und Widersehen (Arnim) **159**:17, 19, 21
"La semaine Sainte" (Lamartine) **11**:245, 264, 269
Semeinaia khronika (Aksakov) **2**:11-18; **181**:4, 6, 13-14, 16, 24, 28-35, 37-39, 42, 45, 49-50, 57, 65-67
"Semele" (Cooke) **110**:9
Semeynaya kartina (Ostrovsky) **30**:101; **57**:195, 206-8
The Semi-Attached Couple (Eden) **10**:103-08, 110
The Semi-Detached House (Eden) **10**:103, 105-10
"Semper eadem" (Verlaine) **51**:387
"Sen" (Mickiewicz) **101**:161, 164, 185-86
"Sen Cezary" (Krasiński) **4**:306, 313
Sen srebrny Salomei (Slowacki) **15**:348, 352, 371, 378, 380
"Sending" (Arnold) **6**:67
Sendung (Goethe)
See *Theatralische Sendung*
Senhora (Alencar) **157**:9, 31, 39-41
Senilia (Turgenev)
See *Stikhotvoreniya v proze*
El señor Saco con respecto a la revolución de cuba (Villaverde) **121**:335
"Sensation" (Rimbaud) **4**:467, 478; **35**:275, 282
"Sensation Novels" (Oliphant) **221**:281
Sense and Sensibility (Austen) **1**:30, 32-4, 37, 39, 41, 44, 46-7, 50-1, 53-4, 59-61, 63-4, 66; **13**:67, 73, 76, 96-8, 106-07; **19**:4, 6, 32, 38, 42, 44; **33**:66, 68-9, 74, 76, 90-3, 96; **51**:12, 16, 47, 55; **81**:1-90; **95**:2-3, 11-12, 16-17, 21, 56, 74, 76, 79-80; **119**:14, 17-18, 21, 24-5, 27, 34-5, 37, 39, 42, 45, 48, 51; **150**:14, 19, 21, 25, 37, 45, 67, 70, 72; **222**:6, 19, 30, 36, 52, 88
Sensibility (More) **27**:332, 336; **141**:231-32

"The Sensitive Man and the Cold Man" (Karamzin) **3**:281
"The Sensitive Plant" (Shelley) **18**:319, 330, 334, 339, 343-44, 349, 358-59, 362-63; **175**:199, 240
"Sensitiveness" (Newman) **38**:343-44
"The Sensory and Motor Nerves" (Lewes) **25**:287
"The Sentences" (Patmore) **9**:330-31
"A Sentiment of Spring" (Zhukovsky) **35**:403, 407
"Sentimental Colloquy" (Verlaine)
See "Colloque sentimental"
Sentimental Education: A Young Man's History (Flaubert)
See *L'éducation sentimentale: Histoire d'un jeune homme*
"Sentimental Walk" (Verlaine)
See "Promenade sentimentale"
"Sentimentalisme" (Villiers de l'Isle Adam) **3**:590
"Sentimentality" (Villiers de l'Isle Adam)
See "Sentimentalisme"
"El sentimiento religioso" (Martínez de la Rosa) **102**:254
"The Sentry" (Leskov)
See "Chelovék na chasákh"
The Sentry, and Other Stories (Leskov) **25**:230-31
"Separate Ways" (Ichiyō)
See "Wakare-Michi"
The Separated Wife (Sacher-Masoch) **31**:290-91, 297-98, 301
The Separation (Baillie) **2**:40-41; **151**:55, 114
"Separation of Church and State" (Brownson) **50**:51
The Separation of Mother and Child by the Laws of "Custody of Infants" Considered (Norton) **205**:75-76, 85, 136
I sepolcri (Foscolo) **8**:262, 264-65, 267-70, 272; **97**:50-2, 55, 57-9, 62-4, 67-8, 78, 83-4, 86-7, 97-9
Les sept cordes de la lyre (Sand) **2**:588; **42**:314, 368-73
"Les sept vieillards" (Baudelaire) **6**:79, 116, 129-30; **29**:100, 104, 114; **55**:16, 19, 28, 35, 37-42, 67; **155**:3-4, 6-7
"September" (Clare) **9**:112, 116; **86**:130
"September" (Lampman) **194**:92
"September, 1802" (Wordsworth) **206**:308
"September Gale" (Holmes) **14**:101
"September in Australia" (Kendall) **12**:183, 185-86, 191, 199-201
"September in Toronto" (Crawford) **127**:198-99
"Septembermorgen" (Mörike) **10**:448; **201**:369
"September's Baccalaureate" (Dickinson) **21**:67
"September's End" (Petofi)
See "Szeptember végén"
Septet (Beethoven) **227**:6
Septimius Felton, or the Elixir of Life (Hawthorne) **2**:307-08, 315, 319-21, 324, 335
"Septuagesima Sunday" (Keble) **87**:172, 202
The Sepulchres (Foscolo)
See *I sepolcri*
"Sequel" (Mallarmé) **41**:254
"A Sequel to an Evening at a Caucasian Spa in 1824" (Bestuzhev)
See "Sledstvie vechera na kavkazskikh vodakh v 1824 godu"
Sequel to Drum-Taps (Whitman) **4**:580; **205**:341
A Sequel to Early Lessons (Edgeworth) **51**:81
"La sera del dí di festa" (Leopardi) **129**:229, 232
"The Seraph and the Poet" (Barrett Browning) **61**:43
"The Seraphim" (Barrett Browning) **1**:122; **61**:4-5, 48, 52-7, 61; **66**:71
The Seraphim (Barrett Browning) **170**:103, 105-6, 108, 110, 112
The Seraphim, and Other Poems (Barrett Browning) **1**:112, 126; **61**:4, 8, 41-2, 48, 50-3, 61; **66**:44, 83; **170**:3, 25, 27, 86, 104-5, 107, 109
"Seraphina" (Wieland) **177**:265
Séraphita (Balzac) **5**:46, 49, 81; **35**:55; **53**:28, 31; **153**:65, 108, 116, 119, 124-28, 130
The Serapion Brethren (Hoffmann)
See *Die Serapions Brüder*
"The Serapion Brothers" (Hoffmann)
See *Die Serapions Brüder*
Die Serapions Brüder (Hoffmann) **183**:165-66, 184-85, 187-88, 195, 233, 267, 278, 298
A Serbian Book of Folk Songs (Karadzic)
See *Narodna srbska pjesnarica*
Serbian Dictionary (Karadzic)
See *Srpski rjeĉnik*
Serbian Grammar (Karadzic)
See *Srpska gramatika*
"Serenada" (Pavlova) **138**:4, 50
"Serenade" (Allingham) **25**:6
"A Serenade" (Brontë) **105**:55
"La sérénade" (Nerval) **67**:306
"A Serenade" (Pavlova)
See "Serenada"
"Serenade" (Pinkney) **31**:268, 273-74, 279
"Serenade" (Timrod) **25**:366, 385
"Sérénade" (Verlaine) **230**:166
"A Serenade at the Villa" (Browning) **19**:127
Serenades in Ritor Nelles (Muller) **73**:352
Series of Lay Sermons (Hogg) **109**:231
A Series of Plays: In Which It Is Attempted to Delineate the Stronger Passions of the Mind, Each Passion Being the Subject of a Tragedy and a Comedy (Baillie) **2**:31-32, 39-43, 30-31, 38-43, 36, 39-43; **71**:1-2, 16, 19, 28, 31-32, 51-53; **151**:4, 8-11, 13-15, 17, 22-23, 25, 52, 56, 71, 77, 88, 94, 98, 106-8, 113-18, 122, 127
A Series of Popular Essays, Illustrative of Principles Essentially Connected with the Improvement of the Understanding, the Imagination, and the Heart (Hamilton) **153**:277, 308-10, 348, 350-54
Sermon in a Churchyard (Macaulay) **42**:116
"A Sermon of Merchants" (Parker) **186**:207
A Sermon of Slavery (Parker) **186**:132, 163
"The Sermon of St. Francis" (Longfellow) **45**:139
A Sermon of War, Preached at the Melodeon, on Sunday, June 7, 1846 (Parker) **186**:164
"A Sermon on Village Slander" (Brackenridge) **227**:104, 117
"Sermon Record Book" (Parker) **186**:205
Sermons (Arnold) **18**:3, 18, 27
Sermons (Maturin) **169**:46, 56-57
The Sermons and Devotional Writings of Gerard Manley Hopkins (Hopkins) **189**:23-25, 29-31, 35, 39, 41, 44-45, 48, 55-56, 62, 91, 93, 115-16, 118, 139-40, 142-43, 146-47
Sermons and Tracts (Channing) **17**:4
Sermons Bearing on Subjects of the Day (Newman) **38**:304, 306-07, 309; **99**:224
"Sermons in Favor of the Federal Constitution" (Brackenridge) **227**:115, 117-18
Sermons of Blair (Blair) **75**:116, 123, 129-32
Sermons of Theism, Atheism, and the Popular Theology (Parker) **186**:126, 148, 168, 212, 215, 222
Sermons Preached on Various Occasions (Newman) **38**:309-11
"Le Serpent" (Sade) **47**:313, 351
"The Serpent" (Very) **9**:387
"The Serpent Is Shut Out from Paradise" (Shelley) **93**:307-08
"Le serpent qui danse" (Baudelaire) **55**:9, 28-9
The Serpent Woman (Gozzi)
See *La donna serpente*
"La Serre" (Maupassant) **83**:229
The Servant (Shevchenko)
See *Naimychka*
The Servant Girl (Shevchenko)
See *Naimychka*
"La servante au grand coeur" (Baudelaire) **29**:80; **55**:23, 64
La servante du roi (Musset) **7**:258
"Servaz und Pankraz" (Gotthelf) **117**:44, 51, 56-8
Servian Folks' Songs (Runeberg) **41**:309
"The Service" (Thoreau) **7**:379-81; **138**:70, 117, 119, 123
Servitude et grandeur militaires (Vigny) **7**:467-68, 471-74, 476-78, 485; **102**:336-37, 353, 378
"Ses purs ongles, très haut" (Mallarmé) **210**:241
"Ses purs ongles très haut dèdiant leur onyx" (Mallarmé)
See "Sonnet en -yx"
"Seth Woodsum's Wife" (Smith) **187**:319
Seth's Brother's Wife (Frederic) **10**:182-83, 187-88, 191, 193-95, 200-04, 207, 209-13, 216; **175**:149, 154, 158
"The Setting of the Moon" (Leopardi)
See "Il tramonto della luna"
"The Setting Sun" (Clare) **86**:156
"The Settle an' the Girt Wood Vire" (Barnes) **75**:70, 77, 82
"The Settlement" (Slowacki)
See "Posielenie"
"The Settler, or the Prophecy Fulfilled" (Richardson) **55**:299
"Settlers at Home" (Martineau) **26**:323
The Settlers at Home (Martineau) **137**:256, 260
"The Settlers Settled; or, Pat Connor and His Two Masters" (Traill) **31**:326
Seven Brothers (Kivi)
See *Seitsemän veljestä*
The Seven Champions of Christendom (Planché) **42**:290, 293, 301
Seven Gables (Hawthorne)
See *The House of the Seven Gables: A Romance*
The Seven Hills (De Mille) **123**:123
782 (Dickinson) **77**:151
715 (Dickinson) **77**:163
757 (Dickinson) **77**:50
745 (Dickinson) **77**:64
709 (Dickinson) **77**:71
791 (Dickinson) **77**:150
797 (Dickinson) **77**:92, 95
738 (Dickinson) **77**:63
712 (Dickinson) **77**:49, 96, 163, 173
728 (Dickinson) **77**:95
721 (Dickinson) **77**:140, 144
722 (Dickinson) **77**:84
Seven Legends (Keller)
See *Sieben Legenden*
"The Seven Old Men" (Baudelaire)
See "Les sept vieillards"
"Seven Sisters" (Wordsworth) **12**:393
The Seven Strings of the Lyre (Sand)
See *Les sept cordes de la lyre*
"The Seven Vagabonds" (Hawthorne) **2**:305
"The Seven Wonders of the World" (Cranch) **115**:42
1754 (Dickinson) **77**:132
Seventeen Hundred and Ninety-One: A Poem, in Imitation of the Thirteenth Satire of Juvenal (Murphy) **229**:225
"17 oktiabra A. N. Maikovu" (Aksakov) **181**:61
1720 (Dickinson) **77**:119
"Seventh Satire" (Adams) **175**:46, 49, 51-52
Seventh Symphony (Beethoven) **227**:6
76 (Dickinson) **77**:74
72 (Dickinson) **77**:121-22
Seventy-Six (Neal) **161**:279, 285-86, 290-91, 299-300, 318-19, 323, 325
"Seven-year-old Poets" (Rimbaud)
See "Les poètes de sept ans"
"Severed and Gone" (Brontë) **71**:106
"Severed Selves" (Rossetti) **77**:313
"Severer Service of myself" (Dickinson) **171**:199
"The Sewing Bird" (O'Brien) **21**:234
"The Sexton's Adventure" (Le Fanu) **9**:321

"The Sexton's Daughter" (Shevchenko)
See "Tytarivna"
"The Sexton's Hero" (Gaskell) **137**:4, 38
Sexual Inversion (Symonds) **34**:343
"Sfinks" (Pavlova) **138**:13, 33, 48
A Shabby Genteel Story (Thackeray) **5**:482, 506; **14**:402, 408; **43**:359; **169**:242; **213**:238
"The Shadow" (Andersen)
See "Skyggen"
"The Shadow" (Clough) **27**:55, 79, 87
"A Shadow" (Longfellow) **45**:121
"Shadow, a Parable" (Poe) **1**:497-98, 513; **16**:306, 331; **117**:268
"The Shadow and the Light" (Whittier) **8**:493
The Shadow of Ashlydyat (Wood) **178**:288, 291, 314, 335
Shadow Tree Shaft (Robertson) **35**:330, 333, 335-36, 356, 369
"Shadows" (Milnes) **61**:145
"Shadows All" (Hayne) **94**:166
Shadows and Sunbeams (Parton) **86**:350-52
Shadows of Society (Sacher-Masoch) **31**:294
"Shadows of Taste" (Clare) **9**:104; **86**:113, 130
Shadows of the Clouds (Froude) **43**:192-93, 209
"Shadows of the Mountain Pine" (Cooke) **5**:132
"Shadows of the Pine Forest" (Cooke) **5**:132
Shadowy images of a journey to the Harz Mountains and Saxony (Andersen) **79**:79
"Shaftesbury Feäir" (Barnes) **75**:67, 98
"The Shaker Bridal" (Hawthorne) **2**:327; **10**:316; **158**:253, 255
"Shakespear" (Herder) **8**:315; **186**:13, 18, 84, 87, 91
Shakespear Illustrated (Lennox) **23**:228, 231, 261-65; **134**:271, 292
"Shakespeare" (Arnold) **29**:4, 35; **89**:95
"Shakespeare" (Blind) **202**:57
"Shakespeare" (Longfellow) **45**:186
"Shakespeare" (Very) **9**:370, 379, 382
"Shakespeare, a Poet Generally" (Coleridge) **99**:87
Shakespeare and His Forerunners: Studies in Elizabethan Poetry and Its Development from Early English (Lanier) **6**:240, 245; **118**:290, 294
Shakespeare as Actor and Critic (Lewes) **215**:131
The Shakespeare Head Brontë (Brontë) **217**:100-101, 106
Shakespeare in the Shades (Cumberland) **167**:107, 136
"Shakespeare Once More" (Lowell) **2**:509
"Shakespeare; or, The Poet" (Emerson)
See "Shakespeare, the Poet"
Shakespeare Papers (Maginn) **8**:435, 440
"Shakespeare, the Poet" (Emerson) **1**:295; **98**:70, 108, 112
"Shakespeare und kein Ende!" (Goethe) **154**:279
Shakespearean Criticism (Coleridge) **99**:102, 105; **197**:241, 272
Shakespeares Behandlung des Wunderbaren (Tieck) **5**:520, 526; **46**:332
"Shakespeare's Judgment Equal to His Genius" (Coleridge) **99**:86
Shakespeares Mädchen und Frauen (Heine) **4**:244, 246, 265; **147**:177
Shakespeare's Treatment of the Marvelous (Tieck)
See *Shakespeares Behandlung des Wunderbaren*
Shakespeare's Vorschule (Tieck) **5**:511, 520; **46**:359
Shakespeare-Studien (Ludwig) **4**:351-52, 358, 366, 368
"Shakespeare—the Man" (Bagehot) **10**:57
"The Shaking of the Pear Tree" (Craik) **38**:119
"Shakspeare's Critics, English and Foreign" (Lewes) **25**:285, 305
"Shameful Death" (Morris) **4**:426
"Shameless" (Thomson) **18**:411
"Shampooing the English" (Haliburton) **149**:295
"Shamus O'Brien" (Le Fanu) **9**:298-99
"Shane Fadh's Wedding" (Carleton) **3**:89-90, 92; **199**:33, 56
"Shanid Castle" (Griffin) **7**:194, 196
Shannondale (Southworth) **26**:431
"Shared" (Larcom) **179**:174
"The Shark" (Solomos)
See "O pórphyras"
"Sharp Snaffles" (Simms) **3**:508
Sharps and Flats (Field) **3**:209
The Shaughraun (Boucicault) **41**:27-30, 34, 39, 43, 49, 51, 53
Shawl Straps (Alcott) **83**:34
"Shchi" (Turgenev) **122**:308, 312
She and He (Sand)
See *Elle et lui*
"She bore it till the simple veins/Traced azure on her hand" (Dickinson) **77**:162-63
"She Came and Went" (Lowell) **90**:214
The She-Devils (Barbey d'Aurevilly)
See *Les diaboliques*
"She Died at Play" (Dickinson) **21**:55
"She Dwelt among the Untrodden Ways" (Wordsworth) **206**:224, 281
"She dwelt among th'untrodden ways" (Wordsworth) **111**:323, 327-28
"She Is Far from the Land" (Hood) **16**:236
"She Is Far from the Land" (Moore) **6**:391
"She Lay as If at Play" (Dickinson) **21**:42-3; **171**:161
"She loves him yet" (Osgood) **141**:321
"She Sleeps!" (Isaacs)
See "Ella duerme!"
"She Was a Phantom of Delight" (Wordsworth) **206**:225
"She Was Good for Nothing" (Andersen)
See "Hun duede ikke"
"She Was No Good" (Andersen)
See "Hun duede ikke"
"She Was not There" (Willis) **194**:305
A Sheaf Gleaned in French Fields (Dutt) **29**:120, 127-28
"Shed No Tear!" (Keats) **8**:360
"The Sheep and the Dogs" (Krylov) **1**:435
"A Sheepsheering Song" (Thelwall) **162**:328-30, 336
The Sheik of Alexandria and His Slaves (Hauff)
See *Der Scheik von Alessandria und seine Sklaven*
"The Shekh" (Taylor) **89**:302-03
"A Shelf in my Bookcase" (Smith) **59**:307, 309-10, 315, 317, 323, 337
"The Shell" (Chivers) **49**:71
"Shelley" (Thomson) **18**:406, 414
Shelley's Poetry and Prose (Shelley) **175**:301, 303
Shelley's Prose (Shelley) **143**:244; **175**:300-301, 307
"Shelley's View of Nature Contrasted With Darwin's" (Blind) **202**:46, 52
"The Shepherd" (Blake) **37**:3, 38, 57, 65, 72, 78, 92
"The Shepherd and His Dog Rover" (Bloomfield) **145**:154-55
"The Shepherd Girl" (Kivi)
See "Paimentyttö"
"The Shepherd of King Admetus" (Lowell) **90**:194
The Shepherd of Salisbury Plain (More) **27**:333, 338, 347-49, 358; **141**:167, 188, 191, 269-70, 288-89, 300
The Shepherd Prince (Mapu)
See *Ahavat Zion*
"Shepherd Sandy" (Krylov) **1**:439
"The Shepherdess and the Chimney Sweep" (Andersen) **7**:22, 34; **79**:23, 40, 42, 58, 87; **214**:48, 55, 59-60
"The Shepherdess and the Sheep" (Andersen)
See "Hyrdinden og Skorsteensfeieren"
"The Shepherd's Brow, Fronting Forked Lightning, Owns" (Hopkins) **17**:246, 262
The Shepherd's Calendar (Hogg) **109**:202, 256
The Shepherd's Calendar, with Village Stories, and Other Poems (Clare) **9**:78-79, 84, 96, 103-04, 106-07, 111-12, 114, 116, 123; **86**:93-105, 110, 125, 130, 154, 156, 160, 165, 168-69, 174
"The Shepherd's Dog" (Robinson) **142**:137
"The Shepherd's Dream" (Bloomfield) **145**:158
"The Shepherd's Hut" (Vigny) **7**:474
"Shepot grustnyj, govor tajnyj" (Pavlova) **138**:54
Sheppard Lee (Bird) **1**:84-86, 88, 91
Sheppard Lee. Written by Himself ... (Bird) **197**:14, 43-45, 49, 68
"Sheridan" (Landor) **14**:166
Sheridan (Oliphant) **221**:233
The Sheriff's Ball (Barham) **77**:6
"She's All My Fancy Painted Him" (Dodgson) **139**:33
"She's Up and Gone, the Graceless Girl" (Hood) **16**:219
The Shield (Cooper) **129**:67
Shifting for Himself; or, Gilbert Greyson's Fortunes (Alger) **8**:16, 43
"Shikubi no egao" (Ueda Akinari) **131**:21-22, 57-58, 88
"Shinel" (Gogol) **5**:218-20, 227, 229-30, 235-36, 238-39; **31**:88; **162**:8, 12, 14, 19, 27, 29-30, 37, 39-44, 46, 51, 63-64, 81-86, 96, 126
"The Ship of Earth" (Lanier) **6**:236; **118**:217
"The Ships of San Juan" (Silva)
See "Los maderos de San Juan"
"A Shipwreck" (Osgood) **141**:326
The Shipwreck (Mackenzie) **41**:184
"Shiramine" (Ueda Akinari) **131**:13, 24-25, 27, 32, 38, 40-41, 46, 48-49, 53, 64-65, 69, 87
Shirley: A Tale (Brontë) **3**:46-9, 52, 55-7, 59-61, 64-5, 67, 69-71, 74-6; **8**:54-5; **33**:103, 117-18, 122, 129, 143; **58**:153-246; **105**:2, 6, 54-56, 73; **155**:158-59, 163-64, 178, 225-27; **217**:4-5, 7-8, 11-12, 19, 22, 25, 32, 92, 118-23, 125, 153, 155-57, 162-63; **229**:4, 15-16, 19, 32, 34, 38, 85, 160-61, 164, 178-79, 182, 200
"The Shirt Collar" (Andersen)
See "Flipperne"
Shodo kikimimi sekenzaru (Ueda Akinari) **131**:18, 45, 60, 86
"The Shoes of Fortune" (Crawford) **127**:188
Shoes of Fortune (Andersen) **79**:3
"The Shoes That Were Danced to Pieces" (Grimm Brothers) **3**:227
"Shooter's Hill" (Bloomfield) **145**:133
"Shooter's Hill—Topographical Digressions" (Thelwall) **162**:307
"The Shooting Match" (Longstreet) **159**:123, 131, 133-34, 143-44, 146-47, 149, 154, 159, 161, 164-67, 180, 185, 202, 204
"Shooting Niagra: And After?" (Carlyle) **70**:93
"Shop" (Browning) **19**:87, 96
The Shopkeeper turned Sailor; or, the Folly of going out of our Element (More) **141**:179
"Shops and Their Tenants" (Dickens) **187**:26
"Short but Typical Scene" (Laforgue)
See "Pierrots"
A Short Consecutive Account of the Chronicle of the World (Grundtvig)
See *Kort Begreb af Verdens Krønike i Sammenhæng*
"Short Prose" (Silva)
See "Prosas breves"
Short Prose Poems (Baudelaire)
See *Le spleen de Paris, petits poèmes en prose*
A Short Sketch of the World's Chronicle (Grundtvig)
See *Kort Begreb af Verdens Krønike i Sammenhæng*
Short Stories by Alexandre Dumas (Dumas) **71**:219

Short Studies on Great Subjects (Froude) **43**:178-79, 189-90, 203-04
"Short Unpretentious Prayer" (Laforgue)
See "Petites prière sans prétention"
Shorter Novels of Herman Melville (Melville) **193**:52
Shorter Prose Writings (Schiller)
See *Kleinere prosaische Schriften*
Shorter Works and Fragments (Coleridge) **177**:160; **197**:310-11; **231**:140-41
"The Shot" (Pushkin)
See "Vystrel"
The Shot from the Pulpit (Meyer)
See "Der Schuß von der Kanzel"
"Should We Temper Our Words" (Eminescu) **131**:326
Shou-tzu p'u (Li Ju-chen) **137**:206
"Shponka's Dream" (Gogol) **15**:89
Shriften II (Novalis)
See *Blüthenstaub*
Shriften III (Novalis)
See *Randbemerkungen zu Friedrich Schlegels 'Ideen'*
"Shrodon Feäir" (Barnes) **75**:77
"The Shrubbery" (Cowper) **8**:138
"Shu Dhu, or, the Dark Day" (Carleton) **199**:4
"Shut Not Your Doors" (Whitman) **205**:217
"Shut Out" (Rossetti) **186**:265
"The Shumanite" (Willis) **194**:306
"The Shy Man" (Barnes) **75**:8-9
"Si j'étais petit oiseau" (Beranger) **34**:44
"Si l'aurore" (Leconte de Lisle) **29**:235
"Si vienes a mi campo" (Isaacs) **70**:309
"Siberia" (Mangan) **27**:296, 298, 311-13
"Sibrandus Schafnaburgensis" (Browning) **19**:96; **79**:94, 99, 101
Sibylline Leaves: A Collection of Poems (Coleridge) **9**:137, 139, 146, 159; **54**:121; **111**:292; **197**:192, 236, 267, 271, 313; **231**:18, 38, 151
"Sibyl's Leaves" (Hopkins)
See "Spelt from Sibyl's Leaves"
"Sic Itur" (Clough) **27**:108
"Sic Semper Liberatoribus, March 13, 1881" (Lazarus) **109**:343
"'Sic transit gloria mundi'" (Dickinson) **21**:62
"Sic Vita" (Thoreau) **138**:75, 117
"The Siciliam Captive" (Hemans) **71**:296
A Sicilian Romance (Radcliffe) **6**:406, 409-15, 419-20, 424, 426, 444-45; **55**:225, 229-31, 242-4, 278; **106**:349; **223**:184, 189-90, 210-13, 217, 240, 242, 256, 258, 285-86, 288-89, 296-97, 309, 311, 313, 320, 322, 324, 327, 338
The Sicilian Vespers (Scribe)
See *Les vêpres siciliennes*
"Sicily Burns's Wedding" (Harris) **23**:155, 159, 161-62; **165**:181, 184, 191, 196, 200, 225, 231, 236, 242, 244, 252, 254-55, 270, 274, 286
"The Sick Author" (Freneau) **111**:134
"A Sick Bed" (Bryant) **6**:165; **46**:22
"The Sick in Heart" (Lenau) **16**:276
"The Sick King in Bokhara" (Arnold) **6**:72; **29**:26, 35; **218**:132
"The Sick Rose" (Blake) **37**:16, 26, 42-3, 50, 57, 82, 84-7, 92, 96-7; **173**:105
"The Sick Stockrider" (Gordon) **21**:149-51, 154-55, 158-59, 161, 163, 166, 170-72, 174-77, 181-83, 187
The Sickness unto Death (Kierkegaard)
See *Sygdommen til Døden*
"Sideboard" (Rimbaud)
See "Le buffet"
Sidney (Symonds) **34**:342
"Sie erlischt" (Heine) **147**:184
Sie trägt die Schuld (Arnim) **123**:8
"Sie, und nicht Wir" (Klopstock) **225**:330
Sieben Legenden (Keller) **2**:411-12, 414, 416
Siebenundsiebzig Gedichte aus den hinterlassenen Papieren eines reisenden Waldhornisten (Muller) **73**:368
"Les siècles maudits" (Leconte de Lisle) **29**:224
Der Sieg der Natur über die Schwärmerei; oder, die Abenteuer des Don Sylvio von Rosalva (Wieland) **177**:251-52, 284-87, 289-90, 294, 299-301, 303-5, 330-31, 335, 339, 342, 351-59
The Siege (Baillie) **2**:36; **71**:5-6, 12; **151**:115
"The Siege of Ancona" (Landor) **14**:183
The Siege of Corinth (Byron) **2**:63, 72, 89, 95-96; **12**:139; **109**:102
The Siege of Derry; or, Sufferings of the Protestants: A Tale of the Revolution (Tonna)
See *Derry: A Tale of the Revolution in 1688*
"The Siege of Roxburgh" (Hogg) **109**:204
The Siege of Valencia (Hemans) **29**:196, 201; **71**:261, 267, 269, 275-76, 278, 291
"The Siege of Vienna" (Chivers) **49**:69
Siegesbogen und Sternbild (Schumann) **143**:84
Siegfried (Wagner) **9**:417, 441, 448-49, 454-55, 459, 464, 466, 469-70; **119**:180, 186, 197, 205-10, 213, 222, 228-31, 268, 274, 278-79, 282, 289, 305-06, 321, 345
"Siegfried's Death" (Wagner)
See *Siegfrieds Tod*
Siegfrieds Tod (Hebbel) **43**:235, 238
Siegfrieds Tod (Wagner) **9**:445, 463; **119**:186, 316
"Siempre contigo" (Isaacs) **70**:308
"Sierra Morena" (Karamzin) **3**:285, 287-89; **173**:342
"The Siesta" (Bryant) **6**:172
"Sieste Eternelle" (Laforgue) **221**:19
"The Sifting of Peter" (Longfellow) **45**:128, 131
"Sigh" (Mallarmé)
See "Soupir"
"Sigh On, Sad Heart" (Hood) **16**:218
"Sighing for Retirement" (Clare) **9**:120
"Sight" (Lampman) **194**:33, 74, 90
"A Sight in Camp in the Daybreak Gray and Dim" (Whitman) **31**:403, 431; **81**:323, 331
"Sight of the Hills from the Kozłlowa Steppes" (Mickiewicz)
See "Widok gór ze stepów Kozłlowa"
"The Sight of the Ocean" (Very) **9**:376
"A Sight to Camp in the Daybreak Gray and Dim" (Whitman) **205**:339
"Sights from a Steeple" (Hawthorne) **2**:291-92; **23**:170; **191**:215
"The Sightseer" (Krylov) **1**:435
"El Siglo en blanco" (Larra) **130**:196
"The Sign" (Villiers de l'Isle Adam)
See "L'intersigne"
"Sign from the West" (Cranch) **115**:51
"Signalement" (Laforgue) **221**:89
"Signatur des Zeitalters" (Schlegel) **45**:338
"The Signet Ring" (Baratynsky) **103**:2
"The Significance of Swedish Poverty" (Almqvist)
See "Svenska fattigdomens betydelse"
Significance of the Alphabet (Peabody) **169**:202-3
La Signora Fantastici (Staël-Holstein) **91**:360
"Signs of the Times" (Carlyle) **70**:7, 39, 44, 73-74, 78, 80-82
Sigurd der Schlangentöter (Fouqué) **2**:265, 267
Sigurd Ring (Stagnelius) **61**:253, 257-8
Sigurds Rache (Fouqué) **2**:265
Sila de Jouy (Heredia) **209**:119
"Sila spomina" (Preseren) **127**:298, 323
Silas Marner, the Weaver of Raveloe (Eliot) **4**:99-100, 102-03, 106, 109-11, 114, 117, 119, 121, 123, 126-27, 131, 147-52; **13**:289, 291, 293; **23**:51, 56-7, 80; **41**:55-155; **49**:197, 213; **89**:215, 239; **118**:40, 43, 49, 59-60, 104-5, 107-8; **183**:151; **199**:215
Die silberne Hochzeit (Kotzebue) **25**:141
Silcote (Kingsley)
See *Silcote of Silcotes*
Silcote of Silcotes (Kingsley) **107**:189, 192-93, 209, 221-24, 226, 228
Silcotes (Kingsley)
See *Silcote of Silcotes*
"Le Silence" (Mallarmé) **210**:250
"Silence" (Nekrasov) **11**:406
"Le silence" (Vigny) **7**:481
"Silence, a Fable" (Poe) **1**:513; **16**:306, 312, 331, 336; **94**:240; **117**:268, 281, 283, 308
"The Silence of Faith" (Harpur) **114**:144
"The Silent Cell" (Jones) **222**:173, 176
"The Silent Melody" (Holmes) **14**:109
"Silent Noon" (Rossetti) **4**:514; **77**:312
"Silent O Moyle" (Moore) **6**:391
"Silent Sea" (Mickiewicz)
See "Cisza morska"
"Silentium" (Tyutchev) **34**:381, 386, 412
"Silenus in Proteus" (Beddoes) **154**:79
"Silford Hall; or, The Happy Day" (Crabbe) **26**:136; **121**:4
"Silhouettes" (Kierkegaard) **125**:205-9, 214, 248, 250-51
"Silly Novels by Lady Novelists" (Eliot) **23**:98; **118**:188-89; **183**:68
"Silly Novels by Lady Novelists" (Eliot) **209**:77
"Silly Shore" (Crabbe) **26**:102
"Silly Steve" (Petofi)
See "Bolond Istók"
"Silva a la Agricultura de la Zona Tórrida" (Bello) **131**:93-94
Silva de romances viejos (Grimm Brothers) **3**:221
"Silva to the Agriculture of the Torrid Zone" (Bello)
See "Silva a la Agricultura de la Zona Tórrida"
Silvas Americanas (Bello) **131**:92-93, 109
The Silver Acre and Other Tales (Carleton) **199**:54
The Silver Box (Dumas) **9**:234
The Silver Dream of Salomea (Slowacki)
See *Sen srebrny Salomei*
"The Silver Mine" (Hale) **75**:297, 362
Silver Mines (Alencar) **157**:9
The Silver Mines (Alencar)
See *As Minas de Prata*
"Silver Wedding" (Clough) **27**:106
The Silverado Squatters (Stevenson) **193**:213, 220, 238, 327
"A Silvia" (Leopardi) **129**:219, 228-29, 328, 343, 350, 357-58
Simhat hanef (Smolenskin) **30**:189-90, 195-96
Simon (Sand) **2**:589, 599
"Simon Gets a 'Soft Snap' out of his Daddy" (Hooper) **177**:207, 211
"Simon Lee" (Wordsworth) **12**:387, 428, 434, 445-46; **111**:198-200, 202, 211, 224, 228, 248, 251, 253, 277, 279-83, 287, 314, 323, 348-50, 359-60, 366-67, 369; **166**:235, 320
"Simon Lee, the Old Huntsman" (Wordsworth)
See "Simon Lee"
"Simon Plays the 'Snatch Game'" (Hooper)
See "Introduction—Simon Plays the 'Snatch' Game"
"Simon Speculates Again" (Hooper) **177**:207-9
"Simon Starts Forth to Fight the 'Tiger'" (Hooper) **177**:214
"Simon Suggs Attends a Camp-Meeting" (Hooper) **177**:178-79, 183, 200-201, 212
Simon Verde (Caballero) **10**:72
"Simone" (Musset) **7**:256, 258
"Simple agonie" (Laforgue) **5**:280; **53**:289; **221**:48, 82, 91
"Simple Death-Pangs" (Laforgue)
See "Simple agonie"
"Simply Dying" (Laforgue)
See "Simple agonie"
"Simple Frescoes" (Verlaine)
See "Simples Fresques"
"Simples fresques I" (Verlaine) **230**:155

"A Simple Heart" (Flaubert)
See "Un coeur simple"
"Simple Simon" (Andersen) **7**:34; **79**:25
A Simple Story (Inchbald) **62**:131-40, 142, 149, 154-6, 158-9, 163-8, 178-81, 186, 188, 191
"The simple Story of my own first Love" (Carlyle) **181**:133, 136, 138
"Simple Susan" (Edgeworth) **1**:265; **51**:79
Simple Tales (Opie) **65**:171, 174, 179-81, 197
"Simples Fresques" (Verlaine) **51**:370, 381-82
The Simpleton (Reade) **2**:541, 545, 549; **74**:255, 257, 260, 263-65, 284
Simsone Grisaldo (Klinger) **1**:429
Sin and Sorrow Are Common to All (Ostrovsky)
See *Grekh da beda na kogo ne zhivyot*
"The Sin of a Father" (Gaskell)
See "Right at Last"
"Sin un cuarto" (Alarcón) **219**:53
"Since Dawn Grows Large . . ." (Verlaine)
See "Puisque l'aube grandit . . ."
"Sincere Anguish" (Laforgue)
See "L'Angoisse sincère"
Sincerity (Rowson) **182**:356
"Sincerity and Hypocrisy" (Newman) **38**:306
"Sindhu" (Dutt) **29**:124-25, 127, 129-30
"Sinfonia Eroica" (Levy) **59**:109
"Sing On, Sad Heart" (Hood) **16**:233
"Sing, Sweet Harp" (Moore) **110**:186
"The Singer" (Zhukovsky) **35**:384-85
"The Singer in Prison" (Whitman) **205**:207
"The Singer in the Kremlin" (Zhukovsky) **35**:379
"The Singer in the Prison" (Whitman) **4**:561
"The Singers" (Longfellow) **2**:491-92
"The Singers" (Turgenev) **21**:413, 418, 420; **37**:379; **122**:280
"The Singing, Soaring Lark" (Grimm Brothers) **3**:227
"The Singing Spirit" (Ridge) **82**:183-84
The Single Hound (Dickinson) **21**:22-3, 29-30, 33; **171**:90, 92
Singleheart and Doubleface (Reade) **2**:547, 549; **74**:260, 263
"Singlethought" (Leskov)
See "Odnodum"
Sing-Song: A Nursery Rhyme-Book (Rossetti) **2**:557, 565, 571; **50**:271, 288-9, 301, 304-7; **66**:330, 341; **186**:229, 234-39, 266-67, 269, 296
"Singular Advantage of Being an R.A." (Haydon) **146**:141
"Singular Dream from a Correspondent" (Hogg) **109**:279
"Singular Passage in the Life of the Late Dr. Harris" (Barham) **77**:36
"Singularities of War" (D'Israeli) **217**:334
Sink or Swim; or, Harry Raymond's Resolve (Alger) **8**:36, 42-43
"The Sinking of the Merrimack" (Larcom) **179**:169, 177
"The Sinking Ship" (Rimbaud)
See "L'eclatante victoire de Saarebrück"
Das Sinngedicht (Keller) **2**:412, 414, 416, 421-23
Sins of Government, Sins of the Nation (Barbauld) **50**:4
Sins of the Government, Sins of the Nation (Barbauld) **185**:43-45, 58, 94-95, 117, 119, 121, 141-42, 149
Sintram and His Companions (Fouqué) **2**:261-63, 265, 268
"Siope" (Poe) **16**:292; **94**:240
Sir Andrew Wylie of That Ilk (Galt) **1**:329, 332-33, 335, 337; **110**:77-80, 84-6, 95-6
"Sir Brasil's Falcon" (O'Brien) **21**:234, 242
Sir Brook Fossbrooke (Lever) **23**:292, 303, 308
Sir Charles Grandison, or The Happy Man (Austen) **119**:30-1
"Sir David Graeme" (Hogg) **109**:268
Sir Eldred of the Bower (More) **27**:332, 336
Sir Eldred of the Bower and the Bleeding Rock: Two Legendary Tales (More) **141**:203, 231, 255-57, 311
"Sir Eustace Grey" (Crabbe) **26**:78-9, 81, 111, 118, 123, 126, 134; **121**:5, 9-10, 24, 26, 34
"Sir Federigo's Falcon" (Longfellow)
See "The Falcon of Ser Federigo"
"Sir Galahad" (Tennyson) **30**:223; **65**:305; **202**:218
"Sir Galahad: A Christmas Mystery" (Morris) **4**:426, 431, 444
"Sir Giles' War-Song" (Morris) **4**:444
Sir Harry Hotspur of Humblethwaite (Trollope) **6**:460, 470, 484; **101**:251, 309, 312-13
Sir Henry Tunstall (Brontë) **109**:29
"Sir Hubert" (Patmore)
See "The Falcon"
"Sir Humphrey Gilbert" (Longfellow) **2**:493; **45**:153
Sir James Mackintosh (Macaulay) **42**:115, 122
Sir Jasper Carew (Lever) **23**:292
Sir John Chiverton (Ainsworth) **13**:15
Sir John Eliot (Forster) **11**:102, 115
"Sir Lancelot and Queen Guinevere" (Tennyson) **65**:376; **202**:218
"Sir Maurice" (Baillie) **2**:42; **151**:43-5
"Sir Peter Harpdon's End" (Morris) **4**:423, 425-26, 432, 441, 444
Sir Ralph Esher; or, Memoirs of a Gentleman of the Court of Charles II (Hunt) **1**:410
Sir Robert's Fortune (Oliphant) **61**:203, 210-1
"Sir Thomas Browne" (Pater) **90**:337
Sir Thomas More; or, Colloquies on the Progress and Prospects of Society (Southey) **8**:462-65, 467; **97**:266, 286
Sir Tom (Oliphant) **61**:204, 211
Sir Tristrem (Scott) **209**:196
Sir Walter Finch et son fils William (Charriere) **66**:124-5, 137, 161, 164
"Sir Walter Raleigh" (Thoreau) **138**:120, 123
"Sir Walter Scott" (Carlyle) **70**:7
"Sir William Montague" (Austen) **119**:13
"The Sire de Malétroit's Door" (Stevenson) **5**:394, 408, 415, 431; **193**:256
The Siren (Sacher-Masoch) **31**:301
"Síri dal" (Madach) **19**:369
"Sirius" (Lampman) **194**:30
The Sister (Lennox) **23**:231
"Sister Anne" (O'Brien) **21**:236, 243-44
Sister Anne (Kock)
See *Soeur Anne*
"Sister Helen" (Barrett Browning) **1**:124
"Sister Helen" (Rossetti) **4**:491, 493, 497-99, 505-07, 512, 514, 518-19, 523, 526-27, 529-30; **77**:337, 348
Sister Maggie (Eliot)
See *The Mill on the Floss*
"Sister Maude" (Rossetti) **2**:555, 575; **50**:270; **66**:312, 352
"The Sister of Charity" (Griffin) **7**:196, 202
Sister Philomene (Goncourt and Goncourt)
See *Soeur Philomène*
"Sister St. Luke" (Woolson) **82**:273, 302
"The Sisters" (Crabbe) **26**:118, 130
"The Sisters" (Mörike)
See "Die Schwestern"
"The Sisters of Albano" (Shelley) **59**:151
"Sisters of Charity" (Rimbaud)
See "Les soeurs de charité"
Sisters of Charity Abroad and at Home (Jameson) **43**:305, 327
"The Sister's Trial" (Alcott) **83**:8
"Sistrum" (Fuller) **50**:247-8
"Sita" (Dutt) **29**:126
Sitaram (Chatterji) **19**:210-11, 213-14, 216-22, 224
Situation (Liszt)
See *De la situation des artistes et de leur condition dans la société*
"Situation of the House" (Gilpin) **30**:40
The Six Chief Lives from Johnson's "Lives of the Poets" (Arnold) **218**:168
689 (Dickinson) **77**:66
640 (Dickinson) **77**:64, 67, 96
646 (Dickinson) **77**:131
690 (Dickinson) **77**:119
698 (Dickinson) **77**:89
692 (Dickinson) **77**:163-64
670 (Dickinson) **77**:97
673 (Dickinson) **77**:94
664 (Dickinson) **77**:63
613 (Dickinson) **77**:81
634 (Dickinson) **77**:101
636 (Dickinson) **77**:51
603 (Dickinson) **77**:184
612 (Dickinson) **77**:131
629 (Dickinson) **77**:121
627 (Dickinson) **77**:80
622 (Dickinson) **77**:162
Six Lectures to Working Men (Huxley) **67**:59
Six Moral Tales from Jules Laforgue (Laforgue)
See *Moralités légendaires*
"Six Plain Sermons for the Times" (Parker) **186**:207
Six Political Discourses Founded on the Scripture (Brackenridge) **7**:44; **227**:48, 105
"The Six Servants" (Grimm Brothers) **3**:227
Six to One: A Nantucket Idyll (Bellamy) **4**:30; **86**:9-11, 79
"Six Weeks at Heppenheim" (Gaskell) **5**:201-02; **70**:187
"Sixt und Clärchen" (Wieland) **177**:265
1651 (Dickinson) **77**:92, 95
1604 (Dickinson) **77**:93
1607 (Dickinson) **77**:149
1670 (Dickinson) **77**:148
1677 (Dickinson) **77**:92
1660 (Dickinson) **77**:140
1620 (Dickinson) **77**:119
"The Sixteenth Century and the Nineteenth" (Gladstone) **213**:112
"The Sixth Sunday after Epiphany" (Keble) **87**:203
"The Sixth Sunday after Trinity" (Keble) **87**:177, 202
Sixth Symphony (Beethoven) **227**:33
67 (Dickinson) **77**:119
"A Sixty-Drop Dose of Laudanum" (Mangan) **27**:291, 303
"The Size of the World" (Schiller) **39**:336
"Sizhu zadumchiv i odin" (Tyutchev) **34**:399
Skabelsen, mennesket, og messias (Wergeland) **5**:536, 538-42
Skällnora kvarn (Almqvist) **42**:19
Skällnora Mill (Almqvist)
See *Skällnora kvarn*
"Skaz o tul'skom kosom Levse i o stal'noj bloxe" (Leskov) **174**:77
"Skazanie o Fedore-khristianine i o druge ego Abrame-zhidovine" (Leskov) **174**:105, 116
"Skazanie o Fedore-khristianine i o druge ego Avrame-zhidovine" (Leskov) **25**:245, 265, 267
"Skazanie o Fyodore—Khristianine i o druge ego Abrame—zhidovine" (Leskov)
See "Skazanie o Fedore-khristianine i o druge ego Avrame-zhidovine"
Skazhi, Kakoi sud'boi (Pushkin) **83**:333
Skazka dlya detey (Lermontov) **126**:136, 138-39, 154
"Skazka o Mertvoy Tsarevne" (Pushkin) **3**:446; **83**:281
"Skazka o Rybake i Rybke" (Pushkin) **3**:446; **83**:284-85
"Skazka o Tsare Sultane" (Pushkin) **3**:443, 446; **83**:278-79
"Skazka o Zolotom Petushke" (Pushkin) **27**:379; **83**:277-80, 282-85
Skazki (Pushkin) **3**:446, 459

Skazki (Saltykov) **16**:346, 349, 351, 373-75
"The Skeleton in Armor" (Longfellow) **2**:472, 493; **45**:99, 103, 110, 116, 144, 153
"The Skeleton Priest, or The Marriage of Death" (Dacre) **151**:149
"The Skeleton's Cave" (Bryant) **6**:180-81
"Skeptical Christmas" (Laforgue)
See "Noël sceptique"
"The Skeptics" (Lenau) **16**:276
"A Sketch" (Byron) **109**:82
"The Sketch" (Jones) **222**:124
"A Sketch" (Rossetti) **186**:262
A Sketch (Halleck) **47**:57
Sketch (Sigourney)
See *Sketch of Connecticut, Forty Years Since*
The Sketch Book (Irving)
See *The Sketch Book of Geoffrey Crayon, Gent.*
The Sketch Book of Geoffrey Crayon, Gent. (Irving) **2**:365-77, 379-84, 386-90, 392; **19**:326-51; **95**:223, 226-28, 232, 234, 236-38, 240, 243, 245, 249, 264-69, 273-80, 291, 293-94, 296-97
"A Sketch in the Manner of Hogarth" (Patmore) **9**:329
Sketch of 1842 (Darwin)
See *On the Origin of Species by Means of Natural Selection or the Preservation of Favoured Races in the Struggle for Life*
Sketch of Connecticut, Forty Years Since (Sigourney) **21**:301, 313-16; **87**:320, 338-39, 341-43
"Sketch of the Present Situation of America, 1794" (Murray) **63**:213
"Sketches" (Clare)
See "Sketches in the Life of John Clare"
Sketches (Crèvecoeur)
See *Sketches of Eighteenth Century America: More "Letters from an American Farmer"*
Sketches (Newman)
See *Historical Sketches*
Sketches (De Quincey)
See *Autobiographic Sketches*
Sketches (Sigourney) **21**:289; **87**:321
Sketches (Trollope)
See *Travelling Sketches*
Sketches (Willis) **194**:295, 301, 304
Sketches After English Landscape Painters (Thackeray) **213**:242-43
Sketches among the Poor (Gaskell) **70**:185, 193; **137**:38, 47, 54
Sketches and Essays (Hazlitt) **29**:148
Sketches and Studies in Italy (Symonds) **34**:333, 364
Sketches and Studies in Italy and Greece (Symonds) **34**:333, 337, 364
Sketches by Boz, Illustrative of Every-Day Life, and Every-Day People (Dickens)
See *Sketches by Boz of Every-Day Life and Every-Day People*
Sketches by Boz of Every-Day Life and Every-Day People (Dickens) **3**:138; **8**:200; **37**:165, 168, 176-77, 180, 183-85, 187, 195, 198-99; **105**:353; **113**:63, 91, 98, 118, 124; **187**:25-26; **203**:188, 190, 250, 255; **206**:26, 131; **211**:26; **219**:151; **231**:205
Sketches from a Hunter's Album (Turgenev)
See *Zapiski okhotnika*
"Sketches from the Country" (Moodie) **14**:231
"Sketches in the Life of John Clare" (Clare) **86**:152-53, 155, 170-75
"Sketches of a History of Carsol" (Brown) **74**:49
Sketches of American Character (Hale) **75**:296, 319, 349
"Sketches of American History" (Freneau) **111**:166
Sketches of American Policy . . . (Webster) **30**:403
Sketches of Eighteenth Century America: More "Letters from an American Farmer" (Crèvecoeur) **105**:102-06, 122, 124-25, 127, 139, 152, 157, 162-64, 182
Sketches of English Character (Gore) **65**:21
Sketches of English literature: With Considerations on the Spirit of the Times, Men, and Revolutions (Chateaubriand)
See *Essai sur la littérature Anglaise et considérations sur le génie des hommes, des temps et, des révolutions*
"Sketches of Female Biography" (Rowson) **5**:318; **69**:115-16; **182**:252, 254, 256-57, 259, 261
Sketches of History (Godwin) **14**:53
"Sketches of India" (Lanier) **118**:214-15
"Sketches of my Life" (Clare)
See "Sketches in the Life of John Clare"
Sketches of Provincial Life (Saltykov)
See *Gubernskie ocherki*
"Sketches of Russian Life in the Caucasus" (Lermontov)
See *Geroi nashego vremeni*
Sketches of Spain and Portugal (Beckford)
See *Italy: With Sketches of Spain and Portugal*
Sketches of Switzerland (Cooper) **54**:256
Sketches of the Gogol Period of Russian Literature (Chernyshevsky) **1**:160-61, 166
Sketches of the Principal Picture Galleries in England (Hazlitt) **82**:156-58, 161
Sketches of the State of Manners and Opinions in the French Republic, Towards the Close of the Eighteenth Century in a Series of Letters (Williams) **135**:260, 302, 304-6, 335
Sketches of Young Gentlemen (Dickens) **219**:197
"Sketches on Different Subjects" (Freneau) **111**:129
"Skipper Ben" (Larcom) **179**:167
"Skipper Ireson's Ride" (Whittier) **8**:493, 496, 506, 508-10, 513, 515-16, 519, 521-22, 526, 530; **59**:356-8, 360, 365, 371
"Das Sklavenschiff" (Heine) **147**:139-43
"Skomorokh Pamfalon" (Leskov) **174**:7, 67
"Skomorox Pamfalon" (Leskov) **25**:239, 245-46
"The Skull" (Baratynsky)
See "Cerep"
"Skulls" (Turgenev) **21**:452
"Skul'ptor" (Baratynsky) **103**:29
Skupoi rytsar (Pushkin) **3**:433-34, 447-48, 452, 454; **83**:263-64, 285-88, 338-39, 351, 353
"The Sky A-Clearèn" (Barnes) **75**:17
"The Sky Is Low, the Clouds Are Mean" (Dickinson) **21**:7
"Sky-Blue Flower" (Eminescu)
See "Floare albastra"
"Skyggen" (Andersen) **7**:23, 26, 37; **79**:23, 28, 40, 42, 51, 53, 63, 66, 68, 72; **214**:9, 33, 40, 61, 75
"The Skylark" (Hogg) **109**:200-01
"The Skylark Leaving Her Nest" (Clare) **9**:80, 94, 117
"The Skylark Sings" (Petofi)
See "Pacsirtaszót hallok megint"
"Skyrockets" (Baudelaire)
See "Fusées"
Sky-Walk, or the Man Unknown to Himself (Brown) **22**:28; **74**:15, 54, 67-8, 76, 92, 133, 155, 175; **122**:116
"Slander" (Osgood) **141**:325-26
Slander (Scribe)
See *La calomnie*
"Slang in America" (Whitman) **4**:576; **81**:286
"The Slantèn Light o' Fall" (Barnes) **75**:7
The Slaughter House (Echeverria)
See "El matadero"
"The Slave" (Horton) **87**:102, 104
"The Slave Ship" (Castro Alves)
See "O Navio Negreiro"
"The Slave Ships" (Whittier) **8**:489, 509-10, 515
"The Slave Singing at Midnight" (Longfellow) **103**:290
"The Slave Trade" (Williams) **135**:255, 286, 300
"The Slaveholder" (Very) **9**:383
"Slaveholder's Sermon" (Douglass) **7**:123
The Slave-King (Hugo)
See *Bug-Jargal*
"The Slaver" (Allingham) **25**:6
"The Slaver" (Castro Alves)
See "O Navio Negreiro"
"Slavery" (Haliburton) **149**:344
"Slavery" (Horton) **87**:99, 102
Slavery (Channing) **17**:24, 32, 35
Slavery (More) **141**:234, 267
"Slavery in Massachusetts" (Thoreau) **7**:386; **21**:329-31, 370; **207**:264, 281-82, 319, 335, 337-39
"Slavery in New England" (Sedgwick) **98**:317
The Slavery of Husbands (Ostrovsky) **30**:96
The Slaves (Castro Alves)
See *Os escravos*
Les Slaves (Mickiewicz) **101**:166-73
"The Slave's Complaint" (Horton) **87**:94, 98, 101, 109-10
"The Slave's Dream" (Longfellow) **45**:155
Slaves in Algiers; or, A Struggle for Freedom (Rowson) **5**:309-10, 313, 318; **69**:103, 140-46, 157-63; **182**:253-54, 257-59, 276-81, 313, 333, 343-45, 353, 357
"The Slaves of Martinique" (Whittier) **8**:510
"A Slave's Reflections the Eve Before His Sale" (Horton) **87**:102
"The Slave's Story" (Harpur) **114**:144, 148-50, 152
"Slavyanka" (Zhukovsky) **35**:403, 405-06
The Slaying of Meghanada (Dutt)
See *Meghnādbadh Kābya*
"Slaying of Tamatea" (Stevenson) **193**:215
"Sledstvie vechera na kavkazskikh vodakh v 1824 godu" (Bestuzhev) **131**:156
"Sleep" (Mickiewicz)
See "Sen"
"Sleep and Poetry" (Keats) **8**:343, 345, 354-55, 364-65, 368, 391; **73**:142, 152, 157-58, 174, 181-82, 203, 206-208, 214, 216, 225-26, 254-56, 260, 311, 322, 324, 339; **121**:100-102, 105-6, 118, 122, 136-37, 141, 147-48, 215; **225**:141, 162, 165-66, 186, 225-26, 244, 262
"Sleep Did Come Wi' The Dew" (Barnes) **75**:101
"Sleep let me sleep, for I am sick of care" (Rossetti) **186**:282
"The Sleep of Sigismund" (Ingelow) **39**:258
"The Sleeper" (Poe) **1**:512; **55**:181; **117**:192, 196, 217, 221, 233, 278, 281-82, 298, 334
"The Sleeper" (Thomson) **18**:417
"The Sleepers" (Whitman) **4**:571, 579, 584, 596, 602; **31**:404-05, 412-14, 416-19, 421-25, 433; **81**:236, 258, 320, 342, 351; **205**:191-94, 212, 226, 228, 230-33, 300-302, 309, 332-36, 340-42
"Sleeping at Last" (Rossetti) **66**:343; **186**:309-10, 312-15
The Sleeping Bard (Borrow) **9**:54
Sleeping Beauty in the Wood (Feuillet)
See *Belle au Bois Dormant*
The Sleeping Beauty in the Wood (Planché) **42**:273, 277, 279, 288-89, 294, 296
The Sleepwalker (Scribe)
See *La somnambule*
"A Sleep-Walking Incident" (Harris) **165**:188
"Sleepy Hollow" (Irving)
See "The Legend of Sleepy Hollow"
"The Sleigh-Bells" (Moodie) **113**:346
"Slepaya" (Shevchenko) **54**:367, 376, 386, 391
"A Slight Error" (Leskov)
See "Malen' kaja ošibka"
"A Slip of the Pen" (Levy) **59**:113
"Slip-Slopperies of Correspondence" (Willis) **194**:319

"Slipyi" (Shevchenko) **54**:388-9
"Slovo od mladosti" (Preseren) **127**:293, 297, 329-30, 332, 334
Slow and Sure; or, From the Street to the Shop (Alger) **8**:45
Śluby panieńskie; czyli, Magnetyzm serca (Fredro) **8**:285-87, 289-90, 292-93
"The Sluggish Smoke Curls Up from Some Deep Dell" (Thoreau) **7**:383
"A Slumber Did My Spirit Seal" (Wordsworth) **206**:225, 286
"A Slumber Did My Spirit Steal" (Wordsworth) **111**:323-24, 328
"Small Autumnal Wretchednesses" (Laforgue) See "Petites misères d'automne"
"Small Family Memories" (Cooper) **129**:4, 15, 41, 66
The Small House at Allington (Trollope) **6**:457-58, 463, 470, 486, 491, 497, 499-502, 509, 515, 517; **101**:235, 237-38, 266, 306, 308, 313, 319, 321; **215**:202-4, 208, 215, 308
The Small Life of Poe (Chivers) **49**:66
Smarh (Flaubert) **2**:255; **62**:72; **135**:172
Smarra; ou, Les démons de la nuit (Nodier) **19**:377-78, 381-83, 387-89, 392, 398-401, 404
"Smekh i gore" (Leskov) **174**:16, 32, 52-53, 59
"Smert" (Baratynsky) **103**:7, 10, 16
"Smert' poeta" (Lermontov) **5**:295; **47**:158, 166; **126**:144, 218, 224
The Smiles Gone (Keller) See *Das Verlorene Lachen*
"The Smiling Death's-Head" (Ueda Akinari) See "Shikubi no egao"
"Smoke" (Thoreau) **7**:355, 370; **207**:234
Smoke (Turgenev) See *Dym*
The Smoker Mixer (Jerrold) **2**:403
"Smotri kak na rechnom prostore" (Tyutchev) **34**:399
"Smugglers and Poachers" (Crabbe) **121**:6
"Smuggler's Leap" (Barham) **77**:36
"Snachala mysl', voploshchena" (Baratynsky) **103**:47
"The Snail and the Rosebush" (Crawford) **127**:188
"The Snake of the Cabin" (Simms) **3**:501
"The Snake-Bit Irishman" (Harris) **23**:159; **165**:187, 233, 254, 265
The Snark (Dodgson) See *The Hunting of the Snark: An Agony in Eight Fits*
Snarleyyow; or, The Dog Fiend (Marryat) **3**:317, 319-21
"Sneedronningen" (Andersen) **7**:22-3, 28, 34; **79**:23, 26-7, 59; **214**:23-24, 26-27, 48, 50-51, 53, 55, 72-73, 75, 77-80, 83-84, 86
"Sneewittchen" (Grimm Brothers) **3**:224-25
Snegurochka (Ostrovsky) **30**:97, 104, 111, 119; **57**:206-7, 220-3
"Snip-Snap" (Cooke) **110**:35
The Snob Papers (Thackeray) See *The Book of Snobs*
"The Snob Royal" (Thackeray) **43**:388
The Snobs of England (Thackeray) See *The Book of Snobs*
"Snoring for the Millions" (Dickens) **219**:188
"La snova zdes! pod sen'iu krova" (Pavlova) **138**:15
"Snow" (Lampman) **25**:204; **194**:86
"The Snow Drop" (Robinson) **142**:111-13, 115
"The Snow Image: A Childish Miracle" (Hawthorne) **2**:311, 322, 329, 332; **39**:236; **158**:243, 246
The Snow Image and Uncollected Tales (Hawthorne) **158**:368
The Snow Maiden (Ostrovsky) See *Snegurochka*
"The Snow Queen" (Andersen) See "Sneedronningen"
"The Snow Queen, a Folk Tale in Seven Parts" (Andersen) See "Sneedronningen"
"Snow Shower" (Bryant) **6**:165, 169; **46**:4, 21
"Snow Song" (Moodie) **14**:218
"Snow Storm" (Clare) **9**:123; **86**:110, 167-69
"The Snow Storm" (Emerson) **1**:295; **98**:46, 177, 179, 181
"The Snow Wreath" (Haliburton) **149**:291
The Snowball (Tamayo y Baus) See *La bola de nieve*
Snow-Bound: A Winter Idyl (Whittier) **8**:496, 501-03, 508-11, 513-14, 516, 518-20, 522-24, 526, 530-32; **59**:354, 356-8, 360-1, 366, 371-2, 374-6, 378-80, 385-91
"The Snowdrop" (Allingham) **25**:14
"Snowfall" (Vigny) See "La neige"
"Snowflakes" (Hawthorne) **2**:298, 305
"Snow-flakes" (Longfellow) **45**:130
"The Snow-Image" (Hawthorne) See "The Snow Image: A Childish Miracle"
The Snow-Image, and Other Twice-Told Tales (Hawthorne) **226**:118
The Snow-Image and Uncollected Tales (Hawthorne) **171**:343
"The Snow-Messengers" (Hayne) **94**:167-68
"The Snows" (Webster) **230**:313
"A Snowshoer's Halt" (Lampman) **194**:79
"The Snowstorm" (Aksakov) **181**:50
"The Snowstorm" (Pushkin) See "Metel"
"Snow-White" (Grimm Brothers) See "Sneewittchen"
"A Snowy Day" (Ichiyō) See "Yuki no Hi"
"Snowy Mountains" (Tyutchev) **34**:389
"Snubbing a Snob" (Haliburton) **15**:136
"So again I see you" (Tyutchev) See "Itak, opyat uvidelsya ya s vami"
"So Fresh and Frail" (Eminescu) See "Atît de frageda"
"So Help Me, Thou, O Lord!" (Slowacki) **15**:365
"So I Pull My Stockings Off" (Dickinson) **21**:58
"So Let It Be" (Osgood) **141**:324-25
"So Long!" (Whitman) **31**:433; **81**:338; **205**:158, 202, 224-26, 235-36, 243, 259, 267-70, 279-80
"So, there are moments in life" (Tyutchev) See "Tak, v zhizni est mgnoveniya"
"The Soaring Swan" (Chivers) **49**:48, 52
The Sob of the Earth (Laforgue) See *Le sanglot de la terre*
"Sobaka" (Turgenev) **21**:399, 409, 415, 420, 431, 440-41; **122**:241-42, 244, 265, 267-68, 293, 310, 337, 342, 344, 348-49, 365, 368-70, 377-78
"Sober Reflections on the Seditious and Inflammatory Letter of the Rt. Hon. Edmund Burke to a Noble Lord" (Thelwall) **162**:313
"Soberba" (Castro) **78**:2
"Sobiranie babochek" (Aksakov) **181**:20, 22, 65
"Soborjane" (Leskov) **174**:11
Soborjane (Leskov) **25**:228-29, 232, 234, 238-39, 268; **174**:5, 8-17, 23, 38, 42, 58-59, 61-63, 65, 95-101, 120-21, 123-24, 126
Sobranie russkikh stikhotvorenii (Zhukovsky) **35**:394
Sobranie sochinenii (Aksakov) **181**:46
Sobranie sochinenii v odinnadtsati tomakh (Leskov) **174**:82-85, 87-88
Sobranie sochinenii v shesti tomakh (Leskov) **174**:83-86
Sobranie socinenij (Leskov) **174**:60, 72, 77, 82-83
Sobranie socinenij v cetyrex tomax (Lermontov) **126**:189-92
"Sobre la indolencia de los Filipinos" (Rizal) **27**:410, 419, 425, 427
De sobremesa (Silva) **114**:262-63, 267, 274, 276-77, 280, 284, 286-90, 292, 294, 296, 299-300, 303-5, 308, 315-22
Sochineniya v dvukh tomakh (Bestuzhev) **131**:178-87
Sochineniya v dvukh tomakh, Vol. 1 (Bestuzhev) **131**:209, 211-13
"Social Aspects of the German Romantic School" (Boyesen) **135**:6
The Social Cancer (Rizal) See *Noli me tangere*
The Social Compact exemplified in the Constitution of the Commonwealth of Massachusetts (Adams) **175**:62
Social Strugglers: A Novel (Boyesen) **135**:14, 22-23, 31, 42-43, 62-63
"The Social War" (Mérimée) **6**:353
"Socialism: Its Growth and Outcome" (Morris) **4**:425
Socialism: Utopian and Scientific (Engels) See *Die Entwicklung des Sozialismus von der Uopie zur Wissenschaft*
"Society" (Thoreau) **138**:116
Society (Robertson) **35**:330, 333-34, 336, 338, 340-41, 345, 347, 349, 352-53, 355-57, 360, 362, 363, 365-72
"Society and Solitude" (Emerson) **98**:68
Society and Solitude (Emerson) **1**:280; **38**:209; **98**:54
Society in America (Martineau) **26**:307, 309, 311, 314, 318, 322, 334-38, 355, 357-58; **137**:236, 281, 302, 304, 306, 309, 312, 315-24, 327-30, 332-33, 358, 360-61
"Society in the Bush" (Traill) **31**:327
Society the Redeemed Form of Man, and the Earnest of God's Omnipotence in Human Nature: Affirmed in Letters to a Friend (James) **53**:193, 204-5, 207-8, 210, 212, 228, 230, 233, 236, 240
Sočinenija (Pisarev) **25**:344
"Socrates" (Heredia) **209**:129
Socrates Out of His Senses, or Dialogues of Diogenes of Sinope (Wieland) See *Sokrates Mainomenos; oder, Die Dialogen des Diogenes von Sinope*
"Socrates und Alcibiades" (Hölderlin) **187**:303
Sodome et Gomorrhe (Sade) **3**:482
Soeur Anne (Kock) **16**:245, 249, 251-53
"Soeur Louise de la Misericorde" (Rossetti) **66**:305
Soeur Philomène (Goncourt and Goncourt) **7**:151-52, 161, 175-76, 181, 187, 189
"Les soeurs de charité" (Rimbaud) **4**:455; **35**:280-82, 290-91; **82**:230, 233
"Les soeurs Rondoli" (Maupassant) **83**:194-95, 201, 203
"The Sofa" (Cowper) **8**:110-11, 120, 128-29; **94**:30, 124
Sofonisba (Alfieri) **101**:13, 15, 18-19, 39
"Softer-Mother's Tale" (Wordsworth) **12**:386
"Soggarth Aroon" (Banim and Banim) **13**:128-29
Die Söhne des Thales: Ein dramatisches Gedicht (Werner) **189**:317-19, 321, 328, 330-31, 359-60, 363, 365-66
"Die Söhne Haruns" (Meyer) **81**:209
"Sohrab and Rustum" (Arnold) **6**:31, 34, 42, 44, 50, 54, 66, 68, 72; **29**:23, 32, 37; **89**:14, 28; **218**:115, 134, 139, 151, 155, 176, 188, 190
"Soia" (Castro) **78**:42
"Le soir" (Lamartine) **11**:245, 264, 269
"Sois de bronze . . ." (Verlaine) **230**:169
"Soir de carnaval" (Laforgue) **221**:84-85, 87
"Le soir de la jeunesse" (Sainte-Beuve) **5**:347
"Un soir d'octobre" (Verlaine) **230**:161
"Soir historique" (Rimbaud) **35**:323; **82**:232, 248; **227**:203, 210, 239, 261, 263, 309
Les Soirées de St. Petersbourg ou entretiens sur le gouvernement temporel de la

Providence (Maistre) **37**:282, 284, 286, 292, 294-95, 297-98, 300, 305-08, 313-18, 322
Sokrates Mainomenos; oder, Die Dialogen des Diogenes von Sinope (Wieland) **177**:243, 286-87, 320, 331, 363, 365-66
"Sokrates und Alkibiades" (Hölderlin) **16**:162
"Sokratics in the Strand" (Levy) **59**:86, 94, 108-9, 111
"Sol natal" (Desbordes-Valmore) **97**:18-19
"Der Soldat" (Eichendorff) **225**:7
"Le Soldat laboureur" (Verlaine) **230**:163
"Die Soldatenbraut" (Mörike) **201**:252-53, 294
"Soldatgossen" (Runeberg) **41**:312, 316, 325, 328
"Solde" (Rimbaud) **35**:290, 309, 312, 322-23; **227**:298, 323
"The Soldier" (Hemans) **71**:279
"The Soldier and the Pard" (Taylor) **89**:301
"The Soldier Boy" (Maginn) **8**:434
"The Soldier Boy" (Runeberg)
See "Soldatgossen"
"A Soldier is the Noblest Name" (Rowson) **182**:281
The Soldier of Seventy-Six (Dunlap) **2**:211, 213, 218
"The Soldier Ploughman" (Verlaine)
See "Le Soldat laboureur"
"The Soldier's Betrothed" (Mörike)
See "Die Soldatenbraut"
"The Soldier's Dream" (Campbell) **19**:179, 181, 187, 193
"The Soldier's Funeral" (Southey) **97**:312, 315
"The Soldier's Grave" (Landon) **15**:161
"The Soldier's Home" (Bloomfield) **145**:158
"The Soldier's Return" (Opie) **65**:158
"Soldier's Song" (Taylor) **89**:309-10
"The Soldier's Tomb" (Isaacs)
See "La tumba del soldado"
"The Soldier's Well" (Shevchenko)
See "Moskaleva Krynycja"
"The Soldier's Widow" (Willis) **194**:297, 306
"The Soldier's Wife" (Southey) **97**:312, 315
"Le soleil" (Baudelaire) **29**:100; **55**:15, 35-6, 56, 65; **155**:3-5, 7-8, 25
"Soleil couchant" (Banville) **9**:31
"Soleil couchant" (Laforgue) **221**:92
"Soleil et chair" (Rimbaud) **4**:455, 485; **35**:280, 282; **82**:230; **227**:208, 236-37
Le Soleil était encore chaud (Rimbaud)
See *Prologue*
"Soleils couchants" (Verlaine) **2**:631; **51**:385
"A Solemn Thing It Was I Said" (Dickinson) **21**:57; **77**:67
"Solemnity" (Mallarmé)
See "Solennité"
"Solennité" (Mallarmé) **41**:254-55, 282-83; **210**:251
Soliloquies (Schleiermacher)
See *Monologen: Eine Neujahrsgabe*
"Soliloquy" (Yearsley) **174**:316
"Soliloquy of Mr. Broadbrim" (Parton) **86**:352
"Soliloquy of the Spanish Cloister" (Browning) **79**:163, 165, 170
"Le solitaire" (Lamartine) **11**:255
"Les Solitaires de Normandie" (Genlis) **166**:32
"The Solitary Life" (Leopardi)
See "La vita solitaria"
"The Solitary Reaper" (Wordsworth) **12**:431, 456, 463-66; **166**:264; **206**:250, 336
"The Solitary Sparrow" (Leopardi)
See "Il Passero Solitario"
"Solitary Stanzas" (Castro Alves)
See "Estrofes do Solitário"
"La solitude" (Baudelaire) **155**:124
"Solitude" (Clare) **9**:77-78
"Solitude" (Dodgson) **139**:30
"La solitude" (Lamartine) **11**:245; **190**:236
"Solitude" (Lampman) **25**:208-09; **194**:20, 75, 100
"Solitude" (Maupassant) **42**:202-03
"Solitude" (Sigourney) **21**:310
"Solitude" (Thoreau) **7**:352, 408
"Solitude" (Warton)
See "Ode to Solitude"
Soll und Haben (Freytag) **109**:144-45, 147-54, 157-62, 164-67, 172, 177, 180-83
Soll und Haben, der klassische Kaufmannsroman (Freytag)
See *Soll und Haben*
Le solliciteur; ou, L'art d'obtenir des places (Scribe) **16**:382
"Solo amistad?" (Isaacs) **70**:308
"Solo de lune" (Laforgue) **5**:277; **53**:293; **221**:21, 23, 48, 62, 64-65
"Solomon" (Woolson) **82**:286, 293, 333
Solomon (Klopstock) **11**:226
"Solovei i Kukushka" (Pushkin) **83**:304
"Solution" (Emerson) **38**:192
"Solvet seclum" (Leconte de Lisle) **29**:222
"Las sombras" (Heredia) **209**:154, 165-66
"Sombre récit, conteur plus sombre" (Villiers de l'Isle Adam) **3**:589-90
"Sombre Tale, Sombre Teller" (Villiers de l'Isle Adam)
See "Sombre récit, conteur plus sombre"
El sombrero de tres picos (Alarcon) **1**:12-13, 15-18; **219**:4, 7-9, 17, 19-29, 32-40, 51
"Some Account of my Kin, my Tallents and Myself" (Clare) **86**:173
"Some Account of Stonehenge, the Giant's Dance" (Poe) **94**:229
Some Account of the Christian Poets (Barrett Browning)
See *The Book of the Poets*
Some Account of the Greek Christian Poets (Barrett Browning) **66**:44
"Some Account of the Latter Days of Richard Marston, of Dunoran" (Le Fanu)
See "Some Account of the Latter Days of the Hon. Richard Marston of Dunoran"
"Some Account of the Latter Days of the Hon. Richard Marston of Dunoran" (Le Fanu) **58**:272
"Some Account of Thomas Tucker" (Cooke) **110**:20, 43, 48-9
Some Accounts of the Frolics of Idle Jack Brown (More) **141**:179
Some Adventures of Captain Simon Suggs, Late of the Tallapoosa Volunteers; Together with "Taking the Census," and Other Alabama Sketches (Hooper) **177**:171, 173-75, 177-84, 188-91, 193-94, 198, 201, 207-12
"Some Arrows Slay but Whom They Strike" (Dickinson) **21**:56
Some Articles on the Depreciation of Silver and on Topics Connected with It (Bagehot) **10**:20
"Some Aspects of Robert Burns" (Stevenson) **193**:275
"Some Comments on Didacticism in Stories and Novels" (Dobrolyubov) **5**:140
"Some Feasts and Fasts" (Rossetti) **50**:285
"Some Hints & Observations concerning the civilization of the Indians, or Aborigines of America" (Bartram) **145**:3, 121
"Some Observations on Diaries, Self-Biography, and Self-Characters" (D'Israeli) **217**:321
"Some Observations on the Historical Development of Honour" (Herzen) **61**:101
"Some Passages in the Life of a Lion" (Poe) **16**:322
Some Passages in the Life of Mistress Margaret Maitland of Sunnyside (Oliphant)
See *Passages in the Life of Mrs. Margaret Maitland of Sunnyside, Written by Herself*
Some Passages in the Life of Mr. Adam Blair, Minister of the Gospel at Cross-Meikle (Lockhart) **5**:286, 288, 292, 294-96, 302-03, 306-07, 310-13
"Some Strange Disturbances in an Old House on Augier Street" (Le Fanu) **9**:317
"Some Thoughts on the Abodes, Life and Social Conditions of the Poor, especially in Dorsetshire" (Barnes) **75**:102
"Some War Memoranda" (Whitman) **4**:554
Some Words on the Countryside, Folk Character, and Way of Life in Saarijärvi Parish (Runeberg)
See *Några ord om nejderna, folklynnet och levnadssättet i Saarijärvi socken*
"Some Words with a Mummy" (Poe) **94**:240; **211**:224, 297-98, 304, 307
"Some Work for Immortality" (Dickinson) **21**:38
Somebody's Neighbors (Cooke) **110**:19, 21, 26, 33-6, 39, 43-4
"Something" (Andersen)
See "Noget"
"Something about the Sciences, Arts and Enlightenment" (Karamzin)
See "Nechto o naukakh, isskustvakh i prosveshchenii"
"Something Beyond" (Larcom) **179**:176
"Something Concerning the first Human Society According to the Proscriptions of the Mosaic Law" (Schiller) **166**:145
"Something Gathers Up the Fragments" (Traill) **31**:328
"Something on the Sciences, Arts, and Enlightenment" (Karamzin)
See "Nečto o naukax, iskusstvax, i proveščenii"
"Something to Write About" (Andersen) **79**:30
"Sometimes a light surprises" (Cowper) **94**:69
"Sometimes with One I Love" (Whitman) **4**:554
"Somewhere or Other" (Rossetti) **50**:295
"Sommeil" (Corbière)
See "La litanie du sommeil"
"Le sommeil du condor" (Leconte de Lisle) **29**:210, 212, 216-17, 223
"Ein Sommer tagstraum" (Droste-Hülshoff) **3**:203
"Sommerfuglen" (Andersen) **79**:69
Sommergeschichten und Lieder (Storm) **195**:92
"Das Sommermärchen" (Wieland) **177**:233
"Die Sommernacht" (Klopstock) **11**:220, 236
Die Sommernacht (Klopstock) **225**:298
"Sommernacht" (Meyer) **81**:151
"La Somnambule" (Vigny) **102**:335
La somnambule (Scribe) **16**:382, 391
"Son" (Bestuzhev) **131**:151
"Son" (Shevchenko) **54**:379-80, 382
"Son" (Turgenev) **21**:415, 435, 441, 452; **122**:243, 245-47, 266-67, 269, 364-65, 368, 371, 375-78
"The Son" (Very) **9**:378
"Le son du cor s'afflige vers les bois" (Verlaine) **51**:355
A Son Excellence Reschid-Pascha ancien grand vizir de l'Empire Ottoman (Comte) **54**:211
"Son na more" (Tyutchev) **34**:389, 404, 408-09
"The Son of Arminius: A Tale of Ancient Rome" (Moodie) **113**:310
The Son of Cromwell (Scribe)
See *Le fils de Cromwell; ou, Une Restauration*
"The Son of Darkness" (Krasiński)
See "Syn cieniów"
The Son of his Father (Oliphant) **61**:203, 205, 210
"The Son of Man" (Lazarus) **109**:337
A Son of the Forest: The Experience of William Apes, a Native of the Forest (Apess) **73**:4-5, 7-10, 14-15, 27-28, 31
The Son of the Soil (Oliphant) **11**:446, 449; **61**:203
Sonata in A flat, op. 110 (Beethoven) **227**:7, 34
Sonata, op. 27 (Beethoven) **227**:22
Sonata, op. 132 (Beethoven) **227**:34
"Sonderbarer Rechtsfall" (Kleist) **37**:237

Sonetje nesreče (Preseren) **127**:295-96, 304, 330
"Sonetni venec" (Preseren) **127**:293, 295, 298, 305, 308
"Sonetos negros" (Silva) **114**:301
"Sonette 4" (Eichendorff) **225**:45
Sonety Krymskie (Mickiewicz) **3**:389-90, 393-94, 399, 402-05; **101**:157, 183, 187, 190-92
"Song" (Blake)
See "Bard's Song"
"Song" (Browning) **79**:94, 101, 174
"Song" (Clare) **86**:114
"Song" (Coleridge) **90**:27
"Song" (Lampman) **194**:39
"The Song" (Longstreet) **159**:118, 133, 137, 144, 147-48, 176, 185-86, 199-202
"Song" (Moore) **110**:192
"Song" (Pinkney) **31**:273-74, 277, 280
"Song" (Poe) **117**:280
"Song" (Rossetti) **2**:575; **50**:288-89; **186**:269-72, 279-80, 332
"A Song" (Shevchenko)
See "Dumka"
"Song" (Taylor) **89**:300
"Song" (Tennyson) **30**:245, 276, 279
"The Song" (Very) **9**:380
"Song 1" (Barbauld)
See "Hymn I"
"Song 4" (Barbauld)
See "Hymn IV"
"Song 6" (Barbauld)
See "Hymn VI"
"Song and Praise" (Very) **9**:376
"Song at Sunset" (Whitman) **4**:601; **31**:391; **205**:162, 165
"Song by Julius Angora" (Brontë) **16**:79, 121
"Song by Siegfried" (Beddoes) **3**:34
"Song by Thanatos" (Beddoes) **154**:79
"Song for a Highland Drover" (Bloomfield) **145**:129, 154
"Song for All Seas, All Ships" (Whitman) **31**:431
"Song for Autumn" (Lenau) **16**:276
"A Song for Occupations" (Whitman) **4**:577; **31**:419, 425, 443, 445; **81**:246, 250, 322, 342, 363; **205**:162-63, 191-94, 204, 211, 218, 226, 237-39, 241, 246, 301, 325
"A Song for the Future" (Harpur) **114**:166
"Song for the New Year's Eve" (Bryant) **6**:165
"Song for the Night of Christ's Resurrection" (Ingelow) **39**:266; **107**:148
"A Song for the Ragged Schools of London" (Barrett Browning) **61**:67
"A Song from 'Disguises'" (Webster) **230**:239
"Song from the HIghest Tower" (Rimbaud)
See "Chanson de la plus haute tour"
"Song from the Inner Life" (Chivers) **49**:72
"Song I am wearing away like the Snow in the Sun" (Opie) **65**:166
"Song III" (Barbauld) **50**:14
"Song Last Day" (Clare) **86**:114, 153
"A Song of Autumn" (Gordon) **21**:151, 155-56, 159-60, 176, 188
The Song of Bacchus (Pushkin) **83**:279
"The Song of Elaine" (Lanier) **118**:241
"A Song of Eternity in Time" (Lanier) **6**:244
"The Song of Fionnuala" (Moore) **6**:399
The Song of Hiawatha (Longfellow) **2**:477, 481, 483-84, 486-87, 494-96, 498; **45**:102-03, 106, 110-11, 114, 119-20, 128, 134, 136, 139, 144-45, 147, 149-150, 157-59, 166-69, 171-80, 187-88, 190; **101**:93-150; **103**:277, 283-84, 301, 304, 308
"Song of Isbrand" (Beddoes) **3**:34; **154**:38
"A Song of Joys" (Whitman) **4**:577, 601; **205**:211, 226
"The Song of Lamech" (Prescott) **163**:50
"Song of LeVerrier on Discovering a New Planet" (Chivers) **49**:72
"A Song of Liberty" (Blake) **13**:169, 184, 214, 221; **57**:29-30, 40, 58; **190**:14, 162
A Song of Liberty (Blake) **201**:20
The Song of Los (Blake) **13**:184-85, 192-93, 221-22, 226-27; **37**:35; **173**:9, 81; **190**:11, 14, 28; **201**:32
"Song of Love" (Lamartine)
See "Chant d'amour"
"A Song of Love" (Lanier) **118**:217
"A Song of Love Triumphant" (Turgenev)
See "Pesn' torzhestvuyushchey lyubvi"
"The Song of Marion's Men" (Bryant) **6**:165, 169, 172, 182
"Song of Melancholy" (Dacre) **151**:186
"The Song of Morphine" (Casal)
See "La canción de la morfina"
"Song of My Cid" (Bello) **131**:92
"The Song of My Heart" (Kivi) **30**:51
"Song of Myself" (Whitman) **31**:368-70, 375-76, 378-80, 385-87, 389-90, 392-93, 401-05, 409, 411-13, 416-21, 424-29, 435-36, 441, 443, 445; **4**:544, 562-63, 568, 571, 576, 579, 581-84, 589, 593-600, 602-04; **81**:23, 239-40, 247-8, 250, 258, 261-3, 269, 271, 276, 279-82, 299, 302-03, 307-8, 310, 312-13, 315-16, 318-20, 322, 327, 333, 340; **205**:157, 159-62, 164, 172-73, 190-94, 197, 201-2, 204,
"The Song of Ninian Melville" (Kendall) **12**:191
"Song of Occupations" (Whitman)
See "A Song for Occupations"
"The Song of Pan" (Lampman) **25**:167
"Song of Pitcairn's Island" (Bryant) **6**:172
"Song of Praise" (Clare) **9**:76
"Song of Prudence" (Whitman) **81**:338; **205**:174
"The Song of Rahéro: A Legend of Tahiti" (Stevenson) **5**:410, 428; **193**:215
"The Song of Scandinavian Warriors" (Tyutchev)
See "Pesn skandinavskix voinov"
"Song of Slaves in the Desert" (Whittier) **59**:369, 372
The Song of Solomon, Newly Translated (Percy) **95**:313, 320, 336, 338, 360
"Song of Songs" (Barnes) **75**:99
Song of Songs (Daudet) **1**:237
"Song of Sorrow" (Keats) **73**:152
"Song of the African" (Castro Alves)
See "Canção do Africano"
"Song of the Answerer" (Whitman) **4**:591; **31**:425, 431; **205**:157, 191-92, 194, 204, 218, 226
"The Song of the Axe" (Crawford) **12**:158
"Song of the Banner at Daybreak" (Whitman) **4**:576; **81**:317; **205**:158-59
"Song of the Bard" (Blake)
See "Bard's Song"
"The Song of the Bell" (Schiller)
See "Das Lied von der Glocke"
"Song of the Body Electric" (Whitman)
See "I Sing the Body Electric"
"The Song of the Bower" (Rossetti) **4**:491, 496-97, 510; **77**:328
"Song of the Broad-Axe" (Whitman) **4**:567, 571-72, 580; **31**:387, 392-93; **81**:322; **205**:157-58, 162-63, 211, 226
"The Song of the Cattle Hunters" (Kendall) **12**:179, 183, 191, 195
"The Song of the Chattahoochee" (Lanier) **6**:236, 238-39, 249, 264-65, 270; **118**:203, 232, 238, 240, 265, 268, 275
"The Song of the Croaker" (Alger) **8**:16; **83**:112
"Song of the Dead" (Novalis)
See "Lier der Toten"
"The Song of the Dogs" (Petofi)
See "A kutyák dala"
"The Song of the Earth" (Boker) **125**:7, 78
"Song of the Exposition" (Whitman) **4**:601; **205**:158, 196, 203-4, 208, 211, 226, 324
The Song of the Factory Slave (Jones) **222**:115
"A Song of the Future" (Lanier) **6**:244
"The Song of the Greek Amazon" (Bryant) **6**:172; **46**:7
"Song of the Greeks" (Campbell) **19**:179
"The Song of the Hunter" (Mörike)
See "Jägerlied"
"Song of the Lithuanian Legion" (Slowacki) **15**:349
Song of the Low (Jones) **222**:131
The Song of the Merchant Kaláshnikov (Lermontov)
See *Pesnya pro tsarya Ivana Vasilievicha, molodogo oprichnika i undalogo kuptsa Kalashnikova*
"Song of the Middle Watch" (Ingelow) **107**:124
Song of the Night (Leopardi)
See "Canto notturno di un pastore errante dell'Asia"
"Song of the Open Road" (Whitman) **4**:582, 592, 596; **31**:387, 393, 431, 443; **81**:257, 278, 299, 314; **205**:172, 226
"The Song of the Philaretians" (Mickiewicz) **3**:398
"Song of the Pixies" (Coleridge) **197**:215
"The Song of the Poor Man" (Zhukovsky) **35**:402
"Song of the Redwood Tree" (Whitman) **4**:579; **31**:392; **205**:208, 211, 226
"A Song of the Rolling Earth" (Whitman) **4**:576; **31**:391; **81**:329; **205**:160, 205, 211, 226, 262
"Song of the sea" (Meyer)
See "Der Gesang des Meeres"
"Song of the Shingle Splitters" (Kendall) **12**:191, 195
"The Song of the Shirt" (Hood) **16**:205, 207-10, 212, 215, 220-21, 224-28, 231, 233-34, 236-38; **35**:227
"Song of the Sower" (Bryant) **6**:165; **46**:19
"Song of the Stars" (Bryant) **6**:161, 178, 190; **46**:6, 39
"Song of the Stream-Drops" (Lampman) **25**:200; **194**:60-61
"Song of the Stygian Naiades" (Beddoes) **3**:32, 34, 41
"The Song of the Surf" (Gordon) **21**:150, 154, 160, 164, 166, 176
"The Song of the Treadmill" (Holmes) **14**:99
"The Song of the Triumphant Love" (Turgenev)
See "Pesn' torzhestvuyushchey lyubvi"
Song of the Tsar Ivan Vasilievich, the young oprichnik and the bold Merchant Kalashnikov (Lermontov)
See *Pesnya pro tsarya Ivana Vasilievicha, molodogo oprichnika i undalogo kuptsa Kalashnikova*
"Song of the Universal" (Whitman) **31**:389-90; **205**:203, 208
"The Song of the Vermonters" (Whittier) **8**:526
"Song of the Wanderer" (Nekrasov) **11**:407
"The Song of the Willi" (Blind) **202**:10, 12-15, 17-18, 27-30, 32
"Song of the Wind" (Mörike)
See "Lied vom Winde"
"The Song of the Wolves" (Petofi)
See "A farkasok dala"
"Song of Two at Night" (Mörike)
See "Gesang zu zweien in der Nacht"
The Song of Tzar Ivan Vasiljevich, His Young Life-Guardsman, and the Valiant Merchant Kaláshnikov (Lermontov)
See *Pesnya pro tsarya Ivana Vasilievicha, molodogo oprichnika i undalogo kuptsa Kalashnikova*
"Song on Captain Barney's Victory" (Freneau) **1**:319
"Song: Rarely, Rarely, Comest Thou, Spirit of Delight" (Shelley) **18**:340, 344, 372
"The Song Sparrow" (Lampman) **194**:51
"Song to a City Girl" (Clare) **9**:77
Song to Joy (Schiller)
See *Lied an die Freude*
"Song to the Men of England" (Shelley) **175**:240, 325
"Song, Venus" (Lazarus) **8**:426

"Song, Was it for this I dearly loved thee" (Opie) **65**:160
"Song, Yes, thou art changed" (Opie) **65**:160
"Le songe" (Sainte-Beuve) **5**:346
"Le songe de Polyphile" (Nerval) **67**:335
"Le Songe du Reviewer" (Musset) **150**:309
Songes (Almqvist) **42**:15-16, 20
"Songs" (Chivers)
See "Songs of the Heart"
"Songs" (Taylor) **89**:300
Songs, by the Ettrick Shepherd (Hogg) **109**:250
"Song's Eternity" (Clare) **9**:88, 97, 124
Songs For Children (Hale) **75**:286
Songs for Her (Verlaine)
See *Chansons pour elle*
"Songs for Strangers and Pilgrims" (Rossetti) **50**:286
"Songs for the Soldiers" (Crawford) **127**:153, 220-21
Songs from the Gulf of Salerno (Muller)
See *Lieder aus dem Meerbusen von Salerno*
Songs from the Mountains (Kendall) **12**:185, 187, 192, 197
"Songs in a Cornfield" (Rossetti) **50**:288
Songs of a Semite: The Dance to Death, and Other Poems (Lazarus) **8**:415, 421, 423-24; **109**:289, 297, 304, 310, 318, 326-27, 331, 343-44
Songs of a Troubadour (Zorrilla y Moral)
See *Cantos del trovador*
"Songs of Aldhelm" (Lanier) **118**:217
"Songs of Beulah" (Blake) **173**:111
Songs of Ensign Stål (Runeberg)
See *Fänrik Ståls sägner*
Songs of Experience (Blake) **13**:159, 163, 165, 172, 202, 218-22, 226, 240-43, 254; **57**:49; **127**:40, 75, 80; **173**:10, 16-17, 28, 108; **190**:17-18, 61, 64; **201**:18, 47, 63, 65, 123, 129
Songs of Innocence (Blake) **13**:159, 162, 171-72, 179-82, 191, 210-11, 218-19, 221, 239-43, 250-51; **57**:26; **127**:31, 75; **190**:14-15, 61, 94; **201**:47, 65, 74, 85, 104
Songs of Innocence (Child) **173**:108
Songs of Innocence and of Experience: Shewing the Two Contrary States of the Human Soul (Blake) **13**:159, 163, 184, 188-89, 218; **37**:1-99; **57**:50, 57, 93; **127**:75, 79, 82; **201**:18, 47, 63, 65, 123, 129
Songs of Labor, and Other Poems (Whittier) **8**:495, 500-01, 506, 512, 517; **59**:350, 355, 357-8, 370
"The Songs of our Fathers" (Hemans) **71**:264
"Songs of Parting" (Whitman) **4**:546; **205**:224, 226
"Songs of Semite" (Lazarus) **109**:341, 344
"Songs of Seven" (Ingelow) **39**:257, 264; **107**:119-20, 122, 146
"Songs of the Affections" (Hemans) **71**:261, 289
Songs of the Affections (Hemans) **71**:275, 277, 279, 293, 303-04, 307
Songs of the Army of the Night (Adams) **33**:2-8, 10-13, 15-18, 22, 24-5
Songs of the Domestic Affections (Hemans) **29**:205
"Songs of the Heart" (Chivers) **49**:48, 57
"Songs of the Ingenues" (Verlaine)
See "La chanson des ingénues"
"Songs of the Months" (Martineau) **26**:309
"Songs of the Night Watches" (Ingelow) **39**:264
Songs of the Occident (Blind)
See *Birds of Passage: Songs of the Orient and Occident*
"Songs of the Pixies" (Coleridge) **99**:18, 54
"Songs of the Voices of Birds" (Ingelow) **39**:264-65; **107**:122-23
Songs of the Western Slavs (Pushkin) **3**:452
Songs of Travel (Stevenson) **5**:419, 428
"Songs of Twilight" (Hugo) **3**:261
"Songs with Preludes" (Ingelow) **39**:264; **107**:119
Songs without Words (Verlaine)
See *Romances sans paroles*
"Song—Sweet Indian Maid" (Ridge) **82**:181
Sonhos d'ouro (Alencar) **157**:30, 41
The Son-in-Law of M. Poirier (Augier)
See *Le gendre de Monsieur Poirier*
Sonnailles et clochettes (Banville) **9**:20, 30-31
Die Sonnenfinsternis (Stifter) **198**:276-77
Die Sonnenjungfrau (Kotzebue) **25**:135-37, 147
Sonnenklarer Bericht, A Report, Clear as the Sun, for the General Public on the Real Essence of the Latest Philosophy: An Attempt to compel the Reader to Understand (Fichte) **62**:4, 34
"Sonnet" (Cranch) **115**:6
"Sonnet" (Hayne) **94**:160-61
"Sonnet" (Keats) **8**:343, 349
"Sonnet" (Musset) **150**:232
"Sonnet" (Rimbaud) **227**:333-35
"Sonnet" (Tennyson) **30**:205
"Sonnet 1" (Barrett Browning) **170**:28-30
"Sonnet 1" (Smith) **115**:152, 156
"Sonnet 2" (Barrett Browning) **170**:29
"Sonnet 2" (Smith) **115**:124, 204-5, 215
"Sonnet 3" (Barrett Browning) **170**:25, 29
"Sonnet 3" (Smith) **115**:153
"Sonnet 4" (Barrett Browning) **170**:12, 25, 28
"Sonnet 4" (Smith) **115**:153, 173, 177, 180, 202-3
"Sonnet 5" (Barrett Browning) **170**:25
"Sonnet 5" (Smith) **115**:154, 177-78
"Sonnet 8" (Barrett Browning) **170**:28, 53
"Sonnet 9" (Barrett Browning) **170**:53
"Sonnet 9" (Smith) **115**:156
"Sonnet 10" (Barrett Browning) **170**:53
"Sonnet 10" (Smith) **115**:177
"Sonnet 11" (Barrett Browning) **170**:53
"Sonnet 12" (Barrett Browning) **170**:53
"Sonnet 12" (Smith) **115**:154, 218
"Sonnet 13" (Barrett Browning) **170**:28, 53
"Sonnet 13" (Webster) **230**:332
"Sonnet 14" (Barrett Browning) **170**:29
"Sonnet 14" (Webster) **230**:330
"Sonnet 16" (Barrett Browning) **170**:28
"Sonnet 16" (Webster) **230**:330
"Sonnet 17" (Webster) **230**:331
"Sonnet 18" (Barrett Browning) **170**:54
"Sonnet 18" (Webster) **230**:331
"Sonnet 21" (Barrett Browning) **170**:13, 55
"Sonnet 22" (Barrett Browning) **170**:26, 29
"Sonnet 25" (Barrett Browning) **170**:28-29
"Sonnet 26" (Barrett Browning) **170**:29-30
"Sonnet 26" (Smith) **115**:178
"Sonnet 27" (Barrett Browning) **170**:28, 30
"Sonnet 27" (Smith) **115**:177
"Sonnet 30" (Smith) **115**:178
"Sonnet 31" (Smith) **115**:206
"Sonnet 32" (Smith) **115**:152, 178, 215
"Sonnet 33" (Smith) **115**:178
"Sonnet 34" (Smith) **115**:177
"Sonnet 35" (Barrett Browning) **170**:26, 28
"Sonnet 36" (Smith) **115**:125, 154
"Sonnet 40" (Barrett Browning) **170**:30
"Sonnet 42" (Smith) **115**:206
"Sonnet 43" (Barrett Browning) **170**:10, 28-30, 56
"Sonnet 44" (Barrett Browning) **170**:10
"Sonnet 44" (Smith) **115**:123, 153-54, 197-99, 205
"Sonnet 45" (Smith) **115**:178
"Sonnet 47" (Smith) **115**:153, 176-77
"Sonnet 48" (Smith) **115**:154, 182
"Sonnet 55" (Smith) **115**:177
"Sonnet 57" (Smith) **115**:212, 217
"Sonnet 62" (Smith) **115**:217
"Sonnet 66" (Smith) **115**:176-77, 216
"Sonnet 67" (Smith) **115**:216
"Sonnet 68" (Smith) **115**:152
"Sonnet 70" (Smith) **115**:199
"Sonnet 77" (Smith) **115**:153
"Sonnet 79" (Smith) **115**:177, 218-19
"Sonnet 83" (Smith) **115**:210
"Sonnet 84" (Smith) **115**:177, 182
"Sonnet 89" (Smith) **115**:216
"Sonnet 90" (Smith) **115**:153, 216
"Sonnet 91" (Smith) **115**:216
"Sonnet 92" (Smith) **115**:210, 216
"Sonnet 116" (Barrett Browning) **170**:28-29
"Sonnet à Sir Bob" (Corbière) **43**:13
"Sonnet allégorique de lui-même" (Mallarmé) **41**:289, 291-92; **210**:241
"Sonnet boiteux" (Verlaine) **2**:631; **230**:154
"Sonnet CCLIV" (Boker) **125**:89
"Sonnet CCLXIII" (Boker) **125**:89
"Sonnet CCLXXI" (Boker) **125**:89
"Sonnet CCLXXV" (Boker) **125**:90
"Sonnet CCLXXX" (Boker) **125**:91
"Sonnet CCLXXXII" (Boker) **125**:91
"Sonnet CCXXXIX" (Boker) **125**:89
"Sonnet CCXXXVIII" (Boker) **125**:89
"Sonnet CIX" (Boker) **125**:89
"Sonnet CLXXX" (Boker) **125**:89
"Sonnet CXLVIII" (Boker) **125**:90
"Sonnet CXXIII" (Boker) **125**:84
"Sonnet CXXIV" (Boker) **125**:84
"Sonnet CXXXII" (Boker) **125**:90
"Sonnet CXXXIII" (Boker) **125**:90
"Sonnet CXXXIV" (Boker) **125**:90
"Sonnet CXXXVI" (Boker) **125**:90
"Sonnet en -yx" (Mallarmé) **4**:389; **41**:242-43, 289, 292-93; **210**:240-41, 243-44
"Sonnet: England in 1819" (Shelley) **18**:375; **175**:325
"Sonnet from the Psalms" (Rossetti) **186**:278
"Sonnet II" (Boker) **125**:90
"Sonnet II" (Norton) **205**:142
"Sonnet III" (Norton) **205**:142
"Sonnet IV" (Robinson) **142**:142-43
"Sonnet LIV" (Boker) **125**:89
"Sonnet LXIV" (Boker) **125**:85
"Sonnet LXX" (Boker) **125**:88
"Sonnet LXXI" (Boker) **125**:89
"Sonnet LXXII" (Boker) **125**:89
"Sonnet LXXIV" (Boker) **125**:89
"Sonnet LXXVIII" (Boker) **125**:89
"Sonnet LXXXVIII" (Boker) **125**:89
"Sonnet No. Three" (Smith) **59**:332
"Sonnet on Leaving Winchester" (Bowles) **103**:68
"Sonnet, On Seeing Miss Helen Maria Williams Weep at a Tale of Distress" (Wordsworth) **206**:297
"Sonnet on the Approach of Autumn" (Opie) **65**:160
"Sonnet on the Fate of Poetic Genius in a Sordid Community" (Harpur) **114**:102
"Sonnet on the Mexican War" (Cranch) **115**:22
"Sonnet on the Nile" (Hunt) **70**:248
"Sonnet on the Ryne" (Bowles) **103**:85
"Sonnet pour éventail" (Laforgue) **221**:83
"Sonnet to Flib" (Lippard) **198**:133
"Sonnet to Haydon" (Reynolds) **146**:166
"Sonnet to Hope" (Williams) **135**:255
"Sonnet to My Brothers" (Keats) **8**:345
"Sonnet to My Country" (Isaacs) **70**:306
"Sonnet to Solitude" (Keats) **8**:345
"Sonnet: to the Autumnal Moon" (Coleridge) **197**:215
"Sonnet to the Moon" (Williams) **135**:255
"Sonnet to Twilight" (Williams) **135**:255, 333
"Sonnet to Zante" (Poe) **117**:217
"Sonnet Written at Tinemouth, Northumberland" (Bowles) **103**:85, 87, 90, 92-4
"Sonnet XIV" (Robinson) **142**:143
"Sonnet XIV" (Webster) **230**:323
"Sonnet XLII" (Boker) **125**:88
"Sonnet XLV" (Boker) **125**:89
"Sonnet XV" (Robinson) **142**:143
"Sonnet XV" (Webster) **230**:320-23
"Sonnet XVI" (Webster) **230**:321
"Sonnet XVII" (Webster) **230**:321

"Sonnet XXIII" (Boker) **125**:85
"Sonnet XXV" (Boker) **125**:85
"Sonnet XXVI" (Webster) **230**:319
"Sonnet XXVII" (Boker) **125**:84
"Sonnet XXXI" (Boker) **125**:89
"Sonnet XXXVI" (Robinson) **142**:143
Sonnets (Foscolo) **97**:62
Sonnets (Mallarmé) **4**:380
Sonnets (Mickiewicz)
See *Sonety Krymskie*
Sonnets: A Sequence on Profane Love (Boker) **125**:82-83
Sonnets and Canzonets (Alcott) **1**:22, 25; **167**:11, 72
Sonnets, and Other Poems (Hayne) **94**:138-39
"'Sonnets, attempted in the Manner of 'Contemporary Writers'" (Coleridge) **111**:353
"Sonnets by Nehemiah Higginbottom" (Coleridge) **111**:353
"Sonnets Dedicated to Liberty" (Wordsworth) **206**:296
"Sonnets for Pictures" (Rossetti) **77**:303, 344
Sonnets from the Crimea (Mickiewicz)
See *Sonety Krymskie*
Sonnets from the Portuguese (Barrett Browning) **1**:115, 122-4, 129; **16**:130-54; **61**:34, 43; **66**:44, 90-1; **170**:10-12, 14, 24-26, 28, 31, 53-57, 67, 69-71, 86, 116
The Sonnets of Michelangelo and of Campanella (Symonds) **34**:334, 336
Sonnets of Petrarch (Liszt) **199**:307
Sonnets of Unhappiness (Preseren)
See *Sonetje nesreče*
The Sonnets of William Wordsworth (Wordsworth) **12**:414
Sonnets on Art (Schlegel) **142**:300
Sonnets on the War (Dobell) **43**:62
Sonnets on the War (Smith) **59**:293, 312, 319-20
Sonnets, written chiefly in Picturesque Spots (Bowles)
See *Sonnets written chiefly on Picturesque Spots during a Tour*
Sonnets written chiefly on Picturesque Spots during a Tour (Bowles) **103**:59-60, 72, 78, 85-7
"Sonnet—Silence" (Poe) **1**:528
"Sonnet—To Science" (Poe) **117**:215, 227, 231-32, 234, 242, 260, 281; **211**:226, 248
"Le Sonneur" (Mallarmé) **41**:250, 281, 290; **210**:217, 244
"Der Sonntag des Grossvaters" (Gotthelf) **117**:6
"Sonntags" (Meyer) **81**:205
Sons of Kings (Gobineau)
See *Les pléiades*
Sons of the Valley (Werner)
See *Die Söhne des Thales: Ein dramatisches Gedicht*
Sons of Tupã (Alencar)
See *Os filhos de Tupã*
"Sons of Tupan" (Alencar)
See "Filhos de Tupan"
The Sons of Usna (Chivers) **49**:76, 78-9
"Soothsay" (Rossetti) **4**:509, 514, 518
Sophia (Lennox) **23**:228-29, 233-34; **134**:271
Sophie ou les sintiments setrcts (Staël-Holstein) **91**:326-27, 340, 358
Sophonisba (Alfieri)
See *Sofonisba*
"Sopra il monumento di Dante" (Leopardi) **129**:219, 316, 328
"Sopra il ritratto di una bella donna" (Leopardi) **129**:226, 246, 289, 291, 310
The Sorceress (Oliphant) **11**:454
La sorcière (Michelet) **31**:208, 220, 222-24, 230, 245, 258
"Sorcières espagnoles" (Mérimée) **6**:366
Sordello (Browning) **19**:75, 77-8, 102, 105, 109-10, 118, 120, 149-51; **79**:96, 132, 140, 146-47, 149, 164, 180-82, 185-86, 189-90
Søren Kierkegaard's Journals and Papers (Kierkegaard)
See *Papirer*
Soren Kierkegaards Samlede Vaerker (Kierkegaard) **78**:157-66, 168-69; **125**:260, 265
Sorgen ohne Noth und Noth ohne Sorgen (Kotzebue) **25**:145, 147
"Sorochinskaia iarmarka" (Gogol) **5**:218, 250, 256; **31**:110; **162**:61, 92, 95, 121-22
"Sorochintsy Fair" (Gogol)
See "Sorochinskaia iarmarka"
"Sorocinskaja jamarka" (Gogol)
See "Sorochinskaia iarmarka"
"Sorrow" (Lampman) **25**:187
The Sorrows and Joys of a Schoolmaster (Gotthelf)
See *Leiden und Freuden eines Schulmeisters*
"Sorrows for the Death of a Favourite Tabby Cat" (Clare) **9**:77
"The Sorrows of Chatterton" (Harpur) **114**:137, 145
"The Sorrows of Rosalie" (Norton) **47**:239, 246, 248; **205**:86, 128-29
The Sorrows of Rosalie: A Tale with Other Poems (Norton) **205**:67
The Sorrows of Rosalie and other Poems (Norton) **47**:251, 260
The Sorrows of Switzerland (Bowles) **103**:54, 70
The Sorrows of Werter (Goethe)
See *Die Leiden des jungen Werthers*
The Sorrows of Yamba (More) **141**:269
The Sorrows of Young Werther (Goethe)
See *Die Leiden des jungen Werthers*
"Sortes Virgilianæ" (Timrod) **25**:361
Sortilege and Astrology (De Quincey) **4**:78
"Sotnyk" (Shevchenko) **54**:368
"Les Soucis matériels" (Baratynsky) **103**:16
"Soul and Country" (Mangan) **27**:296, 300
"The Soul Has Bandaged Moments" (Dickinson) **21**:76, 81; **77**:97; **171**:104
"A Soul in Prison" (Webster) **230**:231, 233, 248-49
"Soul of Poets" (Keats) **8**:360
"The Soul of the Revolution" (Martí) **63**:166
"The Soul of the Rose" (Silva)
See "El alma de la rosa"
"The Soul of Wine" (Baudelaire)
See "L'ame du vin"
"The Soul Selects Her Own Society" (Dickinson) **21**:43; **171**:108, 178, 213
"The Soul should always stand ajar" (Dickinson) **77**:157
"Soul toward God, think of me" (Verlaine)
See "Âme vers Dieu, pensez à moi"
"The Soul Would Like to Be a Star" (Tyutchev) **34**:389
"Soul-Advances" (Hayne) **94**:138
"Soul-Drift" (Blind) **202**:52
"Soul's Beauty" (Rossetti) **4**:514-15; **77**:326
"The Soul's Expression" (Barrett Browning) **61**:5, 9, 43; **66**:85; **170**:109
"Souls of Songs" (Meyer)
See "Liederseelen"
"The Soul's Opportunities" (Very) **9**:388
"The Soul's Superior instants" (Dickinson) **171**:157, 179-80
"A Soul's Tragedy" (Browning) **19**:102, 113; **79**:153-54
"The Soul's Travelling" (Barrett Browning) **170**:106
"Soul-Sickness" (Very) **9**:397
"Sound Morality: Or, Practical Religion as distinguished from Theoretical Religion" (Hogg) **109**:231
"Sound o' Water" (Barnes) **75**:88
"The Sound of Home" (Lenau) **16**:277
"Sound Sleep" (Rossetti) **50**:267
Sound Softly, My Song (Liszt)
See *Kling leise, mein Lied*
Soundings From the Atlantic (Holmes) **81**:102, 104
"Sounds" (Barrett Browning) **170**:106
"Sounds" (Thoreau) **7**:392, 402-4
"Soup from a Sausage Skewer" (Andersen)
See "How to Cook Soup upon a Sausage Pin"
"Soup of the Day" (Verlaine)
See "La Soupe du jour"
"La Soupe du jour" (Verlaine) **230**:163
"La Soupe du soir" (Verlaine) **230**:164, 166
"La Soupe et les nuages" (Baudelaire) **155**:23, 25, 95
"Soupir" (Mallarmé) **41**:250, 267-72, 279, 281; **210**:235-36
"La source" (Leconte de Lisle) **29**:245
"La source dans les bois" (Lamartine) **11**:279
Source of Positive Pleasure (Polidori)
See *Essay on the Source of Positive Pleasure*
"The Sources of Danger to the Republic" (Douglass) **7**:126
"Sous la table, dialogue bachique sur plusieurs questions de haute morale" (Gautier) **59**:10, 27
"Sous l'èpais Sycomore" (Leconte de Lisle) **29**:224
"Le sous préfet aux champs" (Daudet) **1**:238, 252
"Sous un portrait de Corbière" (Corbière) **43**:31, 33
"Sous-préfet in the Fields" (Daudet)
See "Le sous préfet aux champs"
Le Souterrain, ou Matilde (Lee)
See *The Recess, or, A Tale of Other Times*
"The South" (Lazarus) **8**:420
South Africa (Trollope) **215**:218
South Carolina Exposition and Protest (Calhoun) **15**:26-7, 50, 55
"South Carolina to the States of the North" (Hayne) **94**:144, 148
"The South Devil" (Woolson) **82**:272, 301
"The South Sea House" (Lamb) **10**:415, 435-36; **113**:199, 224, 235, 244, 267
"A South Sea Islander" (Adams) **33**:4
South Sea Letters (Stevenson)
See *In the South Seas*
"The South Sea Sisters" (Horne) **127**:260
South Sea Tales (Stevenson) **193**:358
The South Seas (Stevenson)
See *In the South Seas*
"The Southdown Shepherd" (Jefferies) **47**:134
"A Southern Night" (Arnold) **6**:72; **29**:26-7; **218**:119, 150
"Southern Prose" (Lanier) **6**:267
"Southey and Landor" (Landor) **14**:166, 195
"Southey and Porson" (Landor) **14**:194-95
"Southey's Edition of the *Pilgrim's Progress* " (Macaulay) **231**:278
Soutien de famille (Daudet) **1**:251
"A Souvenir" (Holmes) **14**:100
"Souvenir" (Maupassant) **83**:181
"Souvenir" (Musset)
See "Le souvenir"
"Le souvenir" (Musset) **7**:258, 263, 272, 275, 280; **150**:276-81, 307, 315, 318-9, 327-8
"Souvenir de la nuit du quatre" (Hugo) **3**:262
"Le souvenir d'enfance; ou, La vie cachée" (Lamartine) **11**:255, 269-70, 278-79; **190**:192, 225, 233, 263
"Souvenir des Alpes" (Musset) **150**:318-19
Souvenir des vielles guerres (Hugo) **3**:264
Souvenirs (Goncharov) **63**:3
Souvenirs (Renan) **145**:358
Souvenirs de Alexis de Tocqueville (Tocqueville) **7**:426-29, 446, 454-56; **63**:299, 304, 335, 369, 371
Souvenirs de jeunesse (Nodier) **19**:376, 384-85
Souvenirs de la révolution (Nodier) **19**:385
Souvenirs de la Révolution française (Williams) **135**:285, 289-90, 315-20, 336

Souvenirs de voyage (Gobineau) **17**:79-80, 93, 103
Souvenirs dégotisme (Stendhal) **23**:410, 411-12; **178**:156, 218
Souvenirs d'enfance et de jeunesse (Renan) **26**:382, 386-87, 391-93, 398, 405-06, 408, 413, 415, 418, 421-22
Les Souvenirs d'un étudiant pauvre (Vallès) **71**:363
Souvenirs d'un homme de lettres (Daudet) **1**:241
"Souvenirs d'un vieux professeur allemand" (Renan) **26**:413
Souvenirs d'une favorite (Dumas) **71**:218
Souvenirs, impressions, pensées, et paysages pendant un voyage en Orient, 1832-1833; ou, Notes d'un voyageur (Lamartine) **11**:249, 251, 267, 289; **190**:172, 174-75, 184, 186, 191, 194-95, 209, 215, 226, 264
"Souvenirs occulte" (Villiers de l'Isle Adam) **3**:589-90
"Souvenirs sur Leconte de Lisle" (Verlaine) **230**:162
"The Sovereignty of Ethics" (Emerson) **98**:66
"The Sovereignty of Love" (Dacre) **151**:170
"Sovremennoe" (Tyutchev) **34**:396
Sovremyonnaya idilliya (Saltykov) **16**:359, 361, 369, 373-74
"The Sower" (Very) **9**:384
Sowers Not Reapers (Martineau) **137**:267, 269
Sowing the Wind (Linton) **41**:157, 164-166, 170-71
The Spaewife (Galt) **1**:333-34
The Spagnoletto (Lazarus) **8**:418-19, 421, 425; **109**:289
Spain (Gautier)
See *España*
"Spain—The Confessional" (Browning) **79**:94
"The Spaniand" (Wergeland)
See "Spaniolen"
"The Spaniards in Denmark" (Mérimée)
See "Les Espagnols en Danemark"
Spaniards in Odense (Andersen) **79**:11
The Spaniards in Peru; or, The Death of Rolla (Kotzebue)
See *Die Spanier in Peru, oder Rollas Tod*
Die Spanier in Peru, oder Rollas Tod (Kotzebue) **25**:130, 141, 144-45, 148-49
"Spaniolen" (Wergeland) **5**:536, 540
"Spanische Atriden" (Heine) **147**:229, 231
Spanisches Theater (Schlegel) **15**:230
The Spanish Curate (Planché) **42**:273
The Spanish Drama: Lope de Vega and Calderon (Lewes) **25**:285, 324
The Spanish Father (Mackenzie) **41**:184, 208-12
Spanish Grammar (Bello) **131**:93
The Spanish Gypsy (Eliot) **4**:102-04, 107, 109, 113-15, 140; **13**:333-34; **23**:52, 67, 88; **118**:58, 130, 166, 173
The Spanish Gypsy: A Poem (Eliot) **183**:29, 65; **199**:286
The Spanish Gypsy: A Poem (Eliot) **209**:100
"A Spanish Love Song" (Kendall) **12**:181, 193
"The Spanish Military Nun" (De Quincey) **87**:15, 55-7
The Spanish Moors (Pixérécourt)
See *Les maures d'espagne; ou, Le pouvoir de l'enfance*
"The Spanish Nun" (De Quincey) **4**:74-75
The Spanish Story of the Armada and Other Essays (Froude) **43**:187
The Spanish Student (Longfellow) **2**:480, 482, 484, 497; **45**:113-14, 133, 135, 144, 148
"The Spanish Theatre" (Schlegel)
See "Über das spanische Theater"
"The Sparrow" (Isaacs)
See "El gorrión"
"The Sparrow" (Turgenev) **21**:452; **122**:289, 293
"The Sparrow's Nest" (Wordsworth) **12**:431
Spartacus, A Roman Story (Moodie) **113**:310, 319
"The Spartan Boy" (Lamb) **125**:348
"The Spartan Mother and Her Son" (Hemans) **71**:271
"The Spasmodic or German School" (Dodgson) **139**:125
"Spätboot" (Meyer) **81**:203
Späte Rosen (Storm) **195**:4, 26, 39, 41, 95
"Spätjahr" (Meyer) **81**:140-41, 145-46, 148-50, 155
"Der Spaziergang" (Schiller) **39**:305, 337, 380; **166**:103-4
"Speak roughly to your little boy" (Dodgson) **139**:29
Speaking Likenesses (Rossetti) **50**:271, 276, 301; **66**:331; **186**:229, 233, 238-43, 252, 255-59, 264, 266, 296
"A Spec in China" (Horne) **127**:260
"Special Message to Congress" (Lincoln)
See "Message to Congress in Special Session, July 4, 1861"
"Special Pleading" (Lanier) **6**:238, 242, 247; **118**:203, 215
"Special Report" (Arnold) **89**:110
Specimen (Cowper) **94**:82-3
Specimen Days (Whitman) **4**:577-78, 582, 588; **31**:403; **81**:275, 316-18, 338, 358, 369
Specimen Days & Collect (Whitman) **205**:185, 197, 251-53
"Specimen of an Induction" (Keats) **8**:345; **73**:151, 311; **225**:263
"Specimen of an Induction to a Poem" (Keats) **73**:158
Specimens of a New Version of Telemachus. To which is prefixed, A Defence of Poetry. Address to Henry James Pye, Esq. (D'Israeli)
See *A Defence of Poetry. Addressed to Henry James Pye, Esq. To which is added, A Specimen of a New Version of Telemachus*
Specimens of English Dramatic Poets Who Lived About the Time of Shakespeare (Lamb) **10**:391, 398, 405, 421-22, 427, 431-32, 434-35, 438; **113**:230, 255-59, 278
Specimens of the British Poets, with Biographical and Critical Notices, and an Essay on English Poetry (Campbell) **19**:171, 175, 200
Specimens of the Later English Poets (Southey) **97**:267
Specimens of the Table Talk of the Late Samuel Taylor Coleridge (Coleridge) **9**:157, 159; **29**:141, 147, 167, 169, 171, 187; **82**:88, 90, 115, 142, 144, 146; **197**:225, 235, 237; **231**:20-22, 25, 102, 104, 106, 122
Un spectacle dans un fauteuil (Musset) **7**:260, 267; **150**:300, 304, 311, 313, 319, 343, 347
Spectacle in an Armchair (Musset)
See *Un spectacle dans un fauteuil*
"Un Spectacle interrompu" (Mallarmé) **210**:206-7, 249, 254-55
"Le spectacle interrompu" (Mallarmé) **4**:371
"Spectacle rassurant" (Hugo) **3**:273
"The Spectacles" (Poe) **55**:147; **117**:322
"The Spectre around Me" (Blake) **13**:181, 232
"The Spectre Bridegroom" (Irving) **2**:382-83; **19**:327-29, 341, 344, 348
The Spectre Lover (Southworth) **26**:434
"The Spectre of Tappington" (Barham) **77**:4, 7, 10, 35, 41
"The Spectre of the Cattle Flat" (Harpur) **114**:141, 148-50
"The Spectre Pig" (Holmes) **14**:101, 121, 127-28
"The Spectre Ship" (Whittier) **8**:485
"Spectre Warriors" (Whittier) **8**:485
"Spectres" (Leconte de Lisle) **29**:224
Speculations on Metaphysics (Shelley) **93**:354-55
"Speculations on Morals" (Shelley) **93**:374; **143**:244
"Speculative Theism regarded as a Theory of the Universe" (Parker) **186**:127
"The Speculator" (Smith) **187**:319-20
"Speech at Chicago, Illinois" (Lincoln)
See "Speech in Reply to Douglas at Chicago, Illinois"
"Speech at Columbus, Ohio" (Lincoln) **201**:223
"Speech at Indianapolis, Indiana" (Lincoln) **201**:223
"Speech at Peoria" (Lincoln)
See "Peoria Speech"
"Speech Concerning Mythology" (Schlegel)
See "Die Rede über Mythologie und symbolische Anschaung"
"Speech Delivered at Kalamazoo, Michigan" (Lincoln) **201**:163, 206
Speech for Shakespeare's Anniversary (Goethe)
See *Rede zum Schäkespears Tag*
"Speech in Reply to Douglas at Chicago, Illinois" (Lincoln) **201**:165, 207
"Speech in Reply to Douglas at Springfield, Illinois" (Lincoln) **201**:165
"Speech of a Water Nymph" (Darwin)
See "Address of a Water Nymph"
Speech of Abraham Lincoln, of Illinois, Delivered at the Cooper Institute, Monday, Feb. 27, 1860 (Lincoln) **201**:156-57, 161-63, 166, 169, 207-8, 219-23, 225
Speech of Hon. Abraham Lincoln, before the Republican State Convention, June 16, 1858 (Lincoln) **201**:162-64, 166, 169, 187, 198, 200, 206-7, 219, 222-23, 225
"Speech on Government" (Macaulay) **231**:302
Speech on the Joint Resolution for Distributing Rations to the Distressed Fugitives from Indian Hostilities (Adams) **175**:74
Speeches and Writings (Lincoln)
See *Abraham Lincoln: His Speeches and Writings*
Speeches by Lord Macaulay with His "Minute on Indian Education" (Macaulay) **231**:324-28
The Speeches of Charles Dickens (Dickens) **206**:142
Speeches on Religion (Schleiermacher)
See *Über die Religion: Reden an die Gebildeten unter ihren Verächtern*
Speeches on Religion to Its Cultured Despisers (Schleiermacher)
See *Über die Religion: Reden an die Gebildeten unter ihren Verächtern*
"Speeches to the Basle Congress" (Bakunin) **58**:132
The Spell (Brontë) **33**:127
"Spell-Bound" (Morris) **4**:419
A Spelling Dictionary (Rowson) **69**:115; **182**:356
A Spelling-Book, with Appropriate Lessons in Reading and with a Stepping Stone to English Grammar (Cobbett) **49**:160
"The Spells of Home" (Hemans) **71**:264
"Spelt from Sibyl's Leaves" (Hopkins) **17**:198, 231, 238, 243, 246-48, 255-56; **189**:26, 28, 38, 41-42, 46, 48, 54, 91, 115, 120, 125-32
The Spendthrift (Ainsworth) **13**:41
The Spendthrift (Jerrold) **2**:402
The Spendthrift (Leskov)
See *Rastočitel*
The Spendthrift (Raimund)
See *Der Verschwender*
"Spenser" (Boker) **125**:35
"Speranza" (Ingelow) **39**:258
"Sperm" (Silva)
See "Zoospermos"
"The Spermaceti Papers" (Lippard) **198**:134, 143, 163-67, 173, 181, 189, 208
"The Sphere of Sense and Logic of Feeling" (Lewes) **215**:158
"The Sphinx" (Emerson) **1**:285, 289, 295-96; **38**:169, 187, 189; **98**:177-86
"The Sphinx" (Pavlova)
See "Sfinks"

"The Sphinx" (Poe) **16**:332
Le Sphinx (Feuillet) **45**:77, 79, 82, 87, 89
Le Sphinx rouge (Dumas) **71**:220
"Sphinx-Money" (Blind) **202**:54
"The Sphinx's Children" (Cooke) **110**:3, 18-19
The Sphinx's Children (Cooke)
See *The Sphinx's Children and Other People's*
The Sphinx's Children and Other People's (Cooke) **110**:19, 21, 26, 33-7, 39, 43
"A Spider Sewed at Night" (Dickinson) **21**:76
Der Spiegel des Cyprianus (Storm) **195**:14, 23-25, 32, 35, 42, 66, 72-73
"Das Spiegelbild" (Grillparzer) **102**:174
Der Spiegelritter (Kotzebue) **25**:146
"Spiel mannslied" (Keller) **2**:421
"Spielerglück" (Hoffmann) **2**:342
Spielmann (Grillparzer)
See *Der Arme Spielmann*
Spillner (Mörike) **201**:253, 255, 257, 288-89, 293, 299
"Der Spinnerin Lied" (Brentano) **1**:96, 102, 105; **191**:45-46, 48-49, 61
"Der Spinnerin Nachtlied" (Brentano)
See "Der Spinnerin Lied"
Spinning-Wheel Stories (Alcott) **58**:50-1
"Spinoza and the Bible" (Arnold) **29**:55
Spinoza: Ein historischer Roman (Auerbach) **171**:14, 22, 47-48, 54
Spinoza, the Life of a Thinker (Auerbach)
See *Spinoza: Ein historischer Roman*
"Spinoza's Life and Works" (Lewes) **215**:142-43
"Spinozianism" (Schleiermacher) **107**:328
"The Spinster's Sweet-Arts" (Tennyson) **202**:291
Spiridion (Sand) **2**:582, 585, 587, 598, 600; **42**:319-20, 372; **57**:315, 360, 375
Spirit (Coleridge)
See *Inquiring Spirit*
"A Spirit Haunts the Year's Last Hours" (Tennyson) **30**:211
"Spirit Independent of Matter" (Murray) **63**:207
Spirit of Christianity (Hegel) **151**:302-3, 305
Spirit of Discovery (Bowles) **103**:54-5
The Spirit of Hebrew Poetry (Herder)
See *Vom Geist der ebräischen Poesie*
Spirit of Peers and People: A National Tragi-Comedy (Horne) **127**:252-53, 256, 263
"The Spirit of Poetry" (Osgood) **141**:320
"The Spirit of the Age" (Kennedy) **2**:432
"The Spirit of the Age" (Mill) **11**:369
The Spirit of the Age (Hazlitt) **29**:148, 152, 164, 166-67, 170, 174, 188; **82**:102-03, 106, 108-09, 112-13, 123, 125, 127
The Spirit of the Age (Horne) **127**:236, 239-40, 245
Spirit of the Age (Martínez de la Rosa)
See *Espíritu del siglo*
"The Spirit of the Glen" (Hogg) **109**:203
"The Spirit of the Reeds" (Bird) **197**:6
The Spirit of the Reeds (Bird) **1**:87
"Spirit Whose Work Is Done" (Whitman) **4**:543; **81**:315
Spirite (Gautier) **1**:345, 352, 354-55; **59**:12-14, 33-6, 39, 42, 44, 71
"The Spirit's Blasted Tree" (Scott) **15**:255
"Spirits Everywhere" (Mangan) **27**:273
"Spirits of the Dead" (Poe) **117**:264, 280
"A Spirit's Return" (Hemans) **71**:303
"The Spirit's Trials" (Froude) **43**:192
Spiritual Creation (James) **53**:195, 204, 233
"Spiritual Diary" (Cowper) **94**:27, 30
"Spiritual Laws" (Emerson) **38**:149, 174, 224, 226-27; **98**:37, 107, 110-11
Spiritual Songs (Novalis)
See *Geistliche Lieder*
"Spiritual Torment" (Leskov)
See "Tomlenie Dukha"
"Spiritualism and Materialism" (Lewes) **25**:314; **215**:140-41
Der spiritus familiaris des Rosstäuschers (Droste-Hülshoff) **3**:196, 200-01
"The Spiteful Letter" (Tennyson) **202**:278, 280, 284
"Der Spitzwegsche Rahmen" (Gotthelf) **117**:55
"Le spleen" (Baudelaire)
See *Le spleen de Paris, petits poèmes en prose*
"Spleen" (Baudelaire)
See *Le spleen de Paris, petits poèmes en prose*
"Spleen" (Laforgue) **221**:73, 75, 78
"Spleen" (Verlaine) **51**:383
Le spleen de Paris (Baudelaire)
See *Le spleen de Paris, petits poèmes en prose*
Le spleen de Paris, petits poèmes en prose (Baudelaire) **6**:84, 86-87, 90, 103, 111; **29**:68, 75, 79, 83-84, 87, 103, 108, 110-12; **55**:13, 43, 46-52 61, 65, 70; **155**:21-23, 28-29, 39, 41, 45, 47, 56-57, 70, 72-74, 76-77, 79-81, 86, 89-91, 94-95, 104, 106-7, 110, 113-15
"Spleen et Idéal" (Baudelaire) **55**:15, 51, 56-66, 73; **155**:44, 113
"Spleen I" (Baudelaire) **55**:44, 64
"Spleen II" (Baudelaire) **55**:44
"Spleen IV" (Baudelaire) **55**:44-6
"Les Spleens exceptionnels" (Laforgue) **221**:86
Splendeurs et misères des courtisanes (Balzac) **5**:63, 75-76; **153**:9, 66, 69-75, 79, 82, 147, 149, 153, 158
"The Splendor Falls on Castle Walls" (Tennyson) **202**:179
"Splendor of Falling Day" (Whitman) **4**:544
Splendors and Miseries of a Courtesan (Balzac)
See *Splendeurs et misères des courtisanes*
"The Splenetic Indian" (Freneau) **111**:133
"Split the Lark—and you'll find the Music" (Dickinson) **171**:96, 143, 179-82
"The Spoken Thought Becomes a Lie" (Tyutchev)
See "Silentium"
"Sponsa Dei" (Patmore) **9**:339, 352, 354, 359, 361-62
Sponsalizio (Liszt) **199**:307
"Spontaneity or Instinct" (Emerson) **1**:293
"Spontaneous Me" (Whitman) **31**:372
Sporting and Social Recollections (Surtees) **14**:377
"Sporting Epistles from East Tennessee" (Harris) **165**:198
The Sportsman's Miscellany (Aksakov)
See *Rasskazy i vospominaniia okhotnika o raznykh okhotakh*
A Sportsman's Sketches (Turgenev)
See *Zapiski okhotnika*
A Sportsman's Stories and Memoirs on Various Kinds of Sport (Aksakov)
See *Rasskazy i vospominaniia okhotnika o raznykh okhotakh*
"Spot Resolutions" (Lincoln)
See "Resolutions to the United States House of Representatives, December 22, 1847"
"The Spotted Dog" (Trollope) **101**:235
The Spouter; or, the Triple Revenge. A Comic Farce in Two Acts. As it was Intended to be Perform'd. With the Original Prologue. Written by the author; and intended to be spoken by Mr. Garrick, dress'd in black (Murphy) **229**:241
"Spravedlivyj čelovek" (Leskov) **25**:228
"Sprich aus der Ferne" (Brentano) **1**:104
"Spring" (Baratynsky)
See "Vesna, vesna! kak vozdukh chist!..."
"Spring" (Barnes) **75**:34
"Spring" (Blake) **13**:182; **37**:3, 9, 13, 41, 61, 71-2, 74-6, 92
"The Spring" (Derzhavin)
See "Kliuch"
"Spring" (Hood) **16**:235
"Spring" (Hopkins) **17**:191, 220; **189**:5-7, 52-53, 81-82, 84, 107, 113, 135
"Spring" (Hunt) **1**:417
"Spring" (Lanier) **118**:259
"Spring" (Osgood) **141**:324
"Spring" (Rossetti) **2**:575; **186**:283
"Spring" (Thoreau) **7**:399, 404-5; **138**:95-6, 129, 186, 192
"Spring" (Timrod) **25**:364, 372, 376, 382-83, 386, 388
"Spring" (Tyutchev)
See "Vesna"
"Spring and Boils" (Shaw) **15**:335
"Spring and Fall" (Hopkins) **17**:236, 243-44, 246, 256; **189**:53, 82-83, 126
"Spring and Tyranny" (Lanier) **118**:217
"Spring Calm" (Tyutchev)
See "Vesennee uspokoenie"
"A Spring Chanson" (Smith) **59**:308, 321
Spring Freshets (Turgenev)
See *Veshnie vody*
"Spring in Town" (Bryant) **6**:161
"Spring is Come" (Allingham) **25**:9
"The Spring Is Here" (Willis) **194**:306
"Spring Longing" (Lazarus) **109**:292
"Spring on the River" (Lampman) **194**:59
"Spring Quiet" (Rossetti) **2**:574
"The Spring returns, the pewit screams" (Clare) **86**:90
"Spring Songs" (Clare) **9**:121
"Spring Songs" (Symonds) **34**:323
"Spring, spring! how pure the air!..." (Baratynsky)
See "Vesna, vesna! kak vozdukh chist!..."
"Spring Storm" (Tyutchev) **34**:288, 389, 401
"Spring Waters" (Tyutchev) **34**:389, 391
The Spring Wreath (Arnim)
See *Clemens Brentanos Frühlingskranz aus Jugendbriefen ihm geflochten, wie er selbst schriftlich verlangte*
"The Springs" (Hale) **75**:300
"Spring's Bedfellow" (Morris) **4**:434
The Springtime of Love (Schumann) **143**:139
"Springtime's Glances" (Lenau) **16**:276, 278
Spring-Torrents (Turgenev)
See *Veshnie vody*
"Sputnica feia" (Pavlova) **138**:16, 49
The Spy (Cooper) **203**:4, 6, 8, 46-48, 50, 74, 84-86, 88-89, 91-96
The Spy (Hogg) **109**:200, 203-04, 246, 258, 261-62
The Spy: A Tale of the Neutral Ground (Cooper) **1**:194-97, 200, 202, 207, 221-23; **27**:123-24, 137, 171; **54**:249, 251-2, 264-5, 273, 277, 280, 287, 299-300
"The Squabble of the Sea Nymphs; or, The Sacrifice of the Tuscararoes" (Warren) **13**:412, 414, 431; **226**:261, 264
The Squanders of Castle Squander (Carleton) **199**:10, 20, 56, 80, 83, 97, 100
The Squandors of Castle Squandor (Carleton) **3**:85-86, 89-90
The Square Table (Sigourney) **87**:325
"Squaudered Lives" (Taylor) **89**:309
"Le squelette laboureur" (Baudelaire) **29**:101, 103; **55**:12, 35; **155**:3, 7
The Squire (Krasicki)
See *Pan Podstoli*
Squire Arden (Oliphant) **61**:216
"The Squire in the poem" (Crabbe) **121**:65
"Squire Maurice" (Smith) **59**:321, 331, 333
"Squire Paine's Conversion" (Cooke) **110**:24, 33-4
"Squire Thomas; or, The Precipitate Choice" (Crabbe) **26**:93; **121**:40
"Squire Toby's Will" (Le Fanu) **9**:312
"The Squire's Story" (Gaskell) **70**:188
The Squire's Story (Barham) **77**:4
Srpska gramatika (Karadzic) **115**:83
Srpske narodne pjesme (Karadzic) **115**:77-80, 100, 112

Srpske narodne poslovice (Karadzic) **115**:78-9
Srpski rječnik (Karadzic) **115**:83
SS (Parton)
See *Shadows and Sunbeams*
St. Agnes (Keats)
See *The Eve of St. Agnes*
"St. Agnes Eve" (Tennyson) **115**:235; **202**:334
"St. Alban's Abbey" (Radcliffe) **6**:412; **55**:224
"St. Alexius" (Webster) **230**:231
"St. Andrew's Anniversary" (Brackenridge) **7**:56
"St. Augustine in April" (Lanier) **6**:232; **118**:212
St. Bartholomew's Eve (Newman) **99**:249
"St. Brandan" (Arnold) **6**:44, 66
St. Cecilia, or the Power of Music (Kleist)
See *Die heilige Cäcilie; oder, die Gewalt der Musik*
"St. Clair Flats" (Woolson) **82**:272, 285, 293, 333
St. Clair; or, The Heiress of Desmond (Morgan) **29**:389-90
"St. Coutt's" (Jones) **222**:169
St. Cupid (Jerrold) **2**:402-03
St. Domingo: Its Revolutions and Its Patriots (Brown) **2**:47-48, 52
"St. Edmond's Eve" (Shelley) **18**:342
"St. George's Hospital" (Landon) **15**:161
St. Giles and St. James (Jerrold) **2**:398-400, 402, 405
St. Irvyne; or, The Rosicrucian (Shelley) **18**:307, 341
St. Ives: Being the Adventures of a French Prisoner in England (Stevenson) **5**:419
"The St. James Phenomenon" (Hunt) **1**:423
St John in Patmos (Bowles) **103**:54-5, 61
"St. John's Eve" (Gogol)
See "Večer nakanune Ivana Kupala"
"St. John's Eve" (Jones) **222**:158
"The St. Lawrence" (Willis) **194**:282
St. Leon: A Tale of the Sixteenth Century (Godwin) **14**:37, 40, 42, 44-5, 47, 50, 52, 55-6, 58-60, 68-78, 80-3; **130**:29, 60, 151, 169
"St. Luke the Painter" (Rossetti) **77**:308
"St. Margaret's Eve" (Allingham) **25**:7
St. Martin's Eve (Wood) **178**:278, 288, 291, 320
"St. Martin's Summer" (Browning) **19**:88
"St. Mary of the Lowes" (Hogg) **109**:202
"St. Michael's Chapel" (Lazarus) **109**:297
St. Michael's Mount (Bowles) **103**:54, 60, 70
St. Patrick's Day; or, The Scheming Lieutenant (Sheridan) **91**:240-41
"St. Paul and Protestantism" (Arnold) **126**:109
St. Paul and Protestantism; with an Introduction on Puritanism and the Church of England (Arnold) **29**:8, 15-16, 20; **126**:63-64, 89-90
St. Paul and Protestantism, with an Essay on Puritanism and the Church of England (Arnold) **218**:111, 121, 178
"St. Paul's Characteristic Gift" (Newman) **38**:305
"St. Peter's Denial of Christ" (Baudelaire)
See "Le reniement de Saint-Pierre"
"St. Petersburg" (Mickiewicz) **3**:401
St. Ronan's Well (Scott) **15**:277, 289; **209**:216
"St. Simeon Stylites" (Tennyson) **30**:279, 281; **65**:270; **202**:299, 335
"St. Valentine's Day" (Patmore) **9**:343, 349, 357
St. Valentine's Day; or, The Fair Maid of Perth (Scott) **15**:270, 283, 300, 309, 313; **69**:313, 369; **209**:182, 184-85, 250
"St. Winefred's Well" (Hopkins) **17**:185, 190
Stadier paa Livets Vej (Kierkegaard) **34**:200-01, 222-223, 238, 261, 263; **78**:173, 178, 181, 227, 238; **125**:184-85, 190-92, 198, 201, 209, 248, 258-68
"Die Stadt" (Storm) **1**:547; **195**:61
Die Stadt Lucca (Heine) **147**:167-68
"The Staff and Scrip" (Rossetti) **4**:505, 518-19, 523, 527, 529-31; **77**:326, 328-30, 348
The Stag King (Gozzi)
See *Il re cervo*
"The Stage and the Spirit of Reverence" (Dodgson) **53**:122
"The Stage Coach" (Irving) **19**:328
"Stage Illusion" (Lamb) **10**:410, 432, 434
Stages on Life's Way (Kierkegaard)
See *Stadier paa Livets Vej*
"The Stag-Eyed Lady" (Hood) **16**:234-35
"Stagnant Waters" (Pisarev) **25**:338
"Stained Glass Rose" (Laforgue)
See "Rosace en vitrail"
Les stalactites (Banville) **9**:2, 14, 18-19, 26, 28-29
"Stalwart the Bushranger" (Harpur) **114**:136
"Stances" (Musset) **150**:232
"Stances à la Malibran" (Musset) **7**:261-62, 280
"Stand by the Flag" (Foster) **26**:288
"The Standard of Liberty" (Rowson) **182**:279
The Standard of Liberty (Brackenridge) **227**:105, 108, 110
"The Standards" (Patmore) **9**:334, 339-40, 359, 362
Ständchen in Ritornellen aus Albano (Muller) **73**:362
"Den standhaftige Tinsoldat" (Andersen) **7**:23, 28-9, 34, 37, 39; **79**:21, 23, 33, 40, 51, 58, 62-4, 70-1, 76, 82
"Stangers Yet" (Milnes) **61**:136, 141-2, 152
"Stansy" (Baratynsky) **103**:8-9
"Stantsionnyi smotritel" (Pushkin) **3**:435, 464; **83**:272, 323, 327-29, 337, 354-55
"Stanza" (Clare) **9**:111
"Stanzas" (Baratynsky)
See "Stansy"
"Stanzas" (Cranch) **115**:32, 35
"Stanzas" (Moore) **110**:177
"Stanzas" (Poe) **117**:264
"Stanzas from the Grande Chartreuse" (Arnold) **29**:4, 6-7, 28, 32-3, 38; **89**:46, 51-2, 88, 96-7; **218**:117, 122, 125, 160-62, 177, 187-88, 190, 276, 279
"Stanzas in Memory of Edward Quillinan" (Arnold) **29**:22, 37
"Stanzas in Memory of the Author of 'Obermann'" (Arnold) **29**:4, 6-7, 22-3, 31, 36, 38; **218**:117, 119, 126, 155, 177, 179, 183, 188-89
"Stanzas Meditated in the Cloisters of Christ's Hospital" (Dyer) **129**:96
"Stanzas Occasioned by certain absurd, extravagant, and even blasphemous panegyrics and encomiums on the character of the late gen. Washington" (Freneau) **111**:160
"Stanzas Occasioned by the Ruins of a Country Inn" (Freneau) **111**:145
Stanzas of Woe (Yearsley) **174**:298, 316-18, 335
"Stanzas on Coming of Age" (Hood) **16**:236
"Stanzas on Peele Castle" (Wordsworth) **12**:431, 436, 447, 469
"Stanzas on the Battle of Navarino" (Campbell) **19**:183
"Stanzas On the Decease of Thomas Paine" (Freneau) **111**:160
"Stanzas on the Fate of Henry Percy" (Brontë) **105**:55
"Stanzas on the Great Western Canal of the State of New York" (Freneau) **111**:102
"Stanzas on the Threatened Invasion" (Campbell) **19**:191
"Stanzas Subjoined to the Yearly Bill of Mortality of the Parish of All Saints, Northampton" (Cowper) **8**:119
"Stanzas to Cynthio" (Opie) **65**:160
"Stanzas To F S O" (Poe) **55**:212
"Stanzas to Malibran" (Musset)
See "Stances à la Malibran"
"Stanzas to the Memory of Gen. Washington" (Freneau) **111**:160
"Stanzas to the Memory of Richard Allen" (Reynolds) **146**:186
Stanzas to the Memory of the Late King (Hemans) **29**:192
"Stanzas to Tolstoi" (Pushkin) **83**:256
"Stanzas Written at the Island of Madeira" (Freneau) **111**:105
"Stanzas Written in Dejection" (Shelley)
See "Stanzas Written in Dejection-December 1818, Near Naples"
"Stanzas Written in Dejection-December 1818, Near Naples" (Shelley) **18**:344, 370-71, 373; **93**:308; **175**:273
Stanzas written on the Road between Florence and Pisa (Byron) **149**:54
"Stanzas written under Aeolus's Harp" (Opie) **65**:156
"Stanzas.—April, 1814" (Shelley) **93**:307
"Stapfen" (Meyer) **81**:199, 204-05, 209
"The Star and the Water-Lily" (Holmes) **14**:128
The Star Chamber (Ainsworth) **13**:45
"The Star Gazer" (Cranch) **115**:5, 40
"Star in the East" (Paine) **62**:325
"The Star of Cuba" (Heredia)
See "La estrella de Cuba"
The Star of Seville (Kemble) **18**:179-80
"The Star of Venus" (Heredia)
See "La estrella de Venus"
"Staratelno my nablyudaem svet..." (Baratynsky) **103**:9
"Starinnaia povest'—Roman i Ol'ga" (Bestuzhev) **131**:167, 175, 182-83
"The Starless King's Son" (Eminescu) **33**:264
"Starlight in the Odenwald" (Taylor) **89**:298
"The Starlight Night" (Hopkins) **17**:185, 191, 195, 216, 247; **189**:53, 106-7, 145
"Starosvetskie Pomeščiki" (Gogol) **5**:209, 218-19, 231, 245-47, 254-55; **162**:17, 54, 95, 99, 121
"The Stars Are with the Voyager" (Hood) **16**:222
"Starting from Paumanok" (Whitman) **4**:568-600, 603; **31**:389-90, 392-93, 398; **81**:246, 265, 319, 353; **205**:202, 204, 217, 224, 226, 239, 256, 260, 336-37
"Starukha" (Pavlova) **138**:12, 54
"Starye gody v sele Plodomasove" (Leskov) **174**:11, 13, 62, 120, 123
Starye gody v sele Plodomasove (Leskov) **25**:228, 232
"Starye portrety" (Turgenev) **21**:453-54; **122**:246
"State and Religion" (Wagner) **9**:414
The State in Its Relations with the Church (Gladstone) **213**:116, 118, 120
"The State of German Literature" (Carlyle) **70**:39, 63, 94
State Papers vol.13, Children's Employment (Horne) **127**:266
"The Stately Homes of England" (Hemans) **71**:283, 305
"States" (Laforgue)
See "Etats"
"Statesman and Thinker" (Krylov) **1**:439
The Statesman's Manual; or, The Bible the Best Guide to Political Skill and Foresight: A Lay Sermon (Coleridge) **9**:135; **197**:240, 266; **177**:76; **231**:51, 83, 86, 101, 121-22
"The Statesman's Secret" (Holmes) **14**:128
The Statesmen of the Commonwealth of England: With a Treatise on the Popular Progress in English History (Forster) **11**:115
"The Stationmaster" (Pushkin)
See "Stantsionnyi smotritel"
Statism and Anarchism (Bakunin) **25**:47, 49; **58**:144, 146
"La Statue amoureuse" (Gautier) **59**:35, 38-40
"The Statue and the Bust" (Browning) **19**:79, 114, 127, 129, 131

The Statue Guest (Pushkin)
See *Kamennyi gost'*
Statute Establishing Religious Freedom in Virginia (Jefferson) **103**:123, 221, 223
Statute of Virginia for Religious Freedom (Jefferson)
See *Statute Establishing Religious Freedom in Virginia*
"Stay, Summer Breath" (Foster) **26**:287
The Steadfast: Story of A Saint and A Sinner (Cooke) **110**:21, 24, 39, 50, 56, 58, 66
"The Steadfast Tin Soldier" (Andersen)
See "Den standhaftige Tinsoldat"
"The Stealing Magpie" (Herzen) **10**:334, 350; **61**:108
"The Stealthy School of Criticism" (Rossetti) **77**:341-42
The Steam boat (Galt) **1**:333, 335; **110**:84-6, 114
"The Steamboat" (Baratynsky)
See "Piroskaf"
"The Steamer" (Baratynsky)
See "Piroskaf"
"La steaua" (Eminescu) **33**:251
Der Stechlin (Fontane) **26**:234, 241, 243-45, 248, 256-57, 261, 269-71, 275, 278; **163**:162, 168-69, 196-98, 200, 203, 220, 248, 286
"The Steed and Its Rider" (Krylov) **1**:435
"The Steed and the Rider" (Jones) **222**:169
"Steele and Addison" (Landor) **14**:165
Steht Homer z. Ex. unterm Spruch des Aristoteles & Compagnie? (Claudius) **75**:196
Stein und Rose (Storm)
See *Hinzelmeier*
"Das Steinerne Herz" (Hoffmann) **183**:194-95
"Stella" (Mowatt) **74**:219, 234-35
"Stella" (Nin) **7**:23, 29
Stella (Goethe) **4**:164, 174, 219-20; **34**:71-2
"Stella Maris" (Symonds) **34**:323, 338-39, 350-51
Stello: A Session with Doctor Noir (Vigny)
See *Les consultations du Docteur Noir: Stello; ou, les diables bleus, première consultation*
Stello, ou les Diables bleus (Vigny)
See *Les consultations du Docteur Noir: Stello; ou, les diables bleus, première consultation*
Stendhal: Romans (Stendhal) **178**:214, 224-25
Sténie (Balzac) **5**:88
Stenka Razine (Mérimée) **65**:85
Stephen Calvert (Brown)
See *Memoirs of Stephen Calvert*
Stephen, M. D. (Warner) **146**:261
Stephen of Leon, A Tale of Peru (Bird)
See *Fedalla, A Tale of Peru*
Stephen the Great (Eminescu) **131**:292
Stephen the Younger (Eminescu) **33**:264-65
"The Step-Mother" (Parton) **86**:349
"Stepnoj korol' Lir" (Turgenev)
See "Son"
"Stepnoy Korol 'Lir" (Turgenev) **21**:401, 408, 414, 416-17, 420, 422, 427, 435, 440-41; **122**:264, 266, 268
"The Steppes of Akkerman" (Mickiewicz)
See "Stepy Akermańskie"
"Stepy Akermańskie" (Mickiewicz) **3**:404
"Die sterbende Meduse" (Meyer) **81**:207
"Stérilités" (Laforgue) **221**:92
"Stern Disappointment" (Moodie) **113**:348
"Die Sternbilder des Tierkreises" (Schlegel) **142**:324
Sterne's Maria (Dunlap) **2**:213
"The Stethoscope Song" (Holmes) **81**:107
"The Steward" (Turgenev) **21**:377
"Steyermark" (Taylor) **89**:298
Stick to Your Own Station (Ostrovsky)
See *Ne v svoi sani ne sadis!*
"Stikhi na rozhdenie v Severe porfirorodnago otroka" (Derzhavin) **215**:12-15, 22-23, 33, 52
Stikhotvoreniia (Pavlova) **138**:34
Stikhotvoreniia Poèmy Proza Pis'ma (Baratynsky) **103**:47
Stikhotvoreniya v proze (Turgenev) **21**:414, 420, 431, 441, 452-55; **37**:443; **122**:243, 280, 283, 289, 293, 306-8, 312
"Still and bright, in twilight shining" (Brontë) **109**:28, 36
"The Still Small Voice" (Ridge) **82**:181
"The Still Small Voice" (Very) **9**:387
"Stillborn" (Baratynsky)
See "Nedonosok"
"The Still-Born" (Very) **9**:378
Stille Liebe (Hauff) **185**:321
Ein Stiller Musikant (Storm) **1**:540; **195**:18, 53, 57
"A still-Volcano-Life" (Dickinson) **77**:145-46
Stilpo und seine Kinder (Klinger) **1**:429
"Stimme des Kindes" (Lenau) **16**:281
"Stimme des Volks" (Hölderlin) **16**:191; **187**:187, 215
Stimmen der Völker in Liedern (Herder)
See *Volkslieder*
"Stimmung" (Meyer) **81**:152
Stine (Fontane) **26**:235-36, 240, 244, 248, 251-53, 258-59, 270-71; **163**:216
"The Stinger" (Leskov)
See "Jazvitel' nyj"
"The Stirrup-Cup" (Lanier) **6**:236, 249, 254; **118**:238, 273, 275
Stockholm, Fountainebleau, et Rome (Dumas)
See *Christine; ou, Stockholm, Fountainebleau, et Rome*
"Stoic and Hedonist" (Lampman) **25**:165, 190, 219
"Stojit' v seli Subotovi" (Shevchenko) **54**:382
The Stolen Child (Galt) **1**:334
"A Stolen Letter" (Collins) **1**:187
"Stolen Waters" (Dodgson) **139**:30, 126-27
"The Stolen White Girl" (Ridge) **82**:175, 180
The Stone Guest (Pushkin)
See *Kamennyi gost'*
"Stone of Night" (Blake) **37**:80
"Stonehenge" (Radcliffe) **6**:412
"The Stone-Pit" (Clare) **9**:117
Stones of Many Colors (Stifter)
See *Bunte Steine*
"Stopal'scik" (Leskov) **174**:37
"Stoppenaalen" (Andersen) **79**:23, 34, 69, 89; **214**:59-60
The Store Boy (Alger) **83**:112
"Den Store Søslange" (Andersen) **214**:61-62
Storia compendiosa della vita di Lorenzo da Ponte (Da Ponte) **50**:97
"Storia del genere umano" (Leopardi) **129**:243, 265, 297
Stories (Andersen)
See *Eventyr, fortalte for bøorn*
Stories for Persons of the Middle Rank (More) **141**:191
Stories from Carleton (Carleton)
See *Tales from Carleton*
Stories from the Italian Poets, with Lives of the Writers (Hunt) **1**:413
"Stories of Authority" (Multatuli) **165**:336
Stories of Ensign Stål (Runeberg)
See *Fänrik Ståls sägner*
Stories of the Canadian Forest (Traill)
See *Lady Mary and Her Nurse; or, A Peep into the Canadian Forest*
Stories of the Old Dominion (Cooke) **5**:125, 127, 131
Stories of the Orphan Petrush (Shevchenko)
See *Povisty o besrodnom Petrush*
Stories of the Seen and the Unseen (Oliphant) **221**:244
Stories of the Study (Galt) **1**:334; **110**:114
Stories to a Child (Ingelow)
See *Stories Told to a Child*
Stories Told for Children (Andersen)
See *Eventyr, fortalte for bøorn*
Stories Told to a Child (Ingelow) **39**:264; **107**:119, 161, 163-64
"The Storks" (Andersen) **7**:29; **79**:23
"The Storm" (Baratynsky)
See "Burya"
"Storm" (Lampman) **25**:193, 207, 220; **194**:24, 31
"The Storm" (Mickiewicz)
See "Burza"
The Storm (Ostrovsky)
See *Groza*
"The Storm" (Webster) **230**:311
Storm als Erzieher (Storm) **195**:20
"Storm in the Fens" (Clare) **86**:110
"A Storm in the Mountains" (Harpur) **114**:96, 98, 105, 120-21, 125, 144, 158, 161-62, 164
"Storm of Thunder among Mountains" (Hogg) **109**:202, 206
"Storm on Lake Asquam" (Whittier) **8**:520
"The Storm Rages Ever More Violently" (Tyutchev)
See "Vse bešennej burja"
"Storm Song" (Taylor) **89**:300
"Storm Voices" (Lampman) **194**:29
Storm-beat Maid (Baillie) **71**:53-4,
Storming the Bastille (Dumas)
See *Ange Pitou*
"The Stormy Morning" (Muller)
See "Der stürmische Morgen"
"A Story" (Pavlova)
See "Razskaz"
"Story for a Child" (Lermontov) **5**:288
"A Story from the Dunes" (Andersen)
See "En Historie fra Klitterne"
"The Story of a Civil Servant Who Stole Overcoats" (Gogol)
See "Shinel"
The Story of a Famous Old Jewish Firm (Thomson) **18**:426
"Story of a Feather" (Jerrold) **2**:395-96, 399, 401-02, 404
"The Story of a Lie" (Stevenson) **193**:221, 279, 281-82
"The Story of a Mother" (Andersen)
See "Hisbrien om en Moder"
The Story of a Puppet (Collodi)
See *Le Avventure di Pinocchio*
"The Story of a Russian Officer in Captivity among the Mountaineers" (Bestuzhev)
See "Rasskaz ofitsera, byvshego v plenu u gorcev"
"The Story of a Shipwreck" (Gordon)
See "From the Wreck"
The Story of a Town (Saltykov)
See *Istoriya odnogo goroda*
"A Story of a Wedding Tour" (Oliphant) **61**:205, 210-11
"The Story of an Affinity" (Lampman) **25**:199, 201, 219-20; **194**:18, 20-22, 27, 31-32, 42
The Story of an Affinity (Lampman) **194**:105-7, 109, 111-12
"The Story of an Outcast" (Boyesen) **135**:11, 20-21, 25
Story of Belkis and Solomon (Nerval) **1**:475
"A Story of Doom" (Ingelow) **39**:256, 262, 265
A Story of Doom and Other Poems (Ingelow) **39**:257, 264, 266; **107**:118, 124, 147, 149, 155-57, 159
"The Story of Father Alexis" (Turgenev)
See "Rasskaz ottsa Aleksaya"
A Story of Franics Villon (Stevenson)
See *A Lodging for the Night: A Story of Francis Villon*
"The Story of Gamber-Ali" (Gobineau)
See "Histoire de Gambèr-Aly"
"The Story of Glaucus the Thessalian" (Hayne) **94**:144, 153-54, 156-59
The Story of Goethe's Life (Lewes)
See *The Life and Works of Goethe*
The Story of Hester Wilmot (More) **141**:169

"The Story of Honest Casper and Fair Annie" (Brentano)
See "Geschichte vom braven Kasperl und dem schönen Annerl"
"The Story of How Ivan Ivanovich Quarreled with Ivan Nikiforovich" (Gogol)
See "The Tale of How Ivan Ivanovich Quarrelled with Ivan Nikiforovich"
The Story of Juliette; or, Vice Amply Rewarded (Sade)
See *Juliette; ou, Les prospérités du vice*
"The Story of Julius" (Brown) **74**:140
The Story of Kennett (Taylor) **89**:311, 343, 346-50
"The Story of Lieutenant Ergunov" (Turgenev)
See "Istoriya leytenanta Ergunova"
"The Story of Margaret" (Wordsworth)
See "The Ruined Cottage"
Story of Margaretta (Murray) **63**:174, 176-78, 190, 209-14
The Story of My Heart (Jefferies) **47**:94-6, 101, 105, 111, 115, 119, 121, 123-25, 129, 132-34, 136-38, 143
The Story of My Life (Andersen)
See *Mit Livs Eventyr*
The Story of My Life (Sand)
See *Histoire de ma vie*
"The Story of Noble Kasperl and Pretty Annerl" (Brentano)
See "Geschichte vom braven Kasperl und dem schönen Annerl"
The Story of Norway (Boyesen) **135**:8
"A Story of Pennsylvania" (Taylor) **89**:359
The Story of Pretty Lau (Mörike)
See *Historie von der schönen Lau*
"The Story of Prince Alasi and the Princess Firouzkah" (Beckford) **214**:104
"A Story of Psyche" (Griffin) **7**:214
"The Story of Rhodope" (Morris) **4**:417, 447
"The Story of Rimini" (Hunt) **1**:410-12, 414, 421
The Story of Rimini (Hunt) **70**:250, 253, 263, 267, 282
The Story of Sigurd the Volsung, and the Fall of the Niblungs (Morris) **4**:417-18, 420-21, 428, 430-33, 435, 443
"Story of the Bandbox" (Stevenson) **193**:252-53, 256, 280
"Story of the Fallen Master" (Werner) **189**:317
"The Story of the Forest" (Eminescu) **131**:296
"The Story of the Four Little Children Who Went Round the World" (Lear) **3**:297
"The Story of the Glittering Plain, Which Has Been Also Called the Land of Living Men or the Acre of the Undying" (Morris) **4**:425, 436-37, 440
"Story of the House with the Green Blinds" (Stevenson) **193**:252, 254-55, 279
"Story of the Island of Cuba" (Bryant) **6**:181
"The Story of the Just Caspar and Fair Annie" (Brentano)
See "Geschichte vom braven Kasperl und dem schönen Annerl"
"The Story of the Just Casper and Fair Annie" (Brentano)
See "Geschichte vom braven Kasperl und dem schönen Annerl"
"Story of the Lost Reflection" (Hoffmann)
See "Das Verlorene Spiegelbild"
"Story of the Physician and the Saratoga Trunk" (Stevenson) **5**:394; **193**:252, 294, 316
"The Story of the Seven Families from the Lake Pipple-Popple" (Lear) **3**:307
"The Story of the Star-Travelling Magus" (Eminescu)
See "The Tale of the Magus Travelling in the Stars"
"The Story of the Three Bears" (Southey) **8**:470, 475; **97**:271, 289-90, 292, 323-29
"The Story of the Two Ivans" (Gogol)
See "The Tale of How Ivan Ivanovich Quarrelled with Ivan Nikiforovich"
"The Story of the Unknown Church" (Morris) **4**:429
"The Story of the Wind" (Andersen) **214**:55-56
"The Story of the Young Italian" (Irving) **2**:370, 382, 390; **19**:332
"Story of the Young Man in Holy Orders" (Stevenson) **193**:251
"Story of the Young Man with the Cream Tarts" (Stevenson) **5**:394, 413; **193**:251-53
"The Story of the Young Robber" (Irving) **2**:390; **19**:344
"The Story of Toby" (Melville) **45**:204
"Story of Two Highlanders'" (Hogg) **109**:248
The Story of Venus and Tannhäuser (Beardsley) **6**:137-38, 144-47, 149-50, 152-54
"The Story Teller" (Hawthorne) **79**:320
"The Story Teller at Fault" (Griffin) **7**:198
The Story Without a Name (Barbey d'Aurevilly)
See *Une histoire sans nom*
"A Story without a Tail" (Maginn) **8**:438-39
"The Stout Gentleman" (Irving) **2**:389; **95**:227
The Stout Gentleman (Irving) **95**:226
Strafford (Browning) **19**:75, 78, 102; **79**:146, 189
"Die Sträflinge" (Auerbach) **171**:8, 67
"The strains we hear in foreign lands" (Moodie) **113**:344
The Strait Gate and the Broad Way (More) **141**:175
Strandbakken ved Egeløkke (Grundtvig) **158**:138
The Strange Case of Dr. Jekyll and Mr. Hyde (Stevenson) **5**:398, 400, 402-05, 408, 413, 415, 418, 421, 427, 429, 433-37; **14**:311-40; **63**:261, 269; **193**:204, 208-10, 212, 216, 218-19, 222, 225-26, 238, 249-50, 259, 263, 265-67, 269-71, 274, 283, 287, 304, 310, 313, 353, 357, 360-64, 366-68
"The Strange Child" (Kuhatschek)
See "Das Fremde Kind"
"Strange Disturbances on Aungier Street" (Le Fanu)
See "Some Strange Disturbances in an Old House on Augier Street"
"A Strange Event in the Life of Schalken the Painter" (Le Fanu) **9**:312, 314, 318-20, 322
"Strange Fits of Passion Have I Known" (Wordsworth) **12**:445, 464; **111**:226, 323-24, 327-28
The Strange Gentleman (Dickens) **37**:153
A Strange History (Lewes) **25**:291
"The Strange Lady" (Bryant) **6**:186; **46**:4
A Strange Manuscript Found in a Copper Cylinder (De Mille) **123**:107 , 108-19, 123-24, 126, 128-34, 138-42, 144, 146-49, 151, 153, 158, 160
"A Strange Story" (Turgenev)
See "Strannaya istoriya"
A Strange Story (Bulwer-Lytton) **1**:150-51; **45**:22-3, 47
The Strange Story of Dr. Jekyll and Mr. Hyde (Stevenson)
See *The Strange Case of Dr. Jekyll and Mr. Hyde*
"The Strange Story of Korah, Dathan, and Abiram, Numbers, Chap. XVI, Accounted For" (Paine) **62**:325
"Strange Tales" (Gaskell) **214**:333
"Strange to Say, on Club Paper" (Thackeray) **213**:305
"The strange year when Copenhagen got gas lights" (Andersen)
See "Gudfaders Billedbog"
"The Stranger" (Baudelaire)
See "L'étranger"
"The Stranger" (Lewis) **11**:302
The Stranger (Bird) **1**:90
The Stranger (Kotzebue)
See *Menschenhass und Reue*
Stranger (Sheridan) **5**:362
"The Stranger: Being a Further Portion of the Recluse, A Poem" (Hogg) **4**:282; **109**:192, 247
"The Stranger in Louisiana" (Hemans) **71**:264
"A Stranger Minstrel" (Robinson) **142**:115
"The Stranger's Vision" (Brady) **41**:312-13
"Strannaya istoriya" (Turgenev) **21**:399, 408, 416, 435, 441, 453; **122**:242, 365, 369, 371, 378
"Strannik" (Pavlova) **138**:14
"Strannost" (Karamzin) **173**:285
"Strashnaia mest" (Gogol)
See "Strašnaja mest"
"Strashnoe gadanie: Rasskaz" (Bestuzhev) **131**:149, 156, 158-59, 210, 212-13
"Strašnaja mest" (Gogol) **5**:218, 223-25, 230-31, 249, 251, 256-57; **31**:76, 120; **162**:27, 92-95, 98-99, 111-13, 117, 123, 125
"Strast' sprosit" (Bestuzhev) **131**:165
"Stratford-on-Avon" (Irving) **2**:381; **19**:327, 347; **95**:265-67
"Stratton Water" (Rossetti) **4**:506, 518, 523; **77**:326, 337-38
"Straw in the Streets" (Levy) **203**:343
"Stray Echoes from the Elder Sons of Song" (Kendall) **12**:197
"Stray Walks" (Clare) **86**:142
"The Strayed Reveller" (Arnold) **6**:44, 51, 70-71, 74; **29**:25-6, 29, 35; **89**:91; **126**:111; **218**:112
The Strayed Reveller, and Other Poems (Arnold) **6**:28, 30-31, 70; **29**:34; **89**:88; **218**:184
"The Stream of Life" (Bryant) **46**:7
"The Stream's Secret" (Rossetti) **4**:492, 495, 501, 505, 510, 513, 518, 520, 525-27; **77**:308, 338, 357-58, 361
"The Street" (Kendall) **12**:183
"The Street of the Hyacinth" (Woolson) **82**:275, 293, 296-97, 308
"Streets" (Verlaine) **51**:374
The Streets of London (Boucicault) **41**:32
Streets of the World (Sala) **46**:246
"The Street-Singer" (Allingham) **25**:6
Der Streit über das Judenthum in der Musik (Freytag) **109**:180
Stretton (Kingsley) **107**:188-89, 192-93, 197, 209, 212, 227-28
"The Stricken South to the North" (Hayne) **94**:144
"The Strictness of the Law of Christ" (Newman) **38**:305
"Strictures for Pictures" (Thackeray) **213**:329
Strictures on the Modern System of Female Education (More) **141**:209-12, 220-21, 223, 233, 271-73, 281, 303, 307-9
Strictures on the Modern System of Female Education, with a View of the Principles and Conduct Prevalent among Women of Rank and Fortune (More) **27**:333, 339, 341, 350, 353, 355
"Strife and Peace" (Ingelow) **39**:263
Strife and Peace; or, Scenes in Norway (Bremer) **11**:17, 19, 22, 24
String Quartet in A Major, op. 18 (Beethoven) **227**:34
String Quartet in A Minor, op. 132 (Beethoven) **227**:34
String Quartet in B-flat Major, op. 130 (Beethoven) **227**:34
String Quartet in F Minor, op. 95 (Beethoven) **227**:23
"The String that tied my Lady's Shoe" (Willis) **194**:301
"The String Token" (Barnes) **75**:36
"The Striped Snaik" (Shaw) **15**:335
The Stripling (Baillie) **2**:40-41; **71**:7
Striving for Fortune (Alger) **8**:30

"The Stroll to Grasmere" (Wilson) **5**:561
Strong and Steady; or, Paddle Your Own Canoe (Alger) **8**:43, 46; **83**:104, 107, 145
Strong as Death (Maupassant)
See *Fort comme la mort*
"Stronger Lessons" (Whitman) **31**:434
"Stronger than a Man" (Hugo) **161**:222
"Struck, Was I, Nor Yet by Lightning" (Dickinson) **21**:54
"The Struggle for Existence in Human Society" (Huxley) **67**:28, 97-8, 105, 109
"The Struggle for Kansas" (Hughes) **207**:125-29
"Struggle for Life" (Daudet) **1**:238
"The Struggle for Life" (Pisarev)
See "Bor'ba za žizn"
"The Struggle for Parliamentary Reform" (Beddoes) **154**:74
"Struggle for Survival" (Pisarev)
See "Bor'ba za suščestvovanie"
The Struggles of Brown, Jones, and Robinson (Trollope) **6**:460, 514
"The Struggles of Conscience" (Crabbe) **26**:93; **121**:40
Struggling Upward, and Other Works (Alger) **8**:20-21, 31, 36; **83**:94
Stuart of Dunleath (Norton) **47**:247-49, 255, 257-58
Stuart of Dunleath: A Story of Modern Times (Norton) **205**:59, 67-68, 71-72, 82-83, 85-87
"Stučit!" (Turgenev)
See "Stuk...stuk...stuk"
The Student (Freytag)
See *Die Gelehrte*
"The Student of Salamanca" (Irving) **2**:368, 387, 389-90
"The Student of the Dead Languages" (Freneau) **1**:317
"Studentenfahrt" (Eichendorff) **225**:6-7
"A Student's Diary" (Brown) **74**:35
Studien (Hauff) **185**:319-21, 323-24
Studien (Novalis)
See *Fichte-Studien*
Studien (Stifter) **41**:359-60, 366-69, 375-77, 384, 391; **198**:258-60, 275, 298
Studien und Anmerkungen zu Lessings Nathan der Weise (Auerbach) **171**:38, 55, 57
"Studierzimmer II" (Goethe) **154**:326
Studies (Ludwig) **4**:348-49
Studies (Stifter)
See *Studien*
"Studies by the Sea" (Smith) **115**:119
Studies for Stories (Ingelow) **39**:259, 264; **107**:119
"Studies for Two Heads" (Lowell) **2**:507; **90**:220
Studies from Life (Craik) **38**:119
Studies in Animal Life (Lewes) **25**:288, 296-97, 310-11; **215**:86, 122
Studies in German Literature (Taylor) **89**:340
Studies in Religious History (Renan)
See *Etudes d'histoire religieuse*
Studies in the History of the Renaissance (Pater)
See *The Renaissance: Studies in Art and Poetry*
Studies of Plant Life in Canada; or, Gleanings from Forest, Lake and Plain (Traill) **31**:316-17, 328
"Studies of Roman History" (Mérimée) **6**:352
Studies of the Greek Poets (Symonds) **34**:332-33, 337, 351, 356, 366, 371
Studies on Homer and the Homeric Age (Gladstone) **213**:116, 125-28, 135-41
"Studies on the Situation" (Eminescu) **33**:273; **131**:328
"Studium-Aufsatz" (Schlegel)
See "Über das Studium der griechischen Poesie"
"Study of Hands: Hands of an Empress and of an Assassin Contrasted" (Gautier) **1**:342
"The Study of Poetry" (Arnold) **6**:55, 57-58, 69, 72; **29**:42-3, 45-6, 59; **89**:32, 38, 85-6, 89, 100, 112; **126**:114-15; **218**:141, 143, 201, 205
"A Study of Provincial Life" (Eliot)
See *Middlemarch: A Study of Provincial Life*
The Study of Psychology (Lewes) **215**:88, 96
"Stuk...stuk...stuk" (Turgenev) **21**:401, 416, 420, 441; **122**:243-44, 264, 364
"Eine Stunde ein Jude" (Auerbach) **171**:75, 78
"Die Stunden der Weihe" (Klopstock) **11**:234; **225**:282, 327
"Ein Stündlein wohl vor Tag" (Mörike) **201**:252-53, 294, 303-4
"Les stupra" (Rimbaud) **35**:291, 296
Sturm und Drang (Klinger) **1**:429-31
"Der stürmische Morgen" (Muller) **73**:384, 392
"Stutgard" (Hölderlin) **16**:161, 163
The Stuttgart Brownie (Mörike)
See *Das Stuttgarter Hutzelmännlein*
"Das Stuttgarter Hutzel männlein" (Mörike) **10**:447, 456-57
Das Stuttgarter Hutzelmännlein (Mörike) **201**:252-53
"The Stwonen Porch" (Barnes) **75**:103
"Stygmat" (Norwid) **17**:370-71, 379, 381
"Style" (De Quincey) **4**:61
"Style" (Lampman) **25**:213
"Style" (Pater) **7**:299, 308, 324-25, 328, 339; **90**:241, 251, 323; **159**:233, 239-40
"Style" (Stevenson) **193**:214
"Le Style épistolaire" (Maupassant) **83**:228
"Sub Rosa-Crux" (Fuller) **50**:245, 249
"Sub tegmine fagi" (Castro Alves) **205**:4
"The Subjection of Women" (Neal) **161**:336
The Subjection of Women (Mill) **11**:349, 356, 360, 366, 375, 388-89, 392-93; **58**:360, 379; **179**:201, 318-20, 323-24, 333
Subjective Logic (Hegel)
See *Wissenschaft der Logik*
"Subjugation of Switzerland" (Wordsworth) **12**:431
"Sublime Was the Warning" (Moore) **110**:182
"Sublimity of Composition" (Beattie)
See *Dissertations Moral and Critical: On Memory and Imagination; On Dreaming; The Theory of Language; On Fable and Romance; On the Attachments of Kindred; Illustrations on Sublimity*
Suborneur (Sade) **47**:361
"Substance and Shadow" (Newman) **38**:344-45
Substance and Shadow; or, Morality and Religion in Their Relation to Life: An Essay upon the Physics of Creation (James) **53**:199-200, 204, 217, 228-30, 236
"The Substance of a Diary of Sickness" (Willis) **194**:298
"The Suburbs of the Capital" (Mickiewicz) **3**:401
"Success" (Dickinson) **171**:87
Success (Alcott) **58**:37
"Success in Fiction" (Oliphant) **61**:221
Success in Literature (Lewes)
See *The Principles of Success in Literature*
"Success Is Counted Sweetest" (Dickinson) **21**:73
Success, or a Hit If You Like It (Planché) **42**:290
"The Succession of Forest Trees" (Thoreau) **7**:411; **207**:199
"Successors of Pan" (Lampman)
See "Favourites of Pan"
"Le succube" (Balzac) **5**:78
Such Stuff as Dreams are made on (FitzGerald) **153**:186
Such Things Are (Inchbald) **62**:142-3, 145-9, 147, 149, 184-5
"Sudden Life" (Rossetti) **4**:516
"Sueño de gloria: Apoteosis de Gustavo Moreau" (Casal) **131**:219, 224, 228-29, 236, 244, 266, 268-69
"Sueta suet" (Baratynsky)
See "Vanitas Vanitatum"
The Suffering of Young Werther (Goethe)
See *Die Leiden des jungen Werthers*
"A Suffolk Ballad" (Bloomfield) **145**:177
"The Sugar-Plum Tree" (Field) **3**:206
"Suggested By Matthew Arnold's 'Stanzas from the Grande Chartreuse'" (Thomson) **18**:406, 414, 424
Suggestions for Establishing an English Art Theatre (Planché) **42**:276
"Suggestions on Arithmetic" (Parton) **86**:375
Suggestions Respecting Improvements in Education (Beecher) **30**:2, 14, 23
"The Suicide" (Adams) **175**:29
The Suicide Club (Stevenson) **5**:393-94, 403, 408, 417; **193**:204, 212, 219, 250-52, 256-57, 294-95, 298-99, 313, 315-16
Le suicide; ou, Le vieux sergent (Pixérécourt) **39**:287
"Suil Dhuv the Coiner" (Griffin) **7**:197, 201, 207, 212, 217
"Suis-je" (Laforgue) **221**:74, 83-85
A Suitable Match (Fontane)
See *Irrungen, Wirrungen*
A Suitable Place (Ostrovsky)
See *Dokhodnoye mesto*
The Suitors (Gogol) **162**:18
"The Suliote Mother" (Hemans) **71**:295
"Sullen Clouds Have Disappeared from the Fair Sky" (Mickiewicz) **3**:398
Sultan Wampum, oder Die Wünsche (Kotzebue) **25**:147
"Sultry Day" (Meyer)
See "Schwüle"
"The Sumac Gatherers" (Cooke) **5**:133
Sumerki (Baratynsky) **103**:12, 16, 26, 28, 46
"Summa" (Hopkins) **189**:113
A Summary View of the Rights of British America (Jefferson) **11**:166, 173, 179, 192, 199; **103**:144, 210-11
"Summer" (Bloomfield) **145**:152
"Summer" (Bryant) **46**:9
"Summer" (Clare) **9**:119; **86**:97
"The Summer Bower" (Timrod) **25**:364, 367, 372
"Summer by the Lakeside" (Whittier) **8**:519-20
"The Summer Camp" (Taylor) **89**:300-01
"A Summer Day" (Baillie) **151**:41, 86, 88-89, 93-94
"Summer Days or, the Young Wife's Affliction" (Parton) **86**:346
"Summer Evening" (Clare) **86**:131
"A Summer Evening" (Lampman) **25**:183, 211
"Summer Evening" (Tyutchev)
See "Letnij vecer"
"A Summer Evening Churchyard" (Shelley) **93**:307, 326
"A Summer Evening's Dream" (Bellamy) **4**:31; **86**:75
"A Summer Idyl" (O'Brien) **21**:246
"Summer Images" (Clare) **9**:80, 86, 96, 105, 117, 119
Summer in London (Fontane) **26**:233
A Summer in Skye (Smith) **59**:295, 299, 303, 311-2, 314, 316, 319, 321-3, 333-4, 337, 340
A Summer in the Sahara (Fromentin)
See *Un été dans le Sahara*
"Summer Longings" (Foster) **26**:289, 295
"A Summer Mood" (Hayne) **94**:144, 159, 161
"Summer Morning" (Clare) **9**:72, 74, 119; **86**:130
"A Summer Night" (Arnold) **6**:72; **29**:25-6, 31, 34, 36; **89**:98
"A Summer Night" (Kivi)
See "Kesäyö"
"Summer Night" (Klopstock)
See "Die Sommernacht"
A Summer Night (Krasiński) **4**:306
"Summer Night. Variations of Certain Melodies" (Taylor) **89**:318-19

Summer on the Lakes, in 1843 (Fuller) **5**:154-55, 157-58, 163-64, 168, 170; **50**:235-8, 241-4, 217-8; **211**:91-92, 113, 123, 127, 129, 183, 188, 201-3
"A Summer Pilgrimage" (Whittier) **59**:366
"A Summer Ramble" (Bryant) **6**:187; **46**:2
Summer Rambles (Jameson)
See *Winter Studies and Summer Rambles in Canada*
"Summer Retreat in Arkansas" (Thorpe) **183**:357
"The Summer Sea" (Kingsley) **35**:226
"Summer Storm" (Lowell) **2**:507
"Summer Wind" (Bryant) **6**:159, 168, 176; **46**:6, 43
"A Summer-Night" (Arnold) **218**:114, 119, 149-50, 178, 190, 276
"A Summer's Evening Meditation" (Barbauld) **185**:29, 35, 37-38, 138-39, 145
The Summer's Tale (Cumberland) **167**:118, 132, 136, 146, 154, 187
"Summer—We All Have Seen" (Dickinson) **21**:69
"The Sun" (Baudelaire)
See "Le soleil"
"Sun and Flesh" (Rimbaud)
See "Soleil et chair"
"The Sun Cup" (Lampman) **194**:48, 79, 82, 92, 139
"The sun has gone down" (Clare) **86**:118
"The Sun kept setting-setting-still" (Dickinson) **77**:163-64
La Sunamite (Staël-Holstein) **91**:359-60
"The Sunbeam" (Hemans) **71**:264
"Sunbeams and Shadows" (Hugo) **3**:261
"Sunday" (Kivi)
See "Sunnuntai"
"Sunday Afternoon" (Dickinson)
See "From All the Jails the Boys and Girls"
"Sunday at Hampstead" (Thomson) **18**:391-92, 395, 397, 409, 411-12, 417
"Sunday at Home" (Hawthorne) **2**:291-92; **39**:230; **191**:215
"A Sun-Day Hymn" (Holmes) **81**:100, 107
The Sunday School (More) **27**:345; **141**:173, 176, 192, 219
"Sunday up the River" (Thomson) **18**:390-92, 395-97, 404-05, 408-09, 411-12, 414, 417, 421
"Sunday Walks" (Clare) **86**:142
"A Sunday with Shepherds and Herdboys" (Clare) **9**:117
"The Sundering Flood" (Morris) **4**:424-25, 438
"Sundown" (Longfellow) **45**:130
"Sun-Down Poem" (Whitman) **4**:546; **205**:330
"Sunlight and Flesh" (Rimbaud)
See "Soleil et chair"
"Sunlight in a London Square" (Jefferies) **47**:95, 136
"Sunlight on the Sea" (Gordon) **21**:150, 160, 175
"Sunnuntai" (Kivi) **30**:51
Sunny Memories of Foreign Lands (Stowe) **3**:547
"Sun-Painting and Sun-Sculpture" (Holmes) **81**:102
"Sunrise" (Lanier) **6**:237-38, 240, 243, 246-47, 253-54, 256, 265, 268, 281; **118**:204, 219, 221, 223-24, 232, 239-40, 268-71, 273, 275
"Sunrise" (Lazarus) **8**:420
"Sunrise" (Tyutchev) **34**:404
A Sunrise Song (Lanier) **118**:224
"The Sun's Shame" (Rossetti) **4**:491, 499
"A Sunset" (Clare) **9**:121
"Sunset" (Laforgue)
See "Soleil couchant"
"Sunset" (Lampman) **194**:81-82
"Sunset" (Lanier) **118**:238
"Sunset and Sunrise on Lake Ontario: A Reminiscence" (Traill) **31**:328
"Sunset at les Eboulements" (Lampman) **25**:179, 185-86, 190; **194**:7, 99-100
"Sunset in the Forest" (Meyer)
See "Abendrot im Walde"
"Sunset Visions" (Clare) **9**:121
"Sunshine and Young Mothers" (Parton) **86**:350
Sunshine through the Clouds (Lewes) **25**:291
Sunt lacrymae rerum, En mode hongrois (Liszt) **199**:307
"Sunthin' in the Pastoral Line" (Lowell) **2**:520, 522
"The Superannuated Man" (Lamb) **10**:392, 415; **113**:198-99, 248
The Supernaturalism of New-England (Whittier) **8**:487, 509
"A Superscription" (Rossetti) **4**:491; **77**:357
"Superstition" (Hogg) **109**:244
"Supper at the Mill" (Ingelow) **39**:255-56, 262-65, 268; **107**:119, 122
"Supplement to the Travelling Sketches" (Heine)
See "Nachträge Zu den Reisebildern"
"Supposed Confessions of a Second-Rate Sensitive Mind not in unity with itself" (Tennyson) **30**:252; **65**:270, 274, 368; **115**:237, 239
"The Supreme Sacrifice" (Lazarus) **109**:337
"Supreme Surrender" (Rossetti) **4**:498
"Sur Catherine de Médicis" (Balzac) **153**:94
"Sur la Conversion des Rentes" (Lamartine) **190**:171
"Sur la destruction des monuments en France" (Hugo) **21**:221; **161**:145
"Sur la femme" (Laforgue) **53**:291
"Sur la Liberté du Commerce" (Lamartine) **190**:171
"Sur la Naissance du Conte de Paris" (Musset) **150**:309
Sur la politique rationelle (Lamartine) **190**:204
"Sur le système continental" (Schlegel) **142**:308
Sur l'eau (Maupassant) **1**:446, 451, 453; **83**:163, 201
Sur les générations actuelles (Senancour) **16**:438, 441, 445-47
"Sur les Lettres de deux Grecs" (Chateaubriand) **134**:8
"Sur les œuvres complètes de Byron" (Vigny) **102**:379
"Sur l'herbe" (Verlaine) **2**:628-30; **51**:378, 387
"Sur l'image du Christ écrasant le mal" (Lamartine) **11**:279
"Sur Madame Georgette Leblanc" (Mallarmé) **210**:232
"Sur un album" (Gautier) **59**:18
"Sur une défunte" (Laforgue) **5**:280; **53**:292; **221**:62, 65-67
Sur une statue de Ganymede (Verlaine) **51**:363
Surfaceism; or, the World and its Wife (Gore) **65**:21
"The Surgeon's Daughter" (Scott) **15**:308-09
"Surgi de la croupe et du bond" (Mallarmé)
See "Une dentelle s'abolit"
"Une Surprise" (Maupassant) **83**:182
"Surprised by Joy" (Wordsworth) **12**:466; **166**:205
Surrey of Eagle's-Nest; or, The Memoirs of a Staff Officer Serving in Virginia (Cooke) **5**:124, 126-35
"Sursum Corda" (Emerson) **1**:296
"Sursum Corda" (Rossetti) **50**:313
Sursum corda (Liszt) **199**:307
"Sûryâ" (Leconte de Lisle) **29**:241
Susan (Austen) **119**:17-18, 45
"Susan Yates" (Lamb)
See "First Going to Church"
"Susan's Bird" (Mörike)
See "Suschens Vogel"
"Suschens Vogel" (Mörike) **201**:280, 294
"Suspects His Constancy" (Robinson) **142**:175
"Suspense" (Dickinson)
See "Elysium Is as Far as To"
Suspiria de profundis (De Quincey) **4**:61, 63-64, 66, 80, 83, 86-87, 89; **87**:3-16, 22, 31, 33, 36-7, 52, 75, 77; **198**:3, 41, 46, 48, 51, 58-59, 64, 67, 88
"Susquehanna" (Crèvecoeur) **105**:152-55, 157-60
"Sut at a Negro Night Meeting" (Harris) **165**:191, 236, 238-39, 242-43, 254, 290, 292-94
Sut Lovingood (Harris)
See *Sut Lovingood: Yarns Spun by a "Nat'ral Born Durn'd Fool"*
"Sut Lovingood, A Chapter from His Autobiography" (Harris) **23**:160
"Sut Lovingood at Bull's Gap" (Harris) **165**:209, 213, 216-17, 224
"Sut Lovingood Come to Life" (Harris) **23**:151; **165**:168, 233
"Sut Lovingood, His Autobiography" (Harris) **165**:224, 226
"Sut Lovingood Lands Old Abe Safe at Last" (Harris) **23**:159
"Sut Lovingood Lands Ole Abe Safe at Last" (Harris) **165**:183
"Sut Lovingood, on the Puritan Yankee" (Harris) **23**:151, 153; **165**:165; **165**:233
"Sut Lovingood Reports What Bob Dawson Said, After Marrying a Substitute" (Harris) **165**:216
Sut Lovingood, Yarns Spun by a "Nat'ral Born Durn'd Fool" (Harris) **165**:162-64, 177, 181, 183-84, 187, 198-202, 204, 206, 210-12, 219, 223, 225-30, 235, 240-41, 244-45, 247-56, 258, 260-62, 264-68, 270-73, 275-80, 282-83, 286-87, 293, 295
Sut Lovingood: Yarns Spun by a "Nat'ral Born Durn'd Fool" (Harris) **23**:133, 135, 137-40, 142, 144-49, 156-57, 159-60, 162-64; **165**:176, 178, 184, 187, 189, 198, 213, 232, 253, 258, 266, 285-87
"Sut Lovingood's Adventures in New York" (Harris) **23**:149, 160; **165**:184
"Sut Lovingood's Allegory" (Harris) **23**:152; **165**:170, 233, 295-96
"Sut Lovingood's Big Dinner Story" (Harris) **23**:160; **165**:209
"Sut Lovingood's Big Music Box Story" (Harris) **23**:160
"Sut Lovingood's Chest Story" (Harris) **23**:159; **165**:191, 200, 216, 232, 266, 271
"Sut Lovingood's Daddy 'Acting Horse'" (Harris) **23**:139, 141, 153, 158, 161, 163-64; **165**:181, 196, 198-99, 201, 207, 229, 241-42, 252, 254-57, 277
"Sut Lovingood's Dog" (Harris) **23**:157, 159; **165**:211, 254, 260
"Sut Lovingood's Dream" (Harris) **165**:287
"Sut Lovingood's Hog Ride" (Harris) **23**:160; **165**:210, 227
"Sut Lovingood's Love Feast ove Varmints" (Harris) **23**:150
"Sut Lovingood's Sermon" (Harris) **23**:159; **165**:226, 244, 261, 275
Sut Lovingood's Travels with Old Abe Lincoln (Harris) **23**:137
Sut Lovingood's Yarns (Harris)
See *Sut Lovingood, Yarns Spun by a "Nat'ral Born Durn'd Fool"*
"Suteishimaru" (Ueda Akinari) **131**:21-22, 58
Sutherland As It Was And Is; Or How A Country May Be Ruined (Miller) **143**:13
"Sutherland's Grave" (Kendall) **12**:181, 199
"Sut's New-Fangled Shirt" (Harris) **23**:140, 158, 163; **165**:181, 205, 226, 229, 241-42, 258-59, 277-78
"Sut's Sermon" (Harris) **165**:280
"The Suttee" (Cooke) **110**:9
"Suzon" (Musset) **7**:256, 267; **150**:310
"Svalen" (Wergeland) **5**:536, 541
"Svartsjukans nätter" (Runeberg) **41**:309, 317
Svea (Tegner) **2**:611-14
"Sveaborg" (Runeberg) **41**:312, 323-24
"Svedger" (Stagnelius) **61**:248

Svegder (Stagnelius) **61**:253, 258-9
"Sven Duva" (Runeberg) **41**:315, 322, 325, 328
"Svenska fattigdomens betydelse" (Almqvist) **42**:14, 18-19
"Sventura" (Foscolo) **8**:266
"Svetlana" (Zhukovsky) **35**:379, 389, 394, 398, 400-01
"Svidanie" (Turgenev) **122**:264
"Svinedrengen" (Andersen) **7**:23, 32, 34, 32, 34; **79**:23-4, 30, 40-2, 51-2, 64, 70-2; **214**:37-38, 40, 76
"Svoenravnoe prozvanie..." (Baratynsky) **103**:11
Svoi lyudi—sochtemsya! (Ostrovsky) **30**:97-9, 104-05, 109-13, 117; **57**:195, 197, 199, 207-8, 213-4, 218-21
Svoia sem'ia, ili Zamuzhniaia nevesta (Griboedov) **129**:172-73
"Svyataya noch na nebosklon vzoshla" (Tyutchev) **34**:393, 397, 405
"Swabian Popular Song" (Mangan) **27**:290
"The Swallow" (Derzhavin) **215**:30
"The Swallow" (Smith) **115**:119
"Swallow" (Tennyson)
See "O Swallow, Swallow"
"The Swallow" (Wergeland)
See "Svalen"
Swallow Barn; or, A Sojourn in the Old Dominion (Kennedy) **2**:428-35
"The Swallow Leaves Her Nest" (Beddoes) **3**:34
"Swamp Robin" (Lanier) **118**:242
"The Swan" (Baudelaire)
See "Le cygne"
"The Swan" (Derzhavin)
See "Lebed"
"The Swan" (Hemans) **71**:270
"The Swan" (Tyutchev)
See "Lebed"
"Swan Song" (Brentano)
See "Schwanenlied"
"The Swan's Nest" (Andersen) **7**:21
"The Swans of Lir" (Griffin) **7**:198
"Swart Among the Buckeyes" (Boyesen) **135**:12, 19
"Swarthy Wastelands, Wild and Woodless" (Kendall) **12**:179
"The Swashbuckler" (Turgenev)
See "The Duelist"
"Swayne Vonved" (Borrow) **9**:54
Swear Not at All (Bentham) **38**:92, 97
"Swedenborg; or, The Mystic" (Emerson) **98**:92, 100
"Sweep Song" (Blake) **13**:161
"The Sweep's Complaint" (Hood) **16**:236, 239
"Sweet and low" (Tennyson) **202**:179
"Sweet Death" (Rossetti) **186**:332-33
"Sweet Mary Dove" (Clare) **86**:89
"Sweet Meat Has Sower Sauce or, the Slave-Trader in the Dumps" (Cowper) **94**:32
"Sweet Sunday Bells" (Allingham) **25**:24-5
"Sweet Susan" (Clare) **86**:89
"The Sweethearts" (Andersen) **79**:58, 66
"The Sweethearts, or the Top and the Ball" (Andersen) **214**:72
"Sweetness and Light" (Arnold) **218**:197, 216
"The Sweetness of Life" (Lampman) **25**:188; **194**:70, 75, 77-80, 82-84, 91-92
Swellfoot (Shelley)
See *Oedipus Tyrannus; Or Swellfoot the Tyrant*
Swellfoot the Tyrant (Shelley)
See *Oedipus Tyrannus; Or Swellfoot the Tyrant*
Świeczka zgasta (Fredro) **8**:285
"The Swift" (Very) **9**:387
"The Swiftest Runners" (Andersen) **7**:25
"The Swilcar Oak" (Darwin)
See "Address to the Swilcar Oak"
"Swilcar Oak" (Darwin)
See "Address to the Swilcar Oak"
"The Swimmer" (Castro Alves)
See "O nadador"
"The Swimmer" (Gordon) **21**:151, 156-57, 160, 163, 167, 176, 183, 187-88
"The Swimmer" (Pavlova)
See "Plovets"
"The Swineherd" (Andersen)
See "Svinedrengen"
"Swineherd" (Crawford) **127**:188
"The Swing" (Kivi)
See "Keinu"
"The Swiss Artist" (Brontë) **109**:35
The Swiss Family Robinson (Wyss)
See *Der Schweizerische Robinson; oder, Der schiffbrüchige Schweizerprediger und seine Familie*
Switrigail oder Beiträge zu der Geschichte von Lithauen, Russland, Polen, und Preussen (Kotzebue) **25**:140
"Switzerland" (Arnold) **6**:44; **29**:34; **89**:14-20, 48; **218**:122, 151
"The Switzer's Wife" (Hemans) **71**:275, 291
"The Sword" (Crawford) **127**:171
The Sword and the Distaff; or, "Fair, Fat, and Forty" (Simms)
See *Woodcraft; or, Hawks about the Dovecote*
"Sxolastiki xix veka" (Pisarev) **25**:337, 345
"A s'y méprendre" (Villiers de l'Isle Adam) **3**:590
"Syberie" (Norwid) **17**:373
Sybil; or, The Two Nations (Disraeli) **2**:144-45, 147-54; **39**:4, 6, 9-12, 15-17, 19-20, 22-7, 30-31, 33-5, 38, 41, 44-51, 56-59, 61-4, 69, 73, 75-6, 78, 80; **79**:195-97, 199, 212-13, 222, 234-36, 238-39, 244-45, 247-50, 252-55, 257-59, 261-64, 269, 271, 279, 281-82
"Sybil Swallow's Wit" (Brentano)
See "Sybille Schwalbenwitz"
"Sybille" (Mitford) **4**:400
Sybille (Feuillet)
See *Histoire de Sybille*
"Sybille Schwalbenwitz" (Brentano) **191**:136
"The Sycamores" (Whittier) **8**:516
"The Sydney International Exhibition" (Kendall) **12**:187, 191, 200, 202-03
Sygdommen til Døden (Kierkegaard) **34**:178, 192, 200, 224, 226-29, 231-32, 238, 264; **78**:124-27, 140-43, 152, 175, 182-83, 185-86, 188-90, 193, 195, 238, 242; **125**:206, 241, 244, 253, 256, 284
"The Sylphid" (Robinson) **142**:105, 115, 206
"The Sylphs of the Seasons" (Allston) **2**:19, 21-22, 24, 26
The Sylphs of the Seasons, with Other Poems (Allston) **2**:19-21, 24
"Sylvan Musings. In May" (Hayne) **94**:160
Sylvandire (Dumas) **71**:203
"Sylvia" (Musset) **7**:258
Sylvia; or, The May Queen (Darley) **2**:125-27, 129-30, 133
Sylvia's Lovers (Gaskell) **5**:185, 188, 190, 192, 196-98, 201, 204-06; **70**:120, 123-24; 129, 132-33, 185, 187, 189, 196, 198, 200-02, 205-06, 209, 212-13; **137**:3-4, 40; **214**:190, 332, 342, 344
Sylvie and Bruno (Dodgson) **2**:106-8, 111, 115, 117, 121-2; **53**:40, 56-7, 84, 86, 89-90, 104-9, 113, 115; **139**:4-5, 21-27, 45, 52-53, 89, 120, 126, 136-37, 139, 147
Sylvie and Bruno Concluded (Dodgson) **2**:107, 111, 115, 121-2; **53**:105; **139**:4-5, 14, 21-22, 45, 53, 89, 139
Sylvie: Recollections of Valois (Nerval) **1**:475-80, 482, 485, 487, 489; **67**:303-04, 311, 315, 318, 320, 323-25, 333-35, 348, 351, 354, 356-57, 360, 363
Sylvoe (Herder) **8**:299
"The Symbol and the Saint" (Field) **3**:205
Symbolic Logic (Dodgson) **53**:110, 122
Symbolic Logic, Part I: Elementary (Dodgson) **139**:8-9, 80, 84, 145
"Symbolism and Language" (Cranch) **115**:9
"Sympathy" (Lazarus) **109**:295
"Sympathy" (Thomson) **18**:400-01
"Sympathy" (Thoreau)
See "Elegy"
Symphonic Poems (Liszt) **199**:303-4
"Symphonic Studies" (Lazarus) **109**:291-92
"Symphonie en blanc majeur" (Gautier) **59**:19
Symphonie littéraire (Mallarmé) **4**:396; **41**:269, 278
"The Symphony" (Lanier) **6**:232, 235, 237-38, 243-44, 248-49, 251, 253-54, 257-59, 263, 265, 269, 274, 277, 279; **118**:203, 206-7, 213, 218, 223-24, 229, 236-38, 240, 259-62, 265, 267-68, 270, 279
Symphony in C Major (Wagner) **119**:189
Symphony in C Minor (Beethoven)
See *Fifth Symphony*
Sympneumata (Oliphant) **47**:289-93, 295
"Symptoms of Love" (Opie) **65**:156
"Syn ceniów" (Krasiński) **4**:306, 313
"Synet" (Grundtvig) **158**:182
Synspunktet for min Forfatter-Virksomhed (Kierkegaard) **34**:201, 203-05, 238, 248, 250-55, 257-58; **78**:121, 181, 197, 215, 238; **125**:176, 209, 229, 234
Synthèse Subjective ou Système universel des conceptions propres a l'état normal de l'Humanité (Comte) **54**:211, 214
Synthetic Philosophy (Brownson) **50**:27
Synthetic Psychology (Brownson) **50**:27
"The Syrens" (Lowell) **2**:502, 507
"Syrinx" (Kendall) **12**:192
Syskonlif (Bremer) **11**:23-24, 34-35
System der gesammten Philosophie und der Naturphilosophie insbesondere (Schelling) **30**:175-77
Das System der Sittenlehre nach den prinzipen der Wissenschaftslehre (Fichte) **62**:30, 34, 47, 58
System der Wissenschaft: 1. Theil. Der Phänomenologies des Geistes (Hegel) **46**:60-1, 70, 73-4, 86, 89-90, 102, 104-06, 108, 112, 140, 147, 150, 162, 164-73, 175-78, 187, 189
System des transcendentalen Idealismus (Schelling) **30**:122-24, 126-28, 146, 155, 166, 176-81
A System of Christians Ethics on the Principles of the Evangelical Church (Schleiermacher)
See *Der christliche Glaube nach den Grundsäzen der evangelischen Kirche im Zusammenhange dargestellt*
"The System of Doctor Tarr and Professor Fether" (Poe) **16**:312; **55**:147
"The System of Elementary Facts and Principles, by which the Phenomena of Human Utterance are explained, and the Rules for the just delivery of Eloquence are taught" (Thelwall) **162**:340
The System of Ethical Theory according to the Principles of Wissenschaftslehre (Fichte)
See *Das System der Sittenlehre nach den prinzipen der Wissenschaftslehre*
A System of Logic, Ratiocinative and Inductive: Being a Connected View of the Principles of Evidence and the Methods of Scientific Investigation (Mill) **11**:329-30, 332, 337, 339, 341, 349-51, 358, 365, 375-76, 380, 383; **58**:319, 321-4, 327, 337, 341, 375; **179**:206, 211, 220, 289-90, 294, 311-12, 315, 319, 321, 354; **223**:93, 108-10, 124
System of Positive Philosophy (Comte)
See *Système de Politique Positive ou Traité de Sociologie instituant la Religion de l'Humanité*
"System of the Heavens" (De Quincey) **87**:7
"System of the Heavens as Revealed by Lord Rosse's Telescope" (De Quincey) **198**:90

System of Transcendental Idealism (Schelling)
See *System des transcendentalen Idealismus*
A System of Vegetables (Darwin) **106**:232, 274
Systema Representative (Alencar) **157**:5
Système de Logique Positive ou Traité de philosophie mathématique (Comte) **54**:211
Système de Politique Positive ou Traité de Sociologie instituant la Religion de l'Humanité (Comte) **54**:199, 203, 205, 210, 212, 235-8, 241-2, 244
Syzygies (Dodgson) **139**:57
"Szabadság, szerelem" (Petofi) **21**:279
"A szájhösök" (Petofi) **21**:280
"Szczęsacliwość filutów" (Krasicki) **8**:407
"Széchenyi emlékezete" (Arany) **34**:16
"Szécsi Mária" (Petofi) **21**:264, 267
"Szene aus meinen Kinderjahren" (Brentano) **191**:118
"Szeptember végén" (Petofi) **21**:260, 285
"A szerelem, a szerelem" (Petofi) **21**:283
"Szerelem átka" (Petofi) **21**:264
Szerelem Gyöngyei (Petofi) **21**:285
"Szeretlek, kedvesem" (Petofi) **21**:285
"Szomjas ember tünödése" (Petofi) **21**:283
"Szondi két apródja" (Arany) **34**:15, 20
"Szüleim halálára" (Petofi) **21**:286
"Ta voix" (Banville) **9**:29
"Taarnvægteren" (Andersen) **79**:77
"Tabakadelsgesellschaft" (Beddoes) **154**:26
"A táblabíro" (Petofi) **21**:277
A Table of the Springs of Action (Bentham) **38**:55-7, 84, 90
Table Talk (Coleridge)
See *Specimens of the Table Talk of the Late Samuel Taylor Coleridge*
Table Talk (Cowper) **94**:19, 51-3, 58-9
Table Talk (Pushkin) **3**:436; **83**:270, 274
The "Table Talk" and "Omniana" of Samuel Taylor Coleridge (Coleridge) **177**:127-29
The Table Talk of Samuel Taylor Coleridge (Coleridge) **177**:34, 159
Le Tableau de Paris (Vallès) **71**:342-43, 373
Tableau historique et critique de la poésie Française et du théâtre Français au seizième siècle (Sainte-Beuve) **5**:338, 349
Tableaux de la nature (Humboldt) **170**:181
Tableaux de siège (Gautier) **1**:344
"Tableaux parisiens" (Baudelaire) **6**:113, 115, 122-24; **55**:15-16, 35, 37-42, 65-6, 73
Tableaux parisiens (Baudelaire) **155**:44, 113
"The Tables Turned" (Wordsworth) **111**:202, 209, 225, 255, 281, 283, 285, 314; **206**:318, 334
"Table-Talk" (Cowper) **8**:110, 120; **94**:25-8, 112, 129
Table-Talk (Alcott) **1**:21, 23-26; **167**:72, 85-86, 89, 92
Table-Talk (Coleridge)
See *Specimens of the Table Talk of the Late Samuel Taylor Coleridge*
Tablets (Alcott) **1**:23-26; **167**:17, 72, 85, 89
Tablettes romantiques (Nodier) **19**:378
"Tábori képek" (Madach) **19**:369
"Tact" (Emerson) **1**:285
Tafellieder (Muller) **73**:353, 387
"Ein Tag aus Noltens Jugendleben" (Mörike) **10**:451-52
"Tag, schein' herein" (Meyer) **81**:143
"Tag und Nacht" (Mörike) **201**:250, 300-301
Tagalog Nobility (Rizal) **27**:420
Tagebuch (Beethoven) **227**:32-35
Tagebuch aus Wien. Von Latour bis auf Windischgrätz (Auerbach) **171**:35
Tagebuch einer Reise durch die Schweitz (La Roche) **121**:242, 299, 301
Tagebuch einer Reise durch Holland und England (La Roche) **121**:242, 299, 302-6
Tagebücher (Grillparzer) **102**:101-02, 105-07, 111, 168-72
Tagebücher (Hebbel) **43**:252-53, 255, 261, 263
Der Tagebücher des Dichters Zacharias Werner (Werner) **189**:364
"Einem Tagelohner" (Meyer) **81**:155
"Täglich zu singen" (Claudius) **75**:190
"Ta-Hsüeh" (Clague)
See "The Latest Decalogue"
Le tailleur de pierres de Saint-Point (Lamartine) **11**:286
"The Tain Quest" (Ferguson) **33**:278-79, 283, 289, 293
Taine's On Intelligence (Taine)
See *De l'intelligence*
"Tajemnica Lorda Singleworth" (Norwid) **17**:369, 379, 382
"Tak, v zhizni est mgnoveniya" (Tyutchev) **34**:399
"Take delight: all passes by!" (Baratynsky)
See "Naslazhdaytes: vsyo pokhodit!..."
"Take Your Heaven Further On" (Dickinson) **21**:54, 57
Takekurabe (Ichiyō) **49**:331, 336-37, 341, 344-47, 350, 353
"Taken from my Mothers singing" (Clare) **86**:108
Taking by Storm (Lewes) **25**:291
"The Taking of the Redoubt" (Mérimée)
See "L'enlèvement de la rédoute"
"Taking the Census in Alabama. By a Chicken Man of 1840" (Hooper) **177**:183-84, 193, 213
"Taking up the Fair Ideal" (Dickinson) **21**:56
Talanty i poklonniki (Ostrovsky) **30**:103, 111, 115, 117; **57**:212-4, 216-7, 220
Talbot Harland (Ainsworth) **13**:36
"Tale" (Rimbaud)
See "Conte"
"A Tale" (Verlaine)
See "Un conte"
The Tale (Eminescu) **33**:266
"A Tale about Myself" (Herzen) **61**:108
"A Tale. Addressed to a Sybarite" (D'Israeli) **217**:305
"Tale for Girls" (Rossetti) **50**:289
A Tale from the Paris Exposition 1867 (Andersen)
See *Dryaden. Et Eventyr fra Udstillingstidin i Paris 1867*
"The Tale of a God-pleasing Skomorokh" (Leskov) **174**:68
A Tale of a Man of Valour (Ueda Akinari)
See *Masurao monogatari*
"The Tale of a Trumpet" (Hood) **16**:218-19, 235
"The Tale of Fedor the Christian and Avram the Jew" (Leskov)
See "Skazanie o Fedore-khristianine i o druge ego Avrame-zhidovine"
"The Tale of Fedor the Christian and His Friend Abraham the Jew" (Leskov)
See "Skazanie o Fedore-khristianine i o druge ego Abrame-zhidovine"
The Tale of Gockel, Hinkel & Gackeliah (Brentano)
See *Gockel, Hinkel und Gackeleia: Märchen, wiedererzählt*
"The Tale of Good Queen Bess" (Hogg) **4**:283
"The Tale of Honest Casper and Fair Annie" (Brentano)
See "Geschichte vom braven Kasperl und dem schönen Annerl"
"The Tale of How Ivan Ivanovich Quarrelled with Ivan Nikiforovich" (Gogol) **2**:228, 234, 250; **31**:110-11, 114, 117, 119; **5**:219, 227, 231, 242, 249-51; **162**:15, 17, 27, 52, 54, 58, 62, 67, 82, 86, 94-95, 98, 119
"A Tale of Jerusalem" (Poe) **55**:185
A Tale of Manchester Life (Gaskell)
See *Mary Barton: A Tale of Manchester Life*
A Tale of Mystery (Holcroft) **85**:199, 212, 224-25, 235, 237
A Tale of Paraguay (Southey) **8**:460; **97**:264, 273, 276
"Tale of Romance" (Keats) **8**:322
"A Tale of Terror" (Hood) **16**:221
"Tale of the Crucifixion" (Multatuli) **165**:319-20
"The Tale of the Dead Princess and the Seven Heroes" (Pushkin)
See "Skazka o Mertvoy Tsarevne"
"The Tale of the Fisherman and the Fish" (Pushkin)
See "Skazka o Rybake i Rybke"
The Tale of the Golden Cockerel (Pushkin)
See "Skazka o Zolotom Petushke"
A Tale of the House of the Wolfings and All the Kindreds of Mark (Morris) **4**:425
"Tale of the Indians" (Maturin) **6**:325, 334
"Tale of the Inmate of the Cottage" (Wordsworth) **166**:340-41
"The Tale of the Lime Tree" (Eminescu) **33**:247
"The Tale of the Lover to his Mistress" (Beddoes) **154**:78
"Tale of the Lucky Purse" (Arnim)
See "Der Heckebeutel"
"The Tale of the Magus Travelling in the Stars" (Eminescu) **33**:246, 264; **131**:287
"The Tale of the Monk and the Jew Versified" (Paine) **62**:321
"Tale of the Monk Felix" (Longfellow) **45**:113
"A Tale of the Passions" (Shelley)
See "A Tale of the Passions; or, The Death of Despina"
"A Tale of the Passions; or, The Death of Despina" (Shelley) **14**:267
"A Tale of the Ragged Mountains" (Poe) **55**:201; **94**:240; **211**:253
"Tale of the Spaniard" (Maturin) **6**:334
"The Tale of the Squint-Eyed Left-Handed Smith from Tula and the Steel Flea" (Leskov)
See "Levša"
"The Tale of the Three Pictures" (Fouqué) **2**:266
"Tale of the Tsar Berendeia" (Zhukovsky) **35**:390
"The Tale of the Tsar Sultan" (Pushkin)
See "Skazka o Tsare Sultane"
A Tale of the Tyne (Martineau) **137**:264, 267
"The Tale of Theodore the Christian and His Friend Abraham the Jew" (Leskov)
See "Skazanie o Fedore-khristianine i o druge ego Avrame-zhidovine"
"A Tale of Trials" (Opie) **65**:171
A Tale of Two Cities (Dickens) **3**:154-55; **8**:168; **18**:114, 120, 131; **26**:168, 171, 178, 228; **86**:186-267; **105**:254; **113**:20, 53-4, 103, 118; **187**:27; **203**:250; **206**:114; **211**:34; **217**:218; **230**:82, 89, 91-2, 141-42; **231**:182
"The Tale of Two Ivans" (Gogol)
See "The Tale of How Ivan Ivanovich Quarrelled with Ivan Nikiforovich"
"The Talent for Silence" (Lewes) **25**:290
Talents and Admirers (Ostrovsky)
See *Talanty i poklonniki*
Tales (Cowper) **8**:103
Tales (Crabbe) **26**:93, 102, 111, 114, 119, 128, 130-31, 134-35, 138, 148, 150-51; **121**:4-6, 10-11, 25, 43, 61, 73-4, 78, 83-4
Tales (Hogg)
See *The Works of the Ettrick Shepherd*
Tales (Poe)
See *Poetry and Tales*
Tales (Runeberg)
See *Fänrik Ståls sägner*
Tales (Wilson) **5**:564, 567
"Tales and Essays for Children" (Sigourney) **87**:321
"Tales and Historic Scenes" (Hemans) **71**:261
Tales and Historic Scenes in Verse (Hemans) **29**:192, 202; **71**:274-76, 289, 291, 293-95
Tales and Reminiscences of a Hunter on Various Types of Hunting (Aksakov)
See *Rasskazy i vospominaniia okhotnika o raznykh okhotakh*

Tales and Sketches (Miller) **143**:9, 48
Tales and Sketches (Norton) **47**:246, 248
Tales and Sketches (Sedgwick) **19**:440
Tales and Sketches, Illustrating the Character, Usages, Traditions, Sports, and Pastimes of the Irish Peasantry (Carleton) **199**:21, 43
Tales and Stories (Shelley) **14**:264; **59**:155
Tales and Stories by Mary Wollstonecraft Shelley (Shelley)
See *Tales and Stories*
Tales by Belkin (Pushkin)
See *Povesti Belkina*
Tales by Edgar A. Poe (Poe) **1**:495; **16**:293-94, 296
Tales by the O'Hara Family (Banim and Banim) **13**:116-32, 141
Tales for the Common People (More) **141**:191, 271
Tales for the Pemberton Children (Opie) **65**:173
Tales from Carleton (Carleton) **199**:29, 80
Tales from Shakespear (Lamb) **125**:301-7, 320, 352, 354, 358
Tales from Shakespeare, Designed for the Use of Young Persons (Lamb) **10**:386, 402, 406, 417, 420, 422, 439; **113**:159, 199, 278, 286
Tales from Two Hemispheres (Boyesen) **135**:8, 12, 24-26, 30
Tales in Verse (Crabbe) **121**:34, 36, 39-40, 65
Tales in Verse (Holcroft) **85**:199-200, 212-13
Tales of a Grandfather (Scott)
See *The History of Scotland*
Tales of a Traveller (Irving) **2**:369-71, 374, 379, 381-82, 384, 387, 389-90; **19**:331-33, 341, 344; **95**:280
Tales of a Wayside Inn (Longfellow) **2**:481, 484, 487-88, 492, 495-96; **45**:113-14, 119, 124, 128, 132, 137-38, 140, 144-45, 147, 149, 160, 162, 185, 187-88
Tales of All Countries (Trollope) **215**:208, 221
"Tales of an Englishman" (Brontë) **109**:47
The Tales of Belkin (Pushkin)
See *Povesti Belkina*
Tales of Ensign Stål (Runeberg)
See *Fänrik Ståls sägner*
Tales of Fashionable Life (Edgeworth) **1**:257, 261, 267-68; **51**:75, 89, 93, 130, 137, 140; **158**:19, 46, 52, 69
Tales of Hoffmann (Hoffmann)
See *Hoffmann's Fairy Tales*
Tales of Ireland (Carleton) **3**:83, 88, 91; **199**:9, 53, 58, 65
The Tales of Ivan Belkin (Pushkin)
See *Povesti Belkina*
Tales of My Landlord (Scott) **15**:259, 304, 309-10, 321-22; **69**:299; **209**:173-74, 178, 199-201, 219, 253, 262-63, 272
Tales of My Neighborhood (Griffin) **7**:215, 218
Tales of Mystery and Imagination (Poe) **16**:309, 311
Tales of Old Travel Re-Narrated (Kingsley) **107**:209
Tales of Orris (Ingelow) **39**:263
Tales of Real Life (Opie) **65**:171
Tales of Spain and Italy (Musset)
See *Contes d'Espagne et d'Italie*
Tales of the Court of Vienna (Sacher-Masoch) **31**:294
Tales of the Folio Club (Poe) **55**:185
Tales of the Grotesque and Arabesque (Poe) **1**:492-93, 520-21; **16**:291-92, 296; **55**:132; **94**:239
Tales of the Hall (Crabbe) **26**:100, 103, 108, 115-16, 128-31, 134, 136, 142, 149; **121**:6, 12, 14, 34, 84
Tales of the Heart (Opie) **65**:164, 171, 174, 179, 197-8
"Tales of the Inn Kitchen" (Irving) **19**:328
Tales of the Juryroom (Griffin) **7**:204
Tales of the Munster Festivals (Griffin) **7**:193, 197, 204, 207, 210-12, 216-17
Tales of the Phantasus (Tieck)
See *Phantasus*
"Tales of the Province House" (Hawthorne) **2**:303
Tales of the Queen of Navarre (Scribe)
See *Les contes de la reine de Navarre*
Tales of the Russian Court (Sacher-Masoch) **31**:294
Tales of the Spring Rain (Ueda Akinari)
See *Harusame Monogatari*
Tales of the Wars of Montrose (Hogg) **4**:279
Tales of Wonder (Lewis) **11**:296-97, 302
Tales Told for Children (Andersen)
See *Eventyr, fortalte for bøorn*
"Taliessin" (Tennyson) **30**:294
"Le talion" (Leconte de Lisle) **29**:225-26
"Le Talion" (Sade) **47**:313
Der Talisman (Nestroy) **42**:220-21, 223, 232, 239, 242, 245-47, 249, 251-53, 264
The Talisman (Scott) **15**:312; **69**:303-04, 313-14, 316, 319, 328, 332-34; **209**:182
"Talk and Talkers: A Sequel" (Stevenson) **193**:275-76, 281-82
"A Talk on What Is a Son of the Motherland" (Radishchev) **190**:314
"The Talking Lady" (Mitford) **4**:401, 408
"The Talking Oak" (Holmes) **14**:109
"Talking Oak" (Tennyson) **30**:215
"Tall Ambrosia" (Thoreau) **7**:384
"The Tall Woman" (Alarcon)
See "La mujer alta"
"The 'Tallapoosy Vollantares' Meet the Enemy" (Hooper) **177**:208
"Taller moderno" (Silva) **114**:299, 301
"Talleyrand" (Landor) **14**:166
"Tam o' the Lin" (Baillie) **151**:86, 92
Tamakatsuma (Motoori) **45**:277
Tamakushige (Motoori) **45**:276-79
"Taman" (Lermontov) **5**:290-91, 295, 297, 300-02, 305-06; **126**:145, 150-51, 153-54, 157, 195-96, 199
"Tamango" (Mérimée) **6**:354, 360, 365-6, 369; **65**:56, 60, 66, 113
Tamaris (Sand) **57**:316
"Tamarlane" (Poe) **1**:492, 527; **117**:195, 224-25, 227, 244, 260, 264, 266, 269, 280
Tamarlane, and Other Poems, By a Bostonian (Poe) **1**:514; **55**:207; **117**:224
"Der Tambour" (Mörike) **201**:294
The Tambov Treasurer's Wife (Lermontov)
See *Tambovskaya kaznacheysha*
Tambovskaya kaznacheysha (Lermontov) **126**:134, 136
"Tamerlane" (Poe) **211**:249
"Tamerton Church-Tower" (Patmore) **9**:328-29
Tamerton Church-Tower, and Other Poems (Patmore) **9**:328, 348
"The Taming of the Shrew" (Lamb) **125**:305
"The Tampa Resolution" (Martí)
See "Resoluciónes tomadas por le emigracion cubana de Tampa"
"Tampa Robins" (Lanier) **6**:236, 238-39, 243, 255; **118**:273, 275
The Tamworth Reading Room (Newman) **38**:324; **99**:261, 273, 278-79, 301
"Tan solo dudas y terrores sieto" (Castro) **78**:41
Tancred; or, The New Crusade (Disraeli) **2**:140-41, 144-45, 147-48, 150-54; **39**:3-4, 6, 16-17, 20, 23-4, 26-7, 29-31, 34-5, 39-42, 44-5, 47, 50-1, 56, 64, 69, 75-7, 80; **79**:195, 212-15, 222, 232-33, 235, 239, 257-60, 263-64, 266-67, 269, 276
Tandai shoshin roku (Ueda Akinari) **131**:20, 51, 60, 81-83
Tändeleien und Erzählungen (Claudius) **75**:191-92
The Tangled Skein (Dodgson) **2**:107
A Tangled Tale (Dodgson) **139**:57
Tanglewood Tales for Girls and Boys: Being a Second Wonder-Book (Hawthorne) **2**:302, 306, 313; **17**:149-50; **23**:214; **226**:118, 135
Tanhauser (Wagner)
See *Tannhäuser*
"Tannhaüser" (Lazarus) **8**:412-14, 420, 425-26; **109**:289-90, 294, 319, 321
Tannhäuser (Nestroy) **42**:225
Tannhäuser (Wagner) **9**:401, 403, 406, 414-16, 418-19, 421, 434, 437, 450, 452, 454-55, 462-63, 469, 473-74; **119**:172, 176, 178, 181, 185, 192, 195, 198, 240, 244, 267-68, 274, 302, 328
"Tannhäuser and the Faithful Eckbert" (Tieck)
See "Der Getreue Eckart und der Tannen häuser"
"Tante Tandpine" (Andersen) **79**:66, 73-77; **214**:41-42, 58, 60
"Tanto e tanto nos odiamos" (Castro) **78**:2
"Der Tanz" (Schiller) **166**:94, 103-4
Das Tanzlegendchen (Keller) **2**:416
Tarantella (Liszt) **199**:307
Tarantella, a Romance (Blind) **202**:3-4, 31-32
Tarare (Da Ponte) **50**:83-4
Taras Bulba (Gogol) **5**:209, 218-20, 227, 230, 240, 242, 248-49, 251, 256; **31**:122; **162**:11-12, 25, 32-35, 37-40, 42, 44, 95, 98, 100, 104, 108
"Tarasova nic" (Shevchenko) **54**:360, 371-4
"La tarde azul" (Isaacs) **70**:304
"Tardy George" (Boker) **125**:33, 39, 81
"Tarr and Fether" (Poe)
See "The System of Doctor Tarr and Professor Fether"
"The Tartars" (De Quincey) **4**:75
"The Tartarus of Maids" (Melville)
See "The Paradise of Bachelors and the Tartarus of Maids"
"Tartuffe's Punishment" (Rimbaud)
See "Le châtiment de Tartuff"
The Tashkentsians (Saltykov)
See *Gospoda Tashkentsy*
The Task (Cowper) **8**:96-97, 99, 102-06, 109-20, 122-23, 125, 127-29, 132-33, 138; **94**:46-51, 65, 76-7, 79, 84, 92-6, 98, 100-01, 119-120, 124, 126-30
Task of the Historian (Humboldt)
See *Über die Aufgabe des Geschichtschreibers*
Tasso (Liszt) **199**:329
Tasso (Shelley) **175**:202
"Tasso and His Sister" (Hemans) **71**:306-07
"Tasso to Leonora" (Thomson) **18**:396
Taste (Coleridge) **231**:27
"'Tas-tis, tas-tis' na silenciosa noite" (Castro) **78**:41
"Tat'jana Borisovna i ee plemjannik" (Turgenev) **122**:264
The Tatler (Hunt) **70**:288
Tatsachen des Bewusstseins (Fichte) **62**:34
Tattered Tom; or, The Story of a Street Arab (Alger) **8**:42, 45; **83**:129, 140, 145
"Der Taucher" (Schiller) **39**:330, 388; **166**:106-7, 115
Taugenichts (Eichendorff)
See *Aus dem Leben eines Taugenichts und Das Marmorbild: Zwei Novellen nebst einem Anhange von Liedern und Romanzen*
"Taurus in Lynchburg Market" (Harris) **23**:159, 163; **165**:210, 225, 229, 255-56, 258-60
"Taüschung" (Muller) **73**:366, 383, 390, 392-93, 396-97
"Távolból" (Petofi) **21**:276
Tawny Rachel; or, the Fortune Teller (More) **141**:190, 193, 270
Tchitchikoff's Journey; or Dead Souls (Gogol)
See *Mertvye dushi*
"De Te" (Gordon) **21**:155, 159-60, 164, 176, 183
"Le Te Deum du Ier Janvier" (Hugo) **3**:276
Te Deum zur Feyer der Einnahme von Paris durch die zum heiligen Kriege verbündten Heere (Werner) **189**:357
Tea Table (Coleridge) **90**:20

"Tea-Ballad" (Warren) **13**:414
"Teachers' Migration" (Sarmiento) **123**:274
"The Teaching and Sayings of Bacon" (Bestuzhev)
See "Uchenie—aforizmy iz Bekona"
"Teapots and Quails" (Lear) **3**:306
"The Tear of a Wife" (Parton) **86**:350
"Tears" (Tyutchev) **34**:387-88
"Tears" (Whitman) **4**:567, 571, 580; **31**:431; **205**:158, 160, 309
Tears (Desbordes-Valmore)
See *Les Pleurs*
"Tears and Roses" (Muller) **73**:352
"Tears, Idle Tears" (Tennyson) **30**:246, 248, 279, 283; **115**:364, 366; **202**:174, 193, 196, 198, 243
"Teatral'nyi raz'ezd posle predstavleniia novoi komedii" (Gogol) **5**:254; **15**:83-84, 98, 106, 108, 110; **31**:98, 103; **162**:60
"Teatros" (Larra) **130**:228, 247-48, 273
"Tece voda v synje more" (Shevchenko) **54**:372
"Technical Education" (Huxley) **67**:55-6
Technik des Dramas (Freytag)
See *Die Technik des Dramas*
Die Technik des Dramas (Freytag) **109**:137, 140-43
Technique of the Drama (Freytag)
See *Die Technik des Dramas*
Teckningar utur hvardagslifvet (Bremer) **11**:33, 35
Tecumseh; or, The Warrior of the West: A Poem of Four Cantos with Notes (Richardson) **55**:293, 302, 311-3, 317, 329-32, 335, 343
"Tegnér's Drapa" (Longfellow) **45**:132, 155, 190
Tékéli; ou, Le siège de Montgatz (Pixérécourt) **39**:274, 277, 279, 283-84, 287
"Telegram to General Hooker" (Lincoln) **201**:168
"The Telegraph and Telephone" (Cranch) **115**:42
Telemachus (Planché) **42**:273, 278, 286, 298-99
Telie (Bird) **197**:32
"Telka" (Field) **3**:210
"Tell All the Truth but Tell It Slant" (Dickinson) **21**:75; **77**:160
Tell Truth and Shame the Devil (Dunlap) **2**:214, 217
"Telling the Bees" (Whittier) **8**:493, 506, 509-10, 513, 517, 519-21, 531; **59**:356, 358, 360, 369, 371, 373-4
"The Tell-Tale Heart" (Poe) **1**:500; **16**:295, 301, 303, 309-10, 315-16, 319, 328-29, 331-32, 336; **55**:172, 202; **78**:256-63, 265-70, 272-75, 277-86, 289-90, 294, 296-300; **97**:180; **117**:320, 322-23; **211**:254-55, 273, 277, 280
"The Temeraire" (Melville) **123**:258
Temper (Morgan) **29**:390
Temper, or, Domestic Scenes (Opie) **65**:169, 173-4, 179
"Temperance Address Delivered before the Springfield Washington Temperance Society" (Lincoln) **18**:278
"Temperance Movement" (De Quincey) **4**:61
"The Tempest" (Barrett Browning) **61**:35-7
"The Tempest" (Lamb) **125**:303
"Un tempête sous un crâne" (Hugo) **10**:354, 357, 366, 378
The Templars in Cyprus: A Dramatic Poem (Werner)
See *Die Söhne des Thales: Ein dramatisches Gedicht*
"Le temple" (Lamartine) **11**:269
The Temple (Darwin)
See *The Temple of Nature; or Origin of Society*
The Temple of Independence (Dunlap) **2**:213
"The Temple of Infamy" (Harpur) **114**:144
Temple of Nature (Horne Tooke) **195**:301, 305
The Temple of Nature; or Origin of Society (Darwin) **106**:185-86, 190-92, 195-97, 199-200, 203, 207, 209-10, 212, 214, 216, 218, 221, 228-29, 232-34, 237, 239-40, 242, 244-45, 247-52, 254-56, 259-60, 262-66, 269, 274, 277-78
"The Temple Pyramid of Cholula" (Heredia)
See "En el Teocalli de Cholula"
"The temple soared" (Fuller) **50**:246
Die Templer auf Cypern (Werner)
See *Die Söhne des Thales: Ein dramatisches Gedicht*
Templos de España (Bécquer)
See *Historia de los Templos de España*
The Temptation (Krasiński) **4**:306
Temptation and Atonement (Gore) **65**:21
The Temptation of Pescara (Meyer)
See *Die Versuchung des Pescara*
The Temptation of Saint Anthony (Flaubert)
See *La tentation de Saint Antoine*
The Temptation of St. Anthony (Flaubert)
See *La tentation de Saint Antoine*
"10 de octubre!" (Martí)
See "October 10!"
Ten Letters to Dr. Joseph Priestly, in Answer to His Letters to the Inhabitants of Northumberland (Webster) **30**:405
"Ten piedad de mi" (Isaacs) **70**:310-11
Ten Sermons of Religion (Parker) **186**:168
Ten Tales (Maginn) **8**:440, 442-43
"Ten Theses" (Coleridge) **231**:99, 103, 106
"Ten Years Ago" (Clarke) **19**:233
Ten Years' Exile (Staël-Holstein)
See *Dix années d'exil*
Ten Years from the Life of a Woman; or, Bad Advice (Scribe)
See *Dix ans de la vie d'une femme; ou, Les Mauvais Conseils*
"The Tenant" (Very) **9**:376
The Tenant of Wildfell Hall (Brontë) **4**:38-43, 47-54, 56; **71**:73-74, 90, 104-5, 109-10, 112, 126, 134, 137, 141, 143-45, 147, 154-55, 157, 159, 164, 167, 169, 174, 179; **102**:1-73
Tenants of Malory (Le Fanu) **9**:301, 302, 304, 311; **58**:271, 295, 303
"Tendenzen" Fragment (Schlegel) **226**:174-75
"Tender Friendship in the Lower Estate" (Karamzin)
See "Nezhnost' druzhby v nizkom sostoianii"
The Tender Recollections of Irene McGillicuddy (Oliphant) **47**:288
"Les Ténèbres" (Baudelaire) **55**:10
"Tènébres" (Gautier) **1**:340, 350
Une ténébreuse affaire (Balzac) **5**:74; **153**:69
"Tengerihántás" (Arany) **34**:21
"Tennyson" (Mill) **179**:349-50
"Tennyson's Poems" (Mill) **58**:368
"The Tent on the Beach" (Whittier) **8**:509, 520; **59**:350
The Tent on the Beach, and Other Poems (Whittier) **8**:501
Tentation (Feuillet) **45**:87-90
La tentation de Saint Antoine (Flaubert) **2**:220, 227, 229-31, 233-4, 236-9, 243-6, 255-6; **10**:125, 132, 155-6; **19**:278; **62**:69, 76, 79, 82, 90-2, 96, 98-9, 111; **66**:262, 269-72; **135**:77, 84, 126, 172; **185**:189, 223, 245
"Les Tentations" (Baudelaire) **155**:105-10
The Tenth Haycock (Martineau) **137**:250
"El teocalli de Cholula" (Heredia)
See "En el Teocalli de Cholula"
"Teon i Eskhin" (Zhukovsky) **35**:379, 398
Teplitzer Fragmente (Novalis) **178**:24, 90
"The Terek's Gifts" (Lermontov) **126**:142
"Teresa" (Isaacs) **70**:306
Térésa (Dumas) **11**:42-43, 47, 67
"Teresa di Faenza" (Lazarus) **109**:292
"A természet vadvirága" (Petofi) **21**:278
"Terminus" (Emerson) **1**:279, 289, 296; **98**:177, 184
Ternove (Gobineau) **17**:79
"Terpsichore" (Holmes) **14**:101
Terpsichore (Herder) **8**:313
"The Terrace at Berne" (Arnold) **6**:44; **29**:34; **89**:4, 7
La terreur prussienne (Dumas) **71**:210
"A Terrible Disappointment" (Petofi)
See "Irtóztató csalódás"
"The Terrible Divination: A Story" (Bestuzhev)
See "Strashnoe gadanie: Rasskaz"
"The Terrible Doubt of Appearances" (Whitman) **4**:562
"A Terrible Night" (O'Brien) **21**:236, 245-46, 252
A Terrible Temptation (Reade) **2**:541, 546, 549; **74**:243, 248-49, 255, 263-64, 284
"A Terrible Vengeance" (Gogol)
See "Strašnaja mest"
"A Terribly Strange Bed" (Collins) **93**:64
Tessa (Laforgue) **221**:39
"Tessa's Surprise" (Alcott) **6**:16
"The Test" (Bestuzhev)
See "Ispytaniye"
Test (Murphy) **229**:234-35, 239
The Test of Honour (Rowson)
See *Mary; or, The Test of Honour, A Novel. By a Young Lady*
"Le testament" (Maupassant) **1**:458
"Testament" (Shevchenko)
See "Zapovit"
Testament (Comte) **54**:213
A Testament (Sacher-Masoch) **31**:295
"Testament de Champavert" (Borel) **41**:5-7
Le Testament d'un blagueur (Vallès) **71**:357
"The Testament of Cathaeir Mor" (Mangan) **27**:297-98
"El testamento" (Larra) **130**:249
Testigo de bronce (Zorrilla y Moral) **6**:523
"A Testimony" (Rossetti) **186**:277, 332
The Testimony of the Rocks; or, Geology and Its Bearings on the Two Theologies (Miller) **143**:6, 17, 33, 40, 57
"The Tests of Progressive Science" (Hopkins) **189**:112
"Tête de faune" (Rimbaud) **4**:458
"Tête-à-tête Confessions" (Willis) **194**:298
"La tête de Kenwarc'h" (Leconte de Lisle) **29**:225
La tête de mort; ou, Les ruines de Pompeïa (Pixérécourt) **39**:272, 278-79, 283, 289-90
"Tetemrehívás" (Arany) **34**:21
"Les Têtes de morts" (Laforgue) **221**:82, 84
Les têtes du serail (Hugo) **3**:234
Tetralogy (Wagner) **9**:437
Teutonic Mythology (Grimm Brothers)
See *Deutsche Mythologie*
Teverino (Sand) **2**:589, 599; **42**:310, 320; **57**:315-6
"Text zum Oratorium von Ett" (Brentano) **191**:37
"A Textbook of Literature for Russian Youth" (Gogol) **31**:95, 106, 125, 136; **162**:32, 35, 72-73
Textbook on World History (Grundtvig)
See *Lærebog i Verdenhistorien*
"Tezkomyslnot" (Macha) **46**:202
Thackeray (Trollope) **101**:345
Thalaba the Destroyer (Southey) **8**:447-49, 451, 453, 456, 461, 474, 476-77; **97**:260-61, 268, 275, 278-79, 281, 293-97, 307, 322, 332, 336
"Thamurīos Marching" (Browning) **79**:106, 113, 115-16, 174
"Thamyris" (Lampman) **194**:38
"Thanatopsis" (Bryant) **6**:158-60, 163-65, 168-74, 176-79, 182-83, 187-90, 192; **46**:2-4, 8-9, 17, 19-23, 29, 34, 37, 41, 44, 49-51, 53
"Thanatos to Kenelm" (Beddoes) **154**:79
"Thank God, I Glory in Thy Love!" (Osgood) **141**:353
"Thanks in Old Age" (Whitman) **31**:434
"Thanks to Felitsa" (Derzhavin)
See "Blagodarnost' Felitse"
"Thanks to meddling malice" (Baratynsky) **103**:47-9

"Thanks to the Soldier" (Lincoln) **201**:154
"A Thanksgiving" (Larcom) **179**:175, 178
"Thar's More in the Man Than Thar Is in the Land" (Lanier) **6**:264; **118**:227-28, 230, 235
That Boy of Norcott's (Lever) **23**:292
"That Enough Is as Good as a Feast" (Lamb) **10**:428
"That Letter" (Bellamy) **4**:30-31
"That Nature Is a Heraclitean Fire and of the Comfort of the Resurrection" (Hopkins) **17**:190, 214, 244, 246, 250, 253, 256; **189**:26, 32, 48, 71, 77, 92, 115, 120, 139, 146
"That Pig Morin" (Maupassant) **1**:460
"That Shadow My Likeness" (Whitman) **205**:326
"Thatchen O' the Rick" (Barnes) **75**:77
"Thaw" (Dacre) **151**:148
Theages oder Unterredungen von Schönheit und Liebe (Wieland) **17**:401, 419
Theaterg'schichten (Nestroy) **42**:243
Theatralische Sendung (Goethe) **90**:102-04
Théatre (Musset) **150**:340-41
Théâtre choisi (Pixérécourt) **39**:278, 280-83, 288
Théâtre de Clara Gazul (Mérimée) **6**:350, 353-4, 356, 362; **65**:44, 49, 54-6, 63, 79-82, 85, 87, 90, 95
Théâtre d'Eugène Scribe, dediéà ses collaborateurs (Scribe) **16**:381
Théâtre mystère comédies et ballets (Gautier) **59**:35
Théâtre pour l'usage des jeunes personnes (Genlis) **166**:33
Theatrical Mission (Goethe)
See *Theatralische Sendung*
The Theatrical Recorder (Holcroft) **85**:235
"Thébaide" (Gautier) **1**:350
"The Theban Sphinx" (De Quincey) **87**:53, 57
"Thee God I come from" (Hopkins) **189**:114
"Their Height in Heaven Comforts Not" (Dickinson) **21**:38
"Theism" (Mill) **11**:358, 378-79; **179**:210-11, 293
Theism, Atheism, and the Popular Theology (Parker)
See *Sermons of Theism, Atheism, and the Popular Theology*
"Thekla at her Lover's Grave" (Hemans) **71**:303
"Thekla's Answer" (Arnold) **29**:35
"Thekla's Song" (Harpur) **114**:144
Thel (Blake)
See *The Book of Thel*
"Them Ku Klux" (Lanier) **118**:227, 231
"Themself Are All I Have" (Dickinson) **21**:58
"Then She Bore Pale Desire" (Blake) **13**:240
"Les thénardiers" (Hugo) **10**:375
"Theodicaea Novissima" (Hallam) **110**:120, 141-46
Theodor Storm, Sämtliche Werke (Storm)
See *Sämtliche Werke*
Theodora Desanges (Linton)
See *The Second Youth of Theodora Desanges*
"Théodore de Banville" (Mallarmé) **41**:281
"Theodric: A Domestic Tale" (Campbell) **19**:175, 179, 181, 184, 190, 193, 197
Theodric: A Domestic Tale, and Other Poems (Campbell) **19**:175
Theogonie nach den Quellen des classischen, hebräischen und christlichen Alterthums (Feuerbach) **139**:242
Theokritos, Bion, und Moschos (Mörike) **10**:449
The Theological Works of Thomas Paine (Paine) **62**:325
Theology Explained and Defended in a Series of Sermons (Dwight) **13**:265, 269, 272
"The Theology of the Seven Epistles of St. Ignatius" (Newman) **38**:311
"Theon and Aeschines" (Zhukovsky)
See "Teon i Eskhin"
"A Théophie Gautier" (Banville) **9**:26, 28
"Théophile Gautier" (Baudelaire) **29**:70
Theophrastus Such (Eliot) **118**:118
Théorie de conte (Balzac) **153**:147
Théorie de l'unité universelle (Fourier) **51**:161
Théorie des quatre mouvements (Fourier) **51**:156, 161, 163, 171, 174
Theorie und Geschichte der Red-Kunst und Dicht-Kunst (Wieland) **17**:417, 419
"Theories of Food" (Lewes) **25**:287
Theories of Surplus Value (Marx) **114**:8, 70
Theory and History of the Fine Arts (Schlegel) **142**:302
Theory of a True Poetical Language (Chivers) **49**:54
"Theory of Colours" (Goethe) **4**:209-10
"Theory of Greek Tragedy" (De Quincey) **87**:74-5, 78; **198**:58
Theory of Legislation (Bentham) **38**:66, 68, 70
Theory of Life (Coleridge)
See *Hints towards the Formation of a More Comprehensive Theory of Life*
"A Theory of Poetry" (Timrod) **25**:365, 373, 378, 380
The Theory of Science in its General Lines (Fichte)
See *Die Wissenschaftslehre in ihrem allgemeinen Umrisse*
"Theory of the Vertebrate Skull" (Huxley) **67**:4
"Theosophie des Julius" (Schiller) **166**:154-55
"Theosophy" (Novalis) **13**:404
"Therania" (Allingham) **25**:9, 18
"There" (Herzen)
See "Elena"
"There" (Verlaine) **51**:371-72
"There Are Those Favorites of Inspiration" (Pavlova)
See "Est! liubimtsy vdokhnovenii"
"There Are Thousands" (Petofi)
See "Ezrivel terem"
"There came a day at summer's full" (Dickinson) **77**:58, 156
"There Came a Wind Like a Bugle" (Dickinson) **21**:81; **77**:97
"There Goes, There Drones the Green Noise, the Noise of Spring" (Nekrasov) **11**:411
"There Had Been Wars" (Shevchenko)
See "Buvaly voiny"
"There is a bondage which is worse to bear" (Wordsworth) **206**:301
"There Is a Fountain" (Cowper) **8**:127
There is a Time to Plant (Smolenskin)
See *Et la-ta'at*
"There Is a Sky above the Roof" (Verlaine) **230**:220
"There Is Another Loneliness" (Dickinson) **21**:69
"There Is in the Light of Autumn Evenings" (Tyutchev) **34**:393
"There is melody in the sea waves" (Tyutchev)
See "Pevuchest est v morskikh volnakh"
"There Is Mist on the Mountain" (Scott) **15**:318
"There is no God the wicked saith" (Prescott) **163**:6
There Is No Natural Religion (Blake) **37**:55; **57**:53, 91; **127**:5, 31, 123; **173**:9; **190**:50; **201**:34, 48, 142
"There Is Not a Spot in this Wide Peopled Earth" (Moodie) **113**:308
"There Should Have Been Roses" (Jacobsen) **34**:170-72
"There Stands in the Village of Subotiv" (Shevchenko)
See "Stojit' v seli Subotovi"
"There Was a Boy" (Wordsworth) **38**:405, 408; **166**:295; **206**:336
"There Was a Child Went Forth" (Whitman) **4**:584, 602; **31**:403-04, 425, 445; **81**:314, 358-59, 364, 368; **205**:191-92, 194, 217, 301, 309
Therefore (Mallarmé)
See *Igitur*
"There's a Certain Slant of Light" (Dickinson) **21**:42, 75; **171**:104-5, 111, 135-36, 177
"There's a Good Time Coming" (Foster) **26**:295
"There's a rare Soul of Poetry which may be" (Harpur) **114**:115
"There's Been a Death in the Opposite House" (Dickinson) **21**:43
"There's Danger in Old Chairs!" (Harris) **165**:188
"There's Dr. Clash" (Blake) **37**:29
"There's Rest" (Moodie) **113**:345
"Theresa" (Keller) **2**:412
Thérèse Aubert (Nodier) **19**:376, 381, 384-85
"Thermopylae" (Brontë) **109**:28
"These and Those" (Verlaine)
See "Les Uns et les autres"
"These are the days when birds come back" (Dickinson) **171**:105
"These Are the Nights that Beetles Love" (Dickinson) **21**:82
"These Carols" (Whitman) **4**:602
"These I Singing in Spring" (Whitman) **31**:387
"These Prairies Glow with Flowers" (Bryant) **6**:165
"These Sad But Glorious Days": Dispatches from Europe (Fuller) **211**:210, 214-16
"The Theses of Erastus" (Gladstone) **213**:111, 120
Theses on Feuerbach (Marx) **114**:36, 69
Theseus and Ariadne (Planché) **42**:287
Thessalonica (Brown) **74**:15, 49, 82-3; **122**:119
"Thestylis" (Leconte de Lisle) **29**:219
"They Desire a Better Country" (Rossetti) **186**:259
"They Put Us Far Apart" (Dickinson) **21**:38
"They Taught Me, and It Was a Fearful Creed" (Bryant) **46**:21
"They Teach" (Laforgue)
See "Dimanches"
"Thick-Headed Thoughts" (Gordon) **21**:168
"Thick-Sprinkled Bunting" (Whitman) **81**:318
"The Thief" (Nekrasov) **11**:407
Things As They Are; or, The Adventures of Caleb Williams (Godwin) **14**:36, 40-5, 47-53, 55-9, 61-2, 68-85, 87, 92-3; **130**:1-190
"Things Necessary to the Life of a Woman" (Warren) **13**:412, 415
"Things of August" (Laforgue) **221**:19
Things Seen (Hugo)
See *Choses vues*
"Think of It, O Soul" (Mörike)
See "Denk' es, o Seele"
"Think of the Soul" (Whitman) **205**:162, 164, 202
The Thinker (Liszt)
See *Il Pensieroso*
"Thinking Proletariat" (Pisarev) **25**:339
Thiodolf, the Islander (Fouqué) **2**:266, 268
"The Third Day" (Longfellow) **45**:138
"The Third Epistle" (Eminescu)
See "Scrisoarea a treia"
"The Third Fytte" (Beddoes) **154**:12
"Third Letter to Marcie" (Sand) **42**:358
"The Third of February, 1852" (Tennyson) **30**:294
"The Third Part of Christabel" (Maginn) **8**:438
"Third Sunday in Advent" (Keble) **87**:177
"Third Sunday in Lent" (Keble) **87**:157
Third Symphony (Beethoven) **227**:4
"The Third Voice" (Dodgson) **139**:128
"The Thirteen" (Balzac)
See "Histoire des treize"
The Thirteen-Book Prelude (Wordsworth) **206**:287
1356 (Dickinson) **77**:89
1347 (Dickinson) **77**:94
1377 (Dickinson) **77**:153
1364 (Dickinson) **77**:123
1339 (Dickinson) **77**:96
1331 (Dickinson) **77**:77
"Thirteenth Satire" (Adams) **175**:46-47, 49, 51-52

"Thirty-five" (Willis) **194**:307
"The Thirty Flasks" (Mangan) **27**:291, 302
Thirty Poems (Bryant) **6**:165
Thirty Years Later, the War, or Insurrection of El Chacho (Sarmiento) **123**:274
Thirty Years of Paris and of My Literary Life (Daudet)
See *Trente ans de Paris*
This Book Belongs to the King (Arnim)
See *Dies Buch Gehört dem König*
"This City and This Country" (Blake) **37**:29
"This Compost" (Whitman) **31**:368, 370, 402, 404, 408; **81**:258
"This Frog He Would Awooing Ride" (Blake) **37**:29
"This Is My Letter to the World" (Dickinson) **171**:217
"This is the land the sunset washes" (Dickinson) **171**:89
"This Life" (Arany)
See "Ez az élet"
"This Lime-Tree Bower My Prison" (Coleridge) **54**:71; **99**:2, 28, 37, 101, 104; **197**:243, 326; **231**:17, 79, 110, 130, 132
"This living hand" (Keats) **225**:248, 254-56
This Must Be Said, So Let It Be Said (Kierkegaard) **34**:238
"This twilight seems a veil of gause and mist" (Clare) **86**:120, 129
"This Was a Poet" (Dickinson) **171**:185
"This World is not Conclusion" (Dickinson) **171**:222
"Tho' the Last Glimpse of Erin" (Moore) **110**:186, 194, 198
Thomas à Becket (Darley) **2**:128, 130
Thomas Abbts Schriften (Herder)
See *Ueber Thomas Abbts Schriften*
"Thomas Carlyle" (Thoreau) **207**:257
Thomas Carlyle (Froude) **43**:181, 189, 197-98, 215-221
"Thomas Carlyle and His Works" (Thoreau) **138**:124, 127
Thomas Chalmers, Preacher, Philosopher, and Statesman (Oliphant) **221**:233
"Thomas Davis: An Elegy" (Ferguson) **33**:288
"Thomson and Cowper" (Hazlitt) **29**:166
"Thoralf and Synnöv" (Boyesen) **135**:10, 18
"Thora's Song" (Gordon) **21**:173
"Thoreau" (Emerson) **98**:73
"Thoreau" (Lowell) **90**:202, 206, 220-21
"The Thorn" (Wordsworth) **12**:386-87, 403, 430, 445; **111**:200-3, 207-8, 210-12, 223, 244, 263, 283, 291-92, 294, 312-13, 315-16, 338, 356, 367-69; **166**:244; **206**:234, 312, 336
"Thorns for the Rose" (Parton) **86**:347
"The Thorns in the Geate" (Barnes) **75**:73
"The Thorny Path of Honor" (Andersen) **7**:21; **79**:84, 89
"Thorp Green" (Brontë) **109**:38
"Those Evening Bells" (Moore) **110**:197
"Those Waiting for the Moving of the Water" (Leskov)
See "Cajuscie dvizenija vody"
"Those Who Have Perished and Those Who Are Perishing" (Pisarev)
See "Pogibšie i pogibajuščie"
Those Who Were Overlooked (Leskov)
See *Obojdennye*
"Thou Art Indeed Just, Lord" (Hopkins) **17**:225; **189**:52, 85-86, 139
"Thou Art the Eyes by Which I See" (Very) **9**:384
"Thou Art the Man" (Poe) **211**:253
"Thou camest to thy bower my love" (Tennyson) **202**:189
"Thou little Child" (Wordsworth) **206**:271
"Thou Mother with Thy Equal Brood" (Whitman) **4**:586; **31**:390; **205**:203, 208, 226
"Thou Orb Aloft Full-Dazzling" (Whitman) **31**:391
"Thou Shalt Hear the Judgement of the Fool" (Turgenev) **37**:385
Thou Shalt Not Lie (Grillparzer)
See *Weh dem, der lügt!*
"Thou who dost smile" (Boker) **125**:82
"Thought" (Allston) **2**:26
"Thought" (Lermontov) **47**:166
"Thought for Michael Angelo" (Horne) **127**:255, 271
"Thought May Well Be Ever Ranging" (Clough) **27**:105
"A Thought of Columbus" (Whitman)
See "A Prayer of Columbus"
"The Thought of Death" (Symonds) **34**:323
"A Thought on Book-Binding" (Melville) **123**:255
"A Thought on Thoughts" (Barrett Browning) **61**:22
"Thought while Making the Grave of a New Born Child" (Willis) **194**:307
"The thoughtful dragon" (Lonnrot) **53**:339
"The Thoughtful Ones" (Almqvist)
See "De fundersamme"
"Thoughts" (Amiel)
See "Pensées"
"Thoughts" (Arany)
See "Gondolatok"
"Thoughts" (Beddoes) **154**:56
"Thoughts" (Whitman) **31**:433
Thoughts (Joubert)
See *Pensées, essais, maxmimes, et correspondance de Joseph Joubert*
"Thoughts 1" (Whitman) **205**:162, 165
"Thoughts 2" (Whitman) **205**:162, 165
Thoughts, A Series of Sonnets (Harpur) **114**:95, 105, 107-8, 120, 138
"Thoughts and Doings" (Huxley) **67**:49
"Thoughts and Fancies" (Coleridge) **90**:26-7
"Thoughts at the Funeral of a Respected Friend" (Sigourney) **21**:309
"Thoughts at the Grave of Sir Walter Scott" (Sigourney) **21**:301
"Thoughts for Mourners" (Sigourney) **87**:337
"Thoughts from Various Authors" (Bestuzhev)
See "Mysli iz raznykh avtorov"
Thoughts in verse on Christian children; their ways and their privileges (Keble)
See *Lyra Innocentium: Thoughts in Verse on Christian Children, Their Ways, and Their Privileges*
Thoughts of a Recluse (Wright) **74**:362
"Thoughts on a Tomb" (Zhukovsky) **35**:377, 402-03, 405
Thoughts on African Colonization (Garrison) **149**:237, 246-48, 250, 257
Thoughts on Art, Philosophy, and Religion (Dobell) **43**:60
"Thoughts on Beauty and Art" (Barnes) **75**:28, 55, 65-6
Thoughts on English Prosody (Jefferson) **11**:190; **103**:105
Thoughts on Government (Adams) **106**:11, 13
Thoughts on Man: His Nature, Productions, and Discoveries (Godwin) **14**:50, 62, 66; **130**:26-27, 36-37, 40
"Thoughts on My Sick-Bed" (Wordsworth) **138**:284-85, 313
"Thoughts on Myth, Epic, and History" (Grimm Brothers) **3**:219
Thoughts on Parliamentary Reform (Mill) **179**:227, 313
"Thoughts on Poetry and Its Varieties" (Mill) **179**:208, 211, 338
Thoughts on Purity of Election (Milnes) **61**:138
"Thoughts on Reading" (Whitman) **81**:239
"Thoughts on Sunday Morning" (Fuller) **5**:170
Thoughts on the Condition of Women, and on the Injustice of Mental Subordination (Robinson) **142**:153, 157-59, 173, 198, 202-4, 208, 226, 241, 247
"Thoughts on the Devotional Taste and on Sects and Establishments" (Barbauld) **185**:52, 118, 120
"Thoughts on the Enfranchisement of the Negroes" (Brackenridge) **227**:116
Thoughts on the Importance of the Manners of the Great to General Society (More) **27**:332-33, 337; **141**:164, 170, 233, 269, 306
"Thoughts on the Inconsistency of Human Expectations" (Barbauld) **185**:7, 26
"Thoughts on the Inequality of Conditions" (Barbauld) **185**:149, 156
"Thoughts on the Present Indian War" (Brackenridge) **227**:73
"Thoughts on the Soul" (Dana) **53**:158, 175
"Thoughts on True Freedom" (Karamzin)
See "Mysli ob istinnoy svobode"
"Thoughts Suggested at the Bazaar at Kingston House" (Barnes) **75**:42
"Thousand-and-Second Tale of Scheherazade" (Poe) **94**:240
"Thousands of Years from Now" (Andersen)
See "Orn Aartusinder"
Thraliana: The Diary of Mrs. Hester Lynch Thrale (Later Mrs. Piozzi), 1776-1809 (Piozzi) **57**:236, 240, 251-3, 257-9, 261, 263, 265-70, 284, 287-91, 293, 297, 299, 304
"Thränenregen" (Muller) **73**:364, 370-72, 375
"Thrawn Janet" (Stevenson) **5**:403, 431, 434; **63**:228, 274; **193**:204, 216, 228-29, 231-34, 238-41, 279
3 (Dickinson) **77**:120
"The Three" (Wergeland) **5**:537
Three Ages (Martineau) **137**:269
"The Three Bears" (Southey)
See "The Story of the Three Bears"
The Three Clerks: A Novel (Trollope) **6**:453, 463, 465, 470-71, 492, 499-500, 511-12, 514; **101**:235, 253, 266, 275, 329, 333; **215**:208-9, 215, 226, 230, 299, 302-3, 306, 337
The Three-Cornered Hat (Alarcón)
See *El sombrero de tres picos*
The Three Cousins (Trollope) **30**:330
Three Cutters (Marryat) **3**:317, 320
"Three Encounters" (Turgenev)
See "Three Meetings"
"The Three Enemies" (Rossetti) **2**:562-3, 576; **50**:272; **66**:305; **186**:318
"Three epilogues by way of Farewell to Personal Literature" (Verlaine)
See "Trois épilogues en manière d'adieux à la littérature personnelle"
"The Three Eras of Libbie Marsh" (Gaskell)
See "Libbie Marsh's Three Eras"
Three Essays on Picturesque Beauty (Gilpin) **30**:41-3
Three Essays on Religion (Mill)
See *Nature, the Utility of Religion, and Theism*
"The Three Fishers" (Kingsley) **35**:218, 226, 232
"The Three Flowers" (Allingham) **25**:8
"The Three Friends" (Gordon) **21**:149, 151, 155, 161, 163
"The Three Friends" (Lamb) **10**:389
"Three Friends of Mine" (Longfellow) **2**:492; **45**:132
The Three Friends—A Socialist Tragedy (Horne) **127**:255
"Three Gipsies" (Lenau) **16**:264
"Three Graces of Christian Science" (Martineau) **26**:349
"The Three Graves" (Coleridge) **9**:148; **111**:291-92; **177**:17, 122, 159-60; **231**:72
"The Three Graves" (Wordsworth) **111**:291-92
The Three Guardsmen (Dumas)
See *Les trois mousquetaires*
"The Three Guides" (Brontë) **4**:45
The Three Gypsies (Liszt)
See *Die drei Zigeuner*
"The Three Half Crowns" (Mangan) **27**:303

Time Works Wonders (Jerrold) **2**:395, 397, 401-06
"The Time-Piece" (Cowper) **8**:110-11, 115, 128-29; **94**:27, 30, 120
"The Times" (Barbauld) **185**:31
"The Times" (Barnes) **75**:23, 43-4, 96, 101, 105, 108-09
"Times o' Year" (Barnes) **75**:20, 26, 68
"Time's Revenges" (Browning) **79**:94, 102
Timoleon (Melville) **3**:351, 363, 379; **91**:184; **157**:212; **181**:297
Timoleone (Alfieri) **101**:8, 32, 38, 42
"Timon of Athens" (Lamb) **125**:304
Timon of Athens (Cumberland) **167**:143, 154, 157, 187-88
Timothy Crump's Ward (Alger) **8**:41; **83**:96, 142, 146
Timour the Tartar (Lewis) **11**:306
The Tin Box (Alger) **8**:43-44; **83**:92
"The Tin Soldier" (Andersen)
See "Den standhaftige Tinsoldat"
"The Tinder Box" (Andersen)
See "Fyrtøiet"
"The Tinker" (Wordsworth) **111**:203-4
"The Tint I Cannot Take—Is Best" (Dickinson) **21**:83
"A tintásüveg" (Petofi) **21**:283
"Tintern Abbey" (Wordsworth)
See "Lines Composed a Few Miles above Tintern Abbey, on Revisiting the Banks of the Wye during a Tour, July 13, 1798"
"The Tippler and His Horse" (Muller) **73**:353
"The Tippler to His Bottle" (Horton) **87**:89
"Le tir et le cimetière" (Baudelaire) **155**:23, 27-28
"The Tired" (Webster) **230**:233-34, 253
"Tired Memory" (Patmore) **9**:349, 358
"Tiresias" (Tennyson) **30**:235, 280, 293; **202**:293-97, 335
Tiresias, and Other Poems (Tennyson) **202**:288-91, 293
Tiriel (Blake) **13**:183, 218-21; **37**:14, 20, 22; **173**:128; **190**:11, 14
Tirocinium; or, Review of Schools (Cowper) **8**:98; **94**:8-9, 14-16, 19-21
'Tis All for the Best (More) **141**:282
"'Tis April and the morning, love" (Clare) **86**:87
"Tis Finished" (Very) **9**:387
"Tis not that Dying hurts us so" (Dickinson) **171**:142, 176
"Tis Opposites Entice" (Dickinson) **21**:69
"Tis Sixty Years Since" (Oliphant) **221**:242
'Tis Sixty Years Since (Scott)
See *Waverley; or, 'Tis Sixty Years Since*
"Tis so appalling-it exhilirates sic" (Dickinson) **77**:75-76
"Tis the Last Glass of Claret" (Maginn) **8**:441
"Tis the Last Rose of Summer" (Moore) **6**:397; **110**:196
"The Tisza" (Petofi) **21**:285
"Le Titan" (Hugo) **189**:235
Titan (Jean Paul) **7**:226, 232-33, 236, 238-40
The Tithe Proctor (Carleton) **199**:8, 10, 12, 20, 24-25, 46, 56, 80, 97
The Tithe Proctor: Being a Tale of the Tithe Rebellion in Ireland (Carleton) **3**:85-86, 90
"Tithon" (Tennyson) **202**:335
"Tithonus" (Tennyson) **30**:220, 239, 279-80, 283; **65**:358-9; **115**:237, 240; **202**:242, 280
"Titmouse" (Emerson) **1**:284, 296; **38**:186; **98**:184
Tiw: or, a View on the Roots and Stems of the English as a Teutonic Tongue (Barnes) **75**:26-7, 40, 65
"To" (Halleck) **47**:57
"To ——" (Keats) **73**:154
"To ——" (Lanier) **6**:237
"To ——" (Moore) **110**:177
"To ——" (Osgood) **141**:326, 352, 354-55
"To ——" (Pinkney) **31**:276
"To ——" (Poe) **55**:214; **117**:242, 280
"To ——" (Smith) **59**:320
"To ——" (Willis) **194**:287, 301
"To ——, After Reading a Life and Letters" (Tennyson) **65**:381
"To a Bavarian Girl" (Taylor) **89**:298
"To a Bunch of Grapes" (Beddoes) **154**:56
"To a Caty-Did" (Freneau) **1**:317, 322; **111**:141
"To a Certain Civilian" (Whitman) **31**:360; **81**:314; **205**:339
"To a Child" (Baillie) **151**:46
"To a Child" (Longfellow) **2**:493; **45**:155
"To a China Tree" (Chivers) **49**:48
"To a City Pigeon" (Willis) **194**:297, 302
"To a Cloud" (Bryant) **6**:161
"To a Comet" (Harpur) **114**:144
"To a Common Prostitute" (Whitman) **31**:403, 428, 432
"To a Comrade" (Corbière) **43**:14
"To a Dead Woman" (Meyer)
See "Einer Toten"
"To a Dear Sister" (Osgood) **141**:353
"To a False Friend" (Hood) **16**:216
"To a Flower" (Lampman) **194**:8
To a Former Goethe Disciple (Heine)
See *An einen ehemaligen Goetheaner*
"To a Fragment of Cotton" (Sigourney) **87**:346-48
"To a Friend" (Arnold) **6**:44; **29**:35
"To a Friend" (Keats) **73**:147, 231-32
"To a Friend" (Novalis) **13**:364
"To a Friend Who Asked How I Felt When the Nurse First Presented My Infant to Me" (Coleridge) **99**:37
"To a Friend Who Sent Me Some Roses" (Keats) **225**:224
"To a Fringed Gentian" (Bryant) **6**:169, 172, 193; **46**:7-9
"To A. G. A." (Brontë) **16**:122
"To a Gentleman Who Requested a List of the Articles Which Female Vanity Has Comprized Under the Head of Necessaries" (Warren) **226**:263, 291
"To a Gipsy Child by the Sea-shore" (Arnold) **29**:4, 35; **89**:95; **218**:147
To a Great Nation (Barbauld) **185**:44, 58-59, 142
"To a Highland Girl" (Wordsworth) **12**:434
"To a Historian" (Whitman) **205**:162, 165, 197
"To a Honey Bee" (Freneau) **1**:315
"To A. I. Kaznacheevu" (Aksakov)
See "A. I. Kaznacheevu"
"To a Katydid" (Holmes) **14**:100
"To a Lady, on being asked by reasons or quitting England in the spring" (Byron) **149**:163
"To a Lady, with Some Painted Flowers" (Barbauld) **185**:27, 35, 37, 92, 113, 122, 154-55
"To a Lofty Beauty Edith Southey, from her Poor Kinsman" (Coleridge) **90**:6, 26
"To a Magnate" (Pushkin) **3**:443
"To a Maniac" (Opie) **65**:160
"To a Millionaire" (Lampman) **25**:194; **194**:10, 24, 61, 118-19
"To a Mocking Bird Singing in a Tree" (Ridge) **82**:184
"To a Moralist" (Schiller) **39**:339
"To a Mosquito" (Bryant) **6**:161, 167; **46**:7
"To a Mountain" (Kendall) **12**:185, 187, 189-90, 198, 200
"To a Nightingale" (Aksakov)
See "K solov'iu"
"To a Nightingale" (Karamzin)
See "K solov'iu"
"To a Nightingale" (Smith)
See "Sonnet 3"
"To a Nun" (Solomos) **15**:393
"To a Passing Woman" (Baudelaire)
See "À une passante"
"To a Patriotic Gentleman" (Warren) **226**:261
"To a Persian Boy" (Taylor) **89**:357
"To a Polish Mother" (Mickiewicz) **3**:398
"To a Republican Friend" (Arnold) **29**:34
"To a Rosebud in Humble Life" (Clare) **9**:74
"To a Russian Landowner" (Gogol) **31**:138
"To a Shred of Linen" (Sigourney) **21**:299, 301, 310; **87**:346-48
"To a Skylark" (Shelley) **18**:319, 329, 336, 355, 361-62; **175**:214, 264
"To a Southern Statesman" (Whittier) **8**:519
"To a Spindle" (Bloomfield) **145**:174
"To a Star Seen at Twilight" (Ridge) **82**:184
"To a Stream" (Darley) **2**:133
"To a Waterfowl" (Bryant) **6**:158, 162-63, 168-70, 172-74, 177, 183-84, 190, 192; **46**:3, 6, 23, 32, 41, 43-4, 47, 53-4
"To a Western Boy" (Whitman) **4**:575
"To a Winter Scene" (Clare) **86**:110
"To a Young Ass" (Coleridge) **54**:71; **231**:60
"To a Young Gentleman Residing in France" (Warren) **13**:413
"To a Young Lady" (Warren) **226**:261
"To a Young Lady on Showing an Excellent Piece of Painting, Much Faded" (Warren) **13**:413
"To a Young Lady Who Requested the Author to Draw Her Character" (Trumbull) **30**:345, 349
"To All" (Very) **9**:383
"To Albert Mérat" (Verlaine)
See "À Albert Mérat"
"To Allegra Florence in Heaven" (Chivers) **49**:38, 40, 51, 56
"To Allegra in Heaven" (Chivers)
See "To Allegra Florence in Heaven"
"To Amine" (Mangan) **27**:278
"To an Aeolian Harp" (Mörike) **10**:446
"To an Angry Zealot" (Freneau) **111**:113
"To an Äolian Harp" (Mörike)
See "An eine Äolsharfe"
"To an Apostate" (Heine) **147**:202
"To an April Daisy" (Clare) **9**:74
"To an Author" (Freneau) **111**:142, 181
"To an Echo on the Banks of the Hunter" (Harpur) **114**:107-8, 115, 117, 144
"To an Enthusiast" (Dyer) **129**:107
"To an Insect" (Holmes) **14**:128
"To an Insignificant Flower" (Clare) **9**:123
"To an Old Man" (Freneau) **111**:144
"To an Ultra-Protestant" (Lampman) **25**:194; **194**:21, 28
"To an Unfaithful One" (Aksakov)
See "K nevernoi"
"To an Unknown Friend" (Nekrasov) **11**:418
"To Anna" (Opie) **65**:160
"To Anna" (Rowson) **182**:254, 257
"To Asra" (Coleridge) **231**:124
"To Autumn" (Keats)
See "Ode to Autumn"
"To Autumn Robin" (Clare) **9**:80
"To Baratynsky" (Pavlova)
See *A. D. Baratynskoy*
"To Bayard Taylor" (Lanier) **6**:248
"To Be or Not to Be" (Blake) **37**:29
"To Beethoven" (Lanier) **118**:286
"To Blazes!" (Petofi)
See "Lánggal égo"
"To Bogdanovic" (Baratynsky)
See "Bogdanovicu"
"To Brighton" (Jefferies) **47**:134-35
"To Brødre" (Andersen) **214**:62
"To Brown Dwarf of Rügen" (Whittier) **8**:529
To Buonaparte, the Liberator (Foscolo) **97**:49
"To Byron" (Jones) **222**:160
"To Byron" (Keats) **73**:145, 148
"To Carmen Sylva" (Lazarus) **109**:339
"To Cecilia" (Chivers) **49**:71
"To Charles Cowden Clarke" (Keats) **73**:318, 331; **225**:139, 225
"To Charles Knight" (Dickens) **230**:20
"To Charlotte Cushman" (Lanier) **118**:215
"To Chaucer" (Lampman) **25**:172, 184, 193, 217; **194**:29, 36, 55, 132

"To Cole, the Painter, Departing For Europe" (Bryant) **46**:55
"To Consoling Rays . . ." (Laforgue)
See "Aux rayons consolants . . ."
"To Constantia Singing" (Shelley) **18**:344, 370
"To Count Razumsky" (Pushkin) **83**:272
"To Cuba" (Manzano) **155**:289
"To Cuban Women" (Gómez de Avellaneda)
See "A las cubanas"
"To Damascus" (Kendall) **12**:181, 192
"To Death" (Lampman) **194**:129, 131
"To Death" (Shelley) **18**:342
"To Delvig" (Baratynsky) **103**:10
"To Dependence" (Smith)
See "Sonnet 57"
"To Die Takes Just a Little While" (Dickinson) **21**:42; **77**:163
"To Don Quixote" (Verlaine)
See "À Don Quichotte"
"To Dr. Aikin ..." (Barbauld) **185**:31-32, 38, 122, 128
"To Dr. Moore" (Williams)
See "An Epistle to Dr. Moore"
"To Dr. Priestley" (Barbauld) **185**:90, 144
"To Dr. Thomas Shearer" (Lanier) **118**:219
"To E" (Levy) **59**:94, 102, 120
"To E. FitzGerald" (Tennyson) **30**:280
"To E. Milkeev" (Pavlova) **138**:14
"To E—, with the foregoing Sonnets" (Reynolds) **146**:213
"To Ebert" (Klopstock)
See "An Ebert"
"To Edward Williams" (Shelley) **18**:369
"To Eliza" (Horton) **87**:110
"To Elizabeth Linley" (Sheridan) **91**:232
"To Ellen" (Emerson) **38**:189
"To Emilia" (Heredia)
See "A Emilia"
"To Emir Abdel-Kader" (Norwid) **17**:368
"To England" (Adams) **33**:4
"To England" (Boker) **125**:31, 33
"To Ennui" (Halleck) **47**:76
"To Ermengarde" (Willis) **194**:305
"To Ernest Delahaye" (Verlaine)
See "À Ernest Delahaye"
"To Eugene. Life at Zvanka" (Derzhavin)
See "Evgeniu. Zhizn' Zvanskaya"
"To Eugénie" (Verlaine)
See "À Eugénie"
"To Eva" (Emerson) **98**:92, 96
"To Evening" (Foscolo)
See "Alla sera"
To Every Sage His Share of Folly (Ostrovsky)
See *Na vsyakogo mudretsa dovolno prostoty*
"To F. W. N." (Newman) **38**:343
"To Fancy" (Keats) **8**:355
"To Fancy" (Neal) **161**:319
"To Fancy" (Smith)
See "Sonnet 47"
"To Fanny" (Keats) **8**:362; **73**:154
"To Fausta" (Arnold) **29**:35
"To Fidelio, Long Absent on the Great Public Cause, Which Agitated All America in 1776" (Warren) **13**:413
"To Fight Aloud Is Very Brave" (Dickinson) **21**:37, 56
"To Florence" (Foscolo) **8**:278
"To Foreign Lands" (Whitman) **31**:426; **205**:217
"To Genius" (Neal) **161**:319
"To Gentlemen: A Call to Be a Husband" (Parton) **86**:362
"To George Cruikshank..." (Arnold) **29**:4
"To George Eliot" (Woolson) **82**:311
"To George Felton Mathew" (Keats) **225**:225, 251
"To George Sand: A Recognition" (Barrett Browning) **61**:5
"To (Georgiana)" (Pinkney) **31**:280
"To Get the Final Lilt of Songs" (Whitman) **31**:434
"To Gladstone" (Crawford) **127**:223
"To God" (Blake) **190**:6
"To Gogol" (Shevchenko)
See "To Hohol"
"To Governor Johnstone, one of the British Commissioners, on his late letters and offers to bribe certain eminent characters in America, and threatening afterwards to appeal to the public" (Paine) **62**:321
"To Hampstead" (Hunt) **70**:291, 293-94, 297
"To Harriet" (Shelley) **18**:358
"To hear an Oriole sing" (Dickinson) **77**:110
"To Helen" (Poe) **1**:492, 528; **16**:330; **117**:196, 207-10, 212, 227, 231, 235-37, 242-44, 280-82, 287, 309, 332; **211**:249
"To Henrique. Pray and Hope!" (Isaacs)
See "A Henrique. Ora y espera!"
"To Henry" (Opie) **65**:160
"To Henry George in America" (Adams) **33**:25
"To Him that Was Crucified" (Whitman) **31**:372; **205**:172
"To Him Who Says He Loves" (Dacre) **151**:170
"To His Distant Lady" (Foscolo)
See "Alla sua donna lontana"
"To His Friend on Her Recovery" (Foscolo)
See "All' amica risanata"
"To his lady" (Leopardi)
See "Alla sua donna"
"To His Watch" (Hopkins) **17**:235; **189**:113, 146
"To Hohol" (Shevchenko) **54**:380
"To Homer" (Keats) **73**:194; **121**:129, 141
"To Honoria, on Her Journey to Dover" (Warren) **13**:413
"To Hope" (Beethoven) **227**:26
"To Hope" (Hood) **16**:234
"To Hope" (Keats) **73**:311, 334
"To Hope" (Smith) **115**:156
"To Hope" (Williams) **135**:336
"To Ianthe: With Petrarca's Sonnets" (Landor) **14**:199
"To Imitators" (Baratynsky)
See "Podrazhatelyam"
"To Iurev" (Pushkin) **83**:308
"To J. W." (Emerson) **1**:296; **98**:179
To James Russell Lowell on his Fiftieth Birthday (Cranch) **115**:35
"To Jane: The Invitation" (Shelley) **18**:357-58, 362, 369, 371-73; **93**:309
"To Jane: The Keen Stars Were Twinkling" (Shelley) **18**:369-70; **93**:309
"To Jane: The Recollection" (Shelley) **18**:357-58, 362, 369, 371-73; **93**:309
"To Jarifa in an Orgy" (Espronceda)
See "A Jarifa en una orgía"
"To Joachim Lelewel" (Mickiewicz) **3**:398
"To Joanna" (Wordsworth) **111**:219
"To John Ruskin" (Adams) **33**:25
"To Joseph Brenan" (Mangan) **27**:301
To Joy (Schiller)
See *Lied an die Freude*
"To Julia" (Barnes) **75**:70
"To Julia" (Boker) **125**:82
"To K.A. Sverbeevaya" (Baratynsky) **103**:10
"To know just how He suffered-would be dear" (Dickinson) **77**:162
"To Konsin" (Baratynsky)
See "K Konsinu"
"To Ladies' Eyes" (Moore) **110**:185
"To Lady H—, On an Old Ring Found at Tunbridge-Wells" (Moore) **110**:177
"To Lallie" (Levy) **59**:110
"To Laura" (Kendall) **12**:183
"To Laura" (Sheridan) **91**:232
To Laura (Foscolo) **97**:48-9
"To Laura, and a Love Elegy to Laura" (Opie) **65**:160
"To Laura, Melancholy" (Schiller) **39**:339
"To Leigh Hunt" (Keats) **73**:312
"To Lenore" (Osgood) **141**:325
"To Liberty" (Robinson) **142**:132
"To Lindorf" (Dacre) **151**:148
"To Literary Aspirants" (Parton) **86**:374
"To Lizzie" (Ridge) **82**:180
"To Lorenzo" (Opie) **65**:160
"To Lothario" (Opie) **65**:160
"To Louis Napoleon" (Boker) **125**:25
"To Lucy" (Derzhavin) **215**:19
"To Luigia Pallavicini, Thrown from Her Horse" (Foscolo)
See "A Luigia Pallavicini caduto da cavello"
"To Luxury" (Thelwall) **162**:308
"To M—, from Abroad" (Willis) **194**:300
"To M. ł. on the Day of Taking Her Holy Communion" (Mickiewicz) **3**:399-400
"To M. L. S." (Poe) **117**:242, 280
"To Madeline" (Tennyson) **202**:337
"To Maidens and Youths" (Stevenson)
See "Virginibus Puerisque"
"To Marcia" (Freneau) **111**:133
"To Marguerite" (Arnold) **89**:19; **218**:147, 190, 275-76
"To Marie with a Copy of the Translation of Faust" (Taylor) **89**:326
To Marry or Not to Marry (Inchbald) **62**:144-6, 185
"To Mary" (Cowper) **8**:116, 123; **94**:34
To Matija Čop (Preseren)
See *Matiju Čopu*
"To Meet So Enabled a Man" (Dickinson) **21**:50
"To Melancholy" (Smith)
See "Sonnet 32"
"To Members of Parliament, the Prince and the Nation" (Haydon) **146**:141
"To Mercy" (Karamzin)
See "K milosti"
"To Meta: The Cloister" (Arnold) **218**:275
"To M.H." (Wordsworth) **111**:219
"To Mie Tirante" (Darley) **2**:133
"To Mihril" (Mangan) **27**:290
"To Mira, on the Care of her Infant" (Yearsley) **174**:317
"To Miss Macartney" (Cowper) **94**:23, 26
"To Miss R. B." (Fuller) **5**:169
"To Mr. —" (Warren) **13**:431; **226**:261
"To Mr. ****, An Unlettered Poet, On Genius Unimprov'd" (Yearsley) **174**:306, 338
"To Mr. Arthur Aikin" (Dyer) **129**:136, 138-40, 143-44
"To Mr. R—, on His Benevolent Scheme for Rescuing Poor Children from Vice and Misery by Promoting Sunday Schools" (Yearsley) **174**:316
"To Mr. S. T. Coleridge" (Barbauld) **185**:89, 143
"To Mr. West on his Translation of Pindar" (Warton) **118**:356
"To Mrs Henry T—ghe, On Reading Her 'Psyche'. 1802" (Moore) **110**:178
"To Mrs. King" (Cowper) **94**:27
"To Mrs. P." (Barbauld) **185**:129, 133
"To Mrs. Priestley, with some Drawings of Birds and Insects" (Barbauld) **185**:34, 37, 128, 151
"To Mrs. Siddons" (Baillie) **151**:86, 114
"To Mrs. V-N" (Yearsley) **174**:299
"To Muscovite Friends" (Mickiewicz)
See "Do przyjaciól Moskali"
"To My Brother George" (Keats) **73**:331; **225**:139, 141-42, 186-87
"To My Class, On Certain Fruits and Flowers Sent Me in Sickness" (Lanier) **118**:218-19
To My Convalescent Friend (Foscolo)
See *Ode all'amica risanata*
"To My Daughter C." (Isaacs)
See "A mi hija Clementina"
"To My Father" (Stevenson) **5**:401
"To My Father on His Birthday" (Barrett Browning) **61**:27, 30, 34
"To My Fellow Countrymen" (Shevchenko)
See "Poslaniie"
"To My First Neighbour" (Derzhavin) **215**:6
"To My Friend, the Poet" (Pushkin) **83**:271
"To My Friends" (Pushkin) **83**:256

"To My Friends, on Sending Schiller's 'Ode to Joy'" (Tyutchev) **34**:392, 395
"To my Friends, who ridiculed a tender Leave-taking" (Arnold) **89**:20
"To My Lyre" (Smith) **115**:155-56
"To My Mother" (Chivers)
See "To My Mother in Heaven"
"To My Mother" (Hayne) **94**:160
"To My Mother" (Poe) **117**:227, 242
"To my Mother" (Rossetti) **186**:309
To My Mother (Castro)
See *A mi madre*
To My Mother (Hayne) **94**:134
"To My Mother from the Apennines" (Willis) **194**:307
"To My Mother in Heaven" (Chivers) **49**:50, 70
"To My Muscovite Friends" (Mickiewicz)
See "Do przyjaciól Moskali"
"To My Native Land" (Mangan) **27**:296, 299
"To My Niece" (Wordsworth) **138**:310
"To My Old Friend Peter Schlemihl" (Chamisso) **82**:9
"To My Old Oak Table" (Bloomfield) **145**:132
"To My Old Readers" (Holmes) **14**:128
"To My Old Schoolmaster" (Whittier) **59**:360, 371-3
"To My Sister" (Gordon) **21**:154, 160-61, 173
"To My Sister" (Whittier) **59**:371, 387
"To My Sister" (Wordsworth) **12**:445; **206**:274
"To My Son" (Arany)
See "Fiamnak"
"To My Wife" (Heredia) **209**:123
"To My Wife" (Verlaine)
See "À ma femme"
"To Myself" (Derzhavin) **215**:19
"To N." (Tyutchev) **34**:389
"To N. M. Yazykov" (Baratynsky) **103**:4
"To N. V. Gogol, 3 July 1847" (Belinski) **5**:101, 110-11
"To Nature" (Coleridge) **231**:152
"To Night" (Shelley) **18**:362
"To Nina" (Derzhavin) **215**:11, 18
"To N.N." (Tyutchev) **34**:394
"To Oblivion" (Smith)
See "Sonnet 90"
"To Old Roscoff" (Corbière)
See "Au vieux Roscoff"
"To One Afar" (Taylor) **89**:298
"To One in Paradise" (Poe) **117**:217, 227, 233, 237, 243, 280-81, 299, 308; **211**:246
"To One Who Has Been Long in City Pent" (Keats) **225**:243
"To One Who Is Too Cheerful" (Baudelaire) **155**:40
"To Osnovjanenko" (Shevchenko)
See "Do Osnovjanenka"
"To Our Ladies of Death" (Thomson) **18**:392, 397-98, 403, 409, 412-13, 418, 421, 424
"To Peter Porcupine" (Freneau) **111**:129
"To Phaon" (Robinson) **142**:175
"To Poesy" (Beddoes) **154**:56
"To Potentates and Judges" (Derzhavin)
See "Oda. Prelozhenie 81-go psalma"
"To Princess Roukin" (Verlaine)
See "À la Princesse Roukhine"
"To Princess Z.A. Volkonskaya" (Baratynsky)
See "Knyagine Z.A. Volkonskoy"
"To R. B." (Hopkins) **17**:225, 260, 262
"To Reshemysl" (Derzhavin) **215**:26, 28, 40, 42, 46
"To Rev. W. L. Bowles" (Coleridge) **231**:109
"To Rhea" (Emerson) **38**:169, 191
"To Richard Wagner" (Lanier) **118**:217, 286
To Romance (Byron) **149**:56
"To Rulers and Judges" (Derzhavin)
See "Oda. Prelozhenie 81-go psalma"
To Russian, Polish and All Slav Friends (Bakunin)
See *To the Russian, Polish, and All the Slav Countries*
"To Sarah" (Fuller) **50**:247
"To Sarah" (Osgood) **141**:320-21
"To Science" (Poe) **55**:151; **78**:282
"To Seem the Stranger Lies My Lot" (Hopkins) **17**:192, 261-62; **189**:4, 26, 77, 83-84, 146
"To Sensibility" (Williams) **135**:255
"To Silence" (Beddoes) **154**:10
"To Silvia" (Leopardi)
See "A Silvia"
"To Simplicity of Manners" (Thelwall) **162**:309
"To Sir Robert Smyth: What is Love" (Paine) **62**:324
"To Sleep" (Keats) **73**:196-97; **225**:135
"To Sleep!" (Tennyson) **202**:291
"To Solitude" (Warton)
See "Ode to Solitude"
"To Some Ladies" (Keats) **73**:311; **225**:242
"To Spring or Concerning the Antique Fables" (Leopardi)
See "Alla primavera o delle favole antiche"
"To Stella" (Yearsley) **174**:333, 337
"To Superstition" (Warton)
See "Ode to Superstition"
"To Sylvia" (Levy) **59**:95
"To Sympathy" (Dacre) **151**:148
"To Tartar, A Terrier Beauty" (Beddoes) **154**:47, 49
"To the Apennines" (Bryant) **6**:164; **46**:47
"To the Apollo on my pin" (Fuller) **50**:246
"To the Aurora Borealis" (Cranch) **115**:8, 32, 54
"To the Body" (Patmore) **9**:339, 354, 359, 363
"To the British Democracy" (Jones) **222**:131
"To the Cam" (Dyer) **129**:93
"To the Canary Bird" (Very) **9**:380, 390-91
"To the Chartist Body" (Jones) **222**:139
To the Citizens of the United States (Paine) **62**:271
"To the Coat of Arms of New Granada" (Isaacs)
See "Al escudo de armas de Nueva Granada"
"To the Coterie" (Baratynsky)
See "Kotterii"
"To the Cricket" (Lampman) **25**:208
"To the Critic of Barry's Works in the Edinburgh Review, Aug. 1810" (Haydon) **146**:139
"To the crowd life's daily cares are sweet" (Baratynsky)
See "Tolpe trevozhny den' priveten"
"To the Daisy" (Wordsworth) **12**:395; **206**:245
"To the Dandelion" (Lowell) **90**:190, 215
"To the Dead and the Living" (Shevchenko)
See "Poslaniie"
"To the Driving Cloud" (Longfellow) **45**:168; **101**:122; **103**:282
"To the Duke of Wellington" (Arnold) **29**:35
"To The Dying Clad" (Longfellow) **101**:122
"To the Eternal Memory of Kotljarevs'kyj" (Shevchenko)
See "Na vicnu pamjat' Kotljarevs' komu"
"To the Evening Star" (Blake) **37**:40
"To the Evening Star" (Campbell) **19**:188
"To the Evening Wind" (Bryant) **6**:159, 169, 176, 183
"To the Face seen in the Moon" (Fuller) **50**:249-50
"To the Flowers of Heidelberg" (Rizal)
See "A las flores de Heidelberg"
"To the Fossil Flower" (Very) **9**:376, 380
"To the Friend F. I." (Eminescu) **131**:294, 297
"To The Fringed Gentian" (Bryant) **46**:3
"To the Girls" (Preseren)
See "Dekletam"
To the Goddess Misfortune (Foscolo) **97**:52
"To the Goddess of Botany" (Smith)
See "Sonnet 79"
To the Gold Coast for Gold (Burton) **42**:40
"To the Grasshopper and the Cricket" (Hunt) **70**:263
"To the Great Metropolis" (Clough) **27**:103, 114
"To the Great Metropolis" (Prescott) **163**:35-36
"To the Hesitating Purchaser" (Stevenson) **63**:229
"To the Hon. J. Winthrop, Esq." (Warren) **13**:413, 431; **226**:257, 261, 264
"To the Hon Mrs Norton, the Poetess, on Meeting Her at Frampton House" (Barnes) **75**:85
"To the Honourable H—e W—e, on Reading The Castle of Otranto. December, 1784" (Yearsley) **174**:307
"To the Humming Bird" (Very) **9**:379
"To the Hungarian Youth" (Petofi)
See "A magyar ifjakhoz"
"To the Immortal Memory of the Halibut on which I dined This Day" (Cowper) **94**:122
"To the Infant Hampden" (Thelwall) **162**:317-20, 322-25
"To the Infant Princess" (Hunt) **70**:259
"To the Ingleeze Khafir Calling Himself Djaun Bool Djenkinzun" (Mangan) **27**:284, 311-13
"To the King" (Krasicki)
See "Do króla"
"To the King of England" (Paine) **62**:322, 324
"To the Ladies: A Call to Be a Wife" (Parton) **86**:363
"To, 'The Lady Geraldine'" (Osgood) **141**:327
"To the Lady in the Chemisette . . ." (Willis) **194**:307
"To the Leaven's Soil They Trod" (Whitman) **81**:313
"To the Lord Viscount Forbes" (Moore) **110**:171
"To the Lyre" (Derzhavin)
See "K lyre"
"To the Magnolia Grandiflora" (Cranch) **115**:46
"To the Man-of-War Bird" (Whitman) **205**:158, 254
"To the Memory of Bem, a Funeral Rhapsody" (Norwid)
See "Bema pamięci żałobny rapsod"
To the Memory of Canning (Coleridge) **90**:16
"To the Memory of Iu. P. Vrevskaia" (Turgenev)
See "Pamiati Iu. P. Vrevskoi"
"To the Memory of the Brave Americans" (Freneau)
See "The Prophecy—To the Memory of the Brave Americans under General Greene, Who Fell in the Action of September 8, 1781"
"To the Men of Kent, October 1803" (Wordsworth) **206**:301-2
"To the Miss Websters, with Dr. Aikin's 'Wish,' which They Expressed a Desire to Have a Copy of" (Barbauld) **185**:92
"To the Moon" (Leopardi)
See "Alla Luna"
"To the Moon" (Smith)
See "Sonnet 4"
"To the Moon" (Zhukovsky)
See "K mesyatsu"
"To the Muse" (Foscolo)
See "Alla musa"
"To the Nation" (Petofi)
See "A nemzethez"
"To the National Assembly" (Petofi)
See "A nemzetgyüléshez"
"To the New Type of the Morning Post" (Robinson) **142**:166
"To the Nightingale" (Clare) **9**:123
"To the Nightingale" (Cowper) **8**:120
"To the Nightingale" (Lamartine)
See "Au rossignol"
"To the Ottawa River" (Lampman) **25**:184, 210
"To the Past" (Bryant) **6**:162
"To the People" (Hugo) **3**:262
"To the Philosopher" (Baratynsky)
See "Mudrecu"
"To the Poet" (Preseren)
See "Pevcu"
"To the Poet" (Pushkin) **83**:249, 257

"To the Poet Coleridge" (Robinson) **142**:94, 97, 111, 247-48
To the Poet in Whittier (Hayne) **94**:144
"To the Poets Who Only Read and Listen" (Holmes) **14**:132
"To the Poor" (Barbauld) **185**:143, 157
"To the Portrait of 'A Lady'" (Holmes) **14**:99
"To the Prophetic Soul" (Lampman) **25**:216; **194**:45, 120-21
To the Public (Villaverde) **121**:335
"To the Pure All Things Are Pure" (Very) **9**:385
"To the Queen" (Blake) **16**:182
"To the Queen" (Hunt) **70**:259
"To the Queen" (Tennyson) **202**:206-7, 215, 254
"To the Rainbow" (Campbell) **19**:181-82, 192, 198
"To the Reader" (Baillie) **151**:73, 75, 115, 117
"To the Reader" (Baudelaire)
See "Au lecteur"
"To the Recording Angel" (Sheridan) **91**:232
"To the Republicans of North America" (Shelley) **175**:281
"To the Rescue" (Dodgson) **2**:107
"To the River Cherwell, Oxford" (Bowles) **103**:79-80, 82, 88-9, 92, 94
"To the River Itchin, Near Winton" (Bowles) **103**:72, 76, 80, 83-4, 86
"To the River Otter" (Coleridge) **99**:17
"To the River Wainsbeck" (Bowles)
See "To the River Wensbeck"
"To the River Wensbeck" (Bowles) **103**:72, 80
To the Russian, Polish, and All the Slav Countries (Bakunin) **25**:64; **58**:135
"To the Sayers of Words" (Whitman) **81**:329
"To the Sea!" (Isaacs)
See "Al mar!"
"To the Sea" (Pushkin)
See "K moriu"
"To the Shade of Mary Robinson" (Dacre) **151**:198, 213
"To the Small Celandine" (Wordsworth) **12**:395; **206**:245
"To the Snipe" (Clare) **86**:144
"To the Sons of Labor" (Adams) **33**:25
"To the South Downs" (Smith)
See "Sonnet 5"
"To the Spirit of Keats" (Lowell) **2**:522
"To the Spirit of Poesy" (Harpur) **114**:94, 144
"To the Star" (Eminescu) **33**:246
"To the States" (Whitman) **31**:426
"To the Sultan's Accession" (Pushkin) **83**:272
"To the Sun" (Heredia)
See "Al sol"
"To the Sun" (Smith)
See "Sonnet 89"
"To the Tsar once was it said" (Pushkin) **83**:272
"To the Unknown Eros" (Patmore) **9**:339, 359, 364
"To the Utilitarians" (Wordsworth) **12**:446
"To the Warbling Vireo" (Lampman) **25**:207; **194**:140
"To the Warsaw Critics" (Mickiewicz)
See "O Krytykach i Recenzentach"
"To the Working-Classes of Great-Britain" (Engels) **85**:184
"To the Young Poets" (Hölderlin)
See "An die jungen Dichter"
"To Think of Time" (Whitman) **4**:600; **31**:419, 421, 424-25, 443; **81**:342, 361-62; **205**:191-94, 226, 335
"To Think of You" (Whitman) **205**:300
"To Those Who Accuse the Author of Ingratitude" (Yearsley) **174**:337
"To Time" (Clare) **86**:160
"To Tirzah" (Blake) **13**:202, 221, 243; **37**:44, 47, 49, 53, 57, 90-1; **173**:28; **190**:42; **201**:65-66
"To Torrismond" (Warren) **13**:430; **226**:261, 265
"To Turgenev, in Answer to His Letter" (Zhukovsky) **35**:402
"To Two Friends" (Tyutchev) **34**:388, 395
"To Two Sisters" (Tyutchev) **34**:394
"To V. and R." (Isaacs)
See "A Virginia y Rufino"
To Verdener (Jacobsen) **34**:158, 168, 172
"To Vernon Lee" (Levy) **59**:120
"To Virgil" (Tennyson) **30**:286; **202**:294
"To Virtue" (Karamzin)
See "K dobrodeteli"
"To W. Wordsworth" (Coleridge) **177**:155
"To What Serves Mortal Beauty" (Hopkins) **17**:197, 243; **189**:66, 92, 126, 135
"To Whom This May Come" (Bellamy) **4**:30; **86**:70, 75
"To Wilhelmina" (Lanier) **6**:237
"To William Cromartie Yearsley" (Yearsley) **174**:317
"To William Wordsworth Composed on the Night after His Recitation of a Poem on the Growth of the Individual Mind" (Coleridge) **54**:127; **99**:104; **231**:131, 135
"To Winter" (Blake) **13**:219
"To Wisdom" (Barbauld) **185**:30-31, 33
"To Wordsworth" (Hemans) **71**:288
"To Wordsworth" (Landor) **14**:198
"To Wordsworth" (Reynolds) **146**:204
"To Working Men" (Dickens) **187**:172
"To Yazykov" (Baratynsky)
See "To N. M. Yazykov"
"To You" (Silva)
See "A tí"
"To You" (Whitman) **31**:426; **205**:227, 313
"To Zante" (Foscolo)
See "A Zacinto"
"To Zante" (Poe) **117**:308
"A Toast" (Preseren)
See "Zdravljica"
"Le toast des gallois et des bretons" (Lamartine) **11**:271
"Toast funèbre" (Mallarmé) **4**:387-89, 396; **41**:272; **210**:241
"Tobias Correspondence" (Maginn) **8**:439
"Tobler's Ode to Nature" (Goethe)
See "Goethe's Botany: The Metamorphosis of Plants"
"Toccata" (Schumann) **143**:73
"A Toccata of Galuppi's" (Browning) **19**:117, 153; **79**:106, 108-09, 164
"Der Tochter der Heide" (Mörike) **201**:292
"Toc...toc...toc" (Turgenev)
See "Stuk...stuk...stuk"
Der Tod Adams: Ein Trauerspiel (Klopstock) **11**:218, 231; **225**:279, 289
Der Tod am Hochzeitstage (Nestroy) **42**:224, 229
"Der Tod, das ist die kühle Nacht" (Heine) **4**:256
Der Tod des Dichters (Tieck) **46**:397
Der Tod des Empedokles (Hölderlin) **16**:162; **187**:191, 252, 304
"Der Tod des Erzbischofs Engelbert von Köln" (Droste-Hülshoff) **3**:197, 202
"Der Tod fürs Vaterland" (Hölderlin) **16**:174
"Tod Lapraik's Tale" (Stevenson) **193**:238
"To-Day" (Hugo) **3**:253
"To-Day" (Krasiński) **4**:307
"Today" (Very) **9**:378
"Todesgedanken" (Mörike) **201**:303
"Tofenfeier" (Schiller) **39**:386
The Toiler of the Sea (Hugo)
See *Les travailleurs de la mer*
The Toilers of the Field (Jefferies) **47**:112, 119, 137
The Toilers of the Sea (Hugo)
See *Les travailleurs de la mer*
"Toilette of a Hebrew Lady" (De Quincey) **4**:69
"La toison d'or" (Gautier) **1**:345, 350; **59**:13, 31-2
A Token of Friendship for All Seasons (Osgood) **141**:341
Toldi (Arany) **34**:4-6, 10-11, 14, 16, 18, 20, 23
Toldi estéje (Arany) **34**:4, 6, 8, 10, 14, 16, 18
Toldi szerelme (Arany) **34**:4, 10, 14, 18
"A tölgyek alatt" (Arany) **34**:21
Der tolle Invalide (Arnim) **159**:10, 14-16, 31, 95
"Der Tolle Invalide auf dem Fort Ratonneau" (Arnim) **5**:13, 15-16, 18, 21-24
"Der Tolpatch" (Auerbach) **171**:69
"Tolpe trevozhny den' priveten" (Baratynsky) **103**:16-17
Tom Brace (Alger) **8**:43
Tom Brown at Oxford (Hughes) **207**:106, 115, 131-32, 135, 139, 141, 146-47, 151-55
Tom Brown's School Days (Hughes) **207**:102-4, 106, 108-24, 129, 136-38, 140-45, 150, 152, 155, 159, 161-65, 167, 170
Tom Burke of "Ours" (Lever) **23**:285, 292, 299-301, 303, 305-07, 309
"Tom Fane and I" (Willis) **194**:282
"Tom Owen, the Bee-Hunter" (Thorpe) **183**:355, 357
Tom Temple's Career (Alger) **8**:34
Tom the Bootblack; or, The Road to Success (Alger)
See *The Western Boy; or, The Road to Success*
Tom Tracy (Alger) **83**:113
"The Tomb at San Praxed's" (Browning)
See "The Bishop Orders His Tomb at San Praxed's"
"The Tomb of B." (Isaacs)
See "La tumba de Belisario"
"The Tomb of Charlemagne" (Taylor) **89**:298
"The Tomb of Edgar Poe" (Mallarmé)
See "Le tombeau d'Edgar Poe"
"The Tomb of Madame Langhans" (Hemans) **71**:304
"Les tombales" (Maupassant) **83**:171-72, 194, 197
"La Tombe lointaine" (Desbordes-Valmore) **97**:7
Un tombeau d'Anatole (Mallarmé)
See *Pour un tombeau d'Anatole*
"Le tombeau d'Edgar Poe" (Mallarmé) **4**:376; **41**:280, 289, 291
"Le tombeau d'Edgard Poe" (Mallarmé)
See "Le tombeau d'Edgar Poe"
"Le tombeau d'une mère" (Lamartine) **11**:270; **190**:179, 263
Un tombeau pour Anatole (Mallarmé) **41**:248, 251, 275, 289
"Tombeaux" (Mallarmé) **210**:241
"The Tombs in the Abbey" (Lamb) **10**:408; **113**:173, 177, 179
"The Tombs of the Kings" (Blind) **202**:6, 55, 57
"Tomlenie Dukha" (Leskov) **174**:7
"Tommatoo" (O'Brien) **21**:234, 239, 242-43
"Tommelise" (Andersen) **7**:28-29; **79**:23, 31, 50, 58, 70-71, 76, 81; **214**:54
"Tommy's Dead" (Dobell) **43**:48
"Tomorrow" (Edgeworth) **51**:88-9
"To-morrow" (Longfellow) **45**:121
"To-morrow" (Sigourney) **21**:298
"Tomorrow" (Tennyson) **202**:291
"Tom's Garland" (Hopkins) **17**:189, 225
"The Tone of a Koto" (Ichiyō)
See "Koto no Ne"
"Die Tonwelt" (Schumann) **143**:73, 80, 130
"Tony Blink's Class Book, No. 1" (Lippard) **198**:133
Tony Butler (Lever) **23**:292, 303
"Too Late" (Arnold) **89**:49
"Too Late" (Browning) **19**:131
"Too Late" (Cooke) **110**:20, 30, 34, 37, 43-4, 47, 49
"Too Late" (Laforgue)
See "Trop tard"
"Too Late" (Lenau) **16**:276
"Too Long, O Spirit of Storm" (Timrod) **25**:362, 373
The Too Many (Alfieri)
See *I troppi*

"Too Much" (Mörike) **10**:446
"Too Ready Writer" (Eliot) **183**:64
"Too Soon" (Jones) **222**:128
"The Top and the Ball" (Andersen) **79**:23, 34, 69; **214**:59
"Topografía de la Provincia de Cumaná" (Bello) **131**:129
"Topography of the Province of Cumaná, Venezuela" (Bello)
See "Topografía de la Provincia de Cumaná"
"Topolja" (Shevchenko) **54**:373, 389
Topsy Turvy Talk (Fredro)
See *Trzy po trzy*
"The Torch" (Whitman) **4**:592
Torlogh O'Brien (Le Fanu) **58**:275
"The Torn Hat" (Willis) **194**:297
Törnrosens bok (Almqvist) **42**:4, 9-10, 15
"The Torpedoes of Progress" (Fourier) **51**:180
Torquato Tasso (Goethe) **4**:162-63, 166-67, 169, 172, 190, 192, 211, 218-21; **34**:75, 90; **154**:231, 233, 237, 262, 310, 312, 317
"Torquemada" (Longfellow) **2**:481; **45**:137, 145, 161
Torquemada (Hugo) **3**:261, 264, 269-70; **161**:236
"Torquil and Oona" (Smith) **59**:333
"The Torrent" (Blind) **202**:41
The Torrents of Spring (Turgenev)
See *Veshnie vody*
Torrismond (Beddoes) **3**:29, 32, 34, 36, 38-39; **154**:9-10, 12-13, 45-46
Torso (Herder) **8**:313
Tortesa; or, the Usurer Matched (Willis) **194**:292, 304, 308-10, 329
"La tortuga y la hormiga" (Lizardi) **30**:68
"La torture par l'espérance" (Villiers de l'Isle Adam) **3**:587
"The Tortured Heart" (Rimbaud)
See "La coeur volé"
"Tory Pledges" (Moore) **110**:172
"Toryism, Whiggism, and Radicalism" (De Quincey) **198**:107-8
"To—'s Picture" (Moore) **110**:177
"Der tote Achill" (Meyer) **81**:199, 206, 209
"Die Tote Clarissa" (Klopstock) **11**:240
"Das tote Kind" (Meyer) **81**:143
"Die toten Freunde" (Meyer) **81**:199, 203
"Touch My Honour, Touch My Life" (Griffin) **7**:215
"Touching 'Never'" (Rossetti) **50**:298
"The Touchstone" (Allingham) **25**:6
"The Tough Yarn" (Smith) **187**:320
La tour de Nesle (Dumas) **11**:42-43, 47, 57, 63, 75, 79, 89-90; **71**:184, 186, 190, 193, 209, 232, 249
La tour de Percemont (Sand) **2**:596
"Tour en Belgique" (Gautier) **1**:352
A Tour of Switzerland, or a View of the present State of the Governments and Manners of those Contons, with comparative Sketches of the present State of Paris (Williams) **135**:260, 302, 306, 334-35, 342
"A Tour of the Forest" (Turgenev) **21**:415, 420, 441
A Tour on the Prairies (Irving) **2**:372, 376-77, 380, 382; **95**:253, 280
Tour to the Lakes (Gilpin) **30**:28, 43
"Tourmaline" (Stifter) **41**:357, 360-62, 364
"Tournament at Reval" (Bestuzhev)
See "Revel'skii turnir"
"The Tournament: Joust First Being the Right Pleasant Joust betwixt Heart and Brain" (Lanier) **6**:254; **118**:238, 259-60
"Toussaint l'ouverture" (Whittier) **8**:515; **59**:364
Toussaint l'ouverture (Lamartine) **11**:258
Tout (Balzac) **153**:150
"Tout entière" (Baudelaire) **55**:29
"Tout Orgueil fume-t-il du soir" (Mallarmé) **210**:241, 244-45
"Toute mon âme" (Banville) **9**:29
La Tovr Saint-Jacques (Dumas) **71**:193
"Towards a History of Religion and Philosophy in Germany" (Heine)
See "Zur Geschichte der Religion und Philosophie in Deutschland"
"Towards Democracy" (Whitman) **31**:371
Tower Hill (Ainsworth) **13**:36, 40
The Tower of London (Ainsworth) **13**:26, 28, 31-6, 39-40, 43-44, 48-49
The Tower of Nesle (Dumas)
See *La tour de Nesle*
"The Tower of the Dream" (Harpur) **114**:99-100, 105, 144
"The Town" (Martineau) **26**:353
"The Town" (Pushkin)
See "Gorodok"
Town and Country (Trollope) **30**:330-31
"A Town and Country Mouse" (Cooke)
See "A Town Mouse and a Country Mouse"
Town Geology (Kingsley) **35**:232
"A Town Mouse and a Country Mouse" (Cooke) **110**:34, 42, 44
The Town of Lucca (Heine) **54**:319
The Town of the Cascades (Banim) **13**:130
"The Toys" (Patmore) **9**:343, 349, 358
"Tract" (Newman)
See *Tracts for the Times*
"Tract 73" (Newman) **99**:220-22
"Tract 83" (Newman) **99**:220, 222
"Tract 85" (Newman) **99**:221, 225
Tract 90 (Newman) **38**:291, 294, 299-300, 315, 318, 320-21
"Tract One" (Newman)
See *Tracts for the Times*
"Tract XC" (Newman)
See *Tracts for the Times*
Tracts (Keble)
See *Tracts for the Times*
Tracts (Newman)
See *Tracts for the Times*
The Tracts (Newman)
See *Tracts for the Times*
"Tracts and Essays on Several Subjects" (Freneau) **111**:132
Tracts for the Times (Keble) **87**:132, 192-93, 199
Tracts for the Times (Newman) **99**:220, 264
Tracts of the Times (Newman)
See *Tracts for the Times*
Tracy's Ambition (Griffin) **7**:197-98, 201, 209, 213-14, 216, 218
"Trades" (Crabbe) **26**:140
"The Tradesman's Daughter" (Jones) **222**:146
Traditions of Palestine (Martineau) **26**:309-10, 326; **137**:336
"Traduzione de'due primi canti dell'Odissea di Ippolito Pindemonte" (Foscolo) **97**:89
"Tragédia no Lar" (Castro Alves)
See "O Navio Negreiro"
"Tragédia no Mar" (Castro Alves)
See "O Navio Negreiro"
"Una tragedia y un ángel" (Bécquer) **106**:144
The Tragedies of Maddelen, Agamemnon, Lady Macbeth, Antonia, and Clytemnestra (Galt) **1**:327
The Tragedy of Count Alarcos (Disraeli) **39**:67; **79**:269, 277-78
"The Tragedy of Donohoe" (Harpur) **114**:94, 114, 138
The Tragedy of Man (Madach)
See *Az ember tragédiája*
Tragedy of the Conspiracy of Venice (Martínez de la Rosa)
See *La conjuración de Venecia*
"The Tragic" (Emerson) **38**:193-94
"Tragic Demise of Temporal Love" (Brentano) **191**:97
"The Tragic Drama, The Apostate, a Tragedy in 5 Acts. R. L. Sheil" (Maturin) **169**:46
"The Tragic in Ancient Drama Reflected in the Tragic in Modern Drama" (Kierkegaard) **125**:198, 203, 205-6, 208, 212-14, 248, 280
Der Tragödie erster Teil (Goethe)
See *Faust. Die Erster Teil*
Traidor, inconfeso, y mártir (Zorrilla y Moral) **6**:523
"Trailing Arbutus" (Cooke) **110**:9, 15
Train Boy (Alger) **83**:142
"A Train went through a burial gate" (Dickinson) **171**:87
"The Training" (Whittier) **59**:364, 373
Training in Christianity (Kierkegaard) **78**:124-25, 154-55, 229, 238
"Training in Relation to Health" (Lewes) **25**:310
Traité de l'association domestique-agricole (Fourier) **51**:156, 161, 172
Traité des écritures cunéiformes (Gobineau) **17**:65
Traité sur les Sacrifices (Maistre) **37**:308
"Le traitement du docteur Tristan" (Villiers de l'Isle Adam) **3**:590
Traités de Législation civile et pénale (Bentham) **38**:24-5, 66
"The Traitor" (Bestuzhev)
See "Izmennik"
"Traits" (Sigourney)
See *Traits of the Aborigines of America*
Traits and Stories of the Irish Peasantry (Carleton) **3**:85, 83-86, 88-94; **199**:3, 6-12, 14-16, 18, 21, 23, 25, 27-31, 33-34, 38, 43, 46, 48, 54, 56, 58-66, 75-76, 89-93, 95, 101-2
Traits of American Life (Hale) **75**:296, 319, 349, 356-62
"Traits of Indian Character" (Irving) **95**:265-66, 269
Traits of the Aborigines of America (Sigourney) **21**:304; **87**:340-42
"Tramps of the Night" (Bertrand) **31**:54
"Tranquilization" (Tyutchev) **34**:389
"La transaction" (Balzac) **153**:151
"Transcendency" (Emerson) **1**:282
Transcendental Philosophy (Schelling)
See *System des transcendentalen Idealismus*
"Transcendental Wild Oats" (Alcott) **58**:12, 69; **83**:35
"'Transcendentalism'" (Browning) **19**:131; **79**:141-42
"Transcendentalism" (Cranch) **115**:32, 64
Transcendentalism. A Lecture (Parker) **186**:124
"The Transcendentalist" (Emerson) **38**:209, 227-30; **98**:114
"A Transcript and a Transcription" (Webster) **230**:303
"Transfiguration" (Alcott) **167**:51
"Transformation" (Shelley) **14**:264, 267; **59**:154-5; **103**:344
The Transformation (Brown)
See *Wieland; or The Transformation*
Transformation; or, The Romance of Monte Beni (Hawthorne)
See *The Marble Faun; or, The Romance of Monte Beni*
The Transient and Permanent in Christianity (Parker)
See *A Discourse on the Transient and Permanent in Christianity*
"The Transient and the Permanent in the Sick-Room" (Martineau) **137**:283
"Transition" (Emerson) **38**:190
Transitory Flowers (Manzano)
See *Flores pasajeras*
Translation of the Letters of a Hindoo Rajah (Hamilton) **153**:265-66, 268, 291-92, 294, 297-98, 308, 322, 327-28, 337-45, 356-58, 360-65
Translations from Alexander Petőfi, the Magyar Poet (Petofi) **21**:259
Translations from Camoens and Other Poets, with Original Poems (Hemans) **29**:192
Translations from Horace (Brontë) **109**:26
"The Transmigration of Souls" (Baratynsky) **103**:3

"The Transmigrations of Indur" (Barbauld) **185**:131
"Transplanted" (Dickinson)
See "As If Some Little Arctic Flower"
"A Transplanted Boy" (Woolson) **82**:276, 297, 344-45
"A Transport One Cannot Contain" (Dickinson) **21**:79
"Transpositions" (Whitman) **205**:157, 162, 164-65
"Transpositions d'art" (Gautier) **59**:19
Tran-Tran (Tamayo y Baus) **1**:571
"Trapping a Sheriff" (Harris) **23**:159, 161, 163; **165**:163, 201, 227, 242, 271-72, 280, 285
"Le Trappiste" (Vigny) **102**:335, 367
"Tras una enfermedad" (Casal) **131**:239
"Die Traube" (Meyer) **81**:146, 149-50
"Trauerode" (Schiller) **39**:386
Trauerspiel in Sizilien (Hebbel)
See *Ein Trauerspiel in Sizilien: Tragicomödie in einem Act, nebst einem Sendschreiben an H. T. Rötscher*
Ein Trauerspiel in Sizilien: Tragicomödie in einem Act, nebst einem Sendschreiben an H. T. Rötscher (Hebbel) **43**:237, 257, 275
Die Trauerspiele des Sophokles (Hölderlin) **187**:281
Der Traum (Klopstock) **225**:298
"Der Traum der Wüste" (Brentano) **191**:68, 70
Der Traum ein Leben (Grillparzer) **1**:384-85, 390, 398; **102**:93, 105, 107, 110-12, 115-17, 172, 185, 187
"Traum und Erwachen" (Chamisso) **82**:27
"Traumbilder" (Heine) **4**:248-49, 257, 259
"Der traurige Krönung" (Mörike) **201**:292, 298
Les travailleurs de la mer (Hugo) **3**:248-50, 252-53, 255, 258-59, 264, 267, 270-71; **10**:367; **21**:195, 199, 213; **161**:202, 204, 207-8, 214-20; **189**:179, 221, 223, 248, 295
Travel Journal (Herder)
See *Journal meiner Reise im Jahr*
Travel Letters (Petofi)
See *Úti levelek*
Travel Writing (Shelley) **170**:336
"The Traveler" (Hölderlin)
See "Versöhnender, der du nimmer geglaubt ..."
The Traveller Returned (Murray) **63**:184-5, 193, 195, 199, 201, 214
The Travellers (Sedgwick) **19**:447
"The Traveller's Story of a Terribly Strange Bed" (Collins)
See "A Terribly Strange Bed"
Travelling (Dickens)
See *Pictures from Italy*
"The Travelling Companion" (Andersen)
See "Reisekammeraten"
"Travelling in England in the Old Days" (De Quincey) **198**:24, 105
"Travelling in Victoria" (Kingsley) **107**:232, 240
Travelling Sketches (Trollope) **215**:218, 221
Travels (Bartram) **145**:3, 5-9, 11, 13, 15, 18-21, 23-26, 28-29, 32, 34-35, 37-38, 41-49, 52, 61-63, 65-67, 69-82, 85-92, 95-96, 100-103, 105, 107-9, 111, 114-22
Travels (Burton) **42**:36
Travels (Sarmiento)
See *Viajes*
Travels from Hamburg, through Westphalia, Holland, and the Netherlands, to Paris (Holcroft) **85**:198-99, 207, 212, 215, 235
Travels from Moscow through Prussia, Germany, Switzerland, France, and England (Karamzin)
See *Pis'ma Russkogo puteshestvennika*
Travels in America (Chateaubriand)
See *Voyage en Amérique*
Travels in Georgia and Florida, 1773-74: A Report to Dr. John Fothergill (Bartram) **145**:43, 47, 75, 78, 105, 107-9, 115, 117-19
Travels in Greece, Palestine, Egypt, and Barbary, during the Years 1806 and 1807 (Chateaubriand)
See *Itinéraire de Paris à Jérusalem et de Jérusalem à Paris, en allant par la Grèce, et revenant par l'Egypte, a Barbarie, et l'Espagne*
Travels in Italy (Goethe)
See *Italienische Reise*
Travels in New-England and New-York (Dwight) **13**:267-69, 271-73, 276-77
Travels in the East, including a Journey to the Holy Land (Lamartine)
See *Souvenirs, impressions, pensées, et paysages pendant un voyage en Orient (1832-1833); ou, Notes d'un voyageur*
"Travels in the Land of Not" (Emerson) **1**:308
Travels of an Irish Gentleman in Search of a Religion (Moore) **6**:396
Travels round the World (Chamisso) **82**:5
Travels through North and South Carolina, Georgia, East and West Florida, the Cherokee Country, the Extensive Territories of the Muscogulges, or Creek Confederacy, and the Country of the Chactaws (Bartram)
See *Travels*
Travels to the Holy Land (Lamartine)
See *Souvenirs, impressions, pensées, et paysages pendant un voyage en Orient (1832-1833); ou, Notes d'un voyageur*
Travels with a Donkey in the Cévennes (Stevenson) **5**:387-88, 397, 410; **193**:204-5, 213, 220-21, 353-57
"Travels with Abe" (Harris) **165**:233
"A través de la ciudad. El centro de dependientes" (Casal) **131**:274, 280
The Treasure (Mörike)
See *Der Schatz*
Treasure Island (Stevenson) **5**:394, 397, 399-400, 402-5, 407, 409, 415, 417, 422, 425, 429-39; **14**:318; **63**:220-76; **193**:204, 210-15, 220-24, 241, 250, 256, 258, 274, 282, 287, 294-96, 304, 313, 324-27, 329-33, 344
"The Treasure of Franchard" (Stevenson) **193**:209-10, 280, 282
"The Treasures of the Deep" (Hemans) **71**:264
"Treatise on a Pair of Tongs" (Mangan) **27**:291
A Treatise on Ancient and Modern Literature (Staël-Holstein)
See *De la littérature considérée dans ses rapports avec les institutions sociales*
A Treatise on Cobbett's Corn (Cobbett) **49**:110, 114, 151-52
The Treatise on Despair (Kierkegaard)
See *Sygdommen til Døden*
Treatise on Domestic and Agricultural Association (Fourier)
See *Traité de l'association domestique-agricole*
A Treatise on Domestic Economy for the Use of Young Ladies at Home and at School (Beecher) **30**:14-15, 17-24
Treatise on Method (Coleridge) **197**:285
"Treatise on Morals" (Shelley) **18**:376; **93**:340
A Treatise on the Influence of the Passions upon the Happiness of Individuals and Nations (Staël-Holstein)
See *De l'influence des passions sur le bonheur des individus et des nations*
Treatise upon the Origin of Language (Herder)
See *Abhandlung über den Ursprung der Sprache, walche den von der Königl*
"The Treaty of Friendship" (Andersen) **79**:89
Trébutien (Barbey d'Aurevilly)
See *Lettres à Trébutien*
"The Tree" (Very) **9**:380, 387, 391
"Tree Burial" (Bryant) **46**:4, 19, 22
"The Tree of Liberty" (Harpur) **114**:166
"The Tree of Life" (Beddoes) **154**:77
"The Tree of Life" (Dutt) **29**:122
"Trees Be Company" (Barnes) **75**:36
"Treinta años" (Manzano) **155**:277, 297, 305, 307, 309-10
"Treize ans" (Barbey d'Aurevilly) **1**:76; **213**:74
The Tremendous Adventures of Major Gahagan (Thackeray) **5**:470
Tremordyn Cliff (Trollope) **30**:319
Trente ans de Paris (Daudet) **1**:236
Trente-six ballades joyeuses (Banville) **9**:18, 25
Tres amores (Gómez de Avellaneda) **111**:28, 53
"Tres Fechas" (Bécquer) **106**:97, 99, 103, 106, 115, 120, 130-32, 149, 156, 159
"Los tres no son más que dos y el que no es nada vale por tres—mascarada política" (Larra) **130**:195-96, 223, 254
Le trésor d'Arlatan (Daudet) **1**:251-52
"Le trésor de al caverne d'Arcueil" (Borel) **41**:13
Trésor des fèves et fleur des pois (Nodier) **19**:385
"Très-sourd" (Laforgue) **221**:87
"Treu Kätchen" (Ludwig) **4**:353
"Treue" (Eichendorff) **225**:45
Ein Treuer Diener Seines Herrn (Grillparzer) **1**:384, 387; **102**:90, 111, 168, 172, 180, 184
Der Treulose (Nestroy) **42**:257
"Tri dushi" (Pavlova) **138**:32-34, 50
"Tri palmy" (Lermontov) **5**:287, 295; **126**:142
"Tri portreta" (Turgenev) **21**:377, 414, 417-18; **122**:241, 266, 350
"Tri putnika" (Zhukovsky) **35**:398
"Tri vstreči" (Turgenev) **122**:268
"A Triad" (Rossetti) **2**:561; **50**:298, 321-22; **66**:330
"The Triad" (Wordsworth) **206**:306
The Trial (Baillie)
See *The Tryal*
The Trial of Abraham (Wieland) **17**:390
"The Trial of Mamachtaga" (Brackenridge) **7**:55
"The Trial of the Dead" (Sigourney) **21**:299
The Trial of Theodore Parker, for the "Misdemeanor" of a Speech in Faneuil Hall against Kidnapping, before the Circuit Court of the United States, at Boston, April 3, 1855 (Parker) **186**:132, 162, 172-73
"Trials of a Travelling Musician" (Moodie) **14**:235
"The Trials of Arden" (Brown) **74**:186
The Trials of Margaret Lyndsay (Wilson) **5**:547-49, 554, 558, 561, 564, 567, 569
"Trials of Temper" (Hogg) **4**:283
Trials of the Human Heart (Rowson) **5**:311-12, 314, 316, 319; **69**:103-05, 113, 136-39; **182**:255, 258-59, 261, 263, 280, 313, 353
The Tribes of Ireland (Mangan) **27**:314-15
Tribulat Bonhomet (Villiers de l'Isle Adam) **3**:583, 586, 588
"Tribuneaux rustiques" (Maupassant) **1**:448; **83**:174
"Tribute to the Memory of a Dog" (Wordsworth) **12**:430
"La tricoteuse" (Crawford) **12**:169-70
The Trident of Albion (Thelwall) **162**:339-40, 342-43
"Trifles" (Emerson) **38**:145
Trifles from Episcopal Life (Leskov)
See *Meloci archierejskoj zizni*
Trilby (Du Maurier) **86**:278-81, 285-88, 292, 294, 296-307
Trilby; ou, Le lutin d'Argail (Nodier) **19**:377, 381, 384-86, 388, 392-93, 395, 400-01
Trilogie der Leidenschaft (Goethe) **4**:201
"Trinitas" (Whittier) **59**:356
"Triomphe" (Banville) **9**:31
"A Trip from Åbo" (Runeberg) **41**:313
"A Trip to Ischia" (Taylor) **89**:313
A Trip to Niagara; or, Travellers in America (Dunlap) **2**:212-13
A Trip to Parnassus; or the Judgement of Apollo on Dramatic Authors and Performers (Rowson) **69**:109-11, 117, 141

A Trip to Parnassus; or, The Judgment of Apollo on Dramatic Authors and Performers (Rowson) **182**:262, 273-76, 352
A Trip to Scarborough (Sheridan) **5**:359, 382; **91**:242
"A Trip to Stony Lake" (Moodie) **113**:348
Trip to the Orient (Nerval)
See *Voyage en Orient*
"A Trip to Walpole Island and Port Sarnia" (Richardson) **55**:314, 317
"Tripetown: Twenty Minutes for Breakfast" (Harris) **23**:159; **165**:261, 275
Triptyque (Mallarmé) **210**:156, 241, 244
"Tristram and Isolt" (Arnold) **218**:115, 132, 138, 151, 188-89
Tristan and Isolde (Wagner)
See *Tristan und Isolde*
Tristan de Roux (Dumas) **9**:234
Tristan und Isolde (Wagner) **9**:404, 406, 408, 412-13, 416, 419, 421, 439-40, 442-43, 446, 450, 452-58, 460, 464-65, 467, 470; **119**:172, 182, 185, 198, 210, 228, 240, 244-46, 268-69, 293, 295-96, 303, 312-15, 349
"Triste" (Silva) **114**:294
"Triste, triste" (Laforgue) **221**:76-77, 84
"Los tristes" (Castro) **78**:21
"Tristesse" (Desbordes-Valmore) **97**:6, 29
"Tristesse" (Gautier) **1**:350
"Tristesse" (Lamartine) **11**:254
"Tristesse" (Musset) **7**:275; **150**:307, 310, 328
"Les tristesses de la lune" (Baudelaire) **6**:80
Tristia ex Ponto (Grillparzer) **102**:174
"Tristissima nox" (Casal) **131**:267
"Tristitia" (Patmore) **9**:349, 358
Tristram and Iseult (Arnold) **6**:32, 34, 42, 44, 54, 66-68, 72-75; **29**:6-7, 23, 31, 33, 35; **89**:3-12
"Trisyllabic Feet" (Bryant) **6**:178
"Der Triumf der Liebe" (Schiller) **39**:386
"Triumph Der Empfindsamkeit" (Goethe) **4**:200
The Triumph of Infidelity (Dwight) **13**:263, 269-70, 272-73, 278-79
"The Triumph of Life" (Shelley)
See *The Triumph of Life*
The Triumph of Life (Shelley) **18**:326, 329, 336, 339, 346, 349-53, 355, 360-65, 373, 379, 382-83; **93**:322, 333, 341, 344, 354; **143**:247; **175**:241, 293, 311, 319
"The Triumph of Mind Over Body" (Brontë) **109**:30
"The Triumph of Pleasure" (Dacre) **151**:214-15
"The Triumph of Poetry" (Dyer) **129**:97
"The Triumph of Woman" (Southey) **8**:447
"Triumphal Arch" (Meyer)
See "Der Triumphbogen"
"A Triumphal Arch, Erected in Honor of Kotzebue" (Schlegel) **15**:223
"The Triumphal Banquet" (Schiller) **39**:305
"Der Triumphbogen" (Meyer) **81**:140, 153-54, 156, 199
"The Triumphs of Bacchus" (Pushkin) **3**:415
"Trockne Blumen" (Muller) **73**:363, 365, 373
Les trois amoureux (Balzac) **5**:39; **153**:62, 64, 66-69, 71, 75, 77, 153
Trois ans en Asie (Gobineau) **17**:71
Trois contes: Un coeur simple; La légende de Saint-Julien l'hospitalier; Hérodias (Flaubert) **2**:227, 233, 257-9; **62**:108; **135**:93, 109, 145
"Trois épilogues en manière d'adieux à la littérature personnelle" (Verlaine) **230**:162
Les Trois Femmes (Charriere) **66**:124-6, 134, 136-7
"Les trois filles de Milton" (Villiers de l'Isle Adam)
See "Les filles de Milton"
Les Trois Maupin; ou, La Veille de la Régence (Scribe) **16**:412-13
Les trois mousquetaires (Dumas) **11**:50, 52, 58, 63-65, 68, 70, 72-73, 75-76, 80, 86-90; **71**:184, 186, 188-89, 198, 201, 209-10, 228, 232
"Trojka" (Nekrasov) **11**:412
"The Troll Garden" (Kingsley) **35**:240
"Trop tard" (Laforgue) **221**:88
"Tropical Landscape" (Silva)
See "Paisaje tropical"
Les tros mosquetaros (Dumas)
See *Les trois mousquetaires*
"The Trosachs" (Wordsworth) **12**:417
"The Trossachs" (Wordsworth) **206**:240
"Trost" (Mörike) **201**:279
"Le trou du serpent" (Gautier) **1**:350
The Troubadour, Catalogue of Pictures, and Historical Sketches (Landon) **15**:161, 166, 168
"Troubadour Song" (Hemans) **71**:275
La troublante (Dumas) **9**:246
"Troubled about Many Things" (Dickinson)
See "How Many Times These Low Feet Staggered"
"Troubles of the Day" (Barnes) **75**:20
A Troublesome Lodger (Mayhew) **31**:158
Trouled Waters (Ichiyō)
See *Nigorie*
"Troy Town" (Rossetti) **4**:492, 498, 505, 511, 518, 526-27, 530; **77**:326-28, 330, 337, 340
Les Troyens (Scribe) **16**:407
"The Truce of Piscataqua" (Whittier) **59**:371
"True" (Cooke) **110**:57
"True and False Comforts" (Cowper) **94**:72
"The True and Froggy Art of Swimming" (Horne) **127**:262
The True and the False (Tennyson) **65**:379
The True and the False Waldemar (Arnim)
See *Der Echte und der falsche Waldemar*
"True Considerateness" (James) **206**:197
The True Heroes; or, The Noble Army of Martyrs (More) **141**:191
The True History of Joshua Davidson, Christian and Communist (Linton) **41**:167, 169-70
"The True in Dreams" (Cranch) **115**:22
"The True Life" (Lampman) **25**:219; **194**:11-12, 43-44
"The True Light" (Very) **9**:372, 385, 390
The True Messiah; or, The Old and New Testaments, Examined According to the Principles of the Language of Nature (Peabody) **169**:200
The True Remedy for the Wrongs of Woman (Beecher) **30**:16, 24-5
The True Story of My Life (Andersen) **7**:15, 23
"A True Tale of the Wiltshire Labourer" (Jefferies) **47**:116, 119
"True Woman" (Rossetti) **77**:312
True Womanhood (Neal) **161**:291
"True Worshippers" (Martineau) **26**:309
"Truls, the Nameless" (Boyesen) **135**:11, 19
"A Trumpet of Our Own" (Ridge) **82**:195
"The Trumpeter, an Old English Tale" (Robinson) **142**:136
"Der trunkene Gott" (Meyer) **81**:207
"Truth" (Baratynsky)
See "Istina"
"The Truth" (Blake) **13**:165
"The Truth" (Cowper) **8**:110, 120; **94**:26, 28-9, 111-12, 114
"Truth" (Cowper) **94**:10, 14, 16, 51, 53-5, 58-9
"Truth" (Lampman) **25**:163
"The Truth" (Lampman) **25**:160-61, 194, 199, 212, 218
"The Truth About the United States" (Martí) **63**:167
Truth and Method (Keats) **225**:196
"Truth as the Fountain of Beauty in Dramatic Literature" (Tamayo y Baus) **1**:565
"Truth Crushed to Earth" (Bryant) **6**:165
"Truth of Intercourse" (Stevenson) **5**:389; **63**:271, 275; **193**:214
"Truxton's Victory" (Rowson) **5**:322
Try and Trust (Alger) **83**:92
The Tryal (Baillie) **2**:31, 43; **71**:1, 6, 51, 56, 59-67; **151**:14, 27, 31, 33-38, 114
"Tryzna" (Shevchenko) **54**:379, 386, 390-2, 395
Trzy myśli pozostale po ś.p. Henryku Ligenzie (Krasiński) **4**:306, 313
Trzy po trzy (Fredro) **8**:287-90, 293
Trzy poemata (Slowacki) **15**:358
"Tsar'-Devitsa" (Derzhavin) **215**:32
"The Tsar, Knitting his brows" (Pushkin) **83**:272
"Tsar, nash, nemets russkiy . . ." (Bestuzhev) **131**:181
"Tsar Nikita" (Pushkin) **3**:443, 451
"Tsar Sultan" (Pushkin)
See "Skazka o Tsare Sultane"
"Tschia" (Lamartine) **11**:245, 270, 283
Tsuzurabumi (Ueda Akinari) **131**:20
Tsyganka (Baratynsky)
See *Nalozhnitsa*
Tsygany (Pushkin) **3**:409-12, 416, 421, 424, 433, 444-45, 447-48, 451, 453, 458-59, 462; **27**:386, 392; **83**:243, 245, 250, 334, 357
"Tu es beau comme le desert, avec toutes ses fleurs et toutes ses brises" (Dacre) **151**:148, 184
"Tu imagen de María" (Isaacs) **70**:309
"Tu mettrais l'univers entier dans tu ruelle" (Baudelaire) **29**:103; **55**:56
"Tu n'es pas du tout . . ." (Verlaine) **230**:170
"Tu sèmes au hasard la joie et les désastres" (Baudelaire) **155**:98
"Tubber Derg; or, The Red Well" (Carleton) **3**:85, 89, 92, 96; **199**:5, 11, 18, 65, 76
"Tuci" (Lermontov) **126**:190-91
"Tudor Tramp" (Crawford) **12**:169-70
"Tuesday before Easter" (Keble) **87**:177
The Tuggses at Ramsgate and Other Sketches Illustrative of Every-Day Life and Every-Day People (Dickens)
See *Sketches by Boz, Illustrative of Every-Day Life and Every-Day People*
La tulipe noire (Dumas) **11**:60, 68, 74, 77
Tullach (Oliphant)
See *Memoir of the Life of John Tullach*
"La tumba de Belisario" (Isaacs) **70**:312
"La tumba del soldado" (Isaacs) **70**:311
"Tündérálom" (Petofi) **21**:264, 279
Tündérálom (Madach) **19**:371
"The Tune of Seven Towers" (Morris) **4**:419, 426, 431-32
"Tupejnyi xudožnik" (Leskov) **25**:239
"Tupejnyj chodoznik" (Leskov) **174**:37
Turandot (Gozzi) **23**:107, 112-14, 119-23, 125-29
"Le turco" (Banville) **9**:16
"The Turf" (Longstreet) **159**:123, 136, 144, 146, 161, 176, 182, 184, 199, 202
"Turgenev, Pisemsky, and Goncharov" (Pisarev)
See "Pisemskij, Turgenev, i Goncarov"
"The Turkish Lady" (Campbell) **19**:179, 181
The Turkish Wonder (Gozzi)
See *Il mostro turchino*
"Turmalin" (Stifter)
See "Tourmaline"
Turmalin (Stifter) **198**:283
"The Turn of the Day" (Barnes) **75**:33
"The Turn Out" (Longstreet) **159**:118, 133-34, 144, 161, 184, 192, 203
Turn the Carpet (More) **141**:171
"Turnerlust" (Hauff) **185**:353
"Turner's Old Téméraire, under a Figure Symbolizing the Church" (Lowell) **2**:512
"The Turn-Out" (Martineau) **26**:309; **137**:251, 264-65
"The Turnstile" (Barnes) **75**:8
"El turpial" (Isaacs) **70**:303
"Turtle Soup" (Dodgson) **139**:37
"The Tuscan Maid" (Allston) **2**:21, 26
Tutte le opere (Leopardi) **129**:313, 315-16
Tutte le opere (Manzoni) **29**:306; **98**:214
"Twaddle on Tweedside" (Wilson) **5**:550

"Twas a Long Parting—But the Time" (Dickinson) **21**:56, 79
Twas All for the Best (Bird) **1**:87, 89, 93
"Twas but a Babe" (Sigourney) **21**:309
"Twas like a Maelstrom" (Dickinson) **77**:114-15
"twas warm-at first-like Us" (Dickinson) **77**:162-64
"The Tweed Visited" (Bowles) **103**:80
"Tweil" (Barnes) **75**:7, 79
The Twelfth of August; or, the Feast of Freedom (More) **141**:235
1258 (Dickinson) **77**:81
1254 (Dickinson) **77**:68
1247 (Dickinson) **77**:109
1209 (Dickinson) **77**:89
1210 (Cantor) **77**:93
1225 (Dickinson) **77**:75
Twelve Original Hibernian Melodies (Morgan) **29**:390
Twelve Sermons (Cobbett) **49**:110, 114, 123, 152, 156, 160
"The Twelve Sleeping Maidens" (Zhukovsky) **35**:379, 389, 391, 398
Twelve Years (Northup)
See *Twelve Years a Slave, Narrative of Solomon Northup, a Citizen of New York, Kidnapped in Washington City in 1841, and Rescued in 1853, from a Cotton Plantation Near the Red River in Louisiana*
Twelve Years a Slave, Narrative of Solomon Northup, a Citizen of New York, Kidnapped in Washington City in 1841, and Rescued in 1853, from a Cotton Plantation Near the Red River in Louisiana (Northup) **105**:358-94
"Twenty Ballads by a Swiss" (Meyer)
See "Zwanzig Balladen von einem Schweizer"
25 Years After (Andersen) **79**:11
Der 24. Februar (Werner)
See *Der vierundzwanzigste Februar: Eine romantische Tragödie in einem Akt*
Le 24 février (Dumas) **71**:192
"Twenty Golden Years Ago" (Mangan) **27**:281, 292, 296, 298
Twenty Poems in Common English (Barnes) **75**:40
Twenty Years After; or, The Further Feats and Fortunes of a Gascon Adventurer (Dumas)
See *Vingt ans après*
Twenty-Five Village Sermons (Kingsley) **35**:205
24 (Dickinson) **77**:84
The Twentyfourth of February: A Tragedy in One Act (Werner)
See *Der vierundzwanzigste Februar: Eine romantische Tragödie in einem Akt*
"The Twenty-Second of December" (Bryant) **46**:47
"Twenty-Seventh Letter" (Schiller) **166**:104
"Twenty-Third Letter" (Schiller) **166**:108
"Twenty-third Sunday after Trinity" (Keble) **87**:177
"Twice" (Rossetti) **2**:565, 570; **50**:267, 287, 313, 318; **66**:342; **186**:268
Twice Round the Clock, or the Hours of the Day and Night in London (Sala) **46**:232-33, 237, 244-50
"The Twice-Revised Code" (Arnold) **218**:240
Twice-Told Tales (Hawthorne) **2**:291-94, 299, 303, 305, 319, 321-22; **10**:272, 274; **39**:235-36; **79**:295-96, 307-09; **95**:106, 111; **171**:342-43; **191**:257; **226**:118
"Twilight" (Halleck) **47**:57, 61
"Twilight" (Levy) **59**:94; **203**:345
"Twilight" (Norton) **47**:238, 240
"Twilight" (Silva)
See "Crepúsculo"
"Twilight" (Tyutchev) **34**:402
"Twilight" (Whitman) **31**:434; **81**:370
Twilight (Baratynsky)
See *Sumerki*
"Twilight Calm" (Rossetti) **2**:576
"Twilight Night" (Rossetti) **50**:288
The Twilight of the Gods (Wagner)
See *Die Götterdämmerung*
"The Twin Brothers" (Eminescu) **33**:265
Twin Roses (Mowatt) **74**:221
"Twinkle, twinkle little Bat" (Dodgson) **139**:29
"The Twins" (Eminescu) **131**:286-87, 290-91, 296, 346
The Twins (Shevchenko)
See *Blyzniata*
"Twins of Macha" (Ferguson) **33**:279, 285
Twist (Dickens)
See *Oliver Twist*
"A Twist-Imony in Favour of Gin-Twist" (Maginn) **8**:441
2 (Dickinson) **77**:120
The Two Admirals (Cooper) **1**:208, 221; **54**:258, 263; **203**:74
Two Ages (Kierkegaard)
See *En literair Anmeldelse. To Tidsaldre*
Two Ages: The Age of Revolution and the Present Age, a Literary Review (Kierkegaard)
See *En literair Anmeldelse. To Tidsaldre*
"The Two April Mornings" (Wordsworth) **12**:420; **111**:325, 349-50; **166**:235
"The Two Armies" (Timrod) **25**:361, 388
"Two Augurs" (Villiers de l'Isle Adam)
See "Deux augures"
"Two Brothers" (Andersen)
See "To Brødre"
"Two Brothers" (Baillie) **2**:42
"The Two Brothers" (Dodgson) **139**:33-34
"The Two Butlers of Kilkenny" (Maginn) **8**:440
"Two Canadian Poets" (Lampman) **25**:213-14, 216
The Two Chiefs of Dunboy (Froude) **43**:192-96
"The Two Children" (Brontë) **16**:93
"Two Choices" (Rossetti) **50**:310
"Two Cities—Two Books" (Oliphant) **221**:298-300
"Two Countrymen" (Krylov) **1**:439
"Two Days' Solitary Imprisonment" (Bellamy) **4**:30
"The Two Deserts" (Patmore) **9**:358
Two Discourses at the Communion on Fridays (Kierkegaard) **34**:205, 239
"The Two Dogs" (Grillparzer)
See "Die beiden Hunde"
"The Two Dragoons" (Runeberg) **41**:314
Two Dramas from Calderón (FitzGerald) **9**:276
"The Two Drovers" (Scott) **110**:232; **209**:284, 289-93, 338
"Two Early French Stories" (Pater) **7**:338; **159**:256-57, 265, 278, 295-96, 300, 321, 323-25
Two Edifying Discourses (Kierkegaard) **34**:224, 258; **125**:210
The Two Emilys (Lee) **191**:316
"The Two Enthusiasts" (Reynolds) **146**:172
"Two Farms in Woone" (Barnes) **75**:43-4, 93, 101
"Two Fates" (Baratynsky)
See "Dve doli"
"The Two Fishermen" (Moodie) **14**:231
The Two Foscari (Byron) **2**:66, 79-80, 92; **109**:99, 102; **149**:44
Two Foscari (Mitford) **4**:403
Two Friends (Turgenev) **21**:418; **37**:435; **122**:246, 350
"The Two Generals" (Trollope) **101**:264
"The Two Gentlemen of Verona" (Lamb) **125**:304-5
"The Two Graves" (Bryant) **46**:3
"The Two Grenadiers" (Heine) **4**:242-43
"2 Harps" (Allingham) **25**:7
"The Two Heirs" (Mérimée) **6**:354
"The Two Herberts" (Fuller) **211**:92
"The Two Herd-Boys" (Taylor) **89**:342
280 (Dickinson) **77**:76
288 (Dickinson) **77**:112
281 (Dickinson) **77**:75
286 (Dickinson) **77**:91
283 (Dickinson) **77**:66
211 (Dickinson) **77**:149
258 (Dickinson) **77**:84
255 (Dickinson) **77**:163
251 (Dickinson) **77**:152
253 (Dickinson) **77**:119
252 (Dickinson) **77**:119
249 (Dickinson) **77**:149
241 (Dickinson) **77**:162
246 (Dickinson) **77**:65
296 (Dickinson) **77**:63, 147
293 (Dickinson) **77**:50, 64
271 (Dickinson) **77**:67
273 (Dickinson) **77**:184
272 (Dickinson) **77**:68
216 (Dickinson) **77**:71
239 (Dickinson) **77**:96
232 (Dickinson) **77**:173
"Two in the Campagna" (Browning) **19**:112; **79**:162
"The Two Islands" (Castro Alves)
See "As duas ilhas"
"The Two Ivans" (Gogol)
See "The Tale of How Ivan Ivanovich Quarrelled with Ivan Nikiforovich"
"The Two Kinds of Poetry" (Mill) **58**:321-2, 324, 329, 363; **179**:343, 347, 350
"Two Landowners" (Turgenev) **122**:293, 350
"Two Lengths Has Every Day" (Dickinson) **21**:77
"Two Letters to Lord Byron" (Bowles) **103**:54
"The Two Little Skeezucks" (Field) **3**:208
"Two Maidens" (Andersen) **214**:55
The Two Martyrs (Chateaubriand)
See *Les martyrs; ou, Le triomphe de la religion Chrétienne*
The Two Mentors (Reeve) **19**:408, 412, 415
Two Minor Ethico-Religious Treatises (Kierkegaard) **78**:238
"Two Mollies: A City Sketch" (Boyesen) **135**:13
"Two Muses" (Klopstock) **11**:231
"Two National Songs to the Same Measure" (Harpur) **114**:144
Two Nights Before the Full Moon (Ichiyō)
See *Jusan'ya*
"The Two Pages of Szondi" (Arany)
See "Szondi két apródja"
"The Two Painters" (Allston) **2**:20-21
"The Two Peacocks of Bedfont" (Hood) **16**:218
The Two Piccolomini (Schiller)
See *Wallenstein*
"The Two Pigeons" (Laforgue)
See "Les Deux Pigeons"
"The Two Poplar Trees" (Desbordes-Valmore)
See "Les Deux peupliers"
"The Two Portraits" (Timrod) **25**:361
"Two Pursuits" (Rossetti) **66**:305
"Two Quatrains" (Turgenev)
See "Dva chetverostishiia"
"The Two Races" (Jones) **222**:125, 157
"The Two Races of Men" (Lamb) **10**:392, 409-11, 428, 436; **113**:173-75, 199
"Two Red Roses across the Moon" (Morris) **4**:426, 431, 444
"The Two Rivers" (Longfellow) **45**:130
Two Rivulets (Whitman) **205**:212, 226, 317
"Two Roses and a Ring" (Crawford) **127**:189
"Two Sails" (Meyer)
See "Zwei Segel"
"Two Saints" (Cooke) **110**:16, 55, 57-8
The Two Scars (Fredro)
See *Dwie blizny*
"Two Scenes from the Life of Blondel" (Lowell) **2**:511
"Two Scenes in a Post Office" (Lippard) **198**:133
Two Sermons on the Interpretation of Prophecy (Arnold) **18**:18

The Two Shoemakers (More) **27**:345, 358; **141**:167, 169, 281, 288
"The Two Sides of the River" (Morris) **4**:421
"Two Sides to a Tortoise" (Melville) **3**:383
"Two Sisters" (Stifter)
See "Zwei Schwestern"
"Two Sisters of Mercy" (Baudelaire)
See "Les Deux Bonnes Soeurs"
"The Two Skulls" (O'Brien) **21**:242
The Two Soldiers (More) **141**:172
"Two Sonnets" (Thomson) **18**:392
"Two Sonnets: Harvard" (Holmes) **14**:129
"The Two Sons" (Opie) **65**:173
"The Two Spirits: An Allegory" (Shelley) **18**:362; **93**:304
Two Stories of the Seen and Unseen (Oliphant) **61**:174
"The Two Swans" (Hood) **16**:218, 227, 231
"Two Swimmers Wrestled on the Spar" (Dickinson) **21**:63
"The Two Temples" (Melville) **157**:111; **193**:146, 149-51
"The Two Terrors" (Levy) **59**:94; **203**:351
"The Two Thieves" (Wordsworth) **111**:235
Two Thoughts of Death (Rossetti) **50**:287
"The Two Travellers" (Bryant) **46**:42
"Two Trees Were We" (Barnes) **75**:70
"The Two Villages" (Cooke) **110**:3, 9, 41
"Two Voices" (Ferguson) **33**:290
"The Two Voices" (Ingelow) **39**:256
"The Two Voices" (Tennyson) **30**:226-28, 233, 253, 276-77, 281; **65**:241, 243, 249, 267, 270-1; **115**:236-37, 252, 256-57, 261; **202**:242
"The Two Watchers" (Whittier) **8**:493
"Two Ways of Telling A Story" (Ingelow) **107**:150
The Two Wealthy Farmers (More) **27**:345
"The Two Widows of Hunter's Creek" (Traill) **31**:324
Two Wolves and a Lamb (Webb) **143**:325, 337, 351, 357
Two Women (Gómez de Avellaneda)
See *Dos mujeres*
"The Two Worlds" (Newman) **38**:345
"Two Worlds" (Winthrop) **210**:301, 304
Two Worlds (Jacobsen)
See *To Verdener*
Two Years Ago (Kingsley) **35**:208, 211, 215, 220, 230-32, 235, 241-42, 244, 246-49, 251, 253-57
"The Two-Days-Old Baby" (Blake)
See "Infant Joy"
A Twofold Life (Pavlova)
See *Dvoinaia zhizn!*
"Two-Part Prelude" (Wordsworth) **206**:287
Two-penny Trash (Cobbett)
See *Cobbett's Twopenny Trash*
"Ty skazhi, govori . . ." (Bestuzhev) **131**:181
"Ty, utselevshii v serdtse nishchem" (Pavlova) **138**:21, 55
"Ty vse, chto serdtsu milo" (Pavlova) **138**:11
"Ty zrel ego v krugo bol shogo sveta" (Tyutchev) **34**:389, 404
"The Tyger" (Blake) **13**:180-81, 222, 227-29, 231-33, 243, 247; **37**:3-4, 7, 10, 13, 18, 27, 33, 43, 49, 51, 54-7, 62, 69, 77-8, 82, 84-5, 93; **190**:32
Tylney Hall (Hood) **16**:201, 205
Typee (Melville)
See *Typee: A Peep at Polynesian Life, During a Four Months' Residence in a Valley of the Marquesas*
Typee: A Peep at Polynesian Life (Melville)
See *Typee: A Peep at Polynesian Life, During a Four Months' Residence in a Valley of the Marquesas*
Typee: A Peep at Polynesian Life, During a Four Months' Residence in a Valley of the Marquesas (Melville) **3**:325-30, 332-34, 337-42, 344, 347, 349, 355-56, 359-60, 363-65, 370-71, 384; **12**:255, 257, 259; **29**:323-24, 331, 335, 338, 354, 367-68; **45**:193-257; **49**:391; **91**:9, 33, 42, 44-5, 55, 63, 122, 212; **123**:187, 192-93, 211, 232, 238-39, 251-52; **157**:64, 68; **181**:154, 164, 189, 204, 212, 214, 230, 263, 327-29, 331; **221**:100, 104, 108, 116, 118, 122, 140, 147-48, 157, 167-68, 191-92, 194, 196, 198
Les Types de Paris (Mallarmé) **41**:249
"Tyranny" (Lanier)
See "Spring and Tyranny"
"The Tyranny of Love" (Robinson) **142**:175
"Tyrant's Work. Russian Pictures in the East See Region" ("Irodova raboma. Russkiie karminy v Osmziejskom kraie") (Leskov) **174**:129
Tyrocinium (Cowper)
See *Tirocinium; or, Review of Schools*
"Tytarivna" (Shevchenko) **54**:389
"U Boha za dvermy lezhala sokyra" (Shevchenko) **54**:390
"Den uartige Dreng" (Andersen) **79**:76
"Über alte und neue Kirchenmusik" (Hoffmann)
See "Alte und neue Kirchenmusik"
"Über Anmut und Würde" (Schiller) **166**:120, 135, 146, 171
Über Anmut und Würde (Schiller) **69**:206
"Über das Dirigiren" (Wagner) **9**:475
"Über das Erhabene" (Schiller) **39**:363, 367, 380-81, 386-86; **69**:209-10, 266; **166**:108, 121, 144-46, 176, 181
Über das Genie (Claudius) **75**:195-96, 205, 209-10, 212-14, 219
"Über das Marionettentheater" (Kleist) **2**:446-47, 451, 454-55, 458, 461-62; **37**:226-27, 233, 246, 249-50, 264-65, 267; **222**:188, 198, 203, 208, 210, 212-15, 222, 263
"Über das Pathetische" (Schiller) **39**:377
"Über das spanische Theater" (Schlegel) **142**:301, 319
"Über das Studium der griechischen Poesie" (Schlegel) **45**:310-12, 319-20, 326-27, 331, 342, 357-60, 366; **226**:164, 241
"Über das Tragische" (Hölderlin) **187**:252
"Über das Verhältnis des Angenehmen und Schönen zum Nützlichen" (Wieland) **177**:297, 363
Über das Wesen der menschlichen Freiheit (Schelling)
See *Philosophische Untersuchungen über das Wesen der menschlichen Freiheit und die damit zusammenhängende Gegenstände*
"Über das Wesen des Drama" (Grillparzer) **102**:104
"Über den Ausbruck: 'Stilles Verdienst'" (Claudius) **75**:211
Über den Begriff der Wissenschaftslehre (Fichte) **62**:29
"Über den Dualis" (Humboldt) **134**:199
"Über den Entwurf zu einer neuen Konstitution für die Juden" (Humboldt) **134**:208, 210
"Über den Fleis in mehreren gelehrten Sprachen" (Herder) **186**:78-81
"Über den freien Gebrauch der Vernunft in Glaubenssachen" (Wieland) **177**:244
"Über den Gebrauch des Chors in der Tragödie" (Schiller) **69**:181
"Über den Geist der Menschheit" (Humboldt) **134**:194
Über den Geschlechtsunterschied und dessen Einfluss auf die organische Natur (Humboldt) **134**:171
"Über den Hang der Menschen an Magie und Geistererscheinungen zu glauben" (Wieland) **177**:367
Über den Nationalcharakter der Sprachen (Humboldt) **134**:206
"Über den Unterschied der Dichtarten" (Hölderlin) **187**:205, 231
"Über den Unterschied der Dichtungsarten" (Hölderlin) **16**:177
Über den Ursprung der Sprache (Herder)
See *Abhandlung über den Ursprung der Sprache, walche den von der Königl*
Über den Zusammenhang der tierischen Natur des Menschen mit seiner geistigen (Schiller) **39**:394; **166**:116
"Über die allmähliche Verfertigung der Gedanken beim Reden" (Kleist) **2**:458; **37**:225, 250-2; **222**:200, 202, 256, 259-60, 278
Über die ästhetische Erziehung des Menschen in einer Reihe von Briefen (Schiller) **166**:90-91, 93-94, 121, 135, 160-61, 163
"Über die Aufführung der Schauspiele des Calderon de la Barca auf dem Theater in Bamberg" (Hoffmann) **183**:180
Über die Aufgabe des Geschichtschreibers (Humboldt) **134**:157
"Über die Diotima" (Schlegel) **45**:358, 373; **226**:197
"Über die Grenzen des Schönen" (Schlegel) **45**:357
"Über die Heide" (Storm) **1**:548
"Über die Ideale der Alten" (Wieland)
See "Gedanken über die Ideale der Alten"
"Über die Kupferstiche" (Tieck) **5**:520
Über die männliche und weibliche Form (Humboldt) **134**:171
Über die neuere deutsche Litteratur. Fragmente (Herder) **186**:13-14, 16, 18-20, 35, 65
Über die nothwendigen Grenzen beim Gebrauch schöner Formen (Schiller) **69**:250
"Uber die Philosophie" (Schlegel) **226**:222
Über die Philosophie der Sprache, und des Worts (Schlegel) **45**:301
Über die Religion: Reden an die Gebildeten unter ihren Verächtern (Schleiermacher) **107**:262, 265-66, 274, 318-19, 331-32, 334-36, 339, 343, 345, 347-51, 353, 355-56, 358, 361, 376, 382-83, 396-98, 401, 405, 408-09
Über die Schriften des Lukas: Ein kritischer Versuch (Schleiermacher) **107**:268, 369
Über die Sprache und Weisheit der Indier (Schlegel) **45**:288, 300, 316
"Über die Unsterblichkeit der Seele" (Claudius) **75**:210, 216
"Über die Unverständlichkeit" (Schlegel) **45**:335, 343, 375-76, 379, 381-82; **226**:171-74, 176, 221-22, 224, 226, 242
"Über die Verfahrungsweise des poetischen Geistes" (Hölderlin) **16**:177; **187**:226, 230, 255-57, 259, 263-65, 271
"Über die verschiedenen Arten zu dichten" (Hölderlin) **16**:177
Über die Verschiedenheiten des menschlichen Sprachbaues (Humboldt) **134**:206
Über die vierfache Wurzel des Satzes vom zureichenden Grunde (Schopenhauer) **51**:278, 328; **157**:246, 264, 284-85, 321
"Über die von J. J. Rousseau vorgeschlagenen Versuche, den wahren Stand der Natur des Menschen zu entdecken" (Wieland) **177**:258
"Über die weiblichen Charaktere in den griechischen Dichtern" (Schlegel) **45**:358
Über die Wirkung der Dichtkunst auf die Sitten der Völker in alten und neven Zeiten (Herder) **8**:316
"Über die wissenschaftlichen Behandlungsarten des Naturrechts" (Hegel) **46**:110
Über dramatische Kunst und Litteratur (Schlegel) **142**:294-95, 301, 311-12, 321, 342, 346, 348
"Über ein Sprichwort" (Claudius) **75**:213
Über Garantien (Eichendorff) **8**:220
"Uber Goethes *Meister* " (Schlegel) **226**:222, 246
"Über Lessing" (Schlegel) **45**:359

"Über naïve und sentimentalische Dichtung" (Schiller) **39**:337, 347, 366, 370, 381, 391; **69**:187, 208, 257; **166**:121, 132-33, 159-60, 173
"Über Ossian und die Lieder alter Völker" (Herder)
See "Auszug aus einem Briefwechsel über Ossian und die Lieder alter Völker"
"Über Poesie, Silbenmaß und Sprache" (Schlegel) **142**:316
Über Polen (Heine) **54**:336
Über Recensenten Unfug (Kotzebue) **25**:135
"Über Religion" (Hölderlin) **187**:239-40, 248
Über Religion (Humboldt) **134**:192
"Über Romeo und Julia" (Schlegel) **142**:344
"Über Schädelnerven" (Büchner) **146**:16, 65, 91
"Über schöne Literatur and Kunst" (Schlegel) **142**:319
Über Sprach und Dichtkunst (Klopstock) **11**:228, 233-34
"Über weibliche Bildung" (Wieland) **177**:312
Ubezhishche Monrepo (Saltykov) **16**:345, 358, 373-75
Ubirajara (Alencar) **157**:9, 12-13, 15, 20, 27
"Übungen im Stil" (Claudius) **75**:210, 218
"Uchenie—aforizmy iz Bekona" (Bestuzhev) **131**:165, 168
Udolpho (Radcliffe)
See *The Mysteries of Udolpho*
Udsigt over Verdens-Krøniken fornemmelig i det Luthreske Tidsrum (Grundtvig) **158**:140-41, 147-54
Udvalgte Skrifter (Grundtvig) **158**:148, 150, 152-55, 175-76, 181, 183-85
Ueber das Wesen des Gelehrten (Fichte) **62**:35
Ueber den Grund unseres Glaubens an eine göttliche Weltregierung (Fichte) **62**:34
Üeber die französische Bühne (Heine) **147**:220, 228
"Ueber die Glaubwürdigkeit Lucians in seinen Nachrichten vom Peregrinus" (Wieland) **177**:336
"Ueber die innige Verwandschaft der Poesie und Tonkunst" (Schumann) **143**:73
Ueber die Seelenwandrung. Drei Gespräche (Herder) **186**:18, 100, 102
"Ueber die Zufälligkeit und Nichtigkeit des Nachruhms" (Schumann) **143**:73
Ueber dramatische Kunst und Litteratur (Schlegel) **15**:205, 209, 212, 218, 223, 228, 230-35, 241
Ueber Polen (Heine) **147**:218
Ueber Thomas Abbts Schriften (Herder) **186**:14-15, 20
Ueda Akinari zenshu (Ueda Akinari) **131**:21
"Uezdnyj lekar" (Turgenev) **122**:264-65
Ugetsu Monogatari (Ueda Akinari) **131**:2-6, 9, 12-17, 19, 21-23, 30-31, 35-39, 41, 45-53, 57, 60-64, 67-70, 72-74, 76-77, 85-88
"The Ugly Duckling" (Andersen)
See "Den grimme Ælling"
"The Ugly Princess" (Kingsley) **35**:206
"Ugolino" (Mickiewicz) **101**:162-64
Uiyamabumi (Motoori) **45**:277
"Ukazi" (Preseren) **127**:298
"Ukha bez ryby" (Leskov)
See "Uxa bez ryby"
"Ukrainian Duma" (Slowacki) **15**:368
"Ulalume" (Poe) **1**:503, 509, 512, 519; **16**:305; **55**:141, 160; **94**:233; 192, 195-96, 207, 211, 217, 221, 226-27, 236-40, 242-43, 246-47, 264, 277-78, 280-81, 288, 297-98, 309-11, 316, 334; **211**:312
Ulfhild (Grundtvig) **158**:135
"Der Uli" (Meyer) **81**:140, 146, 148
Uli der Knecht: Elin Volksbuch (Gotthelf)
See *Wie Uli der Knecht glücklich wird*
Uli der Pächter (Gotthelf) **117**:4, 6-8, 17-18, 24, 27, 32-3, 35, 39
"Ulmarra" (Kendall) **12**:192
"Uloola" (Kendall) **12**:192, 201
Ulric the Farm Servant: A Story of the Bernese Lowlands (Gotthelf)
See *Wie Uli der Knecht glücklich wird*
Ulrich der Empfindsame (Tieck) **5**:519
"La última calaverada" (Alarcón) **219**:52-53
"Ultima canto di Saffo" (Leopardi) **129**:340
"La última ilusión" (Casal) **131**:242
"Ultimatum" (Kierkegaard) **125**:202, 210, 213, 234, 254
Ultime lettere di Jacopo Ortis (Foscolo) **8**:260-65, 267, 269, 273, 275, 277-8; **97**:49-50, 53, 62, 70-80, 82-4, 88, 97
"El último adiós y nosotros, inos morimos o qué hacemos?" (Larra) **130**:205, 231, 241, 243
"El último arrebol" (Isaacs) **70**:308
"Ultra cœlos" (Leconte de Lisle) **29**:226, 228, 235
"Ulysses" (Tennyson) **30**:213, 223, 239, 242, 257, 276, 279-80, 283; **65**:376; **115**:235, 240, 275; **202**:188, 280, 289, 335
Ulysses (Lamb) **113**:278
"Umeršee soslovie" (Leskov) **25**:258
"Die ummauerte Seele und der Epheu" (Brentano) **191**:72
"Umoregi" (Ichiyō) **49**:334, 342
Umsonst (Nestroy) **42**:242, 245, 250
"A un vincitore nel pallone" (Leopardi) **129**:328
"A una dama burlada" (Espronceda) **39**:116
"A una estrella" (Espronceda) **39**:86, 100, 102-04, 108-11, 113, 116, 118-19
"The Unbaptized Priest" (Leskov)
See "Nekrescenyj pop"
Der Unbedeutende (Nestroy) **42**:220, 244, 246-47, 263
Das Unbehagen (Grillparzer) **102**:216
"The Uncanny Guest" (Hoffmann)
See "Der Unheimliche Gast"
"Uncle and Aunt" (Barnes) **75**:13, 48
"Uncle and Nephew" (O'Brien) **21**:236, 247
"The Uncle and Nephew" (Opie) **65**:159
"Uncle Arly" (Lear)
See "Incidents in the Life of My Uncle Arly"
"Uncle Ben's Attack of Spring Fever, and How He Got Cured" (Parton) **86**:351
"Uncle Jack" (Nekrasov) **11**:421
"Uncle Jim's Baptist Revival Hymn" (Lanier) **118**:227, 235
"Uncle Joe and His Family" (Moodie) **14**:231
"Uncle Josh" (Cooke) **110**:43
"Uncle Out O' Debt and' Out O' Danger" (Barnes) **75**:70
Uncle Silas: A Tale of Bartram-Haugh (Le Fanu) **9**:299-314, 316-17; **58**:251, 254, 256, 266, 269-71, 274-5, 286-9, 291-303, 306-13
Uncle Tom's Cabin; or, Life among the Lowly (Stowe) **3**:537-53, 555-61, 563; **50**:328-407; **195**:148-281
"Uncle's Dream" (Dostoevsky) **2**:168, 203
The Uncollected Poetry and Prose of Walt Whitman (Whitman) **205**:253-54, 322
The Uncollected Writings of Charles Dickens (Dickens) **217**:247
"Uncommercial Traveller" (Dickens) **217**:267
The Uncommercial Traveller (Dickens) **18**:111; **113**:68
"The Unconscious Life" (Cranch) **115**:68
Under a Mask (Boker)
See *The World a Mask*
Under Ground (Dodgson)
See *Alice's Adventures Under Ground*
"Under the Cloudy Sky" (Eminescu) **33**:265
"Under the Glacier" (Boyesen) **135**:13, 19, 27
Under the Hill (Beardsley)
See *The Story of Venus and Tannhäuser*
Under the Hill, and Other Essays in Prose and Verse (Beardsley) **6**:147
"Under the Light, yet under" (Dickinson) **171**:101
Under the Lilacs (Alcott) **6**:18, 20; **58**:41, 49-50
"Under the Oaks" (Arany)
See "A tölgyek alatt"
Under the Pine (Hayne) **94**:136
"Under the Pine. To the Memory of Henry Timrod" (Hayne) **94**:159, 165
"Under the Rose" (Rossetti)
See "The Iniquity of the Fathers upon the Children"
"Under the Violets" (Holmes) **14**:109, 128, 132
"Under the Willow" (Andersen) **7**:21, 29, 32
"Under the Willow She's Sleeping" (Foster) **26**:295
Under the Willows, and Other Poems (Lowell) **2**:509; **90**:198
"Under the Willow-Tree" (Andersen) **79**:82
"Under the Window" (Preseren)
See "Pod oknom"
Under Which Lord? (Linton) **41**:167
"An Undertaker" (Hood) **16**:206
"The Undertaker" (Pushkin)
See "Grobovshchik"
Underwoods (Stevenson) **5**:400-01, 428; **63**:239-40; **193**:205, 210, 215
"Undine" (Eminescu) **131**:286-87
"Undine" (Rossetti) **186**:275-76
Undine (Fouqué) **2**:262-63, 265-69
Undine (Hoffmann) **2**:345; **183**:181, 198, 222, 228
The Undivine Comedy (Krasiński) **4**:300, 302-09, 311-22
"Undue Significance" (Dickinson) **171**:176, 191
"The Undying One" (Norton) **47**:233, 239, 251; **205**:45, 67, 69-70, 86, 127-28, 138
The Undying One and Other Poems (Norton) **47**:235, 246, 252, 260; **205**:122
"A une heure du matin" (Baudelaire) **155**:46-47, 107
"A une jeune tribun" (Gautier) **59**:18
"A une mendiante rousse" (Baudelaire) **155**:4-5
"A une passante" (Baudelaire) **155**:4-5, 7, 9
Unexplored Syria (Burton) **42**:37
"The Unexpress'd" (Whitman) **31**:435
"The Unfaithful Servants" (Very) **9**:383
"The Unfaithful Village Girl" (Isaacs)
See "La aldeana infiel"
"An Unfinished Draft" (Beddoes) **154**:78
"The Unfinished Poem" (Krasiński) **4**:304, 307
"The Unforeseen" (Baudelaire)
See "L'imprévu"
"Unforgotten" (Rossetti) **186**:270
"The Unfortunate" (Shevchenko)
See "Tryzna"
"The Unfortunate" (Turgenev)
See "Neschastnaya"
"The Unfortunates" (Nekrasov)
See "Nesžastnye"
"Ungeduld" (Muller) **73**:364, 370-71
Die Unglücklichen (Kotzebue) **25**:146-47
"Unha vez tiren un cravo" (Castro) **78**:41
"The Unhappiest Man" (Kierkegaard) **125**:207-9
"The Unhappy" (Nekrasov) **11**:404-05
"An Unhappy Girl" (Turgenev)
See "Neschastnaya"
Unhappy Valley (Burton)
See *Scinde; or the Unhappy Valley*
Die unheilbringende Zauberkrone (Raimund) **69**:8, 12, 16, 22, 24, 27, 36-38, 44-6, 48-9, 52
"Der Unheimliche Gast" (Hoffmann) **2**:342, 353; **183**:196-97, 204-5
Die Uniform des Feldmarschalls Wellington (Kotzebue) **25**:136
"Union Means Power" (Eminescu) **33**:272
"Union of Church and State" (Brownson) **50**:54
"The Unioners" (Barnes)
See "The Times"
"Unitarian Christianity: Discourse at the Ordination of the Rev. Jared Sparks" (Channing) **17**:34
"Unitarian Christianity Most Favorable to Piety: Discourse at the Dedication of the

Second Congregational Unitarian Church in New York" (Channing) **17**:35, 39
"L'Univers 1854" (Chaadaev) **197**:133
"Universal Goodness" (Clare) **9**:120
"Universal Money" (Bagehot) **10**:31
"The Universe" (Poe) **117**:304, 309, 320
"Universities: Actual and Ideal" (Huxley) **67**:92
"University Preaching" (Newman) **38**:302, 304
"University Sermon" (Newman) **99**:298
"University Sermon X" (Newman) **99**:298
"University Sermon XI" (Newman) **99**:298
"University Sermon XII" (Newman) **99**:298
"University Sermons" (Newman)
See *Fifteen Sermons Preached before the University of Oxford*
"University Subjects" (Newman)
See *The Idea of a University, Defined and Illustrated*
"The Unknown" (Hale) **75**:358, 361-2
"The Unknown Dead" (Timrod) **25**:360, 388
The Unknown Eros (Patmore)
See *The Unknown Eros, and Other Odes I-XXXI*
The Unknown Eros, and Other Odes I-XXXI (Patmore) **9**:333, 336-39, 342-43, 346-47, 352, 354-55, 357-59, 361-62, 364
"The Unknown Masterpiece" (Balzac)
See "Le Chef-d'oeuvre inconnu"
"The Unknown Way" (Bryant) **6**:175; **46**:38, 42, 48
"The Unknown Woman" (Villiers de l'Isle Adam)
See "L'inconnue"
"Unmaßgebliche Betrachtung" (Kleist) **37**:274
"The Unmarried Mother" (Preseren)
See "Nezakonska mati"
"Ünneprontók" (Arany) **34**:5
L'uno (Alfieri) **101**:45, 73
"The Unparalleled Adventure of One Hans Pfaall" (Poe) **1**:500; **16**:292, 300, 303, 313, 321, 335
"Unparteyische Betrachtungen über die dermalige Staats-Revolution in Frankreich" (Wieland) **177**:277
"An Unprotected Female at the Pyramids" (Trollope) **101**:233, 235
Unpublished Letters of Samuel Taylor Coleridge (Coleridge) **197**:307; **231**:36
Unpublished Poems (Desbordes-Valmore)
See *Poésies inédites*
"Unquiet Sleeper" (Whittier) **8**:845
"Unreal Words" (Newman) **38**:304
"The Unreaped Row" (Nekrasov) **11**:409
"Unrest" (Lampman) **25**:187
"Les Uns et les autres" (Verlaine) **230**:161
"Unseen Buds" (Whitman) **31**:435
The Unseen Friend (Larcom) **179**:173
"The Unseen Playmate" (Stevenson) **193x'**:205
"Unseen Spirits" (Willis) **194**:292, 331
"Unshriven" (Gordon) **21**:160
Die Unsichtbare Loge (Jean Paul) **7**:232, 238, 240
"Unspoken Language" (Sigourney) **21**:298
The Unstable Man's Morning Hymn (Werner)
See *Unstäts Morgenpsalm*
"Unsre Sprache" (Klopstock) **225**:297, 318
"The Unstamped Press in London" (Horne) **127**:253
Unstäts Morgenpsalm (Werner) **189**:325
"Unsterbliche Geliebte Letter" (Beethoven) **227**:18
Das unsterbliche Leben: Unbekannte Briefe von Clemens Brentano (Brentano) **191**:34, 68
"The Untainted Heart" (Preseren)
See "Neiztrohnjeno srce"
Unter dem Tannenbaum (Storm) **195**:94
"Unter den Sternen" (Meyer) **81**:147
"Unter Sternen" (Keller) **2**:421
Unterhaltungen deutscher Ausgewanderten (Goethe) **4**:196
Unterm Birnbaum (Fontane) **26**:236, 243, 272; **163**:161, 215
"Eine Unterredung über die Rechtmässigkeit des Gebrauchs, den die Französische Nazion dermahlen von ihrer Aufklärung und Stärke macht. Geschrieben im August 1789" (Wieland) **177**:274
"Unterricht" (Klopstock) **11**:238
"Unterwelt" (Heine) **147**:196
"Until the Very End" (Arany)
See "Mindvégig"
"Unto Like Story—Trouble Has Enticed Me" (Dickinson) **21**:64
"'Unto Me?' I Do Not Know You" (Dickinson) **21**:58; **77**:160
"Unto Myself I Reared a Monument" (Pushkin) **83**:249
"Die unüberwindliche Flotte" (Schiller) **39**:388
"An Unusual Story" (Goncharov)
See "Neobyknovennaya istoriya"
"Unveiled" (Hayne) **94**:148-49, 166
Unverhofft (Nestroy) **42**:220
Die Unvermählte (Kotzebue) **25**:145
"Unwahrscheinliche Wahrhaftigkeiten" (Kleist) **37**:237
Unwiederbringlich (Fontane) **26**:234, 236-37, 239-40, 244, 251-53, 259-60; **163**:161, 198, 215, 250
"Unwritten Music" (Willis) **194**:297
"Unwritten Philosophy" (Willis) **194**:296
"Unwritten Poetry" (Willis) **194**:296
"Der Unzufriedene" (Grillparzer) **102**:192
"Up at a Villa-Down in the City, as Distinguished by an Italian Person of Quality" (Browning) **79**:170
"Up Hill" (Rossetti) **2**:555, 562, 572, 575; **50**:272, 283, 317; **66**:301; **186**:265, 332
"Up in the Blue Ridge" (Woolson) **82**:273, 299, 302
"Up the Airy Mountain" (Allingham)
See "The Fairies"
"Up the Country": Letters Written to Her Sister from the Upper Provinces of India (Eden) **10**:103-04
Up the Rhine (Hood) **16**:229
"Up to the Star" (Eminescu)
See "La steaua"
"The Upas Tree" (Pushkin)
See "Anchar"
Upbuilding Discourses (Kierkegaard) **125**:233
"An Up-Country Township" (Clarke) **19**:250
The Upholsterer; or, What News? A Farce, in Two Acts, As it is Performed at the Theatre-Royal, in Drury-Lane (Murphy) **229**:234
"Uplifting" (Lampman) **194**:47
"Upon a fitful dream of passion" (Taylor) **89**:300
"Upon a Mother's Grave" (Lamartine)
See "Le tombeau d'une mère"
"Upon a Very Ancient Dutch House on Long Island" (Freneau) **111**:148, 151
"Upon his Saddle sprung a Bird" (Dickinson) **171**:180
"Upon parting" (Preseren)
See "K slovesu"
"Upon the Anatomy and Affinities of the Medusae" (Huxley) **67**:4
"Upon the Bank at Early Dawn" (Thoreau) **7**:383
"Upon the Lonely Moor" (Dodgson) **139**:34
"Upon the Strange Attempt Made on the Lives of Her Majesty" (Hunt) **70**:259
"Upon This Bank at Early Dawn" (Thoreau)
See "Upon the Bank at Early Dawn"
"Upon Westminster Bridge" (Wordsworth) **166**:295
The Upper Rhine: The Scenery of Its Banks and the Manners of Its People (Mayhew) **31**:192
The Upright Men (Tamayo y Baus)
See *Los hombres de bien*
The Uprising in the Cévennes (Tieck)
See *Der Aufruhr in den Cevennen*
Uramurasaki (Ichiyō) **49**:349
Urania: A Rhymed Lesson (Holmes) **14**:100
"Uranii" (Tyutchev) **34**:387-88
"Uranothen" (Chivers) **49**:50
"Urara" (Kendall) **12**:192
"Ur-Don Karlos" (Schiller) **166**:126
Urdu-i-M'ualla (Ghalib) **39**:161
Urfaust (Goethe) **4**:204; **34**:68, 73, 85-6, 94-5, 121-24, 127
"Uriel" (Emerson) **98**:177, 179-81
Urizen (Blake)
See *The Book of Urizen*
"Urn" (Keats)
See "Ode on a Grecian Urn"
"La urna" (Casal) **131**:255
Urne (Feuillet) **45**:88
Ursachen des gesunkenen Geschmacks (Herder) **186**:18
Der Ursprung der Familie, des Privateigenthums und des Staats (Engels) **85**:6, 9, 12-13, 15, 19, 31, 94-97, 118; **114**:83
Ursprung der Sprache (Herder)
See *Abhandlung über den Ursprung der Sprache, walche den von der Königl*
Ursula (Keller) **2**:412
Ursule Mirouët (Balzac) **53**:8; **153**:66-69, 76
"Das Urteil des Paris" (Wieland) **17**:427, 429
"Urteil und Sein" (Hölderlin) **187**:231, 240, 248, 292-95, 297
"Urtheil und Seyn" (Hölderlin)
See "Urteil und Sein"
"Der Urwald" (Lenau) **16**:269, 278, 283
L'Uscoque (Sand) **174**:289
"The Use and Abuse of Political Terms" (Mill) **58**:320
"The Use of Conflict" (Bagehot) **10**:45
Used Up (Boucicault) **41**:30
Useful and Instructive Poetry (Dodgson) **139**:32, 61
Useless Memoirs of the Life of Carlo Gozzi (Gozzi)
See *Memorie inutili della vita di Carlo Gozzi*
"Uses of Great Men" (Emerson) **98**:68, 70, 72
"Usher" (Poe)
See "The Fall of the House of Usher"
Ustep (Mickiewicz)
See *The Digression*
"The Usurer" (Lampman) **194**:10
Usurpation (Constant)
See *De l'esprit de conquête et de l'usurpation dans leurs rapports avec la civilisation européenne*
"The Usurpations of Reason" (Newman) **38**:304, 307
"Uta no homare" (Ueda Akinari) **131**:21-22, 52, 59
Úti jegyzetek (Petofi) **21**:277-78, 280
Úti levelek (Petofi) **21**:277-78, 280
"Utilitarian Theory of Government" (Macaulay) **231**:294, 304
Utilitarianism (Mill) **11**:372, 378, 380, 385; **58**:319, 333-4, 342, 350, 379; **179**:207, 294, 308-10, 328-31, 333-34, 337
"Utility of Religion" (Mill) **11**:358, 378; **58**:327; **179**:210-11, 308, 310, 329, 331-32
"Utopie" (Lamartine) **11**:271
"Utoplena" (Shevchenko) **54**:360, 389-90
"Utrumque Paratus" (Arnold) **29**:35
"Utsusemi" (Ichiyō) **49**:354
"Uxa bez ryby" (Leskov) **25**:265, 267; **174**:105
"Uzhin Polliona" (Pavlova) **138**:13, 50
"Uznik" (Pushkin) **83**:351
"Uznik" (Zhukovsky) **35**:398
V chuzhom piru pokhmelye (Ostrovsky) **30**:100, 102-03, 110, 113, 115
"V den' imenin" (Bestuzhev) **131**:150
"V derevne" (Tyutchev) **34**:414

"V dni bezgranichnykh uvlecheniy..." (Baratynsky) **103**:4, 21
"V doroge" (Nekrasov) **11**:412, 420
V srede umerennosti i akkuratnosti (Saltykov) **16**:345, 358, 374
"V tarantase" (Leskov) **174**:24, 26-28
"V tolpe. . ." (Pavlova) **138**:20
"V. V.: or, Plots and Counterplots" (Alcott) **218**:84
Les vacances de Pandolphe (Sand) **42**:346-47, 349
Väd är kärlek? (Almqvist) **42**:17
Vade-Mecum (Norwid) **17**:365, 371-74, 377, 379, 386
Vadim (Lermontov) **5**:294, 296; **47**:162-63, 191-92, 224; **126**:156, 214
"Vadimov" (Bestuzhev) **131**:161
"Vadrózsák" (Madach) **19**:368
"Vae Victis" (Gordon) **21**:164
"Vagabond" (Rimbaud) **227**:270, 334
Vagabond Tales (Boyesen) **135**:13, 29-30
"Vagabonds" (Rimbaud) **4**:477, 482; **35**:293-94, 322; **82**:226
Vagabunduli Libellus (Symonds) **34**:337, 365
"The Vagrant" (Lampman) **194**:18
"Vain" (Robinson) **142**:175
"The Vain Flight" (Lampman) **194**:129, 131
"The Vain Owl and the Elf" (Crawford) **12**:172; **127**:181-82, 184, 189
"Vain Virtues" (Rossetti) **4**:491, 499
"Les Vaincus" (Verlaine) **230**:210
Les Vaincus (Verlaine) **230**:210, 213
Vala (Blake)
See *The Four Zoas: The Torments of Love and Jealousy in the Death and Judgement of Albion the Ancient Man*
"Válasz kedvesem levelére" (Petofi) **21**:285
"Valdek" (Macha) **46**:201
"Valdemar" (Poe)
See "The Facts in the Case of M. Valdemar"
"Valdice" (Macha) **46**:201
"The Vale of Esthwaite" (Wordsworth) **111**:293
"Vale of Tears" (Leskov)
See "Judol'"
"The Vale of Tears" (Leskov)
See "Judol'"
"The Valediction" (Cowper) **94**:25
"Valedictory Address" (Gladstone) **213**:129
"Valedictory Address" (Haliburton) **149**:340
"Valedictory Stanzas to Kemble" (Campbell) **19**:179, 191
Valentin: A French Boy's Story of Sedan (Kingsley) **107**:192-93, 209
"A Valentine" (Poe) **117**:242
Valentine (Sand) **2**:581, 585-86, 588-89, 596-98, 604-07; **42**:314-15, 317, 335, 339-40, 349, 354, 356, 357, 386; **57**:311-33, 316-20, 327-28, 333, 335-37, 339, 347-48, 350, 355, 368, 371; **174**:167
Valentine M'Clutchy, the Irish Agent; or, Chronicles of the Castle Cumber Property (Carleton) **3**:83, 85-87, 89-90, 94-96; **199**:5, 8-9, 12, 19-20, 22, 24-25, 40-41, 43, 46, 51, 63-67, 80-81
Valentine; ou, Le séduction (Pixérécourt) **39**:272, 277, 279, 284
Die Valentine: Schauspiel in fünf Aufzügen (Freytag) **109**:138
"Valentines" (Allingham) **25**:24
"Valentine's Day" (Lamb) **10**:436; **113**:245
"Valentine's Day; or, A Lover's Reminiscences" (Osgood) **141**:357
Valentine's Eve (Opie) **65**:162, 173-4, 179, 197
Valeria oder Vaterlist (Brentano)
See *Ponce de Leon*
Valérie (Scribe) **16**:386-88
"Valerik" (Lermontov) **5**:295; **126**:189
Valerius: A Roman Story (Lockhart) **6**:287, 292-96, 302, 310-12
Valet an meine Leser (Claudius) **75**:198, 214-16
Le Valet du Fermier (Bloomfield) **145**:136
"Valete Omnia" (Chivers) **49**:74
"The Valiant Soldiers" (Truth) **94**:338
Valkyrie (Wagner)
See *Die Walküre*
Valla, or the death and judgment of the Ancient Man: a dream of Nine Nights (Blake)
See *The Four Zoas: The Torments of Love and Jealousy in the Death and Judgment of Albion the Ancient Man*
"La Vallée de la Scarpe" (Desbordes-Valmore) **97**:6
Vallée d'Obermann (Liszt) **199**:307
Valles (Jules)-Séverine: Correspondance (Vallès) **71**:374, 376
"The Valley of Baca" (Lazarus) **109**:337
"The Valley of the Shadow of Death" (Dodgson) **139**:29-30, 126
"The Valley of Unrest" (Poe) **117**:264, 272-75, 281-82, 306-8
"Le vallon" (Lamartine) **11**:269, 282; **190**:192, 221, 234, 251
Valperga; or, The Life and Adventures of Castruccio, Prince of Lucca (Shelley) **14**:252-53, 261, 265, 267, 270-71, 274-75, 289-90, 292-93; **59**:144, 154, 192-3; **103**:331-32, 335, 338-40, 342, 346; **170**:303
"Value of a Newspaper" (Brackenridge) **227**:114, 116
Value of Criticism (Sacher-Masoch) **31**:286
Value, Price, and Profit (Marx) **114**:10
Valvèdre (Sand) **42**:312, 335, 340; **57**:311
"Vamos bebendo" (Castro) **78**:2
"The Vampire" (Baudelaire)
See "Les métamorphoses du vampire"
"Le Vampire" (Baudelaire)
See "Les métamorphoses du vampire"
The Vampire (Boucicault) **41**:32
Le Vampire (Dumas) **71**:210-11, 213-15
Le vampire (Nodier) **19**:378, 383
Le Vampire nouvelle traduite de l'anglais de Lord Byron (Polidori)
See *The Vampyre: A Tale*
Der Vampyr Eine Erzahlung aus dem Englischen des Lord Byron Nebst einer Schilderung seines Aufenthaltes in Mytilene (Polidori)
See *The Vampyre: A Tale*
The Vampyre (Byron) **109**:121
The Vampyre: A Tale (Polidori) **51**:193-96, 199, 201-05, 207-09, 211-29, 231-32, 234, 237-41
"Van Baer on the Development Hypothesis" (Lewes) **215**:147
"Vancenza" (Robinson) **142**:148
Vancenza; or, The Dangers of Credulity (Robinson) **142**:95, 157, 183
Vanda (Norwid) **17**:366-67, 369, 379
"Vanddraaben" (Andersen) **79**:68, 74, 89; **214**:61
"Vande Mataram" (Chatterji) **19**:216, 220, 222, 227
"Vane's Story" (Thomson) **18**:396-97, 400-01, 403, 405-06, 408, 411-13, 420, 424
Vane's Story, Weddah and Om-el-Bonain, and Other Poems (Thomson) **18**:392
"Vanhest" (Brackenridge)
See "The Cave of Vanhest"
Vanina Vanini (Stendhal) **23**:408; **46**:294, 307
"The Vanishers" (Whittier) **59**:375-7
"Vanitas Vanitatum" (Baratynsky) **103**:29
Vanitas Vanitatum (Brontë) **71**:91
"Vanities" (Barrett Browning) **170**:106
Vanity Fair: A Novel without a Hero (Thackeray) **5**:444-50, 452-54, 457-61, 464, 466-69, 471-78, 480, 482-84, 486-90, 492-95, 497-501, 503-04, 506; **14**:387-439; **43**:349-50, 356-57, 361-62, 368, 372, 374, 376-77, 379, 389, 393; **169**:208-343; **213**:199, 202-4, 211, 213, 217, 238-40, 242, 247, 260, 263, 266, 270-71, 275, 281-85, 290, 298, 301, 314-15, 317-19, 323, 328, 333, 337-41, 343-47
"The Vanity of Existence" (Freneau) **1**:317; **111**:141, 144
"Vanity of Vanities" (Rossetti) **186**:277-78
"Vanna's Twins" (Rossetti) **66**:330; **186**:233
The Variation of Animals and Plants under Domestication (Darwin) **57**:147, 168, 170
"Variations" (Schumann) **143**:120
"Variations lyriques" (Banville) **9**:16
Variations sur un sujet (Mallarmé) **41**:249; **210**:210, 243
"Variété d l'idéal" (Laforgue) **221**:42
Varieties in Prose (Allingham) **25**:15
"Varios caracteres" (Larra) **130**:193
"Various Verses" (Silva)
See "Versos varios"
"Various Wines" (Derzhavin) **215**:17
Varnak (Shevchenko) **54**:392-3
"Vásárban" (Arany) **34**:21
Vasconselos (Simms) **3**:507-08
"Le vase" (Leconte de Lisle) **29**:239
"Le vase étrusque" (Mérimée) **6**:352-4, 360, 367, 369-70; **65**:55, 57-8, 62-3, 100, 102, 104, 113, 128
"The Vase of Ibu Mokil" (Lampman) **25**:167
"Vashti the Queen" (Crawford) **12**:155
Vasilisa Melentyevna (Ostrovsky) **30**:101; **57**:206-7
Vassall Morton (Parkman) **12**:346, 349
"Vastness" (Tennyson) **30**:228, 280; **115**:341-42; **202**:289
"Vaterländische Gesänge" (Hölderlin) **16**:180
Vathek (Beckford) **16**:15-25, 27-39, 41-7, 49-57, 59; **214**:91-92, 98, 101, 103, 107-15, 117, 119-24, 126-27, 130, 134, 138-40, 142-43, 145-46, 148-49, 151-54, 157-61, 165, 167-70, 172-74
The Vatican Decrees in their Bearing on Civil Allegiance: A Political Expostulation (Gladstone) **213**:116
"The Vaudois' Wife" (Hemans) **71**:303
"Vaudracour and Julia" (Wordsworth) **166**:305, 308
Vaurien: or, Sketches of the Times: Exhibiting Views of the Philosophies, Religions, Politics, Literature, and Manners of the Age (D'Israeli) **217**:292-93, 308-9
Vautrin (Balzac) **5**:75
"Vdol' Fontanki-reki" (Bestuzhev) **131**:181
"Ve, pensamiento!" (Isaacs) **70**:305
"The Veairies" (Barnes) **75**:75
"Večer nakanune Ivana Kupala" (Gogol) **5**:231, 236, 251; **162**:18, 92-93, 95
"Vecher na bivuake" (Bestuzhev) **131**:175, 185, 210
"Vecher na kavkazskikh vodakh v 1824 godu" (Bestuzhev) **131**:156, 158
Vecher v Sorrente (Turgenev) **21**:428
Vechera ná khutore bliz Dikanki (Gogol) **5**:209, 218-19, 227, 231, 235, 242, 248-49; **15**:95, 98; **162**:16-17, 26-27, 29, 44, 53, 60-61, 67, 90-100, 111, 121-23
Vechny muzh (Dostoevsky) **2**:168, 175, 188, 203; **33**:178; **119**:156; **167**:334
"Veder Napoli poi Mori" (Corbière) **43**:33
"The Veiled Hippolytus" (Pater) **7**:303
"The Veiled image of Sais" (Schiller)
See "Das Verschleierte Bild von Sais"
"The Veiled Prophet of Khorassan" (Moore) **6**:379, 381, 393; **110**:203-4, 210, 212, 214, 216-17, 221, 224-25
"Veiled Prophet of Korassan" (Moore)
See "The Veiled Prophet of Khorassan"
"La Veillée" (Maupassant) **83**:172, 228
"La veillée" (Sainte-Beuve) **5**:347
"Veillée d'avril" (Laforgue) **221**:85
"La veillée de Vincennes" (Vigny) **7**:478
"Veillées" (Rimbaud) **35**:311; **82**:230, 232; **227**:297, 309-10
Veillées des Antilles (Desbordes-Valmore) **97**:12
Les veillées du château, ou Cours de morale à

l'usage des enfans (Genlis) **166**:7, 9-11, 28-29, 31-35, 53-54
"Veils" (Cranch) **115**:26-9, 35
Veinte años despues (Dumas)
See *Vingt ans après*
"Vejeces" (Silva) **114**:299, 301-3
Velikosvetskii raskol (Leskov) **174**:109
"Vellen O' the Tree" (Barnes) **75**:76, 95
"Vel'mozh" (Derzhavin) **215**:37, 39, 42, 44, 46-48
"Die Veltlinertraube" (Meyer) **81**:141-42, 150, 155
"Velykyj l'ox" (Shevchenko) **54**:368, 381, 388
"The Venale Muse" (Baudelaire)
See "La Muse vénale"
"Vendanges" (Verlaine) **230**:153, 164-65
La Vendée: An Historical Romance (Trollope) **6**:514; **33**:417; **101**:264; **215**:208
"Une vendetta" (Maupassant) **1**:469; **83**:208, 210-12, 222
"La vendetta revenge" (Balzac) **153**:151
"A vendre" (Maupassant) **83**:181
"Venecïia" (Pavlova) **138**:16, 49
"Venedigs erster Tag" (Meyer) **81**:209
"Venere" (Eminescu) **33**:265
"Veneris pueri" (Landor) **14**:181
Venetia (Disraeli) **2**:138-39, 143, 149; **39**:22, 24-5, 29, 40, 46, 52, 65-8, 75; **79**:223-28, 230, 233, 269, 272-73, 276-77
The Venetian Bracelet, The Lost Pleiad, A History of the Lyre, and Other Poems (Landon) **15**:158, 161, 166
Venetian Epigrams (Goethe) **4**:173
A Venetian Night (Musset)
See *La nuit Vénitienne; ou, Les noces de laurette*
Venezia e Napoli (Liszt) **199**:307
Vengeance (Fredro)
See *Zemsta*
"La vengeance d'une femme" (Barbey d'Aurevilly) **1**:75, 77-78; **213**:16, 18, 56-61, 68
Vengeance d'une Italienne (Scribe) **16**:381
The Vengeance of the Covenant (Smolenskin)
See *Nekam berit*
The Vengeance of the Goddess Diana (Hayne) **94**:144
"The Vengeance of the Welshmen of Tirawley" (Ferguson) **33**:278, 289, 294, 301, 305
"Venice" (Longfellow) **45**:121
"Venice" (Pavlova)
See "Venecïia"
"Venice" (Rogers) **69**:71
"Venice, an Italian Song" (Longfellow)
See "Venice"
"Venice in the East End" (Jefferies) **47**:95, 136
"Venice's First Day" (Meyer)
See "Venedigs erster Tag"
"Venise" (Musset) **150**:232
Venoni; or, The Novice of St. Mark's (Lewis) **11**:305
"Le vent dans la plaine Suspend son haleine" (Verlaine) **230**:185
"Le vent froid de la nuit" (Leconte de Lisle) **29**:222, 228, 235-36
"La venta de los gatos" (Bécquer) **106**:97, 99
"Ventajas de las cosas a medio hacer" (Larra) **17**:275; **130**:197, 223
"La ventana" (Silva) **114**:271, 301, 303
"Une vente" (Maupassant) **1**:448
La Vénus à la fourrure (Sacher-Masoch)
See *Venus im Pelz*
"Venus Anadeomena" (Casal) **131**:236, 267
"Vénus anadyomène" (Rimbaud) **4**:471
"Venus and Madonna" (Eminescu) **131**:287, 330-31
"La Vénus de Milo" (Leconte de Lisle) **29**:222, 224, 238-39
"La Vénus d'Ille" (Mérimée) **6**:353-5, 357, 359, 361, 363, 366, 368-71; **65**:50, 52-4, 56-61, 87, 96, 98, 100-01, 103, 114-15, 118, 123, 129-32, 140
Venus im Pelz (Sacher-Masoch) **31**:285, 287-88, 291-94, 296-98, 300-03, 305, 307, 309-12
Venus in Furs (Sacher-Masoch)
See *Venus im Pelz*
"The Venus of Ille" (Mérimée)
See "La Vénus d'Ille"
"La venus rustique" (Maupassant) **1**:455
"Venus's Looking-Glass" (Rossetti) **2**:561, 576
"Der Venuswagen" (Schiller) **39**:339
Les vêpres siciliennes (Scribe) **16**:408
"Ver erat" (Rimbaud) **227**:208
"Véra" (Villiers de l'Isle Adam) **3**:581, 590
"Vera i neverie. Stsena iz poemy" (Baratynsky) **103**:8
"Vérandah" (Leconte de Lisle) **29**:215
"Die Verbannten" (Droste-Hülshoff) **3**:193
Die Verbannten Gotter (Heine) **4**:235, 239-40, 267-68; **147**:136, 147
Die Verbannung aus dem Sauberreiche (Nestroy) **42**:224
"Verborgenheit" (Mörike) **10**:458
"Verdad y poesía" (Casal) **131**:259
"The Verdict" (Dostoevsky)
See "Prigover"
"El verdugo" (Espronceda) **39**:85, 100, 107-09, 113-14, 118
El verdugo (Balzac) **5**:78; **53**:25; **153**:149, 151
"Véres napokról álmodom" (Petofi) **21**:286
Verflucht sei der Acker um deinetwellen (Claudius) **75**:191
Der Verfolgte (Fouqué) **2**:266
"Vergänglichkeit" (Lenau) **16**:282
"Die Vergeltung" (Klopstock) **11**:238
Der verhängnisvolle Faschingsnacht (Nestroy) **42**:225-26, 228-29, 240
Die Verkehrte Welt (Tieck) **5**:517, 522-24, 529-30, 532
Die Verkennung (Klopstock) **225**:298
Die Verkleidungen des französischen Hofmeisters (Arnim) **159**:95
"Das verlassene Mägdlein" (Mörike) **201**:252-53, 268, 272, 280, 288, 298-99, 301, 303, 305, 369, 371
"Der Verlassene Mägdlein" (Mörike) **10**:453
Die Verlobung (Tieck) **5**:514
"Die Verlobung in St. Domingo" (Kleist) **222**:228, 230, 233, 259
Die Verlobung in St. Domingo (Kleist) **2**:456, 462; **37**:245, 247-49, 253-55
Die verlorene Handschrift (Freytag) **109**:153, 158, 175, 177-78
Das Verlorene Lachen (Keller) **2**:415, 421, 423
"Verlorene Posten" (Heine) **147**:235
"Das verlorene Schwert" (Meyer) **81**:209
"Das Verlorene Spiegelbild" (Hoffmann) **2**:341
"Vermächtnis" (Goethe) **4**:172
Vermischte Schriften (Heine) **4**:235, 240, 256, 265; **147**:200
Vermischte unphysiognomische Regeln (Lavater) **142**:13-14
"The Vernal Ague" (Freneau) **111**:153-54
Verner's Pride (Wood) **178**:270, 272, 320, 325
Veronika (Storm) **1**:539-40; **195**:7, 17, 95
Le Verre d'eau; ou, Les Effets et les causes (Scribe) **16**:388-89, 395-96, 401-03, 405-07, 413-14
"Le Verrou" (Maupassant) **83**:176
Vers de circonstance (Mallarmé) **41**:247-50; **210**:197, 240-41
"Vers dorés" (Nerval) **1**:476, 478, 486; **67**:307
"Vers dorés" (Verlaine) **230**:162
"Vers en assonances" (Verlaine) **230**:168
Vers et prose (Mallarmé) **210**:214, 264
"Vers nouveaux et chansons" (Rimbaud) **82**:240
Vers pour être calomnié (Verlaine) **51**:362
"Verschiedenartige Geschichtsauffassung" (Heine) **147**:190, 230
Verschiedene (Heine) **4**:249-50
"Verschiedene Deutung" (Lenau) **16**:269, 283
"Das Verschleierte Bild von Sais" (Schiller) **166**:107, 112
Der Verschwender (Raimund) **69**:5-6, 8-10, 13, 15, 18, 26, 38, 43-6, 48, 50-3
"Verschwiegene Liebe" (Eichendorff) **225**:7
Der Verschwiegene wider Willen (Kotzebue) **25**:136
Die Verschwörung des Fiesco zu Genua (Schiller) **39**:309-12, 323, 327, 334, 361, 368, 375, 392-94; **69**:169, 239, 263
Verse and Reverse (Alencar)
See *Verso e Reverso*
"Verse Epistle to Sara" (Coleridge) **231**:65-66
Verse Tales (Desbordes-Valmore)
See *Contes en vers*
Verses (Rossetti) **2**:559, 561, 576; **50**:271, 284-6
"Verses Addressed to Laura" (Sheridan) **91**:233
"Verses by Lady Geralda" (Brontë) **71**:165
"Verses for Being Vilified" (Verlaine) **51**:372
"Verses, Made at Sea, in a Heavy Gale" (Freneau) **111**:147, 178-81
The Verses of Frederick the Great (Sacher-Masoch) **31**:291
"Verses on the Birth in the North of a Porphyrogennete Child on the Twelfth Day of December, on Which the Sun Begins his Return from Winter to Summer" (Derzhavin)
See "Stikhi na rozhdenie v Severe porfirorodnago otroka"
"Verses on the Death of Prince Meshchersky" (Derzhavin)
See "Na smert ' kniazia Meshcherskogo"
Verses on the Death of the Revd Mr Charles Churchill (Beattie) **25**:122, 124
"Verses on the Exile of the Prince Imperial" (Jefferies) **47**:121
"Verses on the New Year" (Webster) **30**:421
Verses on Various Occasions (Newman) **38**:314; **99**:256
"Verses on War" (Paine)
See "Verses to a Friend After a Long Conversation on War"
Verses. Reprinted from Called to be Saints, Time Flies, The Face of the Deep (Rossetti) **186**:310, 313, 332, 334, 336, 343, 346-47
Verses Supposed to be Written by Alexander Selkirk (Cowper) **94**:32-38
"Verses to a Friend After a Long Conversation on War" (Paine) **62**:322
Verses to John Howard (Bowles) **103**:54, 70
"The Verses to Memory of a Young Friend" (Lamb) **113**:193
"Verses to the Memory of Garrick" (Sheridan) **91**:234
"Verses written at Bath on Finding the Heel of a Shoe" (Cowper) **94**:119
"Verses Written in a Alcove" (Barbauld) **185**:34-35, 37
"Verses Written in the Leaves of an Ivory Pocket-Book, Presented to Master Turner" (Barbauld) **185**:92
"Verses Written on the Back of an Old Visitation Copy of the Arms of Dr. Priestley's Family, with Proposals for a New Escutcheon" (Barbauld) **185**:92
Versi inediti (Manzoni) **98**:276
"Versions from the Irish" (Ferguson) **33**:287
Verso e Reverso (Alencar) **157**:5
"Versöhnender, der du nimmer geglaubt ..." (Hölderlin) **16**:162, 166, 168-69, 171, 176; **187**:233
Der versöhnte Menschenfeind (Schiller) **166**:130-31, 133
Die Versöhnung, oder Bruderzwist (Kotzebue) **25**:147, 155
"Versos enscritos en una tempestad" (Heredia)
See "En una tempestad"
Versos Libres (Martí) **63**:105-6
Versos sencillos (Martí) **63**:63, 105, 107-10, 167
"Versos varios" (Silva) **114**:300
"Verstand und Herz" (Herder) **186**:18

Versuch einer Geschichte der lyrischen Dichtkunst (Herder) **186**:37
Versuch einer Kritik aller Offenbarung (Fichte) **62**:8, 33, 40
Versuch einer Theorie der elektrischen Erscheinungen (Arnim) **159**:46
"Ein Versuch in Versen" (Claudius) **75**:193
"Versuch über das deutsche Singspiel" (Wieland) **177**:330, 336
Versuch über das Sein (Herder) **186**:34, 63
"Versuch über den verschiedenen Styl in Goethe's früheren und späteren Werken" (Schlegel) **45**:309, 327
Versuche des Ignaz Mácha, Die (Macha) **46**:200
"Versuch über den Begriff des Republikanismus" (Schlegel) **226**:232
Versuche über die gereizte Muskel- und Nervenfaser nebst Vermuthungen über den chemischen Process des Lebens in der Thier- und Pflanzenwelt (Humboldt) **170**:145
Die Versuchung des Pescara (Meyer) **81**:135-37, 153, 164, 166-67, 181, 194
"Vertige" (Rimbaud) **4**:462
Vertrauliche Briefe über das vormalige staatsrechtliche Verhältnis des Waadtlandes zur Stadt Bern: Aus dem Franz. eines verstorbenen Schweizers (Hegel) **151**:258
Vertraute Briefe über Friedrich Schlegels Lucinde (Schleiermacher) **107**:268, 325, 376, 379, 382
Die Verwandlung (Klopstock) **225**:296, 300
Die Verwandtschaften (Kotzebue) **25**:145
Verwickeltegeschicht (Nestroy) **42**:234-35
"Der verwundete Baum" (Meyer) **81**:200
"Verwünschung" (Grillparzer) **102**:174
Very Hard Cash (Reade)
See *Hard Cash: A Matter-of-Fact Romance*
"The Very Image" (Villiers de l'Isle Adam)
See "A s'y méprendre"
Very Young and Quite Another Story (Ingelow) **39**:264
"Veselie i gore" (Baratynsky) **103**:11
"Vesennee uspokoenie" (Tyutchev) **34**:411
Veshnie vody (Turgenev) **21**:399-401, 411, 413-14, 416, 419, 431, 435, 437-41; **37**:424; **122**:242, 245, 247, 249, 265-67, 326-31, 338, 348, 362, 364
"Vesica piscis" (Patmore) **9**:359
"Vesna" (Baratynsky)
See "Vesna, vesna! kak vozdukh chist!..."
"Vesna" (Tyutchev) **34**:388, 398, 400, 405
"Vesna, vesna! kak vozdukh chist!..." (Baratynsky) **103**:11, 13
Vešnie vody (Turgenev)
See *Veshnie vody*
The Vespers of Palermo (Hemans) **29**:196, 201, 206; **71**:261, 267
"Vestíbulo: Retrato de Gustavo Moreau" (Casal) **131**:219, 223, 227-29, 236, 266, 268-70
"The Veteran" (Runeberg)
See "Veteranen"
"Veteranen" (Runeberg) **41**:321
The Veto on Love (Wagner) **9**:414
"Vezde i vsegda" (Pavlova) **138**:4, 17, 52
"Vézelay" (Pater) **159**:257
VI Etudes de Concert (Schumann) **143**:120
Via crucis (Liszt) **199**:348
Viaggo sentimentale di yorick lungo la Francia e l'Italia (Foscolo) **8**:263-64
Viajes (Sarmiento) **123**:273-74
Viajes por España (Alarcon) **1**:12; **219**:18
Viajes por Europa, África i América, 1845-1847 (Sarmiento) **123**:282, 322, 330, 347, 378
Vicaire des Ardennes (Balzac) **5**:58
The Vicar of Bullhampton (Trollope) **6**:465; **101**:235, 312, 319, 342
The Vicar of Wrexhill (Trollope) **30**:308, 319
"The Vices of the Constitution" (Madison) **126**:296
"Vices of the Political System of the United States" (Madison) **126**:297
"Vicksburg" (Hayne) **94**:149
Le Vicomte de Bragelonne (Dumas) **71**:184, 189, 222, 242
"The Victim" (Tennyson) **202**:278-82
The Victim of Prejudice (Hays) **114**:174-75, 182, 189, 191, 197, 200, 206-8, 210, 215-16, 218-20, 222-23, 226-30, 233-34, 251-57
"The Victim of the Deep" (Sigourney) **87**:332-33
"Victims of Progress" (Boyesen) **135**:49
"Victor and Vanquished" (Longfellow) **45**:139
"Victor Hugo's Romances" (Stevenson) **5**:415; **63**:239-40
Victor; ou, L'enfant de la forêt (Pixérécourt) **39**:273, 276
Victor Vane, the Young Secretary (Alger) **8**:17, 46
Victoria (Rowson) **5**:309, 315, 321; **69**:99, 102-03, 105, 111, 119-22, 125, 127, 135, 141; **182**:254, 257-60, 263, 351
The Victorian Age of English Literature (Oliphant) **221**:238, 264
"A Victorian Rebel" (Morris) **4**:436
"Victoria's Tears" (Barrett Browning) **61**:8, 61
The Victories of Love (Patmore) **9**:349, 352
"Victorieusement fui" (Mallarmé) **41**:291
"Victory" (Lazarus) **8**:419
The Victory and Death of Lord Nelson (Cumberland) **167**:140
"Victory Comes Late" (Dickinson) **21**:39
"Victory in Defeat" (Patmore) **9**:358, 365
Vida de Abrán Lincoln (Sarmiento) **123**:274-75
Vida de Dominguito (Sarmiento) **123**:319, 338
"Vida de Quiroga" (Sarmiento) **123**:378
Vida y hechos del famoso caballero Don Catrín de la fachenda (Lizardi) **30**:69-73, 78-9
"Videnie" (Tyutchev) **34**:389, 404-05, 407-09
"Videnie Murzy" (Derzhavin) **215**:13, 16, 26, 44, 57-59, 61
"Vid'ma" (Shevchenko) **54**:368, 389
Une vie (Maupassant) **1**:442, 445-46, 452-54, 456, 463, 465-69; **42**:167-69, 174, 189; **83**:169, 172, 182, 227, 230
"La Vie antérieure" (Baudelaire) **6**:83; **55**:5
"Vie de Byron" (Lamartine) **11**:270
Vie des grands hommes (Lamartine)
See *Le Civilisateur: Histoire de l'humanité par les grands hommes*
Vie de Henri Brulard (Stendhal) **23**:352, 368, 376, 378-79, 410-12, 416, 422; **46**:261, 270, 277, 281, 320, 325; **178**:156, 171, 217-18, 220-22, 226-27
La vie de Jésus (Renan) **26**:365, 367-72, 377, 401-5, 407-11, 414, 418, 420; **145**:272-366
"Vie de Joseph Delorme" (Sainte-Beuve) **5**:346
La Vie de Polinchinelle et ses Nombreuses Aventures (Feuillet) **45**:93
Vie de Rancé (Chateaubriand) **134**:15, 18, 99
Vie de Rossini (Stendhal) **23**:352; **178**:173, 190, 192, 231
"La vie de voyage" (Gobineau) **17**:69-70, 104
La vie d'une comédienne (Banville) **9**:19
"La vie et la mort du Capitaine Renaud; ou, La canne du jour" (Vigny) **7**:473, 478
Vie, poésies, et pensées de Joseph Delorme (Sainte-Beuve) **5**:335, 346
"Vieille chanson du jeune temps" (Hugo) **3**:263
"La vieille fille" (Balzac) **5**:33-4, 46, 65, 71; **53**:29; **153**:94-95, 147, 152
Une vieille maîtresse (Barbey d'Aurevilly) **1**:70
"Viel kraftzfüsselnder Bücklinge" (Preseren) **127**:315
Viel Lärmen um Nichts (Eichendorff) **225**:9, 22
"Vields By Watervalls" (Barnes) **75**:31
Une vielle maîtresse (Barbey d'Aurevilly) **213**:5, 39, 45-48, 62, 68
"Viendome perseguide por la alondra" (Castro) **78**:40
Vienna and the Austrians (Trollope) **30**:310
"Vier Jahreszeiten" (Goethe) **4**:193
Vier Schauspiele von Shakespeare (Tieck) **5**:520
"Vierge folle" (Rimbaud)
See "Délires I"
"Le vierge, le vivace et le bel aujourdhui" (Mallarmé) **210**:219, 244
Der vierundzwanzigste Februar: Eine romantische Tragödie in einem Akt (Werner) **189**:316, 330, 334, 344-48, 350-52, 355, 363, 367
"Der vierzehnte Julius" (Wieland) **177**:281
"Vies" (Rimbaud) **82**:242; **227**:211, 293, 309
"Vies I" (Rimbaud) **35**:322
"Vies II" (Rimbaud) **35**:297, 322
Vies de Haydn, de Mozart, et de Métastase (Stendhal)
See *Lettres écrites de Vienne en Autriche, sur le célèbre compositeur Jh Haydn, suivies d'une vie de Mozart, et de considérations sur Métastase et l'état present de la musique en France et en Italie*
Vies de quelques hommes illustres (Lamartine) **190**:253-60
"Le vieux drapeau" (Beranger) **34**:28, 38, 44
"Le vieux saltimbanque" (Baudelaire) **155**:57, 113
"Le vieux vagabond" (Beranger) **34**:38
"The View" (Hölderlin) **187**:213
A View of General Tenour of the New Testament Regarding the Nature and Dignity of Jesus Christ: Including a Collection of the Various Passages in the Gospels, Acts of the Apostles, and the Epistles... (Baillie) **151**:106
A View of the English Stage (Hazlitt) **29**:174, 188; **82**:125
"View of the Mountains from the Kozlov Steppes" (Mickiewicz)
See "Widok gór ze stepów Kozłowa"
"A View on Russian Literature in 1847" (Belinski) **5**:99, 109, 105, 108-09, 116
Views Afoot: or Europe seen with Knapsuck and Staff (Taylor) **89**:297, 363
The Views and Reviews in American History, Literature, and Fiction (Simms) **3**:501
Views of Labour and Gold (Barnes) **75**:23, 40, 51-2, 60, 66, 102, 107
"Views of Life" (Brontë) **4**:45
Views of Society and Manners in America (Wright) **74**:373, 377-78
"The Vigil in Aiden" (Chivers) **49**:71, 73
"Vigil of the Annunciation" (Rossetti) **50**:291
"Vigil Strange I Kept on the Field One Night" (Whitman) **81**:301, 321-22, 330; **205**:160, 309, 339
"Vigils" (Rimbaud)
See "Veillées"
"La vigne de Naboth" (Leconte de Lisle) **29**:215, 226-28
"La vigne et la maison" (Lamartine) **11**:272, 284-85, 289; **190**:209, 219, 225, 227, 263
"Vigny" (Mill) **58**:333
Vijnan rahasya (Chatterji) **19**:225
"Világosságot!" (Petofi) **21**:285
"Le vilain" (Beranger) **34**:28
"De vilde Svaner" (Andersen) **7**:26, 29, 32-3; **79**:23-4, 63, 76, 88; **214**:55, 75
Vilette (Brontë) **155**:158-59, 166, 177-78, 211, 227
Villa Eden (Auerbach)
See *Das Landhaus am Rhein*
The Villa on the Rhine (Auerbach)
See *Das Landhaus am Rhein*
"The Village" (Pushkin) **83**:333
"The Village" (Turgenev)
See "Derevnia"
The Village (Crabbe) **26**:77-81, 83, 86, 101-02, 106, 110-11, 116-18, 120, 122, 124, 127,

131-34, 137, 140-41, 143, 145-48, 151; **121**:8-10, 16, 18, 26, 28-30, 52, 59, 63-66, 72-7373, 75, 83-84, 88
Le Village (Feuillet) **45**:75, 88-9
"The Village Band" (Krylov) **1**:439
"The Village Beau" (Mitford) **4**:401
"The Village Blacksmith" (Hayne) **94**:144
"The Village Blacksmith" (Longfellow) **2**:472-73, 493; **45**:99, 116, 135, 148, 152, 179; **103**:285, 293, 295
"The Village Churchyard" (Zhukovsky)
See "Thoughts on a Tomb"
The Village Coquette (Dickens) **37**:153
Village Disputants (More) **27**:359
"Village Doctor" (Turgenev) **21**:378
The Village Fete (Cumberland) **167**:201-2
The Village Fool (Arany)
See *A falu bolondja*
"The Village Garden" (Levy) **59**:89, 102; **203**:339, 343-44
"A Village Holiday and Wedding" (Karamzin)
See "Sel'skii prazdnik i svad'ba"
"A Village Lear" (Turgenev)
See "Stepnoy Korol 'Lir"
"Village Lovers" (Turgenev) **21**:378
"The Village Merchant" (Freneau) **1**:314
"Village Minstrel" (Clare) **9**:76-77, 97, 102, 113; **86**:129, 157
The Village Minstrel, and Other Poems (Clare) **9**:76-78, 84, 97, 112, 115; **86**:89-90, 103, 108, 110, 113, 125, 154, 159-60, 173-74
"The Village of Balmaquhappel" (Hogg) **4**:284
"Village of Goryukhino" (Pushkin)
See *Istoriia sela Goriukhino*
The Village of Stepanchikovo (Dostoevsky)
See *The Friend of the Family*
"The Village on the Heath" (Stifter)
See "Das Haidedorf"
Village Politics (More) **141**:164, 166-67, 171, 179, 189-90, 199, 224, 267, 269-70, 281, 286-87, 299, 301, 310
Village Politics, by Will Chip (More) **27**:333, 342-45, 349, 359
"The Village Register" (Crabbe)
See "The Parish Register"
A Village Romeo and Juliet (Keller)
See *Romeo und Julia auf dem Dorfe*
The Village Verse-book (Bowles) **103**:54
"Ville" (Rimbaud) **227**:209, 236, 238-40, 247, 271, 334
"La ville enchantée" (Banville) **9**:16
La Ville Noire (Sand) **42**:312-13
"Villes" (Rimbaud) **4**:473; **35**:269, 290, 322; **82**:238
"Villes I" (Rimbaud) **35**:309, 313; **82**:232; **227**:204, 206, 209-11, 241-42, 247, 271
"Villes II" (Rimbaud) **227**:204, 206, 209-11, 242, 271, 296, 309-11
Villette (Brontë) **3**:49-61, 63-4, 67-74, 76, 80; **8**:54-5, 72, 75; **33**:102-57; **58**:171, 179, 187, 194-96, 199, 205; **105**:4, 6-7, 45-6, 64, 66, 71, 73, 75; **217**:15, 22, 25, 37, 41-45, 48-57, 59, 61-68, 87-92, 96, 100-107, 110-16, 119, 125, 154, 174-76, 178-81; **229**:1-214
Le vin (Baudelaire) **6**:116, 122, 124; **55**:62, 66; **155**:44, 113
"Le vin de l'assassin" (Baudelaire) **29**:104; **55**:62
"Le vin des amants" (Baudelaire) **29**:104-05; **55**:43-4
"Le vin des chiffoniers" (Baudelaire) **6**:96; **29**:112
"Vinden fortæller om Valdemar Daae og hans Døttre" (Andersen) **79**:77
"Vindicación" (Larra) **17**:273
Vindication (Hays) **114**:231
A Vindication of a Natural Diet (Shelley) **175**:321
A Vindication of Catholic Morality (Manzoni)
See *Osservazioni sulla morale cattolica*
Vindication of Congress (Hamilton)
See *A Full Vindication of the Measures of Congress*
Vindication of the English Constitution (Disraeli) **39**:6, 25-6; **79**:211, 215, 269-70, 275
Vindiciae Ecclesiae Anglicanae (Southey) **97**:265-66
The Vindictive Man (Holcroft) **85**:199, 212-13, 237
"Vineta" (Muller) **73**:352, 359
Vingt ans après (Dumas) **11**:58, 63, 65, 68, 73-74, 76; **71**:203
Vingt jours en Sicile (Renan) **26**:417
"Vino" (Nekrasov) **11**:412, 414
The Vintage of Burgundy (Rogers) **69**:66-7, 73
Viola tricolor (Storm) **1**:540; **195**:4, 18
"La viole de gamba" (Bertrand) **31**:47, 49
"The Violet" (Brontë) **229**:200
"The Violet" (Very) **9**:376, 380
"The Violet and the Rose" (Webster) **230**:309-10, 313
"The Violin" (Cranch) **115**:6
"Violin Sonata in D minor" (Schumann) **143**:115
Violin Sonata in G Major, op. 96 (Beethoven) **227**:18
"Violina" (O'Brien) **21**:249-50
"The Violinist" (Lampman) **25**:167, 204
A Viovinha (Alencar) **157**:15-18
Virgil (Warton)
See *Works of Virgil*
"The Virgin" (Meyer)
See "Die Jungfrau"
"The Virgin" (Thoreau) **7**:383
The Virgin and the Nun (Keller)
See *Die Jungfrau und die Nonne*
The Virgin as Knight (Keller)
See *Die Jungfrau als Ritter*
"The Virgin Mary to the Child Jesus" (Barrett Browning) **61**:8, 10, 61; **170**:105
"Virgin Mother Mary mild" (Fuller) **50**:245, 247
Virgin Soil (Turgenev)
See *Nov'*
Virginalia or Songs of My Summer Nights (Chivers) **49**:43, 47-9, 52, 73-6
Virginia (Alfieri) **101**:8, 38, 42-3
Virginia (Macaulay) **42**:111
Virginia (Tamayo y Baus) **1**:570-71
Virginia: A History of the People (Cooke) **5**:127, 131, 135
Virginia and Magdalene (Southworth) **26**:432
"Virginia and Paul" (Villiers de l'Isle Adam)
See "Virginie et Paul"
The Virginia Bohemians (Cooke) **5**:125, 127, 131-32, 135
"La 'Virginia' del Páez" (Isaacs) **70**:308
"The 'Virginia' of the Páez River" (Isaacs)
See "La 'Virginia' del Páez"
Virginia; or, The Roman Father (Mackenzie) **41**:207-09
"A Virginia Romana" (Leopardi) **129**:329, 332
"A Virginia y Rufino" (Isaacs) **70**:311
The Virginian Comedians; or, Old Days in the Old Dominion (Cooke) **5**:121, 123, 126-35
The Virginians: A Tale of the Last Century (Thackeray) **5**:460-61, 481, 485, 488, 500; **14**:452; **43**:363, 388; **213**:316
"Virginia—the West" (Whitman) **205**:159
"Virginibus Puerisque" (Stevenson) **193**:274-76, 279, 281-82
Virginibus Puerisque, and Other Papers (Stevenson) **5**:388-90, 395, 397, 402-05, 410, 413-14, 425; **193**:203, 206, 210-14, 219, 221, 276
"Virginie et Paul" (Villiers de l'Isle Adam) **3**:590
La Virtù indiana (Leopardi) **129**:347
"Virtue" (Lampman) **194**:27
"Virtue and Vice" (Thomson) **18**:392
"A Visão dos Mortos" (Castro Alves) **205**:3, 13, 24
Vishavriksha (Chatterji) **19**:204-06, 209, 212-15, 217-21
"The Visible Church for the Sake of the Elect" (Newman) **38**:305
"The Vision" (Adams) **175**:41, 43, 45
"A Vision" (Clare) **9**:100, 102-03; **86**:87, 90, 114
"The Vision" (Grundtvig) **158**:182
"Vision" (Heredia) **209**:130
"Vision" (Lampman) **194**:17, 67-68, 90, 92
"A Vision" (Peabody) **169**:194-98
"The Vision" (Southey) **97**:281
"Vision" (Tyutchev)
See "Videnie"
The Vision (Beckford) **16**:37, 47-50
"The Vision Beautiful" (Longfellow) **45**:128
"La vision de Brahma" (Leconte de Lisle) **29**:222-23, 241-42
"La vision de Charles XI" (Mérimée) **65**:48, 53-4, 57-8, 87, 99, 115
La vision de Dante (Hugo) **3**:270
"La vision de Snorr" (Leconte de Lisle) **29**:225, 227
"La visión del Castillo" (Isaacs) **70**:308-09
"La visión del poeta compuesta en un Ingenio de fabricar azúcar" (Manzano) **155**:307-10
The Vision, Liber Vertatis (Beckford) **214**:101-3, 105-7, 138, 140-42
The Vision of Columbus (Barlow) **23**:3, 12, 14-16, 18-20, 22, 26, 29, 32, 37, 40, 42; **223**:9-10, 13, 19-22, 24-25, 27, 34-37, 40, 42, 45, 52-53, 59-60, 73, 78-79, 84
"A Vision of Connaught in the Thirteenth Century" (Mangan) **27**:296, 298, 301, 311-13
"A Vision of Conor O'Sullivan" (Mangan) **27**:308
"The Vision of Don Quixote" (Eminescu)
See "Viziunea lui don Quijote"
The Vision of Don Roderick: A Poem (Scott) **209**:307
"The Vision of Dry Bones" (Moodie) **113**:316-17
"Vision of Hell" (Borrow) **9**:54
"A Vision of Horns" (Lamb) **10**:411
The Vision of Judgement (Byron) **149**:10
The Vision of Judgment (Byron) **2**:67, 72, 75, 78, 81, 91-94; **12**:102, 138; **109**:105
A Vision of Judgment (Southey) **8**:458, 461, 463-64; **97**:259, 264, 273, 277
"Vision of Kubla Khan" (Coleridge)
See "Kubla Khan"
"A Vision of Poesy" (Timrod) **25**:361, 364-66, 369, 372-74, 378, 383-84
"A Vision of Poets" (Barrett Browning) **1**:113, 115, 117, 127; **61**:4; **170**:56
"A Vision of Purgatory" (Maginn) **8**:440
"The Vision of Sin" (Tennyson) **30**:223, 233, 249-50, 254; **115**:236
"The Vision of Sir Launfal" (Lowell) **2**:507, 515, 516, 522; **90**:193, 209-10, 215-17
"The Vision of Sudden Death" (De Quincey) **4**:82-83; **198**:46
"The Vision of the Castle Ranch" (Isaacs)
See "La visión del Castillo"
"Vision of the Dead" (Castro Alves)
See "A Visão dos Mortos"
"The Vision of the Fountain" (Hawthorne) **2**:298
"The Vision of the Goblet" (Boker) **125**:78
A Vision of the Last Judgment (Blake) **13**:219, 246; **37**:4, 28; **57**:24, 67, 74, 79; **127**:7, 16, 71, 125, 127, 131, 137; **173**:8, 18, 47, 51, 104, 120-21, 123, 132-33, 153; **190**:98; **201**:41, 113
"A Vision of the Mermaids" (Hopkins) **17**:190-91, 195, 215, 222; **189**:10-12, 87, 91, 97
"The Vision of the Mirza" (Derzhavin)
See "Videnie Murzy"

"The Vision of the Night, A Fragment" (Freneau) **111**:152
"A Vision of the Sea" (Shelley) **175**:195, 198
"A Vision of Twilight" (Lampman) **25**:204; **194**:19, 21, 24-25, 30, 38, 54
"The Vision of Vanity" (Mackenzie) **41**:184
"The Vision; or, Prospect of the Future Happiness of America" (Dwight) **13**:270, 272, 276, 278-79
"The Visionary" (Brontë) **16**:74-5, 86
"Visions" (Turgenev)
See "Prizraki. Fantaziya"
Visions (Borrow) **9**:54
"Visions: A Fantasy" (Turgenev)
See "Prizraki. Fantaziya"
"Visions in the Smoke" (Gordon) **21**:160-61, 165, 180
Visions of the Daughters of Albion: The Eye Sees More Than the Heart Knows (Blake) **13**:163, 183, 218, 220-21, 223, 232-33, 251-52; **37**:22; **127**:11, 60, 82; **173**:42, 61, 105, 152, 157; **190**:11, 14, 61, 94, 98; **201**:1-150
Visions of the Past (Dutt) **118**:31
"The Visit" (Austen) **119**:13
"The Visit" (Very) **9**:378
"Visit in Urach" (Mörike)
See "Besuch in Urach"
"The Visit of the Gods" (Coleridge) **197**:215; **231**:151
"A Visit to Grosse Isle" (Moodie) **14**:243
A Visit to India, China and Japan in the year 1853 (Taylor) **89**:346
"A Visit to Portugal" (Andersen) **79**:79
"Visit to Ranelagh" (Bloomfield) **145**:133
"A Visit to the Autocrat's Landlady" (Holmes) **81**:98
Une visite à Bedlam (Scribe) **16**:391
"La Visite au hameau" (Desbordes-Valmore) **97**:8
Une visite de Noces (Dumas) **9**:223, 225-26, 230, 232-33, 242
"Visites" (Verlaine) **230**:168
Visitor of the Poor (Peabody) **169**:147
"Visitors" (Irving) **2**:372
"Visits" (Verlaine)
See "Visites"
Visits and Sketches at Home and Abroad (Jameson) **43**:304, 317, 320, 323, 337
"Visits to St. Giles" (Tonna) **135**:204
"Visszatekintés" (Arany) **34**:16, 19
Vita (Alfieri) **101**:14, 25, 41, 52, 56-7, 59, 64-5, 67-70, 73, 75, 78-80, 83
"La vita solitaria" (Leopardi) **129**:229-33
"Vitre bujnyj" (Shevchenko) **54**:375
"Vittoria Accoramboni" (Symonds) **34**:348
Vittoria Accorombona (Tieck) **5**:517, 532; **46**:365, 374-76, 381, 397
"Vitzliputzli" (Heine) **147**:139, 159-60, 163, 217
La viuda de Padilla (Martínez de la Rosa) **102**:226, 230, 245, 252
"La vivandière" (Beranger) **34**:29
"Vive la Révolution!" (Baudelaire) **155**:18
Vivia; or, The Secret of Power (Southworth) **26**:438
"Vivia Perpetua" (Lampman) **25**:169, 220; **194**:21, 68, 77-78
Vivian (Edgeworth) **1**:267-68; **51**:88-90; **158**:46-50, 52
Vivian Grey (Disraeli) **2**:136-39, 142-43, 145-46, 148-50; **39**:3, 20-2, 24-5, 30-3, 39-40, 42, 44-6, 50-2, 65-6, 74-5, 78; **79**:199-202, 214, 218, 226-27, 232, 257, 270-72, 274, 276, 279
"Vivian to His Correspondents" (Lewes) **25**:290
Viviparous Quadrupeds of North America, The (Audubon) **47**:13, 33-8, 45-6, 51-2
"The Vixen" (Clare) **9**:117; **86**:131
"Vixerunt" (Herzen) **10**:338
"Viy" (Gogol) **5**:224, 226-27, 242, 248-49, 251, 256-58; **31**:120, 122; **162**:12, 15, 27, 54, 96, 98, 104
"Viziunea lui don Quijote" (Eminescu) **131**:348
"Vladimir Beltov" (Herzen) **61**:109
Vladimir den Store (Stagnelius) **61**:248, 251, 261, 263
Vladimir the Great (Stagnelius)
See *Vladimir den Store*
"Vladyčnyj sud" (Leskov) **25**:258-59, 265-67; **174**:38, 46, 105-7, 109-12, 114-16
"Vlas" (Nekrasov) **11**:400, 407, 412-13, 421
"Vlastiteliam i sudiiam" (Derzhavin)
See "Oda. Prelozhenie 81-go psalma"
Vließ (Grillparzer)
See *Das goldene Vließ*
"Vocalism" (Whitman) **205**:162, 165
The Vocation of Man (Fichte)
See *Die Bestimmung des Menschen*
"Vodopad" (Derzhavin) **215**:10, 22-23, 28, 32, 34-35, 39, 53-56
"Vœu" (Verlaine) **230**:165, 194-95
"La vœu suprême" (Leconte de Lisle) **29**:228, 235
"La voeux stériles" (Musset) **7**:256
"Les Voeux Stériles" (Musset) **150**:225, 234, 321-22
Voevoda: Son na Volge (Ostrovsky) **57**:206-7
"Die Vogelhütte" (Droste-Hülshoff) **3**:197
"Der Vogelsang, oder die drei Lehren" (Wieland) **177**:265, 294-97
Die Vogelscheuche (Tieck) **5**:519
"The Voice" (Arnold) **29**:35
"The Voice and the Peak" (Tennyson) **30**:271-72
"A Voice from the Dungeon" (Brontë) **4**:44
A Voice from the Factories (Norton) **47**:260; **205**:67, 86, 144
"A Voice from the Nile" (Thomson) **18**:421
"A Voice from the World" (Hopkins) **189**:142
"The Voice in the Pines" (Hayne) **94**:144, 149
"The Voice in the Wild Oak" (Kendall) **12**:189
"The Voice of a Spirit" (Schiller) **39**:306
"The Voice of Autumn" (Bryant) **6**:176
"Voice of By-Gone Days" (Foster) **26**:287
"A Voice of Encouragement—A New Year's Lay" (Mangan) **27**:300, 317
The Voice of Flowers (Sigourney) **87**:321
"A Voice of Nature" (Clare) **9**:110
The Voice of Nature (Dunlap) **2**:211
"Voice of Spring" (Hemans) **29**:200
"The Voice of the Ancient Bard" (Blake) **13**:181; **37**:19, 45, 72; **173**:17
"The Voice of the Native Oak" (Harpur) **114**:116
"Voice of the People" (Hölderlin)
See "Stimme des Volks"
"The Voice of Things" (Silva)
See "La voz de las cosas"
"The Voice of Thought" (Chivers) **49**:58, 72
"Voice out of the Sea" (Whitman) **4**:546
"The Voice that Stands for Floods to Me" (Dickinson) **21**:77
A Voice to America (Thorpe) **183**:336
"The Voiceless" (Holmes) **14**:109, 132; **81**:97
"Voices from the Canadian Woods: The White Cedar" (Traill) **31**:327
"Voices of Africa" (Castro Alves)
See "Vozes d'Africa"
"Voices of Earth" (Lampman) **25**:194, 204; **194**:30, 79, 102
Voices of Freedom (Whittier) **8**:489, 495, 504-05, 509-16; **59**:353, 357-8
"Voices of the Contraband" (Winthrop) **210**:275
"Voices of the Night" (Longfellow) **2**:471; **45**:112, 115, 127, 131, 133-34, 151-52, 154, 183-84; **103**:293, 295
Voices of the Peoples in Songs (Herder)
See *Volkslieder*
"Voices of the Pines" (Hayne)
See "The Voice in the Pines"
"The Voices that Be Gone" (Barnes) **75**:59
"Void in Law" (Barrett Browning) **61**:7, 45, 66
Les voiles nors (Gobineau) **17**:104
"Voitel' nica" (Leskov) **25**:228, 235, 238-39, 246, 260, 263-65; **174**:10, 40
"Voitel-nitsa" (Leskov)
See "Voitel' nica"
La voiture de masques (Goncourt and Goncourt) **7**:153
"La Voix d'un ami" (Desbordes-Valmore) **97**:28
"La Voix perdue" (Desbordes-Valmore) **97**:6-7
"Vojtina ars poetikájából" (Arany) **34**:16
Vol. 1 (Sochineniya v dvukh tomakh) (Bestuzhev)
See *Sochineniya v dvukh tomakh, Vol. 1*
Vol. I (Prosas) (Casal)
See *Prosas*
Vol. II (Prosas) (Casal)
See *Prosas*
Vol. III (Prosas) (Casal)
See *Prosas*
"Les Voleurs" (Mérimée) **65**:121-2
Volki i ovtsy (Ostrovsky) **30**:100, 103, 113, 115; **57**:213-4, 220
"Der Volksglaube im katholischen Deutschland" (Storm) **195**:95
"Volksglauben in den Pyrenäen" (Droste-Hülshoff) **3**:203
Volkskalender (Auerbach) **171**:39
Volkslieder (Herder) **8**:299, 310, 315; **186**:82, 87, 107
Volksmärchen (Tieck) **46**:334
Volledige Werken (Multatuli) **165**:330, 342, 344
Vollständige Ausgabe durch einem Verein von Freunden des Verewigten (Hegel) **46**:139
Vollständige ausgabe letzter Hand (Goethe) **34**:125
"Vol'nost': Oda" (Pushkin) **3**:455; **83**:253, 305
"Voltaire" (Carlyle) **70**:61
Volume the First (Austen) **1**:46; **119**:13; **222**:107
Volume the Second (Austen) **119**:13
Volume the Third (Austen) **119**:13
"Voluntaries" (Emerson) **1**:279, 285, 290, 296; **98**:39, 177, 182-83
"The Volunteer" (Hood) **16**:237
The Volunteers (Bird) **197**:24, 29
The Volunteers (Rowson) **69**:140-41; **182**:280-81, 353
"La volupté" (Baudelaire) **55**:74
Volupté (Sainte-Beuve) **5**:328, 333, 335, 337, 348, 351
"The Voluptuary Cured" (Griffin) **7**:214
Voluptuousness (Sainte-Beuve)
See *Volupté*
"Vom Abgrund nemlich ..." (Hölderlin) **187**:218
Vom andern Ufer (Herzen) **10**:326-7, 332, 334-7, 339-40, 344, 346
"Vom ästhetischen Werte der griechischen Komödie" (Schlegel) **45**:312, 324, 334, 358
"Vom dem traurigen Untergang Zeitlicher Liebe" (Brentano) **191**:70
"Vom deutschen Hexameter" (Klopstock) **225**:338-39
"Vom Erhabenen" (Schiller) **166**:143-44
Vom Erkennen und Empfinden der meschlichen Seele (Herder) **186**:14-15, 17-18, 20, 93-94
Vom Geist der ebräischen Poesie (Herder) **8**:297, 300, 303, 305-06, 316; **186**:18, 85, 98
"Vom Gewissen: In Briefen an Andres" (Claudius) **75**:218
Vom Ich als Princip der Philosophie (Schelling) **30**:128, 164
"Vom Sieben-Nixen-Chor" (Mörike) **201**:272, 292, 298
"Vom Vaterunser" (Claudius) **75**:217
"Vom Wert des Studiums der Griechen und Römer" (Schlegel) **45**:310, 357
"Von Ähnlichkeit der mittlern englischen und deutschen Dichtkunst" (Herder) **186**:17
"Von den abwechselnden Verbindungen und dem Worte 'Verstehen" (Klopstock) **225**:336
Von den Lebensaltern einer Sprache (Herder) **8**:317

Von der Auferstehung als Glauben, Geschichte, und Lehre (Herder) **186**:48
"Von der Darstellung" (Klopstock) **225**:335-40
"Von der Heiligen Poesie" (Klopstock) **225**:291
Von der Physiognomik (Lavater) **142**:57
"Von der Seele" (Schlegel) **45**:338
"Von der Sprache der Poesie" (Klopstock) **225**:293, 340
"Von der Überlegung: Eine Paradoxe" (Kleist) **37**:249, 266; **222**:205
Von der Verschiedenheit des Geschmacks und der Denkart unter den Menschen (Herder) **186**:36
"Von der Wahrheit" (Hölderlin) **187**:264
Von deutscher Art und Kunst (Herder) **8**:309-10
"Von Essen" (Runeberg) **41**:314
Von heut und ehedem (Storm) **1**:544
"Von hohen Menschen" (Jean Paul) **7**:240
Von Jenseit des Meeres (Storm) **195**:5, 14, 19-20, 42, 70
"Von Jung" (Poe) **16**:322
"Von Kempelen and His Discovery" (Poe) **16**:313
"Von Konow" (Runeberg) **41**:314
"Von Projekten und Projektmachern" (Claudius) **75**:203
Von Ranke (Macaulay)
See *Essay on Ranke*
"Von Törne" (Runeberg) **41**:314
"Von Volksliedern" (Arnim) **159**:43, 57-58
Von Zwanzig bis Dreissig (Fontane) **26**:235, 247-49
Vor dem Sturm (Fontane) **163**:161-62, 169, 197, 245
Vor dem Sturm: Roman aus dem Winter 1812 auf 13 (Fontane) **26**:236-37, 243, 250-52, 261, 267, 270-71, 274-75, 278
"Vor dem Tor" (Goethe) **4**:215, 221
"Vor der Ernte" (Meyer) **81**:146, 152-53, 157, 206
"Vor einer Büste" (Meyer) **81**:207
"Vor Gericht" (Goethe) **34**:71
Vorarbeiten zu verschiedenen Fragment Sammlungen (Novalis) **178**:127-28
"Vord lys!" (Wergeland) **5**:539
"Vorläufige Thesen zur Reform der Philosophie" (Feuerbach) **139**:293, 331
Vorlesung über das Wesen der Religion: Nebst Zusätzen und Anmerkungen (Feuerbach) **139**:289, 293
Vorlesungen über die Aesthetik (Hegel) **46**:181-2, 186-7; **151**:238, 292-6, 342, 372
Vorlesungen über die Geschichte der Philosophie (Hegel) **46**:166, 192; **151**:237, 239-40, 323, 325-26, 328, 330-31, 338, 341, 345
Vorlesungen über die Methode des academischen Studium (Schelling) **30**:167
Vorlesungen über die Philosophie der Geschichte (Hegel) **46**:110
Vorlesungen über die Philosophie der Religion, nebst iener Schrift über die Beweise vom Dasein Gottes (Hegel) **46**:162, 186; **151**:238
Vorlesungen über die Philosophie der Weltgeschichte (Hegel) **46**:119, 125, 128-30, 156-57; **151**:239, 281-85, 323, 326, 330-31
"Die vorörtliche Krankheit" (Beddoes) **154**:29, 32
"Vörös Rébék" (Arany) **34**:21
Vorrede (Herder) **186**:18
"Vorrede in Form eines Prologs" (Werner) **189**:329
Vorschule der Aesthetik: Nebst einigen Vorlesungen in Leipzig über die Parte ien der Zeit (Jean Paul) **7**:223, 225-26, 234, 237-38, 242
"Vorspiel auf dem Theater" (Goethe) **154**:192-93, 218-19, 228, 237, 241, 261, 264, 315, 324, 326
Vorstenschool (Multatuli) **165**:331, 349
Vortesungen über die Naturphilosophie als der Encyklopädie zweiter Theil (Hegel) **151**:241-47
"Vorwurf an Laura" (Schiller) **39**:357
"Vorzeichen" (Grillparzer) **102**:175
Vospitannitsa (Ostrovsky) **30**:98-9, 102, 104, 111, 115; **57**:198, 209-10, 218-20
Vospominanie ob Aleksandre Semenoviche Shishkove (Aksakov) **181**:60, 68
"Vospominanie v Tsarskom Sele" (Pushkin) **3**:423; **83**:258
Vospominaniia prezhei zhizni (Aksakov) **2**:13-14; **181**:4, 10, 13-16, 45, 49-50, 60, 65-66, 68
"Vostochnaia Legenda" (Turgenev) **122**:312
"Vot rodina moia" (Aksakov) **181**:61
"Vot vernyi spisok vpechatlenii" (Baratynsky) **103**:47
"Votive Offering" (Meyer)
See "Weihgeschenck"
"Vous êtes calme . . ." (Verlaine) **230**:168
"The Vow" (Fouqué) **2**:266
"The Vow of the Chrysanthemum" (Ueda Akinari)
See "Kikuka no chigiri"
"Vox Ecclesiae, Vox Christi" (Rossetti) **77**:292-93, 295, 297
"Vox Populi" (Longfellow) **45**:134
"Vox populi" (Villiers de l'Isle Adam) **3**:590
"Le voyage" (Baudelaire) **6**:90, 93, 101, 109, 116-17, 123-24; **29**:78, 90, 105, 107; **55**:3-4, 6, 12, 26, 29, 43, 49-50, 52-53, 65-8, 73, 78; **155**:17, 32-36, 116
"The Voyage" (Irving) **95**:265
Voyage (Crèvecoeur)
See *Voyage dans la Haute Pennsylvanie et dans l'Etat de New-York not generally known; and conveying some idea of the late and present interior circumsances of the British Colonies in North America...*
"Voyage à Cythère" (Baudelaire) **155**:12, 60
"Le voyage à Cythère" (Baudelaire) **6**:91, 109, 116-17; **29**:74, 84, 104; **55**:4, 29, 31, 33, 73-6, 78-80
Voyage aux eaux des Pyrénées (Taine) **15**:411, 431, 450, 452
Voyage dans la Haute Pennsylvanie et dans l'Etat de New-York not generally known; and conveying some idea of the late and present interior circumsances of the British Colonies in North America... (Crèvecoeur) **105**:94-5, 104
Voyage de Humboldt et Bonpland (Humboldt) **170**:180-81, 187
"Voyage de Noce" (Maupassant) **83**:173
"Voyage du jeune anacharsis" (Nerval) **67**:320
Voyage en Amérique (Chateaubriand) **3**:134; **134**:41-45, 47, 80, 95, 127
Voyage en Egypte (Fromentin) **10**:229; **125**:106-7, 109-11, 139-40
Voyage en Espagne (Gautier) **1**:339, 341, 344
Voyage en Italie (Chateaubriand) **134**:18, 20, 92
Voyage en Italie (Gautier) **59**:47-55
Voyage en Italie (Taine) **15**:417, 452
Voyage en Orient (Flaubert) **62**:113-5, 117, 123
Voyage en Orient (Lamartine)
See *Souvenirs, impressions, pensées, et paysages pendant un voyage en Orient (1832-1833); ou, Notes d'un voyageur*
Voyage en Orient (Nerval) **1**:475-76, 479-80, 483, 485; **67**:302-03, 312, 323, 333-34, 336, 357, 363-64, 366-72, 375
Voyage en Russie (Gautier) **1**:344
The Voyage of Captain Popanilla (Disraeli) **2**:149, 153; **39**:3, 33, 39, 46, 48-9, 52-5, 72-3, 75; **79**:269-71
The Voyage of Columbus (Rogers) **69**:68, 70-1, 74, 83
"The Voyage of Maeldune" (Tennyson) **30**:223
"The Voyage of Telegonus" (Kendall) **12**:181, 190, 192, 201-02
The Voyage of the Beagle (Darwin)
See *The Zoology of the Voyage of the Beagle*
The Voyage of the Fregate Pallada (Goncharov) **1**:366, 370, 373; **63**:3-4, 27
"The Voyage of Timberoo-Tabo-Eede, an Otaheite Indian" (Freneau) **111**:133
A Voyage to Arzrum (Pushkin) **3**:436
A Voyage to Boston (Freneau) **111**:139
"Voyage to Cythera" (Baudelaire)
See "Le voyage à Cythère"
"Voyage to England" (Irving) **19**:328, 350-51
A Voyage to the Holy Land (Slowacki)
See *Podróż na Wschód—Podróż do Ziemi Swietej z Neopolu*
"The Voyager's Song" (Pinkney) **31**:273, 279
Voyages (Flaubert) **135**:84; **185**:188, 219
Voyages (Gautier) **59**:51
Voyages and Travels . . . (Galt) **1**:327; **110**:76, 94
"Voyance" (Verlaine) **51**:382
"Voyant letters" (Rimbaud)
See "Lettres du voyant"
"Les Voyelles" (Rimbaud) **4**:452-53, 469, 472, 475, 482; **35**:323; **82**:227, 248, 256, 258; **227**:198, 280
Voyevoda (Ostrovsky)
See *Voevoda: Son na Volge*
"La voz de las cosas" (Silva) **114**:299, 301
"La voz del silencio" (Bécquer) **106**:112, 114
"Vozes d'Africa" (Castro Alves) **205**:5, 9, 11, 17, 23, 33, 35
Vrajānganān Kāvya (Dutt) **118**:5
"Vse bešennej burja" (Tyutchev) **34**:415
"Vse mysl' da mysl'!..." (Baratynsky) **103**:25-9
"Vsegda i vezde" (Bestuzhev) **131**:150
"Vstrecha s Martinistami" (Aksakov) **181**:68
"Vuelta al sur" (Heredia) **209**:126, 135
La vuelta de Martín Fierro (Hernández) **17**:162-69, 171-72, 176-79
"La vuelta del combate" (Bécquer) **106**:110
"La vuelta del recluta" (Isaacs) **70**:305
"Vuelva ud. mañana" (Larra) **130**:230
Vues des Cordillères et monumens des peuples indigènes de l'Amérique (Humboldt) **170**:170
The Vultures (Becque)
See *Les corbeaux*
"V.V.: or Plots and Counterplots" (Alcott) **58**:39; **83**:6
Vybrannye mesta iz perepiski s druzyami (Gogol) **5**:212, 230, 238, 243, 257; **15**:100; **31**:111, 120, 127, 129, 133, 135-36, 139; **162**:13, 15, 30-31, 51, 68-69, 74, 79, 87-89, 97, 106, 130
"Vystrel" (Pushkin) **3**:435, 452; **83**:272, 323-27, 337, 354
"Vyzdorovlenie" (Karamzin) **173**:347
"Vzoshla zaria..." (Zhukovsky) **35**:406
"Waarheid in Legende" (Multatuli) **165**:326
"Wachusett" (Thoreau)
See "A Walk to Wachusett"
Waclaw (Slowacki) **15**:348, 358
Wacousta; or, The Prophecy: A Tale of the Canadas (Richardson) **55**:288, 290, 292, 294, 299-300, 303-5, 312-27, 329, 332-40, 342-4, 346-65, 369-76
Wage-Labor and Capital (Marx) **114**:10
Die Wage: Zeitschrift für Bürgerleben, Wissenschaft und Kunst (Börne) **193**:5, 17, 45
"The Wager" (Crabbe) **26**:93; **121**:4-5
A Wager (Tamayo y Baus) **1**:571
"Wages" (Tennyson) **202**:278, 280, 284-85
"The Waggon A-Stooded" (Barnes) **75**:78
The Waggoner (Wordsworth) **12**:409, 422, 451
"Wahlesel" (Heine) **147**:229
Die Wahlverwandtschaften (Goethe) **4**:168, 172-73, 176, 178, 188, 193, 201, 223; **34**:98; **154**:202, 205, 210, 237
Die Wahlverwandtschaften (Grillparzer) **102**:172

Wahrheit aus Jean Paul's Leben (Jean Paul) **7**:229-30
"The Waif" (Longfellow) **2**:474
"The Waif Woman" (Stevenson) **193**:280-81
"The Wail and Warning of the Three Khalandeers" (Mangan) **27**:278, 284-85
Wait and Hope (Alger) **8**:44
"Waiting by the Gate" (Bryant) **6**:193
"Waiting for Dead Men's Shoes" (Moodie) **14**:236
"A Waitress" (Woolson) **82**:290
"Wakacje" (Norwid) **17**:373
"Wakaremichi" (Ichiyō)
See "Wakare-Michi"
"Wakare-Michi" (Ichiyō) **49**:336-37, 347-48, 350-51, 353-54
"The Wake" (Shevchenko)
See "Tryzna"
The Wake (Hogg)
See *The Queen's Wake*
"Wakefield" (Hawthorne) **2**:292
"Wakerejimo" (Ichiyō) **49**:341
"Waking Dream in Sickness" (Willis) **194**:307
"Walcourt" (Verlaine) **51**:370, 382, 384; **230**:163, 187
"Wald und Höhle" (Goethe) **4**:214
Der Waldbrunnen (Stifter) **41**:375, 379
Waldeinsamkeit (Tieck) **5**:519
"Waldemar Daa and His Daughters" (Andersen)
See "The Wind Tells of Valdemar Daae and His Daughters"
Walden; or, Life in the Woods (Thoreau) **7**:349-53, 357, 361, 363, 369-70, 373-7, 379-82, 385-411; **21**:319-20, 322, 328-30, 340, 343-5, 350-3, 358, 360-1, 369-70, 372; **61**:278-390; **138**:66-68, 74-75, 78, 80, 82-85, 87-89, 95-97, 99, 102-3, 115, 119, 123-26, 128-31, 134, 137, 140-41, 144, 146-50, 155-58, 162, 164, 166-67, 170, 177, 182-83, 186, 188-89, 191-93; **207**:181, 187, 189-90, 196-97, 201-3,
Waldfried (Auerbach) **171**:11-12, 16, 20
"Der Waldgänger" (Stifter) **41**:343, 353; **198**:260
"Wald-Idylle" (Mörike) **10**:449; **201**:343, 345, 366-70
"Die Waldkapelle" (Lenau) **16**:278
"Waldplage" (Mörike) **201**:318, 345, 370
Der Waldsteig (Stifter) **41**:361, 366, 377; **198**:260, 275-76, 284
Waldszenen (Schumann) **143**:140
Waldwinkel (Storm) **1**:540; **195**:4, 127, 130
"A walesi bárdok" (Arany) **34**:8, 10, 15, 21
"The Walk" (Schiller)
See "Der Spaziergang"
"A Walk at Sunset" (Bryant) **46**:3, 13
"Walk in the Woods" (Clare) **9**:123
"A Walk Through the Franconian Switzerland" (Taylor) **89**:308
"The Walk to Dummer" (Moodie) **14**:231, 239
"A Walk to Railway Point" (Traill) **31**:327
"A Walk to Wachusett" (Thoreau) **21**:372; **138**:106, 118, 120, 124, 159-63, 165-67
"Walking" (Thoreau) **7**:394; **21**:372; **138**:71, 135, 162, 167; **207**:264, 266
"Walking in Scotland" (Keats) **8**:360
"Walking to the Mail" (Tennyson) **115**:240
A Walking Tour (Andersen)
A Walking Tour from the Holmen Canal to the Eastern Point of Amager (Andersen)
See *Fodrejse fra Holmens Canal til Østpynten of Amager*
"Walking Tours" (Stevenson) **5**:413
"Walking with God" (Cowper) **94**:73
"Walks in the Wheat-fields" (Jefferies) **47**:140, 143
Die Walküre (Wagner) **9**:409, 414, 416-17, 419, 448, 454, 456, 459, 466, 469-70, 473; **119**:186-87, 201-07, 222, 228-31, 277, 282, 309, 320, 347, 349-51, 354-55
"A Wall Flower" (Levy) **59**:92
"Wallace" (Baillie)
See "William Wallace"
"Wallace" (Hemans) **71**:261
"Wallace" (Hogg) **109**:200
Walladmor (De Quincey) **198**:88
Wallenrod (Mickiewicz)
See *Konrad Wallenrod*
Wallenstein (Coleridge) **111**:232
Wallenstein (Schiller) **39**:314, 316, 318-20, 322, 324, 326, 328, 337, 341-46, 348, 352, 361, 364, 367-69, 372-73, 375-78, 380, 385; **69**:169, 189, 194, 243-44, 272, 275; **166**:76-86, 141, 143, 146, 159, 186-94
Wallenstein's Camp (Schiller)
See *Wallenstein*
Wallenstein's Death (Schiller)
See *Wallenstein*
Wallenstein's Lager (Schiller)
See *Wallenstein*
Wallenstein's Tod (Schiller)
See *Wallenstein*
"The Wallflower" (Wergeland) **5**:538
The Walloons (Cumberland) **167**:122, 140, 148, 157, 189-90
Wallstein (Constant) **6**:213, 224; **182**:197, 202-4, 206
"The Walnut Coffin Papers" (Lippard) **198**:134, 143, 163
"Walpurgisnacht" (Goethe) **4**:214-15
"The Walrus and the Carpenter" (Carroll) **2**:112; **53**:40, 43, 54, 73, 93, 96, 113; **139**:29, 38, 137
"The Walse" (Sheridan) **91**:233
Walsingham; or, The Pupil of Nature (Robinson) **142**:113, 119-29, 153, 184, 202, 226-27, 230-32, 234-36, 257-58, 261, 263, 265-66, 269
"Walstein's School of History" (Brown) **74**:170, 172, 175-76
Walt and Vult; or, The Twins (Jean Paul)
See *Flegeljahre: Eine Biographie*
"Walt Whitman" (Whitman)
See "Song of Myself"
Walt Whitman: A Study (Symonds) **34**:365
"Walt Whitman, an American" (Whitman) **4**:540, 545-46, 548, 556
Walt Whitman's Leaves of Grass: The First (1855) Edition (Whitman)
See *Leaves of Grass*
Walt Whitman's Workshop (Whitman) **205**:251
"Walter" (Droste-Hülshoff) **3**:195-96
Walter (Herder) **186**:10
"Walter and Jane: or, The Poor Blacksmith" (Bloomfield) **145**:128-30, 151-52
Walter Pieterse: A Story of Holland (Multatuli)
See *De Geschiedenis van Wouertje Pieterse*
Walter Savage Landor (Forster) **11**:102-03, 120, 125-27, 129-31
Walter Scott et La Princesse Clèves (Stendhal) **23**:392
Walter Sherwood's Probation; or, Cool Head and Warm Heart (Alger) **8**:24, 43
"Walter Wilson" (Hale) **75**:298
"Wanda" (Vigny) **7**:473, 478, 484; **102**:380
Wanda, Königin der Sarmaten: Eine romantische Tragödie mit Gesang in fünf Akten (Werner) **189**:330-31, 363
"Wandelnde Glocke" (Goethe) **4**:192
"Der Wanderer" (Hölderlin)
See "Versöhnender, der du nimmer geglaubt ..."
"Wanderer" (Pavlova)
See "Strannik"
"The Wanderer" (Pushkin) **83**:279
"The Wanderer" (Wordsworth) **166**:215, 263; **206**:243
The Wanderer (Brontë) **109**:29
The Wanderer (Sacher-Masoch) **31**:291-92
The Wanderer and His Home (Lamartine)
See *Nouvelles Confidences: Avec une partie entièrement inédite*
A Wanderer Astray on the Path of Life (Smolenskin)
See *ha-To'eh be-darke ha-hayim*
"The Wanderer from the Fold" (Brontë) **16**:86
"The Wanderer of the Wold" (Lewis) **11**:302-03
The Wanderer; or, Female Difficulties (Burney) **12**:19, 21-2, 28, 30, 32-4, 46-7, 51-4, 56-9, 62-4; **54**:18-19, 21, 25-7, 29-31, 36-9, 50-2; **107**:10, 13, 16
"The Wanderers" (Morris) **4**:427
"Wander-füße" (Meyer) **81**:155
The Wandering Boys (Pixérécourt)
See *Le pèlerin blanc; ou, Les orphelins du hameau*
The Wandering Heir (Reade) **2**:541-42, 547, 549; **74**:256, 263-65
"The Wandering Jew" (Muller) **73**:351
The Wandering Jew (Sue) **1**:555-60
"Wandering Knight's Song" (Lockhart) **6**:297
The Wandering Minstrel (Mayhew) **31**:156, 158-59
Wandering Recollections of a Somewhat Busy Life (Neal) **161**:319-21, 332, 334
"Wandering Willie" (Stevenson) **5**:428
Wanderings in Spain (Gautier)
See *Voyage en Espagne*
Wanderings in Three Continents (Burton) **42**:35
"The Wanderings of Cain" (Coleridge) **54**:79; **111**:240, 291; **197**:201, 215, 311-12
The Wanderings of Ulysses (Lamb) **10**:406
The Wanderings of Warwick (Smith) **23**:323; **115**:166
Wandering—with Pleasure but not without Morals (Shevchenko)
See *Matros*
Wanderjahre (Goethe)
See *Wilhelm Meisters Wanderjahre; oder, Die Entsagenden*
Wanderlieder (Muller) **73**:365-67, 387
Wanderlieder eines rheinischen Handwerksburschen (Muller) **73**:362, 380
"Das Wandern der Künste und Wissenschaften" (Arnim) **159**:95
"Das Wandern ist des Müllers Lust" (Muller) **73**:350, 379, 381, 383
"Der wandernde Musikant" (Eichendorff) **225**:58
"Wanderschaft" (Muller) **73**:364, 368
"Wanderschaft, Wandernder Dichter" (Eichendorff) **8**:213
"Die Wanderung" (Hölderlin) **16**:174-76
Wanderungen durch die Mark Brandenburg (Fontane) **26**:234, 261, 263, 270; **163**:168, 238
"Der Wandrer" (Goethe) **4**:211, 214
"Wandrers Nachtlied" (Mörike) **201**:309
"Wandrers Sturmlied" (Goethe) **4**:212
Wandsbeck, eine Art von Romanze (Claudius) **75**:196
Der Wandsbecker Bote (Claudius) **75**:192, 195, 201
"The Waning Moon" (Bryant) **46**:4
Wann-Chlore (Balzac)
See *Jane la pâle*
"Wann der jüngste Tag wird werden" (Brentano) **191**:65
The Wants of Life (D'Israeli) **217**:304
"The Wants of the Times" (Brownson) **50**:47
"War" (Channing) **17**:33
"War" (Crawford) **12**:174; **127**:215, 218-19, 221, 227
"War" (Lampman) **25**:167, 203; **194**:15
"War" (Rimbaud)
See "Guerre"
War (Robertson) **35**:335, 354, 361, 364-65
"The War against Books" (D'Israeli) **217**:285
"War and Folk Songs" (Hauff) **185**:351, 353
"War and Peace: A Poem" (Hemans) **71**:272-73
"The War and the Commune" (Mazzini) **34**:281
"War Essentially Wrong" (Garrison) **149**:256
War Memoranda (Whitman) **81**:317

War of 1812 (Richardson) **55**:301-2, 311-2, 317, 330, 347
The War of Chocim (Krasicki)
See *Wojna Chocimska*
War of the Mascates (Alencar) **157**:9
War of the Norns and the Asas (Grundtvig) **1**:401
"The War of the Turcomans" (Gobineau)
See "La guerre des Turcomans"
"The War Pipe" (Auerbach) **171**:50
"War Song" (Moore) **6**:398
War Sonnets (Smith)
See *Sonnets on the War*
The War Widow (Frederic) **10**:188
War with the Saints (Tonna) **135**:207
Warbeck (Schiller) **69**:169
Warbeck: A Pathetic Tale (Lee) **191**:316
The Ward (Ostrovsky)
See *Vospitannitsa*
The Warden (Trollope) **6**:452-53, 464-66, 470-71, 476, 494, 497, 499, 510, 512, 514, 517; **33**:362, 365, 374-75, 382, 387-88, 395-96, 416, 418-20, 424; **101**:232, 235, 243, 253, 263, 266, 275, 280, 287, 307, 318, 329, 30; **215**:199, 207-9, 213, 231-32, 282, 336-37, 341
"Wardour Street" (Morris) **4**:434
"Ward's Ideal of a Christian Church" (Gladstone) **213**:112
"Ware kara" (Ichiyō) **49**:336-37
"Waring" (Browning) **79**:100
The Warlord: Dream on the Volga (Ostrovsky)
See *Voevoda: Son na Volge*
"Warning" (Grillparzer)
See "Warnung"
"The Warning" (Longfellow) **45**:147, 155
"The Warning Voice" (Mangan) **27**:296, 299-300, 316
"Warnung" (Grillparzer) **102**:175
"Warren Hastings" (Macaulay) **231**:301-6, 309-10
"The Warrigal—Wild Dog" (Kendall) **12**:183
"The Warrior's Return" (Opie) **65**:160-1, 175
"Warsaw" (Grillparzer)
See "Warschau"
"Warschau" (Grillparzer) **102**:175
War-Song for the Scanian Reserves (Tegner) **2**:613
War-songs for Freemen (Child) **173**:210
"Warum gabst du uns" (Goethe) **4**:193
"Was ist deutsch?" (Wagner) **119**:291
"Was ist Wahrheit?" (Wieland) **177**:245, 267-71
"Was My Brother in the Battle" (Foster) **26**:288
"Was soll geschehen im Glücke" (Arnim) **159**:59
"Was the Earl of Beaconsfield a Representative Jew?" (Lazarus) **8**:419, 424; **109**:297, 302-03, 306, 319, 327
"Was Thy Wrath against the Sea?" (Rossetti) **186**:336
"Was wär' ich ohne dich gewesen?" (Novalis) **13**:362
"Was war und bleibt die Schillerfeier" (Auerbach) **171**:39
"Was will der Franzos? und Was will der Deutsche?: Eine Auntwort aus dem Schwarzwald" (Auerbach) **171**:40
Was wir bringen (Goethe) **154**:262
"The Washers of the Shroud" (Lowell) **2**:514; **90**:193, 198
"Washing-Day" (Barbauld) **50**:14-16; **185**:58, 96, 114-15, 133-34, 154
"A Washington" (Gómez de Avellaneda) **111**:4
"Washington" (Landor) **14**:166
Washington and His Generals; or, Legends of the Revolution, by George Lippard. With a Biographical Sketch of the Author, by Rev. C. Chauncey Burr (Lippard) **198**:118, 123, 125, 173, 181, 189, 209-10, 216
"Washington as a Camp" (Winthrop) **210**:271, 275, 280, 296
Washington Irving Journals and Notebooks, Vol. II (Irving) **95**:276, 278-79
Washington Irving Letters Volume I 1802-23 (Irving) **95**:273-79
"Wasps in a Garden" (Lamb) **125**:346, 360
"Wasserflut" (Muller) **73**:384, 396
Der Wassermensch (Tieck) **5**:519
"Die Wassernot im Emmental" (Gotthelf) **117**:4
"Waste Not, Want Not" (Edgeworth) **1**:265; **51**:87
The Wastrel (Leskov)
See *Rastočitel*
"Wat o' the Cleuch" (Hogg) **109**:246, 249
Wat Tyler (Southey) **8**:455, 458, 467; **97**:250, 259, 263-64, 267, 293, 312-17
"The Watch" (Mickiewicz) **3**:398
"The Watch" (Turgenev)
See "Časy"
The Watch Dog (Fredro)
See *Brytan bryś*
"The Watcher" (Le Fanu)
See "The Familiar"
"The Watching of the Falcon" (Morris) **4**:416, 447-48
The Watchman (Coleridge) **111**:253; **197**:310-12; **231**:58-59, 160
"The Water Colley" (Jefferies) **47**:136
"Water Color" (Verlaine)
See "Aquarelles"
"The Water Craft of the Back-woods" (Thorpe) **183**:358
"The Water Crowfoot" (Barnes) **75**:22, 28, 37
"The Water Crowvoot" (Barnes)
See "The Water Crowfoot"
Water Drops (Sigourney) **87**:321
"Water Flows into the Blue Sea" (Shevchenko)
See "Tece voda v synje more"
"The Water Lady" (Hood) **16**:225
"The Water Lillies" (Moodie) **113**:316
"The Water Nymph" (Lermontov)
See "Rusalka"
The Water Nymph (Pushkin)
See *Rusalka*
"The Water of Life" (Grimm Brothers) **3**:222
"The Water of the Wondrous Isles" (Morris) **4**:425, 436, 438
The Water Witch (Cooper) **203**:85
The Water-Babies: A Fairy-Tale for a Land-Baby (Kingsley) **35**:220, 227, 232, 235, 246, 249, 251, 254-55, 258-60
"Watercolor in Five Minutes" (Laforgue)
See "Aquarelle en cinq minutes"
"The Waterfall" (Baratynsky) **103**:6, 10
"The Waterfall" (Derzhavin)
See "Vodopad"
"The Waterfall and the Eglantine" (Wordsworth) **111**:323
"Water-Lilies" (Clare) **9**:117
"The Waterlily" (Crawford) **12**:172; **127**:181-86, 189, 193-94
"The Water's Flow" (Muller)
See "Wasserflut"
The Water-Witch; or, The Skimmer of the Seas (Cooper) **1**:200, 207-08, 221-22; **54**:255
Watkins Tottle and Other Sketches Illustrative of Every-Day Life and Every-Day People (Dickens)
See *Sketches by Boz, Illustrative of Every-Day Life and Every-Day People*
The Watson (Austen) **207**:46
The Watsons (Austen) **1**:36, 42, 46, 50-52, 54, 60; **13**:99; **119**:18, 26, 30, 45-6; **210**:132
Wau-Nan-Gee; or, The Massacre at Chicago (Richardson) **55**:304, 313, 321
"Wava, The Fairy of the Shell" (Crawford) **127**:181-84, 189, 193
Waverley Novels (Scott) **15**:275-76, 278-79, 284, 289, 292, 294-95, 300, 306-07, 309-10, 318, 320-22, 325; **209**:195, 201, 216, 218-19, 224, 240-42, 250, 252-53, 257, 262, 273, 277, 280, 283, 285-86, 314-15, 319, 329-30, 344-45, 352
Waverley; or, 'Tis Sixty Years Since (Scott) **15**:257-59, 263, 266-67, 269-70, 274-75, 285-87, 289, 300-03, 307, 310, 313, 315-16, 318, 321, 323; **69**:296-97, 299-300, 303-04, 308, 318-20, 378, 391; **110**:230-345; **209**:194, 211-12, 215-19, 222-24, 230, 235, 238, 240, 242-43, 245-47, 249-50, 252-59, 262-63, 271, 278-82, 286, 299, 304-5, 314-15, 319, 333, 349-51
"The Waves" (Rossetti) **186**:234
"The Waves" (Taylor) **89**:300
The Waves (Grillparzer) **1**:385
"The Waves of this Troublesome World" (Rossetti) **186**:233, 237
"The Waving of the Corn" (Lanier) **6**:238; **118**:203
"The Wax Works" (Longstreet) **159**:123, 125, 144, 151, 161, 176, 182, 184
'Way Down East (Smith)
See *The Life and Writings of Major Jack Downing of Downingville, Away Down East in the State of Maine, Written by Himself*
"Way Down upon the Swanee River" (Foster)
See "Old Folks at Home"
"Way of the Soul" (Tennyson) **115**:313
"The Way of the World" (Rossetti) **66**:342
The Way to Keep Him. A Comedy in Three Acts. As it is Perform'd at the Theatre-Royal in Drury-Lane (Murphy) **229**:222-23, 234
The Way to Plenty . . . Written in 1795, the Year of Scarcity (More) **141**:189, 282, 300
The Way towards the Blessed Life; or, The Doctrine of Religion (Fichte)
See *Die Anweisung zum seligen Leben, oder auch die Religionslehre*
The Way We Live Now (Trollope) **6**:460-61, 464, 471, 477, 480, 482, 487, 489, 497, 500, 507, 511-13; **33**:417, 424; **101**:216, 221, 251, 253, 256, 266, 273, 275, 279-81, 283, 286-88, 290, 292, 308, 311-12, 319, 326-28; **215**:324, 334
"Wayconnell Tower" (Allingham) **25**:8
Wayfaring Songs (Eichendorff) **225**:4
The Ways of Manhattan (Cooper)
See *The Ways of the Hour*
The Ways of the Hour (Cooper) **1**:220; **54**:259, 262-3, 300; **203**:22-31, 49
"The Wayside Dream" (Taylor) **89**:298-99
"Wayside Flowers" (Allingham) **25**:14
"The Wayside Inn" (Turgenev)
See "The Inn"
Wayside Inn (Longfellow)
See *Tales of a Wayside Inn*
"The Wayside Well" (Allingham) **25**:6, 8, 24
We and Our Neighbors; or, The Records of an Unfashionable Street: A Sequel to "My Wife and I" (Stowe) **3**:554, 562
"We Are Coming Father Abraham, 300,000 More" (Foster) **26**:298
"We Are Seven" (Wordsworth) **12**:387, 414, 430; **111**:202, 209, 223, 228, 252, 314, 316, 348, 358; **166**:235; **206**:275, 309, 312
"We Break the Glass" (Pinkney) **31**:279-80
"We May Roam Through the World" (Moore) **110**:185
"We Part for Ever!" (Osgood) **141**:354
"We Parted" (Lermontov) **5**:299
"We Play at Paste" (Dickinson) **21**:43
"We studiously observe the world..." (Baratynsky)
See "Staratelno my nablyudaem svet..."
"We Too Shall Sleep" (Lampman) **194**:129, 131
"We Two" (Webster) **230**:313-14
"We Two, Each Other's Only Pride" (Sheridan) **91**:232
"We Two, How Long We Were Fool'd" (Whitman) **4**:601; **31**:389
"We Watched Her Breathing" (Hood) **16**:233
"The Weaker Vessel" (Parton) **86**:350
"The Weaker Vessel" (Patmore) **9**:340, 344

"Weal and Woe in Garveloch" (Martineau) **26**:336; **137**:240, 250
"Wealth" (Crawford) **127**:215-16, 218-19
"Wealth" (Emerson) **98**:8-9, 113, 135
"Wealth and Poverty" (Ueda Akinari)
See "Himpukuron"
"Weariness" (Longfellow) **45**:116-17, 131
Wearing of the Gray (Cooke) **5**:130, 135
"Weary in Well-Doing" (Rossetti) **50**:268, 316
"Weary of the Bitter Ease" (Mallarmé)
See "Las de l'amer repos"
"A Weary Pund of Tow" (Baillie) **151**:92
"The Weary Soul" (Milnes) **61**:136
"The Weathercock" (Muller) **73**:385
"The Weaver" (Lampman) **25**:206, 216
"The Weavers" (Heine)
See "Die schlesischen Weber"
"Wechsel" (Hölderlin) **16**:185
"Wechsel der Töne" (Hölderlin) **187**:296-98
"Wechselgesang in der Nacht" (Mörike) **201**:299
"Weddah and Om-el-Bonain" (Thomson) **18**:392, 397, 401, 403, 405, 408
"The Wedding" (Lamb) **10**:410
"Wedding and Funeral" (Hale) **75**:296
The Wedding Day (Inchbald) **62**:144, 150
"Wedding Hymn" (Lanier) **6**:237; **118**:242
"The Wedding Knell" (Hawthorne) **2**:291; **10**:316; **79**:296; **95**:105
"The Wedding of Maksim Crnojević" (Chappel) **115**:92
"The Wedding of Marko Kraljeviĉ" (Karadzic) **115**:91
Weder Lorbeerbaum noch Bettlestab (Nestroy) **42**:239-40
"Wednesday" (Thoreau) **7**:352
"Wednesday Before Easter" (Keble) **87**:201
"The Wee Pickle Tow" (Baillie) **151**:92
"Wee Wee Husband" (Rossetti) **186**:238
Weeds and Wildings, with a Rose or Two (Melville) **3**:379-80; **157**:212
"A Week in a Village" (Clare) **86**:92
"A Week on Capri" (Taylor) **89**:313
A Week on the Concord and Merrimack Rivers (Thoreau) **7**:348, 352, 361, 369-70, 375, 377-8, 381, 388-90, 400, 405, 410-1; **21**:322, 344-6, 369-70, 372; **61**:283, 288, 296-7, 302, 306, 309, 315, 326, 335, 339, 342-3, 348, 352, 375; **138**:66-67, 71-72, 74-81, 83-92, 94-109, 111-12, 114-31, 133-42, 144-45, 148-53, 155-63, 165-67, 169-71, 174-78, 182-86, 188-92; **207**:188, 202-3, 208-11, 219-20, 232-33, 244, 255-57,
Weekly Political Register (Cobbett)
See *Cobbett's Weekly Political Register*
"Weep On, Weep On" (Moore) **110**:187
"The Weepen Leady" (Barnes) **75**:76
"The Weeping Savior" (Barrett Browning) **170**:106
"Weeping Willow" (Sigourney) **87**:321
"Der Wegweiser" (Muller) **73**:391, 393, 396-97
Weh dem, der lügt! (Grillparzer) **1**:384; **102**:106, 131, 139, 168, 172, 184, 186, 188, 190, 192
Wehmüller (Brentano)
See *Die mehreren Wehmüller und ungarischen Nationalgesichter: Erzählung*
"Das Weib des Admirals" (Meyer) **81**:142
"Das weiBe Spitzchen" (Meyer) **81**:144
Der weibliche Jakobiner-Klubb (Kotzebue) **25**:143, 147
"Weighed in the Balance" (Woolson) **82**:322
"A Weight with Needles on the Pounds" (Dickinson) **21**:64
Weihe der Kraft (Werner)
See *Martin Luther, oder die Weihe der Kraft: Eine Tragödie vom Verfasser der Söhne des Thales*
Die Weihe der Unkraft: Ein Ergänzungblatt zur deutschen Haustafel (Werner) **189**:322, 326, 347, 358
"Der Weiher" (Droste-Hülshoff) **3**:203
"Weihgeschenck" (Meyer) **81**:199, 205, 209
"Weihgeschenk" (Mörike) **201**:345-46
"Weihnachtsabend" (Storm) **195**:53
Die Weihnachtsfeier: Ein Gespräch (Schleiermacher) **107**:268, 350, 363, 376, 398, 400
"Weimar and its Dead" (Taylor) **89**:308
"Weimar in June" (Taylor) **89**:325
Weimar's Dead (Liszt)
See *Weimars Toten*
Weimar's September Festival in Celebration of the hundredth Birthday of Carl August (Liszt) **199**:305
Weimars Toten (Liszt) **199**:308
"Der Weingott" (Hölderlin) **16**:176
"Weinhtrunk an die toten Freunde" (Klopstock) **11**:236-37
"Weinsegen" (Meyer) **81**:146
Weir of Hermiston (Stevenson) **5**:416-19, 427, 429-34; **193**:223, 229, 254, 274, 279, 313
Weir of Hermiston: An Unfinished Romance (Stevenson)
See *Weir of Hermiston*
"Weird Gathering" (Whittier) **8**:485
"The Weird Lady" (Kingsley) **35**:218
Weird Women (Barbey d'Aurevilly)
See *Les diaboliques*
"Weis Rosen" (Storm)
See "Ein Buch der weisen Rose"
Weisthümer (Grimm Brothers) **3**:216
"Welcome" (Very) **9**:388
"Welcome and Parting" (Goethe)
See "Willkommen und Abschied"
"The Welcome Home" (Opie) **65**:172
"Welcome joy, and welcome sorrow" (Keats) **225**:143
"Welcome to Egypt" (Blind) **202**:52, 55
"Welcome, Wild North-Easter!" (Kingsley) **35**:212, 219
"The Well at the World's End" (Morris) **4**:424-36, 438
"Well! Dad's Dead" (Harris) **23**:142, 146, 160; **165**:170, 175, 183, 196, 265
"The Well of Pen-Morfa" (Gaskell) **5**:205; **70**:185, 190
We'll Settle It Among Ourselves (Ostrovsky)
See *Svoi lyudi—sochtemsya!*
"Well! Thou Art Happy" (Byron) **2**:77
"Welland River" (Morris) **4**:431, 444
"Welldean Hall" (Hogg) **4**:283; **109**:203, 279
"Wellington's Funeral" (Rossetti) **4**:518; **77**:296-7
Welsh Melodies (Hemans) **29**:205; **71**:261
"The Welshmen of Tirawley" (Ferguson)
See "The Vengeance of the Welshmen of Tirawley"
Die Welt als Wille und Vorstellung (Schopenhauer) **51**:245, 249, 270-71, 287, 292, 294, 302, 311-12, 315-16, 318, 321, 324, 344-46; **157**:217, 220, 229-30, 234, 240, 242-48, 259-68, 271-72, 275-76, 278-81, 284, 299-300, 302-6, 308, 312-13, 315-16, 318-19, 322, 329-33, 337-38, 340-42, 344-46, 350-56
Die Weltalter (Schelling) **30**:141, 170
"Die Welten" (Klopstock) **225**:305-11
Weltgeschichtliche Bertrachtungen (Burckhardt) **49**:5, 7-9, 16, 19, 22
"Weltlauf" (Heine) **147**:229
"Weltlich Recht" (Brentano) **191**:25
"Die Weltweisen" (Schiller) **166**:121
"Wen Gott betrügt, ist wohl betrogen" (Clough) **27**:103, 107
"Wenden Castle" (Bestuzhev)
See "Zamok Venden"
"Wenn der lahme Weber träumt, er webe" (Brentano) **1**:105
"Wenn der Sturm das Meer umschlinget" (Brentano) **1**:104
Wenn die Äpfel reif sind (Storm) **195**:94
"Went Hwome" (Barnes) **75**:53
The Wept of Wish Ton-Wish (Cooper)
See *The Borderers*
The Wept of Wish-ton-Wish (Cooper) **1**:199, 221-22; **54**:255, 262
"Wer ist der Verräter?" (Goethe) **4**:194
Wer ist schuldig? (Grillparzer) **102**:78
"Die Werbung" (Lenau) **16**:264, 285
"Das Werden im Vergehen" (Hölderlin) **16**:178
"Werden im Vergehen" (Hölderlin) **187**:247
"We're a Million in the Field" (Foster) **26**:288
Werke (Arnim) **159**:95-99
Werke (Brentano) **191**:34, 36-42, 67, 90-92, 118-22, 128-33
Werke (Goethe) **154**:218, 220-21, 270-72, 276-79, 315-17, 337, 342-43
Werke (Hauff)
See *Sämtliche Werke in drei Bänden*
Werke (Herder) **186**:34
Werke (Kleist)
See *Sämtliche Werke und Briefe*
Werke (Mörike) **201**:299-300, 303, 359
Werke (Storm)
See *Sämtliche Werke*
Werke (Wieland) **177**:359
"Werke: Hamburger Ausgabe" (Goethe) **90**:42-4, 103, 106-07
Werke, Schriften und Briefe (Fontane) **163**:240-41
Werke und Briefe (Arnim) **38**:12
Werke und Briefe: Historisch-kritische Gesamtausgabe (Stifter) **198**:310, 314-15
Werner (Byron) **2**:67, 79-80, 90
"An Werther" (Goethe) **154**:277
Werther (Arnim) **159**:73
Werther (Goethe)
See *Die Leiden des jungen Werthers*
Werther (Hays) **114**:177
Das Wesen der Religion (Feuerbach) **139**:241-42, 289, 293
Das Wesen des Christentums (Feuerbach) **139**:236, 242, 246, 251-53, 260, 266, 271, 274-81, 283, 286-87, 289-90, 293-94, 297-98, 309, 313, 316-25, 329, 334, 337, 339, 343
"West End Fair" (Barbauld) **185**:57
"West India Emancipation" (Garrison) **149**:258-59
"West Indian" (Cumberland) **167**:128
The West Indian (Cumberland) **167**:111, 119, 122, 127-28, 131, 133-34, 137, 142, 146, 150, 152-55, 158, 160-61, 163, 166, 175, 177-79, 181, 186-89, 191, 202-5
The West Indies and the Spanish Main (Trollope) **215**:218
"West London" (Arnold) **218**:147
"The West Shetucket Railroad" (Cooke)
See "The West Shetucket Railway"
"The West Shetucket Railway" (Cooke) **110**:18, 32, 44
"The West Wind" (Bryant) **6**:176; **46**:45
Westbrook, The Outlaw; or, The Avenging Wolf. An American Border Tale (Richardson) **55**:304, 364-6
West-Eastern Divan (Goethe)
See *West—östlicher Divan*
The Western Boy; or, The Road to Success (Alger) **8**:20, 33, 45; **83**:142, 148
Western Clearings (Kirkland) **85**:260, 263, 265, 270, 284, 301
Western Home, and Other Poems (Sigourney) **87**:326
The Western Journals of Washington Irving (Irving) **2**:382
"Westminster Abbey" (Irving) **2**:381; **19**:347
"Westminster Bridge" (Wordsworth) **12**:431
West—östlicher Divan (Goethe) **4**:173, 193; **154**:180, 315-16
Westward Ho! (Kingsley) **35**:209, 211, 215-18, 220, 222, 228-31, 233, 235, 241, 243-44, 249, 252, 255-57
Westward Ho! (Paulding) **2**:527-30

"Wetterleuchten" (Meyer) **81**:153, 199, 204, 209
"Wettgesang" (Schlegel) **15**:229
"Der Wettpflüger" (Auerbach) **171**:75, 80
"Weyla's Song" (Mörike)
See "Gesang Weylas"
"Weymouth" (Dacre) **151**:149
The Whale (Melville)
See *Moby-Dick; or, The Whale*
"The Wharf Rat" (O'Brien) **21**:234
"What?" (Rossetti) **186**:294
"What Am I without Thee?" (Lanier) **118**:231
"What Animals are Made for" (Barbauld) **185**:126, 131
"What are Heavy? Sea-Sand and Sorrow" (Rossetti) **186**:237
"What Befell" (O'Brien) **21**:245
"What Can an Old Man Do But Die?" (Hood) **16**:219
"What Can It Mean?" (Delany) **93**:157
"What Daddy Does Is Always Right" (Andersen)
See "What Father Does is Always Right"
"What Dick and I Did" (Barnes) **75**:78
"What Do Poets Want with Gold?" (Lampman) **25**:160, 188, 200, 216
"What Does an Author Need?" (Karamzin)
See "Chto nuzhno avtoru"
"What Does It Mean?" (Delany) **93**:157
"What Father Does" (Andersen)
See "What Father Does is Always Right"
"What Father Does is Always Right" (Andersen) **7**:34; **79**:88; **214**:58
"What, For Us, My Heart . . ." (Rimbaud)
See "Qu'est-ce pour nous"
"What for Us, My Heart, Are Pools of Blood" (Rimbaud) **4**:486
"What Had I Been If Thou Were Not?" (Novalis)
See "Was wär' ich ohne dich gewesen?"
"What I Lived For" (Thoreau) **7**:352, 381
"What if I say I shall not wait?" (Dickinson) **171**:96
"What Is a Classic" (Sainte-Beuve) **5**:350
"What is Beauty?" (Child) **73**:77
What Is Enlightenment? (Kant) **27**:219, 231, 237
"What Is Fancy?" (Lamb) **125**:354
"What Is Happiness?" (Auerbach) **171**:48
"What Is He?" (Disraeli) **79**:215
"What Is Heaven" (Dickinson)
See "What Is 'Paradise'"
"What is Life?" (Chivers) **49**:69
"What is Life?" (Clare) **86**:156
"What is Life?" (Coleridge) **231**:84-85
What is Love? (Almqvist)
See *Väd är kärlek?*
"What Is Oblornovism?" (Dobrolyubov) **5**:140-41, 145, 147, 149, 151
What Is Orientation in Thinking? (Kant) **27**:220
"What Is 'Paradise'" (Dickinson) **21**:41
"What Is Past, What Is Lost, What Is Gone" (Pavlova) **138**:34
"What Is Poetry" (Mill) **11**:384; **58**:319, 323-5, 329, 332, 363, 366, 368; **179**:343, 345, 351
"What is Poetry?" (Timrod) **25**:380
"What Is Really My Belief?" (Landor) **14**:201
"What Is Said to the Poet About Flowers" (Rimbaud)
See "Ce qu'on dit au poète à propos de fleurs"
"What is the People?" (Hazlitt) **29**:184
"What is the preferable method or system for writing history?" (Martínez de la Rosa)
See "¿Cuál es el método o sistema preferible para escribir la historia?"
"What Is There in the Distant Hills" (Clare) **9**:124
What Is to Be Done? Tales about New People (Chernyshevsky)
See *Chto delat'?*
"What Mr. Robinson Thinks" (Lowell) **90**:218
"What Must a Fairy's Dream Be" (Foster) **26**:287
"What mystery pervades a well" (Dickinson) **171**:103, 181
What Never Dies (Barbey d'Aurevilly)
See *Ce qui ne meurt pas*
"What old Johanne told" (Andersen)
See "Hvad gamle Johanne fortalte"
"What One Says to the Poet on the Subject of Flowers" (Rimbaud)
See "Ce qu'on dit au poète à propos de fleurs"
"What Santa Claus Brought Me" (O'Brien) **21**:246
"What Shall I Call You" (Petofi)
See "Minek nevezzelek"
"What shall I do for the land that bred me" (Hopkins) **189**:126
"What Ship Puzzled at Sea" (Whitman) **31**:388
"What should happen with a fortunate turn of fate" (Arnim)
See "Was soll geschehen im Glücke"
"What strains are these?" (Baratynsky)
See "Chto za zvuki?"
"What the Birds Said" (Whittier) **8**:517; **59**:358
"What the Black Man Wants" (Douglass) **7**:130
"What the Lord Lyndhurst Really Was" (Bagehot) **10**:58
"What the Moon Saw" (Andersen)
See "Billedbog uden Billeder"
"What the Old Man Does is Always Right" (Andersen)
See "What Father Does is Always Right"
"What the Tortoise said to Achilles" (Dodgson) **139**:80, 83
"What the Voice Said" (Whittier) **8**:530
"What the Whole Family Said" (Andersen) **214**:48
"What, Then, Does Dr. Newman Mean?" (Kingsley) **35**:229
"What Things Exist?" (Bentham) **38**:93
"What Think You I Take My Pen in Hand" (Whitman) **205**:220
"What Use Are Black Brows to Me?" (Shevchenko) **54**:374
"What Use are you, Days" (Baratynsky)
See "Na chto vy, dni"
"What Was It? A Mystery" (O'Brien) **21**:235-36, 238, 240, 242, 245-46, 248-51, 253
What We Must All Come To. A Comedy in Two Acts. As it Was Intended to be Acted at the Theatre-Royal in Covent-Garden (Murphy) **229**:223, 234, 254
What We Offer (Goethe)
See *Was wir bringen*
"What we, when face to face we see" (Prescott) **163**:6, 50
What Will He Do with It? (Bulwer-Lytton) **1**:151; **45**:22, 69
"What Would I Give?" (Rossetti) **2**:575; **186**:265
"Whatever Happened to Me?" (Rossetti) **186**:269
"What's This?" (Corbière)
See "Ça?"
"What's This Uproar Again?" (Petofi)
See "Mi lárma ez megént?"
The Wheel of Fortune (Cumberland) **167**:111, 122, 127, 131, 140, 142, 144, 150, 172-73, 190-92
"When All the World is Young, Lad" (Kingsley) **35**:227
"When Even the Voice of Thoughts Is Silent" (Eminescu) **33**:247
"When from Afar" (Hölderlin) **187**:212
"When He Who Adores Thee" (Moore) **6**:391
"When I Am Dead, My Dearest, Sing No Sad Songs for Me" (Rossetti) **2**:563
"When I have borne in memory what has tamed" (Wordsworth) **206**:301
"When I Have Fears That I May Cease to Be" (Keats) **73**:161, 193-94, 256; **225**:205, 210-11, 220
"When I Heard at the Close of Day" (Whitman) **81**:330
"When I Saw You" (Eminescu) **33**:265
"When I was a youth my shouts..." (Baratynsky)
See "Byvalo, otrok, zvonkim klikom..."
"When I Was Young" (Parton) **86**:373
"When I was young, with ringing call..." (Baratynsky)
See "Byvalo, otrok, zvonkim klikom..."
"When in Death I Shall Calm Recline" (Moore) **6**:389
"When Israel Came Out of Egypt" (Clough)
See "The New Sinai"
"When Lilacs Last in the Dooryard Bloom'd" (Whitman) **4**:544, 559, 561, 569, 571, 579-80, 582, 592, 595, 602; **31**:368, 370, 385, 388-91, 404-05, 408, 432; **81**:255, 257-58, 268, 271, 331, 366-70; **205**:159-60, 225, 237, 309, 313, 335, 337-40
"When Lilacs Last in the Dooryard Bloomed" (Whitman)
See "When Lilacs Last in the Dooryard Bloom'd"
"When my heart is vexed I will complain" (Rossetti) **186**:314
"When Old Corruption First Begun" (Blake) **13**:182; **37**:29
"When Our Deteriorating Strength" (Tyutchev)
See "Kogda drjaxlejušcie sily"
"When our two souls stand up erect and strong" (Barrett Browning) **170**:57
"When Panting Sighs the Bosom Fill" (Clough) **27**:52, 106
"When Soft September" (Clough) **27**:104
"When Sparrows Build" (Ingelow) **39**:268; **107**:122
"When the Blacksmith Leaves his Forge..." (Bestuzhev)
See "Kak idyot kuznets da iz kuznitsy . . ."
"When the Kye Comes Hame" (Hogg) **4**:286; **109**:269
When the Spaniards Were Here (Andersen) **79**:16
"When the Yellowing Fields Billow" (Lermontov) **5**:295
"When to Great Chastisers" (Pavlova)
See "Kogda karateliam velikim"
"When We Husked the Corn" (O'Brien) **21**:245
"When will the darkness disappear..." (Baratynsky)
See "Kogda ischeznet omrachenie"
"When Will the Day Come?" (Dobrolyubov) **5**:140, 149
"When You Tell Me . . ." (Verlaine)
See "Quand tu me racontes . . ."
"When Youthful Hope Is Fled" (Lockhart) **6**:296
"Whenever I Remember" (Eminescu) **131**:296
"Where?" (Heine)
See "Wo?"
"Where am I now?" (Crabbe) **121**:82
"Where Be You Going, You Devon Maid?" (Keats) **8**:360
"Where Does the Day Begin?" (Dodgson) **53**:51
"Where Gleaming Fields of Haze" (Thoreau) **7**:384
"Where I Have Lost, I Softer Tread" (Dickinson) **21**:55
"Where is the sweet whisper..." (Baratynsky)
See "Gde sladkiy shyopot..."
Where It Is Thin, There It Breaks (Turgenev) **21**:428, 432
"Where Liberty Was Born" (Chivers) **49**:51
"Where Shall We Bury Our Shame?" (Moore) **110**:186
"Wherefore" (Lazarus) **8**:418
"Wherefore" (Lermontov) **5**:299

"Wherefore should a slave" (Baratynsky)
See "K chemu nevolniku mechtania svobody?..."
"Wherein All Nature is the Theatre to Her Sorrow" (Liszt) **199**:307
"Wherein He Expatiates Upon Love's Paradoxes" (Liszt) **199**:307
"Where's Agnes?" (Barrett Browning) **61**:45; **170**:122
"Whereto?" (Preseren)
See "Kám?"
"Wherever I Go and Look" (Eichendorff) **8**:210
"Which Is the True One?" (Baudelaire)
See "Laquelle est la vraie?"
Whigs and Whiggism: Political Writings by Benjamin Disraeli (Disraeli) **39**:69; **79**:269
"Whigs und Tories" (Fontane) **163**:200
Whims and Oddities (Hood) **16**:202, 205, 208, 213, 219
Whimsicalities (Hood) **16**:217, 238
"A Whirl-Blast from behind the Hill" (Wordsworth) **12**:446
"A Whisper in the Dark" (Alcott) **58**:75
"Whisperings in the Wattle-Boughs" (Gordon) **21**:154, 160-61, 173, 181
"Whispers of Heavenly Death" (Whitman) **81**:309; **205**:226, 330, 335, 340-41
Whispers to a Bride (Sigourney) **87**:321-22, 338
"White an' Blue" (Barnes) **75**:17, 22, 46
The White Banner (Lippard) **198**:123, 182, 211, 226-27, 229
The White Cat (Planché) **42**:273, 288-89
"The White Chip Hat" (Willis) **194**:307
"The White Doe of Rylstone" (Wordsworth)
See *The White Doe of Rylstone; or, The Fate of the Nortons*
The White Doe of Rylstone; or, The Fate of the Nortons (Wordsworth) **12**:400, 407-8, 422, 460, 466; **166**:210, 235, 268; **206**:258
"The White Eagle" (Leskov)
See "Belyj orel"
"White Exploit" (Dickinson) **77**:68
"A white hen sitting" (Rossetti) **186**:235
"White Lies" (Opie) **65**:162, 171, 179
White Lies (Reade) **2**:534, 536, 549; **74**:245, 258, 264-64, 312
"White Margaret" (Lampman) **25**:183, 220
"White Mountains" (Whittier) **8**:485
"White Nights" (Dostoevsky) **33**:201; **167**:243
"The White Old Maid" (Hawthorne) **2**:292, 322
"White Pansies" (Lampman) **194**:129-31
"White Peak" (Ueda Akinari)
See "Shiramine"
"The White Road up Athirt the Hill" (Barnes) **75**:87
"The White Rose" (Martí)
See "La Rosa Blanca"
"The White Ship" (Rossetti) **4**:499-500, 506-08, 518, 525-26, 532
The White Woman (Scribe)
See *La dame blanche*
Whitehall; or, The Days of George IV (Maginn) **8**:432, 436, 441
White-Jacket; or, The World in a Man-of-War (Melville) **3**:328, 332-34, 337, 339, 342, 345, 347-49, 359-61, 363, 365, 371, 373; **12**:281; **29**:318, 322, 325, 327-28, 331-34, 340-41, 345, 348, 350, 354, 358, 360-64, 367-69, 372, 374, 378; **45**:243, 254; **49**:391-92; **91**:42-3, 45, 55, 186; **123**:177, 184, 204, 211, 232, 235, 239; **157**:109; **181**:144, 154, 156-57, 160, 164, 186, 200, 204; **193**:107, 130, 146, 148; **221**:96-221
Whiteladies (Oliphant) **11**:441, 446; **61**:212; **221**:225
"Whiteness" (Isaacs)
See "Albor"
"The Whitewashed Cottage of the Susquehannah, An Indian Story" (Bird) **197**:32
"Whither?" (Muller)
See "Wohin?"
"Whitsun Eve" (Rossetti) **186**:340, 346
"Whitsuntide an' Club Walken" (Barnes) **75**:95
"The Whitsuntide Fire" (Kivi)
See "Helavalkea"
Whittier on Writers and Writings (Whittier) **59**:364
"Who Can Be Happy and Free in Russia?" (Nekrasov)
See "Komu na Rusi zhit khorosho"
"Who curseth Sorrow knows her not at all" (Crawford) **127**:151-52
"Who goes to dine must take his Feast" (Dickinson) **171**:202
"Who Has Seen the Wind" (Rossetti) **50**:306
"Who Hath Ears to Hear Let Him Hear" (Very) **9**:381
Who Is Guilty? (Grillparzer)
See *Wer ist schuldig?*
"Who is Now Reading This?" (Whitman) **81**:332; **205**:206
"Who Is the People?" (Hazlitt) **82**:129
"Who Is This Woman...?" (De Quincey) **4**:88
Who Is to Blame? (Herzen)
See *Kto vinovat?*
"Who Killed Zebedee?" (Collins) **1**:188
"Who Learns My Lesson Complete" (Whitman) **31**:419, 425; **205**:191-92, 214
"Who Shall Deliver Me?" (Rossetti) **2**:572; **186**:332
"Who shaped these walls has shewn" (Hopkins) **189**:135
"Who Was Lost and Is Found" (Oliphant) **61**:202, 222
"Who was She?" (Taylor) **89**:325
"Who Will Say the World is Dying?" (Kingsley) **35**:219
"Who Would be the Last Man" (Parton) **86**:351
"Whoever Wants to Wander to Foreign Lands" (Eichendorff) **8**:210
"Whoever You Are Holding Me Now in Hand" (Whitman) **205**:243-44, 262, 309
Whom to Marry and How to Get Married! or, The Adventures of a Lady in Search of a Good Husband (Mayhew) **31**:160-61, 178, 191
Who's to Blame? (Newman) **38**:324
Who's Your Friend (Planché) **42**:278
"Why Are There Few Writers of Talent in Russia?" (Karamzin)
See "Ot chego v Rossii malo avtorskikh talantov"
"Why did baby die" (Rossetti) **186**:237
"Why Did I Laugh Tonight" (Keats) **73**:173, 194, 202, 217
"Why Distant Objects Please" (Hazlitt) **82**:158
"Why Do Ye Call the Poet Lonely?" (Lampman) **25**:216
"Why I Am a Liberal" (Browning) **19**:110
"Why I Wrote Looking Backward" (Bellamy) **147**:71-72, 78-79, 85, 89
"Why Lombard Street Is Sometimes Highly Excited and Sometimes Very Dull" (Bagehot) **10**:22
"Why Mr. Disraeli Has Succeeded" (Bagehot) **10**:31, 58
"Why Should a Slåve" (Baratynsky)
See "K chemu nevolniku mechtania svobody?..."
"Why Should We Hurry—Why Indeed?" (Dickinson) **21**:66
"Why Should We Weep for Those that Die?" (Tennyson) **202**:289
"Why the Heroes of Romances Are Insipid" (Hazlitt) **29**:148
"Why the Little Frenchman Wears His Arm in a Sling" (Poe) **16**:292, 323-24
"Why the Little Frenchman Wears His Hand in a Sling" (Poe) **211**:250
"Why Was She Blonde?" (Alarcón)
See "¿Por qué era rubia?"
"Why—Do They Shut Me Out of Heaven" (Dickinson) **21**:53, 56
"Wi! lang-legged Tam the bruise I tried" (Baillie)
See "My Nanny O"
The Wide, Wide World (Warner) **31**:332-33, 337-41, 343-49, 352-55; **146**:218-352
Wider Unser. Gedenkblätter zur Geschichte dieser Tage (Auerbach) **171**:40
"Widok gór ze stepów Kozłowa" (Mickiewicz) **3**:404; **101**:188-89
"The Widow" (Southey) **97**:315
"The Widow and her Hour-Glass" (Bloomfield) **145**:129-30, 152
"The Widow and Her Son" (Irving) **19**:327, 348; **95**:232, 237
The Widow Barnaby (Trollope) **30**:314, 319-20
"The Widow Goe" (Crabbe) **26**:132
The Widow Grey (Crabbe) **121**:33
The Widow Lerouge (Gaboriau)
See *L'affaire Lerouge*
The Widow Married: A Sequel to the Widow Barnaby (Trollope) **30**:314, 320, 322
"The Widow McCloud's Mare" (Harris) **23**:159; **165**:254
"The Widow of Crescentius" (Hemans) **71**:293
The Widow of Delphi (Cumberland) **167**:148, 157, 189-90
Widow of Padilla (Martínez de la Rosa)
See *La viuda de Padilla*
"The Widow of Zarephath" (Sigourney) **21**:309
The Widow; or, a Picture of Modern Times (Robinson) **142**:132, 184
The Widow Rugby's Husband, A Night at the Ugly Man's, and Other Tales of Alabama (Hooper)
See *A Ride with Old Kit Knucker, and Other Sketches, and Scenes of Alabama*
"The Widow's Home" (Robinson) **142**:136-37, 249, 278
The Widow's Marriage (Boker) **125**:21, 36, 58
"The Widow's Mite" (Trollope) **215**:212
The Widow's Only Son (Cumberland) **167**:198-99
"The Widow's Son" (Irving)
See "The Widow and Her Son"
The Widow's Son (Southworth) **26**:433
"Widow's Song" (Pinkney) **31**:270
"The Widow's Tale" (Crabbe) **26**:93, 129-30, 135
"A Widow's Tale" (Oliphant) **61**:205, 209, 211-2
"The Widow's Trials" (Parton) **86**:347
The Widow's Vow (Inchbald) **62**:143, 145-6, 148
Wie Anne Bäbi Jowäger haushaltet und wie es ihm mit dem Dokterngeht (Gotthelf) **117**:5, 7-8, 15, 17, 19, 23, 32, 35, 38-9, 52
"Wie Christen eine Frau gewinnt" (Gotthelf) **117**:6, 25
"Wie die Philosophie zum Besten des Volkes allgemeiner und nützlicher werden kann" (Herder) **186**:64
"Wie fünf Mädchen im branntwein jämmerlich umkommen" (Gotthelf) **117**:44, 51, 58
"Wie Joggeli eine Frau sucht" (Gotthelf) **117**:6, 35
Wie Uli der Knecht glücklich wird (Gotthelf) **117**:4, 7-8, 18, 24, 32, 35-6, 38, 40, 43
"Wie wenn am Feiertage ..." (Hölderlin) **16**:161, 173, 175, 190-91, 195; **187**:202-3, 205-6, 208, 224, 283
"Wiederkehr" (Hölderlin) **16**:185
"Wiegenlied eines jammernden Herzens" (Brentano) **191**:31-32
Wieland; or The Transformation (Brown) **22**:4-8, 11-14, 16-17, 19-20, 22-31, 33-40, 48-52, 54-5; **74**:4-7, 9-10, 13, 15-18, 21, 36-7, 41, 46-7, 49-51, 53-6, 60-1, 64, 68-70, 75-7, 80, 82-3, 92-5, 98, 103-05, 107-08, 110-12, 117, 120, 122-26, 129-30, 133-34, 137, 141-47, 149-50, 155-56, 159, 161,

163-64, 196-203; **122**:1-168
Wielands Gesammelte Schriften (Wieland) **177**:284
Wielands Werke (Wieland) **177**:243, 268, 284
Wielki cztowiek do matych interesbw (Fredro) **8**:285
"Wielkie-słowa" (Norwid) **17**:374
"The Wife" (Irving) **2**:376-77, 392; **19**:327-28, 331, 334, 348, 350; **95**:232, 237, 249, 265, 277
The Wife (Norton) **47**:248, 255; **205**:81, 85
"The Wife A-Lost" (Barnes) **75**:7, 73
"Wife and Two Children, Sleeping in the Same Chamber" (Hood) **16**:216
"The Wife A-Prais'd" (Barnes) **75**:73
"A Wife at Daybreak I Shall Be" (Dickinson) **77**:143
Wife Murderer; or, The Clemenceau Tragedy (Dumas)
See *L'affaire Clémenceau: Mémoire de l'accusé*
"The Wife of Asdrubal" (Hemans) **71**:294
"The Wife of Brittany" (Hayne) **94**:148-149, 153-58
The Wife of Claude (Dumas)
See *La femme de Claude*
"Wife to Husband" (Rossetti) **50**:267; **186**:262
"The Wife's Appeal" (Willis) **194**:302, 304
"A Wife's Duty" (Opie) **65**:171-3, 179, 182
The Wife's Trial (Lamb) **10**:404
The Wigwam and the Cabin (Simms) **3**:501-02, 505-06, 508, 510
"Wild Apples" (Thoreau) **7**:378; **207**:188, 197
The Wild Ass' Skin (Balzac)
See *La peau de chagrin*
The Wild Ass's Skin (Balzac)
See *La peau de chagrin*
Wild Bee of Australia: A Series of Poems with Prose Notes (Harpur) **114**:120, 122
"Wild Flower of Nature" (Petofi)
See "A természet vadvirága"
"Wild Flowers" (Campbell) **19**:181
"Wild Flowers" (Jefferies) **47**:102, 137
Wild Flowers (Bloomfield) **145**:148, 156-57, 160, 167-68, 176
The Wild Goose Chace (Dunlap) **2**:213-14
"The Wild Honey Suckle" (Freneau) **1**:314-17, 322-23; **111**:133, 141, 159
The Wild Irish Boy (Maturin) **6**:317, 322, 328, 331, 336, 341-42, 346; **169**:18, 20-23, 46, 48, 50, 74, 101-2, 114, 118, 120-29
The Wild Irish Girl (Morgan) **29**:386, 388-91
"Wild Kangaroo" (Kendall) **12**:191
Wild Life in a Southern County (Jefferies) **47**:88, 96-97, 103, 105, 108, 111-12, 121, 133, 136-37, 142
Wild Money (Ostrovsky)
See *Beshenye dengi*
"Wild Nights!" (Dickinson) **171**:96
"Wild Nights—Wild Nights" (Dickinson) **21**:43, 49, 58, 77; **77**:149
"Wild Oats" (Alcott)
See "Transcendental Wild Oats"
Wild Roses of Cape Ann and Other Poems (Larcom) **179**:171, 173-74
"The Wild Swans" (Andersen)
See "De vilde Svaner"
"Wild Turkey Hunting" (Thorpe) **183**:356
Wild Wales: Its People, Language, and Scenery (Borrow) **9**:45-49, 51, 54-56, 66
"Wild Wind" (Shevchenko)
See "Vitre bujnyj"
"Wild-Cat Hunting" (Thorpe) **183**:356
"The Wilderness and Our Indian Friends" (Moodie) **14**:231
Der Wildfang (Kotzebue) **25**:133, 145, 155
Wildfell Hall (Brontë)
See *The Tenant of Wildfell Hall*
"The Wild-Flower Nosegay" (Clare) **9**:84
"Wildflower Song" (Blake) **13**:173
"Wildgoose Lodge" (Carleton) **3**:85, 91, 96; **199**:18, 25, 33-34, 56, 103
"Die Wildschützen" (Ludwig) **4**:365
"An Wilhelm Hartlaub" (Mörike) **201**:271
Wilhelm Meister (Goethe) **90**:47-52, 57-64, 79-82, 85-6, 88, 102, 105
Wilhelm Meister (Gotthelf) **117**:22
Wilhelm Meister's Apprenticeship (Goethe)
See *Wilhelm Meisters Lehrjahre*
Wilhelm Meisters Lehrjahre (Goethe) **34**:59, 74-5, 88-9, 133; **90**:38-122
Wilhelm Meister's Travels (Goethe)
See *Wilhelm Meisters Wanderjahre; oder, Die Entsagenden*
Wilhelm Meisters Wanderjahre (Goethe)
See *Wilhelm Meisters Wanderjahre; oder, Die Entsagenden*
Wilhelm Meisters Wanderjahre; oder, Die Entsagenden (Goethe) **34**:73-4, 88-9, 94; **90**:43, 105; **154**:182-4, 203, 209-10, 233, 242, 271
Wilhelm Tell (Schiller) **39**:306, 321-22, 325, 330, 337, 346-47, 361, 368, 372, 377, 380, 385; **69**:168-283; **166**:146, 159, 173, 190
"Wilhelm von Schwerin" (Runeberg) **41**:312, 325-26
"Wilhemina" (Woolson) **82**:272, 286, 305, 307, 333
"The Will" (Edgeworth) **51**:89-90
"Will" (Hayne)
See "The Will and the Wing"
"The Will" (Very) **9**:387
A Will (Sacher-Masoch) **31**:287
"The Will and the Wing" (Hayne) **94**:145
The Will and the Wing (Hayne) **94**:134, 160
"The Will as Vision" (Pater) **7**:336
The Will in Nature (Schopenhauer)
See *Der Wille in der Natur*
"Will o' the Mill" (Stevenson) **5**:415, 418, 424, 431; **193**:209, 255, 277-78, 281
"A Will of Iron" (Leskov)
See "Zheleznaia volia"
"The Will of the People" (Boker) **125**:39
"Will Waterproof's Lyrical Monologue" (Tennyson) **30**:234
Der Wille in der Natur (Schopenhauer) **51**:294, 296-97; **157**:218, 235, 316, 318, 338
William Allair; or, Running Away to Sea (Wood) **178**:304
"William Bailey" (Crabbe) **26**:109
"William Bond" (Blake) **13**:172; **37**:22
"William Cowper" (Bagehot) **10**:40
William Lovell (Tieck) **5**:513, 515, 517-18, 522-23, 525, 527-28; **46**:375, 382, 384, 397-401, 409-11
"William Penn" (Herzen) **10**:348
William Shakespeare (Hugo) **3**:258, 273-74; **161**:193, 200-202; **189**:251, 255
"William Tell" (Bryant) **46**:47
William Tell (Schiller)
See *Wilhelm Tell*
"William the Silent" (Douglass) **7**:126
"William Wallace" (Baillie) **151**:121-2
"William Wilson" (Poe) **1**:492, 506; **16**:303, 314-16, 319, 329, 331, 336; **55**:194-5; **78**:260; **97**:180; **117**:213; **211**:253
"William's Views" (Hazlitt) **29**:144
"Willie and Katie, A pastoral" (Hogg) **109**:268
"Willie Has Gone to the War" (Foster) **26**:285
"Willie was a Wanton Wag" (Baillie)
See "The Merry Bachelor"
"Willie We Have Missed You" (Foster) **26**:298
"Willie Winkie" (Andersen)
Willing to Die (Le Fanu) **9**:299; **58**:273-5, 295, 301, 303
"Willkommen und Abschied" (Goethe) **4**:195
"The Willow and the Red Cliff" (Morris) **4**:429
"Willowwood" (Rossetti) **4**:496, 500-01, 512; 77;313, 339, 358
"Will's Will and His Two Thanksgivings" (Cooke) **110**:35
"Willst du, ich soll Hütten bauen?" (Grillparzer) **102**:174
"Willy Gilliland" (Ferguson) **33**:299
"Willy of the Dale" (Rowson) **182**:282
Willy Reilly and His Dear Coleen Bawn (Carleton) **3**:85, 87, 90
Willy Reilly and his dear Colleen Bawn (Carleton) **199**:10, 20, 97
"Wilson" (Poe)
See "William Wilson"
"Wilt Thou Be Gone, Love?" (Foster) **26**:298
"Wilton Harvey" (Sedgwick) **19**:445
"Winckelmann" (Pater) **7**:305, 312, 339; **90**:273, 296, 298, 300-01, 303, 305-06; **159**:295, 315-20, 324, 327
"Wind" (Dobell) **43**:46
"The Wind" (Morris) **4**:419, 423, 431-32, 444
"The Wind and Stream" (Bryant) **6**:165, 176; **46**:20
"Wind and Wave" (Patmore) **9**:349, 357
"The Wind Flower" (Very) **9**:372, 380
"Wind of the West Arise" (Darley) **2**:128
"The Wind Tells of Valdemar Daae and His Daughters" (Andersen) **7**:33, 35
"The Wind Tells the Story of Valdemar Daa and his Daughters" (Andersen)
See "The Wind Tells of Valdemar Daae and His Daughters"
"The Wind Waves o'er the Meadows Green" (Clare) **9**:111
"Wind-Clouds and Star-Drifts" (Holmes) **14**:125, 129; **81**:103, 105
"Windfield Plain" (Robinson) **142**:104
"The Windhover" (Hopkins) **17**:185, 198, 206, 211, 216, 221, 225, 232, 236-39, 246, 254-55, 257-60; **189**:5-7, 9, 29, 35, 47, 52, 60-64, 66-68, 75, 81, 90, 94, 110, 114, 145
"The Winding Banks of Erne" (Allingham) **25**:18, 20-21
"Windlass Song" (Allingham) **25**:8
"The Window" (Silva)
See "La ventana"
"Window Wat's Courtship" (Hogg) **4**:283
"Windows" (Hunt) **1**:417
"The Windows" (Mallarmé)
See "Les fenêtres"
"The Winds" (Bryant) **6**:175-76; **46**:7, 47
"The Winds drew off" (Dickinson) **171**:91
"Winds of Heaven" (Jefferies) **47**:101
"The Wind's Story" (Andersen) **7**:29
"The Wind's Tale" (Andersen)
See "The Wind Tells of Valdemar Daae and His Daughters"
"The Wind's Tidings in August, 1870" (Webster) **230**:240
Windsor Castle (Ainsworth) **13**:28, 31-2, 34, 36, 40, 43, 47-48
"A Windy Day in Summer" (Hopkins) **189**:88
Wine (Baudelaire)
See *Le vin*
"The Wine Bibber's Glory" (Maginn) **8**:441
"Wine Harvesting" (Verlaine)
See "Vendanges"
"Wine of Cyprus" (Barrett Browning) **61**:43
"The Wine of the Assassin" (Baudelaire)
See "Le vin de l'assassin"
Wine, Women, and Song (Symonds) **34**:323, 337
The Wing-and-Wing (Cooper)
See *Jack-o'-Lantern*
The Wing-and-Wing; or, Le Feu-Follet (Cooper) **1**:221-22; **54**:258
"Winged Hours" (Rossetti) **4**:498
"Winged Sphynx" (Fuller) **50**:247-8
Wingolf (Klopstock) **11**:235, 237; **225**:282-84, 286, 288, 297-98, 321
"Wings" (Lazarus) **8**:420
Wings for an Angel (Alencar)
See *Azas de Um Anjo*
"Winke zur Fortsetzung" (Hölderlin) **187**:241
"Winter" (Blind) **202**:30-31
"Winter" (Bloomfield) **145**:141
"Winter" (Clare) **9**:106; **86**:98, 110, 160-61
"Winter" (Lampman) **25**:189, 204; **194**:24, 52
"Winter" (Patmore) **9**:349, 357
"Winter" (Smith) **59**:315-6, 322

"Winter Coming" (Laforgue)
See "Derniers vers I"
"Winter-Break" (Lampman) **194**:52
"A Winter Day" (Leskov)
See "Zimnij den'"
Winter Day (Baillie) **71**:52; **151**:41, 86, 88-9, 93-4
"The Winter Evening" (Cowper) **8**:120, 128; **94**:23, 26, 28, 30, 44, 127, 129-30
"Winter Evening" (Lampman) **25**:180, 197, 204, 211; **194**:18, 29, 47, 51, 99
"Winter Evening" (Pushkin)
See "Zimniy Vecher"
Winter Evening Tales: Collected among the Cottagers in the South of Scotland (Hogg) **4**:276
"Winter Fields" (Clare) **86**:160
"Winter Hues Recalled" (Lampman) **25**:160, 164, 181, 192, 194, 200; **194**:30, 42, 52-53, 100, 103, 138
"Winter Hunt" (Grillparzer)
See "Jagd im Winter"
Winter Idyl (Whittier)
See *Snow-Bound: A Winter Idyl*
A Winter in Russia (Gautier)
See *Voyage en Russie*
"A Winter in the Country" (Hale) **75**:298
The Winter Journey (Muller)
See *Die Winterreise*
"Winter Joys" (Hale) **75**:294
"The Winter Landscape" (Mitford) **4**:401
"Winter Morning" (Mörike)
See "An einem Wintermorgen"
"Winter Morning's Walk" (Cowper) **8**:119, 129; **94**:24, 27
"Winter: My Secret" (Rossetti) **50**:299, 312; **186**:304
"A Winter Night" (Barnes) **75**:15, 97
"Winter Night" (Lenau) **16**:276
"The Winter Night" (Very) **9**:387
Winter Notes on Summer Impressions (Dostoevsky)
See *Zimnie zametki o letnikh vpechatleniiakh*
"A Winter Piece" (Bryant) **6**:168-69; **46**:43, 45, 47
A Winter Piece: Being a Serious Exhortation, with a Call to the Unconverted, and a Short Contemplation on the Death of Jesus Christ (Hammon) **5**:262-63, 265
"Winter Rain" (Rossetti) **2**:575
"A Winter Scene" (Bryant) **46**:21
"Winter Solitude" (Lampman) **194**:99
"The Winter Song" (Bloomfield) **145**:131
"Winter Song" (Bloomfield) **145**:154-55
"Winter-Store" (Lampman) **25**:183, 187, 204; **194**:17, 20, 23, 48, 51, 68, 70, 74, 81-82, 90-92, 139
Winter Studies and Summer Rambles in Canada (Jameson) **43**:304, 312, 321, 323, 328-45
"The Winter Theatres" (Lewes) **25**:291
"Winter Thought" (Lampman) **25**:166
"Winter Uplands" (Lampman) **25**:172, 185, 200, 210; **194**:87, 99, 101
"Winter Visitors" (Thoreau) **7**:378, 408
"A Winter Walk" (Thoreau) **138**:121
"The Winter Walk at Noon" (Cowper) **94**:27, 29-30
"Winter Winds Cold and Blea" (Clare) **9**:111
"Winter with the Gulf Stream" (Hopkins) **189**:120
"Winterfreuden" (Klopstock) **225**:310
Der Wintergarten (Arnim) **159**:18, 35, 42, 57-60, 62, 68, 84, 95-96, 99
Wintermarchen (Heine)
See *Deutschland: Ein Wintermärchen*
"Winternacht" (Keller) **2**:421
Die Winterreise (Muller) **73**:350-52, 360, 365-66, 373, 375, 380, 382-84, 387-96
"A Winter's Day" (Leskov)
See "Zimnij den'"
"Winter's gone the summer breezes" (Clare) **86**:87
"A Winter's Ramble in Grasmere Vale" (Wordsworth) **25**:421
"A Winter's Ramble in Grasmere's Vale" (Wordsworth) **138**:229-32
Winter's Tale (Heine)
See *Deutschland: Ein Wintermärchen*
"The Winter's Walk" (Norton) **47**:238, 241, 245
Winterslow: Essays and Characters Written There (Hazlitt) **29**:148
"Wintertag" (Meyer) **81**:147
"Wirkung in die Ferne" (Goethe) **4**:192
Der Wirrwarr (Kotzebue) **25**:142
"Das Wirtshaus" (Muller) **73**:394, 396
Das Wirtshaus im Spessart (Hauff) **185**:318, 334, 356
Wisbur (Stagnelius) **61**:253, 256-7
"Wisdom" (Cowper) **94**:75
Wisdom (Verlaine)
See *Sagesse*
"Wisdom and Innocence" (Newman) **38**:308
Wisdom and Language of India (Schlegel)
See *Über die Sprache und Weisheit der Indier*
"Wisdom as Contrasted with Faith and with Bigotry" (Newman) **38**:307
"The Wisdom of Ali" (Taylor) **89**:302, 304
"The Wise Delights of Love" (Patmore)
See "Deliciae Sapientiae de Amore"
"Wise in her Generation" (Levy) **59**:92, 95, 112; **203**:351, 353
The Wise Man of the East (Inchbald) **62**:144, 146-8
"A Wish" (Arnold) **29**:34
"The Wish" (Eminescu) **131**:287
"The Wish" (Lermontov) **126**:142
"A Wish" (Rogers) **69**:67, 79
"Wish" (Verlaine)
See "Voeu"
Wishing-Cap Papers (Hunt) **1**:417; **70**:279, 282
Wissenschaft der Logik (Hegel) **46**:190; **151**:237-38, 273, 276, 288-89, 348-54, 372
Die Wissenschaftslehre in ihrem allgemeinen Umrisse (Fichte) **62**:34
Wit and Wisdom from West Africa: A Collection of 2,859 Proverbs, Being an Attempt to Make Africans Delineate Themselves (Burton) **42**:35
"A Witch" (Barnes) **75**:75
"The Witch" (Shevchenko)
See "Vid'ma"
The Witch (Lamb) **10**:401
The Witch (Michelet)
See *La sorcière*
"Witch Aunt" (Lamb) **10**:402
"A Witch in the Nursery" (Horne) **127**:268
"The Witch of Atlas" (Shelley) **18**:326-27, 329, 345, 357-58, 362-63; **175**:232
"The Witch of East Cliff" (Moodie) **14**:231
"Witch of Fife" (Hogg) **4**:275, 280, 282-83, 285; **109**:240, 243, 248, 270, 279
"The Witch of Fyfe" (Southey) **8**:472
"The Witch of Hebron" (Harpur) **114**:99, 105, 144-46
"The Witch of Inky Dell" (Haliburton) **149**:285-87
"The Witch of Wenham" (Whittier) **8**:509, 529
"The Witch-Bride" (Allingham) **25**:18
Witchcraft (Baillie) **2**:40-41; **151**:11, 13, 55, 75, 117
"Witches, and Other Night Fears" (Lamb) **10**:410, 429, 437; **113**:173, 177-78, 200, 219, 250-51
The Witches' Frolic (Barham) **77**:7, 9, 41
"The Witches of Traquir" (Hogg) **109**:279
"A Witch's Chant" (Hogg) **4**:282; **109**:201
"The Witch's Daughter" (Whittier) **8**:515; **59**:351, 356, 371
"With a Flower" (Dickinson)
See "I Hide Myself within My Flower"
"With a Guitar, to Jane" (Shelley) **18**:362, 369-70
"With a lively sense of greeting" (Tyutchev)
See "Zhivym sochuvstviem priveta"
"With a Rose That Bloomed on the Day of John Brown's Martyrdom" (Alcott) **58**:48
"With Antecedents" (Whitman) **81**:335; **205**:162, 164, 202, 205
"With Garments Flowing" (Clare) **86**:87
"With Graceful Seat and Skilful Hand" (Clough) **27**:106
"With Muted Strings" (Verlaine) **51**:374
"With Pinions of Disdain" (Dickinson) **171**:216
"With the Night" (Lampman) **194**:52, 81-82
With Trumpet and Drum (Field) **3**:205-06
"With Two Words" (Meyer)
See "Mit zwei Worten"
"With Whom Is No Variableness, Neither Shadow of Turning" (Clough) **27**:84, 100
"Withdrawal" (Mörike)
See "Verborgenheit"
"Within a Budding Grove" (Browning) **79**:167
Within Living Memory (Grundtvig)
See *Mands Minde*
"Within my Garden, rides a Bird" (Dickinson) **77**:121; **171**:132-33
Within the Precincts (Oliphant) **61**:204, 209, 240, 243
"Without a Cent" (Alarcón)
See "Sin un cuarto"
Without a Dowry (Ostrovsky)
See *Besprídannitsa*
"Without Her" (Rossetti) **4**:514
"Withstanders" (Barnes) **75**:9
Witiko (Stifter) **41**:337, 339, 344, 346, 356, 358-60, 364, 369-75, 391; **198**:283-87
The Witlings (Burney) **54**:35
"A Witness From Beyond the Grave in Defense of Women" (Leskov)
See "Zagrobnyj svidetel"
"The Witnesses" (Longfellow) **2**:483; **45**:123, 155; **103**:290
"Der Witwer in der Brüdergemeinde" (Werner) **189**:330
"Wives" (Irving) **95**:235, 237
Wives and Daughters: An Every-Day Story (Gaskell) **5**:185-86, 188, 190, 192-93, 197-98, 201, 203-06; **70**:120, 123, 129, 132, 182, 185, 187, 193, 197, 199-200, 214; **97**:110, 113, 124; **137**:54, 167; **214**:188, 190-91, 193, 241-50
Wives as They Were and Maids as They Are (Inchbald) **62**:144-9, 185
"The Wives of the Dead" (Hawthorne) **2**:322
The Wizard's Son (Oliphant) **11**:442-3, 446-9, 454; **61**:216
"Wo?" (Heine) **147**:129
"Wo schlägt ein Herz, das bleibend fühlt?" (Brentano) **191**:67-68
"Woak Hill" (Barnes) **75**:8, 13, 46, 48
"Woak Wer Good Enough Woonce" (Barnes) **75**:69, 82
Woe from Wit (Griboedov)
See *Gore ot Uma*
"Woe to the Double-Tongued" (Tennyson) **30**:293
"Wohin?" (Muller) **73**:350, 363-64, 369, 374
"Wohlan! so bin ich deiner los" (Brentano) **191**:120
Wojna Chocimska (Krasicki) **8**:398
"A Wold Friend" (Barnes) **75**:9
"The Wold Waggon" (Barnes) **75**:82-3
"The Wold Wall" (Barnes) **75**:20, 26, 67-8
"Wolf and Hound" (Gordon) **21**:155, 158-59, 164-65, 176, 183, 188
"The Wolf and the Cat" (Krylov) **1**:435
"The Wolf Screamed" (Rimbaud)
See "Le loup criait"
"Wolfert Webber" (Irving) **2**:390; **19**:337
"Wolfert's Roost" (Irving) **2**:384; **19**:331
The Wolf-Leader (Dumas)
See *Le Meneur de Loups*

Wolves and Sheep (Ostrovsky)
See *Volki i ovtsy*
The Wolves and the Lamb (Thackeray) **213**:322-25
"Woman" (Baillie) **151**:41
"Woman" (Crabbe) **26**:78
"Woman" (Emerson) **98**:166-69, 171-72
"Woman" (Gogol)
See "Zhenshchina"
"Woman" (Halleck) **47**:57, 78, 81
Woman (Michelet)
See *La femme, la famille, et le prêtre*
"Woman and Fame" (Hemans) **71**:296-97
Woman and Her Master (Morgan) **29**:396-97
"Woman . . . Apple of Discord" (Eminescu) **131**:288
A Woman Hater (Reade) **2**:547, 549; **74**:254-57, 264-65, 284, 289
Woman in the Nineteenth Century (Fuller) **5**:156-57, 163-65, 168, 171-73; **50**:217, 228-235, 243, 245-51, 253-60; **211**:91-93, 100, 105, 117, 123, 130, 135-38, 140-43, 146-52, 155-58, 162-63, 165, 171, 173-75, 177-78, 183, 185, 187, 190-91
"Woman in the Year 2000" (Bellamy) **147**:96
"The Woman in White" (Dumas) **71**:185
The Woman in White (Collins) **1**:173-75, 178-83, 187-88, 191; **18**:61, 63-5, 67, 69, 72, 78-9; **93**:2-3, 7-12, 14, 19-20, 24-7, 30, 33-4, 46-7, 50, 52-6, 58-9, 61-3, 65-6, 86-91
The Woman Never Vexed (Planché) **42**:273
"Woman of Arles" (Daudet) **1**:238
The Woman of Paris (Becque)
See *La Parisienne*
The Woman of the Pharisees (Caballero)
See *La Farisea*
A Woman of Thirty (Balzac)
See "La femme de trente ans"
"The Woman of Three Cows" (Mangan) **27**:283, 310-11
"The Woman of Zakynthos" (Solomos)
See "I gynaika tis Zakynthos"
"Woman on the Field of Battle" (Hemans) **71**:275, 293
Woman; or, Ida of Athens (Morgan) **29**:386, 396
"Woman Question" (Brownson) **50**:56
Woman Snake (Gozzi)
See *La donna serpente*
"A Woman Sold" (Webster) **230**:228
A Woman Sold (Webster) **230**:226, 260, 263-67
A Woman Sold, and Other Poems (Webster) **230**:227
The Woman Taken in Adultery (Fontane)
See *L'adultera*
"Woman the Poet of Nature" (Hale) **75**:324-25
"A Woman Waits for Me" (Whitman) **31**:402; **81**:329; **205**:219
"Woman! when I behold thee" (Keats) **73**:147
Womanly Profiles (Alencar) **157**:9
"Woman's Christmas" (Larcom) **179**:170
"Woman's Easter" (Larcom) **179**:170
The Woman's Kingdom (Craik) **38**:122, 132
"A Woman's Last Word" (Browning) **19**:127, 131, 155, 158; **79**:163
A Woman's Life (Maupassant)
See *Une vie*
"The Woman's Parliament" (Neal) **161**:336
Woman's Record; or, Sketches of All Distinguished Women, from "The Beginning" Till A.D. 1850. (Hale) **75**:280, 283, 303-05, 307-09, 317, 335-42, 349, 353, 355, 360-61
"A Woman's Revenge" (Barbey d'Aurevilly)
See "La vengeance d'une femme"
The Woman's Reward (Norton) **47**:248, 255; **205**:81, 85-86, 131-32
"Woman's Rights—and Woman's Wrongs" (Neal) **161**:334
"A Woman's Shortcomings" (Barrett Browning) **61**:43
A Woman's Thoughts about Women (Craik) **38**:126-27, 129, 130
Woman's Wrongs: A Series of Tales (Jones) **222**:134, 139-41, 144-47
"Women" (King)
See "La mujer"
"Women and Club Life" (Levy) **59**:92; **203**:353-54
"Women and Money" (Parton) **86**:351
"Women and Roses" (Browning) **19**:127
"Women As They Are" (Rowson) **69**:129; **182**:257, 260
Women as They Are; or, The Manners of the Day (Gore) **65**:20, 22
Women in Sacred History (Stowe) **195**:161
"Women Looking for Lice" (Rimbaud)
See "Les chercheuses de poux"
"Women of Cairo" (Nerval) **1**:475
The Women of the North (Stagnelius) **61**:248, 253
Women; or, Pour et contre (Maturin) **6**:320-23, 328, 332-33, 335, 340-43, 347; **169**:18, 22-23, 46, 48-50, 74, 114, 120, 122-23, 126-29
"Women Politicians" (Maupassant)
See "Politiciennes"
"Women's Dignity" (Schiller)
See "Würde der Frauen"
"A Women's Love and a Wife's Duty" (Opie) **65**:172
Women's Songs (Karadzic)
See *Ženske pjesme*
"Wonder is not precisely Knowing" (Dickinson) **77**:77
Wonder Stories Told for Children (Andersen)
See *Eventyr, fortalte for bøorn*
Wonder Tales Told for Children (Andersen)
See *Eventyr, fortalte for bøorn*
A Wonder-Book for Girls and Boys (Hawthorne) **2**:299, 301, 306, 313; **17**:149-50; **23**:214; **158**:233
The Wonderful Advantages of adventuring in the Lottery!!! (More) **141**:179
Wonderful Adventures of Mrs. Seacole in Many Lands (Seacole) **147**:253-54, 256-57, 260, 262-64, 267, 273, 281-82, 289-90, 292-96, 304, 310, 312-15, 321-27, 329-34, 337-38
"A Wonderful Case of General Perplexity" ("Udivimielsoftnyj sluchaj vsieobshchiego niedoumieniya") (Leskov) **174**:141
The Wonderful History of Peter Schlemihl (Chamisso)
See *Peter Schlemihls Wundersame Geschichte*
Wonderful Stories for Children (Andersen)
See *Eventyr, fortalte for børn*
Wonderful Tales (Andersen)
See *Eventyr, fortalte for børn*
Wonderful Tales for Children (Andersen)
See *Eventyr, fortalte for børn*
Wonderland (Dodgson)
See *Alice's Adventures in Wonderland*
The Wonderous Tale of Cocky, Clucky, and Cackle (Brentano)
See *Gockel, Hinkel und Gackeleia: Märchen, wiedererzählt*
"The Wondersmith" (O'Brien) **21**:234-39, 242, 249-51, 253
"A Wondrous City" (Baratynsky)
See "Chudnyy grad poroy solyotsya..."
"A wondrous city at times emerges..." (Baratynsky)
See "Chudnyy grad poroy solyotsya..."
The Wondrous Tale of Alroy (Disraeli) **2**:138; **39**:3, 22, 24, 39-40, 42, 46, 66; **79**:202-07, 211, 214-18, 227-28, 233, 269, 273-74, 282
The Wondrous Tale of Ikey Solomons (Barham) **77**:6
"The Wood" (Reynolds) **146**:173
"The Wood beyond the World" (Morris) **4**:425, 437
The Wood Daemon (Lewis) **11**:305
Wood Magic (Jefferies) **47**:93-94, 101, 112, 124-27, 129-31, 137
"The Wood Nymph" (Andersen) **79**:82, 84
"The Wood of Saint John" (Silva)
See "Los maderos de San Juan"
"Woodcock Fire-Hunting" (Thorpe) **183**:357
Woodcraft; or, Hawks about the Dovecote (Simms) **3**:507-09, 513-14
"The Woodcutter" (Leskov)
See "Povest' o bogougodnom drovokole"
"The Woodcutter's Hut" (Lampman) **25**:186, 188, 202, 218
"Wooden Steeds" (Verlaine)
See "Chevaux de bois"
"Woodland Hallo" (Bloomfield) **145**:133
The Woodlands; or, A Treatise on the Preparation of the Ground for Planting (Cobbett) **49**:110, 114, 132, 151
"The Woodlark" (Lanier) **118**:241
"The Woodman and the Nightingale" (Shelley) **18**:373
"The Woodman's Daughter" (Patmore) **9**:327, 348
"Woodnotes" (Emerson) **1**:296-99; **38**:169, 178
"Woodnotes II" (Emerson) **38**:184, 186-87; **98**:179
"The Woods" (Ridge) **82**:185
The Wood-Spirit: A Novel (Jones) **222**:116, 157
"The Woodspurge" (Rossetti) **4**:491, 512, 516, 526; **77**:308
Woodstock (Scott) **15**:309, 316; **69**:304
"The Woody Hollow" (Barnes) **75**:95
"The Wooing of Gheezis" (Crawford) **127**:214
"The Wooing of Hallbiorn" (Morris) **4**:421, 434
The Woolgatherer (Hogg) **4**:285
"Woone smile mwore" (Barnes) **75**:7
"A Word about America" (Arnold) **126**:95
"A Word About Lomonosov" (Radishchev) **190**:313
"A Word About Rhyme" (Verlaine)
See "Un mot sur la rime"
"A Word about Tom Jones" (Lewes) **25**:306
"The Word 'Aesthetic'" (Peabody) **169**:202
"A Word dropped careless on a Page" (Dickinson) **77**:107
A Word for Nature (Cumberland) **167**:193-97
"A Word for the Novel Writers" (Moodie) **113**:296
"A Word More About America" (Arnold) **218**:258, 261
"A Word on Fools" (Bestuzhev)
See "Nechto o gluptsakh"
"A Word on the Annuals" (Thackeray) **213**:327
"A Word on the Drama" (Hebbel)
See "Mein Wort über das Drama"
"A Word Out of the Sea" (Whitman) **205**:336
"A Word to the Elect" (Brontë) **4**:51
"A Word to the Public" (Bulwer-Lytton) **1**:155
"A Word to the Sun to Begin With" (Laforgue)
See "Un Mot au Soleil pour commencer"
"Word to Two Young Ladies" (Bloomfield) **145**:154
Wordless Romances (Verlaine)
See *Romances sans paroles*
Words (Whitman) **81**:286-87
"The words of delusion" (Schiller)
See "Die Worte des Wahns"
"Words of Encouragement" (Garrison) **149**:258
"The words of faith" (Schiller)
See "Die Worte des Glaubens"
"The Words of Rosalind's Scroll" (Barrett Browning) **61**:69
"Words to the Reader" (Jones) **222**:131
"Wordsworth" (Arnold) **89**:86
"Wordsworth" (Pater) **7**:306, 338; **90**:296, 298, 305; **159**:226
"Wordsworth" (Whittier) **59**:364
"Wordsworth, Tennyson, and Browning; or, Pure, Ornate, and Grotesque Art in Poetry" (Bagehot) **10**:30, 57, 62
"Wordsworth's Poetry" (De Quincey) **4**:61

"Wordsworth's Thanksgiving Ode" (Reynolds) **146**:206
"Work" (Lamb) **10**:405
Work (Alcott)
See *Work: A Story of Experience*
Work (Barrett Browning) **66**:44
Work: A Story of Experience (Alcott) **6**:16; **58**:10-5, 17-9, 21-3, 28, 37, 49, 69, 81-5, 87-8; **83**:6, 9, 30, 33, 57; **218**:7, 23, 37, 40, 42-43, 47-49
"Work and Contemplation" (Barrett Browning) **61**:43
"The Work and Mission of My Life" (Wagner) **119**:189
"Work without Hope" (Coleridge) **9**:159; **197**:215
"Workers" (Rimbaud)
See "Ouvriers"
"The Workhouse Clock" (Hood) **16**:209, 228, 235, 239
Working Notes (Dickens) **113**:130, 133, 137
"The Workingman's Drink" (Baudelaire) **6**:83
"The Working-Man's Wife" (Jones) **222**:144-47
Works (Baillie) **71**:16-17; **151**:113
Works (Byron) **109**:123, 126
Works (Eminescu) **131**:295, 297, 319
Works (Hazlitt) **82**:97-101
Works (Lanier) **118**:248
Works (Mackenzie) **41**:184, 213
Works (Moore) **110**:181
Works (Pisarev)
See *Sočinenija*
Works (Poe)
See *The Collected Works of Edgar Allan Poe*
Works (Rimbaud)
See *Oeuvres complètes*
Works (Tonna)
See *The Works of Charlotte Elizabeth*
Works IV, Posthumous Poems (Eminescu) **33**:266
Works V (Eminescu) **33**:266
"Works and Days" (Emerson) **1**:280, 290; **38**:150
The Works and Life of Walter Bagehot (Bagehot) **10**:31
Works, 1899 (Thackeray)
See *The Works of William Makepeace Thackeray*
Works, 1908 (Thackeray)
See *The Oxford Thackeray*
The Works of Alexander Hamilton (Hamilton) **49**:308
The Works of Arthur Murphy, Esq. In Seven Volumes (Murphy) **229**:229, 234, 236, 239
The Works of Charles and Mary Lamb (Lamb) **10**:389
The Works of Charles and Mary Lamb (Lamb) **125**:345-50, 375
The Works of Charles Lamb (Lamb) **113**:180-81, 184, 186, 202-05, 279-81
The Works of Charlotte Elizabeth (Tonna) **135**:193, 195
The Works of Francis Parkman (Parkman)
See *France and England in North America*
The Works of Gerald Griffin (Griffin) **7**:196
Works of Hannah More (More) **141**:217, 219, 224, 267, 279-82, 303
Works of Jeremy Bentham (Bentham) **38**:53-4, 80, 90, 92
The Works of Joel Barlow (Barlow) **223**:73-85
The Works of John C. Calhoun (Calhoun) **15**:25
Works of Love (Kierkegaard)
See *Kjerlighedens Gjerninger*
Works of Love: Some Christian Reflections in the Form of Discourses (Kierkegaard)
See *Kjerlighedens Gjerninger*
The Works of Maria Edgeworth (Edgeworth) **1**:258
Works of Peter Porcupine (Cobbett)
See *Porcupine's Works*
Works of Shakespeare (Blair) **75**:129-30, 132
The Works of the Ettrick Shepherd (Hogg) **4**:279; **109**:192, 200-01, 203-05, 207, 274
The Works of Thomas Carlyle (Carlyle) **70**:64
Works of Thomas De Quincey (De Quincey) **198**:4
The Works of Thomas Lovell Beddoes (Beddoes) **154**:86, 89-90
Works of Virgil (Warton) **118**:337, 353
The Works of William Blake, Poetic, Symbolic, and Critical (Blake) **127**:3
The Works of William Carleton (Carleton) **199**:38, 45
The Works of William Makepeace Thackeray (Thackeray) **213**:262, 265-67
"The World" (Rossetti) **2**:561; **66**:305; **186**:304-5
"The World" (Very) **9**:387
The World a Mask (Boker) **125**:20-21, 28, 36, 58, 82
"The World and the Quietist" (Arnold) **29**:34-5
"The World and the Soul" (Harpur) **114**:100, 126, 166
The World as Will and Idea (Schopenhauer)
See *Die Welt als Wille und Vorstellung*
The World as Will and Representation (Schopenhauer)
See *Die Welt als Wille und Vorstellung*
The World before Them (Moodie) **14**:226
"The World Below the Brine" (Whitman) **31**:431
"A World for a Sonnet" (Isaacs)
See "Un mundo por un soneto"
The World in a Man-of-War (Melville)
See *White-Jacket; or, The World in a Man-of-War*
"The World of Dreams" (Crabbe) **26**:118, 126, 139; **121**:81-2
"The World. Self-Destruction" (Rossetti) **50**:285
The World Well Lost (Linton) **41**:166
"The World-feels Dusty/When We stop to Die" (Dickinson) **77**:163
Worldly Apes with a Smattering of Various Arts (Ueda Akinari)
See *Shodo kikimimi sekenzaru*
Worldly Monkeys with Ears for the Arts (Ueda Akinari)
See *Shodo kikimimi sekenzaru*
"The World's Convention" (Whittier) **8**:491
World's End (Jefferies) **47**:93
"The World's Epigram" (Allingham) **25**:6
"The World's Justice" (Lazarus) **109**:311, 336-37
"The World-Soul" (Emerson) **1**:296
"Wormwood and Night-Shade" (Gordon) **21**:150, 154, 160, 167, 181
"Worship" (Emerson) **38**:149
"Die Worte des Glaubens" (Schiller) **39**:388; **166**:122
"Die Worte des Wahns" (Schiller) **166**:122
"The Worth of Hours" (Milnes) **61**:136
The Worthies of Yorkshire and Lancashire (Coleridge) **90**:15
Worthy of Pity (Fredro)
See *Godzien litości*
Wotton Reinfred (Carlyle) **70**:44
"Would I Die or Should You Die" (Eminescu) **131**:294
"Would I Knew" (Allingham) **25**:7, 18
"Wound in the Side" (Meyer)
See "Die Seitenwunde"
"The Wound-Dresser" (Whitman) **4**:558, 582; **81**:313, 320-22; **205**:159, 339
"A Wounded Deer—leaps highest—" (Dickinson) **171**:112, 161, 167
"The Wounded Hussar" (Campbell) **19**:190, 193
"Wounded in the House of Friends" (Whitman) **205**:312
Woyzeck (Büchner) **26**:4, 7, 9-11, 14, 16-22, 25-7, 35-9, 41-2, 45-7, 49, 55-7, 62, 65, 67, 69; **146**:3-4, 7-12, 15-16, 18-20, 22-24, 38, 40, 44, 51-58, 63, 65-66, 91, 93, 95-103, 106-7
"The Wraith of the Rose" (Osgood) **141**:331-32
"The Wrath of Samson" (Vigny)
See "La colère de Samson"
"The Wreath and the Chain" (Moore) **110**:177, 180
"Wreath of Sonnets" (Preseren)
See "Sonetni venec"
A Wreath of Wild Flowers from New England (Osgood) **141**:319-20, 323, 330, 341, 354-55
"Wreath the Bowl" (Moore) **110**:190
"The Wreck" (Tennyson) **202**:291
"The Wreck" (Wergeland) **5**:537
"The Wreck of Rivermouth" (Whittier) **8**:506, 509, 513, 529
"The Wreck of the Deutschland" (Hopkins) **17**:183-84, 186, 188, 194-95, 202, 207-09, 215, 217, 220, 222, 224-25, 229-32, 238-39, 242-43, 245-46, 250-58, 260; **189**:5, 10, 12, 16, 19-20, 22, 46-48, 51-52, 54, 62, 74, 76, 83-84, 88-90, 105, 109, 115, 120, 135, 138-39, 142-45
"Wreck of the Emelie" (Clare) **9**:125
"The Wreck of the Hesperus" (Longfellow) **2**:472, 493; **45**:99, 116, 135, 140, 144, 153, 155, 158, 179-80; **103**:298
The Wrecker (Stevenson) **5**:411, 415, 522; **193**:211-12, 214, 216, 221, 223-24, 346
The Wretched (Hugo)
See *Les misérables*
"Wretched! All Gifts . . ." (Verlaine)
See "Malheureux! Tous les dons . . ."
"The Wretched Dionysos" (Eminescu)
See "Sarmanul Dionis"
"A Writer's Confession" (Gogol) **162**:27, 30-31
A Writer's Diary (Dostoevsky)
See *Dnevnik pisatelya*
Writer's Diary (Dostoevsky)
See *Dnevnik pisatelya*
"Writing Under Difficulties" (Parton) **86**:373
Writings (Hallam) **110**:120
Writings (Jefferson) **103**:195, 198
Writings (Lowell) **90**:220
Writings (Novalis)
See *Schriften*
The Writings of Henry David Thoreau (Thoreau) **138**:67; **207**:191, 219-20, 222, 224, 227, 231-35
The Writings of James Madison (Madison) **126**:278
The Writings of John Greenleaf Whittier (Whittier) **8**:506
Writings of Thomas De Quincey (De Quincey)
See *De Quincey's Writings*
Writings on India (Mill) **179**:356, 361
"Written at Bamborough Castle" (Bowles) **103**:67
"Written at Bignor Park in Sussex, in August, 1799" (Smith)
See "Sonnet 92"
"Written at Exmouth, midsummer 1795" (Smith)
See "Sonnet 68"
"Written at Midnight" (Rogers) **69**:68
written at midnight on the River St. Lawrence (Moodie) **113**:345
"Written at Ostend. July 22, 1787" (Bowles) **103**:68, 72
"Written at Rome, 1833" (Emerson) **38**:190
"Written at the Close of Spring" (Smith)
See "Sonnet 2"
"Written at Tinemouth" (Bowles)
See "Sonnet Written at Tinemouth, Northumberland"
"Written at Tinemouth, Northumberland, After a Tempestuous Voyage" (Bowles)
See "Sonnet Written at Tinemouth, Northumberland"
"Written in a Bible" (Coleridge) **90**:32
"Written in a tempestuous night, on the coast of Sussex" (Smith)
See "Sonnet 66"

"Written in a Thunderstorm" (Clare) **9**:102
"Written in Autumn" (Clare) **9**:121
"Written in Emerson's Essays" (Arnold) **29**:34
"Written in Farm Wood, South Downs, in May 1784" (Smith)
See "Sonnet 31"
"Written in Germany, On one of the coldest days of the Century" (Wordsworth) **111**:235
"Written in Spring" (Allston) **2**:26
"Written in the Church-Yard at Middleton in Sussex" (Smith)
See "Sonnet 44"
"Written in the Cloisters of Christ's Hospital" (Dyer) **129**:148
"Written in the First Leaf of a Child's Memorandum-Book" (Lamb) **125**:347, 361
"Written on a Marble" (Barbauld) **50**:16; **185**:92-93
"Written on the Day" (Keats) **73**:147, 253, 332
"Written on the sea shore.—October, 1784" (Smith)
See "Sonnet 12"
The Wrong Box (Stevenson) **5**:409; **193**:287-99
The Wrongs of Woman (Tonna) **135**:195-96, 199-200, 207-17, 220-21, 223-25
The Wrongs of Woman, Part I (Tonna)
See "Milliners and Dressmakers"
The Wrongs of Woman, Part II (Tonna)
See "The Forsaken Home"
The Wrongs of Woman, Part III (Tonna)
See "The Little Pin Headers"
The Wrongs of Woman, Part IV (Tonna)
See "The Lace Runners"
The Wrongs of Women (Tonna)
See *The Wrongs of Woman*
"The Wryneck's Nest" (Clare) **86**:133
"Wstęp do bajek" (Krasicki) **8**:402
"Die wunderbare Rede" (Meyer) **81**:154
Wunderhorn (Brentano)
See *Des Knaben Wunderhorn: Alte deutsche Lieder*
Die Wunderkinder (Schumann)
See *Florestan*
"Die wunderliche Prinzessin" (Eichendorff) **225**:44
"Die Wunderlichen Nachbarskinder" (Goethe) **4**:196
"Wunsch" (Meyer) **81**:150
"Wünschelrute" (Eichendorff) **225**:51-53
"Würde der Frauen" (Schiller) **166**:141
"Die Wurmlinger Kapelle" (Lenau) **16**:275, 282
Wuthering Heights (Brontë) **16**:63-9, 71-5, 77-8, 80, 82-3, 85-6, 88-90, 92-7, 100-01, 103, 105-17, 122-26; **35**:107-97; **165**:1-159
Wyandotté (Cooper) **203**:39, 46-47, 74-75, 86-87
Wyandotté; or, The Hutted Knoll (Cooper) **1**:204-05, 217; **54**:258, 277, 280
Wych Hazel (Warner) **146**:235, 261
Wychowanka (Fredro) **8**:293
Wylder's Hand (Le Fanu) **9**:299, 301-03, 309, 311-12, 316-18; **58**:251, 266, 268-9, 271-4, 288-9, 301
"Wynken, Blynken, and Nod" (Field) **3**:205-06, 209-10, 212
"Wyoming" (Halleck) **47**:65, 71
The Wyvern Mystery (Le Fanu) **58**:273-4
"Xan" (Castro) **78**:2
"Xantippe" (Levy) **59**:92, 102, 104, 106-7; **203**:328-30, 332-33, 335, 350
Xantippe and Other Verse (Levy) **59**:86, 92, 106-7
Xenien (Goethe) **4**:193
Xenien (Schiller) **39**:362
"Xenophanes" (Emerson) **1**:297; **98**:179
"Xenophanes" (Lampman) **25**:184; **194**:34, 38
"Xigante scos olmos" (Castro) **78**:3
"Ximenes" (Polidori) **51**:233
Ximenes, The Wreath, and Other Poems (Polidori) **51**:201
Xudoznik (Shevchenko) **54**:362, 365, 371, 381, 387, 390, 392, 396-8
"A xusticia pola man" (Castro) **78**:42
"A XXX dedicándole estas poesías" (Espronceda) **39**:108-09
Yager's Songs and Poems of the War of 1813 (Fouqué) **2**:267
"Yak by vy znaly panychi" (Shevchenko) **54**:394
Yakov Pasynkov (Turgenev) **21**:414, 418; **122**:242, 245, 268
"Yale Commencement Poem" (Barlow) **223**:60
"Yamiyo" (Ichiyō) **49**:353
"Yamizakura" (Ichiyō) **49**:334, 341
"A Yankee Christmas" (Smith) **187**:319
Yankee Chronology (Dunlap) **2**:211, 213, 218
"Yankee Eating and Horse Feeding" (Haliburton) **149**:296
A Yankee in Canada, with Anti-Slavery and Reform Papers (Thoreau) **7**:361; **21**:347, 353; **61**:339; **207**:191, 213, 321
The Yankey in London (Tyler) **3**:571-72, 574
"Yardley Oak" (Cowper) **8**:102, 116, 118-23, 139-40; **94**:39, 119
Yarns (Harris)
See *Sut Lovingood: Yarns Spun by a "Nat'ral Born Durn'd Fool"*
"Yarrow Revisited" (Wordsworth) **166**:213
"Yarrow Unvisited" (Wordsworth) **166**:213
"Yarrow Visited" (Wordsworth) **166**:213
"Yarrows" (Wordsworth) **12**:431
Yasaisho (Ueda Akinari) **131**:19, 45
Yasumikoto (Ueda Akinari) **131**:20, 51
"Yazykovu" (Baratynsky)
See "To N. M. Yazykov"
"Ye Mariners of England" (Campbell) **19**:165, 168, 179, 181-82, 185, 190-93, 195-96
"Ye Wearie Wayfarer" (Gordon) **21**:159-61, 173, 177, 179-80
A Year at Hartlebury; or, The Election (Disraeli) **39**:74
"The Year Clock" (Barnes) **75**:32
"A Year in Heaven" (Larcom) **179**:177
A Year in the Sahel (Fromentin)
See *Un année dans le sahel*
"The Year LVII of the Republic, One and Indivisible" (Herzen) **10**:338
A Year of Consolation (Kemble) **18**:182-83
The Year of Our Lord (Droste-Hülshoff) **3**:194
"A Year's Courtship" (Timrod) **25**:361-62
A Year's Life (Lowell) **2**:502, 515; **90**:221
Years of Boyhood (Leskov)
See *Detskie gody*
Years of Childhood (Aksakov)
See *Detskie gody Bagrova-vnuka*
The Years of Childhood of Bagrov, the Grandson (Aksakov)
See *Detskie gody Bagrova-vnuka*
A Year's Residence in the United States (Cobbett)
See *A Year's Residence in the United States of America*
A Year's Residence in the United States of America (Cobbett) **49**:110, 113, 120, 153
"A Year's Spinning" (Barrett Browning) **66**:60
"Years, You Years to Come" (Arany)
See "Evek, ti még jövendőévek"
"Yeast" (Huxley) **67**:83
Yeast (Kingsley) **35**:202-04, 209, 211-15, 219-22, 226-28, 230-31, 233-36, 241-42, 244, 246-53, 255
The Yellow Dwarf (Planché) **42**:273, 278-79, 288-89, 292, 294, 296
The Yellow Mask (Collins) **1**:180
"The Yellow Violet" (Bryant) **6**:158, 169, 193; **46**:3, 6, 25, 40-1
"The Yellow Violet" (Very) **9**:372
"Yellow Wagtail's Nest" (Clare) **9**:85
"Yellowhammer's Nest" (Clare) **9**:85
The Yellowplush Correspondence (Thackeray)
See *The Yellowplush Papers*
The Yellowplush Papers (Thackeray) **5**:444, 447, 450, 465, 469, 481, 506; **14**:420; **43**:381; **169**:242; **213**:207, 285, 346
The Yemassee (Simms) **3**:499-500, 502, 506-08, 511-12, 514
"Yermolai and the Miller's Wife" (Turgenev)
See "Ermolaj i mel'ničicha"
"Yermolay and the Miller's Wife" (Turgenev)
See "Ermolaj i mel'ničicha"
"Yes, lower to the level" (Osgood) **141**:321
"Yes, You Inspire Me . . ." (Verlaine)
See "Oui, tu m'inspires . . ."
"Yeshcho listok iz dnevnika gvardeyskogo ofitsera" (Bestuzhev) **131**:186
Yestereve came a knock on the portals of Hell (Grundtvig)
See *I Kvæld blev der banket paa Helvedesport*
Yesteryear and Latterday (Verlaine)
See *Jadis et naguère*
Yet Another Philosophy of History (Herder)
See *Ideen zur Philosophie der Geschichte der Menschheit*
"Yet—If There were . . ." (Laforgue)
See "Pourtant!—S'il y avait . . ."
"Les yeux des pauvres" (Baudelaire) **155**:86-89
Yevgeny Onegin (Pushkin) **3**:409-15, 417-18, 421-25, 431-34, 436-48, 451, 455, 459, 461-62, 464; **27**:361-405; **83**:243, 245-47, 249-51, 269-70, 304-05, 308, 318-19, 323, 33, 334-38, 350, 353-54, 357, 361, 372-73
"The Yew Tree" (Wordsworth)
See "Lines Left upon a Seat in a Yew-tree"
"The Yew Trees" (Wordsworth) **12**:452
"Yew-tree Seat" (Wordsworth)
See "Lines Left upon a Seat in a Yew-tree"
"Yey" (Bestuzhev) **131**:150
"Yid Somersault" (Leskov)
See "Židovskaja kuvyrkalegija"
Yin-chien (Li Ju-chen) **137**:206
"Yo cantar, cantar, canté" (Castro) **78**:55, 59
Yö ja päivä (Kivi) **30**:53
"Yo quiero ser cómico" (Larra) **130**:248-49
"Yoke and Star" (Martí)
See "Yugo y Estrella"
"The Yonghy-Bonghy-Bò" (Lear)
See "The Courtship of the Yonghy Bonghy Bo"
"Yonnondio" (Whitman) **31**:434; **81**:345, 347
"Yorktown Centennial Lyric" (Hayne) **94**:145
"You Add Tomorrow to Your Days" (Eminescu) **33**:246
"You Are All That Is Dear To My Heart" (Pavlova)
See "Ty vse, chto serdtsu milo"
"You are calm . . ." (Verlaine)
See "Vous êtes calme . . ."
"You are not at all . . ." (Verlaine)
See "Tu n'es pas du tout . . ."
"You are old Father William" (Dodgson) **139**:29
"You Ask Me, Why, Though Ill at Ease" (Tennyson) **30**:293
You Can't Live As You Want To (Ostrovsky)
See *Ne tak zhiví kak khóchetsya*
"You, dead, dead, dead" (Verlaine) **51**:372
"You Felons on Trial in Courts" (Whitman) **31**:372
"You Incorrigible . . ." (Verlaine)
See "Incorrigible, toi . . ."
"You Lingering Sparse Leaves of Me" (Whitman) **31**:434
"You saw him in society circles" (Tyutchev)
See "Ty zrel ego v krugo bol shogo sveta"
"You saw him in the mundane spheres" (Tyutchev)
See "Ty zrel ego v krugo bol shogo sveta"
"You So Much Tortured Me with Words of Love" (Eminescu) **131**:287
You Suffer Through No Fault of Your Own (Ostrovsky) **57**:209-10
"You Who Have Lived on in My Beggarly Heart" (Pavlova) **138**:34

"You Will Hear the Judgment of a Fool" (Turgenev) **122**:283
"You Would Place the Whole Universe in Your Alley" (Baudelaire)
See "Tu mettrais l'univers entier dans tu ruelle"
"Yound Death" (Rossetti) **50**:292
"Young Achilles" (Symonds) **34**:356
The Young Acrobat (Alger) **83**:118
The Young Adventurer; or, Tom's Trip across the Plains (Alger) **8**:25
"Young America" (Halleck) **47**:71
Young America (Halleck) **47**:80
Young and Handsome (Planché) **42**:275, 288
The Young Bank Messenger (Alger)
See *A Cousin's Conspiracy*
"The Young Bear Hunter" (Kivi)
See "Nuori Karhunampuja"
Young Benjamin Franklin (Mayhew) **31**:193
The Young Countess; or, Love and Jealousy (Trollope) **30**:330
The Young Duke (Disraeli) **2**:137, 144, 146, 147; **39**:3, 22, 24-6, 28, 30-1, 33, 39-40, 45-6, 51-2, 65-8, 75-6; **79**:200-202, 214-15, 227, 239, 270-71
The Young Emigrants; or, Pictures of Canada, Calculated to Amuse and Instruct the Minds of Youth (Traill) **31**:320-21
The Young Explorer (Alger) **8**:43
"A Young Fir-Wood" (Rossetti) **4**:491
"The Young Giant" (Grimm Brothers) **3**:227
"Young Goodman Brown" (Hawthorne) **2**:293, 297-98, 310, 317, 324, 327, 329, 331, 333; **10**:300; **17**:137; **23**:202; **39**:180; **79**:311, 317-18; **95**:91, 93-8, 100, 105, 107-10, 112, 114-16, 118-20, 123-29, 132-34, 137-40, 146-48, 150-51, 155-60, 162-63, 167-70, 176-80, 184, 186, 188, 190, 192-93, 195-96, 198, 204, 210, 213; **158**:336; **171**:327, 342-43; **191**:189, 215
Young Heads and Young Hearts (Desbordes-Valmore)
See *Jeunes Têtes et jeunes coeurs*
"The Young Heir's Death Bed" (Norton) **205**:82
"Young Household" (Rimbaud)
See "Jeune ménage"
"The Young Italian" (Irving)
See "The Story of the Young Italian"
"Young Kennedy" (Hogg) **109**:280
"The Young Lady-Peasant Girl" (Pushkin)
See "Baryshnia-krest'ianka"
Young Love (Trollope) **30**:329
"The Young Mahometan" (Lamb)
See "Margaret Green: The Young Mahometan"
The Young Married Couple (Griboedov)
See *Molodye suprugi*
The Young Master Carpenter (Tieck)
See *Der junge Tischlermeister*
Young Men and Old Women (Inchbald) **62**:144-5
"Young Men's Lyceum Speech" (Lincoln)
See "Address before the Young Men's Lyceum of Springfield, Illinois"
"The Young Milliner" (Jones) **222**:146-47
The Young Miner (Alger) **8**:40
Young Mrs. Jardine (Craik) **38**:122
Young Musgrave (Oliphant) **11**:446
The Young Musician (Alger) **8**:43
The Young Outlaw (Alger) **8**:42
The Young Philosopher (Smith) **23**:326, 330, 333; **115**:136, 144, 147-48
"Young Poet" (Crabbe) **26**:102
"The Young Queen" (Barrett Browning) **61**:61
"The Young Robber" (Irving)
See "The Story of the Young Robber"
The Young Salesman (Alger) **8**:46; **83**:114
The Young Sculptor (Mayhew) **31**:159
"The Young Serf" (Taylor) **89**:342
"Young Soult" (Brontë)
See "Young Soult's Poem"
"Young Soult's Poem" (Brontë) **109**:35
"Young Tirel" (Meyer)
See "Jung Tirel"
Young Tom Hall (Surtees) **14**:351, 378-80
Young Wives (Griboedov)
See *Molodye suprugi*
The Younger Son (Trelawny)
See *Adventures of a Younger Son*
"Your Brother Has a Falcon" (Rossetti) **186**:236
"Your Image of Mary" (Isaacs)
See "Tu imagen de María"
"Your love to me appears in doubtful signs" (Boker) **125**:82
"Youth" (Rimbaud)
See "Jeunesse"
"Youth and Age" (Coleridge) **9**:159; **231**:87
"Youth and Art" (Browning) **19**:131
"Youth and Calm" (Arnold) **6**:75; **29**:31, 37; **89**:25
"Youth and Love" (Stevenson) **5**:428
"Youth and Manhood" (Timrod) **25**:381
"Youth, Day, Old Age, and Night" (Whitman) **205**:211
Youth of Jefferson (Cooke) **5**:121, 124, 128-29
"The Youth of Man" (Arnold) **6**:51; **29**:27, 34; **218**:156-58
"The Youth of Nature" (Arnold) **6**:51, 56; **29**:34, 36; **89**:99; **218**:119, 149, 156-57, 183
"The youth once gaily cried" (Baratynsky)
See "Byvalo, otrok, zvonkim klikom..."
"Youth, thou art fled" (Coleridge) **90**:27
The Youthful Days of Mr. Mathews (Reynolds) **146**:193
"Youthful Dreams" (Lenau) **16**:277
"Youth's Agitations" (Arnold) **29**:27; **218**:116
Youth's First Step in Geography (Rowson) **69**:116; **182**:356
The Youth's Magic Horn (Arnim)
See *Des Knaben Wunderhorn*
"You've seen Balloons set" (Dickinson) **171**:174
"Yudol" (Leskov)
See "Judol'"
Yugalanguriya (Chatterji) **19**:217-19
"Yugo y Estrella" (Martí) **63**:87
"Yuki no Hi" (Ichiyō) **49**:335, 342, 353
"Yuku Kumo" (Ichiyō) **49**:344, 353
"Yunost" (Bestuzhev) **131**:150
"Yveline Samoris" (Maupassant) **83**:194-96, 220-21
"Yvette" (Maupassant) **1**:443, 457, 463-64; **83**:194-96, 220
"Z. Marcas" (Balzac) **5**:51; **153**:94, 149, 153
"Z pamiętnika" (Norwid) **17**:375
"Za bairakom bairak" (Shevchenko) **54**:389
"Za chainym stolom" (Pavlova) **138**:22-27, 35-36, 47
Za kulisami: Tyrtej (Norwid) **17**:379
"Zabytaja derevnja" (Nekrasov) **11**:412-13
Zacharias Werners ausgewählte Schriften (Werner)
See *Ausgewählte Schriften*
Zafira (Manzano) **155**:277, 297
"Zagadka" (Norwid) **17**:373
Zagadocnyj celovek (Leskov) **174**:38, 53
"Zagon" (Leskov) **25**:258; **174**:30, 32, 36-37, 53
"Zagrobnyj svidetel" (Leskov) **174**:6-7, 83
Zahme Xenien (Goethe) **4**:173, 193
"Zaiachii remiz" (Leskov)
See "Zajačij remiz"
Zaidee (Oliphant) **221**:226, 230
"Zajačij remiz" (Leskov) **25**:229, 231-32, 234, 238-39; **174**:20-21, 38-41, 90
Zakhudalyj rod (Leskov)
See *Zaxudalyj rod*
"Zakoldovannoe mesto" (Gogol) **5**:231; **31**:120; **162**:93-94
Zametki neizvestnogo (Leskov) **174**:129-31, 133-34, 136-42
"Zamok Eyzen" (Bestuzhev) **131**:175, 184, 187, 208-10, 213
"Zamok Neigauzen" (Bestuzhev) **131**:171, 183, 185, 209
"Zamok Venden" (Bestuzhev) **131**:169, 175, 183-84, 208-10
Zampa der Tagdieb (Nestroy) **42**:225
Zanoni (Bulwer-Lytton) **1**:140-41, 147, 150, 153; **45**:3, 5-7, 19, 23, 47-54, 69-70
Zanzibar; City, Island, and Coast (Burton) **42**:40-1
El zapatero y el rey (Zorrilla y Moral) **6**:523, 525-26
"Zapechatlennyi angel" (Leskov) **25**:228, 233, 238; **174**:5, 9, 16, 41-42
Zapiska o drevnej i novoj rossii (Karamzin)
See *O drevnei i novoi Rossii v ee politicheskom i grazhdanskom otnosheniiakh*
Zapiski iz mertvogo doma (Dostoevsky)
See *Zapiski iz podpol'ya*
Zapiski iz podpol'ia (Dostoevsky)
See *Zapiski iz podpol'ya*
Zapiski iz podpol'ya (Dostoevsky) **2**:160-63, 168, 172, 184, 189, 195, 201-03; **7**:80, 90, 106-7, 116; **21**:107, 1146; **33**:158-243; **43**:92, 122, 164; **119**:90, 147, 156; **167**:241, 278, 303, 328, 336; **202**:75-76, 81
Zapiski ob uzhen'e (Aksakov)
See *Zapiski ob uzhenyi ryby*
Zapiski ob uzhenyi ryby (Aksakov) **2**:16; **181**:18-26, 45-49, 51-53, 59, 63-64
Zapiski okhotnika (Turgenev) **21**:378, 388, 399-400, 406, 409, 413, 416-18, 420-21, 432, 435, 437, 441, 446-48, 451, 454; **37**:364, 379, 393, 401-02, 430, 438; **122**:241, 247, 256, 260, 263-66, 275-76, 279, 293-94, 306, 348, 350
Zapiski ruzheĭnogo okhotnika Orenburgskoĭ gubernii (Aksakov)
See *Zapiski ruzheynago okhotnika*
Zapiski ruzheynago okhotnika (Aksakov) **2**:16; **181**:18-24, 26, 45-47, 49, 51-52, 57, 64-65
Zapiski starucha (Fredro) **8**:293
Zapisnaia knizhka (Leskov) **174**:88
Zapolya: A Christmas Tale, in Two Parts (Coleridge) **9**:143, 159; **231**:58-59
"Zapovit" (Shevchenko) **54**:384, 390
"Zapustenie" (Baratynsky) **103**:11-12
Zaputannoye delo (Saltykov) **16**:368
"Zara" (Rossetti) **186**:275-76
Zaragoza (Martínez de la Rosa) **102**:225
Zastrozzi (Shelley) **18**:306, 341-42; **93**:272
"Zatiš'e" (Turgenev) **122**:268
"Die Zauberei im Herbste" (Eichendorff) **8**:226; **225**:9
"Die Zauberin im Walde" (Eichendorff) **225**:43, 45, 54-56
"Zauberlehrling" (Goethe) **4**:192
"Der Zauberleuchtturm" (Mörike) **10**:455; **201**:273, 298
Der Zauberring (Fouqué) **2**:265-68
"Zaunno" (Bestuzhev) **131**:172
Zavtrak u predvoritelya (Turgenev) **21**:432
Zawisza czarny (Slowacki) **15**:371-72, 380
Zawisza the Black (Slowacki)
See *Zawisza czarny*
Zaxudalyj rod (Leskov) **25**:228, 232, 238, 245; **174**:16, 31, 38, 62, 65
"Zdes, gde tak vyalo svod nebesnyy" (Tyutchev) **34**:400
"Zdravljica" (Preseren) **127**:299, 329, 332, 334
"Zeal and Love" (Newman) **38**:343
"Żegluga" (Mickiewicz) **3**:403
"Die Zeichen" (Meyer) **81**:155
Zeim, re dei genii (Gozzi) **23**:119
"Zeinab and Kathema" (Shelley) **93**:336
Die Zeit Constantins des Grossen (Burckhardt) **49**:10, 15-6, 23, 32-4
"Zeitbilder" (Droste-Hülshoff) **3**:193, 200
Zeitgedichte (Heine) **54**:345, 348; **147**:193
"Der Zeitgeist" (Hölderlin) **16**:191
Zeitgeist und Bernergeist (Gotthelf) **117**:4, 6-7, 14-15, 17-18, 22, 32, 34

Zeitung für Einsiedler (Brentano) **191**:35
"Železnaja volja" (Leskov) **25**:239; **174**:32, 34-35, 90
"Zelyóny shum" (Nekrasov) **11**:413, 417, 420-21
"Zemcuznoe ozerel'e" (Leskov) **174**:24
The Zemganno Brothers (Goncourt)
See *Les frères Zemganno*
Zemsta (Fredro) **8**:285-87, 289-90, 292-93
The Zenana, and Minor Poems of L. E. L. (Landon) **15**:161
Zenobia. A Tragedy. As It Is Performed at the Theatre-Royal in Drury-Lane. By the Author of The Orphan of China (Murphy) **229**:234
Ženske pjesme (Karadzic) **115**:112
"Zephyrus and Flora" (Barbauld) **50**:13
Der Zerbrochene Krug (Kleist) **2**:439-41, 443-45, 454, 457, 461, 463; **37**:226, 229, 233, 237, 239, 241, 243-44, 253-55, 267, 270-73; **222**:185, 205, 233, 236, 255-56, 285, 287
"Der zerbrochene Ringlein" (Eichendorff) **225**:7
Zéro (Balzac) **153**:150
Der Zerrissene (Nestroy) **42**:220, 223, 251, 257
Zerstreute Blätter (Herder) **8**:313; **186**:13-14, 99-100
Zerstreute Kapitel (Storm) **195**:89
Die Zerstreuten (Kotzebue) **25**:136
"Zgubljena vera" (Preseren) **127**:298, 323
"Zhelanie" (Zhukovsky) **35**:403, 407
"Zheleznaia volia" (Leskov) **174**:47-48, 50
Zhenit'ba (Gogol)
See *Zhenit'ba; Sovershenno neveroyatnoye sobitye*
Zhenit'ba; Sovershenno neveroyatnoye sobitye (Gogol) **5**:218, 224, 231, 251; **15**:84-85, 98; **162**:3, 18-19, 63, 107
"Zhenshchina" (Gogol) **5**:258; **31**:137; **162**:129-30
"Zhidovskaia kuvyrkollegiia" (Leskov)
See "Židovskaja kuvyrkalegija"
Zhitie Fedora Vasil'evicha Ushakova, s priobshcheiem nekotorykh ego sochinenii (Radishchev) **190**:276, 300-303, 306-8, 314, 318-19, 331-32, 336
"Zhivym sochuvstviem priveta" (Tyutchev) **34**:404
Zibaldone (Leopardi) **129**:222-23, 225-26, 228, 230, 234-39, 241-43, 248, 255-60, 264-68, 272, 276-77, 279-82, 291, 295-96, 298, 302-6, 314, 316-19, 322-26, 330-32, 339-41, 343, 346-48
"Zid" (Turgenev) **122**:267
"Židovskaja kuvyrkalegija" (Leskov) **25**:265-67; **174**:105
"Die Zigeuner und ihre Musik in Ungarn" (Liszt) **199**:298
"Die Zigeunerin" (Ludwig) **4**:353
Zigzags (Gautier)
See *Caprices et zigzags*
"The Zilver-Weed" (Barnes) **75**:38
Zimnie zametki o letnikh vpechatleniiakh (Dostoevsky) **2**:195; **33**:234; **119**:73, 132; **167**:336
"Zimnii den" (Leskov)
See "Zimnij den'"
"Zimnij den'" (Leskov) **25**:232; **174**:38, 53, 90
"Zimniy Vecher" (Pushkin) **3**:443
The Zincali; or, An Account of the Gypsies of Spain (Borrow) **9**:36-40, 42, 66
Zinzendorff, and Other Poems (Sigourney) **21**:292, 307; **87**:321, 326, 337, 340, 342
Žitie Fëdora Vasil'evica Ušakova (Radishchev)
See *Zhitie Fedora Vasil'evicha Ushakova, s priobshcheiem nekotorykh ego sochinenii*
"Zitie odnoj baby" (Leskov) **174**:64, 120-21, 123, 135
Zitie odnoj baby (Leskov) **174**:52
"Zitten Out the Wold Year" (Barnes) **75**:77
"Ziua de mâine" (Eminescu) **131**:361
Zivopisnaja Ukraina (Shevchenko) **54**:379
Zivot i obicaji naroda srpska (Karadzic) **115**:79
Zizine (Kock) **16**:248
Złota czaszka (Slowacki) **15**:352, 354, 371
"Znakomstvo s Derzhavinym" (Aksakov) **181**:60, 68
Zoas (Blake)
See *The Four Zoas: The Torments of Love and Jealousy in the Death and Judgment of Albion the Ancient Man*
La Zobeide (Gozzi) **23**:108, 119, 123, 126
Zofloya; or, the Moor: A Romance of the Fifteenth Century (Dacre) **151**:139-40, 142-43, 145-48, 150-52, 155-56, 159-62, 164, 174-78, 180, 190-92, 196-206, 215-16, 218-19, 224-27
"Żona modna" (Krasicki) **8**:403, 407
"A Zong" (Barnes) **75**:71
The Zoology of the Voyage of the Beagle (Darwin) **57**:113, 116
The zoonomia; or, Laws fo Organic Life (Darwin) **106**:185-86, 191-92, 203, 205, 208-11, 216-21, 228, 233-34, 236, 240, 242, 245, 247, 252, 260, 269, 274-78
"Zoospermos" (Silva) **114**:263, 319
Zoospermos (Silva) **114**:273
"Zoraida" (Isaacs) **70**:310
Zrzędnosc i przecora (Fredro) **8**:284-85
"Zu der Edlen Jagd" (Gordon) **21**:159
"Zu Bacharach am Rheine" (Brentano) **191**:119
Zu ebener Erde und erster Stock (Nestroy) **42**:231-32, 236, 238-41, 257
"Zu viel" (Mörike) **201**:280
"The Zucca" (Shelley) **18**:370
"Zueignung" (Arnim) **159**:58
"Zueignung" (Goethe) **154**:191-92, 249, 273
"Der Zufall. Geschichte der Mrs. Ligh" (Arnim) **159**:84
"Zufällige Gedanken über die Abschaffung des Erbadels in Frankreich" (Wieland) **177**:280
"Zukunftsmusik" (Wagner) **119**:198
Zulma (Staël-Holstein) **91**:340, 358
Zum ewigen Frieden: Ein philosophischer Entwurf (Kant) **27**:228-29, 236, 238
"Zum neven Jahr" (Mörike) **10**:455
Zum Sinn des Gefühls (Herder) **186**:64
"Zum Titelblatte des Republikaners für 1836" (Beddoes) **154**:25, 30, 32
"Zummer" (Barnes) **75**:6
"Zummer an'Winter" (Barnes) **75**:9 32
"Zummer Stream" (Barnes) **75**:22, 59
"Zummer Thoughts in Winter Time" (Barnes) **75**:22, 32
"Zunsheen in the Winter" (Barnes) **75**:32
Zur Chronik von Grieshuus (Storm) **1**:540-41, 546; **195**:5, 72
"Zur Geschichte der neueren romantischen Poesie in Deutschland" (Eichendorff) **225**:46
Zur Geschichte der neuern schonen Literatur in Deutschland (Heine) **147**:149-51, 166-68, 189, 191, 198, 216-17, 245
"Zur Geschichte der Religion und Philosophie in Deutschland" (Heine) **4**:255, 263, 264, 266; **54**:321, 336-7, 340; **147**:188, 190-91, 204, 216, 230, 233, 245
"Zur Geschichte des Elefanten" (Schlegel) **142**:324
Zur kritik der politischen Ökonomie (Marx) **17**:289, 302, 304, 318, 321-22, 335; **114**:8, 10, 37, 70, 78, 80, 82, 84-5
Zur Philosophie und Wissenschaft der Nature (1) (Schopenhauer) **51**:297
Zur "Wald- und Wasserfreude" (Storm) **195**:5, 131
Die Zürcher Novellen (Keller) **2**:412, 414, 416, 422
"Zürchersee" (Klopstock) **11**:234, 237-38; **225**:297, 315, 330
ZurFarbenlehre (Goethe) **154**:199-200, 202, 204, 206, 210-12, 324, 329
Eine zurückgezogene Vorrede aus dem Jahre 1881 (Storm) **195**:20-21
Die Zurückkunft des Vaters (Kotzebue) **25**:140
Zusätze (Hegel) **151**:242, 244, 370-71
"Zver'" (Leskov) **25**:239; **174**:7, 37
"Zvezdocka" (Baratynsky) **103**:28
"Zwanzig Balladen von einem Schweizer" (Meyer) **81**:199, 209
"Zweckprosa" (Gotthelf) **117**:92
"Zwei Feuerreiter" (Auerbach) **171**:75
"Zwei Johannes würmchen" (Klopstock) **11**:238
"Zwei Polen" (Lenau) **16**:286
"Zwei Schwestern" (Stifter) **41**:334, 343, 366
Zwei Schwestern (Stifter) **198**:260, 276-77
"Zwei Segel" (Spencer) **81**:201
"Die Zweifler" (Lenau) **16**:272, 275, 287
"Die Zweikampf" (Kleist) **222**:207, 236, 238, 259
Der Zweikampf (Kleist) **2**:456, 458, 461; **37**:237-38, 246, 249, 253-55
"Die Zweite Unterredung mit dem Pfarrer von ***" (Wieland) **177**:285
Zwerg Nase (Hauff) **185**:335-37, 339-42, 356-60
Zwey Hundert Christliche Lieder (Lavater) **142**:12
"Die zwey wichtigsten Ereignisse des vorigen Monats" (Wieland) **177**:279
"Zwiegesprach" (Meyer) **81**:147
"Zwielicht" (Eichendorff) **225**:55-56
Die Zwillinge (Klinger) **1**:429
Zwischen Himmel und Erde (Ludwig) **4**:346-50, 354-55, 357-58, 360-61, 363-64, 367-68
Zwölf Gedichte (Schumann) **143**:139
Zwölf Mädchen in Uniform (Nestroy) **42**:236
Zwölf moralische Briefe (Wieland) **17**:417-18
Zwolon (Norwid) **17**:367, 371, 379
"Zyuleyka, S persidskogo" (Bestuzhev) **131**:150